Twentieth-Century Literary Criticism

Guide to Gale Literary Criticism Series

For criticism on	Consult these Gale series
Authors now living or who died after December 31, 1959	*CONTEMPORARY LITERARY CRITICISM (CLC)*
Authors who died between 1900 and 1959	*TWENTIETH-CENTURY LITERARY CRITICISM (TCLC)*
Authors who died between 1800 and 1899	*NINETEENTH-CENTURY LITERATURE CRITICISM (NCLC)*
Authors who died between 1400 and 1799	*LITERATURE CRITICISM FROM 1400 TO 1800 (LC)* *SHAKESPEAREAN CRITICISM (SC)*
Authors who died before 1400	*CLASSICAL AND MEDIEVAL LITERATURE CRITICISM (CMLC)*
Black writers of the past two hundred years	*BLACK LITERATURE CRITICISM (BLC)*
Authors of books for children and young adults	*CHILDREN'S LITERATURE REVIEW (CLR)*
Dramatists	*DRAMA CRITICISM (DC)*
Hispanic writers of the late nineteenth and twentieth centuries	*HISPANIC LITERATURE CRITICISM (HLC)*
Poets	*POETRY CRITICISM (PC)*
Short story writers	*SHORT STORY CRITICISM (SSC)*
Major authors from the Renaissance to the present	*WORLD LITERATURE CRITICISM, 1500 TO THE PRESENT (WLC)*

ISSN 0276-8178

Volume 53

Twentieth-Century Literary Criticism

**Excerpts from Criticism of the
Works of Novelists, Poets, Playwrights,
Short Story Writers, and Other Creative Writers
Who Lived between 1900 and 1960,
from the First Published Critical
Appraisals to Current Evaluations**

Laurie Di Mauro
Editor

**Jennifer Gariepy
Christopher Giroux
Margaret A. Haerens
Marie Lazzari
Thomas Ligotti
David Segal**
Associate Editors

Gale Research Inc. • *DETROIT* • *WASHINGTON, D.C.* • *LONDON*

STAFF

Laurie Di Mauro, *Editor*

Giroux, Margaret A. Haerens, Marie Lazzari, Thomas Ligotti, David Segal,
Associate Editors

Pamela Willwerth Aue, Christine Bichler, Martha Bommarito, Nancy Dziedzic, Ian A. Goodhall, Matthew McDonough,
Assistant Editors

Jeanne A. Gough, *Permissions & Production Manager*
Linda M. Pugliese, *Production Supervisor*
Donna Craft, Paul Lewon, Maureen A. Puhl, Camille P. Robinson, Sheila Walencewicz, *Editorial Associates*

Sandra C. Davis, *Permissions Supervisor (Text)*
Maria L. Franklin, Josephine M. Keene, Michele Lonoconus, Shalice Shah, Kimberly F. Smilay, *Permissions Associates*
Jennifer A. Arnold, Brandy C. Merritt, *Permissions Assistants*

Margaret A. Chamberlain, *Permissions Supervisor (Pictures)*
Pamela A. Hayes, Arlene Johnson, Keith Reed, Barbara A. Wallace, *Permissions Associates*
Susan Brohman, *Permissions Assistant*

Victoria B. Cariappa, *Research Manager*
Maureen Richards, *Research Supervisor*
Maria Bryson, Mary Beth McElmeel, Donna Melnychenko, Tamara C. Nott, Jaema Paradowski, *Editorial Associates*
Julie A. Kriebel, Stefanie Scarlett, *Editorial Assistants*

Mary Beth Trimper, *Production Director*
Catherine Kemp, *Production Assistant*

Cynthia Baldwin, *Art Director*
Barbara J. Yarrow, *Graphic Services Supervisor*
Sherrell Hobbs, *Desktop Publisher*
Willie F. Mathis, *Camera Operator*

Library of Congress Catalog Card Number 76-46132
ISBN 0-8103-2431-8
ISSN 0276-8178

Printed in the United States of America
Published simultaneously in the United Kingdom
by Gale Research International Limited
(An affiliated company of Gale Research Inc.)
10 9 8 7 6 5 4 3 2 1

I(T)P™

The trademark **ITP** is used under license.

Contents

Preface vii

Acknowledgments xi

Preface

Since its inception more than fifteen years ago, *Twentieth-Century Literary Criticism* has been purchased and used by nearly 10,000 school, public, and college or university libraries. *TCLC* has covered more than 500 authors, representing 58 nationalities, and over 25,000 titles. No other reference source has surveyed the critical response to twentieth-century authors and literature as thoroughly as *TCLC*. In the words of one reviewer, "there is nothing comparable available." *TCLC* "is a gold mine of information—dates, pseudonyms, biographical information, and criticism from books and periodicals—which many libraries would have difficulty assembling on their own."

Scope of the Series

TCLC is designed to serve as an introduction to authors who died between 1900 and 1960 and to the most significant interpretations of these author's works. The great poets, novelists, short story writers, playwrights, and philosophers of this period are frequently studied in high school and college literature courses. In organizing and excerpting the vast amount of critical material written on these authors, *TCLC* helps students develop valuable insight into literary history, promotes a better understanding of the texts, and sparks ideas for papers and assignments. Each entry in *TCLC* presents a comprehensive survey of an author's career or an individual work of literature and provides the user with a multiplicity of interpretations and assessments. Such variety allows students to pursue their own interests; furthermore, it fosters an awareness that literature is dynamic and responsive to many different opinions.

Every fourth volume of *TCLC* is devoted to literary topics that cannot be covered under the author approach used in the rest of the series. Such topics include literary movements, prominent themes in twentieth-century literature, literary reaction to political and historical events, significant eras in literary history, prominent literary anniversaries, and the literatures of cultures that are often overlooked by English-speaking readers.

TCLC is designed as a companion series to Gale's *Contemporary Literary Criticism*, which reprints commentary on authors now living or who have died since 1960. Because of the different periods under consideration, there is no duplication of material between *CLC* and *TCLC*. For additional information about *CLC* and Gale's other criticism titles, users should consult the Guide to Gale Literary Criticism Series preceding the title page in this volume.

Coverage

Each volume of *TCLC* is carefully compiled to present:

- criticism of authors, or literary topics, representing a variety of genres and nationalities

- both major and lesser-known writers and literary works of the period

- 10-15 authors or 4-6 topics per volume

- individual entries that survey critical response to each author's work or each topic in literary history, including early criticism to reflect initial reactions; later criticism to represent any rise or decline in reputation; and current retrospective analyses.

Organization of This Book

An author entry consists of the following elements: author heading, biographical and critical introduction, list of principal works, excerpts of criticism (each preceded by an annotation and followed by a bibliographic citation), and a bibliography of further reading.

- The **Author Heading** consists of the name under which the author most commonly wrote, followed by birth and death dates. If an author wrote consistently under a pseudonym, the pseudonym will be listed in the author heading and the real name given in parentheses on the first line of the biographical and critical introduction. Also located at the beginning of the introduction to the author entry are any name variations under which an author wrote, including transliterated forms for authors whose languages use nonroman alphabets.

- The **Biographical and Critical Introduction** outlines the author's life and career, as well as the critical issues surrounding his or her work. References to past volumes of *TCLC* are provided at the beginning of the introduction. Additional sources of information in other biographical and critical reference series published by Gale, including *Short Story Criticism, Children's Literature Review, Contemporary Authors, Dictionary of Literary Biography,* and *Something about the Author,* are listed in a box at the end of the entry.

- Most *TCLC* entries include **Portraits** of the author. Many entries also contain reproductions of materials pertinent to an author's career, including manuscript pages, title pages, dust jackets, letters, and drawings, as well as photographs of important people, places, and events in an author's life.

- The **List of Principal Works** is chronological by date of first book publication and identifies the genre of each work. In the case of foreign authors with both foreign-language publications and English translations, the title and date of the first English-language edition are given in brackets. Unless otherwise indicated, dramas are dated by first performance, not first publication.

- Critical excerpts are prefaced by **Annotations** providing the reader with information about both the critic and the criticism that follows. Included are the critic's reputation, individual approach to literary criticism, and particular expertise in an author's works. Also noted are the relative importance of a work of criticism, the scope of the excerpt, and the growth of critical controversy or changes in critical trends regarding an author. In some cases, these annotations cross-reference excerpts by critics who discuss each other's commentary.

- **Criticism** is arranged chronologically in each author entry to provide a perspective on changes in critical evaluation over the years. All titles of works by the author featured in the entry are printed in boldface type to enable the user to easily locate discussion of particular works. Also for purposes of easier identification, the critic's name and the publication date of the essay are given at the beginning of each piece of criticism. Unsigned criticism is preceded by the title of the journal in which it appeared. Some of the excerpts in *TCLC* also contain translated material. Unless otherwise noted, translations in brackets are by the editors; translations in parentheses or continuous with the text are by the critic. Publication information (such as footnotes or page and line references to specific editions of works) have been deleted at the editor's discretion to provide smoother reading of the text.

- A complete **Bibliographic Citation** designed to facilitate location of the original essay or book follows each piece of criticism.

- An annotated list of **Further Reading** appearing at the end of each author entry suggests secondary sources on the author. In some cases it includes essays for which the editors could not obtain reprint rights.

Cumulative Indexes

- Each volume of *TCLC* contains a cumulative **Author Index** listing all authors who have appeared in Gale's Literary Criticism Series, along with cross references to such biographical series as *Contemporary Authors* and *Dictionary of Literary Biography*. For readers' convenience, a complete list of Gale titles included appears on the first page of the author index. Useful for locating authors within the various series, this index is particularly valuable for those authors who are identified by a certain period but who, because of their death dates, are placed in another, or for those authors whose careers span two periods. For example, F. Scott Fitzgerald is found in *TCLC,* yet a writer often associated with him, Ernest Hemingway, is found in *CLC*.

- Each *TCLC* volume includes a cumulative **Nationality Index** which lists all authors who have appeared in *TCLC* volumes, arranged alphabetically under their respective nationalities, as well as Topics volume entries devoted to particular national literatures.

- Each new volume in Gale's Literary Criticism Series includes a cumulative **Topic Index,** which lists all literary topics treated in *NCLC, TCLC, LC 1400-1800,* and the *CLC* yearbook.

- Each new volume of *TCLC,* with the exception of the Topics volumes, includes a **Title Index** listing the titles of all literary works discussed in the volume. In response to numerous suggestions from librarians, Gale has also produced a **Special Paperbound Edition** of the *TCLC* title index. This annual cumulation lists all titles discussed in the series since its inception and is issued with the first volume of *TCLC* published each year. Additional copies of the index are available on request. Librarians and patrons will welcome this separate index; it saves shelf space, is easy to use, and is recyclable upon receipt of the following year's cumulation. Titles discussed in the Topics volume entries are not included *TCLC* cumulative index.

Citing *Twentieth-Century Literary Criticism*

When writing papers, students who quote directly from any volume in Gale's literary Criticism Series may use the following general forms to footnote reprinted criticism. The first example pertains to materials drawn from periodicals, the second to material reprinted from books.

[1]T. S. Eliot, "John Donne," *The Nation and the Athenaeum,* 33 (9 June 1923), 321-32; excerpted and reprinted in *Literature Criticism from 1400 to 1800,* Vol. 10, ed. James E. Person, Jr. (Detroit: Gale Research, 1989), pp. 28-9.

[2]Clara G. Stillman, *Samuel Butler: A Mid-Victorian Modern* (Viking Press, 1932); excerpted and reprinted in *Twentieth-Century Literary Criticism,* Vol. 33, ed. Paula Kepos (Detroit: Gale Research, 1989), pp. 43-5.

Suggestions Are Welcome

In response to suggestions, several features have been added to *TCLC* since the series began, including annotations to excerpted criticism, a cumulative index to authors in all Gale literary criticism series, entries devoted to criticism on a single work by a major author, more extensive illustrations, and a title index listing all literary works discussed in the series since its inception.

Readers who wish to suggest authors or topics to appear in future volumes, or who have other suggestions, are cordially invited to write the editors.

Acknowledgments

The editors wish to thank the copyright holders of the excerpted criticism included in this volume, the permissions managers of many book and magazine publishing companies for assisting us in securing reprint rights, and Anthony Bogucki for assistance with copyright research. We are also grateful to the staffs of the Detroit Public Library, the Library of Congress, the University of Detroit Mercy Library, Wayne State University Purdy/Kresge Library Complex, and the University of Michigan Libraries for making their resources available to us. Following is a list of the copyright holders who have granted us permission to reprint material in this volume of *TCLC*. Every effort has been made to trace copyright, but if omissions have been made, please let us know.

COPYRIGHTED EXCERPTS IN *TCLC*, VOLUME 53, WERE REPRINTED FROM THE FOLLOWING PERIODICALS:

Agora, v. 2, Fall, 1973.—*American Literature,* v. XXX, November, 1958. Copyright © 1958, renewed 1986 Duke University Press, Durham, NC. Reprinted by permission of the publisher.—*Colby Library Quarterly,* s. XXIII, June, 1987. Reprinted by permission of the publisher.—*Dutch Quarterly Review of Anglo-American Letters,* v. 20, 1990. Reprinted by permission of the publisher.—*Encounter,* v. XLIV, February, 1975.—*English Literature in Transition: 1800-1920,* v. 19, 1976. Copyright © 1976 *English Literature in Transition: 1880-1920.* Reprinted by permission of the publisher.—*The German Quarterly,* v. LV, November, 1982. Copyright © 1982 by the American Association of Teachers of German. Reprinted by permission of the publisher.—*Journal of European Studies,* v. 14, December, 1984.—*The Midwest Quarterly,* v. XXX, Autumn, 1988. Copyright, 1988, by *The Midwest Quarterly,* Pittsburgh State University. Reprinted by permission of the publisher.—*Modern Fiction Studies,* v. XVII, Spring, 1971. Copyright © 1971 by Purdue Research Foundation, West Lafayette, IN 47907. All rights reserved. Reprinted with permission.—*Modern Language Studies,* v. 21, Fall, 1991 for "The Transparent Eyes of May Welland in Wharton's 'The Age of Innocence' " by Evelyn E. Fracasso. Copyright, Northeast Modern Language Association, 1991. Reprinted by permission of the publisher and the author.—*The New Republic,* v. 132, June, 1955. © 1955, renewed 1983 The New Republic, Inc. Reprinted by permission of *The New Republic.*—*New York Herald Tribune Books,* October 30, 1932. Copyright 1932, renewed 1960 New York Herald Tribune Inc. All rights reserved. Reprinted by permission.—*The New York Times Book Review,* October, 17, 1920; June 20, 1948; November 20, 1949. Copyright 1920, renewed 1948; copyright 1948, renewed 1976; copyright 1949, renewed 1977 by The New York Times Company. All reprinted by permission of the publisher.—*The Quarterly of Film, Radio and Television,* v. IX, Winter, 1954. Copyright 1954 by The Regents of the University of California. Reprinted by permission of the publisher.—*The Quarterly Journal of Speech,* v. 63, February, 1977 for "Mythic Rhetoric in 'Mein Kampf': A Structuralist Critique" by Michael McGuire. Copyright 1977 by the Speech Communication Association. Reprinted by permission of the publisher and the author.—*Research Studies,* v. 38, March, 1970 for " 'The Age of Innocence': Art of Artifice?" by James W. Gargano. Reprinted by permission of the author.—*San Jose Studies,* v. 11, Fall, 1985 "Expressionism and 'Nosferatu' " by Bert Cardullo. © San Jose State University Foundation, 1985. Reprinted by permission of the publisher and the author.—*The Saturday Review of Literature,* v. XV, January 30, 1937. Copyright 1937, renewed 1964 *Saturday Review* magazine. Reprinted by permission of the publisher.—*Sight and Sound,* v. 36, Summer, 1967. Copyright © 1967 by The British Film Institute. Reprinted by permission of the publisher.—*The Slavonic and East European Review,* v. 64, July, 1986. © University of London (School of Slavonic and East European Studies) 1986. Reprinted by permission of the publisher.—*Soviet Literature,* n. 2, 1968. © *Soviet Literature,* 1968. Reprinted by permission of the publisher.—*Studies in American Fiction,* v. 6, Spring, 1978. Copyright © 1978 Northeastern University. Reprinted by permission of the publisher.—*Studies in Short Fiction,* v. V, Fall, 1967; v. VIII, Spring, 1971. Copyright 1967, 1971 by Newberry College. Both reprinted by permission of the publisher.—*Studies in the Novel,* v. XXIII, Summer, 1991. Copyright 1991 by North Texas State University. Reprinted by permission of the publisher.—*Studies in Twentieth Century Literature,* v. 7, Fall, 1982. Copyright © 1982 by *Studies in Twentieth*

Century Literature. Reprinted by permission of the publisher.—*Victorian Poetry,* v. 29, Spring, 1991; v. 30, Summer, 1992. Both reprinted by permission of the publisher.—*Wascana Review,* v. 22, Fall, 1987. Copyright, 1987 by *Wascana Review*. Reprinted by permission of the publisher.

COPYRIGHTED EXCERPTS IN *TCLC*, VOLUME 53, WERE REPRINTED FROM THE FOLLOWING BOOKS:

Alexander, Michael. From "Hardy Among the Poets," in *Thomas Hardy After Fifty Years*. Edited by Lance St. John Butler. Rowman & Littlefield, 1977. Chapter 5 © Michael Alexander 1977. All rights reserved. Reprinted by permission of the publisher.—Andrew, Dudley. From *Film in the Aura of Art*. Princeton University Press, 1984. Copyright © 1984 by Princeton University Press. All rights reserved. Reprinted by permission of the publisher.—Barlow, John D. From *German Expressionist Film*. Twayne, 1982. Copyright © 1982 by G. K. Hall & Co. Reprinted with the permission of Twayne Publishers, an imprint of Macmillan Publishing Company.—Bayley, John. From "The Child in Walter de la Mare," in *Children and Their Books: A Celebration of the Work of Iona and Peter Opie*. Edited by Gillian Avery and Julia Briggs. Oxford at the Clarendon Press, 1989. © The Several Contributors 1989. All rights reserved. Reprinted by permission of Oxford University Press.—Beach, Joseph Warren. From *The Twentieth Century Novel: Studies in Technique*. Appleton-Century Crofts, Inc., 1932. © 1932, renewed 1960. Reprinted by permission of the Literary Estate of Joseph Warren Beach.—Bergstrom, Janet. From "Sexuality at a Loss: The Films of F. W. Murnau," in *The Female in Western Culture: Contemporary Perspectives*. Edited by Susan Rubin Suleiman. Cambridge, Mass.: Harvard University Press, 1986. Copyright © 1985, 1986 by the President and Fellows of Harvard College. All rights reserved. Excerpted by permission of the publisher and the author.—Bhattacharya, France. From "The Supernatural in Tagore's Short Stories," in *Rabindranath Tagore: Perspectives in Time*. Edited by Mary Lago and Ronald Warwick. The Macmillan Press Ltd., 1989. © Mary Lago and Ronald Warwick 1989. All rights reserved. Reprinted by permission of Macmillan, London and Basingstoke.—Boydston, Jeanne. From " 'Grave Endearing Tradition': Edith Wharton and the Domestic Novel," in *Faith of a (Woman) Writer*. Contributions in Women's Studies, No. 86. Edited by Alice Kessler-Harris and William McBrien. Greenwood Press, 1988. Copyright © 1988 by Hofstra University. All rights reserved. Reprinted by permission of Greenwood Publishing Group, Inc., Westport, CT.—Briggs, Julia. From *Night Visitors*. Faber, 1977. © 1977 Julia Briggs. All rights reserved. Reprinted by permission of Faber & Faber Ltd.—Brown, Edward J. From *Russian Literature since the Revolution*. Revised edition. Collier Books, 1969. Copyright © 1963 by The Crowell-Collier Publishing Company. © 1969 Macmillan Company. All rights reserved. Reprinted by permission of the Literary Estate of Edward J. Brown.—Burke, Kenneth. From *The Philosophy of Literary Form: Studies in Symbolic Action*. Third edition. University of California Press, 1973. Copyright © 1973 by The Regents of the University of California. Reprinted by permission of the publisher.—Dolan, Paul J. From *Of War and War's Alarm: Fiction and Politics in the Modern World*. The Free Press, 1976. Copyright © 1976 by Paul J. Dolan. All rights reserved. Reprinted with the permission of Macmillan Publishing Company.—Downs, Robert B. From *Books that Changed the World*. Second edition. American Library Association, 1978. Copyright © 1956, 1961, 1964, 1970, 1978 by the American Library Association. All rights reserved. Reprinted by permission of the publisher.—Eisner, Lotte H. From *The Haunted Screen: Expressionism in the German Cinema and the Influence of Max Reinhardt*. Translated by Roger Greaves. Thames & Hudson, 1969. Translation and new material © Thames & Hudson 1969. Reprinted by permission of the publisher.—Folsom, James K. From *The American Western Novel*. NCUP, Inc. (Formerly New College & University Press), 1966. Copyright © 1966 by New College and University Press, Inc. All rights reserved. Reprinted by permission of the publisher.—Gaston, Edwin W., Jr. From *Eugene Manlove Rhodes: Cowboy Chronicler*. Steck-Vaughn Company, 1967. Reprinted by permission of the publisher.—Greenberg, Martin. From *The Terror of Art: Kafka and Modern Literature*. Basic Books, Inc., Publishers, 1968. © 1965, 1966, 1968 by Martin Greenberg. Reprinted by permission of Basic Books, a division of HarperCollins Publishers, Inc.—Greene, Graham. *Collected Essays*. The Viking Press, 1969. Copyright 1951, © 1966, 1968, 1969 by Graham Greene. All rights reserved. Reprinted by permission of Viking Penguin, a division of Penguin Books USA, Inc. In Canada by Laurence Pollinger Ltd. for Graham Greene.—Hutchinson, W. H. From "Virgins, Villains, and

PHOTOGRAPHS AND ILLUSTRATIONS APPEARING IN *TCLC*, VOLUME 53, WERE RECEIVED FROM THE FOLLOWING SOURCES:

Dale Carnegie

1888-1955

(Born Dale Breckenridge Carnagey) American nonfiction writer and biographer.

INTRODUCTION

Carnegie is best remembered for his self-improvement book *How to Win Friends and Influence People* and for creating the Dale Carnegie Course in Public Speaking and Human Relations. His methods are credited with helping millions of people learn to speak more confidently in public. While some critics have characterized Carnegie's advice and techniques as manipulative, others contend, and he himself asserted, that his guidelines for success consisted of wholly positive ideals and basic principles of common sense.

Carnegie was born near Maryville, Missouri. His father was a hardworking but financially unsuccessful farmer and his mother a devout Methodist who hoped her son would become a missionary, minister, or teacher. Encouraged by his mother, Carnegie gained his earliest oratorical experience reciting poetry at church and Sunday school gatherings during his boyhood. Later, as a student at tuition-free Warrensburg State Teachers College, he won numerous declamatory and debate contests. Fellow students began to seek his advice and tutelage, and he developed a reputation for infusing even the most reticent students with enough confidence to successfully complete their declamation and elocution requirements. After he left the college in 1908, Carnegie tried a variety of sales jobs, moved to New York City, studied acting, and enrolled in a writing course. Utilizing his experience as a speech tutor, Carnegie began teaching night classes in public speaking at the YMCA, hoping to earn enough money to spend his days writing. By 1914, still dreaming of publishing a best-selling novel, he was earning nearly five hundred dollars a week writing human interest stories for magazines and teaching his public speaking classes. In 1915 he published his first book, *The Art of Public Speaking*.

In 1919 Carnegie changed the spelling of his name, possibly to exploit the aura of success associated with industrialist Andrew Carnegie. During the next few years he lived in Europe, where he worked with broadcaster Lowell Thomas, met and married a German woman who claimed to be a countess, and, in one of the great disappointments of his life, wrote a novel so fiercely rejected by editors and his literary agent that he never attempted to publish it or write another. Carnegie and his wife returned to New York, where he once again began teaching and writing articles. He was asked to provide corporate training for salesmen and executives, and soon he was hiring and training additional teachers and standardizing his entire

public speaking program, using his book as a guide to the course. His marriage, an unhappy partnership from the start, ended in 1931. Business grew rapidly with the publication of Carnegie's surprise bestseller *How to Win Friends and Influence People* in 1936. By this time he had also written *Lincoln the Unknown*, which he would later call his favorite of his own books, and the first of three volumes of biographical sketches. Until shortly before his death, Carnegie remained active as a seminar speaker, radio talk show guest, and newspaper columnist. During his lifetime, *How to Win Friends and Influence People* sold nearly five million English language copies. More than twice that number have sold since Carnegie's death in 1955, and his course in public speaking is still popular in more than sixty countries.

As the first commercially successful book of its kind, *How to Win Friends and Influence People* launched the now-familiar genre of the motivational handbook. Carnegie's folksy, midwestern manner made his methods for achieving success in personal and professional relationships seem readily accessible to everyone, regardless of economic status, social class, or educational background. Carnegie's philosophy of success comprised three principles: get people to like you, gain their cooperation, and change their attitudes and behavior. These effects were achievable, Carnegie believed, by being pleasant, respectful, and encouraging in one's dealings with other people. This simple prescription prompted much negative commentary from critics accustomed to more sophisticated ideas. In his own defense, Carnegie once remarked at a gathering of publishers and editors: "Gentlemen, I've never claimed to have a new idea. . . . I present, reiterate, and glorify the obvious—because the obvious is what people need to be told. . . . The ideas I stand for are not mine. I borrowed them from Socrates, I swiped them from Chesterfield, I stole them from Jesus, and I put them in a book."

PRINCIPAL WORKS

The Art of Public Speaking [with J. Berg Esenwein] (lectures and speeches) 1915

Public Speaking: A Practical Course for Business Men (nonfiction) 1926

Public Speaking and Influencing Men in Business (nonfiction) 1931

Lincoln the Unknown (biography) 1932

Little-Known Facts about Well-Known People (sketches) 1934

How to Win Friends and Influence People (nonfiction) 1936

Five Minute Biographies (sketches) 1937

Biographical Roundup (sketches) 1945

How to Stop Worrying and Start Living (nonfiction) 1948

CRITICISM

Allan Nevins (essay date 1932)

[*Nevins was an American historian and educator who published numerous studies of the Civil War era. In the following review, he characterizes Carnegie's* Lincoln the Unknown *as a sentimental portrait.*]

Frankly admitting that until several years ago he had known little about Lincoln, Mr. Carnegie tells us that his book [*Lincoln the Unknown*] rests upon intensive study since then and upon a feeling for the subject so profound that he wrote most of the chapters where Lincoln had lived and moved. The sight in London of a chance article by T. P. O'Connor on Ann Rutledge first stirred his curiosity. After three years work in Europe and New York he threw away his manuscript. Going to Illinois, he lived among the people whose fathers had known Lincoln intimately, labored for months among newspapers and court

records, and spent a summer in Petersburg, a mile from Lincoln's New Salem. Under the same white oaks which Lincoln knew he set up his typewriter, and half the book was composed there, with the winding Sangamon flowing beside him and the hayfields musical with meadow-larks and bob-whites. When he came to write of Ann Rutledge, he drove with a typewriter and folding table "through a hog-lot and a cow pasture until I reached the quiet, secluded spot where Ann Rutledge lies buried, and there, where Lincoln came to weep, was set down the story of his grief." Other chapters were written in the sitting room of the Lincoln house in Springfield—some at the desk where he composed his first inaugural address. These are curious literary methods.

It will at least be seen that Mr. Carnegie has brought genuine feeling to his story of Lincoln, and this feeling shows in all his pages. The book is short. It is unpretentious, making no claim to new information or to any new interpretations of importance. The title is infelicitous, for at this time there can be no Lincoln the unknown. Indeed, in various essential features Mr. Carnegie draws his Lincoln after the portrait made so many years ago by W. H. Herndon, and so largely confirmed by the exhaustive researches of Albert J. Beveridge. Such few merits as the volume possesses are due in large part to the warmth of the author's feeling for Lincoln, and to his instinct for graphic human detail. It also has a quick narrative flow. Despite the handicap of jerky sentences and paragraphs and the familiarity of the contents, these three qualities give the book a certain vitality and will perhaps carry the reader—particularly the ordinary reader who does not know more than Mr. Carnegie did a half dozen years ago—through to the end.

Viewed critically, the book has two great and innumerable minor defects: it over-simplifies the portrait of Lincoln, and it heavily sentimentalizes the man. The author is intent above everything else upon drawing Lincoln as a tragic figure, buffeted at every step through life and sunk in melancholy. For this purpose he treats Ann Rutledge's death as an appalling blow to Lincoln, though Mr. Beveridge pretty conclusively showed there was no real evidence for such a view. With the same object he treats Lincoln's marriage as an unrelieved tragedy, ignoring the fact that it gave him social position, assisted in his political rise, and yielded long periods of content if not happiness. To accentuate the pathos, he emphasizes Lincoln's poverty, his uncouthness, the contempt with which he was sometimes treated by others, and his "failure" in middle age. At forty-nine, we are told, "in business he has been a failure"; "in marriage he has found stark, bleak unhappiness"; "in politics and the cherished desires of his heart he has met with frustration and defeat." To describe the Lincoln of 1858 in these terms is, to say the least, something of an exaggeration. In the treatment of the White House years we might expect a sturdier tone, but again the same note is repeatedly struck. Almost nothing is said of Lincoln's ebullitions of humor, while the infinite complexity of the man is not revealed. Undoubtedly he played the game of politics joyously, assiduously, and expertly, and undoubtedly in Washington he sometimes felt the elation of mastery. His varied intellectual and moral qualities—his shrewdness, his insight, his craft, his magnanimity, his caution, his tenderness, his occasional inflexibility—cannot be drawn in a few broad and pathetic strokes.

When we say that Mr. Carnegie has an instinct for graphic human detail, we do less than justice to one of his traits. He has a bizarre taste in details. It interests him that the Springfield druggist refused to sell perfume to Mrs. Lincoln on credit; that the boarding house where Lincoln lived as a Congressman in Washington had no plumbing and a goose-pen in the back yard; that garden-seeds sprouted on the dusty bookcases in Lincoln's law offices; that when Willie died in the White House Lincoln had the body twice exhumed for a farewell look; that John Wilkes Booth when shot carried the pictures of five sweethearts; that when Lincoln's coffin was opened in 1901 there was a spot of mould on his tie. In a book of three hundred pages, he gives forty to the pursuit of Booth and to the various efforts to carry off Lincoln's body. When he comes to describe Lincoln's Secretary of War, it is in these terms, all too characteristic of the style of the volume:

> Short, heavy-set, with the build of a bull, Stanton had something of that animal's fierceness and ferocity.
>
> All his life he had been rash and erratic. His father, a physician, hung a human skeleton in the barn where the boy played, hoping that he too would become a doctor. The young Stanton lectured to his playmates about the skeleton, Moses, hell-fire, and the flood; and then went off to Columbus, Ohio, and became a clerk in a drug store. He boarded in a private family, and one morning shortly after he left the house, the daughter of the family fell ill with cholera, and was dead and in her grave when Stanton came home for supper that night.
>
> He refused to believe it.
>
> Fearing that she had been buried alive, he hurried to the cemetery, found a spade, and worked furiously for hours, digging up her body.
>
> Years later, driven to despair by the death of his own daughter, Lucy, he had her body exhumed after she had been buried thirteen months, and kept her corpse in his bedroom more than a year.
>
> When Mrs. Stanton died, he put her nightcap and nightgown beside him in bed each night, and wept over them.
>
> He was a strange man.

It might be thought that, with so much that is really excellent upon Lincoln in print, we had reached a point where a new book upon him really had to present a fairly good excuse for being. But the "literature of the subject" will no doubt continue to be enriched year after year, with just such volumes as this.

Allan Nevins, "A Portrait of Lincoln," in The Saturday Review of Literature, *Vol. VIII, No. 30, February 13, 1932, p. 522.*

Carmel O'Neill Haley   (essay date 1932)

[*In the following review, Haley offers a flattering consideration of* Lincoln the Unknown.]

If Dale Carnegie's avowed purpose in **Lincoln the Unknown** was to lift the mists which six thousand volumes on him and the lapse of sixty-five years have generated, he certainly has succeeded—and he has given us a corking good story into the bargain. There is not one uninteresting page in the three hundred odd which tell the tale.

One ugly word, the name of the sin Lucy Hanks committed, might well have been deleted. Abraham Lincoln's mother was the result of her second slip from virtue. His grandfather was a gentleman who employed Lucy Hanks as domestic. He might have married her but for social considerations. She married later on and had eight children, thus retrieving her social position, poverty-stricken though she remained.

Headgear played an important rôle in the biography, although it is no *Sartor Resartus*. A squirrel-skin cap covered the touseled head of young Abe while he attended school off and on until fifteen; at that age the man whose classic letter of condolence to Mrs. Bixby now hangs on the walls of Oxford University, had learned to read but he could not write. Under his hat, Lincoln, as postmaster of Salem village, carried the mail. From it like a conjurer he drew letters instead of rabbits. Into his hat he thrust the scraps of paper on which he jotted down some of the famous sentences he hurled at Stephen A. Douglas, his dressy political opponent. Carried about in his top hat, on a sheet of rough blue foolscap paper, was scribbled the priceless Gettysburg address. Abe fished it out now and then to give it "another lick." On the top of his silk hat the gruff, tempestuous Secretary of War, Stanton, dashed off his orders as he sat by the side of his fallen chief.

Out of this unusual biography comes the speech of Stanton, overheard by Lincoln: "I will not associate with such a damned, gawky, long-armed ape as that. If I can't have a man who is a gentleman in appearance with me in the case, I will abandon it." But Lincoln forgave this insult, as he overlooked the insults of McClellan.

Out of this tale emerges clear and distinct the rugged, homespun Lincoln, full of puns and pathos and deepest melancholy—a Lincoln patiently pursuing his education through the books which fell his way, rereading and memorizing whole passages of Shakespeare, Blackstone's *Commentaries on Law,* Parson Weems's *Life of George Washington.* The last cost him three days' hard labor for the neighbor from whom he borrowed it (the book got soaked through the chinks of his log cabin). He shouted Cicero and Demosthenes to the echoing woods and to such rude companions as he had about him.

There was also a tender side to his studies; he could recite Poe's "Annabel Lee" and "Oh why should the spirit of mortal be proud?" His early dead love, Anne Rutledge, doubtless was identified in his mind with the lost Annabel Lee.

She who became Mrs. Lincoln gets rather a rough deal, apparently well deserved. The author calls her a "mean, common, envious, affected, mannerless virago," and he isn't quoting, either. It must be confessed that for an ambitious woman to marry a man who had once left her flat, all bedecked in her wedding finery—but also a man in whom she recognized presidential timber—and to have him sprawl on the hall floor with an overturned chair for a head rest, to press his tie and lay out his clothes for the famous debate with her erstwhile admirer, Stephen Douglas, and to have him turn up on the platform one gallus hitching up his trousers over his collarless shirt, would try even a less high-spirited woman than Mary Todd. Lincoln with saintly patience bore with her fits of temper and called her "Mother." But did not this modern Xantippe by her restless ambition help to develop the giant whom all nations revere?

The author was born on a farm in Missouri and understands the man of the hoe and the chopping-block, and as he is also an instructor in public speaking he brings forth that which is arresting. Lincoln and his associates, both in the written words of the book and in its underlying moods, stand forth with the clarity of a starry night. (pp. 22-3)

> Carmel O'Neill Haley, "Father Abraham," in The Commonweal, Vol. XVI, No. 1, May 4, 1932, pp. 22-3.

James Thurber   (essay date 1937)

[*James Thurber was a celebrated American humorist best-known for his essays, stories, and cartoons published in the* New Yorker *magazine during the 1930s and 1940s. In the following review, he probes the literary and philosophical merits of Carnegie's* How to Win Friends and Influence People.]

Dale Carnegie, according to his friend and pupil, Mr. Lowell Thomas, who wrote the preface to [*How to Win Friends and Influence People*] was born on a Missouri farm forty-six years ago. He went to State Teachers' College, riding horseback the three miles from the farm. At home he did the heavy chores, studied by a coal-oil lamp till midnight, got up at three to feed his father's pedigreed pigs. He was mainly interested in logic, argumentation, and debate. He got so he won, finally, "every speaking contest in college." After some years as a crack salesman of correspondence courses, and of bacon, soap, and lard, he studied at the American Academy of Arts in New York and "toured the country playing the role of Dr. Hartley in *Polly of the Circus.*" He went from that into selling trucks and then he began to teach public speaking in the Y.M.C.A. schools of New York. "Today," says Mr. Thomas, "far more adults come to Dale Carnegie for training in public speaking than go to all the extension courses in public speaking conducted by all the twenty-two colleges and universities located in New York City." Mr. Thomas says that Carnegie has criticized 150,000 speeches, or "one for almost every day that has passed since Columbus discovered America." During the past twenty-five years Mr. Carnegie has trained more than 15,000 business and professional men, including employees and executives of the Westinghouse Company, the

Brooklyn Union Gas Company, and the New York Telephone Company.

"In preparation for this book," writes Mr. Carnegie, "I read everything that I could find on the subject—everything from Dorothy Dix, the divorce-court records, and *The Parents' Magazine,* to Professor Overstreet, Alfred Adler, and William James. . . . I hired a trained research man to spend one and a half years in various libraries reading everything I had missed . . . erudite tomes on psychology, hundreds of magazine articles . . . countless biographies. . . . I personally interviewed scores of successful people . . . Marconi, Franklin D. Roosevelt, Owen D. Young, Clark Gable, Mary Pickford. . . ."

In this book you will find the secret of Jim Farley's success, the turning point in Hall Caine's life, why Andrew Carnegie paid Charles Schwab a million dollars a year, and Adela Rogers St. John's analysis of the Mdivani charm for women. At the end there is a list of nine books on sex life and marriage and ten rules for wives and ten for husbands. Everywhere there are things like this: "The next time we are tempted to give somebody 'hail Columbia' let's pull a five-dollar bill out of our pocket, look at Lincoln's picture on the bill, and ask, 'How would Lincoln handle this problem if he had it?' " And this: "Flattery is from the teeth out. Sincere appreciation is from the heart out. No! No! No! I am not suggesting flattery! Far from it. I'm talking about a new way of life. Let me repeat: *I'm talking about a new way of life.*" That new way of life is incorporated in a set of rules, of which these are a few: "Smile," "Remember that a man's name to him is the sweetest and most important sound in the English language," "Make the other person feel important and do it sincerely," "Never tell a man he is wrong," "Get the other person saying 'yes, yes' immediately." One chapter is entitled "How to Make People Like You Instantly," another "A Quick Way to Make Everybody Happy." I think that gives you the idea.

Mr. Carnegie prints proudly this case history of one of his pupils, "a sophisticated, worldly-wise stockbroker."

> I have been married for over eighteen years and in all that time I have seldom, until last week, smiled at my wife or spoken two dozen words to her from the time I got up until I was ready to leave for business. . . . Since you asked me to make a talk about my experience with smiles, I thought I would try it for a week. So the next morning . . . I looked at my glum mug in the mirror and said to myself, "Bill, you are going to wipe the scowl off that sour puss of yours today." . . . I greeted my wife with a "Good morning, my dear," and smiled as I said it. You warned me that she might be surprised. Well, you underestimated her reaction. She was bewildered. She was shocked.

I think that also gives you the idea.

Mr. Carnegie loudly protests that one can be sincere and at the same time versed in the tricks of influencing people. Unfortunately, the disingenuities in his set of rules and in his case histories stand out like ghosts at a banquet. Mr. Carnegie, I gather, is a bit touchy on this point. He relates that, in addressing an audience one night, he told them of how he had once, out of sheer kindliness, said to a postoffice clerk, "I certainly wish I had your head of hair." One of Mr. Carnegie's listeners, who had apparently come to learn about how to influence people, how to get what you're after, asked, naturally enough, it seems to me, "What did you want to get out of him?" Writes Mr. Carnegie: "What was I trying to get out of him!!! Great God Almighty!!!" Steady on, Mr. Carnegie. Remember "Smile," and some of your other rules, and also one of mine: exclamation points, even three in a row, do not successfully convey depth of sincerity or intensity of feeling.

> *James Thurber, "The Voice with the Smile,"*
> *in* The Saturday Review of Literature, *Vol.*
> *XV, No. 14, January 30, 1937, p. 6.*

Carnegie on making friends:

If we want to make friends, let's put ourselves out to do things for other people—things that require time, energy, unselfishness, and thoughtfulness. . . .

For years I have made it a point to find out the birthdays of my friends. How? Although I haven't the foggiest bit of faith in astrology, I begin by asking the other party whether he believes the date of one's birth has anything to do with character and disposition. I then ask him to tell me the month and day of his birth. If he says November 24, for example, I keep repeating to myself, "November 24, November 24." The minute his back is turned, I write down his name and birthday and later transfer it to a birthday book. At the beginning of each year, I have these birthday dates scheduled in my calendar pad, so they come to my attention automatically. When the natal day arrives, there is my letter or telegram. What a hit it makes! I am frequently the only person on earth who remembers.

> *Dale Carnegie, in his* How to Win Friends and Influence
> People, *1936.*

Thomas Lask   (essay date 1948)

[*In the following review of* How to Stop Worrying and Start Living, *Lask characterizes Carnegie's book as a collection of anecdotal platitudes.*]

Mr. Carnegie's latest blueprint for a social Garden of Eden [*How to Stop Worrying and Start Living*] is so choked with formula, exhortation and case history that no reader will go entirely unrewarded. And with the world spinning to a fare-thee-well, there's no hurt in hearing Mr. Carnegie say again that worry wastes energy, fritters away lives and leads to physical ills. He urges you to unwind, relax, take the long view, pray and learn from others. Especially the latter. In fact he offers so many success stories that after a while his book reads like a revival meeting wherein every one present trots down to the pulpit and tells how he was saved. It was not only the weight of the evidence but the changeless bill that got us down. Just for seasoning, it would have been nice to read about a man, say, who worried twenty years, used so-and-so's formula, which didn't help him a nickel's worth and who just went on worrying.

Our author is not afraid to apply his propositions to specific areas of human conduct as a slight listing of his chapter heads will show: "How to Keep From Worrying About Insomnia," "How the Housewife Can Avoid Fatigue," "How to Lessen Your Financial Worries," and "How to Add an Hour to Your Waking Day." Or to call on William James, the latest book on psychosomatic medicine, memories of his boyhood on a Missouri farm or what Jeanette MacDonald does when she is depressed and worried. If you are interested, Miss MacDonald reads the Twenty-third Psalm.) And to show that both the problems and the solutions are as old as man, he has culled a Bartlett-full quota of sayings, from Marcus Aurelius to Babe Ruth, which acts as plaster of paris to bind the whole thing together. In the hour of quotation Dale Carnegie will not fail you. Indeed, you don't even have to worry about his book. If, he says frankly, after you have read to Page 44 you find that matters are not working out as they should—just throw the book into the ash can.

> *Thomas Lask, in a review of "How to Stop*
> *Worrying and Start Living," in* The New York
> Times Book Review, *June 20, 1948, p. 14.*

Donald Meyer   (essay date 1965)

[*Meyer is an American historian and educator. In the following excerpt, he examines the flaws in Carnegie's philosophy of success in* How to Win Friends and Influence People.]

[*How to Win Friends and Influence People*] is one of those pulse points in modern American popular culture where the murmers and racing of hidden currents can be discerned.

Of the book's influence, one can say only that it no doubt confirmed as much as it stimulated broad feelings. We do know the book was no lucky accident. Carnegie had been refining his lore through the twenties, in instructions to businessmen about practical, effective human relations, and his manual *Public Speaking and Influencing Men in Business* had been itself a success among a specialized audience. In any case, whether leading or following popular sentiments, Carnegie performed the task of scripturizing them. Thereby they came to constitute a "mind," with its own inherent logic—and problems.

In his advice to young men [in *The Outlook for the Average Man*], Albert Shaw had been hazy about the characterological style the average young man should nourish—or affect. The closest he came to enjoining any particular trait was in his recommendation of "cooperation." In the old ethic, the value of "cooperation" had been ambiguous. Naturally, Alger-style heroes had had sufficient interpersonal competence to impress rich benefactors, and certainly in the Protestant praise of "trade" from the time of Daniel Defoe, a psyche able, even willing, to please, stood posited. Yet "cooperation" hardly could count as more than an ornament, as the subtle dialectic of a master competitor and aggressor, such as Franklin, who never disguised the fact that the cooperation he commended was manipulation. Cooperation in the old ethic, in short, attested the strength of the old character structure to accommodate a deal of duplicity, insincerity, hypocrisy.

It was Dale Carnegie's business to transform the ornament into the keystone, to bring the occasion of insincerity into the heart—and make it sincere.

His favorite hero was a man of the transition, Charles Schwab, rising in the age of creation, arriving in the age of administration. Schwab, as was reiterated time out of mind on the luncheon circuits, was a man who knew how to handle men. He was an expert in human relations. He knew how to get men to want to do what he wanted them to do. Schwab's enormous ideological reputation was symptomatic. He had not, after all, been the "original" hero of his own tale. That had been Andrew Carnegie, who had picked Schwab to run his, Carnegie's, creations. Schwab was the most famous early success in a new sort of job—executive management. Neither building steel companies in ambitious passion nor juggling them in financial empires, he was their immanent genius, the first hero-bureaucrat. Over the long run it would be seen that bureaucrats need not, and should not, be heroes, except to themselves. But Schwab's reputation facilitated the new role-identification.

A man chosen by another man: one could take this as the crux of the new gospels of success. In Horatio Alger's tales young lads were chosen by older men upon their display of courage, pluck or industry, though of course it is well to note how much luck had to do with these decisive choices: what if the girl one rescued was not a merchant's daughter? Still, these displays presumably revealed total character: one was chosen for what one really was. Schwab's secret, according to Dale Carnegie, was a prodigiously winning smile—a smile "worth a million dollars." Was this the revelation of Schwab as a man? Interestingly, the favorite anecdotes about Schwab portrayed his capacity for charming workers in the mill rather than in more usual executive scenes. If the smile revealed character, evidently there were some power-interests at stake as well. Smiles might defeat unions. Anyway, had Andrew Carnegie chosen Schwab because he, Carnegie, had found Schwab's smile irresistible? It seemed unlikely; but perhaps Carnegie knew workers found it so. Schwab's symbolic status was not due to the specter of labor problems, however. It was due to the need . . . for believing in personal significance among the successful.

Dale Carnegie's book was full of salesmen, many identified by name. It was suggestive that none had real stature as culture heroes. . . . Nevertheless, though incapable of producing culture heroes, salesmanship had become a critical phase of the economy. Salesmen sold things to people. Frank Haddock's warning [in his *The Power of Will*] not to sell people things they did not really want evinced an old spirit about to be engulfed in a new dilemma. Could the economy safely rely upon "natural" demands alone? As long as 130 years before, Joel Barlow, the Jeffersonian advocate of unJeffersonian economic expansion, had urged the deliberate cultivation of "artificial" wants as necessary stimulus to progress and prosperity. But, heir of

the fabled Yankee trader, the modern salesman might still find himself, among people still inhibited by ascetic thrift and frugality, regarded as the Yankee had been, a man who could make you buy despite yourself, who could get inside you somehow, manipulate you, get the "better" of you by seducing the worst in you. In this ultimate salesmanship between retailer and consumer there assuredly lurked a nest of questions about sincerity, curling and uncurling about each other. But this was not the salesmanship discussed by Carnegie at all.

One section of his book—Part Five, "Letters That Produced Miraculous Results"—defined his focus. The two letters Carnegie discussed were both written by a man named Ken R. Dyke, sales-promotion manager of the Johns-Manville Company. What were the miraculous results? Dyke's letters went out, not to customers, but to dealers in Johns-Manville products, asking them simply to tell him whether the sales campaign being carried on by the company was doing any good. Miraculously, 42.5 per cent of the dealers actually did reply to tell him. The ordinary return on such requests ran, apparently, from 5 to 8 per cent. The second letter went to architects, inquiring whether the company's catalogue was any good. Dyke got back a little less than 50 per cent returns, as against ordinary returns of 2 to 5 per cent.

What Dyke's letters overcame—temporarily, of course— was a kind of organizational noise, or friction, or better still, automatism. With the establishment of national bureaucratic organizations, naturally the problem of communications became immense. Dyke himself had no product to sell, no sales resistance to overcome. He was trying to help dealers and architects to sell. But ordinarily not even self-interest overcame the routine and security of the system. Letters by the thousands vanished into the void, moths beating for attention against the screens of standard operating procedure. Relationships had become distant, mechanical, abstract.

The job of the manager was to repersonalize, rehumanize, reanimate this world of increasing rote. This was Dyke's talent. Of course, the point at which the salesman had to do this most specifically was the point of contact with the ultimate consumer, by linking commodities with symbols—of status, of success, of character, of power, of belonging, of mortality, of patriotism, of potency. But the salesmanship taught by Carnegie was salesmanship within the system itself, the salesmanship of the system selling itself to itself. And in this regard, the book was witness to the collapse of older theories of economic behavior, theories assuming that economic self-interest is rational and decides. Why did more than half the dealers fail to respond even to Ken R. Dyke's seductive appeal to their self-interest?

What did decide? Feelings, and more precisely, a certain feeling. The deepest urge in human nature is the "desire to be important," Carnegie said, and this explained the success of Charles Schwab and Ken R. Dyke. They made men feel important. (Though he might as well have credited any number of sages over the centuries, Carnegie attributed this insight to John Dewey.) What in Frank Haddock had been only a peripheral intimation now became the center: organization is people and people want to feel they count. One plain implication of Carnegie's book was that the system had not been making people feel they did count. Something was needed. Carnegie's prescription was simple. Smile. Be like Charles Schwab.

It hardly took modern psychology to explain the cogency of smiles in improving human relations, or of some of Carnegie's other recommendations: extend "lavish praise"; offer "hearty approbation"; talk about what people are interested in; let them think new ideas are their ideas; be interested in them. All this helps them feel important. This in turn, in some way, helps you.

But just how does it help you?

Carnegie's rules were clear and commonsensical with respect to the object, the man smiled at, the man whose name is remembered, the man allowed to imagine the idea is his. What was not so clear was the position of the subject, the man who smiles.

Why does a person smile? Because, perhaps, he is happy. Perhaps he already feels important and therefore can smile. But Carnegie was not writing his book for people who already were smiling. He wrote it for people who evidently were not smiling and needed to be told to do so. What reasons would they have? As in the psychological sequence pointed out by William James, that wondrous technique of acting "as if" . . . it was possible to smile in order to feel happy. The idea attracted Carnegie as well, who . . . quoted James frequently. But this was not Carnegie's main lesson. By that logic a person could make himself feel important and have an end with it. Carnegie's emphasis fell upon people's need to be smiled at by other people.

A man might smile at other people because he was glad to see them, was interested in them, did find them important. Here was Carnegie's chance to propose the soft liberal Protestant answer to all problems of human relations. Really love other people. Everyone is sacred. The richest field of experience is the community of others, of brotherhood, teamwork, the group. Really be a member of the family of man. But this was not Carnegie's strategy. Far from displaying any hint of the liberal faith that in their deepest selves people *are* loving, Carnegie worked instead from a harsh principle. "People are not interested in you. They are not interested in me. They are interested in themselves—morning, noon, and after dinner."

A Hobbesian view that people are universally self-centered and selfish logically implied the Hobbesian predicament, the war of all against all. Quite consistently with his original premise, Hobbes escaped it by invoking the action of rational self-interest which would lead people to see that in self-protection they must accept authority and order. Rejecting the evangelical liberal Protestant effort to break the premise by winning people from selfishness to love, and the humanist liberal denial of the premise, Carnegie's answer was to substitute smiles for Hobbes's political authority. This, too, was consistent, presumably. To feel important, one must be smiled at. Therefore one smiles in order to elicit smiles.

But instantly, this raised a problem Hobbes had not had to face. "No! No! No! I am not suggesting flattery," Carnegie admonished. "An insincere grin? No. That doesn't fool anybody. We know it is mechanical and we resent it. I am talking about a real smile, a heart-warming smile, a smile that comes from within. . . ." "Make the other person feel important—and do it sincerely."

Hobbesians had a perfectly rational basis for sincerely committing their safety to the autocrat. Unfortunately, one thing missing in *How to Win Friends and Influence People* was instruction in how sincerely to like people, sincerely to be interested in them, and sincerely to find them important.

Naturally, Carnegie could not help vitiating his exhortations to sincerity a bit. What was a "real" smile? One that was "heart-warming," yes—though that did not prove it came from a warm heart; one that "came from within," yes—though "within" was not necessarily always sincere; but then also, in a transition to which Carnegie himself was obviously insensible: "the kind of smile that will bring a good price in the market place." There was nothing subtle about the trouble here. Heart-warming smiles worth good prices which nevertheless did not come from warm hearts were easily imaginable. Such were learned routinely by professional actors, for instance, for whom, according to some schools of dramatic science (though denied by others), to have to feel the emotion one believably projects is an interference. Carnegie's real—though hidden, since he could not face the issue—point was not that the smiles of non-professionals would be so crude as not to work, for there were many talented amateurs. It was rather that the man who used smiles must believe in his smiles in order to believe in the smiles directed at him. His sincere smile was his allegiance to the system of smiles.

In Carnegie's world, people did not seek importance by seeking some power. They did not seek importance by doing something important. They did not seek importance by giving themselves to some important process. Where sincerity became an issue was where people lacked these sorts of importance. Sincerity was a problem for the weak. In accord with Carnegie's Hobbesian assumptions, the purpose of the smile was to disarm others, to remove from them their reality as power, and this could be done only if one believed in one's own smiles, only if one believed that one really did like the other, that is, that the other was truly smiling, likable, and therefore as innocent as oneself. What one achieved by smiling was not power but the neutralization of power, so long as one smiled sincerely.

In the long run this was a self-consuming logic. It was not the potential hypocrisy and cynicism that vitiated the method. It was rather that trying to solve the problem of sincerity by self-manipulation involved one in an infinite regression, an endless effort to disarm oneself as well as others. The idea that liking people would serve the purpose of influencing people ran onto the reef that the purpose for having influence was disintegrated. What happened when likable people met? They could only seek to resemble each other, concealing their ulterior purpose of exerting influence not only from each other but from themselves. Of such a situation it would not be enough to say that character had become "personality" . . .—a mask, a pose—because the fact that the mask was a mask was forgotten. The one purpose that seemed to remain clear was, of course, to make money. But money, an impersonal symbol, now symbolized precisely the impersonality of personality, that is, the dependent reflection in everyone of everyone else. Implicitly, Carnegie here did have the medium which buoyed up his logic. Money, he clearly assumed, did not have to be in short supply; smiles could earn it, and everyone could smile—even more easily than everyone could have right thoughts. The indefinite regression of smiling disarmament could proceed so long as the money lasted.

Still, likability was victimized, not just by the suspicion that there were those playing the game insincerely, but by the stress of being likable. To be a mirror in which others might find themselves important, to commit oneself sincerely to what one appeared to be, to consist primarily of behavior, talk and smiles that others liked was to become still more vulnerable, exposed still more to what lay outside, when it was precisely to disarm outside power that one smiled. It was to engage in the disintegration of one's own awareness of reality, one's own ego-consciousness, one's own integration as a self.

Carnegie on making a speech:

You have been invited to make a speech, and have come to me with perplexing questions. I'll try to answer them.

"What shall I talk about?" Talk about what interests you—from pouter pigeons to Julius Caesar; speak with enthusiasm and you are sure to interest your audience. I have seen that happen thousands of times. I know a man who could hold you and 5000 other people spellbound by talking about his hobby of collecting Oriental rugs. You may know more about catfish or cyclones or cleaning fluids than anyone else in the audience. If so, that may be a good topic for you. Don't try to get a topic out of the newspapers or the encyclopedia or a book of speeches. Dig your topic—or, if your subject is assigned, your approach—out of your own head and heart.

"How shall I deliver my talk?" Speak sincerely, from the heart. You may make blunders, but you can hardly fail to make an impression. The most difficult problem I face in training men is to blast them out of their shells and inspire them to speak with genuine earnestness. That is probably the most important rule in delivery. Your audience must feel that you know what you are talking about, that you mean it and have an intense desire to tell about it.

"How long shall I talk?" Stop when people are eager to have you go on. Stop before they want you to. Lincoln made the most famous speech in the world at Gettysburg; and he did it with ten sentences and spoke less than five minutes. Unless you are very much better than you think you are, and unless your subject is extremely important, you had better not take more than twice as much time as Lincoln took.

Dale Carnegie in The Rotarian, *1936.*

As for winning friends, one of the peculiarities of the famous book was that it had practically nothing to say of friendship.

It may be wondered whether Carnegie's book was primarily about gaining success after all. To be sure, for men of an older, work-oriented, tool-oriented temper, it could come as a revelation to be told that smiles were helpful. If such men could learn the lesson, they might well smile their way higher up some one or another ladder than their technical competence might have carried them. But Carnegie never realistically asked just where and to what extent in the business world smiles did count. Were there no gruff or impersonal or strictly analytical or even sour-tempered successes left? There were, and it was not at all clear that some of them were not still the men of real power. The business of smiling did correspond to a shift in the nature of the business world, but it was also very much a betrayal of uncertainty and sometimes schism in the sense men had of themselves and their worth. Perhaps men still sure of themselves, men who already felt important, were the ones who, even in the personalized bureaucracy, smiled most influentially because they smiled only when they really did mean it. (pp. 180-88)

> *Donald Meyer, "Spiritual Automation, New Style," in his* The Positive Thinkers: Religion as Pop Psychology from Mary Baker Eddy to Oral Roberts, *second edition, Pantheon Books, 1980, pp. 177-94.*

Giles Kemp and Edward Claflin   (essay date 1989)

[*Kemp, an American businessman, and Claflin, a contemporary American writer, are both graduates of the Dale Carnegie Course in Public Speaking and Human Relations. In this excerpt from their biography of Carnegie, they suggest that Carnegie's classes provided his most effective forum for the expression of his ideas and explain his major principles for success in both personal and professional relationships.*]

Dale Carnegie may have been his own worst enemy. Famed for his courses on public speaking, his own speaking style was rambling, his accent a midwestern twang. When he was the number one best-selling author in America, he gave interviews in which he expressed astonishment at his fame and insisted that he had nothing profound to say to people.

Although his courses inspired some of the foremost political leaders, broadcast journalists, and inspirational speakers of his time, he staunchly insisted that his methods were only common sense and that his teachings were for the common man.

Dale Carnegie was also a man misunderstood by many who saw only his public image and had no direct experience with his teachings.

Although he advocated spontaneity and sincerity, many saw him as the proponent of methods that were cynical, conniving, and manipulative.

One of the great teachers of all time—whose teaching techniques have spread across the globe and whose message touched millions of lives—he was, at best, shrugged off by academics and, at the worst, heartily scorned.

A man who dedicated his life to giving hope to everyday working people, he was often derided by intellectuals as a pandering preacher of blind acceptance.

A writer who dealt frankly and openly with agnosticism, emptiness, psychosomatic illness, and suicide, he was branded a starry-eyed optimist.

Although his course had been in existence for twenty-four years when his first popular book was published, *How to Win Friends and Influence People* was the key to Dale Carnegie's fame. First published in 1936 by Simon & Schuster, it became an overnight success. It went on to sell more than 15 million copies.

To someone who has never encountered Dale Carnegie's prose before, it seems a curious book to be a best-seller. Its language, message, and examples are rooted in the vernacular of the nineteen twenties and thirties. Anyone looking at the four sections of the book will see that, yes, this is a book on how to manipulate people. These sections are "Fundamental Techniques in Handling People," "Six Ways to Make People Like You," "How to Win People to Your Way of Thinking," and "Be a Leader: How to Change People Without Giving Offense or Arousing Resentment." Chapter titles reveal the homespun nature of the Dale Carnegie philosophy, with phrases such as "If You Want to Gather Honey, Don't Kick Over the Beehive," "If You're Wrong, Admit It," and "No One Likes to Take Orders."

Are these the keys to the Dale Carnegie kingdom?

And, if so, what was all the excitement about?

More to the point, are such common-sense aphorisms still relevant today?

The answers are certainly not to be found in the writing. The text is appealing enough, the stories have a certain quaint charm, and the quotations are apt. The principles that serve as action steps are about what you would expect to find in most self-help psychology books today. But Dale Carnegie's prose certainly isn't brilliant. He repeats himself. He contradicts himself.

Nor was it the man, apart from the book, who made the sales figures soar. This was no Bill Cosby or Lee Iacocca. He was never on a par with the most popular communicators of his time, men like Lowell Thomas and Edward R. Murrow. In his radio appearances no charisma came through—because it wasn't there. He seemed like a good guy, sincere enough, a little schoolmarmish at times, though harmless and well-meaning for all that.

If it was not the book who made the man, and not the man who made the book, then what *was* going on?

We wondered.

And then we began to look at the course.

The Dale Carnegie Course in Public Speaking and Human Relations was begun in 1912 by Carnegie (his last name was then spelled Carnagey) in a YMCA night school on 125th Street in New York's Harlem. With only a few interruptions (World War I, a bout of novel writing that took him to Europe, and a venture with Lowell Thomas), Carnegie continually taught, refined, and promoted the course up until his death in 1955.

More than three million men and women have graduated from the fourteen-week, fourteen-session program. In 1988 there were over 165,000 graduates of the Dale Carnegie Course in the United States alone, and the course is conducted in more than sixty other countries around the world.

The list of esteemed graduates is long. Many of those graduates say that the course changed their lives. Among the recent notables are Lee Iacocca ("To this day, I'm a great believer in the Dale Carnegie Institute. . . . I've sent dozens of introverted guys to Dale Carnegie at the company's expense."); Linda Gray (of "Dallas" fame); Tom Monaghan (founder of Domino's Pizza); John Emery (of Emery Air Freight); and Stew Leonard (who owns the largest dairy store in the world). The list of entrepreneurs, executives, politicians, and performers is extensive. Perhaps even more significant, the course, in the nineteen eighties, has experienced a surge of popularity. Many of tomorrow's speakers, politicians, sales professionals, and business leaders are taking the course today.

As students of the Dale Carnegie phenomenon, the authors became interested in the course both for what it is—which is a unique group experience—and for what it says about Dale Carnegie.

In Dale Carnegie, we finally concluded, we have the unique situation of a man who best expressed himself *through a course that was a living experience.* But the course was also an invention that the inventor could not escape. Throughout his life, there were times when Carnegie attempted to leave his invention behind and go on to other accomplishments. After each hiatus, however, Carnegie returned to the course—partly out of necessity (he could always make a living teaching "Dale Carnegie" classes) and partly because it was, simply, what he did best. So it became the repository of all the aspirations that he had in other areas—as an orator, a salesman, an actor, a novelist, a theatrical producer, and a businessman.

Dale Carnegie made the course his lifework. In it he concentrated his life experiences. The course was his laboratory with people. Because it was his own creation, he could alter the format. He worked out ways to increase positive reinforcement. He created new environments where people would experiment, reach out, and take risks. His participants were the congregation for the country preacher in him, the restless masses responding to a missionary message. The nation's readers made an author of him; the listeners made a philosopher of him.

Through the years, he experimented, explored new techniques, and added different experiences. He was a perfectionist who never stopped trying to improve the course. He threw away what did not work, while holding on to those elements that continued to inspire. The course was not only his creation but his best means of expression. Everything that he wanted to say to people was relayed in the form of a fourteen-week experience. The course was more powerful than any of his speeches, more lasting than any of his books, more meaningful than the total sum of words he borrowed from worldly pundits and philosophers. (pp. 1-5)

To Carnegie, there were essentially three levels of leadership. The first, and easiest, was getting people to like you. The concept sounds basic, but many people are never taught how to do it.

Take, for instance, Peter Albrecht, a recent graduate of a prestigious business school. Smart, hard-working, and capable, he could not understand why he was being ignored by his colleagues at a large advertising agency. He had heard about the MBA syndrome, where graduate students newly minted as Masters of Business Administration had trouble fitting into organizations, but he hadn't imagined it happening to him. Albrecht had enrolled in the Carnegie course to sharpen his presentation skills. When it came time to make a commitment to become a friendlier person, he chose to apply the principles at the office.

His strategy was simple. He would try to be friendlier in the morning. Instead of rushing in at 8:30 and heading straight for his office to enjoy a cup of coffee and review his mail, he would make a point of smiling at people, greeting them by name and spending a little time chatting. This was the only conscious change he tried to make in his behavior. But after three weeks, he felt he was starting to fit in more. Don, from down the hall, had pointed out to him a project deadline that he had been unaware of. Albrecht would have looked bad if he hadn't met it. Tom, another account executive, asked him to join in a new client presentation that had exciting potential.

Albrecht found himself looking forward to coming to the office. "Maybe these things would have happened anyway," he told the class when he reported on his commitment. "But I don't think so. So, if you want to have a better time at work, use people's names. And smile."

Nancy Arbor is another class member who found that working at being a friendlier person made a difference in the way she felt about her job. The credit manager in a large publishing company, she had been in her job for over five years. She was good at it and thought she enjoyed it, but was frustrated that most of her contact with people was over the phone. There was significant turnover in her company, so she decided to take it upon herself to introduce herself to every newly hired person on her floor. The day someone started, she would stop in for ten or fifteen minutes, get acquainted, and answer questions about the company.

The results? She felt good doing it because people seemed so appreciative that she had made the effort. She also felt that it was nicer to be able to walk down the halls and know who everybody was. Plus, one of the new employees ended up a lastminute replacement for a share in the summer house Nancy rented with four other women.

Smiling, not criticizing, using people's names, being a good listener, giving sincere appreciation are the common-sense techniques that Carnegie advocated to become a friendlier person. Once class members became exposed to the techniques, they usually find them easy and worthwhile to follow.

Establishing a friendly rapport is only the first of three leadership levels in the Carnegie method. The second level is gaining someone's cooperation.

American business seems plagued by bosses who have a very low opinion of the productivity of their secretaries and administrative assistants. Frequently, the attitude is returned. Or so you might conclude from sitting in on Dale Carnegie classes.

When class members make a commitment to gain someone's enthusiastic cooperation, they're often talking about job-related activities. A boss, for instance, resolves to get his or her secretary to do a better job by beginning in a friendly way. He might let the secretary feel that the idea is his or her own, or might throw down a challenge. For many, these resolutions signify a departure from the "when I say jump, please jump" school of management.

Class member Al Benjamin was put out with his secretary Janine. Her typing was full of errors. She rushed out at 5:00 no matter what Al still had to accomplish. She was behind in her filing. They barely spoke to each other, and Al was about to call personnel to ask for a replacement.

But he decided to try some of the Carnegie principles. He started making a point of asking Janine about her family and her hobby of designing clothes. He looked for things he could praise in her work. And one day at 4:30 when a project was dumped on his desk to be done by the next morning, he asked Janine for her suggestions as to how he could get it done.

After talking for several minutes about alternatives, Janine suddenly said, "You know, that's silly. I can get it done faster myself. I'll do it." So she stayed until 7:00 and finished it. Looking back at his experience, Al said the improvement in Janine's work pleased him and that working together had become much more pleasant. (pp. 94-7)

The third and toughest level of leadership is changing someone's attitude or behavior. Sometimes this is the same as getting a lackadaisical worker to become an enthusiastic worker. Other times it has nothing to do with enthusiasm. An effective instructor will demonstrate how to change someone's behavior through his or her teaching techniques. For although Carnegie didn't want his instructors to criticize, he did expect them to change behavior in class members.

John Stevens tells a story about an accident that happened on a summer vacation. In the first thirty seconds of his two-minute talk, he sets the scene chopping wood at a campground by Vermont's Lake Champlain. But he is not getting into the story fast enough. His instructor, Robin Peters, speaks up from the back of the room:

"John, strong topic, but now *show* us."

John begins to pantomime swinging the ax. She encourages him, "That's it—good action."

John acts out the story and holds the class's attention.

When he sits down, Robin asks, "Did you feel how much more natural and effective you were when you started acting out the story?"

Robin's coaching technique was an example of several of the techniques Carnegie advocated for changing people. She began with praise ("strong topic"). She led John to put more action into his talk. Then she closed with encouragement and praise. Some instructors call this the sandwich technique: Praise goes on both sides of constructive criticism. The technique works primarily because a skillful instructor makes the class member feel happy through recognizing that the change is an improvement.

Toward the end of the course's fourteen sessions, class members make a commitment to change someone's attitude or behavior. The choices are almost endless. A boss resolves to put an error-prone trainee at ease by talking about all the mistakes he made when he was started. A twenty-eight-year-old owner of a duplex decides to surprise her upstairs tenants by being very friendly and asking them if it wouldn't be more sensible to turn the thermostat down than to open the window. The mother of a teenage boy is going to stop nagging her son about studying. She's going to seek ways she can use positive reinforcement.

As class members report successful experiences in changing people's behavior and attitudes, they achieve a greater sense of control. They observe that it is possible to accomplish changes that previously might have seemed unattainable. They also see that the process must begin with setting a goal that has a payoff for everyone.

For instance, both the boss and the trainee will benefit if the trainee makes fewer errors. Why should the boss try to score points at the expense of the trainee or make him feel badly? Just finding fault is unlikely to improve overall performance.

Principles such as "Call attention to people's mistakes indirectly," and "Let the other person save face," sound like common sense. They appear brand new, however, to many class members. Business education is far more popular today than when Carnegie started his course. Nonetheless, very few undergraduate or MBA programs teach these mundane details of how to deal with people.

You won't find a copy of *How to Win Friends* at Harvard Business School's Baker Library, the largest business library in the country. Until recently, there wasn't even a course at Harvard that dealt with the importance of interpersonal relationships and leadership. Then, Professor John Kotter introduced a course called "Power and Influence." Not surprisingly, the course became very popular, for it recognized that doing well in leadership jobs, regardless of level or formal title, required paying attention to relationships and the process of getting cooperation.

Kotter's course and his book, also called *Power and Influence,* encourage people to think about work in terms of their relationships at work and to recognize the significance of leadership issues. But he stops short of providing nuts-and-bolts suggestions for implementing the ideas. In other words, he makes the student and reader consider the key question. How do you learn to lead?

Only recently are writers on management focusing on the nitty-gritty. Thomas J. Peters, who has achieved extraordinary popularity through books such as *In Search of Excellence, A Passion for Excellence,* and *Thriving on Chaos,* does give advice on how a manager should lead. Like Carnegie, he gives a shopping list of simple principles that anyone can use to deal with the people in the office.

Today, middle managers must typically concern themselves with their relationships with peers, with people in other departments and divisions, and with people outside the company. Many jobs require complex leadership skills. At lower levels there may be fewer people to manage, but there is also likely to be less formal authority. So the individual who has developed his or her leadership skills has increasing value to the organization.

The Carnegie course does not pay much attention to management theory. Theory X and Theory Y; MBO (Management by Objectives); ZBB (zero-based budgeting); CPM (Critical Path Method); and other techniques of management science never get mentioned. The principles of leadership used in the course have not changed since Carnegie first published them in 1936. But the recognition in corporate America that the course gets people to change the way they deal with other people is a major reason corporations pay for 75 percent of tuitions and that Carnegie course business has boomed in recent years. (pp. 98-100)

Giles Kemp and Edward Claflin, in their Dale Carnegie: The Man Who Influenced Millions, *St. Martin's Press, 1989, 214 p.*

FURTHER READING

Criticism

Conniff, Richard. "The So-So Salesman Who Told Millions How to Make It Big." *Smithsonian* 18, No. 7 (October 1987): 82-93.

>   Profiles the Dale Carnegie Course, exploring the reasons for its continuing appeal to contemporary American business leaders.

Huber, Richard M. "How to Win Friends and Influence People." In his *The American Idea of Success,* pp. 226-50. New York: McGraw-Hill Book Co., 1971.

>   Overview of Carnegie's best-selling book, including biographical anecdotes and a brief history of the evolution of American success literature.

Walter de la Mare

1873-1956

(Full name Walter John de la Mare; also wrote under the pseudonym Walter Ramal) English poet, novelist, short story writer, critic, essayist, anthologist, and playwright.

The following entry presents criticism of de la Mare's short stories. For discussion of de la Mare's complete career, see *TCLC*, Volume 4.

INTRODUCTION

De la Mare was one of the chief exemplars of the romantic imagination in modern literature. In his poetry and fiction he explored such characteristic romantic concerns as dreams, death, and the fantasy worlds of childhood. Critics often focus on de la Mare's short fiction, especially his numerous tales of supernatural horror, as his most accomplished and enduring work.

De la Mare began writing short stories and poetry while working as a bookkeeper in the London offices of the Anglo-American (Standard) Oil Company during the 1890s. His first published short story, "Kismet," appeared in the journal *Sketch* in 1895. In 1902 he published his first major work, the poetry collection *Songs of Childhood,* which was recognized as a significant example of children's literature for its creative imagery and variety of meters. Critics often assert that a childlike richness of imagination influenced everything de la Mare wrote, emphasizing his frequent depiction of childhood as a time of intuition, deep emotion, and closeness to spiritual truth. In 1908, following the publication of his novel *Henry Brocken* and the poetry collection entitled *Poems,* de la Mare was granted a Civil List pension, enabling him to terminate his corporate employment and focus exclusively on writing. He died in 1956.

As a short story writer, de la Mare is frequently compared to Henry James, particularly for his elaborate prose style and his ambiguous, often obscure treatment of supernatural themes. This latter quality is particularly apparent in de la Mare's frequently discussed short story "The Riddle," in which seven children go to live with their grandmother after the death of their father. The grandmother warns the children that they may play anywhere in the house except in an old oak chest in one of the spare bedrooms. Nevertheless, the children are drawn by ones and twos to play in the trunk, where they mysteriously disappear. While the meaning of their disappearance remains enigmatic, commentators have generally interpreted the events as a symbolic presentation of aging and death.

Criticism of de la Mare's short stories often focuses on his characters, who are invariably peculiar and frequently attributed with demonic powers. Discussing de la Mare's characters, David Cecil has explained that there is "al-

ways something odd about them. . . . The children are queer children, with their demure manners and solemn eyes and heads buzzing with fancies; the bachelors and old maids are solitary, eccentric, often a trifle crazy; the landladies and shopkeepers are 'character parts,' as full of grotesque idiosyncrasy as the personages of Dickens." Among the most memorable of these personages is the title character of "Seaton's Aunt." At the beginning of the story the narrator describes one of his schoolmates, Arthur Seaton, who lives with his aunt. The narrator accepts an invitation to visit Seaton's home, where he senses the intangible, though nonetheless threatening, power the boy's aunt has over him. Some years later Seaton invites the narrator to his aunt's house to meet his fiancée. The narrator experiences the same sense of menace that existed on his previous visit, and Seaton expresses his fear that something terrible is about to happen to him, presumably caused by his aunt. Several months afterward the narrator learns that Seaton has died under mysterious circumstances shortly before his wedding. The subtlety and artistry of this narrative are foremost among those literary qualities that account for de la Mare's high stature as an author of supernatural fiction. In addition, critics have praised de la Mare's adept rendering of uncanny subject matter using realistic narrative techniques. As Doris Ross McCrosson has observed: "De la Mare's settings are firmly anchored in reality, his characters are credible, and the situations in which they find themselves are easily possible. At least, this is so at the beginning of the tales; and, by the time de la Mare ventures into the incredible, the reader has, in Coleridge's phrase, willingly suspended disbelief."

PRINCIPAL WORKS

Songs of Childhood [as Walter Ramal] (poetry) 1902
Henry Brocken (novel) 1904
Poems (poetry) 1906
The Return (novel) 1910; revised editions 1922, 1945
The Three Mulla-Mulgars (novel) 1910; also published as *The Three Royal Monkeys*, 1935
A Child's Day (poetry) 1912
The Listeners, and Other Poems (poetry) 1912
Peacock Pie (poetry) 1913
Motley, and Other Poems (poetry) 1918
Crossings (drama) 1919
Memoirs of a Midget (novel) 1921
The Veil, and Other Poems (poetry) 1921
Down-Adown-Derry (poetry) 1922
Stuff and Nonsense and So On (poetry) 1922
The Riddle, and Other Stories (short stories) 1923
Ding Dong Bell (short stories) 1924; enlarged edition, 1936
Broomsticks, and Other Tales (short stories) 1925
The Connoisseur, and Other Stories (short stories) 1926
The Captive, and Other Poems (poetry) 1928
On the Edge (short stories) 1930
Poems for Children (poetry) 1930
The Fleeting, and Other Poems (poetry) 1933
The Lord Fish (short stories) 1933
The Wind Blows Over (short stories) 1936
This Year, Next Year (poetry) 1937
Memory, and Other Poems (poetry) 1938
Pleasures and Speculations (essays) 1940
Bells and Grass (poetry) 1941
The Burning Glass, and Other Poems (poetry) 1945
Collected Stories for Children (short stories) 1947
Winged Chariot (poetry) 1951
O Lovely England, and Other Poems (poetry) 1953
Private View (essays) 1953
Selected Poems (poetry) 1954
A Beginning, and Other Stories (short stories) 1955
Eight Tales (short stories) 1971
The Collected Poems of Walter de la Mare (poetry) 1979

CRITICISM

The Times Literary Supplement   (essay date 1926)

[*In the following review, the critic praises the imaginative qualities of the stories collected in* The Connoisseur, and Other Stories.]

Mr. de la Mare has the poet's imagination, and it is a poetic emotion that delights us in his stories. At the same time he takes kindly to the humours and liberties, even the lengths, of prose; for the nine tales contained in *The Connoisseur, and Other Stories* are longer than those of *The Riddle,* and, whatever one may think about expansion as against compression, he certainly advances with a freer movement. The magic of his vision, unaltered, takes us into enchanted air. Thence comes the transmuting thrill; and yet as we read him the intensity of the experience, like the artistry of his method, seems to reveal itself at the point where our commonplace world shades into the other—in those moments when, as the teller of his first story puts it, "the natural edges off into the unknown." In that story, **"Mr. Kempe,"** one notes the finely graded process. The landscape of an English sea-coast merges by steps in a more exotic one; the physical terror of the man clinging to the cliff-face is barbed with a sense that something is watching him which he cannot see. And then, when we have discovered the strange hermit, Mr. Kempe, and the heart of the story seems to lie in his quest of the soul—so ingeniously inwoven with that terror of the cliffs—the hypnosis of Mr. de la Mare's subject takes him a stage farther and Kempe becomes a sinister madman, yet of so rugged a character that he holds his ground.

We have left the actual; but more than one story in the book makes us wonder whether a criticism often lodged against Mr. de la Mare—that he doffs the world aside and seeks an escape from "reality" by means of incantations—is really fair. For the easy objection seems to miss the point. How can you be said to be fleeing the real, or the actual, when you are merely opening your eyes to what the simplest fragment of it, on your view, involves? Mr. de la Mare begins and ends in wonder. Objects and incidents, the face of a friend or stranger, suggest not only a possible enchantment but a question. And this, so far from being an evasion, is precisely the question of reality. Where does it rise and whence, and what hidden significance may there be in this haphazard world of things which we are mainly bent on turning into tools of use? Beauty itself is one experience which stays our hand, as it were, and marks the real. And Mr. de la Mare's answer is to let his vision project itself into the same crystal air; which, in the best of his stories, so finely blends the distinctness of precision with the apprehension of mysteries that we cannot see. His answer is the imaginative creation in itself. But what we have got from it is an intense experience, an emotion fusing one surmise after another about the uncomprehended limits of our world.

One might say, again, that the terror as well as the beauty of it is a sign of the compulsive way it comes. Mr. de la Mare excels in depicting the subtleties of fear. We might almost go further and say that he believes in fear, not merely as a means for imaginative effects, but as a sense which lifts the veil of the unknown, or at least feels that the unknown is there. **"Mr. Kempe"** had its alarms; but there is a deeper and more powerful modulation in **"All Hallows,"** which is not only the best story in the book, but perhaps the finest piece of imaginative prose that Mr. de la Mare has written. The remote cathedral, stranded by the sea-shore almost out of touch of men, is an intense and lovely vision; its haunted mystery, as imparted by the faithful, prophet-like old verger, is a strangely vital one. A series of subtle, dream-like touches conveys the menace of "our ghostly enemy," but nothing could be more banefully real. The same delicacy of touch amidst horror can be felt in **"The Wharf "**—a story of an actual dream, the spell of which disolves pleasantly among countryfolk and fields. Throughout the book, indeed, the spectral is balanced by the human. One lights with reassurance on Mr. Thripp, the humanly angelic father of a rather trying family in a humdrum setting. Yet Mr. Thripp is no mere innocent; and there are several other stories in which the queer predicament, whatever it may be, is but a foil for the workings of personality and temperament. The scrutiny of men and women here is both keener and wider.

As compared with Mr. de la Mare's last book of stories, these seem to belong more to the imagination and less to fancy. Not that the sheer invention of fancy is otherwise than lively here; the parrot's startling blend of accomplishments in **"Pretty Poll"** is a case in point, and so still more is the malign strategy in **"All Hallows."** But it has gone deeper. In the intriguing, Dostoevsky-like narrative of **"Missing"** the human depths become, indeed, a little difficult; the harried stranger who tells the tale is hard to place, and we are not sure of the real object of the story. This is partly a result of the technique. Mr. de la Mare does spend a good deal of himself on building up a tale; and a possible reason for this may be that he often seems unwilling or unable to provide an ending. Yet "beginning" and "end" may be crude terms to apply to something really timeless. The permeating atmosphere and the mystery it holds are themselves the source of his enchantment; and it is because they have called all his faculties into play in this volume that it is a book not of charm only, but of power.

"The Connoisseur," in The Times Literary Supplement, *No. 1272, June 17, 1926, p. 412.*

P. C. Kennedy   (essay date 1926)

[*In the following review of* The Connoisseur, and Other Stories, *Kennedy criticizes the prose style in de la Mare's short stories.*]

It may be, of course, that the capacity to enjoy Mr. de la Mare's prose is a special gift, rare yet authentic, a sort of overtone or bloom of appreciation, beyond the mere straightforward judgment of those who ordinarily know good prose when they see it. On the other hand, it may be that Mr. de la Mare can't really write prose at all, and that the admiration expressed for his stories is nothing but an unconscious overflow from the admiration which all of us feel for his poems. What is certain is that he does not write what can be considered good prose by any of the accepted canons. Personally, I am always willing to reject canons which seem more accepted than acceptable: I am all for your wild untameable exceptions, your errant splendours, your Blakes, Whitmans and Merediths. But your exception, no less than your rule, must survive the test of detailed examination. Let us apply that test to this new volume by Mr. de la Mare.

The first story is called **"Mr. Kempe,"** and is about loneliness and terror: it is supposed to be told by a schoolmaster who, on a dangerous piece of cliff, was threatened with the hospitality of a madman. The madman's hobby was the soul; he conducted researches into the question of the soul's existence; and he did so (apparently) by murdering his occasional guests. The schoolmaster tells the story in a public-house, and comic relief is provided by a gentleman with eyes like plums in a pudding. It is easy enough to unravel the technique here; Mr. de la Mare is trying to make his horror more real by putting it cheek by jowl with the commonplace. Unfortunately, he has less then no gift for comic relief, and his bright angelic mind is dreadfully ill at ease with the commonplace. As for his ability to handle the language—on his very first page, in trying to tell us that "autumnal scents, failing day, rain so gentle and persistent," make one feel sleepy, he says: "Such phenomena as these have a slightly soporific effect on the human consciousness." It is incredible, but it is so. A few pages further on, he is trying to express a more complicated idea (he has explained that an old woman thought there was "a something marked on the map"):

> Sure enough there was; though unfortunately long wear of the one I carried had not only left indecipherable more than an Old English letter or two of any record of it, but had rubbed off a square half-mile or so of the country round about it.

It is clear what is meant. It is meant that a letter or two, but no more, could still be deciphered; but what is said is something quite different. Again a few pages, and we find this statement about Nature: "Like the ants and the aphides and the elvers and the tadpoles, she produces us humans in millions." But ants don't, and Mr. de la Mare does not think or mean that they do. Again, what he means is as clear as his inability to say it.

It may be argued that it is possible to write very badly and still be effective, as it is possible to bat very badly and still make a lot of runs. There are instances: Charlotte Brontë is one of them. But Charlotte Brontë does at least appear to be at home among her own pomposities and primnesses: Mr. de la Mare seems all the time unhappily squandering himself on a sort of thing for which he knows that he is too good. Take the next story, **"Missing"**; I will not attempt to analyse its plot, because I am not sure what its plot is—nor does it matter: in this sort of narrative, atmosphere is everything and fact nothing. This story is told in a tea-shop, by a man of whom we learn:

> Even a Chelsea psychic would have been compelled to acknowledge that this particular human being had either disposed of his aura or had left it at home.

Surely it would be impossible to strike a more rapid succession of obviously false notes; and the falsity gets worse; we are to understand that the un-aura'd gentleman has foxy eyes:

> I have never heard though that the fox is a dangerous animal even in a corner; only that he has his wits about him and preys on geese—*whereas my stranger in the tea-shop had been refreshing himself with Osborne biscuits.*

Could ineptitude or irrelevance go further? The italics are mine. Alas that the words italicised should be Mr. de la Mare's!

"The Connoisseur," the third story, which gives its name to the whole, is chaotic and ambitious: here indeed the test must be of the actual writing. Either the spirit is lifted by sheer power of words, or it isn't. To quote long passages is often a bad way of criticism; it is a way I like to avoid whenever possible; but here it is the only way of doing my author justice. The effect at which he is aiming could not by anybody be rendered in a few lines: it must depend on architecture, the kind of architecture we get in clouds and sunsets; wings lifted beyond spires, and buttresses literally flying. I will quote, then, a long passage from Mr. de la Mare; I will quote also, for comparison, a famous passage in which, I feel, is done the thing that Mr. de la Mare is attempting. I will not give a name to either (though indeed the famous passage is *so* famous that I cannot hope to make much mystification); and I will respectfully leave my readers to judge if the comparison is a fair one, and what it tells. Here is one passage:

> Its last filmy wreaths of sulphurous smoke had centuries before ceased to wreathe themselves from Ajubajao's enormous womb. Leagues distant though its cone must be, its jagged outlines were sharply discernible, cut clean against that southern horizon. The skies shallowly arching the plain of lava that flowed out annularly from its base in enormous undulations, league on league, until its margin lay etched and fretted against the eastern heavens—this low-hung firmament was now of a greenish pallor. In its midst the noonday's sun burned raylessly like a sullen topaz set in jade.
>
> But utterly lifeless though the plain appeared to be, minute susurrations were occasionally audible, caused apparently by scatterings of lava dust lifted from their hollows on heated draughts of air. These gathering in volume, raised at last their multitudinous voices into a prolonged hiss, a sustained shrill sibilation as if the silken fringes of an enormous robe were being dragged gently across this ink-black Sahara.
>
> As they subsided once more, drifting softly to rest, a faint musical murmur followed their gigantic sigh, like that of far-distant drums and dulcimers from a secret and hidden borderland. Then this also ceased, and only the plaintive horns of the midges and the scurry of beetles scuttling beneath their shards to and fro in their haunts in the crevices of the lava broke the hush.

And here is the other:

> I thought that it was a Sunday morning in May;

that it was Easter Sunday, and as yet very early in the morning. I was standing, as it seemed to me, at the door of my own cottage. Right before me lay the very scene which could really be commanded from that situation, but exalted, as was usual, and solemnised by the power of dreams. There were the same mountains, and the same lovely valley at their feet; but the mountains were raised to more than Alpine height, and there was interspace far larger between them of savannahs and forest lawns; the hedges were rich with white roses; and no living creature was to be seen . . .

Each describes height and contrasted lowland: the Sahara of the one balances the Alps and savannahs of the other: each gives the sense of silence as prelude to some music or movement that is to come. Yet one passage affects me with a sense of almost intolerable beauty: the other, though it uses the appropriate words, leaves me utterly cold—it is the sort of *made* rhetoric which I cannot without an effort compel myself to read. This is a purely subjective reaction; I make no other claim for it. And those who honestly get from Mr. de la Mare a thrill which I have missed are presumably in the right of it.

Only—and this is my reason for discussing the matter at such length—wherever a great reputation exists, there is immediately the danger that many will delude themselves into the belief that they are thrilled when they aren't. It becomes "bad form" to question the idol: and literary taste loses integrity. Mr. de la Mare is, through no fault of his own, the victim of this idolatry. To stand up against it is invidious: to protest one's sorrow at having to stand up against it makes one sound like Uriah Heep. But what is the wretched critic to do? If the short passages which I have quoted from **"Mr. Kempe"** and **"Missing"** are not awkward and ugly—if the long passage I have quoted from **"The Connoisseur"** is not formal and lifeless—I will eat my hat. I should be only too glad to eat my words.

Mr. de la Mare, it must be remembered, is making in these stories an extraordinarily high claim. He is not proposing just to pass the time for us. He is assaulting one of the loftiest citadels of art, attempting one of the most sacred retreats of emotion. Just because his stories are difficult to understand—just because, at the precise edge where the ordinary story-teller would be expected to give us definition and conclusion, they fade away into airy fantasy and confound us with the implication of inexplicable meanings—he must succeed *absolutely,* or he fails. The stuff must be sheer beauty, or it is nothing. The thrill must be the thrill that poetry gives us. Well, not all men can have, or can expect to have, all gifts. Mr. de la Mare thrills us all right when he writes poetry in verse: I cannot think it is his line to write poetry in prose.

The three tales which I have named are typical. There are six more in the book, and the least ambitious are the best. **"Disillusioned"** and **"The Wharf"** are keen studies of psychological states: **"All Hallows,"** on the other hand, and **"The Lost Track"** are involved, and seem to depend for the lightening of their obscurity upon some distant and difficult revelation of connections—a revelation which never comes. **"Pretty Poll"** is about a parrot with two voices, one of a devil, one of an angel; and about a young man who ruined his life by seeking for the original teacher of the angelic tones. The writing of this story in particular reflects the artificial awkwardness of the theme: "You dark taciturn angel," says one woman to another; and there is perhaps more revelation than is intended when she says also: "He *is* being rather a long time coming to what I suppose will be the point." That might stand for a criticism of all these tales.

There is a detail of minor interest in Mr. de la Mare's style; but perhaps it is illuminating. He is fond of incorporating in his own sentences the great imaginative phrases of others: "For when the slow dark hours begin"; "intense inane"; "romantic chasm." It is not a bad habit, this of concealed quotation: it is even a good one, if the phrases chosen are really apt to their context: but when they are *not,* they have a disruptive effect! And a curious comment on them is supplied by the following passage, where the quotations are unconcealed:

> "Better not," she said, and for the first time smiled. "That would be four to one." The words haunt me.

> But then so, too, do those of "O Keith of Ravelston, the sorrows of thy line!" and so, too, do "Bare ruined choirs where late the sweet birds sang," and so, too, do "Cover her face; mine eyes dazzle; she died young." What are we to make of ourselves while we are the slaves of such incantations as these?

What are we to make of a writer—an admired writer, a beloved writer, an admittedly great writer—who can compare his own phrase to the almost incomparable incantations? It is nothing worse than odd that Mr. de la Mare, having occasion to quote the most famous lines of Keats, should destroy them by misquotation, as he does when he writes: "My heart aches and a drowsy numbness fills my sense, as though of hemlock I had drunk." But that deliberate comparison is no such slip of the pen: it is surely the anxious effort of a magic-maker, half-conscious that in the medium he has here chosen the magic won't work. (pp. 328-29)

P. C. Kennedy, in a review of "The Connoisseur, and Other Stories," in New Statesman, *Vol. XXVII, No. 688, July 3, 1926, pp. 328-29.*

Forrest Reid   (essay date 1929)

[*In the following excerpt, Reid provides a survey of de la Mare's short stories.*]

[De la Mare's later stories are collected in the volumes *Crossings, The Riddle, Broomsticks, Two Tales, The Connoisseur,* and *At First Sight.* For the purpose of discussion] I must make a selection from them, and for the sake of convenience shall divide them (very loosely) into four groups.

To the first group I allot those stories in which the subjects are drawn from real life and kept there.

In Group Two I place the six tales of the supernatural—

'Seaton's Aunt', 'Out of the Deep', 'All Hallows', 'The Green Room', 'A Recluse', and 'Miss Jemima'. The reader, I dare say, may be surprised that this group is not larger, and of course there are many children's stories that have to do with magic and fairies, but that is not just the same thing. In these lighter tales the author is playing with ideas that in the stories of our second group he takes seriously; their aim is but to beguile the fancy, and I shall regard them therefore as constituting Group Three, which, on the whole, I consider to be the least important section of Mr. de la Mare's work. Even that lovely little play, *Crossings,* must be relegated to this group, since the supernatural element in it does not proceed from, and is not addressed to, the deeper, questioning imagination, but is introduced solely for an artistic purpose—to charm, to amuse.

Our fourth and widest group is more difficult to define. The stories in it, when they are stories at all, hover on the edge of a world that is neither dreamland nor matter-of-fact. Such things as 'The Creatures', 'Visitors', 'The Tree', 'Maria Fly', would, we feel, be fairy stories if they weren't something quite different—something that is rooted in reality.

> One of the very last things that Tom Nevis was to think about in this world was a sight he had seen when he was a child of about ten. Years and years were to pass by after that March morning; and at last Tom was far away from home and England in the heat and glare of the tropics. Yet this one far-away memory floated up into his imagination to rest there in its peace as a planet shining in its silver above the snows of remote hills. It had just stayed on in the quiet depths of his mind—like the small insects that may be seen imprisoned in lumps of amber, their wings still glistening ages after they were used in flitting hither and thither in their world as it then was.

> Most human beings have little experiences similar to Tom's. But they come more commonly to rather solitary people—people who enjoy being alone, and who have daydreams.

So begins the quaint and charming tale called 'Visitors', and it is, one suspects, just such little experiences that many of the compositions in Group Four commemorate. The characters too, I should say, are as a rule drawn from within. Often the story is of the slightest, but the author has so keen a sense of everything that is touching, humorous, picturesque, or poetic in it, he bathes it in such a richness of tone and fills it out with such a wealth of meaning, that we ask for nothing more. In such things as 'Disillusioned', 'The Vats', 'The Creatures', 'Alice's Godmother', 'Selina's Parable', there is positively no story at all in the ordinary sense. I do not dare to suggest that this is partly why we return to them so often, but we really do get a fuller, and sometimes even a different impression from each renewed excursion into their quiet paths. To mention the subjects of these tales may throw a light on the author's mind, but very little on the tales themselves. A momentary flash of sympathy between an eminent physician and the patient who has come to consult him ('Disillusioned'); the sight of two vast primeval cisterns on an empty plain ('The

Vats'); a glimpse of two slightly but far from unpleasantly abnormal children on a lonely farm ('**The Creatures**'); a farmyard on a summer afternoon ('**Selina's Parable**'): these are the 'insects' imprisoned in the amber of memory and imagination. '**Disillusioned**' consists primarily in what is left *unsaid* during a strangely suggestive but non-committal conversation: the effect of '**Lispet, Lispett & Vaine**' depends largely on our grasping the fact that Maunders is *improvising* the whole thing: the author of such tales surely is paying the highest compliment he can to his reader's intelligence. As for '**The Thief**', it is less a story than an early Flemish picture glowing in jewelled colours: Bloudie Jacke of Shrewsberrie possessed no rarer collection.

. . . . .

> The real represents to my perception the things we cannot possibly *not* know, sooner or later, in one way or another; it being but one of the accidents of our hampered state, and one of the incidents of their quantity and number, that particular instances have not yet come our way. The romantic stands, on the other hand, for the things that, with all the facilities in the world, all the wealth and all the courage and all the wit and all the adventure, we never *can* directly know; the things that can reach us only through the beautiful circuit and subterfuge of our thought and our desire.

The author of this passage can readily be guessed, and while, as a definition, it does not cover the whole ground, since there is also a habit of mind, a point of view, we can only call romantic (Conrad's, for instance, who rarely if ever wrote of what he did not 'directly know'), it may at least serve to introduce the particular group of Mr. de la Mare's tales I have described as tales of real life. If those we shall discuss later stand, in Henry James's words, 'for the things that, with all the facilities in the world, we never can directly know, the things that can reach us only through the beautiful circuit and subterfuge of our thought and our desire', these—containing, among one or two minor pieces, '**The Lost Track**', '**Disillusioned**', '**At First Sight**', '**The Nap**', '**Pretty Poll**', '**Mr. Kempe**', and '**Missing**'—are composed of material quite within the grasp of experience. True, the subject of one of them, '**Mr. Kempe**', has the strangeness, the fearful allurement of the abnormal ('**Mr. Kempe**' is the study of a disordered mind), but it is only an accident if Mr. Kempe or some one like him has not yet come our way: as for Mr. Bleet, the hero of '**Missing**', he is not only sane but a person of marked sobriety, who, we can easily imagine, would be highly censorious of any infraction of social conventions.

'**Missing**' is among Mr. de la Mare's masterpieces. It is not a pleasant story, and it is remarkable that its sinister quality springs largely from its reticence. Mr. Bleet tells his interlocutor nothing alarming; Mr. Bleet is a victim of circumstances fortuitous and hostile. A chance encounter on a stifling Saturday afternoon in a second-rate London teashop having provided him with a confidant, he simply takes advantage of the fact. It is the confidant who describes their meeting.

> I gave my order, and sat back exhausted in a list-
less vacancy of mind and body. And my dazed eyes, having like the flies little of particular interest to settle on, settled on the only fellow reveller that happened to be sitting within easy reach. At first glimpse there could hardly be a human being you would suppose less likely to attract attention. He was so scrupulously respectable, so entirely innocent of 'atmosphere'. . . .

> He wore a neat—an excessively neat—pepper-and-salt tweed suit, the waistcoat cut high and exhibiting the points of a butterfly collar and a triangle of black silk cravat slipped through a gold mourning ring. His ears maybe were a little out of the mode. They had been attached rather high and flat on either side of his conical head with its dark, glossy, silver-speckled hair.

> The nose was straight, the nostrils full. They suggested courage of a kind; possibly, even, on occasion, bravado. He looked the kind of man, I mean, it is well to keep out of a corner. But the eyes that were now peering vacantly down that longish nose over a trim but unendearing moustache at the crumbs on his empty plate were too close together. . . . Those eyes gave this spruce and respectable person just a hint, a glint of the fox.

And one or two other little physical peculiarities become apparent—the *glitter* in the 'close-neighbouring eyes', the hands, powerful and hairy.

What follows is an interesting talk in which Mr. Bleet, who has been rather deprived of companionship of late, does most of the talking. His listener has time to speculate, and the result somehow for us is that Mr. Bleet's conversation assumes a more and more ghastly complexion, while behind it we watch a soul, tormented, half-developed, and singularly unprepossessing.

The technique of the thing is superb; it is impossible to say at what moment our first vague suspicions of Mr. Bleet turn to certainties. The fatal word is never mentioned by either him or his companion, but no detailed description of an unusually savage murder could produce quite the dire effect of Mr. Bleet's picture of a blameless life in that 'nice little place' 'about seventy miles from London', where he resided with a half-witted sister and a paying guest, the buxom and comparatively opulent Miss Dutton.

The story is terrible, because below all that is being said the spirits of both narrator and listener are shuddering away from a glimpse of some awful thing their words deny. On the face of it, Mr. Bleet treats his companion to no more than a spectacle of self-pity, broken by an occasional outburst of resentment or defiance. But he is not an engaging person naturally, nor would be even had he happier memories of which to unburden himself than his tortuous and cautious account of the 'Enquiry'. The 'Enquiry' was concerning Miss Dutton, who was 'missing'. Yet even the 'Enquiry', for all its callousness, never went so far as to mention murder. Moreover Mr. Bleet completely cleared himself, we gather; left that room without a stain on his character: except, of course, in the jaundiced view of the obstinately malicious, who unfortunately comprised the majority of his neighbours. He clears himself anew on this breathless, enervating afternoon; and at the same time there grows up in the thickening air behind him a scene that becomes more and more vivid with every indignant protest he utters—a picture of a deliberate but ferocious act, and of all the grisly business connected with the subsequent disappearance of Miss Dutton—a picture of Miss Dutton herself, or rather of her remains, a little messy now, but still plump, blonde, slightly common though 'quite the lady'—of her very clothing. And, I repeat, not one word of these things exists on the printed page.

What does exist is the vulgarity of Mr. Bleet, his occasional slips in grammar, the disagreeable condition of his half-melted vanilla ice. Yes, the vanilla ice too contributes to the reality and repulsiveness of Miss Dutton's 'tragedy'; insensibly we have grown as prejudiced as the neighbours.

We are unfair in more ways than one, for there is no doubt that what most disgusts us, most alienates our sympathy, is not Mr. Bleet's wickedness, or supposed wickedness (after all the vanilla ice is hardly evidence), but something ugly that surrounds and emanates from him: it is as if this ugliness composed the greater part of his sin, and all its horror. For sheer suggestiveness I question if even 'Seaton's Aunt' surpasses this story. And its effect is the more desolating because we dimly feel that Mr. Bleet really is suffering in an inarticulate, incomplete fashion (though certainly not suffering from remorse), and that we *ought,* perhaps, to be pitying instead of detesting him. If he were quite without a soul, if he were not human, it would be so much simpler: it is the glimpses we get of that mis-shapen, hunted, jaunty yet abject spirit, that are so disquieting. After all, we don't really care a straw about Miss Dutton, who was vulgar, pretentious, and amorous. If she had forced her company upon *us,* and we could by a mere effort of will have caused her to be 'missing', 'missing' she infallibly would have been. So we bolster up our self-respect by casting fresh aspersions at Mr. Bleet. There is the disagreeable feature that he benefited financially by Miss Dutton's disappearance. And then—the ears—the glitter in the eyes—the powerful hairy hands. . . . It won't bear thinking about: we are not in the least like that. And it is the most appalling murder story ever written.

Let me turn, after this, if only for a moment, to a contemplation of the marvel of the writing; and there is a way in which I think it is more marvellous here than in any other of the stories. To explain what I mean I must mention the great difficulty that sometimes exists of adapting a highly individual style to realistic dialogue. I say 'sometimes', because for writers like Flaubert or Anatole France—writers whose style, though completely individual, keeps closely to the idiom of actual speech—the difficulty is at least greatly minimized. But for Henry James in his last period, to take the most extreme example I can think of, the difficulty was insurmountable. *Nobody* ever talked (except possibly on occasion their author himself) as *everybody* talks in the later Jacobean novels and stories. But they *had* to talk in that way, they *had* to conform to the Jacobean idiom and rhythm, otherwise each of their remarks would have produced the distressing effect of those sudden lapses into the spoken phrase we find in old-fashioned opera. The convention must be accepted as frankly as it is accepted

in opera, in the dialogues between Tristan and Isolde. And though in the work of Mr. de la Mare it is carried to nothing like the same pitch, now and again here to owe must be prepared to accept it. It may be so skilfully disguised that we don't notice it: still the translation or adaptation is there. Everything said by Mrs. Thripps (the charwoman in **'Out of the Deep'**), for instance, is true to the mind and heart of Mrs. Thripps, but no actual talk of a charwoman could possibly be fitted just as it is into a de la Mare score. Mrs. Thripps's words, if you examine them, you will find to have been recast. But the most subtle example of speech modulation I can think of is furnished by the talk of Mr. Bleet in this story, **'Missing'**, where it is managed so perfectly that we seem to be, and indeed *are,* listening to the very voice of the man, and yet listening to music. Miraculous as it may sound, vulgarity and commonness unutterable have lost not a shade of their identity, and yet are inseparable from beauty.

. . . . .

In the tales of the supernatural the realistic method is maintained, and what *can* be observed is shown with an unfailing mastery of description. Some feature in the scene evoked may even symbolize the kind of adventure that is to follow. The picture of the slimy pond swarming with tadpoles at the beginning of **'Seaton's Aunt'** is of this sort. It prepares us for the house we have not yet seen, but which is, in its turn, swarming with a kind of spiritual larvæ. All the material objects in **'Seaton's Aunt'** are solid, palpable, casting heavy shadows that somehow carry the imagination into regions of ghostly terror. In fact, in this particular story the only ghosts *are* these shadows—not so much as a glimpse of a vanishing apparition ever crosses the vision of either Seaton or his friend. What they see with their eyes is nothing more alarming than the Aunt herself, or her vast empty bed in 'the feeble clearness of a nightlight': the whole drama emerges, deepens, darkens, in a succession of hints and omens. To this end the first appearance of Miss Seaton is masterly.

> We were approaching the house when Seaton suddenly came to a standstill. Indeed, I have always had the impression that he plucked at my sleeve. Something, at least, seemed to catch me back, as it were, as he cried, 'Look out, there she is!'
>
> She was standing at an upper window which opened wide on a hinge, and at first sight she looked an excessively tall and overwhelming figure. This, however, was mainly because the window reached all but to the floor of her bedroom. She was in reality rather an under-sized woman, in spite of her long face and big head. She must have stood, I think, unusually still, with eyes fixed on us, though this impression may be due to Seaton's sudden warning and to my consciousness of the cautious and subdued air that had fallen on him at sight of her. I know that without the least reason in the world I felt a kind of guiltiness, as if I had been 'caught'. There was a silvery star pattern sprinkled on her black silk dress, and even from the ground I could see the immense coils of her hair and the rings on her left hand which was held fingering the small jet

buttons of her bodice. She watched our united advance without stirring, until, imperceptibly, her eyes raised and lost themselves in the distance, so that it was out of an assumed reverie that she appeared suddenly to awaken to our presence beneath her when we drew close to the house.

No more than this picture, but what a huge push forward it gives to the story. The uneasiness Miss Seaton inspires in the two schoolboys is contagious. It is heightened by the equivocal nature of its cause, and reaches its climax of sheer terror when they become aware that she is listening outside their bedroom door at night. But it is still more amazing, perhaps, how a sombre beauty flushes through this dreadful creation of a spiritual vampire, whose unnatural appetite has created a charnel-house atmosphere, the alluring reek of which has emptied the churchyard of its ghosts. Poor Withers's attempts—in self-defence—to take it all calmly, rationally—to regard Seaton's Aunt merely as a cynical, rather gross and greedy old lady with an unpleasant nephew and a disconcerting taste for ponderous irony—poor Withers's attempts, in short, to be an aloof little man of the world, are far from successful. Everything that happens is quite ordinary, or very nearly ordinary, and yet, as if by remorseless predestination, everything that happens tends to the sinister. The first thing the boys do when they reach the village where they are to pass their half-term holiday with Miss Seaton is to stop at a chemist's: 'We descended the two steps into his dusky and odorous interior to buy, I remember, some rat poison.' And a little later they pause at the tadpole pond to allow Seaton to examine his pets: 'I can see his absorbed face now as he sat on his heels and fished the slimy things out in his sallow palms.' Such incidents are nothing when taken separately; it is their cumulative effect that gets on Withers's nerves. Even the room Miss Seaton has allotted to him—the, at first sight, so 'jolly little bedroom, with a brass fender and rugs and a polished floor'—suddenly reveals the peculiar 'touch' of his hostess. 'Over the washstand was a little black-framed water-colour drawing, depicting a large eye with an extremely fish-like intensity in the spark of light on the dark pupil; and in "illuminated" lettering beneath was printed very minutely, "Thou God Seest ME", followed by a long looped monogram, "S.S.", in the corner. . . . "This is the room, Withers, my brother William died in when a boy. Admire the view!"' The 'jolliness', for poor Withers, dies out on the instant.

Seaton, as he stands that night in his pyjamas by his chum's dressing-table, supplies the finishing touch. "'Even this room's nothing more than a coffin. I suppose she told you—'It's all exactly the same as when my brother William died'—trust her for that! And good luck to him, say I.'"

There is something at once pathetic and repugnant about the nervous and furtive Seaton. He has the two qualities shared by all Mr. de la Mare's boys, of being at once strange and absolutely convincing. He has more pocket-money, larger hampers of food than his schoolfellows, and yet he dimly knows, and we know too, that he is doomed. He is exactly like a little rat swimming round and round in a water-trap, and we watch him growing feebler and feebler but still swimming, swimming, while his Aunt's big face leans in gloating interest over the abominable spectacle.

The thing is superbly done; the effect aimed at is that of terror, and this effect is achieved as elsewhere, I think, only in *The Turn of the Screw* and one or two stories by Edgar Poe. Everything contributes to it, from Miss Seaton's sarcasms to her nephew's behaviour at school: everything, from the swarming tadpole pond to the unfinished game of chess, is accepted by the imagination as a symbol, and fulfils its purpose.

One secret of the story's power lies in the very absence from it of a visible ghost. I do not mean that the effect of an apparition presented objectively need necessarily fall flat, though the stories in which this sudden collapse does *not* occur might be numbered on the fingers of one hand. The ghost story, in truth, if it is not merely to be crude and silly, demands a very special technique quite beyond the reach of the average concoctor of horrors. It is significant that the only successful experiments I can recall exhibit a marked element of beauty—the last quality one would look for in sensational fiction. But in such things as *The Turn of the Screw,* or Meade Falkner's *The Lost Stradivarius,* the drama might very nearly be described as a conflict between beauty and ugliness. At all events, any fond idea that the ghost in itself can constitute interest must result in failure. The mere presence of a ghost, decked in however grisly trappings, can only interest the extremely artless. What may be of the *intensest* interest, on the other hand, is the presentation of a normal mind terrified, or revolted by, or simply struggling against the influence of, such an apparition. It is not the ghost but the person who sees the ghost that matters, therefore the finer the mind shown as reacting to such phenomena the richer will be our impression. *The Turn of the Screw* is the most moving and terrifying ghost story ever written simply because the *human* drama in it is the most poignant; and what would 'Seaton's Aunt' be if the characters were the commonplace puppets of the ordinary 'thriller'?

In the de la Mare tales of the supernatural the effect aimed at is, characteristically, more lyrical than dramatic. From one of the most beautiful—'All Hallows'—drama is completely absent, and even in 'Seaton's Aunt', which probably is the best 'story as a story', there is no dramatic climax comparable to that in *The Turn of the Screw*. The concluding scene of 'Seaton's Aunt' is a rounding-off of what has gone before: the tension is relaxed, it is pitched on a slightly lower key, and the end is brought about when the strings finally cease to vibrate; whereas in *The Turn of the Screw* they suddenly snap when emotion has reached its highest point, and the terrible cry of despair torn from the lost and dying boy still rings on in our ears after the book is closed.

In **'Out of the Deep'** (originally called **'The Bell'**) the ending is on the first page, and the story is told backwards. Here the hauntings actually materialize, impress themselves on sight, hearing, and even on the sense of smell. It is true that Jimmie's state of mind is abnormal. Disease and the ravages of a reckless life have broken down certain barriers, and it is because these barriers no longer exist that when he rings the bell in his empty house it is answered by such attendants. None the less, the implication remains that the attendants are real. They are not, I mean, to be taken as the visions of his fever, though Mrs. Thripps, the charwoman who comes in each day to tidy up and cook for him, can find no trace of their activities in the morning. Yet neither are they ordinary ghosts. The ghosts visiting Jimmie (dying lonely and disgraced in his hated Uncle's old house, even in his hated Uncle's 'prodigious yet elegant Arabian bed')—the ghosts, literally called up by him, have a relation to him on some mysterious spiritual plane, correspond to the moral condition of his mind at the moment when he tugs 'the sumptuous crimson pleated silk bell-pull'.

Jimmie is another example of the value of the human element in these excursions into the super-normal. His life has been deplorable. 'Even in his first breeches he was never what could be called a nice little boy.' But he has grown up since then, and the 'not-niceness' of thirty or so is a rather different matter from the 'not-niceness' of even the least desirable kind of little boy. For one thing it implies a whole world of experience the little boy at his worst can only be reaching out to; and this perhaps is why we are never placed on quite such intimate and confidential terms with Jimmie as we were with our Craftsman—why, when it comes to confidences, we return *to* his boyhood. An odious butler had been the bane of *his* early years too. Soames is more sanctimonious than Jacobs, but he is of the same kidney. 'Soames used frequently to wring Jimmie's then protuberant ears. Soames sneaked habitually; and with a sort of gloating piety on his drooping face, was invariably present at the subsequent castigation.' In a few pages the picture of a tarnished, loveless childhood is complete; its very comedy is tragic; and we watch that shivering little wretch—obdurate, sullen, unhappy, an infallible liar—standing as if detected in secret depravity while his Aunt Charlotte reproves him for being 'so wickedly frightened of the dark'. 'You know very well your dear Uncle will not permit gas in the attic, so there's no use asking for it. You have nothing on your conscience, I trust?'

Aunt Charlotte might be forgiven much for the sake of that remark; and she is nearer the truth than she imagines, for poor Jimmie has always had a good deal on his conscience and always will have; but the small, flickering flame of beauty in his spirit (without which he could not be a de la Mare hero), of that Aunt Charlotte and Uncle Timothy will never be aware.

From tiny wandering seeds may spring marvellous plants, and from a sentence in a Welsh Guide-Book, describing the situation by the sea of St. David's Cathedral, sprang the tale of **'All Hallows'**. The real St. David's (the outside of which on inspection proved disappointing) was not visited till after the story was written: the whole thing therefore—story and scene—is the creation of the writer.

'All Hallows' is not a ghost story; it is the account of an invasion by the powers of darkness of an ancient Christian stronghold now weakened through its garrison's lack of faith. The demons of the air, riding in from the sea on storm and cloud and mist, have found an entrance, and this once holy temple is being altered to their unholy pur-

pose. Only the old sexton remains faithful, and it is he who tells the strange narrative to a sympathetic tourist, who, tired and dusty after a long tramp, finds himself towards the close of an August afternoon within the besieged precincts. **'All Hallows'** is a wonderful piece of writing. This cathedral not built of hands comes to life literally to the sound of music. Out of music it rises before us in its vastness and beauty, its wind-swept fairness. At first, with the weary grateful traveller, we simply gaze at it in admiration, rejoicing in its dream of quietness and beauty; and once only an uneasy question arises as to whether all is well. The momentary doubt is dismissed; but when the traveller has passed through a side door into the actual building, and finds himself suddenly listening to an incredible history, a vague fear begins to stir in the deepening twilight.

The grandeur remains, a sense of colossal yet delicate beauty, of wide spaces and the coolness and whiteness of sculptured stone. Unlike the tales of human hauntings, there is no ugliness here. The haunters have the dark majesty of fallen Angels and Principalities, and the two humans who spy on them are in comparison mere creeping things, safe so long as they hide themselves, do not come out into the open.

The traveller listens courteously; but what crazed, impossible secrets are these that are being poured into his ears! He is sceptical, curious, sympathetic—and gradually the narrative becomes less impossible, and then not impossible at all, as he becomes aware of evidence. Those great carved figures of saints that had looked so innocent from where he had first beheld them, as he emerges on the roof to a closer inspection reveal anything but saintly features and expressions. The work of alteration has not only begun but has proceeded far. And they must not linger too long, now that the light is failing: once—once the sexton had been nearly caught.

> 'In this very gallery. They nearly had me, sir. But by good fortune there's a recess a little further on—stored up with some old fragments of carving, from the original building, sixth-century, so it's said: stone capitals, heads and hands, and suchlike. I had had my warning, and managed to lep in there and conceal myself. But only just in time. Indeed, sir, I confess I was in such a condition of terror and horror I turned my back.'
>
> 'You mean, you heard, but didn't look? And—something came?'
>
> 'Yes, sir, I seemed to be reduced to no bigger than a child, huddled up there in that corner. There was a sound like clanging metal—but I don't think it was metal. It drew near at a furious speed, then passed me, making a filthy gust of wind. For some instants I couldn't breathe; the air was gone.'
>
> 'And no other sound?'
>
> 'No other sound, sir, except out of the distance a noise like the sounding of a stupendous kind of gibberish. A calling; or so it seemed—no human sound. The air shook with it. You see,

sir, I myself wasn't of any consequence, I take it—unless a mere obstruction in the way. But—I have heard it said somewhere that the rarity of these happenings is only because it's a pain and torment and not any sort of pleasure for such beings, such apparitions, sir, good or bad, to visit our outward world.'

It is evident that a story like this must either succeed or utterly fail: there can be no half measures, because the drop from the sublime to the ridiculous—or shall I in this case say to the merely sensational?—is precipitous. 'All Hallows', to my mind, succeeds. The achievement is worthy of the conception, and leaves in memory that sense of a unique and beautiful experience which is produced more frequently by a fine poem than by fiction.

'The Green Room' is less striking in theme, and at first sight may appear to be in the tradition of the ordinary ghost story. In two respects, indeed, it is: the apparition appears in the accustomed way, and the young man who sees it is unimportant. Alan is a naïve and pleasant but rather colourless youth, his only claim to distinction being a certain delicacy of feeling. It might be argued that he is at least as interesting as the humans in 'All Hallows', but then the humans in 'All Hallows' hardly count, the cathedral itself is the hero of that composition, and in a way that certainly cannot be claimed for the second-hand bookshop which is the scene of 'The Green Room'. What the story does express, and very pleasantly, is a fragile, lingering, half-pathetic sense of the past. Moreover, there is something ghostly in the very weakness and futility of Alan's frail and damaged wraith; but it is pity, not fear, she arouses even in him. Just for a moment perhaps there is horror—in a veiled and terrible suggestion of an appetite existing beyond the grave. But it is no more than a hint, the dramatization of *that* particular idea would have led to a very different tale.

Alan's ghost is the phantom of a woman betrayed and deserted, one whom suffering did not ennoble, and who eventually committed suicide. Once she had lived in this very house where the shop is—lived here in a relationship that remains undefined with a certain Dr. Marchmont. Dr. Marchmont, whether lover or brother, belonged to the last, unrecorded phase of her life; and we get just a tiny glimpse of what that household may have been from a few books left behind—books of the kind described in catalogues as 'curious'. The lady herself left a manuscript volume of verses in the manner of Acton Bell, but commemorating an experience Acton would never have commemorated. Alan at any rate finds the verses, and with them a photograph—not of his ghost, but of what she once had been in the days of innocence. That the innocence was lost, and possibly even derided, is revealed gradually to him—the full, shocking understanding only coming when, after he has had her verses printed, he learns that this sentimental kindness is not in the least what she really wants of him. It is all, as I say, hinted rather than stated, with infinite subtlety and ingenuity. The quoted verses themselves are a marvel of ingenuity, of the gift of getting outside one's own skin and into that of a completely different person.

As a story, 'The Green Room' produces no such electrical

effect as 'Seaton's Aunt' and some of the other tales. It is very quiet, and I should hesitate to say that the last drop of intensity had been squeezed out of the strange situation. For *that,* I rather think, it would have been necessary to have faced the uncompromisingly unpleasant, and had he done so Mr. de la Mare could not have kept his story in tone with the delicate, slightly faded colouring of the old-fashioned room, with the scent of antique bindings and the fairness of black type on ancient pages, which all through it has been his aim to do.

The reader who would sup on horrors must turn to 'A Recluse'—the the nearest approach to a 'shocker' the author ever wrote. By this I mean that if it scares us it has fulfilled all its purpose. Far be it from me to breathe a word against such a purpose. It is not the highest, but only a pedant or a prig will deny that he enjoys being thrilled, and our superior attitude towards sensational fiction is adopted largely because the blatant and the crude *fail* to produce this effect. The method in 'A Recluse' is akin to the method in 'Seaton's Aunt', but the result is different. The strangeness is here, but somehow not the beauty. And yet the material used is no uglier than the material used in several tales—in 'Missing', for example, or 'An Ideal Craftsman': it is simply that it has not undergone the spiritual transmutation we find in these stories—is used to a different end: there is no conflict between beauty and ugliness; nothing, as it were, to mark the spiritual values; the story is launched directly at our nerves.

And it succeeds: we can trust Mr. de la Mare's skill for that: the horror thrusts through, though I am doubtful if anything else does, if there *is* anything else, and we cannot be blamed if our author has taught us to look for more. Mr. Bloom, at all events, is an acquaintance who will not quickly be forgotten. He is a spiritualist who has carried things rather far—to a point, in fact, when those whom he has been accustomed to summon no longer wait to be summoned. Mr. Bloom emphatically is *there;* and, more unaccountably, so to a great extent is the young man, now deceased, who was his secretary, though of him we are shown nothing but his clothes and the aspect of his bedroom, which Mr. Bloom's reluctant guest for one night only wakes up to take due stock of. The effect is distinctly gruesome; the whole tale is gruesome—so much and so *physically* so that we quite understand and share the guest's loss of appetite when he sits down to the tempting supper provided for him. Ugliness somehow exudes from everything remotely connected with Mr. Bloom (from his rare old furniture and Waterford glass to his chickens in their white sauce and all the other baked meats provided at that ample and faintly disgusting feast), or rather it exudes from Mr. Bloom himself, and rests on his possessions like the smear of a greasy hand.

But the story reaches our nerves, grips us closely even while some of its ramifications are not clearly grasped. Our first suspicion, for instance, when Mr. Bloom by tampering with his unwilling visitor's car, tricks him into spending a night at Montrésor—our first suspicion that he wants him for some sinister experiment, proves mistaken. Yet if Mr. Bloom *merely* was terrified at the thought of spending a night alone in Montrésor (his own house, which he is preparing to leave), surely we should be given a very cogent reason for his being obliged to do so: as it is, there seems to have been nothing to prevent him from leaving the house in the afternoon and returning to it next morning. Nor is the climax of the story quite clear: I mean the scene where the visitor, waking at dawn and hearing strange noises overhead, goes to Mr. Bloom's room.

> What I was not prepared for was the spectacle of Mr. Bloom's bed. When I entered the room, I am perfectly certain there had been nothing abnormal about that—except that it had not been slept in. True, the light had meanwhile increased a little, but not much. No—the bed had been empty.
>
> Not so now. The lower part of it was all but entirely flat, the white coverlid over it was drawn almost as neat and close from side to side of it as the cover of a billiard table. But on the pillow, the beard protruding over the turned-down sheet, now showed what appeared to be the head and face of Mr. Bloom. With head jerked back, I watched that face steadily, transfixedly. It was a flawless facsimile, waxen, motionless; but it was not a real face and head. It was an hallucination. How induced is quite another matter. No spirit of life, no livingness had ever stirred those soaplike, stagnant features. . . . It was merely a mask, a lifelike mask (past even the dexterity of a Chinese artist to rival), and—though I hardly know why—it was inconceivably shocking.

Well, we know why it is shocking. It is because it is ugly—so ugly that it becomes obscene. It is meant to shock, and it succeeds; but what *is* this counterfeit Mr. Bloom?

It may be that I do wrong to criticize **'A Recluse'**, for as yet it has been published only in Lady Cynthia Asquith's *Ghost Book* of 1926. I pass therefore the more readily to **'Miss Jemima',** which, though it is the slightest of all these tales, is definitely in the first rank. I have detached it from the collection of children's stories called ***Broomsticks*** where it is placed, because, though it too certainly is a children's story, the author here believes every word he writes. It is a story told to a little girl called Susan by her granny, and the relation between this happily assorted pair contributes an exquisitely domestic charm to what is really a narrative of spiritual danger. When Susan's granny was a little girl she was very nearly lured beyond the boundary we are forbidden to pass; only the merest chance saved her, a single tiny peep, coming just not too late, into the true nature of the lovely being who wanted her.

'Miss Jemima' is so delightful a thing, so essentially fine and true, that to mention Susan's two 'exacalys' and her one 'quincidence' as having aroused a momentary uneasiness goes very much against the grain. All the rest of Susan's conversation is beautifully right—which is just the reason why I *do* mention these doubtful locutions. Susan, indeed, may have used them, though children even at the age of six or seven (and she is older than that) are generally absurdly pedantic about the pronunciation of a long or unfamiliar word. It probably doesn't—the word, I mean—always come right, but on the other hand, in my experience, it rarely if ever comes in the manner of Susan's 'exa-

calys' and Ann's 'stremelys' (Ann of *Crossings*), possibly because individuals have individual tricks of speech, and these are established literary forms. Whether right or wrong, however, was not quite my point. When I said that these speeches aroused uneasiness, it was because they seemed to me to constitute an appeal—such as we do not expect from Mr. de la Mare. He never makes that appeal when he is writing about little boys: them we have to take on their merits be they never so slender.

. . . . .

Through these two girls, Susan and Ann, we reach our third group of stories, in which I include *Crossings,* though it is written in dramatic form. That beautiful play of ghosts and fairies, butchers, bakers and candlestick-makers, must have been conceived and carried out in a singularly happy mood. It is a blend of magic, fun, and poetry, and its setting is a world of dusk and silver, where houses, woods, and people are all exactly as we should like them to be. If I place it in Group Three, indeed, it is only because there is no symbol in its dreaming; all belongs frankly to 'once-upon-a-time'. The plot is fantasy. The children escape from a grim Bayswater Aunt, and in the country, at Crossings,—an old house with a ghost and a mouse or two—live for a while by themselves; and the youngest child, Ann, is stolen by fairies and brought back again.

I am completely ignorant of the problems of dramatic production, but it seems to me *Crossings* would present far fewer difficulties in its actual mounting than, say, [Maurice Maeterlinck's] *The Blue Bird,* while the play itself is infinitely fresher and more charming. There might be some trouble in finding an Ann, but so long as the school-boy brother was not represented by a plump little person bulging out of her Etons in curves fatal to illusion we could accept an Ann older than the author's portrait, and all the rest would be plain sailing.

At any rate, as a poem, as a story, as an arm-chair drama, the thing is exquisite. It is fooling of course, lovely midsummer night's fooling, but the touch is so deft, the spirit so gravely humorous and tender, that at the time we take it half seriously. The very fact that the characters are so much de la Mare characters, the house so much a de la Mare house, gives it, as a play, the rarest charm of familiarity in strangeness.

And several of the fairy tales proper—**'The Dutch Cheese', 'The Sleeping Boys of Warwickshire', 'The Lovely Myfanwy',** to pick out two or three examples—are also first-rate things of their kind. It is not a kind wholly suited to Mr. de la Mare. The fairy tale (and it must be remembered I am speaking now of the old-fashioned fairy tale of Perrault and Grimm) depends for success almost as much on ingenuity of plot as does the mystery story. The plot must have a beginning, middle, and end, and the end must come in the nature of a surprise, a climax, the excitement must be steadily progressive. Certainly the three stories by Mr. de la Mare I have mentioned fulfil these conditions, but there are others which do not. **'Wages',** for instance, an attempt in the same genre, appears to me not so much a story as a group of incidents for a story which has still to be invented. In both **'Wages'** and **'John Cobler'** (they will be found in the *Joy Street* annuals), after an excellent start the tale carries on for a little; then gradually loses its momentum, and ceases languidly. As for that long Hoffmannesque fantasy, **'A Nose'**, even the beginning seems to me unpromising. I may be advertising my own heaviness, but I confess I see nothing amusing in the idea of a person growing up from childhood in the belief his nose is made of wax: at any rate it is not in this kind of thing that we need look for the true quality of our author.

The children's stories that are really his, and which I would place in my last group, strike an entirely different note. It is the old difference, I suppose, between fancy and imagination. **'Maria Fly'**, **'Visitors'**, **'Alice's Godmother'**, **'Broomsticks'**: from such tales all the ingredients of the traditional fairy tale are conspicuously absent. They are not dependent on plot (at least not on any ingeniously arranged plot), they depend on the quality of the imagination in them—the imagination that creates reality. So, with our little friend Maria Fly: 'On purpose she didn't even glance again at the Fly. She most particularly (though she didn't know why) wished not to see it again. So she walked sidelong a little, her head turned to one side, too, so that no part of her eye should see the fly again even by accident.' Those sentences have very much the value of the picture of Seaton hovering over his pond of tadpoles. They have, indeed, an effect less startling than, but not dissimilar in kind from that of the sudden clear ringing of a telephone bell in the dead stillness of night. They create instantly an alertness: create, too, that reality—however far removed from normal experience—I have spoken of as characteristic of all Mr. de la Mare's most authentic work.

The line of division, in fact, between the best of these children's tales, and stories like **'The Creatures'**, **'The Tree'**, or even **'The Vats'**, is of a gossamer thinness: we might say the latter would be unlikely to appeal to a child, but that is all. I choose these three so different compositions because their underlying theme is an old de la Mare theme—more or less disguised in the two first, but in **'The Vats'** expressed directly, if whimsically; and with the unhurried gravity of a bygone century echoing in the elaborate imagery and full, solemn chords of its prose.

> We had frittered away, squandered so many days, weeks, years—and had saved so little. Spendthrifts of the unborrowable, we had been living on our capital—a capital bringing in how meagre an 'interest'—and were continually growing poorer. Once, when we were children, and in our own world, an hour had been as capacious as the blue bowl of the sky, and of as refreshing a milk. Now its successors haggardly snatched their way past our sluggard senses like thieves pursued. . . .
>
> We came at once to a standstill amid the farflung stretches of the unknown plateau on which we had re-found ourselves, and with eyes fixed upon these astonishing objects, stood and stared. I have called them Vats. Vats they were not; but rather sunken Reservoirs; vast semi-spherical primeval Cisterns. . . . They wore that air of lovely timelessness which decks the thorn, and

haunts for the half-woken sense the odour of sweet-briar; yet they were grey with the everlasting, as are the beards of the patriarchs and the cindery craters of the Moon. Theirs was the semblance of having been lost, forgotten, abandoned, like some foundered Nereid-haunted derelict of the first sailors, rotting in dream upon an undiscovered shore. They haunched their vast shapes out of the green beneath the sunless blue of space, and for untrodden leagues around them stretched like a paradisal savanna what we poor thronging clock-vexed men call Silence. Solitude. . . .

> They called to mind some hidden being within us that, if not their coeval, was at least aware of their exquisite antiquity. Whether of archangelic or daemonic construction, clearly they had remained unvisited by mortal man for as many centuries at least as there are cherries in Damascus or beads in Tierra del Fuego. . . . Yet within the lightless bellies of these sarcophagi were heaped up, we were utterly assured (though *how*, I know not) floods, beyond measure, of the waters for which our souls had pined. Waters imaginably so clear as to be dense, as if of melted metal more translucent even than crystal; of such a tenuous purity that not even the moonlit branches of a dream would spell their reflex in them; so costly, so far beyond price, that this whole stony world's rubies and sapphires and amethysts of Mandalay and Guadalajara and Solikamsk, all the treasure-houses of Cambalech and the booty of King Tamburlane would suffice to purchase not one drop.

(pp. 206-43)

Forrest Reid, in his Walter de la Mare: A Critical Study, *Henry Holt and Company, 1929, 256 p.*

De la Mare on darkness and the imagination:

The imagination bestirs itself in the dark; the serpent sloughs its daily skin. And perhaps because night actually attracts less kindly phantom fauna than the day, evil and disaster are associated with darkness: dark thoughts, a darkened outlook, dark deeds, the night of the soul. The imaginative writers have given the sharpest edge to the word. What is called realism is usually a record of life at a low pitch and ebb viewed in the sunless light of day—so often a drab waste of grey and white, and an east wind blowing. But imaginative evil, either in thought or act or art is an evil that is rare and may be almost past endurance—there is an evil dream in Dostoevski, there are drawings of Goya's—and this, like the funguses, flourishes in the dark.

Walter de la Mare, in his introduction to Behold, This Dreamer, *1939.*

Arthur Machen (essay date 1930)

[*Machen was a Welsh short story writer and novelist best known for his tales of bizarre occurrences and supernat-*

ural horror. In the following review of On the Edge, *he focuses on "The Recluse," questioning whether or not de la Mare's characteristic obscurity contributes to or detracts from the success of this story.*]

When the hour sounds from the belfry, the strokes sound clear, definite and distinct in the air. Everyone can hear that it is one, or seven, or twelve, as it may be; and there the matter ends for most of us. But if we listen more curiously, and forget about dinner time and appointments kept or missed, we shall hear between the master strokes of the bell a melodious humming murmur, and this in its turn may be resolved into notes mounting the scale in a fixed and certain order, mounting and still mounting into worlds beyond our sense, into eternity. These sounds are the overtones; they have their analogies in the region of the arts, with a difference. For in the affair of the bell founders, the overtones are only of this importance, that the tuners have to take them into account if the bell is to be perfectly in tune; otherwise they are a mere by-product of the great stroke; incidental, not essential. But the arts exist for their overtones; it is by their presence or absence that we distinguish genius from talent. It is the main business, nay the only business, of the bell to tell us that it is twelve o'clock, but it is not the main business of Tennyson to tell us that Ulysses and his companions came into the land of the lotus eaters at some time after that hour. In the one case, the overtones are accidental; in the other, they are essential. It is the affair of the clock to tell us the time; it is the affair of the arts to take us out of time into eternity, into that region which is beyond the world of the logical understanding, beyond the power of direct utterance.

And yet, in the art of literature certainly, in the arts of painting and sculpture probably, the great stroke—to continue this bell analogy—must be clearly enunciated, with no doubtful sound. It is hard to believe that the Augustus John portrait of Madame Suggia suffers in any way from its being, quite evidently and undeniably, a picture of a woman playing the violoncello; it is hard to think it would have been a still greater masterpiece if it had looked rather like a tiger under a palm tree. But however this may be with painting and sculpture, it is certainly true in prose literature: the finest work is defined. It need not be scientifically true. It is not scientifically true, as it happens, that human eyes and bones, when submerged at a depth of thirty feet become pearls and coral; but the poet, though mistaken, is clear and definite in his statement. Poetry, it is true, has a larger licence in this matter than prose, since poetry is a near approach to that primitive incantation from which all literature proceeds. There is a certain confusion in the narrative of "Kubla Khan"; and the magic casements charmed by the song of the nightingale are misty. And it might be urged, perhaps, in some quarters that Mr. de la Mare has availed himself of his poet's licence in writing some of the curious and beautiful short stories in *On the Edge.* There is an everlasting question that besets not the minor but the major decisions of criticism. It is a simple thing to dismiss "Standing at the buffet in immaculate evening dress he selected a dozen of the succulent bivalves." It is more difficult to decide whether a clearer definition would have improved **"A Recluse,"** one of the most singular of these singular studies.

In this tale the narrator, "Mr. Dash," is motoring one May evening along a country road, when he is strangely drawn by the appearance of a house seen through high gates of wrought iron. Mr. Dash, I say, was drawn to this house, but hardly by the attraction of love. It had about it those veils of mystery, that sense of *aliquid latet,* which haunt certain visible things: houses, trees, gardens, the shape of hills, secret and silent valleys:

> To all appearance it was vacant, but if so, it could not have been vacant long. The drive was sadly in need of weeding; though the lawns had been recently mown. High-grown forest trees towered round about it, overtopping its roof—chiefly chestnuts, their massive lower branches drooping so close to the turf they almost brushed its surface. They were festooned from crown to roof with branching candelabra—like spikes of blossom. Now it was daylight; but imagine them on a still, pitch-black night, their every twig upholding a tiny, phosphoric cluster of tapers.

Mr. Dash drives his car past the iron gates, and strolls by the terrace of the quiet red-brick Georgian house, with its singular hint of undefined mystery, and discovers that, after all, it is still tenanted. The owner, Mr. Bloom, a heavy, stooping, bearded man, is standing at the threshold; a bald man, with a domed brow. He greets Mr. Dash courteously, but that gentleman "wanted to shake him off, to go away. He was an empty-looking man . . . if his house had suggested vacancy, so did he; and yet, I wonder."

It is impossible to summarise Mr. de la Mare without committing outrage and injustice; but it must be said that Mr. Bloom lures Mr. Dash into his hall, strangely occupied with a hugger-mugger of fine old furniture, as if an antique dealer were about to flit. Mr. Bloom leaves his guest in the library for a moment, and when he returns Mr. Dash, distressed, uneasy, he knows not why, shakes hands, and in spite of protestations, makes his way to his car. The gear-key is missing; the nearest town is seven miles away; and Mr. Dash must be Mr. Bloom's guest for the night. The two dine together, simply and choicely; and Mr. Bloom speaks of his dead secretary who has been of great use to him in his "literary work"; and then the literary work becomes "little experiments," which yielded "the most curious and interesting results"; and the little experiments are at last defined as the processes of the séance of the spiritualists. Mr. Dash had dabbled a little in spiritualism and thought poorly enough of the results, and spoke of it all as a silly and dangerous waste of time; and his host grew grey with rage. The evening wears on; it becomes apparent that there was some hideous mystery about the death of Mr. Champneys, the secretary; and it is into the bedroom of the dead man that Mr. Dash is shown. The servant who prepared the dinner is gone for the night: Mr. Dash and Mr. Bloom are the only tenants of the house. Mr. Dash falls asleep, and wakes suddenly with the dawn; and looking about him sees the room as it were drenched in terror: "this is how Mr. Champney's room would appear to anyone who had become for some reason or another intensely afraid."

And then he heard voices speaking, echoing hollow in

some distance of the house; one of the voices Mr. Bloom's, the other like it; and there was the sound of hurrying feet overhead. Mr. Dash goes into the study, and sees there a small bed, and on a table beside it the contents of Mr. Bloom's pocket, among them Mr. Dash's missing gear-key. And the bed:

> The lower part of it was all but entirely flat, the white coverlid having been drawn almost as neat and close from side to side of it as the carapace of a billiard table. But on the pillow—the grey-flecked brown beard protruding over the turned-down sheet—now showed what appeared to be the head and face of Mr. Bloom . . . It was a flawless facsimile, waxen, motionless; but it was not a real face and head. It was an hallu-cination . . . it was inconceivably shocking.

Mr. Dash flees the abhorred, infested house.

I should have made it clear that Mr. Bloom detained Mr. Dash because he was human, because the horrors that the necromancer had summoned from the depths pressed now so thick about him that even his foul soul was shaken and aghast. I should have mentioned also a faint hint that there was some tincture of corruption in the personality of Champneys, the dead secretary: medium, it is to be sup-posed, was his true title. Such, then, in crude outline, is the story of **"A Recluse."** Would it have been a better tale if it had been told more definitely? I leave that an open question.

Is the purely personal objection valid? I am not quite clear as to this; but I am bound to confess that I have such an objection to make against **"A Recluse."** It is this. The word of the enigma is, clearly, spiritualism; and no struc-ture built on that basis can appal me, or enchant me, or make my breath come quickly, or, indeed, win the faintest interest from me. I take the word of the spiritualists them-selves, that the séance is a homely, friendly, and helpful institution; that the spirits are as harmless and playful as kittens, and, sometimes, as helpful as big St. Bernards and Church Workers. No tale that begins with a planchette, a hidden slate, or a rapping table can make me quail. Whereas another of the stories in the book, **"Crewe"**—. In that tale there is a scarecrow which is luminous, but not in the light of the sun—a hideous terror. (pp. vi, viii)

Arthur Machen, *"The Line of Terror,"* in *New Stateman, Vol. XXXVI, No. 911, October 11, 1930, pp. vi, viii.*

Graham Greene   (essay date 1948)

[*An English man of letters, Greene is generally consid-ered one of the most important Catholic novelists of the twentieth century. In his major works, he explored the problems of spiritually and socially alienated individu-als living in corrupt and corrupting societies. As a book reviewer at the* Spectator, *Greene was deemed a shrewd literary critic with a taste for the works of neglected au-thors. In the following essay, which was originally pub-lished in 1948, he comments on the recurring railway and travel motifs in de la Mare's short stories and favor-ably compares him with the renowned supernatural fic-tion writer M. R. James.*]

Every creative writer worth our consideration, every writ-er who can be called in the wide eighteenth-century use of the term a poet, is a victim: a man given over to an ob-session. Was it not the obsessive fear of treachery which dictated not only James's plots but also his elaborate con-ceits (behind the barbed network of his style he could feel really secure himself), and was it not another obsession, a terrible pity for human beings, which drove Hardy to write novels that are like desperate acts of rebellion in a lost cause? What obsession then do we find in Mr de la Mare—one of the few living writers who can survive in this company?

The obsession is perhaps most easily detected in the sym-bols an author uses, and it would not be far from the truth—odd as it may seem on the face of it—to say that the dominant symbol in Mr de la Mare's short stories is the railway station or the railway journey: sometimes the small country railway station, all but deserted except by a couple of travellers chance met and an aged porter, at dusk or bathed in the quiet meditative light of a harvest afternoon: sometimes the waiting room of a great junction with its dying dusty fire and its garrulous occupant. But if not the dominant symbol at least this symbol—or rather group of symbols—occurs almost as frequently as do the ghosts of his poems—the ghosts that listen to the mother as she reads to her children, the lamenting ghosts that rat-tle the door like wind or moisten the glass like rain. Prose is a more intractable medium than verse. In prose we must be gently lured outside the boundaries of our experience. The symbol must in a favourable sense of the word be pro-saic.

> One hasty glance around him showed that he was the sole traveller to alight on the frosted tim-bers of the obscure little station. A faint rosiness in the west foretold the decline of the still wintry day. The firs that flanked the dreary passenger-shed of the platform stood burdened already with the blackness of coming night. (**'The Tree'**)

> When murky winter dusk begins to settle over the railway station at Crewe its first-class wait-ing-room grows steadily more stagnant. Particu-larly if one is alone in it. The long grimed win-dows do little more than sift the failing light that slopes in on them from the glass roof outside and is too feeble to penetrate into the recesses be-yond. And the grained massive black-leathered furniture becomes less and less inviting. It ap-pears to have been made for a scene of extreme and diabolical violence that one may hope will never occur. One can hardly at any rate imagine it to have been designed by a really *good* man! (**'Crewe'**)

> . . . at this instant the sad neutral winter land-scape, already scarcely perceptible beneath a thin grey skin of frozen snow and a steadily de-scending veil of tiny flakes from the heavens above it, was suddenly blotted out. The train lights had come on, and the small cabin in which the two of them sat together had become a cage of radiance. How Lavinia hated too much light. (**'A Froward Child'**)

> She was standing at the open window [of the

train], looking out, but not as if she had ever entirely desisted from looking in—an oval face with highish cheekbones, and eyes and mouth from which a remote smile was now vanishing as softly and secretly as a bird enters and vanishes into its nest. ('A Nest of Singing Birds')

The noonday express with a wildly soaring crescendo of lamentation came sweeping in sheer magnificence of onset round the curve, soared through the little green empty station—its windows a long broken faceless glint of sunlit glass—and that too vanished. Vanished! A swirl of dust and an unutterable stillness followed after it. The skin of a banana on the platform was the only proof that it had come and gone. Its shattering clamour had left for contrast an almost helpless sense of peace. 'Yes, yes!' we all seemed to be whispering—from the Cedar of Lebanon to the little hyssop in the wall—'here we all are; and still, thank heaven, safe. *Safe!*' ('Ding Dong Bell')

It is surely impossible not to feel ourselves in the presence of an obsession—the same obsession that haunts the melancholy subtle cadences of Mr de la Mare's poetry. Such trite phrases as 'ships that pass', 'travellers through life', 'journey's end' are the way in which for centuries the common man has taken a sidelong glance at the common fate (to be here, and there, and gone)—and looked away again. But every once in a while, perhaps only once or twice in a century, a man finds he cannot so easily dismiss with a regulation phrase what meets his eyes: the eyes linger: the obsession is born—in an Emily Brontë, a Beddoes, a James Thomson, in Mr de la Mare.

> '*Mors.* And what does *Mors* mean?' enquired that oddly indolent voice in the quiet. 'Was it his name, or his initials, or is it a charm?' 'It means—well, sleep,' I said. 'Or nightmare, or dawn, or nothing, or—it might mean everything.' I confess, though, that to my ear it had the sound at that moment of an enormous breaker, bursting on the shore of some unspeakably remote island and we two marooned. ('Ding Dong Bell')

One thing, it will be noticed in all these stories, *Mors* does not mean; it does not mean Hell—or Heaven. That obsession with death that fills Mr de la Mare's poetry with the whisper of ghosts, that expresses itself over and over again in the short story in the form of *revenants,* has never led him to accept—or even to speculate on—the Christian answer. Christianity when it figures in these stories is like a dead religion of which we see only the enormous stone memorials. Churches do occur—in 'All Hallows', 'The Trumpet', 'Strangers and Pilgrims', but they are empty haunted buildings.

> At this moment of the afternoon the great church almost cheated one into the belief that it was possessed of a life of its own. It lay, as I say, couched in its natural hollow, basking under the dark dome of the heavens like some half-fossilized monster that might at any moment stir and awaken out of the swoon to which the wand of the enchanter had committed it. ('All Hallows')

What an odd world, to those of us with traditional Christian beliefs, is this world of Mr de la Mare's: the world where the terrible Seaton's Aunt absorbs the living as a spider does and remains alive herself in the company of the dead. 'I don't look to flesh and blood for my company. When you've got to be my age, Mr Smithers (which God forbid), you'll find life a very different affair from what you seem to think it is now. You won't seek company then, I'll be bound. It's thrust on you'; the world of the recluse Mr Bloom, that spiritualist who had pressed on too far ignoring the advice that the poet would have given him.

> Bethink thee: every enticing league thou wend
> Beyond the mark where life its bound hath set
> Will lead thee at length where human pathways
>   end
> And the dark enemy spreads his maddening net.

How wrong, however, it would be to give the impression that Mr de la Mare is just another, however accomplished, writer of ghost stories, yet what is it that divides this world of Mr Kempe and Mr Bloom and Seaton's Aunt, the dubious fellow-passenger with Lavinia in the train, the stranger in Crewe waiting room from the world of the late M. R. James's creation—told by the antiquary? M. R. James with admirable skill invented ghosts to make the flesh creep; astutely he used the image which would best convey horror; he was concerned with truth only in the sense that his stories must ring true—while they were being read. But Mr de la Mare is concerned, like his own Mr Bloom, to find out: his stories are true in the sense that the author believes—and conveys his belief—that this is the real world, but only in so far as he has yet discovered it. They are tentative. His use of prose reminds us frequently of a blind man trying to describe an object from the touch only—'this thing is circular, or nearly circular, oddly dinted, too hard to be a ball: it might be, yes it might be, a human skull'. At any moment we expect a complete discovery, but the discovery is delayed. We, as well as the author, are this side of Lethe. When I was a child I used to be horrified by Carroll's poem *The Hunting of the Snark.* The danger that the snark might prove to be a boojum haunted me from the first page, and sometimes reading Mr de la Mare's stories, I fear that the author in his strange fumbling at the invisible curtain may suddenly come on the inescapable boojum truth, and just as quickly vanish away.

For how they continually seek their snark, his characters—in railway trains, in deserted churches, even in the bars of village inns. Listen to them speaking, and see how all the time they ignore what is at least a fact—that an answer to their questions has been proposed: how intent they are to find an alternative, personal explanation: how they hover and debate and touch and withdraw, while the boojum waits.

> There's Free Will, for example: there's Moral Responsibility; and such little riddles as where we all come from and where we are going to, why, we don't even know what we are—in ourselves, I mean. And how many of us have tried to find out? ('Mr Kempe')

> 'The points as I take it, sir, are these. First,' he

laid forefinger on forefinger, 'the number of those gone as compared with ourselves who are still waiting. Next, there being no warrant that what is seen—if seen at all—is wraiths of the departed, and not from elsewhere. The very waterspouts outside are said to be demonstrations of that belief. Third and last, another question: What purpose could call so small a sprinkling of them back—a few grains of sand out of the wilderness, unless, it may be, some festering grievance; or hunger for the living, sir; or duty left undone? In which case, mark you, which of any of us is safe?' (**'Strangers and Pilgrims'**)

'My dream was only—*after;* the state after death, as they call it. . . .' Mr Eaves leaned forward, and all but whispered the curious tidings into her ear. 'It's—it's just the same,' he said. (**'The Three Friends'**)

There is no space in an essay of this length to study the technique which does occasionally creak with other than the tread of visitants; nor to dwell on the minor defects—the occasional archness, whimsicality, playfulness, especially when Mr de la Mare is unwise enough to dress his narrator up in women's clothes (as he did in *The Memoirs of a Midget.* Perhaps we could surrender without too much regret one third of his short stories, but what a volume would be left. **'The Almond Tree,' 'Seaton's Aunt,' 'The Three Friends,' 'The Count's Courtship,' 'Miss Duveen,' 'A Recluse,' 'Willows,' 'Crewe,' 'An Ideal Craftsman,' 'A Froward Child,' 'A Revenant,' 'The Trumpet,' 'Strangers and Pilgrims,' 'Mr Kempe,' 'Missing,' 'Disillusioned,' 'All Hallows'**—here is one man's choice of what he could not, under any circumstances, spare.

In all these stories we have a prose unequalled in its richness since the death of James, or dare one, at this date, say Robert Louis Stevenson. Stevenson comes particularly to mind because he played with so wide a vocabulary—the colloquial and the literary phrase, incorporating even the dialect word and naturalizing it. So Mr de la Mare will play consciously with clichés (hemmed like James's between inverted commas), turning them under-side as it were to the reader, and showing what other meanings lie there hidden: he will suddenly enrich a colloquial conversation with a literary phrase out of the common tongue, or enrich on the contrary a conscious literary description with a turn of country phrase—'destiny was spudding at his tap root'.

With these resources at his command no one can bring the natural visible world more sharply to the eye: from the railway carriage window we watch the landscape unfold, the sparkle of frost and rain, the glare of summer sunlight, the lights in evening windows; we are wooed and lulled sometimes to the verge of sleep by the beauty of the prose, until suddenly without warning a sentence breaks in midbreath and we look up and see the terrified eyes of our fellow-passenger, appealing, hungry, scared, as he watches what we cannot see—'the sediment of an unspeakable obsession', and a certain glibness would seem to surround our easy conscious Christian answers to all that wild speculation, if we could ever trust ourselves to urge that cold comfort upon this stranger travelling 'our way'. (pp. 141-48)

Graham Greene, "Walter de la Mare's Short Stories," in his Collected Essays, *The Viking Press, 1969, pp. 141-48.*

De la Mare on seeing ghosts:

Though positive 'scientific' proof of any experience in the nature of the ghostly is usually and of necessity impracticable, since it is apt to be unique, traces of such experiences themselves are by no means rare. A quiet inspection of matter itself through the eyes of the physicist tends to cut away the ground from under the sceptic's feet. And even though a few moments' listening lightless solitude in any house in the night hours may fall far short of any positive intimation that that house is haunted, it will hardly fail to hint that the imagination is.

On the other hand, the percipient may coldly decline to respond even to what appears to be a definite overture of this nature. Not many months ago, in a house reputed to be haunted (it would have bettered the experience if I had been unaware of this before I went to bed!), I awoke, not only convinced that there stood a ghost in my room, but by no means anxious to share its company. Fully conscious, but with my eyes shut—though I knew it was early morning—I argued with myself: 'Now, if I turn my head, open my eyes, and look, and *there* it is, whatever else may happen, it will certainly be hours before I get to sleep again. Better pay no attention.' This dismal counsel prevailed, my eye-lids remained shut, and to sleep again I went. But how abject a welcome was this to one who (perhaps) meant me no harm, and in all probability will never visit me again!

Walter de la Mare, in his introduction to They Walk Again: An Anthology of Ghost Stories, *1942.*

John H. Wills (essay date 1964)

[*In the following essay, Wills provides an overview and assessment of de la Mare's major stories.*]

Walter de la Mare is the most underrated short story writer in the English language. He belongs in the company of the masters: of Hawthorne, James, Conrad, Joyce, Mansfield, Lawrence, Hemingway, and Eudora Welty. And he deserves high position among these; for with the possible exception of James, de la Mare probably wrote more first-rate stories than any one of them. Over a sixty-year period—from 1896 to 1959—de la Mare wrote over eighty short stories, at least forty of which no student of the short story can afford to ignore. The best are perhaps **"The Riddle," "The Almond Tree," "Miss Duveen," "The Bowl," "Seaton's Aunt," "Out of the Deep," "The Creatures,"** and **"The Tree"** from *The Riddle* (1923); **"Lucy," "Maria-Fly,"** and **"Visitors"** from *Broomsticks* (1925); **"The Connoisseur," "The Wharf," "The Nap,"** and **"All Hallows"** from *The Connoisseur* (1926); **"A Recluse," "At First Sight,"** and **"An Ideal Craftsman"** from *On the Edge* (1930); and **"Physic," "Miss Miller,"** and **"The Trumpet"** from *The Wind Blows Over* (1936).

Few American critics know these stories. If they were

known, one would encounter them in the anthologies and read of them in the periodicals. Perhaps we cannot give attention to a belated Romantic poet turned story writer—especially to one pigeon-holed as fuddy-duddy and queer upstairs. Perhaps we cannot take seriously an author who wrote almost half of his books for children.

Even the British know de la Mare principally as a children's writer and lyric poet—as the kindly, sage, whimsical author of **"The Lord Fish,"** *The Three Mulla-Mulgars, Peacock Pie;* and as the mystical, somewhat antiquated lyrist of **"The Veil," "The Listeners," "Nod," "Silver,"** etc. There are, however, a few discriminating devotees of de la Mare's stories—men who have admired the right stories for the right reasons. R. L. Mégroz wrote a fine pioneer study of de la Mare [*Walter de la Mare: A Biographical and Critical Study*] as early as 1924, and in 1933 contributed additional remarks in his *Five Novelist-Poets of Today.* Mégroz makes very high claims for the stories, in one place asserting that de la Mare "has James' insight with more poetic imagination, being capable of a deeper passion of awareness," and in another, that his "sense of evil is as profound as James' or Conrad's." The second full-length study [*Walter de la Mare: A Critical Study*] (also finely sensitive) was written by Forrest Reid, and again the name Reid most often invokes in discussing de la Mare's stories is that of James.

In comparatively recent years the stories have received further serious attention. In the Prefatory Note to his critical monograph, *Walter de la Mare: An Exploration* (1947), John Atkins concludes with the statement that "Mr. de la Mare's fame will ultimately rest on his magnificent stories and two very interesting novels [*The Return* (1910) and *Memoirs of a Midget* (1921)], not on his accomplished but minor verse." In 1948 Lord David Cecil and Graham Greene wrote two highly laudatory essays on his stories for Faber and Faber's *A Tribute to Walter de la Mare on his Seventy-Fifth Birthday.* Cecil's tribute is filled with superlatives:

> No one has ever described certain aspects of English landscape as well as he: character, especially child character, is drawn with a wonderfully intimate insight, made warm by countless strokes of tender and humorous observation. As for his command over the world of dream and spirit, it is unsurpassed in literature. He has a Coleridge-like faculty for giving a local habitation and a name to those basic nameless terrors and ecstacies and bewilderments which lurk far below the level of consciousness. It does not matter if we do not accept his interpretation of these phenomena. The rationalist may admire these beautiful enigmatic disquieting stories simply for the true picture they give of the movements of the subconscious mind. Understood, as Mr. de la Mare intends us to understand them, they reveal a penetration into the spiritual regions of man's experience deeper than is to be found in the work of any other contemporary author.

Greene is equally as enthusiastic, particularly concerning de la Mare's manipulation of language. After listing seven-

teen of the stories—"one man's choice of what he could not, under any circumstances, spare"—Greene adds:

> In all these stories, it seems to this admirer that we have a prose unequaled in its richness since the death of James, or dare one, at this date, say Robert Louis Stevenson. Stevenson comes particularly to mind because he played with so wide a vocabulary—the colloquial and the literary phrase, incorporating even the dialect word and naturalizing it. So Mr. de la Mare will play consciously with clichés (hemmed like James' between inverted commas), turning them underside as it were to the reader, and showing what other meanings lie there hidden . . .

There have been other important tributes in comparatively recent years—particularly those by Edward Wagenknecht, Kenneth Hopkins, Dylan Thomas, and H. C. Duffin. And of the short stories, these critics also speak with enthusiasm.

It is apparent that Walter de la Mare was no accidental genius. Among the great story writers in English only James and Joyce combine such literary erudition with conscious craftsmanship. After reading his two collections of critical essays and the lengthy introductions and copious footnotes to the five anthologies he compiled, one comes away with the idea that de la Mare read much. And the notion never leaves one. Another notion that remains is that de la Mare consciously placed himself, by the nature of his enthusiasms and the manner in which he wrote, squarely within the major tradition of the short story—the tradition which began and came to flower in the work of three Americans: Poe, Hawthorne, and James.

These writers were often on de la Mare's lips, and he learned much from them: among other things, the importance of atmosphere from Poe, of ambiguity from Hawthorne, and of a controlled character point of view from James. He learned something even more important from the American masters, something vital to the very structure of the short story. What he said of James, he might have said of himself:

> the more one reads of poetry and fiction the more evident it becomes that the still and lucid atmosphere in which the truly imaginative flourishes is that of dream, and childhood is in a sense a dream, disturbed by nightmare maybe, from which consciousness gradually awakens. In that visionary atmosphere everything that Mr. James wrote is suffused.

The idyllic dream, the horrors of nightmare, and the awakening consciousness—what has commonly been referred to as the story of initiation—from these elements the great tradition of the short story in English has evolved: in stories of childhood and adolescence, like "My Kinsman, Major Molineux," "Araby," "The Garden Party," "The Killers," "The Basement Room," "Blackberry Winter," and "Barn Burning"; and in stories of adulthood, like "The Fall of the House of Usher," "The Beast in the Jungle," *Heart of Darkness,* "The Man Who Died," "Pale Horse, Pale Rider," and "The Death of a Travelling Salesman." Nearly all of de la Mare's best stories recount the initiation of children, adolescents, or adults to one sort of reality or another. In each there is a dreamlike innocence, a nightmarish revelation of horrors or at least wonders, and a readjusted scale of values.

The modernity of de la Mare as a writer of short stories is apparent in the ways that count: in his fascination with the suggestibility of language; in his deliberate employment of ambiguity, paradox, and irony; in his structural use of myth, fairy tale, ghost story, and dream; in his expert manipulation of first and third person character point of view; in the dialectical configuration of his imagery; in his repeated probings into the labyrinths of the unconscious or dreaming mind; in his obsessive and enduring interest in the nature of time; and above all, in his organic conception of art—repeatedly displayed in his thematically and atmospherically unified stories. In Cecil's words de la Mare is indeed "in the truest sense of a misused overworked word, a symbolist."

But, to be first-rate, a writer must be more than a symbolist: he must be able to write well. And de la Mare wrote very well. At its best (and that is quite often) his prose displays the freshness of Welty's, the sonorousness of Stevenson's, and the orchestral complexity of James'. **"All Hallows"** begins like this:

> It was about half past three on an August afternoon when I found myself for the first time looking down upon All Hallows. And at first glimpse of it, every vestige of fatigue and vexation passed away. I stood "at gaze," as the old phrase goes—like the two children of Israel sent in to spy out the Promised Land. How often the imagination transcends the real. Not so All Hallows. Having at last reached the end of my journey—flies, dust, heat, wind—having at last come limping out upon the green sea-bluff beneath which lay its walls—I confess the actuality excelled my feeble dreams of it.
>
> What astonished me most perhaps was the sense not so much of its age, its austerity, or even its solitude, but its air of abandonment. It lay couched there as if in its narrow sea-bay. Not a sound was in the air; not a jackdaw clapped its wings among its turrets. No other roof, not even a chimney, was in sight; only the dark-blue arch of the sky; the narrow snow-line of the ebbing tide; and that gaunt coast fading away into the haze of a west over which were already gathering the veils of sunset.
>
> We had met them at an appropriate hour and season. And yet—I wonder. For it was certainly not the "beauty" of All Hallows, lulled as if into a dream in this serenity of air and heavens, which was to leave the sharpest impression upon me. And what kind of first showing would it have made, I speculated, if an autumnal gale had been shrilling and trumpeting across its narrow bay—clots of wind-borne spume floating among its dusty pinnacles—and the roar of the sea echoing against its walls! Imagine it frozen stark in winter, icy hoar-frost edging its every boss, moulding, finial, crocket, cusp!

The initial paragraphs of **"Seaton's Aunt"** exhibit a more racy, down-to-earth idom:

I had heard rumours of Seaton's aunt long before I actually encountered her. Seaton, in the hush of confidence, or at any little show of toleration on our part, would remark, "My aunt," or "My old aunt, you know," as if his relative might be a kind of cement to an *entente cordiale.*

He had an unusual quantity of pocket-money; or, at any rate, it was bestowed on him in unusually large amounts; and he spent it freely, though none of us would have described him as an "awfully generous chap." "Hello, Seaton," we would say, "the old Begum?" At the beginning of term, too, he used to bring back surprising and exotic dainties in a box with a trick padlock that accompanied him from his first appearance at Gummidge's in a billycock hat to the rather abrupt conclusion of his schoolboy days.

From a boy's point of view he looked distastefully foreign, with his yellow skin, and slow chocolate-coloured eyes, and lean weak figure. Merely for his looks he was treated by most of us true-blue Englishmen with condescension, hostility, or contempt. We used to call him "Pongo," but without much better excuse for the nickname than his skin. He was, that is, in one sense of the term what he assuredly was not in the other sense, a sport.

Often, as in the following passages from **"The Creatures,"** his style is as rich, as resonant, as metaphysically provocative as, say, Melville at his best:

> I would start off after morning, bread and cheese in pocket, from the bare old house I lodged in, bound for that unforeseen nowhere, for which the heart, the fantasy aches. Lingering hot noondays would find me stretched in a state half-comatose, yet vigilant, on the close-flowered turf of the fields or cliffs, on the sun-baked sands and rocks, soaking in the scene and life around me like some pilgrim chameleon. It was in hope to lose my way that I would set out. How shall a man find his way unless he lose it? Now and then I succeeded. That country is large, and its land and sea marks easily cheat the stranger. I was still of an age, you see, when my "small door" was ajar, and I planted a solid foot to keep it from shutting. But how could I know what I was after? One just shakes the tree of life, and the rare fruits come tumbling down, to rot for the most part in the lush grasses.
>
> . . . . .
>
> What was most haunting and provocative in that far-away country was its fleeting resemblance to the country of dream. You stand, you sit, or lie prone on its bud-starred heights, and look down; the green, dispersed, treeless landscape spreads beneath you, with its hollows and mounded slopes, clustering farmstead, and scatter of village, all motionless under the vast wash of sun and blue, like the drop-scene of some enchanted playhouse centuries old. So, too, the visionary bird-haunted headlands, veiled faintly in a mist of unreality above their broken stones and the enormous saucer of the sea.
>
> . . . . .

You cannot guess there what you may not chance upon, or whom. Bells clash, boom, and quarrel hollowly on the edge of darkness in those breakers. Voices waver across the fainter winds. The birds cry in a tongue unknown yet not unfamiliar. The sky is the hawks' and the stars'. *There* one is on the edge of life, of the unforeseen, whereas our cities—are not our dessicated jaded minds ever continually pressing and edging further and further away from freedom, the vast unknown, the infinite presence, picking a fool's journey from sensual fact to fact at the tail of that he-ass called Reason? I suggest that in that solitude the spirit within us realizes that it treads the outskirts of a region long since called the Imagination. I assert we have strayed, and in our blindness abandoned—

Creating unforgettable characters is another of de la Mare's talents. He is especially adept at Dickensian grotesques, apparent in the opening passages of **"The Tree."** The Philistine merchant is on his way to collect a debt from his half-brother, an indigent artist:

Encased in his dingy first-class railway carriage, the prosperous Fruit Merchant sat alone. From the collar of his thick frieze greatcoat stuck out a triangular nose. On either side of it a small, bleak, black eye gazed absently at one of the buttons on the empty blue-upholstered seat opposite to him. His breath spread a fading vapour in the air. He sat bolt upright, congealed in body, heated in mind, his unseeing eye fixed on that cloth button, that stud.

There was nothing else to look at, for his six narrow glass windows were whitely sheeted with hoar-frost. Only his thoughts were his company, while the coach, the superannuated coach, bumped dully over the metals. And his thoughts were neither a satisfaction nor a pleasure. His square hard head under his square hard hat was nothing but a pot seething with vexation, scorn, and discontent.

De la Mare is especially good at lonely and curious children like little Maria. Here she is learning about the nature of reality by observing a housefly on a door-jamb:

For some reason this particular fly was different; and Maria sat watching it with the closest attention. It seemed to be that just as Maria herself was one particular little girl, so this was one particular fly. A fly by itself. A fly living its own one life; confident, alert, alone in its own Fly World.

To judge from its solitude, and the easy careless busy way in which it was spending its time, it might be supposed it was Sirius—and not another star in the sky. And after a while, so intent did Maria become that she seemed to be doing a great deal more than merely watching the fly. She became engrossed.

She was now stooping together in her chair almost as if she was a pin-cushion and her eyes were black-headed pins in it. She seemed almost to have *become* the fly—Maria-Fly. If it is possible, that is, she had become two things at once, or one thing at twice. It was an odd experience

and it lasted at least three minutes by the little gold clock, with the gilt goggling fish on either side its dial under the glass case on the chimney-piece. Three minutes, that is, of ordinary clock time.

For when Maria herself came-to, it seemed she had been away for at least three centuries—as if, like the stranger in the rhyme, she had been with her candle all the way to Babylon; ay, and back again: as if she had gone away Maria, came back Maria-Fly; and now was just Maria again. But yet, when she came-to, everything was a little different.

Maria's outward personality is seen in her relationships with the various adults around the house who know nothing (or, better, have forgotten everything they knew) about the Fly World. De la Mare is always good with "queer" matronly ladies. Here is Maria's encounter with her friend, Miss Salmon:

On the way back along the corridor Maria passed the door of the work-room; it was ajar, and she peeped in. Miss Salmon, in her black stuff dress, sat there beside a table on which stood a sewing-machine. At this moment she was at work with her needle. She always smelt fresh, but a little faint; though also of camphor. She had an immensely long white face—white forehead and chin—with rather protruding eyes and elbows; and she and Maria were old friends.

"And what can I do for you Madam, this morning?" she cried in a deep voice like a man's.

"Well, I just looked in, Madam, to tell you I seen a fly."

"If you was to look through the eye of the smallest needle in that work-basket you would see the gates of Paradise," said Miss Salmon, stitching away again with a click that sounded almost as loud as if a carpenter were at work in the room.

"Give it to me," said Maria.

"Ah ha!" cried Miss Salmon, "such things need looking for."

"Ah ha!" chirped Maria, "and that means tidying all the basket up."

"Nothing seek, nothing find," cried Miss Salmon, "as the cat said to the stickleback, which is far better than Latin, Madam. And what, may I ask, was the name of Mr. Jasper Fly Esquire? If you would kindly ask the gentleman to step this way I will make him a paper house with bars to it, and we'll feed him on strawberries and cream."

Maria's spirits seemed to sink into her shoes. "It was not that kind of a fly at all," she said, "and—and I don't wish to tell you the name, thank you very much."

"Good morning," said Miss Salmon lifting her needle and opening wide her eyes, "and don't forget closing time's at seven."

Scraps of description or characterization are not worth

very much in themselves. The whole of any one of de la Mare's better stories is worth far more than the sum of its parts. **"The Wharf"** will do as well as any to demonstrate how rich and tightly knit these stories are.

"The Wharf" is a story of about 6,000 words (rather short for de la Mare) written from the limited omniscient, or third-person character, point of view. The focal character is a young mother, and the major part of the story concerns her memories of the terrifying ordeal she underwent seven years earlier as a result of a nightmare she had had. Notice the insight de la Mare displays in tracing the progress of her breakdown; and notice also the magnificently sustained atmosphere of the dream:

> It had begun in the March by her being just "out of sorts," overtired and fretful. But she had got better. And then, while she was going up to bed that night—seven years ago now—her candle had been blown out by a draught from the dark open landing window. Nothing of consequence had happened during the evening. Her husband had been elated by a letter from an old friend of his bachelor days, and she herself had been doing needlework. And yet, this absurd little accident to her candle had resembled the straw too many on the camel's back.

> It had seemed like an enemy—that puff of wind: as if a spectre had whispered, "Try the dark!" And she had sat down there on the stairs in the gloom and had begun to cry. Without a sound the burning tears had slowly rolled down her cheeks as if from the very depths of her life. "So *this* was the meaning of everything!" The fit was quickly over. The cold air at the landing window had soothed her, and in a moment or two she had lit her candle again, and, as if filled with remorse, had looked in on her two sleeping children, and after kissing them, gone to bed.

> And it was in the middle of that night her dream had come. After stifling in her pillow a few belated sobs, lest her husband should hear her, she had fallen asleep. And she had dreamed that she was standing alone on the timbers of a kind of immense wharf, beside a wide, sluggish stream. There was no moon, and there were no stars, so far as she could remember, in the sky. Yet all around her was faintly visible. The water itself as if of its own slow moving darkness, seemed to be luminous. She could see that darkness as if by its own light: or rather was conscious of it, as if all around her was taking its light from herself. How absurd!

> The wharf was built on piles that plunged down into the slime beneath. There were flights of stone steps on the left, and up there, beyond, loomed what appeared to be immense unwindowed buildings, like warehouses or granaries, but these she could not see very plainly. Confronting her, further down the wharf, and moored to it by a thick rope, floated on the river a huge and empty barge. There was a wrapped figure stooping there, where the sweeps jut out, as if in profound sleep. And above the barge, on the wharf itself, lay a vague irregular mass of what apparently had come out of the barge.

> It was at the spectacle of the mere shape of this foul mass, it seemed, that she had begun to be afraid. It would have horrified her even if she had been alone in the solitude of the wharf—even in the absence of the gigantic apparition-like beings who stood around about it; busy with great shovels, working silently in company. They, she realized, were unaware of her presence. They laboured on, without speech, intent only on their office. And as she watched them she could have not conceived it was possible to be so solitary and terrified and lost.

> There was no Past in her dream. She stood on this dreadful wharf, beside this soundless and sluggish river under the impenetrable murk of its skies, as if in an eternal present. And though she could scarcely move for terror, some impulse within impelled her to approach nearer to discover what these angelic yet horrifying shapes were at. And as she drew near enough to them to distinguish the faintly flaming eyes in their faces, and the straight flax-coloured hair upon their heads, even the shape of their enormous shovels, she became aware of yet another presence standing close beside her, more shadowy than they, more closely resembling her own phantom self.

> But though it was beyond her power to turn and confront it, it seemed that by its influence she realized what cargo the barge had been carrying up the stream and had disgorged upon the wharf. It was a heap, sombre and terrific, of a kind of refuse. The horror of this realization shook her even now, as she knelt there, the flames of the kitchen fire lighting up her fair blond face. For, as if through a whisper in her consciousness from the companion that stood beside her—she knew that this refuse was the souls of men; the souls not of utterly vile and evil men (if such there were; and no knowledge was given to her of where *their* souls lay or where the blessed) but of ordinary nondescript men, "wayfaring men, though fools." Yet nothing but what seemed to be a sublime indifference to their laborious toil and to its object showed on the faces of the labourers on the wharf.

> Perhaps if there had been any speech among them, or if any sound—no more earthly than echo in her imagination—of their movements had reached her above the flowing of that vast dark stealthy stream, and above the scrapings of the timbers of the shovels, almost as large as those used in an oast-house, she would have been less afraid.

> But this unfathomable silence seemed to intensify the gloom as she watched; every object there became darker yet more sharply outlined, so that she could see more clearly, up above, the immense steep-walled warehouses. For now their walls too seemed to afford a gentle luminosity. And one thought only was repeating itself again and again in her mind: The souls, the souls of men! *The souls, the souls, of men!*

> And then, beyond human heart to bear, the secret messenger beside her let fall into her con-

sciousness another seed of thought. She realized that her poor husband's soul was there in that vast nondescript heap; and those of loved-ones gone, wayfarers, friends of her childhood, her girlhood, and of those nearer yet, valueless, neglected—being shoveled away by these gigantic, angelic beings.

"Oh, my dear, my dear," she was weeping within. And, as if with afflicted lungs and bursting temples she continued to gaze, suddenly out of the nowhere of those skies, two or three angle-winged birds swooped down and alighting in greed near by, covertly watched the toilers.

And one, bolder than the rest, scurried forward on scowering wing, and leapt back into the air burdened with its morsel out of that accumulation. The sight of it pierced her being in this eternity as if that morsel were her own. And suddenly one of the shapes, and not an instant too soon, had lifted its shovel, brandishing it on high above his head, with a shrill resounding cry—"Harpy!"

The cry shattered the silence, reverberated on and on, wharf, warehouse, starless arch, and she had awakened: had awakened to her small homely bedroom. It was bathed as if with beauty by the beams of the night-light that shone on a small table beside her bed where used to sleep her three-year-old. It was safety, assurance, peace; and yet unreal. Unreal even her husband—his simple face perfectly still and strange in sleep—lying quietly beside her.

The word "unreal" here provides a key to the complexity of the story. Earlier, before recalling her dream, she had also questioned the reality of her present waking life. " 'Was what she had seen real?' she asked, '*Was* there such a place? Were there such dreadful beings? After all, places you could not see had real existence—think of the vast mountainous forests of the world and the deserts and all their horrors! And perhaps after death?' " Then, at the conclusion of the story, even after she has presumably been cured of her nerve-shattering depression, and been healthy of mind for seven years, she once again questions the reality of the waking world—specifically, of the farmer who effected her cure and of the farm where her cure was effected. As she tells her husband: "I've been daydreaming—just thinking: *you* know. How queer things are! Can you really believe that Mr. Simmonds is at the farm *now,* this very moment? . . . It's all snow; and soon it will be getting dark; and the cows have been milked; and the fields are fading away out of the light; and the ponds with the reeds. . . . It's still; like a dream. . . ."

In that section of the story treating of the woman's cure (if one can call it that), de la Mare displays real understanding. He displays also his symbolic design in action, especially in his daring use of the stable manure as a foil to the heaped-up souls on the wharf.

Shortly following her terrifying dream, the distraught young mother, at the advice of her physician, goes alone to a private farm not far from London. At first she cannot forget her nightmare, but then one day while she is pursuing Nellie, Farmer Simmond's cow, she comes upon a mound she had several times earlier seen from a distance lying in the corner of the barnyard:

> She could not even (more than vaguely, like reflection in water) see those shapes with the shovels simply because what she now saw in actuality was so vivid and lovely a thing. It was a heap of old stable manure; and it must have lain there where it was for a very long time, since it was strayed over in every direction, and was lit up with the tufted colours of at least a dozen varieties of wild flowers. Her glance wandered to and fro from bell to bell and cup to cup; the harsh yet sweet odour of the yard and stables was in her nostrils: that of hay was in the air; and into the distance stretched meadow and field under the sky, their crops sprouting, their green deepening.

> And as she stood, densely gazing at this heap, she herself it had seemed became nothing more than that picture in her eyes. And then Mr. Simmonds had come out and across the yard, his flannel shirtsleeves tucked up above his thick sun-burned arms, and a pitchfork in his hand. He had touched his hat with that almost schoolboyish gentle grin of his; then when he noticed that she was trying to speak to him, had stood beside her, leaning on his pitchfork, his glance following the directions of her eyes.

A moment later Simmonds begins, in reply to her "disjointed curious questions," to talk about the manure and its flowers:

> It was just "stable-mook"; and the older that is, of course, the better. It would be used all right some time, he assured her. The wild flowers, pretty creatures, wouldn't harm it; not they. They'd fade by the winter and *become* it. . . .

> And still she persisted, struggling as it were in the midst of the dream vaguely hanging its shrouds in her mind, as if towards a crevice of light to come out by. And Mr. Simmonds had been patience and courtesy itself. He had told her about the various chemical manures they used on the crops. That was one thing. But there was, she gathered, what was called "nature" in *this* stuff. It was not exactly the very life of the flowers, for that came you could not tell whence, it is the "virtue" in it. It and the rain and the dew was just as much and as little as their lifeblood—their sap—as the drink and victuals of humans and animals are. "If you starve a lad, ma'am, keep him from his victuals, he don't exactly flourish, do he?"

> Oh yes, he agreed such facts were strange, and, as you might say almost unacknowledgeable. A curious thing, too, that what to some seems just filth and waste and nastiness should be the very secret of all that is most precious in the living things of the world. But then, we don't all think alike; "'t wouldn't do, d'ye see?" Why, he had explained and she had listened to him as quietly as a child at school, the roots of a tree will bend at right angles after the secret waters underneath. He crooked his forefinger to show her how. And the groping hair-like filaments of the

shallowest weed would turn towards a richer food in the soil. "We farmers couldn't do without it, ma'am. If the nature's out of a thing, it is as good as dead and gone, for ever. Wasn't it now the "good-nature" in a human being that made him what he was? That and what you might call his very life. "Look at Nellie, there! Don't her just comfort your eye in a manner of speaking?"

And whether it was Mr. Simmond's words, or the way he said them, as if for her comfort—and they were as much a part and parcel of his own good-nature as were his brown hairy arms and his pitchfork and the creases on his round face; or whether it was just the calm copious gentle sunshine that was streaming down on them from across the low heavens, and on the roofs and walls of the yard, and on that rich brown and golden heap of stable manure with its delicate colonies of live things shedding their beauty on every side, nodding their heads in the lightest of airs; she could not tell. At that very moment and as if for joy a red cock clapped his wings on the midden, and shouted his *Qui vive.*

At this, a whelming wave of consolation, and understanding seemed to have enveloped her very soul. Mr. Simmonds may have actually seen the tears dropping from her eyes as she turned to smile at him, and to thank him. She didn't mind. It was nothing in the world in her perhaps that he would ever be able to understand. He would never know, never even guess that he had been her predestined redemption.

But the symbolism is more complex than I have suggested. The flower imagery, for instance, extends, ramifies, enriches the story's meaning. The story is framed in present time. At the time of her recollection, the young woman has three girls, the last of whom was born after her breakdown. The two older daughters are fair, healthy, "normal" children; the youngest is dark, strange, wild, excitable, like her mother. At the outset of the story the three children are going to a party (it is after they have gone that the mother, staring into the kitchen fire, recalls her ordeal), and the mother is admiring her youngest daughter's new frock. "With that wearer in it," she muses, "it looked for all the world like the white petals of a flower; its flashing crimson fruit just peeping out from beneath. It looked like spindle-tree blossom and spindle berries both together." Is not the mother here somehow unconsciously drawing a parallel between her daughter and the flowers of the "stable-mook"? And, if she is, is she considering herself to be the "mook" of the barnyard or the "mook" of the Wharf? Both, I think. Depending upon her mood at the moment. Shortly after the children go, and before reliving her dream, she reveals the basic instability of her mind, and thus the incompleteness of her cure:

> She was happy now. But thinking too much was unwise. That had been at the root of Uncle Willie's malady. He could not rest, and then had become hopelessly 'silly'—then, his 'visitors!' What a comfort to pretend for a moment to be like one of those empty jugs on the dresser; or rather, not quite empty but with a bunch of flowers in one! And a fresh bunch every day. If you

remain empty, ideas come creeping in—as sleep, too; one's mind is empty, waiting for dreams to well in. It is always dangerous leaving doors ajar.

This mental instability is stressed in the concluding lines of the story when her husband returns home and asks her whether the children had not been a handful in getting off to the party: "He smoothed her hair with his hand. But she seemed still too deeply immerged and far-lost in her memory of the farm to answer for a moment, and then her words came as if by rote." " 'A handful?' They *were*—and that tiny thing!—I am sometimes, you know, Jim, almost afraid of those wild spirits—as if she might—just burst into tiny pieces—into bits some day—like glass. It's such a world to have to be careful in!"

The theme of **"The Wharf"** resembles the theme of Conrad's *Heart of Darkness*: if one wishes to be happy in this world he had better live in the spirit of his illusions, for reality (with all its "horrors") will not bear looking into. Now, **"The Wharf"** is not so complex as *Heart of Darkness,* but it is as profound, as brilliantly conceived, as well written (with "less adjectival insistence"), and as thematically unified. In short, it can bear comparison with the best stories in the language. But so can **"All Hallows," "The Nap," "Seaton's Aunt," "The Connoisseur," "The Creatures,"** and, with only the slightest presumption, twelve or fifteen of de la Mare's other stories. Is it not ridiculous that, with the exception of those in two small collections, all of de la Mare's short stories are out of print? And is it not doubly ridiculous that since his death in 1956 not one extended study of these stories has appeared? (pp. 85-91)

> *John H. Wills, "Architecture of Reality: The Short Stories of Walter de la Mare," in* North Dakota Quarterly, *Vol. 32, No. 4, Autumn, 1964, pp. 85-92.*

Julia Briggs   (essay date 1977)

[*Briggs is an English critic. In the following essay, she examines de la Mare's stories of the supernatural.*]

The most interesting ghost stories written after the Great War were those of the poet Walter de la Mare (1873-1956). They had little in common with others of their time, though the influence of Henry James was discernible, contributing a complexity, intensity and literary seriousness only rivalled by the great nineteenth-century masters of the form, Scott, Dickens, Le Fanu and James himself. Modern criticism has consistently neglected de la Mare's work, particularly his prose writings. They have been excluded from the accepted canons of important literature, receiving only an occasional accolade, and that mainly from fellow-authors. As a result, most of them have long been out of print, although single pieces often reappear in anthologies of ghost stories. It is to be hoped that his reputation is merely undergoing a temporary recession and that before too long that delicate yet powerful vision will receive the recognition it deserves.

The tendency to omit any reference to his remarkable short stories in literary histories is probably due to a sense

De la Mare in 1922.

that they are old-fashioned, even out-of-date in character. The world depicted is not the familiar urban landscape of pylons, airports and motorways, but a never-never land, a romantic vision of a lovely England, long lost if it ever existed at all. There is some justification for such a view: although the modern world intrudes occasionally—there is a tube train in **'Bad Company'**, a car in **'A Recluse'**, and elsewhere trains, buses, pubs and teashops—de la Mare prefers a simplified setting that conforms to poetic universals or is generalized by the enduring influence of nature. He looks over his shoulder to a dateless, idealized Victorian era where private incomes and servants were the norm rather than the exception, a world whose demise ultimately prevented his contemporary, E. M. Forster, from writing any more novels. Even worse, de la Mare is felt to have avoided the main issues of fiction by presenting love with all the evasiveness of a Victorian, and by not treating social life at all. Professor Robson has commented: 'The traditional subjects of the novel—manners, social criticism, studies of moral conduct—are not at the centre of his interests.' It might be argued that such concerns are less appropriate to the short story than the novel. De la Mare scores by presenting brilliantly illuminated fragments of experience. His imaginative world is essentially subjective, an intensifying gaze focused on a sequence of curious, perhaps inexplicable events.

Ironically it is these qualities that make his work modern. As the novel and drama become increasingly concerned to pursue in depth the nature of private fantasy and obsession, so de la Mare's stories may be seen to anticipate more recent poetic explorations of loneliness, silence and death, so remarkable in Beckett and Pinter, for example. Like them, he writes of the absurdity or total failure of communication in settings whose historical time or place are kept deliberately vague. His heroes, like theirs, grope their way through the metaphysical uncertainties of a universe in which they can never hope to be more than 'strangers and pilgrims', and the highest aim is merely to survive.

De la Mare's stories pose a series of questions about the nature of life itself, some of which are actually asked in the course of the tales, while others remain implicit. There are no assertions and no solutions here, only an endless sequence of explorations of ever-increasing delicacy. Although many of his ghost stories are very powerful, they seldom have a clearly defined climax, and in this respect his work resembles that of E. T. A. Hoffmann, another explorer at the remoter edges of human life. All Walter de la Mare's narratives are hedged about with doubts and uncertainties: his characteristic narrator is an odd person met on a train or a railway platform, in a teashop or a pub, whose references can never be checked. When the story is told in the first person or the narrator of the uncanny events is shown in sharper focus, the experience itself then becomes elusive, a series of strange, often unpleasantly suggestive incidents which might nevertheless sustain a more prosaic explanation than is liable to occur to the reader.

Nor is it only the characters and events of these stories which refuse to be pigeon-holed. Over and over again the writer asks, implicitly or explicitly, 'What indeed constitutes the *reality* of any fellow creature?' or more simply, 'Was what she had seen real?' In an important sense his short stories form a continuous spectrum in which the distinction between the 'real' and the supernatural is at best an artificial one. There is nothing as horrifying among the ghost stories as **'In the Forest'**, a totally plausible narrative, while the daylight mystery of **'Missing'** is more appalling than that of **'Crewe'**, which it otherwise closely resembles, because of what is left unsaid and unadmitted. Both relate a brief encounter with a sinister individual who tells a story of betrayal and virtual murder. Yet although **'Missing'** is set on a bright summer day, and has none of the supernatural overtones of **'Crewe'**, the speaker's pathetic attempts to conceal his crime make him even more horrifying. In the de la Mare universe objective experience and objectivity in general seems to hold little interest; what matters is the subjective truth. It may be broken into small fragments, highly coloured by the minds of those who experience it, but it is small enough to be free from any distortion, other than the imposed colouring of the mind through which it comes. His stories are deliberately limited in scope and length, but their accuracy and integrity give them an importance far beyond the immediate impact; they require several readings before their possible meanings will be exhausted.

The deliberate limiting of the areas of experience to be explored is reflected in the techniques he used for looking at them: 'the eye of childhood' is a favourite device, both in the non-supernatural tales, and in such ghost stories as **'Seaton's Aunt'.** Closely related to the little world of the child is the physically limited adult world of **'At First Sight'** (*On the Edge,* 1930) where the hero cannot raise his eyes above knee level, or that of Miss M in *Memoirs of a Midget* (1921). The theme of visual distortion is combined with the child's eye view in the tragic story, **'The Guardian'** (*A Beginning,* 1955), whose prosaic narrator is the last of a long line of selfish and possessive protectors. When her little nephew, Philip, swivels his eyes to the corner of his head, he catches a glimpse of a dreadful crouching figure that reminds him of 'that horrid, horrid Satan'. Like the hero of **'At First Sight'**, little Philip may have some genuine ocular disability. His aunt later wonders that it never occurred to her to consult an oculist. At the end of the story the dying child's eyes 'moved to their extreme angle' to behold, not a demon this time, but the angelic dormitory maid whose serene face 'vaguely recalled some old picture'. The guardian of the title thus refers not only to the crabbed narrator, but also to the guardian angel that she had hesitated to recommend to the frightened child, but whom he finally meets in the person of the sick-room maid. For de la Mare, the horrors and glories lurk at the edge of our vision, and are only beheld by the few who are painfully sensitive to them. He may well have known the physiological fact that objects glimpsed at the edge of the field of vision act as warnings to the brain, thus producing sensations of fear. It lends an added point.

The child-observer is a most useful device in fiction since his sharp observation, but lack of total comprehension, requires the reader to supply much of the interpretation himself. Walter de la Mare may have learnt this technique from Henry James, who uses it so effectively in his novel *What Maisie Knew.* De la Mare's admiration for James both as a ghost story writer and, more generally, as a stylist, is evident in much of his work, but while, like James, he often uses language to express thought in motion, he avoids the tendency to thickness and 'clotting' which sometimes makes James difficult to read. As one would expect of a poet, he pays the closest attention to language at all times, and uses it with a sense of irony and aptness that repays the reader's full attention.

One respect in which Walter de la Mare surpasses his master is in the use of language to establish character. An obvious comparison here might be with Kipling, but the use of the monologue for self-revelation, such an integral part of de la Mare's art, is perhaps more reminiscent of Browning, a distant relative of his. Yet again such a comparison fails to do justice to the vividly colloquial quality of the language. The unforgettable way in which it reaches out to the unknown, as well as its frequent content of self-delusion, seem to point forward to modern dramatists such as Harold Pinter. Here is an example from **'Crewe'** (*On the Edge,* 1930), a tale where even the setting, an empty waiting room, seems to belong to a Pinter dialogue:

> 'And talking of that, now, have you ever heard say that there is less risk sitting in a railway carriage at sixty miles an hour than in laying alone, safe, as you might suppose, in your own bed?

That's true, too.' He glanced round him. 'You know where you are in a place like this, too. It's solid, though—' I couldn't catch the words that followed, but they seemed to be uncomplimentary to things in general.

'Yes,' I agreed, 'it certainly looks solid.'

'Ah, "looks",' he went on cantankerously. 'But what *is* your "solid", come to that? I thought so myself once.' He seemed to be pondering over the *once.* 'But now,' he added, 'I know different.'

Henry James and Walter de la Mare both differ from the majority of ghost story writers in that they used the supernatural not merely as an end in itself, but also as a subordinate element in their fictions. Many of James's short stories such as 'Owen Wingrave' and 'Sir Edmund Orme' are centered not on the ghost, but on a human drama played out in the foreground. So too are a number of Walter de la Mare's tales, though with this difference, that his writing is never wholly free from a sense of wonder and mystery and so his minor ghosts often fit more naturally into their background. For example in **'The Trumpet'** (*The Wind Blows Over,* 1936) there is more than a hint that the terrified Philip sees the spirit of his half-brother, Dick, entering the church on All Saints Eve, even while the boy clambers precariously to the roof within. What else could it be, since 'it isn't a man and it isn't a woman'? Such an interpretation is further suggested by the children's speculations on the nature of death and the meaning of the motto, *resurgam.* Nevertheless the story is primarily concerned with the relationship between Philip and Dick, and the appearance of the ghost is not crucial, but merely characteristic of a world where anything may happen.

Two other stories, **'A Froward Child'** and **'The Face'**, show how supernatural experiences may bring about the estrangement of a young couple. Here the emphasis falls on the breakdown of the relationship rather than on the girl's strange experience, the significance of which lies—in both stories—in the fact that she cannot convey it to her stolid, unimaginative fiancé. **'Cape Race'** presents a similar situation but without the element of the supernatural, and the inadequate relationship is ultimately accepted. In **'A Froward Child'** and **'The Face'** the supernatural experiences of Lavinia and Nora deepen, rather than lessen, their individual isolation. In **'Cape Race'** Lettie's encounter with the land-bird is strangely liberating, yet she is able to accept the differences between herself and her dull fiancé as Lavinia and Nora were not. **'An Anniversary'** (from *A Beginning*) is also about estrangement, but this time the parting is more than earthly, for a dead lover returns to reclaim his mistress, now Aubrey's unhappy wife. It is difficult to decide whether the supernatural or human interest predominates here, since the real horror lies in Aubrey's consuming and degrading jealousy, not in the visitation of his dead rival. De la Mare's trick of irony runs riot in Aubrey's consciousness, and the total effect has something of the savagery and unrestrained bitterness of Chaucer's *Merchant's Tale,* although the explicit references are, not unnaturally, to *Othello* and the horror of being Iago.

Where the supernatural is made to contribute to larger effects and employed generally as part of the writer's equipment, it may be used for light-hearted pieces, such as Henry James's 'The Third Person' and de la Mare's '**A Revenant**', or for lyrical and mysterious studies such as '**The Looking Glass**' or '**The Riddle**'. The fairy-tale mood of these two stories dominates the collection entitled *The Riddle* (1923) but subsequently was chiefly limited to his stories for children. On the whole de la Mare's ventures into the regions of fantasy are more surefooted than James's because his work deals, not with society and its values, but rather with loneliness and isolation, areas where relative views and the individual imagination assume greater importance. In James's world, where essentially human values and ethics predominate, the ghost is often felt to be an intrusion; de la Mare's universe is far more internal and spiritual, and his ghosts consequently gain more from their settings. In those stories where the supernatural puts in a fleeting, even a doubtful appearance (as in '**The Trumpet**', '**Mr Kempe**' or '**Bad Company**' for example) the prevailing atmosphere and the surrounding discussion greatly enhance the ghostly effect. Perhaps this is because, as Dylan Thomas observed, 'His subject, always, is the imminence of spiritual danger.'

Yet if spiritual danger is the predominant theme, it is only another aspect of that obsession with death which underlies all Walter de la Mare's writing, both in prose and verse, and which makes him find in the ghost story a natural medium for his speculations on the subject. The phenomenon of death, and what may lie beyond, is seen as crucial to an understanding of life, and as possibly conferring meaning on it, if only the evidence could be interpreted aright:

> 'MORS. And what does MORS mean?' enquired that oddly indolent voice. . . . 'It means—well, sleep,' I said. 'Or nightmare, or dawn, or nothing or—it might mean everything.'

> (*Ding Dong Bell*, 1924)

But herein lies the difficulty—death is also the most extreme form of those breakdowns in communication which are often present, always implicit in his stories. It is, or should be 'the bourne from which no traveller returns', yet only too many of de la Mare's characters are anxious to prise open its uncertainties and violate its quiet (for him, as for M. R. James, necromancy is always a deplorable activity). In de la Mare's work, death has taken over the rôle which love traditionally plays in fiction, as the most central and significant experience of life, which must illuminate and confer meaning on everything. Love is secondary, and only too frequently itself leads to death or to one of those eternal partings that are even more unbearable. Sometimes, as in '**Seaton's Aunt**', death so deeply overshadows the lovers that their relationship scarcely comes to life at all. For the reader as for the narrator, Arthur Seaton 'had never been much better than "buried" in my mind.'

De la Mare's concern with the nature and meaning of death was not limited to his fiction. In a conversation with Lord Brain, recorded at the end of his life, he remarked *à propos* of a head injury he had sustained, 'It means, doesn't it, that our whole perception depends on our body, so that when we die we lose not only our bodies but our

whole apparatus of thought; we leave two vacua.' His restless and enquiring mind could not remain secure in the easy answers of religion (Graham Greene remarked on how odd his world appeared 'to those of us with traditional Christian beliefs'). Yet if he was certain of anything it was of the spiritual nature of life and of the universe, the quality to which G. K. Chesterton paid tribute in calling him a mystic. This certainty gave him a detachment and serenity when writing of the physical aspect of death that provides a striking contrast to the morbidness of Poe, a writer whom he much admired. In '**The House**', Mr Asprey, approaching death and chasing away some cockroaches is 'aware at the same moment of the surmise that his next abode might be frequented by another species of vermin'; yet his attitude is one of realistic acceptance, rather than gloomy self-indulgence. In de la Mare's cupboards there are no decaying corpses or skeletons. The most physical of his ghosts resembles a scarecrow, while most of them prefer to be heard and not seen, confiding their activities to voices and perhaps 'a light footfall'. Ugliness is essentially a human attribute, and the dead, if well content, may exert the wholesome influence of a country churchyard on a summer night, such as provides the setting of '**Benighted**'.

Ding Dong Bell, the book of epitaphs which includes '**Benighted**', conveys the peace of death, as well as its terrors, and in this respect forms a useful corrective to the sinister graveyard of Widderstone in *The Return* (1910). The very name here seems significant, halfway between 'widdershins' (a favourite word in de la Mare's poetry) and 'wither-stone' or perhaps 'whither?-stone'. Here the exhausted Lawford becomes possessed by a seventeenth-century suicide, Sabathier. Much of this short novel is taken up with discussions on the nature of death between Lawford and the strange hermit, Herbert Herbert, who lives beside the graveyard and eventually reconciles Lawford to death and to what has happened to him. Many of de la Mare's most characteristic themes, the inadequacy of traditional religion in the face of spiritual distress, the loss of an ideal loved one, as well as a prolonged discussion on the nature and meaning of death, are to be found in this strange and fascinating book. Several of his short stories, also, are concerned with similar speculations, on death and what lies beyond—for example '**The Three Friends**' and '**The Bird of Travel**'. '**The Vats**' is a meditation on the nature of eternity and in '**The Wharf**', a dung-heap becomes a highly original symbol of salvation. None of these are strictly ghost stories, though '**The Three Friends**' might be described as 'on the edge'. The ghost stories themselves frequently explore the same topics: the narrator of '**Crewe**', Mr Blake, voices a number of opinions on the subject: 'It's my belief there's some kind of ferry plying on that river. And coming back depends on what you want to come back *for*.'

Perhaps the most lengthy and varied discussion of the meaning of death takes place in '**A Recluse**', where all the apparently random incidents of the leisurely opening contribute in one way or another to the total atmosphere. Returning from a visit to a friend who had been at death's door and is gradually recovering, the narrator encounters a strange horseman carrying a cardboard box—a grotesque cross between Alice's White Knight and the horseman of Death in the Apocalypse. That this character should warn him with a gesture against the house 'Montresor' seems to make it both more sinister and more fascinating. Here the narrator meets Mr Bloom, the horrible occupant, who tries to keep him there and keep him awake because he is afraid of—what? Mr Bloom is a dabbler in the occult, and it seems that he fears the very forces he has aroused. Mr Dash, the narrator, has had some experience of psychic investigation through an old family friend, and finds the whole thing 'a silly and dangerous waste of time'. His experiences at Montresor do not prove him wrong, though they give him a closer glimpse of its workings. Everything that Mr Dash encounters increases his uneasiness, the ugly dog, the secretary's diary, the horrible mask of Mr Bloom and the discovery of his stolen gear key, the voices, and the last figure glimpsed in the shrubbery as he drives away. Even the music Mr Bloom plays him, Ravel's *Gaspard de la Nuit,* is satanic. Like Seaton's aunt, whom he resembles in more than one respect, Bloom has filled the house with horrid inhabitants, although unlike her, he seems somewhat daunted by their presence.

The language of the whole story is shot through with irony. Such a sentence as 'it was not only that Mr Bloom's manner was obviously a mask'—clearly anticipates the central episode, when the narrator finds a mask of Bloom lying on his bed. This event, in turn, causes the reader to wonder whether the visual appearance of Mr Bloom is not entirely assumed, and as easily cast on or off as the boots which intrigue the narrator so much. Like everything else about Mr Bloom, these boots do not seem to be entirely real, for they are 'adorned with . . . imitation laces'. Their emptiness, as they stand by Mr Bloom's bed, is curiously disquieting. The word 'ghost' itself is used with a special sense of its significance: the dead secretary's diary yields a few last scrawled and ominous words, and 'the ink . . . had left its ghost on the blank page opposite'. Not merely the ink, but the writer too, perhaps, has left a ghost in the haunted 'Montresor'. As the narrator comments,

> I had long suspected that Mr Bloom's activities may have proved responsible for guests even more undesirable than myself, even though . . . they may, perhaps, have been of a purely subjective order.

Similarly in **'Seaton's Aunt'**, the narrator, Withers, fails to send his old school friend Seaton 'the ghost of a wedding present', appropriately enough since the intended recipient has in fact died. At their final dinner party together, the aunt teases her wretched nephew Arthur with the ominous and prophetic words 'I shall have memory for company . . . the ghosts of other days.'

As a child, Arthur Seaton seemed pathetically afraid of his grotesque and sinister aunt and guardian, even suspecting her of being a witch, a notion pooh-poohed by Withers. There is certainly no tangible evidence of her supernatural powers, and yet the horrible atmosphere of the house and the aunt's final mistaking of Withers for Arthur *after* the latter's death combine to convince us that he was after all right and that there will be no peace for her nephew even in the grave. The language throughout is dense with sug-

gestion as when at their last dinner together Withers observes, 'I could scarcely see her little glittering eyes under their penthouse lids.' The sentence recalls the witch's words from *Macbeth,* themselves conveying something of what she has done to her hapless nephew:

> I shall drain him dry as hay.
> Sleep shall neither night or day
> Hang upon his pent-house lid;
> He shall live a man forbid.

The reference has a further point in context because the aunt's tiny glittering eyes, which seem to see in the dark and even at a distance, penetrate the house. Eyes (like mirrors) are favourite symbols for de la Mare. Philip's troubles in **'The Guardian'** are first revealed when he describes how the gas-bead at night looks like a watchful eye. In **'Seaton's Aunt',** the watchful eye is symbolized by a painting 'depicting a large eye with an extremely fishlike intensity . . . beneath was printed very minutely, "Thou God, seest ME".' The unhappy Seaton assures Withers 'There's hundreds of eyes like that in this house; and even if God does see you, He takes precious good care you don't see Him.' On Wither's first visit to the house, as a schoolboy, the aunt's 'chocolate eyes . . . were more than half-covered by unusually long and heavy lids'. On his second visit, the occasion of the dinner party, 'her eyelids . . . hung even a little heavier in age over their slow-moving inscrutable pupils'. On his final visit, 'the old eyes had rather suddenly failed'. The aunt's terrifying eyes are somehow related to her vampirish watch over Seaton, which continues even after his death and her blindness.

Seaton's aunt, Mr Bloom and Mr Kempe in the story of that name are consumed by an insatiable desire to pry into death's well-kept secrets, so that they become ghouls and necromancers, though the exact extent of Mr Kempe's investigations is left vague. He is probably innocent of calling up the dead, but he appears to have attempted to prolong the lives of those at the point of death (his wife, the fallen climbers) in the hope of extracting from them the truth about 'the other side'. A glimpse of his dropped photographs is enough for the narrator, who flees without further delay. Although Walter de la Mare's warlocks are far more highly individualized than their traditional prototypes, and themselves become objects of pathos to a certain degree, his uncompromising horror of such dabbling is in itself traditional.

The spirits summoned up by Mr Bloom and Seaton's aunt are apparently hapless wretches like Bloom's ex-secretary, Sidney Champneys, or Arthur Seaton himself, pathetically incapable of self-assertion, but not all ghosts are like this. Some may demonstrate a more active malevolence, like the gardener, Mr Menzies, who comes back for George in **'Crewe'**, or the frustrated poetess, Esther F., in **'The Green Room'**, like Sabathier in *The Return* or Beverley's old aunt in **'The Quincunx'.** These last two use possession in order to gain their ends, but perhaps the most sinister possession described is not on a human scale at all. It is that of the great cathedral, **'All Hallows'**, which is being 're-edificated and restored by some agency unknown'. This story uses a number of features that occur elsewhere: an atmosphere of oppressive heat (as in **'Miss-**

ing'), and the narrative of a strange old man, in this case the cathedral verger, who has been looking for an outsider to whom he may unburden himself. The counterpart of the satanic take-over of **'All Hallows'** is the strange and beautiful haunting of the house by the sea in **'Music'**, where, it seems, one may hear the music of the spheres. This story is from his last collection, *A Beginning* (with characteristic irony) and the imagery is often, and no doubt intentionally, redolent of Shakespeare's last play *The Tempest,* with its unearthly music:

> Sometimes a thousand twangling instruments
> Will hum about mine ears.

Both the cathedral of All Hallows and the house in **'Music'** stand on the shore, in positions of maximum exposure to the sea; both are full of the sound of the sea, perhaps the most ancient metaphor for man's last voyage. It is this unobtrusive and traditional use of symbolism that makes de la Mare's work so effective.

One pattern of correspondence which occurs frequently is the reflection of the owner in his house. Even the name, 'Montresor' smacks of the preciosity of Mr Bloom while the Seatons' home is all gloom, and seems to age and decay in mystic sympathy with its owner. But the two stories where the analogy between house and owner is made most explicit are **'Out of the Deep'** and **'The House'**. The latter might be read as a simple allegory of the soul departing from its tenement of clay:

> If positive landlord there were (himself perhaps
> the architect) Mr Asprey of late years had sel-
> dom 'called on' him, even in a merely metaphor-
> ical sense. And now—well, the one thing certain
> was that he had been given notice to quit.

Mr Asprey's inspection of his rooms, and his constant note-taking represent useless and belated attempts to 'put his house in order' before his departure. Yet the central episode, in which a dead maid appears and he presents her with the wallet she apparently once took remains elusive and unexplained—does he merely give her 'alms for oblivion'?

'Out of the Deep' (*The Riddle,* 1923) also leaves a number of questions unresolved, and here again there is a close similarity between the old and haunted house, and the tubercular Jimmie, who inherits it and has to exorcize the ghosts of his unhappy childhood before he can die peacefully, with the bell-rope looped safely out of his reach. Each time he rings the bell, something comes up from the servants' quarters below, up out of the deep well of the unconscious:

> Thinking was like a fountain. Once it gets going
> at a certain pressure, well, it is almost impossible
> to turn it off. And, my hat! what odd things
> come up with the water!

The figures who appear are essentially Jimmie's own creations, rather than the ghosts of the servants, now dead, who once persecuted him there, but he attempts to equate his visions with his persecutors. The young man who appears and shows 'just a flavour, a flicker . . . of resemblance to himself' Jimmie christens 'Soames Junior', as if he were really an emanation of the cruel old butler he once

knew. He refuses to admit that these servants are entirely of his own making, and his jeers and scorn therefore rebound only on himself and are bound up with his self-contempt and self-loathing. When he learns to live amicably with them, and thus with his own subconscious life, he is able to die peacefully in the attic where he had suffered so horribly from childhood nightmares. His efforts to punish the dead, both actual (his sale of his uncle's treasures) and imaginary (in ringing the bells for the departed servants) have failed and are succeeded by acceptance. The house itself has become the arena for Jimmie's internal battle, and hence, by extension, his mind; horrors come up from 'below stairs', yet Jimmie finally dies in the attic, the upper region where reason, or perhaps even the elusive soul may dwell.

Among de la Mare's many powerful ghost stories, perhaps the most unforgettable is also the quietest, the most oblique and delicate: **'Strangers and Pilgrims'** was first printed in the American edition of *The Wind Blows Over* and then added to a new edition of *Ding Dong Bell* (1936), as it is set in a cemetery and includes a number of epitaphs. At a superficial level this story describes a protracted and rather unsatisfactory encounter between an old verger closing up his church for the evening and a stranger in search of a particular grave which he fails to find. The deeper implication, however, is that it is his *own* grave for which he is searching. The visitor is undoubtedly strange in more than the obvious sense of the word:

> Clothes, manner, gait, speech—never in his long
> experience had any specimen of a human being
> embodied so many peculiarities. And there was
> yet another, pervading all the rest, yet more elu-
> sive.

Like Sabathier in *The Return,* he seems to have been a suicide and as the conversation turns towards ghosts he briefly alludes to his own fate:

> 'And assuredly,' he hesitated, 'if, at the end,
> there had been extreme trouble and—horror.'
>
> The harsh screaming of the swifts coursing in
> the twilight . . . was for the moment the only
> comment on these remarks.

Most disturbing of all is the entry in the Church Register which gives, under the date 1880, the dead man's name followed by the cryptic comment 'Nothing known. Not buried here.' One wonders on how many previous occasions the stranger had made the same useless pilgrimage to that cemetery to prompt such a note.

The epitaphs scattered through the story provide a commentary on certain aspects of death, in particular the finality of its partings, both for husband and wife, and even more poignantly for mother and child. The title as well as the course of the conversation also invites a further consideration of the relationship between the living and the dead, and the way in which the impenetrable mystery of death casts disturbing shadows over our conception of life. The revenant, a stranger and pilgrim under an inexplicable compulsion, might equally serve as a representative of the living, themselves strangers and pilgrims in a universe whose total meaning death makes incomprehensible. For the riddle of life is death, and our conception of existence as ordered or absurd turns on what its termination signifies. This is what makes death de la Mare's central concern (just as, though he treats it very differently, it is also Samuel Beckett's). What makes him such an important and stimulating writer of ghost stories is that he uses the form to pose a question it is supremely well-suited to ask—what is the meaning of death, and therefore of life? The figure of Ambrose Manning, remorselessly driven on by his search for his mortal remains, for the little that is left of himself, seems to suggest that death too is equivocal, mysterious, unknowable. Ultimately there is no answer to de la Mare's 'Qui vive?' thrown out across the great unknown but an echo. (pp. 182-95)

> *Julia Briggs, "On the Edge: Walter de la Mare," in her* Night Visitors, *Faber, 1977, pp. 182-95.*

John Bayley   (essay date 1989)

[*An English poet, novelist, and critic, Bayley is best known for his critical studies of Thomas Hardy, Alexander Pushkin, and Leo Tolstoy. In the following essay, he examines de la Mare's view of childhood as expressed in his fiction, focusing primarily on the short stories "A Recluse" and "Seaton's Aunt."*]

In *The Turn of the Screw* Henry James could be said to have invented, inadvertently, a new concept of children. By some sort of intuitive process of his art he conveyed their essential dissimilarity from adults, and the way they live naturally in a world of their own, however ready they may be to seem to accommodate themselves to the ideas of grown-ups. His discovery is a by-product of the tale's technique, for in manipulating the ghostly atmosphere and apparatus he requires the behaviour of the two children exposed to it to seem curious and suspicious—even eerie to their elders, and to their new governess in particular. Today we should think nothing of it; indeed it might be regarded as virtually the norm of childish behaviour, especially for children brought up as little Miles and Flora have been.

The further slant in the tale is that the ghosts—that sinister pair, the former valet and governess—seem, by dying, to have entered the childish world. They share the same dismaying inaccessibility as the couple who were once their young charges, and seem to merge into their ambiguous being. What frightens and horrifies the new governess seems quite normal and cosy to the children, an accepted part of their daily life, with its own small secret inventions and assumptions. Ghosts and children seem to understand each other, and to live on the same level of being, observing and frequenting the same covert runways. Walter de la Mare must have unconsciously absorbed this point. Children and the unseen live in the same world with him too. We know how much he admired James's stories, and his own reveal their unmistakable influence.

None more so than his masterpiece, **'A Recluse'**, from the collection called **On the Edge**. The sinister thing about this wonderfully bland and intricate tale, in which the young narrator has an involuntary experience in the house

of a Mr Bloom, is that the theme of *The Turn of the Screw* is both exploited and reversed. Mr Bloom, big, sly, ineffectual, copious of speech and manner, is an appalling parody of childhood, and its proper distance from the adult world. He plays a trick on Mr Dash, the brashly unsuggestible narrator, who has been drawn by what seems the deserted beauty of an English country house to do a bit of harmless trespassing. Sitting in his little sports car he contemplates the Palladian porch and the gracious front door, and suddenly there is Mr Bloom, materialized in its opening, contemplating him, and presently inviting him in to see the house. After a few moments of Mr Bloom's overwhelming affability Mr Dash is conscious above all of an equally overwhelming desire to escape. He himself is like the child now who longs to get away from a particular sort of 'grown-up' atmosphere; and this disturbing alternation of roles will continue throughout the story. The children's trick the old creature plays on his young visitor, and which the latter never for a moment suspects, is to purloin the ignition key of his sports car, and thus to acquire him as an unwilling guest for the night. Company is what Mr Bloom inordinately desires, for the 'company' that attends him in the house, as a result of his psychical research with the planchette and other false childish devices, he has found to be not the kind to be left alone with.

The point about these disquieting and enchanting stories of de la Mare is that they mingle, with great ease and a kind of eerie and dreamy naturalness, the world of childhood and adulthood, with an imaginative dimension in which both partake, but to which both are always having to say goodbye. No state in life is fixed: we live like strangers and revenants between the state of being old and being young; and in de la Mare's art we experience both in a poetic form to which we can uniquely respond. The poem **'The Listeners'** carries its own gloss on this atmosphere, for who in it is what? The traveller is himself a ghost and the listeners are the vanishments of his own sensibility, to which return is only possible through the medium of art, frail but vivid. Like children listening on the stairs the disembodied ones can overhear the sounds of perpetual departure, and how the silence surges softly backwards.

In the best stories this commingling has the relish but also the power of parody. If the word were not so incongruous for the sensibility of de la Mare one would say that he positively gloats over it. The house, Montresor, in **'A Recluse'** has all the aesthetic possibility of Henry James's Bly in *The Turn of the Screw*. Its details are suave and pastoral— 'lush, tepid, inexhaustible'—in an English May; and its master has, no doubt by intention, the physical stance, speech, and manner of James himself, James in whom the 'small boy—and others' acquires a new and disquieting perspective of meaning. To Mr Dash it seems incredible that this great simpering disconcerting creature could ever have been a little boy playing childish games at Montresor, but into the reader's reception the idea slips totally, for a version of those games is still going on.

The parody, and as it were the fixity of childhood, when that evanescent state should long have departed into consciousness and recollection, gives to Mr Bloom, as to Seaton's Aunt in the story of that title, something pathetic but also potentially appalling. Mr Dash escapes from the world of Mr Bloom, who is left in his gracious but also 'swarming' domain until the news of his decease comes in some oblique way to the young narrator. Arthur Seaton, already adult in childhood from his experiences, never escapes from the monstrous aunt who seems to have invested in herself the secret arrogance and egoism of one kind of childish world. He seeks to grow up and to enter the adult world of marriage and normality, but in some unnamed and unnameable way she destroys him. Yet he is not entirely 'worsted', for his presence remains to haunt her too, in the dreadful literalness of a perpetual intimacy. When the narrator, Seaton's one-time school-friend, calls at the house after his death, it seems quite natural that the rasping old voice should float down over the banisters saying 'Arthur? Is that you, Arthur?' In the same way the voice of Mr Bloom is heard in the small hours in the passages of Montresor, querulously calling 'Coming—coming' . . . at the behest of some domineering presence. The game in which adult, child, and 'presence' meet and conjoin was played too in the house and bedroom of Seaton's Aunt, when the old lady's dressing-gown was heard swishing softly back to her bedroom, and the two children fled into the cupboard where, as she lay serenely on her great bed, she knew very well they were hiding.

Childhood, for de la Mare, is a state of acceptance—acceptance of power and evil, joy and woe, the real and the feigned, the natural and supernatural—inhabiting the same dimension. Because, in consciousness, we never leave the childhood world, there is no special enclave for children. They take the adult world for granted, without attempting to understand it. The special intimation in both **'A Recluse'** and **'Seaton's Aunt'** is an exploring of this. Mr Bloom, whom the narrator finds impossible to imagine as a child, in fact has the childish faculty of acceptance to a most unnerving degree. Montresor, and its swarm of inhabitants and presences, is—or was—as natural to him as the book world of Henry Brocken was to him in de la Mare's early 'novel' of that name. Brocken was not in the least surprised to be talking to the girls from Herrick's poems, and to Gulliver in his stockade among the Houyhnhnms. Of course there is something slightly self-conscious about this, an echo of the deliberate 'for children—and also for adults' technique of Kipling's *Puck of Pook's Hill* and *Rewards and Fairies*. De la Mare's later stories are much odder and more business-like. Mr Bloom is indeed not a 'child'; but his activities and the atmosphere that surrounds him are seen as if through a child's sense of things—the grown-up perquisites, keys, and loose change lying on a dressing table, loose capacious armchairs of worn vermilion leather, seeming to blend with the presences who have come to live among them—the man with his back turned glimpsed standing under a tree outside, the beings to whom Mr Bloom querulously responded with his 'Coming—coming'—as if he were an adult summoned by a child, or a child by an adult. All this seems lost on young Mr Dash, the narrator, through whose medium it none the less becomes visible, and audible. When he wakes in the night, everything about him in the room looks peculiar, and he realizes it is as if seen by someone intensely afraid; yet he has himself no sense of

fear. In the same way the writer manages it so that everything in the story is as if seen by a child, although there are no children in it, and no suggestion of their presence, no emphasis on their style of awareness.

Something of the same sort takes place in **'Seaton's Aunt'**, where the old woman, like Mr Bloom, seems isolated in a terrible parody of childhood. Both may remind us of the former governess and valet in *The Turn of the Screw*, who are united with the children, as Mr Bloom with his ghosts and Seaton with his infernal aunt. All three stories imagine with great skill and delicacy that debatable land where childhood and adulthood are joined by the nature of the imagination itself, a land from which the narrator in each tale is formally excluded. De la Mare has, in a sense, taken further the involuntary *trouvaille* made by James in the working out of his subject. If James perceived the difference of children, de la Mare's art sees the difference between all persons who still exhibit, in whatever context, the behaviour and assumptions of the childish condition, and those who do not. All three stories take it invisibly for granted, and in the most matter-of-fact way, that there is nothing serene or innocent in the child's world of vision, that anything seemingly angelic in it may belong to dark angels as well as bright ones. In the world of that imagination no distinction can nor need be made between the light and the dark. It is a pre-moral world, rather than a morally ambiguous one, in which monstrosity appears only in the eye of the narrator-beholder. The light and dark exist in their vividness, and their own matter-of-factness. There is something unnerving in all these stories, but there is also the deep satisfaction of something unswervingly true, rigorously unsentimental.

That lack of sentiment is a function of the fact that the three stories take childhood for granted, even as they 'expose' it. The stories are neither for children, nor about children, and yet they can only be fully appreciated by those readers by whom the child's world is naturally and involuntarily understood. When I said that Henry James accidentally invented the modern child in a literary context I also implied the paradox that it is *because* childhood is different that it cannot be isolated, contained, and understood by the vision in art of the adult world. That is exactly what the governess is attempting to do in *The Turn of the Screw*, and its sub-text tells how she fails. It is also what the narrators are seeking to do in **'A Recluse'**, and in **'Seaton's Aunt'**; and there too the memorable figures in the tales elude the narrator, remaining for the reader (and no doubt for the writer too) in their own peculiar and compelling worlds of being.

There is another feature to the paradox. Because children are different, what they read is the same. They are falsified by stories intended for children and they falsify themselves (which they are generally perfectly willing to do) by accepting the idea of 'children's stories'. Naturally little actors, as the governess in *The Turn of the Screw* finds out, they will accept any version of themselves, in literature as in life, but their real appetite is for whatever is read by persons who are both child and adult, that large category which only excludes (and there only notionally) James's governess and de la Mare's narrators. What matters is the sense in which we are all children when we read; and children as readers are, as it were, the same only more so.

The reader becomes child as he reads, and hence 'different'. That is perhaps the crux of the matter; and it is the matter which is in a sense analysed by the nature of the three tales I have discussed. Their form of secret imaginative analysis explains their peculiar resonance, and its success. De la Mare is a striking example here, because his work shows so subtly, and so conclusively, the difference between stories of childhood and 'children's stories'. The latter category, and the poems he wrote of the same kind, are frankly potboilers with their own sort of individuality and charm, but artistically not in the same class as his best poetry and prose. Many of his best stories, like '**Miss Duveen**' and '**The Almond Tree**', are specifically for and about childhood, but their art is far removed from his tales for children. *The Three Royal Monkeys* (or *The Three Mulla-Mulgars* as it was in the first edition) is a far better book than C. S. Lewis's *The Lion, the Witch and the Wardrobe,* with which it has something in common, notably the landscape in which summer has been transformed, as if by malign magic, into wintry snow. (Lewis may well have copied this or had an unconscious memory of it.) But although *The Three Royal Monkeys* is full of wonderfully memorable and imaginative scenes—like the great Gunga with his bow, the mountain Mulgars, and their subterranean cousins who impassively watch the voyage of the three travellers through the underground river—it suffers both from a repetition of the motifs and traditions of such books, from *The Swiss Family Robinson* to *The Coral Island,* and from an almost inevitable handing on of their general moral tone.

That general moral tone is one that might be considered suitable for 'children of all ages', a somewhat ominous concept, and one very different from the much more complex and indefinable feeling, which de la Mare's best stories give us, that children are different, and that we are sharing—even embodying—that difference in the act of reading. 'Children's stories' give us in a sense the feeling that we are all the same, all little adults, good, civic, virtuous, collective. That collective and communal atmosphere is common to *The Lord of the Rings, The Swiss Family Robinson, The Coral Island, Swallows and Amazons,* and most other such quest adventure tales, not excluding *The Three Royal Monkeys* and even *The Wind in the Willows,* although Kenneth Grahame's classic has the brilliant notion of isolating Toad from his civic-minded fellows. The wholly authentic aspect of *The Wind in the Willows,* which has kept it fresh for so long, is the perception that children take adult class attitudes and social activities for granted, as the reader takes those of the 'animals' in the story. Thus the animals appear like adults to the reader, who is not—by virtue of being reader—assumed to belong to the jolly gang involved, as he is in our other examples, but to accept them almost incuriously as creatures inhabiting the grown-up world of parties, clubs, and country houses. The irony of Toad's conversion at the end is that he has been the 'child' in the tale, and that he is now definitively joining the grown-up world, not by moral choice but because he has no choice. The book ends with the end of childhood, and the notional perpetuating of the 'grown-up' animal regime.

The most imaginative thing in *The Three Royal Monkeys* is somewhat similar. Nod, the youngest of the three, is accidentally captured by a human castaway, Ben Battle, and frightens him by imitating the sounds of his voice. Nod, like a young child, is not just imitating, as would a parrot or mynah bird, but is naming after the man the things indicated by him. Battle's fear and wonder is caused by the unexpected loss of his own solitude, which seems threatened by the signs of independent intelligence in Nod, whom he had wanted as a pet, to be talked to but to remain uncomprehending. Nod's company, like that of the presences in '**A Recluse**', or that of the children in *The Turn of the Screw,* suddenly seems to enter the realm of the uncanny. This goes to the heart of de la Mare's vision of childhood as a solitary state only imaginable in its aspect of solitude. When two solitudes meet, however reluctantly, 'strangeness' begins. This occurs in '**Miss Duveen**', between the mad woman and the child, and in '**Seaton's Aunt**', not only between the two persons named in that phrase, but between aunt and narrator. The process is most elaborately displayed in '**A Recluse**', with its strong element of parodic buried humour where Mr Bloom talks interminably to his captive guest, majestically resenting any attempt by the guest to talk back. The real anguish which is so moving in that story—moving like a big fish far down in deep water—is Mr Bloom's adult imprisonment in a childhood solitude, once so exciting and so much to be revelled in. It seems like de la Mare's recognition of what is secretly equivocal—a possible source of deep personal trouble—in his own sources of literary inspiration. Like other writers for 'children'—Beatrix Potter for instance—he both displayed and relieved in the process something sad about himself. James, too, gives us the feel both of exclusion and of tenderness where children are concerned.

Yet de la Mare's story is also filled with a childish zest, a kind of private enthusiasm not unlike the one that lurks at times even in the most banal of de la Mare's 'children's' tales. What reader of the story can afterwards forget the wonderful supper conjured up by Mr Bloom for his reluctant guest? Mentally cursing the inexplicable loss of the essential car key, Mr Dash gloomily contemplates the deep green parterres from the terrace porch, and sourly imagines his insufferable host 'contemplating the broken meats in the great larder'. Mr Bloom had apologized in advance for what must of necessity be 'a lamentably modest little meal', but as usual he had shown himself to be incapable of 'facing facts'. Cold bouillon is followed by a pair of spring chickens, the white sauce on their breasts decorated in lozenges of cucumber and basil, 'hapless birds' who seem to have fed on the herbs of paradise. They are accompanied by an asparagus salad, 'so cold to the tongue as to suggest ice' and followed by a noble stilton and a bowl of dark rich wine jelly, thickly clotted with cream. 'After the sherry champagne was our only wine, and it was solely due to my abstemiousness that we failed to finish the second bottle.'

Children are fascinated by food in stories, but this is no childish meal. By what agency is it provided?—the old housekeeper vaguely mentioned by Mr Bloom as attending to his daily needs and departing well before evening? Why not, and yet there is more than a suggestion that some more magical and sinister agency must be involved. Everything in the fine old house is gracious and conventional and timeless, and yet everything is possessed by some occult force which never explains itself except through oblique hints and disquieting manifestations. The reassurance, the enchanted fixity of childhood, is suffused with some other force, which produced both childish excitement and absorption and a sense of some void beneath, the jaws of indifference into which everything is about to drop. De la Mare's inspiration, as always, is excited by the supernatural and yet finally disillusioned by it. Mr Bloom reminds him of a solitary spinster cousin with whom he used to play the planchette game, and it is her haunted yearning eyes which are the image in the story's last sentence. Wholly 'adult' as it is, the excitements and disillusionments of childhood underlie the story and insensibly penetrate all its levels.

And the food? Yes, food is magically important in this context. Ben Battle's homely supper, and how he eats it, is dwelt on at length in **The Three Royal Monkeys,** and both it and Mr Bloom's feast may remind us of those splendid matter-of-fact meals in *The Wind in the Willows*—the picnic, the extemporized Christmas dinner in the Mole's old home, the glorious pheasant stew Toad cajoled from the gipsy, the simple but sustaining lunch— 'bacon and broad beans and a macaroni pudding'—eaten by the animals after Toad's return, before the serious business of recapturing Toad Hall. But it is vital to the enthralment of childhood that these should be all *grown-up* meals. I recall at an early age being attached to a book for children by Stanley Rogers, who wrote sea stories. It described the adventures of two boys who found themselves back in the past and aboard an Elizabethan galleon, commanded, rather improbably, by Sir Richard Grenville. They are offered a sumptuous meal 'in the cuddy', at which, as the captain explains, the fish only looks like fish but is really 'frozen lemon jelly'. (Curious, the association of ice with magical meals.) I remember at this point, however, my total disgust and disillusionment with the author's intention and method: he was writing for children and this was a children's tea-party. How could one go on any longer believing in the galleon and her crew and business?

De la Mare's characters, whether man, child, or beast, inhabit a very different world. **'Who said Peacock Pie?'**— the poem and its query come from a collection of verses for children, but its sense is both complex and mysterious. The old king who uttered those ironic words to the sparrow makes one of the many confrontations which move the poet's imagination. The little poem **'Crazed'** has three such—a blazing flower meadow, a nocturnal pool, a face that looks briefly out from the lattice of a toiling windmill:

Crazed
I know a pool where nightshade preens
Her poisonous fruitage in the moon;
Where the frail aspen her shadow leans
In midnight cold a-swoon.

I know a meadow flat with gold—
A million million burning flowers
In moon-sun's thirst their buds unfold
Beneath his blazing showers.

I saw a crazed face, did I,
Stare from the lattice of a mill,
While the lank sails clacked idly by
High on the windy hill.

And no confrontation is stranger, or more rich in what it implies, than the child's with the man; or either with some force that dispossesses them from their normal state and status. A sense of ghostliness may do it. In any case what matters is that when immersed in de la Mare's world the reader loses distinction between a childish self and any other kind. When this magic fails, as it does in many of the poems and stories, the product becomes creepy or quaint in much the same way as with less individual and less original authors. Any undue emphasis on the nature or quality of childhood is usually fatal, dispelling that sense of a life lived naturally in a world of the seen and unseen. Forrest Reid is a writer with his own kind of originality and his own sense of childhood, but when he collaborated with de la Mare in a story called **'An Ideal Craftsman'** the result was disastrous. The idea of a boy who 'arranges' a death in the most realistic and convincing manner may have appealed to the authors' more commonplace sense of the macabre, but it exaggerates and vulgarizes an original perception in much the same way as horror stories and films about childhood do today.

Children are more alienated from this world even than our adult selves. That is one paradox which the best stories suggest, however lightly, even in the midst of delineating a consciousness which seems to take the seen and the unseen equally for granted. Sadness in that sense of things is almost indistinguishable from joy. When the traveller in **Ding Dong Bell** sees a human figure in the snow by a churchyard he knows it to be a version of himself, blessedly dispossessed from living, even as he assumes its ordinariness as a fellow mortal. Angels are creations of our own sense of not belonging where we are. De la Mare's best art is about that, as it relates to all our ages. (pp. 337-48)

John Bayley, "The Child in Walter de la Mare," in Children and Their Books: A Celebration of the Work of Iona and Peter Opie, *edited by Gillian Avery and Julia Briggs, Oxford at the Clarendon Press, 1989, pp. 337-49.*

FURTHER READING

Criticism

Clark, Leonard. "The Storyteller." In his *Walter de la Mare,* pp. 54-71. London: Bodley Head, 1960.
    Discusses de la Mare's stories for children and adults.

Hopkins, Kenneth. *Walter de la Mare.* London: Longmans, Green & Co., 1953, 44 p.

Includes commentary on de la Mare's short stories.

Kennedy, P. C. Review of *Broomsticks, and Other Tales,* by Walter de la Mare. *The New Statesman* XXVI, No. 659 (12 December 1925): 273-74.

Argues that the children's stories collected in *Broomsticks, and Other Tales* are unlikely to appeal to young readers.

McCrosson, Doris Ross. *Walter de la Mare.* New York: Twayne, 1966, 170 p.

Includes a chapter examining the point of view, settings, and characterization of de la Mare's short stories.

Mortimer, Raymond. Review of *The Riddle, and Other Stories,* by Walter de la Mare. *The New Statesman* XXI, No. 528 (26 May 1923): 201.

Finds the stories collected in *The Riddle* "a little monotonous" in their cumulative effect but praises the characterization and restrained morbidity and mysticism of de la Mare's tales.

Oliver, Edith. "De la Mare at Home." *The Nation and Athenaeum* XLVIII, No. 2 (11 October 1930): 54, 56.

Favorable review of *On the Edge.*

Penzoldt, Peter. "Walter de la Mare." In his *The Supernatural in Fiction,* pp. 203-27. London: Peter Nevill, 1952.

Examines de la Mare's supernatural fiction and compares "Out of the Deep" with Henry James's novella *The Turn of the Screw.*

Punter, David. "The Ambivalence of Memory: Henry James and Walter de la Mare." In his *The Literature of Terror: A History of Gothic Fictions from 1765 to the Present Day,* pp. 291-313. New York: Longman, 1980.

Comparative study of supernatural elements in short fiction by Henry James and Walter de la Mare. Punter comments: "The central point of comparison which I want to emphasise between James's *Turn of the Screw*

and de la Mare's stories is their insistence on the connexion between fear and self-delusion. Where their narrators and story-tellers profess to see the world as haunted, we as readers are being constantly required to reassess these hauntings in terms of the deficiencies of the narrators themselves."

Sykes, Gerald. "Walter de la Mare." *The Nation* (New York) 132, No. 3430 (1 April 1931): 356.

Praises de la Mare's treatment of sentimental themes in *On the Edge.*

"The Connoisseur." *The Times Literary Supplement,* No. 1272 (17 June 1926): 412.

Praises the imaginative qualities of the stories in *The Connoisseur, and Other Stories.*

"Creatures of Dream." *The Times Literary Supplement,* No. 2798 (14 October 1955) 597-99.

Review praising the characterization and dialogue of the stories collected in *A Beginning, and Other Stories.*

Wagenknecht, Edward. "Walter de la Mare's 'The Riddle': A Note on the Teaching of Literature with Allegorical Tendencies." *College English* 11, No. 2 (November 1949): 72-80.

Analyzes "The Riddle," focusing on the allegorical aspects of the story.

————. Introduction to *The Collected Tales of Walter de la Mare,* by Walter de la Mare, pp. vii-xxi. New York: Alfred A. Knopf, 1950.

Discusses de la Mare's reputation as a short story writer.

————. Introduction to *Eight Tales,* by Walter de la Mare, pp. vii-xx. Sauk City, Wis.: Arkham House, 1971.

Discusses de la Mare's early short stories.

Additional coverage of de la Mare's life and career is contained in the following sources published by Gale Research: *Children's Literature Review,* Vol. 23; *Concise Dictionary of British Literary Biography,* Vol. 6.; *Contemporary Authors,* Vols. 110, 137; *Dictionary of Literary Biography,* Vol. 19; *DISCovering Authors; Major Authors and Illustrators for Children and Young Adults; Short Story Criticism,* Vol. 14; *Something about the Author,* Vol. 16; *Twentieth-Century Literary Criticism,* Vol. 4; and *World Literature Criticism.*

Aleksandr Fadeyev

1901-1956

(Pseudonym of Aleksandr Aleksandrovich Bulgya; also transliterated as Fadayev, Fadeev, and Fedeyev) Russian novelist, essayist, nonfiction writer, and short story writer.

INTRODUCTION

A leading proponent of Socialist Realism in Soviet literature during the Stalinist period, Fadeyev is best known for his civil war novel *Razgrom* (*The Nineteen*). Incorporating stylistic techniques employed by Leo Tolstoy, Fadeyev's fiction is noted for its focus on psychological realism and Marxist ideology. Fadeyev was also an influential literary official in the Stalin regime and subsequently played an integral role in the regimentation of Soviet literature in the twentieth century.

Fadeyev was born in Kimry, Tver, and raised in Siberia. He fought with Bolshevik forces in eastern Russia during the Revolution and became a member of the Communist Party in 1918. After the war, Fadeyev attended business school in Vladivostock and a mining school in Moscow, publishing the short stories "Protiv techenia" ("Against the Current") and "Razliv" ("The Flood") in the early 1920s. Active in the Communist Party, Fadeyev rose to prominence in the Russian Association of Proletarian Writers and became a board member of the Writer's Union in 1934. As general secretary of the Writer's Union, an appointment he received in 1946, Fadeyev wielded great influence over Soviet writers. Advocating the need for social realism in literature, Fadeyev urged Soviet artists to imitate established Russian authors writing in the realist tradition, to eliminate romanticism and formalism from their writings, and to infuse their work with Marxist doctrine and ideology. After Josef Stalin's death in 1953, Fadeyev lost favor with the Communist Party's Central Committee and was demoted to chairman of the Writer's Union. He committed suicide in 1956.

Significantly influenced by Tolstoy, Fadeyev is known for his realistic portrayal of individual psychology and morality. His first novel, *The Nineteen,* depicts the conflicts of a doomed company of Communist guerrillas fighting the White Cossacks and the Japanese in Siberia during the Russian Revolution. The narrative introduces several characters who became widely imitated in Soviet literature during Stalin's rule: the simple, courageous proletariat, Morozka; his girlfriend, Varya, a strong, kind-hearted nurse; the weak intellectual, Mechik, who betrays the company; and Levinson, the complex, pragmatic leader who attempts to retain control over the company and his own fear and insecurities. Fadeyev's impartial portrayal of individual motivation was considered innovative for that period and was well-received critically—Levinson is often considered one of the first "positive" heroes in Rus-

sian literature—but some commentators suggested that Fadeyev's characterization of the untrustworthy intellectual, Mechik, was biased by Marxist ideology.

Soviet history and politics are also integral to Fadeyev's other novels, *Posledniy iz Udege* and *Molodaya gvardiya* (*The Young Guard*). In the unfinished work *Posledniy iz Udege,* Fadéyev chronicled the repercussions of the revolution on the lives of the Udeges, a nearly extinct Far Eastern tribe. *The Young Guard* documents partisan resistance in the Ukraine to German occupation during World War II. *The Young Guard* initially earned Fadeyev a Stalin Award for literature but was later denounced for "serious ideological and artistic errors." Fadeyev consequently rewrote the novel to present a more flattering portrait of the Soviet people and the role of the Communist Party in the resistance movement.

Evaluations of Fadeyev's literary status have historically been informed by his politics. In the Soviet Union, particularly after Stalin's death, Fadeyev's writings were often considered suspect due to their political content, but the 1970s witnessed a renewed interest in his work. In 1974 the Soviet government established the Fadeyev Medal to honor authors whose works depict the "heroic achievements of the Soviet people in the defense of its socialist homeland." Western critics have faulted Fadeyev for sacrificing literary aesthetics to political doctrine, yet they continue to praise his treatment of the individual. As Edward J. Brown observed: "The important thing for Fadeyev is the political idea of the book, and he exercises what literary skill he has to express that idea in terms of individual human experience."

PRINCIPAL WORKS

Razgrom   (novel) 1928
[*The Nineteen,* 1929; also published as *The Rout,* 1956]
Posledniy iz Udege. 4 vols.   (unfinished novel)   1930-40; revised edition, 1957
Leningrad v dni blokady (nonfiction) 1944
[*Leningrad in the Days of the Blockade,* 1946]
Molodaya gvardiya (novel) 1945; published in journal *Znamya;* revised edition, 1951
[*The Young Guard,* 1958]
Za tridtsat' let   (essays, speeches, and letters)   1957; revised edition, 1959
Sobranie sochinenii. 7 vols.   (short stories, novels, essays, speeches, and letters) 1969-71
Pis' ma, 1916-56   (letters)   1967; enlarged edition, 1973

CRITICISM

Arthur Ruhl   (essay date 1930)

[*In the following review, Ruhl offers a positive assessment of* The Nineteen.]

[**The Nineteen**] is the story of a troop of Communist "partisans"—guerilla volunteers—fighting in eastern Siberia during the revolutionary civil-war period, against the Japanese and Kolchak. There is only one woman among the named characters; a sort of camp-follower nurse, a big-hearted, animal-like female, who mothers her men, as they seem to need mothering, and is possessed from time to time by various of them. All the rest are fighting-men—a handful of peasants and mine-workers, with their sabres and rifles and horses, slogging more or less blindly about in the wilderness of the Siberian *taiga,* now toward, now away from a vague but stronger enemy, almost as a herd of buffalo or wild cattle might turn, now this way, now that, as hunger or thirst or danger might pull or drive them.

But it isn't quite so blind and animal-like as that. They have a leader, a Jew named Levinson, in whom is personified all those qualities that make a man leader of other men; through whom, although it is never expressed in intellectual, political terms, we are expected to feel the passionate faith of the proletarian zealot, giving everything to the cause. He is one of those made by the revolution which he himself is making; a man who otherwise might have been quite small and ordinary, transfigured in the revolutionary fire.

And the drive and bigness which the little story has, comes partly from the fact that there is no controversy this way or that, no localization of person or place. But for a passing reference to "Maximalists"—a very "Left" but not quite orthodox wing, to which the young trooper through whose eyes most of the scenes are seen, had formerly belonged—there is no mention of any of the parties, personalities, and controversial questions which usually obtrude even into revolutionary novels written by Russians inside Russia. Everything of that sort is taken for granted. We start simply with the troop as it stands, as with so many men on a storm-tossed ship; a little splotch of humanity, flickering back and forth across mountains, rivers, through deep, still valleys; fighting, dying, dodging this way and that, drinking and loving when the chance offers, all the time held together and driven forward by that never discussed but indomitable force, until only the nineteen are left, and these, bloody, beaten, go riding ahead—"for it was necessary to live and a man had to do his duty."

It might appear from this that Fedeyev's narrative is merely a sort of epic of the animal will-to-live; something in the Jack London vein, for instance. But curiously, or possibly subtly, enough, it is much more than that. Its outstanding quality, in spite of the raw flesh of which it seems superficially to be made, and its absence of sentimentality, and even, for the most part, of conventional sentiment, is its compassion and rough tenderness; the human warmth of this gang of roughnecks; the dewy beauty of the natural world through which they go blundering and killing and being killed. For Fedeyev is a poet, in spite of himself, so to say; however cautious a Communist writer must be not to express his poetry in the "wrong" way.

I have said that there is no discussion or argument. In general, this is the case, but once, when Levinson, racking his brains as to how "these millions of people who have lived for centuries under an indolent sun, in dirt and poverty, ploughing with primitive tools, believing in a vindictive and foolish God," how, out of these can be made "a new, fine, vigorous man," indulges in a moment of recollection and introspection, which, in a word, embodies the whole Communist ideology:

> The only thing that came back to his mind was an old photograph of a sickly little Jewish boy with big, ingenuous eyes, wearing a black jacket, who looked with surprising, unchildish intentness at the spot where he had been told a pretty bird would fly out. But the bird didn't fly out . . . and he remembered that he had almost cried with disappointment. How many further such disappointments he had suffered before he had finally been convinced that "things aren't like that!" And when he was really convinced he understood what dangers and evils befall men because of these lying tales about pretty little birds—pretty little birds which will fly out from

somewhere or other—and he realized how many of them spend their lives in fruitless expectation. . . . No, he had no further need of these birds! He had relentlessly suppressed all sweet and vain regrets for them; he had crushed in himself everything that he had inherited from past generations brought up on those lying tales of pretty little birds! . . . "To see everything as it is, in order to change everything that is, to control everything there is"—Levinson had achieved this wisdom, the simplest and the most difficult a man can achieve.

This one passage is the nearest to "propaganda" that the little story ever gets. For the rest, it is a straight narrative of the day to day lives of the fighting "partisans"—told with extreme brevity and simplicity, with beauty and tenderness. (pp. 917-18)

> Arthur Ruhl, "Fighting 'Partisans'," in The Saturday Review of Literature, *Vol. VI, No. 38, April 12, 1930, pp. 917-18.*

Aleksandr Fadeyev   (essay date 1932)

[*In the following essay, which was originally read at a Moscow city district meeting in 1932, Fadeyev discusses the composing of* The Nineteen, *the work's themes, and its characters.*]

The books *The Nineteen* and *The Last of the Udeghe* were written on the basis of Civil War material: I passed through the school of the Civil War myself, in particular I took part in the partisan struggle. I had no idea at the time that I would ever become a writer, but my memory stored away impressions of the events I witnessed. Evidently some things in the struggle in which I was taking part created a deeper impression, some aspects of it attracted my special attention, while other things I disregarded and forgot without realizing it. If I had thought then that I would become a writer I would evidently have made many notes hot on the tracks of the events. But even so I would hardly have known in advance how the notes would be utilized.

In the initial stage of creative work, which I find it most difficult to describe, images flit about chaotically in the artist's mind in utter confusion; instead of ordered, integrated images there is only the raw material of life—faces, characters, events, isolated facts, natural settings, etc.—which have created the greatest impression on him. At this stage of his work the artist has no definite idea of what will emerge from his observations and studies of life. It is very difficult, in fact impossible, to describe how the material takes shape and is sifted in this melting pot, how a tentative outline of the subject and plot develops. After a while the random images begin to fall into some sort of pattern—as yet far from comprehensive. Certain landmarks of the work begin to take shape in the mind; this is the stage when the artist can start writing down episodes and chapters and draw up a general plan of work. The time comes when you can get down to intense conscious work: you select the most pertinent material out of the vast amount of impressions and images retained by the memory, take what you need, reject the superfluous, condense facts and impressions with the purpose of expressing, conveying as comprehensively and vividly as possible the principal idea of the book, which crystallizes more and more clearly in the mind. This is the second stage of the writer's work.

I conceived the theme of *The Nineteen* long before I got down to the actual writing. The main contours took shape in my mind as far back as 1921 or 1922, but I began writing the book only in 1925. At the time (1921-1922) the themes of *The Nineteen* and *The Last of the Udeghe* mingled in my mind, and I did not yet contemplate writing two books. I thought it would be one novel. But in the process of sifting the material I realized that it comprised two books, and I purposefully proceeded to work in both directions, attempting to formulate the main thought, the main idea of each and to determine the means I would employ for their imaginative expression.

As concerns the themes of *The Nineteen* and the *Last of the Udeghe,* I was at the time going through the second stage of creativity, when the subjects and individual story lines began to take shape in my imagination. I began consciously to consider by what artistic means I would express them.

At this stage you think a lot about the plot, that is to say, in what way, through what events and through what sequence of these events you can best convey the essential thoughts and ideas of the work. . . .

What are the essential ideas of *The Nineteen*? I can define them as follows. The first and fundamental idea: human material is being sifted in the Civil War, the revolution sweeps away everything hostile, all that is incapable of genuine revolutionary struggle, all that has accidentally found its way into the revolutionary camp is winnowed away, while all that has risen from the genuine roots of the revolution, from the millions-strong masses of the working people, is tempered, grows and develops in the struggle.

The tremendous remoulding of people which is taking place is successful because the revolution is led by the foremost representatives of the working class—the Communists, who clearly see the goal towards which they are advancing and who lead the more backward and help them re-educate.

This is how I can define the basic theme of the novel.

There are also several incidental themes. One of them consists in the following: I observed that in stories about the partisan movement the latter was represented as purely spontaneous, as an independent peasant movement hardly influenced by the city and the workers. But my own experience of partisan struggle had shown me that, in spite of the considerable spontaneous element, the decisive, organizing role in the partisan movement was played by Bolshevik workers. It was this idea that I wished to stress in *The Nineteen,* in refutation of what had been written about the partisan movement by others.

Simultaneously I wished to develop the idea that there is no such thing as an abstract, "generally human" eternal morality. . . .

That is why two characters were brought forth—Morozka and Mechik. Morozka's life was a hard one, he went through a bitter school of life before the revolution. He could steal, swear profanely, deal rudely with a woman; he had vague notions about many things, he could lie and drink heavily. All these traits of his character are doubtlessly derogatory. But in difficult, decisive moments of the struggle he acted for the good of the revolution, overcoming his weaknesses. His participation in the revolutionary struggle was a process in which his personality was moulded, in which he was liberated from the evil heritage of the past and acquired new qualities of a revolutionary fighter. He was unable to complete the road of development because he was killed early.

Mechik, another hero of the novel, is very "moral" from the point of view of the Ten Commandments: he is "sincere," does not "commit adultery," "does not steal," "does not swear," but these are purely superficial qualities, which conceal an inner egotism, an absence of his fidelity to the working class' cause, his petty individualism. When put to the revolutionary test Morozka turns out to be a loftier human type than Mechik, for his aspirations are loftier—and they determine his development as a loftier personality.

These are approximately the main ideas I wanted to convey in *The Nineteen*. What factual material did I have with which to express these thoughts and ideas? I was mainly assisted by my personal observations of Bolsheviks, of workers, of intellectuals both during the Civil War and after it.

Thus, in *The Nineteen* I attempted to present more or less generalized characters, to create characters which would not simply reproduce this or that living person of the Civil War period, but would also constitute a condensed sociopsychological image.

The story line of *The Nineteen* is quite simple. The main ideas are conveyed through an account of the fate of an isolated detachment, an account of how the Whites pursue it, how it resists the Whites, how it is hunted and attacked and how, in the end, it breaks out of the encircling Whites, losing many of its men but ready for new battles. The events of the novel and the actions of its characters take place over a short period of time. The novel presents a step-by-step account of all the detachment's engagements, starting from the beginning of its rout and ending with its final breaking through the encircling Whites. In this short period of time people reveal their various fundamental qualities: some are revolutionaries, others are hostile to, or at best unsuitable for, the Revolution. Thanks to the grit and stamina of such men as Levinson and Baklanov, the reader is left with a realization and feeling of the strength of the revolution, in spite of the detachment's defeat.

It took me two years to write the novel. What were the main principles which guided me? First of all, as distinct from the mannered language of my first work, **"The Flood,"** I tried to write as simply as possible and express my ideas as clearly as possible. I subordinated all my work to the task of writing so as to convey precisely and con-

vincingly all I see, all I imagine. The habits acquired in my earlier work made themselves especially felt in the first few chapters, when I had not yet learned to do away with superficial verbal embellishments. As the work progressed I gradually got rid of this fault. . . . I worked a lot on the novel, rewriting various chapters many times. There are chapters which I rewrote more than twenty times (for example, "On the Road" and "The Burden"). There is not a chapter which I didn't rewrite four or five times.

As you know, critics have noted that *The Nineteen* reveals the influence of the great Russian writer, Leo Tolstoy. This is true in part, but only in part. It is not true in the sense that there is not a trace of the Tolstoyan philosophy in the book. However, I have always been charmed by the vividness and veracity of Tolstoy's characters, the exactitude and sensual tangibility of the depicted events and his great simplicity. In working on *The Nineteen* I occasionally involuntarily followed certain characteristic features of Tolstoy's language in rhythmic pattern and phrase construction.

This does not worry me much, for any artist, when he begins to work, necessarily derives from past experiences.

While working on *The Nineteen* I found for myself that many of the preconceived ideas did not fit into the book, and that in the process of work new points arose, not envisaged before. For example, initially my idea had been that Mechik was to commit suicide; but when I began working on this character I gradually came to the conclusion that he could not and should not do so.

Mechik's behaviour all through the novel was such that I realized that he was incapable of self-destruction. Suicide would give him a halo of petty-bourgeois "heroism" or "martyrdom" quite out of keeping with his character, for in actual fact he is a shallow, cowardly fellow and his sufferings are extremely superficial, shallow and petty.

Originally I had planned Metelitsa as a secondary character, just one of the platoon commanders; but in the process of the work, when I reached the third part of the novel, I felt compelled to dwell on this figure at much greater length, I realized that the character of Metelitsa was important for the characterization of Levinson. I felt it necessary to present in Metelitsa those traits which Levinson lacked, and this compelled me to develop his character much more fully. The difficulty was that there was nothing of the sort in the original plan. So a delay occurred in my work, between the second and third parts. I was unable to go on. I just could not follow the original plan and I did not at once realize the cause of my difficulty.

Only in the course of the work, and after further analysis, did I realize that I had to develop the character of Metelitsa more fully. Had I thought of this before I would have dwelt longer on Metelitsa in the earlier chapters. It was too late to redo everything, which is why the episode with Metelitsa in the beginning of the third part stands out so prominently, disturbing somewhat the harmony of the book.

It was as a result of this work that *The Nineteen* appeared, with all its merits and demerits. (pp. 140-44)

Aleksandr Fadeyev, "My Work on 'The Nine-teen'," translated by Vladimir Talmy, in *Soviet Literature, No. 2, 1968, pp. 140-44.*

Rufus W. Mathewson, Jr.   (essay date 1958)

[*Mathewson was an American critic and professor of Russian and comparative literature. In the following excerpt, he provides a character sketch of Levinson, the protagonist of* The Nineteen.]

[**The Nineteen**] does not differ in kind from dozens of later Soviet novels, but achieves a certain plausibility by muting the note of political evangelism. The human material is thin, and the situations are severely limited as means of exposing character. But Fadeev has concentrated on this dimension to the nearly complete exclusion of political matters, and further has tried hard to remain true to it.

The wanderings of a doomed company of mounted guerrillas in the back country of the Far Eastern Maritime Provinces provides a setting remote from the main revolutionary struggle. The novel is organized around two human situations: the first is a political-sexual triangle in which a shopworn but kindhearted camp-follower and nurse, Varya, moves between two men, her "husband," Morozka, a confused coal miner, and Metchik, an oversensitive, self-pitying intellectual. Varya's final reunion with Morozka, whose attitudes have been clarified by the influence of the more steadfast of his fellow miners, is intended to make a political point. Metchik is never able to become a part of the unit, never perceives its inner human "mechanism," and expresses his intellectual's selfishness in a final moment of cowardice that destroys the entire company. Varya's return to Morozka is a return at the same time to the selfless fraternity of her own kind, in response to a *mystique* of class solidarity.

The second situation, less schematic than the first, deals with the inner drama of the company's leader, the hunched, "gnome-like" Jewish Communist, Levinson. He struggles to retain "control" over men, over events, and over himself, and, what is genuinely refreshing, loses out in a certain sense on all these scores. We cannot know Fadeev's intention in this matter, but there is a suggestion, at least, that Levinson's "inappropriateness," because he is a Jew, and is physically deformed, implies that the leader is an isolated, special kind of being, who is crippled in more than a physical sense. Levinson's solitude is established as a primary condition of his existence. He is entirely cut off from his family. At one moment of great fatigue he notes that one of his troopers has the same beautifully rounded head as his son, but a moment later the impression vanishes. The very fact that it occurs to him represents a lapse in control, because of his delirious state of fatigue.

Earlier, long before the crisis that ends in the unit's defeat, a letter from his wife, containing nothing but bad news, provokes Levinson to write a reply:

> At first he was reluctant to break the circle of thought enclosing this side of his life, but little by little he penetrated it, his face softening; he covered two sheets with his small, scarcely legi-

ble handwriting, and in them were many words which few people who knew him would have expected from him.

Then the "circle" is closed as Levinson gallops off to inspect the sentries, and is not opened again. He is cut off, too, by the nature of his detached guerrilla command from whatever spiritual nourishment he might derive from association with his political brotherhood. He is cut off, too, from his past. The only reference he makes to his childhood concerns the illusions which clouded his view of the world. There is a glimpse of the big-eyed Jewish boy, waiting in vain for the photographer's "pretty little bird" to fly out of the camera, and then mastering his disappointment, as he was to do on countless later occasions, when he had been deceived by false promises and attractive illusions. He had finally learned to distrust them all:

> And when he was really convinced he understood what dangers and evils befall men because of these lying tales about pretty little birds . . . and he realized how many of them spend their lives in fruitless expectation. . . . No, he had no further need of those birds! He had relentlessly suppressed all sweet and vain regrets for them; he had crushed in himself everything that he had inherited from past generations brought up on these lying tales of pretty little birds.

The most significant measure of his solitude is the distance separating him from his men. Levinson feels that an inscrutable façade and a cultivated air of certainty about all decisions, even when they are wild guesses, are indispensable for maintaining command over his volunteer crew. He needed to struggle remorselessly with his own weaknesses, but those he could not overcome had to be hidden:

> From the hour that Levinson had been elected commandant, nobody could think of him in any other capacity. It seemed to each one of them that the distinctive thing about Levinson was that he was made to command the company. If he had told them how, in his childhood, he had helped his father in a secondhand furniture business, how his father all his life had dreamed of becoming rich, but was afraid of mice and played the violin very badly—all of them would have thought it a bad joke. Levinson never spoke of such things. Not that he deliberately avoided them, but he knew that everybody looked on him as an exceptional type of person. He realized his own weaknesses and the weaknesses of others; and he thought that, if one was to lead other people, one must above all make them aware of their weaknesses whilst suppressing and hiding one's own.

This glimpse behind the hero's façade, of course, is never permitted his men. When the military situation is confused, Levinson's

> whole attitude . . . was calculated to convey the impression that he understood perfectly how these things had come about, that he knew where they were heading, that there was nothing unusual or terrifying about them, and that he, Levinson, had long ago decided upon a safe, infallible plan for their salvation.

Actually the exact opposite is the case: "In point of fact, not only had he no such plan, but he was completely lost, as perplexed as a schoolboy."

The necessary deceptions of leadership, certainly not unique to Bolshevik guerrilla leaders, impose certain extra burdens on Levinson. The men of this detachment, with its nucleus of class-conscious miners, are not disposed to question their cause, but neither are they likely to consult it very often to find reasons for endurance. Levinson is made the custodian of their collective conscience, longings, and anxieties. But he does not doubt their steadfastness. It was rooted in an "instinct" as strong as self-preservation:

> Because of this instinct every thing they had to suffer, even death, was justified by the ultimate cause, and without it not one of them, he knew, would have voluntarily chosen to die in the Ulahinsk *taiga*. But he also knew that this profound instinct dwelt in men under a thick covering of the commonplace, of the trivial necessities of daily life, and of all the cares and anxieties for one's own insignificant but vital being; they had all to eat and sleep, and the flesh was weak.

Levinson and his lieutenants took on all these burdens, looking after the physical comforts, as well, of these simple partisans, "all of them conscious of their own weakness," as importunate as children. The parental responsibilities Levinson assumes have a sanction, Fadeev tells us, in the needs of "the children," who collaborate willingly in the manufacture of the myth of Levinson's infallibility. Under the pressure of events, however, his mask of mocking self-assurance is no longer adequate. An act of open defiance by one of his men is met by Levinson with his Mauser in his hand. They are volunteers, after all, in history's cause, bound to it by an instinct as strong as self-preservation. Strong measures are necessary to remind the errant one of his obligation. But such measures are costly:

> When Levinson looked round at his men they were all staring at him in fear and with respect, but that was all. There was no sympathy in their eyes. At that moment he felt that he was a hostile force raised above the company. But he was ready to go on; he was convinced that this force was right.

Defeat was in the air, morale had declined, Levinson had become harsher: "Every day unseen ties—ties which linked him to the heart of the company—snapped." His authority came to depend more and more on the force of his will. As his words lost their effect, the premium on the toughness and rectitude of his personal example increased. He was in the forefront of all the fighting; he dreaded compromising the image of himself at the head of the column by dozing and slumping in the saddle. As the company moves blindly toward annihilation, the final contest begins between Levinson's "control" over himself and the weakness of his flesh, as his body disintegrates under the nervous and physical strain.

Levinson's is not the simple drive of class instinct. The combination of knowledge, doctrine, and emotion which power every Marxian activist has an interesting configuration in him. Almost nothing is said of doctrine; there is very little in his behavior that is tactically motivated. On the one occasion when orders come from higher authority, Levinson rejects four of the five paragraphs as nonsensical, and proceeds to carry out the one he agrees with. There is no "political work" in his detachment, no agitation, pamphlets, commissars, or amateur theatricals. The morale problem of the men is solved, as we have seen, by Levinson's custodianship of their unarticulated aspirations and by the rigorous example of his own conduct. The source of his own strength is to be found in a creed which has echoes in it of classical Marxian humanism, of the Leninist revision of that ethos, and of Chernyshevsky's—and many other Russians'—belief in the eventual appearance of a new kind of man.

A conversation with the self-centered Metchik provokes the central moment of speculation in the novel:

> Only with us . . . could such lazy and spineless creatures, so futile and worthless, be found; only in our own country, where millions of people have lived for centuries under an indolent sun, in dirt and poverty, ploughing with primitive tools, believing in a vindictive and foolish God— only in such a country, where there is so little store of wisdom, could they exist.

Levinson is here echoing the ancient complaint of Russian men of conscience: Russia's tragic backwardness, above all her *human* backwardness, is the truest measure of her degradation. Belinsky's letter to Gogol in 1848 is as much the source of these thoughts as Marx's essays on the factory system. Levinson's goals and his deepest beliefs display the same double origin, recalling the dreams of the radical democrats a good deal more vividly, perhaps, than Marx's vision of the human creature restored to wholeness. We are close now to the heart of his credo:

> And Levinson was moved, because these were his deepest and most intimate beliefs; because the inner meaning of his life lay in overcoming this poverty and ignorance; because otherwise he would not be Levinson at all, but someone else; because he was urged by an overpowering desire, stronger than any other of his desires, to help create a new, fine, vigorous man. But how could one talk of a new, fine man when numberless millions of people still lived such wretched, poverty-stricken, primitive lives?

For the interim man there is Engels's freedom and Lenin's activist ethic:

> "To see everything as it is, in order to change everything that is, to control everything there is"—Levinson had achieved this *wisdom*, the simplest and the most difficult a man can achieve.

To overcome all enemies, to dispel all illusions, to surmount all obstacles, he has built his life around a core of revolutionary virtues: clarity of vision and inflexibility of will. If we recall the critique of the radical personality in the nineteenth century, these virtues are sources as well of his crippling alienation from his fellows. From time to time, like his predecessor, he needs to consult his vision of the future to find the strength to bear the unpromising and intolerable present:

> He went on without caring where; the cold, dewy branches freshened his face; he felt a rush of unusual strength, which seemed to carry him high above the actual moment (might it not be toward the new man of whom he dreamt with all the strength of his soul?) and from this vast height, earthly and human, he mastered his enemy, his own weak flesh.

Levinson is not the "new man" himself, as he clearly understands, but he sometimes senses his kinship with him. In preserving the mold of the leader, and passing it on to hand-picked successors, he feels that he is keeping alive the strain that will ultimately issue in the higher human type he dreams of. He carefully refrains from discouraging his assistant Baklanov, who imitates his every act, intonation, and gesture—even the physical movements that result from Levinson's bodily deformation. Baklanov will learn in his own time about the deception of leadership. It is more important to preserve the chain of virtuous being:

> As a young man, Levinson had also copied those who instructed him, and they had seemed to him as admirable and right-minded as he apparently seemed to Baklanov. When he was older he understood that his teachers were not what he had supposed them, and he was none the less grateful to them. After all, Baklanov not only copied his mannerisms, but drew on his whole experience of life—his methods of fighting, of working, of living. And Levinson knew that the mannerisms would pass with the years, while the other things, enriched by his own experience, would pass on to new Levinsons and Baklanovs; and that, he felt, was important, that was as it should be.

Levinson's "control," which depends on his own recognition and definition of necessity, is put to a number of minor tests. When it becomes "necessary" to poison a fatally wounded partisan, Metchik, indifferent to the "necessity," is horrified. Not Levinson, who, though troubled by the decision, falls back on his basic standard of virtue: "If it's necessary, it can't be helped . . . can it?" This answer is made easier by the victim's concurrence in his own death. His men look away while an impoverished Korean peasant weeps at Levinson's feet, pleading to be allowed to keep his last pig. Levinson is affected, but necessity's answer is all he heeds. His men are starving.

These decisions have no after effects because history, after all, justifies them. But when his control is threatened by a set of overwhelming circumstances, Levinson is thrown into the ultimate conflict of the Bolshevik saint: his body and his nervous system are subject to relentless pressure, increasing until the breaking point is reached. What is engaging in Levinson's drama is the fact that he *does* break.

After a hideous night of pursuit through a forest bog, the battered column of partisans emerges with the daylight on a peaceful forest road, sparkling with autumn frost. Levinson's brain is reeling with fatigue (it is at this moment that the image of his son's head appears to him). He is con-

scious of a strong feeling of affection for his men but his control has finally deserted him:

> He no longer led them, and it was only they themselves who were unaware of his powerlessness, and continued to follow him like a herd accustomed to its leader. And it was precisely this terrible thing that he had feared most of all in the early morning hours.

When the Cossack ambush is announced by shots down the road, Levinson betrays his helplessness by two physical movements which pass unobserved:

> He looked back helplessly, searching for the first time for support from others; but in the partisans' despairing, dumbly pleading faces, which seemed to melt under his gaze into a single face, pale, white, questioning, he read only helplessness and fear. . . . "Here it is, here's what I feared," Levinson thought, and he flung out a hand as though he sought something to hold on to.

A glance at the simple, resolute face of his lieutenant inspires a last act of will and he leads his company deliriously to its doom.

At this moment Fadeev might have ended his epic, with Bolshevik virtue convincingly intact, and with a sense of men having died not badly for aspirations which, for all their incoherence, did them no dishonor. A handful, however, nineteen in all, survived, and through them Fadeev contrives a swift moment of catharsis, ending with the obligatory note of uplift. For a while, Levinson automatically enacts his role as leader before the surviving handful:

> Levinson rode a little in front of the others, thoughtful, his head drooping. Sometimes he looked back helplessly, as if he wanted to ask something and could not remember what; he looked at them all with a prolonged unseeing stare, his glance strange and suffering.

At last understanding dawns on him and with it the last shred of his Bolshevik control departs:

> Levinson's eyes remained fixed for several seconds on the men. Then all at once he somehow collapsed and shrank, and everybody at once noticed that he had become weaker and much older. He was no longer ashamed of his weakness and he no longer tried to hide it; he sat huddled up in his saddle, slowly blinking his long wet lashes, and the tears ran down his beard. . . . The men turned aside in fear that they might lose control of themselves.

Here again Fadeev might have ended his tale with the pathos of loss still uppermost, with Levinson reduced at last to his human dimensions, but more plausible because of it. But this unpretentious novel, not distinguished for its depth of insight or richness of character, yet sound enough up to this moment because of its response to the inner logic of its elements, must now proceed to its directed conclusion. This characteristic moment of the Soviet novel deserves a careful look. The standard mechanism is the verbal coda, presented most often in the form of a flat declaration of faith or belief. Fadeev relies rather on the transfiguring effect of a natural landscape, and thus approaches by indirection his final statement of affirmation.

Levinson is weeping uncontrollably, the others are silent when they finally ride out of the forest:

> The forest came to an end in front of them quite unexpectedly, merging into the vastness of the high blue sky and the bright russet-colored earth bathed in the sunshine; the harvested fields spread out on either side.

The valley is full of the voices and the movements of people, "resounding with a joyful, busy life of their own." In the final poetic lunge, Fadeev reaches for the transfiguring note:

> Behind the river, propping up the sky, rose the blue mountains, and from their sharp peaks, which seemed to grow out of the sky, a transparent foam of pinkish-white cloud, salted by the sea, poured into the valley, foaming and speckled like new milk.

Levinson is delivered from his lapse into the human, as if by magic, and returned to his political matrix, and to his master image of control:

> Levinson looked silently, with eyes which were still wet, at this vastness of earth and sky, promising bread and rest, at these distant people on the threshing-ground whom he would soon have to make his own—as near to him as were the eighteen men who followed him in silence. He ceased crying; it was necessary to live and a man had to do his duty.

It requires care to decide what the grounds are for questioning this resolution. It is possible, of course, that this final paragraph is not a response to the formula but was intended simply as a conventional and rather noncommittal contrasting of a vulnerable character with the "eternal" aspects of life, in order to give Levinson a final poignancy. If this is so, the effect is certainly too abrupt—not deep enough (or relevant to what we know of Levinson) to be a religious experience—and not pointed enough to be ironic. We have not, after all, known Levinson very well. But that is the novelist's fault, in the end. And there are grounds within the novel for pronouncing its ending false. Levinson's abrupt recovery may be taken as a possible response of the politically obsessed personality, or it may be explained simply as a shallowness of affect on Levinson's part. But this is unkind to the image we already have of him. We have seen him stretched to the limit of his endurance, and have not the evidence to term him any more than an ordinarily limited man, with ties to the nourishing commonplaces of human experience that have not yet been snapped. The "fault" and the violation of the material's logic are Fadeev's in the end. To suggest that "life" for Levinson involves a simple return to the political image of himself, or to imply that the prolonged suffering he has undergone can be assimilated through the restorative effects of nature, is to betray the integrity of his image. To ignore entirely the inference that if "life" means the repetition of what Levinson has just gone through, it forecasts a downward progress toward aridity, exhaustion, and death, is simply to write badly. Or it is to impose on the reader the dictum that the cause matters above all things and its casualties will be forgotten. (pp. 242-53)

> *Rufus W. Mathewson, Jr., "Leather Men," in his* The Positive Hero in Russian Literature, *Columbia University Press, 1958, pp. 227-67.*

On *Posledniy iz Udege*:

Fadeyev's limitations were clearly revealed in his first large-scale, multi-volume work, the novel *Posledniy iz Udege* (*The Last of the Udege*), which he began writing parallel with *The Rout* (he even thought of incorporating the latter as an episode in the novel). The title must have been suggested to Fadeyev by James Fenimore Cooper's *The Last of the Mohicans* (the Udege are a curious, almost extinct native tribe of Siberia). The novel was planned as an ambitious social-psychological novel with a multitude of characters and a complex, multiplanar plot, involving the Siberian intelligentsia, coal miners, members of the Communist party, and some representatives of the Udege. One of the themes of the novel is the cultural "rehabilitation" of the Udege by the Soviet government and their incorporation into the collective-farming system. In the first volumes the action takes place during the Civil War in the Far East (with some flashbacks into the pre-Revolutionary period); in the concluding volume the transformation wrought by the Revolution was to be shown. Fadeyev himself said that the Udege theme of the novel was suggested to him by Engels' *The Origin of the Family, Private Property, and the State*.

The novel was planned in six parts, or volumes. The first installments were published in 1930, and the completed four parts appeared in book form in 1930, 1933, 1935, and 1940. Some chapters of Part 4 were published in 1956, and in 1957 appeared a posthumous revised edition of all that had been written. The earlier parts had in the meantime undergone considerable revision. As late as 1951, Fadeyev voiced his dissatisfaction with the novel, saying that, while it had been meant as a historical novel, it did not contain enough history. Earlier he had said that he had found the work on this novel very difficult going: "Evidently one must possess a greater artistic experience than I have to write a big novel with a complex idea, such as I have planned."

> *Gleb Struve, in* Russian Literature under Lenin and Stalin, 1917-1953, *1971.*

Edward J. Brown   (essay date 1969)

[*Brown is an American educator and critic who has written extensively on post-Revolution Soviet literature. Notable among his studies is* Russian Literature since the Revolution *(1963), which some critics consider the definitive work on the period. In the following excerpt from a revised edition of that study, he provides an overview of Fadeyev's career and major works.*]

Fadeyev (1901-1956), who was a native of Siberia and the son of a village doctor, joined the Communist Party at the age of seventeen, fought in Siberia against Admiral Kolchak, the Japanese, and Semyonov's Cossacks, published his first stories **"The Flood"** and **"Against the Current"** in

1923, and at last settled in Moscow to become a close collaborator of Leopold Averbakh, the leader of the Russian Association of Proletarian Writers (RAPP). Fadeyev was from the start a writer with a mission. Though his first novel *The Nineteen* (1927) was a success in the Communist and proletarian milieu, he early showed a preference for the writing of resolutions, speeches, and essays on the theory of proletarian literature. (p. 172)

Fadeyev's insistent emphasis on the portrayal of "living men" in their complex psychological reality was solidly based on Marxist doctrine. Marx and Engels had provided texts suitable for use in the ideological struggle against those relentless "human streams" and romanticized heroes of the early proletarian period. Because Marx, Engels, and Lenin had at times expressed a preference for writers of the realistic school, the words "reality" and "realism" came to be clothed with mystical authority. Fadeyev took upon himself the task of liquidating romanticism. He was an enemy, also, of formalism, stylization, "factography," anything, indeed, that smacked of "modernism." He developed the argument that "realism" is the literary expression of a materialist philosophy and devised a slogan to be used against romantics: "Down with Schiller!"

Fadeyev and his friends in their position as lawgivers to

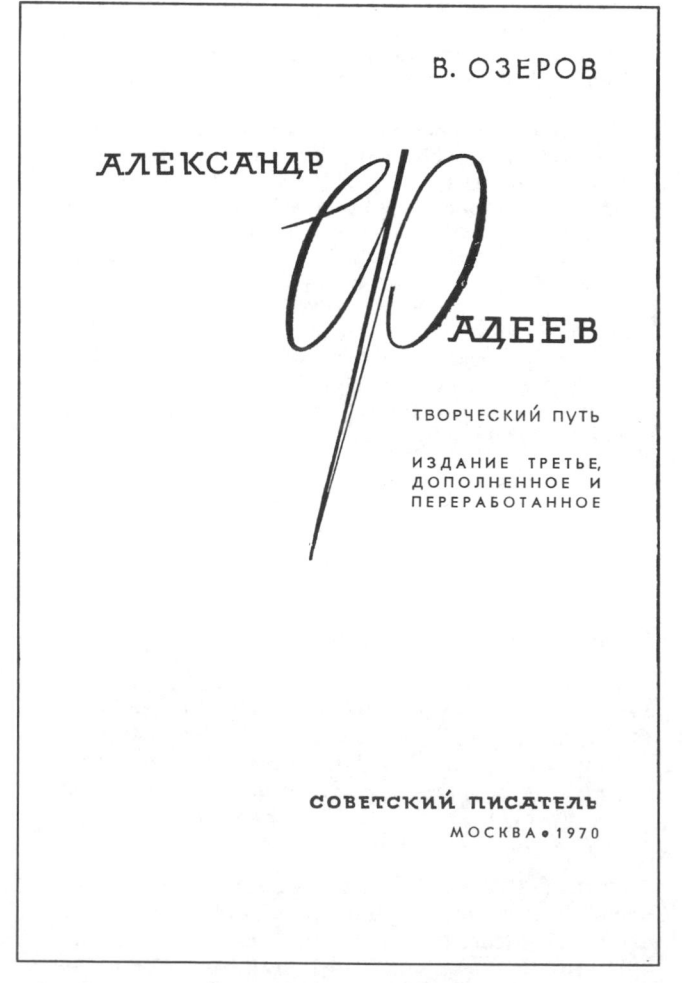

Cover to Fadeyev's first novel.

proletarian writers urged upon them the value of a realistic approach to individual psychology and prescribed models for them to imitate. The importance of the "classics" and the need to learn from them were a steady refrain. What "classics" did they have in mind? Not even the Proletcult or the Smithy had succeeded in producing a totally new literature, and all proletarian writers had in some degree been learning from past masters. The question clearly was "which classics" should be imitated, and for Fadeyev, the "classics" added up to one author, Leo Tolstoy. Rebelling against the modernism of Bely and Pilnyak, which had infected even proletarian writing, Fadeyev, and with him the leading proletarian writers, reverted to the style of their "grandfathers," the great masters of classical realism.

Tolstoy was made to order for the proletarians. His approach to character seemed "rational" in that his probing tended to reveal the motivation of behavior in terms of environment, memory, hidden needs, and desires. His method had solid sanction from the nineteenth-century socialist critic Chernyshevsky, who called him a "dialectician of the human psyche," and from Lenin, who admired his ability to "remove the masks" from social convention. And his artistic means are so simple and economical in appearance that it would seem anyone might use them with profit. Fadeyev reported that before writing his novel, *The Nineteen,* he reread *War and Peace* in its entirety.

The Nineteen reveals hardly a trace of "Pilnyakian" device. It is free of excited lyrical digressions. Its language is a smooth instrument of communication featuring matter rather than manner. Syntactic distortion, verbal play, self-conscious ornamentation are scrupulously avoided, almost for the first time in Soviet prose. The important thing for Fadeyev is the political *idea* of the book, and he exercises what literary skill he has to express that idea in terms of individual human experience. The result is a novel which, in spite of its reversion to an earlier realistic style, struck the Soviet reader as a new departure, for it described real people rather than a clash of primitive forces or the inexorable historical march of "masses."

The political purpose of the novel is to show, in a small band of guerrillas operating in parts of Siberia controlled by the Whites and the Japanese, the nexus of relations binding together the social forces which made the Revolution. The band contains peasants, workmen, professional revolutionaries, "*lumpen* proletarians," students, intellectuals. The psychology of each "class" is presented in the inner thoughts and feelings of a particular representative. Thus the peasant has a violent hatred of farmer landlords, but so strong a love for his own little plot of ground that he fails to understand larger issues; the youthful intellectual Mechik has a romantic attachment to "the workers" and "the Revolution" but can't be relied upon in a crisis; the unruly proletarian anarchist Morozka develops loyalty and discipline in association with the band. And it is the "real" worker, the miner Dubov, who understands most clearly the great issues of the time, and the leader of the band, the Jew Levinson, lays his greatest reliance on Dubov and his men.

In Levinson Fadeyev created a new kind of hero. Levinson

has all the square-jawed ruthlessness of Kozhuk in *The Iron Flood* or Gleb Chumalov in *Cement,* and he presents to his men the image of unbreakable resolve. But he also has a secret inner life and a consciousness of his own weaknesses. The techniques for revealing the private as well as the public thoughts of his characters Fadeyev learned from Tolstoy. He confessed, "When working on *The Nineteen* I often found myself subconsciously imitating Tolstoy even in my choice of words and in the rhythm of my sentences."

Examples of the Tolstoyan technique of the "inner monologue" and other Tolstoyan devices are common in the novel. The young intellectual Mechik muses about his working-class girl friend, Varya:

> His thoughts carried him far away into the bright days of the future, and in consequence they were light and airy, dissolving of their own accord like the soft, rosy clouds over the plains of the taiga. He thought how he would return with Varya to the town in a cushioned, jolting train with open windows, through which they would see just such soft, rosy clouds sailing over the darkening chain of mountains in the distance. They two would sit at the window, very close to each other, Varya murmuring soft words to him, he stroking her head, and her braids would shine like gold, like the noonday sun. . . . The Varya of his daydreams bore little resemblance to the round-shouldered woman of the pump at No. 1 Pit, since all his imaginings were remote from actual things and embodied only what he longed to see.

Mechik sees Morozka and Varya return from a tryst in the woods:

> When he saw Morozka again, returning so soon from the forest (the orderly was swinging his arms as he walked, his steps heavy and slow), Mechik, with the subconscious assurance which is based on no concrete fact, but which does not permit of doubt, realized that "nothing had happened" between Morozka and Varya, and that he, Mechik, was the cause. An uneasy joy and an inexplicable feeling of guilt woke in him, and he began to be afraid of encountering Morozka's murderous glance.

The adjutant Baklanov involuntarily reveals his reverence for the leader:

> "What? . . . " Baklanov asked again in threatening tones, turning his whole body to the man in the way Levinson would (Baklanov thought that Levinson did this in order to emphasize the importance of his questions, but in point of fact Levinson twisted in this manner because he had been wounded in the neck and could not turn round in any other way).

Fadeyev's novel is simple in its plot and straightforward in its execution. Levinson's band, trapped and hopelessly outnumbered, is beaten and decimated. Only nineteen men escape, and they go on, defeated but not demoralized, ready to fight again for the Revolution. The revelation of that leader's human weaknesses, his fear in battle, his secret failures in self-confidence, and the near collapse of his strength and will in the face of disaster was the new touch that added to Fadeyev's proletarian novel the fillip of human verisimilitude. Fadeyev claimed to have created, in Levinson, not a saint but a "living man." He did succeed, in any case, in jolting the reader with this picture of an abject and miserable commander surveying the poor remnant of his band:

> Levinson's eyes remained fixed for several seconds on the men. Then all at once he somehow collapsed and shrank, and everybody at once noticed that he had become weak and much older. He was no longer ashamed of his weakness and he no longer tried to hide it; he sat huddled up in the saddle, slowly blinking his long wet eyelashes, and the tears ran down his beard. . . . The men turned aside in fear that they might lose control of themselves.
>
> Levinson turned his horse and slowly went on ahead. The company followed him.
>
> "Don't cry! . . . What good . . . will that do?" Gontcharenko said humbly, raising Varya by the shoulder.
>
> Whenever Levinson forgot himself he started to look behind him in uncertainty; remembering that Baklanov was not there, he began to cry again.
>
> So they rode out from the forest—the nineteen.

Fadeyev's second novel was planned as an ambitious fictional effort to be published in six substantial parts. Only the first four parts had been completed at his death in 1956, and he was at that time engaged in writing the fifth part, of which one chapter was published. *The Last of the Udegs* has, like *The Nineteen,* an idea which gives it form and content. The Udegs, a remote nomadic tribe of the Russian far east, whose contacts with twentieth-century civilization have been sporadic and brief and whose culture is still on the level of primitive Communism, are suddenly confronted with the "Communism" of a modern world state. Fadeyev planned to demonstrate in telling their story the thesis that an extremely primitive people under the guidance of the Soviet government may experience a leap from tribal Communism to the complex collective organization of the twentieth century, skipping over the intervening "historical stages": family, private property, slavery, feudalism, capitalism and socialism. Lines from Engel's *Origin of the Family, Private Property, and the State* stood as an epigraph in an early edition of the novel. But to describe the novel solely in terms of ideology does less than justice to a work over which Fadeyev labored for thirty years and to which he gave his best as a writer. Uneven though it is, *The Last of the Udegs* contains some of Fadeyev's best pages, and the fact that he spent his energies on literary administration rather than on the completion of this novel is a minor tragedy. In concept it was to be, in a sense, an experiment in the juxtaposition and contrast of various stages in the development of human societies, and each "stage" had its representative in a particular person. There are a dozen or more clearly delineated characters, the merchant-capitalist, the radical intellectual, the peasant revolutionary, the proletarian socialist, the Chinese merchant, and, last, the members of the primitive Udeg community itself whose way of life was to be radically altered through contact with "history" in the form of collectivized farming.

When Fadeyev describes in translucent prose the simple way of life of the Udeg tribes, their adjustment to cruel seasonal changes, their hunting expeditions, the education of their young, their courtship and marriage customs, he covers very skillfully ground which has, no doubt, been gone over before. And yet the story of these simple but hardly innocent people abruptly confronted with the weapons and the violent issues of modern Europe has a power of historical drama not wholly dampened by the author's insistent Marxist message.

The Young Guard, a novel about the guerrilla resistance to the German occupation during the Second World War, has had a sorry fate. Published in 1946, it was awarded a Stalin prize, first class. In the same year a dramatization was presented in Leningrad. Discussion of the novel took place in factories, at meetings of the Young Communist League, and in the Writers' Union. Defects were pointed out, the presence of which Fadeyev acknowledged. In a letter covering his "errors" Fadeyev said:

> I was criticized not because the underground fighters were poorly described, but because I should have given a broader picture of the activity of our Party in the underground, and because I should have shown not only Bolsheviks who were weakly organized and who failed, but chiefly such as were capable of organizing a genuine resistance to the German occupationists. The latter were of course more typical, and I shall take this advice.

A "revised and enlarged" edition of the novel was published in 1951. A comparison of the two versions shows that Fadeyev included "new material" giving credit to the centralized Party apparatus for a movement that had in the first edition been presented as a spontaneous manifestation in the young of Soviet patriotism.

The operation performed on *The Young Guard* damaged but did not destroy it. Fadeyev displays in it a stylistic virtuosity that was absent from both *The Nineteen* and *The Last of the Udegs.* An occasional note of romanticism recalls the early Civil War novels, and elements of the heroic national saga have reminded some critics of [Nikolai] Gogol's *Taras Bulba.* As in so many of the Civil War novels, including his own *The Nineteen,* the most powerful scenes, those labored over with special devotion and skill, are scenes of disorganization and defeat. Quite possibly the best writing in *The Young Guard* is to be found in those pages which describe the retreat of the Red Army before the Germans and the confused and tragic evacuation of the civilian population.

A study of Fadeyev's career as a writer and as a literary official would throw much light on Soviet society. He was another of the young Red Army commissars who entered proletarian literature in the early twenties with firm convictions and great plans. He was one of the principal leaders of the Russian Association of Proletarian Writers and, along with Averbakh and Libedinsky, devised its literary platform and fought its literary battles. When RAPP was liquidated in 1932 and his comrades fell into disgrace, Fadeyev himself wrote a series of earnest articles (*Old and New*) in support of the new regime in literature. He survived the purges of 1936-1938 while many of those same comrades were shot or sent into exile. His role during this period is impossible to assess on the basis of information we now have. From 1939 to 1954 he was Secretary of the Executive Board of the Union of Soviet Writers. He was thus directly involved in policies that led to the debasement of Soviet literature, and he was the official spokesman of its Stalinist period. He was not re-elected as Secretary of the Union at the Second Congress of Soviet Writers held in 1954, after the death of Stalin. There is evidence that he suffered from alcoholism, and had undergone hospital treatment for that ailment. In May, 1956, early in the de-Stalinization period, he shot himself. Probably the most honest words spoken in public about him were those of the novelist [Mikhail] Sholokhov at the Twentieth Congress of the Communist Party:

> Why couldn't someone long ago have said to Fadeyev: "The thirst for power is a contemptible thing in the writers' world. The Writers' Union is not a military body, nor is it a punitive battalion, and no writer need stand at attention before you, Comrade Fadeyev. . . . " For a great many years Fadeyev was a "general secretary" and gave his time exclusively to such business. The result is that we lost a good writer, and now we have also lost a "general secretary. . . . "
>
> (pp. 172-79)
>
> *Edward J. Brown, "The Proletarians II," in his* Russian Literature since the Revolution, *revised edition, Collier Books, 1969, pp. 162-93.*

Helen von Ssachno   (essay date 1975)

[*In the following excerpt, Ssachno discusses the creation of the Fadeyev Medal and examines Fadeyev's writing career within the context of the Stalinist regime and its political policies.*]

It was announced on the front page of the Soviet *Literaturnaya Gazeta* early last year: the establishment of an Alexander Fadeyev award for outstanding work in the field of "War Literature", consisting of gold and silver medals to be awarded by the secretariat of the Soviet Writers' Union in association with the political Commissars of the Red Army and Navy. The award was intended as a mark of recognition of the patriotism, political commitment, and artistic qualities of writers who convincingly portrayed the "heroic achievements of the Soviet people in defence of its socialist homeland." Nothing surprising here. But that it should have been named after Alexander Fadeyev, the former secretary-general of the Soviet Writers' Union who committed suicide in May 1956, could have (and probably did) raise a few eyebrows.

Fadeyev's lifelong combination of the roles of writer and politician puts his whole career in an ambiguous light and was ultimately disastrous to both. He was sixteen when the Revolution (*i.e.* the October seizure of power) broke out, and was a pupil at the commercial school at Vladivostok. He fired a pistol at the picture of the Tsar in his parents' home and then pointed it at his own reflection in the mirror—a histrionic gesture of whose symbolical nature he was well aware, and a kind of dress rehearsal of the real tragedy of 13 May 1956. Then, no less melodramatically, the boy burnt his poems and left home to join a band of Bolshevik militants. The three years of partisan warfare that followed were reflected in his short novel *Rasgrom* (*The Massacre*), on which his reputation as a Soviet writer was to be based; it is undoubtedly one of the most colourful literary documents of the early period of War Communism.

He did not write a great deal more. There is an uncompleted novel called *The Last of the Udege Tribe,* a description of the Soviet nationality policies in Siberia; and in 1944 he published a collection of War dispatches. Then there are the first few chapters of a similarly uncompleted novel, *Black Metallurgy;* and finally his chief work, *The Young Guard,* a novel about the partisans in the Second World War (which he had to rewrite completely at Stalin's bidding). This took him some four years, and in the end "Stalin's battle" was given its literary apotheosis.

> Stalingrad is the most tremendous manifestation of brilliant generalship. . . . Stalingrad is the most priceless fruit of the genius whose name the town bears. . . .

Then there began the phase of total subjection that was to be ultimately so disastrous. So completely did Fadeyev identify himself with Stalin's personal dictatorship that after the latter's death he became a symbol of the personality cult. For this he had more than ample opportunity. With the exception of a few years during the Second World War, he remained president of the Writers' Union (he was Maxim Gorky's successor) until his death. He was a member of the Party's Central Committee for 16 years. He was also a member of the committee that granted the Stalin Prize (of which he was himself a winner). He was president of the Soviet Peace Council and vice-president of the World Peace Council. He travelled from country to country, made innumerable speeches, issued orders and laid down the law.

How could all this not affect a writer? His character changed out of all recognition. He knew that his career as an author was over, and that henceforth he could be nothing but a faithful police-dog in the most exposed cultural-political position that the Soviet Union had to offer; and it was this knowledge which began slowly to gnaw away at him. He became an alcoholic, and certain neurotic signs more and more characterised his public appearances. When Stalin died he had long been a dead man himself. As president of the Writers' Union he had to pronounce political judgment on every suspicious literary tendency, and his judgments inevitably carried awesome weight. And now, suddenly, he became the personification of a period that was officially denounced as—criminal! At the 20th Party Congress he was not re-elected to the Central Committee, and his enemies started harrying him.

Mikhail Sholokhov—he was not yet the political watch-dog which he became after his speech at the 23rd Party Congress (1966) in which he demanded the death penalty for Andrey Sinyavsky and Juli Daniel—publicly attacked him.

> After Gorky's death we sought with Comrade Fadeyev to establish a kind of collective leadership in the Writers' Union. Nothing came of that. Fadeyev turned out to have such a domineering trend that he could not be converted to the principle of collegiality. This state of affairs lasted for fifteen years. Today I ask myself: Why did we not tell Fadeyev at the outset that the Writers' Union is not an army—and certainly not a prison chain-gang—and that we writers did not propose to stand to attention in front of you, Comrade Fadeyev? . . .

It is hard to guess what would have become of him if he had not committed suicide. He might have been sacrificed as a scapegoat of the Personality Cult, or he might have been only temporarily shelved. At all events, after his death a slow process of resurrection began, with the publication first of his very meagre posthumous works; and then, at intervals of several years, of his correspondence.

As a letter-writer Fadeyev was unknown to his contemporaries; in their eyes the President of the Writers' Union was the most corrupt of the corrupt. But now, when the various phases of his corruption were revealed by the publication of his certainly more than carefully edited correspondence, many of these contemporaries were forced at least to reconsider the matter. Here was a man on whose actions and passions the state had secured a monopoly, and whose life had nevertheless ended in disaster. He had faithfully followed the ideological phases of Russian Communism and had been ruined by the changes that followed Stalin's death. His letters revealed that he could not face up to the process of moral destruction that these dialectical leaps had involved. On 29 April 1956, two weeks before his death, he wrote to a friend:

> I am ill and, as always during an illness, all my private and official affairs have got into a hopeless state of confusion. Meanwhile so much that is basically new has happened that my novel will presumably once more have to be thoroughly rewritten. At all events I am trying to pull myself together to regain at least a certain equilibrium. . . .

Today patriotic rubbish is being honoured in his name. At all events, there is little to be said for the works for which Fadeyev Prizes have been awarded. A gold medal has gone to Sholokhov's still uncompleted novel *They Fought for Their Homeland,* which is war literature at the level of low journalism. Another gold medal has gone to Fadeyev's temporary successor in the Writers' Union, Alexei Surkov, for his quite insipid war poetry. A silver medal went to Anatoly Ananiev who since Vsevolod Kochetov's death has been editor of the down-the-line orthodox literary journal *October.* The last martial mediocrity to be honoured is Victor Kondratyenko, editor of the Kiev literary journal *The Rainbow.*

Undoubtedly there are good war-writers in the Soviet Union, such as Victor Nekrasov, who has fallen out of favour (and has now obtained a visa and left for the West);

or Konstantin Simonov, Grigori Baklanov, Yuri Bondariov, or Vassily Bykov, who continue to write nothing but "war books" nearly thirty years after the end of World War II. The same applies to the war poems of Vinokurov or Slutzky: no trace there of inflated emotionalism or party-line pathos. But what is wanted by the authorities, or at any rate so it seems after these awards, is martial claptrap, aggressive, verbal strong-arm stuff.

On Fadeyev and the probable reasons for his suicide:

I remember him at the Peace Congress at the Waldorf only seven years ago. A man like a thick, hardwood tree, a soldier standing hands clasped behind back and feet apart in the position called parade rest. So gifted, so unbreakable. What happened to his gifts? Why did he break? The wind of revelation did not uproot him, and yet the trunk snapped. Could it be because, for all his bravery, he could not bend? Bending, too, is wisdom for the tree. . . .

Had Fadayev given up writing? (Organizing, criticizing, concretizing are not writing. Believe it or not, they are easier.) The question, if relevant, is secondary. What is pertinent is that he was persuaded—allowed himself to be—that, if writers were engineers of the soul, necessity had elected him to be a kind of chief engineer. In a concocted atmosphere of permanent crisis, which the facts did not warrant and the Soviet people at large did not feel, he was to be the sturdy sergeant of the cultural sector of the line. The dean of writers, the instrument of policy, the strategic tool in the construction of the new man. That was the image others planted in him, and for whose conduct he was to be responsible. Forthright as always, he embraced it consciously, though surely not aware of where the choice would lead. (Later to learn that strategy hid self-interest, that policy meant the power of persons, and that history explains much but does not justify everything.)

Henceforth, artists were to be told how far it was proper for their insight to delve, and what it was safe to show a citizenry which had borne two world wars and accomplished the greatest revolution in history. The writer was to lead men through the forest of passions to the promised land of reason by hacking down the trees and erasing the footprints of the march. The instructions of Plato were revived: strangle instinct and perception and lie simply for the benefit of the perplexed. From this to silent discretion before the murder of one's own colleagues, the Yiddish writers, was a long, long step, more like an exile, but Fadayev, prisoner of his image, had to take it. And how many more! Could that have been where he began to die?

So we blame Fadayev. No, no. Do you peck at the protagonist of tragedy? Do you mock Othello from the middle rows? For, like that hero, Fadayev died enraged. He thought himself clothed in theory, to see himself in the end naked of fact. He was proud ("I have done the state some service"), and found himself alone. Out of loyalty, he allowed others to be his fate, only to realize what he, fighter and novelist, once knew: Fate is ourselves, too.

Charles Humboldt, in his "Fadayev," in Masses and Mainstream, *July 1956.*

How bitter that Alexander Fadeyev should be resurrected for this purpose! It is surely some chilling mockery—after all, the things for which gold and silver medals are being awarded in his name were his tragic undoing. The award of an "Alexander Fadeyev Gold Medal" to Mikhail Sholokhov belongs to the same category of black humour. One wonders: whose brain-child was this joke? One suspects a bitter Russian wit has been at work. (pp. 56-8)

Helen von Ssachno, "Two Russian Writers: Fadeyev & Tvardovsky," in Encounter, *Vol. XLIV, No. 2, February, 1975, pp. 56-60.*

Nicholas Rzhevsky   (essay date 1983)

[*Rzhevsky is an Austrian-born American educator, translator, critic, and director. In the following excerpt, he analyzes the influence of Socialist Realism, Soviet ideology, and Leo Tolstoy on Fadeyev's fiction.*]

If the creative responses to ideology, on the suggested terms of individuality and identity, are indeed integral components of the Russian writer's vitality and insight, then a condition of ideological deprivation, it would have to follow, would critically injure the important textual attributes. The tragic misfortune of Russian culture, of course, is that such a measure is provided in the twentieth century through the evolution of ideas and letters in the Soviet Union.

There has been much of lasting value produced in the Soviet period, it is true, and a number of writers have continued the proud traditions of Russian literature after 1917. Bulgakov, Pasternak, Zamyatin, Sholokhov, and Solzhenitsyn, or even the less-talented Fedin, Leonov, Katayev, Kaverin, and Gorky offer ample evidence of both literary vitality and insight. The truly Soviet literature, however—in a sense impossible for the nineteenth century when there was no "Russian" literature attached to a homogeneous sociopolitical program—is quite a different order of art. This body of fiction is represented by Alexander Fadeyev, Dmitry Furmanov, Fedor Gladkov, Semen Babayevsky, Boris Polevoi (Kampov), and other writers, whose texts are marked by sterility and banality and who provide the key examples of socialist realism, the officially sanctioned aesthetic program of the USSR throughout much of its history.

One typical explanation of the inadequacy of socialist realism—that it is *too* ideological, too committed to society, politics, and moral rhetoric—fails to take into account the actual internal relationship of the Soviet writer with his culture. Differences of achievement between past and present Russian texts only become more puzzling in this view, for contact with moral and sociopolitical issues enhanced rather than detracted from the typical Russian vitality. Indeed, the telling weakness of Soviet fiction lies not in its social or moral commitments but in the prohibitions which make a true self-involvement in ideology impossible. Soviet literature is not unlike the Soviet constitution in this regard in that its principal failure is the spirit rather than the letter of the law. For in spite of a very sound system of legal codes, everyone in the Soviet judiciary recognizes his impotence before orders issued from someone higher in the bureaucracy, just as every Soviet writer knows that the values he expresses in his fiction are ultimately determined not by his own moral interests and beliefs but by the current program of the party. Deming Brown's thorough and penetrating study of literature after Stalin [*Soviet Russian Literature since Stalin*] reaches a similar judgement in suggesting that the avoidance of "serious ideological confrontations" and the absence of "questions of ideological belief" are indications of what has gone wrong. It would be more appropriate, in this regard, to speak of the ideological hypocrisy, rather than the ideological enthusiasm, of Soviet fiction. The distinction is important to make because it helps us not only to justify our value judgements about the soundness of Russian literature and the relative weakness of orthodox Soviet texts, but also suggests a definition of the internal mechanisms and core formulations of a unique and cautionary literary process in the twentieth century.

A clear view of socialist realism from within is provided by the evolution of basic Russian values during its tenure. The native responses to love, brotherhood, sacrifice, and humility are no longer present as a spiritual moral reference brought into fiction by writers, but are evoked, frequently by order of committee, for purposes of propaganda and social control. Most typically, brotherhood, courage, and humility are used by protagonists who argue for some form of sacrifice by citizens and consumers to the larger needs of the state and the future, while inclinations to protest are channeled into the uncomfortable fictional positions of villainous selfishness and egoism which the reader is warned in various ways to avoid. The moral platitudes and external features of Soviet positive heroes are thus related, as in the instance of older Russian positive types, to the perennial kenotic standards, except that they are cynically used in literature, as in various social mechanisms, for political domination rather than for moral catalysis and self-confrontation.

Such ideological hypocrisy is most clearly evident in Soviet responses to the individual. While the rights of the self and personality are strongly defended in media and literature, it is ultimately understood by all except the most naive that the individual is not an independent value standing outside historical and economic forces, but is the tool of government policy. A pioneering student of Soviet literature, Ernest J. Simmons, has described the effect on fictional processes [in his *Russian Fiction and Soviet Ideology*, 1958] as follows: "Perhaps for the first time in the history of literature art has utterly repudiated the subjective . . . and the artist has been forced to kill within himself the desire to convey a personal vision of humanity in his work. The primary purpose of literature in the Soviet Union is to instruct, and the obligation of the writer is to employ his medium to instruct in conformity with the spirit and letter of the latest ideological position of the Communist party." This is not to say that there are no Soviet writers who believe in Marxism-Leninism and who make it their own ideology (although, in fact, very few of the minimally talented ones ever did), but that a true creative commitment even to orthodox doctrine is impossible because the government does not allow any ideology except its own. Vladimir Mayakovsky, one writer who believed in communism and attempted to make it an active

part of his poetry, ultimately committed suicide—in large part, we can assume, because of government prohibitions which prevented him from true ideological expression. Such political impositions from the outside had strong technical implications for literary procedure. For the writer's inability to involve his own self in ideology created difficulties of aesthetic discovery and inspiration which lead directly to the sterility of style and form in socialist realist texts.

The acute problem for those Soviet authors who wanted to continue writing after the relatively free environment of the twenties gradually passed into history must have been how to create metaphors, characters, and plots without the active and honest involvement of their own thought and emotional commitments. The practical solution that was agreed upon, I would like to suggest, can be understood in the socialist realist response to Russian literary tradition. Just as the use of older, native values for purposes of social and political control, the development of the formal properties of Soviet literature—as, for that matter, all other aesthetic technique whether it be in the ballet, architecture, painting, or music—ultimately came to depend on a gross imitation of methods and style created in the past. In his "On Socialist Realism," Andrei Sinyavsky, writing under the pseudonym of Abram Tertz, defined the result as a "loathsome literary salad [in which] characters torment themselves though not quite as Dostoevsky's do, are mournful but not quite as Chekhov's, create happy families which are not quite like Tolstoy's, and, suddenly becoming aware of the time they are living in, scream at the reader the copybook slogans which they read in Soviet newspapers, like 'Long live world peace!' or 'Down with the warmongers!'" It can be postulated that by disrupting the normal interaction of a writer and his culture through the interjection of politics into the creative process, socialist realism prevented the kind of intense personal commitment to art which inspires experiment and new literary forms, and forced instead a dulled imitation of already available plots, characters, metaphors, and stylistic devices. The two major characteristics of socialist realism, in fact, can be seen to be the repetition of whatever government policy is current—to the extent, as Sholokhov, Fadeyev, and a number of other writers knew, of rewriting already published novels to adjust for changes in the political situation—and the imitation of past stylistic and thematic conventions to decorate an impersonal ideology.

The suggested literary procedures can be found in most Soviet fiction, but a particularly useful example is provided by the process through which Alexander Fadeyev created ***Razgrom (The Rout)***. Written in 1926-27, the novel portrays the adventures of a Bolshevik troop of soldiers in the period of communist consolidation after the revolution. The principal characters are all stock figures: Levinson, a commissar and positive hero; Morozka and Metelitsa, courageous Soviet guerrillas; Metchik, a representative of the intelligentsia and a foil for Fadeyev's polemic with it; Goncharenko, a factory worker; and Varya, a peasant girl who provides love interest. The troop fails, as can be expected from the title, but their defeat is not consequential and is only meant to illustrate the trials and hardships that communists must go through before the inevitable so-cialist victory. The importance of this novel should not be gauged only by this dubious thematic structure, for Fadeyev's key role in the politics which impregnated Soviet culture, as well as his methods of using literature, had larger repercussions in the course of socialist realism. Indeed, *The Rout*'s essential contribution was to demonstrate a practical way of imitating one particular writer taken from the Russian fictional heritage. The writer was Leo Tolstoy, and it was his stylistic examples and literary devices which allowed Fadeyev to provide an important model for those who remained within the ideological pale created by the government. Such a response to Tolstoy helped produce key components of socialist realism by demonstrating a two-step process of following an older writer's fictional technique while criticizing his ideology and interjecting in its place some of the major tenets of Lenin's party.

Although the published references which Fadeyev made to Tolstoy before and during the period when *The Rout* was being written are very sparse, they demonstrate a thorough knowledge of his work. Among these is a citation taken from Tolstoy's texts which appeared in Fadeyev's notebooks for 1927 (March 3) and, in April of the same year, a note on literary method in **"Hadji Murat."** In 1928, when *The Rout* was already finished, Fadeyev mentioned Tolstoy in **"Against Superficiality,"** an article aimed at M. Semenov's critical analysis. It "should and could" be shown, he writes, "what is the nature of Tolstoy's world view . . . , how Tolstoy was limited by his class." Much later in 1944 and then in 1955, Fadeyev revealed his intimate knowledge of Tolstoy's diaries, although it would be difficult to establish when he read them. In 1955-56, Fadeyev also examined Tolstoy's use of a number of themes to illuminate one central idea and concluded that such stylistic procedure should be "a canon of artistic work."

However, it was in 1932, approximately six years after finishing *The Rout* and in a time of decisive importance for Soviet literature, that Fadeyev gave the clearest signs of his particular preoccupation with Tolstoy. In the article **"About Socialist Realism"** he writes: "The contradiction is well known between the idealistic philosophic views of L. Tolstoy and the basic realistic tendency of his work; it is this [contradiction] that has enabled us to call his work 'a step forward in the creative maturity of humanity.' " Two aspects of the statement should be stressed. First, the citation is from Lenin and it shows that Fadeyev knew he could use Tolstoy for his own purposes supported by the most important political authority. Second, in this passage Fadeyev takes his first firm step in separating form and ideology, a separation that was an integral part of his reaction to the past. That same year, in the article **"My Literary Experience—To the Beginning Author,"** he went on to give the best exposition of such a process:

> I wrote this novel [*The Rout*] in two years. What basic principles did I use for the work? First of all, in contrast to the pretentious language of my first piece ("The Overflow"), I attempted to write much more simply, to express my thoughts clearly. I subjected the entire work to this task:

> write it so that it would more clearly, persuasively, exactly, show all of what I see, what I conceive. . . .

> As you know, critics have noted that *The Rout* was influenced by a great Russian writer, Leo Tolstoy. This is partially true, partially not. It is not true in the respect that there is not a trace of Tolstoy's world view in this work. But Tolstoy always captivated me by the life and validity of his artistic images. . . . While working on *The Rout,* I involuntarily assumed certain characteristic elements of Tolstoy's language, of the rhythm of a phrase. This circumstance doesn't worry me particularly: any artist who is beginning to work depends on the experience of the past. . . . If an artist succeeds in revealing new elements of reality, in developing new ideas, then the influence which the more experienced master has exerted on him in the process of study, does not affect his independence, and it becomes more and more solid during the artist's growth. Undoubtedly, for each of us who learns his trade from a classic writer, it is necessary to study critically both the ideological content of [that writer's] legacy and [his] formal method of artistic expression.

A discrepancy here should be singled out. Fadeyev was not beginning his literary career and his own remarks about an abrupt change in style from his early work to *The Rout* point to this earlier fiction. But *The Rout* was, in a certain sense, a new departure for him, for the political conditions which helped create this novel did not strongly affect his earlier texts, nor did they affect the ornamentally rich fiction of Boris Pilnyak, Artyom Vesyoly (Kochkurov), Babel, and Vsevolod Ivanov. The reason for the error is understandable because Fadeyev is speaking of a literature in which he is beginning to work and which differs markedly from the daring and highly individualistic literary responses to the communism of the twenties. Furthermore, perhaps as a result of the creative vacuum fostered by the change in political conditions, he goes on to offer a practical method of promulgating the new type of fiction. And as can be seen from the second part of the citation, this method hinged on utilizing the past in terms of the dichotomy discussed earlier.

The reaction of one writer, no matter how important his position in literary circles or in the circles that exercise literary control, does not, of course, entirely explain the drastic change in the mode of Soviet fiction in the 1930s; the demand for simplicity and unsophisticated prose undoubtedly reflected five-year-plan sensibilities which needed propaganda and feared the nonutilitarian. But the fact that an ornamental style had not been noticeably present in Russian culture since the period of the baroque, with the possible exception of Gogol, and was consequently a step toward creative independence from the established tradition of the past century, could not fail to influence the Soviet writer in his search for a workable solution to totalitarianism. It can be ventured that while the spirit of innovation and experiment in twentieth-century ornamentalism demanded a commitment to art which was rapidly becoming impossible, the past century offered a familiar and rich store of literary formalities which could easily, with a minimum of intellectual labor, be called upon. Indeed, as Fadeyev hastens to point out, the only problem was maintaining the separation of ideological content and formal method as a precaution against any alien intellectual moments in the work of the classics. Thus, we can expect *The Rout* to mimic Tolstoy's literary devices and to interject current sociopolitical doctrine where Tolstoy would depend on his powers of speculation.

Perhaps the most obvious use of Tolstoy's work can be seen in the syntactical structure adopted in *The Rout.* Typical of *War and Peace, Anna Karenina,* and most of Tolstoy's fiction are phrases, sentences, or even paragraphs which convey the sense that "a given situation happened not because . . . but because." Syntax, in this instance, clearly reflects attempts to discard the false core of things and to get at the real principles of life. The beginning of the short story "After the Ball," for one example, shows a character at the height of such a process: "You say that man can not understand by himself what is good, or what is bad, that everything depends on the event. . . . I will tell you of myself. . . . My whole life has been formulated, one way or another, not by the environment but from something completely different." Obviously, Fadeyev could not accept the idea of this particular paragraph: to say that man is not created by his environment would be too contrary to the spirit of Marxism-Leninism. But Fadeyev does accept the bare form, and we can trace numerous instances in *The Rout*:

> He went on even more carefully and warily, not because he wanted to remain unobserved, but so that he might not frighten the smile off the guard's face.
>
> . . . . .
>
> When he recognized Levinson, Metchik was embarrassed, not so much because his rifle was out of order, but because he had been taken unawares with such thoughts.
>
> . . . . .
>
> Stashinsky could see that he praised Levinson not only because Levinson was clever, but because it pleased the man to ascribe to somebody qualities he himself did not possess.
>
> . . . . .
>
> It seemed to her that he alone, so good-looking, so modest and tender, could satisfy her yearning for motherhood, and that she had fallen in love with him for no other reason. (In reality this feeling had arisen in her only after she had fallen in love with Metchik, while her infertility had physical reasons behind it which did not depend on personal desires.)

Another link between Fadeyev's and Tolstoy's literary devices can be seen in the psychological approach to characterization used by both men. Particularly relevant are the frequent internal monologues that are often found in *The Rout.* Metchik, Morozka, Levinson, and other protagonists all carry on unmistakably Tolstoyan conversations with themselves. Not only are they depicted through a method of characterization typical of Tolstoy's texts, but

their very thoughts carry the unmistakable tone of Tolstoy's characters. The "smoke of gunpowder and heroic deeds" of Metchik's dreams and their contrast to the brutal reality of war bear an obvious resemblance to young Petya Rostov's flights of imagination. The Soviet warrior's reaction to the first horse given to him ("What am I—a little boy?") is colored by the same childish desire to be accepted as a grown man which worries Petya and the protagonist of *Childhood, Boyhood, Youth.* Metelitsa, once he realizes that death is imminent, accepts his fate in a manner virtually identical to Prince Andrey's: "However, he groped on and on until he eventually realized with final, desperate certitude that this time there was no chance of escape. And once he was convinced of this, the question of his own life and death ceased to interest him."

But there is a further parallel which can be drawn between Metelitsa's death and Tolstoy's work. The particular chapter in which Metelitsa is shot is entitled "Three Deaths," the title which Tolstoy gave to one of his stories. Tolstoy was largely concerned with showing the differences between the deaths of a noblewoman and a peasant. The peasant accepts his fate and faces death calmly and without futile struggle, to the point of giving away his boots on the condition that the recipient erect a tombstone over his grave. The noblewoman does not accept her fate, cannot face the thought of her death, and dies foolishly, striving to the end to find a miraculous cure which will save her life. In the process she betrays her human dignity and makes life miserable for all around her. Metelitsa, like the peasant and unlike the noblewoman, dies a brave death. In contrast, a man shot in reprisal by Levinson's partisans dies ingloriously, pleading for his life. Thus, in all probability, the idea of presenting a positive virtue through the "proper" sacrificial death of a partisan came out of Tolstoy's story, although the exploration of ultimate experiential issues was replaced by Fadeyev with the current political demand for sacrifice and defense of the party.

Another law of psychological dynamics which we can observe in Tolstoy's characters is the sudden, abrupt nature of changes in their feelings. It is typical for Tolstoy's heroes to be suddenly struck by something, to sharply change their intentions under the jolting awareness of some essential truth. Pierre's reawakening to his love of Natasha is of this nature. Pierre has no thoughts about his feelings till he meets Natasha at Princess Marya's residence:

> But at that moment Princess Marya said, "Natasha!" And the face with the intent eyes—painfully, with effort, like a rusty door opening—smiled, and through that opened door, there floated to Pierre a sudden, overwhelming rush of long-forgotten bliss, of which, especially now, he had no thought. It breathed upon him, overwhelmed him and swallowed him up entirely. When she smiled, there could be no doubt. It was Natasha, and he loved her.

This abrupt awareness of a profound thought, of real feeling, is also typical of Fadeyev's characters. For one example, Varya's thoughts about Metchik go through this process:

And suddenly she felt that she did not at all want to harbor resentment and evil notions directed against him, or to suffer from them herself when everybody around was so contented and nobody worried their heads about anything, and when she too might be thoughtlessly happy. There and then she made up her mind to cast all other things from her head and to go to Metchik; now she no longer saw anything humiliating about such a step.

Metchik himself undergoes a sudden emotional reaction which smacks of Tolstoy's method of characterization: "Metchik's chance remark had evidently awakened a host of unwanted memories in Baklanov. With sudden passion, Metchik began to argue that it was not in the least a bad thing, but quite good, that Baklanov had not been in high school." The difference between the two sets of responses is that in Tolstoy's texts the character's sudden realization led to basic truths and complex issues of experience the writer wants to confront; in Fadeyev's work the shock of awareness introduces banal notions of feminine sexuality and social class. Both Varya's and Metchik's platitudes are derived from Marxist-Leninist doctrine; Varya is stimulated by a sexual drive based on the most vulgar of materialistic views of personality, and Metchik defends, with a gross Marxian sentimentalism, the rights of the lowly and uneducated.

In striking out for the new ways of literature, Fadeyev argued against the persistent lyrical descriptions of nature which created much of the beauty of early Soviet prose. The Soviet critic Bushmin was entirely right when he wrote [in *Voprosy Sovetsko: literatury,* 1953] that "the author of *The Rout* followed the traditions of the old masters of realism in his methods of description." Fadeyev's nature, in the main, is simple and uncolored by extreme flourishes in language. Bushmin describes this particular aspect in detail and there is no need for extensive analysis. But Bushmin does not clarify a major characteristic of Fadeyev's style and its origins in Tolstoy. Strikingly enough, Fadeyev himself pointed out where he was remiss to Bushmin after reading his critical essay. In a letter of 11 October 1948, Fadeyev writes: "The landscape often serves [Tolstoy] the function of expressing a deep thought (remember Prince Andrey and the old oak, and later this same oak, covered with green) and—even more than with Turgenev—serves to express feelings which give emotional color to the condition of characters."

Fadeyev was focusing on a literary technique that he had already incorporated into his own text using Tolstoy's method of introducing environment and setting to develop characterization. The following example from *The Rout* is typical:

> Every morning when they were carried out of the stuffy barrack hut, the quiet fair-bearded old man Pika came up to Metchik. He made Metchik see an old forgotten picture: in tranquil stillness, near an ancient, moss-grown hermitage, a quiet and clear-browed old man wearing a calotte sits fishing on the emerald-green bank of a lake. A peaceful sky above the old man's head; fir trees, peaceful and languorous, all

around; the peaceful lake overgrown with rushes. Peace, dreams, silence . . .

Bushmin cites this passage in his article but does not explain that the rustic scene is clearly supposed to reflect Fadeyev's criticism of Metchik's impractical, idealistic character, as does this following excerpt:

> His thought carried him far away—into the radiant days of the future; they were light and airy and melted imperceptibly like the gentle, rosy clouds over the glades of the taiga. He pictured himself returning together with Varya to the town in a jolting train with open windows, beyond which clouds as gentle and rosy as these would sail above the distant, hazy mountain ranges. The two of them would sit at the window, side by side, very close to each other, Varya murmuring soft words to him, he stroking her head and her plaits, as golden as burning daylight. . . .

After Morozka realizes that Varya loves Metchik, we read: "He felt forsaken and lonely. It seemed to him that he was sailing over a huge, deserted field and its terrifying emptiness only accentuated his loneliness."

Tolstoy's work further served Fadeyev in constructing a new type of protagonist—the political commissar or party representative—who would be used throughout socialist realist fiction to argue for immediate government goals. Earlier, writers such as Vsevolod Ivanov and Dmitry Furmanov had created amazing Bolshevik heroes—Nikita Vershinin, Chapayev, Serafimovich's "Iron-Jaw" Kozhukh—who were hardly credible but strikingly forceful giants fighting for the glorious future. Such fictional types were all too representative of poetic fancy and unbridled literary imagination to be the reliable spokesmen of government needs. Some one stock protagonist was needed for this function and Fadeyev provided a solution by using Tolstoy's fiction to invent Levinson, a much more ordinary, "realistic" protagonist who directly interjects party ideas into the text. Below, I will examine Levinson as a particularly representative model of technical imitation and ideological sterility but first I would like to show some of the typical modes of description taken from Tolstoy which are shared by almost *all* of Fadeyev's protagonists.

In 1935, Fadeyev made the following notation after reading Stanislavsky's *My Life in Art:* "An example of the approach from the external to the internal: one half of the mustache pasted higher than the other helped to reveal a character. (L. Tolsoy—the role of a stearine spot in one of the works of the artist Mikhailov in *Anna Karenina*)." In other words, our writer's notebooks show that he related the use of a particular detail in characterization—a stearine spot, a mustache—to the work of Tolstoy. Indeed, one of Tolstoy's favorite devices was to force the impression of one particular element of a character's physique on the reader's awareness. We remember Elena most vividly for her "white shoulders," her brother for his harelip and idiotic speech, Pierre for his huge clumsy figure, Kutuzov for his tired old face. Tolstoy selects one or two physical details and by constantly repeating them in the activity of his characters, creates a central leitmotif of description from which the reader can generalize to the entire nature of a personality. As Fadeyev points out, each of these external details carries with it a higher, "internal" meaning. Elena's white shoulders symbolize her depravity and sexuality; her brother's grotesque lip, the nature of court figures whom Tolstoy thoroughly satirizes; Pierre's bearlike clumsiness, his groping and awkward search for the meaning of life; Kutuzov's tired face, the acceptance of fate and the understanding that men do not determine the course of events. Fadeyev carries this technique into his own work.

A typical physical detail which is used extensively throughout *The Rout* involves the eyes of the characters. We read of Levinson's "foreign, big eyes," Morozka's "green-hazel!" and Varya's "smoky" ones, and of Metchik's "poor, lost look." Varya's and Morozka's eyes are also used to convey the feeling of a particular moment. After one of their excursions into the forest, the two return "hiding their eyes from each other, tired and languid." These "tired and languid" eyes are indications, we can assume, not only of the essence of their sexual experience but also of the nature of their entire relationship and Varya's escape from it in Metchik's arms.

There are numerous other details which serve the same function of characterization. Interesting in *The Rout* are Goncharenko's "large, knotty hands." While Varya's large hands, like her large bosom, should convey her primitive, peasant nature, Goncharenko's hands help to establish his love for work and proletarian determination. Morozka's disobedient locks of hair crudely prepare us for his thievery and reckless spirit. Metelitsa's "sharp nostrils" characterize his keen mind and lithe body. Doctor Stashinsky's unbending figure and rigidly tough spine form the physical detail which is best supposed to predispose the reader to understand the doctor's unwavering act of mercy killing. Finally, Levinson's small body is an important part of Fadeyev's differences with the conventions of early Soviet literature. For in this period, it is not the "iron jaw" of Kozhukh or Chapayev's legendary figure which would lead the party to victory but the ideas of Marxism-Leninism which govern Levinson's puny physique. Thus, we are brought to the question of Fadeyev's response to Tolstoy's ideological heritage; as we have seen, the formal side of Tolstoy's fiction was imitated directly and without embarrassment.

During his career as a cultural bureaucrat Fadeyev was chairman of a committee which was preparing Tolstoy's work for publication. In March of 1949, he wrote out a list of suggestions to its members. One suggestion was:

> It is doubtful that one can put out the texts of even Tolstoy's fictional work without a short introduction which will help the reader to understand and judge properly Tolstoy's ideological-artistic development. . . . It is impossible, for instance, not to comment on the challenging, 'aristocratic,' remarks of Tolstoy. . . . It is no less important to contrast the first variations of Kutuzov's and Bagration's images with the final embodiment of their images in the novel. Such differences present a particularly good opportu-

nity to place Tolstoy's views on the historic role of these generals under criticism. . . .

In 1950, Fadeyev repeated the same demand after V. F. Lebedev naively submitted his memoirs of Tolstoy for comment. Fadeyev returned the manuscript with this criticism: "Insofar as your meeting with Tolstoy was connected with his religious search, one just cannot write that the reason for the meeting was Tolstoy's book *God's Kingdom is within You;* one must dwell longer on Tolstoy's religious views, they must be explained and they must be criticized." As we will see, Fadeyev had much earlier attempted his own criticism in the figure of Levinson.

The one particular motif of Tolstoy's thought which Fadeyev, as a good party member with a firm knowledge of Lenin, could not possibly admit, was the wavering and seemingly inconclusive historical determinism of *War and Peace.* For Tolstoy, as we have seen, many causes, many elements, went into shaping the course of things. The major ideological argument of *War and Peace* was directed at the historians, writers, and politicians who saw history not in the many unexplainable causes which really determine events but through the simplified view of a predetermined future. Tolstoy's devastating portrayal of Napoleon and of the generals on both sides who thought they controlled the flow of battle was created with such a polemic in mind. Obviously, given Lenin's history-creating vanguard, with its finger supposedly placed firmly on the pulse of the world, Fadeyev could either pretend not to notice this aspect of Tolstoy's work or directly pick up the gauntlet. In the figure of Levinson, we see that he chose the latter path.

Levinson stands opposite to the hero of *War and Peace* in one vital respect: General Kutuzov feels he does not control events; Levinson knows he does. Because Fadeyev maintains his formal debt to Tolstoy in creating Levinson no less than in the depiction of the other protagonists we noted, his character structure is one of the most obvious examples of the separation between literary convention and ideology which took place in the creative process that brought forward *The Rout.* For instance, Levinson has Kutuzov's "rare patience and doggedness," the same ability to communicate with soldiers and peasants, the same sly approach to his subordinates. In order to inspire confidence in his men, he, like Kutuzov, pretends to have a sure draft to the fate of his soldiers. Both, in reality, have none. As we will see, later Fadeyev does give Levinson the power to understand and control events; here, however, Levinson is identical to the Russian general in his ability to put up a good bluff. Another technique meant to build morale in Levinson's soldiers is taken straight out of *War and Peace.* After Borodino, Kutuzov's famous response was "The battle is won," although nothing of the sort had happened. Levinson gives commands with the same assurance and the same neglect of cold facts. Last of all, in a scene strikingly reminiscent of the legendary Council of Tilsit, Levinson, like Kutuzov, listens calmly to the various arguments of his lieutenants and, when all are finished, gives his unequivocal decision to retreat. The formal similarities that exist between the two leaders are obvious, and it is not too extreme to say that one appears to be the caricature of the other.

Monument to Fadeyev.

historical context that Tolstoy undertook in protagonists like Pierre Bezukhov.

Most of such examples serve to illustrate a crucial pattern of Soviet aesthetic reaction to an environment which prohibited the natural relationship of ideology and literary form. It is true that the correlation between the death of creative formal experiments and literary technique and the imposed end of ideology is not necessarily direct, and the purpose of this essay was not to establish irrevocable proof of a direct relationship. Moreover, no attempt to demonstrate a unique influence on Fadeyev's work was intended since other writers could have been used to provide similar material for imitation. But I would like to suggest that the outlined reaction to the past is, at the very least, an indication of an abnormal development of literature—of an environment which spoiled the intellectual reservoirs of its writers, forced a rabid dependence on the purely mechanical elements of its legacy, and prohibited the normal reformulation and growth of its complete heritage. By speaking of this total heritage, I do not mean to say that Fadeyev should have mimicked or even concerned himself with Tolstoy's philosophy but that the results of his labor would have surely been more valuable to the existence of literature as a living, ever-changing force if he, like Tolstoy, had been allowed to extend his own mind and vision beyond the boundaries established by the state. The telling examples of a literature in which ideology is deprived of the writer's identity can only remind us again of the decisive role played by values of the self in past literary achievements. (pp. 133-48)

Nicholas Rzhevsky, "Ideology as Control: Tolstoy and Fadeyev," in his Russian Literature and Ideology: Herzen, Dostoevsky, Leontiev, Tolstoy, Fadeyev, *University of Illinois Press, 1983, pp. 133-48.*

Roger Cockrell   (essay date 1986)

[*In the essay below, Cockrell evaluates Fadeyev as a literary theorist.*]

In November 1926, at the plenary meeting of VAPP in Moscow, the young Aleksandr Fadeyev, the author of **Razgrom,** was elected to membership of the Association's secretariat and bureau. [The critic adds in a footnote: 'VAPP (Vserossiyskaya Assotsiatsiya proletarskikh pisateley) had become by 1926, the largest and most influential of all the various proletarian literary organizations. Two years later, as part of a general reorganization of such groupings, it was retitled RAPP (Rossiyskaya Assotsiatsiya proletarskikh pisateley), under which name it remained until its final dissolution in 1932.'] Behind him lay two years of valuable experience as party journalist and activist in the south of Russia. In Krasnodar and particularly in Rostov, where he had been appointed the editor of the Party section of the newspaper *Sovetskiy yug,* his outstanding organizational abilities and talents as forceful spokesman for the proletarian cause in Soviet literature had swiftly been recognized. In January 1925 the Rostov Proletarian Writers' Association had elected him, together with the dramatist and future RAPP leader

On the other hand, Kutuzov's success in *War and Peace* was due entirely to the fact that he did not attempt to understand or control the stream of events. Fadeyev provides the opposite argument for Levinson:

> Not that he believed, either then or now, that an individual was incapable of influencing events in which masses of men were involved—no, this view seemed to him the worst sort of human hypocrisy, a camouflage for the weakness of those who had recourse to it, for their lack of the will to action. . . . In this second period he acquired the power to direct events; the more clearly and accurately he divined their genuine course and the mutual relation of forces and of the men involved—the more complete and more successful was this power of his.

The passage is all dead weight in the ideological sense; it is an insertion into the text, without any intellectual work on the part of the author, of Lenin's theory of the conscious vanguard. Levinson's power and will to action are ultimately hypocritical, in the sense of ideological hypocrisy noted previously, for they are not independent, self-explored values but are shown to be valid only in expressing the victory of the party and the inevitable triumph of Marxism-Leninism. The character's spiritually emasculated political meaning is a far cry, of course, from the personally felt, ideological exploration of the individual and

V. M. Kirshon, as delegate to the First All-Union Conference of Proletarian Writers in Moscow; and in April of the same year he had been appointed, again with Kirshon, to the editorial board of the Rostov region's first literary journal *Lava*. Although his activities were concerned for the most part with local and regional affairs it is clear that this period had served as an invaluable apprenticeship for the tasks and the posts Fadeyev was later to assume.

By the time Fadeyev joined the higher echelons of VAPP, the Association's new leadership which had arisen from the split within its ranks following the Party Resolution on Literature of July 1925 had been able to establish itself. The old leadership—men such as Vardin, Lelevich, and Rodov who had advocated such a vigorously hostile view towards the idea of any accommodation with the fellow-travellers—now formed the 'left' opposition within the Association. The new-style VAPP, led by Averbakh, Libedinsky, and Raskol'nikov, was now firmly oriented along the lines laid down by the Party Resolution which, while reasserting the basic concept of eventual proletarian hegemony in literature, advocated the principle of co-operation with the fellow-travellers. As a result of this change in orientation greater emphasis was placed on more literary, as opposed to merely ideological, criteria in the Association's pronouncements—a shift which was reflected in the change of title of its journal, in May 1926, from *Na postu* to *Na literaturnom postu*. This somewhat more relaxed and 'literary' approach seems to have struck a responsive chord in Fadeyev. This can be deduced firstly from his own stories which had already been published and which had revealed the temperament of an author whom it would be difficult to describe as a harsh and uncompromising ideologue; secondly, from his own account of his experience at the January 1925 Conference of proletarian writers in which he had attempted to soften the harsh anti-fellow-traveller line put forward by Vardin.

Further evidence for Fadeyev's advocacy of co-operation with other than purely proletarian writers can be seen in the first edition of the journal *Lava,* of which he was on the editorial board and which appeared three months before the 1925 Party Resolution. This contained an article by Kirshon, a writer who, from an ideological point of view, was very close to Fadeyev, in which the author stated categorically that the policy towards the fellow-travellers should be to strive to bring them closer to proletarian ideals, rather than to hound them.

Whatever the truth of Fadeyev's position before 1926, it is quite clear where his sympathies lay by the end of that year. Firmly committed to a policy which was both orthodox from the Party point of view and at the same time reasonably moderate and centrist, he quickly consolidated his position within the VAPP leadership to become, by the end of the decade, one of its most powerful and influential figures. In 1927 he was appointed to the editorial board of one of the Association's two literary journals, *Oktyabr'*, and, the following year, to the second, *Na literaturnom postu;* in addition he was appointed in 1931 to be chief editor of *Krasnaya nov',* the journal which had been founded and edited by Voronsky during the 1920s.

As the author of ***Razgrom***, which rapidly came to be viewed as one of the seminal works of early Soviet literature, Fadeyev had acquired considerable prestige and respect within proletarian literary circles across a broad spectrum of opinion, excluding the extreme left. Once established in Moscow at the centre of power, he was to further that reputation, this time as a literary theorist, with a whole series of keynote speeches and articles which appeared between the years 1927 and 1932. Contemporaries testify to the particular impact which Fadeyev made on his mainly youthful audiences. From the first he seems to have been marked out as one of the leaders of his generation of writers.

This [essay] has a fourfold purpose: first, to identify the major themes contained in these speeches and articles; secondly, to evaluate Fadeyev's contribution as a literary theorist during the period under question; thirdly, to attempt to establish his position in the literary spectrum of the late 1920s; and finally, to comment on the relationship between the two aspects of Fadeyev as literary theorist on the one hand and creative author on the other.

In 1928 an article by Fadeyev entitled '**Protiv verkhoglyadstva**' appeared in the journal *Revolyutsiya i kul' tura.* It was a reply to an earlier article in the same journal by someone writing under the pseudonym of Semyonov. According to Fadeyev, Semyonov's article amounted to a series of platitudes, pseudo-truths and distortions of the position taken by proletarian writers such as Libedinsky and Fadeyev himself at the VAPP conference earlier in the year. Fadeyev uses his reply as an opportunity not simply to defend the VAPP standpoint, but also to unleash the full weight of his invective and sarcastic rhetoric against Semyonov—thereby revealing himself as a formidable and dangerous opponent. The article, peppered with caustic comments, concludes, in the best rhetorical tradition, with a biting peroration inviting Comrade Semyonov to mount his emaciated and vulgar camel and return to the remote deserts of Central Asia where he belongs.

After taking up the challenge on Libedinsky's behalf in the first section of the article Fadeyev turns to Semyonov's charge that his, Fadeyev's, use of the slogan 'living man' is harmful because it does not emphasize the fact that people must be portrayed in the light of Marxism and Bolshevism; it would therefore be acceptable to writers across a wide ideological spectrum including some who are hostile to socialism:

> Comrade Semyonov naively supposes that artistic creativity is a process which can be developed by the use of slogans. As a consequence he brandishes the slogan: 'Living people must be depicted in the light of Marxism and Bolshevism!!' My dear comrade Semyonov! For Bolshevik proletarian writers this goes absolutely without saying. The point is, by what artistic method are we to portray 'living people' in the light of Marxism and Bolshevism?

'*How* is the new proletarian writer to depict "living people" in his works?' The problems faced by Fadeyev in attempting to answer this crucial question were manifold and complex. The battle he was fighting had to be waged on two fronts: on the one hand he was setting out not only to establish the basic principles underlying the new proletarian literature but also to present it as a qualitative step forward in the cultural evolution of mankind; on the other he had to defend his position and that of like-minded proletarian critics from attack by hostile critics of many different ideological persuasions who viewed it as flawed or even untenable; such critics had, in turn, to be counterattacked.

Fadeyev did not underestimate the task confronting him. He was well aware of the almost total lack of a firm theoretical basis on which the whole concept of proletarian literature was to be founded. He recognized that, in trying to grapple with the problem of how to create believable heroes and characters within the context of an ideologically committed society, he was in practically unknown territory:

> . . . It turns out that our question on the depiction of living people in literature is an extremely simple and comprehensible one. For the fact of our posing it basically means that we are on such a low level, artistically speaking, that we have still not learnt to depict flesh-and-blood people; instead, we portray them schematically. But we need to depict them so that the reader can *believe* that such people really exist.

This acknowledgement of the relatively primitive nature of proletarian literary theory forms a constant theme in Fadeyev's theoretical writings. Echoing Lenin's view of the extremely low level of culture and literacy in the country and his exhortation to 'Study, study and study', he pointed out that proletarian writers were still at the kindergarten stage and he repeatedly stressed the necessity and primacy of education as an essential factor in their development. Lenin's exhortation to study had indeed been reflected in the 1925 Party Resolution which had specifically warned proletarian writers and critics against the sins of arrogance and communist conceit (*komchvanstvo*). In the final paragraphs of his speech **'Stolbovaya doroga proletarskoy literatury'**, Fadeyev was to develop this idea, urging his listeners to study firstly from life itself ('moguchaya, polnokrovnaya, mnogo obraznaya zhizn'') and secondly from the classics of realistic literature.

Of the two major tasks—the establishment of a new proletarian literary theory on the one hand and the assault on what he considered to be hostile theories on the other—it was the second to which Fadeyev, in the years up to 1932, devoted more time and with which he dealt more convincingly. Indeed, an analysis of these early speeches and articles shows that the stance which he adopted was more negative than positive—negative in the sense that he seemed generally concerned more to attack others, to analyse the past, particularly the French realistic literature of the nineteenth century, and to present contemporary problems, rather than positively to point the way ahead. It was only after 1932, with the emergence of the newly accepted creed of socialist realism, that he was to turn to a consistent and systematic presentation of his views on the form and content of the new socialist literature.

This general pattern is revealed in Fadeyev's keynote speech **'Stolbovaya doroga proletarskoy literatury'**. After

a few introductory remarks he launches into his main theme—the creation of 'living people', illustrating, with a quotation from Libedinsky, his contention that proletarian writers are still at a very primitive stage of development:

> This is how we portray people—a commissar, for example. Such a person should possess certain specific features, and so we give him these features and away he goes. Or a bourgeois—he too has his specific features. An intellectual— just the same thing, all in a predetermined mould, and it's done.

Fadeyev then proceeds to examine the realistic writers of the nineteenth century, taking Flaubert, Tolstoy, and Zola as his examples. Nineteenth-century realism possessed the enormous virtue, in his view, of describing people as they are, but as a method it suffered from two outstanding faults: first, from the social orientation of the writers concerned—the fact that in their works they inevitably expressed, albeit unconsciously, the views of the ruling class and bourgeoisie; and secondly, from its failure to depict individuals as part of a whole, as determined by a whole network of social relationships. (As support for this second point Fadeyev quotes directly from Plekhanov's *Iskusstvo i obshchestvennaya zhizn'* (1911-12), from which Fadeyev derived many of his ideas.) Fadeyev concludes this section with the generalized platitude that it is only the new proletarian art which is capable of depicting real people in terms of their social relationships, since the subjective hopes, expectations, and interests of the proletariat coincide, for the first time in history, with the objective process of historical development.

This is classic Marxist territory, of course, based on the premise that literature, as one part of the superstructure, is a reflection of the economic base: once the exploitation of the many by the few has been removed, then the conflicts and contradictions which have characterized all previous societies will inevitably begin to disappear. The exact process, however, by which, as Fadeyev claims, the proletariat become the masters of genuinely realistic characterization remains unclear and he is unable or unwilling, at least at this stage, to throw any further light on the matter.

Fadeyev turns instead to an examination of those methods, both historical and contemporary, which are hostile to what he terms the 'proletarian materialist' method. These methods he divides into two basic camps—the 'irrationalists' and the 'ultra-rationalists'. The first group, which includes the 'idealists' Gippius and Leonid Andreyev as well as their more contemporary irrationalist brethren such as Vsevolod Ivanov, distorts reality through an excessive, not to say obsessive, use of the subconscious and intuitive in their presentation of characters. Under the influence of Freud and Bergson, these writers exaggerate this intuitive 'psychical' element to such an extent that the reader is unable to discern any objective laws governing human motivation whatsoever. Characters move in a seemingly random way, the motivation for their actions wrapped in a fog of mystification.

On much the same grounds Fadeyev attacks the Pereval

theoreticians, Lezhnev and Gorbov, for giving undue weight to the role of subconscious processes in literature as a means of revealing the truth. In many respects, Fadeyev claims, the method championed by the Pereval group is so close to that of the irrationalists that it is indistinguishable from it. Neither method is capable of giving any more than a distorted and one-sided picture of reality.

Having dealt with one end of the literary spectrum, Fadeyev now switches his line of attack to the opposite extreme, the ultra-rationalists in LEF (Levyy front iskusstva). Early in 1928 LEF had made a categorical statement on its position with its championing of the 'precise fixation of facts' as the fundamental artistic principle. To this Fadeyev retorts that the contraposition of fact with art is a method which can lead only to absurdity. What is meant by the term 'precise fixation of facts'? What view of reality can be gained by a simple mechanical description of an object or a character? Turning once more to Lenin, Fadeyev uses the Bolshevik leader's argument that even such a simple object as a glass is the summation of an infinite number of relationships and qualities which depend on its function. 'Fixation of the facts' as a literary method is wrong, in other words, on two important counts: first, because it gives merely a one-sided, superficial and therefore non-essential view of reality; and secondly, because it does not take into account the point of view of the observer. The reduction by LEF writers and critics of the subconscious to the purely biological and mechanical, moreover, renders the idea of beauty and the emotional apprehension of reality superfluous.

Here we have come full circle, for with Fadeyev's emphasis on the need for the subconscious approach and the necessity of 'looking into the psyche' of characters in order to portray reality, he is apparently advancing arguments and methods which he has already scornfully rejected in the first section of his speech. The whole thrust of his argument, however, is not that the 'intuitive' approach, or indeed the 'rationalist' approach, is wrong in itself, but, rather, that it is incorrect to elevate it to a position where it constitutes the only artistic method. Each of the two extremes, in his view, is guilty of making the fundamentally false 'metaphysical' polarization between the unconscious and the conscious, intuition and reason, and the irrational and rational. These elements should not be seen as mutually exclusive but should, rather, be combined and synthesized to form what he considers to be the only genuinely realistic method.

The ideas which Fadeyev expresses in **'Stolbovaya doroga'** form the basis for his literary theory which he is to develop subsequently. The argument is a simple one: proceeding from a recognition of the inadequacy and flaws inherent in purely idealist and rational methods, proletarian writers, through studying both from life as well as from the works of classical literature, should now fashion a method which will represent a totally new type of literature—a higher reformulation and synthesis of existing methods, combined within a fundamentally proletarian world-view.

But if the statement of the task confronting the proletarian writer is relatively simple, its realization, as Fadeyev himself recognized and emphasized on many occasions, presents him with formidable difficulties; what is demanded is the ability, through the process of careful selection of material, to reveal the essential characteristics of human personality and behaviour within the framework of a story that satisfies both the reader and also ideological criteria. Of crucial importance here is the whole relationship of the writer with the reality he is describing; to what extent are the terms 'realism' and 'romanticism' applicable to the new proletarian literary method? It is to this question in particular that Fadeyev addressed himself in his article **'Protiv verkhoglyadstva'** (1928), and his speech of the following year at the plenary meeting of RAPP, **'Doloy Shillera!'**.

'Protiv verkhoglyadstva' is, as we have shown, primarily a defence of the views expressed by Fadeyev himself and his fellow-writer Libedinsky at the 1928 VAPP conference. But Fadeyev uses the opportunity to develop important, if largely unoriginal, ideas which are to influence profoundly the future course of proletarian literary theory. He takes as his starting-point Libedinsky's dictum that art reproduces reality in the form of immediate impressions of that reality; without such immediacy of impressions a 'work of art' can no longer be defined as such. To the extent to which a decadent art form, such as cubism, loses its ability to create the illusion of reality through the reflection of immediate impressions—to that extent it ceases to be art. But true art, so Fadeyev's argument continues, does not merely consist in the immediate reflection of reality; it arises as a result of the artist distinguishing between what is merely superficial and commonplace on the one hand and what is essential and universal on the other. He does this above all by a process of rejection (*ottalkivaniye*); the truth is revealed precisely by 'removing the covers' from reality and by unmasking everything that is false and inessential.

According to this line of reasoning, therefore, all true art has adopted the method of depicting reality first through the assimilation of immediate impressions and then through some kind of filtering process, as a result of which these processes are either unmasked or idealized. This is, moreover, a process which has occurred throughout the history of civilization—with the exception of the very earliest forms of art, such as that of the Greeks who, as a result of their primitive child-like stage of social development, had no need either to unmask or to idealize. The apotheosis of this cultural development will prove—and here Fadeyev repeats almost word-for-word the claim that he has already made in **'Stolbovaya doroga . . . '**—to be the representation of reality by proletarian artists who, because of their unique and unprecedented social circumstances, possess the only correct method for its cognition.

Even if we leave to one side this last highly dubious and dogmatic claim—which can be seen, ironically, as one more form of 'idealization', to use Fadeyev's own term—there are clearly many more questions to be answered. One of these questions concerns the problem of romanticism. What exactly was Fadeyev's attitude to the romantic school of the nineteenth century and what is its relationship to the new proletarian art of the twentieth century?

If there is, as we shall see, a great deal of confusion surrounding this question it is a state of affairs for which Fadeyev himself is partly responsible. On the one hand, he claims first that idealization gives a false view of reality, and secondly that such a method is an inherent characteristic of 'all types of romantic schools of literature'; on the other hand, however, he goes on to deny that he is talking about romanticism generally.

What, then, is Fadeyev's position? To throw some light on this we must turn to a speech which he made in 1929, to which he gave the provocative and somewhat arrogant title of **'Doloy Shillera!'**.

After some introductory remarks in which Fadeyev makes a careful and pointed distinction between so-called literary specialists on the one hand and writers on the other—the first are interested in a work of art as a finished product, the second as a creative process—he then poses what for him is the key question: how does the writer relate to reality: through what kind of spectacles does he view the world?

In answering this Fadeyev once again takes his examples from nineteenth-century literature. On the one hand, there are those writers such as Stendhal, Flaubert, Balzac, the Goncourt brothers, Zola, and Maupassant who, for all the differences in their approach and for all their limitations—and here Fadeyev repeats the already familiar quotations from Plekhanov—may be classed as materialist: materialist in the sense that they were able to remove the covers from superficial reality and thereby to reveal the objective truth underlying it. The German writer Schiller, on the other hand, is an illustration of a totally contrary tendency. Quoting once again from Plekhanov, as well as from Marx, Fadeyev sets out to prove Schiller's fundamentally idealistic approach:

> Take his characters William Tell or Karl Moor. They wear heroic clothes and the hats of hunters and brigands; at every step they take they declaim freedom. But take their heroic clothes away, consider their declarations carefully, and you will see the figure of a revolutionary German shopkeeper whose shouts for freedom mask the basic desire of all shopkeepers—the freedom of the market-place.

The method of idealist writers such as Schiller, in other words, is the reverse of the materialists' method; instead of peeling away everything that is false and superficial to reveal the bedrock of hard reality beneath, the idealists clothe this reality in all kinds of mystifying and romantically heightened garments in order to conceal it.

Up to this point there has been apparently little change in the line of argument which Fadeyev has put forward previously. But now he turns his attention to something new, by beginning finally to examine—rather than merely repeat ritualized platitudes—how the new proletarian literature relates to this nineteenth-century pattern. His view, characteristically, is that proletarian writers should be neither 'naive realists' nor 'false romantics', but should adopt a method which is, in effect, a synthesis of these two major streams; they should, in other words, proceed dialectically:

> . . . unlike the great realists of the past the proletarian writer will see the process of social development and the forces underlying this process and determining its development; he will, that is to say, be able to portray the birth of the new in the old, of tomorrow in today, the struggle and victory of the new over the old. And this means that such an artist will not only explain the world more than any artist of the past, but will consciously serve the process of change.

These ideas—of seeing 'tomorrow' in 'today' and of the function of the artist not merely as an interpreter but as a creative, transforming agent—show Fadeyev's commitment to what can only be seen as a type of romanticism: the visionary dreams of a glorious future, based not on concealing present reality but, on the contrary, on a precise awareness of the present coupled with a perspective of the future:

> Once the artist has mastered this method he will be able to portray the phenomena of life . . . in the light of what 'ought to be'. In this sense the proletarian artist will be not merely the most sober of realists but also the greatest of dreamers . . .

Fadeyev is here in fact juggling with two different kinds of romanticism: on the one hand the false type of romanticism as exemplified by Schiller and, on the other, the idea of revolutionary romanticism, the literary method which, with its merging of vision with reality, was to become one of the central tenets of socialist realism. The failure to understand this crucial point has led to incorrect assessments of Fadeyev's position during the late 1920s. The short-lived opposition group within the proletarian literary movement, Litfront, for example, was to castigate Fadeyev for not championing the romantic element in literature. Among more recent Soviet critics the generally percipient Sheshukov makes the common error of stating that Fadeyev came to appreciate the importance of romanticism as part of the socialist literary method only as late as the 1950s. And when H. Ermolaev writes [in his *Soviet Literary Theories, 1917-1934,* 1963] that—

> In this discourse the Onlitguardists saw only what they wanted to see: the realistic quality of the dreaming. Lenin's appeal contained nothing romantic for Fadeyev; just the opposite: it was 'a most profound materialistic slogan' that must be 'raised as a banner for all our proletarian literature' . . .

and, later, that—

> With Fadeyev's article the RAPP leaders' opposition to any brand of romanticism in proletarian literature reached its peak. They continued to act as indefatigable champions of realism . . .

he is distorting Fadeyev's views by taking just one strand of Fadeyev's argument, the rejection of Schillerian romanticism, and elevating it to the single, most important point. Of all the critics, Kiselyova [in her *Tvorcheskiye iskaniya A. Fadeyeva,* 1965] is the most interesting in this debate: beginning by apparently agreeing with Ermolaev, when she writes that the development of Fadeyev's art was characterized by a movement away from the complete rejection of romanticism to a complete acceptance of it, she then contradicts herself:

> Besides, Fadeyev's rejection of romanticism, was not absolute . . . it was a rejection of romantic form and style, but not of the idea of perspective, of dreaming of that which we have come to see as a fundamental feature of socialist realism—revolutionary romanticism.

This is surely the point. In his speeches and articles from 1932 right up to the end of his life Fadeyev's view of proletarian literature as forming some kind of synthesis between reality and vision is a development of the ideas he expressed in 1929 and not a contradiction of them. The fact that after 1932 he uses the term 'revolutionary romanticism' approvingly represents a change of terminology rather than of substance. The essential argument that the artist must depict the embryonic future within the context of present reality remains constant.

The common—one might even say prevalent—assessment of Fadeyev's position in the late 1920s as that of a dogmatic and essentially narrow-minded ideologue needs, therefore, to be challenged. The real picture is both more complex and less harsh. It is certainly true that he revealed in these speeches and articles many of the less attractive qualities which characterized the proletarian literary movement as a whole during these years. But these lie at the periphery rather than the centre of his literary theory. If we focus our views on his search for a new method of literature in which the contrasting principles of realism and romanticism would be reconciled, a very different picture emerges. It reveals someone who to a certain extent stands outside the RAPP position and close to the broader sympathies of the Pereval critics. Ironically, Ermolaev's insistence on the contrary—that Fadeyev, as an Onlitguardist, was fundamentally opposed to the Pereval line—only serves to prove the point. In his analysis of the views of one of the leading Pereval critics, Lezhnev, Ermolaev writes:

> . . . unlike Fadeyev, the Pereval critic saw no unbridgeable gap between realism and romanticism. Contrary to the Onlitguardists' peculiar dismissal of romantic art, he championed revolutionary romanticism as an indispensable component of proletarian literature, as an expression of revolutionary enthusiasm, zest for life and dreams of the future, for 'a revolutionary cannot but be a dreamer'. Here Lezhnev demonstrated not only that his conception of proletarian literature was much broader than that of the RAPP leaders but also he was more orthodox than they, for revolutionary romanticism later became an ingredient of socialist realism.

With this statement Ermolaev has again fallen into the trap of focusing only on Fadeyev's diatribe against Schiller (the 'peculiar dismissal of romantic art') and ignoring all those points which identify Fadeyev's position with that of Lezhnev; if it is true that Lezhnev not only championed the cause of revolutionary romanticism but also, in so doing, anticipated one of the main tenets of socialist realism then this is true in equal measure, as we have shown, of Fadeyev.

In more general terms Ermolaev's careful distinction between the principles subscribed to by Pereval and those by RAPP, of which he considered Fadeyev a typical member, needs to be treated with caution.

> Pereval's theories, although founded on Marxist principles, were marked by considerable broad-mindedness, respect for art and the writer's individuality, demand for artistic integrity, and a notable absence of ideological dogmatism. These traits favourably set Pereval apart from RAPP. Both championed psychological realism. Pereval's conception of this realism, however, was broader and acknowledged the need for revolutionary romanticism.

If we exclude the absence of ideological dogmatism, the demarcation line between Pereval and at least some members of RAPP, including Fadeyev and Libedinsky, is more blurred than this assessment suggests.

The faults inherent in an excessively rigid assessment of Fadeyev's views are further revealed in the clear, if largely unacknowledged, link between them and those of Aleksandr Voronsky, the influential critic and editor of *Krasnaya nov'*, who, although not formally a member of Pereval, played a very large part in determining Pereval's theories.

It would be difficult to overestimate the importance of the role played by Voronsky on the literary stage directly during the first half of the 1920s and indirectly for many years after. Although he retained nominally the editorship of *Krasnaya nov'* for a short while after the Party Resolution on Literature in 1925, he was soon ousted from this position and, with the rise of Stalin during the last half of the decade, his name and reputation, coupled increasingly with Trotsky's, swiftly passed into disfavour; he was arrested during the purge in 1937 and died in 1943, almost certainly in a Stalinist labour camp. The journal which he founded, *Krasnaya nov'*, lived on after his departure from it until 1942, although freed from its 'Voronskiist' errors.

As a member of the Bolshevik intelligentsia Voronsky was on generally goods terms with many of the Bolshevik leaders immediately after the Revolution; it was Lenin indeed who had initiated and encouraged the founding of *Krasnaya nov* and Voronsky's association with it. But temperamentally and ideologically he stood on the right wing of the Party, advocating a tolerant attitude towards the fellow-travellers. He cultivated a deliberate policy of publishing in his journal writers who represented a broad spectrum of views. Like Lenin, he believed in the importance of basic cultural education and the significant role literature had to play in this process; like Trotsky, he believed that 'proletarian' art did not exist in Soviet Russia and that it would be wrong to seek specifically to promote it.

The special impact of Voronsky's views on literature derives not so much from any particular originality as from the intellectual force and vigour with which he put them across and from the at least partly hostile context within which he operated. His early theories of art come largely from Plekhanov out of Belinsky; included amongst these are first his insistence that art should not be seen merely as an instrument or weapon in the ideological struggle but that it has two components, or 'values': a sociological, or subjective value, and an aesthetic, or objective value; and secondly, his belief that whereas art and science share the same aim in that the object for both of them is the cognition and understanding of reality, they are none the less two fundamentally different processes: the artistic process, on the one hand, entails synthesis, sensuous nature, images and intuition; whereas the scientific process, on the other, entails analysis, mind, ideas and rational thought. Apart from devoting much attention to such universal principles as the role and function of art, Voronsky was also concerned with the more specific problems related to the creative process and, in particular, the portrayal of ideologically committed, yet artistically believable heroes. He arrives, however, at no clear resolution of this perhaps insoluble problem: the 'new man' still lies hidden in the mists of the Communist future. But he undoubtedly comes down on the side of psychological realism and of portraying people in the round with all their inconsistencies, faults, and contradictions; the intuitive and rational sides of man must be depicted not as separate but as constituent interlocking parts of a whole. Writers were to arrive at the truth by studying Tolstoy's method of constructing a world of 'hidden, secret, unconscious intentions that man usually does not even suspect' beneath the world of 'external actions and utterances'.

Even this somewhat cursory account of Voronsky's literary theories shows many points of contact with Fadeyev. We have already seen the latter's fundamental concern with the creation of a new type of hero, his championing of the Tolstoyan method as an example to be studied and followed, and his belief that reality could be revealed by uncovering the truth that lay beneath the superficial facts of experience. Both Voronsky and Fadeyev maintained that it was the duty of the more ideologically committed to assimilate the fellow-travellers rather than to foster a spirit of antagonism between them. Again, both of them recognized the miserably low level of culture in the country and expressed the view that one of the most important aims of art was to remedy this situation. One of Voronsky's starting points indeed had been the idea of the writers' dissatisfaction with reality and the need to bridge the gap between the ideal and reality. In an early article he had illustrated this in a passage which directly anticipates Fadeyev's own formulation:

> When a poet or writer is dissatisfied with external reality he naturally strives to depict it not as it is but as it should be; he tries to lift the curtain of the future and to depict man as an ideal. He begins to view today's reality through the prism of the 'ideal' tomorrow.

Finally we should remember Voronsky's generally very positive opinion of Fadeyev's novel **Razgrom** which, although it had not appeared in *Krasnaya nov,* represented, in his view, an almost uniquely successful attempt to portray characters with a convincing blend of both 'activist' and 'contemplative' elements.

Nothing that has been said about Fadeyev's literary theories has been intended to gloss over the many obvious neg-ative aspects which characterize this part of his career. He shared in full measure at least some of the worst features of the RAPP mentality, and much of what he said and wrote reflected that association's dogmatic and intolerant approach. Neither can it be claimed that his views were particularly profound or original; quite the contrary. Compared with someone such as Voronsky, his arguments were repetitive and for the most part rather superficial, lacking real intellectual substance; and they were arguments indeed which derived largely from others—from historical figures such as Belinsky, Hegel, Marx, and Engels, from Plekhanov and Lenin, and from his contemporaries both within and outside of RAPP, such as Libedinsky and Voronsky. As in his creative writing, so in his theoretical statements his talent lay in highlighting and synthesizing existing ideas rather than in any particularly innovative qualities.

This talent should not however be underestimated. In an atmosphere of extreme belligerence and hostility he proved himself to be a formidable opponent and showed that he was capable of expressing his views in a consistent and forceful manner. More than that, he showed, too, the ability to understand what was needed, for the line that he adopted in the late 1920s in the face of much opposition and criticism even from some Party organizations, came to be enshrined in the official doctrine of socialist realism a few years later. As Kiselyova points out:

> As we can see, as early as 1929 Fadeyev was singling out from contemporary literature those features which later, in 1934, during the first Congress of Soviet Writers, would be used in one form or another to define the method of socialist realism; the link with tradition, especially with realism; historical awareness and the sense of perspective; the portrayal of life in its development; the direct relationship between the artist and life, and the active function of art.

Among the more positive aspects of Fadeyev as literary theorist we should remember, too, his genuine interest in the creative process and the development of a new type of socialist literature, together with his concern for literary standards. He sought above all to achieve a blend and reconciliation of existing contrasting elements which, from a more philosophical standpoint, could be termed intuitivism and rationalism and, from a more literary point of view, the realistic and the romantic. He argued consistently that whereas a synthesis of these elements, coupled with the 'correct', i.e. 'proletarian', viewpoint on the part of the writer, formed the only possible basis for the new literary method, an excessive emphasis on one of them alone not merely represented a distortion but was basically inimical to this method.

Neither should Fadeyev's practical experience as the author of **Razgrom** and other stories be forgotten. The difficulties he encountered in creating 'living people' such as Levinson, Mechik, and Morozka, are reflected implicitly throughout his attempts to arrive at a formula for a new literary method. In each case, as author as well as theorist, he is striving for a grand reconciliation of contrasting elements and a whole world-view—(*tselostnoye mirovozzreniye*). This, moreover, for Fadeyev, was not just a literary or theoretical problem; the oscillation and clash between 'realism' and 'romanticism' in his theoretical writings were paralleled by the fundamental dualism within his own nature and temperament. It was a conflict indeed which contributed in no small measure to his eventual disintegration and tragic end. (pp. 339-54)

> *Roger Cockrell, "Aleksandr Fadeyev and Literary Theorist, 1927-1932," in* The Slavonic and East European Review, *Vol. 64, No. 3, July, 1986, pp. 339-54.*

FURTHER READING

Reavey, George. "The War in Fiction—The Tolstoyan Approach." In his *Soviet Literature To-day,* pp. 82-4. New York: Greenwood Press, 1947.
>   Briefly discusses Fadeyev's novels *Posledniy iz Udege* and *The Young Guard,* placing these works within "the Tolstoyan method . . . of realism and psychology."

Struve, Gleb. "Fadeyev" and "War Fiction." In his *Russian Literature under Lenin and Stalin, 1917-1953,* pp. 134-36, pp. 319-22. Norman: University of Oklahoma Press, 1971.
>   Provides short overview of Fadeyev's fiction.

Trilling, Lionel. "The Social Emotions." In *Speaking of Literature and Society,* edited by Diana Trilling, pp. 34-6. New York: Harcourt Brace Jovanovich, 1980.
>   Review of *The Nineteen* originally appearing in *The New Freeman* in July 1930. Trilling praises the novel's focus on emotion and social action.

Additional information on Fadeyev's life and career is contained in the following source published by Gale Research: *Contemporary Authors,* **Vol. 117.**

Thomas Hardy

1840-1928

English poet, novelist, playwright, short story writer, and essayist.

The following entry presents criticism of Hardy's poetry. For information on Hardy's complete career, see *TCLC*, Volumes 4 and 10; for discussion of his novel *Tess of the D'Urbervilles*, see *TCLC*, Volume 18; for discussion of his novel *The Mayor of Casterbridge* see *TCLC*, Volume 32; for discussion of his novel *The Return of the Native*, see *TCLC*, Volume 48.

INTRODUCTION

Highly acclaimed for his novels, which include *Tess of the D'Urbervilles*, *The Return of the Native*, and *The Mayor of Casterbridge*, Hardy is also a major figure in English poetry. Hardy's verse, like his novels, reflects the influence of Charles Darwin and other nineteenth-century scientists and philosophers in its portrayal of a mechanistic universe in which existence is a constant struggle for survival. While Hardy's unsentimental depictions of nature and the human condition were frequently condemned as pessimistic during his own lifetime, modern commentators have generally praised him for his honesty and compassion.

Hardy was born and raised in Dorset, which became the basis for the Wessex countryside of his poetry and fiction. Educated in local schools until the age of sixteen, Hardy did not attend a university but taught himself by reading in poetry, philosophy, and science. During the 1860s Hardy commenced upon a literary career, submitting essays and poetry to various magazines. After having these works repeatedly rejected, Hardy began writing novels, publishing *Desperate Remedies* in 1871. *Under the Greenwood Tree*, published a year later, was the first of Hardy's novels that was both a critical and commercial success. While he was publishing novels from the 1870s to the 1890s, Hardy continued to write poetry. Negative public and critical reaction to *Jude the Obscure* caused Hardy to stop writing novels and focus on poetry. *Wessex Poems*, published in 1898, collects works written years earlier with newer poems, as do all of Hardy's subsequent volumes of poetry. These include *Poems of the Past and Present*, *Time's Laughingstocks, and Other Verses*, and *Satires of Circumstance*. Hardy published eight poetry collections and an epic narrative poem, *The Dynasts: A Drama of the Napoleonic Wars*, during his lifetime. Hardy's last collection, *Winter Words*, appeared posthumously. He died in 1928.

Hardy called himself a meliorist, one who believes that individuals are powerless to affect their own lives, and that only by accepting this fact can they have any hope of happiness. In contrast to the Victorian ideal of progress,

Hardy's novels and poetry portray human beings at the mercy of forces that they have no ability to control, primarily nature, society, and internal compulsions. Hardy's pessimistic philosophy is evident in such poems as "The Subalterns," in which various forces of nature "speak," presenting themselves as the mere servants of a blind, irresistible, and irrational higher power. Though faulted for their sometimes clumsy structure, these poems are often praised for a lyric power unique in its particular blend of traditional and experimental forms.

Hardy's last major work, *The Dynasts*, was designed as a summation of his views on existence. Juxtaposing the historical drama of the Napoleonic wars with a Greek chorus made up of "Phantom Intelligences" such as the Spirits Ironic and Sinister, this work is the author's ultimate statement concerning the forces that influence life. Thematically central to this work is the concept of Immanent Will, an omnipresent force that is indifferent to human affairs and blindly generates conscious and unconscious life out of an unknown, self-sustaining necessity. Many critics consider *The Dynasts* more successful as an examination of Hardy's philosophy than as dramatic poetry, finding it vital for a complete understanding of Hardy's ideas. For the integrity of his moral and philosophical views, and for the imaginative achievement of the world of Wessex, Hardy continues to receive undiminished acclaim from critics, scholars, and the reading public.

PRINCIPAL WORKS

Desperate Remedies (novel) 1871

Under the Greenwood Tree (novel) 1872

A Pair of Blue Eyes (novel) 1873

Far from the Madding Crowd (novel) 1874

The Hand of Ethelberta (novel) 1876

The Return of the Native (novel) 1878

The Trumpet-Major (novel) 1880

A Laodicean; or, The Castle of the De Stancys (novel) 1881

Two on a Tower (novel) 1882

The Mayor of Casterbridge (novel) 1886

The Woodlanders (novel) 1887

Wessex Tales, Strange, Lively, and Commonplace (short stories) 1888

A Group of Noble Dames (short stories) 1891

Tess of the D'Urbervilles: A Pure Woman Faithfully Presented (novel) 1891

Life's Little Ironies (short stories) 1894

Jude the Obscure (novel) 1895

The Well-Beloved (novel) 1895

Wessex Poems, and Other Verses (poetry) 1898

Poems of the Past and the Present (poetry) 1902

The Dynasts: A Drama of the Napoleonic Wars. 3 vols. [first publication] (poetry) 1904-08

Time's Laughingstocks, and Other Verses (poetry) 1909

A Changed Man, the Waiting Supper, and Other Tales (short stories and novel) 1913

Satires of Circumstance (poetry) 1914

Moments of Vision, and Miscellaneous Verses (poetry) 1917

*Tess of the D'Urbervilles [first publication] (drama) 1924

Human Shows, Far Phantasies, Songs, and Trifles (poetry) 1925

Late Lyrics and Earlier, with Many Other Verses (poetry) 1925

Collected Poems (poetry) 1926

Winter Words (poetry) 1928

**An Indiscretion in the Life of an Heiress (novel) 1934

---

*This drama is an adaptation of the novel *Tess of the D'Urbervilles.*

**This work is a revision of *The Poor Man and the Lady,* an unpublished novel.

CRITICISM

Sir Arthur Quiller-Couch   (essay date 1918)

[*Quiller-Couch was an English man of letters who is especially noted as the editor of the* Oxford Book of English Verse *(1900) and of several other distinguished anthologies. He also wrote many novels and short stories, the most famous of which was* The Golden Spur *(1889), a novel which, like much of his fiction, is set in his native Cornwall. A contributor to various English periodicals, Quiller-Couch published many of his magazine essays under the pseudonym "Q." In the following excerpt from a lecture that was first published in 1918, Quiller-Couch provides an overview of Hardy's poetry, praising the poet's compassion and authentic depiction of country life.*]

Thomas Hardy (long may he live!) is my elder, and so much my elder that for thirty years I have reverenced him as a master: that is, as a master of the Novel. His first novel *Desperate Remedies* dates back to 1871: his first artistic triumph *Under the Greenwood Tree,* to 1872. Pass intervening years and come to the grand close in *Tess of the D'Urbervilles* (1891), *Jude the Obscure* (1895): on that last date his career as a novelist ceases, and at the age of fifty-five. Three years later, in 1898, he publishes his first book of verse. Now any pettifogging fellow can point out that this volume, entitled *Wessex Poems,* contains many poems composed long before 1898—some so far back as 1865; and the more easily because Hardy is careful to print the dates. So for that matter do some of Hardy's later volumes contain early poems, either printed as first written, or as revised. But no petty fog can obscure the plain fact that in 1895, or a little later, Hardy definitely turned his back on prose fiction and started to appeal to a new generation in verse; as a writer of high poetical verse if the gods should allow. To this purpose he has held. A second volume, *Poems of the Past and the Present* followed in 1901; *The Dynasts,* Part I in 1903, Part II in 1906, Part III in 1908, *Time's Laughing Stocks* in 1909. *Satires of Circumstance* were collected in 1914. His latest volume *Moments of Vision* appeared but the other day, and bears 1917 on its title-page. So, seeing that all this, including that great epical drama, *The Dynasts,* falls within the ken of the last twenty years, and not without it, you may allow perhaps that it concerns men of your age and mine, equally if not similarly.

Ah, but you may answer, 'By all means let it concern you. The point is, can a man of Thomas Hardy's age write what appeals to *us?'* Well, yes, I think his poetry may appeal to you, as it certainly concerns you. That his Muse is predominantly melancholy I brush aside as no bar at all. If youth do not understand melancholy, why then the most of Shelley, the most of Byron, a great part of Keats, or—to come to later instances—a great, if not the greater, part of Francis Thompson and Yeats and most of the young poets of the Irish school, is closed to it: which is absurd. 'No, no! go not to Lethe' for Melancholy. She dwells neither there nor with middle-age:

> She dwells with Beauty—Beauty that must die;
> And Joy, whose hand is ever at his lips

Bidding adieu; and aching Pleasure nigh,
Turning to poison while the bee-mouth sips:
Ay, in the very temple of Delight
Veil'd Melancholy has her sovran shrine,
Though seen of none save him whose strenuous
    tongue
Can burst Joy's grape against his palate fine;
His soul shall taste the sadness of her might,
And be among her cloudy trophies hung.

No, no: it is proper to youth to know melancholy as it is to have raptures. But only to middle-age is it granted to be properly cheerful. Yes, there are compensations! Let us assure you that only towards middle-age will you burst upon a palate fine the true juice of Chaucer's *Prologue,* written in *his* middle-age, or of Montaigne, or of Molière: as in youth you will choose Rossetti, but later transfer your choice to William Morris, least sick or sorry, best of cheer among the poets of his time.

As for Hardy's pessimism, that, to be sure, does not consort well with youth. But, as I shall hope to show, it always challenges youth; it is never faded, jejune, effete; it never plays—or, to be accurate, it seldom plays—with old mere sentimentalities. Even when it plays with commonplaces it never leaves them conventions. In his depths the man is always thinking, and his perplexities, being all-important and yet unsolved, are by your generation to be faced, whether you solve them or not.

For another point, close beside and yet more important, we have talked of insensibility to poetry and how with the years it may steal upon the reader. Now most of you remember, I daresay, Matthew Arnold's late and mournful lines on the drying up of poesy in the writer:

Youth rambles on life's arid mount,
And strikes the rock, and finds the vein,
And brings the water from the fount,
The fount which shall not flow again.

The man mature with labour chops
For the bright stream a channel grand,
And sees not that the sacred drops
Ran off and vanish'd out of hand.

And then the old man totters nigh
And feebly rakes among the stones.
The mount is mute, the channel dry;
And down he lays his weary bones.

Well, at any rate Thomas Hardy contradicts, and in practice, *that* rather cheap kind of pessimism. (There was always, I think, in Matthew Arnold a tendency to be Wordsworth's widow, and to fall rather exasperatingly 'a-thinking of the old 'un,' who undoubtedly did in later life, for some thirty years 'rake among the stones' and died in the end, as the country practitioner put it, 'of nothing serious.')

I am aware that to support this theory of desiccation in poets many startling instances may be cited. But without saying yea or nay, or supposing it symptomatic of our age, I cannot think it quite accidental that out of the small number of poets I have been privileged to know personally, two should have tapped, quite late in life, a well of poetry abundant, fresh, pure; of *lyrical* poetry, too, fresher, purer and far more abundant than ever they found as

young men. It happened so, at all events, with an old schoolmaster of mine, the late T. E. Brown, whose quality and whose performance are now generally admitted. It has happened so with Thomas Hardy. His first poems—or, to say it more accurately, the poems in his first-published volume—were stiff, awkward. They often achieved a curious, haunting, countrified lilt; they worked always true to pattern: you felt about them, too, that the verses held the daemon of poetry, constricted, struggling for expression. But in form they resembled the drawings with which the author illustrated that first volume. They were architectural draughts (Hardy had been an architect). When they told a story, you wondered why he, so well able to do it, had not written this particular story in prose. The poetic thought was there: but the words were hard and precise, sometimes scientifically pedantic. For instance, in the last poem I shall read today he drags in the word 'stillicide,' which means the drip of water in a cavern, or from eaves. Stevenson has recorded his mingled feelings on discovering, in the process of his scientific studies, that 'stillicide' was not a crime. The early poems faceted no rays, they melted into none of those magical, chemical combinations out of which words became poetry and a new thing, 'half angel and half bird.'

Years pass, with their efforts; and then in his latest volume, published by this man at the age of seventy-seven, he discovers a lyrical note which I shall quote to you, not at all because its theme is characteristic—for it is not—as not at all because it is deep and wonted—for it is not. It is, if you will, 'silly sooth, and dallies with the innocence of love.' Yes, just for that reason I quote it, and because in a poet of ordinary evolution it would fall naturally among the *Juvenilia:*

Lalage's coming:
Where is she now, O?
Turning to bow, O,
And smile, is she,
Just at parting,
Parting, parting,
As she is starting
To come to me?

Lalage's coming,
Nearer is she now, O,
End anyhow, O,
Today's husbandry!
Would a gilt chair were mine,
Slippers of air were mine,
Brushes for hair were mine
    Of ivory!

What will she think, O,
She who's so comely,
Viewing how homely
A sort are we!
Nought here's enough for her,
All is too rough for her,
Even my love for her
    Poor in degree.

. . . . .

Lalage's come; aye,
Come is she now, O!
Does Heaven allow, O,

A meeting to be?
Yes, she is here now,
Here now, here now,
Nothing to fear now,
Here's Lalage!

If that be too trivial, take another—remembering that I give them only as metrical specimens, merely to show how this poet, whose metrical muscles were stiff and hard at fifty-odd has at seventy-odd (the date is 1913) worked them supple, so that now the verse cadences to the feeling:

Out of the past there rises a week—
Who shall read the years O!
In that week there was heard a singing—
Who shall spell the years O!—
In that week there was heard a singing,
And the white owl wondered why.
In that week there was heard a singing,
And forth from the casement were candles fling-
ing
Radiance that fell on the deodar and lit up the
path thereby.

Or take him on a lower note:

I need not go
Through sleet and snow
To where I know
She waits for me;
She will wait me there
Till I find it fair,
And have time to spare
From company . . .

. . . . .

What—not upbraid me
That I delayed me,
Nor ask what stayed me
So long? Ah, no!—
New cares may claim me,
New loves inflame me,
She will not blame me,
But suffer it so.

I reserve for the while the most individual quality in Hardy's versifying (to me an individual excellence) which has given it character from the first—I mean his country lilt; because I must approach it, and the man, and his philosophy of life, all three by one path.

First of all, and last of all, he is a countryman. And the first meaning of this is that his mind works like most country minds in this great little island. They are introspective *because* insular: and their soil is cumbered, piled with history and local tradition: a land of arable inveterately and deeply ploughed; of pastures close-webbed at the root by rain and sun persistently reviving the blade which the teeth of sheep and cattle persistently crop; of its heaths—such as Newmarket—where racehorses in training gallops beat their hoofs in the very footprints of Boadicea's mares and stallions; of mines, working yet, that paid their first-fruits to Sidon and Carthage, choked harbours, dead empires. In this land of ours, I say, the mind of a native must dig vertically down through strata. Though it be the mind of a farm labourer, it knows its acres intimately; not only their rotation of crops, and slant to wind or sun, but their several humours, caprices, obstinacies of soil; and, always

with an eye to windward, hopes for the weather it knows likeliest to profit them. So when, as with Hardy, a countryman has the further knowledge that comes of booklearning, and acquires with it the historical sense, that sense still feels vertically downwards, through soil and subsoil, through the mould of Norman, Dane, Saxon, Celt, Iber, and of tribes beyond history, to the geological formations layered over by this accumulated dust.

Further, you know that the tales of old time which haunt a true countryman's imagination are tales of violence, of lonely houses where suppressed passions inhabit to flame out in murder or suicide, to make a legend, to haunt a cross-road or a mile-post: fierce, primitive deeds breaking up through the slow crust of custom: unaccountable, but not unnatural. Along the king's highway, a gibbet where sheepstealers used to swing: in such and such a copse a tree, on that tree such and such a branch where a poor girl hanged herself for love: at the three roads by the blacksmith's a triangle of turf still called 'Betsy Beneath' because there they buried her uncoffined and drove a stake through her.

Further, if you know your rural England, you will know that every village in it is a small shop of gossip. 'Have you heard? Young Peter Hodge is at upsides with his wife? yes, already, and her only expectin'.' 'They tell me Farmer So-and-so have a mortgage, if you'll believe, on the Lower Barton Farm.' 'So, that girl Jenny is in trouble as I always foretold.' Vengeance o' Jenny's case!

Well as I interpret this most genuine, most autochthonous of living writers, I see him leaning over the gate of a field with a wood's edge bordering it. He knows the wood so intimately that his ear detects and separates the notes of the wind as it soughs in oak, hornbeam, pine (see the opening of *Under the Greenwood Tree,* or *The Woodlanders, passim*). Of the sheep on the pasture he knows when their lambs will fall. He judges the grass, if it be sufficient. He knows that breast-shaped knob on the knap of the hill and how many centuries have worn to this what was the high burial mound of a British chieftain: he knows the lias beneath the chief's grave, and the layered rock still deeper—that is, he knows as near as geologists can tell. He knows, having a boy's eye for this, where a nest is likeliest to be, and of what bird. But what more intrigues him than any of these things—still as he follows the line of the hedge—is that under one innocent-looking thorn such and such a parish tragedy was enacted. Just here, they tell, two brothers quarrelled and one smote the other with a reaping-hook; just there was lovers' bliss and just there, a brief while later the woman's heart broke.

For (you must know) though a gossip's, this countryman's heart is strangely tender. Let me pause for proof, by one short poem, that even Blake's heart was not tenderer than Hardy's. It is called

The Blinded Bird

So zestfully canst thou sing?
And all this indignity,
With God's consent, on thee!
Blinded ere yet a-wing
By the red-hot needle thou,

I stand and wonder how
So zestfully thou canst sing . . .

. . . . .

Resenting not such wrong,
Thy grievous pain forgot,
Eternal dark thy lot,
Groping thy whole life long,
After that stab of fire;
Enjailed in pitiless wire;
Resenting not such wrong!

Who hath charity? This bird.
Who suffereth long and is kind,
Is not provoked, though blind
And alive ensepulchred?
Who hopeth, endureth all things?
Who thinketh no evil, but sings?
Who is divine? This bird.

Above all, his pity is for women, partly for the fate that
condemns their bloom to be brief and evanescent (unless
written in time on a man's heart where it never grows
old)—so brief the chance, with no term to the after-pain!
But he pities them more because he sees the increase of our
race to rest on an unfair game, in which, nine throws out
of ten, the dice are loaded against the woman; a duel of
sex, almost at times an internecine duel, which his soul
grows to abhor: for

Victrix causa deis placuit, sed victa Catoni,

and, looking up, he sees God, or whatever gods may be,
deriding the victim. We are all flies to these gods who tease
us for their sport. Even if man labour and profit his fellows
with an idea, yet, in Milton's phrase (as quoted by Hardy)

Truth like a bastard comes into the world
Never without ill-fame to him who gives her
    birth.

But, for women, who, nine times out of ten, pay the price
of the great jest, Hardy feels most acutely. 'Poor wounded
name,' he quotes and inscribes on the title-page of *Tess*

Poor wounded name! my bosom as a bed
Shall lodge thee . . .

and in the last sentence of his most sorrowful tale he flings
his now famous taunt up at 'the President of the Immortals,' even as passionately as did Cleopatra for her own
loss:

Iras. Madam!
Charmian. O madam, madam, madam!
Iras. Royal Egypt!
    Empress!
Charmian. Peace, peace, Iras!
Cleopatra. No more but e'en a woman, and com-
    manded
By such poor passion as the maid that milks

(Tess was a dairy-maid)

And does the meanest chares. It were for me
To throw my sceptre at the injurious gods;
To tell them that this world did equal theirs
Till they had stol'n our jewel.

Say what you will, this indignation in Hardy is noble, is

chivalrous, and, as the world is worked, it has much reason at the back of its furious 'Why?—Why?—Why?' It has
great excuse when it sours down to bitterest irony, as in
this early ditty of two country-bred girls meeting in London—and you will note how the old market-jog of rhythm
and rhyme *ache* themselves into the irony:

'O 'Melia, my dear, this does everything crown!
Who could have supposed I should meet you in
    Town?
And whence such fair garments, such prosperi-
    ty?'—
'O didn't you know I'd been ruined?' said she.

—'You left us in tatters, without shoes or socks,
Tired of digging potatoes, and spudding up
    docks;
And now you've gay bracelets and bright feath-
    ers three!'—
'Yes: that's how we dress when we're ruined,'
    said she . . .

. . . . .

—'I wish I had feathers, a fine sweeping gown,
And a delicate face, and could strut about
    Town!'—
'My dear—a raw country girl, such as you be,
Isn't equal to that. You ain't ruined,' said she.

Women (I think) are more impatient of irony than men:
and when Hardy turns his irony upon them—as he often
does in his novels—I have observed that they eye it suspi-
ciously, restively; they would be undetected in their devices, hate instinctively that which shows their secret ways
of power at work under show of servility. Hardy, their
champion, would break down the servility: and they distrust him for it.

Well—and though they be ungrateful—perhaps their instinct is true and his is a childless creed: and for men,
though it be manly to face it out and test it, an unhopeful
creed. For women it must be certainly unpromising to
read the doctrine of *Jude the Obscure,* which works out
to this, that man's aspirations to make the world better are
chiefly clogged by the flesh, and that flesh is woman. To
man it can scarcely be less heartening to be barred with
the question

Has some Vast Imbecility,
Mighty to build and blend,
But impotent to tend,
Framed us in jest, and left us now to hazardry?

Or come we of an Automaton
Unconscious of our pains?
Or are we live remains
Of Godhead dying downwards, brain and eye
    now gone?

Well, when it comes to this, I for one can only answer that,
if it were, we must yet carry on somehow, sing a song on
the raft we cannot steer, keep a heart of sorts, and share
out the rations to the women and children. But that word
recalls me. It is a *childless* creed. It has no more evidence
than Meredith's: intellectually viewed, I find them equal:
but Meredith has hope, hope for the young: and I must put
my money on hope.

Further, when I consider, these poems—as those novels—crowd the sardonic laughter of the gods too thickly. There is irony enough in life, God wot: but here is a man possessed with it. All men, all stories, tramp with him to his titles *Life's Little Ironies, Satires of Circumstance, Time's Laughing Stocks.* So one hesitates and asks: Is life, after all, a parish full of bad practical jokes? *Is* catholic man like *this*? No: as we take up poem after poem in which human loves and aspirations find themselves thwarted, set astray, or butting against some door that, having opened a glimpse of paradise, shuts by some power idiotically mischievous if not malignant—shuts with a click of the latch and a chuckle of mocking laughter—we tell ourselves, 'These things happen: but in any such crowd they never and in no life happen.' And while we debate this, Hardy confounds us, spreading out his irony upon one grand ironic drama, *The Dynasts.*

I suppose *The Dynasts* to be—and I shall not allow for rival Doughty's noble but remote, morose, almost Chinese, epic, *The Dawn in Britain* (this, too, a product of a man well past meridian)—I suppose *The Dynasts* to be the grandest poetic structure planned and raised in England in our time. In the soar and sweep of that drama the poet—whom, a moment ago, we were on the point of accusing for provincial, lays Europe beneath us 'flat, as to an eagle's eye'—a map with little things in multitudes, ants in armies, scurrying along the threads which are roads, violently agitated in nodules which are cities. But let me quote one or two of Hardy's own stage directions and thereby not only save myself the vain effort to do what has been perfectly done for me, but send you, if you would practise the art of condensed and vivid description, to models as good as can be found in English prose. Imagine yourselves, then, an audience aloft and listening to the talk of such Spirits as watch over human destinies.

> The nether sky opens, and Europe is disclosed as a prone and emaciated figure, the Alps shaping like a backbone, and the branching mountain-chains like ribs, the peninsular plateau of Spain forming a head. Broad and lengthy lowlands stretch from the north of France across Russia like a grey-green garment hemmed by the Ural mountains and the glistening Arctic Ocean.

> The point of view then sinks downward through space, and draws near to the surface of the perturbed countries, where the people, . . . are seen writhing, crawling, heaving, and vibrating, in their various cities and nationalities.

(A picture of Europe today.) Then

> A new and penetrating light descends on the spectacle, enduing men and things with a seeming transparency, and exhibiting as one organism the anatomy of life and movement in all humanity and vitalized matter included in the display.

So the focus slides down and up and again down: it narrows on the British House of Commons, or on a village green, or on a bedroom in a palace: it expands to sweep the field of Austerlitz. I ask you to turn for yourselves to one marvellous scene of a cellar, full of drunken deserters,

looking out on the snow-tormented road along which straggles the army of Sir John Moore and struggles for Coruña. . . . But here is a passage in the retreat from Moscow:

> What has floated down from the sky upon the Army is a flake of snow. Then come another and another, till natural features, hitherto varied with the tints of autumn, are confounded, and all is phantasmal grey and white.

> The caterpillar shape still creeps laboriously nearer: but instead of increasing in size by the rules of perspective, it gets more attenuated, and there are left upon the ground behind it minute parts of itself, which are speedily flaked over, and remain as white pimples by the wayside.

> Pines rise mournfully on each side of the nearing object. . . . Endowed with enlarged powers of audition as of vision, we are struck by the mournful taciturnity that prevails. Nature is mute. Save for the incessant flogging of the wind-broken and lacerated horses there are no sounds.

The diction of the poem itself seldom rises to match its conception. In the rustic scenes we get that incomparable prose, nervous, and vernacular, yet Biblical, which Hardy has made out of his native dialect: but the major human characters talk in verse which is often too prosy, and the watching Spirits attain but spasmodically to the height of their high argument. Their lips are not touched by any such flame as kindles (for example) the lips of the watching Spirits in *Prometheus Unbound*. But we must not judge a poem of *The Dynasts'* range and scope apart from its total impression: and *that*, in *The Dynasts* is tremendous. And I at this moment am committing a deadly artistic sin against proportion in attempting to talk of it in a part of a lecture. It should have two lectures to itself.

As for its philosophy, one naturally compares it with that of Tolstoy's great novel *War and Peace*. But whereas Tolstoy and Hardy both see Napoleon as a puppet under Heaven—as Plato pronounces Man to be 'at his best a noble plaything for the gods'—the one, being Russian and an idealist, sees the little great man's ends shaped by a Divinity, watching over Sion, having purpose: the other, a most honest pessimist, can detect no purpose, or no beneficent one. For all he can see, God works—if He work—a magnipotent Will, but

> Like a knitter drowsed,
> Whose fingers play in skilled unmindfulness,
> The will has woven with an absent heed
> Since life first was; and ever will so weave.

And there for today we must leave it. (pp. 181-97)

> *Sir Arthur Quiller-Couch, "The Poetry of Thomas Hardy," in his* Studies in Literature, *first series, Cambridge at the University Press, 1937, pp. 178-99.*

J. Middleton Murry   (essay date 1919)

[*Murry is recognized as one of the most significant En-*

> The originality of Hardy's poetry lies in the fact that it bears everywhere upon it the impress of a master of prose fiction.
>
> —Lytton Strachey, "Mr. Hardy's New Poems," in New Statesman, December 19, 1914.

glish critics and editors of the twentieth century. Anticipating later scholarly opinion, he championed—through his positions as founding editor of the Adelphi, and as a regular contributor to the Times Literary Supplement, among other periodicals—the writings of Hardy, Marcel Proust, James Joyce, Paul Valéry, and D. H. Lawrence. As with his magazine essays, Murry's book-length critical works are noted for their impassioned tone and startling discoveries; such biographically centered critical studies as Keats and Shakespeare: A Study of Keats' Poetic Life from 1816-1820 (1925) and Son of Woman: The Story of D. H. Lawrence (1931) contain esoteric, controversial conclusions that have angered scholars who favor more traditional approaches. Notwithstanding this criticism, Murry is often cited for his perspicuity, clarity, and supportive argumentation. His early exposition on literary appreciation, The Problem of Style (1922), is considered an informed guidebook for both critics and general readers to employ when considering not only the style of a literary work, but also its theme and viewpoint. In it Murry espouses the theoretical premise underlying all his criticism, that in order to evaluate fully a writer's achievement, the critic must search for the crucial passages which effectively "crystallize" the writer's innermost impressions and convictions. In the following essay, Murry praises Hardy's poetry for its style and compassionate treatment of human suffering.]

One meets fairly often with the critical opinion that Mr Hardy's poetry is incidental. It is admitted on all sides that his poetry has curious merits of its own, but it is held to be completely subordinate to his novels, and those who maintain that it must be considered as having equal standing with his prose, are not seldom treated as guilty of paradox and preciousness.

We are inclined to wonder, as we review the situation, whether those of the contrary persuasion are not allowing themselves to be impressed primarily by mere bulk, and arguing that a man's chief work must necessarily be what he has done most of; and we feel that some such supposition is necessary to explain what appears to us as a visible reluctance to allow Mr Hardy's poetry a clean impact upon the critical consciousness. It is true that we have ranged against us critics of distinction, such as Mr Lascelles Abercrombie and Mr Robert Lynd, and that it may savour of impertinence to suggest that the case could have been unconsciously pre-judged in their minds when they addressed themselves to Mr Hardy's poetry. Nevertheless, we find some significance in the fact that both these critics are of such an age that when they came to years of discretion the Wessex Novels were in existence as a corpus.

There, before their eyes, was a monument of literary work having a unity unlike that of any contemporary author. The poems became public only after they had laid the foundations of their judgment. For them Mr Hardy's work was done. Whatever he might subsequently produce was an interesting, but to their criticism an otiose appendix to his prose achievement.

It happens therefore that to a somewhat younger critic the perspective may be different. By the accident of years it would appear to him that Mr Hardy's poetry was no less a corpus than his prose. They would be extended equally and at the same moment before his eyes; he would embark upon voyages of discovery into both at roughly the same time; and he might find, in total innocence of preciousness and paradox, that the poetry would yield up to him a quality of perfume not less essential than any that he could extract from the prose.

This is, as we see it, the case with ourselves. We discover all that our elders discover in Mr Hardy's novels; we see more than they in his poetry. To our mind it exists superbly in its own right; it is not lifted into significance upon the glorious substructure of the novels. They also are complete in themselves. We recognise the relation between the achievements, and discern that they are the work of a single mind; but they are separate works, having separate and unique excellences. The one is only approximately explicable in terms of the other. We incline, therefore, to attach a signal importance to what has always seemed to us the most important sentence in Who's Who?—namely, that in which Mr Hardy confesses that in 1868 he was compelled—that is his own word—to give up writing poetry for prose.

For Mr Hardy's poetic gift is not a late and freakish flowering. In the volume into which has been gathered all his poetical work with the exception of The Dynasts, are pieces bearing the date 1866 which display an astonishing mastery, not merely of technique but of the essential content of great poetry. Nor are such pieces exceptional. Granted that Mr Hardy has retained only the finest of his early poetry, still there are a dozen poems of 1866-7 which belong either entirely or in part to the category of major poetry. Take, for instance, 'Neutral Tones':—

> We sood by a pond that winter day,
> And the sun was white, as though chidden of
>   God
> And a few leaves lay on the starving sod;
> —They had fallen from an ash, and were gray.
>
> Your eyes on me were as eyes that rove
> Over tedious riddles long ago;
> And some winds played between us to and fro
> On which lost the more by our love.
>
> The smile on your mouth was the deadest thing
> Alive enough to have strength to die;
> And a grin of bitterness swept thereby
> Like an ominous bird a-wing. . . .
>
> Since then keen lessons that love deceives
> And wrings with wrong, have shaped to me
> Your face, and the God-curst sun, and a tree
> And a pond edged with grayish leaves.

That was written in 1867. The date of *Desperate Remedies,* Mr Hardy's first novel, was 1871. *Desperate Remedies* may have been written some years before. It makes no difference to the astonishing contrast between the immaturity of the novel and the maturity of the poem. It is surely impossible in the face of such a juxtaposition then to deny that Mr Hardy's poetry exists in its own individual right, and not as a curious simulacrum of his prose.

These early poems have other points of deep interest, of which one of the chief is in a sense technical. One can trace a quite definite influence of Shakespeare's sonnets in his language and imagery. The four sonnets, **'She to Him'** (1866), are full of echoes, as:—

> Numb as a vane that cankers on its point
> True to the wind that kissed ere canker came.

or this from another sonnet of the same year:—

> As common chests encasing wares of price
> Are borne with tenderness through halls of state.

Yet no one reading the sonnets of these years can fail to mark the impress of an individual personality. The effect is, at times, curious and impressive in the extreme. We almost feel that Mr Hardy is bringing some physical compulsion to bear on Shakespeare and forcing him to say something that he does not want to say. Of course, it is merely a curious tweak of the fancy; but there comes to us in such lines as the following an insistent vision of two youths of an age, the one masterful, the other indulgent, and carrying out his companion's firm suggestion:—

> Remembering mine the loss is, not the blame
> That Sportsman Time rears but his brood to kill,
> Knowing me in my soul the very same—
> One who would die to spare you touch of ill!—
> Will you not grant to old affection's claim
> The hand of friendship down Life's sunless hill?

But, fancies aside, the effect of these early poems is twofold. Their attitude is definite:—

> Crass Casualty obstructs the sun and rain
> And dicing time for gladness calls a moan . . .
> These purblind Doomsters had as readily
>   thrown
> Blisses about my pilgrimage as pain.

and the technique has the mark of mastery, a complete economy of statement which produces the conviction that the words are saying only what poet ordained they should say, neither less nor more.

The early years were followed by the long period of the novels, in which, we are prepared to admit, poetry was actually if not in intention incidental. It is the grim truth that poetry cannot be written in between times; and, though we have hardly any dates on which to rely, we are willing to believe that few of Mr Hardy's characteristic poems were written between the appearance of *Desperate Remedies* and his farewell to the activity of novel-writing with *The Well-Beloved* (1897). But the few dates which we have tell us that **'Thoughts of Phena,'** the beautiful poem beginning:—

> Not a line of her writing have I,

> Not a thread of her hair. . . .

which reaches forward to the love poems of 1912-13, was written in 1890.

Whether the development of Mr Hardy's poetry was concealed or visible during the period of the novels, development there was into a maturity so overwhelming that by its touchstone the poetical work of his famous contemporaries appears singularly jejune and false. But, though by the accident of social conditions—for that Mr Hardy waited till 1898 to publish his first volume of poems is more a social than an artistic fact—it is impossible to follow out the phases of his poetical progress in the detail we would desire, it is impossible not to recognise that the mature poet, Mr Hardy, is of the same poetical substance as the young poet of the 'sixties. The attitude is unchanged; the modifications of the theme of 'crass casualty' leave its central asseveration unchanged. There are restatements, enlargements of perspective, a slow and forceful expansion of the personal into the universal, but the truth once recognised is never suffered for a moment to be hidden or mollified. Only a superficial logic would point, for instance, to his

> Wonder if Man's consciousness
> Was a mistake of God's,

as a denial of 'casualty.' To envisage an accepted truth from a new angle, to turn it over and over again in the mind in the hope of finding some aspect which might accord with a large and general view is the inevitable movement of any mind that is alive and not dead. To say that Mr Hardy has finally discovered unity may be paradoxical; but it is true. The harmony of the artist is not as the harmony of the preacher or the philosopher. Neither would grant, neither would understand the profound acquiescence that lies behind 'Adonais' or the 'Ode to the Grecian Urn.' Such acquiescence has no moral quality, as morality is even now understood, nor any logical compulsion. It does not stifle anger nor deny anguish; it turns no smiling face upon unsmiling things; it is not puffed up with the resonance of futile heroics. It accepts the things that are as the necessary basis of artistic creation. This unity which comes of the instinctive refusal in the great poet to deny experience, and subdues the self into the whole as part of that which is not denied, is to be found in every corner of Mr Hardy's mature poetry. It gives, as it alone can really give, to personal emotion what is called the impersonality of great poetry. We feel it as a sense of background, a conviction that a given poem is not the record, but the culmination of an experience, and that the experience of which it is the culmination is far larger and more profound than the one which it seems to record.

At the basis of great poetry lies an all-embracing realism, an adequacy to all experience, a refusal of the merely personal in exultation or dismay. Take the contrast between Rupert Brooke's deservedly famous lines: 'There is some corner of a foreign field . . .' and Mr Hardy's **'Drummer Hodge'**:—

> Yet portion of that unknown plain
> Will Hodge for ever be;
> His homely Northern heart and brain

> Grow to some Southern tree,
> And strange-eyed constellations reign
> His stars eternally.

We know which is the truer. Which is the more beautiful? Is it not Mr Hardy? And which (strange question) is the more consoling, the more satisfying, the more acceptable? Is it not Mr Hardy? There is sorrow, but it is the sorrow of the spheres. And this, not the apparent anger and dismay of a self's discomfiture, is the quality of greatness in Mr Hardy's poetry. The Mr Hardy of the love poems of 1912-13 is not a man giving way to memory in poetry; he is a great poet uttering the cry of the universe. A vast range of acknowledged experience returns to weight each syllable; it is the quality of life that is vocal, gathered into a moment of time with a vista of years:—

> Ignorant of what there is flitting here to see,
> The waked birds preen and the seals flop lazily,
> Soon you will have, Dear, to vanish from me,
> For the stars close their shutters and the
>   Dawn whitens hazily.
> Trust me, I mind not, though Life lours
> The bringing me here; nay, bring me here again!
> I am just the same as when
> Our days were a joy and our paths through flow-
>   ers.

We have read these poems of Thomas Hardy, read them not once, but many times. Many of them have already become part of our being; their indelible impress has given shape to dumb and striving elements in our soul; they have set free and purged mute, heart-devouring regrets. And yet, though this is so, the reading of them in a single volume, the submission to their movement with a like unbroken motion of the mind, gathers their greatness, their poignancy and passion, into one stream, submerging us and leaving us patient and purified.

There have been many poets among us in the last fifty years, poets of sure talent, and it may be even of genius, but no other of them has this compulsive power. The secret is not hard to find. Not one of them is adequate to what we know and have suffered. We have in our own hearts a new touchstone of poetic greatness. We have learned too much to be wholly responsive to less than an adamantine honesty of soul and a complete acknowledgment of experience. 'Give us the whole,' we cry, 'give us the truth.' Unless we can catch the undertone of this acknowledgment, a poet's voice is in our ears hardly more than sounding brass or a tinkling cymbal.

Therefore we turn—some by instinct and some by deliberate choice—to the greatest; therefore we deliberately set Mr Hardy among these. What they have, he has, and has in their degree—a plenary vision of life. He is the master of the fundamental theme; it enters into, echoes in, modulates and modifies all his particular emotions, and the individual poems of which they are the substance. Each work of his is a fragment of a whole—not a detached and arbitrarily severed fragment, but a unity which implies, calls for and in a profound sense creates a vaster and completely comprehensive whole. His reaction to an episode has behind and within it a reaction to the universe. An overwhelming endorsement descends upon his words: he

traces them as with a pencil, and straightway they are graven in stone.

Thus his short poems have a weight and validity which sets them apart in kind from even the very finest work of his contemporaries. These may be perfect in and for themselves; but a short poem by Mr Hardy is often perfect in a higher sense. As the lines of a diagram may be produced in imagination to contain within themselves all space, one of Mr Hardy's most characteristic poems may expand and embrace all human experience. In it we may hear the sombre, ruthless rhythm of life itself—the dominant theme that gives individuation to the ripple of fragmentary joys and sorrows. Take '**The Broken Appointment**':—

> You did not come,
> And marching Time drew on, and wore me
>   numb.—
> Yet less for loss of your dear presence there
> Than that I thus found lacking in your make
> That high compassion which can overbear
> Reluctance for pure lovingkindness' sake
> Grieved I, when, as the hope-hour stroked its
>   sum,
> You did not come.
>
> You love not me,
> And love alone can lend you loyalty
> —I know and knew it. But, unto the store
> Of human deeds divine in all but name,
> Was it not worth a little hour or more
> To add yet this: Once you, a woman, came
> To soothe a time-torn man; even though it be
> You love not me?

On such a seeming fragment of personal experience lies the visible endorsement of the universe. The hopes not of a lover but of humanity are crushed beneath its rhythm. The ruthlessness of the event is intensified in the motion of the poem till one can hear the even pad of destiny; and a moment comes when to a sense made eager by the strain of intense attention it seems to have been written by the destiny it records.

What is the secret of poetic power like this? We do not look for it in technique, though the technique of this poem is masterly. But the technique of 'as the hope-hour stroked its sum' is of such a kind that we know as we read that it proceeds from a sheer compulsive force. For a moment it startles; a moment more and the echo of those very words is reverberant with accumulated purpose. They are pitiless as the poem; the sign of an ultimate obedience is upon them. Whence came the power that compelled it? Can the source be defined or indicated? We believe it can be indicated, though not defined. We can show where to look for the mystery, that in spite of our regard remains a mystery still. We are persuaded that almost on the instant that it was felt the original emotion of the poem was endorsed. Perhaps it came to the poet as the pain of a particular and personal experience; but in a little or a long while—creative time is not measured by days or years—it became, for him, a part of the texture of the general life. It became a manifestation of life, almost, nay wholly, in the sacramental sense, a veritable epiphany. The manifold and inexhaustible quality of life was focused into a single revelation. A critic's words do not lend themselves to the neces-

Hardy's sketch of his birthplace in Brockhampton.

sary precision. We should need to write with exactly the same power as Mr Hardy when he wrote 'the hope-hour stroked its sum,' to make our meaning likewise inevitable. The word 'revelation' is fertile in false suggestion; the creative act of power which we seek to elucidate is an act of plenary apprehension, by which one manifestation, one form of life, one experience is seen in its rigorous relation to all other and to all possible manifestations, forms, and experiences. It is, we believe, the act which Mr Hardy himself has tried to formulate in the phrase which is the title of one of his books of poems—*Moments of Vision.*

Only those who do not read Mr Hardy could make the mistake of supposing that on his lips such a phrase had a mystical implication. Between belief and logic lies a third kingdom, which the mystics and the philosophers alike are too eager to forget—the kingdom of art, no less the residence of truth than the two other realms, and to some, perhaps, more authentic even than they. Therefore when we expand the word 'vision' in the phrase to 'æsthetic vision' we mean, not the perception of beauty, at least in the ordinary sense of that ill-used word, but the apprehension of truth, the recognition of a complete system of valid relations incapable of logical statement. Such are the acts of unique apprehension which Mr Hardy, we believe, implied by his title. In a 'moment of vision' the poet recognises in a single separate incident of life, life's essential quality. The uniqueness of the whole, the infinite multiplicity and variety of its elements, are manifested and apprehended in a part. Since we are here at work on the confines of intelligible statement, it is better, even at the cost of brutalising a poem, to choose an example from the book

that bears the mysterious name. The verses that follow come from **'Near Lanivet, 1872.'** We choose them as an example of Mr Hardy's method at less than its best, at a point at which the scaffolding of his process is just visible.

> There was a stunted hand-post just on the crest,
> Only a few feet high:
> She was tired, and we stopped in the twilight-
> time for her rest,
> At the crossways close thereby.
>
> She leant back, being so weary, against its stem,
> And laid her arms on its own,
> Each open palm stretched out to each end of
> them,
> Her sad face sideways thrown.
>
> Her white-clothed form at this dim-lit cease of
> day
> Made her look as one crucified
> In my gaze at her from the midst of the dusty
> way,
> And hurriedly 'Don't,' I cried.
>
> I do not think she heard. Loosing thence she
> said,
> As she stepped forth ready to go,
> 'I am rested now.—Something strange came into
> my head;
> I wish I had not leant so!' . . .
>
> And we dragged on and on, while we seemed to
> see
> In the running of Time's far glass
> Her crucified, as she had wondered if she might
> be

Some day.—Alas, alas!

Superstition and symbolism, some may say; but they mistakenly invert the order of the creative process. The poet's act of apprehension is wholly different from the lover's fear; and of this apprehension the chance-shaped crucifix is the symbol and not the cause. The concentration of life's vicissitude upon that white-clothed form was first recognised by a sovereign act of æsthetic understanding or intuition; the seeming crucifix supplied a scaffolding for its expression; it afforded a clue to the method of transposition into words which might convey the truth thus apprehended; it suggested an equivalence. The distinction may appear to be hair-drawn, but we believe that it is vital to the theory of poetry as a whole, and to an understanding of Mr Hardy's poetry in particular. Indeed, in it must be sought the meaning of another of his titles, 'Satires of Circumstance,' where the particular circumstance is neither typical nor fortuitous, but a symbol necessary to communicate to others the sense of a quality in life more largely and variously apprehended by the poet.

At the risk of appearing fantastic we will endeavour still further to elucidate our meaning. The poetic process is, we believe, twofold. The one part, the discovery of the symbol, the establishment of an equivalence, is what we may call poetic method. It is concerned with the transposition and communication of emotion, no matter what the emotion may be, for to poetic method the emotional material is, strictly, indifferent. The other part is an æsthetic apprehension of significance, the recognition of the all in the one. This is a specifically poetic act, or rather the supreme poetic act. Yet it may be absent from poetry. For there is no necessary connection between poetic apprehension and poetic method. Poetic method frequently exists without poetic apprehension; and there is no reason to suppose that the reverse is not also true, for the recognition of greatness in poetry is probably not the peculiar privilege of great poets. We have here, at least a principle of division between major and minor poetry.

Mr Hardy is a major poet; and we are impelled to seek further and ask what it is that enables such a poet to perform this sovereign act of apprehension and to recognise the quality of the all in the quality of the one. We believe that the answer is simple. The great poet knows what he is looking for. Once more we speak too precisely, and so falsely, being compelled to use the language of the kingdom of logic to describe what is being done in the kingdom of art. The poet, we say, knows the quality for which he seeks; but this knowledge is rather a condition than a possession of soul. It is a state of responsiveness rather than a knowledge of that to which he will respond. But it is knowledge inasmuch as the choice of that to which he will respond is determined by the condition of his soul. On the purity of that condition depends his greatness as a poet, and that purity in its turn depends upon his denying no element of his profound experience. If he denies or forgets, the synthesis—again the word is a metaphor—which must establish itself within him is fragmentary and false. The new event can wake but partial echoes in his soul or none at all; it can neither be received into, nor can it create a complete relation, and so it passes incommensurable from limbo into forgetfulness.

Mr Hardy stands high above all other modern poets by the deliberate purity of his responsiveness. The contagion of the world's slow stain has not touched him; from the first he held aloof from the general conspiracy to forget in which not only those who are professional optimists take a part. Therefore his simplest words have a vehemence and strangeness of their own:—

> It will have been:
> Nor God nor Demon can undo the done,
> Unsight the seen
> Make muted music be as unbegun
> Though things terrene
> Groan in their bondage till oblivion supervene.

What neither God nor Demon can do, men are incessantly at work to accomplish. Life itself rewards them for their assiduity, for she scatters her roses chiefly on the paths of those who forget her thorns. But the great poet remembers both rose and thorn; and it is beyond his power to remember them otherwise than together.

It was fitting, then, and to some senses inevitable, that Mr Hardy should have crowned his work as a poet in his old age by a series of love poems that are unique for power and passion in even the English language. This late and wonderful flowering has no tinge of miracle; it has sprung straight from the main stem of Mr Hardy's poetic growth. Into 'Veteris Vestigia Flammæ' is distilled the quintessence of the power that created the Wessex Novels and *The Dynasts;* all that Mr Hardy has to tell us of life, the whole of the truth that he has apprehended, is in these poems, and no poet since poetry began has apprehended or told us more. *Sunt lacrimæ rerum.* (pp. 121-37)

> *J. Middleton Murry, "The Poetry of Mr Hardy," in his* Aspects of Literature, *W. Collins Sons & Co. Ltd., 1920, pp. 121-38.*

Joseph Warren Beach   (essay date 1936)

[*Beach was an American critic and educator who specialized in American and English literature of the Romantic and Victorian eras. Of his work, Beach noted: "I do not aim so much to render final judgments and deliver certificates of greatness, which is something manifestly impossible and a trifle ridiculous, as to analyze and interpret stories and poems as expressions of our humanity and as effective works of art." In the following essay, Beach argues that Hardy's poetry is antithetical to the nature poetry of the Romantic Era.*]

Thomas Hardy heralds the disappearance from English poetry of nature with a capital N. Even more vigorously than Tennyson he denies the benevolence of nature conceived as the unity of things personified or as the sum of natural laws. And since he has no religious power, like Tennyson's God, to set up in contrast to nature, as a guarantee of happiness for spiritual beings, nothing is left in him of the optimistic *Weltansicht* characteristic of the palmy days of nature-poetry. He has neither the naturalism of Wordsworth nor his religion-inspired optimism.

First and last, in his poems and novels, he has many references to what, as he says in *The Dynasts,*

> Men love to dub Dame Nature—that lay-shape
> They use to hang phenomena upon—
> Whose deftest mothering in fairest spheres
> Is girt about by terms inexorable!

But Hardy seems to be clear enough through all his writing that nature is nothing more than a lay-shape, or convenient personification, and that she is strictly conditioned by "terms inexorable" which have no reference to our human notions of goodness and benevolence.

It is true that, especially in his earliest work, he sometimes refers to nature in a conventional way as the course of things which, if it could be left unopposed by artificial human arrangements, would naturally work for good ends. Thus in the earliest dated of his poems in which he uses the term nature, the sonnet **"Discouragement":**

> To see the Mother, naturing Nature, stand
> All racked and wrung by her unfaithful lord,
> Her hopes dismayed by his defiling hand,
> Her passioned plans for bloom and beauty
>   marred:
>
> Where she would mint a perfect mould, an ill;
> Where she would don divinest hues, a stain,
> Over her purposed genial hour a chill,
> Upon her charm of flawless flesh a blain:
>
> Her loves dependent on a feature's trim,
> A whole life's circumstance on hap of birth,
> A soul's direction on a body's whim,
> Eternal Heaven upon a day of Earth,
> Is frost to flower of heroism and worth,
> And fosterer of visions ghast and grim.

It is interesting to find Hardy thus referring to the scholastic *natura naturans* ("Naturing Nature"), whose passioned plans are for bloom and beauty, and echoing Wordsworth's complaint of "what man has made of man." But even here there are suggestions of flaws inherent in the natural design itself, such that man could hardly be expected to be happy in following his impulse—"Her loves dependent on a feature's trim"—"A soul's direction on a body's whim." In a poem of the same period, Hardy describes a meeting of two lovers in a church. The man is going to die; the woman to comfort him protests that she loves him; but struck by the tragic irony of the case, she could not prize—

> A world conditioned thus, or care for breath
> Where Nature such dilemmas could devise.

Another poem records the passing of Hardy's illusions in regard to nature. The glory has departed, and the poet looks back sadly on the time when he—

> Wrought thee (nature) for my pleasure,
> Planned thee as a measure
> For expounding
> And resounding
> Glad things that men treasure.

"In a Wood" (1887-96) records his discovery that the vegetable world is, like the world of men, a scene of fighting and mutual destruction. In **"Nature's Questioning"** Hardy quite reverses Wordsworth's procedure. Instead of going to "field, flock and tree" for an answer to his own questions about the universe, he represents these natural creatures as coming to him for light on questions that leave them entirely bewildered. In **"The Bullfinches,"** the poet informs the birds that while "all we creatures" are, according to the faeries of Blackmoor Vale, under the care of "the Mother," yet she never tries to protect us from danger, but works on dreaming and heedless. The indifference of "the Matron," or "the Great Dame," to her children's fate is expressed in **"At a Bridal"** and **"To an Orphan Child"**; her blindness and unconsciousness in **"The Lacking Sense," "Doom and She," "The Sleep-Worker."**

The altered feeling towards Dame Nature is strikingly exhibited in Hardy by the type of landscape, season, weather, which dominates his poetry and prose. The gentle, the sublime, the luxuriant, the cheerful aspects of nature have largely given place to the severe, the sombre, the meagre. An unusually large number of pieces is devoted to aspects of weather hostile to man and beast—**"Winter in Durnover Field," "A Backward Spring," "A Wet August," "If It's Ever Spring Again," "An Unkindly May," "Snow in the Suburbs,"** and a whole series of snow pieces. The romantic and picturesque landscapes of "Alastor" and "Endymion" have given place to **"Winter's Dregs"** and "the land's sharp features." The soaring ecstasy of Shelley's skylark and the "shadows and sunny glimmerings" of Wordsworth's green linnet have given place to—

> An aged thrush, frail, gaunt and small,
> In blast-beruffled plume.

The sombre philosophy of Hardy harmonizes with the prevailing sombreness of nature, whether in his poems or novels. And in the reciprocal action of his philosophy and his temperament, gravely musing and saturnine, it is impossible to say which has more affected the other. At any rate, he appears to have a natural preference in taste for aspects of nature which reflect the modified gloom of his intellectual outlook. His own rationale of this is given in a classic passage in his famous description of Egdon Heath.

> Indeed, it is a question if the exclusive reign of this orthodox beauty is not approaching its last quarter. The new Vale of Tempe may be a gaunt waste in Thule: human souls may find themselves in closer and closer harmony with external things wearing a sombreness distasteful to our race when it was young. The time seems near, if it has not actually arrived, when the chastened sublimity of a moor, a sea, or a mountain will be all of nature that is absolutely in keeping with the moods of the more thinking among mankind. And ultimately, to the commonest tourist, spots like Iceland may become what the vineyards and myrtle-gardens of South Europe are to him now; and Heidelberg and Baden be passed unheeded as he hastens from the Alps to the sand-dunes of Scheveningen.

In his novels Hardy's references to personified nature exhibit the same general attitude as in his poems. There is this one apparent exception to be noted, that, where there is opposition between natural impulse and the restrictions of law and convention, natural impulse is assumed to be right. This opposition is strongest in *Tess of the D'Urbervilles* (1891) and *Jude the Obscure* (1894-95).

Tess, about to bear her illegitimate child in the rural seclusion of Blackmoor, reproached herself for her guilt, as if she were out of harmony with the world. She was terrified without reason by "a cloud of moral hobgoblins."

> Walking among the sleeping birds in the hedges, watching the skipping rabbits on a moonlit warren, or standing under a pheasant-laden bough, she looked upon herself as a figure of Guilt intruding into the haunts of Innocence. But all the while she was making a distinction where there was no difference. Feeling herself in antagonism, she was quite in accord. She had been made to break an accepted social law, but no law known to the environment in which she fancied herself such an anomaly.

So in ironic vein the author refers to her short-lived infant as "that bastard gift of shameless nature who respects not the civil law." When Angel Clare made love to her later at the dairy farm, she felt in honor bound to reject his suit, but this was against nature. "Every see-saw of her breath, every wave of her blood, every pulse singing in her ears, was a voice that joined with Nature in revolt against her scrupulousness." Her very instinct not to tell him of her "past" was "her instinct of self-preservation." After their marriage, when she had at length told him, Clare could not bear to go on living with her "while that [other] man lives, he being your husband in the sight of Nature, if not really." But this appeal to nature seems to the author perverse; he suggests on the contrary: "Some might risk the odd paradox that with more animalism he would have been the nobler man."

In *Jude* there is a considerable number of references to nature as running counter to the religious restrictions upon the sex-impulse. Gibbon is quoted on "insulted nature" in reference to the excessive chastity of the early saints. Sue's sticking to her husband, whom she loathes, is by Jude ruled to be wrong, "speaking from experience and unbiassed nature." Of her marriage to himself, Jude declares, "Nature's own marriage it is, unquestionably!" But though they were legally married, Sue, taking the high ecclesiastical point of view, protests that this is not "Heaven's marriage." In the eyes of God she considers herself still married to her first husband. And in this whole debate there is no doubt that Hardy's sympathy is on the side of nature as against the notions of conventional religion. Jude reflects as follows on his frustrated career:

> Strange that his first aspiration—towards academical proficiency—had been checked by a woman, and that his second aspiration—towards apostleship—had also been checked by a woman. "Is it," he said, "that the women are to blame; or is it the artificial system of things, under which the normal sex-impulses are turned into devilish domestic gins and springes to noose and hold back those who want to progress?"

And Sue, before she turns religious, reflects thus upon her own dilemma: "It is none of the tragedies of love that's love's usual tragedy in civilized life, but a tragedy artificially manufactured for people who in a natural state would find relief in parting!"

But while Hardy recognizes, like every one else, the dis-

Hardy, age 19.

tress caused when natural impulse is balked by artificial codes of conduct, none realizes more acutely than he that nature herself is full of cruelty. Social codes are themselves a part of nature; and, beyond all that can be controlled by social codes, are the infinitely complicated lines of circumstance which tend to make impossible the attainment of happiness by any created being.

> In the ill-judged execution of the well-judged plan of things, the call seldom produces the comer, the man to love rarely coincides with the hour for loving. Nature does not often say "See!" to a poor creature at a time when seeing can lead to happy doing; or reply "Here!" to a body's cry of "Where?" till the hide-and-seek has become an irksome, outworn game.

Men's harshnesses towards women are but an outgrowth of "the universal harshness . . . the harshness of the position towards the temperament, of the means towards the aims, of to-day towards yesterday, of hereafter towards to-day." Thus in the interplay of human desire and aspiration with the circumstances under which they are to be gratified, there is an inherent want of adjustment which, in many different ways, determines their frustration and disappointment.

The very natural impulses which Hardy champions against the conventions of society bring misery with them. Referring to the half-dozen Durbeyfield children condemned by nature to sail along in one ship with their heedless parents, Hardy remarks:

> Some people would like to know whence the poet whose philosophy is in these days deemed as profound and trustworthy as his song is sweet and pure, gets his authority for speaking of "Nature's holy plan."

Referring to the hopeless passion of the dairy maids for Clare, he speaks of "cruel Nature's law." Tess, after making her confession to Clare, still looked absolutely pure, "Nature, in her fantastic trickery, had set such a seal of girlishness upon [her] countenance."

In *Jude* the principal characters are unanimous in finding nature indifferent or hostile to man. Jude often felt "the scorn of Nature for man's finer emotions, and her lack of interest in his aspirations." Phillotson, reflecting on the misery of Sue, declares: "Cruelty is the law pervading all nature and society; and we can't get out of it if we would!" Sue finds that "Nature's law [is] mutual butchery." And the author in his own person, referring to the weakness of women as a sex, declares that they "by no possible exertion of their willing hearts and abilities could be made strong while the inexorable laws of nature remain what they are." Above all, the young Jude is revolted by his realization that, in nature's plan, the lower animals must be the victims of man, through that "flaw in the terrestrial scheme, by which what was good for God's birds was bad for God's gardener."

This idea of a flaw in the terrestrial scheme is everywhere present in Hardy's writing. Thus in *The Return of the Native* (1878), he speaks of the "long line of disillusive centuries" which have permanently displaced the cheerful Hellenic idea of life. "That old-fashioned revelling in the general situation grows less and less possible as we uncover the defects of natural laws, and see the quandary that man is in by their operation."

Nature is but one of many alternative terms used by Hardy for designating the unity of process and the directing power in the world. Fate and destiny are words found more often in the mouths of the characters, who reflect the superstitious philosophy of untrained country-people. God and providence are terms they take up from their religious culture. Chance, hap, circumstance are words suggestive of the seeming capriciousness of events, their irrelevance to human aims and direction. None of these terms is to be regarded as indicating that Hardy seriously adhered to the philosophy implied in its use. At no period of his writing did Hardy share the religious views of his characters, and God or the gods, providence, chance, fate, must all be taken in a figurative and dramatic sense, as reflecting the point of view of human beings caught in a web too large and complicated for mortal understanding.

That Hardy was a scientific determinist in his interpretation of how things come about is evident from many passages in the novels. Thus, in *The Mayor of Casterbridge* (1886), he comments as follows on the seeming element of chance in a certain act of Lucetta, involving a striking coincidence.

> That she had chosen for her afternoon walk the road along which she had returned to Casterbridge three hours earlier in a carriage was curious—if anything should be called curious in concatenations of phenomena wherein each is known to have its accounting cause.

Again, he comments on Henchard's superstitious notion of the intervention of a sinister intelligence.

> Henchard, like all his kind, was superstitious, and he could not help thinking that the concatenation of events this evening had produced was the scheme of some sinister intelligence bent on punishing him. Yet they had developed naturally.

His explanation of how these events came about is immediately followed by reference to the "mockery" of the case and "this ironical sequence of things"; and so we know that the mockery and the irony are not in nature, but simply in the relation of certain natural events to man's intentions, as seen from the point of view of the man himself. So in *The Woodlanders* (1887) a certain fateful letter of Marty South is called "the tiny instrument of a cause deep in nature." Of men's attitude towards a causality which they cannot trace Hardy speaks in the same book.

> The petulance that relatives show towards each other is in truth directed against that intangible Causality which has shaped the situation no less for the offenders than the offended, but is too elusive to be discerned and cornered by poor humanity in irritated mood.

In *Tess,* again, Hardy speaks of Tess and Clare balanced on the edge of passion. "All the while they were none the less converging, under the force of irresistible law, as surely as two streams in one vale."

That the doings of individuals form a part of the entire pattern of cause and effect which makes up the universe is a point often emphasized.

> Hardly anything could be more isolated or more self-contained than the lives of these two walking here in the lonely antelucan hour, when gray shades, material and mental, are so very gray. And yet, looked at in a certain way, their lonely courses formed no detached design at all, but were part of the pattern in the great web of human doings then weaving in both hemispheres, from the White Sea to Cape Horn.

In this web, since all happens naturally and according to law, nothing comes about capriciously. But in the relation between outward circumstances and the needs and desires of men, there is infinite possibility for what men call accident, chance, fate, destiny, and the irony of circumstances that throw jeering reflections on one another. (pp. 503-11)

By fate or destiny Hardy means the course of a man's life as determined by all the antecedent circumstances in the chain of causality. There is nothing here of the Greek religious conception of fate, or of a destiny or nemesis having us individually in mind. Fate is not arbitrary, being only another name for natural causality. The seeming arbitrariness of fate is an illusion of men; it overrules our will because, in its large and impersonal working, it has no reference to our will. An accident is a mere crossing of two sets of circumstances, an intersection of two orbits, which registers as an interference. Circumstances are the separate moments in the chain of causation. Circumstance is another name for the conditions under which we carry on our lives—most noted when unfavorable.

Throughout Hardy's work the emphasis is thrown, both by the author and by the characters of his fiction, on those elements in circumstance which are unfavorable to men's hopes.

> "There's a back'ard current in the world, and we must do our utmost to advance in order just to bide where we be." . . . "Having found man's life to be a wretchedly conceived scheme, I renounce it." . . .
>
> [*Desperate Remedies*]

Too numerous to mention are the instances in the poems of this hostility of circumstance to men's desires and aspirations. Whole volumes are devoted to its exemplification, as indicated by the titles, *Satires of Circumstance, Time's Laughingstocks.* The upshot of volumes of poems is stated in general terms in **"Yell'ham-Wood's Story."** Yell'ham-Wood is one of Hardy's many impersonations of nature, and the general lesson of nature as stated by the voice of this forest is as follows:

> It says that Life would signify
> A thwarted purposing:
> That we come to live, and are called to die.
> Yes, that's the thing
> In fall, in spring,
> That Yell'ham says:—
> "Life offers—to deny!"

Hardy does not believe in any God, or gods, or providence having regard for men or other creatures. But he recognizes the anthropomorphic disposition to invent gods and blame them for the ills of life. He expressly declares that his characters are mistaken in doing so; and when he himself uses these terms, it is clear that it is ironically and satirically.

> "Providence, whom I had just thanked, seemed a mocking tormentor laughing at me." [*Desperate Remedies*] . . . Even then Boldwood did not recognize that the impersonator of Heaven's persistent irony towards him, who had once before broken in upon his bliss, scourged him, and snatched his delight away, had come to do these things a second time. [*Far from the Madding Crowd*] . . . But Providence is nothing if not coquettish; and no sooner had Eustacia formed this resolve than the opportunity came which, while sought, had been entirely withholden. . . . Yet, instead of blaming herself for the issue she laid the fault upon the shoulders of some indistinct, colossal Prince of the World, who had framed her situation and ruled her lot. [*The Return of the Native*] (pp. 511-13)

The final term chosen by Hardy for designating the unity and the directing power of the universe is one taken, in all probability, from Schopenhauer,—the Immanent Will. Mr. Ernest Brennecke, in *Thomas Hardy's Universe,* has drawn many parallels between Hardy's philosophy in *The Dynasts* and that of Schopenhauer in *Die Welt als Wille und Vorstellung;* and he and Mr. Stevenson have traced through the poems the gradual replacement of Chance, Circumstance, God, Providence, Nature, and other unsatisfactory terms, by the more satisfactory—but still admittedly tentative and groping term—the Immanent Will. Hardy's characterization of the Immanent Will in *The Dynasts*—in many ways identical with his earlier characterization of God in the poems—will make clear why it was that the sometimes alternative term nature had ceased to have for him the cheerful and mystical significance it had for poets like Wordsworth and Shelley and later for poets like Emerson, Whitman, Swinburne and Meredith— had altogether ceased indeed to be a term to conjure with.

Mr. Brennecke is at some pains to make us understand that Schopenhauer's Will—and more dubiously, Hardy's—implies an idealistic metaphysic. The term will, taken from man's conscious and purposive action, is extended to cover all operations of the organic and inorganic world. But it amounts to no more than an urge in things which gives them the direction and the form which they have. The idealism is found altogether in the formative, the organizing character of this urge, which follows certain patterns vaguely suggestive of the world-patterns of Aristotle and Plato. Whatever may be the case with Hardy, Schopenhauer had a growing aversion to materialistic systems as incapable of explaining the organizing and formative character of this power. The behavior of the universe as a whole and in all its parts is the expression of an inherent, and as we might say, protoplasmic nature, an inner urge, and not merely the result of impulsion from without. In this sense the system of Schopenhauer, and of Hardy after him, is idealistic.

But the idealism of Schopenhauer and Hardy, as I understand it, is distinguished from most idealistic systems by the fact that it does not imply rationality. Hardy, at any rate, does not attribute intelligence to the universal Will, or assume the existence of any intelligent supreme being lying back of or explaining the Will. Intelligence is a late and secondary development, to a large extent a delusion, and at any rate following upon the urge and action of the Will. Consequently the teleology of these men is sharply distinguished from that of most idealists, and in particular from that of writers like Cudworth and the eighteenth-century natural theologians. The Will follows unconsciously a plan inherent in itself, and the universe is purposive in that in every detail it carries out the original plan. But that this original plan implies the special adjustment of each part, of each organ and each organism, to the rôle it is to play in the universe, is certainly not remotely suggested in Hardy's writing; there is no suggestion that living creatures, including man, were destined to happiness under this plan; that it is benevolent in its particular dispositions; or that—as in the favorite eighteenth-century systems, in Shaftesbury, Pope, Wordsworth—the particular dispositions, however unsatisfactory by themselves, may be conceived of as building up in a whole which is harmonious and good taken altogether.

The word Will in Hardy and Schopenhauer carries for the most part implications quite the contrary of what it carries for religious thinkers like Coleridge. It is not the expression of intelligent thought, of "spirit," but of an unconscious impulse, better described in terms of animal instinct, vegetable irritability, and the insensitive—though formal—operations of inorganic matter, in the formation of crystals, the phenomena of electricity, etc. The impersonal and automatic working of this Will leaves no place for freedom in the action of men, so that the system is thoroughly unmoral and deterministic or necessarian.

Thus the Spirit of the Years describes the working of the will in human history.

> So the Will heaves through Space, and moulds
>   the times,
> With mortals for Its fingers! We shall see
> Again men's passions, virtues, visions, crimes,
> Obey resistlessly
> The purposive, unmotived, dominant Thing
> Which sways in brooding dark their wayfaring!

The unconsciousness of the Will is again stated thus:

> In that immense unweeting Mind is shown
> One far above forethinking; purposive,
> Yet superconscious; a Clairvoyancy
> That knows not what It knows, yet works there-
>   with.

Again, of the Immanent Will:

> It works unconsciously, as heretofore,
> Eternal artistries in Circumstance,
> Whose patterns, wrought by rapt æsthetic rote,
> Seem in themselves Its single listless aim,
> And not their consequence.

There is something to remind us of Cudworth's Plastic Nature in this Immanent Will, which works purposively and esthetically but without consciousness of what it does, proceeds like a thinking being but without thought—

> Which thinking on, yet weighing not Its
>   thought,
> Unchecks Its clock-like laws.

But in Cudworth the Plastic Nature is purposive and organizing in character by virtue of the Supreme Intelligence whose agent it is, whereas in Hardy the unconscious and unintelligent Will is the supreme principle of the universe, and—as the Spirit of the Years declares:

> In the Foretime, even to the germ of Being,
> Nothing appears of shape to indicate
> That cognizance has marshalled things terrene,
> Or will (such is my thinking) in my span.
> Better they show that, like a knitter drowsed,
> Whose fingers play in skilled unmindfulness,
> The Will has woven with an absent heed
> Since life first was; and ever will so weave.

The mechanism of this Will and of the human beings and other forms of vitalized matter which form a part of it is figured, poetically, in terms derived from anatomy, as a gigantic brain, more suggestive of materialistic science, it seems to me, than of the vague metaphysical idealism which Mr. Brennecke ascribes to Hardy. It is "a seeming transparency . . . exhibiting as one organism the anatomy of life and movement in all humanity and vitalized matter included in the display." Strange waves pass back and forth along gossamer-like threads.

> These are the Prime Volitions,—fibrils, veins,
> Will-tissues, nerves, and pulses of the Cause,
> That heave throughout the Earth's compositure.
> Their sum is like the lobule of a Brain
> Evolving always that it wots not of;
> A Brain whose whole connotes the Everywhere,
> And whose procedure may not be discerned
> By phantom eyes like ours; the while unguessed
> Of those it stirs, who (even as ye do) dream
> Their motions free, their orderings supreme . . .

Throughout **The Dynasts** terms are used for designating this Will which emphasize the deterministic character of its action, making mere puppets of men, and its want of consciousness and intelligence. "It is," Mr. Brennecke notes, "the Great Necessitator, the Eternal Urger, the High Influence that sways the English realm with all its homuncules, the Master-Hand that plays the game alone, the Back of Things that hauls the halyards of the world.'" In the After Scene, with which the drama closes, it is called the Great Foresightless, the Inadvertent Mind, and—

> . . . the dreaming, dark, dumb thing
> That turns the handle of this idle show.

It is expressly stated here, and elsewhere, that this Will, being foresightless and inadvertent, has no concern with the sufferings of mortals—though obviously it is responsible for them—and that the entire universe, like the small part of it exhibited in this epic of the Napoleonic wars, is, so far as one can make out by reason, "inutile all." The only hope for souls who would like to think well of the universe is that, as man in the course of the ages has evolved consciousness, so conceivably might the supreme will, with happy results for the creation—

> Consciousness the Will informing, till It fashion
>   all things fair!

This mitigating concession, made virtually without preparation at the end of a uniformly hopeless chronicle, is not to be regarded seriously as an element in Hardy's philosophy. It is radically inconsistent with the general concept of the Immanent Will, which expressly rules out the notion of a spirit external to the universe, being conceived as the mere principle of action inherent in the behavior of things. Altogether the Immanent Will is not a concept to arouse the enthusiasm of mortals like the Christian God or the nature of eighteenth-century poetry. It is nothing more than a metaphysical convenience,—a term for expressing the unity and pattern of existing things.

The Darwinian theory of evolution was from the beginning assumed by Hardy, and it underlies all his general speculation. As he wrote in 1876, "the evolution of species seems but a minute and obvious process" in the general world-movement, in which "all things merge into one another—good into evil, generosity into justice, religion into politics, the years into the ages, the world into the universe." But the concept of evolution gave him none of the comfort that it did Meredith—quite the contrary. Mr. Stevenson remarks that certain of Hardy's poems have the air of direct rebuttals to Meredith's hopeful evolutionary teaching. Hardy is, for the most part, doubtful of the possibility of any man's contributing to the progress of the race. Heredity, he finds, works "according to mechanical principles, beyond the control of human will." Nature shows no intention of improving the race by the process of reproduction. Hardy fails to find any general tendency to good in the world. In **"Nature's Questioning,"** field, pool, and tree interrogate the poet on the ruling power of the world, reviewing the various alternatives. Is it some "vast Imbecility," good at building but "impotent to tend"; or an "Automaton unconscious of our pains"; or is there some "high Plan as yet not understood," which involves so much suffering as incident to its operation?

The evolution of thought and sensibility, on which Meredith relies for his hopeful view of man's destiny, and for his entire ethical system, is with Hardy the main evidence of the blundering ineptitude of nature or God. It has occasioned untold suffering in both man and the lower animals. This view is more than once expressed by Hardy in his notebooks at different periods.

> Law has produced in man a child who cannot but constantly reproach its parent for doing much and yet not all, and constantly say to such parent that it would have been better never to have begun doing than to have *over*done so indecisively; that is, than to have created so far beyond all apparent first intention (on the emotional side) without mending matters by a second intention and execution, to eliminate the evils of the blunder of overdoing. The emotions have no place in a world of defect, and it is a cruel injustice that they should have developed in it. . . . A woeful fact—that the human race is too extremely developed for its corporeal conditions, the nerves being evolved to an activity abnormal in such an environment. Even the higher animals are in excess in this respect. It may be questioned if Nature, or what we call Nature, so far back as when she crossed the line from invertebrates to vertebrates, did not exceed her mission. This planet does not supply the material for happiness to higher existences. Other planets may, though one can hardly see how.

Hardy's most impressive statement of this view in poetry is in **"The Mother Mourns."** Here for the nonce the poet assumes, what he for the most part denies, that Mother Nature is aware of the sufferings of her creatures, and he represents her as regretting her evolutionary experiment, which has given man intelligence capable of judging and condemning her plan.

> "I had not proposed me a Creature
> (She soughed) so excelling
> All else of my kingdom in compass
> And brightness of brain
>
> "As to read my defects with a god-glance,
> Uncover each vestige
> Of old inadvertence, annunciate
> Each flaw and each stain

. . . . .

> "Why loosened I olden control here
> To mechanize skywards,
> Undeeming great scope could outshape in
> A globe of such grain?
>
> "Man's mountings of mind-sight I checked not,
> Till range of his vision
> Has topped my intent, and found blemish
> Throughout my domain.
>
> "He holds as inept his own soul-shell—
> My deftest achievement—
> Contemns me for fitful inventions
> Ill-timed and inane:
>
> "No more sees my sun as a Sanct-shape,
> My moon as the Night-queen,
> My stars as august and sublime ones
> That influences rain:
>
> "Reckons gross and ignoble my teaching,
> Immoral my story,
> My love-lights a lure, that my species
> May gather and gain."

This poem, in which the evolution of the mind is represented as a sheer blunder, is, as Mr. Stevenson suggests, a blasting reply to Meredith's "Earth and Man." In this one poem, for dramatic purposes, nature is figured as a conscious and planning goddess. But, in the group of poems printed with it in *Poems of the Past and Present* (**"The Lacking Sense," "Doom and She," "The Sleep-Worker," "The Bullfinches," "God-Forgotten," "The Bedridden Peasant to an Unknowing God"**), Mother Nature, or the alternative God, is shown as blind and dumb, a mere somnambulist. This is the price which Hardy pays—like Mill before him—for his supposition that the ruling power is not the deliberate planner of mortal miseries. The ruler of the universe, as they both hold, cannot be benevolent and omniscient at the same time.

Strictly speaking, in Hardy, the ruling power is neither omniscient nor benevolent. It is blind and indifferent. The Immanent Will, or Fundamental Energy, is no more than the sum total of all the activity in the universe. In the development of man's intelligence it works by natural selection, which is carried out by mere "random sequence" of events.

> The cognizance ye mourn, Life's doom to feel,
> If I report it meetly, came unmeant,
> Emerging with blind gropes from impercipience
> By random sequence—luckless, tragic Chance,
>
> If ye will call it so. 'Twas needed not
> In the economy of Vitality,
> Which might have ever kept a sealed cognition
> As doth the Will Itself.

It will be observed what an extremely attenuated version of teleology it is that will consist with this Epicurean-Lucretian notion of luckless Chance as the conductor of evolution. Nothing remains of purposiveness but the vague esthetic recognition of unity and pattern in things. Conscious design, providence, harmony, benevolence have all evaporated from the concept of nature. As a subject for poetic exaltation it no longer has any value; and inevitably it goes into the discard, together with concepts more strictly theological. Thomas Hardy sounds the death-knell of the old nature-poetry. (pp. 513-21)

Joseph Warren Beach, "Hardy," in his The Concept of Nature in Nineteenth-Century English Poetry, *1936. Reprint by Russell & Russell, 1966, pp. 503-21.*

Delmore Schwartz (essay date 1940)

[*Schwartz was an American poet, short story writer, and critic. In the following essay, which was originally published in 1940, he analyzes the effects of Hardy's personal beliefs upon his poetry and his readership.*]

It is natural that beliefs should be involved in poetry in a variety of ways. Hardy is a rich example of this variety. For that reason, it would be well to distinguish some of the important ways in which belief inhabits poetry.

Some poetry is written in order to state beliefs. The purpose of the versification is to make the doctrine plain. Lucretius is the obvious and much-used example, and Dante is probably another, although there is some dramatic justification for most passages of philosophical statement and discussion in the *Paradiso*.

Some poetry employs beliefs merely as an aspect of the thoughts and emotions of the human characters with which it is concerned. Almost every dramatic poet will serve as an example of this tendency. Human beings are full of beliefs, a fact which even the naturalistic novelist

Hardy, age 21.

cannot wholly forget; and since their beliefs are very important motives in their lives, no serious poet can forget about beliefs all the time. One doubts that any serious poet would want to do so.

It is not difficult to distinguish the two poetic uses of belief from each other. The first kind is generally marked by the forms of direct statement, the second kind by a narrative or dramatic context. And when there is a shift in purpose, when the dramatic poet begins to use his characters merely as mouthpieces to state beliefs, the shift shows immediately in the surface of the poetry. The poet's use of his medium and his attitude toward his subject are always reflected strikingly in the looking glass of form.

Between these two extremes, there exist intermediate stages of which Hardy provides a number of examples. It is commonplace, in addition, that a poet may begin with the intention of stating a belief—or perhaps merely some observation which interests him—and conclude by modifying belief and observation to suit the necessities of versification, the suggestion of a rhyme or the implication of a metaphor.

But there is a prior way in which beliefs enter into a poem. It is prior in that it is inevitable in the very act of writing poetry, while the previous two ways may conceivably be avoided. The poet's beliefs operate within his poem whether he knows it or not, and apart from any effort to use them. This fundamental operation of belief can be seen when we consider a Christian poet's observations of Nature, and then compare them to similar observations on the part of a Romantic poet, such as Wordsworth or Keats. The comparison can be made more extreme with ease, if we substitute a Russian or a Chinese poet, using descriptive passages. It should be evident that poets with different beliefs when confronted with what is nominally the same object do not make the same observations. The same shift because of belief occurs in the slightest detail of language; such common words as *pain, animal, night, rock, hope, death,* and *sky* must of necessity have different powers of association and implication for the Christian poet and one whose beliefs are different. It is a simple fact that our beliefs not only make us see certain things, but also prevent us from seeing other things; and in addition, or perhaps one should say at the same time, our understanding of the language we use is changed.

In Hardy's poetry these three functions of belief all have an important part. Another and equally important factor is at work also. With the tone, the attitude implied by the tone, and often with the explicit statement of his poem, Hardy says with the greatest emphasis: "You see: this is what Life is." And more than that, he says very often: "You see: your old conception of what Life is has been shown to be wrong and foolish by this example."

One hesitates to make a simple synopsis of Hardy's beliefs. It is not that there is anything inherently obscure in them, but that they exist in his poetry so close to the attitudes, feelings, tones, and observations which make them different from their abstract formulation. For the purpose of lucidity, however, it is worth while saying that Hardy believed, in the most literal sense, that the fundamental factor in the nature of things was a "First or Fundamental Energy," as he calls it in the foreword to *The Dynasts.* This Energy operated without consciousness or order throughout the universe and produced the motions of the stars and the long development of the forms of life upon our own planet. Hardy did not hold this view simply, though on occasion he stated it thus. Stated thus, his writing would be an example of philosophical poetry. But this view is only one moment of his whole state of mind and does not by any means exist by itself. It is a view which Hardy affirms in active opposition, first of all, to the view that an intelligent and omnipotent Being rules the universe; second of all, in active opposition to what he knew of the nature of human life as something lived by human beings who in their conscious striving blandly disregarded the fact that they were merely products of the First or Fundamental Energy. Thus Hardy's state of mind is one example of the conflict between the new scientific view of Life which the nineteenth century produced and the whole attitude toward Life which had been traditional to Western culture. Hardy is a partisan of the new view, but acutely conscious always of the old view. He holds the two in a dialectical tension. Indeed there are moments when it seems that Hardy is merely taking the Christian idea of God and the world, and placing a negative prefix to each of God's attributes. The genuine atheist, by contrast, is never so concerned with the view which he has rejected. Or if he is so concerned, he is, like Hardy, a being who is fundamentally religious and essentially possessed by a state of mind in which an old view of Life and a new one contest without conclusion.

There are certain poems in which this conflict is stated explicitly. In the lyric called **"A Plaint to Man,"** the false God of Christianity is personified and given a voice, and with that voice he addresses mankind, resuming the doctrine of evolution:

> When you slowly emerged from the den of Time,
> And gained percipience as you grew,
> And fleshed you fair out of shapeless slime,
>
> Wherefore, O Man, did there come to you
> The unhappy need of creating me—
> A form like your own—for praying to?

This false God, being told that mankind had need of some agency of hope and mercy, tells mankind that he, God, dwindles day by day "beneath the deicide eyes of seers," "and tomorrow the whole of me disappears," so that "the truth should be told, and the fact be faced"—the fact that if mankind is to have mercy, justice, and love, the human heart itself would have to provide it.

In another poem, **"God's Funeral,"** the ambiguity of Hardy's attitude becomes increasingly evident. The God of Christianity is being escorted to his grave by a long train of mourners who are described in Dantesque lines and who have thoughts which are overheard by the protagonist of the poem and which rehearse the history of monotheism from the standpoint of a higher criticism of the Bible. Among the funeral throng, however, the protagonist sees many who refuse to believe that God has died:

> Some in the background then I saw,

> Sweet women, youths, men, all incredulous,
> Who chimed: "This is a counterfeit of straw,
> This requiem mockery! Still he lives to us!"
>
> I could not buoy their faith: and yet
> Many I had known: with all I sympathized;
> And though struck speechless, I did not forget
> That what was mourned for, I, too, long had
> prized.

This confession that Hardy, too, had prized what he was so concerned to deny must be remembered for the light it gives us upon Hardy's poetry as a whole. In other poems, the wish to believe in the dying God is frankly declared. **"The Oxen,"** a poem which will require detailed attention, tells of an old Christmas story that the oxen kneel at the hour of Christ's nativity, and the poet declares in the most moving terms that if he should be asked at Christmas to come to the pen at midnight to see the oxen kneel, he would go "in the gloom," "Hoping it might be so"! In *The Dynasts,* this desire is given the most peculiar and pathetic form of all. The hope is stated at the very end that the Fundamental Energy which rules the nature of things will continue to evolve until It takes upon Itself the attribute of consciousness—"Consciousness the Will informing till It fashions all things fair!"—and thus, or such is the implication, becomes like the God of Christianity, a God of love, mercy, and justice.

At the same time, there is a decisive moment of Hardy's state of mind which is directly opposed to this one. Hardy works without end to manipulate the events in the lives of his characters so that it will be plain that human life is at the mercy of chance and the most arbitrary circumstances. Hardy not only makes his Immanent Will of the universe an active power of evil, but he engages his characters in the most incredible conjunctions of unfortunate accidents. There is such an intensity of interest in seeing chance thwart and annihilate human life that the tendency of mind seems pathological until one remembers that chance and coincidence have become for Hardy one of the primary motions of the universe. It is Providence, which is functioning in reverse; the poet has attempted to state a definite view of life in the very working out of his plot.

And at the same time also, the older and stronger view of Life inhabited the poet's mind at a level on which it was not opposed. Hardy inherited a substratum of sensibility of a definite character and formed by definite beliefs which denied the scientific view his intellect accepted. He inherited this sensibility from his fathers, just as he inherited the lineaments of his face, and he could as soon have changed one as the other. Hardy was convinced that the new scientific view was the correct one; he was convinced intellectually, that is to say, that Darwin, Huxley, Schopenhauer, Hartmann, and Nietzsche had attained to the truth about Life. But at the same time, he could not help seeing Nature and human life in the light which was as habitual as walking on one's feet and not on one's hands. He could not work as a poet without his profound sense of history and sense of the past, his feeling for the many generations who had lived and died in his countryside before him; and his mind, like theirs, naturally and inevitably recognized human choice, responsibility, and freedom, the irreparable character of human acts and the undeniable necessity of seeing life from the inside of the human psyche rather than from the astronomical-biological perspective of nineteenth-century science. But more than that, he could not work as a poet without such entities as "spectres, mysterious voices, intuitions, omens and haunted places," the operations of the supernatural in which he could not believe.

The cosmology of nineteenth-century science which affected Hardy so much has had a long and interesting history in the culture of the last forty years. Its effects are to be seen in the novels of Theodore Dreiser, in the plays of Bernard Shaw, the early philosophical writing of Bertrand Russell, the early poetry of Archibald MacLeish, and the poetry of Robinson Jeffers. A prime American example is Joseph Wood Krutch's *The Modern Temper,* where it is explicitly announced that such things as love and tragedy and all other specifically human values are not possible to modern man. The example of Bertrand Russell suggests that of I. A. Richards, whose sincerity ritual to test the genuineness of a poem works at least in part by envisaging the "meaninglessness" of the universe which follows or seemed to follow from the scientific view; and the example of Krutch suggests some of the best poems of Mark Van Doren, where the emptiness of the sky, the departure of the old picture of the world, is the literal theme. This array of examples, and the many others which might be added, should not only suggest how modern a poet Hardy is; they should also suggest how variously the scientific view may enter into the poet's whole being, what different attitudes it may engender, and how differently the poet's sensibility may attempt to handle it.

It is nothing if not fitting that I. A. Richards should look to Hardy for his perfect example in *Science and Poetry,* the book he has devoted to precisely this question, the effect of the scientific view upon the modern poet. Mr. Richards is at once very illuminating, I think, and very wrong in what he says of Hardy. It would not be possible for anyone to improve upon the appreciation of Hardy's virtues implicit in the three pages Mr. Richards devotes to him; but it would be equally difficult to invert the truth about Hardy as completely as Mr. Richards does in the interests of his general thesis. He quotes a remark about Hardy made by J. Middleton Murry: "His reaction to an episode has behind it and within it a reaction to the universe." And then his comment is: "This is not as I should put it were I making a statement; but read as a pseudo-statement, emotively, it is excellent; it makes us remember how we felt. Actually it describes just what Hardy, at his best, does not do. He makes no reaction to the universe, recognizing it as something to which no reaction is more relevant than another."

On the contrary, Hardy is almost always bringing his reaction to the universe into his poems. It is true that he sees the universe as something to which no reaction is more relevant than another; but it is just that view of the neutral universe which prepossesses Hardy almost always and gives much of the power to the most minute details of his poems. Perhaps one ought to say not Hardy's beliefs, but Hardy's disbeliefs; whichever term is exact, the fact is that his beliefs or disbeliefs make possible the great strength of his verse. We can see that this is so if we examine some of the poems in which Hardy's beliefs play a direct part.

The Oxen

Christmas Eve, and twelve of the clock.
"Now they are all on their knees,"
An elder said as we sat in a flock
By the embers in hearthside ease.

We pictured the meek mild creatures where
They dwelt in their strawy pen,
Nor did it occur to one of us there
To doubt they were kneeling then.

So fair a fancy few would weave
In these years! Yet, I feel,
If someone said on Christmas Eve,
"Come; see the oxen kneel,

"In the lonely barton by yonder coomb
Our childhood used to know,"
I should go with him in the gloom,
Hoping it might be so.

The belief in this poem is of course a disbelief in the truth of Christianity. The emotion is the wish that it were true. But it must be emphasized that this emotion, which obviously motivates the whole poem, depends upon a very full sense of what the belief in Christianity amounted to; and this sense also functions to provide the poet with the details of the Christmas story which serves as the example of Christianity. It is Hardy's sensibility as the son of his fathers which makes possible his realization of the specific scene and story; this sensibility itself was the product of definite beliefs, to refer back to the point made at the beginning that we see what we do see because of our beliefs. But for the whole poem to be written, it was necessary that what Hardy's sensibility made him conscious of should be held against the scientific view which his intellect accepted. Both must enter into the poem. This is the sense in which a reaction to the universe, if one must use Mr. Murry's terms, is involved in Hardy's reaction to the Christmas story. Hardy, remembering the Christmas story of childhood, cannot help keeping in mind the immense universe of nineteenth-century science, which not only makes such a story seem untrue, but increases one's reasons for wishing that it were true. His sensibility's grasp of the meaning of Christmas and Christianity makes such a choice of detail as calling the oxen "meek mild creatures" likely, perfectly exact, and implicit with the Christian quality of humility. His intellectual awareness of the new world-picture engenders the fullness of meaning involved in the phrase, which is deliberately emphasized by the overflow, "In these years!" A reaction to the universe is involved in this phrase and in addition a reaction to a definite period in Western culture.

If we take a negative example, one in which Hardy's beliefs have operated to produce a poor poem, this function of belief will be seen with further definition. The following poem is as typical of Hardy's failures as **"The Oxen"** is of the elements which produced his successes:

The Masked Face

I found me in a great surging space,
At either end a door,

And I said: "What is this giddying place,
With no firm-fixéd floor,
That I knew not of before?"
"It is Life," said a mask-clad face.

I asked: "But how do I come here,
Who never wished to come;
Can the light and air be made more clear,
The floor more quietsome,
And the door set wide? They numb
Fast-locked, and fill with fear."

The mask put on a bleak smile then,
And said, "O vassal-wight,
There once complained a goosequill pen
To the scribe of the Infinite
Of the words it had to write
Because they were past its ken."

Here too Hardy's picture of the universe is at work and Hardy is intent upon declaring his belief that Life is beyond human understanding. But there is a plain incongruity between the vaguely cosmological scene which is declared to be Life in the first stanza and the stenographic metaphor for human life in the last stanza, which, apart from this relationship, is grotesque enough in itself. There is no adequate reason in the poem why a giddying place with no firm-fixéd floor should be beyond understanding, and it is not made so by being entitled: Life. It reminds one rather of the barrel-rolls at amusement parks and by no means of the revolutions of day and night which Hardy presumably had in mind. The masked face is probably intended to designate the Immanent Will; but here again, there is a gulf between what Hardy meant by that Will and any speaking face, and the gulf cannot be annulled merely by the device of personification. Moreover, it is difficult enough to see the human being as a goosequill pen; when the pen complains, the poem collapses because too great a weight of meaning has been put upon a figure which was inadequate at the start.

In poems such as these, and they are not few, Hardy has been merely attempting to versify his beliefs about the universe, and neither his mastery of language nor his skill at versification can provide him with all that he needs. He needs his sensibility; but his sensibility works only when the objects proper to it are in view. When it is required to function on a cosmological scene, it can only produce weak and incommensurate figures. It is possible for a poet to make poetry by the direct statement of his beliefs, but it is not possible for such a poet as Hardy. The true philosophical poet is characterized by an understanding of ideas and an interest in them which absorbs his whole being. Hardy was interested in ideas, too; but predominantly in their bearing upon human life. No better characterization could be formulated than the one Hardy wrote for his novel *Two on a Tower:* "This slightly-built romance was the outcome of a wish to set the emotional history of two infinitesimal lives against the stupendous background of the stellar universe, and to impart to readers the sentiment that of these contrasting magnitudes the smaller might be the greater to them as men."

Hardy failed when he tried to make a direct statement of his beliefs; he succeeded when he used his beliefs to make significant the observations which concerned him. This contrast should suggest that something essential to the nature of poetry may very well be in question. It is a long time since the statement was first made that poetry is more philosophical than history; the example of Hardy provides another instance of how useful and how illuminating the doctrine is. The minute particulars of Hardy's experience might have made a diary, history, or biography; what made them poetry was the functioning of Hardy's beliefs. The function of belief was to generalize his experience into something neither merely particular, which is the historian's concern; nor merely general, which is the philosopher's; but into symbols which possess the qualitative richness, as Mr. Ransom might say, of any particular thing and yet have that generality which makes them significant beyond their moment of existence, or the passing context in which they are located. And here again an examination of a particular poem will make the discussion specific:

A Drizzling Easter Morning

And he is risen? Well, be it so. . . .
And still the pensive lands complain,
And dead men wait as long ago,
As if, much doubting, they would know
What they are ransomed from, before
They pass again their sheltering door.

I stand amid them in the rain,
While blusters vex the yew and vane;
And on the road the weary wain
Plods forward, laden heavily;
And toilers with their aches are fain
For endless rest—though risen is he.

It is the belief and disbelief in Christ's resurrection which not only make this poem possible, but make its details so moving. They are not only moving; the weary wain which plods forward heavily and the dead men in the graveyard are envisaged fully as particular things and yet become significant of the whole experience of suffering and evil just because the belief exists for Hardy and provides a light which makes these particular things symbols. *Without the belief, it is only another rainy morning in March or April.* In passing, it should be noted that both belief and disbelief are necessary; the belief is necessary to the disbelief. And both are responsible here as elsewhere for that quality of language which is Hardy's greatest strength. The mere use of such words as *men, doubting, door, rain,* has a richness of implication, a sense of generations of human experience behind it; this richness is created immediately by the modifying words in the context, *pensive, weary, plod, vex, heavily,* and other workings of the words upon each other; but fundamentally by Hardy's ability to see particulars as significant of Life in general. He would not have had that ability without his beliefs and disbeliefs, though it is true that other poets get that ability by other means and other beliefs.

Once we remember that good poems have been produced by the use of different and contradictory beliefs, we are confronted by the problem of belief in the modern sense.

There are good reasons for supposing that this is not, in itself, a poetic problem. But at any rate, it is true enough that many readers are profoundly disturbed by poems which contain beliefs which they do not accept or beliefs which are in direct contradiction to their own. Hardy's beliefs, as presented explicitly in his poems, offended and still offend his readers in this way.

In turn, the poet is wounded to hear that his poems are not enjoyed because his beliefs are untrue. Throughout his long career, both as poet and as novelist, Hardy was intensely disturbed by criticism on such a basis.

In the "Apology" to *Late Lyrics and Earlier,* Hardy spoke out with the tiredness and anger of an author who has suffered from reviewers for fifty years. His answer is curious and defective, however. He points out that the case against him is "neatly summarized in a stern pronouncement . . . 'This view of life is not mine.' " But instead of defending himself by pointing to all the great poetry which would be eliminated if it were judged merely on the basis of its agreement with the reader's beliefs, Hardy concedes the basic issue to his critics by claiming that his beliefs are better than they have been painted. He defends himself by saying that he is not a pessimist, but "an evolutionary meliorist." No one but another evolutionary meliorist could be persuaded by this kind of argument.

On another occasion, in the introduction to *The Dynasts,* Hardy attempts to solve the problem by requiring Coleridge's temporary "suspension of disbelief which constitutes poetic faith." But this formula would seem to provide for no more than the convention of theatrical or fictive illusion. When the curtain rises, we must suspend disbelief as to whether we see before us Elsinore, a platform before the castle. If we do not, then there can be no play. The case seems more difficult, at least on the surface, when we are asked to accept alien beliefs.

Now there are two ways in which we tend to handle alien beliefs. One of them is to reject those poems which contain beliefs we regard as false. This is an example of judging poetry in terms of its subject, considered in abstraction; and the difficulties are obviously numerous. For one thing, as has been said, we would have to reject most great poetry. Certainly we would have to do without Homer, and without Dante or Shakespeare.

The other alternative, which is in any case preferable to the first, is to judge poetry wholly in terms of its formal character. But this is an act of unjustifiable abstraction also. For it is evident that we enjoy more in a poem, or at least the poem presents more to us, than a refined use of language.

What we need, and what we actually have, I think, is a criterion for the beliefs in a poem which is genuinely a poetic criterion. In reading Hardy when he is successful, in **"A Drizzling Easter Morning,"** we find that the belief and disbelief operate upon the particular *datum* of the poem to give it a metaphorical significance it would not otherwise have. To repeat, without both belief and disbelief it is only another rainy morning in the spring. Conversely, in **"The Masked Face,"** the asserted belief, instead of generalizing the particulars of the poem, merely interferes with them and fails to give them the significance they are intended to have.

In both instances, we are faced with a relationship between the belief in the poem and its other particulars. This is a relationship *internal* to the poem, so to speak. It is not a question of the relationship of the poet's beliefs to the reader's. In **"The Masked Face,"** for example, the inadequacy proceeds from the relationship between the belief that Life is beyond human understanding, and the goose-quill pen which is required to represent the human mind.

It might be objected that this internal relationship between the belief and the rest of the poem is in turn good, or not good, in terms of what the given reader himself believes. Thus it might seem that for a reader who shares Hardy's beliefs, the goose-quill pen was an adequate figure for the human mind. Actually this cannot be so, unless the reader is not interested in poetry but merely in hearing his beliefs stated. If the reader is interested in poetry, the poem itself cannot give him the poetic experience of Life as beyond human understanding, which is its intention. The details of the poem, as presented in the context which the belief and the versification provide, do not do the work in the reader's mind which is done by such an element in **"A Drizzling Easter Morning,"** as the weary wain, which plods forward, laden heavily. And one reason why they lack that energy is their relationship, within the poem, to the belief the poem asserts. Whether or not the reader shares Hardy's beliefs, even if he shares them completely, the goose-quill pen is an inadequate figure for what it is intended to signify in the context. The belief in the poem fails to make it adequate, and this is a poetic failure, just as, in **"The Oxen,"** the kneeling animals are a poetic success because of the disbelief, whether the reader himself disbelieves in Christianity or not.

And again, it might be objected that only valid beliefs, in the end, can operate successfully upon the other elements of any poem. Once more we must refer back first to the fact that poets have written good poetry based upon opposed beliefs, and then to the point made at the start, that there is a basic way in which beliefs have much to do with the whole character of a poet's sensibility, with what he sees and does not see. The subject of poetry is experience, not truth—even when the poet is writing about ideas. When the poet can get the whole experience of his sensibility into his poem, then there will be an adequate relationship between the details of his poem and the beliefs he asserts, whether they are true or not. For then he is getting the actuality of his experience into his poem, and it does not matter whether that actuality is illusory or not; just as the earth may be seen as flat. The functioning of his sensibility guarantees his asserted beliefs; it guarantees them as aspects of experience, though not as statements of truth. The philosophical poet, as well as any other kind, must meet this test. The details of his poem are neither dramatic, nor lyrical, but there is the same question of the relationship between his asserted ideas and the language, tone, attitude, and figures which constitute the rest of the poem.

At any rate, by adopting this point of view, we avoid the two extremes, the two kinds of abstraction, which violate the poem as a concrete whole. And it is especially necessary to do this in Hardy's case, for it is unlikely that many readers will hold Hardy's beliefs as he held them. In the future we are likely to believe less or more; but we will not be in the same kind of intellectual situation as Hardy was.

The important thing is to keep Hardy's poetry, to keep as much of it as we can, and to enjoy it for what it is in its utmost concreteness. And if this is to be accomplished, it is necessary that we keep Hardy's beliefs *in* his poetry, and our own beliefs outside. (pp. 334-45)

> *Delmore Schwartz, "Poetry and Belief in Thomas Hardy," in* Critiques and Essays in Criticism, *1920-1948,* Representing the Achievement of Modern British and American Critics, *edited by Robert Wooster Stallman, The Ronald Press Company, 1949, pp. 334-45.*

So far as it is possible to be a poet without having a singing voice, Hardy is a poet, and a profoundly interesting one.

—*Arthur Symons, "Thomas Hardy," in* The Dial, *January, 1920.*

Michael Alexander   (essay date 1977)

[*Alexander is an English educator, critic, and translator of Old English literature. In the following essay, he examines Hardy's importance in the context of modern English poetry.*]

Prose was his trade, poetry his art, and yet, after fifty years, critics are still showing us along the beaten track to the monuments of trade. Our attention is drawn to major novels such as *Jude the Obscure* and to influences on Hardy's thought, while the bulk of his poetry remains unread and its worth unestimated. Poets have neglected him less, and the New Oxford Books of English and of Twentieth Century English Verse give him greatly enlarged room. Yet while his name is held in affectionate respect, it does not raise the critical wind that has blown those of Yeats and Eliot into modern esteem. Notwithstanding his late *floruit* as a poet (*Poems of 1912-13* is contemporary with Yeats's *Responsibilities* and Pound's *Lustra*) Hardy remains one of the Old rather than the Modern Masters.

A memorial essay might aspire to be modest and minute, and could in any case scarcely affect the cultural predispositions that lead to Hardy's popular fiction being better known to critics than his poetry. Yet a few commonplaces and some blunt assertions may indicate starting-points for the sorting-out and critical estimate that wait to be undertaken. . . .

1. Hardy thought of himself as a poet rather than a novelist. Victorian England produced better novelists, but the superiority of another English poet flourishing between 1837 and 1978 would have to be argued.

2. His position as the last great English poet seems unlikely to be threatened by Ted Hughes.

3. Whatever the insufficiencies of Hardy's ideas of God, of probability and of baronets, his verse makes him a dangerous subject for the kinds of patronage once extended to him as a poor provincial, for example by James, Eliot and even Leavis.

4. The selections in anthologies, though they have recently improved, do no kind of justice to his one thousand poems. Though the collected editions are often muddling, the widespread rumour that most of Hardy's poems are bad cannot survive any sort of a careful reading.

5. Hardy was not a philosopher. He does not seem even to have convinced many people that he was, as he claimed to be, a 'meliorist'. His ideas about 'the President of the Immortals' and the 'purblind Doomsters' are not what make him an interesting writer.

6. Hardy was a countryman and a nature poet, and he was born and died in the same parish. Yet he spent a surprising amount of time in London. He had a good schooling, which he improved on, read several languages, travelled, and was something of an antiquarian. He was proficient in music, draughtsmanship and architecture. Though he warbled native woodnotes, he had early learned from William Barnes to do so to Persian and other tunes. He was deeply versed in English poetry. Apart from his well-recorded knowledge of the classics, the Bible and Shakespeare, he was from his first writings deeply indebted to the literature of country life in Wordsworth, and even Gray, as well as Shakespeare. Though partly self-taught, he was in no way a yokel or a naïve genius.

Though this last point may be accepted—and there is no space here to argue the others—it does not banish the image of Hardy as the gloatingly malign rustic pessimist—a distorted image, for which the distortion of his writing career is in part responsible. The circumstances of this career are well enough known, though the following account of it may be less familiar, and I quote it, for, despite its ripeness of manner, it has the right emphases. It comes in Ford Madox Ford's *The March of Literature;* he is engaged in a contrast of Hardy with Whitman.

> As an interpreter of our modern day whose motto really is the French peasant's 'La vie, voyez vous, n'est jamais si bonne ni mauvaise que l'on ne croit', Whitman has to stand down before Hardy. Hardy, in fact, was the ideal poet of a generation. He was the most passionate and the most learned of them all. He had the luck, singular in poets, of being able to achieve a competence other than by poetry and then to devote the ending years of his life to his beloved verses. All the while he was making a living and then a competence sufficient to keep him during the closing years of his life, he was, on the side, practising verse-writing, learning the prosodies of every nation that had ever had a prosody. He disliked novel-writing but he made a small fortune by it.
>
> It takes a man with a determination like that to make a great poet. If he has to use that grim de-

termination first to another end, when he is at last released he will write a *Dynasts.*

The novelist's view of Hardy's career is shrewd, and I find a corrective value in the emphases on passion, learning, determination and release. Before the 'release' from prose, Hardy had already stepped out of the shade of the Greenwood Tree, having booby-trapped the Wessex of the endpaper maps with the corpses of Tess and Jude. Wessexlovers caught sight of a sardonic expression on the mild features, and wondered, with Gosse, what Providence had done to Mr Hardy that he should rise up in the arable land of Wessex and shake his fist at his Creator. This Tolpuddle curmudgeon is not, of course, Thomas Hardy, but the image has stuck. The public could not have expected that a poet should emerge from this septuagenarian chrysalis, especially after *The Dynasts,* nor were his achievements much remarked. Other axes were being noisily ground, and after the war Hardy was a Grand Old Man. His last visit to London was in 1925 (for Harold Macmillan's wedding), by which time modern poetry had usurped the throne.

Yet Providence had played a part in Hardy's career. The publisher's readers to whom *Desperate Remedies* was sent were John Morley and George Meredith; and Alexander Macmillan's letter to Hardy in 1870, though it recommended a cosier tone to the aspiring novelist, is a reminder of nobler days. The timing of Hardy's second début, as poet, was less auspicious; in 1912, according to Ezra Pound, nobody paid any attention to Hardy's verse. In 1908 Ford had founded the *English Review,* in order, as he quixotically claimed, to print a poem which Hardy could not get published anywhere in England. The *English Review* marvellously united the old and the new writers in a way that was soon to become impossible; it is important on the present occasion to recognise that Hardy also united the old and the new. His presence has haunted almost all subsequent English poets, and it can now be seen that the modern English poetic tradition flowed, or oozed wistlessly, through him.

This may seem improbable. In 'An Ancient to Ancients' Hardy wrote:

> The bower we shrined to Tennyson, Gentlemen,
> Is root-wrecked, damps there drip upon
> Sagged seats, the creeper-nails are rust,
> The spider is sole denizen.

The rhyme alone might seem to disqualify him from being a hander-on of anything, yet Pound, for example, a blithe bower-wrecker, had the deepest respect for Hardy and expressed it throughout his career. His retrospect of 1964 is particularly apposite; I reproduce a few of his dicta: 'No man ever had so much Latin and so eschewed the least appearance of being a classicist on the surface.' 'Contemporary for a long time with Browning on whom he improves at his, Hardy's, best, taking over the marrow of the tradition . . . ' 'No one trying to learn writing in regular, formed verse can learn better than in observing what Thomas Hardy accepted from Browning and what he pruned away from his more busteous or rambunctious predecessor.' 'Nobody, on occasion, ever used rhyme with less insult to statement. . . . ' 'The poems of 1912-13 lift

him to his apex, sixteen poems from **"The Going"** to **"Castle Boterel"**, all good, and enough for a lifetime. **"The Waterfall"** is the lead-up, at the end of the volume just precedent.' Thinking about Hardy's comment on his own *Homage to Sextus Propertius,* Pound is struck by 'the degree in which Hardy would have had his mind on the SUBJECT MATTER, and how little he cared about manner, which does not in the least mean that he did not care about it or had not a definite aim.'

The remarks on Latin, metre, rhyme, on Browning and subject-matter, are not, from Pound, surprising. More notable here are the stresses on 'the tradition' and on the *Poems of 1912-13.* I suggest later in this essay that Hardy, countrified rhymester though he may have seemed through Vorticist spectacles, conformed before it was articulated to Pound's demand for 'direct treatment of the object'—the 'natural object' which, in Pound's view, was 'the proper and perfect symbol'.

I also find it helpful to see Hardy as carrying on not only the dramatic tradition of Browning, but the main lyric tradition of the expression of personal emotion, within which Browning is a variant, as well as the deeper pastoral bias in English poetry going back beyond Wordsworth. Or, as Ford put it, concluding his comparison with Whitman in his most Corinthian manner for the benefit of his American audience:

> He had a peasant intelligence; so he was wise. He resembled the root of a four-hundred-year-old tree; he resembled a moss-covered rock that has lain for four hundred years in a forest. So he knew that destiny attends on chance since chance is always characteristic of the circumstances in which it takes part. Beside him, Whitman was an hysteriac. He was not wise. The essential townsman can never be wise because he cannot see life for the buildings. Whitman saw factories rise and was excited over the future of the race. Hardy saw factories smudge his rural scene, and was merely depressed. He knew that the human heart remained the essential stamping ground of the poet.

If T. S. Eliot had a stamping ground it may indeed have been the human heart, but he made it known that he did not stamp there personally. He had, in an extreme form, the reserve that made Hardy say, in the preface to *Wessex Poems:* 'the pieces are in a large degree dramatic and personative in conception: and this even where they are not obviously so.' Yet Eliot recoiled from the directness with which Hardy dealt with 'personative' emotional situations that were also transparently personal. In the wake of Eliot's impersonal strategy for poetry, with its associated irony, ambiguity and symbolic complexity, modern critics have found little to say about poetry which is not complex in this way. As Pound noted, 'When a writer's matter is stated with such entirety and with such clarity there is no place left for the explaining critic.' The 'matter' Hardy 'states' is not primarily English country life—the background of his novels and earlier verse—but the emotional realities of individual lives.

Considering the expression of powerful feeling in poetry, one cannot evade Wordsworth, though in their reforming criticism Eliot and Pound treat his name as taboo. It is interesting, then, to find Pound reproducing, from Hardy's Prefatory Apology to *Late Lyrics and Earlier* (1922), the passage from Wordsworth's Preface rebutting the supposition 'that by the act of writing in verse an author makes a formal engagement that he will gratify certain known habits of association: that he not only thus apprises the reader that certain classes of ideas and expressions will be found in his book, but that others will be carefully excluded." Hardy's Apology also invokes the phrases 'obstinate questionings' and 'blank misgivings', taking it for granted that the reader will know their source in the Immortality Ode. He later calls on Wordsworth a third time. Indeed, the inclusion of unwonted 'ideas and expressions' in his verse is only one aspect of Hardy's allegiance to Wordsworth. If Crabbe invented peasant tragedy, Wordsworth ennobled it, and Hardy chose it as his first stamping ground. The endurance of elemental feeling in 'natural' lives is the presupposition of all his work: Gabriel Oak, as both his names suggest, is a matinée version of Wordsworth's Michael. Hardy says that in his youth Wordsworth was the norm of poetry, and indeed his first poem, **'Domicilium'**, is steeped in Wordsworth, both in its verse and its feeling. The machinery and melodrama of Hardy's tales, though like *Michael* they are related 'For the delight of a few natural hearts', weakens them; but the best of his poems are worthy of his allegiance. The *Poems of 1912-13* are in the tradition created by the Lucy poems, particularly **'A slumber did my spirit seal'**. The personal loss is less concealed, more narrowly autobiographical, but the poet's personal experience is raised into a representative myth—which is the essence of Wordsworth's development of the English poetic tradition. Again, the source of Hardy's imagery is predominantly 'the natural object', or complex of natural objects, to which Wordsworth ultimately returns, as in the celebrated passage on the restoration of the imagination in Book XIII of the *Prelude*:

> The single sheep and the one blasted tree,
> And the bleak music from that old stone wall.

To be sure, one does not imagine Hardy, on his bicycle, 'grasping at a wall or a tree to recall himself from the abyss of idealism to the reality', or not so frequently as Wordsworth; for all his ghosts and his moments of vision, he has a more literal eye—and a more exactly specific turn of phrase. For Hardy the milk 'purrs into the pail', the morning 'hardens against the wall'—one is aware that these are impinging on the privacy of a highly idiosyncratic consciousness, that it is a Thomas Hardy who records this. But his poetry, like Wordsworth's, moves from observation and description to a more generally symbolic presentation. The relative ease and informality both of Hardy's natural observation, and of the ways in which he invests it with significance, are due in part to the speeding-up of expressive conventions established by Wordsworth.

'An August Midnight' may furnish some evidence to test these large suggestions:

I

A shaded lamp and a waving blind,
And the beat of a clock from a distant floor:

On this scene enter—winged, horned, and
      spined—
A longlegs, a moth, and a dumbledore;
While 'mid my page there idly stands
A sleepy fly, that rubs its hands. . . .

II

Thus meet we five, in this still place,
At this point of time, at this point in space.
—My guests besmear my new-penned line,
Or bang at the lamp and fall supine.
'God's humblest, they!' I muse. Yet why?
They know Earth-secrets that know not I.

The observation here is more casual, minute, even trivial, than Wordsworth's, and might at first seem not far from Yeats's parody of a modern poem: 'I am sitting in a chair, there are three dead flies on a corner of the ceiling.' Yet its particularity does not reflect a vacancy. There is a dramatic novelist's skill in the scene-setting; then the distracted eye focuses on to the hands of this unlikely Hamlet; and the mind floats out to consider time and space. The musing that follows might strike an unaccustomed reader as overcondensed, or a blasé reader as sententious and even morbid. Yet Hardy believed that 'unadjusted impressions have their value', and the musing has dramatic congruity. It may be that the moral (an intimation of mortality) is not quite adequate to all the alarms set off by 'At this point of time, at this point in space'. Even this inadequacy may be seen as Wordsworthian. More clearly in the tradition of Wordsworth is the diapason from tiny and transient to mortal and cosmic—as with the violet and the star in **'She dwelt among untrodden ways'**—and, again, the way the tables are turned on the writer, his realisation that his initial reading is quite outflanked by a bleaker natural reality. There are many differences—no immortality here—and this is a slight piece, but the ancestry of the mode of the poem is not in doubt. Hardy's particularity and queerness do not make the pattern of the poem, the way it develops its symbolic extension, different in kind from the Wordsworthian model.

Tributary influences on Hardy's tradition are the dramatic, from Browning, and the narrative, and these complicate the inheritance. Eliot's charge that Hardy is self-absorbed (again, not unlike Wordsworth) overlooks the detachment with which Hardy notes events that impinge on his consciousness; it also neglects his 'personative' ability—seen in 'we five'—to enter into the viewpoint of persons, animals and natural forces at points in time and space very different from his own. Several early poems are called **'She, to Him'**, **'He, to Her'**; others take the different corners of emotional triangles, or tell more tangled tales. This develops later into an ability to dramatise and embody his own predicaments, and also to give them a narrative rather than a merely expressive interest. In *Poems of 1912-13* Hardy presents himself as a character in a drama, almost like an Elizabethan. This set of poems is the easiest extended text to take from the poems as they are arranged at the moment; and one of the most important of them, **'After a Journey'**, may serve as a familiar example to try out some of these suggestions.

The death of his first wife, Emma Lavinia, took place on 27 November 1912, at which point in Hardy's notebook we find: 'Sent £20 to the Pension Fund, Society of Authors, making £25 in all.' We know that the marriage had not turned out happily—'Summer gave us sweets, but autumn wrought division'—and that Emma's death revived with astonishing force the ardour of Hardy's early love. The 1912-13 poems (and many others on the same subject) are poems of love as well as loss. The epigraph, *veteris vestigia flammae,* is a well-known tag from the opening of the fourth book of the *Aeneid,* yet poignantly apt. The widowed Dido recognises the traces of the long-quenched flame of passion now rekindled by the sight and story of Aeneas. The bereaved Hardy is likewise consumed by the painful memories aroused by all the vestiges of Emma—memories of disappointment mixed with guilt, which he seeks to appease by retracing his *footsteps* ('Down the years, down the dead scenes I have tracked you') to the scenes of their courtship in Cornwall in March 1870. 'After a Journey' begins 'Hereto I come to view a voiceless ghost'—a ghost which appears in several of the poems, and not unlike the ghost of Dido encountered by Aeneas in Hades.

This journey back to 'Lyonnesse' is inscribed in the memorable landscape of the early romance, *A Pair of Blue Eyes* (1873), Hardy's later preface to the book, dated March 1895, ends:

> The place is pre-eminently (for one person at least) the region of dream and mystery. The ghostly birds, the pall-like sea, the frothy wind, the eternal soliloquy of the waters, the bloom of dark purple cast, that seems to exhale from the shoreward precipices, in themselves lend to the scene an atmosphere like the twilight of a night vision.

> One enormous sea-bord cliff in particular figures in the narrative; and for some forgotten reason or other this cliff was described in the story as being without a name. Accuracy would require the statement to be that a remarkable cliff which resembles in many points the cliff of the description bears a name that no event has made famous.

This is Beeny Cliff, revisited in March 1913, as the poem of that title relates, and the scene also of 'After a Journey' and 'At Castle Boterel'. Hardy had earlier written 'The shore and country about Castle Boterel . . . is the furthest westward of all those convenient corners wherein I have ventured to erect my theatre for these imperfect little dramas of country life and passions.' Like some of his less imperfect ones, *A Pair of Blue Eyes* contains great scenes, in one of which Hardy contrives that Knight, an amateur geologist, hanging by his fingernails from the top of Beeny Cliff, should find himself face to face with the fossil of a Trilobite; whereupon 'Time closed up like a fan before him. He saw himself at one extremity of the years, face to face with the beginning and all the intermediate centuries simultaneously.'

Again and again in *Poems of 1912-13* Time closes up like a fan, though by means of conjunctions and coincidences less contrived than in the romances and most of the novels. Hardy's little dramas move from scene to scene, and in the romances the links between them are perfunctory,

for the scenes exist to set up the 'moments of vision' that they embody; these moments of vision are remarkable for their subjective intensity, their feeling of fatality, not for their circumstantial probability or objective necessity. Thus at the beginning of *Two on a Tower* there is a chance fatality about Lady Constantine's wish to visit the tower; or of Elfride's wish to walk around the top of another tower in *A Pair of Blue Eyes;* or about Gabriel Oak's presence at the haystack fire. In later novels the concatenation is riveted more carefully, so that Tess's choice, led up to by a series of forced choices, determines the rest of her life. These fatal conjunctions are hung, sometimes unhappily, on a temporal sequence; and the more characters, the more obvious the scaffolding of chance.

In poetry Hardy could dispense with the temporal sequence and the furniture of novels and still have the concentrated character-revelations at moments of crisis, for the sake of which his narratives were constructed. Hence the superiority of the poetry: the novels crank themselves up to dramatic situations whereas the poems grow out of them. The dramatic or personative poems can begin in the middle of the meeting and work outwards, backwards or forwards in time. Hardy's eye for place and scene allows him to create firmly and economically the background which produces the unique moment. In the novels, the firmness of the scene-setting often contrasts strangely with the shakiness of the plot-machinery. In Hardy the presence and energy of places—'interlune' on Egdon Heath, for example—can convincingly determine the action of persons. This energy between places and persons is generated in a neater and more controlled form in the poems, as in 'An August Midnight'; in his own experience and under the stress of his own emotions, Hardy had no need to manufacture artificially dramatic situations. The sleepy fly appears more naturally than the Trilobite.

Theatre conventions, however, remain useful to Hardy in his later poetry. 'After a Journey', for example, can be described in theatrical terms: 'Enter poet, advance stage front, addresses audience, turns to wife's ghost, addresses it indirectly, questions it directly.' Stanza two contains her imagined reply. There are also stage-directions: 'up and down', 'facing round about me everywhere', 'leading me on', 'I now frailly follow', 'here' and 'here'. Time and place appear very naturally and vividly, and the poem owes much of its immediacy and authenticity to the practised ease with which Hardy deploys these conventions, themselves as old as the Shakespearian soliloquy—'Is this a dagger that I see before me', for example, contains all necessary indications of gesture and movement. Equally stage-hallowed is the convention that the voiceless ghost, besought to speak, shows the courting place, and must disappear before dawn. The apostrophes and rhetorical questions, the 'answers' and the final protestation are likewise traditional, even stagy, but appear natural. Such conventions articulate and dramatise what would otherwise be mere autobiographical utterance, and we eavesdrop on Hardy's colloquy with his dead wife without feeling its improbability.

This self-dramatisation—'Yes: I have re-entered your old haunts at last'—is rescued from melodrama by the specific way in which the night landscape and its visitor are realised, both in its actual detail and in his idiosyncratic perception of it; thus 'soliloquies' was revised to 'ejaculations', 'viewed' to 'scanned'. Equally precise and peculiar to Hardy's eye and locution are 'nut-coloured hair', 'there's no knowing', 'wherein' and the extraordinary

> Ignorant of what there is flitting here to see,
> The waked birds preen and the seals flop lazily.

The credible, authentic and particular coexist in the poem, however, with the general, the eloquent, the Shakespearian, as in 'Time's derision', 'Life lours' and, especially, her imagined words and his closing declaration. Here we touch the critical problem of Hardy's diction and style, never adequately described. Too much has been made of his oddness or inelegance, not enough of his strength and eloquence. Much of his language is idiomatic everyday speech: 'the spots we knew', 'the cave just under', 'I am just the same'. Yet he easily and unselfconsciously uses the traditional language of poetry: 'olden haunts', 'twain', 'Time', and, quaintly, 'the stars close their shutters'. Both ordinary and poetic speech are used firmly, even roughly, unaesthetically, and what is literary in his style is old, absorbed, time-honoured. Not that Hardy lacks finesse—*haunted* in line 18 is perfectly calculated—but he deliberately avoided the appearance of finish, he concealed his art; his wood needed no veneer. Not that Hardy is a *plain* writer: he certainly works nearer the staple of English than, say, Hopkins, but on the other hand he is capable of the (entirely successful) grand rhetoric of **'Beeny Cliff'**.

The genuineness of the feeling in **'After a Journey',** the lack of sentimentality even in his gallant final sentiment, has made it admired, and this must be due to its solidity and simplicity: it unfolds from a single impulse. We are moved partly because we are so clearly and specifically presented with what it is that we are to be moved by; and we believe in Hardy as a character and in the reality of his world. Given the eloquence to which he can rise, as at the end, this may seem enough. It could be argued, however, that this is successful dramatisation of an essentially private emotion—a remarkable achievement but still a limited, individual one. Such I take it is Eliot's objection, recently raised again by Donald Davie.

I believe that, within his realistic mode of presentation, Hardy successfully invests his experience with wider meaning. Where he strives to provide symbols for the larger entities who have to stand in for an absent God, as in **The Dynasts** and other cosmic fables, he is normally not successful, and I am surprised to see anthologists preferring such poems. Apart from Father Time in **Jude,** he does not characteristically go in for symbols in the way of Ibsen or Lawrence: if Egdon Heath, or the Shearing Barn, or, say, the Darkling Thrush are symbols, they are simple, innocent and effective. He does not essay the more refined, flexible and enigmatic symbolism of Chekhov. Indeed, he is not a conscious symbolist at all: it is more his way to begin with the local, actual and particular and to arrange them so as to bring out a natural meaning and significance which can, however, achieve a much more universal resonance than is suggested by dwelling on his idiosyncratic language and observant eye. Less of an idealist and more

of a sceptic than Wordsworth, his secularised religious feeling finds its way back into awe at the universe and its inhabitants.

This feeling for the presences in Man, in Nature and in Human Life, far more than the avowed pessimism, meliorism, Darwinism or determinism which war with it, is Hardy's underlying religion; and it is for this that he is read—an unofficial trust in the imagination, which, alongside his realistic bleakness, reaffirms his inheritance from Wordsworth. For all his conscientious clutches at positivism, he at last remained mercifully unconfined by the advanced ideas of his day.

This awe or unofficial imagination gives his realism the resonance to raise it beyond the interest attaching to an individual's 'unadjusted impressions' of three dead flies on a corner of the ceiling. Though Hardy consciously renounces the vague glamour and consolations of ideal and symbolic systems, his sensibility is permeated by them. The empirical modern English poet, his successor, has likewise forsworn the heroic imaginative codes of Yeats and Eliot, but cannot do without them. Again, Pound's precepts for modern poetry, where they are not merely technical, are realist and even positivist in their assumptions: but he too remained a transcendentalist at heart.

The third stanza of **'After a Journey'** may serve as example of what Wordsworth calls a fair train of imagery. The waterfall, the mist-bow, the cave and the voice all seem to me exactly the kind of natural symbols that Pound asked for, though more solid and traditional than his own early choices. All, apart from the 'voice', are actual phenomena. All, like the word 'haunted', possess a latent symbolic suggestion, not forced upon us but activated by the context. The waterfall may suggest beauty, passion and transience, the mist-bow a hope with some fragility, the cave oracular prophecy. Yet each remains itself and does not become an emblem.

The association of ambiguous oracular prophecy with the cave might seem too classical to be likely in Hardy, were it not that the 'voice' is 'hollow' and its echoes are redoubled in 'ago', 'aglow', and 'follow'. A mist-bow is not a rainbow, and may likewise seem a natural phenomenon here, without a literary or a classical association. But, in the closely related **'Beeny Cliff'**, we find that over the lovers 'there flew an *irised* rain'. It may be that as, for Hardy, life and love flattered only to deceive, rainbows should suggest to him delusive hope. (It may even be in his mind that at the end of *Aeneid* IV it is Iris who cuts the thread of Dido's life in which case an analogy with Aeneas and Dido might be conscious, and the cave would also suggest love, sin and betrayal.) The waterfall is, clearly, just a waterfall; any suggestions of beauty and transience are entirely natural. The poem Pound picked out, **'Under the Waterfall'**, makes it explicit that for Hardy this waterfall directly symbolised the high romance of his courtship. This ingenuously symbolic poem, which is partly in doggerel, tells us that the waterfall was 'About three spans wide and two spans tall', which may or may not be a sincere form of flattery, but certainly shows a Wordsworthian baldness of style and acceptance of 'the natural object'. It begins:

Hardy's first wife, Emma Lavinia Gifford, 1870.

Whenever I plunge my arm, like this,
In a basin of water, . . .

So the waterfall, mist-bow and cave provided a magic and a secluded place for the lovers' picnic forty years before, and now, in the haunted night, form a complex symbol both of promise and of hollowness. But the 'then fair hour' and the 'hollow' voice are the only pointers to remoter symbolic associations of mist-bows or voices from caves, and the success of the stanza does not depend on such recognitions. Hardy's symbolism, then, is latent, unassertive, optional. His urgent juxtaposition of the fairness of 'then' and the frailty of 'now', and his success at conveying what in **'Places'** he calls the 'beneaped and stale' quality of quotidian experience, exemplified here in the heavy ignorance of the flopping seals, indicates that he conversely wished to invest the 'then fair hour' with all the symbolic radiance and splendour of Wordsworth's Immortality Ode.

'Afterwards' is often anthologised, and its imagery provides a final example of Hardy's modulation of natural description into symbolic suggestion. In it Hardy wonders whether after he is dead the sight of natural things will recall him to the minds of those who knew him. Many poems bear witness to his concern that the dead are soon quite forgotten—the second death, he calls it—and he was a great frequenter of churchyards. The English have traditionally domesticated the classical preoccupation with immortality and fame in their country churchyards; Gray's *Elegy* supplied Hardy with much more than the title of *Far from the Madding Crowd*. Hardy once said that it

would have been possible for Wordsworth to see him in his cradle, as for Thomas Gray to have seen Wordsworth in his. This choice of fairy godfathers is revealing, as, ever since Wordsworth disliked Gray's poetic diction, we are used to connecting the artificial *Elegy* with *Lycidas* or *The Scholar Gypsy,* and a natural poem like **'Afterwards'** with Wordsworth. But Hardy, like Gray, was interested in fame and obscurity as well as in graves.

I have long thought that the *Elegy* may have contributed to **'Afterwards'**, especially from the quatrains that so moved Johnson ('For who to dumb forgetfulness a prey') to the end. Particularly apposite to the query repeated in the refrain of **'Afterwards'** is Gray's imagined interview between 'some kindred spirit' and 'some hoary-headed swain':

> For thee who, mindful of the unhonoured dead,
> Dost in these lines their artless tale relate;
> If chance, by lonely Contemplation led,
> Some kindred spirit shall inquire thy fate,
>
> Haply some hoary-headed swain may say,
> 'Oft have we seen him at the peep of dawn
> Brushing with hasty steps the dews away
> To meet the sun upon the upland lawn. . . . '

The conventional pastoral scenes where the swain missed the youth are quite different in purpose from Hardy's realistic vignettes, but their pattern is similar, and one or two details have tiny echoes—'customed'/'customary'; 'upland lawn'/'upland thorn'. The epitaph which Gray sympathetically provides for himself contains the lines:

> Fair Science frowned not on his humble birth
> And Melancholy marked him for her own.

They eminently apply to the creator of *Jude the Obscure.*

Each stanza of **'Afterwards'** asks the same question in a slightly different way, and the poem deepens as the relation of refrain to stanza develops. The elaborate fine image of the first stanza is flattened by the mundane tone of 'Will the neighbours say . . . '. This ordinariness, found again in 'must have been a familiar sight' and the slight bathos of the hedgehog stanza, is eventually purged by the power of the images, and the 'unadjusted' refrains lose their apparent clumsiness. This strain between the mundane and the transcendent is a calculated effect.

Consideration of the imagery discloses the changing backgrounds of a day in May, a summer dusk, a dark summer night, a clear winter night, and, finally, an unspecified gloom. The leading image of each stanza is, in turn, a butterfly, a hawk, a hedgehog, stars, the bell. The processes of a parish, a countryside and a whole year seem to be brought in to the poem. Hardy's mild hope that he will be remembered as a man who used to notice such things fades under the inclusiveness of this revolving cycle of life and death: the butterfly and hedgehog are prey to the larger agencies of the hawk, the bell and the stars, and we are kindred to them. This kinship is suggested by subtle relationships in the imagery: the arrival of the ephemeral wings and leaves of May hints also at the tremulous departure of the soul from its chrysalis; the ominous hawk 'crosses the shades'; the hedgehog's transit is mortal, the neighbours 'stand at the door' to say farewell, but also to leave; their thoughts 'rise' on them as the stars rise into the sky. Everything in the world of the poem is intrinsicate.

The last stanza, particularly the line 'Till they rise again, as they were a new bell's boom', raises in acute form the possibility that the imagery of the poem, so far from being leaves from a country-lover's notebook, has a consistent symbolic dimension involving metaphors of a sort not to be expected from a naturalist, still less an atheist. Mythical and classical literature provide many associations for the figures Hardy employs in the poem: if the hawk and the hedgehog suggest a Darwinian mortality, the butterfly, the stars and the bell suggest, repsectively, the immortality of the soul, stellification and resurrection. There are suggestions that death is final ('he is gone', 'he hears it not now'); that it is a change of form ('stilled'); and even that it is the prelude to immortality (stanzas I and 5). The pragmatic neighbours of stanza I fade away, via 'a gazer', 'one' and 'those', to 'any', whereas the *things* remain, and the certainty of 'he hears it not now' hangs rather thinly in the air. Agnostic and sceptical though it is, **'Afterwards'** is not good evidence that Hardy believed that there was no afterlife. The impotence prosaically expressed in stanza 3 is followed by the exaltation of stanza 4 and the enigmatic hints of stanza 5. The irony of the last line includes the neighbours, just as in the last line of **'The Darkling Thrush'** it includes the poet.

Over the page from **'Afterwards'** is the Apology, where Hardy rebuts the attribution to him of 'a view of life', claiming that the 'said "view" ' was really 'a series of fugitive impressions which I have never tried to coordinate.' With one or two exceptions, this seems to me quite fair, certainly as a comment on **'Afterwards'**. (It is to be followed later by a complimentary reference to Cardinal Newman.) If, as Davie says, Hardy's example has been so important to recent English poetry, the intellectual and emotional shortcomings of that poetry are not to be found in Hardy, despite his positivism and liberalism, for in his poetry these are subverted by something far more deeply interfused.

I have suggested that Hardy's poetry has a modern as well as a traditional aspect, recognised at the time by Pound. It is clear that he is the last *English* poet that English poets have felt able to look back to with confidence. He has enjoyed the high esteem of such very different poets as Lawrence, Graves, Auden, Betjeman, Davie and Larkin. Many active English poets apart from Larkin have rejected the experimental and intellectual poetry that now seems historically associated with international modernism, and are no happier with the extremism of the confessional, surreal or expressionist schools. Hardy is honest with personal experience, and is the last major English practitioner of autobiographical poetry in a traditional form. His technical skill and restraint are the formal counterparts to the stoicism and reserve with which he treats his emotions. It would be pleasant to be able to record that English reluctance to join the modern movement had been accompanied by an imaginative use of English poetic traditions, or by the practice of those skills of versification

which are perhaps Hardy's most available legacy. (pp. 49-63)

> *Michael Alexander, "Hardy among the Poets," in* Thomas Hardy after Fifty Years, *edited by Lance St. John Butler, Rowman and Littlefield, 1977, pp. 49-63.*

A superior metaphysical validity belongs to Hardy's lyrics and little narratives in that the particularity of their detail is sharp and local.

—John Crowe Ransom, "Honey and Gall," The Southern Review, *1940.*

Vern B. Lentz   (essay date 1987)

[*In the following essay, Lentz explores the function of ghostly or disembodied voices in Hardy's shorter poems.*]

Thomas Hardy was fond of a particular kind of poem: the poem in which the words of authority are spoken by a spirit or ghost. Typically, these poems present a problem, and a spirit or ghost speaks words which offer a solution. By rough count, 46 of Hardy's more than 900 poems employ such a disembodied voice. This seems odd, for Hardy was a rationalist and empiricist who did not rely on the supernatural as an answer to any problem. But there they are: 46 poems in which the words of authority are spoken by a disembodied voice. This seems more like Yeats than the agnostic and Darwinian Hardy. What distinguishes this device in Hardy is not that a spirit simply speaks but that its words are authoritative. When Hardy wanted to give speech a special standing he would, frequently, put that speech in the mouth of a spirit; in a Hardy poem ghosts *know* more than mortal humans. Seldom in Hardy's poetry—there are exceptions—does a disembodied voice speak words that are playful, mistaken, or reflective of merely "personal" limitations. Frequently these voices play a didactic role. When Hardy wanted to offer advice or deliver a message he had a spirit deliver that message; when Hardy felt awkward about intruding a comment he apparently felt it was less awkward to have a spirit speak. In one way, these disembodied voices are similar to a moralizing and intrusive narrator in fiction: they offer generalized commentary from an omniscient position. Despite his fondness for ghosts and spirits in poetry, however, Hardy never uses them in fiction. Perhaps this says something about Hardy's notion of the difference between prose and verse: poetry allowed him to be as imaginative and inventive as he chose; prose fiction bound him to the reality of the empiricists.

The best explanation for this rationalist's use of the supernatural lies in H. L. Weatherby's observation [in *Sewanee Review* (1985)] that there are "two Hardys": the agnostic, alienated modern Hardy and the Hardy of traditional vision. The first Hardy is "the London and Max Gate Hardy" and the second is "the man who walked to Higher Bockhampton every Sunday and listened to his mother's stories." This second Hardy is quite at ease with spirits and ghosts and naturally expects that humans will hear voices from a supernatural source. In this traditional vision the ghostly voices will have more than human authority. Weatherby argues convincingly that "Hardy is John Keble and D. H. Lawrence by turns and never recognizes (or acknowledges) the contradiction: both facets of his character seem to have intensified with age."

Hardy was fascinated by ghosts in yet another way: he liked to imagine himself as a spectre. This manner of regarding himself is seen in a curious passage from his autobiography, *The Life and Works of Thomas Hardy*:

> For my part, if there is any way of getting a melancholy satisfaction out of life it lies in dying, so to speak, before one is out of the flesh; by which I mean putting on the manners of ghosts, wandering in their haunts, and taking their views of surrounding things. To think of life as passing away is a sadness; to think of it as past is at least tolerable. Hence even when I enter into a room to pay a simple morning call I have unconsciously the habit of regarding the scene as if I were a spectre not solid enough to influence my environment; only fit to behold and say, as another spectre said: "Peace be unto you!"

To consider himself in this way gave not only satisfaction but a god-like perspective from which to comment on the affairs of men and women; in his poems Hardy frequently assumes this perspective and speaks with the voice of a spirit when he wishes to make a generalizing remark. And when spectral aloofness was his dominant mood Hardy could remove himself as far from life as it was possible to go: into the voice of a bodiless intelligence.

Hardy's poems contain a mix of distinct voices that Hardy assumed, voices that converse with each other. Hardy is chameleon-like in his assumption of discrete voices, no one of which is the sole voice of "the poet." One of these voices is the disembodied voice of the ghost, or, more accurately, various individual spirits populate the poems and generalize on human affairs. Paul Zietlow and Frederick W. Shilstone have explained with precision and comprehensiveness how separate voices interact, i.e., converse, with each other through the whole of Hardy's canon. [In his *Moments of Vision: The Poetry of Thomas Hardy*] Zietlow elucidates Hardy's aesthetic and indicates that the poems represent an interplay of various voices and recognizes how Hardy's poetic sensibility manifests itself in a variety of identities:

> The poet's commitment, then, is not to a sustained interpretation of life, but to moments of experience and to the accurate recording of them. . . . As the speaker in a poem, his identity is defined by the nature of the impression and its means of conveyance, and may bear little relationship to any "real," historical identity: he writes "dramatic monologues by different characters."

This theory justifies the more playful or fanciful flights of the imagination that often occur in Hardy's poetry. But the theory also sanctions deeply serious modes, because a full response to the unique moment brings the poet's self into temporary focus. For a moment, the poet achieves a clear, fixed identity, crystallized from the surging, contradictory being of his consciousness. . . . At such a moment one becomes a reality—not the totality of what one could be, but a single aspect of that potential . . .

[In "Conversing Stances in Hardy's Shorter Poems," *Colby Library Quarterly* (1976)] Shilstone stresses the way in which these voices talk to each other. His argument is that Hardy became increasingly uncomfortable with the ironic stance to which his fiction had forced him by the time of *Jude the Obscure.* The irony of Hardy's fictional narrators became so sardonic and aloof from human concerns, Shilstone writes, that this narrative voice was devoid of sympathy and compassion, hardened by tragedy into an unfeeling remoteness from life. Such remoteness, and the irony that comes from it, indeed represents one aspect of Hardy's character. Another aspect of Hardy's mind, however, insisted on compassion and what Hardy called "loving-kindness." Hardy's desire to separate himself from life manifested itself in irony; his "loving-kindness" manifested itself in a desire to identify himself with the lives and sufferings of fellow humans. In the poetry Hardy's complex character takes the form of separate voices, the speakers of various poems. Hardy was able to move rapidly away from a too cruel irony in one poem to the voice of a different human character in another poem. The disembodied voices represent except in the *Poems of 1912-13*—the cold and ironic aspect of their creator. But Hardy was not always comfortable with this side of himself and, by placing the irony in the voices of ghosts and spirits, detaches himself from the cruelty of that irony by locating its voice elsewhere. All of these various disembodied voices stand outside the flow of time and natural process and offer ironic comment on mortals who are trapped within "the cell of Time." The irony is a product of the timeless perspective of the spirits on the temporal concerns of humans. Recognizing this, it is important to acknowledge, firstly, that Hardy's irony appears in voices other than disembodied ones, and, secondly, that in the poems Hardy employs other voices than those of the ironist.

A basic principle of Hardy's art was his aesthetics of disjunction. The disjunctions of the poems using a disembodied voice involve the juxtaposition of the voices of the living with the voices of the dead, the physical with the spiritual, and, most importantly, the temporal with the timeless. Hardy was quite willing to distort reality as a means of achieving a poetic effect. The disjunctive mode is one in which distortion or disunity of form is a calculated technique designed to convey a truth about the human condition. In his autobiography Hardy discusses this disjunctive mode at several points. In an entry headed "Reflections on Art" he writes that "Art is a disproportioning—(i.e., distorting, throwing out of proportion)—of realities, to show more clearly the features that matter in those realities." And elsewhere, in discussing "the constructional part" of his writing, he says that "the adjustment of things unusual to things eternal and universal" is "the key to the art." Even at those times when the voices of the living seem to converse most naturally and easily with the voices of the dead Hardy is aware that he brings together two presences which are basically dissimilar. [In his *Craft and Character*] Morton Dawen Zabel noticed these " 'startling touches of weirdness' " in discussing the way in which discordance is central to all of Hardy's poetry and fiction. Hardy was both the modern empiricist and the poet of traditional vision: because of these contradictory facets of his own sensibility it was easy for him to bring together in his verse the living and the spectral to establish an ironic perspective.

Another principle of Hardy's aesthetic underlies his fondness for disembodied voices. In the "Apology" to *Late Lyrics and Earlier* he writes that "the real function of poetry [is] the *application* of ideas to life [in Matthew Arnold's familiar phrase]" (emphasis mine). That Hardy repeats Arnold's rather mechanical term "application" to describe the way in which poetic ideas bear upon life is significant. In this formulation "ideas" come from the world of the spirits and are "applied" to "life"—the world of mortal humans. The two elements are brought together by the poet and they don't quite fit; a dissimilarity is present that may grate upon the reader. As in the aesthetics of disjunction a discordance exists, a sense of the poet fusing together two realities which are unlike in kind.

The first, in the order of publication, of Hardy's poems using a spectral voice is **"A Christmas Ghost-Story,"** one of the poems that Hardy wrote on the occasion of the Boer War. The poem sets a pattern for Hardy's other poems employing a ghostly voice as it begins with a description of ordinary, particularized reality which is then juxtaposed with the voice of a "phantom" who makes a generalizing comment. This poem has a significant place in the group of poems which Hardy titled *War Poems* for it sums up all the rest. The words of the phantom are authoritative; undoubtedly the ghost speaks for Hardy. This disembodied voice is the one voice amongst all those in the *War Poems* that is most clearly the poet's. One other poem in the group does employ a disembodied voice: in **"The Souls of the Slain"** a "senior soul-flame" addresses other ghosts and makes a statement on personal immortality. This poem also begins with a concrete description of the actual world—Hardy even employs a footnote to identify the exact place—after which "A dimdiscerned train / Of sprites without mould" appears, speaks, and thus sets the stage for the authoritative words of their leader.

In **"Lausanne: In Gibbon's Old Garden"** Hardy writes of a place he visited and imagines the ghost of Gibbon speaking. Again, the setting is specific and the words of the spectre make a generalizing comment. The juxtaposition is that of the past with the present as well as the solid, physical world with the world of Gibbon's spirit. Hardy was also willing to use disembodied voices for humorous effect; both **"The Levelled Churchyard"** and **"Ah, are you digging on my grave?"** use the voice from the grave to mock the self-centered concerns of individuals. **"Her Father"** and **"The Moth-Signal"** use spectral voices to comment rudely and tauntingly on the romantic affairs of men

and women. In both poems the ghost speaks only at the end; and in each poem the ghost's voice is a jarring intrusion into a dramatized human situation. Hardy's aesthetics of disjunction function here as the poet insists on the discordance between the timeless and the temporal.

A favorite motif of Hardy's is that the dead are better off than the living. In three poems Hardy has ghosts speak from under the sod to explain to the living that death is preferable to life. In all three of these poems the words of the ghosts have authority; the message that spectral voices deliver is conclusive. And it gains significance as it is repeated through Hardy's canon. In **"Voices from Things Growing in a Churchyard"** several representative voices speak from the grave to deliver the message that all is well with the dead. The voices of the dead in **"While Drawing in a Churchyard"** speak the same sentiments and conclude: " 'That no God trumpet us to rise / We truly hope.' " In **"Jubilate"** the dead show as much with their dancing as they put into words; but their one line message to the living, " 'We are out of it all!—yea, in Little-Ease cramped no more,' " confirms what Hardy's ghosts have said elsewhere.

In a number of poems the dead and the living converse; they speak to each other, frequently in a pattern of question and answer. **"Night in the Old Home"** presents a speaker who is "A thinker of crooked thoughts upon Life in the sere" who questions "my perished people" and hears them advise him to:

> "Enjoy, suffer, wait: spread the table here freely
>   like us,
> And, satisfied, placid, unfretting, watch time
>   away beamingly!"

Here there is not a jarring disjunction between death and life. The words of the dead come in an easy conversational answer to the question of the living. **"The To-Be-Forgotten"** follows a similar pattern as the living voice questions the dead and receives the dead's answer. In this poem, as in **"Night in the Old Home,"** the spectral voices are not simply overheard by the speaker but their words come in response to the speaker's questioning; they form a conversation between life and death. The theme of **"The To-Be-Forgotten"** is the same as that of **"The Souls of the Slain"**: immortality is remembrance in the minds of the living. **"The Dead and the Living One"** presents two ghosts and one living voice who, all three, enter into conversation. Here, again, the ghosts speak with authority and the mortal is naive. The poem closes with the female ghost's mordant laugh which is as conclusive as speech, and which serves the same function as the Ancient Briton's grin in **"The Moth-Signal"** and the words of the "cynic ghost" in **"Her Father."**

In Hardy's poetry ghosts can be victims as well as advisors. In **"Spectres that Grieve"** the restless "phantoms of the gone" respond to a human's question, explaining that because they are misrepresented in the memory of mortals they must wander as "shaken slighted visitants" instead of enjoying the relief of death. The ghosts of **"Family Portraits,"** ancestors of the speaker, appear and act out a drama which, if completed, would explain the speaker's "blood's tendance." The fearful speaker interrupts and the ghosts withdraw with a reproach and a warning. In all these poems where the living and the dead converse it is the living who have questions and the dead who speak the answers; the condition of death appears to insure inviolability and authority.

But Hardy writes other poems in which the dead are as perplexed and uncomfortable as the living, even a few poems in which the living answer the questions of the dead. In **"I rose up as my custom is"** and **"The Woman I Met"** discontented ghosts appear to the living. In the first of these poems the ghost receives a lecture from a living woman who has the authority within the poem. In the second a female ghost appears to the speaker; the ghost's purpose is not to make a pronouncement but to express feelings which she kept to herself when living. This ghost has a complex and vulnerable character. In **"Something tapped"** a lonely and helpless ghost complains bitterly to the living; in **"An Upbraiding"** an angry ghost berates a mortal; this ghost speaks its mind but its words carry no special authority; instead, these spectres reveal very "human" and intimate concerns. In similar poems the speaking ghosts are not greatly different from other personae; they reveal personalities like human personalities. These poems emphasize what the living and the dead have in common and grant no special insight to the dead. The female ghost of **"The Monument Maker"** flirts with the sculptor as if she were alive; the ghostly speaker of **"Not only I"** regrets the loss of life, something ghosts rarely do in Hardy's poems, and enumerates the various aspects of its temporal existence which are now "doomed awhile to lie / In this close bin with earthen sides." The speaker of **"Regret not me"** assures the living that death is peaceful; nevertheless, the poem consists of a listing of the charming experiences of its life and, by implication, indicates the same sense of loss that pervades **"Not only I."**

Hardy also uses disembodied voices which are not the ghosts of individuals but disembodied intelligences which voice a poem's most conclusive words. **"The Musical Box"** is one of the most important poems in the Hardy canon, a poem which identifies the precondition which must exist if humans are to enjoy happiness or satisfaction. And while the speaker of the poem is human, it is "a spirit" that enunciates the words which the speaker must grasp: " 'O value what the nonce outpours' " and again: " 'O make the most of what is nigh!' " In **"The Clock of the Years"** the speaker and a "spirit" converse. The spirit is laconic; but he voices the wisdom of the poem. In a similar manner **"At the Entering of the New Year"** uses a spirit to speak the words of authority within the poem. In both **"There seemed a strangeness"** and **"A Night of Questionings"** more talkative spirits, identified as "a Voice" and "the wind," philosophize on the human predicament. In all of these poems understanding, the answers to human questions, comes from a source somewhere between the human and the divine. A somewhat different use of the disembodied voice comes in two of Hardy's poetic fantasies: **"Aquae Sulis"** and **"The Graveyard of Dead Creeds."** In each poem the voice of an extinct religion is overheard and the imagined voices of the religions pronounce their own doom.

In the *Poems of 1912-13* Hardy makes direct use of a disembodied voice twice and twice more refers to "hearing" the voice of his deceased wife, Emma. The ghost of Emma speaks in **"His Visitor"** as the spectre returns to Max Gate to observe and comment on the changes that have taken place. This ghost is different from Hardy's other phantom appearances; a different spectral sensibility exists here. Emma speaks of the domestic details of her old home; she comments on the everydayness and circumstantiality of things in a very specific, almost empirical, manner. This phantom refers to two shared lives: the very ordinariness of the items that hold her attention invoke a shared experience. Here the disembodied voice does not make pronouncements or offer insights; instead, her consciousness registers the concrete details of her household economy. Emma's spirit speaks again in **"The Haunter"** to say that she is closer to her spouse now than when living. The pair were estranged when Emma was alive; but now, her ghost explains, "If he but sigh since my loss befell him / Straight to his side I go." This spectre talks about intimacy, the intimacy of death with life. The speaker of **"Your Last Drive,"** who is undoubtedly close to Hardy himself, addresses his words to a "dear ghost." He imagines the ghost speaking to him and quotes her words. What the phantom says is that, in contrast to the words of **"The Haunter,"** a vast chasm exists between death and life; no separation can be more absolute:

> But I shall not know
> How many times you visit me there,
> Or what your thoughts are, or if you go
> There never at all. And I shall not care.

The speaker of **"The Voice"** hears the sound of the dead: "Woman much missed, how you call to me, call to me." This poem lays equal stress on separation and intimacy: the speaker cannot quote her words, what the voice says is not fully articulated and the speaker even wonders whether the sound he hears is only the wind. And yet, "faltering forward," he cannot rid himself of the voice which, in one way, is even closer to him than the phantom of **"The Haunter"** who cannot make herself heard. The ghostly voices of the *Poems of 1912-13* are the voices of a highly individuated woman who Hardy knew intimately. This ghost is too much of an actual person to have the kind of authority possessed by the more ethereal presences who speak to humans from a spiritual realm. Even after her death, Emma was too human to possess the authority of a spirit.

The fact that Hardy used the disembodied voice so frequently is striking. It does seem to have allowed him to occasionally do in verse what he was used to doing in his fiction: offer commentary from an omniscient position. But this is only one of the functions of the disembodied voice. For a writer who was acutely aware of time and natural process, the voice of a spirit was one way to escape from that process and bring a timeless perspective to bear on human life. In the shorter poems, Hardy uses disembodied voices in at least three ways. The most familiar is the anonymous spirit who makes generalizing and ironic comments on human situations. Frequently, the anonymous spirits answer the direct questions of men and women, thus entering into a conversation with the living.

The message that these anonymous ghosts have for humans is that the dead are content, that death is a relief, that the dead have no desire to return to life. These spirits speak with authority: wisdom is gained in death and humans can trust that the words that come from beyond the grave carry the authority of a spiritual world. Another type of ghost is fitful and bewildered. Death has not brought relief to these spirits and they wish to make contact with the living to have questions answered and situations resolved. The third use of the disembodied voice is in the *Poems of 1912-13,* where the spirit of Emma Hardy visits her former home and her former husband apparently motivated by a simple, and almost human, need for companionship. This ghost is different from the others in that she has an individual personality not greatly different from the personality that was hers when alive. Emma's ghost does not offer understanding or make statements. It seems that she only wants to visit, to establish some kind of contact with her living husband, that loneliness may be her most urgent motivation.

Hardy, then, was fond of writing poems which employ the disembodied voice of a spirit or ghost. These poems are found throughout his canon; they are not clustered in any particular volumes of his verse. The ghostly perspective intrigued Hardy: in his autobiography he writes of regarding himself as a spectre "not solid enough to influence my environment" even in the midst of social visits. Hardy was both the advanced thinker and the poet of traditional vision. This traditional vision, his interest in the folklore of Wessex, made it easy for him to use spirits who speak words of authority to humans. On the other hand, his use of spirits to supply the answers to human problems may be an agnostic's way of indicating that there are no answers. Hardy's aesthetics of disjunction was a fundamental principle of his art, a mode he used throughout his poetry and fiction. This principle made it natural for him to conjoin two separate worlds—the world of the living and the world of the dead—for ironic effect. In the disembodied voice poems, the irony is a product of the difference between the two perspectives. On a less theoretical level, Hardy loved the odd and the unusual; he was fascinated by queer twists. A spectral perspective enabled him to exploit oddities and underline coincidences. Paul Zietlow and Frederick W. Shilstone have elucidated Hardy's use of various speaking voices throughout his poetry: Hardy's usual manner of composition was to create a voice not his own to speak in his poems which, he insisted, were "dramatic monologues by different characters." The disembodied voices are one set of voices which recur again and again amongst the variety of personae in Hardy's canon. (pp. 57-64)

> Vern B. Lentz, "Disembodied Voices in Hardy's Shorter Poems," in Colby Library Quarterly, *series XXIII, No. 2, June, 1987, pp. 57-65.*

Lloyd Siemens   (essay date 1987)

[*In the following essay, Siemens analyzes the process by which Hardy's poetry, harshly criticized for its pessi-*

mism during the poet's lifetime, has gained acceptance and praise from modern poets and critics.]

When Hardy confided late in life that he had always been considered "the Dark Horse of contemporary English literature" he was commenting, with a touch of bitterness, on the decade of public adulation that had crowned a quarter century of critical indifference or abuse. The author who, in his middle years, described himself as one of the "most abused of living writers" had, by the 1920s, tasted honors that none of his contemporary poets could boast: an Order of Merit, Honorary Fellowships at Cambridge and Oxford, five honorary degrees and the offer of a knighthood.

In spite of these formal public tributes, Hardy could not have foreseen that after his death in 1928 his reputation as a poet would undergo a critical re-assessment that is virtually unparalleled in English literary history. The poet who could not find a reliable publisher for his verse for over thirty years has come to be heralded by some scholars as the father of modern verse. The young architect who desired nothing more than to have one of his poems anthologized in Palgrave's *Golden Treasury* is more generously represented in the *New Oxford Book of English Verse* (ed. Helen Gardiner) than any other poets except Shakespeare and Wordsworth. The aging poet who moaned "Why did I ever write a line?" is given more space in *The Oxford Book of Twentieth-Century English Verse* (ed. Philip Larkin) than any other poet.

This astounding critical re-evaluation invites answers to some fundamental questions about Hardy's career as novelist and poet. Why did Hardy abandon the writing of prose fiction at the height of his powers as a novelist? How did his poetic themes—so offensive to his earliest reviewers—acquire relevance and even respectability during his lifetime? What qualities endeared Hardy to the poets of the succeeding generation and why does his poetry continue to win such a warm reception from poets and critics of the 1980s? How, in short, does one account for the "Hardy phenomenon"?

Hardy's own "dark horse" metaphor is highly apt in describing his literary status in the last decade of the nineteenth century. Although, with the publication of *Tess of the d'Urbervilles* and *Jude the Obscure,* Hardy had won international recognition as the foremost English novelist of the day, he had alienated those segments of his national audience (i.e. "pulpit" and "press") that would seriously undermine his reputation and drive him away from prose fiction. By treating the novel as a serious form for the frank examination of cherished institutions and respectable Victorian assumptions, Hardy had offended against the Laws of Mrs. Grundy: he had said what he believed to be true about false morality, prudery and moral humbug. As Hardy recorded in **"In Tenebris II,"** he was a writer "born out of due time" whose candid exploration of social and moral hypocrisies had "disturbed the order" of his smug Victorian contemporaries.

Public reaction was immediate and cruel. *Tess* was denounced as a "clumsy, sordid tale of brutality and lust"— as a revolting illustration of what the *Daily News* labelled

"Tessimism"—and removed from public libraries. *Jude* was declared to be "immoral trash," full of "barnyard matters, manners and morals," and contemptuously retitled *Jude the Obscene*. Nothing short of a book-burning, presided over by Bishop How, was sufficient to purge Victorian parlors of Hardy's heretical views on marriage and divorce. The *Edinburgh Review,* appropriating Holy Writ in its campaign for righteousness, declared "Swinburne planteth, Hardy watereth, and Satan giveth the increase." This spectacle of the British public "in one of its periodical fits of morality" was enough, said Hardy, to "make one sick in a corner."

Hardy drafted an article of reply to his critics, but decided against publishing it. To his friends he confided, "Never retract. Never explain. Get it done and let them howl," but in spite of the show of stoic indifference, the private hurt ran deep. It is recorded in the suicidal utterance of a poem such as **"In Tenebris."** On one point he was definite. He would never again provoke the wrath of the bishops in prose: "A man must be a fool to deliberately stand up to be shot at." Indeed, in the last three decades of his life he showed little or no interest in his fiction; he had had his final say in *Jude* and did not wish to talk any more about his "nearly forgotten art in fiction," his "mere journeywork," as he called it.

In an attempt to escape the wrath of the bishops, Hardy turned his artistic efforts to poetry, to what he insisted on describing as his "more mature and serious work." Poetry had always been his first love but, perhaps more importantly, Hardy saw in poetry a subtle and subversive weapon against the hypocrisy of late Victorian attitudes and utterances. "Write a list of things that everybody thinks and nobody says; and a list of things that everybody says and nobody thinks" runs a note-book entry. Literature in the 1880s was merely transcribing and so perpetuating comforting clichés in prose and verse; its besetting sin, Hardy believed, was its insincerity. And the critics did not criticize a "particular man's artistic interpretation of life," but kept a secret eye on [his] theological and political propriety. In spite of such frank distrust of critics, Hardy hoped that in verse he would be able to express with candor "ideas and emotions which run counter to the inert crystallized opinion—hard as rock—which the vast body of men have vested interests in supporting." He speculated that if Galileo had written a poem (not a prose treatise) about the earth's movement around the sun the Inquisition would not have taken notice.

To the delight of Hardy's detractors, many of his early poems *did* run counter to established and comforting views, for the poems were interrogative rather than declarative and assuring. Through ironic debate, satiric inversion, parody and burlesque they challenged and embarrassed optimistic assumptions about Providence, Progress and Nature—the very assumptions upon which the often smug literature around him was based.

The most pervasive of these assumptions was that the universe is superintended by a beneficent deity, an anthropomorphic and personal God who intervenes providentially in human affairs. Hardy countered by illustrating in verse (as he had already done in the novels) the blind, mechanical force of chance as postulated by Darwin—**"Hap"** and **"The Convergence of the Twain"** are examples—and by substituting for Tennyson's God of Love a bumbling and forgetful chief executive who is ignorant of teleology and ethics and totally indifferent to the affairs of men.

Hardly calculated to endear him to a Victorian audience was Hardy's interrogation of a whole nexus of philosophical certitudes promulgated by Browning. The superior morality attributed to man by dualism (and celebrated by Browning) is an illusion, for man is capable of cruelties beyond the scope of animals. Again, human consciousness, which Browning elevates as the highest product of a teleological process is, from Hardy's point of view, a tragic accident and a curse. Nor can suffering and failure be rationalized as paradoxical proofs of success, as they so often are in Browning, for there are no divine contraries in Hardy's poetry. Hardy could no more give assent to Browning's "robustious, swaggering optimism," or his "juggling and metaphor," than to Tennyson's philosophy of submissive trust. "Funny man, Browning!" Hardy is reported to have said. "All that optimism! He must have put it in to please the public. He *can't* have believed it."

Even the consolations of the rational Positivists, with whom Hardy was popularly associated, were unacceptable to Hardy. Like George Meredith, Hardy accepted evolutionary process in place of Providential Being, but in many poems he challenges Meredith's optimistic deductions from naturalism. By denying a purposive impulse to Nature, Hardy denies both her beneficence and her plan to "speed the race" through evolutionary meliorism. He deflates Meredith's "religion of Progress" by looking backward to record historical regression or by anticipating a coming Dark Age of universal barbarism.

In his attacks on orthodox Christianity, on the "Magical View" of Nature, and on the religion of Progress, Hardy had carried out a project in spiritual slum-clearing, and he should not have been shocked by the critical hostility. He was, after all, dismantling Victorian systems at the height of Queen Victoria's reign. Many reviewers of the first volume (**Wessex Poems,** 1898) lamented that Hardy should have taken up poetry at all. There was the matter of technique—which most critics declared to be unimaginably gauche but the main charge was levelled at Hardy's philosophical bleakness. The adjectives that fairly ring through the early reviews are *blasphemous, heterodox, unchristian, gloomy, morbid, pessimistic.* This assessment, reflecting "inert" and "crystallized" Victorian opinion, was codified and given status by G. K. Chesterton's portrayal in *The Victorian Age in Literature* (1913) of Hardy as the pathetic village atheist maundering in his ale and botanizing in his spiritual swamp.

One year after Chesterton's unsympathetic dismissal of Hardy, the Christian world went to war. Here was an historical event tragically worthy of Hardy's gloomiest predictions. In one of his best-known poems, **"In Tenebris,"** Hardy had promised to "Take a full look at the Worst." On the subject of war, at least, he kept his word:

> 'Peace upon earth!' was said. We sing it,
> And pay a million priests to bring it.
> After two thousand years of mass

> We've got as far as poison-gas.

What an earlier generation of detractors had decried as perverse pessimism came suddenly to be appreciated as evidence both of Hardy's sensitivity to the currents of historical events and of his absolute philosophical integrity. Those very qualities of Hardy's verse that had most offended readers were recognized, overnight, as among his cardinal virtues.

The tributes that poured in after the outbreak of hostilities pointed the direction that Hardy's literary reputation would take after 1914. In a letter dated November 14, 1914, Sydney Cockerell struck the keynote:

> I have been reading and re-reading your new book of poetry with an admiration which I do not know how to express. Those that I have read before seem to me even better than I thought them. It is perhaps that the war has turned one's mind to a different key and that what in some moods I might have called over-dismal now seems not dismal at all—only forceful and true and stimulating.

One week later, A. E. Housman wrote to say that Hardy's poems were "fuller of matter and sincerity than anyone else's." In the following year Virginia Woolf, in a letter to Hardy, described his latest volume as "the most remarkable book to appear in [her] lifetime." At war's end some fifty poets, at the suggestion of Siegfried Sassoon, prepared a volume of holograph poems for presentation on Hardy's eightieth birthday. The tribute, wrote Hardy, was almost his "first awakening to the consciousness that an opinion had silently grown up as it were in the night that he was no mean power in the contemporary world of poetry."

The time was clearly ripe for a re-evaluation of Hardy's poetry. Chesterton had summed up and "fixed" Hardy's reputation on the eve of World War I. Eight years after the end of the war, I. A. Richards argued his case for Hardy as the most courageous of the post-Darwinian poets. Commenting on the many "pseudo-statements" about God, the universe and soul that had become for many sincere minds impossible to believe, Richards defined the role of much Victorian poetic statement as analogous to drug-taking. The most striking exception, Richards declared, was Hardy:

> Attempts to use poetry as a denial or corrective of science are very common. One point can be made about them all: they are never worked out in detail. There is no equivalent of Mill's *Logic* expounding any such view. The language in which they are framed is usually a blend of obsolete psychology and emotive exclamation. . . . Hardy is the poet who has most steadily refused to be comforted. The comfort of forgetfulness, the comfort of beliefs, he has put both these away. . . . Only the greatest tragic poets have achieved an equally self-reliant and immitigable acceptance. [*Science and Poetry*]

In the final decade of his life, Hardy grew into a cult figure. Partly because of Richards' crusading efforts, partly because of Hardy's venerable old age, this pariah of Victorian literature came to be known affectionately as "The Wizard of Wessex." Admirers from the world over deluged Hardy with requests for his autograph, his support for a "Cause," an "occasional" poem or speech or article. Hardy's home, Max Gate, Dorchester, became the shrine to which pilgrims made their journeys—some to pilfer souvenirs, some to celebrate him in song and dance, and some (mainly writers) to pay personal homage to the Grand Old Man of English letters. In January, 1928, Hardy's ashes were buried in that monument to respectability, Westminister Abbey. Among the pallbearers were Prime Minister Baldwin, Ramsay MacDonald, J. M. Barrie, John Galsworthy, Edmund Gosse, A. E. Housman, Rudyard Kipling and G. B. Shaw. It was, said Alfred Noyes, like Gibbon being buried in the Holy Sepulchre with Voltaire as pallbearer.

Criticism after 1920 has been little concerned with the great religious and philosophical issues that dominated late Victorian discussions. The "new poets" of the late 1920s and 1930s were interested more in poetic idiom and "manner" than in philosophical "matter," and they turned frequently to Hardy's poems for models of the distinctive modern poetic voice.

In a wide-ranging reminiscence of his formative years, Roy Fuller has recently discussed the basic tenets of the generation of poets who succeeded Hardy:

> One of the effects of the "new" poetry of the early 1930s was to enlarge the area of the "poetic": indeed, the rule became that there was nothing that was not poetic. . . . Everything, no matter how trivial . . . was equally the subject of poetry. As Auden put it in his introduction to the school's anthology of 1935 (*The Poet's Tongue*), poetry is "memorable speech". . . . One of the effects of the coming of Auden . . . was to remove from poetry the obligation to be "beautiful," an obligation perhaps specifically a hangover from the 1890s. . . . The burden laid on [the poet] was to avoid being in the wrong sense "poetic." What is written should still be "speech," however elaborate the form.

What is remarkable about this credo statement is that it summarizes—as it also post-dates by several decades—Hardy's own statements about the kind of poetry he intended to write. More than twenty years before the publication of his first volume of poems, Hardy recorded his intention of avoiding the "poetic veneer" of the "jewelled line" of poetry. The conventional beauties of "false romance" were, he argued, out of harmony with the post-Darwinian world view. The immediate business of the poet was to "find beauty in ugliness," to show "the sorriness underlying the grandest things and the grandeur underlying the sorriest things."

Hardy's practice bears out his theory. His imagery is often spare, stark and unlovely; it seldom soars except for ironic effect. "Hardy," wrote George Moore, "coaxed his readers into drinking from an old tin pot, a beverage that had hitherto been offered to them only in golden and jewelled goblets." The "old tin pot" is Hardy's answer to both the splendours of verse and the states of mind that maintain them. It is as though some urgency of truth had pared off all but the essential. This preference for directness at the expense of constructed ornament (cf. Fuller's "obligation to be 'beautiful'," being in the wrong sense "poetic"), and the ability to render experience through the imagery of what T.E. Hulme has called "small, dry things" are among Hardy's most important legacies to twentieth-century poetry. It is Hardy's direct rendering of experience without imagistic prettiness or distortion that Ezra Pound had in mind when he testified that he had "learned nothing about poetry" since Hardy's death.

Hardy's reaction against the "jewelled line" of poetry is demonstrated also in the aesthetic austerity of a deliberately roughened and a-poetic art. From the beginning of his career as a poet, Hardy sought an idiom that would counter the sensuous music of much nineteenth-century poetry; in his diction, as in his choice of imagery, he rejected Keats' advice to "load every rift with ore" and to "surprise with a fine excess" of visual beauty and verbal melody. To avoid the word-music of conventional poetic diction he appropriated, according to classifications assigned by *The Oxford English Dictionary,* 137 dialect words, and nearly 250 archaic, obsolete or rare usages. He coined over two hundred words and fabricated as many alliterative compounds.

The critics were quick to pounce: "The diction is persistently clumsy, full of ugly neologisms, with neither the simplicity of untutored song nor that of consummate art," wrote the reviewer for *The Athenaeum* in 1902. Even those admirers who have written most sympathetically about Hardy's radicalism in technique have conceded the laboured and wheezy rhythms, and the occasional "accent of a young architect drawing up specifications so that sometimes all the Muses hold their ears in pain."

There is no denying that gaucheries of diction and rhythm are present in each volume of Hardy's verse. What is important for this discussion is that the gaucheries are usually deliberate. One kind of evidence lies in Hardy's many ballads, songs, and "hymns" that are metrically quite regular. Hardy was an accomplished amateur violinist and 'cellist; his lifelong ambition was to be a church organist. Steeped as he was in the ancient music of rural England, as well as in the poetry of Shelley, Keats and Swinburne, Hardy was quite capable of orthodox harmonies when harmony was his intention.

A more important kind of evidence that Hardy was frequently unmellifluous and "a-poetic" by choice can be found in his notes on versification. He will consciously seek to avoid "mimicking the notes" of his Romantic predecessors. What he values most are "those instances of verse that apparently infringe all the rules, and yet bring reasoned conviction that they are poetry." In his own poetry, he will consciously "conceal art," for "the whole secret of a living style lies in being a little careless."

Hardy's greatest contribution to prosody is not to be found, finally, in the roughened syntax, the unconventional diction or the a-poetic imagery. It lies in his creation of a prose rhetoric that moves with a metrical regularity that does not draw attention to itself—in "memorable speech." These colloquial rhythms were more important to Auden (and to the poets of the next generation) than "any of

Eliot's gas-works and rats' feet" because they were "more flexible and adaptable to different themes" [*The Southern Review* (1940)].

The natural rhetoric of a quiet speaking voice that refuses to be hurried and that will not allow words or the demands of metrical tidiness to dictate its meaning lies behind much of the characteristic Hardy rhythm. The intimate colloquial phrases are Hardy's means to a new kind of music, to what he called "the latent music in the utterance of deep emotion . . . which fills the place of the actual word-music in rhythmic phraseology on thinner emotive subjects."

A fine instance of a "latent music" free of conventional poetic words and images is **"The Walk."** The eight lines of the first stanza contain thirty-nine monosyllabic words:

> You did not walk with me
> Of late to the hill-top tree
> By the gated ways,
> As in earlier days;
> You were weak and lame,
> So you never came.
> And I went alone, and I did not mind,
> Not thinking of you as left behind.

This voice is especially effective as it meditates on separation or loneliness, for it compels the reader's acceptance by its absolute fidelity to experience. The diction is neither gauche nor idiosyncratic, but satisfyingly flat:

> And when you'd mind to career
> Off anywhere—say to town—
> You were all of a sudden gone
> Before I had thought thereon,
> Or noticed your trunks were down.

And that "carelessness of common parlance" that Hardy strove to achieve can, even in the "colloquial" poems, be as metrically regular as the cadences in his songs:

> I should not have shown in the flesh,
> I ought to have gone as a ghost;
> It was awkward, unseemly almost
> Standing solidly there as when fresh . . .
> But to show in the afternoon sun,
> With an aspect of hollow-eyed care,
> When none wished to see me come there,
> Was a garish thing, better undone.

The three poems cited, like most of the *Poems of 1912-13* are evidence that Hardy is frequently most moving when he is least obviously and formally "poetic."

Writing of Hardy's influence on the poets of the 1920s and 1930s, A. McDowall concludes [in his *Thomas Hardy*] that Hardy "cast a spell: what he preached by example was poetic honesty." The honesty is of two kinds. Hardy was one of the first poets to recognize the general disruption of civilization and to give that disruption major place in his poetry. The honesty is evident also in the austerities of style through which Hardy uttered his harsh queries and gnarled meditations. Because the "velvet image" and the "lilting measure" could no longer convey his meaning, Hardy dedicated his craft to the search for a new idiom that would reflect the emotional realities of the modern world.

Hardy's popularity with poets and critics of the last several decades has remained undiminished. Such poets as F. M. Ford, Geoffrey Grigson, Dallas Kenmore, Delmore Schwartz, Allen Tate and Mark Van Doren have paid tribute to Hardy's contributions to the "modern" poetic voice and vision. Other poets—notably C. Day Lewis, Philip Larkin, Dylan Thomas, Thom Gunn, and Tom Paulin—have acknowledged Hardy's influence on their own verse.

Recent extended critical assessments of modernism, too, assign preeminence to Hardy. Thus Donald Davie asserts that "in British poetry of the last fifty years . . . the most far-reaching influence, for good or ill, has not been Yeats, still less Eliot or Pound, not Lawrence, but *Hardy*." Among the qualities judged by Davie (as also by Frank Kermode in *Critical Inquiry*) to have been especially influential are Hardy's informal and "private" tone, his modesty, civility and liberal reasonableness. Both Davie and Kermode stress Hardy's "common sense" as it contrasts with the "thrashing presences" of Pound, Eliot and Yeats—three poets who, according to Theodore Weiss, diverted the mainstream of English poetry, or at least made it turbulent. Weiss, like Davie, concedes that Hardy's current fashionableness is related to the "battered 70s," to our desire for naiveté, for an escape from the intellectual forces that "hover so loomingly, so fiercely, so brilliantly as do those that surround Eliot and Yeats."

There is a double irony that is worthy of final mention. The radical Thomas Hardy who was a prophet without disciples in 1898 became, in Gosse's words, "the commander-in-chief" of modernism for the generation of poets who wrote after World War I; to many poets and critics of our own generation, wearied by the heated complexities of Yeats and Eliot, he has become the model of common sense and reasonableness, the acknowledged defender of poetic tradition. (pp. 16-26)

> *Lloyd Siemens, "A Poet 'Born Out of Due Time': Hardy's New Respectability," in* Wascana Review, *Vol. 22, No. 2, Fall, 1987, pp. 16-27.*

We want more from a poet than a theory of life; we want, if such a thing is possible, the look, feel, sound, taste, and even smell of life itself. And that is what Hardy eventually provides, and provides so richly that his name is sure to last.

—Mark Van Doren, "The Poems of Thomas Hardy," in his The Happy Critic, 1961.

Trevor Johnson   (essay date 1991)

[*In the following essay, Johnson examines Hardy's poetic influences.*]

Although it is more than thirty years since I listened to Robert Graves in his capacity as Professor of Poetry at Oxford, I still recall the unholy glee with which he set about demolishing the poetic establishment, to the unconcealed delight of the undergraduates, if not all their seniors, in his packed audiences. Almost alone of Graves's contemporaries, Hardy escaped unscathed, for he was, as Graves's biographer tells us, the one poet he loved unreservedly. Regrettably, Graves never gave an extended critical view of Hardy's verse, but he spoke of him in a significant context during his lecture, to the Oxford Poetry Society, on "The Word Bàraka." This Moorish word, he said, had no true synonym in modern English, though he offered "holy power" as a rough equivalent, going on to speak of those things in his Majorcan home which, for him, possessed this quality:

> If the house seems, to visiting friends, like a museum, that is their mistake: my great-grandfather's silver candlesticks and my great-great-grandfather's spoons, as well as hundred-year-old plates and dishes, are in daily use, and the English poets are ranked round me on bookshelves within easy reach. I feel contemporary with Thomas Hardy, whom I knew well, and through him with Coleridge and Keats, and through them with Shakespeare, Marlowe, Donne, Skelton and Chaucer. Call me a living fossil, if you like.

If Hardy did not know the word *bàraka,* he certainly knew the thing. Indeed, he once wrote that "clouds, mists and mountains are unimportant beside the wear on a threshold or the print of a hand, and a beloved relative's old battered tankard [is entirely superior] to the finest Greek vase." He meant, of course, "superior" in the sense of the evocative power such objects accrue from what Hardy elsewhere defined as "memorial associations." His poem **"Old Furniture"** is really all about Graves's *bàraka:*

> I see the hands of the generations
> That owned each shiny familiar thing
> In play on its knobs and indentations,
> And with its ancient fashioning,
> Still dallying.
>
> Hands behind hands, growing paler and paler,
> As in a mirror a candle-flame
> Shows images of itself, each frailer
> As it recedes, though the eye may frame
> Its shape the same.
>
> On the clock's dull dial a foggy finger,
> Moving to set the minutes right
> In tentative touches that lift and linger
> In the wont of a moth on a summer night,
> Creeps to my sight.

How well those verses display Hardy's own consummate craftsmanship, their delicate, hesitant—one might say "lingering"—movement perfectly complementing the musing, meditative theme. Superficially, the poem is about mutability, but if that is what it attests it is not what it imparts. At a deeper level it is showing us how tradition—here Hardy's personal, private tradition—may arrest the endless flux of Time. These unexceptional domestic objects acquire and carry with them as they are handed on—

the root sense of the Latin *tradere* from which tradition derives—a doubtless indefinable yet also ineluctable essence of their maker's and their successive owners' personalities and predilections. That is the quality Graves maintained was accessible to us, if we are ready to look and listen. And Hardy's study, like Graves's, was full of things which had *bàraka* for him—his father's violin for example—just as those old bone pens lying on his desk in the museum at Dorchester have it so powerfully for us.

Perhaps no English writer has had an ear more closely attuned to the music of time than Hardy: everywhere, in prose and poetry alike, passages start up from the page to attest his continuing awareness of the past as informing, as involved with, the present. Novels and verse are, equally, time-haunted. To such a cast of mind the merely novel or fashionable was never to assume much importance. Gently deprecating vers libre to the young Graves, he said, "All we can do is to write on the old themes in the old styles, and try to do a little better than those who went before us." Graves, then twenty-five, perhaps thought that reactionary; to Hardy at eighty it was simply an unequivocal statement of his faith in the English poetic tradition, with a characteristically modest claim to a place in it, a position he elaborates, with quiet irony, in **"An Ancient to Ancients"**:

> And ye, red-lipped and smooth browed; list,
> Gentlemen;
> Much is there waits you we have missed;
> Much lore we leave you worth the knowing,
> Much, much has lain outside our ken:
> Nay, rush not: time serves: we are going,
> Gentlemen.

It is an admirably poised attitude, courteous and receptive to the "new note" in his eighties Hardy was enjoying Edward Thomas' poetry and Arthur Waley's translations—yet resting upon the past for its ultimate touchstones. Strange then, that for so long after his death even those critics who admired his verse were chary of allowing it a place in the mainstream of English poetry, with the majority following Leavis, Blackmur, Ransom, and even Douglas Brown in conceding quality only to the most exiguous of selections. Many seem to have thought of him as some sort of literary Douanier Rousseau, a primitive whose invincible naiveté was, paradoxically, just what enabled him to concoct a handful of masterpieces, embedded, like so many lucky sixpences, in a hasty-pudding of dull anecdotage and what H. G. Wells's Mr. Polly called "sesquippledan verboojuice."

Nowadays few would take that line. The major conspectual anthologies of the last two decades offer us compact evidence of a radical reassessment. Philip Larkin's firm preferment of Hardy, with twenty-eight poems, to pride of place in his *Oxford Book of Twentieth Century Verse* was only the first among many similar vindications. I know of eight selections from Hardy's verse now in print and there are three complete editions, one in paperback. Of how many of his contemporaries and predecessors can that be said?

An anthology is not an argument, however, and although Samuel Hynes [in "The Hardy Tradition in Modern En-

glish Poetry," in *Thomas Hardy: The Writer and His Background,* Norman Page, ed.] has very cogently established "the nature of the tradition of which [Hardy] was so great an exemplar, and . . . the line of continuity stretching from his work into the present," he does not identify Hardy's literary ancestors, although he recognizes their existence. Nor, as far as I am aware, does anyone else, except occasionally and in passing. I believe that Hardy as a poet really does belong where such anthologists as Larkin, Dame Helen Gardner, and John Wain have placed him, sailing majestically down the broad mainstream of English poetry and not, with whatever vigor and address, paddling his own canoe along some tributary river.

As C. Day Lewis observed [in "The Lyrical Poetry of Thomas Hardy," *Proceedings of the British Academy* (1951)], "Influence spotters don't have a happy time" with Hardy. Of course, it would be strange if in so prodigal and protean an oeuvre there were no footprints in the sands at all. But, even in the nearest thing we have to juvenilia, the mostly early (albeit heavily revised) **Wessex Poems,** where one would expect the sincerest form of flattery to be frequently in evidence, there are only faint, intermittent traces of that overt, if usually unwitting, indebtedness most young poets display.

But if they could not plausibly accuse him of being a sponge, many critics have been eager to fly to the opposite extreme and charge Hardy with being a stone, unaware of or impervious to his predecessors and thus disenfranchising himself from "access to all that is meant by the tradi-

Landscape sketches by Hardy.

tion of craft," to quote Blackmur's formulation, a "naive poet of simple attitudes and outlook," to quote Leavis. Even the perceptive and sympathetic David Wright quite recently defended Hardy on the ground that "his strength is his weakness; . . . like Burns and Clare . . . he was not primarily a literate poet in that his first approach to poetry was by way of an indigenous oral culture" [Introduction to *Thomas Hardy: Selected Poems*]. No one would dispute the importance of that strand in Hardy's poetic make-up, though I think it is demonstrable that "first approach" cannot be sustained either chronologically or quantitatively. But there is overwhelming evidence to show that Hardy's own claim that he "was a born bookworm, that and that alone was unchanging in him" was well founded.

Some, of course, would counter by querying whether Hardy's reading was well directed. T. S. Eliot, no admirer of Hardy, in 1919 propounded the notion that admission tickets to Parnassus should in future only be issued to poets who could produce evidence of exceptionally comprehensive study, in the original, of European literature. "Tradition cannot be inherited," he asserts. "If you want it you can only obtain it by great labour." Only thus is it possible to acquire that "crucial historical sense" which "compels a man to write . . . with the feeling that the whole of the literature of Europe from Homer, and within it the whole of the literature of his own country, has a simultaneous existence, and comprises a simultaneous order." One may think that a tall order, but, even if we concede Eliot's stipulations, Hardy has a better claim to hold European and, a fortiori, English literature "in his bones"—the phrase is Eliot's—than all but a very few other English poets. For Hardy worked his close, critical, extract-making way from Homer and the Athenian dramatists in painfully acquired Greek, via Virgil, Dante (admittedly with a crib), Heine, and Victor Hugo, from both of whom he made translations, ending up with Eliot's own *The Waste Land,* which he read, copied in part, and annotated in his eighties. Bearing in mind Hardy's insatiable appetite for prose of all kinds, attested by Lennart Björk's edition of *The Literary Notes,* not to mention the sheer bulk of his own writing, admiration is an inadequate term for what we feel; something more like awe is called for.

As for English poetry, Hardy tells us that in 1866-67 "I did not read a word of prose . . . except . . . daily newspapers and weekly reviews." The evidence of this voracious consumption of verse is scattered all over his early novels in the shape of quotations and citations from every major English poet except Chaucer and Spenser, many displaying that easy familiarity which derives from repeated reading. Few poets can have known Shakespeare better and perhaps only Milton among laymen had a more intimate knowledge of the Bible (a requirement Eliot omitted to specify in 1919).

Yet though his knowledge of European literature more than measures up to Eliot's exacting, not to say arbitrary, criteria, though he not only read but was personally acquainted with most of his great contemporaries—Browning, Arnold, and Tennyson among them—the notion that he was, as G. M. Young so patronizingly put it, "imperfectly educated" is by no means defunct. The co-

vert premise on which this stricture rests is that Hardy did not go to a university, though we know he dreamed of doing so. Nevertheless, from our point of view, his parents' canny decision to apprentice their rather immature sixteen-year-old to [architect John] Hicks was fortunate. Architecture was then one of the less socially exclusive professions. Hardy's well-educated and older fellow students opened his mind to wider intellectual horizons just as his work opened his eyes first to Wessex and later to London at its apogee of wealth and international power. Inevitably he also came to know whole strata of society quite opaque to those who had scaled the public school/Oxbridge career ladder, acquiring that sense of mankind as a "great web" which is so crucial a component of both prose and poetry. Moreover, his insatiable appetite for books was quite untrammeled by considerations of what might be academically prescribed or proscribed. He could, and did, read what he chose and thus developed a catholicity of taste which was, in what he later termed "Victoria's formal middle time," exceptional.

Although such prose exemplars as, say, Harrison Ainsworth were unhelpful, his eclecticism had a vital, two-fold significance for his poetry. First, supported by his penchant for second-hand books, his reading acquainted the young Hardy with many poets whom the taste of the time either ignored or denigrated, so making a signal contribution to the individuality of his own verse. Secondly, by offering him mentors from an earlier time, it reinforced his instinctive resistance to the voice of the age, always a danger to impressionable young poets, and never more so than when the voice had the hypnotic power of Tennyson's. Hardy certainly did not undervalue Tennyson's poetry. He possessed a well-thumbed selection, much admired *In Memoriam,* read the *Idylls* in the garden of St. Juliot's Rectory with Emma in the fateful year of 1870. Poetry, however, in Hardy's matured judgment, was not meant to provide an escape hatch from the harsher and more mundane concerns of life, to serve, in F. W. Bateson's mordant phrase, as the "quickest way out of Manchester." Despite his high regard for Tennyson's achievement—in **"An Ancient to Ancients"** he laments that, in the 1920s, "The bower we shrined to Tennyson / Is roof-wrecked"— Hardy flatly rejected the theory of the function of poetry which *The Golden Treasury* propounded.

One might fairly call *The Golden Treasury of the Best Songs and Lyrical Poems in the English Language* of 1861 a manifesto disguised as an anthology. Nominally edited by Tennyson's close friend F. T. Palgrave, it was a runaway success, has never been out of print, and has given many generations of the British people their first and often their only overview of English poetry. It was a seminal book for Hardy himself. Horace Moule, his literary mentor, gave him his first copy in 1862; by 1863 he was annotating it and, forty years later, he told Arthur Symons, "There has never been a good [anthology] since the first edition of *The Golden Treasury.*" No one would dispute that the small blue volume contains many great poems; nevertheless its criteria for inclusion are doctrinaire, partisan, and often perverse. And they are Tennyson's criteria. His grandson tells us that he "had a large share in the shaping of the volume, [he] made the final selection of its contents. . . . His was the final verdict." Indeed, he read each poem aloud twice before making his ex cathedra pronouncement.

The dedication and preface make the editors' aims perfectly explicit. They wish to tap a "fountain of innocent and exalted pleasure" and thereby lead their readers "in higher and healthier ways than those of the world." They contend that "great excellence [in verse] . . . has been even more uniform than Mediocrity," from which premise it follows that "more thought than mastery of expression," is a disqualification. Not surprisingly, the upshot is intriguing. Sir Thomas Wyatt has a solitary poem (of which the text is altered). John Donne, obviously far too cerebral, is totally excluded. Herbert, Vaughan, and Crashaw get one poem each. Herrick per contra has seven, which is more than Ben Jonson, Campion, Drayton, and Daniel all put together. To allow Dryden only two poems, Pope a scrap of juvenilia, and Dr. Johnson nothing, while Gray has eight poems, indicates a profound distrust of Augustan values. Then we come to the Romantics and they have—if Shakespeare is excluded—almost as much space as all the other English poets, evidently because they offer us a "bloom in feeling, an insight into the finer passages of the Soul . . . hitherto hardly attained, and perhaps unattainable even by predecessors of not inferior individual genius." Yet even within this section it is curious to find the unexceptional Thomas Campbell elevated to equality with Keats! Palgrave's dedication to his *Lyrical Poems by Alfred, Lord Tennyson* makes the underlying thesis even more categorical. He contends that the natural function of poetry is happy-making; its primary purpose is adding "sunshine to daylight," thereby helping to "lift us out of ourselves."

Hardy's view of the purpose of poetry was diametrically opposed to Tennyson's. In 1877 he wrote, "Nature's defects must be looked in the eye and transcribed." In 1887 he transcribed these lines from Thomson's *Castle of Indolence,*

> Thrice happy he who on the sunless side
> Of a romantic mountain . . .
> Sits coolly calm: while all the world without
> Unsatisfied and sick, tosses at noon,

adding tartly, "instance of a *wrong* (i.e. selfish) philosophy in poetry." A year later he asserted that "to find beauty in ugliness is the province of the poet," and other evidence abounds in the poetry itself—for example, in his acrid vignette of the "stout upstanders" from his **"In Tenebris II."** His quarrel with Quiller-Couch's *Oxford Book of English Verse* of 1900, which he maintained was "biassed in favour of certain [i.e. optimistic] views of life," stemmed from the fact that "Q," who acknowledged a large "debt" to Palgrave, also claimed that his major objective was "to uplift or console," which to Hardy was not the prime, still less the only end in view for a poet. Yet as late as 1907, Edward Thomas felt the need to defend his anthology, for including "sorrowful verse."

Perhaps some of the views expressed by Imlac in Dr. Johnson's *Rasselas,* which Hardy's mother gave him when he was only six or seven, best summarize Hardy's position. The philosopher says, "To a poet nothing can be use-

less. . . . He [must] estimate the happiness and misery of every condition. . . . He must divest himself of the prejudices of his age or country . . . [and] contemn the applause of his own time." Yet, for all Hardy's aversion to what he called "the art of saying nothing with mellifluous preciosity," the idea of poetry exemplified in Tennyson's "The Poet's Mind" had so taken root in the minds of editors and critics as to make it virtually impossible for a new poet who was not content to subscribe to the "golden" ideology to get into print at all. Tennyson's poem depicts poetic inspiration as a "melodious" fountain welling up on "holy ground" (from which "sophists" are warned to keep off) and drawing its "holy water" from the "brain of the purple mountain." Hardy was not, of course, alone in distrusting this kind of magical mystery tour, but simply to reject "golden" poetry was not enough. Young poets have to find a tradition of their craft that will validate their own practice: Hardy needed to hear ancestral voices speaking in tones congenial to him, and in particular to find historical warranty for his deeply felt instinct to avoid "the jewelled line," exactly the concept upon which Tennyson and Palgrave had based their overwhelmingly popular anthology.

Such a tradition, however much neglected at the time, did exist; such voices were still audible if few listened to them, and such a warranty existed in the work of those very poets who were almost excluded from the pages of *The Golden Treasury* because they did not satisfy the criteria set up by Tennyson for admission to his duodecimo Helicon. I contend that Hardy found in them precisely those qualities of "passion, colour, and originality" which Palgrave and his mentor rejected, as they claimed, in favor of "clearness, unity, or truth."

Hardy's position is certainly clear but it may possibly arouse unworthy suspicions of sour grapes, of objections founded upon an incapacity to write "pure poetry" himself. This contention may be concisely disposed of by considering a brief, unequivocally "golden" lyric:

> Frail luckless exiles hither brought!
> Your dust will not regain
> Old sunny haunts of Classic thought
> When you shall waste and wain;
>
> With folded arms I linger not
> To call them back; 'twere vain;
> In this, or in some other spot,
> I know they'll shine again.

The first—and I think better—verse of this collocation is from Hardy's **"To Flowers from Italy in Winter,"** the second from "Why, why repine, my pensive friend?" by Walter Savage Landor, perhaps the last true Romantic. But my point is simply this: without foreknowledge, could you tell? Even Tennyson himself wrote nothing more opulent than Hardy's "O the opal and the sapphire of that wandering western sea" (**"Beeny Cliff "**). Hardy had no objection to opening "magic casements on the foam / Of perilous seas in faery lands forlorn"; he simply considered it of equal importance to open a few windows on Mixen Lane as well, or, in his own aphoristic lines, that "If way to the Better there be / It exacts a full look at the Worse" (**"In Tenebris II"**). How strongly that reminds us of views expressed by one of Hardy's acknowledged poetic ancestors: the young John Donne—at the time as much torn with theological doubt as the young Hardy—advised his readers, and no doubt himself, to

> doubt wisely; in strange way
> To stand inquiring right, is not to stray;
> To sleepe, or runne wrong, is ("Satire III," ll. 77-79)

Hardy would have found such radical skepticism congenial, but neither Donne's sentiments nor his style would have suited the pages of *The Golden Treasury.* For Donne continues:

> On a huge hill,
> Cragged, and steep, Truth stands, and he that will
> Reach her, about must, and about must goe;
> And what the hills suddennes resists, winne so.
> (ll. 79-82)

What those lines assert and the ungainly yet compelling way in which their rhythms enact the struggles inseparable from a quest for truth makes them an appropriate epigraph for the second part of this essay. In it I hope to outline the English poetic tradition which Hardy came to revere, whose exponents he drew on for sustenance, and a knowledge of which helps to elucidate his intentions.

Sir Thomas Wyatt was praised by Puttenham in 1589 as "one of the chief lanternes of light to all other [poets] since." Hardy found him illuminating enough to take epigraphs from his verse for chapters in both *A Pair of Blue Eyes* (1873) and *The Well-Beloved* (1903), which, bearing in mind that he owned an 1854 edition, suggests an enduring preference. Much more significant is the fact that the "best" poem by the eponymous heroine of *The Hand of Ethelberta* (1876) is described as a "whimsical and rather affecting love-lament somewhat in the tone of many of Sir Thomas Wyatt's poems." Whereas her others are mere *"vers de société,"* this one is "very touching" (chap. 2). Regrettably he does not give Ethelberta's poem in the novel, but he wrote at least one which would fill the bill admirably. I quote the first two verses from one of Wyatt's less well-known songs:

> There is no love
> That can ye move,
> And I can prove
> None othre way;
>
> Therefore I must
> Restrain my lust
> Banish my trust
> And welth away.

Now a verse from Hardy's **"I Need Not Go"**:

> When I've overgot
> The world somewhat,
> When things cost not
> Such stress and strain,
> Is soon enough
> By cypress sough
> To tell my Love
> I am come again. (ll. 9-16)

Surely the resemblance is too strong to be altogether coin-

cidental? The decidedly uncommon verse form is identical of course, but the poised, delicate movement, the light, dry touch, the "shrugging" tone are all the same, and study of the full texts reveals how both poets employ a cool urbanity to mask but not wholly conceal deep feeling. Other poems by Hardy reveal a structural debt to Wyatt—compare, for example, Hardy's **"The Self Unconscious"** with Wyatt's "O Goodely Hand"—but such explicit echoes are of much less importance than the widespread and beneficent influence of Wyatt's colloquial vigor in diction, his delight in metrical experiment, and his sometimes passionate, sometimes sardonic investigation of love rejected or unavailing. All these are Hardy's hallmarks too.

Again, the unanimity with which Victorian critics castigated Wyatt's "uncertain accents" and his "awkward technique" is interesting, since these also figure prominently among the critical brickbats later hurled at Hardy. He certainly read Wyatt in Bell's popular Aldine edition of 1854, in which the introduction warmly commends Wyatt's "extensive vocabulary . . . which imparts constant novelty to his verse"—thus, no doubt, encouraging Hardy in his own linguistic idiosyncrasy. More importantly still—and his own vast repertoire of stanzaic forms is the best evidence of this—he must have seen in Wyatt what rich metrical and verse-form resources were available in English outside the narrow confines of the overworked iambic line. Finally, albeit many of his poems were meant for lute accompaniment, Wyatt often comes closer to the authentic rhythms of speech than all but a few of Hardy's contemporaries.

As E. K. Chambers noted [in *Sir Thomas Wyatt and Some Collected Studies*], "It is with Donne that Wyatt's real affinities lie." Though Tennyson had no time for him, Hardy had a text of Donne's poems before 1867, as his own **"1967"**—evidently written in 1867—makes clear. The second verse, depicting the dead lovers as "a pinch of dust or two," echoes Donne's "The Relique" with its exhumed lovers. As Edward Thomas suggests in his essay "Three Wessex Poets," the last verse offers, in its conceit of the shared "worm" an unmistakable analogue for Donne's "The Flea":

> —Yet what to me how far above?
> For I would only ask thereof
> That thy worm should be my worm, Love!

Thomas' acute identification of Hardy's "ability to mingle elements unexpectedly" (which derives from Dr. Johnson's *discordia concors* definition of Metaphysical verse) comes remarkably close to Hardy's own identification of that "principle of spontaneity" which was, he claimed, a leading feature in his verse, whose "cunning irregularity," if it has roots in Gothic architecture, certainly also displays affinities with Donne's inventiveness.

Donne is, indeed, the only poet to whom Hardy overtly acknowledges a debt. In *The Life* he wrote of himself as "in some qualities of his verse, curiously resembling Donne," and he noted in his copy of Samuel Chew's *Thomas Hardy, Poet and Novelist* (1921), at the point where Chew discusses Hardy's "musings on death," "It is curious that the influence of Donne is not mentioned." A very strong case can be made out for Donne as a seminal influence on Hardy, but as I have written at some length on this elsewhere, I shall restrict my remarks here to generalization and a few supplementary observations.

Even if **"1967"** is the solitary instance of the young disciple's overtly imitating his master's voice, the many echoes discernible suggest that Hardy learned from Donne in three major areas: language, theme, and versification. If we take them in order, both poets shared an insatiable appetite for the exotic word-hoard English offers. Significantly, in contrast to this not invariably welcome trait, Hardy also seems to have learned from Donne the art of using the simplest words to excoriating effect. Take that indestructible term of affection and love, "dear." In Donne we find "If yet I have not all thy love, / Deare, I shall never have it all" ("Love's Infiniteness"), "When I dyed last, and, deare, I dye / As often as from thee I goe" ("The Legacie"), and "Deare Love, for nothing lesse than thee / Would I have broke this happy dreame" ("The Dreame"). In Hardy we have "The love-light shines the last time / Between you, Dear, and me" (**"The End of the Episode"**), "Soon you will have, Dear, to vanish from me" (**"After a Journey"**), and "Dear ghost, in the past, did you ever find / The thought 'What profit,' move me much?" (**"Your Last Drive"**). Each time the supremely ordinary word comes home to the heart; each time the stress falls on it with consummate skill. These fragments also serve to show how Hardy found in Donne warranty for his own use of varied, often irregular line-lengths and stress-patterns, in diminishing the dominance of meter over the actuality of speech. For they assert the centrality of what is said, the technique underpinning the candor, just as the lovely curve of the strainer arches in Wells Cathedral is subdued to their supportive function.

Donne and Hardy each wrote more, and more variously, about love than any other English poet, except possibly Yeats. Widely as their approaches often diverge, there is one *topos* both frequently make use of. Its most famous Classical expression is in Petronius Arbiter's poem beginning "Foeda est in coitu et brevis voluptas," of which the conclusion was translated by Helen Waddell as follows:

> Here is, was, shall be, all delightsomeness
> And here no end shall be
> But a beginning everlastingly.

Undoubtedly Donne knew the lines; the conclusion to his "The Anniversary," verse 1, virtually paraphrases them:

> Only our love hath no decay;
> This, no to morrow hath, nor yesterday.
> Running it never runs from us away,
> But truly keeps his first, last, everlasting day.

The idea recurs in several of his other poems. Hardy's markedly autobiographical *A Pair of Blue Eyes* has this authorial interjection at a moment of emotional crisis, when Elfride the heroine and her rival lovers meet in a graveyard: "Measurement of time should be proportioned rather to the intensity of the experience than to its duration. The lovers' glance, but a moment chronologically, was a season in their history." I have little doubt that, after Emma's death, Hardy reread the novel and the idea, lodging in his mind, became a kind of emotional linchpin in

the *Poems of 1912-13* where it is given many expressions, most notably in **"At Castle Boterel," "After a Journey,"** and **"The Phantom Horsewoman."** Certainly, their shared advocacy of love's power to redefine time is a powerful affinity; possibly, in Hardy, it was a conscious debt. Hardy's copy of E. K. Chambers' edition of Donne (1896) quotes, in its eloquent introduction by George Saintsbury, Bossuet's aphorism, *"Nos passions ont quelques choses d'infini."* He adds, "to express infinity is, no doubt, a contradiction in terms, but no poet has gone nearer this infinite quality of passion than Donne." If we would now see Hardy as the inevitable addition, we ought to acknowledge how much he learned from Donne of what makes his verse sui generis.

I can find no evidence that Hardy ever quoted Donne, whose disciple, George Herbert, is only quoted once, in **The Woodlanders** (chap. xliii). Unfortunately, Hardy's pre-1870 text of Herbert does not carry a purchase date, but Herbert was staple fare for Anglicans, several examples of his verse would have been familiar from childhood in hymnals, and he would surely have sung "The Elixir," still widely used today as "Teach Me My God and King" (from its first line). I now set its third verse alongside the first verse of Hardy's well-known **"I Look Into My Glass":**

> A man, that lookes on glasse,
> On it may stay his eye
> Or if he pleaseth, through it passe,
> And then the heav'n espy.
>
>   . . . .
>
> I look into my glass,
> And view my wasting skin,
> And say, 'Would God it came to pass
> My heart had shrunk as thin!'

Even if we discount the identity of verse-form—Hardy often employed the old "common-metre" quatrains elsewhere—a striking similarity remains. But, more importantly, the two poems exemplify the directions in which Hardy could have learned from Herbert, whose disciple Vaughan he also knew and admired. The most obvious affinity is that luminous simplicity of style and diction which the poems share. Herbert has transmuted the complexities of belief, Hardy those of doubt, into a language picked clean of every last shred of rhetoric, a manner eminently plain, direct, and arresting. These features are equally evident in Herbert's lovely "Song" (from "Easter") beginning "I got me flowers to straw thy way" and Hardy's **"On a Midsummer Eve."** Again they share verse-form, both draw their imagery from rural custom, and both tell, with delicate indirectness, of a love in one instance divine and in the other human.

But of equal importance is Herbert's craftsmanship, manifested in a metrical and conceptual sophistication as telling, if not as pyrotechnic, as Donne's. Herbert developed Donne's use of varied verse-lines within the stanza (see, for example, "Longing" and "The Discharge"), a device to which Hardy often also resorts: that great poem **"The Souls of the Slain"** is only one of many which distinguishes his verse from the stately iambic norm exemplified by Tennyson's *Idylls of the King.* Herbert was also a master of what Walter de la Mare termed "onset." His openings frequently exhibit the same, often physical immediacy as Hardy's; that of Herbert's "The Collar," for example, makes an instructive comparison with Hardy's **"Under the Waterfall."** Possibly even more formative was Herbert's penchant for terse, clinching final lines. His "Love III" ends "You must sit down, says Love, and taste my meat: / So I did sit and eat" with a laconic poignancy echoed in Hardy's **"The Voice":** "Wind oozing thin through the thorn from norward. / And the woman calling." In both, the restraint and the deliberate rallentando effect of the long penultimate line are equally notable and effective.

In a deleted passage from **The Life** Hardy ironically advocates, as a highway to critical acclaim, the imitation of famous living or recently dead poets. In his early reading of Wyatt, Donne, and Herbert, I would contend he found a much thornier but ultimately more rewarding path, one leading him to a revived metrical variety, and a renewed intellectual vivacity and unexpectedness. He did not repudiate Wordsworth's advocacy of "a selection of the language really used by men," but there is no trace in him of the "egotistical sublime" and its attendant solemnity (the quality Tennyson indicted as "thick-ankled"). In retrospect one sees that the immense popular and critical enthusiasm for *The Golden Treasury* verse became inhibiting and restrictive; Victorian critics dismissed Wyatt as occasionally "harsh and refractory," Donne as emitting "a unique clangour," Herbert as having "more regard for the quaintness and unexpectedness of a simile than for its beauty or fitness," while I need hardly say what a gaggle of periodical geese shared Lytton Strachey's view that Hardy's verse was "cacophony incarnate." Such shared opprobrium suggests shared convictions, and a line of descent for Hardy which would need more extension, to include, inter alia, Swift, Gray, Crabbe, Coleridge, Clare, Arnold, Barnes, and Meredith. But I shall conclude with some remarks upon one of Hardy's poems which, even by those who only concede him a handful of them, is acknowledged as a masterpiece.

In **"At Castle Boterel,"** a poem so typical of Hardy at his astonishing best, so entirely sui generis, one may also find evidence of how deeply his roots were struck into tradition, how attentively he listened to his ancestral voices. The bone-bare simplicity of Hardy's language, the reverse of "golden" in its avoidance of lush imagery and elevated diction, is immediately striking. The same unaffected sobriety and directness of address that Herbert uses is combined with the same clipped, yet anything but perfunctory concluding lines, which compress and reinforce the feeling of each verse. We also sense an inner dialogue, a debate with himself, which Herbert often employed to such profound effect, and perhaps learned from Donne, whose already cited "The Anniversary" is also constructed on a frame of implicit question and answer. Hardy called such poems "reveries," which brings us to the "argument" of the poem (something Tennyson thought you could easily overdo). Here Hardy asserts that Love can confer upon a moment in time what Henry Vaughan called "bright shoots of everlastingness" ("The Retreate," 1.20). The identical *topos* clinches Donne's "The Anniversary," and had earlier surfaced in Hardy's **A Pair of Blue Eyes.** But here Hardy also propounds a paradox both Donne-like and truly metaphysical. Those very "primaeval rocks" which, to Hardy's post-Darwinian sensibility, reduce Man—like Hardy's alter ego Knight on "The Cliff without a Name" (chap. 21)—to something as insignificant as a trilobite, are defiantly transformed into a "record in colour and cast / That we two passed." So, too, the minatory figure of Time, his scythe implied in "unflinching rigour," suffers an impudent bouleversement, very reminiscent of Donne as he is dismissed by the contemptuous "mindless rote" into the role of pen-pushing Victorian ledger-clerk. Yet the phrase "Time's unflinching rigour" might in itself have come from Shakespeare's sonnets, its somber resonance preparing us for the heroic plainness of the conclusion, so unsparing, so bleak, so truthful, so unsuited to the pages of *The Golden Treasury.*

"At Castle Boterel" also displays what Hardy termed the "unforeseen character of his own metres and stanzas." Its movement, in contrast to its prevailing mood, is—if not gay—certainly lively; a solemn dance rather than a dirge is suggested, an impression reinforced by the feminine rhymes, something of a bêtise in contemporary poetic etiquette where they were deemed suitable only for comic or at best light verse. But there is no hint of a jingle here, any more than in Wyatt's most famous lyric "They flee from me that sometime did me seek," where they are used just as effectively. Like Wyatt, Hardy achieves emphasis by strong but unobtrusive alliteration, sharing also his predecessor's effortless control of pace, slowing or quickening the tempo to suit the tone. Within a verse-form which he seems to have invented for the occasion, he moves with an easy assurance, yet without eccentricity. Like his subject—and Love versus Time is as old as poetry—Hardy's manner is anything but newfangled. He is writing, as he told Graves, "on the old themes in the old styles" and surely also doing rather more than "a little better."

Some might contend that the last two words of the poem are so traditional as to have hardened into cliché. Yet would any of his three ancestors have hesitated to use them? Does anyone really feel that "Never again" as a commonplace? To me it is as if the words had been recharged with all the emotive force they must have had when someone first juxtaposed them. Hardy's power both to use and to renew the roots of English poetry, to re-endow it with that muscularity, that poignancy, and that resonance which are so richly and so variously evinced by Wyatt, Donne, and Herbert, is nowhere better shown than in **"At Castle Boterel."** The time-worn phrase, within its context, exudes just that quality which Robert Graves was talking about—to return to my starting point—when he said, "In poetry it is *bàraka* which casts an immortal spell on the simplest combination of words." For Hardy that enabling power—whatever we agree to call it—derived in no small measure from his intimate and fructifying knowledge of a major, but in his day unjustly neglected, strand in the English poetic tradition. (pp. 47-60)

Trevor Johnson, "'Ancestral Voices': Hardy and the English Poetic Tradition,'" in Victorian Poetry, Vol. 29, No. 1, Spring, 1991, pp. 47-62.

Robert Langbaum   (essay date 1992)

[*Langbaum is a noted American critic whose main critical concern has been to reestablish a vital connection between the literature of the nineteenth and twentieth centuries, to "connect romanticism with the so-called reactions against it." In his best-known work,* The Poetry of Experience *(1957), Langbaum makes a distinction between an older, ordered "poetry of meaning" and a more modern "poetry of experience" in which the imagination and the writing process itself help to shape the meaning of the poem. In the following essay, he discusses Hardy's stature among English poets.*]

When I told the American poet Theodore Weiss that I was writing on Hardy's poetry, he snorted contemptuously saying Hardy was being used nowadays as a stick with which to beat the modernists, such as Yeats, Eliot, and Pound. Weiss argues this view powerfully in the *Times Literary Supplement* of February 1, 1980. Irving Howe, instead, in the *New York Times Book Review* of May 7, 1978, defends the taste for Hardy's poetry in just the terms feared by Weiss:

> As we slowly emerge from the shadowing power of the age of modernism, Hardy's poems can be felt as more durable . . . than those of, say, T. S. Eliot. . . . Reading Eliot (or even Yeats) one may say, "ah, here in fulfillment is the sensibility that formed us." Reading Hardy one may say, "but this is how life is, has always been, and probably will remain."

In his book *Thomas Hardy,* Howe says that Hardy "through the integrity of his negations" helps make possible the twentieth-century "sensibility of problem and doubt," but "he is finally not of [this century]. That his poems span two cultural eras while refusing to be locked into either is a source of his peculiar attractiveness."

Donald Davie, in his *Thomas Hardy and British Poetry* (1972), most acutely defines the crisis for modernism represented in Britain by the "conversion" to Hardy. Davie begins by declaring that "in British poetry of the last fifty years (as not in American) the most far-reaching influence, for good and ill, has been not Yeats, still less Eliot or Pound, not Lawrence, but *Hardy.*" Davie cites as the model for post–World War II British poetry Philip Larkin's significant "conversion . . . from Yeats to Hardy in 1946, after his very Yeatsian first collection." The post–World War II British poets renounced the grand resonances emerging from the modernists' allegiances to the tradition and to various myths—the "common mythkitty," as Larkin put it—settling for the smaller, drier tones of a precisely noted quotidian reality. In learning to read the great modernists we had to assent to mysticisms, religious orthodoxies, and reactionary politics most of us would not dream of living by. But we thought only such views could in our time supply the symbols necessary for great poetry. Here, says Davie, lies Hardy's importance as

"the one poetic imagination of the first magnitude in the present century who writes out of . . . political and social attitudes which a social democrat recognizes as 'liberal.'" Hardy shows that poetry can be made out of the commonsense working ethic of most English-speaking readers—an ethic Davie aptly describes as "scientific humanism," a scientific world-view tempered by humanitarianism, by what Hardy in the "Apology" to *Late Lyrics* (1922) calls "lovingkindness." In the "Apology" Hardy decries the "present, when belief in witches of Endor is displacing the Darwinian theory." Hardy is probably responding to Yeats's occultism.

Most contemporary American poets seem able to reconcile admiration for the modernists with a taste for Hardy. Even in Britain, pre–World War II poets like W. H. Auden and Cecil Day Lewis could admire Eliot without repudiating their earlier passions for Hardy (Day Lewis' passion remained so strong that he had himself buried near Hardy in Stinsford churchyard). Auden tells how Hardy first gave him the sense of modernity: "Besides serving as the archetype of the Poetic, Hardy was also an expression of the Contemporary Scene." Hardy "was my poetical father." A generation earlier Ezra Pound declared the same filial relation to Browning ("Ich stamm aus Browning. Pourquoi nier son père?"), who educated him in the rough diction, broken syntax, and difficult music of modern lyricism. In a generation still earlier Hardy, as we shall see, learned the same things from Browning, while from Swinburne he learned modern ideas delivered in classic meters ("New words, in classic guise").

Davie, however, insists that for post–World War II poets "the choice cannot be fudged" between mythical and realistic poetry. The contemporary poet must decide whether like Yeats to try "to transcend historical time by seeing it as cyclical, so as to leap above it into a realm that is visionary, mythological," or like Hardy to confine himself to "the world of historical contingency [linear time], a world of specific places at specific times." While mainly agreeing with Davie, I find difficulties in his position which I will try to puzzle out.

Having begun by saying that Hardy is the one twentieth-century poet "of the first magnitude" to express the liberal ethos, Davie subsequently casts doubt on whether Hardy's poetry is indeed "of the first magnitude." He goes on to criticize Hardy's too obvious symmetries, attributing them to the hand of an engineer influenced by Victorian technology or to a poet educated in the regularities of architecture (though Hardy spoke of having learned from his experience with Gothic the art of irregularity). Davie uses the question of symmetry as a criterion of evaluation, showing that the best poems display asymmetries that have slipped past the surveillance of the poet's "imperious" will. Despite his high evaluation at the beginning, Davie seems subsequently to approve of Blackmur's argument that Hardy's successes are "isolated" cases, that he had expertise but lacked "technique in the wide sense" because he lacked "the structural support of a received imagination." "Hardy is not a great poet," writes Davie, "because, except in *The Dynasts,* he does not choose to be."

Davie proposes Hardy as a precursor of Larkin and the other contemporary British poets who in reaction against modernism deliberately set out to be precise and minor. Is the implication then that liberal, realistic poets are not first-rate?

While admitting that Hardy is a much larger figure than Larkin, Davie still considers him minor because his poems deliver an untransformed reality. This, however, is the characteristic of Hardy's poetry which, after the transcendentalizing nineteenth century, later poets took over as particularly modern. Thus Yeats, in the one sentence he devotes to Hardy in the Introduction to his *Oxford Book of Modern Verse,* belittles Hardy's "technical accomplishment" but praises "his mastery of the impersonal objective scene." Italy's leading modernist poet, Eugenio Montale, finds Hardy's relation to objects congenial to his own art, as we see by his translation into Italian of Hardy's **"The Garden Seat,"** but Montale wonders at Hardy's "rigidly closed" forms and "impeccably traditional" stanzas. Davie concludes his discussion of Hardy's poems as follows:

> And so his poems, instead of transforming and displacing quantifiable reality or the reality of common sense, are on the contrary just so many glosses on that reality, which is conceived of as unchallengeably "given" and final. . . . He sold the vocation short, tacitly surrendering the proudest claims traditionally made for the act of poetic imagination.

Yet for an atheistic realist Hardy populates his poems with a surprising number of ghosts. And if he does not draw on the "myth-kitty," he does in his poems and fiction draw on observed folklore which, as the mythology of the illiterate, is older and more fundamental than the myths available through the literary tradition. Hardy's ghosts are not only the folklore ghosts of his ballads, but in his lyrics they are also psychological ghosts of Wordsworthian involuntary memory, wrapping the poems in mystery, dissolving fixities of place and time. Even **"The Garden Seat,"** a realistic portrayal of the abandoned garden seat, evokes the ghosts of those who used to sit upon it. The ghost of Hardy's dead wife Emma flits through these pages, as in **"After a Journey"** (which Davie calls a "phantasmagoria"), where the ghost is placeless: "Hereto I come to view a voiceless ghost; / Whither, O whither will its whim now draw me?" or in **"The Voice"** where Emma's ghost is a timeless, placeless auditory experience:

> Woman much missed, how you call to me, call
>   to me, . . .
> Or is it only the breeze, in its listlessness
> Travelling across the wet mead to me here,
> You being ever dissolved to wan wistlessness,
> Heard no more again far or near?
>
> Thus I; faltering forward,
> Leaves around me falling,
> Wind oozing thin through the thorn from nor-
>   ward,
> And the woman calling.

"Or is it only the breeze" continues the romantic tradition of natural-supernaturalism; while the shortened lines and changed meters of the last stanza produce the break in symmetry which by Davie's criteria (and mine) mark this poem as major.

The ghost of involuntary memory is best exemplified in **"During Wind and Rain,"** where scenes from the past rush back with unbearable poignancy to overwhelm a present represented only by wind and rain: "Ah, no; the years O! / How the sick leaves reel down in throngs." In **"Wessex Heights,"** a ghost poem of eschatological magnitude, the heights, realistically evoked by place names, seem to represent a detached state of existence comparable to the afterlife:

> and at crises when I stand,
> Say, on Ingpen Beacon eastward, or on Wylls-
>   Neck westwardly,
> I seem where I was before my birth, and after
>   death may be.

"In the lowlands," instead, "I have no comrade." "Down there I seem to be false to myself, my simple self that was." It seems misleading to try to identify, as does J. O. Bailey in his *Commentary,* the people being accused of betraying him since he accuses himself as well. "Too weak to mend" and "mind-chains do not clank where one's next neighbour is the sky" suggest self-accusation; so does "I am tracked by phantoms" and "I cannot go to the great grey Plain; there's a figure against the moon, / Nobody sees it but I, and it makes my breast beat out of tune." The ghosts who enter the powerful penultimate stanza seem to represent a purgatorial experience:

> There's a ghost at Yell'ham Bottom chiding
>   loud at the fall of the night,
> There's a ghost in Froom-side Vale, thin lipped
>   and vague, in a shroud of white,
> There is one in the railway-train whenever I do
>   not want it near,
> I see its profile against the pane, saying what I
>   would not hear.

The speaker saves himself through the liberating perspective achieved through loneliness on the heights: "And ghosts then keep their distance; and I know some liberty."

There are also poems in which Hardy portrays himself through the analogy to ghostliness. **"He Revisits His First School"** begins:

> I should not have shown in the flesh,
> I ought to have gone as a ghost;
> It was awkward, unseemly almost,
> Standing solidly there.

as though, Hardy says, I still belonged to the same vigorously living species that inhabits this classroom. I should have waited and returned from the tomb. In the comparable "Among School Children," Yeat's strong presence takes over the scene; whereas Hardy projects his relative absence: his ghost would have made a stronger presence. Absence is again projected in **"The Strange House (Max Gate, A. D. 2000),"** in which future inhabitants sense only faint ghostly stirrings of the Hardys' life there. The most uncanny of the ghostly self-portrayals is the early poem, **"I Look into My Glass,"** in which the aged speaker, seeing himself wasted in body and wishing his "heart had shrunk as thin" so he could wait his "endless rest / With equanimity," is horrified by the youthful passions that still shake his "fragile frame"—as though he were a ghost who could not find rest. One wonders how much Hardy's sense of himself as ghostly emerged from his knowledge that he was at birth taken for dead. "For my part," he wrote in his diary,

> if there is any way of getting a melancholy satisfaction out of life it lies in dying, so to speak, before one is out of the flesh; by which I mean putting on the manners of ghosts, wandering in their haunts, and taking their views of surrounding things. . . . Hence even when I enter into a room to pay a simple morning call I have unconsciously the habit of regarding the scene as if I were a spectre not solid enough to influence my environment.

I have cited all these examples to show, in answer to Davie, that many of Hardy's poems do transform reality, even if the poems of commonsense reality, poems like **"A Commonplace Day"** are admittedly most characteristic. Yet even that poem, which contains such finely realistic lines as "Wanly upon the panes / The rain slides," begins with the line, "The day is turning ghost," and opens out in the end to a cosmic speculation that accounts for the speaker's regret over the dying of so commonplace a day. In the "Apology" to *Late Lyrics*, Hardy tries to reconcile the two sides of his work by dreaming of "an alliance between religion . . . and complete rationality . . . by means of the interfusing effect of poetry." And in the *Life* he speaks of his "infinite trying to reconcile a scientific view of life with the emotional and spiritual, so that they may not be interdestructive."

We cannot classify Hardy the poet simply as an antimythic, commonsense realist when his great novels are wrapped in the mystery noted by Virginia Woolf, who, in her essay on him in *The Common Reader*, describes him as a novelist of unconscious intention, and when so many of his plots are modeled on the mythic patterns of Greek and Shakespearean drama. We cannot finally assess Hardy's poems without remembering that he began publishing his poems when already an elderly successful novelist and that readers were first drawn to the poems because of the novels. Too many critics of the poems (Davie included) write as though the novels did not exist.

Davie describes the difficulty of assessing Hardy's poetry. "Affection for Hardy the poet is general," he writes, ". . . but it is ruinously shot through with protectiveness, even condescension. Hardy is not thought of as an intellectual force." "None of Hardy's admirers have yet found how to make Hardy the poet *weigh* equally with Eliot and Pound and Yeats." Davie does not try to accomplish this end. He and other critics have in effect withdrawn Hardy from the competition by judging him according to another scale—as, though most critics avoid the term, a first-rate *minor* poet. John Crowe Ransom, in the *Southern Review* Hardy issue, calls him "a great minor poet."

Most critics note in Hardy's prodigious output an inevitable number of bad poems, a majority of interesting, well-made poems comprising a refreshing variety of subjects,

verse forms, and tones, and a dozen or two major poems. But there is no agreed upon Hardy canon for the poems as there is for the novels. Everyone, of course, agrees upon a few poems as major; otherwise each critic chooses different poems for discussion. Most critics (Yeats is an exception) praise Hardy's craftsmanship, and the question arises whether the major poems are to be viewed as happy accidents or as a main criterion for evaluating his poetry. In speaking of Hardy as ambitious technically but, except in *The Dynasts*, unambitious in every other way, Davie is suggesting that Hardy *chose* to work on a minor scale and that the major poems are happy accidents, moments when the creative impulse escaped from the watchful eye of the technician and the willful self: hence the chapter titles, "Hardy as Technician" and "Hardy Self-Excelling."

Before proposing my own different evaluation, I want to see how far Hardy can be considered minor in a nonpejorative sense, since many minor poets have become classics. The minor scale of Hardy's poetry makes him useful as an influence. His admirers display an intimate affection for him differing from the awe inspired by the great modernists. More recent poets have found Hardy supportive because he points a direction without preempting their own ideas and feelings. He is, in other words, a precursor from whom much can be learned, but not a competitor.

Auden speaks of his debt to Hardy for "technical instruction." Hardy's faults "were obvious even to a schoolboy, and the young can learn best from those of whom, because they can criticize them, they are not afraid." Hardy was useful as a teacher because no other English poet "employed so many and so complicated stanza forms," and because his rhymed verse kept Auden from too early an excursion into free verse which to a beginner looks easy but is really the most difficult of verse forms. Hardy "taught me much about direct colloquial diction, all the more because his directness was in phrasing and syntax, not in imagery"—for example, " 'I see what you are doing: you are leading me on' " [**"After a Journey"**] and " 'Upon that shore we are clean forgot' " [**"An Ancient to Ancients"**]. "Here was a 'modern' rhetoric which was more fertile and adaptable to different themes than any of Eliot's gas-works and rats' feet [imagery] which one could steal but never make one's own." Actually **"An Ancient to Ancients,"** which was first published in 1922, the year of *The Waste Land*, contains modern imagery comparable to Eliot's:

> Where once we danced, where once we sang,
>   Gentlemen,
> The floors are sunken, cobwebs hang,
> And cracks creep; worms have fed upon
> The doors. . . .
>
>   . . . . .
>
> The bower we shrined to Tennyson,
>   Gentlemen,
> Is roof-wrecked; damps there drip upon
> Sagged seats, the creeper-nails are rust,
> The spider is sole denizen.

But Auden's point is that the apprentice can take what he wants from a minor poet while still calling his style his own.

What then is the difference between major and first-rate minor poetry? The difference does not lie in Hardy's unevenness; Wordsworth is more uneven, yet most of us would agree that he is major. Auden, in introducing his anthology of nineteenth-century British minor poets, says that the major poet is likely to "write more bad poems than the minor." As for enjoyment, he says, "I cannot enjoy one poem by Shelley and am delighted by every line of William Barnes, but I know perfectly well that Shelley is a major poet, and Barnes a minor one."

What then is the difference? A major poet seems to me to be one whose world-view and personal character determine each other and determine the diction, imagery, and central myth running through all his poetry. His poetry is thus characteristic down to its unconscious elements; its originality of content and form emerges from its characteristicness or inner compulsion. That is why major poetry gives the impression of unfathomed depths, leaving us with the desire to *re*read as soon as we have read. Not so minor poetry, which, deriving from the poet's will, can usually be understood and enjoyed with one or two readings, though we may return to it many times to enjoy its clarity of meaning and form. The symmetries of minor poems are obvious, sometimes too obvious; whereas major poems favor asymmetries and leave a final impression of openness even though the older poems employ formal closures.

T. S. Eliot tries to define minor poetry in writing about another poet-novelist, Rudyard Kipling, whom Eliot calls a writer of "*great* verse." Kipling exhibits

> that skill of craftsmanship which seems to enable him to pass from form to form, though always in an identifiable idiom, and from subject to subject, so that we are aware of no inner compulsion to write about this rather than that—a versatility which may make us suspect him of being no more than a performer. . . . I mention Yeats at this point because of the contrast between his development, which is very apparent in the way he writes, and Kipling's development, which is only apparent in what he writes about. We expect to feel, with a great writer, that he *had* to write about the subject he took, and in that way. With no writer of equal eminence to Kipling is this inner compulsion . . . more difficult to discern.

Auden, too, employs the criterion of development. "In the case of the major poet," he says in his Introduction to *Minor Poets,*

> if confronted by two poems of his of equal merit but written at different times, the reader can immediately say which was written first. In the case of a minor poet, on the other hand, however excellent the two poems may be, the reader cannot settle their chronology on the basis of the poems themselves.

If we judge by these criteria, most of Hardy's poems would count as minor, but a significant number would count as major. The New Critics—if we take as an example the contributors to the *Southern Review's* Hardy Centennial issue (Summer 1940)—divide evenly between on the one

side Ransom and Tate, who praise Hardy's poetry with qualifications, and on the other Blackmur and Leavis, who have hardly a good word to say about the poetry. Critics of note nowadays, instead, are unqualified in their praise, beginning with Pound, who in *Guide to Kulchur* asks: "When we, if we live long enough, come to estimate the 'poetry of the period,' against Hardy's 600 pages we will put what?" [In "Wanted: Good Hardy Critic" *Critical Quarterly* (1966)] Philip Larkin "would not wish Hardy's *Collected Poems* a single page shorter, and regards it as many times over the best body of poetic work this century so far has to show." "It is generally agreed today," writes J. Hillis Miller [in *The Linguistic Moment: From Wordsworth to Stevens*] "that Thomas Hardy is one of the greatest of modern poets writing in English." [In *A Map of Misreading*] Harold Bloom calls Hardy a *strong* (i.e., a major) poet, "Shelley's ephebe." [in *The New Oxford Book of Victorian Verse*] Christopher Ricks describes "the recovery of the conviction of Hardy's greatness as a poet," but speaks of him as "the poet who owed so much to Browning."

We might reconcile these varying judgments by saying that Hardy is a major poet who chose for long stretches to work in the minor mode, probably because (now that he had given himself the luxury of writing poetry after all the years of writing fiction for money) he wanted to test his skill at as many poetic forms as possible, wanted to indulge in the craft of poetry. Most Hardy poems are successes in the minor mode, in that they make their points completely with symmetries that are obvious, sometimes too obvious. The symmetries of thought and form in **"The Convergence of the Twain"** are in my opinion too obvious. A successful poem like **"His Immortality"** establishes in an unvarying stanza of obvious symmetry a quickly predictable pattern of thought. The poem begins:

> I saw a dead man's finer part
> Shining within each faithful heart
> Of those bereft. Then said I: "This must be His
>   immortality."

Clearly, the dead man's immortality must diminish as the friends who remember him die. Each stanza describes another step in this diminution until in the final stanza the dead man finds "in me alone, a feeble spark, / Dying amid the dark." The imagery, however, springs a surprise in suggesting ironically that the speaker's immortality is equally vulnerable. The completeness of the ironical statement and the fulfillment of our expectations of thought and form make this poem successful in a minor mode.

As for the question of development, it is a commonplace that Hardy the poet—in contrast to Hardy the novelist—shows no *development,* that his volumes of verse mix earlier and later poems with no discernible differences of period, unless dated or distinguished by a subject such as the Boer War. Hardy dated his early poems, suggesting that in his view they differed from the later poems. Yet if an early success like **"Neutral Tones"** were not dated, could we discern its period? Looking back over Hardy's poems in the *Sunday Times* of May 28, 1922, Edmund Gosse concluded that the poetry had "suffered very little modification in the course of sixty years."

Dennis Taylor, however, in his *Hardy's Poetry 1860-1928,*

argues for development, finding it in Hardy's development of the meditative lyric and in the flowering of pastoral poems in his last volumes. While conceding that Hardy's "poetry does not display the obvious and clearly defined stages" of "other poets," Taylor shows that Hardy himself thought his volumes of verse displayed development, writing in his preface to *Time's Laughingstocks* (1909) of the first-person lyrics in that volume: " 'As a whole they will, I hope, take the reader forward, even if not far, rather than backward.' " By the criterion of development Hardy's poetry falls on the border between major and minor poetry. Having myself discerned little development in Hardy's poetry, I did note in my latest reading a steady increase in plain colloquial diction and syntax. Hardy developed, as Samuel Hynes puts it [in *The Pattern of Hardy's Poetry*], "toward a more consistent and more effective control of that tone which we recognize as uniquely his." Most importantly I noted, beginning so late as *Human Shows* (1925), the last volume published during Hardy's lifetime, a new imagist style which projects emotion entirely through closely observed objective correlatives. **"Snow in the Suburbs"** is the best known example: "Every branch big with it, / Bent every twig with it." Objective correlatives to emotion appear later: "Some flakes have lost their way, and grope back upward, when / Meeting those meandering down they turn and descend again." Although written in couplets throughout, the stanzas vary in line lengths and in the last stanza in number of lines, suggesting a freeing up of the verse.

Other examples are **"Green Slates,"** an **"East-End Curate,"** and **"Coming up Oxford Street: Evening"** (1925), which could be early Eliot:

> A city-clerk, with eyesight not of the best,
> Who sees no escape to the very verge of his days
> From the rut of Oxford Street into open ways;
> And he goes along with head and eyes flagging
>   forlorn,
> Empty of interest in things, and wondering why
>   he was born.

These couplets vary in number of syllables, and are much longer than the lines in the previous longer stanza, which vary in number of syllables and rhyme scheme—suggesting again a freeing up of the verse, already seen in such early poems as **"My Cicely"** and **"The Mother Mourns"** with their many unrhymed lines.

Still other examples are **"The Flower's Tragedy"** and **"At the Aquatic Sports,"** which sound like Frost ("So wholly is their being here / A business they pursue"), and in the posthumous *Winter Words* (1928) the admirably restrained **"The New Boots."** In the moving poem **"Bereft"** (dated 1901), a workingman's widow laments his death with the balladlike refrain:

> Leave the door unbarred,
> The clock unwound,
> Make my lone bed hard—
> Would 'twere underground!

In **"The New Boots,"** instead, the widow's grief is projected through a neighbor's description of the boots which the husband bought joyfully but never lived to wear. The widow's grief is all the more apparent because of her mute-

ness: " 'And she's not touched them or tried / To remove them. . . .' "

It is not clear whether Hardy's imagism developed from his own objective realism (already evident in **"On the Departure Platform,"** 1909), or whether he was influenced by the Imagist poets. He appears to have read volumes sent him by Ezra Pound in 1920-21 and by Amy Lowell in 1922, but his responses to these young Imagists do not suggest influence. The phrase in his last volume, "Just neutral-tinted haps" (**"He Never Expected Much"**), explains what he always aimed to convey, so that the neutrality characteristic of imagism was incipient in his early poems **"Neutral Tones"** and **"Hap."** Hardy's objective realism or metonymy is more characteristic of his poetry than are metaphor and symbol.

If we apply to Hardy Eliot's remark about Kipling's variety, we find that as poet Hardy exhibits even more variety than Kipling, in that he passes not only from form to form and subject to subject but also from level to level. For he mixes with humorous verse and melodramatic balladry poems that are serious philosophically and others that are in the full sense "poetry." The difference between Hardy and his older friend, the Dorsetshire dialect poet William Barnes, exemplifies Hardy's ambiguous position between minor and major poet. According to Samuel Hynes, Barnes's poetry is idyllic whereas Hardy introduces into the regional setting modern ideas: "Darwin stands between them" (*Pattern of Hardy's Poetry*).

Yet we do not feel in reading through a Hardy volume the assured pitch of intensity that we feel with indubitably major poets, or the equally assured lightness of versifiers. Hardy's variousness can be entertaining if we are alive to his shifts of tone; otherwise we may become impatient with his skillful ballads and narratives because our standards have been determined by the greater depths of emotion and psychological insights offered in the major poems. When an indubitably major poet relaxes into light verse—as does Eliot in his charming little book on cats—we feel that the playful excursion need not be taken into account for understanding him. But Hardy establishes no such criterion for exclusion. He himself recognized this problem when complaining in the "Apology" to *Late Lyrics,*

> that dramatic anecdotes of a satirical and humorous intention following verse in a graver voice, have been read as misfires because they raise the smile that they were intended to raise, the journalist, deaf to the sudden change of key, being unconscious that he is laughing with the author, and not at him. I admit that I did not foresee such contingencies as I ought to have done, and that people might not perceive when the tone altered.

Eliot's remark that Kipling's poetry "does not revolutionize" (*On Poetry and Poets*) is inapplicable to Hardy as evidenced by his influence on succeeding poets. Although Hardy did not innovate in verse forms, he did innovate in diction, tone, and above all in subject matter. As novelist Hardy was a major innovator, having developed sex and the unconscious as subjects and mythical rendition as technique. These innovations appear also in the poetry, though less conspicuously. To the extent that Hardy innovated, he might be considered a major poet; to the extent that he modernized and transmitted what was usable in nineteenth-century poetry, Hardy might be considered a first-class minor poet.

What is the use, one might well ask, of the distinction I am trying to draw between major and minor poetry? I am, first of all, trying to develop a standard for evaluating Hardy as against the classic modernist poets and to give him his fair place in the competition by showing that he is in most cases successful on another scale. I am also trying to develop criteria for dealing with the great variety of levels and tones in Hardy's poems. To use the word "major" for the best of them is to make clear the extent and mode of their success. To use the words "first-class minor" for many of the others is to recognize their success on another scale. Finally I want to distinguish between Hardy's poems and novels, to argue for the great novels as his most consistently major work, containing, albeit in prose, his most massively major poetry. (pp. 151-61)

> Robert Langbaum, "The Issue of Hardy's Poetry," in Victorian Poetry, Vol. 30, No. 2, Summer, 1992, pp. 151-63.

FURTHER READING

Bibliography

Gerber, Helmut E., and Davis, W. Eugene. *Thomas Hardy: An Annotated Bibliography of Writings about Him,* 2 vols. De Kalb: Northern Illinois University Press, 1973-83.
> Includes a comprehensive list of periodicals and books which discuss Hardy's poetry.

Biography

Hardy, Florence Emily. *The Early Life of Thomas Hardy: 1840-1891.* New York: The Macmillan Co., 1928, 327 p.
> Biography of Hardy's first fifty-one years, composed largely of diary entries, as well as letters and conversations with Hardy. Some critics believe that the biographical works purportedly written by Florence Emily Hardy, Hardy's second wife, were written entirely by Hardy.

——. *The Later Years of Thomas Hardy: 1892-1928.* New York: The Macmillan Co., 1928, 327 p.
> Noncritical account of Hardy's later years. This book incorporates the text of many letters from Hardy to various correspondents.

Millgate, Michael. *Thomas Hardy: A Biography.* New York: Random House, 1982, 637 p.
> Noncritical biography that draws upon diaries, notebooks, letters, and local records previously inaccessible to biographers. Millgate devotes an appendix to the theory that Hardy fathered an illegitimate son with his cousin Tryphena Sparks.

Weber, Carl J. *Hardy of Wessex: His Life and Literary Career.* New York: Columbia University Press, 1965, 324 p.
> Biography based in large part on Hardy's letters, which this prominent Hardy scholar edited for publication.

Criticism

Bailey, J. O. *The Poetry of Thomas Hardy: A Handbook and Commentary.* Chapel Hill: University of North Carolina Press, 1970, 712 p.
> Supplies literary and biographical background to Hardy's complete poems. Bailey maintains that knowledge of Hardy's life is essential to a full understanding of his poetry.

Blackmur, R. P. "The Shorter Poems of Thomas Hardy." In his *The Expense of Greatness,* pp. 37-73. Gloucester, Mass.: Peter Smith, 1958.
> Overview of Hardy's poetry. Blackmur concludes that "Hardy is the great example of a sensibility violated by ideas; and perhaps the unique example, since Swift, of a sensibility great enough—locked enough in life—to survive the violation."

Blunden, Edmund. *Thomas Hardy.* London: Macmillan and Co., 1942, 286 p.
> Critical study of the novels and poetry.

Collins, V. H. "The Love Poetry of Thomas Hardy." *Essays and Studies* XXVIII (1942): 69-83.
> Analyzes Hardy's love poems, with special emphasis placed on *Poems of 1912-13,* Hardy's series of elegies for his first wife.

Cox, R. G., ed. *Thomas Hardy: The Critical Heritage.* New York: Barnes and Noble, 1970, 473 p.
> Useful compendium of early magazine reviews of Hardy's fiction and poetry.

Davie, Donald. *Thomas Hardy and British Poetry.* New York: Oxford University Press, 1972, 192 p.
> Critical study that claims "in British poetry of the last fifty years . . . the most far-reaching influence, for good and ill, has not been Yeats, still less Eliot or Pound, not Lawrence, but *Hardy."* Davie examines Hardy's influence on such authors as W. H. Auden, J. R. R. Tolkien, and Kingsley Amis.

Deutsch, Babette. "A Look at the Worst." In her *Poetry in Our Time,* pp. 1-27. New York: Columbia University Press, 1952.
> Discussion of Hardy's poetry, which Deutsch finds "bridges the gulf between the Victorian sensibility and our own."

Elliot, George R. "Hardy's Poetry and the Ghostly Moving Picture." *South Atlantic Quarterly* XXVII (July 1928): 280-91.
> Examines the pessimistic view of life expressed in Hardy's poetry, focusing on *The Dynasts.*

Grey, Rowland. "Woman in the Poetry of Thomas Hardy." *Fortnightly Review* DCCIX (January 1926): 34-46.
> Explores Hardy's presentation of the "eternal feminine" in his poems.

Howe, Irving. *Thomas Hardy.* New York: Macmillan, 1985, 206 p.
> Critical survey of Hardy's work that includes biographi-

cal material and separate chapters on the lyric poems and *The Dynasts.*

Jacobus, Mary. "Hardy's Magian Retrospect." *Essays in Criticism* XXXII, No. 3 (July 1982): 258-79.

Discussion of Hardy's "literary posthumousness"—his seeming obsession, in the poems from *Wessex Poems* onward, with the form of immortality a writer of lasting literary merit can attain.

Kendall, Mae. "Pessimism and Thomas Hardy's Poems." *London Quarterly Review* CLXXXII, No. 2 (April 1899): 223-34.

Review of *Wessex Poems* that finds Hardy's verse immoral due to the poet's "egotism" and pessimistic outlook.

Leavis, F. R. "Hardy the Poet." In his *The Critic as Anti-Philosopher,* edited by G. Singh, pp. 98-108. Athens: University of Georgia Press, 1983.

Overview of Hardy's poetry. Leavis finds Hardy's poems stylistically deficient, but concludes that "the single-minded integrity of [Hardy's] preoccupation with a real world and a real past, the intentness of his focus upon particular facts and situations, gives his poetry the solidest kind of emotional substance."

Lucas, F. L. "Hardy." In his *Eight Victorian Poets,* pp. 133-51. Cambridge: Cambridge University Press, 1930.

Praises Hardy's poetry for its compassion and technical virtuosity.

Mitchell, P. E. "Music and Hardy's Poetry." *English Literature in Transition* 30, No. 3 (1987): 308-21.

Discussion of the influence of folk music on Hardy's poetry.

————. "Passion and Companionship in Hardy's Poetry." *Victorian Poetry* 27, No. 1 (Spring 1989): 77-93.

Praises Hardy's realistic and unidealized portrayal of marriage and romance in his poetry.

Moore, Marianne. "Memory's Immortal Gear." *Chicago Review* IV, No. 1 (Autumn 1949): 15-19.

Positive assessment of Hardy's poetry.

Morgan, William W. "The Partial Vision: Hardy's Ideal of Dramatic Poetry." *Tennessee Studies in Literature* XX (1975): 100-08.

Explores Hardy's conception of dramatic poetry.

Orel, Harold. *Thomas Hardy's Epic-Drama: A Study of "The Dynasts."* Lawrence: University of Kansas Publications, 1963, 122 p.

Contains chapters on the writing of *The Dynasts,* its philosophical foundations, its relationship to Milton's *Paradise Lost,* and "Hardy's Attitude toward War."

Pinion, F. B. *A Hardy Companion: A Guide to the Works of Thomas Hardy and Their Background.* London: Macmillan, 1968, 55 p.

Survey of Hardy's work and its major influences, with biographical background.

Taylor, Dennis. *Hardy's Poetry, 1860-1928.* New York: Columbia University Press, 1981, 204 p.

Traces the development of Hardy's poetry.

Van Doren, Mark. "The Poems of Thomas Hardy." In his *The Essays of Mark Van Doren,* pp. 107-28. Westport, Conn.: Greenwood Press, 1980.

Positive overview of Hardy's poetry.

Wright, Walter. *The Shaping of "The Dynasts": A Study in Thomas Hardy.* Lincoln: University of Nebraska Press, 1967, 334 p.

Traces the creative evolution of *The Dynasts,* with a textual examination of the various drafts and revisions of the manuscripts.

Mein Kampf

Adolf Hitler

German politician.

The following entry presents criticism of Hitler's *Mein Kampf* (1925; first published in English as *My Battle,* 1933).

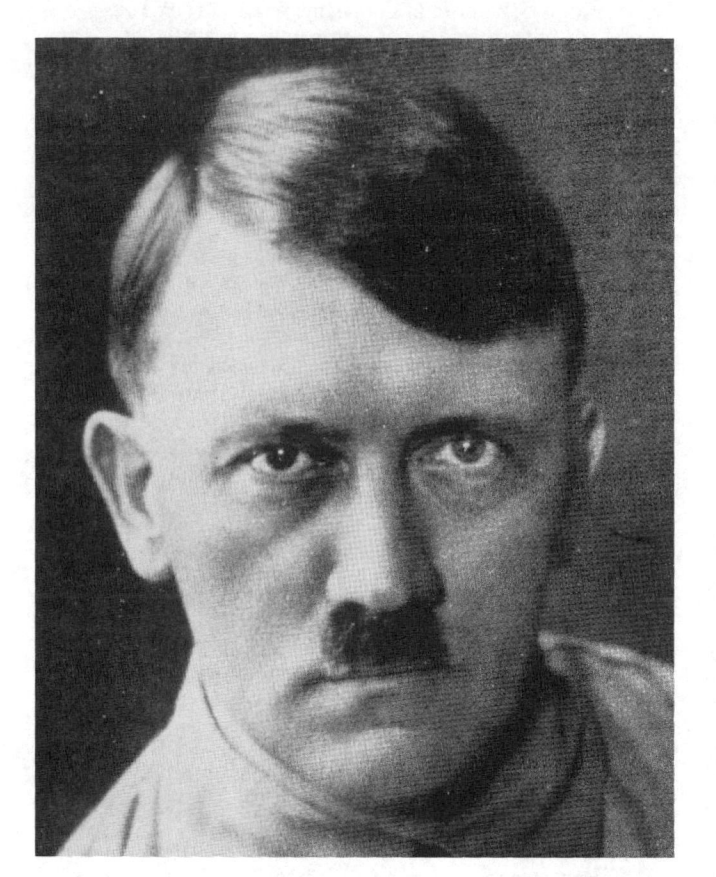

INTRODUCTION

One of the most historically important documents of the twentieth century, *Mein Kampf* outlines the political and social ideology of Adolf Hitler, dictator of Germany from 1933 to 1945. Part autobiography, part despotic manifesto, and, according to most scholars, part fiction, *Mein Kampf* is today considered a work of poorly written megalomaniacal fanaticism, significant more for the tragic and far-reaching effects of its ideas than for the work itself.

Hitler was born in Braunau, Austria, in 1889. His dubious family history, including his father's illegitimacy, was a source of embarrassment to him throughout his life. In 1908 he moved to Vienna—where, he claimed later in *Mein Kampf,* he began forming many of his opinions and ideas—hoping to study art at the Vienna Art Academy. After his application to the school was rejected, he took an interest in politics and began reading voraciously while living on public assistance. In 1913, disgusted with what he considered Viennese hedonism, Hitler moved to Munich, and a year later enlisted in the Bavarian army. Twice decorated with Germany's Iron Cross, Hitler emerged from the military an already powerful speaker and was appointed chairman of the German National Socialist (Nazi) Party in 1921. Rapidly gaining influence, he mounted his infamous Beerhall Putsch in November 1923. The attempted takeover of the German government failed, and Hitler was found guilty of treason and sent to Landsberg prison, serving only nine months of his five-year sentence.

While at Landsberg, Hitler dictated the first volume of *Mein Kampf* to his cellmate Rudolf Hess, who may have had a hand in shaping the content of the book. After his release, Hitler finished the second volume and sought more constitutional means of attaining power. Running on an extreme nationalistic and anti-Semitic platform, he rose again to the position of party leader, re-creating himself through propaganda and rhetoric as the Führer, a self-styled messiah who would lead Germany out of its social and economic morass. In 1933 Paul von Hindenburg, then president of Germany, appointed Hitler cabinet chancellor. Upon Hindenburg's death Hitler succeeded him as president. Flaunting his power, he began a series of antagonistic acts that led ultimately to the outbreak of World War II. In 1942 Hitler and his strategy started to unravel as he became more delusional, insisting on holding direct command of the armed forces. With Germany falling to the Allies, Hitler committed suicide on 30 April 1945.

Mein Kampf was first published in 1925 to a largely unreceptive German audience, selling only 23,000 copies of the first volume and 13,000 of the second up to 1930. However, as Hitler gained political power the Nazis insisted that every German citizen should own a copy. Subsequently, *Mein Kampf* was given as a wedding present to all newly married couples at the Registry Office, to railway officials who demonstrated meritorious service, to all civil servants, and to all school children as a primer on race, genetics, and population. In 1933 alone, almost 1,000,000 copies were sold in Germany. In the United States excerpts from *Mein Kampf* were first translated and published in 1933. Later that year a complete unauthorized translation was published, which led to a legal dispute between Hitler and the publisher, Stackpole and Sons. Afterwards, Hitler ensured that the book could not be completely translated outside of Germany. The most violently racist and inflammatory passages were cut from translations, leaving a seemingly harmless version of the original, until 1939, when Hurst and Blackett published the first unexpurgated English translation. Since then, *Mein*

Kampf has been widely translated worldwide, although sales of the book were forbidden in Germany beginning in October 1945.

The earliest reviews of *Mein Kampf* set the tone for subsequent commentary on Hitler's book, with a 1925 reviewer in the conservative Berlin newspaper *Kreuz-Zeitung* commenting, "The reader looks for the fire of the spirit but only finds arrogance; instead of inspiration, he finds boredom; instead of love and enthusiasm, catchwords; instead of wholesome hatred, nothing but abuse." International critical reaction to *Mein Kampf* began after the publication of the Hurst and Blackett edition. Some commentators believed that the translator, James Murphy, had misread important sections, distorting Hitler's meaning even further than the expurgated editions had. All editions, however, met with an almost universal distaste for Hitler's unwieldy, oratorical style. Dorothy Thompson wrote: "If the world is overthrown by this document and the man behind it, it is overthrown without benefit of grammar or literary style."

Both literary critics and psychologists have analyzed *Mein Kampf* for whatever insight it might provide into the character and actions of its author. Many have found that Hitler created a mythological narrative of his life and his mission in *Mein Kampf,* inventing facts about himself that would aid the rapid dispersion of his messianic doctrine. Kenneth Burke was among the first to comment on Hitler's use of religious symbolism as a propaganda tool. Casting himself as a healer who would unify Aryans, "Hitler found a panacea, a 'cure for what ails you,' a 'snakeoil,' that made such sinister unifying possible within his own nation. . . . This book is the well of Nazi magic; crude magic, but effective." Raymond G. McInnis has observed: "Because of the book's 'turgid,' convoluted style, it suffered the fate of all works purchased out of duty or to show political orthodoxy: it remained largely unread." Few foreign heads of state had read *Mein Kampf* prior to World War II, and most of those who had read it took neither the book nor its author seriously. Even such high-ranking Nazi officials as Josef Goebbels and Hermann Goering acknowledged that they had not read it. Describing the consequences of the unread credo of Nazism, Norman Cousins wrote: "For every word in *Mein Kampf,* 125 lives were to be lost; for every page, 4,700 lives; for every chapter, more than 1,200,000 lives."

CRITICISM

Frederick B. Adams, Jr.   (essay date 1937)

[*In the following excerpt, Adams comments on several early expurgated translations of* Mein Kampf.]

Mein Kampf is the bible of Nazism, and the German text is the basic guide of National Socialist foreign and domestic policy. The book has sold nearly three million copies, and has been translated into at least ten languages, with careful editorial changes. If you are a German living under the influence of the Third Reich, it is good form to have a copy of the book in your library. And if both volumes of your edition are "firsts", published in 1925 and 1927, you have at least circumstantial evidence that you supported Hitler before he came to power, during the trying years when his book helped to unite the factions of the National Socialist movement and actually did much to finance its growth. That is why first editions of *Mein Kampf* are rare outside of Germany, and command a high price in Germany. The trading is largely under-cover, and carried on by Communists.

The German text has been glorified in every conceivable manner. It is part of the curriculum in German schools and universities. The Foreign Ministry has instructed German consuls who perform marriages abroad to give each couple a copy of the book as a wedding present (provided both parties are "Aryans"). Last summer, the Reich League of German Government Officials presented to Hitler an illuminated manuscript of *Mein Kampf* in Gothic script; the volume was the work of seven graphologists who toiled for eleven months to transcribe the text on vellum, after which the leaves were bound in iron (as being the only suitable medium). Visitors to the Olympic Games were astounded to see this monument to propaganda exhibited in the "Hall of Honor" not far from a copy of the Gutenberg Bible. It is scarcely astonishing that German industrialists have considered the printed book a suitable Christmas present for employees.

Mein Kampf is a popular work outside of Germany. It furnishes fuel for many fires of hatred. The Arabs in Palestine are very fond of it. But what the outside world learns about Hitler's ideas and policies is quite different from what the Germans know almost by heart.

Hamilton Fish Armstrong, in his invaluable book *We or They* quotes four times from *Mein Kampf,* but states in a foot-note that only one of the passages quoted is to be found in the American version, published by Houghton Mifflin Company under the title *My Battle.* Mr. Armstrong's three censored passages are

> . . . so-called humanitarianism, that product of a mixture of stupidity, cowardice and superciliousness, [which] will melt away like snow in the March sunshine.

(No use in offending some of the influential brain-trusters.)

> Anyone who really from his heart desires the victory of the pacifist idea in this world should support by every means the conquest of the world by the Germans.

Hitler hopes for peace, but a peace

> established by the victorious sword of a master-nation which leads the world to serve a higher culture.

(You couldn't ask for anything more peaceful than a victorious sword.)

Another commentator, Otto D. Tolischus, writing in *The New York Times Magazine* for October 18, 1936, says:

> The worst example [of translations edited with a view to softening the rough spots] is the English translation published in London. It has eliminated most of the passages referring to France; it has even eliminated the justification of war cited in the opening of the book and toned down the language to the point of falsification.
>
> France, the country most affected by the book, has no translation of it at all. Hitler has steadily refused to authorize a French translation, and an unauthorized translation issued in Paris was suppressed on the ground of copyright violation after an appeal to the French commercial courts by Hitler's publishing house.
>
> The authoritative explanation of [the existence of] the embarrassing passages is that they were written at a time of special stress when Germany was suffering from African troops in the Rhineland, from the Ruhr occupation, and reparations.

Hitler, in other words, doesn't mind repeating his old slurs on France for the ears of his own people, but he doesn't want the French to suspect that he's doing it.

What do you suppose the Chinese translation says?

Here, it seems to me, is a legitimate subject for study by some modern language seminar. I may be the only person who thinks so, and the whole story may never be told. To be sure, Dr. Goebbels ought to be able to supply all the clues to the puzzle, but somehow or other, I doubt if he would. (pp. 467-68)

> *Frederick B. Adams, Jr., "The Crow's Nest,"*
> *in* The Colophon, *Vol. II, Part 3, Summer,*
> *1937, pp. 465-79.*

R. C. K. Ensor   (essay date 1939)

[*Ensor was an English journalist, educator, poet, and author of works on history and politics. Below, a transcription of Ensor's lecture on* Mein Kampf, *delivered on 4 May 1939, is followed by a summary of the discussion that took place after the lecture. In the address, Ensor outlines Hitler's foreign policy in* Mein Kampf *and discusses how the employment of this policy would affect European affairs.*]

Very few great men of action have ever disclosed beforehand so clearly as Adolf Hitler the principles and purposes that guide their acts. Building up a mass movement almost from the bottom, he had to be exceptionally frank with his disciples from quite an early stage. After the European War he began looking very far ahead. He sought to create, not an ordinary political party which might play a give-and-take rôle among a lot of others, but a revolutionary party which should sweep the national board and brush all the other parties away. Nor was even that revolution the goal of his aims. He desired power not so much for its own sake as for the subsequent course of national policy upon which it would enable him to launch the German people. When it is said sometimes that Hitler is sincere,

I think that that is what is meant, and I think it is true. His course, as we shall see, would necessitate the people being ready to endure hardship, to strain every muscle, and eventually to fight a great war. It was not in Hitler's creed that a mass of 60 or 80 million human beings could be carried successfully through an ordeal like that in ignorance. If they were to achieve the journey they must know why they marched. He must enable them to adopt his motives as their own. Therefore he had got to show them what his motives were. It meant much more than attracting them to a political programme in the ordinary sense. He had to give them a whole new *Weltanschauung,* a new way of viewing the universe; a new interpretation, that is, of the meaning of life and the objects of national policy. Of that *Weltanschauung*—pardon my using the word, but there is no compact word in English that quite gives the meaning—*Mein Kampf* is the exposition. It is not, on the face of it, a systematic exposition. It was written in two parts, separately; the first in 1924, during a period of detention in a fortress to which Hitler was sentenced for his part in the Munich *Putsch* fiasco of November 1923; and the second after his liberation. The last page of it is dated November 1926.

It is a hotch-potch of the most varied ingredients. Much of it is autobiography, much is doctrine, a good deal is history (often bad history) and much is polemics (usually very abusive polemics). Hitler's powerful mind never underwent in his youth any higher education. In adult life he undoubtedly has read a great deal, besides arguing and making speeches. But his lack of formal intellectual discipline shows itself in a marked incapacity to arrange his material. He jumps from one topic to another, like the open-air speaker that he used to be. He is full of repetitions and digressions. And though he does, of course, make some show of grouping particular subjects in particular chapters, it is broadly true to say of the book that any subject may turn up on almost any page. That renders it confusing and boring to the foreign reader, and explains why so few foreigners have, I think, effectively read it. And yet it really is a very powerful book, not merely because, if you read it in the German, the terse, harsh staccato rhetoric gives you the sense of a very strong personality, but because, while it lacks logical sequence, it by no means lacks logic. Its varied themes do cohere, and are masterfully bound together to form a single network of wide-reaching yet consistent argumentation.

Another hindrance to the foreign reader is that without a knowledge that in most cases he will not possess he can hardly appreciate the interest of the autobiographical part. And yet that is a very important part. Hitler himself says expressly that the key to his whole mental development lies in his pre-War experiences at Vienna; and it is clear that, at any rate on the emotional side, his guiding hates were derived from that—hatred of the Habsburgs, of the Czechs, of the Jews, of the Socialists, and of parliamentary institutions. It was from observing the Viennese Socialists, he also tells us, that he learned the methods of terrorisation and gangsterism which he himself adopted and perfected, first for national and later for international purposes. Here are two passages which form an interesting account of that technique. The first runs:—

The mentality of the people at large is not sensitive to anything hesitant and weak. Like a woman whose inner sensibilities are not so much swayed by reason as by a vague emotional longing after the strength that is her complement and who would therefore rather bow to a strong man than lord it over a weak man, so the masses would sooner be bossed than supplicated, and feel more reassured by a doctrine that brooks no rival than by one that offers them a liberal choice. With the latter they scarcely know how to deal; and tend therefore to feel let down. Of the barefaced intimidation practised on their minds, or the violent outrage committed upon their human liberty, they are no more conscious than they are of the whole doctrine's fallacies. They see only the ruthless force and brutality of its determined utterances, to which in the end they always succumb.

There you see a view of human nature like that expressed in three well-known lines of Browning:

Oh, the crowd must have emphatic warrant!
Right arm's rod-sweep, tongue's imperial fiat!
Never dares the man put off the prophet.

Hitler does not put off the prophet. He has based his practice on that principle, and his book exemplifies it at every turn. And yet such is its extraordinary candour in this and in many other matters that even while doing so it admits what it is doing.

Here is my second passage:—

The Social Democrats would pick out the adversary whom they thought most formidable [this is an account of the Social Democrats in Vienna and their technique for dealing with political enemies] and on a given signal discharge against him a regular drumfire of lies and slanders. They went on with it, until the nerves of the other side broke down and to get some peace they sacrificed the victim. Only they never got their peace, the fools! The same tactics were repeated over and over again until fear of the mad dogs exercised through suggestion the effect of paralysis.

Well, you could scarcely get a better description of how Hitler himself has dealt with his opponents—first in internal German politics, and then in the international field with such men as Schuschnigg and Beneš. He tells us quite frankly in the book how, observing what the Socialists did, he resolved to copy them and was confident he could better their example.

But let us return to our main track. To follow Hitler's argument in all its branches would be a task far beyond our scale and scope to-night. What I propose to attempt here is to give the briefest outline that I can contrive of his general *Weltanschauung,* and then in more detail show how he applies it in the field of politics and particularly in that of foreign policy.

He starts with a theory, largely false but fanatically believed in, of race. Mankind consists of many and varied races, but the law of higher life and progress, whether spiritual, artistic, economic, is due to one of them only—variously called Aryan or Nordic. This race has acted and

re-enacted, countless times over in history, a particular drama. Members of it having, in virtue of their native superiority, overrun large non-Aryan regions and subdued the non-Aryan inhabitants to their purposes, have built up on the basis of the non-Aryans' brute labour a great edifice of civilisation. These edifices have in turn decayed and collapsed. Why? Hitler's answer is: through miscegenation. The conquering ruling minority has intermarried with its subjects, and being much fewer than they has had its blood swamped by theirs. Only by keeping its blood pure could it have preserved and extended the civilisation, which sprang from its hereditary racial qualities and from them alone. The business therefore of a modern Nordic nation whose blood is that of the supreme race, is to keep that blood pure, and at the same time to maximise its pure offspring in every possible way and to quarter it out over the face of the earth as strongly as possible. Its spread and its dominance are desirable, not only in its own interests, but in those of the rest of mankind, who can hope to derive progress and civilisation from no other source.

Now when you ask what modern nations find themselves in this exalted position of duty and privilege, the answer first and foremost is: the Germans. Germany is the Nordic Great Power. The only other great European nation with any comparable claim is the British. Our past success in quartering out a largely Nordic stock over vast areas of the world outside Europe always evokes Hitler's sincere respect; as you remember it did in his last speech to the German Parliament. But no such even partial equality is conceded to any of Germany's chief neighbours. The French were always a people of mongrels, and are now on the way to becoming a "mulatto empire." As for the Slavs, of whatever kind, they belong to a totally inferior order of humanity and have, as against Germans, no moral rights. If a German ruler conquers Slav land and dispossesses its Slavs in order to settle Germans on it, he is doing not merely a patriotic but a highly moral act; since it is the interest of humanity as a whole that the habitat of the higher race should be extended. A logical but rather unexpected corollary of the same theory is that it is wrong to Germanise subject Slavs. Hitler inveighs against the policies of Habsburg rulers like Joseph II who tried to make the Czechs speak German. For him it is the race that is vital, not the language, and a German speaking Slav is a danger to race purity. It is one of the few glaring inconsistencies in his book that while inveighing against the Habsburgs on that score he also blames bitterly the Badeni language decrees and other concessions to the Slav languages made under Francis Joseph. But that indeed, like much else of his intense hatred of the Habsburgs, seems to be mere blind prejudice inherited from his youthful activity as a follower of pan-Germanism in pre-War Vienna.

The general picture, then, is of one strong creative race and a varied lot of weak non-creative races, who are as wax for the strong race to mould. But there is yet another race to be accounted for, whose faults are not negative but positive, a sort of Satan among the nations. It is active, aggressive, it has no *Lebensraum* of its own, but preys parasitically on that of others, and even permeates the Nordic paradise itself, poisoning, polluting, paralysing. That race is the Jews. The difference between them and races like the

Slavs is that while the latter may be quite useful in the German habitat, if they are kept down in a servile capacity, the Jews cannot be tolerated in any capacity. The only way to deal with them is to get rid of them altogether.

Now these doctrines may sound crude; as indeed they are. But they were exceedingly well-suited for German consumption after the War. To begin with, it is and has long been an almost universal habit among Germans to regard themselves as a race naturally gifted above all other races, a sort of top and crown of mankind. No other great people, I think, has quite an equivalent habit. French, British, Americans, each commonly believe that their particular nation has the greatest record in the world, and are ready to strain history to prove it. But you do not find them feeling that their race is a separate species of humanity, superior to any other. The Germans do. There are some fairly obvious reasons for it, I think. For French, British and Americans the political unit, the nation, is what unites. But the Germans before Bismarck never had been a nation in the political sense, and even Bismarck brought only about three-quarters of them under a common flag. Hence they thought of themselves not as a nation but as a people, a *Volk,* and so, if you like, a race, scattered about Europe under many flags, and everywhere far superior to the people among whom they lived. Note, too, that their sense of superiority was not unplausible. Everywhere in Central and Eastern Europe the German populations can be seen by the naked eye to be hard-working, thrifty, honest, progressive, with clean persons, clean houses, decent sanitation and well-attended schools. By contrast the Slavs (the Czechs alone excepted) have much lower standards, and appear in the mass as being backward, thriftless, shifty, dirty, verminous, insanitary and illiterate. "Where Germanism ends," a German once said to me, "the louse and the bug begin." The reasons for this difference are not really race, of course, but may be found much more in history, tradition, religion, economics and other things. But the difference is there, and race pride was not a surprising result.

That is why the Eastern post-War settlements rankled so bitterly in Germany. Even Liberal Germans thought that the freedom of Poles or Czechs was too dearly purchased, if it entailed putting German minorities under them. They felt rather as Americans would if a foreign conqueror were to put the Southern States under negro rule. Even in 1927, when Germany was perhaps more peaceful and more republican than at any other time, and when there happened to be some small controversies with Poland, I could not, on a visit, find anyone who would discuss the Poles on any other hypothesis than that they were in effect sub-human. When, therefore, Hitler proclaimed the Germans a ruling race, and denounced the post-War Treaties as an infamous violation of the rights of the ruling race, and insisted not only on abrogating them but on aiming to bring all Germans under the German flag and on immensely extending the German habitat, it gave his readers and hearers the same sort of satisfaction that one might imagine a bow feels when its string has been drawn abnormally taut and it is suddenly released to spring away in the other direction.

Let us next examine more specially this question of the German people's habitat, for in it is the key to Hitler's foreign policy. The main discussions about it are in the fourth chapter of the first part and the thirteenth and fourteenth chapters of the second part of his book, but it keeps cropping up all over the book and always in terms that are clear, consistent, fundamental. Every people, says Hitler, if it is to live healthily must have a sufficient area to live in. Further, since as we have seen it is the duty of the Nordic race rapidly to increase its numbers, Germany, as the home of the great Nordic people, must have a large amount of extra space for future expansion. Now, how is she situated in these respects? The answer is that she has nothing like enough land for the present, let alone for the future. With an annual increase given by Hitler as 900,000, she must face famine unless ways and means are found which will forestall the danger of misery and hunger. Four solutions, says Hitler, are possible. (1) Contraceptive limitation of births. That is rejected; being, of course, in complete disagreement with his whole position. (2) "Internal colonisation," a German phrase meaning what we should call a small-holdings movement. This, he says rightly enough, could never cover any large part of the problem. (3) Acquisition of new territory beyond the existing frontiers, enabling more Germans to live by the land. (4) Increase of manufactures for export enabling more Germans to live on the existing territory by foreign trade. The real choice is between (3) and (4). The rulers of pre-War Germany from 1870 onwards chose (4), that is, industrialisation for export. They ought, says Hitler, to have chosen (3)—more peasant production in a greatly enlarged national territory.

Why does Hitler reject the export solution? For three reasons. First, because it involves urbanising and proletarianising the people. Himself a poor country boy driven to Vienna to earn his living, he hates the process. Secondly, because it puts German life at the mercy of vicissitudes in foreign countries which it cannot control. Thirdly, a too compact country is vulnerable in war. A country like Russia or the United States with its population well spread out over a vast area derives defensive strength from its very vastness. A certain size is necessary for the seat of a World Power. At present Germany is not one. But she must become one or perish. What size, then? Well, look at Soviet Russia, says Hitler, look at the British Empire or the United States, China or even the French Empire. Beside any of these Germany's existing territory seems in another class. She must expand. But how? Overseas colonies will not do for this purpose, since none could be obtained suitable for settling millions of white peasants. On the other hand, east of Germany's present living space, in the vast plain of Central and Eastern Europe, immense fertile areas exist as yet thinly populated by inferior peoples. Able to be reached by land, to be conquered and held by the army, and to form with existing Germany a single continuous realm, those areas provide the only and the perfect solution. But how can they be obtained? How, answers Hitler, originally were the two Ostmarks obtained, East Prussia and Austria? How indeed, if you look back far enough, were most of the present German territories obtained? By the German sword followed up by the German plough. Hitler does not flinch from the frank avowal that his policy must be one of annexation by force and that the main victim to be despoiled is Russia. He answers objectors on the first point by saying that all frontiers and all titles to territory were established by force originally, and on the second by pointing to Russia's Bolshevik disorganisation as a providential opportunity for Germany. But the bedrock policy is clear. Germany can only save herself by a vast eastern annexation. She can only achieve the annexation by a European war, and for that war she must start arming herself at top speed at once. Not only limitation of arms but every confining shackle of the Versailles system Germany must in due course ruthlessly strike away. The actual order of the steps taken since 1933— rearmament, remilitarisation of the Rhineland, absorption of Austria, subjugation of Czechoslovakia, and next the prospective subjection of Poland and Roumania—has conformed to a perfectly logical sequence. As to the stage at which Hitler would have to fight his decisive war, it is clear that he hoped, as results proved rightly, that rearmament, remilitarisation of the Rhineland and Austria could be achieved without fighting. The Czechoslovak stage he was bound to assume could not. He was ready to launch the supreme war last September. And to-day it may even be that he feels sorry because, yielding to others, he did not do so.

I am aware that some English experts do not attach all that importance to the idea of *Lebensraum* in Hitler's thinking, but unless he has changed since *Mein Kampf*, of which there is less than no evidence, I think they are clearly wrong. For in the book it is the cardinal concept in foreign policy. It comes out at all sorts of points. It founds, for instance, the whole of the long, vehement and in some ways very acute criticisms, which he passes on Germany's pre-War foreign policies. The real task, he says, for her pre-War statesmen was to provide new *Lebensraum* for Germans; and what they ought to have done was to take advantage of England's long hostility to Russia to ally themselves with her in an anti-Russian war, and get the necessary annexations as the reward of victory. What they did instead was to mess about with colonies, exports and a navy, thereby antagonising England; and to prop up the rotten bulk of Austria-Hungary, which, lying between them and Eastern Europe, actually shut them off from what should have been their goal. In the same way he denounces post-War reversions, like Rapallo, to the old tradition of Prusso-Russian friendship. But it is not merely his thoughts on foreign policy, but his thoughts on home policy also, that are rigidly hitched to this waggon. He is, at heart, as I have said, a countryman. His hatred for the misery and degradation which he saw in working-class Vienna, is blistering. He regards factories and great cities as man-eaters, farms and craft-trades as man-makers. Beyond the industries that are needed to provide war materials, he does not want any more than will create autarkic reciprocity between town and country, each deriving all that it needs from the other and consuming the whole of the other's output. His conception of the future Great Germany is essentially a rural one; and if he were to swerve from his scheme of annexation, he would have not only to eat almost every word that he has written about foreign policy, but to deny all his domestic ideals regarding the basis of what he considers a desirable life for the human race. Over and over again it recurs. Let me just give you some examples: "Frontiers to States are made by men and men can alter them." "The *right* to acquire land and soil can become a *duty,* if without an extension of soil a great people appears doomed to destruction." Or let me read you the conclusion of the matter as expressed on one of the last pages of the book: "The rightness of that foreign policy can only be recognised in a bare century's time, if by then 250 million Germans are living on this continent—and living, not squeezed together as factory coolies for the rest of the world, but as peasants and workers who, through what they produce, reciprocally assure a livelihood to each other." You see the points there. You see first of all the immense figure—250 million Germans in a century. And you see he wants them to be well spread out. Eighty million Germans are at present living on an area that is certainly not more than two-thirds, perhaps not more than half, what it should be in his view. You have got to double the territory and then treble the population. It means an empire something like five or six times the present area of Germany. That, of course, means absorbing not only the Ukraine as it was ceded under the Treaty of Brestlitovsk, but a very much larger area. Mind you, geographically those areas do exist. The Euro-Asiatic land mass is far the most enormous thing in the world, and it is thinly populated; the Germans could spread eastward right over it. Secondly, there is that vivid phrase about factory coolies. There you see the Hitler view (and I venture to say every born countryman's view) of the idea of making a white country the workshop of the world: the *factory coolies* of the rest of the world!

Now those, I think, are key sentences in *Mein Kampf.* Far more so than sayings more often quoted in our newspapers, like that about France as the eternal enemy. As a matter of fact, Hitler himself says about France that he will only be obliged to fight her in order to clear his rear, because he feels sure that she will not stand by and let him seize his prey without interfering.

Ought, then, France—and ought Great Britain—to stand by and give him what has been called a free hand in the east? We know that some influential people, especially in the City of London, have been advocating that in recent years. And indeed to a considerable extent the idea under lay the jettisoning of Czechoslovakia last autumn. But it surely will not pass the test of thought. The new German empire would be so strongly placed, so populous, so rich in every resource and so self-sufficing, so powerful in every way, that no other nation could stand against it. I have heard naïve people object that Great Britain at least could save her Empire by her Navy. They forget that navies today are things of steel, quickly built and quickly outbuilt, and that an impregnable continental block which in manpower, steel-power, coal-power, oil-power, stood to this island as a giant to a pigmy, would not be likely to allow the island very much longer to rule the seas, or indeed to rule anything else. No, when we come to see what is the goal of Hitler's Germany we cannot take refuge in the idea that it does not concern us.

It is a crazy book, *Mein Kampf,* and yet, as I have said, an extremely powerful one. Behind its crudities there is a blend of intense idealism and crabbed argument, a combination that often rather reminds us, though Hitler would abhor the comparison, of St. Paul. In an age of moral relaxation and hedonistic self-seeking Hitler stood out unabashed as the apostle of effort, duty, self-sacrifice, the idealistic subordination of individual interests to those of the community; and he won his power on that appeal. Never did anybody live more emphatically by the belief that spirit dominates matter, that where there is a will there is a way.

Now let me read you just one other passage. Hitler has been saying here that Germany must be armed, and has met with the objection: "How can we rearm? We have no arms; we are surrounded by armed neighbours who do not want us to have any, and have forbidden us to have any; how can we move to do anything?" Hitler says:

> The question of recovering German power is not, "How can we manufacture arms?" but "How can we produce the spirit which makes a people able to carry arms?" If that spirit rules a people, the will finds thousands of ways, any one of which will get the arms for them. Give a coward ten pistols, and when he is attacked he will not be able to fire one shot. Those pistols are of less use to him than a mere blackthorn would be to a brave man.

Well, I do not like Hitler, frankly, and I think he is a world danger. But he is, if ever a man was, *der mutige Mann.*

SUMMARY OF DISCUSSION

DR. G. P. GOOCH (in the Chair) said that it was the first time that a book had been chosen as the subject of an address at the Institute. For this there were many good reasons. *Mein Kampf* stood in a class by itself. Firstly, it was the best best-seller in the world. The sales had already passed the five million mark; Mr. Wells' *Outline of History* was running between the two and three million mark.

Secondly, *Mein Kampf* might be said to have "made history." Politically it was the most influential book which had appeared in any part of the world within the present century, and would probably rank in generations to come with those great explosive works such as *The Communist Manifesto* of Karl Marx, perhaps the most influential political book of the nineteenth century, and Burke's *Reflections on the French Revolution,* of which George III had said in memorable words that every gentleman ought to read it.

Thirdly, *Mein Kampf* was a political autobiography and apologia, and as such only one of a very large family, including Clarendon, Bismarck, von Bülow, Lord Grey and Mr. Lloyd George, not to mention many others; but whereas most of these books were written at the end of a man's life, as a chronicle and a guide for those who should come after him, Hitler's autobiography had been written not after he had finished his work, but just as he was beginning it. Therefore, although the autobiographical part was very interesting, and indeed indispensable to an understanding of one of the most complex figures on the modern stage, more interesting even still was the programme. Already a great deal of that programme had been carried

out. Certainly this book, which was such an extraordinary medley of wisdom and folly, phantasy and statesmanship, could not be ignored, and it was a very good thing that there was now on sale an English translation for those who knew no German.

QUESTION: Where, among the races other than Aryans, had Hitler placed the Italians? Had he spoken of Germany needing allies, and had an Axis ever been contemplated in *Mein Kampf?*

MR. ENSOR said that in *Mein Kampf* Hitler had said that Germany must never again make the mistake she had made in 1914 in getting all the nations against her. She must divide Europe, and some of the peoples must be on her side. In considering those who could be on her side, he had decided upon England and Italy; and since gaining power he had wooed England and won Italy.

QUESTION: How far did the people of Germany really believe in *Mein Kampf?*

MR. ENSOR replied that the extent to which Hitler, at any given moment, was carrying the nation with him was always difficult to estimate, but, broadly speaking, he had swept the country, of that there could be no doubt.

MR. C. H. LUKE asked whether the lecturer would not agree that the philosophy expressed in *Mein Kampf* was no more than the coping-stone of German agitation over the centuries through her philosophers and teachers.

MR. ENSOR said that he had explained that before Hitler had come to power the people of Germany had considered themselves as belonging to a superior race. The reasons for this could be found quite a long way back in their history. Fichte had been partly responsible for it, but it had become very marked since about the middle of the last century, because in the early part of the last century Germany had achieved a very remarkable simultaneity of excellences. There had been the great German universities—scholarship and history practically refounded, philosophy developed beyond anything attempted in any other country, progress, too, in the natural sciences. At the same time the great German musicians had made music appear almost a German monopoly, and simultaneously had come Goethe and Schiller. In the same period Germany had come to the top in war, defeating Napoleon at Leipzig and Waterloo. All these things occurring simultaneously constituted rather a remarkable achievement.

QUESTION: Did not the lecturer think that the desperate solution of Eastern Europe as laid down in the Versailles Treaty had facilitated Hitler's plans to take over the Succession States piecemeal?

MR. ENSOR said that he did not consider the solutions for Eastern Europe contained in the Versailles Treaty as desperate. Broadly speaking, he thought that they had been just solutions. Certain things had been omitted. It would have been a good thing to set up some sort of economic system between the Succession States. Broadly speaking, however, he thought it right that the Poles, the Czechs and the Roumanians should be free.

QUESTION: Had any mention of naval power been made

in *Mein Kampf,* or did Hitler consider that power on land would be sufficient? Had he mentioned possible conflict with any naval Power?

MR. ENSOR replied that Hitler's general argument was that, if land supremacy were secured, then all these things would be added unto it. But in the meantime it was necessary to avoid the mistake made by earlier German statesmen of trying to do the whole thing at once. Pre-War German statesmen had made the great mistake of antagonising Great Britain before they had solved the French and Russian problem.

QUESTION: The lecturer had stated that Hitler had thought that he could get rearmament, the occupation of the Rhineland and the *Anschluss* without war, but that after that point he had been prepared to fight; was this stated in *Mein Kampf*?

MR. ENSOR replied that Hitler had not stated in *Mein Kampf* the exact point at which he would have to fight. It had been his (Mr. Ensor's) diagnosis that he had considered it would be over the question of Czechoslovakia.

QUESTION: Did the lecturer think that, in common with the Poles, the Czechs and the Roumanians, the peoples of Russia should also have been freed under the Versailles Treaty and would this have strengthened the bloc against Germany's eastward expansion?

MR. ENSOR replied that certain parts of Russian territory had been dealt with in the Treaty of Versailles. The Baltic States had been given independence. But the Allies had not been in a position to do more, though they had played with the idea of waging war on Russia and extracting, for instance, the Ukraine.

QUESTION: Had air power been an idea of Herr Hitler or had it been a later idea of General Goering?

MR. ENSOR replied that there was no actual mention of air power in *Mein Kampf.*

QUESTION: Did the lecturer think that it was the logical outcome of *Mein Kampf* for the next step to be taken by Hitler against either Poland or Roumania?

MR. ENSOR replied that certainly the Poles and the Roumanians must be brought under the German wing before she could expand farther east.

QUESTION: Had Herr Hitler spoken in *Mein Kampf* of his forthcoming struggle with Christianity?

MR. ENSOR replied that there was much discussion of religion in *Mein Kampf,* but this was one point where Hitler had gone beyond his book. The pagan, anti-Christian movement in Nazi Germany which had developed since 1933 had gone far beyond *Mein Kampf.* Hitler had even criticised the unwisdom of attempting to interfere with religious bodies. He had criticised the policy of the pan-Germans in pre-War Vienna who had antagonised the Catholic Church. In this matter his book had been more wise than his government.

PROFESSOR R. W. SETON-WATSON said that he was in entire agreement with Mr. Ensor as to the way in which *Mein Kampf* revealed the character of Herr Hitler, as a blend of fanatical idealist and utter cynic. Men who knew him would maintain that utter disbelief in human nature is a dominant trait in that character. Hard times, such as he went through in early life, tended to turn a man either into a disbeliever in humanity or into a saint. The book was also a blend of *Wahrheit* and *Dichtung*—sometimes bordering on the apocalyptic, sometimes containing fantastically false statements, in which, however, Herr Hitler quite obviously believed. Two good examples were his assertion that Francis Ferdinand was making Czech policy, and that the Viennese Jewish Press was working against Berlin, whereas it was, notoriously, in those pre-War years a tool of the Wilhelmstrasse.

The book contained certain fixed ideas. First, Herr Hitler's indictment of the Jews, which was based often on hysteria and fantastic misconceptions. Then his conviction that Marxism was the logical outcome of democracy and parliamentary government. Then again the claim that the Versailles Treaty was one of the greatest crimes in history, and a flagrant violation of the Fourteen Points of President Wilson. In reality only three of the Fourteen Points could even remotely be said to have been violated by the Allies, while many of them related to matters which did not directly affect Germany (Turkey, Russia, etc.). It was, moreover, far too often forgotten that Wilson built up his whole system of the Fourteen Points on a demand for the establishment of Democracy and Pacifism, both of which were anathema to Herr Hitler and constantly denounced by him. This was a fundamental contradiction.

Professor Seton-Watson then referred to Hitler's propagandist methods, based above all on utter contempt for public opinion. In one passage he spoke of the public as "the great stupid flock of sheep"; in another he said his aim is "to force a doctrine upon a whole people," and that "the rightness of propaganda must be judged exclusively by its real effect." In other words, its truth did not matter. "By skilful and sustained use of propaganda one can make a people see even Heaven as Hell, or the most wretched life as paradise." Dr. Goebbels openly declared that propaganda should not be *anständig,* but simply successful. This was what the rest of the world is up against—a solid mass of people who believed that the sole solution for every problem in Germany and in Europe must rest on force.

Herr Hitler followed up *Mein Kampf* by a long series of speeches, containing many misstatements which had gone unchecked. It was high time that they were refuted and challenged, point by point, by responsible statesmen, and not only by a few individuals in opposition. Doubtless a part of the deliberate policy of appeasement was not to answer back or to become involved in polemics: and there was much to be said for this, so long as "appeasement" could be regarded as practicable. But it was only effective when both sides showed the same restraint. When, however, the spokesman of one side poured forth an unending stream of eloquent but false propaganda and got a free advertisement in the world press, while the spokesman of the other remained silent, or was content with a neat phrase about "declamation" or "defence, not defiance," the only possible result was that the undefended thesis should seem to go by default. All the more satisfactory was it to see, at long last, Lord Halifax's refutation of the absurd myth that Britain went to war with Germany in 1914 to ruin her trade (and this refutation was an admirable example of *suaviter in modo*), and again *The Times'* challenge to that other myth that Germany was not beaten in the field but only surrendered on terms which we then failed to observe.

A similar myth was the old charge of encirclement, between 1908 and 1914, and once again to-day. This had been often denied in the House of Commons, but it was necessary that it should be not merely denied, but *refuted,* on the basis of the historical facts, by an official spokesman; and this would be perfectly possible, without undue verbosity or display of academic learning. Explode the pre-war *Einkreisung* myth, and you were in a fair way to exploding the new version (and incidentally, the very dangerous legend that Poland and the Ukraine were thinly populated and therefore suited for alien colonisation, whereas in reality both are very thickly populated). It seemed to him vital that both our statesmen and our historians should take this matter up, and see that the British case was presented, in *German,* on the wireless, to the German public, in urbane, conciliatory, but absolutely firm and concrete form, with chapter and verse for every assertion.

MR. J. A. HUTTON said that the character of Herr Hitler was shown very clearly in *Mein Kampf.* Immediately one saw the contrast between him and his partner in the Axis. Mussolini was the opportunist, pure and simple, whose policy changed from day to day, and who took whatever was offered. Hitler had declared his policy in advance, and it had been there for all to see, though many had been until recently extremely blind. The basis of that policy was Germany's living room; she must expand. If that statement were accepted, Germany was at the moment the victim of a policy of encirclement to prevent her from carrying out this necessary expansion. Right through the book he inveighed against encirclement and stressed the fact that Germany must never again fight on two fronts. The major war must come, but not until Germany was sure of victory. Great Britain was to remain neutral till the minor Powers were destroyed and Germany was powerful enough to dictate to this little island. But by her guarantees to Poland and Roumania Great Britain had suddenly stopped Hitler from marching farther east without having to fight on the west at the same time. The result had been a sudden outburst of anti-British propaganda entirely contrary to the policy outlined in *Mein Kampf.* The speaker foresaw immediate danger to Europe not in the east but in the west, possibly through Spain and Gibraltar. It was not so long since Poland had been one of the wolves round Czechoslovakia. Poland had a desire to become a colonial Power; this could not be achieved as a result of a war with Germany, but could be done by dividing up the British Empire with Germany. So, were hostilities to break out in the west without the east being affected, it might be possible for Germany to maintain neutrality on her eastern front and to seek, first, her living space in the west.

MR. C. H. LUKE said that Herr Hitler had been very for-tunate in the people with whom he had been dealing. He had been surprised at the lecturer's strong statement with regard to German character and ability. Certainly Germany was a great nation, but was any nation really great who could be led by the type of statements made in *Mein Kampf*? He could not see that the world was going to sink under the thunderbolt of a man who spoke as Hitler did in *Mein Kampf.* It should be realised that such plausible statements as that Poland should have peace for twenty-five years if Danzig were allowed to become part of the Reich had a much deeper meaning than at first appeared. There was a quotation in *The Times* of that morning (May 4th, 1939) from the *Osservatore Romano* in which the writer said that the command of Danzig and the mouth of the Vistula was one of the main routes to the hegemony of Europe. If there was talk about whether Danzig was worth a war, it would be desirable to remember that if Danzig went back to the Reich, Hitler would soon be in a position to fortify it and to throttle the nations of Eastern Europe from Poland down to the Black Sea. There was more in the matter than Hitler's command of language and his power over his people. No man would have been able to dominate the United States or the British Empire as Hitler had dominated Germany, and it should be remembered that throughout the ages Germany had never been anything but a nation endeavouring to terrorise somebody. Yet, in spite of this, for hundreds of years she had existed as a number of small States. If Great Britain and America and the other democratic nations were to stand up to Germany and to call Hitler's bluff, then the Reich would soon slip back into the number of small countries into which she had been divided in the past.

MR. G. SOLOVEYTCHIK said that the lecturer had remarked that no nation could maintain a fleet which had not got command of iron and steel. According to *The Daily Telegraph,* Great Britain was at present importing iron and steel from Australia. If with her present industrial apparatus Great Britain needed to import iron and steel, what would be her position if Germany had command not only of the sources on the Continent but also command of the seas? This should be remembered, especially in view of the lecturer's remark that a fleet was not only rapidly built, but rapidly outbuilt.

Concerning Hitler's policy towards Russia, of course *Mein Kampf* did state his desire for the Ukraine and certain parts of Russia, but it should be remembered that up to the signing of the Franco-Soviet Pact Hitler had made friendly overtures to Russia. In an interview with Mr. Ward Price in Berlin in February 1934 he had said that the idea that Germany would take Russian territory was ridiculous. Later, when reviewing his achievements in a speech in the Reichstag, he had emphasised as one of his successes the friendly relations existing between Germany and Russia, and expressed the hope that in spite of ideological differences they would continue to be so. It had not been until July 1934, with the signing of the Franco-Soviet Pact, that he had become so bitterly anti-Russian and presented himself as an anti-Communist crusader. This had certainly served a purpose, particularly with regard to his relations with certain circles in Great Britain, but if the situation were to continue as at present and the negotiations between the latter and the Soviet Union did not result in any definite agreement, it might be that Hitler and Stalin would again be exchanging compliments. It was by no means beyond the realm of possibility that the resignation of Litvinov, which had been described throughout the world press as a great mystery, might be a first move in this direction.

MR. WILSON HARRIS said that great stress had been laid upon the enormous circulation and effect of *Mein Kampf.* It did not, however, necessarily follow that because a book had a vast circulation that it had a vast influence. In Germany every newly married couple had to have a copy of *Mein Kampf,* every member of the Party and every civil servant also was expected to possess a copy; but there was no law requiring it to be read, and it would not be surprising to learn that it had not been read by many of the people who had it in their possession. How, in fact, had Hitler established his ascendancy over the German people and how was it being maintained to-day? He had first persuaded Hindenburg to make him Chancellor. Then one of his entourage had staged the firing of the Reichstag, which had very nearly caused him to win his first election, so nearly that with the Nationalists he had established a majority in the Reichstag. He had used this to excommunicate the Communist Party and thereby secure a majority. During this time he had used his private army to intimidate the population. He had then proceeded to institute a régime of concentration camps. Herr Himmler had begun his great and successful work. He had secured possession of the Press and the radio and had circulated lies and suppressed the truth. Spies had been established in every block of flats and in every factory, letters had been opened and telephone communications listened to; was it astonishing that in these circumstances Herr Hitler had succeeded in dominating the German people?

MR. FRANK HARDIE said that he wished to supplement the point made by Professor Seton-Watson about the importance of refuting the arguments of Herr Hitler by a plain unvarnished statement of the facts over the wireless and in German; he wanted to suggest that there were in Great Britain a great number of distinguished German refugees whose services could be most usefully employed in this connection and who would most willingly give those services.

LIEUT.-COLONEL C. WALEY-COHEN said that it would be very interesting to hear how much of Hitler's foreign policy as contained in *Mein Kampf* was his own and how much had come from his entourage. His ideas concerning a Mittel-Europa were very like those which had had their birth between 1901 and 1913 in Bohemia, which had eventually been absorbed into Czechoslovakia. He had heard the view that a great deal of the detail of Hitler's foreign policy had come from his entourage, and from descendants and successors of those with similar ideas before the War.

MR. ENSOR said that Professor Seton-Watson had contributed an admirable supplement to his own address.

It had been suggested that the refusal of Great Britain to allow Germany to proceed eastwards unchecked might change Hitler's orientation for the time being. This might be so, as he was a very elastic tactician. He had a perfectly clear goal from which he would never swerve, but he would be prepared to approach it from the best possible angle and if he felt the menace in his rear, Great Britain as well as France, to be too great, he might think it a good policy to join with Mussolini and try to isolate the two Western Powers by buying off the Eastern Powers for the time being. It was most probable that he was trying to do that at the present moment. Whether M. Litvinov's resignation indicated a sensational success in this direction was not known, but it was a natural interpretation.

Concerning his statements about German pre-eminence in certain fields, he had not wished to suggest that the Germans were necessarily the greatest people in the world, but that between 1790 and 1830 they had had a great simultaneous flowering in many directions: poets, philosophers, historians, scientists, scholars and musicians. No other nation had ever produced quite so many eminent men and men of genius in so many different fields within so short a space of time.

It was true that Danzig was one of the key points of Europe, and if ever there were such a thing as a people's "living space," then Danzig belonged to Poland. The Poles were the people of the Vistula.

He did not think that much importance need be attached to the fact that Great Britain was importing iron and steel from Australia. A great deal of iron and steel had always been imported by the big iron and steel countries. Before the War Great Britain had tended largely to import German steel to build her ships. This had been more ominous, but there was no reason why she should not now buy some from Australia. A curious thing was that a great deal of the steel with which Germany had carried out her rearmament had been sold to her by England and France; and she was still receiving quite a lot from them.

It might be true that in 1934 Hitler had said that he did not want Russian territory. Later than that he had said that he did not want Czech territory. On the other hand, a Russo-German *rapprochement* was quite possible. After Rapallo there had been a large number of Russian Army officers who had been in close contact with their German opposite numbers; and there had been a good deal of talk about making some sort of bargain over the Ukraine. Very few Russian officers thought that they could stand up to Germany. The earthen pot and the iron pot had often clashed, and always the earthen pot had been broken. This might be to the detriment of Great Britain.

The influence of *Mein Kampf* had certainly been very small outside Germany, but in Germany there was no doubt that its contents were well known and had been swallowed whole by the younger and more active elements in the country. Some months ago he had spoken with a very intelligent German refugee who had left the country only in November. He had said that the educated classes and the great landowners were now bitterly sorry that they had ever allowed the Nazi régime to be established, but the proletariat as a body were for the Government. Those who before had been Communists and Socialists were now Nazis, as were all the youth of the country; and until some disaster changed their outlook they would continue to be so. Of course the régime had been maintained by force. It was the only way in which such a régime could be maintained. Very much the same type of thing had occurred during the régime of Napoleon III. The same type of thing was taking place in Italy.

How many of Hitler's ideas were his own and how many had come from his entourage was an interesting topic for speculation. But the important thing was that he had made those ideas his own. Fundamentally, in that sense, he was sincere. He had a creed which he was prepared to carry through to the end. (pp. 478-96)

R. C. K. Ensor, " 'Mein Kampf' and Europe,"
in International Affairs, *Vol. XVIII, No. 4,*
July-August, 1939, pp. 478-96.

Dorothy Thompson   (essay date 1939)

[*Thompson was an American foreign correspondent and political columnist. In the following review of two unexpurgated editions of* Mein Kampf, *she faults Hitler's writing and his political and economic policies, and discusses his personal background in relation to his racial fanaticism.*]

Americans can now read, in either of two complete, unexpurgated editions [of **Mein Kampf**], 669 pages without annotations (Stackpole edition), or 994 with annotations (Reynal and Hitchcock edition), the text of the book that has shaken Western civilization. The reader will find the English writing rhetorical, turgid, and digressive, and the text disorganized. Do not, however, criticize the translators. Hitler's first battle was with the German language, and this fight at least he has never won. Let it be said that if the world is overthrown by this document and the man behind it, it is overthrown without benefit of grammar or literary style.

I do not mean to quibble, but I do not find this unimportant. The epochal political documents of history, from Plato's *Republic,* through Caesar and Cicero, through the great political literature of the high middle ages and including the political literature of the eighteenth and nineteenth centuries—Voltaire and Montesquieu, Jefferson and the writers of the *Federalist,* Adam Smith and John Stuart Mill—that great body of political writing which has left a permanent mark on history, has combined philosophical content with lucid and elegant form.

But this curious mixture of Austrian pan-Germanism, peculiar personal psychoses, description of revolutionary tactics, amorphous concepts of the state, volubly expressed, does not contain a line of intellectual or spiritual grandeur. Even the fire of hate never burns clear and blue as it does in great polemic.

But this deeply barbarous book may, in its very vulgarity of expression, be in advance of its time. It is perhaps fitting that a movement glorifying the instinctual and the herdlike, and expressing contempt for the intellectual and the differentiated, should, in its most apocalyptical expression, use mass words and debased language, as though to

announce itself as the book to end books; the literature to end literature.

Reading this book through again—I read it first in German in 1927, and often since as a guide to the program of the leader of the Third Reich—several things strike the mind.

One is the total lack of knowledge of, and complete indifference to, economic forces and factors. Politics supersedes economics to the point of ignoring the latter. Hitler does not place politics above economics—he places the latter nowhere at all. When he says, "If a people but desire weapons, weapons will grow in their hands," he expresses a mystical doctrine of will. The whole book is a sort of parable of loaves and fishes. And this gives **Mein Kampf** a dream-like quality—a picture of a world of illimitable possibilities—in which everything can be accomplished and nobody ever has to pay.

This is also its seductiveness. For certainly the man who wrote it has liberated millions from the sense of limitation—as mass men and as individuals. The enormous appeal that religion has, picturing a realm where, after a brief stay in this vale of sorrows, one shall have eternal life and eternal bliss, is transplanted to earth in the Third Reich—Reich being one of those untranslatable German words not limited as is the word "empire" or "nation," but carrying with it the metaphysical idea of a realm transcendant to geography.

Hitler's belief in illimitable possibility is doubtless the outcome of a youth of dreams and fantasies and a manhood which is, in itself, a miracle.

The youth was wretched. His home life was obviously hellish. We know (he does not tell us) that his father was a drunkard (he died of apoplexy, blind-drunk in a pub). His mother was more than twenty years the father's junior, and her own story is dark. She was a distant cousin of her husband's—the story is partly told in notes in the Reynal & Hitchcock edition—and once as a young girl lived as hired help in his first wife's house. Then she left the Danubian village for Vienna and was gone ten years. What experience drove her back home after ten years to marry the elderly, harsh, drunken customs official who was her cousin? Nobody knows.

Alois Hitler, the father, was coarse and brutal toward his son. The fact creeps out, the son's hatred of the father is hardly veiled. The boy wanted to be a painter or an architect—some kind of artist. He ran away from home—again, like his mother, to Vienna. His first, last and overwhelming hate was for the city where his mother had passed those obscure years.

First of all, he hated the squalor of the Vienna slums where he lived. The loathing with which he describes the sodden Vienna working classes is so well remembered and so sincere that one thinks for a moment that out of it must come a people's rebel.

But he loathes not only the dirt, the rags, the lice, but the people under the dirt and rags and lice. He hated the workmen on the buildings where he eventually found employment. Just what sort of employment is not clear. He speaks of working on scaffolds, from which comes the inference that he was a house painter. He hated the workers for lack of national feeling—their internationalism. He hated the Austro-Hungarian empire because non-Germans outnumbered Germans nearly five to one in the Austro-Hungarian empire. Although Slavs were more numerous than Germans, he was against their having any power. He did not want to Germanize them, because "race derives not from language but from soil."

What did he want to do with them? Make them the vassals, apparently, of the "Master Folk"—the Germans! But that is easier said than done, as Hitler may find out one day. In Central and Eastern Europe, the area (exclusive of Russia) where Hitler sees the vision of the great contiguous Continental power, there are, indeed, eighty million Germans. But there are also more than eighty million Poles, North Slavs, South Slavs, Magyars and Rumanians, all very thickly settled and all possessing a curious lack of enthusiasm for being enslaved.

These problems, which the Austrian monarchy sought to solve by tolerance, do not concern the apocalyptic dreamer. His first rage against the Jews was against the liberalism of the Jewish press. The Jewish press supported the empire—thus supporting the racial "Babylon."

It is a curious psychological trauma in which Adolf Hitler finds himself. He hates "dirt," "filth," "scum," "corruption," "pollution," "impurity." It is amazing how often these words and their synonyms occur throughout the book. He longs for "purity," "cleanness." Purity and cleanness become symbolized in his mind by purity of blood—purity of race. The intermingling of races is an unclean thing. The Austro-Hungarian monarchy is doomed because it has sinned. The bloods of races have commingled. The capital is a "Sodom" in which Czechs and Poles, and Magyars and Jews, commingle and corrupt the blood of pure Germans.

Now, all this is very, very queer, and peculiarly so when coupled with what we know of the antecedants and personality of Adolf Hitler.

The drunken father, Alois, was illegitimate. Presumably the grandfather married Alois's mother—but the marriage took place five years after the child's birth. *Perhaps* the father of Alois Schickelgruber was *not* named Hitler—or Hiedler, as the name was originally written, and was not the man who, five years after Alois's birth, married his mother, For, curiously, Adolf's father bore the mother's name until he was forty years old, when his first wife, a woman of some substance, took steps to get her husband legitimized by his step—or natural—father, in order to procure for him a bureaucrat's job.

Surely it is significant that this man, whose agents have snooped into the pedigrees of every German family to discover possible non-Aryan grandparents, has an extremely questionable grandfather, himself!

Why this feeling that a whole nation must expiate racial "crimes"? The purity motif has run through his whole personal life. This man never puts the flesh of animals in his mouth. He is a vegetarian. He never drinks alcohol, nor does he smoke. His footsteps were dogged in his early days by republican journalists, curious and by no means sympathetic, but they could never discover that he had ever had sexual relations with any woman.

But something haunts him. The blood stream of the German race must be purified!

On the subject of eugenics he writes rationally—up to a point. Eugenists all over the world will agree with him that the palpably unfit for reproduction should be sterilized. But the German sterilization laws include habitual drunkards, and it is an amusing thought that had they existed in pre-Hitler Austria Hitler himself would never have been born! (Neither, incidentally, would Beethoven or Nietzsche.)

But what shall one think of the theory advanced, excathedra, without any qualification or doubt whatsoever, that *any* admixture of racial strains breeds schizophrenics and destroys culture?

Germany, according to Hitler (see the chapter "The State"), is already far gone in disintegration because "Nordics" have bred with "easterners" and "westerners," and therefore lack "that sure herd instinct which is rooted in unity of blood and which guards the nation against ruin, especially in dangerous moments, as with such peoples all the minor internal differences usually disappear immediately and the common enemy is confronted by the closed front of a uniform herd."

The German nation has sinned against the blood, and until it expiates that sin it cannot master the earth. That is Hitler's thesis. It must be washed and become clean.

Now, one must emphasize that this is a book of revelation. It is apocalyptical. Hitler has gone through some extraordinary psychic experience in which this fundamental truth has been revealed. He does not make the slightest attempt to prove this—or any other—of his remarkable propositions. They stand above truth, as revelation, vision prophecy. It is of no consequence that the race which Hitler worships does not exist—least of all, as he accurately says—in Germany. Where, in all western civilization, is there a nation in the blood of whose people are not chromosomes of northern barbarians, Romans, Phoenicians, Mediterraneans, Dinarics, Slavs, Teutons, Celts and what not? There is the fact, and most of us feel we can put up with it.

Hitler cannot. It is "impurity." In the orbit of his remarkable psychosis, the laws become merely a symbol. They are really to be a blood sacrifice. The veins of Jews, opened on the sacrificial altar, may furnish the blood letting to wash the sinning races clean.

There is no answer to this because Hitler is completely mediaeval, in the sense that he turns his back on the very concept of rational thinking.

Some of us think that the maintenance of reason—the establishment of criteria, by which ideas are tested empirically and in logic—is the chief thing we are pledged to defend. Some of us think it is the *only* thing worth dedicating one's life to defend. But not Hitler. Hitler thinks that reason itself is a trait of individualism, and individualism is the result of blood mixture. The ideal nation is the herd. The herd is unconquerable, because it moves by common instinct, undeterred by the rationalizations of individuals.

If you are not clear what a herd is, the New Oxford Dictionary defines it as "A company of domestic animals of one kind, kept together by a keeper." The dictionary also—not having consulted *Mein Kampf*—adds, "Said also, contemptuously, of men."

Of course the logic of herd breeding is incest, and again, inbreeding exists in Hitler's family. In the village of Spital, and perhaps as a result of this, he has a first cousin who is a hunchback and an idiot. This fact does not prevent him—does it impel him?—from humiliating, persecuting, psychologically injuring, actually starving, and exiling from their country, straight-limbed, clear-eyed children with high IQs, whose parents or grandparents committed the crime of falling in love outside the herd.

While Hitler was writing this book in the Landsberg prison in Munich (where a weak-minded, tolerant republic imprisoned him for only a few months after he had staged an abortive revolution), in the slummy city of Vienna, where the youth Hitler had suffered, a social democratic government, unaware of its sins against the blood, was tearing down the rabbit warrens of tenements in which Hitler had bitten his fingernails and dreamed of expiation.

Before this book was read by more than a handful of people, these rationalistic individuals had built whole suburbs, complexes of buildings housing thousands, and flooded with light and air. They had put rücksacks and skis on children without investigating their grandmothers, and had built mountain huts for youthful climbers across the Alps. Without bothering about previous racial sins, they had opened public baths and deloused the proletariat.

On Mussolini's orders these rationalists were ousted.

On Hitler's orders their ousters were slain.

From the social democratic Breitner, who believed in the art of possibilities, to the liberator Hitler, who believes in the illimitable will and the blood purge, is six years. It spans, however, the distance between the twentieth century and the tenth—reading from right to left.

So much for the case of Adolf Hitler, though the subject is endlessly fascinating.

As important as Hitler as a case is Hitler as a statesman. The fascination here is that Hitler is not a statesman. He is an anti-statesman, by his own words. The world will one day realize—I think, very soon—that far from being the builder of the modern type of state, Hitler is the greatest nihilist of the century.

For what is a state? Is it not a commonwealth, or polity? The body politic, organized for civil rule and government? The ordering of relations among men, under law, and in a given area? Such it has been from the Greek city states to the United States of America.

But not in Hitler's mind. "The state is a *purpose*" . . .

It is the presumption for the formation of a

higher human culture, but not its cause . . . its end is the preservation and promotion of a community of physically and psychically equal human beings . . . the German Reich, as a state, should include all Germans . . . and lead them gradually and safely to a dominating position. . . .

These words, and the whole context in which they appear, mean simply that the Nazi state exists as a *means* to secure the dominance of the Germanic peoples over the earth—once they have expiated their racial sins.

It is complete dynamism—the perpetual revolution. Nowhere does the Nazi state acquire *status,* come to rest, organize, restrict itself, get down to brass tacks. It is an instrument to bring salvation *to the world.* It is not, in fact, a state at all. It is the nucleus of a movement which is restricted (temporarily at least) only to this planet. A vast struggle is envisaged between the super-men (the Teutons) and the dwarfs (the others). If these supermen didn't happen to have organization, an army, airplanes, and complete life-and-death control over the lives, fortunes and working powers of eighty million people, you would simply ring down the curtain on a mid-season performance of Wagner's Ring of the Nibelungen, take a rest and turn to Mozart. But the stage is not that of the Metropolitan Opera. It is the globe—directed from Berlin with Valkyries yodeling in New York through the German American Bund.

The state as *movement* is something new in the modern world. It was conceived by Mahomet and by Ghengis Khan; Hitler is *their* offspring—not Napoleon's. He is not the bastard child of anything modern. Islam would understand him, and the Hunnish riders, and so, no doubt, do Trotsky and perhaps Stalin.

How fascinating the study would be—were it only a study! We could consider this phenomenon of the three-fold renegade—the renegade patriot, who deserted from his Emperor to join an ally for the purpose of destroying the alliance; the renegade Catholic, who revolted against the universality of the Roman conception and keeps the last Catholic Chancellor of Austria locked up and doped with scopalamine; and, finally, the renegade male, living under an obscure curse which made him elevate to power a pederast and then destroy him, which forbids him to touch a woman, and consecrates him to the purging of the blood!

He is imprisoned by his hates. He describes the methods of the socialists and the Jews—their impertinent use of the lie. Aha! He has learned something! The weapon works! He will use it multiplied a thousand fold! He describes the propaganda of the allied powers. "The Germans were too objective." Aha! He will learn from his enemies! So in the end, his methods are the quintessence of what he describes as most detestable. It is a Dostoievsky legend of total corruption, and salvation through sin, whereby one becomes the very image of the bogey of one's fantasy and is thus redeemed.

And, with all this, lucid moments, lucid passages. The casual reader will pounce upon these. Long passages enunciate banalities, familiar and reasonable. Is not what he writes of parliaments perfectly true? Is not the conception of a sound mind in a sound body perfectly sound? In the midst of this guilt-drenched search for redemption we stumble upon Y.M.C.A. clichés. And then almost lose sight of the fact that the author of *Mein Kampf* has abolished the whole concept of the *citizen* as we have known it from the days of Pericles! In its place is the man of the tribe, ruled by totem and taboo.

Against the instinctualism of this book, against the fetish world, mankind has striven upward, feeling his way step by step through ages. Occasionally he has relapsed—when civilization became too hard. Then we have had a "dark" age.

Are we in for another? I think not.

And where will the fight against the dark blood purge occur?

In Germany.

And how?

By revolution. For Hitler's revelation produced the revolution against which Germany prepares, even now, to revolt. (pp. 3, 20)

> Dorothy Thompson, "Revolution and Revelation, Hitler's Model," in New York Herald Tribune, March 19, 1939, pp. 3, 20.

Max Lerner   (essay date 1939)

[*Lerner was a political scientist, educator, author, and nationally syndicated columnist. His career as a social commentator began in 1927 as an editor for the* Encyclopedia of Social Sciences; *from 1936 to 1939 he served as editor of the* Nation; *and after 1949 he worked as a columnist for the* New York Post. *Throughout his career, Lerner interspersed academic work with his writing. His numerous publications include the popular* It Is Later Than You Think (1938), *a study of contemporary politics, and what he considered his most ambitious work,* America As a Civilization: Life and Thought in the United States Today (1957). *In the essay below, excerpted from his book* Ideas Are Weapons: The History and Uses of Ideas, *Lerner presents an overview of the attitudes and ideas in* Mein Kampf.]

There is no autobiography in history that can match the fantastic quality of *Mein Kampf.* Reading it we are in a universe of grotesque proportions—a nightmare Wonderland in which we are all Alices watching the distorted perspectives. World movements like Christianity, socialism, democracy, are reduced to items in the ego-displacement of a little Austrian water-color dauber. Whole nations and continents become the stamping-ground of his restless personality. His tastes and traumata are expanded into universals to decide the destiny of millions. Here is, in Nietzsche's terms, a "transvaluation of values" with a vengeance. In fact Nietsche often comes to mind in reading these pages. Not Nietzsche the thinker-craftsman, nor the believer in the "European man," nor the creator of the "gay science"—but he of the autobiography, *Ecce Homo,* written in the fitful gleams of sanity preceding his complete collapse. Dostoyevsky also comes to mind, stripped

of his literary genius and the depth of his insights, but the Dostoyevsky of the masochistic rejection of reason and the epileptic trances of the spirit.

There are those who have compared *Mein Kampf* with *Das Kapital* on the ground that both are the bibles of world movements and rationalize the revolutionary impulses of millions. But to compare Hitler's book with Marx's is unfair to both. Marx, for all his vanity, was no megalomaniac; *Mein Kampf* may be described as the anatomy of megalomania. Since Marxism is nothing if not rationalistic, its key-book is a pitiless analysis, in the Ricardian tradition, of the dynamics of our economy. But the key-book of Nazism describes the tempestuous voyage of a tortured mind. It is a mind that has rejected our gods, broken through the taboos that we call civilization, and fashioned a god in its own image and a demonology of its own.

For despite its tirades against individualism, *Mein Kampf* is in reality the individualist dream run amuck. The personality that emerges from its pages is a blending of all that is grandiose in the European Bonapartist tradition with the most fantastic elements of the American success-story. It is a cross between Napoleon and Horatio Alger. It is the Little Corporal dreaming of world empire; it is also the saga of Pluck and Luck, the Boy from Braunau Who Made Good. You have here the apotheosis of sheer individual will imposing itself on the flux of events. Here is a sick mind, a lonely and dwarfed personality, that was able to convert its sickness and frustration into hate, its hate into vengeful ambition, its ambition into cold steel, its steel into an empire and a religion.

The book is at once autobiography, credo, handbook for party leaders, blueprint for world domination. It is the product of an untrained mind—a mind that makes a fetish of external discipline because it could never brook internal discipline. Hitler is neither a systematic nor an original thinker. The unity his book possesses is a psychic unity. He has breathed into his random materials the daemonic force of a great will and a consuming hate. I am reminded of the cosmological theory that an intense sun shining on inert and decayed matter transformed it eventually into reptilian life.

But it will not do on that account to dismiss *Mein Kampf* as a farrago of nonsense, not worth our attention. Its premises are not our own, its reasoning is faulty, its conclusions are hideous to us. Nevertheless its very quality of not making sense is exactly what gives it effectiveness. We must rid ourselves of the view that only logical ideas can be political weapons. Ideas in politics are much like poetry: they need no inner logical structure to be effective. Edward Lear's nonsense verse merely extends a principle inherent in poetry as a whole. And Hitler is, in a sense, the Edward Lear of political thinking. He has taught us that, just as a limerick drives Shakespeare out of our minds, so by a similar Gresham's law illogical political ideas drive out the logical.

And whether or not he makes sense, his book has become the profoundly evocative philosophy of millions of people. The *New Republic* has been running a series on "Books

That Changed Our Minds." Unless the "our" refers to a narrow circle of American intellectuals, *Mein Kampf* should have been included. It has already changed the minds of countless people in France, England, Spain, Denmark, and the Near East, as well as in Germany, Austria, Hungary, Italy.

One may well ask whether Americans will remain immune. Given conditions of decency and social peace, we could afford to laugh at the obsessive intensity with which Hitler rides his anti-liberal, anti-humanitarian, anti-Christian, anti-Semitic, anti-socialist, anti-democratic hobbies. But we do not have the conditions of social peace. Nor do we have the foundations of an enduring social decency. And for millions of people who are ready to cement their collapsing psychic world by hate and illogic, *Mein Kampf* will offer the cement.

. . . . .

Hitler's is a spoken rather than a written book. He dictated the first half of it to his secretary while he was a prisoner at the fortress at Landsberg on the Lech, after the 1923 Beerhall Putsch. And it has all the marks of a book that has been *talked.* It is a congeries of unconnected fragments held together only by the sustained psychic tension of the speaker, rather than something set down reflectively with logic and inter-connection of its parts.

Such surely must have been the talk at the Munich *Stammtische* where *habitués* of all descriptions gathered over their beer and quarreled about the diverse roads to a commonly held Germanic mission. Such must have been the rhapsodic talk that Hanisch, Hitler's companion during the years when his fortune was at its lowest ebb, tells about: Hitler with his emaciated derelict face and his Jewish beard and his long tramp-cassock, declaiming against Marxism in the flophouse at Vienna-Brigittenau; Hitler sitting in the cheap Vienna restaurants while the customers discussed the daily headlines, and holding them spellbound with his attacks on the Jews and the Weimar government. Such must, finally, have been the speeches Hitler made at the huge Zirkuskrone mass-meetings, when the rising young party leader stood for hours on the platform and loosed a wild torrent of talk that swept his listeners along with him.

Among the passages in Hitler's book that ring truest are those in praise of the spoken word and in contempt of the goose-quill. "Every great movement on this globe," he says in his Preface, "owes its rise to the great speakers and not to the great writers." *Mein Kampf* as a spoken book holds the only thinker Hitler ever was—Hitler the talker, projected on the printed page. "Nevertheless the basic elements of a doctrine," he explains in his Preface, "must be set down in permanent form." What are these elements in the case of his own doctrine?

Hitler has urged foreigners to uncover the metaphysical roots of Nazism; and one might well start with his book. To many it will seem incongruous even to think of such a mélange as having serious metaphysical roots. And it is true that Hitler is pitiably amateurish in his handling of political and social concepts. Early in the history of the Nazi Party, Hitler struck an alliance with one of its poets and intellectuals, Dietrich Eckart. From him he may have picked up some of the going ideas of the young conservative intellectuals and some of the patter of their vocabulary. For Hitler, like many other men of action, does not explore ideas but absorbs them. They become part of him not through study and mastery but through a process of osmosis. Yet it is obvious that, if we take metaphysics to mean first principles with respect to thought and society and human beings in it, then even Hitler has a metaphysic. It lies not so much in the articulate doctrine he sets down as in his inarticulate major premises, the things he takes so completely for granted that he finds it unnecessary to do more than allude to them.

The metaphysical roots of Hitler's doctrine must be sought in the soil of the German intellectual tradition. There are two major attitudes current today toward that tradition. One is that we have no quarrel with the German people—that what the Nazis are doing is superimposed on them, and runs counter to every important element in the German past. The second attitude is that our quarrel is exactly with the German people, that they have a Nazi government today because they are Nazi at heart and have always been, and that the whole German intellectual tradition has been building up to Hitler. Neither of these is true. Actually, there are two German traditions, one humanist and the other anti-humanist, one stretching from Goethe and Lessing to Max Weber and Thomas Mann, the other from Fichte and Jean-Paul Richter to Spengler, Carl Schmitt, and Alfred Bäumler. The first stresses freedom, the life of reason, and the possibilities of human existence; the second stresses authority, the brutal and tempestuous in man, and the transcending of the human by the heroic and daemonic. One subordinates the state to culture, the other subordinates culture to the state. One is European, the other fiercely nationalistic; one is democratic, the other feudal. In the great representative Germans the two are intertwined; yet in every German thinker, however complex, an emphasis on the one or the other is unmistakable.

The basic assumptions in *Mein Kampf* are not far from those of the body of Nazi social theory as set forth, for example, in Kolnai's *War against the West,* which—although a very stiff dose for the general reader—deserves much more study by American social scientists than they have thus far given it. They are the assumptions that the masses of men are irrational creatures, acting from deep-lying drives of hunger, fear, imitation, herdism, sadism; that there are natural *Stände,* or gradations of rank, among men, from the slave-mass to the élite and finally to the *Führer* himself; that corresponding to these are varying *Stufe,* or levels of consciousness, forming a mystical base for an eventual caste system; that the social world, like the biological, is a jungle; that man is, in Spengler's terms, "a beast of prey," and that only the strongest are worthy of survival; that where there is no room for the weak, Christianity is a luxury, humanitarianism runs against the grain of life, liberalism is folly, and democracy a crime; that there are sound and healthy tendencies in any community which have been poisoned by the Jews, weakened by Christianity, and undermined by international capitalism and international socialism; that the core of any community (*Gemeinschaft*) is a people around a leader, tied together by idealistic bonds and by a sense of duty to the leader, and that the highest stage of such a community is the *Volksgemeinschaft,* or national community; that communities are not mechanisms but organisms, and that the element of spontaneity and organic growth is the essential element in them; that what is important about them, as about anything, is the *Geist,* or spirit, that informs them; that the *Geist* of a healthy community must run counter to the materialistic spirit of the modern age, and must return to the sense of duty, community honor, and fealty to the leader that characterized the earlier Germanic community; that this *Geist* expresses itself most strongly in a blood-community of race and in adherence to a native and common soil; that in the perception of such values there can be no logical categories but only an intuitionism that is its own principle and its own justification; that in the pursuance of them there will be a return to the basically masculine and military virtues, a substitution of force for the hypocrisy of legality, a substitution of dictatorship for the corruptions of democracy, and the creation of a new élite to replace the massism of the democracies; and that in the achievement of this objective one may count upon the destiny of a people, the divine mission of a leader, and upon the daemonic force within the élite that converts men into heroes.

To understand a body of thought one must always first see it as a systematic unity (even if more systematic than the way in which its proponents themselves see it). In the case of the Nazi doctrine our very aversion to it makes it necessary for us to recognize that it is not all nonsense. I have tried so to state Hitler's metaphysic as to bring out the elements in it that have some strength and some universal appeal.

Leonard Woolf once wrote an absorbing little book called *Quack, Quack,* in which he dealt with the quackeries of men like Keyserling, Spengler, and Bergson in the intellectual field and of Mussolini and Hitler in the political, linking them with the mumbo-jumbo of primitive kingship. But what did not emerge from the book was that Bergson and Spengler, while preparing the ground unconsciously for Hitler, were utterly honest craftsmen; and that Hitler's quackery is not limited to the political field but has deep roots in the intellectual. Nietzsche, for example, talked of the *Übermensch,* or superman; but he was referring to a height of spiritual mastery within the individual, and would have been horrified at the application of the idea in Hitler's book so as to compass the subjection of workers to an employer under the *Führerprinzip.* Spengler talked mystically of race, as Nietzsche did; but Nietzsche would have protested, as Spengler did, against the cry *Juda verrecke* (may the Jews die!) echoed by the Nazi youth, which represents Hitler's application of the race principle. One would look far in the whole anti-humanist intellectual tradition for the elaborate charlatanism of the concepts of *Geist* and *Volk* that one finds in Hitler's book.

In short, Hitler's relation to the German intellectual tradition is that of a quick and mobile intelligence who has picked up some leading ideas and conscripted their intellectual and emotional force skillfully to his own uses.

There are long passages in his book in which he accuses the Jews of being parasites on the host of modern culture; but his own position toward the ideas on which he builds is in the very same sense parasitic.

. . . . .

I have spoken of the ideas that Hitler assumes. How about the ideas he selects for discussion? He has himself given us a clue to his principles of selection which is a thoroughly pragmatic one. "Every great revolutionary movement," he writes, "will untiringly try to make clear to the others the new train of thought, draw them over to its own ground, or at least make them doubtful of their own previous conviction. The propagation of a doctrine . . . has to have a backbone." That is to say, the concepts that Hitler emphasizes in his book are those that will give his propaganda persuasiveness. He looks for the ideas that will be effective in undermining the liberal and democratic beliefs on which the survival of the republic depended, and effective also in meeting the thrust of Marxist beliefs. He has three tasks: he must create a demonology that will unify his followers in a common hatred and a common sense of superiority; he must fight the liberal-democratic and Marxist systems of thought; he must build an intellectual structure of authority and obedience for the Nazi state to come.

The devices that Hitler uses in creating a demonology will appear more relevantly when we discuss Hitler as propagandist. But the theory underlying that demonology, as indeed it underlies the whole of Hitler's intellectual system, is that of blood and race—or better, racism. To an extent, in dealing with the racial interpretation of history, Hitler follows the traditional lines of Count Gobineau, who is the master of all the racial fanatics; Houston Stewart Chamberlain, whose *Foundations of the Nineteenth Century* was probably one of the books Hitler read with more than casualness; Bötticher (who wrote under the name of Paul de Lagarde) and Moeller van den Bruck, whose *Dritte Reich* was one of the Bibles of the pre-Hitler reactionaries; and Rosenberg, whose *Mythus des zwanzigsten Jahrhunderts* was published five years before Hitler wrote his book. Yet when you are dealing with the literature of racial genius, racial purity, racial superiority, you can scarcely trace a direct course. You are on an uncharted sea of mysticism and the subjective, where every mariner steers his own course.

Hitler proceeds by an elaborate division of races into three groups—the culture-creators (only the Aryans belong here), the culture-bearers (for example, the Japanese), the culture-destroyers (presumably only the Jews, yet Hitler includes the Negroes as well). This is a clever classification, for it enables Hitler to specify the perfect race and the parasite race while remaining vague about all the intermediate ones. Even in that paradise of the nebulous, the literature of race, Hitler is unparalleled in his vagueness. He brushes aside as irrelevant all questions of proof, of origins, of race history, of the relation between biological strains and psychological and cultural characteristics. He does not trouble to define race but appeals to the reader's consciousness of its reality. He makes no attempt to place the French, the Italians, the Americans, the English, the

Slavs in his hierarchy: it would be both difficult and dangerous—hence the safe choice of the Japanese for the sterile but harmless "culture-bearers." Above all, despite the fact that he calls his principal chapter on racism "Nation and Race," he nowhere compares the two or distinguishes between them.

Is it because such a distinction might prove inconvenient to Hitler's aims? For the cultural nationalists of the nineteenth century, from Herder and Mazzini to Renan, had talked far more of nation than of race: and where they had talked of race it was as a vague abbreviation of the national character. To perform its function in the wars of liberation, nationalism had to be a unifying concept for the entire population. It could be exclusive in respect to other nationalities but it had to be inclusive in regard to its own. But Hitler's nationalism, since its function in the political revolution was to create both a heroic and a diabolic element, had to be at once unifying and divisive. Having to make use of every device he could lay his hands on, he had to use both the myth of race and the myth of nation and somehow blend them together. The focus of his concept of nationalism is not the German spirit as built up culturally in the history of German institutions, and therefore including all creeds and all biological strains: it is the German spirit as somehow discovered by contrast with its opposite, the Jewish spirit in international history.

So drastic a reversal of the whole European tradition of cultural nationalism would have been almost impossible were it not that Hitler was addressing a bitter and defeated nation. Moeller van den Bruck, whose *Dritte Reich* influenced Hitler deeply, has spoken of the historical function of catastrophe in evoking the great revolutionary energies of a people. Hitler's nationalism is in that sense a nationalism bred of catastrophe. His is a dual appeal to a defeated people: first, to assign the blame to the "November criminals," presumably Marxists and Jews, and thus make the Germans feel that they were betrayed from within rather than defeated from without; secondly, to evoke the energies of a defeated people for a great effort of renascence. His concept of the nation is thus a twisted and stunted one, narrowed down to fit the purposes of a group seeking to lead a humiliated people in a war of *revanche*, and seeking also to turn men's sense of insecurity into the politically profitable channels of counter-revolutionary hate. "From Tacitus to Gobineau," writes Jacques Barzun in his informative book on *Race*, "the great racial ideals have come from disappointed men." He might have added that they have grown up in cultures in despair.

But the contradictions between the race and nation concepts are not the only difficulties Hitler runs into. There is an essential contradiction within the race concept itself. To be unifying, a concept of racism must be idealistic—must stress the spirit of a race, its creativeness, its genius, its invincibility. But to be an effective demonology it must be specific and material, pointing a finger at the impure and the unelect, and devising ways of discovering them infallibly. As long as Hitler talks of the beauty and genius of the Aryan, he is on the spiritual plane; as soon as he talks of the Jews he is on the material plane. It is not sufficiently emphasized that Hitler's race theory was confront-

ed by two traditions—that of the lofty glorification of race, as in Gobineau, Nietzsche, Spengler, Rosenberg; and that of anti-Semitism pure and simple. And confronted by these two traditions he preferred not to choose between them but to combine them. The first was necessary in appealing to ideal strivings; the second was necessary in fixing an object of hatred. Hence the experience the reader of *Mein Kampf* has in moving from misty vaporings about Aryanism to the macabre passages of vivid imagery, such as the famous one about the diabolic black-haired Jewish boy waiting in ambush for the unsuspecting Aryan girl and defiling her with his blood, or the one about the Jews' bringing the Negroes to the Rhine to bastardize the Aryans. But once Hitler is on this plane he has to break with Nietzsche and Spengler and the other race-theorists who were not anti-Semitic. And he is forced also to be specific about tests for Aryanism. Race theorists have always encountered difficulties in creating objective tests for racial purity and impurity. A French physician during the war, avid to give concreteness to the inferiority of the German strain, undertook to prove that you could tell a German through a urinalysis. Similarly in Hitler the genealogical precision of the Nürnberg laws and the movement for sterilization become logical consequences of his doctrine—but they bring it down from the lofty plane on which it started.

Hitler's race doctrine remains, with his anti-Marxism, the most exportable part of the theory of his book. They are the part that can be used best by the Mosleys, the Coughlins and Kuhns. They are the spearhead of the Nazi International. Now that Hitler's power-politics has forced him to drop his anti-Bolshevism, he must rely increasingly on his racism to rationalize his imperialist foreign policy as well as his internal tyranny. In fact, it has always been the blood concept that has linked his domestic with his foreign policy. In the case of anti-Semitism, it is blood-purity; in the case of imperialism, blood-unity. But since Munich and since his attack on Poland, even blood-unity and the need for uniting Germans everywhere under one banner has proved inadequate, for Hitler has been extending the trajectory of his power beyond the boundaries of the countries where there are problems of German minorities. More and more therefore he is likely to move away from the rhetoric of race and blood that fills the pages of *Mein Kampf,* back to the naked imperialist slogan that appears in the book as "the conquest of the world by the Germans." More and more, as Rauschning points out in his *Revolution of Nihilism,* his anti-Semitic theory is likely to become archaic. Its place has already been largely taken by the geopolitics of General Haushofer, and his conception of how geographic and economic strategy can be used to capture further *Lebensraum* and make strong states stronger.

Less archaic is the totalitarian theory in *Mein Kampf.* We use the word "totalitarian" today as loosely as we use the word "ideology"—to refer to any theory we dislike. Actually a totalitarianism may be defined as a social organization in which the government occupies the totality of the field in every area of the individual's life: in politics, in economics, in education, in peace and war, in expression, in religion, in culture. In a long, rambling, and chaotic chapter on "The State," at the beginning of his second volume,

Hitler seeks to construct a rationale for this belief that the state has an exclusive claim to every allegiance of the individual. The state, he says, is quite simply the instrument of the nationality—that is, of the bearers of the national culture. It follows that citizenship is not a matter of course but a privilege to be either denied or granted. There are citizens of the state and subjects of the state. Hitler argues that a mechanical democratic conception bestows citizenship even on the syphilitic: hence the need for rigorous exclusions from citizenship. By a trick of logic he thus manages to lump his political opponents and the vast mass of innocent Jews who were not even his political opponents, with the syphilitic.

And as citizenship may be denied, so too it is granted only on condition of the complete surrender of the individual to the state. Boiled down to its essence, Hitler's whole approach to the state is to see it as an instrument of power to be used by a governing group—a sort of inverted Marxism that substitutes the dominant élite for the dominant class. Hitler shrinks from a cultural approach to the state, as he shrinks from an economic approach. "The quality of a state," he writes, "cannot be evaluated according to the cultural height or the significance of power of this state in the frame of the rest of the world, but exclusively according to the degree of the quality of this institution with regard to the nationality involved in that particular case." Which, translated from its reckless Father Divine slinging-about of words, means probably that a culture (like the German culture under the republic) may rank high in world history yet fail to make full use of the heroic resources of the people. And to do that, says Hitler, it needs order, authority, discipline, leadership. Let it be noted here that those among our own thinkers who in the present crisis stress freedom merely as opposed to authority are playing into Hitler's hands. The intellectual problem of our day is not the opposition between freedom and authority: for the step between "freedom" and "anarchy" is for most people a short one, anarchy being merely the freedom that you don't like; and the association between "authority" and "order" is a close one, order being merely the authority of your own crowd. The antithesis is thus converted from one between freedom and authority to one between anarchy and order. And when that has been done, half the distance toward preparing a people for a totalitarianism has already been traversed. Throughout his book Hitler is careful to associate the images of order and energy with the Nazis and the images of anarchy and exhaustion with the Jews and the socialists and the Weimar regime.

When Hitler speaks of the innate qualities and the energy of the German people, he draws most heavily on the "folk" concept and comes dangerously close to the position of the numerous "folkish" movements in post-war Germany. These movements wanted to move away from the cosmopolitanism of the liberals and socialists to a more severely national culture. Hitler did not want his movement to be associated with theirs in people's minds, yet he was loth to lose the chance of capitalizing on the gains they had made. The result is a weak and wobbly attitude toward them on his part, the gist of which is that if a state is to be a "folkish" state it must not be so as a dreamy concept, but it must be ruthless and disciplined and allow no other allegiance than to itself. It must embody the *Führer-prinzip* in every walk of life—which means in effect the complete control by the party (and therefore by him) of economics, education, propaganda, religion, bureaucracy, and the military. He speaks of this as a process of "integration"—"to integrate through frantic energy the force of a people." Actually it is a process of excluding everyone except his own group from any control over the springs of energy in a culture.

．．．．．

It is when we come to the question of ways and means for capturing power, extending it, consolidating it, that we reach Hitler's only real greatness in the history of thought—a greatness that cannot be denied even by those who hate what he stands for. Hitler is probably the greatest master of propaganda and organization in modern history. To find his equal one must go back to Loyola and the Jesuits. His insights are not insights into theory but into strategy. In fact, it would be possible to follow Kenneth Burke's lead in his brilliant essay, "The Rhetoric of Hitler's 'Battle,' " and regard the whole of Hitler's theory as a set of strategic devices for influencing opinion. Burke's method is nowhere quite as pat and relevant as when applied to Hitler, whose charlatanism as a thinker puts most of his concepts on the plane of manipulation.

What makes him a master in manipulation? "The organizer," he says, and he is speaking of the propagandist as well, "has to be primarily a psychologist." But if we are to speak of Hitler as a psychologist, it is not in the ordinary sense. Professor Gordon Allport has recently told his fellow academic psychologists, in a presidential address, that from the standpoint of understanding how men's minds actually work they are inferior to statesmen and head waiters. Hitler knows nothing of academic lore, nothing of the neurophysiological basis of the mind's behavior, nothing of the refinements of our sensory and motor apparatus. The organizer, Hitler continues, "has to take man as he is. He has to take account of the weakness and of the bestiality equally." He takes men as he has found them empirically and he builds his appeals on his experience with them.

That experience has, in Hitler's case, been a curiously specialized one. He has scarcely ever confronted people except to impress, persuade, browbeat, cajole, rouse them. Even before he became a public figure he had public attitudes. If ever a man since Machiavelli went to the school of power, it was Hitler. The result is that life has presented to him only one mask—the mask of power; and only one problem—how to gain and hold power. And because life has thus limited itself for him, denying him the luxury of experiencing private decency and loyalty and love, he has taken his revenge by forming a low opinion of human nature and using it to the hilt.

He divides men into "the heads and the masses," the leaders and the herd. "Only a fraction of mankind," he says, "is energetic and bold." The rest are cowards and gulls. But the leaders can command the herd only by battering down the walls of opinion and the institutions of state power by which a previous ruling group has surrounded the herd. Hitler understands that the fight for power, whether to capture or retain it, must be conducted on two fronts: in the nerve-centers of men's minds and in the actual nerve-centers of the state—economic, administrative, military, diplomatic. Hence his distinction, in his famous chapter on "Propaganda and Organization" between the members and the followers of a movement. "If a movement," he writes, "has the intention of pulling down a world and of building a new one in its place," it "will have to divide the human material it has won into two great groups: into followers and members." The followers are the mass whose ideas have been changed by the movement and who will in turn change the ideas of other followers. They are the hangers-on; without winning them over or neutralizing them, a movement cannot succeed. The members are the ruthless, disciplined group who will stop at nothing in the struggle for power. The followers should be as numerous as possible, and heterogeneous; the members must be kept few, and as thoroughly disciplined as soldiers. The problem with respect to the first is that of propaganda; with respect to the second, it is organization.

On both scores Hitler and the Nazis borrowed extensively from the Marxist parties, but especially with respect to organization. Hitler studies the Marxists, if not in their literature as he claims, then certainly in their utterances and tactics. It has been pointed out by several critics that Hitler's hatred of the Marxists may have arisen from his inability to answer their arguments in the days when he was trying out his mind against socialist intellectuals and trade-unionists. Time after time he was thrown into confusion among the dialectical windings of a complex intellectual system. Time after time he returned, schooling himself painfully in the art of answering these arguments. "We had a chance," he writes, "to become acquainted with the incredible discipline of our opponents' propaganda, and still today it is my pride to have found the means . . . for beating finally its very makers. Two years later I was master in this craft." It is interesting to note the pride of craftsmanship Hitler shows here, for he is more in his *métier* as a propagandist than as anything else. When he joined the little group of six or seven men that called themselves the German Workers Party and established his place in it, the first job he took for himself was that of propaganda leader. It is here that his combination of imaginative daring, ruthlessness, and startling insight into men's weaknesses was most valuable. When he had to fight the Marxists in order to build his movement he saw that the problem was to play off national feeling against class feeling. When, having been admitted into the government by the von Papen group he had the problem of capturing the government so that he could be the master rather than the prisoner of that group, he did it by the daring coup of the Reichstag fire. When he had the problem of capturing Austria and Czechoslovakia, he did it by playing off the class feeling of the ruling classes in England, France, and even in the victim countries themselves, against their national feeling.

He addressed himself with passion to the task of mastering propaganda. He went to school not only to the Marxists; there are indications in his book that he knew how much was to be learned from other sources as well. He has a great admiration for the organization and methods of the Catholic Church. He speaks again and again of how much he learned by studying the propaganda the British used during the war. And he expresses admiration for American advertising techniques. Put all these together, add the fact that some of the insights of the Freudian school into the "psychology of the depths" must have penetrated to the Nazi circles in their early years, and add finally a mind eager to learn from every experience with men in the mass during the years of war and revolution and reconstruction—and you have the materials out of which Hitler the propagandist and organizer was fashioned.

But these materials would have been nothing had it not been for the fanatical life-and-death earnestness of Hitler himself. This is not the place to explore the psychic springs of this driving will: that must be left to the students of abnormal psychology. But it is clear that very early Hitler mastered the first principle of the success of any movement: that, given a favorable soil and climate for development, a movement is the shadow of a man. Hitler's basic assumption is that in a world of inertia, everything must give way to a driving will; amidst hesitation, assurance will triumph; amidst complexity men will cling to something that is simple; amidst disbelief they are eager for belief, even if externally imposed; in a world of passivity men want the experience of participation; in a world of humanitarian scruples the ruthless use of force will ultimately not be resisted. Finally, that we live by symbols, that the easiest and surest symbol is the person, and that the personification of the leader is at the basis of politics as it is at the basis of religion.

These are the principles on which Hitler's work as propagandist and organizer was based. The specific and rule-of-thumb injunctions with which his book is sprinkled may be traced back to them. They explain the advice he gives that you must always exaggerate your claims, even if fantastically; that you must never concede the slightest justice to your opponent's cause, else men will begin to doubt yours; that your platform, once formulated, must remain fixed; that you must hammer away always at a single idea; that the continued iteration of it will finally induce belief; that there is nothing so likely to be believed in the end as the daring and the unimaginable; that the masses "want the victory of the stronger and the annihilation or the unconditional surrender of the weaker." The principles I have mentioned explain also the tactics that Hitler used in the internal organization of his party: the hierarchy in which the only allegiance is to the leader at the top; the theatrical handling of public meetings; the ritual and insignia of membership; the complete contempt for democratic procedure; the use of drilling and marching; the policing of meetings by storm-troops.

I have spoken of some of the sources of these methods and insights. But in every case Hitler surpassed his masters in boldness, in shrewdness, in scope. He borrowed much from the Marxians, but what he did not borrow was their doctrinairism and their essential belief in men's rationality because they projected their own rationality on others. He copied from the Catholic Church, as well as from the Bolsheviks, the principle of a party ruled by iron discipline, yet neither Loyola nor Lenin made of their followers the completely amoral and inhuman automations that Hitler has made of his. He also took two other principles over from the Catholic Church: from the priesthood the idea of an élite continually renewed by fresh blood; from the Jesuits (perhaps also from the Greeks: see Werner Jaeger's *Paideia*) the strategic political importance of the control of education: yet the uses to which he has put both principles would be unrecognizable by their originators.

In the long run Hitler's reliance is on two things: maintaining an able and disciplined ruling group, and keeping the mass of the population in subjection not only through force but especially through control over every agency of expression and education. Hitler's book is obviously addressed to the young, to their ruthlessness and their sense of frustrated possibilities. The men with whom he surrounded himself were young men: it is perhaps a sign of the slowing up of his movement that more and more there has been a hardening of the Nazi bureaucracy, the growth of vested leadership-interests, a concentration of power in ever fewer hands, a dearth of new faces. The Napoleonic "career open to talent," which furnished no small part of the dynamic of the Nazi movement has given way to a caste system relieved only by the uncertainties of national policy and the turbulence of world political change. The appeal to the young today lies no longer in the depiction of a world ruled by new young gods. It is an appeal based on the imperialist destiny of Germany, on freedom from the old religious ties, but especially on a new sexual freedom.

Hitler's emphasis on the state control of education is so great that much of his chapter on the state is devoted to a minutely detailed agenda of instruction. There is a good deal of talk in it about physical health and physical education: part of this is the "folkish" accent, part a literary carry-over from the Spartan scheme. But in the main Hitler's conception of the educational function of the state is Treitschkean. We are too prone to forget, being Americans and constitutionalists, the strength of the army in the German tradition and the extent to which Hitler is an army man. The young are to be taught military virtues, history bowdlerized by the drill-sergeant, duties and sacrifices. Education is to "find its culmination in branding, through instinct and reason, the race sense and race feeling into the hearts and brains of the youth." Education, in short, is to be narrowed to the purposes of the ruling group, instead of the ruling group being increasingly broadened by education. But even more: hatred is to be raised to the height of the primary educational principle, and thus the primary cohesive force in a community that has no inner principle of cohesion.

. . . . .

Virginia Woolf, in one of her acute critical essays, has a sentence on James Joyce that even more relevantly applies to Hitler. "A desperate man," she calls Joyce, "who feels that in order to breathe he must break the windows." It is not a question here of *Lebensraum* for a nation, but *Lebensraum* for one man: and not all the geographical expanse of the earth and the planetary system would ever medicine him again to a sense of sufficiency. Some men

have had this fanatic desire for personal imperialism and ended either as millionaires or lunatics. Hitler's genius was political, and he had the fortune to live at a time when he could use and be used by the forces of reaction. The intellectual and psychic expression of that role may be found in *Mein Kampf.*

Göring has spoken somewhere of how Hitler proceeds "with the assurance of a somnambulist." If so it is a sleepwalker who has now plunged the world into another war. What the outcome will be, for Germany as well as for the whole of humanist culture, it is too early to know. It would be a good guess however that Hitler's assurance has finally played him false, and fatefully so. He succeeded in Germany so long as he could manipulate his strategy so that he never encountered a superior force. That too has been the secret of his diplomatic successes. Had he been willing to wait after Munich, consolidate his gains, allow the opposition to be split by divisions, he and Nazism might have been able to postpone the reckoning a long time. But the hypnotist came finally to hypnotize himself. The symbols about German destiny and his own which he sold so successfully to the German people he finally sold to himself. He went too far to extricate himself. And the result is a war in which, whatever the outcome from a military standpoint, Nazism as an intellectual system and as a system of values cannot emerge the victor.

The reason is that Hitler's values are life-denying values. Rauschning has called them "nihilism," by which he means the absence of fixed principle. But it is better to call them anti-humanist. For the Rauschnings of this world,

---

Hitler's parentage:

[Hitler's father's] real name was Alois Schicklgruber; he was the illegitimate son of Maria Anna Schicklgruber (1795-1847), who was the daughter of a farmer from Strones in Lower Austria; the father was Johann Nepomuk Hüttler (1807-1888), a farmer in Spital, also in Lower Austria; Alois was christened after his mother. She kept her liaison with Nepomuk a strict secret and in 1842 married her lover's brother. Alois did not change his name to Hitler until 1876 when he was thirty-nine years old. In 1885 he married Clara Pölzl, his own father's granddaughter; to Adolf Hitler, therefore, Johann Nepomuk Hüttler was both paternal grandfather and maternal great-grandfather.

Hitler clearly wished to prevent details of his somewhat questionable past becoming known. Probably for this reason he stated in November 1921 that his father had been a 'Post Office official'—entirely untrue and completely misleading. Very recently (1967) the results of some conclusive research on Hitler's origins have been published; these disprove all the vague suppositions, unproven assertions and statements allegedly backed by 'sources' to the effect that Hitler was possibly of Jewish origin; most of the latter are based upon statements made in Nuremberg in 1946 by Hans Frank, the Nazi Governor-General of Poland.

Werner Maser, in his Hitler's "Mein Kampf": An Analysis, *1970.*

in their desire for the static and their fear of change, pick exactly the strong parts of Hitler's doctrine to oppose. What has given Hitler strength is that there is a good deal of the revolutionist in him. He has promised men to open the windows for them, and they have flocked around him for breath: only to find that when they had smashed the windows he led them into a poisoned room. It is the poison—the anti-humanism, the barbarism—which is the real indictment of Hitler: not the restless desire for change and even for personal aggrandizement. If Hitler is ever defeated it will not be the military strength of the western Allies that will defeat him but the intellectual strength of a humanism which embraces the revolutionary values as well as the permanent. It will not be the war but the peace afterward, provided (what a big proviso!) it is a humane peace and one that does not repeat the follies of Versailles. It will not be the Chamberlains that will ever defeat Hitler but the Thomas Manns. (pp. 356-74)

> Max Lerner, "Some European Thinkers: Hitler as Thinker," in his Ideas Are Weapons: The History and Uses of Ideas, *The Viking Press, 1939, pp. 356-74.*

George Orwell   (essay date 1940)

[*An English novelist, essayist, and journalist, Orwell authored two of the most politically significant novels of the twentieth century:* Animal Farm *(1945) and* Nineteen Eighty-Four *(1949), in which he detailed the oppressive potential of totalitarian systems. In the following review of* Mein Kampf, *Orwell denounces Hitler's policies while acknowledging the power of his appeal.*]

It is a sign of the speed at which events are moving that Hurst and Blackett's unexpurgated edition of **Mein Kampf,** published only a year ago, is edited from a pro-Hitler angle. The obvious intention of the translator's preface and notes is to tone down the book's ferocity and present Hitler in as kindly a light as possible. For at that date Hitler was still respectable. He had crushed the German labour movement, and for that the property-owning classes were willing to forgive him almost anything. Both Left and Right concurred in the very shallow notion that National Socialism was merely a version of Conservatism.

Then suddenly it turned out that Hitler was not respectable after all. As one result of this, Hurst and Blackett's edition was reissued in a new jacket explaining that all profits would be devoted to the Red Cross. Nevertheless, simply on the internal evidence of **Mein Kampf,** it is difficult to believe that any real change has taken place in Hitler's aims and opinions. When one compares his utterances of a year or so ago with those made fifteen years earlier, a thing that strikes one is the rigidity of his mind, the way in which his world-view *doesn't* develop. It is the fixed vision of a monomaniac and not likely to be much affected by the temporary manoeuvres of power politics. Probably, in Hitler's own mind, the Russo-German Pact represents no more than an alteration of time-table. The plan laid down in **Mein Kampf** was to smash Russia first, with the implied intention of smashing England afterwards. Now, as it has turned out, England has got to be dealt with first, because Russia was the more easily bribed of the two. But

Russia's turn will come when England is out of the picture—that, no doubt, is how Hitler sees it. Whether it will turn out that way is of course a different question.

Suppose that Hitler's programme could be put into effect. What he envisages, a hundred years hence, is a continuous state of 250 million Germans with plenty of "living room" (i.e. stretching to Afghanistan or thereabouts), a horrible brainless empire in which, essentially, nothing ever happens except the training of young men for war and the endless breeding of fresh cannon-fodder. How was it that he was able to put this monstrous vision across? It is easy to say that at one stage of his career he was financed by the heavy industrialists, who saw in him the man who would smash the Socialists and Communists. They would not have backed him, however, if he had not talked a great movement into existence already. Again, the situation in Germany, with its seven million unemployed, was obviously favourable for demagogues. But Hitler could not have succeeded against his many rivals if it had not been for the attraction of his own personality, which one can feel even in the clumsy writing of **Mein Kampf,** and which is no doubt overwhelming when one hears his speeches. I should like to put it on record that I have never been able to dislike Hitler. Ever since he came to power—till then, like nearly everyone, I had been deceived into thinking that he did not matter—I have reflected that I would certainly kill him if I could get within reach of him, but that I could feel no personal animosity. The fact is that there is something deeply appealing about him. One feels it again when one sees his photographs—and I recommend especially the photograph at the beginning of Hurst and Blackett's edition, which shows Hitler in his early Brownshirt days. It is a pathetic, dog-like face, the face of a man suffering under intolerable wrongs. In a rather more manly way it reproduces the expression of innumerable pictures of Christ crucified, and there is little doubt that that is how Hitler sees himself. The initial, personal cause of his grievance against the universe can only be guessed at; but at any rate the grievance is there. He is the martyr, the victim, Prometheus chained to the rock, the self-sacrificing hero who fights single-handed against impossible odds. If he were killing a mouse he would know how to make it seem like a dragon. One feels, as with Napoleon, that he is fighting against destiny, that he *can't* win, and yet that he somehow deserves to. The attraction of such a pose is of course enormous; half the films that one sees turn upon some such theme.

Also he has grasped the falsity of the hedonistic attitude to life. Nearly all western thought since the last war, certainly all "progressive" thought, has assumed tacitly that human beings desire nothing beyond ease, security and avoidance of pain. In such a view of life there is no room, for instance, for patriotism and the military virtues. The Socialist who finds his children playing with soldiers is usually upset, but he is never able to think of a substitute for the tin soldiers; tin pacifists somehow won't do. Hitler, because in his own joyless mind he feels it with exceptional strength, knows that human beings *don't* only want comfort, safety, short working-hours, hygiene, birth-control and, in general, common sense; they also, at least intermittently, want struggle and self-sacrifice, not to mention drums, flags and loyalty-parades. However they may be as economic theories, Fascism and Nazism are psychologically far sounder than any hedonistic conception of life. The same is probably true of Stalin's militarised version of Socialism. All three of the great dictators have enhanced their power by imposing intolerable burdens on their peoples. Whereas Socialism, and even capitalism in a more grudging way, have said to people "I offer you a good time," Hitler has said to them "I offer you struggle, danger and death," and as a result a whole nation flings itself at his feet. Perhaps later on they will get sick of it and change their minds, as at the end of the last war. After a few years of slaughter and starvation "Greatest happiness of the greatest number" is a good slogan, but at this moment "Better an end with horror than a horror without end" is a winner. Now that we are fighting against the man who coined it, we ought not to underrate its emotional appeal. (pp. 12-14)

George Orwell, "Review of 'Mein Kampf' by Adolf Hitler," in his The Collected Essays, Journalism, and Letters of George Orwell: My Country Right or Left, 1940-1943, Vol. II, *edited by Sonia Orwell and Ian Angus, Harcourt Brace Jovanovich, 1968, pp. 12-14.*

Kenneth Burke   (essay date 1941)

[*An American critic, poet, and educator, Burke is the author of such works as* A Grammar of Motives *(1945),* A Rhetoric of Motives *(1950), and* The Philosophy of Literary Form: Studies in Symbolic Action, *from which the essay below is taken. In this chapter Burke discusses the rhetoric of* Mein Kampf].

The appearance of ***Mein Kampf*** in unexpurgated translation has called forth far too many vandalistic comments. There are other ways of burning books than on the pyre— and the favorite method of the hasty reviewer is to deprive himself and his readers by inattention. I maintain that it is thoroughly vandalistic for the reviewer to content himself with the mere inflicting of a few symbolic wounds upon this book and its author, of an intensity varying with the resources of the reviewer and the time at his disposal. Hitler's "Battle" is exasperating, even nauseating; yet the fact remains: If the reviewer but knocks off a few adverse attitudinizings and calls it a day, with a guaranty in advance that his article will have a favorable reception among the decent members of our population, he is contributing more to our gratification than to our enlightenment.

Here is the testament of a man who swung a great people into his wake. Let us watch it carefully; and let us watch it, not merely to discover some grounds for prophesying what political move is to follow Munich, and what move to follow that move, etc.; let us try also to discover what kind of "medicine" this medicine-man has concocted, that we may know, with greater accuracy, exactly what to guard against, if we are to forestall the concocting of similar medicine in America.

Already, in many quarters of our country, we are "beyond" the stage where we are being saved from Nazism

by our *virtues*. And fascist integration is being staved off, rather, by the *conflicts among our vices*. Our vices cannot get together in a grand united front of prejudices; and the result of this frustration, if or until they succeed in surmounting it, speaks, as the Bible might say, "in the name of " democracy. Hitler found a panacea, a "cure for what ails you," a "snakeoil," that made such sinister unifying possible within his own nation. And he was helpful enough to put his cards face up on the table, that we might examine his hands. Let us, then, for God's sake, examine them. This book is the well of Nazi magic; crude magic, but effective. A people trained in pragmatism should want to inspect this magic.

Every movement that would recruit its followers from among many discordant and divergent bands, must have some spot towards which all roads lead. Each man may get there in his own way, but it must be the one unifying center of reference for all. Hitler considered this matter carefully, and decided that this center must be not merely a centralizing hub of *ideas,* but a mecca geographically located, towards which all eyes could turn at the appointed hours of prayer (or, in this case, the appointed hours of prayer-in-reverse, the hours of vituperation). So he selected Munich, as the *materialization* of his unifying panacea. As he puts it:

> The geo-political importance of a center of a movement cannot be overrated. Only the presence of such a center and of a place, bathed in the magic of a Mecca or a Rome, can at length give a movement that force which is rooted in the inner unity and in the recognition of a hand that represents this unity.

If a movement must have its Rome, it must also have its devil. For as Russell pointed out years ago, an important ingredient of unity in the Middle Ages (an ingredient that long did its unifying work despite the many factors driving towards disunity) was the symbol of a *common enemy,* the Prince of Evil himself. Men who can unite on nothing else can unite on the basis of a foe shared by all. Hitler himself states the case very succinctly:

> As a whole, and at all times, the efficiency of the truly national leader consists primarily in preventing the division of the attention of a people, and always in concentrating it on a single enemy. The more uniformly the fighting will of a people is put into action, the greater will be the magnetic force of the movement and the more powerful the impetus of the blow. It is part of the genius of a great leader to make adversaries of different fields appear as always belonging to one category only, because to weak and unstable characters the knowledge that there are various enemies will lead only too easily to incipient doubts as to their own cause.
>
> As soon as the wavering masses find themselves confronted with too many enemies, objectivity at once steps in, and the question is raised whether actually all the others are wrong and their own nation or their own movement alone is right.
>
> Also with this comes the first paralysis of their

own strength. Therefore, a number of essentially different enemies must always be regarded as one in such a way that in the opinion of the mass of one's own adherents the war is being waged against one enemy alone. This strengthens the belief in one's own cause and increases one's bitterness against the attacker.

As everyone knows, this policy was exemplified in his selection of an "international" devil, the "international Jew" (the Prince was international, universal, "catholic"). This *materialization* of a religious pattern is, I think, one terrifically effective weapon of propaganda in a period where religion has been progressively weakened by many centuries of capitalist materialism. You need but go back to the sermonizing of centuries to be reminded that religion had a powerful enemy long before organized atheism came upon the scene. Religion is based upon the "prosperity of poverty," upon the use of ways for converting our sufferings and handicaps into a good—but capitalism is based upon the prosperity of acquisitions, the only scheme of value, in fact, by which its proliferating store of gadgets could be sold, assuming for the moment that capitalism had not got so drastically in its own way that it can't sell its gadgets even after it has trained people to feel that human dignity, the "higher standard of living," could be attained only by their vast private accumulation.

So, we have, as unifying step No. 1, the international devil materialized, in the visible, point-to-able form of people with a certain kind of "blood," a burlesque of contemporary neo-positivism's ideal of meaning, which insists upon a *material* reference.

Once Hitler has thus essentialized his enemy, all "proof" henceforth is automatic. If you point out the enormous amount of evidence to show that the Jewish worker is at odds with the "international Jew stock exchange capitalist," Hitler replies with one hundred per cent regularity: That is one more indication of the cunning with which the "Jewish plot" is being engineered. Or would you point to "Aryans" who do the same as his conspiratorial Jews? Very well; that is proof that the "Aryan" has been "seduced" by the Jew.

The sexual symbolism that runs through Hitler's book, lying in wait to draw upon the responses of contemporary sexual values, is easily characterized: Germany in dispersion is the "dehorned Siegfried." The masses are "feminine." As such, they desire to be led by a dominating male. This male, as orator, woos them—and, when he has won them, he commands them. The rival male, the villainous Jew, would on the contrary "seduce" them. If he succeeds, he poisons their blood by intermingling with them. Whereupon, by purely associative connections of ideas, we are moved into attacks upon syphilis, prostitution, incest, and other similar misfortunes, which are introduced as a kind of "musical" argument when he is on the subject of "blood-poisoning" by intermarriage or, in its "spiritual" equivalent, by the infection of "Jewish" ideas, such as democracy. [The critic adds in a footnote: "Hitler also strongly insists upon the total identification between leader and people. Thus, in wooing the people, he would in a roundabout way be wooing himself. The thought might suggest how the Führer, dominating the feminine masses

by his diction, would have an incentive to remain unmarried."]

The "medicinal" appeal of the Jew as scapegoat operates from another angle. The middle class contains, within the mind of each member, a duality: its members simultaneously have a cult of money and a detestation of this cult. When capitalism is going well, this conflict is left more or less in abeyance. But when capitalism is balked, it comes to the fore. Hence, there is "medicine" for the "Aryan" members of the middle class in the projective device of the scapegoat, whereby the "bad" features can be allocated to the "devil," and one can "respect himself" by a distinction between "good" capitalism and "bad" capitalism, with those of a different lodge being the vessels of the "bad" capitalism. It is doubtless the "relief" of this solution that spared Hitler the necessity of explaining just how the "Jewish plot" was to work out. Nowhere does this book, which is so full of war plans, make the slightest attempt to explain the steps whereby the triumph of "Jewish Bolshevism," which destroys *all* finance, will be the triumph of *"Jewish"* finance. Hitler well knows the point at which his "elucidations" should rely upon the lurid alone.

The question arises, in those trying to gauge Hitler: Was his selection of the Jew, as his unifying devil-function, a purely calculating act? Despite the quotation I have already given, I believe that it was *not*. The vigor with which he utilized it, I think, derives from a much more complex state of affairs. It seems that, when Hitler went to Vienna, in a state close to total poverty, he genuinely suffered. He lived among the impoverished; and he describes his misery at the spectacle. He was *sensitive* to it; and his way of manifesting this sensitiveness impresses me that he is, at this point, wholly genuine, as with his wincing at the broken family relationships caused by alcoholism, which he in turn relates to impoverishment. During this time he began his attempts at political theorizing; and his disturbance was considerably increased by the skill with which Marxists tied him into knots. One passage in particular gives you reason, reading between the lines, to believe that the dialecticians of the class struggle, in their skill at blasting his muddled speculations, put him into a state of uncertainty that was finally "solved" by rage:

> The more I argued with them, the more I got to know their dialectics. First they counted on the ignorance of their adversary; then, when there was no way out, they themselves pretended stupidity. If all this was of no avail, they refused to understand or they changed the subject when driven into a corner; they brought up truisms, but they immediately transferred their acceptance to quite different subjects, and, if attacked again, they gave way and pretended to know nothing exactly. Wherever one attacked one of these prophets, one's hands seized slimy jelly; it slipped through one's fingers only to collect again in the next moment. If one smote one of them so thoroughly that, with the bystanders watching, he could but agree, and if one thus thought he had advanced at least one step, one was greatly astonished the following day. The Jew did not in the least remember the day before, he continued to talk in the same old strain as if

nothing had happened, and if indignantly confronted, he pretended to be astonished and could not remember anything except that his assertions had already been proved true the day before.

Often I was stunned.

One did not know what to admire more: their glibness of tongue or their skill in lying.

I gradually began to hate them.

At this point, I think, he is tracing the *spontaneous* rise of his anti-Semitism. He tells how, once he had discovered the "cause" of the misery about him, he could *confront it.* Where he had had to avert his eyes, he could now *positively welcome* the scene. Here his drastic structure of *acceptance* was being formed. He tells of the "internal happiness" that descended upon him.

This was the time in which the greatest change I was ever to experience took place in me.

From a feeble cosmopolite I turned into a fanatical anti-Semite,

and thence we move, by one of those associational tricks which he brings forth at all strategic moments, into a vision of the end of the world—out of which in turn he emerges with his slogan: "I am acting in the sense of the Almighty Creator: *By warding off Jews I am fighting for the Lord's work*" (italics his).

He talks of this transition as a period of "double life," a struggle of "reason" and "reality" against his "heart." It was as "bitter" as it was "blissful." And finally, it was "reason" that won! Which prompts us to note that those who attack Hitlerism as a cult of the irrational should emend their statements to this extent: irrational it is, but it is carried on under the *slogan* of "Reason." Similarly, his cult of war is developed "in the name of" humility, love, and peace. Judged on a quantitative basis, Hitler's book certainly falls under the classification of hate. Its venom is everywhere, its charity is sparse. But the rationalized family tree for this hate situates it in "Aryan love." Some deep-probing German poets, whose work adumbrated the Nazi movement, did gravitate towards thinking *in the name of* war, irrationality, and hate. But Hitler was not among them. After all, when it is so easy to draw a doctrine of war out of a doctrine of peace, why should the astute politician do otherwise, particularly when Hitler has slung together his doctrines, without the slightest effort at logical symmetry? Furthermore, Church thinking always got to its wars in Hitler's "sounder" manner; and the patterns of Hitler's thought are a bastardized or caricatured version of religious thought.

I spoke of Hitler's fury at the dialectics of those who opposed him when his structure was in the stage of scaffolding. From this we may move to another tremendously important aspect of his theory: his attack upon the *parliamentary*. For it is again, I submit, an important aspect of his medicine, in its function as medicine for him personally and as medicine for those who were later to identify themselves with him.

There is a "problem" in the parliament—and nowhere

was this problem more acutely in evidence than in the prewar Vienna that was to serve as Hitler's political schooling. For the parliament, at its best, is a "babel" of voices. There is the wrangle of men representing interests lying awkwardly on the bias across one another, sometimes opposing, sometimes vaguely divergent. Morton Prince's psychiatric study of "Miss Beauchamp," the case of a woman split into several sub-personalities at odds with one another, variously combining under hypnosis, and frequently in turmoil, is the allegory of a democracy fallen upon evil days. The parliament of the Habsburg Empire just prior to its collapse was an especially drastic instance of such disruption, such vocal diaspora, with movements that would reduce one to a disintegrated mass of fragments if he attempted to encompass the totality of its discordancies. So Hitler, suffering under the alienation of poverty and confusion, yearning for some integrative core, came to take this parliament as the basic symbol of all that he would move away from. He damned the tottering Habsburg Empire as a "State of Nationalities." The many conflicting voices of the spokesmen of the many political blocs arose from the fact that various separationist movements of a nationalistic sort had arisen within a Catholic imperial structure formed prior to the nationalistic emphasis and slowly breaking apart under its development. So, you had this Babel of voices; and, by the method of associative mergers, *using ideas as imagery,* it became tied up, in the Hitler rhetoric, with "Babylon," Vienna as the city of poverty, prostitution, immorality, coalitions, half-measures, incest, democracy (i.e., majority rule leading to "lack of personal responsibility"), death, internationalism, seduction, and anything else of thumbs-down sort the associative enterprise cared to add on this side of the balance.

Hitler's way of treating the parliamentary babel, I am sorry to say, was at one important point not much different from that of the customary editorial in our own newspapers. Every conflict among the parliamentary spokesmen represents a corresponding conflict among the material interests of the groups for whom they are speaking. But Hitler did not discuss the babel from this angle. He discussed it on a purely *symptomatic* basis. The strategy of our orthodox press, in thus ridiculing the cacophonous verbal output of Congress, is obvious: by thus centering attack upon the *symptoms* of business conflict, as they reveal themselves on the dial of political wrangling, and leaving the underlying cause, the business conflicts themselves, out of the case, they can gratify the very public they would otherwise alienate: namely, the businessmen who are the activating members of their reading public. Hitler, however, went them one better. For not only did he stress the purely *symptomatic* attack here. He proceeded to search for the "cause." And this "cause," of course, he derived from his medicine, his racial theory by which he could give a noneconomic interpretation of a phenomenon economically engendered.

Here again is where Hitler's corrupt use of religious patterns comes to the fore. Church thought, being primarily concerned with matters of the "personality," with problems of moral betterment, naturally, and I think rightly, stresses as a necessary feature, the act of will upon the part of the individual. Hence its resistance to a purely "environmental" account of human ills. Hence its emphasis upon the "person." Hence its proneness to seek a noneconomic explanation of economic phenomena. Hitler's proposal of a noneconomic "cause" for the disturbances thus had much to recommend it from this angle. And, as a matter of fact, it was Lueger's Christian-Social Party in Vienna that taught Hitler the tactics of tying up a program of social betterment with an anti-Semitic "unifier." The two parties that he carefully studied at that time were this Catholic faction and Schoenerer's Pan-German group. And his analysis of their attainments and shortcomings, from the standpoint of demagogic efficacy, is an extremely astute piece of work, revealing how carefully this man used the current situation in Vienna as an experimental laboratory for the maturing of his plans.

His unification device, we may summarize, had the following important features:

(1) Inborn dignity. In both religious and humanistic patterns of thought, a "natural born" dignity of man is stressed. And this categorical dignity is considered to be an attribute of *all* men, if they will but avail themselves of it, by right thinking and right living. But Hitler gives this ennobling attitude an ominous twist by his theories of race and nation, whereby the "Aryan" is elevated above all others by the innate endowment of his blood, while other "races," in particular Jews and Negroes, are innately inferior. This sinister secularized revision of Christian theology thus puts the sense of dignity upon a fighting basis, requiring the conquest of "inferior races." After the defeat of Germany in the World War, there were especially strong emotional needs that this compensatory doctrine of an *inborn* superiority could gratify.

(2) *Projection* device. The "curative" process that comes with the ability to hand over one's ills to a scapegoat, thereby getting purification by dissociation. This was especially medicinal, since the sense of frustration leads to a self-questioning. Hence if one can hand over his infirmities

The cell at Landsberg prison where Hitler dictated Mein Kampf *to Hess.*

to a vessel, or "cause," outside the self, one can battle an external enemy instead of battling an enemy within. And the greater one's internal inadequacies, the greater the amount of evils one can load upon the back of "the enemy." This device is furthermore given a semblance of reason because the individual properly realizes that he is not alone responsible for his condition. There *are* inimical factors in the scene itself. And he wants to have them "placed," preferably in a way that would require a minimum change in the ways of thinking to which he had been accustomed. This was especially appealing to the middle class, who were encouraged to feel that they could conduct their businesses without any basic change whatever, once the businessmen of a different "race" were eliminated.

(3) Symbolic rebirth. Another aspect of the two features already noted. The projective device of the scapegoat, coupled with the Hitlerite doctrine of inborn racial superiority, provides its followers with a "positive" view of life. They can again get the feel of *moving forward,* towards a *goal* (a promissory feature of which Hitler makes much). In Hitler, as the group's prophet, such rebirth involved a symbolic change of lineage. Here, above all, we see Hitler giving a malign twist to a benign aspect of Christian thought. For whereas the Pope, in the familistic pattern of thought basic to the Church, stated that the Hebrew prophets were the *spiritual ancestors* of Christianity, Hitler uses this same mode of thinking in reverse. He renounces this "ancestry" in a "materialistic" way by voting himself and the members of his lodge a different "blood stream" from that of the Jews.

(4) Commercial use. Hitler obviously here had something to sell—and it was but a question of time until he sold it (i.e., got financial backers for his movement). For it provided a *noneconomic interpretation of economic ills.* As such, it served with maximum efficiency in deflecting the attention from the economic factors involved in modern conflict; hence by attacking "Jew finance" instead of *finance,* it could stimulate an enthusiastic movement that left "Aryan" finance in control.

Never once, throughout his book, does Hitler deviate from the above formula. Invariably, he ends his diatribes against contemporary economic ills by a shift into an insistence that we must get to the "true" cause, which is centered in "race." The "Aryan" is "constructive"; the Jew is "destructive"; and the "Aryan," to continue his *construction,* must *destroy* the Jewish *destruction.* The Aryan, as the vessel of *love,* must *hate* the Jewish *hate.*

Perhaps the most enterprising use of his method is in his chapter, "The Causes of the Collapse," where he refuses to consider Germany's plight as in any basic way connected with the consequences of war. Economic factors, he insists, are "only of second or even third importance," but "political, ethical-moral, as well as factors of blood and race, are of the first importance." His rhetorical steps are especially interesting here, in that he begins by seeming to flout the national susceptibilities: "The military defeat of the German people is not an undeserved catastrophe, but rather a deserved punishment by eternal retribution." He then proceeds to present the military collapse as but a "consequence of moral poisoning, visible to all, the consequence of a decrease in the instinct of self-preservation . . . which had already begun to undermine the foundations of the people and the Reich many years before." This moral decay derived from "a sin against the blood and the degradation of the race," so its innerness was an outerness after all: the Jew, who thereupon gets saddled with a vast amalgamation of evils, among them being capitalism, democracy, pacifism, journalism, poor housing, modernism, big cities, loss of religion, half measures, ill health, and weakness of the monarch.

Hitler had here another important psychological ingredient to play upon. If a State is in economic collapse (and his theories, tentatively taking shape in the pre-war Vienna, were but developed with greater efficiency in post-war Munich), you cannot possibly derive dignity from economic stability. Dignity must come first—and if you possess it, and implement it, from it may follow its economic counterpart. There is much justice to this line of reasoning, so far as it goes. A people in collapse, suffering under economic frustration and the defeat of nationalistic aspirations, with the very midrib of their integrative efforts (the army) in a state of dispersion, have little other than some "spiritual" basis to which they could refer their nationalistic dignity. Hence, the categorical dignity of superior race was a perfect recipe for the situation. It was "spiritual" in so far as it was "above" crude economic "interests," but it was "materialized" at the psychologically "right" spot in that "the enemy" was something you could *see*.

Furthermore, you had the desire for unity, such as a discussion of class conflict, on the basis of conflicting interests, could not satisfy. The yearning for unity is so great that people are always willing to meet you halfway if you will give it to them by fiat, by flat statement, regardless of the facts. Hence, Hitler consistently refused to consider internal political conflict on the basis of conflicting interests. Here again, he could draw upon a religious pattern, by insisting upon a *personal* statement of the relation between classes, the relation between leaders and followers, each group in its way fulfilling the same commonalty of interests, as the soldiers and captains of an army share a common interest in victory. People so dislike the idea of internal division that, where there is a real internal division, their dislike can easily be turned against the man or group who would so much as *name* it, let alone proposing to act upon it. Their natural and justified resentment against internal division itself is turned against the diagnostician who states it as a *fact*. This diagnostician, it is felt, is the *cause* of the disunity he named.

Cutting in from another angle, therefore, we note how two sets of equations were built up, with Hitler combining or coalescing *ideas* the way a poet combines or coalesces *images*. On the one side were the ideas, or images, of disunity, centering in the parliamentary wrangle of the Habsburg "State of Nationalities." This was offered as the antithesis of German nationality, which was presented in the curative imagery of unity, focused upon the glories of the Prussian Reich, with its mecca now moved to "folkish" Vienna. For though Hitler at first attacked the many "folkish"

movements, with their hankerings after a kind of Wagnerian mythology of Germanic origins, he subsequently took "folkish" as a basic word by which to conjure. It was, after all, another noneconomic basis of reference. At first we find him objecting to "those who drift about with the word 'folkish' on their caps," and asserting that "such a Babel of opinions cannot serve as the basis of a political fighting movement." But later he seems to have realized, as he well should, that its vagueness was a major point in its favor. So it was incorporated in the grand coalition of his ideational imagery, or imagistic ideation; and Chapter XI ends with the vision of "a State which represents not a mechanism of economic considerations and interests, alien to the people, but a folkish organism."

So, as against the disunity equations, already listed briefly in our discussion of his attacks upon the parliamentary, we get a contrary purifying set; the wrangle of the parliamentary is to be stilled by the giving of *one* voice to the whole people, this to be the "inner voice" of Hitler, made uniform throughout the German boundaries, as leader and people were completely identified with each other. In sum: Hitler's inner voice, equals leader-people identification, equals unity, equals Reich, equals the mecca of Munich, equals plow, equals sword, equals work, equals war, equals army as midrib, equals responsibility (the personal responsibility of the absolute ruler), equals sacrifice, equals the theory of "German democracy" (the free popular choice of the leader, who then accepts the responsibility, and demands absolute obedience in exchange for his sacrifice), equals love (with the masses as feminine), equals idealism, equals obedience to nature, equals race, nation.

And, of course, the two keystones of these opposite equations were Aryan "heroism" and "sacrifice" vs. Jewish "cunning" and "arrogance." Here again we get an astounding caricature of religious thought. For Hitler presents the concept of "Aryan" superiority, of all ways, in terms of "Aryan humility." This "humility" is extracted by a very delicate process that requires, I am afraid, considerable "good will" on the part of the reader who would follow it.

The Church, we may recall, had proclaimed an integral relationship between Divine Law and Natural Law. Natural Law was the expression of the Will of God. Thus, in the middle age, it was a result of natural law, working through tradition, that some people were serfs and other people nobles. And every good member of the Church was "obedient" to this law. Everybody resigned himself to it. Hence, the serf resigned himself to his poverty, and the noble resigned himself to his riches. The monarch resigned himself to his position as representative of the people. And at times the Churchmen resigned themselves to the need of trying to represent the people instead. And the pattern was made symmetrical by the consideration that each traditional "right" had its corresponding "obligations." Similarly, the Aryan doctrine is a doctrine of resignation, hence of humility. It is in accordance with the laws of nature that the "Aryan blood" is superior to all other bloods. Also, the "law of the survival of the fittest" is God's law, working through natural law. Hence, if the Aryan blood has been vested with the awful responsibility of its inborn superiority, the bearers of this "culture-creating" blood must resign themselves to struggle in behalf of its triumph. Otherwise, the laws of God have been disobeyed, with human decadence as a result. We must fight, he says, in order to "deserve to be alive." The Aryan "obeys" nature. It is only "Jewish arrogance" that thinks of "conquering" nature by democratic ideals of equality.

This picture has some nice distinctions worth following. The major virtue of the Aryan race was its instinct for self-preservation (in obedience to natural law). But the major vice of the Jew was his instinct for self-preservation; for, if he did not have this instinct to a maximum degree, he would not be the "perfect" enemy—that is, he wouldn't be strong enough to account for the ubiquitousness and omnipotence of his conspiracy in destroying the world to become its master.

How, then, are we to distinguish between the benign instinct of self-preservation at the roots of Aryanism, and the malign instinct of self-preservation at the roots of Semitism? We shall distinguish thus: The Aryan self-preservation is based upon *sacrifice,* the sacrifice of the individual to the group, hence, militarism, army discipline, and one big company union. But Jewish self-preservation is based upon individualism, which attains its cunning ends by the exploitation of peace. How, then, can such arrant individualists concoct the world-wide plot? By the help of their "herd instinct." By their sheer "herd instinct" individualists can band together for a common end. They have no real solidarity, but unite opportunistically to seduce the Aryan. Still, that brings up another technical problem. For we have been hearing much about the importance of the *person.* We have been told how, by the "law of the survival of the fittest," there is a sifting of people on the basis of their individual capacities. We even have a special chapter of pure Aryanism: "The Strong Man is Mightiest Alone." Hence, another distinction is necessary: The Jew represents individualism; the Aryan represents "super-individualism."

I had thought, when coming upon the "Strong Man is Mightiest Alone" chapter, that I was going to find Hitler at his weakest. Instead, I found him at his strongest. (I am not referring to *quality,* but to *demagogic effectiveness.*) For the chapter is not at all, as you might infer from the title, done in a "rise of Adolph Hitler" manner. Instead, it deals with the Nazis' gradual absorption of the many disrelated "folkish" groups. And it is managed throughout by means of a spontaneous identification between leader and people. Hence, the Strong Man's "aloneness" is presented as a *public* attribute, in terms of tactics for the struggle against the *Party's* dismemberment under the pressure of rival saviors. There is no explicit talk of Hitler at all. And it is simply *taken for granted* that *his* leadership is the norm, and all other leaderships the abnorm. There is no "philosophy of the superman," in Nietzschean cast. Instead, Hitler's blandishments so integrate leader and people, commingling them so inextricably, that the politician does not even present himself as candidate. Somehow, the battle is over already, the decision has been made. "German democracy" has chosen. And the deployments of politics are, you might say, the chartings of Hitler's pri-

vate mind translated into the vocabulary of nationalistic events. He says *what he thought* in terms of *what parties did.*

Here, I think, we see the distinguishing quality of Hitler's method as an instrument of persuasion, with reference to the question whether Hitler is sincere or deliberate, whether his vision of the omnipotent conspirator has the drastic honesty of paranoia or the sheer shrewdness of a demagogue trained in *Realpolitik* of the Machiavellian sort. Must we choose? Or may we not, rather, replace the "either—or" with a "both—and"? Have we not by now offered grounds enough for our contention that Hitler's sinister powers of persuasion derive from the fact that he spontaneously evolved his "cure-all" in response to inner necessities?

So much, then, was "spontaneous." It was further channelized into the anti-Semitic pattern by the incentives he derived from the Catholic Christian-Social Party in Vienna itself. Add, now, the step into *criticism.* Not criticism in the "parliamentary" sense of doubt, of hearkening to the opposition and attempting to mature a policy in the light of counter-policies; but the "unified" kind of criticism that simply seeks for conscious ways of making one's position more "efficient," more thoroughly itself. This is the kind of criticism at which Hitler was an adept. As a result, he could *spontaneously* turn to a scapegoat mechanism, and he could, by conscious planning, perfect the symmetry of the solution towards which he had spontaneously turned.

This is the meaning of Hitler's diatribes against "objectivity." "Objectivity" is interference-criticism. What Hitler wanted was the kind of criticism that would be a pure and simple coefficient of power, enabling him to go most effectively in the direction he had chosen. And the "inner voice" of which he speaks would henceforth dictate to him the greatest amount of realism, as regards the tactics of efficiency. For instance, having decided that the masses required certainty, and simple certainty, quite as he did himself, he later worked out a 25-point program as the platform of his National Socialist German Workers Party. And he resolutely refused to change one single item in this program, even for purposes of "improvement." He felt that the *fixity* of the platform was more important for propagandistic purposes than any revision of his slogans could be, even though the revisions in themselves had much to be said in their favor. The astounding thing is that, although such an attitude gave good cause to doubt the Hitlerite promises, he could explicitly explain his tactics in his book and still employ them without loss of effectiveness.

[The critic adds in a footnote: "On this point Hitler reasons as follows: 'Here, too, one can learn from the Catholic Church. Although its structure of doctrines in many instances collides, quite unnecessarily, with exact science and research, yet it is unwilling to sacrifice even one little syllable of its dogmas. It has rightly recognized that its resistibility does not lie in a more or less great adjustment to the scientific results of the moment, which in reality are always changing, but rather in a strict adherence to dogmas, once laid down, which alone give the entire structure the character of creed. Today, therefore, the Catholic Church stands firmer than ever. One can prophesy that in the same measure in which the appearances flee, the Church itself, as the resting pole in the flight of appearances, will gain more and more blind adherence.' "]

Hitler also tells of his technique in speaking, once the Nazi party had become effectively organized, and had its army of guards, or bouncers, to maltreat hecklers and throw them from the hall. He would, he recounts, fill his speech with *provocative* remarks, whereat his bouncers would promptly swoop down in flying formation, with swinging fists, upon anyone whom these provocative remarks provoked to answer. The efficiency of Hitlerism is the efficiency of the one voice, implemented throughout a total organization. The trinity of government which he finally offers is: *popularity* of the leader, *force* to back the popularity, and popularity and force maintained together long enough to become backed by a *tradition.* Is such thinking spontaneous or deliberate—or is it not rather both? [The critic adds in a footnote: "Hitler also paid great attention to the conditions under which political oratory is most effective. He sums up thus:

> 'All these cases involve encroachments upon man's freedom of will. This applies, of course, most of all to meetings to which people with a contrary orientation of will are coming, and who now have to be won for new intentions. It seems that in the morning and even during the day men's will power revolts with highest energy against an attempt at being forced under another's will and another's opinion. In the evening, however, they succumb more easily to the dominating force of a stronger will. For truly every such meeting presents a wrestling match between two opposed forces. The superior oratorical talent of a domineering apostolic nature will now succeed more easily in winning for the new will people who themselves have in turn experienced a weakening of their force of resistance in the most natural way, than people who still have full command of the energies of their minds and their will power.

> The same purpose serves also the artificially created and yet mysterious dusk of the Catholic churches, the burning candles, incense, censers, etc.' "]

Freud has given us a succinct paragraph that bears upon the spontaneous aspect of Hitler's persecution mania. (A persecution mania, I should add, different from the pure product in that it was constructed of *public* materials; all the ingredients Hitler stirred into his brew were already rife, with spokesmen and bands of followers, before Hitler "took them over." Both the pre-war and post-war periods were dotted with saviors, of nationalistic and "folkish" cast. This proliferation was analogous to the swarm of barter schemes and currency-tinkering that burst loose upon the United States after the crash of 1929. Also, the commercial availability of Hitler's politics was, in a low sense of the term, a *public* qualification, removing it from the realm of "pure" paranoia, where the sufferer develops a wholly *private* structure of interpretations.)

I cite from *Totem and Taboo:*

Another trait in the attitude of primitive races towards their rulers recalls a mechanism which is universally present in mental disturbances, and is openly revealed in the so-called delusions of persecution. Here the importance of a particular person is extraordinarily heightened and his omnipotence is raised to the improbable in order to make it easier to attribute to him responsibility for everything painful which happens to the patient. Savages really do not act differently towards their rulers when they ascribe to them power over rain and shine, wind and weather, and then dethrone them or kill them because nature has disappointed their expectation of a good hunt or a ripe harvest. The prototype which the paranoiac reconstructs in his persecution mania is found in the relation of the child to its father. Such omnipotence is regularly attributed to the father in the imagination of the son, and distrust of the father has been shown to be intimately connected with the heightened esteem for him. When a paranoiac names a person of his acquaintance as his "persecutor," he thereby elevates him to the paternal succession and brings him under conditions which enable him to make him responsible for all the misfortune which he experiences.

I have already proposed my modifications of this account when discussing the symbolic change of lineage connected with Hitler's project of a "new way of life." Hitler is symbolically changing from the "spiritual ancestry" of the Hebrew prophets to the "superior" ancestry of "Aryanism," and has given his story a kind of bastardized modernization, along the lines of naturalistic, materialistic "science," by his fiction of the special "blood-stream." He is voting himself a new identity (something contrary to the wrangles of the Habsburg Babylon, a soothing national unity); whereupon the vessels of the old identity become a "bad" father, i.e., the persecutor. It is not hard to see how, as his enmity becomes implemented by the backing of an organization, the rôle of "persecutor" is transformed into the rôle of persecuted, as he sets out with his likeminded band to "destroy the destroyer."

Were Hitler simply a poet, he might have written a work with an anti-Semitic turn, and let it go at that. But Hitler, who began as a student of painting, and later shifted to architecture, himself treats his political activities as an extension of his artistic ambitions. He remained, in his own eyes, an "architect," building a "folkish" State that was to match, in political materials, the "folkish" architecture of Munich.

We might consider the matter this way (still trying, that is, to make precise the relationship between the drastically sincere and the deliberately scheming): Do we not know of many authors who seem, as they turn from the rôle of citizen to the rôle of spokesman, to leave one room and enter another? Or who has not, on occasion, talked with a man in private conversation, and then been almost startled at the transformation this man undergoes when addressing a public audience? And I know persons today, who shift between the writing of items in the class of academic, philosophic speculation to items of political pamphleteering, and whose entire style and method changes with this change of rôle. In their academic manner, they are cautious, painstaking, eager to present all significant aspects of the case they are considering; but when they turn to political pamphleteering, they hammer forth with vituperation, they systematically misrepresent the position of their opponent, they go into a kind of political trance, in which, during its throes, they throb like a locomotive; and behold, a moment later, the mediumistic state is abandoned, and they are the most moderate of men.

Now, one will find few pages in Hitler that one could call "moderate." But there are many pages in which he gauges resistances and opportunities with the "rationality" of a skilled advertising man planning a new sales campaign. Politics, he says, must be sold like soap—and soap is not sold in a trance. But he did have the experience of his trance, in the "exaltation" of his anti-Semitism. And later, as he became a successful orator (he insists that revolutions are made solely by the power of the spoken word), he had this "poetic" rôle to draw upon, plus the great relief it provided as a way of slipping from the burden of logical analysis into the pure "spirituality" of vituperative prophecy. What more natural, therefore, than that a man so insistent upon unification would integrate this mood with less ecstatic moments, particularly when he had found the followers and the backers that put a price, both spiritual and material, upon such unification?

Once this happy "unity" is under way, one has a "logic" for the development of a method. One knows when to "spiritualize" a material issue, and when to "materialize" a spiritual one. Thus, when it is a matter of materialistic interests that cause a conflict between employer and employee, Hitler here disdainfully shifts to a high moral plane. He is "above" such low concerns. Everything becomes a matter of "sacrifices" and "personality." It becomes crass to treat employers and employees as different *classes* with a corresponding difference in the classification of their interests. Instead, relations between employer and employee must be on the "personal" basis of leader and follower, and "whatever may have a divisive effect in national life should be given a unifying effect through the army." When talking of national rivalries, however, he makes a very shrewd materialistic gauging of Britain and France with relation to Germany. France, he says, desires the "Balkanization of Germany" (i.e., its breakup into separationist movements—the "disunity" theme again) in order to maintain commercial hegemony on the continent. But Britain desires the "Balkanization of *Europe*," hence would favor a fairly strong and unified Germany, to use as a counter-weight against French hegemony. *German* nationality, however, is unified by the *spiritual* quality of Aryanism (that would produce the national organization via the Party) while this in turn is *materialized* in the myth of the blood-stream.

What are we to learn from Hitler's book? For one thing, I believe that he has shown, to a very disturbing degree, the power of endless repetition. Every circular advertising a Nazi meeting had, at the bottom, two slogans: "Jews not admitted" and "War victims free." And the substance of Nazi propaganda was built about these two "complementary" themes. He describes the power of spectacle; insists

that mass meetings are the fundamental way of giving the individual the sense of being protectively surrounded by a movement, the sense of "community." He also drops one wise hint that I wish the American authorities would take in treating Nazi gatherings. He says that the presence of a special Nazi guard, in Nazi uniforms, was of great importance in building up, among the followers, a tendency to place the center of authority in the Nazi party. I believe that we should take him at his word here, but use the advice in reverse, by insisting that, where Nazi meetings are to be permitted, they be policed by the authorities alone, and that uniformed Nazi guards to enforce the law be prohibited.

And is it possible that an equally important feature of appeal was not so much in the repetitiousness per se, but in the fact that, by means of it, Hitler provided a "world view" for people who had previously seen the world but piecemeal? Did not much of his lure derive, once more, from the *bad* filling of a *good* need? Are not those who insist upon a purely *planless* working of the market asking people to accept far too slovenly a scheme of human purpose, a slovenly scheme that can be accepted so long as it operates with a fair degree of satisfaction, but becomes abhorrent to the victims of its disarray? Are they not then psychologically ready for a rationale, *any* rationale, if it but offer them some specious "universal" explanation? Hence, I doubt whether the appeal was in the sloganizing element alone (particularly as even slogans can only be hammered home, in speech after speech, and two or three hours at a stretch, by endless variations on the themes). And Hitler himself somewhat justifies my interpretation by laying so much stress upon the *half-measures* of the middle-class politicians, and the contrasting *certainty* of his own methods. He was not offering people a *rival* world view; rather, he was offering a world view to people who had no other to pit against it.

As for the basic Nazi trick: the "curative" unification by a fictitious devil-function, gradually made convincing by the sloganizing repetitiousness of standard advertising technique—the opposition must be as unwearying in the attack upon it. It may well be that people, in their human frailty, require an enemy as well as a goal. Very well: Hitlerism itself has provided us with such an enemy—and the clear example of its operation is guaranty that we have, in him and all he stands for, no purely fictitious "devil-function" made to look like a world menace by rhetorical blandishments, but a reality whose ominousness is clarified by the record of its conduct to date. In selecting his brand of doctrine as our "scapegoat," and in tracking down its equivalents in America, we shall be at the very center of accuracy. The Nazis themselves have made the task of clarification easier. Add to them Japan and Italy, and you have *case histories* of fascism for those who might find it more difficult to approach an understanding of its imperialistic drives by a vigorously economic explanation.

But above all, I believe, we must make it apparent that Hitler appeals by relying upon a bastardization of fundamentally religious patterns of thought. In this, if properly presented, there is no slight to religion. There is nothing in religion proper that requires a fascist state. There is much in religion, when misused, that does lead to a fascist state. There is a Latin proverb, *Corruptio optimi pessima,* "the corruption of the best is the worst." And it is the corruptors of religion who are a major menace to the world today, in giving the profound patterns of religious thought a crude and sinister distortion.

Our job, then, our anti-Hitler Battle, is to find all available ways of making the Hitlerite distortions of religion apparent, in order that politicians of his kind in America be unable to perform a similar swindle. The desire for unity is genuine and admirable. The desire for national unity, in the present state of the world, is genuine and admirable. But this unity, if attained on a deceptive basis, by emotional trickeries that shift our criticism from the accurate locus of our trouble, is no unity at all. For, even if we are among those who happen to be "Aryans," we solve no problems even for ourselves by such solutions, since the factors pressing towards calamity remain. Thus, in Germany, after all the upheaval, we see nothing beyond a drive for ever more and more upheaval, precisely because the "new way of life" was no new way, but the dismally oldest way of sheer deception—hence, after all the "change," the factors driving towards unrest are left intact, and even strengthened. True, the Germans had the resentment of a lost war to increase their susceptibility to Hitler's rhetoric. But in a wider sense, it has repeatedly been observed, the whole world lost the War—and the accumulating ills of the capitalist order were but accelerated in their movements towards confusion. Hence, here too there are the resentments that go with frustration of men's ability to work and earn. At that point a certain kind of industrial or financial monopolist may, annoyed by the contrary voices of our parliament, wish for the momentary peace of one voice, amplified by social organizations, with all the others not merely quieted, but given the quietus. So he might, under Nazi promptings, be tempted to back a group of gangsters who, on becoming the political rulers of the state, would protect him against the necessary demands of the workers. His gangsters, then, would be his insurance against his workers. But who would be his insurance against his gangsters? (pp. 191-220)

Kenneth Burke, "The Rhetoric of Hitler's 'Battle'," in his The Philosophy of Literary Form: Studies in Symbolic Action, *third edition, University of California Press, 1973, pp. 191-220.*

Philo M. Buck, Jr.   (essay date 1942)

[*In the essay below, Buck traces many of Hitler's ideas in* Mein Kampf, *including militant devotion to state and leader and the notion of a chosen people, to the principles expressed in the* Old Testament *and the* Koran.]

A few days ago a friend commenting on the accumulation of horror in the day's news exclaimed, 'I wish I could play God for two minutes.' Though a self-convinced unbeliever himself, he is a philosopher and I might gladly have allowed him the role, but only for two minutes. There are only too many playing God. 'I am the greatest German who has ever lived. Mankind, led by the German race is

The basic logic of *Mein Kampf* is one that, when reduced to a brief formulation, horrifies the beholder. Then it fascinates him with the question of how such a logic could have captured the minds of so many people and left most of Europe in shambles before it had run its course.

—*Michael D. Ryan, in his* Hitler's Challenge to the Churches: A Theological Political Analysis of "Mein Kampf," 1974.

now in a period of transition, just as it was when men first began to pass from the ape-like into the human stage. Now they are passing from the human into the super-human stage. I have preceded them. In so far as there is a God in the world, I am He' [quoted by Wickham Steed, from an alleged interview, in *Our War Aims,* Sicker and Warburg]. Megalomania? Psychology can explain it. But psychology alone is helpless to lay this restless spirit and ruthless. It has behind it today a nation in arms, sacrificing itself, and all who oppose, on the altar of the new Deity. No, there are too many mortals affecting to nod and shake the world. Even my philosopher friend might come to take himself seriously.

Playing God, or fancying oneself the mouthpiece of Deity, there is little to choose between them. And of those today who have been called to this role we are fortunate to have the confession of the one whose name to his followers is a greeting and a benediction, Hitler's *Mein Kampf.* It is his confession and his dedication. But it is not the confession, like Saint Augustine's, of one bowed in humility before God, drawn from the well of past offenses and asking for remission and grace. Nor is it a dedication, like that of Isaiah, a man whose unclean lips had been touched by a coal from the altar, standing forth from among a people of unclean lips: 'Here am I, send me.' It is to no power without that this man owes obedience and before whom he bows the knee. The confession is addressed to his world that has gone whoring after false gods, and the only voice to which he hearkens is his own.

The conviction that he was a man apart came early.

But more than once I was tormented by the thought that, if Destiny had put me in the place of those incapable or criminal scamps or incompetents of our propaganda service, a different kind of battle would have been announced to Destiny.

In those months, for the first time, I felt fully the whims of fortune which kept me at the front in a place where any lucky move on the part of a Negro could shoot me down, while somewhere else I would have been able to render a different service to my country.

His life from that moment has been dedicated to his own altar.

His is a new faith for an old people who had known the aftermath of disaster and disillusionment and divided counsels. One thinks of Joan of Arc, but Saint Joan was an instrument and not the agent. One thinks of Mohammed, but the founder of Islam was only the last and chief of the prophets. But the fervor of Hitler's faith and its spectacular success recall some of the most dramatic crises and enthusiasms of history. He is only repeating some of the most interesting and instructive chapters of history— interesting and instructive only in a long and dispassionate perspective.

They are stories of militant enthusiasms, and blazing with fanatical intolerance. The results often seem miraculous. The story of the spread of Mohammedism comes to mind. The utterly inconspicuous region of Mecca and Medina, surrounded by inhospitable desert, the jarring feuds of sparsely scattered tribes whose names had never been written in history; and then Mohammed, and the Koran, and the mind and face of three continents were altered for all time. There is more than a slight parallel between Hitler and the founder of Islam, and between *Mein Kampf* and the Koran. Both men come with the same perfect assurance, and their books become motives for action. Both offer the same alternative to their contemporaries, *Mein Kampf* or the sword. And both promise a heaven of bliss to the faithful. Hitler's progress since he took power has been no less dramatic and startling, and, whatever the final issue, the ideas that gave it motive are worth dispassionate study.

Mein Kampf is a bible; it is more, it has been and still is a best seller. It is a textbook in all German schools, it is being read with anxious curiosity by those who live in its shadow. It is a bible, for it contains maxims of conduct, lessons in art and literary criticism, and an appraisement of nearly all the issues of life today. This man who in forced retirement—he wrote in prison sequestered from his following—passed in review the panorama of his life and of contemporary Germany, pronounced judgment, and delivered his program. It was again like the story of Mohammed, sequestered in Medina during the Hegira from Mecca, composing there the more militant *Suras* of the Koran. He writes to uplift the hearts of the faithful, a discipline that will make them in the fullness of time masters of the earth. It is all there, a book of the law of life.

The ideas are not new. On the contrary it is because they are as old as humanity and as elemental in their simplicity that they are so eagerly embraced. They are a call back to the old tribal loyalties and unquestioning faith in a tribal god and creed. 'And I will take you to me for a people, and I will be to you a god.' Loyalty to the leader, who justifies this loyalty by deeds of self-sacrifice, and as unquestioning faith in the excellence of the tribe, elect and consecrated of old for leadership and a blessing to all people. Hitler gave these ideas, that were not new, to a Germany in the aftermath of the Great War. They are the primitive antithesis of all the ideas of the dignity of man, and individual self-responsibility, and liberal democracy, that the

eighteenth and the nineteenth centuries had cultivated. The days of Germany's and Europe's depression, while Hitler was completing his *Lehrjahre* in Vienna and Munich, had shaken the people's faith in the liberal tradition; when Hitler found his voice the masses were ready. He was not interested in the intellectuals.

It is a return to the primitive, and an extension only of the tribal constitution of the old Germany. The demand for *Lebensraum,* that restless desire for expansion at the expense of neighbors, reminds us of the expedition of Ariovistus, whom Caesar snubbed in his first year in Gaul. Or perhaps better of the Germanic tribes in the weakening days of the Roman Empire that destroyed classical civilization. The divine right of the leader to lead, and the divine obligation of the tribe to follow his star. It is no wonder that the Nazi for his creed goes back in imagination to the days of the sagas of the Nibelungs. Their god is the primitive god of battles, and their heroes the wasters of cities. Intellectual Europe for centuries has been trying to forget this creed. It is no wonder that Hitler was not interested in the intellectuals.

The first article of this creed is the complete authority of the Leader, *Der Führer.* Mankind loves the strong man. Germany adores him.

> Like a woman, whose psychic feeling is influenced less by abstract reasoning than by an indefinable, sentimental longing for complementary strength, who will submit to the strong man rather than dominate the weakling, thus the masses love the ruler rather than the suppliant, and inwardly they are far more satisfied by a doctrine which tolerates no rival than by the grant of liberal freedom; they often feel at a loss what to do with it, and even easily feel themselves deserted.

Whether this idea comes from Nietzsche or from Carlyle makes little difference. Both Carlyle and Nietzsche would be horrified by the romantic excess of its messianic ecstasy, and the cynical materialism of its program. It is messianic in its origin.

> An ingenious idea originates in the brain of a man who now feels himself called upon to transmit his knowledge to the rest of mankind: he now preaches his views and gradually he gains a certain circle of followers. This state of the direct personal transmittal of the ideas of a man to the rest of the world is the most ideal and the most natural one.

Gradually it extends the circle of its influence and gains new adherents. Now it must, as with all religion, have its sacred places and its shrine.

> In connection with this, the geopolitical importance of a center of a movement cannot be overrated. Only the presence of such a center and of a place, bathed in the magic of a Mecca or a Rome, can at length give a movement that force which is rooted in the inner unity and in the recognition of a head that represents this unity.

Never before in the history of a cult or party has the inner story of its rise to power been told with colder impassivity.

It is as though a scientist were analyzing the steps of his experiment, or the astronomer the approach of a new celestial body. The Leader of the new movement seems as inevitable as a law of nature and as little to be questioned. With his appearance all 'waves of free thought' are frozen.

> Therefore, out of the host of sometimes millions of people, who individually more or less clearly and distinctly guess this truth, partly perhaps understand it, *one man* must step forward in order to form, with apodictic force, out of the wavering world of imagination of the great masses, granite principles, and to take up the fight for their sole correctness, until out of the playing waves of a free world of thought a brazen rock of uniform combination of form and will arises.

The order he creates is 'anti-parliamentarian.' It rejects on principle the decision of a majority by which the leader is degraded to the position of the executive of the will and opinion of others. 'All this is a sign of the decay of mankind.' When the Leader once appears he is supreme. And as the prophet of old ascended to Sinai, from whence were delivered the Law and the Commandments, so now this new prophet has built himself a place apart from and above the daily routine of lesser humanity, that from its eminence may be heard the new Law that will create a new people. Like the prophet he had a unique responsibility that cannot be shared. 'He who wants to be the leader, bears, with the highest, unrestricted authority, also the ultimate and the most serious responsibility.'

'The general right for such an activity is based upon its necessity, the personal right on success.' And the Fuehrer has known success. It is only in these last months that this success has been challenged. Is it already too late? Is he the man of destiny to teach the world a new creed?

Make a people believe that they are the people chosen by destiny to re-create the world, and they will, under the leader, accept the mission. So did the Arab tribesmen in the seventh century when they burst out of the desert of Arabia upon an astonished world. So seriously did they take to heart the magic of the Koran. In our own days Jules Romains is looking for 'the men of good will' who will bring a new day to distracted Europe. Who are the elect whom *Mein Kampf* is summoning to make the supreme sacrifice that its new creed may transform a nation and write a new design in history?

'The race question not only furnishes the key to world history, but also to human culture as a whole.' Such is Adolf Hitler's interpretation of the genesis and exodus of civilization. He learned it not in books or from the labors of philosophers. The insight came to him—as it did to the solitary Mohammed—in his communion with himself, part of a reminiscence from the old poetry of the Teutonic past, and part from the reminiscence from boyhood when the Old Testament and the Covenant between Jehovah and the chosen people were read in the home and in the church. A belief in a peculiar heritage and in a people chosen of old for a great cosmic purpose needs no evidence beyond the poetry of an inner conviction.

> God of our fathers, known of old,

Lord of the far-flung battle line,
Beneath whose awful hand we hold
Dominion over palm and pine.

The only difference is that to Kipling the thought brought with it a becoming humility. The Fuehrer so far has shown few traces of this virtue.

Who are the elect? Hitler's idea of the pre-eminence of the Aryan is too much of a commonplace today to need notice. He is convinced of its leadership in history and culture and all the arts. The Aryans are the culture bearers and culture creators, and because of their success destined to rule. But all this is by way of a preface to the selection of the branch of this race that is called now to accept the Covenant and by its discipline make itself ready for the high mission. And here the orthodox Nazi creed sets itself squarely against all newly designed orders for world improvement. Thinkers and planners, like Lenin, Karl Marx, or more modest but no less ardent advocates, dream of humanity as a whole, a world brotherhood or a world federation. Nazism is founded upon the doctrine of one race, one nation, and all who are without are dwellers in darkness and workers of evil.

The state is the race, the extended individual, one in blood, one in creed, one in enthusiasm, one in self-sacrifice. He has adopted as his own a term used before, *Volkische Staat,* the folkish state. For the bond of unity must go deeper than economic and political and even social interests, to the blood. It is again the extended family, the larger tribe, the blood brotherhood where all for one and one for all is an instinctive motive for all action. In the old state 'temples of glory were only erected to merchants and state officials.' Here they will be erected only to 'folkish' leaders.

This is a little different from the idea of the totalitarian state that we see in Italy or Russia, for in both of these, though there is much enthusiasm, there is lacking the mystic doctrine of the sacrament of blood union that makes for all other unions, and much of the mystic devotion that makes sacrifice of self a joy. 'Democracy has no convictions for which people could stake their lives.' Crude and eccentric as Hitler's German is in most of *Mein Kampf,* when he comes to his definition of his state, he grows almost lyrical.

> The State is not an assembly of commercial parties in a certain prescribed space for the fulfilment of economic tasks, but the organization of a community of physically and mentally equal human beings for the better possibility of the furtherance of their species as well as for the fulfilment of the goal of their existence assigned to them by Providence . . . The instinct of preserving the species is the first cause for the formation of human communities. But the State is a folk organism and not an economic organism.

> Thus the most essential supposition for the formation and preservation of a State is the presence of a certain feeling of homogeneity, . . . as well as the readiness to risk one's life for this with all means, something that will lead nations on their own soil to the creation of heroic virtues, but parasites to mendacious hypocrisy and

malicious cruelty . . . Then the best protection will not be represented in its arms, but in its citizens; not fortress walls will protect it, but the living wall of men and women, filled with highest love for the country and with fanatical national enthusiasm.

'Fanatical enthusiasm,' a single will, this in the place of divided counsels, personal fears, and a sense of insecurity, and the inhibitions of action that come with all ideas of personal futility in the present-day chaos. The state authority is directed solely for the purpose of producing a higher personality, healthier, cleaner, and more cultured, more alert, more ready for action. Is it any wonder that on the promise of the new age all young Germany turned to the voice that promised hope and action; that it willingly underwent and undergoes the sternest discipline, hangs the picture of the Leader even in the more intimate regions of the household, and goes forth confidently to a war that will bring it and him glory and justification?

> He who speaks of a mission of the German people on this earth must know that it can exist only in the formation of a State which sees its highest task in the preservation and the promotion of the most noble elements of our nationality which have remained, even of the entire man-kind, unharmed.

The state, the leader who is the state personified, is the God.

Race pride, state pride, these are synonymous. To achieve this again as in the tradition of the Koran, there must be no classes in the state, no unions of workers or of employers, no capitalists and no proletarians. The theory of 'human rights,' which threw a mantle of protection about the individual and gave him certain rights of life, liberty, and the pursuit of happiness, are out of date. The individual has rights only in the rights of All, his liberty is that of co-operating to the measure of his ability with the All, and his pursuit of happiness the quest for the welfare of the All. This is his religion—is it any wonder that in this new state, there can be only one religion?—and all religious dogmas that look elsewhere than to the state for their inspiration are frowned upon and even actively persecuted. You cannot serve God and mammon. To whom is Nazi Germany now erecting an altar?

All who dwell in the state, as all who dwelt in the old state of Judea, are not citizens. Only the elect by race may hope for citizenship, others are 'strangers within thy gates,' who are to be treated as discretion dictates. The pure by blood, disciplined to self-sacrifice and enthusiasm, are the citizens. Others who are less fortunate, though their stay in the land may be one of generations, are subjects—such as the conquered people, like Poles or Czechs. Still farther from the light are aliens, who are only allowed on tolerance, to be treated with hostility, or at best suspicion, for their language and dress betray them, and they may become agents of corruption. Never in European history has the doctrine of the nation received such a downright definition. For its nearest parallel we must look to the constitution of Sparta. But Sparta never dreamed of calling itself anything more than a city-state. The idea of a nation was yet centuries in the future.

It is a stern creed for a stern people, and the definition of a new cult of freedom. 'I shall allow the gospel of the free man to be preached to the man who is master of life and death, of human fear and superstition, who has learned to control his body and muscles and nerves, but remains at the same time impervious to the temptations of the mind and of science presumably free.' What is being done in Germany in the name of education is already well known. Education must be designed only for the 'folkish' mind. As for universal education: 'Universal education is the most corroding and disintegrating poison that Liberation has ever invented for its own destruction.' [The critic adds in a footnote: 'This and the preceding quotation are from Hermann Rauschning, *Hitler Speaks.* Though published by an enemy of the regime, these ideas are perfectly consistent with the spirit of ***Mein Kampf*** and Hitler's published speeches.']

If the Aryans are the superior people, and of these the Germans the elect, who are the inferior? and why Hitler's peculiar and temperamental bitterness against the Jew? 'Therefore, I believe today that I am acting in the sense of the Almighty Creator: by warding off the Jews I am fighting for the Lord's work.' When a conviction like this becomes so deep that it has all the inner convincingness of inspiration, there is little more to be said about it, unless it be to look with the psychiatrist for its source. It is deeply felt. Hence it must be from a super-personal source. It is a religious mandate. When King Saul failed to carry out to the letter the command of Jehovah to exterminate the Amalekites, man, woman, child, and beast, the prophet Samuel ruthlessly allowed him to experience the full enormity of his offense. ***Mein Kampf*** is as ruthless—here pity is dead, there can be no compromise with the foes of the true religion.

For the Jew, by heredity and long environment, is the foe of the 'folkish state.' Self-sacrifice for the good of the All can never become an article in his creed. He is by nature now a seeker of individual power through all the insidious agencies his cunning has devised. One by one he has gained control—so the book alleges—of the agencies that sway public opinion, the press, the theatre, and even the machinery of education. One by one he has climbed into the learned professions—law, medicine, scholarship—until he threatens the very existence of the ideal of the state and patriotism. He cloaks this greed—so the argument runs—with the oily phrases of internationalism and mutual tolerance, only that he may devour the more secretly. All the evils of post-war Germany and the tragedy of the collapse of German civil morale at the end of the war, Hitler has charged against this race. They are the chief enemies of the Lord. Feeling so strangely, we can understand why he acts so ruthlessly.

> Politically he [the Jew] denies to the State all means of self-preservation, he destroys the basis of any national self-dependence and defense, he destroys the confidence in the leaders, he derides history and the past, and he pulls down into the gutter every thing which is truly great. In the domain of culture he infects art, literature, the theater, smites natural feeling, overthrows all conceptions of beauty and sublimity, of nobility and

quality, and in turn he pulls the people down into the confines of his own swinish nature.

There shall be no intercourse in the new state between these deadly parasites and the truly elect. Hence the horror of uncleanness in any mixed marriage. His words of condemnation remind one of the judgment of the stern prophet Ezra:

> And Ezra the priest stood up, and said unto them. Ye have trespassed, and have married strange women, to increase the guilt of Israel. Now therefore make confession unto the Lord, the God of your fathers, and do his pleasure and separate yourselves from the people of the land, and from strange women.

The blood-mixing, however, with the lowering of the racial level caused by it, is the sole cause of the dying-off of old cultures; for the people do not perish by lost wars, but by the loss of that force of resistance which is contained only in the pure blood.

It is an ironic jest of history that the same moral and spiritual indignation of the Old Testament Hebrew, the first Chosen Race, should now be turned against them by the newly Elect. It is the same horror of the unclean thing that the righteous cannot tolerate in their midst, lest their eyes should be tempted and their devotion to their god suffer corruption and they be guilty of sin.

> And what one nation in the earth is like thy people, even like Israel, whom God went to redeem unto himself for a people, and to make him a name, and to do great things for you, and terrible things for thy land.

> And what great nation is there, that hath statutes and judgments so righteous as all this law, which I set before you this day? Only take heed to thy self, and keep thy soul diligently, lest thou forget the things which thine eyes saw.

> Thou shalt be blessed above all people. And thou shalt consume all the peoples which the Lord thy God shall deliver unto thee; thine eye shall not pity them: neither shalt thou serve their gods.

> Every place whereon the sole of your foot shall tread shall be yours—there shall be no man able to stand before you.
> [2 *Samuel* VII, *Deuteronomy* IV, VII, XI]

A faith so potent, a resolution so ruthless, can be kept alive only by constant calls to action. His people are 'believers and fighters.' And here we are reminded of the apparent ruthlessness of Nietzsche's 'blond beast.' 'The world was not meant for cowardly nations.' 'Mankind has grown strong in eternal struggle, and it will perish only through eternal peace.' This does square beautifully with Nietzsche's address by Zarathustra to the soldiers:

> Ye shall love peace as a means to new wars—and the short peace more than the long.

> You I advise not to work, but to fight. You I advise not to peace, but to victory. Let your work be a fight, let your peace be a victory.

> Ye say it is a good cause which halloweth even war? I say unto you: it is the good war which halloweth every cause.

> War and courage have done more great things than charity. Not your sympathy, but your bravery hath hitherto saved the victims.

Hitler and his legions do act like Nietzsche's mythical 'blond beast.' If war is the natural element for a people, how happy Germany should be today! 'The mild Goddess of Peace can march only side by side with the God of War, and that every great deed of this peace needs the protection and help of force.' War must be ruthless, and enemies to be longed for.

> In the ruthless attack upon an adversary the people sees at all times a proof of its own right, and it perceives the renunciation of his destruction as an uncertainty as regards its own right, if not as a sign of its own wrong . . . They must not shun the hatred of the enemies of our nationality and our view of life and its expression, but they should long for it.

The cost of a war will be amply restored later by a higher culture that will come as its blessing. 'No sacrifice to ensure political independence and freedom can be too great. Whatever is withdrawn from general cultural matters by a disproportionate requirement of armament, for the State is later restored in richest measure.' The past twenty years have borne witness, and our children's children will yet be paying the price. 'Their fathers have eaten sour grapes, and the children's teeth are set on edge.' Never perhaps in all literature has the cult of Force been so nakedly displayed, and so shamelessly worshipped. Will cynicism have the last word?

A cynical creed. Human nature is essentially base. The savagery of raw nature in the race for survival, after all these years of so-called civilization and enlightenment, is still unescapable. 'He who wants to live should fight, therefore, and he who does not want to battle in this world of eternal struggle does not deserve to be alive.' Such is the truth that this thinker has distilled from the story of history. There have been others who have shared this creed; but now he is making it the battle-cry of a people in arms. 'But if nations fight for their existence on this planet—that is, if they are approached by the fateful question of "to be or not to be"—all reflections concerning humanity or aesthetics resolve themselves into nothing.'

Here we have it, the note that blends all the miscellaneous verbiage of *Mein Kampf* into a book like the Koran or the Bible: the cynicism of a seer who gives us his measure of human nature; a gospel based on a cynical contempt for all independent human motive. Nowhere is this more apparent than in the methods he lays down for the education of the elect—propaganda for mass education. And with the efficiency of the agencies for direct and constant mass education, the mouth of the leader is ever at the ear of the led.

Hitler early guessed, or saw in a vision, the approach to the mass mind; he shows his genius in the manner in which he proposed to get a hearing and bend to his will the imaginations of millions. His ideas of the state may not be, are not, original. All his devices for the policy of the Third Reich are accepted by him from varied sources. But his is the living imagination which lent them a new persuasiveness, and he it was who conveyed them to the imagination of the country, especially of the youth, and made them the message of a new gospel. One can learn a great deal about propaganda, its use and abuse, from *Mein Kampf.*

It is to be addressed 'only to the masses.' 'It has to appeal forever and only to the masses.' The intellectuals, who are in a hopeless minority, must and should be ignored. Their sympathies may be awakened; but because they have a stake in the old regime, have something to lose by any revolution, they are hopelessly conservative. Propaganda must aim not at enlightenment, but at action. Only the masses who are restless, have nothing to lose, are eager for action, should be the target of any campaign by propaganda that dreams of success. Yet the prophet has his contempt for the masses; there is with him none of the liberal ideology that dreams of the excellence of the nature of the submerged half of a population, none of the glorification of the proletarian that is an essential part of the equipment of the sentimental communist or reformer. Hitler is least of all a sentimentalist, unless it is in his love of that abstraction 'the German people.'

> All propaganda has to be popular and has to adapt its spiritual level to the perception of the least intelligent of those toward whom it intends to direct itself . . . The more modest, then, that its scientific ballast is, and the more it exclusively considers the feelings of the masses, the more striking will be its success . . . The great masses' receptive ability is only very limited, and their understanding is small, but their forgetfulness is great. As a consequence of these facts all effective propaganda has to limit itself only to a very few points and to use them like slogans until even the very last man is able to imagine what is intended by such a word.

Propaganda must be effective, it need not be truthful. 'The task of propaganda is, for instance, not to evaluate the various rights, but far more to stress exclusively the one that is represented by it. It has not to search into truth as far as this is favorable to others, in order to present it then to the masses with doctrinaire honesty, but it has rather to serve its own truth uninterruptedly.' It was with this early insight that he began in the years immediately after the war to build his party. He has not needed to vary his technique. 'Influence on the great masses, concentration on a few points, continuous repetition of the latter, self-assured and confident wording of the texts in the form of apodictic assertion, greatest persistency in spreading, and patience in awaiting the results.' Thus he proceeded, always keeping before him the analogy of a military campaign. 'Concentrate on a single enemy.' Since he began in Vienna in the months immediately after the Great War, the story of his victories is the story of his dramatic and ruthless use of propaganda.

By its means, and the cult of action that is its end, Hitler hopes to found—or he is founding?—a new state. A state of perfect obedience and perfect order. A perfectly homogenous state where all the citizens will be of one race, one idea, one culture, one desire, and ever alert to exterminate the enemy within and hold in lawful subjection the enemy without. A state where the alarm bell is always ringing, and one never goes forth ungirt of his sword. One thinks of the incident in the Old Testament when the Prophet Nehemiah brought back the rejoicing captives to rebuild the sacred city of Jerusalem. Their first work was to restore the walls of the sacred city that they might be a bulwark against the enemy. And everyman at his labor went armed.

> And it came to pass from that time forth, that half of my servants wrought in the work, and half of them held the spears, the shields, and the bows, and the coats of mail; and the rulers were behind all the house of Judah. They that builded the wall and they that bare burdens laded themselves, every one with one of his hands wrought in the work, and with the other held his weapon; and the builders, every one had his sword girded by his side, and so builded.

But there have been those with minds that will not down, whose words come not malapropos at such moments. Montaigne loved his city of Paris. 'I love Paris so tenderly that even her spots, her blemishes, and her warts are dear to me.' But he could also write in a day when it was quite as painful as today to preserve one's faith in human nature: 'I esteem all men as my countrymen; and as kindly embrace a Polonian as a Frenchman.' And of the virtue of perfect obedience he also has a word in passing. 'The commonwealth requireth some to betray, some to lie, some to massacre: leave we that commission to people more obedient and pliable.' Finally of the civic virtue of perfect order: 'There is no course of life so weak and sottish as that which is managed by Order, Method, and Discipline.' These were Montaigne's last words, written at a time when order was seemingly the one thing desired by civil-war torn France. Here again, it may be, we have a good word for war-torn Europe. One can pay too high a price for the blessing of uniformity.

Liberalism as a tradition, from the days of Montaigne, the father of liberal European thought, has placed its hope upon the disciplined and free individual. Hitler's contempt for human nature never grows more bitter than when he speaks of all liberal institutions. It is as though, once a believer in them, he had found his faith shattered in the debris after the Great War, and in despair had turned to a new worship. 'Universal education is the most corroding and disintegrating poison that liberalism ever invented for its own destruction.' This has been quoted before, but it points to the first institution that liberalism holds sacred. 'We set ourselves the task of breeding types, not individualities.' So much for an institution that believes in the sacredness of the individual. He is even more disillusionedly bitter about parliament. 'Parliamentary bed-bugs,' 'parliamentary cattle trading,' parliament, the 'greatest babbling institution of all time,' the 'gravedigger of the German nation and the German Reich.' So much for the second institution of liberal government.

His argument goes even deeper. 'Liberalism is based upon

utterly false assumptions. It rejects the aristocratic principle in nature; instead of the eternal privilege of force and strength, it uses the mass of numbers and their dead weight.' Majority rule, the method of all liberalism, 'sins against the aristocratic basis of nature.' 'A heroic decision is not likely to come from a hundred cowards.' There were events in post-war Germany, as there have been many in all post-war nations, to justify a sweeping inquiry. A diseased society can, if desperate, throw up a fanaticism like this. Only this fanatic is also a genius, a genius with a gift of making himself heard, and he has no scruples. 'I have no scruples, and I will use whatever weapons I please.' National Socialism is a challenge, perhaps to the death, of all that the tradition of liberalism has built in the past three centuries. It is a return to the distant tribal past.

More than once in Germany and in other parts of the world, the ideal of the National Socialist dictator has been compared with the teachings of Carlyle in *Heroes and Hero Worship*. Some professed Carlyle admirers have been abashed at seeing the teaching of their master come to life. And Carlyle's attitude toward the war for liberation of the slaves in America does not add to their comfort. Were Carlyle and then Nietzsche the spiritual ancestors of Hitler and of the intolerance that in its grasping for *Lebensraum* can admit no compromise? The question is an interesting one, but it cannot be answered here. But behind the Carlyle of the *Heroes* and the *Latterday Pamphlets* is also the Carlyle of *Sartor Resartus*. And even in the *Heroes and Hero Worship* there is this sentence, in the chapter that brings the book to a conclusion. It is an imaginary address by Cromwell to Parliament. 'You have had such an opportunity as no Parliament in Europe has ever had! Christ's Law, the Right and True, was to be in some measure made the Law of this land. In place of that, you have got into your idle pedantries, constitutionalities, bottomless cavillings and questionings about written laws for *my* coming here;—and would send the whole matter in chaos again, because I have no Notary's parchment, but only God's voice from the battle-whirlwind, for being President among you.' There is no need for farther comment; to Carlyle Cromwell was leading the English into the Promised Land. To what destination is Hitler leading Germany?

But there are those, and in many places, who are silently or loudly proclaiming National Socialism as a world creed. The thought should give us pause. What would be the world's dilemma if every nation should find a Hitler, and all proclaimed his doctrine of race superiority and the right of the strong to survive? If each nation is a supernation, and each race the elect, what will be the fate of civilization? And one thing more—the paradox, do men gain freedom by sacrificing freedom? There was a day, not long ago, when such questions would have been as fantastic as Gilbert and Sullivan. Today those who answer strike swiftly, armed with the new science and mechanics. (pp. 219-37)

Philo M. Buck, Jr., "The Idol of the Tribe: 'Mein Kampf','" in his Directions in Contemporary Literature, *Oxford University Press, Inc., 1942, pp. 219-38.*

Robert B. Downs   (essay date 1956)

[*Downs is an American critic and educator. In the following essay, originally published in the first edition of* Books That Changed the World *(1956), he discusses the megalomaniacal propaganda in* Mein Kampf.]

The funeral pyre which consumed the mortal remains of Adolf Hitler and Eva Braun on April 30, 1945, deep underground in the Berlin chancellery, was a climax that might have been imagined by the operatic composer Hitler most ardently admired, Richard Wagner, for a new Götterdämmerung, or *Twilight of the Gods*. The scene rang down the curtain on a vast melodrama that had opened a generation earlier, when the future Führer began his march to power.

At the time the Nazi Party under Hitler's leadership took over the reins of government in Germany in 1933 after more than a decade of agitation and violence, the world was appalled by its actions. The regime was coldly ruthless in establishing its control; all vestiges of democratic government were abolished; dissenting views mercilessly suppressed; churches, fraternal orders, and labor unions persecuted or "coordinated"; Jews murdered in large numbers; and territorial threats against ostensibly friendly neighboring nations thundered in waves of propaganda.

Yet, if non-Germans had taken the trouble to peruse a fat tome entitled *Mein Kampf* (*My Struggle*), they would have found the entire program spelled out in all its shocking detail. Thanks to the protection of international copyright, its author had succeeded in restricting the full story to the original German. It is improbable, though, that even if the unexpurgated text had been freely available in English, French, and other languages, many persons would have taken seriously "the fantastic dream of a frenzied visionary"—so vast in scope and incredibly ambitious did it appear. *Mein Kampf* has rightly been called the "propagandistic masterpiece of the age" and, viewed from the standpoint of a trial judge, the "most incriminating book of the twentieth century." A great nation and its allies committed themselves to carrying out the fanatical ideas in the book. By the outbreak of World War II, 5,000,000 copies had been distributed in Germany alone.

Growing up in Vienna (as another Viennese, Sigmund Freud, might have predicted), Hitler formed at a tender age the impressions, prejudices, and hatreds that were to govern him for the remainder of his life. All are poured out in *Mein Kampf*. The opening chapters provide a brief but significant sketch of those early years. Born in 1889, at Braunau, Austria, just across the river from the German border, Hitler always felt himself a German rather than an Austrian, and especially despised the easy-going Viennese. According to his own account, the first years were full of privation, suffering, failure, frustration, and maladjustment. His formal schooling ceased at thirteen, and both parents were lost about the same time. In Vienna, his struggles to become an artist and, failing that, an architect, were handicapped by lack of education and lack of talent.

During the Vienna period, Hitler claims to have read widely, with emphasis on history. His ideas were influenced particularly by a book on the Franco-Prussian War, which inspired in him a fervent pride in the German race and convinced him of the God-given destiny of that people. At the same time he began to form an intense dislike for the Jews, and complete contempt for the Slavs and all other "non-Aryans." The Jew is primarily an international-minded money-maker and exploiter, usually a Socialist or Communist, Hitler declared, while the Slavs are an inferior race, with no culture of their own.

Association with the Social Democrats in Vienna caused Hitler to loathe Socialist and Communist propaganda, and, though he was an apt student of the party's tactics, his hatred of Marxism was lifelong. Despite his omnivorous reading habits, there is no evidence that he ever opened *Das Kapital.* Scarcely less profound was his detestation of democracy and democratic institutions, an aversion which began when he attended sessions of the Austrian Reichsrath in Vienna and observed what he regarded as its inefficient methods.

Finally, no longer willing to breathe the abominable cosmopolitan air of Vienna, Hitler settled in 1912 in Munich, which he called "a thoroughly German city." Two years later, to his delight, the World War came. He enlisted in a Bavarian regiment, and before the war ended had been wounded, gassed, twice decorated, and promoted to the rank of corporal. Germany's defeat both grieved and enraged him—a defeat, he believed, that had been caused by Jews, Marxists, and pacifists. The creation of a democratic German government following the war likewise angered and embittered him. It was then that Hitler resolved to become a politician.

Hitler's entry into politics came after his return to Munich. For a time he served as a paid political informer for the army or *Wehrmacht.* He was invited to, and accepted, membership in a small group called the German Workers' party, soon renamed the National Socialist German Workers' party, the nucleus of the Nazi party. Within a short time, by internal maneuvering, Hitler gained tight control of the organization, and abolished the "senseless" practice of making party decisions by vote of the members. The Party's program, as it developed under Hitler's command, was designed to win the sympathies of the working classes, to exterminate "the international poisoners," to abolish legislative bodies, and to establish the principle of blind, unquestioning obedience to a leader or *Führer.*

By 1923, with 27,000 party members, and supported by a military clique under General Ludendorff, while the Stresemann government appeared to be tottering, Hitler concluded that the time had come to seize power. He had his followers stage the famous Beer Hall Putsch in Munich. The attempt ended in complete fiasco, and sixteen of Hitler's adherents were shot down in the streets. Hitler himself was arrested and sentenced to five years in prison, a term later reduced to one year.

As a prisoner in the Bavarian fortress at Landsberg, Hitler had leisure for the first time to write his autobiography. Actually, *Mein Kampf* is a spoken rather than a written book. Sharing the prison with Hitler was his loyal disciple, Rudolf Hess. To Hess, who typed it directly, Hitler dictat-

ed the first volume of the work. Dedicated to the sixteen Nazis who had fallen in the Munich uprising, the book was originally titled "Four and a Half Years of Struggle Against Lies, Stupidity, and Cowardice." The second volume was completed in 1926 at Berchtesgaden.

Otto Tolischus has described the contents of *Mein Kampf* as "10 per cent autobiography, 90 per cent dogma, and 100 per cent propaganda"—a fair analysis. It seems incredible today that such a crude, long-winded, badly written, contradictory, and repetitious book could have captured the emotions of a highly cultured nation. But the situation was made to order. Ludwig Lore's comments are enlightening:

> The German people in 1933 were in a mood that made them dangerously susceptible to the Fascist bacillus. They had tried to find a way back to normal living and national self-respect and had found the way blocked by prejudice and blind misunderstanding. The great nations were interested only in reparations. The German labor parties which might have helped were split into half a dozen warring camps. All this was played against a background colored by a century of high-pressure nationalism. The German people had reached a point where order and security seemed to matter more than a political freedom that had become synonymous with brawls and bloodshed. Hitler understood these things and used them for his purposes, aided by a phenomenal capacity for organization and propaganda and by the readiness of Germany's great industrialists to finance his campaigns. Once established, the Germans' innate respect for authority made it simple to establish Fascist leadership.

Mein Kampf's theme song, recurring again and again, is race, race purity, race supremacy—though nowhere did Hitler attempt to define race. Mankind, he said, is divided into three groups: the culture-creators, of whom there is only one example, the Aryan or Nordic (more specifically the German); the culture-bearers, such as the Japanese; and the culture-destroyers, e.g., Jews and Negroes. It was never intended by nature, Hitler claimed, that all races should be equal, any more than individuals are equal. Some are created superior to others. The Germans, as the world's strongest race, should rule over the inferior races of the earth. A few characteristic passages from *Mein Kampf* will illustrate Hitler's views on "inferior" races.

Writing of the Austrian Empire:

> I was repelled by the conglomeration of races which the capital showed me, repelled by this whole mixture of Czechs, Poles, Hungarians, Ruthenians, Serbs, Croats, and everywhere, the eternal mushroom of humanity—Jews and more Jews.

About Africans:

> . . . it is criminal lunacy to keep on drilling a born half-ape until people think they have made a lawyer out of him, while millions of members of the highest culture-race must remain in entirely unworthy positions; . . . it is a sin against

the will of the Eternal Creator if His most gifted beings by the hundreds and hundreds of thousands are allowed to degenerate in the present proletarian morass, while Hottentots and Zulu Kaffirs are trained for intellectual professions.

Hindu nationalists "individually always impressed me as gabbling pomposities without any realistic background." Poles, Czechs, Jews, Negroes, and Asiatics are lumped together as unworthy of German citizenship, even though they may be born in Germany and speak the German language. France was regarded with special contempt:

> . . . racially; . . . she is making such great progress in negrification that we can actually speak of an African state arising on European soil. The colonial policy of present-day France cannot be compared with that of Germany in the past. If the development of France in the present style were to be continued for three hundred years, the last remnants of Frankish blood would be submerged in the developing European-African mulatto state.

It is in the attacks on the Jews, however, that Hitler's race prejudice reaches its frenzied height, as, for example, in this passage:

> The Jewish train of thought in all this is clear. The Bolshevization of Germany—that is, the extermination of the national folkish Jewish intelligentsia to make possible the sweating of the German working class under the yoke of Jewish world finance—is conceived only as a preliminary to the further extension of this Jewish tendency of world conquest. As often in history, Germany is the great pivot in the mighty struggle. If our people and our state become the victim of these blood-thirsty and avaricious Jewish tyrants of nations, the whole earth will sink into the snares of this octopus; if Germany frees herself from this embrace, this greatest of dangers to nations may be regarded as broken for the whole world. . . .

> In general, the Jews will always fight within the various national bodies with those weapons which on the basis of the recognized mentality of these nations seem most effective and promise the greatest success. In our national body, so torn with regard to blood, it is therefore the more or less "cosmopolitan," pacifistic-ideological ideas, arising from this fact; in short, the international tendencies which they utilize in their struggle for power . . . until they have turned one state after another into a heap of rubble on which they can then establish the sovereignty of the eternal Jewish empire.

To maintain the pristine purity of the Aryan, i.e., the German master race, there must be no "bastardization" by admixture with inferior stocks. The decline of great nations in the past, asserted Hitler, had invariably resulted from the mixture of blood and the loss of race purity. To prevent such a calamity, it is the state's duty to intervene. Even though "cowards and weaklings" may protest the invasion of their rights, the state must "see that the nation's blood be kept pure so that humanity may reach its highest development. The state must lift marriage from the abyss

of racial shame and sanctify it as an institution for the procreation of likenesses of God instead of monstrosities which are a cross between men and apes."

Fanatically believing in the innate superiority of the Aryan "race" over all others, Hitler preached that it is the duty, and privilege, of the master race to conquer, exploit, dispossess, or exterminate other races for its own advantage. Since Germany was crowded and needed *Lebensraum,* more living space, it was her right, as the great Nordic power, to grab Slavic land, remove the Slavs, and settle Germans on it. All humanity in the long run would benefit through having the habitat of the highest race extended and the scattered Germanic peoples united under one rule. "Only an adequately large space on this earth assures a nation of freedom of existence. . . . Germany will either be a world power or there will be no Germany."

The vast expansion visualized by Hitler would take place principally at the expense of Russia. Looking hungrily to the east, he speculated on what could be accomplished "if the Ural, with its immeasurable raw material and the Ukraine with its immeasurable grain fields lay within Germany." It was Germany's duty to rescue the Russian people from the Bolshevist leaders. "If we speak of soil in Europe today," continued Hitler, "we can primarily have in mind only Russia and her vassal border states. Here Fate itself seems desirous of giving us a sign. By handing Russia to Bolshevism, it robbed the Russian nation of that intelligentsia which previously brought about and guaranteed its existence as a state. . . . The giant empire in the east is ripe for collapse."

Power, Hitler said, is the justification for invasion.

> . . . no people on this earth possesses so much as a square yard of territory on the strength of a higher will or superior right. . . . State boundaries are made by man and changed by man. The fact that a nation has succeeded in acquiring an undue amount of soil constitutes no higher obligation that it should be recognized eternally. At most it proves the strength of the conquerors and the weakness of the nations. And in this case, right lies in this strength alone.

Hitler recognized that there were other possible solutions than territorial expansion to Germany's rapid population growth. One alternative would be contraceptive limitation of births—rejected because it was not in accord with the master race theory. Another, followed by Germany's prewar rulers, was to expand factory production for foreign markets, that is, increased industrialization, a solution not acceptable to Hitler, for he wanted Germany to feed herself and be self-sufficient. Furthermore, he was violently opposed to the creation of a large urban proletariat, the result of a great factory system. A third way out was to increase the productivity of the already available land, but this, argued Hitler, was but a partial and temporary answer. The only real remedy, he concluded, was for Germany to acquire new territory beyond existing frontiers, enabling more Germans to live on the land.

Hitler's long-range goals in population and territory were summarized in this paragraph:

. . . Today we count eighty million Germans in Europe! This foreign policy will be acknowledged as correct only if, after scarcely a hundred years, there are two hundred and fifty million Germans on this continent, and not living penned in as factory coolies for the rest of the world, but: as peasants and workers, who guarantee each other's livelihood by their labor.

In short, Hitler foresaw the German population as more than tripled in the next hundred years, and, per capita, possessing twice as much room as was then available. The idea of a widely spaced population also appealed to Hitler for "military-geographical" reasons, because it would be less vulnerable to an enemy. (Shades of Mackinder-Haushofer!)

To attain the objectives set by his soaring ambition, Hitler proposed to use three methods: propaganda, diplomacy, and force. Nowhere in *Mein Kampf* is the author more revealing of himself and his tactics than in his discussion of propaganda techniques, correctly believed by him to be one of the Nazis' most effective and formidable weapons. Max Lerner called Hitler "probably the greatest master of propaganda and organization in modern history," adding that, "to find his equal one must go back to Loyola and the Jesuits." To perfect his own understanding of the propaganda art, Hitler studied the propaganda techniques of the Marxists, the organization and methods of the Catholic Church, British propaganda of World War I, American advertising, and Freudian psychology. He wrote:

> The function of propaganda . . . is not to weigh and ponder the rights of different people, but exclusively to emphasize the one right which it has set out to argue for. Its task is not to make an objective study of the truth, in so far as it favors the enemy, and then set it before the masses with academic fairness; its task is to serve our own right, always and unflinchingly. It was absolutely wrong to discuss war-guilt from the standpoint that Germany alone could not be held responsible for the outbreak of the catastrophe; it would have been correct to load every bit of the blame on the shoulders of the enemy, even if this had not really corresponded to the true facts, as it actually did. . . . The purpose of propaganda is not to provide interesting distraction for blasé young gentlemen, but to convince, and what I mean is to convince the masses.

The importance of concentration and repetition was stressed.

> The receptivity of the great masses is very limited, their intelligence is small, but their power of forgetting is enormous. In consequence of these facts, all effective propaganda must be limited to a very few points and must harp on these in slogans until the last member of the public understands what you want him to understand by your slogan. As soon as you sacrifice this slogan and try to be manysided, the effect will piddle away, for the crowd can neither digest nor retain the material offered. In this way the result is weakened and in the end entirely cancelled out.

Hitler's faith in propaganda is illustrated by his statement that "It is possible by means of shrewd and unremitting propaganda, to make people believe that heaven is hell—and hell heaven." For its greatest potential, propaganda must be adapted to the most limited intelligence, "aimed always and primarily at the emotions, and very little at men's alleged reason." Propaganda has "no more to do with scientific accuracy than a poster has to do with art. . . . The greater the mass of men to be reached, the lower its intellectual level must be."

Also useful to the propagandist are certain psychological tricks. One should not, for example, attempt to convert a crowd to a different point of view in the morning. Dim lights are useful, and in the evening when people are tired and their powers of resistance low, their "complete emotional capitulation" is relatively easy to achieve. Another mighty tool is mass suggestion, when the mob has a chance to join in parades and spectacular demonstrations, so typical of the Nazi regime. As Hitler put it:

> . . . the gigantic mass demonstrations, these parades of hundreds of thousands of men, which burned into the small, wretched individual the proud conviction that, paltry worm as he was, he was nevertheless a part of a great dragon, beneath whose burning breath the hated bourgeois world would some day go up in fire and flame and the proletarian dictatorship would celebrate its ultimate final victory.

Hitler's supreme contempt for the masses appears again and again, in such phrases as "an empty-headed herd of sheep," "the incarnation of stupidity," and his frequently expressed belief that mankind in the mass is lazy, cowardly, feminine, emotional, and incapable of rational thought.

The ultimate in Hitlerian propaganda technique is the principle of the big lie. The doctrine is "wholly correct," Hitler declared, "that the very greatness of the lie is a factor in getting it believed. . . . With the primitive simplicity of the masses a great lie is more effective than a small one, because they often lie in small matters, but would be too ashamed to tell a great big lie. Hence it will never occur to the broad mass to suspect so large a lie, and the mass will be quite unable to believe that anyone could possibly have the infernal impudence to pervert the truth to such an extent." In brief, the bigger the lie, the more likely it will be believed by the masses.

Another major propaganda principle is that of the single devil. Do not confuse the populace by offering too many enemies for it to hate at the same time. Concentrate upon one adversary, and focus the people's hatred upon this enemy. For Hitler, of course, the Jew served as the universal scapegoat. Regardless of whether he was ranting against democracy, Marxism, the Versailles Treaty, France, or some other favorite target, the Jew was always present, scheming and plotting, trying with devilish ingenuity to undermine Germany and Aryan culture. A sample is this hysterical outburst:

> . . . France is and remains by far the most terrible enemy. This people, which is basically becoming more and more negrified, constitutes in its tie with the aims of Jewish world domination an enduring danger for the existence of the white

race in Europe. For the contamination by Negro blood on the Rhine in the heart of Europe is just as much in keeping with the perverted sadistic thirst for vengeance of this hereditary enemy of our people as is the ice-cold calculation of the Jew thus to begin bastardizing the European continent at its core and to deprive the white race of the foundations for a sovereign existence through infection with lower humanity.

The task of the propagandist is facilitated, Hitler said, by state control of education. Too much book-learning is an error. Physical education and physical health should take first place. Second is the development of character, especially such military virtues as obedience, loyalty, strength of will, self-control, capacity for sacrifice, and pride in responsibility. Relegated to third place is intellectual activity. For girls, training must be for motherhood. The concept of education for all was repugnant to Hitler, who described it as a disintegrating poison invented by liberalism for its own destruction. Each class and each subdivision of a class had only one possible education. He thought that the great mass of people should enjoy the blessings of illiteracy.

For the last group, education is to be limited to an indoctrination with "general ideas, carved by eternal repetition into the heart and memory of the people." Always the guiding principle is that the child belongs to the state, and the sole object of education is to train tools for the state.

Hitler's views on popular education are of a piece with his opinion of democracy in general. At every opportunity he ridiculed the ineffectiveness of the democratic state:

> The Western democracy of today is the forerunner of Marxism which without it would not be thinkable. It provides this world plague with the culture in which its germs can spread. In its most extreme form, parliamentarianism created a "monstrosity of excrement and fire," in which, however, sad to say, the "fire" seems to me at the moment to be burned out. . . . For there is one thing which we must never forget: in this, too, the majority can never replace the man. It is not only a representative of stupidity, but of cowardice as well. And no more that a hundred empty heads makes one wise man will an heroic decision arise from a hundred cowards.

Hitler saw democracy as "the deceitful theory that the Jew would insinuate—namely, the theory that all men are created equal"; while any doctrine of universal suffrage and equal rights is "pernicious and destructive."

Hitler substituted the leader principle for democracy. He put heads over the mass who were supposed to obey orders without question. Over all was the Führer, taking full responsibility for all he did or failed to do.

Having drawn his blueprint for Germany and the world in *Mein Kampf*, Hitler faithfully adhered to it, except for one important, though, as it turned out, temporary deviation—the Nazi-Soviet Pact of 1939. How difficult it must have been for him to swallow the Russian agreement is indicated by this diatribe in *Mein Kampf.*

> Never forget that the rulers of present-day Rus-

sia are common blood-stained criminals; that they are the scum of humanity which, favored by circumstances, overran a great state in a tragic hour, slaughtered and wiped out thousands of her leading intelligentsia in a wild blood lust. . . .

Since Hitler, in *Mein Kampf,* had so plainly revealed his intentions years before he came to power in Germany, and more than a decade prior to the beginning of World War II, why did the statesmen of the world pay so little heed to his warnings? In part, he was ignored because of the general atmosphere of appeasement, wishful thinking, and peace-at-any-price that prevailed. Another factor was an amazing story of international censorship. Because Hitler refused to authorize a complete translation of *Mein Kampf,* only a much expurgated, bowdlerized version was available in English until 1939. In that year, on the eve of war, two American publishers, one with Hitler's approval and one without, brought out uncensored editions. In France, in 1936, Hitler, through his publisher, sued and restrained the issue of a full translation, pleading infringement of copyright. A condensed edition published in London omitted most of the passages attacking France, eliminated a section justifying war, and so softened the tone of the book as to be false and misleading.

Meanwhile, millions of copies of the complete *Mein Kampf* were being sold and circulated in Germany. Every newly married couple was presented with a copy, while every member of the Nazi party and every civil servant was expected to possess the book. Later editions in Germany did, however, leave out the attacks on Russia and France, to conceal Hitler's purposes and to lull potential enemies to sleep.

Viewing *Mein Kampf* retrospectively, historians would maintain that Hitler had no understanding of history, anthropologists that his racial views were nonsense, educators that his theories of education were altogether medieval and reactionary, political scientists would protest his authoritarian doctrines of government and his misrepresentation of democracy, while literary experts would hold that he did not know how to write a paragraph or organize a chapter. Weigert summed it up in this way:

> The half-educated Hitler was a mosaic of influences: the amoral statecraft of Machiavelli, the mystic nationalism and romanticism of Wagner, the organic evolution of Darwin, the grossly exaggerated racialism of Gobineau and Houston Stewart Chamberlain, the messianic complex of Fichte and Hegel, the military braggadocio of Treitschke and Bernhardi, and the financial conspiracy of the Prussian Junker caste. . . . Haushofer served as a channel of unification between theory and action.

And yet, despite such glaring defects, *Mein Kampf* is, as one of its bitterest critics, Hendrik Willem Van Loon, described it, "one of the most extraordinary historical documents of all time," combining "the naiveté of Jean-Jacques Rousseau with the frenzied wrath of an Old Testament prophet." Norman Cousins called it "by far the most effective book of the twentieth century. . . . For every word in *Mein Kampf,* 125 lives were to be lost; for every page, 4,700 lives; for every chapter, more than 1,200,000 lives." Its power was derived, of course, from the fact that it was the political bible of the German people, and guided the policies of the Third Reich from 1933 until the end of World War II.

It is the world's misfortune that Hitler's ideas did not expire with him. Their adherents are still numerous in Germany, while Communist governments have borrowed and are making extensive use of many of them. Dictators everywhere will continue to find primary source material for their evil purposes in *Mein Kampf,* in the same manner that, for the past four centuries, they have been drawing upon Machiavelli. (pp. 274-85)

> *Robert B. Downs, "Study in Megalomania," in his* Books That Changed the World, *second edition, American Library Association, 1978, pp. 274-86.*

Hitler's physical appearance and mannerisms:

Portraits or moving pictures of Hitler are common enough, yet it is well to draw attention to various aspects of his physique. To most non-Nazis Hitler has no particular attraction. He resembles a second-rate waiter. He is a smallish man, slightly under average height. His forehead is slightly receding and his nose somewhat incongruous with the rest of his face. The latter is somewhat soft, his lips thin, and the whole face expressionless. The eyes are a neutral grey which tend to take on the color of their momentary surroundings. The look tends to be staring or dead and lacking in sparkle. There is an essentially feminine quality about his person which is portrayed particularly in his strikingly well-shaped and expressive hands.

Hitler's manner is essentially awkward and all his movements jerky except perhaps the gestures of his hands. 'He appears shy and ill at ease in company and seems seldom capable of carrying on conversation. Usually he declaims while his associates listen. He often seems listless and moody. This is in marked contrast to the dramatic energy of his speeches and his skillful play upon the emotions of his vast audiences, every changing mood of which he appears to perceive and to turn to his own purposes. At times he is conciliatory, at other times he may burst into violent temper tantrums if his whims are checked in any way.

W. H. D. Vernon, in his Hitler, The Man—Notes for a Case History, *1942.*

C. Caspar   (essay date 1958)

> [*In the following essay, Caspar provides a history of the publication and sales of* Mein Kampf.]

Hitler's *Mein Kampf* surely needs no introduction. Even those who have never read the Nazi bible know that its teachings were carried into practice and that millions of innocents suffered and died as a result. But the story of the twenty-year history of the book from the first edition of 10,000 to a total circulation of well over seven million copies is not so well known. These figures have a significance

that reaches beyond the booktrade: they stand as a monument to Nazi crime and also to Western folly. As Sir Winston Churchill remarked in his history of the war, "There was no book which deserved more careful study from the rulers, political and military, of the Allied Powers" [*The Second World War,* 1948]. Yet it was consistently neglected by a generation which had eyes but did not see. In the words of Sir Samuel Hoare, Lord Templewood, the British statesman [in his *Nine Troubled Years,* 1954]:

> We could not believe that the rantings of *Mein Kampf* were a practical manual of daily conduct from which he (Hitler) would never deviate.

GERMAN EDITIONS

Mein Kampf is in two parts, "Eine Abrechnung" and "Die Nationalsozialistische Bewegung," which were written at different times and originally appeared separately. The first part was dictated by Hitler to Rudolf Hess when both were serving a mild term of detention from April 1 to December 20, 1924, at the fortress of Landsberg-am-Lech. Neither the first nor the second part is believed to be wholly Hitler's work, but the exact authorship has never been settled. It seems certain that Father Bernhard Staempfle twice revised the manuscript. Otto Strasser wrote [in his *Hitler and I,* 1940]:

> Good Father Staempfle, a priest of great learning, editor of a paper at Miessbach, spent months rewriting and editing *Mein Kampf.* He eliminated the more flagrant inaccuracies and the excessively childish platitudes. Hitler never forgave Father Staempfle for getting to know his weaknesses so well. He had him murdered by a "special death squad" on the night of June 30, 1934.

According to Strasser's account, Staempfle believed only the chapter on propaganda was Hitler's original contribution. On the other hand, James Murphy, an Irishman who served from 1934 to 1938 as an official in Dr. Goebbels' ministry, stated, on the authority of Hess' younger brother, Alfred:

> Those chapters which deal with the propaganda and organization of the Nazi movement, owe their inspiration to Rudolf Hess, and most of the actual composition was done by him. He was also responsible for the chapters dealing with Lebensraum and the function of the British Empire in the history of the world. [Murphy, *Who Sent Rudolf Hess?,* 1941]

The geo-politician, Karl Haushofer, Hess' tutor, is also said to have had a hand in writing *Mein Kampf.* Thus Edmund A. Walsh, an American student of geo-politics, remarked [in *Total Power,* 1948]:

> The graduation in *Mein Kampf* from rabble-rousing to the elementary stages of geo-politics is too striking and too circumstantial to be a mere coincidence, in view of the type of reading matter that Haushofer admitted he had brought to Hitler and Hess in Landsberg prison. . . . What Haushofer did was to hand a sheathed sword of conquest from his arsenal of scholarly

research. Hitler unsheathed the blade, sharpened the edge and threw away the scabbard.

Haushofer denied the allegation although Walsh attributed a specific chapter—XIV—to him.

Sections of the manuscript were smuggled out of prison by Frau Bechstein who visited Hitler there on the pretext of bringing him phonograph records. She was the elderly wife of a wealthy piano manufacturer who had given financial support to the Nazi movement, and she treated Hitler like a son. The title chosen by Hitler, "Four and a Half Years of Struggle against Lie, Folly and Cowardice: A Reckoning," was changed either by Alfred Rosenberg or by Max Amann. At any rate, the first part, in an edition of 10,000 copies, priced at RM 12 (then about $3.00), appeared as *Mein Kampf* on July 18, 1925. It included an appendix which featured posters advertising 27 meetings in Munich at which Hitler spoke between November 1920 and January 1923. Six months later, on December 2, a second impression brought the total circulation to 18,000. The second part, at the same price, did not appear until December 11, 1926; it sold 13,000 copies within three years. By 1929 the first volume had achieved a total circulation of 23,000.

Even before the manuscript was complete—as far back as May 1924—an agent for the publishers, Messrs. Franz Eher, Nachfolger, G.m.b.H., Munich, systematically canvassed prospective buyers. Of the advance payment of RM 5 collected for a copy of the first volume, the agent received RM 3 commission, the publishers the remainder.

In 1930 the two volumes were superseded by a one-volume "People's Edition," and the original price of RM 24 was reduced to RM 8. As a result of the National Socialist electoral victory on September 14 and the influence of a leaflet drafted by Rudolf Hess ("Wer weiss, was Adolf Hitler will?"), sales that year soared to 62,000. In the following year, however, they slumped to 52,000 but in 1932 reached a peak of 80,000. By the end of 1933, the year of Hitler's rise to power, the total number of copies sold was 1.5 million.

There are discrepancies between the figures quoted above, which were published in 1938 by the Nazi press, and the entries in Messrs. Eher's "Honorar-Buch," the publishers' and the author's royalty ledger (it was confiscated at the end of the war and is now in the Library of Congress). The sales of *Mein Kampf,* each year through November 1933, were recorded as follows in the royalty ledger:

Year	Number of Copies Sold Annually
1925	9,473
1926	6,913
1927	5,507
1928	3,015
1929	7,664
1930	54,086
1931	50,808
1932	90,351
1933	854,127

After 1933 sales of the book reflected the author's political success. Some 30,000 copies were sold monthly in 1934

and 1935; in 1937 more than twice as many. Sales from the original date of publication totaled as follows in the years shown:

Total Number of Copies Sold	
Year	(in thousands)
1935	2,127
1937	3,447
1938	4,000
1940	6,000
1942	7,000

The distribution of *Mein Kampf* was dependent only in part on the publisher's efforts. In 1934 the Prussian Minister of Education ordered the book to be used as a school primer on racial science, heredity and population policy. The Reich Railway Executive in July 1934 selected the book as a reward to its officials when cited for meritorious service. In July 1935 Goering ordered all civil servants to study the book. The Reich Minister of the Interior in April 1936 "recommended" that registrars, including German consuls abroad, present a copy to every bridal couple. Propaganda stimulated sales. A school text, for example, advertised the "classical masterpiece" as follows:

> Boys and girls in their teens must acquire a proper insight in order to understand this new bible of the people. They must become acquainted and familiar with the lines of policy therein traced by the Master's hand. The grown-ups must purify and strengthen their civic consciousness by reading this book. Fathers must teach the thoughts contained in it to their children. [*Dr. Wilhelm Königs Erläuterungen für den Schul- und Hausgebrauch,* 1934]

Yet few of the Nazi elite bothered to read the book. Otto Strasser relates a characteristic incident. At the 1927 Nuremberg Party rally he presented the annual report in which he quoted a few phrases from *Mein Kampf.* Later several colleagues, including some Gauleiters, asked him if he had really read the book "with which none of them seemed to be familiar." Upon further inquiry, "Goebbels shook his head guiltily, Goering burst into loud laughter, and Count Reventlow excused himself on the ground that he had no time." Even Streicher, one of the few friends Hitler actually named in the book, had read "only what concerned the Jewish question"; he had "never read anything else."

Most people simply could not stomach the heavy turgid verbosity, although Hitler claimed that his story was presented as a "series of leading articles in the *Völkischer Beobachter.*" Of those who did wade through the morass, many might have agreed with Fritz Thyssen, the industrialist, who admitted that "*Mein Kampf* revived the insane aspirations of the Pan-Germans," but "not even the most rightist circles in Germany ever took such hysterical ideas seriously." [The critic adds in a footnote: "The conservative *Kreuz-Zeitung* (Berlin) in its review of the first volume of *Mein Kampf,* Oct. 1, 1925, commented: 'The reader looks for the fire of the spirit but only finds arrogance; instead of inspiration, he finds boredom; instead of love and enthusiasm, catchwords; instead of wholesome hatred, nothing but abuse.' "] Dr. Schacht also did not consider "these theoretical extravagances" worthy of attention, citing the fact that the expansion of German Lebensraum in the East, according to *Mein Kampf,* was "made specifically dependent on British acquiescence," and that this should be forthcoming seemed "Utopian."

Meanwhile sales increased steadily. In October 1938 the President of the Reich Chamber of Literature urged booksellers to deal only in new copies, as it was "painful to every National-Socialist-thinking German to see the work of our Führer described in our time as 'second-hand.' " Special editions were produced to supplement the standard "People's Edition" of 1930. A Braille edition, published by the Marburg High School Library for the Blind, was available as early as 1936. Alleged "demands from German-speaking foreigners" were met in 1939 with an edition in Roman type, and for the benefit of the troops a thin paper edition was issued in 1940—like the standard edition but a little smaller in size.

From these various editions Hitler drew a very considerable income. Exact figures for the years 1925 to 1933, given in Messrs. Eher's "Honorar-Buch," reveal that the royalties credited to the author up to November 17, 1933 were as follows in RM:

1925	20,352
1926	14,707
1927	11,494
1928	8,318
1929	15,448
1930	45,472
1931	40,780
1932	62,340
1933	861,146

By 1937 royalties amounted to £50,000 a year, according to G. Ward Price, the British journalist. American royalties totaled $70,000 by 1944, but up to 1939, the author received no more than ten percent due to him.

Hitler's fiftieth birthday in April 1939, coinciding with the sale of the five millionth copy, was marked by the publication of a de luxe edition, bound in dark blue leather, decorated in gold, with the upthrust naked blade of a sword displayed in the center of the cover. The poster appendix found in the first edition was again reproduced, with one significant omission: a poster advertising a rally under the slogan "The Dying Soviet Russia." At this time the first moves toward Nazi-Soviet rapprochement were being made; inclusion of such a poster would clearly have been inopportune.

The text of *Mein Kampf,* however, remained unchanged. Even the Nazi-Soviet pact did not result in a change in the original. There has been an erroneous impression that in the editions issued after 1930 alterations from the original text were introduced. Actually few discrepancies exist. Most are petty points of style, suggesting that a literary hand eliminated crudities. Two of the more important alterations are the following:

1. Standard edition (Munich 1930), p. 722:

> How is it possible for the Jewish press, up to 1918 the faithful champions of Britain's struggle against Germany, now suddenly to break faith and pursue an independent course?

Second edition, II Munich 1929, p. 298:

> How is it possible for the Northcliffe press, up to 1918 . . .

2. Standard edition, p. 723:

> Each year increases the Jewish hold on labor (in the U.S.A.); only a very few still remain independent.

Second edition, II, p. 298:

> . . . one single great man, Ford still remains independent.

With regard to his essential teaching, Hitler did not deny his own pronouncement (p. 513):

> . . . in the wording of its programme, a nationalist movement must never compromise with ideas that may be popular at any one time.

It was as unalterable as Holy Writ, and so of course was the book to be regarded. "We National Socialists know only one Holy Writ, and that is Adolf Hitler's *Mein Kampf,*" Goering declared in 1935 [in *Reden und Aufsätze,* 1938], and this was said by the same man who occasionally

> cursed the tomfoolery of *Mein Kampf;* I'm constantly being asked: "But it says this and the other thing in *Mein Kampf.* Haven't we got to carry that out?" What answer can I give to that? [Hermann Rauschning, *Men of Chaos,* 1942]

Perhaps it was sufficient that Hitler did know all the answers. He took pains to explain away objectionable passages, particularly those concerning France, and in doing so used considerable subterfuge. It was suggested that "after all the book is entitled *My Struggle,* not *My Programme*" [Reuter dispatch from Berlin, in the *Yorkshire Post* (Leeds), Mar. 2, 1936, quoting a German "statesman"]. Hitler's disingenuity in relation to "the German people's relentless moral enemy" was revealed in February 1936 when he was interviewed by M. de Jouvenel, the French journalist, to whom he remarked:

> When I wrote *Mein Kampf* I was in prison. It was the time when French troops occupied the Ruhr district. It was the moment of greatest tension between our two countries. We were enemies . . . But today there is no reason any more for a conflict. You want me to correct my book, like a writer who edits a revised version of his works. But I am not a writer: I am a politician. I do my correcting in my foreign policy itself which is based on Franco-German understanding. If I succeed in bringing about a rapprochement with France, that will be a correction worthy of me.

No Russian journalist was given a similar interpretation: perhaps the news value would not have matched that accorded the interpretation given to the Frenchman. James Murphy, in the introduction to his English translation of *Mein Kampf,* saw no basis for criticizing Hitler's blatant insincerity. As late as 1939 he noted as a serious argument:

> Hitler has declared that, as he was only a politi-

cal leader and not yet a statesman in a position of official responsibility when he wrote his book, what he stated in *Mein Kampf* does not implicate him as Chancellor of the Reich.

TRANSLATIONS

Upon Hitler's rise to power, *Mein Kampf* began to attract attention outside Germany. As early as 1932 the Hearst syndicate offered $25,000 for the rights to the volume. The first translation, in abridged form—there were 297 pages and four photographs—appeared in the United States: *My Battle* (Boston October 1933) was prepared by E. T. S. Dugdale and published by Houghton, Mifflin & Co. In the five years from October 1933 through October 1939, the following sales were reported:

Number of Copies Sold

1933	4,633
1934	931
1935	707
1936	858
1937	1,723
1938	6,500

By September 1940 the total number of copies sold was approximately 100,000.

Subsequently three unabridged editions appeared. One, entitled *Mein Kampf* (669 pp.), which was offered as "the first complete and unexpurgated edition in the English language," was printed late in 1939 by Ludwig Lore, a German-born Social Democrat, who up to 1942 was a columnist of the *New York Post*. Lore used the first German edition and wrote a militant introduction, but revealed neither publisher nor place of publication. Hardly any reference has ever been made to this text. More prominence was attained by two editions which appeared almost simultaneously in 1939, one, an unauthorized version (669 pp.) translated by a scholar whose identity the publishers, Stackpole & Sons, New York, refused to reveal; the other (1,002 pp.), published in New York in collaboration with Reynal & Hitchcock by Houghton, Mifflin & Co., the owners of the American copyright.

The first of the latter translations was a literal version, with "no attempt to make literary English from an original which is . . . verbose, repetitive, ungrammatical and often unintelligible and illiterate." The second was a free translation from the first German edition, with extensive notes designed to clarify obscure passages, sketch the historical background, and check Hitler's predictions against current events. It was the work of an editorial committee headed by Dr. Alvin Johnson, then director of the New School for Social Research, New York, who was assisted by a group including George N. Shuster, John Gunther, and Graham Hutton, the British author. They explained that E. T. S. Dugdale's abridgment, containing less than half of the original, was probably adequate for its time, as "in 1933 it seemed unlikely that any large American public would care to read *Mein Kampf* as a whole," but now "the book has assumed a more urgent character."

Houghton, Mifflin & Co. brought suit against Stackpole & Sons upon the publication of the unauthorized translation. The defendant contended that "the full text should have been published years ago," and they "decided to publish in the public interest," upon counsel's advice that the copyright was faulty: Since Hitler was described as a "Stateless German" in the original copyright application, he could not claim to be a citizen of a country with which the United States had reciprocal arrangements. The Federal Circuit Court of Appeal found against the defendant, holding that their "claim to equity," in the absence of any title or right, was "bold indeed." The court held, further, that a "stateless alien" ought not be left insecure in literary property. If such a condition were permitted, "the United States, contrary to its general policy and tradition, would be putting another obstacle in the way of the survival of homeless refugees of whom many have been students, scholars and writers." The copyright was therefore upheld. Both firms promised that all profits from the sale of the books would be used for the benefit of refugees from Nazi oppression. Approximately 290,000 copies of the various translations were sold by 1942.

My Struggle, under the imprint of Hurst & Blackett, London, priced at 18s., appeared in October 1933, the same month the Dugdale translation was published in the United States. The translator of the English volume (285 pp., including 23 illustrations and the text of the Nazi party programme), who contributed a remarkably unsophisticated preface, chose to remain anonymous. A "Paternoster Library" edition, priced at 5s., with reduced format and illustrations omitted, was published in October 1935. A year later sales of the original edition totaled 5,000 copies, of the Paternoster edition, 14,000 copies. Combined sales of both editions totaled 47,000 copies by August 1938.

My Struggle was described by Professor R. T. Clark, the British historian, as a successful effort to "bowdlerise" and "whitewash" the original text. Robert Dell, the *Manchester Guardian* correspondent, who was one of the first to understand Nazi policy, found it

> difficult to avoid the conclusion that the publication of this translation was an attempt on the part of Hitler and the German Ministry of Propaganda to dupe the English-speaking public

for, he thought, it could be

> no mere coincidence that all, or nearly all, the passages likely to make a bad impression on the English-speaking public and, in particular, all the passages showing Hitler's hatred of France, were omitted. [*Germany Unmasked,* 1934]

The British press, by and large, did not see through the game. *The Times,* which had previously printed extracts from *Mein Kampf,* merely commented that "some of Herr Hitler's historical conclusions" were "extremely ill-digested generalisations of a pseudo-scientific kind." The reviewer for the Conservative *Daily Telegraph* [E. C. Bentley] found the book was "marked by an appalling sincerity" which was "one of the secrets of Herr Hitler's success and the most respectable one." To the avowed champions of Anglo-Nazi cooperation, the merits of the author and his work were even more unusual. Praising Hitler as "by general agreement a profoundly honest man," their monthly journal, the *Anglo-German Review,* described the book as "really quite innocuous" and, where controversial, "a work of amazing moderation."

In January 1939 Hurst & Blackett published a translation by James Murphy of the complete text, using the original German title (567 pp.). According to the *Daily Telegraph,* an unabridged translation had hitherto been withheld on Hitler's order, for he "obviously" wished "to prevent the people of Great Britain from comparing the extravagant bellicosities of his book with the pacific protestations of his speeches as Führer and Reich Chancellor" [J. C. Johnstone, *Daily Telegraph,* 23 March 1939]. *The Times Literary Supplement,* on the other hand, noted that:

> it would not be surprising if this publication increased sympathy for those ideas of Herr Hitler which do not immediately threaten our own interests in the world.

The translator, who contributed occasional explanatory footnotes, also wrote an introduction, to which Hitler surely did not object. Yet copies of this text (as well as of Karl Marx's *Capital*) were among the books officially recommended as gifts to British troops at the front in 1939.

A number of translations appeared in the Scandinavian countries. A Danish translation, *Min Kamp,* by Professor Clara Hammerich, in an edition of 9,000 copies, was circulated also in Norway; the second volume (335 pp.), which was ready first, appeared in 1934, the first volume (380 pp.) in 1936. The publishers were H. Hagerups Forlag, Copenhagen-Oslo. A separate Norwegian edition, translated by Nils Holmberg, appeared in 1941. A Swedish translation, *Min Kamp,* by Anders Quiding and N. P. Sigvard Lind, first was published in 1934 in an edition of 5,000 copies. The two volumes (385 and 336 pp.) were published by Holgar Schildts Forlag, Stockholm. The second Swedish translation, by Holmberg, was issued by Medén Publications and printed in Helsinki in 1941. The Finnish translation by Lauri Hirvensalo was published in the same year by Werner Söderstrom of Helsinki. A second impression brought to 32,000 the number of copies of this translation.

Most of the translations were authorized versions. The Czech translation, *Muj Boy,* which appeared in 1936, was, however, repudiated by the Germans. Two years earlier the German publishers, Messrs. Franz Eher, sued the French publishers, Nouvelles Editions Latines, for infringement of copyright when they published *Mon Combat* in two volumes (368 and 317 pp.), translated by J. Gaudefroy-Demobynes and A. Calmettes. The Paris Court of Commerce ordered the edition to be destroyed and dismissed the defendants' plea that it was in the public interest for every Frenchman to know that Hitler considered France to be Germany's most infamous and dangerous enemy. The court averred that the case would serve as an advertisement should the plaintiffs wish to publish a translation themselves, and hence fixed damages at one franc.

No such translation, however, appeared. The French reader had to be content with secondary explanations of Nazi policy as set forth in *Mein Kampf,* not the primary text itself. Examples are *Hitler par Lui-Même* (174 pp.) by

Charles Appuhin, published in 1933 by Haumont, Paris, and *Que Veut Hitler* (152 pp.) by B. Combes de Patris, published in 1932 by Editions Babu, Paris. Two biographies were also published in 1933 [Michel Gorel's *Hitler sans masque* and "Frateco's" *M. Hitler, Dictateur*], and in 1936 a carefully arranged selection from Hitler's speeches, under the title, *Principes d'Action* (259 pp.), by Arthur S. Pfannstiel. The publishers, Editions Bernard Grasset, Paris, stated that "this first exposition of the Nazi doctrine" was authorized by Hitler.

Another authorized text, published by Messrs. Arthème Fayard, Paris, appeared in 1938 under the title, *Ma Doctrine* (345 pp.). It consisted of translations of selected passages from *Mein Kampf,* extracts from Hitler's speeches and a letter to Mussolini after Austria's Anschluss—in which he vowed that the German frontier with both Italy and France was definitive. The translators, François Dauture and Georges Blond, stated that the volume was "designed to give an exact and complete idea of the present state of Nazi doctrine as devised and applied by Chancellor Adolf Hitler," who "was introducing into Nazi doctrine such elements as would either complete or modify certain doctrinal affirmations in *Mein Kampf,* or even invalidate and replace them."

The political purpose of the volume was made evident by its linking of disjointed extracts from the original text: the first twenty pages were a miscellaneous harvest from the following pages of the standard edition: 95, 84, 88, 97, 410, 96, 92, 93, 98, 99. The particularly anti-French outbursts were omitted from this edition, but not the anti-Jewish passages. The journal of the German-French society in Berlin, *Deutsch-Französische Monatshefte,* far from condemning the anti-French sections of *Mein Kampf,* reproached those who cited them:

> It is not these passages in *Mein Kampf* which concern France and which have been overtaken by the course of events that threaten the foundations of good Franco-German relations, but rather the spiteful propaganda which international hate-mongers carry on in France by using those very passages.

Other European translations included a Dutch translation, *Mijn Kamp,* complete in one volume (852 pp.), by Steven Barends, published in Amsterdam in 1938 by De Amsterdamsche Keurkamer. It had a circulation of between 50,000 to 100,000 copies in 1943. A shortened Italian version of volume II, *La Mia Battaglia,* with a 34-page biography of Hitler and a preface written by him for this edition, was published in 1934 by Messrs. Valentino Bompiani, Milan; the first volume, *La Mia Vita,* appeared four years later. A Spanish edition, *Mi Lucha,* anonymously translated, was published in 1935 by Casa Editorial Araluce, Barcelona. The translator contributed an introduction, commending the Nazis' "constructive and pacifist" ideology. In a second edition (367 pp.), published in Avila late in 1937, the translator spread his admiration evenly over "Hitler, Mussolini, and Franco, the political guides of the new Europe." A complete Portuguese translation, *Minho Luta* (578 pp.), by J. de Mattos Ibiapina, Professor of German at the Escola Militar in Rio de Janeiro, was published in Porto Alegre, Brazil, in 1934 by Edição de Livraria do Globo.

A Hungarian edition, *Harcóm* (504 pp.), prepared by Dr. Istvan Szakáts, who wrote a four-page introduction, was published in Budapest in 1935. It sold 3,300 copies. The Bulgarian text was the work of Christo Kuncheff, leader of the Bulgarian Workers Party. Russian extracts, translated from the German by U. Krusenstern, were published in Shanghai, China, in 1935 by Gong, under the title *Adolf Hitler: Moya Borba. Autobiografiya* (145 pp.).

In the Near East Hitler's polemic was made available in Arabic at an early date. In 1934 the Iraqui periodical, *The Arab World,* of Baghdad, printed several instalments, and in 1935 the Beirut People's Library published *Hitler's Struggle,* 108 pages of selected passages from the original text, translated by Omar Abu-Nassr, with references to Hitler's career drawn from British, American and French sources. The back cover advertised a book in Arabic, entitled, *Hitler the Terror: His Political Police.* Towards the end of 1938 a longer version (250 pp.) was published in Cairo by the Commercial Publishing House. This edition, translated by Ali Mohammed Mahtoub, included the author's full-length portrait and seven pages of photographs illustrating various stages in his career. Hitler was described as "the strongest man in the world," and prominence was given to his threat, "Let the world know that the Germans of Czechoslovakia will not go undefended."

In the Far East a Chinese translation appeared under the auspices of the National Translation Institute at Nanking, with the approval of Dr. Yo Chia Yun, the Chancellor of the National Central University. An abridged Japanese translation (137 + 37 pp.), based on the English translation published by Hurst & Blackett in 1933, appeared in Tokyo in 1938 under the imprint of Herald Magazine, Ltd. The translators, Kanesada Hanazono and Bonzen Komiyama, two university lecturers in English, supplemented the meagre extract from *Mein Kampf* with the full text of the Nazi party programme. In a preface, the well-known nationalist writer, Soho Tokutomi, endorsed Hitler's support of Germany's ancient policy, *Der Drang nach Osten.* Obviously the full implications of this policy were not apparent to the commentator. Yet this volume, which passed through several editions, was suppressed by the Japanese censor, on the ground that it was likely to distort the true intentions of the author. Late in 1938 a complete Japanese translation, prepared by Professor Kinro Gorai, appeared. The translator had applied for the rights as early as 1931. Hitler then demanded ten percent of the royalties, but after Japan joined the Anti-Comintern pact, he agreed to sell the rights for five percent. A Tamil version was reported to have been sold out in Bangkok in 1944.

POST-BELLUM EDITIONS

Since the downfall of Hitler, *Mein Kampf* has had a rather checkered career. In October 1945 an Allied Commission in Berlin formally banned the book for German readers; in 1951, however, second-hand copies were on sale in Hamburg. About the same time Austrian police discovered a recent edition of *Mein Kampf* among a confiscated consignment of books. The demand in Germany, at least at present, does not seem active. A German publisher who advertised for a copy for research purposes received about one hundred offers. The remarkably low average price asked—about DM 2,50—was not a reflection of an overstocked market: though the book had a large circulation in Germany, many copies must have been destroyed either by their owners or by bombing. *Mein Kampf* is simply not much in demand among Germans. [The critic adds in a footnote: "In 1954 German students were urged to read the book by Dr. Hermann Ehlers, then Speaker of the Bundestag, but his reason for doing so, according to the *Frankfurter Allgemeine,* Jan. 21, 1954, was that *Mein Kampf* provided an example of how things must *not* be done."]

Elsewhere the situation varied. In 1952 abridged editions in German, English and Spanish were offered by a publishing house in Madrid. Second-hand copies of the Paternoster Library edition were advertised at 12s. 6d. in the July 21 and 28, 1956 copies of *Union,* the British Fascist weekly paper then published in London.

Arabic "kitbag editions," entitled *Mein Kampf by Adolf Hitler. Hitler and Nazism,* published in 1952, 1954 and 1955 by the Beirut Printing and Publishing House, were found among the personal possessions of some Egyptian officers captured by the Israelis during the Sinai campaign in November 1956. The translator, Louis el Haj, included extracts from *Mein Kampf* and photographs of Hitler and of Nazi party rallies in Nuremberg.

When a Question on the subject was asked in the British House of Commons on February 25, 1957, the spokesman for H. M. Government, Mr. Ian Harvey, Under-Secretary for Foreign Affairs, answered that the use of a book like *Mein Kampf* was entirely contrary to the spirit of the Universal Declaration of Human Rights and of the Genocide Convention. On February 12, Mr. Julian Amery, the Under-Secretary for War, said that while no Arabic copies had been found by British troops, "the book seems to have been in fairly general circulation among officers of the Egyptian Army."

It is then still premature to assume that the final sale of a copy of *Mein Kampf* has been made. (pp. 3-16)

> C. Caspar, " 'Mein Kampf'—A Best Seller," in Jewish Social Studies, *Vol. XX, No. 1, January, 1958, pp. 3-16.*

Michael McGuire   (essay date 1977)

[In the essay below, McGuire provides a structuralist reading of Hitler's use of mythic rhetoric in Mein Kampf.*]*

The topic of Naziism or of Adolf Hitler's rhetoric is neither a new one nor an exhausted one for rhetorical critics, who generally have concentrated on Hitler's speaking and the Nazis' extensively organized system of orators. It is widely known that Hitler and Minister of Propaganda Goebbels believed the spoken word superior to the written word for their revolutionary purposes. Yet the Nazis did not confine their propaganda to oratory: in the Third

Reich journalism, literature, drama, painting, sculpture, architecture, and music all were regulated for use as assertive media to put the Nazis' message in the public eye and mind. And the best substantiated conclusion of scholarly studies of Nazi rhetoric is that in all of its modes the Nazi message is at base the same—and the basis of all Nazi propaganda was Hitler's *Mein Kampf.*

In contrast with the book's evident importance and efficacy are the critical assessments of it from various reviewers. Winston Churchill called it "turgid, verbose, shapeless," [Churchill, *The Second World War,* Vol. I], and William Shirer said [in *The Rise and Fall of the Third Reich*] that *Mein Kampf* "would strike a normal mind of the twentieth century as a grotesque hodgepodge concocted by a half-baked, uneducated neurotic." Hitler's biographer Konrad Heiden said, "Even Hitler's best friends said: Yes, he is an amazing speaker, probably a great leader, perhaps even a political genius—but it's a pity he had to write this stupid book. . . . *Mein Kampf* did little to establish Hitler's intellectual authority in his party" [*Der Fuehrer: Hitler's Rise to Power,* 1944]. Historian Werner Maser adds in *Hitler's Mein Kampf:*

> If *Mein Kampf* had been arranged in any logical, orderly sequence by subject, chapters 6, 7, 9, and 11 (for instance) of Volume 2 would have been included in Volume 1, and, judging by the subject matter, Chapter 11 of Volume 1 would belong to Volume 2, . . . In fact, *Mein Kampf* is nothing but a collection of disconnected speeches, and Hitler's friends and advisors were unable to change its character into anything resembling a systematically laid out and logically constructed book.

Kenneth Burke's critique pointed out that criticisms of *Mein Kampf* have been *vandalistic*—vitrolic but undetailed—but Burke echoed their disgust with Hitler's cumbersome book, calling it "exasperating, even nauseating."

Estimates of *Mein Kampf* minimize its stature especially on account of its structure. *Mein Kampf,* although it is a narrative, ill conforms to the kind of linear, sequential organization expected of a discursive treatise or narrative. My purpose in this essay is to explore the hypothesis that *Mein Kampf* is an encyclopaedic myth which collects at one point all the particulars of the Nazi *Weltanschauung,* and that consequently the meaningful rhetorical structures of *Mein Kampf* must be sought within and between the themes it collects rather than in the sequential on-paper pattern of the text.

Myth is a mode of assertive writing characterized by a superhuman protagonist, narrated by an oracular persona, possessing a unique tense or concept of time, which is offered as a model of reality.

Myths usually resolve contradictions of some sort or address important questions which a culture is asking about itself. Usually the mythic hero, although superior in kind to humans, is a real person in basis—Faust, Jesus, Hercules—whose story is told as a model of social behavior. Besides being grounded in reality through the protagonist, myths generally refer to events alleged to have taken place

in the real historical past; but the myth has rhetorical value because it claims also to be a valid model for the present and future. It is in the sense of myth as model that a notion of a double structure or double tense inheres. A myth often has several text-renderings, as Faust was treated in the medieval chapbooks, by Marlowe, by Goethe, by Mann, even in operas by Berlioz, Busoni, and Gounod. The myth itself is exhausted by none of these texts, but is something greater than and prior to them all. This deep structure of myth is what its numerous versions seek to repeat into clarity.

A method for reading myth to get at both its deep and surface structures is explained by Levi-Strauss [in *Structural Anthropology*]:

> The myth will be treated as an orchestra score would be if it were unwittingly considered as a unilinear series; our task is to reestablish the correct arrangement. Say, for instance, we were confronted with a sequence of the type: 1, 2, 4, 7, 8, 2, 3, 4, 6, 8, 1, 2, 5, 7, 3, 4, 5, 6, 8, . . . , the assignment being to put all the 1's together, all the 2's . . . etc.; the result is a chart.

1	2		4			7	8
	2	3	4		6		8
1	2			5		7	
		3	4	5	6		8

A reconstruction of this kind reveals meaning along the axis of the surface structure—read left to right, top to bottom—and meaning along the axis of the deeper structure, read up and down in a column as a harmonic chord would be read. Thus, such a chart requires the sorting out from Hitler's narrative sentences or fragments which depict events and rearranging them into columns which reveal a common feature. . . .

In this reconstruction all the events in column I are beginnings or births. Column II events all have to do with finding one's mission or the growth and productivity associated with doing the gods' will. Column III contains items which have to do with conditions of decadence, decline and stagnation, and column IV displays events or revelations of death and destruction. Analysis will show that the "deaths" in column IV are not simple terminations, but metamorphoses which collapse into new birth events in column I. Reading this reconstruction across from left to right line after line provides an outline of the narrative sequence, the text structure, of *Mein Kampf.* I hope to show through textual analysis that the pattern of these columns repeats rhythmically in *Mein Kampf* to establish a dialectical confrontation between life and death, good and evil; and that *Mein Kampf* develops a rhetorically elaborate myth.

THE *Mein Kampf* MYTH

"Today I consider it my good fortune that Fate designated my birthplace to be exactly Braunau on the *Inn.* For this small town lies on the border of those two German states whose reunion seems, at least to us of the younger generation, a life-mission to pursue by every means." These first two sentences of *Mein Kampf* set the tone of the entire work. Hitler's birthplace is not something merely men-

Reconstruction of Mein Kampf Myth

I	II	III	IV
Hitler is born	Hitler moves to Vienna.	Hitler suffers poverty; Vienna decays.	Jews and Marxists conspire against German Austria.
Hitler moves to Munich.	World War begins; Hitler enlists.	Offensive halted; Hitler wounded.	
		Propaganda undermines German war effort; home press creates disenchantment.	Munitions workers strike. Marxists dominate labor.
New Western Offensive.		Hitler wounded; Offensive fails.	Revolution, Versailles, and Weimar Govt.
Hitler goes to Munich.		Germany in depression; bourgeois parties and and Weimar Govt. weak.	Bavarian Soviet Revolution.
Hitler enters army political school.	Hitler becomes teacher-orator; joins German Worker's Party.		
Nazis' first mass meeting.	Hitler takes over all party propaganda.	Jews-Marxists and bourgeoisie oppose Nazis. Riots.	Nazi *Putsch* fails; Hitler imprisoned; Party outlawed.
Hitler writes *Mein Kampf.*	Hitler freed; Party ban lifted.	Weimar decays; lives on loans.	

tioned, not accidental, not attributed to his parents, but something carefully determined by Fate—the gods. And this is no case of autobiographical precision; one must note Hitler nowhere gives the date of his birth. In two sentences Hitler establishes a mythic tense—vaguely past but pertinent to the present and prefiguring the future by visions of life-mission and German-Austrian unity—and the entrance of divine will is accomplished. Throughout *Mein Kampf,* events and their causes are depicted in anthropomorphisms which manifest two opposing wills at work; and details are lacking from Hitler's autobiography and historical account, so that, for example, dates often can only be inferred from events. [The critic adds in a footnote: "Hitler also gives some wrong dates. For example, he claims to have moved from Vienna to Munich in 1912, but research indicates 1913."]

Although not all of the events in column I name gods directly, it is the feature of birth or rebirth which is their important connection, and it is easy to show that the gods and goodness are involved. In telling of his move from Vienna to Munich Hitler claims he already knew the city as well as if he had lived within its walls for years, in the capitol of German art, where the dialect was more his own than that of Vienna. In Germany Hitler felt reborn into his homeland: "Inner love seized me for this town more than for any other place known to me from the very first hour of my arrival. A German city!! What a difference from Vienna. I felt sick even thinking about that racial Babylon!" Though Hitler's chapter provides scant details

about his life in Munich, he tells at length about his considerations of proper policy for Germany, particularly with regard to territorial need: "One must cooly and soberly take the position that it certainly cannot be Heaven's will to give one *Volk* fifty times as much land and soil on this earth as another. In this case one must not let himself be kept away from the borders of eternal right by political borders. . . . One should give us the space we need to live . . . and what has been withheld from kindness will have to be taken with the fist."

The new Western offensive, next event in column I, Hitler describes as a march onto sacred soil where his regiment had first received its "baptism of fire." Looking at the reconstruction, Hitler's first move to Munich—his rebirth in Germany—followed the trauma of life in decadent Vienna which he had to leave; and the new Western offensive similarly grew out of the death-like munitions strike in column IV, which, although it caused minimal actual strategic disadvantage to the Germans, must have symbolized to Hitler and other German soldiers the death of their cause or its spirit at home. Similarly, the remaining beginnings in column I stem from events in the final columns of the reconstruction. Hitler returned to Munich after the end of the war; the revolution by communists which formed the Bavarian Soviet government added impetus to provide training for veterans, and Hitler entered army political school. And Hitler's important rebirth in army school was "What I had always suspected earlier without knowing it now came to pass: I could 'speak.' " This orator's birth naturally led to Hitler's teaching, and has an awesome significance in Naziism, as does the Party's first mass meeting, for mass meetings were the Nazi way. The final event in column I is *Mein Kampf:* a beginning because it set down permanently for the first time the Nazi ideology and program in the form of a historical narrative.

All the events in column I are births, rebirths, or beginnings, and the events in column II are related to the births but involve growth or finding divine mission through or after the birth. For example, the first event in column II is Hitler's moving to Vienna after his mother's death. Superficially this event seems the same as going to Munich, but in depth and detail the difference is clear. After losing his mother and failing to gain entrance to the Vienna Academy of Art, Hitler claims to have had to learn about work: "What seemed to me then to be the cruelty of Fate I praise today as the wisdom of Providence. When the Goddess of Misery took me into her arms and often tried to break me, the will to resist grew, and in the end, my will was the victor. I thank those times . . . I praise those times . . . in that they took the mama's boy out of his downy nest and gave him Lady Sorrow for his new mother." Hitler says hunger was his companion, and he tells of living in flop houses and trying to work at odd jobs as well as pursue his artistic ambitions. The Vienna period is presented as a sort of divinely ordered trial by fire for young Hitler. The entire chapter is a lie, actually, but reveals the difference between the author of *Mein Kampf* and its authorial narrating persona-hero. Hitler lived easily off three government pensions and an inheritance, but lived in rooming houses, frequently changing his address, to evade military conscription. Additionally, Hitler's self-chosen mission was art; living in Vienna he began to be interested and aware of politics and propaganda as his circumstance—under the control of Fate, Providence and the Goddess of Misery—forced him to be a worker and to be concerned about issues of economics and politics, his ultimate mission.

Similarly, Hitler's enlistment in the German army at the outbreak of the World War involves deities and mission. Hitler complains that he "often was annoyed at my too late earthly journey and this time of 'peace and order' as an undeserved, mean trick of Fate"; but when war broke out in the Balkans all Europe became eager "that Heaven may finally allow Fate, no longer to be restrained, to run its course." Hitler says the war struck him as "redemption from the annoying frustration of my youth," and in this test or mission Hitler found that he had the courage to be a good soldier, and his political education continued as he reflected on war propaganda and learned psychology. The same Hitler who had refused to serve Austria eagerly followed his German rebirth by joining a Bavarian regiment.

The other events in column II also involve finding of mission and growth. After Hitler's and others' discovery of his speaking ability he became a teacher for the army and was sent out to observe political groups, which was the nature of his first contact with the German Workers' Party. There his own teacher Gottfried Feder gave the premier address, but Hitler's account focuses upon the subsequent discussion period:

Suddenly a "professor" began talking who first questioned the correctness of Feder's reasons, but then—after a very good response by Feder—suddenly stood on the "ground of facts," not, however, without imploring the young party to take up the fight for the "separation" of Bavaria from "Prussia" as an especially important part of its program. The man brazenfacedly asserted that in this case German Austria would immediately attach itself to Bavaria, that the peace would then be much better, and more similar nonsense. I could do nothing else then but proclaim my call to speak and tell this learned gentleman my opinion on this point—with the result that the gentleman who had just spoken left the scene with his tail between his legs even before I was finished. While I spoke they had listened to me with astonished faces, and only as I prepared to say good night to the assembly another man came leaping after me, introduced himself (I did not understand his name completely), and pressed a little booklet into my hand . . . with the urgent request that I read this for certain.

Hitler suggests that he was spiritually compatible with the German Workers' Party, and that its members saw his leadership qualities. The pamphlet, which was Anton Drexler's "My Political Awakening," is described by Hitler as consubstantial with but not as well articulated as his own political philosophy. He claims to have received a membership card in the mail, and would not have attended any meeting, since he would rather start a new party than join one, but curiosity got to him, so he attended the next meeting: "I began to ask questions—outside of a few leading slogans nothing existed: no program, no handbills, nothing printed at all, no membership cards, not even a lousy rubber stamp; only visible good faith and good will." But here again, as whenever Hitler assumes the tone of innocence, destiny helps: "Now Fate itself seemed to give me a sign. I should never have joined one of the existing major parties. . . . This laughable, little foundation with its few members seemed to me to have the advantage of not yet being hardened into an 'organization,' but seemed to offer the chance for real personal activity to the individual." Thus, Hitler's discovery of the German Workers' Party is attributed to Fate.

Naturally, Hitler's assumption of the role and duties of overseeing all the party's propaganda also forms a mission for him and represents the growth of the party which followed. The final item in column II, lifting of the ban on the Nazi Party, is not a rebirth as much as a symptom of increase. The party had not died while its leaders were imprisoned, but it had shared their fate. After *Mein Kampf* (Volume I) had been written recreating the image of the party as a legitimate force, both Hitler and the party were free to pursue their new revolutionary mission together. *Mein Kampf* thus appears as both a product and a statement of the parallel destinies of Hitler and the Nazi Party; it legitimizes Hitler within the party and the party within society.

The events and conditions in column III are not causally related to column II, but stand in contradiction to them; the dialectical tension in Hitler's myth, the contradiction it mediates, is expressed by the interface of columns II and III. For whereas the events in I and II are *life* events attributed to gods and associated with Hitler, events in III and IV are *death* events attributed to the devil and associated with Jew-Marxism. Nonetheless, the revelations to Hitler of the Nazi *Weltanschauung,* which create the oracular persona of *Mein Kampf,* are manifested in these pictures of decrease and descent. The bulk of redundancy picked out by critics consists of repetition and elaboration of the thematic meaning of events and conditions in these negative columns.

The first item in column III—Hitler suffers; Vienna suffers—has special importance to the myth. Sent to Vienna by Fate, Hitler claims to have lived in poverty and suffered much, as did all of Vienna at the time. [The critic adds in a footnote: "Although Hitler actually lies about the extent of his poverty, general conditions in Vienna truly were wretched, including drastic housing shortages, poverty, and epidemic proportions of venereal diseases."] Yet the Providence which sent him to Vienna was not the maker of his suffering, because he tells in detail how he learned the cause of his and his fellow German-Austrians' misery: the Jew-Marxist conspiracy listed as the first item in column IV of the reconstruction. Hitler devotes two long chapters of his first volume to the Vienna period during which he claims to have completed his *Weltanschauung* in that city which was the ideal place to learn about parliaments, Social Democracy, labor, and the Jew. In Vienna Hitler claims to have learned that "nine-tenths of all literary filth, artistic trash, and theatrical nonsense" were produced by the one percent of the population who were Jews; and that "the Social Democratic Press was run by Jews," who are not "Germans of a particular belief, but a separate *Volk.*" For Hitler, Vienna was *the* place where one could learn about the Jewish mind. He says: *"Only the understanding of Jewry provides the key to comprehension of the inner and genuine intentions of Social Democracy.* Whoever knows this *Volk,* for him the veil of false impressions about the goals and spirit of this party is lifted from the eyes, and out of the mist and fog of social phrases arises the grinning, menacing face of Marxism." But Hitler tells us he had to wrestle with his conscience before believing all this evil about the Jews. [The critic adds in a footnote: "This is the biggest lie in *Mein Kampf,* Hitler was raised in an anti-Semitic family, had anti-Semitic teachers in school, and was raised to hate Jews. He did not stumble upon his revelation in Vienna as he claims. Burke, in "The Rhetoric of Hitler's 'Battle'," builds psychological interpretations of Hitler based on the spontaneous rise of his anti-Semitism—which never occurred. Burke also believes Hitler's falsely claimed poverty and manual labor. And Burke makes Hitler's anti-Semitism out to be a product of sexual envy. Facts are, Jew-hating was a life-long habit for Hitler and millions of other Europeans. The sexual tones are, in my opinion, the results of a combination of bad translation and misevaluation. The Austrian press at Hitler's time was dripping with sexual attacks on Jewry, and it is somewhat surprising that Hitler did not more blatantly make such attacks."]

In *Mein Kampf* Hitler narrates a stream of consciousness in which, often only through hard struggle, a naif has hidden secrets of the world revealed to him by Fate, Providence, Dame Sorrow, and the Goddess of Misery. It was not easy to hate Jews; it was not easy to reject the benificence of Social Democracy; it was not easy to decide that parliaments either do nothing or do something wrong; always Hitler claims he had to reverse his prejudices. This tone of confessional reluctance sets forth Hitler's most brutal and hateful beliefs, and at the same time connects him personally with the *Weltanschauung,* which is his revelation.

Hitler also depicts the Aryan very clearly in *Mein Kampf,* and credits the Aryan race with all advances in culture, claiming "What we see before us today of human culture, of the results of art, science and technology is nearly exclusively the product of the Aryan." Obviously, this first establishes the difference of *kind* between the Jew and the Aryan; but Hitler extends the discussion:

> Just as in daily life the so-called genius needs a particular cause, often a formal incentive, in order to be brought to light, so it is in the lives of peoples with the ingenious race. In the monotony of everyday life even important people often tend to seem unimportant and barely rise over the average of their surroundings; yet as soon as they are faced by a situation in which others would despair to go wrong, the ingenious nature grows to light out of the average child, not infrequently to the surprise of those who previously observed him growing up in the narrowness of bourgeois life—hence the prophet is seldom rewarded in his own country. . . . Almost always some kind of shock is needed to call the genius into action. The hammer hit of Fate, which throws one to the ground, suddenly strikes steel in another, and as the shell of mundane life cracks open, the previously hidden kernel lies open before the eyes of the astonished world. The world boggles and does not want to believe that what had seemed to be its own kind is now suddenly a different being: a process which repeats itself in the case of every significant human being.

The Aryan race appears here as an extension of Hitler's self-concept. He slowly reveals for us how the kernel of genius in him was brought to light by intervention of unpersonified gods (Fate, Providence) in crises: his sufferings in Vienna, the World War, and so on. The Aryan is superior to other races in its capacity for genius, and Hitler is one of its geniuses. Hitler's personal superiority of kind over other men would have been harder to assert than the claim that all Aryans are superior. That is, given the shame felt at losing the World War and the genuinely wretched social and economic conditions prevalent in Germany at the time, Hitler's audience was highly susceptible to an appeal which could redefine them positively, and if they were the best people on earth, the mere fact of Hitler's saying so might have sufficed as some proof of his own superiority even without the Aryan race.

Race is the clue to understanding and evaluating a nation and a political philosophy. Hitler says that *"the highest purpose of the state is the care for protection of those same primal racial elements which, as culture giving, forge the beauty and dignity of a higher humanity.*" The state is the container of a natural race, and assumes responsibility for the spiritual and physical well-being of the race. The great failures of Austria-Hungary lay in being insufficiently pro-German; these failures resulted from the parliament, where "the decision is always given by a majority of ignoramuses and incompetents." In contrast, true German democracy is the system in which a genius of Hitler's kind is eagerly followed by the people, who recognize his genius: this *Fuehrer* is solely accountable for policy, whereas parliamentary deputies are never more than one four-hundredth responsible. This decision is presented by Hitler in the same tone as his revelations about the Jews: "I had accepted this opinion with difficulty after two years visiting the Vienna parliament. Then I didn't go any more."

It is rather obvious from the German point of view that the failures on the Western front were conditions of decline, as was Hitler's being wounded a condition of his personal and parallel decline. But of more interest to Hitler were the reasons for the decline, none of which involve the failures of the German army. Hitler claims that the decline was caused by communists at home who manipulated the press (propaganda) to undermine the army: "Right after the first news of victories a certain press began slowly and, maybe at first unrecognizably to many, to pour a few drops of bitterness into the general enthusiasm. This was done behind the mask of a sort of benevolence and good intentions, even a kind of concern. One had doubts about celebrating the victories with too much exuberance. One feared that celebrating in this way was unworthy and inappropriate for so great a nation." This dampening of "enthusiasm" for a fight meant the end to the "intoxication" of the masses with the glorious war. The Jews, by favoring peace, proved their internationalism, their non-German-ness, and their Marxism. Hitler says "the time should have come to proceed against the whole deceitful company of those Jewish poisoners of the *Volk*. . . . If the best fell at the front, then at least one could exterminate the parasites at home." From this bitterness Hitler himself recoils, back to his narrating persona of the naif for revelation:

> But then, of course, a question arose: can spiritual ideas be rooted out at all by the sword? Can one fight a *Weltanschauung* with the application of brute force?
>
> I asked myself this question more than once even then.
>
> From thinking through analogous cases, especially those to be found in history as religious examples, the following fundamental realization arises:
>
> Conceptions and ideas, like movements with a certain spiritual basis, be these true or false, can be broken at a certain stage of their evolution with technological kinds of power only if these physical weapons at the same time are themselves supporters of a new rousing thought, an idea, or a *Weltanschauung.*
>
> . . . Only by constant and consistent application

of the methods [of violence] to suppress a doctrine, etc., can there be any possibility of a successful conclusion. However, as soon as inconstant force alternates with leniency, the doctrine to be suppressed will not only arise again, but it will even be in a position to draw new values from every persecution in that after such a wave of pressure ebbs, indignation over the misery endured drives new adherents to the old doctrine. . . .

> Every *Weltanschauung,* be it more of the religious or the political kind—sometimes the border between the two can scarcely be determined—fights less for the negative annihilation of the opposing world of ideas, but much more for the positive success of its own. That means its fight is less a defense than an attack. That way it has an advantage in the definiteness of its goal, for this goal represents the victory of its own idea, while, the other way around it is very difficult to be certain when the negative goal of annihilation of the enemy doctrine can be seen as completed or assured.

Here Hitler makes it clear that to him a *Weltanschauung* involves a positive and totalistic commitment. The fanaticism he believes necessary for the triumph of any *Weltanschauung* is the element he finds present in "true nationalism," but lacking in the sentiment of patriotism. He claims that the substitution of patriotism for nationalism contributed to the decline of Austria and to the collapse of Germany during the World War.

Hitler's lengthy discussion of the World War (about fifty pages) fails as earlier chapters do to provide details, which, in this case, is especially odd. Hitler was reportedly a good soldier, and a well decorated one, receiving the highest medal possible for an enlisted man: the Iron Cross First Class. But his discussion of the War centers on proving the Jew-Marxist stab in the back. In addition to the Social Democratic (interchangeable with "Jewish" or "Marxist" for Hitler) press undermining the popular will for war, two other actions by the group make the case. First, immediately following the Russian surrender, while Germany prepared to launch a Western counter-offensive, the munitions workers went on strike (Figure, column IV). Indeed, it must have been a bitter pill for the soldier at the front to learn that munitions workers were striking at home; and Hitler notes that although the strike did not substantially affect the army's combat capability, this "Marxist betrayal" totally undermined morale. During that counter-offensive (Figure, column I) back onto the sacred soil where Hitler's regiment had received its "baptism of fire" he was himself a casualty—blinded by British gas and sent to a hospital. It was there that he learned of the second Marxist victory: "One day, suddenly and unexpectedly, the bad news broke in on us. Sailors came on trucks and called out for the Revolution; a few Jew boys were the leaders in this fight for the 'freedom, beauty, and dignity' of our people's existence. None of them had been at the front. By way of a so-called 'gonorrhea hospital' these three orientals were returning home from the base. Now they were raising the red rag in their home town." Whether or not any detail of the episode is true, it calls to mind the mutiny of the German Navy in 1918, and associates that mutiny with Jew-Marxism. Then Hitler tells us that on November 10 a pastor came around and announced the Kaiser's abdication, at which Hitler wept for the first time since his mother's death. In the following days Hitler "became conscious of [his] destiny;" as he concludes his discussion of the war, "I resolved to become a politician."

The events and conditions in columns III and IV of the reconstructed *Mein Kampf* myth are related to each other in the same fashion as events and conditions in columns I and II; but whereas the gods are causal in columns I and II, the anti-will of Jew-Marxism is causal in columns III and IV. Hitler's myth depicts two contradictory wills at work in the world and by doing so it also suggests why the past is valid in the future: life and the world are purposeful and deliberate in this view, and the struggle between these wills cannot stop until one is annihilated. Antipathy exists between the Aryan and the Jew as physical manifestations of these opposing wills: "He who picks up a Jewish newspaper in the morning without seeing himself slandered in it has not spent the previous day usefully," announces Hitler in the next to last of his fourteen points of National Socialism. The concepts, events, and conditions in column III concern decadence brought about by the anti-will, facilitated usually by lack of vigilance or fanaticism on the part of the Aryans. The conditions in column III set up the events in column IV.

The quality of events in column IV is clear: they represent death or anti-life conditions and events. Yet they also lead into the rebirths in column I. Hitler left Vienna after being frustrated totally by the Jewish and Marxist systems of government, labor unions, etc. That ending was necessary for the rebirth in Germany which Hitler sees as the end of idleness and the beginning of activity. The munitions strike, which had to be settled before the New Offensive, proved the need for quick victory or quick peace. The Kaiser's abdication is symbolic of the meaning also of the Versailles Treaty and the Weimar government: the death of the German Empire. With the war ended Hitler had nothing to do but return to Munich. The weakness of the Weimar government led to leftist revolutions, but these afforded new and increased employment for the army—even contributed to Hitler's having ever had the opportunity to attend the army citizenship school and become an agent observing political groups.

The *Putsch* is depicted as the struggle of the Nazis with the "Red Front," and it meant Hitler's imprisonment, a ban on any Nazi meetings, and thirteen deaths (but glorious martyrs). Yet it afforded Hitler the time to write *Mein Kampf* which he never would have had if he and the party had remained active. This termination of the early way of the Nazis also led to rebirth—with one *Fuehrer* and one ideology in *Mein Kampf*. It is in this sense that the deaths in column IV are necessary to the rebirths in column I, and constitute not endings but metamorphoses.

Hitler's second volume is essentially an extension and repetition of themes which were *revealed* to Hitler and to us in the narrative Volume I. Volume II opens with a birth image which parallels that of Volume I, "On February 24, 1920, the first open mass meeting of our young movement took place" in the Munich *Hofbraeuhaus*. Like Volume I,

Volume II is a narrative with substantive digressions elaborating ideational growth. For example, the sixth chapter of Volume II is "the Struggle of the First Period—The Significance of Oratory." As an historical account of the actual rivalry and process of the earliest period of the Nazi party, this chapter is as undetailed as was the Volume I chapter "Years of Suffering in Vienna." Throughout *Mein Kampf* the Nazi *Weltanschauung* is depicted growing out of events, and is verified by explanatory application to events, but always the *Weltanschauung* is emphasized more than events. As narrative, Volume II begins in time before Volume I ends, summarizes its history, and carries forward into the Thousand Year Reich.

In its process of drawing ideas from events and putting ideas into events, Hitler's book can address real world questions which Germans were asking about themselves. Into what psychological, political, and intellectual climates did Hitler speak? The second persona in *Mein Kampf* is a German impoverished economically and patriotically by the World War. He lives surrounded by the opera of Wagner, the fanatical anti-Semitism of Houston Stewart Chamberlain, the nihilism of Nietzsche, the mystical and mythical histories of the Stefan George Circle, the gaudy cabaret and Marlene Dietrich. He looks out upon a Bauhaus world. He lives under a republican government created by foreigners, compelled to national elections almost annually, surrounded by hostile military powers exercising centuries-old grudges, dissolving from within under the strain of leftist and rightist revolutions while relying upon old Prussian, royalist bureaucrats. The German summoned by Hitler belongs with his heart to the German *Volk*, or wants to. Hitler removes his shame by discrediting the "lie of German war guilt;" Hitler offers him pride in the cultural tradition which *Mein Kampf* links to Goethe, Wagner, Frederick the Great, and Bismarck; Hitler tells him, "It is in your blood." To conclusively cement the identity of Germanness with Naziism, Hitler claims such as Bismarck, Fichte, Herder, and Nietzsche as his intellectual precursors.

As a myth, *Mein Kampf* addresses the questions of the Germans and repeats its deep structure into clarity. The basic contradiction which Hitler's myth mediates is the contradiction between life and death, which is associated by pairing with the contradiction between good and evil. The clearest possible explication of the structure of *Mein Kampf* is a reconstruction of the kind performed above in the chart.

CONCLUSIONS AND IMPLICATIONS

The text of *Mein Kampf* is observably disordered, and from its disorder can come an explanation which contributes to our understanding of the workings of the structure which formerly appeared to be an aesthetic defect. *Mein Kampf* achieves meaning not only in telling a story but also in deliberately repeating mythic structures within the encyclopaedic form. In columns I and II harmony is established with a chord including Hitler, Naziism, Aryan purity, Germany, strength, health, and life. The Nazi party and its leader stand for increase and good—the good of the people. The narrative nature of *Mein Kampf* makes dissociating Hitler from Naziism or Naziism from Germany's good impossible, and the gods are invoked as sanctions of this sacred ideology. The opposite of this chord is the harmony between the Jew, democracy, Marxism, Social Democracy, Expressionism, uncertainty, decadence, and death. Columns III and IV have Jew-Marxism stand for decrease in German culture and, therefore, the German people. The Jew cannot be dissociated from Marxist internationalism, which is his invention just as culture is the Aryan's invention. It is easy to settle for suggesting that the Jew was a convenient, tangible enemy or target for the Nazis. But this cannot be all, for the distinguishing thing about the Jew which constitutes a threat to the German *Volk* is metaphysical: namely, the ideology of international Marxism. If the Jew were such a physical target, Hitler would not devote pages of his book to warning against the mistaken belief that Jews are only adherents to a different religion when in fact they are a different race. *Mein Kampf,* an encyclopaedic myth, repeats these meanings into clarity, thus illustrating the contradiction it resolves.

Hitler's ideology does mediate the contradiction it poses. At a certain stage in dialectical progress we may identify the contradiction as between nationalism, represented by Aryan, culture, strength, etc., and socialism, represented by Jew, anti-culture internationalism, the Social Democratic Party, etc. Hitler's solution is National Socialism, in which the State consciously adopts a welfare position

toward its *Volk,* so that the good of each is served by the good of the other—a stronger nation bettering the *Volk,* which, when stronger, strengthens the nation, and so on.

Although this structural interpretation explains how *Mein Kampf* has meaning as an assertive discourse, the book also reveals other acknowledged characteristics of myth. It is set in the past in its narrative origins but extends into the future and explains both, like a model. It is the story of a hero superior in kind to us who nonetheless is a real person acting in a real social setting, not a fictional universe. The gods are present in *Mein Kampf,* although they are not personative gods, and they provide revelations, assistance, and direction to Hitler. He in turn relates to the audience of his myth as a divinely inspired prophet or oracle with answers to disturbing questions and solutions to difficult problems. These features contribute to the rhetorical dimensions of all myths from all cultures. (pp. 1-13)

> *Michael McGuire, "Mythic Rhetoric in 'Mein Kampf': A Structuralist Critique," in* The Quarterly Journal of Speech, *Vol. LXIII, No. 1, February, 1977, pp. 1-13.*

Hans Staudinger   (essay date 1981)

[*In the following excerpt from his book* The Inner Nazi: A Critical Analysis of "Mein Kampf," *Staudinger examines Hitler's racism.*]

According to Hitler the new land (lebensraum) [that he sought to overtake] would help to bring about a racially purified, healthy German people united by sound herd instinct. These basic conditions would guarantee German hegemony in Europe and, above all, enable her to follow the call to fulfill her "mission" in the world. Hitler's aspirations were far from being confined to Europe; he meant to achieve German world domination. Such a world mastery by one nation, he argued, would bring peace to this earth. Yet world conquest and world peace were not, for Hitler, ends in themselves. They were means by which to usher in a new epoch of Aryan culture. For the Germans to become masters of the globe and to give a new culture to this earth—these, indeed, were the real war aims of Hitler. These positive war aims fascinated and inspired German soldier-idealists. Many have discussed Hitler's intentions with regard to the new order in Europe; few realize that this "order" was actually the beginning of a worldwide revolution against the prevailing political and cultural world structure.

In the following discussion I use the terms *nation* and *people* interchangeably since, in the English translation of *Mein Kampf* from which I quote, the English equivalent of *Volk* has been rendered indiscriminately by *nation* and *people; Volkstum* (actually folkdom) and *Volkskörper* (folkish body) have been translated, respectively, as *nationality* and *national body.* In observing this usage of the translation we were aware that we have done away with the distinction, fairly consistently maintained in the original *Mein Kampf,* between *Volk* (people) and *Nation* (nation). In referring to prenational periods Hitler dealt only with the characteristics and the functional relationship of

---

Literary depictions of Hitler:

With respect to Hitler, there has been a poverty and a tyranny of images right from the start. On the popular level, where hyperbole was intended to direct both perception and sentiment, the Führer was exalted as a new Nordic god sent to Germany to lead the country to prosperity and power. The elaborately staged public rallies, the visual blowups of Nazi poster art and propaganda films, the quasi-religious political sermons all projected Hitler as a figure of grandly ceremonious and more than heroic proportions, a new German messiah.

There were, of course, those who were not taken in by these swollen images. Brecht, for instance, preferred to see the Nazi leader in plainer terms and referred to him in his poetry as *der Anstreicher* ("the housepainter"). Hitler's aggressive side is glimpsed in Shaw's *Geneva,* a minor play of 1938 which developed a "Mr. Battler," the pugnacity of the man indicated but also undercut by the touch of conventional stage comedy. Auden sought an image to explain the compelling hold Hitler had over the millions and, in a famous poem, projected him as "a psychopathic god," a phrase later adopted by one of Hitler's biographers. Among the least compromised of his countrymen, Thomas Mann seems not to have known precisely how to understand so vexing and contradictory a figure, at times dismissing him as "our political medicine man" but also acknowledging him as a "genius," albeit genius in a phase of gross decadence and distortion. Mann also denounced him as a "pitiable idler" and "fifth-rank visionary," a "sly sadist and plotter of revenge," but was moved to claim him as "an artist, a brother."

Alvin Rosenfeld, in his Imagining Hitler, *1985.*

---

race, *Volk,* and state; but for modern history he distinguished between nation, *Volk,* race, and state in the following manner: In speaking of a *Volk* living at the present time he thought less of its common political ties, and more of its racial qualities, its common culture and common spirit or soul (*Volksseele*). He gave the concept *Volk* a "folkish" (*i.e.,* romantic) connotation. For Hitler it was the *Volk*—and the *Volk* only—that can possess the herd instinct, that has tradition, language, art, music, "folkways," and mores in common.

In contrast, the modern *nation* meant for Hitler a unit by virtue of a common political history. The nation was expressive of the actual or potential political power of this unit. National consciousness, based on a common political past and common aspirations in the political field, constituted a real nation. The value, the vitality and the strength of the people (*Volk*), Hitler argued, was determined by its racial composition. A nation made up of different peoples, composed of different racial elements, and therefore holding a number of different concepts of life could not endure, unless the core people—the potential master race—with its capacity for organization and its creative gift in the sphere of culture and politics gained the upper hand over the other peoples constituting the nation.

Although race was fundamentally a biological concept for Hitler, it contained, at the same time, an overwhelming historico-metaphysical factor of determinism; the innate qualities of a race determined its political and cultural fate (thus only Aryans were capable of creating culture in this world).

The state arises from conquest. It is a political, protective, and administrative instrument. For Hitler the organic interrelationship between race, *Volk,* nation, and state meant that if a people were racially uniform, it would possess the herd instinct, which, in the long run, would make for a united nation and national (*i.e.,* power) consciousness. The state was the instrument by which to preserve the race, to foster innate capacities of the people, and to increase the power of the nation. "One day there can exist," Hitler wrote [in **Mein Kampf**], "a State which represents . . . a folkish organism: *A Germanic State of the German Nation.*"

Race for Hitler, was the alpha and omega of nature and history: "All great questions of the times," he declared, "are questions of the moment, and they represent only consequences of certain causes. Only one of them is of causal importance, that is the question of the racial preservation of the nationality [*Volkstum*]. In the blood alone there rests the strength as well as the weakness of man." Strength and weakness of nations depended upon their racial composition. The purer a nation in its racial make-up, the stronger it would be. National solidarity was a quality inherent in every nation that retained its original racial purity intact. Such a purebred nation possessed as a natural endowment what Hitler called the herd instinct. He wrote, "sure herd instinct . . . guards the nation [*Nation*] against ruin especially in dangerous moments, as with such peoples all the minor internal differences usually disappear immediately and the common enemy is confronted by the closed front of a uniform herd."

What Hitler called herd instinct must not be confounded with race instinct. The herd instinct of a people described a psychological attitude that could be developed only in the case of a complete racial uniformity (accomplished by the purity of the original race or by a thoroughly mixed and, thus, uniform stock) of all the members of a group. Herd instinct was the psychological attitude characteristic of a homogeneous group, which guaranteed its unity. Race instinct was an instinct inherent in the individual members of a race. By virtue of it the individual was able to sense and to guard against foreign blood. According to Hitler a pure race possessed undiluted herd instinct from which it derived its cohesion and power. But such a race was always threatened with contamination since the individual might be forgetful of his race instinct. If there was race defilement, the racial group would lose its homogeneity and therewith its herd instinct. Disunity and inner conflict would accompany this loss. In order to prevent the loss of racial integrity by the individual, so that the purity of the race would not be endangered, Hitler asked for strong laws against actual or attempted race defilement.

Racial uniformity, for Hitler, was obviously indispensable for the unity of a nation. Yet he recognized in history that very often uniformity of race is not a quality possessed by purebred nations alone. It was equally shared by peoples originally composed of different racial stocks but fused together by intermarriage into a new and homogeneous race. Such a uniform mixture, a product of a final blending over a long series of generations, also engendered that "sure herd instinct which is rooted in the unity of the blood."

Nonetheless, such a crossbred nation, he believed, was at a fateful disadvantage in comparison with a pure race. It paid a terrible price for the uniformity of blood and the herd instinct which it did not possess originally, but had acquired by intense hybridization. Hitler argued that the crossbred progeny was invariably inferior to the parent stock. Hence any hybrid race was doomed to cultural inferiority. Hitler referred specifically to Austria. He discussed the Germanization policy of Joseph II, Emperor of Austria in the Age of Enlightenment. Joseph II made the abortive attempt to impose the German language on his subjects, which included Czechs, Poles, and Croats, to consolidate his empire. Herein, Hitler believed, lay the error of Joseph's policy. Hitler wrote, "Its success would probably have been the conservation of the Austrian State, but also the lowering of the racial level of the German nation [*Nation*] brought about by a linguistic community. In the course of the centuries a certain herd instinct would certainly have crystallized itself, but the herd itself would have become inferior. Perhaps a State people would have been born, but a culture people would have lost."

Hitler argued that the lowering of the cultural and spiritual standard was not the only punishment meted out by nature for the crime of hybridization. A nation made up of hybrids was also bound to succumb in the struggle for existence against a nation of pure race. Suppose, he suggested, that "in the course of thousands of years" there would be formed

> a new mixture in which the original individual elements, in consequence of a thousandfold

crossing, are completely mixed and no longer recognizable. Thus a new nationality [*Volkstum*] with a certain herd-like resistibility would have been formed, but compared with the highest race which helped in forming the first cross-breed, it would be considerably reduced in its spiritual and cultural importance. But also, in this case, the product of the crossing would succumb in the mutual struggle for life, as long as there exists a higher race, that remained unmixed, as opponent. Any herd-like inner completeness of this new national body [*Volkskörper*], formed in the course of a thousand years, would nevertheless, in consequence of the general lowering of the race standard and the diminishing of mental elasticity and creative ability, conditioned by it, not suffice for overcoming victoriously the struggle with an equally uniform but spiritually and culturally superior race.

Thus, according to Hitler, homogeneity of racial elements in the same nation made for national strength, heterogeneity of racial elements made for national weakness. The classical example of a heterogeneous nation was Germany. Originally a nation of pureblooded Germanic-Nordic stock, Germany absorbed many non-Germanic elements into its ethnic body. The German nation was no longer of pureblooded Germanic-Nordic race. Other race elements: "Easterners," "Dinarics," "Westerners," had become parts of the German nation. But these different racial components had never been thrown into the melting pot of a new race: "Unfortunately," wrote Hitler, "our German nationality [*Volkstum*] is no longer based on a racially uniform nucleus," but "the process of the blending of the various primal constituents has not yet progressed so far as to permit speaking of a newly formed race. . . . It is not a new race that results from the fusion, but the racial stocks remain side by side. . . . The racial elements are situated differently, not only territorially but also in individual cases within the same territory. At the side of Nordic people there stand Easterners, at the side of Easterners Dinarics, at the side of both stand Westerners, and in between stand mixtures."

Throughout its history, asserted Hitler, waves of inferior races swept Germany, a "blood-poisoning which affected our national body [*Volkskörper*], especially since the Thirty Years' War." All that "led not only to a decomposition of our blood but also of our soul." Different races lived side by side on German soil tearing it apart and causing it to lose the unity of its national will. Germany fell prey to a superindividualism which found its historical expression in extreme particularism, *i.e.,* the continued existence of independent principalities rather than one united nation.

Hitler considered Germany's lack of racial homogeneity the curse of the past because, in his words, "this side by side placement of our basic racial elements which remained unblended" deprived the German people of its herd instinct, of its unified national will. Hitler believed that had Germany possessed this herd instinct, the old Imperial German Reich would have achieved world domination and would have brought peace unto the world—a

peace under the wings of the German eagle. "If, in its historical development," he declared,

> the German people [*Volk*] had possessed this group unity as it was enjoyed by other peoples, then the German Reich would today be the mistress of this globe. World history would have taken a different course, and no one would be able to decide if in this way there would not have arrived what today so many blinded pacifists hope to beg for by moaning and crying: *A peace, supported not by the palm branches of tearful pacifist professional female mourners, but founded by the victorious sword of a people of overlords* [*Herrenvolk*] *which puts the world into the service of a higher culture.* The fact of the non-existence of a nationality [*Volkstum*] uniform in its blood. . . . has bereft the German people [*Volk*] of its right of mastery.

However, Hitler suggested, the fact that the racial strains remained unblended, so detrimental in the past, held the great promise of the future. "That which has brought us misfortune in the past and in the present," he said,

> can be our blessing in the future. For no matter how detrimental it was on the one hand that a complete mixture of our original racial constituents did not take place, and that by this the formation of a uniform national body [*Volkskörper*] was prevented, it was just as fortunate on the other hand, that by this at least a part of our blood was preserved in purity and escaped racial decline.

> With the complete blending of our original racial elements a closed national body [*Volkskörper*] would certainly have ensued, but, as every racial cross-breeding proves, it would be endowed with an ability to create a culture inferior to that which the highest of the primal components possessed originally. This is the blessing of the failure of complete mixture: that even today we still have in our German national body great stocks of Nordic-Germanic people who remain unblended, in whom we may see the most valuable treasure for our future.

In this manner Hitler argued that the political and cultural mastery in the world which Germany forfeited in the past because of her lack of racial uniformity, was actually no "loss." Germany, as a crossbred nation, might have conquered the world, but she would not have been able to fulfill her cultural mission in history. The great opportunity to become the "noblest" race would have been lost forever. Fortunately, it seemed to Hitler, great reserves of that "noble" stock still existed in Germany, sufficient to carry through a program of biological renaissance of the nation. By newly promoting the Germanic-Nordic stock, Germany could and would regain her original purity and avail herself of the historic certainty to become the "Mistress of the globe." The historic mission that Hitler assigned to the Third Reich was, therefore, not confined to unification of all people of German race into one state and the extension of the German racial frontiers into a new lebensraum, but as well it presupposed the purification of the race. With all these conditions fulfilled, Hitler believed the German Reich could and would rise to world rulership. He wrote:

> Today we know that a complete intermixture of the stocks of our natinal body [*Volkskörper*], in consequence of the unity resulting from this, would perhaps have given us external power, but that the highest goal of mankind would not have been attained, as the only bearer whom Fate has visibly elected for this completion would have perished in the general racial mixture of a uniform people [*einheitavolk*].

> But today, from the viewpoint of our knowledge now gained, we have to examine and to evaluate what, without our contribution, has been prevented by a kind destiny.

> He who speaks of a mission [continued Hitler] of the German people [*Volk*] of this earth must know that it can exist only in the formation of a State which sees its highest task in the preservation and the promotion of the most noble elements of our nationality [*Volkstum*] which have remained, even of the entire mankind, unharmed. . . .

> The German Reich, as a State, should include all Germans, not only with the task of collecting from the people the most valuable stocks of racially primal elements and preserving them, but also to lead them, gradually and safely, to a dominating position.

> By this the State for the first time receives an inner higher goal. In the face of the ridiculous slogan of a safeguarding of peace and order for the peaceful possibility of mutual cheating, the task of the preservation and the promotion of a highest humanity which has been presented to this world by the benevolence of the Almighty, appears a truly high mission.

> Out of a dead mechanism [wrote Hitler] that claims to exist only for its own sake, a living organism has now to be formed with the exclusive purpose of serving a higher idea.

This task had a double aspect: first, the negative measure of eliminating the dysgenic elements in the nation: "He who is not physically and mentally healthy and worthy must not perpetuate his misery in the body of his child;" second, and positively: "the conscious methodical promotion of the fertility of the most healthy bearers of the nationality [*Volkstum*]."

Hitler declared that only this "racially most valuable nucleus of the people"—healthy stock and Nordic stock Hitler obviously assumed to be more or less identical—should be entrusted with the settlement of lebensraum. He wrote:

> The way towards this is above all that the State does not leave the settlement of newly won land to chance, but that it subjects it to special norms. Specially formed race commissions have to issue a certificate of settlement to the individual; but this is dependent on a certain racial purity, to be established. Thus frontier colonies can gradually be formed whose inhabitants are exclusively bearers of highest racial purity and with this of

highest racial efficiency. They are a precious national (*national*) treasure of the entire people [*Volksganzes*]; their growth must fill every national member [*Volksgenosse*] with pride and joyful confidence, as in him there lies the germ for the ultimate great future development of their own people [*Volk*], even of mankind.

Hitler posed the goal of Germany's cultural leadership against what he considered "the ridiculous slogan of the safeguarding of peace and order for the peaceful possibility of mutual cheating," which had been the ideal of the Wilhelmian empire with its talk of peaceful economic conquest. Not pacifism, but continual attack was the watchword for the future:

> Therefore, in the place of a fundamentally stabilized condition appears a period of fighting. But as everywhere and with everything in this world, here too the phrase "who rests—rusts" will keep its validity, and further, that victory is forever contained only in attack. The greater thereby the fighting goal that we have in mind, and the less the understanding of the great masses may be at the moment, the most enormous are, according to world history, the successes—and the importance of these successes if the goal is rightly understood and the fight is carried out with unshakable persistency.

In this great future of the German people, predicted Hitler, the "*superindividualism*" which taken all in all "has deprived us of world domination," will no longer be an obstacle. Such a fighting Germandom, he maintained, of the racial morrow will have the "sure herd instinct" without being subject to the danger of cultural decadence which inevitably would have followed the hybridization of the "Nordic-German" in the general mixture of a uniform people.

Obviously, for Hitler, the final stage of racial "purification" could be achieved only over a period of generations. It would be wrong, however, to draw the conclusion that Hitler, while writing **Mein Kampf,** inferentially ruled out the possibility of German world domination during his lifetime. Hitler found readily at hand an able agency of unification in the Prussian state and above all in the Prussian army, which in the German past had proven capable of artificially overcoming, at least partially, the disintegrating tendencies rooted in Germany's racial heterogeneity. Hitler considered "the organization by the Hohenzollerns of the Brandenburg-Prussian state as a model and crystallization nucleus of a new Reich," one of the great achievements of German history. The creation of the Prussian state precipitated the cultivation

> of a special State conception, as well as of the bringing into organizational form and adaptation to the modern world of the German army's impulse of self-preservation and self-defense. The transformation of the individual defense idea into national defense duty [*Wehrpflicht der Nation*] sprung from this State structure and its new State conception. The importance of this development cannot in the least be exaggerated. Precisely the German nation [*Volk*], superindividualistically disintegrated because of its

jumbled blood, regained from discipline through the Prussian army organism, at least in part, the capacity for organization which it had long missed. What is aboriginally present in other nations [*Völker*] as a result of their herd instinct, we artificially reacquired for our national community [*Volksgemeinschaft*], at least partially, through the process of military training.

In the existence of Prussia, Hitler found the clue to the shortcut which otherwise would have taken generations to fulfill: the state of the Hohenzollerns, with all its shortcomings, merely by means of the Prussian army, succeeded in restoring to the German people, extrinsically, the minimum of unity. Why then should not the "Third Reich," by carrying through the organizational integration of the different German states (Bavaria, Prussia, Brunswick, etc.) in one reich and by using the Prussian military organism with its iron discipline and its leadership principle, succeed in imposing a uniformity of will upon the nation strong enough to overcome the centrifugal forces of the blood? By virtue of such an "emergency" solution, world domination could yet be placed on the agenda of the present instead of a far-distant future.

Hitler's play upon the time factor was one of the most interesting psychological methods for making his thousand-year reich appear as a vision of transcendant value. At the same moment he gave the living Germans the assured hope of actually coming into this reich. He affirmed this hope by glorifying and reawakening the spirit of Potsdam with all its trimmings, from goose step to the glory of war.

Hitler believed that once a fighting Germany, endowed with a healthy and increasingly unified racial stock and led by a state which was the "sovereign incorporation of a nation's [*Volkstum*] instinct of preserving itself on this earth" had gained world domination, then—and only then—could world order be based on pacifism.

> He who actually desires [he wrote] with all his heart, the victory of the pacifistic idea in this world would have to stand up, with all available means, for the conquest of the world by the Germans. . . . Therefore, whether one wanted to or not, if one had the serious will, one would have to decide to wage war in order to arrive at pacifism. . . .
>
> . . . Indeed, the pacifist-humane idea is perhaps quite good whenever the man of the highest standard has previously conquered and subjected the world to a degree that makes him the only master of this globe. Thus the idea is more and more deprived of the possibility of a harmful effect in the measure in which its practical application becomes rare and finally impossible. Therefore, first fight, and then one may see what can be done.

Hitler rejected every idea of cooperation of equal nations through federation in Europe or in the world. He rejected every idea of community or a league of nations. World hegemony and domination by one superior nation was the one possible solution of international integration whereby the nations of kindred race (Aryans) could occupy the preferential positions. He assigned racial kinship the task of ruling over inferior races.

It is necessary to deal here with one more question in order to make clear the relationship of Germany to the Aryan world in Hitler's system. We know of Hitler's eager concern for the future of the Aryan race. What to him is the final court of appeals: the interests of the Aryan or the interests of Germany? The answer may be summed up as follows: Germany's Herculean labors were to be expended first and above all in the struggle for victory, power, position of Germany. But Germany's final triumph resulting in world rulership would at the same time assure the final victory of the Aryan race. The Aryan peoples would live peacefully together protected by the sword of Germany. Germany would be the arbiter of the world.

But in the era that preceded the establishment of the Aryan millennium national clefts necessarily remained within the Aryan world. Fratricidal wars might become inevitable, for in Hitler's words "kinship relations among nations cannot at all eliminate rivalries." It is with reference to this period of transition to world domination that Hitler warned the German youth not to confuse dream ideas of Aryan world brotherhood with the interests of Germany, not to become the knights-errant for other nations, be they Aryan or non-Aryan. "The folkish movement," he asserted, "must not be the attorney for other nations, but the vanguard fighter of its own. Otherwise it is superfluous, and especially has no right to beef about the past. For then it is acting like the past. Much as the old German policy was improperly determined from dynastic viewpoints, equally little must the future be governed by dreamy folkish cosmopolitanism. Above all, however, we are not protective police for the well-known 'poor little nations,' but soldiers of our own nation." Only in the eschatological promise of an Aryan millennium under Germany's aegis, predicted Hitler, would that conflict between the narrower racial group, called the German nation, and the wider racial group of the Aryans find its solution. Not until then would there be world peace and a new era of world culture.

Hitler magnanimously took pains to identify the interest of a world-conquering Germany with the interests of mankind. He asked, what has the world to gain from "the victorious sword of a people of overlords?" Is it only the promised relief from the scourge of the war, the blessings of a world peace? No, Hitler claimed to bear gifts more "precious" than the "Pax Germanica," namely an unprecedented cultural development of the world. This new epoch of world culture would be again, in its essential character, an Aryan culture. Since time immemorial, Hitler declared, it was the Aryan who was the creator of all culture. "What we see before us of human culture today, the results of art, science, and techniques, is almost exclusively the creative product of the Aryan." For, Hitler decreed, culture by definition is Aryan culture. The Aryan "is the Prometheus of mankind, out of whose bright forehead springs the divine spark of genius at all times, forever rekindling that fire which in the form of knowledge lightened up the night of silent secrets and thus made man climb the path towards the position of master of the other beings on this earth. Exclude him—and deep darkness will again fall upon the earth, perhaps even, after a few thousand years, human culture would perish and the world would turn into a desert."

Hitler assigned to the Germans, the "people of overlords," not only the political, but also the cultural leadership among the Aryan peoples. Racially reborn, the German people would represent the noblest branch of the noblest race, the Aryans. The Nordic-Germanic stock was to be the rock upon which Hitler hoped to build the future Germany, "the germ for the ultimate great future development of their own people, even of mankind." In this sense Hitler conceived the mission of Germany to lead the world on the path to the Aryan culture of tomorrow.

According to Hitler it fell upon the Germans to put "the world into the service of a higher culture." This formulation obviously implied the idea of an enslavement of inferior races in the service of the Aryan culture. Such an inference was warranted not only by Hitler's general attitude toward the interior races; it rested also on his description of the origins of Aryan cultures: it was only by the slave labor of the inferior races that the early Aryan cultures were sustained.

> It is no accident [he wrote] that the first cultures originated in those places where the Aryan, by meeting lower peoples, subdued them and made them subject to his will. They, then, were the first technical instrument in the service of a growing culture.

> With this the way that the Aryan had to go was clearly lined out. As a conqueror he subjected the lower peoples and then he regulated their practical ability according to his command and his will and for his aims. But while he thus led them towards a useful, though hard activity, he not only spared the lives of the subjected, but perhaps even gave them a fate which was better than that of their former so-called 'freedom.' As long as he kept up ruthlessly the master's standpoint, he not only really remained 'master' but also the preserver and propagator of the culture. For the latter was based exclusively on his abilities, and with it, on his preservation in purity.

Hitler believed that as long as the Aryan kept his conscious racial superiority and asserted his mastery, culture flowered, even to the benefit of the slaves. But once the Aryan master race gave itself over to the delusion of equality and lowered the racial barriers, its doom was sealed. The Aryan blood fused with that of the inferior slave races.

> But [argued Hitler] as soon as the subjected peoples themselves began to rise . . . the sharp separating wall between master and slave fell. The Aryan gave up the purity of his blood and therefore he also lost his place in the Paradise which he had created for himself. He became submerged in the race-mixture, he gradually lost his cultural ability more and more, till at last not only mentally but also physically he began to resemble more the subjected and aborigines than his ancestors. For some time he may still live on

the existing cultural goods, but then petrifaction sets in, and finally oblivion.

Hitler in formulating a general law of history that culture is Aryan culture, warned Aryan mankind. "Historical experience offers countless proofs of this," he wrote. "It shows with terrible clarity that with any mixing of the blood of the Aryan with lower races the result was the end of the culture-bearer." "For the people do not perish by lost wars, but by the loss of that force of resistance which is contained only in the pure blood. All that is not race in this world is trash. All world historical events, however, are only the expression of the races' instinct of self-preservation in its good or in its evil meaning."

. . . . .

Hitler believed that new land and purification of the race would open the road for the Germans to become the leading nation in the world. But in his mind there existed an antagonist throughout the world—the Jew. Jews, Hitler believed, had strangled the nations of the world and were preparing to make true their age-old dream of world domination.

"The Jewish State," he wrote, "was never spacially limited in itself." The Jewish people have always formed "a State within other States" and made this state "sail under the flag of religion." The Jew is the great "master of lying," Hitler continued, the pure egoist who lives as a parasite in and off the body of other peoples and states. His chief means to enter the national bodies are racial and civil equality, religious tolerance, free press, and above all, democracy. To destroy national unity by class struggle a Jew invented Marxism. Yet to reign internationally, economic and financial power has to yoke in the nations by international treaties and pacifist institutions—all this in order to win real world power by spreading Jewish-Russian bolshevism throughout the world. But the Jew can never hold world power because of his innate destructive nature. He destroys everything in his way and is bound to destroy himself eventually.

Hitler's fantasy of a growing Jewish menace transformed the Jew into a metaphysical abstract, "the personification of the Devil." He described the Jew as the main danger to the Aryan world—to the purity of the Aryan races. The Jew became the prime antagonist of Aryanism. The Aryan was the creator; the Jew was the destroyer. For, declared Hitler, "the Jew possesses no culture-creating energy whatsoever, as the idealism, without which there can never exist a genuine development of man towards a higher level, does not and never did exist in him. His intellect, therefore, will never have a constructive effect, but only a destructive one . . . Any progress of mankind takes place not through him but in spite of him."

Hitler insisted that the possession of enormous economic power as well as the age-old consciousness of being the selected people impelled the Jew. He wrote, "the higher he climbs, the more alluringly rises out of the veil of the past his old goal, once promised to him, and with feverish greed he watches in his brightest heads the dream of world domination step into tangible proximity." In this manner, Hitler imagined that the Jew continuously schemed for world domination. After the Napoleonic War princes and their mistresses tried to divide the world among themselves. Today, argued Hitler, it is the Jew who bids for world domination. "Moreover, times have changed since the Congress of Vienna: princes and the mistresses of princes do not barter and haggle about frontiers, but the implacable world Jew is struggling for dominion over the nations. No nation can dislodge this fist from its throat except by the sword."

The political significance of Judaism in modern times, however, suggested Hitler, began with the emergence of the Jew from the ghetto. First, he tried to remove his political disability. So far he had been deprived of his civil rights and citizenship on religious grounds. The maintenance and further expansion of his economic empire alone made it imperative that he be treated as equal in society, Hitler asserted. "His financial rule of the entire business life has already progressed so far that, without the possession of all the 'civil' rights, he is no longer able to support the whole enormous building, in any case no further increase of his influence can take place." As an entering wedge the Jew cunningly used the Freemasons. "For the strengthening of his political position," wrote Hitler, "he tries to pull down the racial and civil barriers which at first still restrain him at every step. For this purpose he fights with all his innate thoroughness for religious tolerance—and in the completely deteriorated Freemasonry he has an excellent instrument for fighting out and also for 'putting over' his aims. By the strings of Freemasonry the circles of the government and the higher layers of the political and economic *bourgeoisie* fall into his nets without their even guessing this."

Accordingly, the Masonic orders were employed by the Jew to inveigle the upper classes. To beguile the common man the Jew used, Hitler declared, another, coarser instrument, the press. For

> one cannot catch glovemakers and linen weavers in the fine net of Freemasonry; for this one has to apply more coarse but not less thorough means. Thus to Freemasonry the second weapon in the service of Jewry is added; the *press*. He puts himself into possession of it with all toughness, but also with infinite versatility. With it he begins slowly to grasp and to ensnare, to lead and to push the entire public life, because now he is in a position to produce and to conduct the power which under the name of 'public opinion' is better known today than it was a few decades ago.

While in his press, Hitler continued, the Jew preached all those ideals that destroyed race consciousness and national values, the Jew himself anxiously guarded the purity and solidarity of his own race. Wrote Hitler, "While he seems to overflow with 'enlightenment,' 'progress,' 'freedom,' 'humanity,' etc., he exercises the strictest seclusion of his race. Although he sometimes hangs his women onto the coattails of influential Christians, yet he always keeps his male line pure in principle. He poisons the blood of the others, but he guards his own. The Jew does not marry a Christian woman, but always the Christian a Jewess. Yet the bastards take to the Jewish side."

Meanwhile the Jew exercised his newly won influence to prepare the way for democracy. Democracy, Hitler theorized, was based on the principle of majority, and subversive to national strength. The weaker the national will, the easier the way to Jewish world domination. The victory of democracy was therefore, the goal of the Jew in this particular phase of his march to world rule. "His final goal in this state [phase], however," declared Hitler, "is the victory of 'democracy,' or as he understands it: because it eliminates the personality—and in its place it puts the majority of stupidity, incapacity, and last, but not least, cowardice."

While still working for the promotion of democracy, Hitler argued, the Jew was already busy preparing for bolshevism, the next and last stop on his march towards the hoped-for world domination. The Jew became the theorist and organizer of the labor movement. As the era of industrial revolution opened, the Jew cleverly sensed the great political energies which lay dormant in the dissatisfied working class, and slyly he seized the unlimited opportunity for the future that was offered here. The Jew wormed his way into the confidence of the workers, and appealing to their Aryan sense for social justice, he aroused the "have-nots" against the "haves" by way of the Marxian doctrine:

> He approaches the worker [Hitler asserted] pretends to have pity on him, or even to feel indignation at his lot of misery and poverty, in order more easily to gain his confidence in this way. He takes pains to study all the actual (or imagined) hardships of his life—and to awaken a longing for changing such an existence. In an infinitely sly manner, he stimulates the need for social justice, dormant in every Aryan, to the point of hatred against those who have been better favored by fortune, and thus he gives the fight for the abolition of social evils a definite stamp of a view of life. He founds the Marxist theory.

Hitler insisted that the Jew repeated the same trick he had used before when he capitalized on the class struggle between the bourgeoisie and the feudal class. But now the stake he gambled for was infinitely greater. Before his goal was merely full civil rights, now it is rulership. The new proletarian class would serve as his vehicle.

> As soon as, out of the general economic transformation, the new class develops [Hitler predicted], the Jew sees also before him, clearly and distinctly, the new pacemaker of his own further advancement. First he uses the bourgeoisie as the battle ram against the feudal world, then the worker against the bourgeois world. Just as at one time he knew how to gain by sneaking the civil rights for himself in the shadow of the bourgeoisie, thus he hopes now that in the worker's fight for his existence, he will find the way towards a leadership of his own.

Hitler imagined the Jews to be playing a diabolically clever game. With the one hand the Jew organized the capitalist exploitation of the workers; with the other hand he organized the exploited against the capitalists. He led the workers against himself. But this "against himself" is, of course, only metaphorically expressed, for [Hitler claimed] the great master of lies knows how to make himself appear always as the "pure" one and to charge the guilt to the others. As he has the impudence to lead the masses in such a manner, the latter does not even think at all that this could mean the most villainous betrayal of all times. . . .

. . . From now on the worker only has the task of working for the future of the Jewish people. He is unconsciously put into the service of that power which he believes he is fighting. By making him apparently storm against capital, one can most easily make him fight just for the latter. Thus one always cries out against international capital, whereas in reality one means the national economy. The latter is to be demolished so that on its field of carnage the triumph of the international stock exchange may be celebrated.

Hitler insisted that the stronghold from which to rule the world was international finance. He argued that stock exchange Jewry entered the single states and tried to internationalize them in order to dominate the economic and national life. "Jewry," Hitler declared,

will always fight within particular national bodies with those weapons which seem most efficient and promise the greatest success in the light of the well-known mentalities of these nations. Consequently, in our body national, so jumbled from the viewpoint of blood, it uses in its struggle for power the pacifist ideological conceptions sprung from these more or less "cosmopolitan," in short, international, tendencies; in France it employs the well-known and well-understood chauvinism; in England, economic and imperial conceptions; in short, it always utilizes the most essential characteristics exhibited by a people's mentality. Only when by such means it has added a certain luxuriant influence to its wealth of economic and political power does it slough off the hobbles of this transferred weapon and now equally advance the true inner intent of its will and struggle. It begins ever more quickly to destroy, until it thus transforms one State after another into a mass of ruins, on the basis of which shall later be established the sovereignty of the eternal Jewish empire.

Hitler believed that the greatest progress the Jews made toward world cultural decay and at the same time toward world domination occurred close toward the end of the first World War. He wrote, "In Russian bolshevism we must see Jewry's twentieth-century effort to take world dominion unto itself, just as it sought to strive towards the same goal in other periods by other, if inwardly related doings." Jewish bolshevism, by uprooting the Germanic elements, destroyed the Russian empire, which owed its existence not to the "inferior" Russian race, but to the "Germanic nucleus of its superior strata of leaders." "In the surrender of Russia to bolshevism," declared Hitler, "the Russian people was robbed of that intelligentsia which theretofore produced and guaranteed its State stability. For the organization of a Russian State structure was not the result of Russian Slavdom's State-political capacity, but rather a wonderful example of the State-building activity of the German element in an inferior race."

According to Hitler the Jew took the place of the Germanic leadership, but since the strength of the Jewish race lay only in destruction, it would be unable to maintain its rule over Russia. Soviet Russia was, therefore, bound to collapse, although not from inner revolts alone.

Impossible as it is for the Russians alone to shake off the yoke of the Jews through their own strength [asserted Hitler], it is equally impossible in the long run for the Jews to maintain the mighty empire. Jewry itself is not an organizing element, but a ferment of decomposition. The Persian Empire, once so powerful, is now ripe for collapse; and the end of Jewish dominion in Russia will also be the end of the Russian State itself. We have been chosen by Fate to be the witnesses of a catastrophe which will be the most powerful substantiation of the correctness of the folkish theory of race.

Hitler predicted that the next great goal of Jewish bolshevism was Germany. He wrote, "Germany is today the next great battle aim of bolshevism." "The internationalization of our German economy, i.e., the passing of German labor power into the possession of Jewish world finance, can be carried not only in a politically bolshevised State." "The Jewish train of thought is, moreover, clear. The bolshevization of Germany, i.e., the extermination of the national folkish intelligentsia and the exploitation of German labor power in the yoke of world Jewish finance facilitated thereby, is thought of solely as a preliminary to a further extension of this Jewish tendency to conquer the world."

Hitler argued that thus Germany became the pivot in the world struggle between Aryanism and Judaism. But Hitler believed that Jews had to be defeated all over the world. "Thus," he wrote, "as so often in history, the mighty struggle within Germany is the great turning-point. If our people and our State fall victims to this bloodthirsty and moneythirsty Jewish tyrant over nations, then the whole world will fall into this polyp's net; if Germany frees itself from this embrace, this greatest of all dangers to the nations can be regarded as crushed for the entire world." This fight against Jewish bolshevism and international finance was for Hitler one of the great historic tasks of the Germans. Thus, the prevention of Jewish world power with all its institutions, from world finance and Freemasonry to democracy, was the real war aim of Hitler.

According to Hitler, Germany had to begin by cleansing her own body of "Jewish parasites." It is one of the elements of Hitler's foreign policy to free his allies from the Jewish influence. Hitler regarded the destruction of Jewry as one of his main war aims. On the other hand Hitler used this incipient battle against the Jews as one of the major tools in his propaganda in order to awaken and revolutionize the Germans. To Hitler "at all times, the efficiency of the truly national leader consists primarily in preventing the division of the attention of a people, and always in concentrating it in a single enemy." By telling the masses that the Jew was the driving force behind Marxism, democracy, Freemasonry, international finance capital, the League of Nations, French imperialism, and Russian bolshevism—all these enemies were brought under a common denominator. Hitler wrote:

> It is part of the genius of a great leader to make adversaries of different fields appear as always belonging to one category only, because to weak and unstable characters the knowledge that there are various enemies will lead only too easily to incipient doubts as to their own cause.
>
> As soon as the wavering masses find themselves confronting too many enemies, objectivity at once steps in, and the question is raised whether actually all the others are wrong and their own nation or their own movement alone is right.
>
> Also with this comes the first paralysis of their own strength. Therefore, a number of essentially different internal enemies must always be regarded as one in such a way that in the opinion of the mass of one's own adherents the war is being waged against one enemy alone. This strengthens the belief in one's own cause and increases one's bitterness against the attacker.

Little wonder that the Jewish question was given such broad scope in *Mein Kampf.* In the subject index of the German edition of *Mein Kampf,* the references listed under "Judaism" occupy almost a page; only the references listed under the heading of "National Socialism" occupied more space in the index.

Hitler did not bother to mention that the myth of the "chosen people" was developed in Judaism. To avoid this comparison, Hitler shunned the term "chosen people" but nonetheless utilized the concept in a distorted form.

. . . . .

Hitler had clearly indicated as his positive war aims the new German world order and as his negative war aims the destruction of the present national institutions and world relations dominated and shaped, as he saw it, by Jewish machinations. Hitler explained the conditions under which the Germans could take upon themselves this gigantic task. He had opened their eyes to the historic opportunity from the racial as well as from the geographical point of view to become the dominating nation. But his total system was still not closed and conclusive; he had to convince himself and the Germans of the righteousness of the means and the justification of the ways to fulfill these tasks—namely by ruthless war. He revealed to the Germans that the right means were predetermined by the "law of nature," *i.e.,* the right of the stronger to subdue the weaker. According to *Mein Kampf,* violence—from the concentration camps to the battlefield—was the method sanctioned by the law of nature or, as Hitler termed it, "by the law of progress of mankind."

Hitler had imagined that lebensraum would guarantee a healthy balance between industry and agriculture by settling increasing numbers of those of pure German blood. "Destiny" had left to the Germans the historical opportunity to become a pure nation, unified and strong by virtue of sound herd instinct. He believed that it was fortunate for the Germans that they had not mixed their Nordic

stock with inferior races in order to obtain, as a new, thoroughly crossbred national unity—at the cost of a lower level of blood and culture. Thus, according to Hitler, the remaining Nordic stock had the potential basis of a new, purified German nation determined to become "the noblest branch of the noblest race." Such a purified nation had to fulfill the great mission to create and fashion a new Aryan culture. He declared that an awareness of mission must exist in the heart and mind of every young German. This awareness had to be complemented by the moral call to act accordingly. Every young German should be possessed by the indomitable will to power and the stamina to pursue hard struggles for continuous conquest.

Hitler devoted much thought to determining the means to attain this. He found the answer by looking to nature. In the "law of nature" Hitler found the rationale to gain power and utilize it continuously with ruthless force. He justified this mode of life by the "aristocratic" right of the stronger to dominate the weaker. He found this first principle of nature and of history in the expression "the Eternal Will that dominates this universe to promote the victory of the better and stronger," and thereby the demand of "the submission of the worse and the weaker."

This is quite obviously a crude restatement of Darwin's survival of the fittest. In fact, Darwinian influence is prevalent in Hitler's weltanschauung. Hitler adhered to the principle of evolution: "The progress of mankind resembles the ascent on an endless ladder; one cannot arrive at the top without first having taken the lower steps." This evolution was interpreted by Hitler in a teleological fashion, as progress. He spoke of "Nature's will to breed life as a whole towards a higher level." For Hitler the transcendent terms *creator, eternal will,* and *nature* were metaphysical entities by which universe, nature, and culture are determined.

According to Hitler the better and stronger proved his worth in the crucible of the struggle for existence. "Nature"—as a teleological force—presided over this permanent selection by conflict which was intended by her as the prime organ of natural as well as social history. The struggle for existence, *i.e.,* the survival of the fittest, was the agency of all progress in nature as well as in human history. What we find here is a very crude projection from the natural into the social sphere of Darwin's evolutionary hypothesis and of the Darwinian struggle for existence. At the same time Hitler clothed the will to power with an ethical justification. For if it is asserted that the victory of the strongest is the dynamic to which the program of mankind is due, ethical sanction is bestowed on the urge to power, conquest, and domination.

The aristocratic law of nature as accepted and promulgated by the Nazis implied the preordained fundamental inequality of races and individuals. Hitler saw in it not only the "different values of the races, but also the different values of individual man." In other words, Hitler advanced the proposition that the militant selective principle operated in the struggle between race and race as well as between the individuals within each race. From that the führer principle was derived.

On the basis of the preordained inequality of races Hitler categorically asserted a hierarchy of races. Thus the Aryan, by virtue of natural endowment, was superior to the Jew, to the Negro, to the Mongoloid races, and the Nordic, again, was superior to all other Aryans. Human races were considered as species with fixed immutable characteristics. Hitler implied that nature had divided the organic world into species and willed the preservation of their identity; *i.e.,* the purity of races or species. In the animal kingdom, he asserted, every animal of a given species complies with that "brazen basic principle" of Nature. "Every animal mates only with a representative of the same species. The titmouse seeks the titmouse, the finch the finch, the stork the stork, the field mouse the field mouse, the common mouse the common mouse, the wolf the wolf, etc."

Hitler admitted exceptions to that rule, "but then Nature begins to resist this with the help of all visible means." Nature protests against such a violation of her will in two forms: either she limits or denies to the bastard offspring the procreative faculty, or "she takes away the capacity of resistance against disease or inimical attacks." Confronted, in the struggle for existence, with a representative of the higher standard, crossbred races go down in defeat. In this way nature preserves the immutability of the species.

Hitler declared that a mating between higher and lower species was a blatant violation of the "aristocratic" law of nature because, he wrote, it "contradicts Nature's will to breed life as a whole towards a higher level. . . . The stronger has to rule and he is not to amalgamate with the weaker one, that he may not sacrifice his own greatness. Only the born weakling can consider this as cruel . . . for, if this law were not dominating, all conceivable development towards a higher level, on the part of all organically living beings, would be unthinkable for man."

For Hitler any hybridization violated the aristocratic thought of nature. "The result of any crossing, in brief," he said, "is always the following: (a) Lowering of the standard of the higher race, (b) Physical and mental regression, and, with it, the beginning of a slowly but steadily progressive lingering illness. To bring about such a development means nothing less than sinning against the will of the Eternal Creator."

This law applied to all living beings from the titmouse to the Aryan; it applied to individuals and races alike. He explained, "Just as little as Nature desires a mating between weaker individuals and stronger ones, far less she desires the mixing of a higher race with a lower one, as in this case her entire work of higher breeding, which perhaps has taken hundreds of thousands of years, would tumble at one blow. Historical experience offers countless proofs of this. It shows with terrible clarity that with any mixing of the blood of the Aryan with lower races the result was the end of the culture-bearer." Therefore, "the man who misjudges and disdains the laws of race actually forfeits the happiness that seems destined to be his. He prevents the victorious march of the best race and with it also the presumption for all human progress, and in consequence he will remain in the domain of the animal's helpless misery burdened with the sensibility of man."

It becomes clear from the foregoing quotation that "the victorious march of the best race" is not taken by Hitler as a foregone conclusion. If the Aryan peoples allowed themselves to be bastardized or to be blinded by pacifism, the earth might still fall prey to lower races that have preserved their pristine fighting qualities and aggressive spirit.

> As, unfortunately only too frequently, the best nations, or, better still, the really unique cultured races, the pillars of all human progress, in their pacifistic blindness decide to renounce the acquisition of new soil in order to content themselves with "domestic" colonization, while inferior nations know full well how to secure enormous areas on this earth for themselves, this would lead to the following result:

> The culturally superior, but less ruthless, races would have to limit, in consequence of their limited soil, their increase even at a time when the culturally inferior, but more brutal and more natural, people, in consequence of their greater living areas, would be able to increase themselves without limit. In other words: the world will, therefore, some day come into the hands of a mankind that is inferior in culture but superior in energy and activity.

For Hitler there was therefore no comfortable and safe way charted by Providence for the Aryan. If the Aryan lost his urge for self-preservation, he would be doomed. For, Hitler claimed that "in the end, only the urge for self-preservation will eternally succeed. Under its pressure so-called 'humanity,' as the expression of a mixture of stupidity, cowardice and an imaginary superior intelligence, will melt like snow under the March sun. Mankind has grown strong in eternal struggles and it will only perish through eternal peace." Hitler despised pacifists because they were at variance with the design of the "Creator" to set up a pacific world with the palm. A peaceful world, according to Hitler, was only possible as long as a superior race could preserve its strength to subjugate the other races. World peace was a militant peace based on "the victorious sword."

There is a strong activist volitional element in Hitler's theory of struggle for existence. Nature favored the better and the stronger, but no race had a prior claim to the title of the "chosen" race. Every race and nation had to prove its worth in the eternal race struggle. The whole surface of the earth was the arena in which this struggle was fought. Frontiers were man-made. They were not sacred and inviolable by nature's sanction. On the contrary, he wrote, "Nature did not reserve this soil in itself for a certain nation or race as reserved territory for the future, but it is land and soil for that people which has the energy to take it and the industry to cultivate it. Nature does not know political frontiers. She first puts the living beings on this globe and watches the free game of energies. He who is strongest in courage and industry receives, as her favorite child, the right to be the master of existence."

. . . . .

Mein Kampf contains a theory of the workings of nature and, at the same time the inner meaning of history. "Inequality" of the nations and individuals and "purity" of races to accomplish perfection and survival were, according to Hitler, the two great maxims on which nature and history were bound to develop according to the intention of the "Creator." In explaining that the eternal "laws of nature" were simultaneously "laws of history" Hitler claimed to have discovered the meaning of history—the past and the future. Hitler's race concept is not a biological concept only. It asserts that specific innate qualities of specific races enable specific deeds to be accomplished in political and cultural development as well.

For Hitler "culture" was only "Aryan culture." In opposition to "so-called scientists" and experts of "so-called democratic" nations, Hitler "proved" from the pages of history that only purest Nordic stock was endowed to create the highest culture. He insisted that only the Germans had the chance and precondition to fulfill such a "mission." The "Creator" had predetermined the condition (*i.e.,* purity) and the end (*i.e.,* new world culture) attainable under those given conditions. Adolf Hitler had offered his guidance in showing the equally predetermined right means. What was left to the Germans by way of self-determination was the will to fulfill the conditions and to avail themselves of the right means—and the ends would be theirs.

What were these exclusive right means? Nature created unequal specimens. Unequals faced tests and trials on this earth, and only the better and stronger survived. On the basis of this aristocratic law of nature, Hitler developed the "law of progress" in history. Progress resulted from trials and tests, rose from battlefields and bloody sacrifices. The continuation of progress was guaranteed by the domination of the fittest and the subservience of the weaker. The purified Germans had to undergo this ordeal of the "becoming"—since no other way led to progress and world peace. To live up to their predestination, Hitler declared, Germans must be willing to use ruthless power as well as to bring great sacrifices. By such tremendous efforts the Germans signified their choice to become the "chosen" people. (pp. 53-84)

> *Hans Staudinger, "Hitler's Racism and the New World Order," in his* The Inner Nazi: A Critical Analysis of "Mein Kampf," *edited by Peter M. Rutkoff and William B. Scott, Louisiana State University Press, 1981, pp. 53-84.*

FURTHER READING

Bibliography

McInnis, Raymond G. "Adolf Hitler's *Mein Kampf:* Origin, Impact, Criticism, and Sources." *References Services Review* 13, No. 1 (Spring 1985): 15-24.
    Summarizes the content, publishing history, and criticism of *Mein Kampf,* and includes an annotated bibliography of major works on Hitler and nazism.

Biography

Bullock, Alan. *Hitler: A Study in Tyranny.* Rev. ed. New York: Harper and Row, 1964, 848 p.
    Studies Hitler's rise to and fall from political power.

Gervasi, Frank. *Adolf Hitler.* New York: Hawthorn Books, 1974, 279 p.
    Examines Hitler's life in politics and his position as a self-proclaimed prophet and warrior for his cause.

Toland, John. *Adolf Hitler.* New York: Doubleday, 1976, 1035 p.
    Traces Hitler's personal and public life.

Vernon, W. H. D. "Hitler, The Man—Notes for a Case History." *Journal of Abnormal Psychology* 37, No. 3 (July 1942): 295-308.
    Attempts to construct a psychological profile of Hitler based on what was then known about his origins, personal characteristics, sexuality, and "maladjustments," "for if allied strategists could peer 'inside Hitler' and adapt their strategy to what they find there, it is likely that the winning of the war would be speeded."

Woolf, Leonard. "Hitler's Psychology." *The Political Quarterly* XIII, No. 4 (October-December 1942): 373-83.
    Discusses Hitler's political psychology based on *The Speeches of Adolf Hitler, April 1922-August 1939,* translated and edited by Norman H. Baynes.

Criticism

Ensor, R. C. K. "Hitler Unexpurgated." *Spectator* 162, No. 5778 (24 March 1939): 491-92.
    Faults James Murphy for mistranslating much of *Mein Kampf* in the Hurst and Blackett English edition.

Harand, Irene. *His Struggle (An Answer to Hitler).* Chicago: Artcraft Press, 1937, 327 p.
    Argues that anti-Semitism and nazism violate Christian ideals and attempts to explode Hitler's myth of Nordic superiority.

Kennedy, A. L. "Is Hitler a Great Man?" *The Spectator* 161, No. 5760 (18 November 1938): 848-49.
    Early essay discussing Hitler's character as a statesman prior to World War II. Kennedy concludes that, while he admires Hitler's talents as a politician, "whether a quarter of a century hence there will be monuments to him in every large German city . . . I would not care to predict."

Maser, Werner. *Hitler's "Mein Kampf": An Analysis.* Translated by R. H. Barry. London: Faber and Faber, 1970, 272 p.
    Analysis of *Mein Kampf* that examines its origins and structure and the worldview advanced by Hitler in this book.

Rosenfeld, Alvin H. *Imagining Hitler.* Bloomington: Indiana University Press, 1985, 121 p.
    Examines various portrayals of Hitler and nazism in post–World War II popular art and literature, asserting that in creating a myth around Hitler, artists and writers have taken nazism out of its historical context and "transmuted [it] into forms of entertainment and political bad faith."

Ryan, Michael D. "Hitler's Challenge to the Churches: A

Theological Political Analysis of *Mein Kampf.*" In *The German Church Struggle and the Holocaust,* edited by Franklin H. Littell and Hubert G. Locke, pp. 148-64. Detroit: Wayne State University Press, 1974.

Asserts that Hitler directly challenged and threatened German Christianity in his creation of himself as savior of Germany.

Additional coverage of Hitler's life is contained in the following source published by Gale Research: *Contemporary Authors,* Vol. 117.

Violet Hunt

1866-1942

(Born Isobel Violet Hunt; also published under the name
I. V. Hunt) English novelist, biographer, short story writer, and translator.

INTRODUCTION

Hunt is remembered for her highly autobiographical fiction, noted for its focus on women's roles in society, and
for her memoirs of her relationships with popular writers
and artists of Victorian and Edwardian England. Her novels often are viewed as a reaction against the pretentious
social mores, repressive sexuality, and strict adherence to
propriety indicative of Victorian society. A supporter of
the suffrage movement, Hunt epitomized the "new
woman" of 1890s feminism in Britain and was popular for
her psychological portraits of rebellious heroines.

Born in Durham, Hunt was the daughter of watercolorist
Alfred William Hunt and novelist Margaret Raine Hunt.
Through her parents, she became acquainted at an early
age with artists and poets associated with the Pre-
Raphaelite movement: Robert Browning, John Everett
Millais, Edward Burne-Jones, Ford Madox Brown, John
Ruskin, William Morris, and Christina and Dante Gabriel
Rossetti. Hunt studied painting at South Kensington Art
School and, as a teenager, wrote poetry under the guid-
ance of Christina Rossetti. She began writing a column for
the *Pall Mall Gazette* and regularly contributed to popular Victorian periodicals, publishing her first novel, *The
Maiden's Progress,* in 1894. Hunt was notorious for her illicit relationships with literary men, and some of her lovers included novelists W. H. Hudson, Somerset
Maugham, and Oswald Crawford. In 1908 she was hired
as a reader by Ford Madox Ford for *The English Review.*
Ford and Hunt had once met as children, and their reac-
quaintance at *The English Review* had a profound impact
on their personal and professional lives: they collaborated
on several works, including the short story collection *Zeppelin Nights;* they discovered and helped promote the writings of D. H. Lawrence; and they began a long and scandalous love affair. Also well-acquainted with such noted
contemporaries as writer and painter Wyndham Lewis,
poet Ezra Pound, sculptor Henri Gaudier-Brzeska, and
novelists Henry James and Joseph Conrad, Hunt frequently entertained England's cultural elite at her Campden Hill home, which she shared with Ford for several
years. In 1918 Ford left Hunt for her friend Stella Bowen.
In the ensuing years Hunt continued to write fiction, remained active in the feminist movement, and published
her memoirs. Suffering from syphilis, Hunt died in 1942.

The protagonists of Hunt's novels are typically considered
autobiographical and are distinguished by their disdain
for convention and earnest search for passionate relationships. Critics note, however, that in Hunt's first novel, *The
Maiden's Progress,* the heroine succumbs to the traditional
social norms of the Victorian middle class. While expressing ambivalence toward courtship and marriage by playing practical jokes on would-be suitors, the protagonist
worries about being unmarried and subsequently accepts
a conventional lifestyle as a wife. *A Hard Woman,* Hunt's
second novel, affirms a feminist theme through its examination of the exploitation of women by male artists, and
Hunt continued to address issues of sexual politics in her
later fiction. According to Marie Secor, the novel *Unkist,
Unkind!* and the short story collections *Tales of the Uneasy* and *More Tales of the Uneasy* are "psychologically
Gothic," exploring the "neurotic sensibilities of sexually
frustrated women."

Hunt's most popular novel, *White Rose of Weary Leaf,*
concerns a governess who becomes mistress to her pupil's
father. Several critics have compared the book to Charlotte Brontë's *Jane Eyre* (1847), noting parallels between
Hunt's and Brontë's works, the only significant difference
being Hunt's "lack of reticence" in treating sexuality.
White Rose of Weary Leaf was praised for its psychological insight and acuity; critic and friend May Sinclair commented to Hunt that she had "done what Hardy only tried

to do when he wrote [*Tess of the d'Urbervilles*]. It took a woman to do it." Two of Hunt's later novels, *Their Lives* and *Their Hearts,* depart from the romantic plots of her earlier works to explore Victorian family dynamics, particularly the conflicts posed by intergenerational and sibling rivalry. These works are based on Hunt's difficult relationships with her two sisters, who disapproved of her belief in sexual freedom.

Hunt's memoirs and her biography of Elizabeth Siddall, the wife of Pre-Raphaelite poet and painter Dante Gabriel Rossetti, although criticized for being unreliable, have been praised for their intimate depictions of illustrious cultural figures. Hunt is remembered as a chronicler of artistic and social movements who effectively captured the essence of English society at the turn of the century, and her works are often viewed as vehicles that reflected and influenced social change.

PRINCIPAL WORKS

The Maiden's Progress (novel) 1894
A Hard Woman (novel) 1895
Unkist, Unkind! (novel) 1897
The Human Interest (novel) 1899
Affairs of the Heart (novel) 1900
The Celebrity at Home (novel) 1904
Sooner or Later (novel) 1904
White Rose of Weary Leaf (novel) 1908
The Wife of Altamont (novel) 1910
The Doll (novel) 1911
Tales of the Uneasy (short stories) 1911
The Celebrity's Daughter (novel) 1913
*The Governess (novel) 1913
The House of Many Mirrors (novel) 1915
Their Lives (novel) 1916
Zeppelin Nights [with Ford Madox Ford] (short stories) 1916
The Last Ditch (novel) 1918
Their Hearts (novel) 1921
†The Tiger Skin (novel) 1924
More Tales of the Uneasy (short stories) 1925
The Flurried Years (memoirs) 1926; also published as *I Have This to Say,* 1926
The Wife of Rossetti—Her Life and Death (biography) 1932

---

*This novel was begun by Hunt's mother and completed by Hunt.

†This novel is an expanded version of a short story collected in *Tales of the Uneasy* in 1911.

CRITICISM

The Saturday Review, London   (essay date 1908)

[*In the following review, the critic offers a mixed assessment of* White Rose of Weary Leaf.]

[In **White Rose of Weary Leaf** once more] Miss Hunt gives us the love-affairs of a "companion", but the life-story of her Amy Stephens is of a most unusual kind. We are told that she had been a dressmaker and a typewriter, an amanuensis in Russia and a hospital nurse in South Africa, and in the intervals of her experiences as companion to ladies she tried the stage, philanthropic work, and lecturing on social problems! Her outlook on life was unconventional, "she had a good figure, and a bad complexion", she was not in the least mercenary, but had to fight hard for existence. She attracted men, but despised affairs of the heart. And she had such a talent for organisation that she soon came to rule any house of which she was an inmate. An impulse of compassion, combined with lack of prudence, having led her to save from suicide a distinguished public man of bad character, the world assumed quite wrongly that she became his mistress. And so, after all these preliminaries, we find her installed in a Yorkshire country-house with a very odd collection of human beings. Jeremy Dand, the master, was a clever egoist, immoral, or rather a-moral, but not openly disreputable. He was burdened with his mother, his second wife—a pretty, well-meaning, shallow woman—her mother—a heroine of the divorce-court, and the ugly love-sick daughter of his first marriage. All these people Amy managed with skill, until her first adventure in emotion brought her tragedy. The book is clever, well written (the dialogue, and one or two letters, being quite remarkable), and disagreeable. The position of Jeremy and Amy is in essentials so like that of Rochester and Jane Eyre that we cannot help wondering what Charlotte Brontë would think of Miss Hunt's lack of reticence.

> A review of "*White Rose of Weary Leaf,*" in *The Saturday Review,* London, Vol. 105, No. 2735, March 28, 1908, p. 409.

Frederic Taber Cooper   (essay date 1908)

[*An American educator, biographer, and editor, Cooper served for many years as literary critic of the* Bookman, *a popular early twentieth-century literary magazine. In the following review of* White Rose of Weary Leaf, *Cooper argues that, despite its faults, the book contains some "undeniable merit."*]

The White Rose of Weary Leaf, by Violet Hunt, is best defined as a sort of modern *Jane Eyre* story, possessing all the defects of the Charlotte Brontë school and few of its merits. It is sensational, melodramatic, often crude in construction and in character drawing—and nevertheless there is a certain relentless sincerity in the story of the central character, a certain poignant tragedy in her fate that make it a book difficult to lay aside, in spite of one's frequent sense of exasperation, and equally difficult to forget after finishing it. The Jane Eyre of this story is not an inexperienced young girl, but a sad, disillusioned woman, who has long looked the world in the face and expects nothing from it but injustice. The Mr. Rochester has been married, not once, but twice; the surviving wife is not crazed, but simply a self-satisfied little fool. The spectacular tragedy is not a fire, but a railroad wreck, and even here the wife, though badly hurt, insists upon recovering, in spite of the doctor's assurances that she will die. The man, however, allows the other woman to believe that the wife is dead; and from this initial wrong the story moves strongly on to a double expiation, told in a spirit of grim fatalism. It is astonishing that a book so faulty should here and there show streaks of such undeniable merit. (pp. 579-80)

> *Frederic Taber Cooper, in a review of "White Rose of Weary Leaf," in* The Bookman, *New York, Vol. XXVII, August, 1908, pp. 579-80.*

On Hunt's qualities as a writer:

[Violet Hunt's work maddens,] for there are glimpses of brilliance, particularly in her dialogue, and moments of fine humor and social observation, but no sustained, polished effort—her largely instinctive talent remained uncultivated. In her memoir, and in her preface to **More Tales,** Hunt shows sensitivity and insight when discussing other writers' work, but she never touches upon her own: she rarely had time to search for *le mot juste* that she so admired.

> *Jane E. Miller, in her "The Edward Naumburg, Jr., Collection of Violet Hunt,"* Princeton University Library Chronicle, *Winter 1990.*

May Sinclair   (essay date 1922)

[*Sinclair was an English writer and critic who, like Hunt, was an active feminist and member of the suffrage movement. In the following survey of Hunt's novels, Sinclair praises Hunt's rendering of female psychology and her portrayal of tragic heroines.*]

A writer who has once had the misfortune to be called "clever" is damned for all the higher purposes of praise. He may go on adding finer and finer and more and more serious and poignant qualities to his original cleverness, but it will avail him nothing; each new achievement is just another clever trick of his. If the author of *Hamlet* and *King Lear* had been our contemporary and had started by writing, say, *Man and Superman,* he would never have been known as anything but that clever dramatist, Mr. Shakespeare. You may qualify the adjective as you please—brilliantly clever, consummately clever, uncannily clever; the brilliance, the consummation, the uncanniness are forgotten; the cleverness is what sticks.

Let him begin with a reputation for hardness tacked on to his cleverness, and he will never be credited with any tender quality at all.

It was with such a label that Violet Hunt, some time in the early 'nineties, started her career. Her talent was judged to be a merely hard yet superficial cleverness, as of so

much ice for her to skate on; and in spite of the depth and poignancy of *White Rose of Weary Leaf,* of *Their Lives* and *Their Hearts,* in spite of the grim primitive uncanniness of *Tales of the Uneasy,* it is as a brilliant skater on ice that she has passed from that century to this.

To be sure, she has done her best to support the disastrous tradition. She began with the sheer cleverness of *The Maiden's Progress* and *A Hard Woman;* she allowed *The Doll* and *The Celebrity's Daughter* to come after *White Rose of Weary Leaf,* and *The Last Ditch* after *Their Lives;* and she has given us no more *Tales of the Uneasy.* But these beginnings and these relapses are negligible in the face of her positive achievement. If, in the reviewer's well-worn phrase, Violet Hunt had written nothing but *White Rose* and *Their Lives* and *Their Hearts,* these would have been enough to establish a reputation for more than mere cleverness. If only she had written nothing else she would have been recognised as one of the most sincere, uncompromising, and serious of psychological realists.

Unfortunately, *The Maiden's Progress* and *A Hard Woman* came first, and they had a little accomplished air of finality about them. They came in that season of cleverness and hard brilliance, the early 'nineties, the days of the *Pseudonym Library* and *The Yellow Book,* and *The Woman Who Did.*

But already in her youthful work there was, for the discerning, the promise of better things. It is in *The Maiden's Progress.* It is in the last scene of *A Hard Woman.* Possibly this title won for Violet Hunt her celebrity of hardness. On the principle that "Who drives fat oxen must himself be fat," who draws hard women must herself be hard. Yet it was clear even then that Violet Hunt is not on the side of hardness; she is all for the tender and suffering, the sensitive hearts over whom coarse natures ride rough-shod. This novel might have been written to show the horror of hardness. And Moderna in *The Maiden's Progress,* Amy Stephens in *White Rose,* Christina and Orinthia in *Their Lives* and *Their Hearts,* are all vulnerable. They are tortured by a look, by a word said or not said. And Violet Hunt draws them with a superior sympathy and understanding.

So much for the superstition of hardness.

Taken in the bulk, Violet Hunt's work is considerable. There is a record of poems dating from 1879; a long list of novels and short stories dating from '94 to 1921.

There are the first two already mentioned. There is *Unkist, Unkind,* a tale of murder and modern witchcraft, showing a characteristic leaning to the gruesome and uncanny.

There is *The House of Many Mirrors.* This novel is too uneven to be wholly admirable. The end is worked up to a fairly effective climax, but the foregoing parts are poorly constructed. There is an utter lack of cohesion and proportion. Too much importance is given to irrelevant matters—for example, Rosamund Pleydell's traffic in her own cast-off clothing. Action and motive are unrelated. We know that Rosamund is intriguing to get the inheritance for the young husband she adores, over the heads of his two cousins, Lily Mackenzie and Emily Gideon. But it is hard to see how the scheme is furthered by her befriending of the disgraced and disinherited Lily, or by her surreptitious invasion of the Gideons' house. There is no sustained illusion of reality. The situation calls for simplification and compression, but it is spun out and frittered away, and the end comes too late to move us. There is the stuff of tragedy in Rosamund's sublime deception, declaring herself pregnant when she is dying of cancer, and (by a system of posthumously posted letters) pretending to be alive when she is dead. But somehow the thing misses fire.

Not so *The Celebrity at Home* and *The Celebrity's Daughter.* They are very successful and agreeable light comedy. The Comic Spirit, absent from Violet Hunt's other books, plays delightfully round the figure of the Celebrity, exposed in his unclothed reality to the irreverent and precocious eyes of his daughter Tempe.

The Last Ditch marks on the whole a decline from brilliant cleverness to mere smartness; but it has its amusing and redeeming moments; it is more or less true to the spirit of the class that took the Great War light-heartedly, and with a heroic frivolity proved that *"dulce et decorum est,"* et cetera.

There are *Zeppelin Nights* and *The Desirable Alien* and others more negligible.

And there are five outstanding ones. These compel you to remember them: *White Rose of Weary Leaf, Their Lives, Their Hearts, Tales of the Uneasy,* and *Sooner or Later.* This last I should place a little lower than the other four. *White Rose,* even while remembered, can be read again and again with pleasure.

The others must be slightly forgotten to renew their appeal. They should be read separately with a stretch of time between. Taken as the critic must take them, one on the top of the other, their effect is a little stifling. There is a want of perspective and relief. It is like listening to a person with a fixed idea; like looking at repeated portraits of the same figure. There never was such a gallery of English *demi-vierges.*

To be sure, their demi-virginity is purely mental. They are betrayed first by their own minds. There is a *naïveté* about them, an innocent uncertainty. Rosette and Christina offer themselves to their lovers, but they only half know what they are doing; it is partly because they desire to know that they do it. Their passions are too exalted, too pathetic, too foredoomed to count as sensual. Their senses are dumb, unawakened, or superseded. It is their hearts that clamour, unsatisfying and unsatisfied. That is the trouble with them all. One burst of honest sensuality would have settled their business for them and left them calm. But no; they are too subtle for their own or their lovers' satisfaction. They are born to torture and be tortured.

Violet Hunt's hand is masterly in the portrayal of this type. There is nothing in it she is not aware of, nothing that she cannot show. Moderna, Rosette, Orinthia, Christina, are all half-virgins, "born for irregular situations." Orinthia of *Their Hearts* is safely and soundly married, the irreproachable spouse of her cousin, John Dempster

Blenkinsopp. But Orinthia of *Their Lives* is a terror to parents and guardians. In her early and unwholesome teens she strikes up an acquaintance with a seedy, middle-aged stranger, an amatory beach-comber, the prowling male of seaside promenades. The child is innocent enough; but there is a terrible suggestion of what might have happened if the maidservant had not looked over the seawall and caught them sitting side by side on the beach in the dark. And when Orinthia finally marries you feel that her gods have been good to her.

But the gods have no sort of care for Christina. Christina (as Robert Assheton says of Rosette in *Sooner or Later*) is "determined to be ruined." Dull, honest marriage has no attraction for these women; they must gamble with passion, taking big risks. Before they can feel passion they must feel the exciting thrill of danger.

Amy Stephens in *White Rose of Weary Leaf* is another type. She knows no passion but the maternal passion; she is not in love with Jeremy Dand, her middle-aged married lover; she resists him without a struggle until the catastrophe that breaks her nerve. But she, too, abhors marriage and prefers "the irregular situation."

And so they all have the same story. Moderna of *The Maiden's Progress* is an understudy for Christina. Amy is a Christina plus the maternal instinct and minus Christina's talent and her temperament. Rosette is another Christina with another Balfame. They are not content to play with fire at the tips of their fingers; they must throw themselves body and soul into the blaze; and they come out of it scorched and writhing and distorted. They have the qualities of their defects; they are noble and abject, generous and consumed with jealousy; they cling to their disenchanted lovers, and are beaten off, and cling again with a reckless, tactless fidelity. They are heavy-handed and heavy-hearted in loving and have no joy in it; they can neither give happiness nor receive it. They are doomed and know it. Their moment's rapture is spoiled by their premonition of its end. Their lovers' kisses fall on faces wet and salt with tears.

Scenes repeat themselves. Passion, foreboding, reproach, recrimination, repudiation, despair, and more passion. A vicious circle. These figures have no background that counts. Wherever they are, the effect is always the same, of naked passions played out on bare boards before a dark curtain. They may be walking on the Yorkshire moors, or by the bracing north-eastern sea, in woods smelling of damp moss and earth, in gardens by the Solent, and instantly the air is changed; it becomes sultry with passion; it is the air of a stuffy bedroom with the windows tight shut; there is a smell of hair-brushes, cigarette smoke, and warm sachet.

We are least aware of it in *White Rose of Weary Leaf,* because the dominant character, Amy Stephens, is a higher and healthier type. The atmosphere is cleared by conflict, by the beating of her wings as her will resists her lover.

White Rose is perhaps the best book Violet Hunt has written yet; the finest in conception, in form and technique. It is a surprising piece of psychology, male and female. There is no important character in it that does not live, from the amazing and complex Amy Stephens to the too simple and degenerate Dulce Dand, who will go mad if she is not married. Jeremy Dand, Amy's middle-aged married lover, is the one entirely successful male figure that Violet Hunt has created. It is more than a portrait; a portrait is painted in the flat, as are the figures of Robert Assheton and Euphan Balfame, in the two dimensions of brutality and sensual passion. Jeremy Dand is a three-dimensional form that we can walk round; he is not drawn, but hewn, chiselled faithfully in his many-sided detail. He is the average sensual man, but he is never brutal like Assheton and Balfame; Violet Hunt has abandoned the fallacy of the ruling passion and presented him as he is, with all his inconsistencies; selfish and unselfish, generous and mean, faithful and faithless, a human battlefield, till in the end his passion for Amy masters him. Whatever he is at the moment, he is given with an unfaltering rightness. All his mental processes are inevitable.

And the drawing of Amy is as masterly. Nothing she does and feels and says could have been done or felt or said differently. This intricate, utterly feminine soul is laid bare to its last throbbing nerve, its ultimate secret thought. We have the whole of it, all the wonderful detail, its courage, its recklessness, its pity, its scrupulousness, its essential decency, its all but indestructible loyalty, its strength and the infinite pathos of its weakness.

The tragedy is worked out to its end with unrelieved, unrelenting gloom. Every line has the effect of rightness, of a flawless finality. It is so far beyond anything that mere cleverness can do. *White Rose of Weary Leaf* alone should have placed Violet Hunt high in the ranks of the tragic realists.

It was followed by lesser works; and criticism in this country, if not disarmed by a burst of excellence at the start, or a steady rise in merit, is apt to judge novelists by their lapses rather than their achievements.

Then in 1916 came *Their Lives;* and now in 1921 *Their Hearts.* We are back again in the sultry air of *Sooner or Later.* It hangs about Davenant Villa, in the folds of the green and gold Morris curtains, mixed with fumes from the white-globed gaseliers.

Davenant Villa, Kensington, Christina Radmall's home, was an intellectual and artistic centre, where the pre-Raphaelites came and the young æsthetes of the late 'seventies. Christina herself is a poet at sixteen and a journalist at twenty. You gather that if she has a passion for the middle-aged and married Emerson Vlaye and surrenders afterwards to Mr. Balfame (also married and middle-aged) it is not for want of resources in herself. She is clever, witty, she has read enormously if not profoundly, she has innumerable friends who help her in her career. But this heated atmosphere is never cleared by the play of intellect. The pre-Raphaelites might just as well not be there, for all that Christina or Violet Hunt care about them.

And Violet Hunt is right. The pre-Raphaelites do not matter. What matters is Christina's passion; what matters is the jealousy of the three sisters, Christina, Virgilia, and Orinthia, and the drama of their hearts, the whole close, intimate, stifling family scene in which their lives are set.

These inhabitants of Davenant Villa are terrible. The figure of the father, the distinguished painter, Henry Radmall, stands out with a strange incongruous beauty and dignity, untouched by the bickering, the rancour, the combat of mean wills, untouched by the hard, flat, material mind of Victoria Radmall, his wife, who scolds him for saying pounds instead of guineas when he sells his pictures, and for giving away ten-shilling pieces in mistake for sixpences.

True, Mrs. Radmall loves her husband and Christina; Orinthia loves her father; Christina loves her mother, and, when she is old enough to be sorry for her, Orinthia. But between each couple stands Virgilia, complacent, cunning, heartless, utterly selfish, and poisonous with jealousy; Virgilia, who loves nobody but herself, who

> knew how much Papa got for a picture, how much they had a year, how much they had had when they married, the rent of Davenant Villa, what wages the cook got and Trimmer and Grace, and where the principal drains were under the house.

And Christina is jealous of Virgilia. She tries to "keep her down." There is a moment, poignant and unpleasant, when she realises Virgilia's approaching womanhood, that "seemed to put her sister on a pinnacle of elderly mystery, somehow. . . . "

> The curve of Virgilia's hip, spirited, clean cut, with the brown, shiny, spotted material drawn tight over it, reminded the elder sister of the skin and body of an adder she had once come upon in the woods. She had stood and considered it furtively as it lay and sunned itself on a decayed tree-stump, deadly, assured, at ease.

There is another moment, unpleasant but poignant, when Virgilia on the night before her wedding comes into Christina's room, throws herself on the bed in a hysterical state and implores Christina to enlighten her. And Christina, touched by the appeal, her defences broken down, does her best.

> It was half-past twelve. Virgilia rolled over into a sitting posture on the edge of the bed. She yawned, drew herself up:—
>
> "Well, and now I'll go back to my own bed, I think."
>
> Christina was thoroughly awake and rather cross. "Do you feel better," she said, "or," with meaning, "do you want to talk any more?"
>
> Her mistrust of Virgilia was growing, coming back to her in a great traditional flood.

She realises that Virgilia is less innocent than she, that Virgilia has "had" her, and that every word she has said will be used as evidence against her. We do not know that this is so; but we know that Christina feels that it is so.

The marriage of the younger sister is the culminating episode that ends *Their Lives.* It stands for the defeat and doom of Christina. Never, as long as she lives, will she be able to take life like the unscrupulous Virgilia, and, ruthlessly and complacently, conduct it to a successful issue.

The crucial scene is that where Christina, still innocent but infatuated, offers herself to her elderly admirer, the painter, Emerson Vlaye. She does it with a disarming, childlike awkwardness.

> She came up to him close, till her body touched his, her head came just under his chin, so that he could have kissed it or laid his hand upon it. He did neither, he was curious to know what she was about to do or say.
>
> "I'm not an iceberg," she said, doggedly; then, with her head down, "You've no right to say I'm cold."
>
> She repeated, "I'm not, I'm not. . . . Look here, you don't believe in me. . . . But, look here, whatever a woman can give I'll give you. . . . Take me if you care to take me."

But Vlaye does not care. He has no idea of ruining himself for Christina and upsetting the peace of his respectable married *ménage*.

> She . . . stood there irresolute, feeling that what she wanted, really, was to leave him and start fair. . . . But she had not a notion how to do it, how to, even, get out of the room, though the door was not locked. . . .
>
> The painter put his hand to his forehead.
>
> "Put your hat on and run away, there's a good girl," he said.

That is what life does to Christina, who, in her desperate youth, is so reckless and uncompromising, alternately self-betraying and betrayed. It is on Virgilia's wedding-day, in the hall at Davenant Villa, that Christina meets her fate.

> She looked at him coolly, using her own weapon, her large, squarely formed, deep brown disconcerting eyes. . . .
>
> They were, for the moment, pitted against each other. . . .
>
> She criticised his mouth, revealed now in turn as he was speaking to her—jagged and indeterminate at the corners, as if at some time it had been bitted, and pulled and tortured. It was his mouth that had given her the notion that he was bad-tempered. There was a peak in the middle of the upper lip that seemed to shoot forwards rather cruelly when he was saying daring things that he appeared to enjoy saying. . . . He was doing it now.

The second book, *Their Hearts*—hearts of Christina and Orinthia and the hard heart of Virgilia—begins where the first ends, with Virgilia's wedding. Virgilia is removed from the scene; she is henceforth no more than a malignant influence moving in the background, spying on, and more or less plotting against Christina. Of the three sisters, Christina is the only one who possesses any sense of honour. Even Orinthia spies. There is a shocking scene where the youngest Miss Radmall and the servant Grace piece together the fragments of a compromising letter from Balfame to Christina, which Grace has found in the waste-paper basket. But on the whole Orinthia is loyal;

Virgilia removed, there is the truce of God between her and Christina. Moreover, Christina, unmarried and compromised, and tortured by her middle-aged lover, is an object of pity, not of jealousy. And Orinthia marries. Reserving to herself the right of a certain shrewish comment, she becomes Christina's confidant and her protector against Virgilia and Virgilia's husband, the priggish and respectable Dukie Hall.

The story of Christina in *Their Hearts* is the story of Rosette. A more complex and mature Rosette, a Rosette more profoundly understood and more subtly analysed. Comparing *Their Hearts* with *Sooner or Later,* you realise the enormous advance that Violet Hunt has made in the art of portraiture. In *Sooner or Later* she is not only saturated, but swamped and submerged in Rosette's erotics. What with Rosette and Robert Assheton's other mistresses, *Sooner or Later* reeks with one monotonous emotion. It is the least clarified of Violet Hunt's books. There is something compelling in its savage power, its thick, brooding atmosphere. The figures move as in a fog, larger but more indistinct than life, exponents of the one master passion. Violet Hunt herself is overpowered and depressed by the emotions she has evoked. Her style suffers. Except in her dialogue, where she is always brilliant, vigorous, and natural, it is nerveless, monotonous. Yet somehow its nervelessness, its monotony contributes to the effect.

In the two later books we have an infinitely more competent Violet Hunt, mature, detached, consummately observant. Orinthia, Virgilia, Christina, Mrs. Radmall, are drawn with a remorseless sincerity and understanding. Never for one moment does she allow her imagination to do violence to reality. If Christina is her heroine she holds no brief for her; she sees her as she is, with all her cleverness, her frankness and generosity, her boundless capacity for surrender, and with all her stupidity, her self-conscious affectations, her obstinacy, her power to irritate and madden. We see Christina's fascination, but her fascination is not brought forward to obscure her essential tiresomeness. We are made to understand thoroughly why she and Rosette, her prototype, cannot keep their men. Assheton says of Rosette

> This girl I am telling you of was quite the poorest tactician I ever knew. Always driving things into corners, forcing the note, incapable of letting a thing slide. . . . Day by day I watched her knocking nails into her own coffin.

It is all part of their perversity that they should fasten on the kind of man who becomes brutal in the presence of suffering and is implacable to tears.

Only in one respect is the earlier novel superior to its two successors. The figure of the middle-aged lover, Robert Assheton, is positively a finer bit of portraiture than that of Euphan Balfame. He is more distinctly realised in detail; there is more in him; his utterances are more vital and authentic. It is as if Violet Hunt had pulled Robert Assheton to bits, lost most of them, and used the rest to build up Euphan Balfame. He is real as far as he goes, but he does not go quite far enough. He has nothing comparable with Robert Assheton's *cri de cœur:*

"I can't, I can't! Let me go!"

Still, in spite of Balfame's comparative incompleteness, **Their Hearts** remains the more finished and maturer work. It is life seen from more angles than one. There is nothing in **Sooner or Later** to stand beside the portraits of Victoria and Henry Radmall, of Virgilia, of Orinthia. Nothing, not even in **White Rose** (except the great railway accident scene), to compare with the death and burying of Henry Radmall. In the cemetery nobody pays any attention to Christina. Only the old friend of the family, Izzy Farsight, comes up to her where she stands deserted, as everybody is going away.

> Christina did not shrug it off, but endured Miss Izzy's arm around her shoulder, that she stiffened suddenly. . . .
>
> The shadow of a great loneliness fell upon her. Kind friends—yes, but no one who really belonged to her. . . . never. . . . For frankly weeping, tottering a little, leaning on the arms of love that was not disallowed, her two sisters had suffered their husbands to lead them away into the wilderness.

Thus, with an effect of utter predetermined finality, Christina's love-cycle moves between her sister's wedding and her father's funeral.

And the art of it—at first sight there is none. These two books are formless. The story wanders on from time to time and from place to place, moves backwards as much as forwards. The same episodes repeat themselves for no apparent reason. A chance association will fire a train of otherwise irrelevant reminiscence. I have spoken of scenes, but there are no scenes, no big "situations." Nothing is set; there is no working up to a climax. The style is at times jerky; it goes bumping on like a half-filled bus on an uneven road. At times it has the slip-shod ease of a man in a smoke-room, telling his story slangily, ungrammatically, between two whisky-and-sodas. Yet it carries you along; it gets there; the story holds you. The thing is colourless; it has no rhythm, no cadence. But neither has it any affectations or devices; it is the simplest, most innocent style imaginable. There is no beating heart in it, not even the stifled heart-beats of **Sooner or Later.** That is to say, there are no strong emotions.

And yet, by stroke upon little stroke, by touches almost imperceptible, a tremendous, poignant effect of reality is reached. These are the naked thoughts, the naked lives of people we have known; these figures, built up by means so unobtrusive, so inconsiderable, have the solid pressure of flesh and blood. Some of them, George Day, John Dempster, Dukie Hall, Euphan Belfame, may be incomplete, but they are never shadowy. The women are finished to the last eyelash.

Have we any right to complain of a method, a phrasing, that has, after all, done its work so well?

So far we have seen nothing in Violet Hunt but the psychological realist working competently within a narrow range, limiting herself to the presentation of sophisticated urban or suburban types and the society of Bohemia, high or low. There is nothing in these novels to make us suspect the existence in her of a grim northern imagination and of power to deal with the uncanny and the macabre. Nothing by which we might have divined the author of **Tales of the Uneasy.**

When I read these tales I find myself wondering what wild turn Violet Hunt's talent might have taken if she had never lived in London, never seen Fleet Street, but had been brought up, like Emily Brontë, in the Yorkshire country of her people and had never left their moors. **"The Telegram"**, **"The Prayer"**, **"The Barometer"**, **"The Coach"**, **"The Tiger-Skin"** show an imagination of the uncanny that is almost genius. I am told that **"The Prayer"** was the first story she ever wrote. If this was an indication of her true bent, she has been warped from it by education and environment.

"The Barometer", **"The Operation"**, and the **"Tiger-Skin"** are more mature. The first two are terse, swift, concentrated; there is the greatest possible economy of means to ends. **"The Barometer"** is worked up in fifteen short pages to a climax of pity and terror. It is the story of two children terrified by a foreboding. They are afraid of the room they sleep in,

> brooded over by the enormous over-arching elm-tree. Its branches tapped the little skylight panes when it was windy, but now they hung still, like a drooping banner in a calm.

A thunderstorm is brewing. The children implore their mother to take them into her own bed. She refuses. You feel the shuddering of their fear, you hear their crying.

They go up to their bedroom under the sloping roof. In the night the tree draws down the lightning; it strikes through the roof and kills the children. Old Hannah, the servant, goes up to wake them.

> The first thing she saw, before she screamed, was the wide, jagged hole in the rafters above the bed where they still lay in each other's arms, . . . They were quiet and unchanged, except for some little blue marks like shot in the forehead of the one and the breast of the other.

There is not a word that could be added to or taken away from this tale.

And it is so with **"The Operation"**, that powerful story of psychic transference. It is so with **"The Coach"**, that grim essay in the macabre, though here a perverse touch of the old "cleverness" interferes with the authentic thrill.

But no cleverness can spoil the terrible pathos of **"The Tiger-Skin."** It is a study in morbid cruelty; a woman's cruelty to her own child. It is not technically perfect. It would have gained by a greater concentration, yet Violet Hunt has not written anything that so triumphantly and unbearably "comes off."

It is the answer to anybody who still believes in the superstition of her hardness.

I wish she would go on being grim and northern, I wish she would write more uncanny stories. **The Tales** and the novels are in different worlds.

If you care for nothing but beauty, beauty of subject, beauty of form and pattern, beauty of technique, you will not care for the novels of Violet Hunt. But to the lover of austere truth-telling, who would rather see things as they sometimes are than as they are not and cannot be, who prefers a natural ugliness to artificial and sentimental beauty, they will appeal by their sincerity, their unhesitating courage, their incorruptible reality. (pp. 106-18)

> May Sinclair, "The Novels of Violet Hunt," in The English Review, Vol. 34, No. 2, February, 1922, pp. 106-18.

St. John Adcock (essay date 1928)

[*An English author of numerous works, Adcock served as editor of the London* Bookman *from 1923 until his death in 1930. In the following overview of Hunt's life and career, he defines Hunt's "artistic temperament" as one that thrived on the "good society" in which she circulated.*]

It is customary to speak of the artistic temperament as if it had been reduced to a standard pattern—as if it invariably manifested itself in one and the same fashion. This careless attempt to stereotype what is really a most protean spirit has been responsible for misleading many young men who are not artists into adopting the particular (and not always too particular) habits, idiosyncrasies, eccentricities supposed to denote that temperament, under the impression that their having acquired its recognised peculiarities of manner and conduct is in itself evidence that they must also be artistic.

The artistic temperament, however, is no such mechanical and monotonous form of self-indulgence. It develops spontaneously in all who are artists, and can be spuriously developed in many who are not; and when it is the real thing it is as diverse in its ways of asserting itself as are the infinitely varied characters of men and women. It made Milton austere, and Herrick more lively than beseemed one of his cloth; accommodated itself to Byron's vices and to Matthew Arnold's virtues; to Rossetti's Bohemianism and Browning's respectability. It sends one artist into seclusion, another into society; makes one a misanthrope, another a lover of his kind; one a self-centred egoist, dead to all interests but his own, another a genial sentimentalist whose sympathies are ready for all who need them; it afflicts one with a ridiculous conceit of himself, and another with an almost equally ridiculous diffidence and humility.

Difference of sex makes no difference in the workings of this variable artistic temperament. I could tell of how it drives one of the truest of modern women poets to sit and write at her desk for regular hours every morning, and prompts another, who is not more gifted, to write anywhere at any time when inspiration comes to her, and sometimes prevents her from writing anything for weeks together; of how it renders a country quietness and freedom from interruption essential to the work of one accomplished woman novelist, and the stir and friendly neighbourhood and stimulation of town-life or the excitement of travel as essential to that of another.

And Violet Hunt I should guess to be one of these latter. She has for long past made her home in London, and you may frequently meet her here at literary dinners and social gatherings, or at more fashionable salons where men and women distinguished or becoming distinguished in art or letters are wont to congregate and rub shoulders with persons of importance in the business and political worlds. Moreover, you learn from her sometimes elusive, sometimes amazingly candid autobiography, *The Flurried Years,* that she loves and has always loved good society—that is, the society of interesting people who are doing things in the arts, and that she was and is never happier than when she is playing hostess at one of those pleasant, delightfully informal salons of her own. From time to time she has entertained in the drawingroom of her house on Campden Hill, where Gaudier Brjeska's startlingly futurist bust of Ezra Pound is pedestalled in the garden, more famous authors and artists and miscellaneous celebrities than I have space to catalogue; and she opens her 1913 autobiographical chapter with the rapturous ejaculation, "Home, and my yearly garden party never so well attended. Cabinet Ministers, by Jove!" and proceeds to chronicle briefly, "*Fêtes champetres* at the Monds' in Lowndes Square, Henley with the Harmsworths, the Cabaret Club with all the charming artist rabble who were on the top of the vogue." There is a natural exuberance in her enjoyment of these things that reminds you rather of Charles Lamb's almost weeping in the motley Strand for sheer joy in so much life. She notes, immediately after the report of this dazzling social round, that she withdrew to the restfulness of a cottage at Selsey, but even then cannot refrain from adding, "A gorgeous season. I wished my poor mother had been there to see it." No recluse, no hater of madding crowds speaks in all this; and she is too good a conversationalist, who can on occasion administer a caustically witty sting with one of the softest of voices, and is too easily at home among crowds, either as hostess or visitor, not to have given more of her heart to society than to solitude.

Although Violet Hunt was born in the staid old cathedral city of Durham, and in the later years of that Victorian era which is now regarded as dull and prim and dowdily old-fashioned, she has a vivacious unconventionality, an independence and modernity of outlook that seem to make her more of the twentieth than of the nineteenth century. Her father was a well-known artist, her mother a novelist, and she numbered among the friends of her family Browning, Millais, Burne-Jones, Ruskin, the Rossettis—and, by the way, she has been busy for some while past on a book of her Memories of the Rossettis, which will probably have seen the light before these lines are printed.

In 1912 she completed and published a novel called *The Governess,* which had been commenced and left unfinished by her mother long before; but by then she had become a well-known novelist herself. Her own first book, *The Maiden's Progress,* a novel in dialogue, made its appearance in 1894; and before 1912 she had followed it with ten other novels or volumes of short stories including *The Human Interest, A Hard Woman, Unkist, Unkind, Affairs of the Heart, The Celebrity at Home, White Rose of*

Weary Leaf, and in 1910 *The Wife of Altamont* and *Tales of the Uneasy.* To my thinking, the best of these are *White Rose of Weary Leaf* and the brilliant collection of stories in *Tales of the Uneasy.*

The tales in the earlier *Affairs of the Heart* (1900) are unequal as well as varied; they are clever, entertaining stories of *fin de siècle* London life, passionate, bizarre, humorous, but none of them remains so vividly in one's memory as does that bitterly ironic story of the girl who pretends to be a reckless decadent in the hope of pleasing a man who is as decadent as she pretends to be, only to find she has taken the wrong way to charm him and he has fallen in love with a slip of a girl who has all the innocence and simplicity she herself had affected to have lost. But *Tales of the Uneasy* show throughout a surer mastery of the short-story writer's art. Some of these tales, pleasant and unpleasant, of the occult and of real life with the gilt off, are the most brilliant things of the kind Miss Hunt has done—one, that harrowing, haunting story of the eugenist mother and her child, **"The Tiger Skin"**, is a little masterpiece and, as a very long short story, has since been reissued in a book to itself.

The Celebrity at Home, in a lighter vein, is the terribly candid and disrespectful record kept by his daughter of the doings of Mr. Vero-Taylor, a successful dramatist who is a tuft-hunter in high society and neglects his wife and family for the pursuit of those higher things. Much of it is capital farce, and those who coruscate in certain easy-going social circles are depicted with a quietly pungent, genially humorous satire. *White Rose of Weary Leaf* is on larger lines; in design and in characterisation it is a considerable achievement. It holds your interest cunningly, though there is scarcely a likeable person in the book, and one of its triumphs is, that though she is scarcely likeable and brings her worst troubles on herself by her own indiscretions, the chief character in the book, Amy Steevens, is so natural a human creature and goes her way so courageously that the reader is subtly drawn into sympathising with her. She was "constitutionally a rolling stone"; had been assistant in a dressmaker's shop and in a typewriting establishment; secretary to a literary man, and companion to a lady, and had been on the stage. She had been to South Africa and, as a famous man's amanuensis, to Russia. When the novel opens she is serving as governess or companion to the young daughter of an English family staying in Paris. Her native unconventionality is always betraying her into difficulties. When Sir Mervyn Dymond, a worried co-respondent in a divorce suit, attempts to commit suicide, she compromises herself by dashing upstairs and into his bedroom to save him, and is dismissed from her situation accordingly. To atone for this, Sir Mervyn takes her to London as his secretary, and she compromises herself further by staying in his house there, though the relations between them remain on an entirely blameless business footing. Without beauty or passion, she has personality; men are strangely attracted to her, and she has to fight her way very much as Becky Sharp did, and is not always so successful as Becky in contending with the human animals who beset her. Not a pleasant story, but written with imaginative realism and with marked ability.

This book was published in 1908, the year, as Miss Hunt notes in *The Flurried Years,* which began for her "with such high hopes, both personal and literary. . . . As a literary woman, my years of mark and usefulness coincided with a great literary launch, that of the 'greatest Review in the world' ", which proud title she gives to the *English Review,* founded under the editorship of Ford Madox Hueffer in 1908. She touches in some amusing pictures of the unpretentious manner in which the editorial work was carried on in the offices over a poulterer's and fishmonger's shop in Holland Park Avenue. She had written three short stories which an agent had returned to her because he had been unable to sell them and, on the advice of H. G. Wells, she called at the office of the *English Review* and offered them to the editor, and he accepted the second, **"The Coach"**, without reading it.

Presently she became reader for the *Review,* and as such had the luck to discover D. H. Lawrence:

> The editor handed me some manuscript poems, . . . written in pencil and very close, which had come to him from a young schoolmistress in the Midlands. She said that her sweetheart was schoolmaster in the same school. He was the son of a miner, and not very strong, but she had copied out some of his poems, and would the editor give them a glance.

Editor and reader rejoiced in this discovery of a new genius; the poems went into the *Review,* and after some correspondence Lawrence came up to London, abandoned schoolmastering, and started on his literary career. In those days, in addition to being much occupied with the *Review* and with social engagements, Violet Hunt took an active part in the suffragette movement, and tells how she and May Sinclair stood outside High Street, Kensington, railway station with collecting boxes, gathering funds for the cause. In all those *Flurried Years,* when she was busy in these ways, travelling abroad at intervals, and continually worried with the care of an invalid mother and all manner of domestic and other anxieties, though she says nothing of her books, beyond casually mentioning the names of about two of them, she was finding time to write another seven or eight. *The Doll* (1911) was followed by *The Desirable Alien,* which caused the German police to keep a cautious eye on her when she was visiting Germany shortly after its publication in 1913. Then came, in 1915, *The House of Many Mirrors,* and *Their Lives,* in 1916, with its continuation, *Their Hearts,* in 1921, and between these two, *The Last Ditch,* in 1918. Another book of short stories, *More Tales of the Uneasy,* in 1925, was succeeded a year later by that curiously intimate chronicle of her own tumultuous experiences, *The Flurried Years,* which I value most for its interesting personal recollections of so many of her famous contemporaries—of Conrad, Henry James, and more than all, and to say nothing of others, of W. H. Hudson. I don't think Violet Hunt has drawn any character, real or imaginary, with more insight, more beautifully sympathetic understanding than she draws Hudson's in the last twenty pages of this book. Into those few pages she gets a wonderfully living picture of him, his appearance, his way of life, his habits of thought, the resentful mood in which he met old age and the approach of death; these things leading to a poignant account of his dying, of her going to his house, when all the blinds along the street were down, and standing in the unfamiliar silence of the familiar room where he lay dead, and to the final scene of the funeral, where the mourners, little incongruities of incident that edged the solemnity of the occasion, are all etched in with the minutely detailed realism of a Pre-Raphaelite painting. One had not expected so gracious an ending to so bitter and stormy a book as **The Flurried Years,** and it comes there like the windless quiet that fell when last night's storm had worn itself out

> and in one place lay
> Feathers and dust, to-day and yesterday.
>
> (pp. 125-34)

St. John Adcock, "Violet Hunt," in his The Glory That Was Grub Street: Impressions of Contemporary Authors, *The Musson Book Company Limited, 1928, pp. 125-34.*

Hunt's female protagonists:

In her best work, Hunt achieves what Rebecca West called "a cold, white vision of reality," in which the psychological dynamics of sexual relationships are frankly and often painfully dissected. But for all their sophistication, Hunt's modern heroines cannot entirely rid themselves of their romantic illusions, and they are unable to escape in any satisfactory way from the restrictive or destructive relationships they find themselves in.

Jane E. Miller, in her "The Edward Naumburg, Jr., Collection of Violet Hunt," Princeton University Library Chronicle, *Winter 1990.*

Geoffrey Rossetti   (essay date 1932)

[*Rossetti is an English critic. In the following review, he argues that* The Wife of Rossetti *fails as a biography but succeeds as "a Victorian biographical melodrama."*]

That there are but few examples of good biography proves how extremely difficult it is to tell the story of a person's life so as to be faithful at once to art and to truth. Boswell apparently contrived to do both, and so did Tacitus in the "Agricola"—but then both these writers had a strong sense of fact. With them the lawyer or the historian came first, the artist second. In Miss Violet Hunt's life of Elizabeth Siddall [**The Wife of Rossetti—Her Life and Death**] her novelist's imaginative talent comes first and her sense of fact follows very half-heartedly in the rear. The documentation for many hitherto unpublished details in the lives of the well known figures who occur in her book is meagre. The story of the piece of paper which Ford Madox Brown found on the nightdress of Mrs. Rossetti when she was dead surely should receive some documentation. There is probably little doubt that Miss Hunt was told this very interesting detail by someone else. But why is the source not referred to in a foot-note?

Miss Hunt's obvious sympathy with her heroine hardly allows for the fact that Miss Siddall was playing with fire the whole time. From the experience she had had before she married Rossetti, Miss Siddall must have known that he was an odd creature. Indeed she seems to have been no less odd herself, and certainly far more fractious and disagreeable. One's admiration almost goes out to Rossetti for marrying her at all. In such a case many a man would have done a bolt!

Miss Hunt seems to me also most unfair towards the other members of the Rossetti family. It may well be true that they did not like Miss Siddall, and that she was somewhat cold-shouldered. But it should be remembered that Rossetti was one of four children whose parentage was mainly Italian, and that the Italian temperament ran very much in their blood. The feeling for family is very strong in the Italians, and family solidarity was no small feature of this the first generation of the Rossettis in England. When we add that Italians frequently comment on the lack of cohesion in an English family, this different feeling must surely be seen to be partly responsible for the attitude of the rest of his family to Dante Gabriel Rossetti's wife, and possibly for the somewhat indifferent attitude of her own family to her. This aspect of the question might well have been considered by Miss Hunt, as it is an important part of the conflict which undoubtedly took place when the son of the Vastese poet married the daughter of the Sheffield cutler.

But this biography undoubtedly reveals that Miss Hunt has a very strong sense of melodrama. In Sir Hall Caine's biography of Rossetti, and now in Miss Hunt's biography of his wife, there is a strong tendency to exaggerate the melodramatic and the sensational. Nevertheless, we must confess we are becoming a little tired of those "great flares by night in the cemetery" when the coffin was being exhumed, and the anguish of the poet before the dead body of his beautiful young wife. Miss Hunt's story will touch those who are touched by this sort of thing, but to those who are most anxious to know exactly what did occur, and have no wish that any true fact should be concealed, this book will be somewhat disappointing.

Yet it must not be thought that Miss Hunt has produced a worthless or uninteresting piece of work. Her accounts of the Bohemian life led by the various members of the Pre-Raphaelite group are most entertaining.

Perhaps the most charming feature of the book is the very excellent collection of pictures which it contains. These have been selected with great taste, and the delightful pencil portraits of Miss Siddall show what an extremely fine sense of design Rossetti had. Each drawing of Miss Siddall shows her in a new and simple attitude, in which the artist reveals his capacity for elegant design and subtle psychological interpretation. Miss Hunt has attempted a very difficult task and has not been entirely successful, but in so far as she set out to write a Victorian biographical melodrama she has produced a work which is a very considerable achievement.

Geoffrey Rossetti, "The Wife of Rossetti," in The Bookman, *London, Vol. LXXXIII, No. 493, October, 1932, p. 56.*

Evelyn Waugh   (essay date 1932)

[*From the publication in 1928 of his novel* Decline and Fall *until his death in 1966, Waugh was England's leading satirical novelist. In works including* Vile Bodies *(1930),* Scoop *(1938), and* The Loved One *(1948), he skewered such targets as the bored young sophisticates of the 1920s, the questionable values of the British press, and the American commercialization of death. Considered a major Catholic author after his conversion in 1930, Waugh is best known today for his novel* Brideshead Revisited *(1945), which examines the lives of the members of a wealthy Catholic family. In the following review of* The Wife of Rossetti, *he faults the volume's organization and lack of documentation but praises Hunt's attention to detail and treatment of Rossetti's marital life.*]

For many years now it has been no secret that [**The Wife of Rossetti**] was in preparation, and everyone interested in pre-Raphaelite biography has awaited its publication with keen interest. No living writer was better equipped than Miss Hunt for the task; her power of narrative is well known; her upbringing afforded her unique opportunities of collecting information and forming judgements on the principal personalities of the time; to this she has added the fruit of many years unremitting research. Only one who has attempted an excursion into the confused byways of the period can appreciate the importance of this personal acquaintance and tireless investigation. The published sources at the biographer's disposal, though seldom actually untruthful, are riddled through and through with evasions and omissions. Not only are the historians of the brotherhood discreet about intimate personal details whose publication might reasonably be postponed until the reputations and sentiments of the protagonists were no longer vulnerable, but there is also a consistent and ludicrous reluctance on their part to impute such human qualities as undistinguished birth and personal animosity. Left to himself William Rossetti would have preferred to keep the whole of his brother's private life as an obscure legend; his reticence was challenged by William Bell Scott's autobiography and Hall Caine's memoir. He produced an official biography which is a model of subterfuge. Fanny Cornforth, for instance, cannot be wholly disregarded, but she figures in the story under different names and disguises so that no casual reader would recognize her reappearances. For example the nurse who was with Rossetti in Cumberland is nowhere identified with the Cockney who threw nutshells at him in his student days. One of the chief achievements of Miss Hunt's book is to connect and render coherent the innumerable hints and fragmentary revelations of her predecessors. She, for the first time, introduces Annie Miller and explains the origin of Hunt's breach with Rossetti. There is not a page of Miss Hunt's book that does not contain some piece of information enormously significant to the student who has wandered bewildered among the official sources. Here indeed is the weakness of Miss Hunt's book. It is far too full and allusive for the "general reader." Instead of a single, tragic story simply reconstrued, one is confronted by a torrent of invaluable information, fascinating and thrilling reading to someone who knows the six or seven standard works on the subject, but fatally confusing to the uninitiat-

ed. The introductory chapter, with its pedigrees and abrupt changes of subject, might easily discourage the reader. Throughout too there are numerous faults of construction. Miss Hunt continually incorporates phrases and sentences in inverted commas without naming their authors. She is also far too haphazard in her reference to authorities, making no distinction between first- and second-hand information. She several times gives the present reviewer as her reference for statements which, obviously, he can only have made upon higher authority, and for many of her most important revelations, *e.g.,* the note pinned on Miss Siddall's nightgown and removed by Madox Brown, she gives no reference at all. One does not doubt the truth of her story, but it is important to know how the facts reached her—from Brown, Swinburne, unpublished letters or diaries, or at second-hand from her parents.

The book, however, gets clearer and stronger as the story narrows down to the single issue of Rossetti's married life. Elizabeth's Siddall's character, for so long obscured by legend, at last emerges in light—unamiable but convincing. The story of her death is told for the first time, and probably this is the most important single contribution which Miss Hunt makes to her subject. Miss Hunt has stated, with great skill, preserving all the pathos and dramatic force of the incident, what everyone guessed but had not the authority to assert. Hers is an absolutely necessary book, but this one reflexion may be added; it does not seem the final book on the subject. Miss Hunt was in a position, just as was Theodore Watts-Dunton, to write the final book; she has rather chosen to disclose a magnificent treasury of insufficiently correlated fact. The book which will put the whole into literary form has still to be written.

Evelyn Waugh, "Rossetti's Wife," in The Spectator, *Vol. 149, No. 5441, October 8, 1932, p. 449.*

Eda Lou Walton   (essay date 1932)

[*Walton is an American critic. In the review below, she provides a highly laudatory assessment of* The Wife of Rossetti.]

The experience of reading [Violet Hunt's **The Wife of Rossetti**] is very much like spending a week end with a houseful of famous artists and writers, most of whom are strangers to you. You find yourself in a large roomful of people who know each other intimately. You hear first one bit of gossip, then another. Women and men address each other by first names and nicknames. You cannot quite fix any of them at first. All seem to have lived very complicated lives. There are hints of scandal and frequent gossip about a certain tragic suicide—Gabriel's wife—yes. Motives are suggested, then dropped.

You strain your ears trying to determine something about this story: After a few hours of desperate listening you come to the conclusion that every one in the room is just a little mad, after the manner of artists, and that you, yourself a very commonplace person, may turn mad too if you linger long in this fascinating and exotic company. You soon realise that you cannot quite believe all you hear, that tales are contradictory. These people are given to ghosts, too, and hallucinations. How to piece it all together! Truly this is a brilliant gathering. The women in their rich, full, clinging gowns are beautiful in the golden light of the late afternoon. The men, perhaps a little given to eccentricities of manner and egomania, are men of genius.

Well, this is only Saturday, and you will stay till Sunday. Perhaps you will be able to fathom the relationships and the stories.

Violet Hunt's childhood and early girlhood were spent in the midst of the Pre-Raphaelite group:

> With nearly all of the persons concerned in this ancient woe, I have held converse in my degree, except with the chief protagonist, who died before I was born. Her husband I have seen in the street, but his head was muffled up, as it were, in a monk's cowl. But I remember well his sister, Christina, and her broad bosom, in dove-colored silk wreathed with black lace. And his brother, William, with his bold head and red lips. I remember Morris's Viking eyes and Mrs. Morris's hair, her ghostly beauty like a blasted tree or sprig of mistletoe; and Georgie Jones like a little brown bird, and Effie Millais, a handsome Scotch lassie, dressed in her *criardo* crocus gowns. I remember Brown's flowing beard, and Hunt's darling snub nose, and Browning's guttural voice and Millais's hoarse voice a year before he died. And Mr. Scott's wig that he changed monthly to simulate growth, and Theodore Watts with his walrus mustache and gypsy eyes.

And so it is from memory and from the gossipy notebooks and letters of these people, that Miss Hunt reconstructs the innumerable amazing scenes in the lives of the Rossettis and of their many famous friends. The result is a biography which is really a kind of moving picture with sound in which expert photography has caught every gesture, every expression—expert recording, every quality of the voice, even every half-spoken phrase or whisper. The book is tremendously alive, much more dramatic than most more conventionally written biographies. And if the reader is sometimes a little sceptical, a little suspicious of the author's exaggerated sensibility to all that she saw or heard or read about the P. R. B., it is nevertheless this very heightened imagination that makes possible the recapturing of the words, the feelings, the dramatic attitudes of every actor in this most un-Victorian group.

And certainly there is new interpretation in this biography. Whoever caught before Christina Rossetti's sinister cruelty changing slowly to religious intensity? One wishes that Miss Hunt would write Christina's biography. Whoever saw so clearly Rossetti's insatiable need for company, this artist's hunger fed only by new friendships, new loves? Here is the very man, unstable, selfish, blind to everything that did not immediately fulfill his desires. And here is Swinburne, twirling, dancing as if with St. Vitus, drinking more than Elizabeth Siddal wished, always adoring her and capable of understanding her dependency on drugs. Here is Hunt and his wife, too poor to have children and yet attempting parenthood. Here is the ruffian, Morris, whose wife would have preferred a nice modern house, spilling paint from his medieval roof down on the heads of the passers-by.

And here, ever present in all these people's minds, in Elizabeth Siddal ("Sid"—or "Guggums"—to Rossetti), passionate, stubborn, sensuous and virginal, a milliner, a model, then Gabriel's "Queen of Hearts" but not as so many supposed, his mistress, finally his fiancee for almost nine years, and then, too late, his wife. We see her deliberately absorbing Rossetti's vitality, the flame, never warming her for long, writing poetry not unlike his, though much slighter; painting pictures like his too. Once she had cast off her own background and her family for his background and his family (which would not receive her), she tried always to be his shadow. And shortly this shadow grew too pale for the very healthy and restless young fellow, but still it followed him and became his "conscience."

Elizabeth was sick, tubercular, more sick perhaps of "force too long pent up." Only now and then, and in flashes, could there be any release. She was not good at managing situations, but she was very good indeed at resisting all influences against the will in her, flaming, under its suppression, like her own brilliant hair. And so, after nine years, she gets her wish, she is married, almost, it seems, on her death-bed, by a conscience-stricken lover. Two years of marriage, the first, drab and peaceful, the second violently passionate, but without love, and quarrelsome even unto death. Then suicide. An evening at a restaurant with Swinburne, a quarrel on the way home, and the husband leaving the wife to recover her temper while he seeks comfort elsewhere. Later Rossetti returns to find his wife breathing too heavily. She has taken an overdose of laudanum. On her nightgown is pinned the note, not printed by Brown, who discovered it, "My life is so miserable I wish for no more of it." This was a frustrated woman's last stubborn gesture.

Rossetti answered it by laying his book of sonnets (most of which were well memorized by his friends) against his wife's dead cheek, under her burning hair, the hair which he had made the fashion in all London. The whispering and the gossip go on for many years thereafter.

The outlines of this "love" story have been told many times. But no such intuitive, feminine characterisation as Miss Hunt's has been given. Whether or not she is always right, no one can tell us; she is, it must be confessed, very convincing. And what comes through her pages is not the glory of it all, but rather the humor, the pathos, the absurdity, the neurotic madness of it all, and even therein, the terrible humanness. What horrid people, one feels at one moment, how tragically blind and human, he or she is, at the next. And one's mind flashes to Huxley's *Point Counterpoint,* and that novelist's more deliberately satirical analysis of another group of writers and artists, lesser figures, probably, but equally neurotic. Huxley's portraits are deliberately ironic. Miss Hunt's are, I think, not deliberately anything at all, but just people.

The Wife of Rossetti is an absorbing memoir devastatingly analytical at times, richly embroidered in all kinds of carefully searched out details, now and then a little sensational because of its author's superstitious and morbid interest in her heroine. One feels that Violet Hunt might well have been one of these Pre-Raphaelite women herself, she interprets them with such romantic and yet satirical accuracy. They are not pictures to her, they are living women capable of creating glamour, frustration, and bitterness. She understands them even better than she does their more famous husbands. She can follow them into their bedrooms where they giggle and chatter while their husbands argue academically in the studio. Here they all are, tall, full-throated, with heavy-lidded eyes, dressed much alike in the "unstayed" fashion their painter husbands thought medieval and therefore beautiful.

And here, too, presented with a little less penetration, perhaps, are their husbands and lovers, all men obsessed by Art and by themselves, the sensual and yet sensitive Rossetti, the impotent and business-like Ruskin, the strong and slightly inhuman Browning; the weakling Swinburne; the gentle Hunt; the reticent, and wise Allingham, the clumsy Morris. And all these men, being artists, are from a woman's point of view, inept as husbands, and, for the most part, incapable as business men. And so when the week end—on the reading of this memoir—is over, one feels as if one knew every character in this famous Brotherhood and Sisterhood, for it was that, too, almost too intimately, as if one would choose to get off alone for a while and think them over, these people who are bound to haunt one's dreams. (pp. 1, 6)

Eda Lou Walton, "Pre-Raphaelite House Party," in New York Herald Tribune Books, *October 30, 1932, p. 1, 6.*

On Hunt's diaries:

[Hunt's] habit was to jot down notes, arranged by days of the month, and then later—often much later—to write up the occasions in detail; sometimes she never got around to the writing up, but when she did she was frequently highly entertaining about the people she knew, a sharp observer, and a malicious judge. She is also curiously objective in her descriptions of her own conduct, which was usually ill-advised, especially where men were concerned; "I am," she once said, "a sensualist of the emotions," and she seems to have longed almost more for melodramatic situations and scenes than for stable human relationships.

Arthur Mizener, in his "The Lost Papers of Violet Hunt," in The Cornell Library Journal, *Autumn 1967.*

Marie Secor   (essay date 1976)

[*Secor is an American educator and scholar of Pre-Raphaelite literature who has published extensively on Hunt, often in collaboration with Robert Secor. In the essay below, she provides an overview of Hunt's career.*]

If Violet Hunt is remembered at all today, it is as Ford Madox Ford's self-proclaimed wife and only vaguely as a novelist in her own right. Parts of the story of the Ford relationship, which encompassed the years 1908-1918, are told by Violet herself in a Book of memoirs, *The Flurried Years* (1926), published in America under the title *I Have This to Say*. Douglas Goldring, a sub-editor of Ford's *English Review* and long time friend of both Ford and Hunt, talks about her warmly in his memoir, *South Lodge* and Arthur Mizener devotes several chapters to the Ford-Hunt relationship in *The Saddest Story*. What emerges from these sources is a portrait of a well known literary and social figure of her day, whose reputation (both literary and social) declines precipitously following Elsie Martindale Hueffer's 1912 suit over Violet's illegal use of Ford's name. The embarrassment of Elsie's legal victory, followed by the slow, painful disintegration of the affair with Ford, as Stella Bowen replaced Violet, left Violet alone at fifty-five years of age in 1917, with social, professional, and personal wounds from which she never recovered.

Nevertheless, her literary career was long and prolific. She wrote seventeen novels, three collections of stories, two books of autobiographical memoirs, a once popular biography of Elizabeth Siddall in addition to translations, collaborations, and articles in journals. She was also recognized as an important link with the Pre-Raphaelites, whom she knew through her parents, Alfred Hunt, a painter (no relation of Holman Hunt), and Margaret Raine Hunt, a popular novelist. Her parents knew Browning and Tennyson, and Ruskin was godfather to Violet's sister Venice. Her own circle included most of the major literary figures of the early twentieth century: Ford, Wilde (who, in an 1880 letter, calls her "the sweetest Violet in England"), Maugham, Bennett, Wells, James (who called her "Purple Patch"), Conrad, Pound, Wyndham Lewis, Lawrence, and W. H. Hudson. By the time she met Ford in 1908, her best novel *White Rose of Weary Leaf,* had already been published, and with it, Mizener claims, "she became widely recognized as one of the leading women novelists of her time."

Although contemporary reviews of her work were mixed, she was respected by the discerning (Maugham, Lawrence, Bennett, Goldring, Ford, May Sinclair, and Rebecca West) for the very qualities which disturbed the popular reviewers. Reviews of *White Rose,* for instance, praise its cleverness and its dialogue, but find it "disagreeable," "squalidly dreary," and "depressing." Goldring, on the other hand, compares Violet Hunt's work to Colette's (which she knew and admired) and finds it appealing precisely because it introduces "a note of Nastiness in English fiction." By "Nastiness" he seems to mean a frank concern with the sexual psychology of what May Sinclair calls the "English *demi-vierge*," and her refusal to cooperate in the fictional idealization of romantic love and domesticity.

Hunt seems to have suffered by her reputation for wit, both personally and professionally. She was known as a non-stop, brilliant chatterer, apparently inconsequential, but shrewd and humane in her judgments of character. In a 1922 article in the *English Review,* May Sinclair attempts to assess her career and rescue her from the limiting charge of mere cleverness, which she sees as having inhibited recognition of Hunt's major achievement as a "tragic realist" in *White Rose* and her powerful presentation of "the naked thoughts, the naked lives of people we have known" in *Their Lives* and *Their Hearts.* But even this judicious appraisal by a fellow novelist seems to have had little effect on Hunt's reputation. In spite of a 1932 plea by Godfrey Childe for some reprints of her fiction, her novels have almost completely disappeared from circulation. By 1942, the year of her death, the entry in *Twentieth Century Authors* speaks of her work as "very nearly forgotten though it was at once robust and subtle." In the 1955 supplement, Goldring (who wrote the Hunt entry) speculates that if future students of social life and manners are interested in the epoch Violet Hunt represents, "it is difficult to see how Violet's personality—a catfish in that decorous aquarium if ever there was one—can fail to attract attention to herself and her books." Yet twenty more years have brought no revival of interest in her work, in spite of her undeniable talent and her important historical and social position as a "New Woman" with links to an illustrious late Victorian past.

Her career as a novelist spans the years 1894-1925, with her best work appearing from 1904 on. Her early novels, though immature, define some of the themes she pursues more distinctively in her later works. Her first novel, *The Maiden's Progress* (1894) was well received (perhaps partly because of her family's literary and social connections); an early review praises Violet as "one of the smartest dialogue writers of the day." Its heroine, the aptly named Moderna, is like Violet the eldest of three sisters. She is pretty, graceful, and dissatisfied with the prospects of conventional courtship and marriage. Like many of Violet's heroines, she is accused of heartlessness, and even doubts her own capacity for feeling because she finds conventional expectations of young girls unrealistic. After dabbling (without talent or commitment) in the literary-artistic world, she turns to her good suitor, who understands her, waits for her even after she rejects his first proposal, and picks up the pieces when her experiment at freedom fails. Here all is girlish wish-fulfillment: Moderna, at twenty-seven, has her fling, breaks hearts, and finally turns to the good man who has been waiting all the while. Unfortunately, neither Hunt's life nor her later fiction confirm the easy optimism of this adolescent plot.

Although *A Hard Woman* (1895) shares the mannerisms and immaturities of *The Maiden's Progress*—brittle dialogue, self-conscious naughtiness, perfunctory plotting, and weakly characterized men—here Hunt defines her feminist theme more fully. The novel depicts two models of feminine emancipation. Lydia, the wife of an artist, Ferdinand Munday, is an ambitious woman who insists on dominance and independence within marriage, scorning Bohemianism as "declassé." While directing her husband's career, she makes the drawing room her social theater, where she exercises her sharp tongue, her wit and her charm for social and professional advancement. Her opposite is Nevill France, a Bohemian rebel without social grace, but with real beauty and artistic talent. Although Nevill rejects marriage, she retains wholehearted belief in love. Loving Ferdinand and unconcerned about money or appearances, she poses free for him and even sacrifices ca-

reer opportunities for love. Although Lydia has much to learn about feeling, the unconventional Nevill is the novel's true sentimentalist because she cooperates in the Pre-Raphaelite artist's idealization and exploitation of women as decorative objects to be posed with lilies in their hands. Violet herself is torn between these two models in her life: while she longs for the respectability and the social power of marriage, she finds herself victimized by her passion for Ford.

In another early novel, *Unkist, Unkind!* (1897), Hunt abandons the novel of dialogue and dialectical wit for the psychological Gothic, which becomes an important strain in her fiction, lending it its Charlotte Brontë–ish quality. She uses the Gothic to explore the neurotic sensibilities of sexually frustrated women. This novel's psychology is crude and its air of case history does not combine happily with Gothic, but even Hunt's best fiction retains a Gothic sensationalism. Her plots are sometimes sensational; her handling of her characters' emotions, always. She returns to the Gothic tale later in her career with *Tales of the Uneasy* (1911) and *More Tales of the Uneasy* (1925).

These early works reveal Violet Hunt as an immature writer with talent. She arrives as a novelist, not just a bright young woman, in 1904 with two books, *Sooner or Later* and *The Celebrity at Home.* Here she stakes out her two areas of special interest and competence: the sexual psychology of young women and the damage which family life inflicts upon its chief victim, the young girl. The themes are of course related, and she explores their furthest implications in the late autobiographical novels, *Their Lives* and *Their Hearts.*

Sooner or Later, praised highly by Maugham, is also heavily autobiographical, based upon Violet's recently concluded and highly public affair with Oswald Crawfurd, a well known gentleman diplomat, dabbler in literature, and womanizer. He was British consul to Portugal and editor of *The Novel Magazine* and *Black and White,* both of which Violet contributed to frequently. Their affair lasted from 1890 until 1898, during which time Crawfurd was married. After his invalid wife died in 1899, Crawfurd married Lita Brown, a friend of Violet's. He died in 1909, but Violet never forgot him, even though from him she contracted the syphilis which affected her mind later in her life.

Sooner or Later's heroine, Rosette Newall (often called "The Ingenious Ingenue") is bored by her proper, dull suitor and begins an affair with Robert Assheton, an aging rake who represents everything a sheltered girl dreams of: he is a flirtatious, handsome, witty, ruthless sensation seeker, even more fascinating because unavailable for marriage. He finds Rosette's shrewd innocence refreshing; he accuses her of enjoying "taking risks—playing at life." After a mock marriage ceremony, they set up house. In time and inevitably, Rosette becomes possessive; Assheton chafes; she becomes depressed, dependent, accusatory, unattractive. He likens her to "an unpaid bill in the room." The affair winds down in bitter disillusionment. Assheton accuses Rosette of "sexual tactlessness." Like Violet, a poor tactician in all her love affairs, she was always "driving things into corners, forcing a note, incapable of letting a thing slide."

Hunt's characteristic note here is one of emotional sensationalism. The novel is painfully realistic (though not graphic) about sexual relationships; we trace minutely the growth of disgust and revulsion between people who have been disillusioned about each other. Rosette is victimized by her irrational need for Assheton, a need which contradicts objective certainty and moves her to self-destructive perversities in trying to regain the man she knows no longer wants her. We watch her acquire "dreary sexual wisdom." Although obviously not a well distanced work of art, *Sooner or Later* is less brittle and self-consciously smart than the earlier novels; it probes painfully at the realities behind the scenes of drawing room comedy.

The pain of real life, as opposed to life as it appears in novels or in drawing rooms, is also a major theme of the much lighter, more comic *The Celebrity at Home.* Here the point of view is that of fourteen year old Tempe Vero-Taylor, like James's Maisie, the wise innocent, the neglected child moving through the corrupt adult world. Because she is not "out" yet, she observes adult life "through the bannisters," fortunately immune to sexual desire, greed, and the social conventions which move the other characters to foolishness. Her father, George Vero-Taylor, is a novelist of Pre-Raphaelite pretentions who scorns the grubbiness of "suburban" life. Moving in aristocratic circles, passing himself off as single, he ignores the uncomfortable realities and demands of middle-class family life, like daughters who need money for dresses and a son who needs an education. Tempe's mother is an ex-actress, Lucy Jennings, who has wasted away her youth and beauty running the household and waiting for George to come home. Her manager, Mr. Aix, is a "realistic" novelist who seeks out laundresses and shopgirls to "treat" in his fiction, but is helpless dealing with reality. Tempe and her sister Ariadne are left to their own devices by incompetent adults who can deal with reality only through fictional projections. Ariadne, a "nice" conventional girl, finds models of behavior in romantic novels and ultimately gets drawn into the sordid sexual and financial arrangements of her elders. Tempe's needs for affection and stability are simply ignored.

The Celebrity at Home and *Sooner or Later* refine the anti-romantic theme Violet Hunt pursues in all her best fiction. Her young women face life with the support and guidance of families. Pre-Raphaelite idealization of women is exploitive, the prospects of suburban wifeliness unattractive, drawing room cleverness unfulfilling, and romantic heroism unattainable. Sexual liberation may be desirable and political emancipation certainly is (Violet was an ardent supporter of the suffrage movement), but her young women are too conventional to find rebellion thinkable; like their creator, they long for respectability and are ill at ease with Bohemia's self-conscious inversions of conventions.

The novel usually considered her best, *White Rose of Weary Leaf* (1908), presents a fully drawn portrait of an unusual "New Woman" at the beginning of the twentieth century. *White Rose* is a modern governess-novel, the story of a plain girl whose wit, competence, and intelligence fascinate her rich gentleman employer and draw her, fully aware and unrepentant, into an affair with him. The novel was praised for its wit, scored for its sensationalism, and banned by Boots' Circulating Libraries. In response to Boots' attack on her artistic intentions (as well as her social pretensions) Violet defends *White Rose* in a letter, agreeing that it is indeed "not a book for girls," but insisting that "it is a serious attempt to trace out the result of moral deprivation in the character and fate of certain persons with the greatest possible degree of reticence compatible with clearness and an avoidance of all superficial glossing over of main issues of right and wrong." In her characteristically personal and self-aware manner, she concludes her letter with the following appeal: "I am enclosing my photograph and I should like to ask if you think it looks like the authoress of an improper novel."

White Rose's heroine, Amy Stephens, is a modern Jane Eyre—resourceful, intelligent, efficient, outspoken and self-reliant in a world unprotective of young women without money or family. Unlike Jane, however, she is no conventional moralist. She is alone, and her chief concern is survival, not the preservation of a lady's fragile reputation. On the other hand, she is not out for gain or intrigue, or even for sexual gratification. Amy wants only minimal security—a roof over her head and an opportunity to be useful. She is an unlikely, unromantic heroine. Love is not her ruling passion; "at the best it is like olives," she says, "an acquired taste, and very bitter." Even social ambition is irrelevant to her; she has no leisure to cultivate lady-like accomplishments, so unlike most fictional heroines, she is unliterary, unartistic, and unimaginative. In fact, Amy Stephens is cold, unyielding, repressed, and domineering—qualities only slightly warmed by her wit and intellectual acuteness. Most attractive is her determination to survive without compromising her realistic honesty.

With Amy Stephens as its heroine, *White Rose* turns its attack on our inadequate ideas about the relationships between men and women. These relationships are vastly more complex than convention allows. Our laws are concerned with the forms of marriage, fidelity, and legitimacy and our myths with romantic love, but human relationships are by nature shifting and unfixed. Similarly, our fiction attempts to cast fluid relationships in molds which define and limit their meanings; one of the novel's characters is a novelist, Alec Johnson, who is always trying to "fictionalize" the relationships between Amy and her employer-lover, Jeremy Dand.

The characters of *White Rose* are capable of surprising us with their complexity. Dand is Hunt's best male character. He loves Amy passionately, but remains wrapped up in his business, ungenerous to the point of stinginess, and insists he can continue to love his wife. Edith, his wife, is conventional, silly, and not very bright, but not therefore less capable of loving her husband. She has a capacity for understanding and growth, and even comes to accept Amy's presence in her house after she becomes aware of her husband's love for her. Amy, cold and theoretical, becomes Dand's mistress in a moment of carefully defined weakness and without passion; although she submits to an "arrangement" whereby she stays in a rooming house where he visits her, she never feels depraved or fallen.

The novel's power lies in its constantly fresh and surprising dialogue. Like all Hunt novels, it is talky, but here the talk is well focused, the talkers sympathetic. Hunt is at her best dealing with intelligent, verbal, unconventional people in constantly shifting dramatic circumstances. Like most of her heroines, Amy Stephens is perverse and frigid; Violet Hunt has little to say about warm, tender, loving women destined for happiness and fulfillment; but, like the great novelists of the early part of the century—Hardy, James, and Lawrence—she probes compassionately and honestly the sensibilities of young women facing alone a world unconcerned with traditional notions of feminine delicacy.

The Celebrity's Daughter, written in 1913 at the height of the Ford affair, returns to the characters and situation of *The Celebrity at Home* and introduces the theme of feminine self-sacrifice in love. Tempe is now five years older and more resembles James's Nanda Brookenham of *The Awkward Age* than Maisie. Beautiful, generous, sensible, honest and loyal, Tempe is mainly concerned that her father get his divorce so he can do the "right thing," that is marry Lady Scilly, with whom he has been living. Tempe's mother, meanwhile, has resumed her stage career, and Ariadne, her conventional sister with the "political smile," has married the wealthy Simon Hermyre, ex-lover of Lady Scilly, who still provides her with money. In the midst of this disreputable family, Tempe does without the money, clothes, and chaperonage that beautiful young girls need in order to make appropriate matches. She loves Ernie Fynes, an attractive Catholic country gentleman, but her poverty and "impropriety" make it impossible for him to marry her. Like Nanda, she loses the man she loves because he thinks she is not good enough; actually, she is too good, even though she does apparently corrupt things—like taking money from Mrs. Fynes not to marry her son. Tempe is a victim, the only generous person in a selfish world. Like Violet, she craves respectability, but acquires a "reputation" instead.

In Violet Hunt's later novels and tales run two major strains, concern about the impact of World War I on civilian consciousness and a return to her own (fictionalized) childhood and adolescence to explore more fully the interplay between family and individual sensibility. In two long, apparently autobiographical novels, *Their Lives* (1916) and *Their Hearts* (1921), she abandons the self-conscious artifice of her earlier fiction and attempts instead to capture the dense emotional texture of real life, centered largely on family rituals, like coming out parties, engagements, and weddings. The effort is not altogether successful, for both novels are rambling, uneven, and uncertain in focus, but they do constitute a memorable and powerful criticism of late Victorian family life, with its intense rivalries, jealousies, repressions and sexual undercurrents.

The "Lives" and "hearts" which concern her belong to three sisters, Christina, Virgilia, and Orinthia Radmall, daughters of a struggling Pre-Raphaelite artist father. Papa is angelic, but remote from people and uninvolved in the social and moral complexities of raising daughters. "It was Mamma's business to amuse the children, nurse them, scold them, do everything for them; Papa only loved them, and must not be disturbed." A study in frustrated ambition, he paints diligently to support his family, but remains uninvited to join the Royal Academy. Mamma's chief devotion is to Papa's career; she would like to see her daughters properly married off, but lacks the warmth, the insight, and the social grace to handle domestic or emotional complexities. She loves only her middle child, Virgilia, who is most conventionally good. She dislikes her youngest, Orinthia, and even refused to nurse her as a baby. Christina, who resembles Violet, is the eldest. She is artistic, sensitive, precocious, pretty, and flirtatious; her mother fears and humors her, but is unable to provide guidance: "Christina was a bit of a genius. Geniuses did not, but always should, for their own convenience, marry stupid quiet men like George Day, to run their moral errands and do their sublunary housekeeping for them."

In both novels Christina is the center of interest and the other sisters contrast with her. Virgilia is a brilliant portrait of a mean, hard, conventional woman (Christina accuses her of having a "furniture buying mind"). Evidently, much of Violet's resentment of her sister Venice, with whom she has extended unpleasant financial dealings, finds its way into Virgilia's portrait. (Venice is nicknamed "Ice" and called "Goneril" in Violet's memoirs.) Virgilia devotes all her efforts to finding a desirable husband. Ignorant of life, but competent in practical matters, she uses her respectability to bludgeon others, especially Christina. Orinthia, passive, unattractive, and unloved, worships her father silently and incestuously. Permanently wounded by her mother's coldness and further violated by an old man at the beach, she has no chance for life. Marriage only completes her disillusionment. The honeymoon is a nightmare, her husband crude and unfaithful, sex and childbearing repellent. In Orinthia normal feelings are displaced; she dislikes her baby, flirts with her doctor, and after her father's death wants to stay with his corpse all night. She is a victim of sexual ignorance and repression, lacking even Virgilia's worldly competence and determination to acquire things.

Christina, like Violet, is the only sister with charm and artistic talent. Unfortunately, like Violet again, she is self-destructive. After rejecting her proper and dull suitor, she has an affair with an older man, her father's friend and more successful fellow artist, Emerson Vlaye. Vlaye is evidently modelled after George Boughton, a successful landscape painter, Royal Academy associate, and Campden Hill, neighbor of the Hunts. Rejecting her sisters' blind domesticity, Christina seeks freedom by becoming a writer and drifting into Bohemian circles. She also drifts into an affair with her editor, Euphan Balfame, another version of Oswald Crawfurd, an older, married man with an insane wife. The affair proves a dead end; she is without Balfame's love and support when she needs them most and subject to the scorn of others. Caught in the restrictive conventions of illicit love, she must maintain her pose of independence, accept her lover's continuing relationship with his wife, and deal with her own jealousy and attendant powerlessness. Although Christina is brighter and more sensitive than her sisters, she is left a lonely outsider at the scene which concludes *Their Hearts,* her father's funeral. In these novels Violet Hunt comes a long way from the adolescent optimism of her early fiction and even from the disillusioned acceptance of her middle works.

Their Lives and *Their Hearts* are disturbing novels which present no solutions to the problems they raise. Like so many novelists of the late nineteenth and early twentieth centuries, Violet Hunt sees clearly the cultural limitations which restrict her characters' desire for free, honest relationships; she also comes to see as self-destructive the effort to ignore restrictive conventions. In an early review [that was reprinted on the cover of the first edition of *Their Lives*], Rebecca West praises *Their Lives* for the courage of its vision, calling it "an extremely unpleasant book" because of its "profound and reasoned conviction that sweetness and reason are not predominant in human affairs." Neither were sweetness and reason predominant in Violet Hunt's affairs.

Tales of the Uneasy (1911) and *More Tales of the Uneasy* (1925) are collections of stories, some short, some almost novella length, that Hunt wrote over the long span of her career. All are in the mode of the Gothic, dealing with inexplicable, faintly supernatural events. One of them, **"The Coach,"** was admired by James. The Preface to *More Tales* is one of Hunt's best pieces of writing. It recounts charmingly her early meetings with James, evaluates shrewdly his character, acknowledges his mastery of this kind of story, and provides a brilliant explanation of its method and effects, along with what must be the earliest critical analysis of "The Turn of the Screw" as psychological ghost story:

> Henry James was avid of information. He liked to turn over the dust-heaps of other people's minds in his own refined and jackdaw-like manner, very gingerly, for he was desperately afraid of being mixed up in any way with reality. He wanted to see the game—as much of it as was likely to be useful to him—from the stadium reserved for spectators, with good strong railings between tragedy and him. He preferred to stand without wetting his feet on the edge of the turbid stream of existence where men and women floated and swam and strove and drowned—socially—unless they happened to solve their problem, the one that he had in imagination set them, in good time.

Of "The Turn of the Screw" she writes:

> I, myself, think it is just a freak story which rose full-armed from the subliminal consciousness of—as the surface mind goes—a sexually unsophisticated man. . . . He had the simplicity of genius which scorns, or at least is not careful to guard itself from, misunderstanding. He enjoyed the little scandal created by this strongest, most reputation-making outcome of the Jamesian mind. . . . It brought us together in the butterfly days when I danced all night and read all day, lying on a backboard to make my shoulders straight.

The total eclipse of Violet Hunt's reputation as a novelist

has been our misfortune as much as hers. Although many of the important novelists of her era (such as Hardy, Lawrence, Gissing, Bennett, and James) deal probingly and sympathetically with women characters, today we read few women novelists to compare with them. I would suggest, tentatively, that **White Rose of Weary Leaf, Their Lives, Their Hearts,** and some of the stories from **More Tales of the Uneasy,** specifically **"Love's Last Leave,"** **"The Cigaret Case of the Commander,"** and **"The Corsican Sisters,"** are not only well written and readable (claims which could be made for most of Hunt's fiction), but significant both artistically and historically. Artistically, because her young women are accurately, minutely, and passionately drawn, her dialogue at its best both witty and dramatic, and her sense of sexual relationships honestly complex. Historically, because Violet Hunt stands, fully aware and intelligent, between the Pre-Raphaelite age she was born into and brought up in and the early twentieth–century artistic and literary world she participated in so fully through her relationships with Ford, James, and the many important writers connected with the *English Review.*

Her best work has qualities which should admit her to the company of the important Edwardian novelists. She has a keen perception of the social and familial pressures which affect character, accompanied by an understanding of the inadequacy of drawing room psychology. Her young women are created by the nineteenth century, but they face the twentieth with the need to define their moral positions honestly and personally and to break out of the Pre-Raphaelite mold of exploitive idealization. (pp. 25-33)

> *Marie Secor, "Violet Hunt, Novelist: A Reintroduction," in* English Literature in Transition: 1880-1920, *Vol. 19, No. 1, 1976, pp. 25-34.*

FURTHER READING

Miller, Jane E. "The Edward Naumburg, Jr., Collection of Violet Hunt." *Princeton University Library Chronicle* LI, No. 2 (Winter 1990): 210-18.
> Discusses a selection of Hunt's manuscripts and letters in the Naumburg Collection, providing correlative biographical data.

Mizener, Arthur. "The Lost Papers of Violet Hunt." *The Cornell Library Journal* No. 3 (Autumn 1967): 1-6.
> Traces the discovery of Violet Hunt's "lost" papers from Lady Mander and the Newnham College Library Collection in England to their eventual purchase by Cornell University. Providing excerpts from Hunt's diaries, the article includes anecdotes concerning Hunt's relationship with Ford Madox Ford and other prominent literary figures of the day.

Secor, Robert. "Aesthetes and Pre-Raphaelites: Oscar Wilde and the Sweetest Violet in England." *Texas Studies in Literature and Language* 21, No. 3 (Fall 1979): 396-412.

Includes a detailed account of Hunt's friendship with Oscar Wilde.

————. "Henry James and Violet Hunt, the 'Improper Person of Babylon.'" *Journal of Modern Literature* 13, No. 1 (March 1986): 3-36.

Documents Hunt's relationship and correspondence with Henry James.

"In the Penal Colony"
Franz Kafka

Austro-Czech short story writer, novelist, and diarist.

The following entry presents criticism of Kafka's short story "In der Strafkolonie," first published in 1919 and translated into English in 1948 as "In the Penal Colony." For a discussion of Kafka's complete career, see *TCLC*, Volumes 2 and 6; for a comprehensive overview of his novella *Die Verwandlung* (*The Metamorphosis*), see *TCLC*, Volume 13; for a discussion of his novel *Der Prozess* (*The Trial*), see *TCLC*, Volume 29; for a discussion of his novel *Das Schloss* (*The Castle*), see *TCLC*, Volume 47.

INTRODUCTION

"In the Penal Colony" is considered one of Kafka's most important and paradigmatic narratives. This work is typical of Kafka's fiction in the reportorial detachment of its descriptions of nightmarish events and in its enigmatic symbolism. While many critics consider the depiction of brutality and despotism in "In the Penal Colony" to be a harbinger of nazism, criticism of Kafka's story includes a variety of interpretations and perspectives.

"In the Penal Colony" relates the observations of the "explorer," who has been asked to inspect an elaborate execution machine which is zealously maintained and operated by the "officer." As he prepares to execute a bedraggled, submissive prisoner, the officer explains how the "old commandant" designed and constructed the machine, an enormous, box-shaped apparatus which employs a matrix of needles to literally inscribe the criminal's offense into his flesh. The officer informs the explorer that the torture lasts twelve hours and that in the days of the old commandant the spectacle was witnessed by a festive crowd including children. However, the new commandant has adopted more humane methods of punishment, and the officer is the sole remaining advocate of the machine. According to the officer, the machine's victims unfailingly experience a kind of spiritual illumination before they die. While the explorer initially recoils in disgust at the officer's animated entreaties to examine the machine, his attitude manifests subtle alterations as the officer's discourse intensifies, and the fact that he eventually flees the penal colony without delivering his report to the new commandant suggests that he may feel some empathy for the officer, if not for his view of justice. In spite of his wavering sympathies, the explorer finally rebukes the officer, and the latter responds by calmly releasing the prisoner and taking his place on the machine's bed, after adjusting it to inscribe the words "Be Just." To the explorer's astonishment, the machine begins to malfunction, ejecting cogwheels and violently mutilating the officer's body. Upon examination of his corpse the explorer discovers that his face "was as it had

been in life; no sign was visible of the promised redemption."

Criticism of "In the Penal Colony" often focuses on the stark contrast between the old and new commandants, which is frequently interpreted in allegorical terms as a distinction between the patriarchal Judaic God of the Old Testament, a symbol of stern commandments and oppressive justice, and the Christian emphasis on love and forgiveness. In contrast with this theological reading, some critics have argued that "In the Penal Colony" is an essentially secular meditation on the spiritual void created by modern relativism and skepticism. According to this view, the glow of enlightenment in the faces of the machine's victims is evidence that its justice was sanctioned by God. By extension, the absence of illumination in the officer's expression would seem to symbolize the loss of God; suffering and punishment persist but are stripped of their redemptive power in a secular age.

Other critics, while acknowledging the theological dimension of Kafka's fiction, argue that the themes of guilt and redemption do not exclusively refer to God but are defining aspects of a more concrete experience centering upon alienation and persecution within the bureaucratic institutions of modern society. While this socially critical dimension of Kafka's fiction is more explicit in a work like *The Trial*, the sadistic function of the execution machine, coupled with the arbitrary and despotic form of "justice" espoused by the officer, has prompted some critics to view "In the Penal Colony" as a prophecy of the totalitarian regimes of Nazi Germany and the Soviet Union.

The extreme variety of interpretations of "In the Penal Colony" is typical of Kafka criticism. Kafka has been portrayed as a modernist, an existentialist, and a surrealist by critics of diverse theoretical orientations, although there is consensus only on the judgment that he was a profoundly independent and original writer. While most critics concede that there can be no definitive interpretation of "In the Penal Colony," it shares with such works as *The Trial* and *The Metamorphosis* a visionary perception of modern existence and, behind the enigmas of its characters, a disturbing force of recognition.

CRITICISM

Martin Greenberg   (essay date 1965)

[*An American educator, Greenberg is the translator of* Franz Kafka: Diaries, 1914-1923. *In the following excerpt from his* The Terror of Art: Kafka and Modern Literature, *he discusses the religious symbolism of "In the Penal Colony" and concludes that the story's technical flaws render it inferior to Kafka's more mature works, such as* The Trial.]

Kafka failed in *Amerika* for lack of a suitable narrative mode, the subjective mode of the dream story. In the short novel **"In the Penal Colony,"** which he wrote in the fall of 1914, about the same time he began *The Trial,* again he seems to me to fail to master his material. Now, however, the failure is not due to artistic immaturity—now it is the failure of the mature artist to stick with sure instinct to the formal requirements of his own vision. Failure however is too strong a word here. One cannot call such a powerful story a failure. But neither is it a success.

Ideas obtrude in the story with unusual distinctness and in the end the reader is confronted with an intellectual dilemma rather than a living mystery—but not for want of a unitary image through which to tell the story. The image is there, and a very powerful one it is, in the shape of the penal island with its dreadful execution machine squatting in the middle of it—the image of a world under the judgment of the law. Nevertheless, as Austin Warren observes, "this story [is] pretty persistently and consistently allegorical"; that is, it refers one *directly* to ideas. If we examine what the allegory consists in and how it is presented, I think we shall find that the power of the story to disturb is not only due to its artistic power.

The world discovered in the story is in a state of schism, a world divided between the Old and the New. That is the essential allegory. On one side stands the traditional machine of judgment under the law, invented and built by the patriarchal old Commandant, now dead. By an ingenious mechanism of vibrating needles it writes a condemned man's sentence deeper and deeper into his flesh till at the sixth hour "enlightenment comes even to the most dull-witted"; at the twelfth hour he dies. The priest of this cruel rite is the officer-judge, a disciple of the old Commandant; he describes the workings of the machine with enthusiastic pedantry to the visiting explorer. On the other side stands the new Commandant, "always looking for an excuse to attack [the] old way of doing things"; his "new, mild doctrine" prefers humane judicial methods, but he hesitates to affront a venerable institution directly and therefore tries to subvert it by harassment and deliberate neglect.

The old law judged according to the principle that "guilt is never to be doubted"—the guilt of mankind was never to be doubted. Therefore no trial needed to take place. "Other courts cannot follow that principle, for they consist of various opinions and on top of that have higher courts over them." The old court then was absolute—the highest court. In the new, liberal order there is no highest court, only "various opinions."

The old law aimed at being eternal law: "We who were [the old Commandant's] friends," says the officer, "knew even before he died that the organization of the colony was so perfect that his successor, even with a thousand new schemes in his head, would find it impossible to alter anything, at least for many years to come." But the new Commandant cares nothing about eternity; what he cares about, as a man of progress and the times, is "harbor works, nothing but harbor works!" A womanizer, he swims in the atmosphere of a crowd of admiring females; through the "women who influence him" the world is womanized. The old Commandant had "his ladies" too, but there was no petticoat government.

The condemned man vomits when he is strapped down in the machine and takes the felt gag in his mouth, because "the [new] Commandant's ladies stuff the man with sugar candy before he's led off. He has lived on stinking fish his whole life long and now he has to eat sugar candy!" The "new, mild doctrine" is effeminate and, by causing the condemned man to vomit over himself, degrading. But the condemned man vomits too because the felt gag has been chewed by hundreds rather than being changed for every execution as it used to be. So the new regime is callous as well as sentimental.

"How different an execution was in the old days!" exclaimed the officer-judge. Then the whole island gathered together in the true ceremony of belief and the Commandant himself laid the condemned man under the Harrow.

> No discordant noise spoilt the working of the machine. Many did not care to watch it but lay with closed eyes in the sand; they all knew: Now Justice is being done. In the silence one heard nothing but the condemned man's sighs, half muffled by the felt gag. Nowadays the machine can no longer wring from anyone a sigh louder than the felt gag can stifle; but in those days the writing needles let drop an acid fluid, which

we're no longer permitted to use. Well, and then came the sixth hour! It was impossible to grant all the requests to be allowed to watch it from near by. The Commandant in his wisdom ordained that the children should have the preference . . . often enough I would be squatting there with a small child in either arm. How we all absorbed the look of transfiguration on the face of the sufferer, how we bathed our cheeks in the radiance of that justice, achieved at last and fading so quickly! What times there were, my comrade!

Under the old law, *Justice was done.* All shared ritually in the redemption which the condemned man found under the law in death. All stood under the same law and could look forward to the same redemption. Death redeemed. Of course, all this is according to the officer's point of view. But the point is that his is the point of view that excludes "points of view"—he lives the conviction of absolute justice.

That is how things were in the old days. Now, however, the sea of faith has ebbed. When the officer is unable to persuade the explorer, who remains convinced "that the injustice of the procedure and the inhumanity of the execution were undeniable," to side with him against the new Commandant, he lies down with devout determination in the judgment machine to execute himself. But execution according to the old law is no longer possible, a new dispensation has succeeded; the machine can no longer "do Justice." Negated, it spits out its parts and goes to pieces, murdering the officer indecently instead of executing him: " . . . [T]his was no [ceremonial] torture such as the officer desired, this was plain murder." Death no longer redeems:

> [The face of the corpse] was as it had been in life; no sign was visible of the promised redemption; what the others had found in the machine the officer had not found; the lips were firmly pressed together, the eyes were open, with the same expression as in life, the look was calm and convinced, through the forehead went the point of the great iron spike.

As Professor Emrich comments [in his *Franz Kafka*], "The age of redemption is no more. The dead man remains stuck in life. He no longer can cross the boundary into the liberating Beyond. Man is consigned entirely to the earth."

Lawless sentimentality takes the place of implacable judgment, turning the liberated prisoner and his guard into guffawing clowns. The former observes with satisfaction how the officer takes his place in the machine:

> So this was revenge. Although he himself had not suffered to the end, he was to be revenged to the end. A broad, silent grin now appeared on his face and stayed there all the rest of the time.

Justice no longer holds sway, but revenge—an internecine warfare of each against each, in a never-ending pursuit of the upper hand.

In the cavernous, blackened interior of the teahouse, which makes on the explorer "the impression of some his-torical memory or other," so that he feels "the power of past times," the old Commandant lies buried. All that remains of the old order is a prophecy, written on his gravestone, that he "will rise again and lead his adherents from this house to recover the colony. Have faith and wait!"

"In the Penal Colony" takes place in historical time—the colony is a more or less recognizable possession of a European power of the late-nineteenth or early-twentieth century—rather than in the timeless subjective dimension into which the protagonists of Kafka's dream narratives awaken out of historical time. Its subject matter is the religious history of the world, which it recapitulates in terms of the old times and the new times of a penal colony. Like most of Kafka's stories, it is concerned with spiritual need, but it treats this subject in historical terms rather than through an individual who experiences the despair of spiritual darkness in the timelessness of his soul. It is an historical allegory.

It would be a mistake, however, to read too-specific references into the allegory. The old regime of the old Commandant does not, for example, pointedly refer to Old Testament days, it only embraces them in its meaning, along with all the other old regimes that based their authority on a transcendent religious absolute. As an ancient idol which is at the same time a piece of modern machinery, the execution machine reaches from the present all the way back to the most barbarous times of Dagon and the other stocks and stones in whose name our worshiping fathers did absolute justice. The old ends and the new begins at the point at which justice based on supreme authority yields to justice based on "various opinions."

So far I have said little about the explorer, yet as the one through whose eyes the story is narrated and the embodiment of its moral point of view, his role is crucial for the way in which the allegory is presented. A dispassionate observer of the "peculiarities of many peoples," an enlightened modern relativist and naturalist, from first to last he condemns the injustice and the inhumanity of the old law—so much so indeed that he is moved to abandon his attitude of scientific neutrality for once and intervene against the execution. Mixed, however, with his disapproval of the old judicial procedure is a growing admiration for the officer, even though he cannot but deplore his narrow-mindedness. Touched in the end by the officer's "sincere conviction," the explorer decides to do nothing to hinder the operation of the old law, although, by refusing the officer's plea to join forces with him against the new Commandant, he will do nothing to help it either. When the officer lies down under the Harrow to execute himself, he can only approve his decision: "the officer was doing the right thing; in his place the explorer would not have acted otherwise."

What the explorer is confronted with on the penal island is a moral choice between the old law and the new—the story arranges itself as a kind of contest between the two regimes to win his concurrence. The old law is primitive and cruel, yet the explorer must admire the spiritual unity and conviction it begets in its adherents; a conviction which is able to attain ultimate spiritual knowledge in redemption through final judgment under the law. On the other hand, it is just precisely ultimateness that the new law lacks. He despises its effeminate sentimentality, laxity and shallow worldliness. Nevertheless, he must approve its superior humanity: "The injustice of the [old] procedure and the inhumanity of the execution were undeniable." So actually it is not a moral choice that the explorer is faced with, since there is never any question of what his moral judgment is. The choice he faces is between morality and spirituality. The two have come apart. Before this conflict between the moral and the spiritual, the explorer retreats into a neutrality which has nothing to do with his old scientific detachment. His neutrality now expresses the troubled state of mind of someone who has had a glimpse into hitherto undiscerned depths.

And yet the glimpse he gains is historical rather than religious. It is not insight into religious truth but into the religious past. The explorer does not and cannot believe in the truth of the old law; what he sees is the way it was when mankind was ruled by the idea of supreme truth. The execution machine is an historical demonstration to him of the primitive unity of absolute justice and human society, spirit and the world. But that unity explodes under his very eyes when the officer dies unredeemed ("murdered") in the disintegrating machine—redemption under the old law is an exploded (literally exploded!) religious idea. What the explorer feels toward the old law is a mixture of horror and nostalgia: horror at its cruelty, nostalgia for its spirituality. The story is painfully divided between the moral and the religious (or rather between the moral and the religious regarded nostalgically) and in the end the explorer must flee the dilemma the colony presents him with in dismayed haste.

"In the Penal Colony" is not *about* the conflict between the moral and the religious; it falls victim to that conflict. The explorer's dilemma is only a dilemma because the question of the old law's truth has been left aside. Leaving aside the question of truth casts an obscurantist shadow over the whole story, introduces a moral and intellectual equivocation. When the question of truth is not left aside there can be only one choice: we can only choose to be modern and go on from there. There is no going back to the old law, even if only to the extent of choosing to be neutral toward it as the explorer does. One of the reasons why the story is disturbing is this negative one: because it is morally and intellectually equivocal. The allegory teeters on the edge of a familiar snobbery, which was so strong in Prague among the sons of the Jewish middle class at the beginning of the century—the snobbery, as [Franz] Werfel puts it . . . , of "those . . . who run around as mystics and orthodox believers only because every tailor, schoolteacher and journalist is a believing atheist." But working against the impression of snobbish obscurantism is the mute, unpalliated horror of the execution machine. Never do we lose sight of the fact that "the injustice of the procedure and the inhumanity of the execution were undeniable." The positive power of the story to disturb is owing to the image of the execution machine; its finicky details testify incontrovertibly to injustice. The authentic power of the story lies in its image of a religiosity which is as wicked and destructive as it is spiritual.

In the more or less historical framework of the story, on its level of rational consciousness, the old Commandant's religion, as a relic of the past, can only move the explorer nostalgically, it cannot compel him at the center of his being. An outside observer, an onlooker rather than a participant, he is impressed by the old law's spiritual appearance—aesthetically. The explorer does not face a true dilemma in the penal colony, he is spectator at an allegorical confrontation.

The failure of the story is a failure to be subjective—and through subjectivity to reach the truth. In Kafka's dream narrative of the inner self there is no outside observer to whose detached judgment rival historical conceptions are submitted and between which he is challenged to choose. The protagonist in Kafka's dream stories is not confronted with a choice he must intellectually consider; his whole *being* is caught in a situation in which it is impossible for him to *live*. The injustice of the court in *The Trial* is also "undeniable," but its law is established in Joseph K.'s innermost self, not on an island he can sail away from. Joseph K. is caught in the living mystery of concrete existence, he does not stand there weighing modern relative ideas against ancient absolute ones. It is impossible for men to live without a trust in ultimate justice ("something indestructible"), and at the same time ultimate justice is impossible in a world where one must not accept as true what the law says is true, "one must only accept it as necessary"—to quote the priest's last comment to Joseph K. on the parable of the law. In his dream narrative of the inner self, Kafka is able to unite within the one breast of Joseph K. the subservient primitive soul of the condemned man, for whom the authority of the old law is absolute, and the skeptical, yearning modern consciousness of the explorer, for whom the injustice of the old law is undeniable. In the court he is able to unite the cruel mythic absoluteness of the penal colony's old law with the hollowness of its new law. Out of that unity is born the truth of *The Trial*. (pp. 104-12)

> *Martin Greenberg, in his* The Terror of Art: Kafka and Modern Literature, *Basic Books, Inc., Publishers, 1968, 241 p.*

Dale Kramer (essay date 1967)

[*An American educator and critic, Kramer is the author and editor of several books on Thomas Hardy. In the following essay, he interprets the explorer in "In the Penal Colony" as a paragon of "tolerance and suspended judgment in matters of relative morality."*]

Commentators often give attention to Franz Kafka's brilliant imagery, his distortions of reality that project so vividly his vision of a society with grotesque values and goals, and the relationship of his work to clinical psychological theory. Readers attempt to synthesize Kafka's response to the complexities and inanities of modern life by analyzing his esoteric handling of highly personal images of cockroaches, caged circus performers and beasts, and finely sensitized machines that seem to possess a consciousness. Less frequently, however, do the commentators give Kafka credit for the manner in which he marshals and directs his pieces so that the form itself suggests a significance and connotes a meaning beyond—but not contradictory to—the surface rendering of horror and abnormality.

A close reading of what is nearly the paradigmatic Kafka utterance, **"In the Penal Colony,"** reveals a sophisticated and functional artistry. We usually read the story as an allegory of the fate in a changing, unsympathetic world of an old system of belief, either religious or political. This reading is not inaccurate in its broad outlines; indeed, it is hard to conceive of another reading that so well accounts for the variety of allusions in the story. Still, an observation of the progress of events, that is, of the structure, affords considerable clarification of the point regarding the death of the old system that Kafka makes through his tale. Put simply, Kafka urges the desirability of tolerance and suspended judgment in matters of relative morality.

The point is best got at by first noting the end of the story. The New Commandant of the penal colony has asked the foreign explorer, who serves as the focus of narration, to observe an ingenious machine executing a brute of a soldier who had neglected a trifling duty. The officer in charge of the machine attempts to convince the explorer of the value and beauty of the machine, which had been invented by the now-dead Old Commandant. Upon being told that the explorer would not defend the machine to a conference board convening on the morrow, and knowing that his method of punishing guilty persons is therefore doomed, the officer places himself in the machine and dies violently. The explorer visits the burial-place of the Old Commandant, which is below the floor of the colony's teahouse because the priest would not let him be buried in the churchyard; he then leaves the island without paying the expected visit to the New Commandant to give his opinion of the machine. Through this unplanned departure, the explorer expresses some sort of sympathy for the self-immolated officer. That the sympathy has some bearing upon his final response to the ideology of the officer—that is, to the old system of belief—is suggested through his refusal, just before he leaves the colony, to mock the prophecy that the Old Commandant will rise from his grave to "lead his adherents . . . to recover the colony." Of course, the [explorer's] sympathy is far from total. His refusal to defend the machine is not rescinded, even though he knows the officer is about to kill himself because of his refusal. There is, likewise, no indication that the explorer's distaste for the Old Commandant's methods of justice ever lessens. But that there is sympathy for the officer as there is antipathy for his methods Kafka is careful to point out: "If the judicial procedure which the officer cherished were really so near its end, possibly as a result of his [the explorer's] own intervention, as to which he felt himself pledged—then the officer was doing the right thing: in his place the explorer would not have acted otherwise." Just what in the narrative explains the explorer's suddenly leaving the island has never been clearly established. Most critics have overlooked the techniques of fiction as a basis for resolving the issue. Yet such obvious matters as characterization and comparison of details provide a direct apprehension of Kafka's resolution of the conflict between societal beliefs.

The most direct explanation of the explorer's sympathy for the officer is the similarity of their personalities, so close that the explorer becomes the psychological double of the officer. Although they oppose each other in the "matter" of the story, an attitude toward justice, in all other features they are quite alike. First of all, the two men approach the "matter" of the story with similar dedication. Neither is corruptible, the officer by the opprobrium into which his machine has fallen, the explorer by thought of anyone's agreement or disagreement with his ideas. Both are concerned with the honor of their behavior. The officer scrupulously heeds his concept of justice, even towards himself ("Guilt is never to be doubted"); the explorer initially hesitates to express his opinion of the machine for fear of offending either of his hosts, the New Commandant or the officer. Both the explorer and the officer are convinced of the rightness of their stands toward the machine, so much so that each may be thought of as an absolutist personality. The ultimate development in the similarity of the two men has already been noted: the explorer's feeling that if he were in the officer's situation he would also have placed himself in the machine. After the officer is in the machine, and it has begun its aborted performance and is discharging its cogwheels, the explorer feels he should stand by the officer since the officer can "no longer look after himself." After the machine has finished butchering the officer, the explorer alone of the three witnesses feels any compulsion to remove the body from the self-destroyed machine.

This similarity between the two central characters is one of the reasons we come to accept the explorer as the interpreter of the action. In addition, he is not merely a simplistic outsider who judges a social custom on surface qualities. Eclectic and tolerant of national modes, he brings far-reaching sympathies to the evaluation of human behavior that allow him to give more than a limited conventional response to an inhumane procedure. Indeed, he had come into the situation in the penal colony with "no intention at all of altering other people's methods of administering justice"; but his shock upon learning about the harshness of punishment for the smallest offense leads eventually to his determination to condemn the machine to the New Commandant. His climactic fleeing the island as he does marks a return to the detachedness he had displayed when ignorant of the nature of the officer's machine. A basic difference, of course, is that his refusal to become involved initially reflects only professional principle, while at the end it highlights his "learning" Kafka's point.

The sometimes subtle but always consistent parallels between the explorer and the officer reinforce the inevitability of the explorer's final act, which hinges upon the manner of the death of the officer. Immediately before the machine begins to operate on the officer, the explorer is still determined to make clear to the New Commandant his unfavorable opinion of the method of execution that the officer's impassioned explanation has brought him to. He is "resolved to stay till the end" of the self-execution out of respect for the officer's sincerity, but he has not altered his opposition to employment of the machine on unwilling victims. He remains "pledged" to the "intervention" that has led the officer to release the condemned prisoner and to place himself in the machine. Of necessity, then, the explorer's abrupt departure from the island stems at least in part from his response to the officer's death. Kafka does not state directly why the explorer acts as he does, but the details of the machine's handling of the officer as self-sacrificial victim clearly point to the cause.

Upon learning the hopeless prospects for his system of belief, the officer releases the prisoner he had been about to execute, strips himself, and prepares the machine for his own execution. The machine tattoos into its victims' bodies the law they have disobeyed. The released prisoner would have had "HONOR THY SUPERIORS" punched into his body; the officer sets the machine to write "BE JUST" into his own body. The implication is obvious: having executed untold numbers according to his ideal of harsh justice (he is the jury and judge *and* executioner), he is now prepared to die in the machine himself. A goal other than justice is suggested by his envy of the other victims' look of beatitude when they discover (after six hours in the machine) the message that the machine has been writing into their bodies; but this goal does not clearly play a determining role in the officer's suicide.

But rather than execute the officer with slow and exquisite torture, as was customary, the machine begins to operate as if with intentions of its own, spews forth its cogwheels even though working silently, and kills the officer within a very short time. Such an outcome of a conscious effort to achieve a particular kind of death might seem to represent a repudiation of the officer by the system he worshipped, as if to suggest he had perverted the justice he administered. Many considerations, in addition to the explorer's continued sympathy with the officer's action, nullify this possibility, and make the officer's death a vindication, if not of the system he served, at least of his own personal role in that system.

There is no reason to believe that the machine has executed the officer inappropriately. Rather, the variation in the machine's pattern is inevitable, given the conditions of the machine's normal successful operations. In the first place, the officer, unlike the other victims, has not committed a crime against the society supporting the machine; in fact, he is the last self-proclaimed member of that society. Similarly, unlike the other victims, the officer knows what the machine will write on him, thereby obviating the moment of the excruciating illumination for which he had envied those who had previously suffered in the machine. Because he is already an initiate, the "calm and convinced look" that the explorer sees on the face of his corpse is all that the officer could expect to attain to. A third unorthodoxy in the officer's planned self-execution is that the motto "BE JUST" does not signify the law the officer has broken. The officer lacks not justice—he is the walking manifestation of absolute and unflinching justice—but compassion, moderation in guilt-finding, and fellow-feeling. In other words, in his case the machine was asked to perform, ironically, an unjust lettering. The very process of its rebellion suggests the integrity of the system it stands for.

The manner in which the machine varies its pattern of operation is significant. As I have already recounted, in killing the officer the machine starts by itself, runs in defiance of the programmed instructions the officer gave it before he lay in the Bed, and continues to operate even though its internal workings are being discarded. Obviously, Kafka marks out the officer in some way—either as unworthy of the machine, which is hardly likely, or as being beyond the usual educative and punitive function of the machine, which as I point out above is more probable. Through the abnormal action of the machine, which cannot be fully explained by noting inadequate maintenance and the shortage of spare parts, the officer becomes not a victim, not a martyr, but a hero. The special treatment given the officer by the Old Commandant's invention is, in a genuine sense, similar to the special treatment given to Christ at death by the forces of nature that His Father had created. This general echo of an established religion is, of course, in full accordance with the usual reading of **"In the Penal Colony."**

The elements of non-naturalism in the officer's death are paralleled elsewhere in this horrifying but concrete and straightforward narrative only in the prophecy of the Old Commandant's rising from the dead. The misbehavior of the machine adds a measure of credibility to the prophecy. It is upon hearing of the prophecy, after coming from the scene of self-execution, that the explorer turns his steps toward the harbor. These suggestions of a reality stronger than physicality are the structural justifications for the explorer's unexplained sudden rejection of his "pledge" to speak to the New Commandant against the method of execution sponsored by the now-dead officer.

It does not follow, however, that by having the explorer behave as he does at the end of the story, Kafka supports totalitarian "justice." Judgment upon the system of justice itself is essentially incidental to Kafka's allegory of the decay of a social practice. Most allegories are more conventionally and clearly in support of a specific moral belief, but Kafka's highly individualistic employment of imagistic patterns prevents an interpretation obviously applicable to group morality. The dénouement of **Metamorphosis,** for example, creates sympathy for both the pariah Gregor and his innocent but suffering family; it likewise encourages disenchantment both with the selfish, involuted Gregor and with his family that is finally unable to tolerate his uniqueness. In **"In the Penal Colony,"** Kafka is making a case for basic understanding and tolerance. The personality of the explorer implies an amenable morality that survives the decadence of the old system; but it survives without rancor, refusing to placate the New Commandant by attacking the Old at the same time that it refuses to reinstitute the Old. To do either would be to play false to a new insight into the permanent virtues of loyalty and principle in the human personality. (pp. 362-67)

Dale Kramer, "The Aesthetics of Theme: Kafka's 'In the Penal Colony'," in Studies in Short Fiction, *Vol. V, No. 1, Fall, 1967, pp. 362-67.*

Kurt J. Fickert   (essay date 1971)

[*Fickert is a German-born American poet, educator, and*

A short story like Kafka's "In the Penal Colony" has nothing whatever in common with Poe, although scenes of horror occur in it along the same thematic line.

—*Max Brod, in his* Franz Kafka: A Biography, *1947.*

translator. In the following essay, he asserts that a literal interpretation of "In the Penal Colony" reveals Kafka's attitude toward Christian morality and redemption.]

"The secret of Kafka's writing," so one critic has confided, "is its *literalness*" [Kurt Weinberg, *Kafkas Dichtungen*]. This comment seems particularly pertinent to " **In the Penal Colony,**" whose narrative proceeds forcefully and unswervingly toward its conclusion without the circuitousness characteristic of many a Kafka story. **"In the Penal Colony"** depicts straightforwardly a series of events occurring in the colony within a short span of time: a world-traveler is invited to view the performance of a diabolically ingenious execution machine; then the officer, under whose supervision the execution is to be carried out, paradoxically takes the place of the condemned man and is executed, and the traveler flees. Although the sequential and tripartite nature of the story tend to suggest the logicality underlying it and, indeed, its literalness, the many interpreters of **"In the Penal Colony"** have generally failed to consider the story on its own terms and have explicated it in regard to its place in the Kafka canon. For Heinz Politzer, for instance, the essence of **"In the Penal Colony"** is the execution machine, which becomes for him another instance of a symbol for "the tortures to which Kafka, the writer, subjected himself." Walter Sokel in *Kafka—Tragik und Ironie* finds the story "as always" a charade depicting Kafka's most pressing personal problem, the conflict with his father: "the old commandant is quite obviously a variant of the father figure in Kafka's mythic interpretation of his own life." Taking into account the existentialistic agony which cries out to him from the pages of Kafka's work, Wilhelm Emrich [in his *Franz Kafka*] focuses his attention on the meaning of death as it comes on the execution machine: "Man must withstand the ultimate (*absolute*) catastrophe." That **"In the Penal Colony"** has its place in the explication of Kafka's work as an attack against officialdom or fascism or as a sublimation of the pangs of tuberculosis or sexual impotence or as the unsophisticated transcription of dreams has been adequately considered. There remains the possibility of analyzing **"In the Penal Colony"** in terms of the story Kafka tells, of the three episodes he has devised and their interrelationship, and of the plethora of details which make the nightmarish events incontrovertibly real.

The first third of the story centers around the execution machine itself, which is elaborately described. Its resemblance to a guillotine and its presence in a penal colony, located apparently in a remote and tropical region, suggest at least a visual association between Kafka's colony and the once notorious French penal colony of Devil's Island. However, the machine is more sophisticated than a guillotine. Its victim lies spread-eagled on a "bed," over which a press hovers. When lowered, the press tatoos by means of a series of needles a message on the condemned man's back and penetrates his head with a spike. The torture lasts six hours. The description of the machine and its functioning Kafka has carefully integrated into the story itself. The officer in charge of the execution, which the traveler has been intimidated into witnessing, climbs up on the unaccountably high instrument by means of a ladder; up above, he spreads his arms out, and he descends by sliding down a pole. Having prepared the machine to receive its victim, a nondescript soldier guilty of the infraction of some insignificant rule, a "common man," the officer regales the increasingly ill-at-ease observer with the past history of the colony and its sinister machine. It has been designed by the former commandant of the penal colony—"soldier, judge, master-builder, chemist, designer." The officer identifies himself as the agent of this now vanished authority, having come from his side to act in his stead, specifically as a judge. While remembering fondly the old commandant, the officer is particularly scornful of the new one who surrounds himself with fawning women; the traveler himself pictures the present ruler of the penal colony as a kind of Pontius Pilate, appeasing the crowd by asking it for its judgment. At this point in the story of **"In the Penal Colony"** the exposition has been completed and the cue for passion provided: the action has been initiated.

The purport of **"In the Penal Colony"** has already emerged from the situation presented by Kafka and the aggregation of details elaborating on it. That Kafka is dealing with the religious dimension in life, with human guilt and punishment in a sphere removed from the domain of civil justice, is a fact which may be deduced from the exotic setting, the mysterious properties of the machine and its mystical capacity to purify its victims, and the proselyting zeal of the officer, whose filial relationship to the former ruler of the colony and creator of the machine is apparent. In his study of Kafka, Heinz Politzer concedes, while placing the story of the penal colony in the framework of Kafka's guilt complex, the result of his having become a writer, that **"In the Penal Colony"** deals with religion: "he created in the torture machine . . . a metaphor of what religion meant to him." Furthermore, the Christian element in Kafka's consideration of a philosophy of religion is unmistakable; it has been established that the role of the officer is that of a surrogate for God and that the machine is a symbol or relic with redemptive force. Walter Sokel, who otherwise relates **"In the Penal Colony"** to the problem of the father-son conflict, thus summarizes Kafka's concern in the story with the Christian religion: "Essential elements of the ideology of the penal system are closely connected with Christianity. . . . " In regard to its delving into Christian theology **"In the Penal Colony"** is not unique among Kafka's stories, but it alone undertakes a transliteration of the way of the cross.

The second part of the story deals with the sacrificial death of the officer. But first the soldier condemned by the officer has had his travail, has been scourged, has fallen in the procession to the place of execution, has been strapped to the machine, and, while languishing there, has been fed gruel, much as Christ was offered an anesthetic. At the moment when the officer despairs of convincing the traveler of the efficacy of the machine, he suddenly puts an end to the torment of the condemned man and frees him. The officer disrobes; later the condemned man and the soldier assisting with the execution squabble over possession of some of his clothing. Without accounting for his action, the officer stretches himself out on the machine and sets it in motion with the expectation that the press will imprint the message "Be just!" on his back. But the machine malfunctions; the officer is bloodily and unceremoniously executed. His body hangs from the machine and is lifted off by the condemned man and the soldier whom the observer has failed to send away with the command "Go home!" (With one of them kneeling, pleading to be allowed to stay, they present the picture of a Pietà at the base of the machine.) Literally, the central and principal event in **"In the Penal Colony"** is thus the dying of one man, an innocent man, in place of another, a condemned man and an everyman. That a religious concept, that of the salvation of man through the interposition of God Himself between God and man, lies behind this act of self-sacrifice, Kafka makes patently clear by his analysis of the machine in the first part of the story, by his characterization of the officer, and by his choice of and amassing of details obviously consistent with Christian tradition.

In his "Hochzeitsvorbereitungen auf dem Lande" Kafka has dealt directly with the significance of the passion and death of Christ: "We too must suffer what is being suffered around us. Christ suffered for humanity, but humanity must suffer for Him." Kafka's concept of religion emerges as one centered on the individual who must acknowledge his guilt, his having inflicted suffering on God (the Father) and who must reconcile himself to his having to suffer accordingly. In the end the pain of the individual would supposedly have the purpose of purifying him, of redeeming him. Walter Sokel can therefore speak of Kafka's philosophy of religion as a "complex of punishment, self-sacrifice, and purification." Obviously, **"In the Penal Colony"** contains the elements necessary to make possible an understanding of the events of the story in terms of religious beliefs.

Kafka's conclusions on the basis of these premises of guilt and suffering in the religious dimension of man are evolved in the third segment of **"In the Penal Colony."** Following the death of the officer there is a break in the story. The traveler becomes the dominant figure. The text makes clear that he is modern European man ("You are the product of a European philosophy," . . .); that he is a skeptic with a bias in favor of a rationalistic, scientific point of view; and that he is Kafka himself as an objective observer. The traveler flees the scene of the gruesome suicide; the liberated condemned man and the soldier pursue the traveler, as if his effort to put the episode behind him could but be in vain. Exhausted, he takes refuge in an inn which is a cave (Christ was born in the cave-stable behind an inn). Bearded working men are gathered there; an association with the disciples, meeting after the death of

Christ, suggests itself, especially since the traveler in his guilt at having refused to acknowledge the purpose of the machine resembles Peter, having denied his Lord, and since the men move away a table to reveal a tomb. However, the tombstone now brought to light exhibits a message pertaining to the certain return of the old commandant. Although an oblique reference to the Second Coming of Christ might be inferred here, another sphere of religious symbolism might have engaged Kafka's attention at this point, as Kurt Weinberg has proposed in his interpretation of **"In the Penal Colony."** He depicts the bearded men as the Jews and the old commandant as Jehovah; the penal colony represents then the old covenant between God and the Jews, a basis for an order in the world which must be restored. The traveler, having rejected a religion based on guilt and suffering, likewise turns his back on a religion derived from history and tradition. Throwing money among the bearded men to divert their attention, he escapes from the inn; in the boat which will take him to the ship in the harbor which, sailing away, will free him from having to contemplate the penal colony, he throws a rope at the condemned man and the soldier who have pursued him even to the shore. This rope may represent his last ties with traditional religious beliefs. Weinberg emphasizes the negative character of the conclusion and of, indeed, the entire story of **"In the Penal Colony"**; its symbolism represents for him "the protean transformations of *negative* religious concepts, which are no longer considered in all seriousness by the author, but whose peculiar persistence (*unausrottbares Sonderdasein*) in the soul of the modern European cannot be denied."

"In the Penal Colony" ends with a refutation of the premise, symbolized by the machine, with which it began. That God created the world as a penal colony in which man must suffer in order to be redeemed, to be accepted by God, is the article of faith presented in the first part of the story; the traveler is immediately repulsed by this idea. In the second section of the story the suggestion that the suffering is vicarious—a Christian idea—is appended, and the traveler discards it, too. In the conclusion to the story regard for the whole religious dimension in life is warily cast aside. Austin Warren in his interpretation of **"In the Penal Colony"** has pointed out Kafka's inclination to disassociate himself from religious belief: "Kafka, fearful of softening religion, wants to present it in all its rigor, its repellence to the flesh—in its irrationality and inscrutability and uncertainty, too." By careful plotting, a logical arrangement of three episodes with a climax to the events coming in the middle, by the use of pertinent details all drawn from the religious sphere, and by the interplay of characters who have well-defined philosophic and theosophic values (the common man, the savior-prophet, the skeptic), Kafka has written a story which is a work of art in the spirit of the twentieth century. In it the mystical becomes literal; the interpreter of **"In the Penal Colony"** can accept it only on these, on its own terms. (pp. 31-6)

Kurt J. Fickert, "A Literal Interpretation of 'In the Penal Colony'," in Modern Fiction Studies, *Vol. XVII, No. 1, Spring, 1971, pp. 31-6.*

Leonard R. Mendelsohn   (essay date 1971)

[*In the following essay, Mendelsohn argues that the significance of "In the Penal Colony" hinges on an existential dilemma—the explorer's ignorance of his own freedom and the "nothingness" that surrounds it.*]

For the Explorer, hero of Kafka's **"In the Penal Colony,"** revelation held not triumph but terror. Unlike Boethius, he finds no solace in accepting fate. Because he is not chained to the Wheel of Fortune, Kafka's hero discovers, much to his horror, that it is he who must spin a wheel turning not only himself but others as well. And it is neither uncertainty nor mischance that he must fear, but his own unrestrained control, along with the accompanying involvement and responsibility. As a result of this ironic reversal of the medieval dilemma, the heroic enterprise attempts not philosophic resolve, but involves the hero in a futile effort to conceal from himself his own power, and all that it entails. And where Boethius found solutions by rejecting the unreal, which the temporal world was thought to be, Kafka's hero can achieve consolation only by becoming oblivious to his own power. But despite repeated efforts at self-deception, he is inevitably overcome by his irretractable power to manipulate the Wheel of Fortune. Though he might suspend this freedom, it pursues, and finally forces itself upon him.

Throughout the narrative the reader witnesses repeated façades out of which the hero futilely constructs illusions of bondage. He visits a prison isle, a place apparently void of free will, only to discover in its restraint simply a backdrop against which his freedom is all the more evident. His German appellation, *Der Reiseinde,* likewise conveys his frantic efforts at self-deception. He is, as the German suggests, a traveler, and not, as the generally rendered English translation would have it, an explorer. For he has traveled widely—but more in flight than in quest. The opening lines further indicate that he wishes not to explore, only to be free of involvement. He attends the execution not out of curiosity, but for fear that refusal would constitute a breach of etiquette. Contrasting the Officer's devoted elaboration, the hero strives for detachment through a somewhat belabored disinterest. Retreating behind protocol, this fugitive from freedom stifles his revulsion at what he might consider barbarism, should he allow himself the dangerous luxury of an opinion.

Here as elsewhere in **"In the Penal Colony"** personal feelings threaten the security of the hero's illusion. Since the individual controls circumstance, then emotion, leading on to conviction, could push him into the dreaded position of the arbiter—a role ultimately thrust upon him. Even those statements later in the story in which he expresses opinions about the machine, reflect not conviction but desperation as all opportunities for detachment begin to vanish. Any ability to determine circumstances, or even any reminder of this power, constitutes to him the supreme horror. To forestall his emergence as judge, the Explorer employs self-administered confusion. By clouding issues, by forming veils of illusions, he might conceivably escape the freedom to judge. And it is in the Penal Colony, the home of victimizing and regimentation, that he seeks relief from harrying freedom.

For a time his flight from freedom is partly successful. Obscuring the crucial importance of the Explorer's dilemma is the overbearing presence of the infernal machine. It is easy to view the machine as the prime concern of the story, and the central allegorical device. The Officer introduces it in the first sentence and the description and detail concerning it comprise the bulk of the narrative. Furthermore, morbid fascination with its unusual means of executing a capital sentence, and the meticulous and fanatical concern with its operation, command attention which can easily overshadow any other line in the work. It would be folly to suggest that Kafka attempts to deceive the reader by performing some sleight of mind technique while all eyes are on the harrow. It would be more accurate to imply a stylistic parallel linking the reader's plight with that of the Explorer. Both are prone, perhaps even willing, to confuse the essential issue. The misplaced dilemma presents itself as one of the controlling leitmotifs of Kafka's fiction. As the Explorer forgets that he must eventually be condemned to judgment, instead of by it, so the reader is unaware that the crucial dilemma concerns not the art of the infernal machine, but the Explorer's efforts to keep himself free of involvement.

The machine reflects the predicament being thrust upon the Explorer. It becomes progressively evident that the machine is a ritual the performance of which entails death by an unusual, though highly symbolic means. Ignoring the intended victim, who is allowed to roam freely, the Officer expounds upon ceremony and tradition. Never attempting to rationalize the suffering inflicted by the machine, he minutely details the functions of its manifold parts and bewails the difficulty of obtaining workable equipment. Remembering the days when the faithful flocked to the festivities, he recalls the young children, who were accorded the extraordinary privilege of viewing the ritual from up close. As the Officer remembers himself tenderly supporting a young child on knee, with his arm embracing another, warmly and patiently instructing both in the minutiae of the grisly scene on the harrow, mention is made of neither death nor torture. He utters no gory details, nor does it appear likely that any are forthcoming. He needs no justification, as he is unaware that any is necessary. Among these trappings of a catechism for the innocent, it is quite possible to forget momentarily the cruel torment. Any horror that endures in the reader's mind essentially serves as an ironic foil to the Officer's religious devotion to his ritual.

But unless anyone should think the machine is only of historical concern, a relic of barbarism past, another execution impends. The intended victim, however, remains disturbingly unconcerned by the presence of the machine, as he displays a rather stupid curiosity. Significantly, Kafka calls him *Der Verurteilte,* the condemned; for having been judged, he is spared the desperate awareness and enduring agony visited upon those who sit in judgment. Kafka compares the victim to a dog who might be allowed to roam freely through the hills but who would return quickly to the call of his master. He prefers the security represented by the machine to the frightful awareness of his freedom. If freedom could be avoided, then pacific resolve is possible. The victim thus protected is at peace, while the Explorer's apprehension intensifies as it becomes increasingly evident that the fate of the machine is in his hands.

In this, the twilight of the machine's heyday, the Officer remains devoid of sadistic motives. He is a proponent of a liturgy, and as the sole surviving priest, he turns his energies towards reviving the declining ritual. Dispassionate towards suffering, he simply views torture and ultimate death as part of the ceremony. Never does he argue the machine's humaneness, nor does he justify the pain; neither, conversely, does he betray any disjointed enjoyment of the agony visited upon a victim. The victim is merely an essential part of the proceedings, much like wine, wafer, and vestments. Torment and destruction are simply means of achieving desired communion, the goal of the ritual.

It is important to view the machine as a ritual, for it is within the nature of ritual that the concept of enforced freedom arises. The machine in operation serves as the center of the ritual, with the Officer as celebrant and the throng as communicants. In the midst of the frenzied ceremony, it might be possible to forget the unanswered question, with whom is communion to be attained? With this question the full force of gaping emptiness confronts the unfortunately aware. The Officer's prophet, the old commandant, revealed the ritual and little more. The designs of the machine, illegible and useless, alone remain as legacy; and the Officer will allow no tampering, since this might lead to distortions of the original design. The frantic concern with details of the machine and the emptiness attendant upon its decline impart the uncomfortable suggestion that there may be nothing else.

Stranded within a decaying liturgy, a means of communion and nothing with which to commune, we return to the Officer's narration of better times, during the zenith of the popularity of the machine. There we find communion in healthy existence, but still no hint of anything with which to commune. Success or failure of the ritual appear independent of actual communion, and dependent upon the ability to remove the faithful from the question of whether there exists anything beyond the momentary frenzy. At this moment in the history of the penal colony, the situation conveys a gloomily novel function of communion. There is nothing to commune with but the ritual itself. The ritual as spiritual soporific protects celebrant and would-be communicant from the terrors of revealed emptiness.

The ritual need go no further. Communion, in Kafka's world, has become a man-produced, benevolent deception made necessary by a characteristic of the human mind, that property which pictures emptiness while failing to protect the individual from the terrors of his perception. Incomplete communion carries in itself a completed truth—that there is nothing else—and at the same time it provides a means for combating the emptiness revealed. But to remain secure from the terrible knowledge of nothingness would mean to deceive oneself into thinking that a larger power enslaves him, and that he has no choice and no control. Such an illusion protects the Officer and the Condemned, and the Explorer labors desperately to escape any suggestion that he has any control. But despite all efforts, a dire certainty repeatedly emerges, that man is free, that there is no larger restraining power other than voluntary subservience to his own ideas. Encrusted with illusions, he attempts to escape freedom that would release the terrifying revelation that there is nothing else. But freedom pursues and finally dispels all illusion. Unable to remain permanently imprisoned by this consoling deception, the individual must awaken to exercise soul-crippling judgment. Attempting to use this freedom against itself, the observer in the early moments of revelation valiantly tries to reject all choices, hoping to live under the dicta of tyrant or ceremony. But even in this act he acknowledges his control; and as a victim of enforced freedom, he remembers that he must choose, thereby bringing horrible revelation into full blown awareness. Paradoxically, freedom proves a paralyzing power, tempered only by illusions of servitude. But so relentlessly ultimate is this freedom that it expels all illusions and abandons the individual to mercy of his own decisions.

"In the Penal Colony" takes place in the moments when freedom is yet intimation, not awareness; and it centers on the Explorer as he desperately tries to misconceive. Refusing to surrender outright to freedom, he still attempts to create a fortress of deceptions. The machine likewise was such a consoling illusion for its faithful when it was endowed with prophet, celebrant, and believers. But now a solitary priest, served by a few perfunctory assistants, must turn his energies towards preservation rather than amplification of the ritual. Stripped of charisma, the ritual, instead of concealing, now imparts uncomfortable hints of the ceremony's purpose; and the awareness of deception renders the illusion ineffective. Ritual, as suggested by Kafka's machine, is made necessary by the desire to escape the notion that nothing exists beyond the control of man. The failure of the ritual intensifies the agony it sought to hide.

Because it functions to conceal freedom and not as part of a code of behavior, the ritual subordinates all ethics and morality. In fact the machine replaces ethics, so that lingering ethical problems represent incomplete immersion in the ceremony. At the time of the narrative, however, only the Officer retains the full commitment necessary to derive the benefits from the machine. The Soldier and the Condemned exist under the protection of being victimized, but such security is short lived. After the demise of the ritual, they too must face the freedom that makes them attempt to flee the penal colony. But they are rebuffed by a gesture of the Explorer and are turned back to the dismal isle, reverberating with the terrible awareness of their freedom.

The Officer's devotion is complete. Imbued as he is with the ritual, he succeeds in sustaining an illusory loss of freedom. He need concern himself with only one problem, the survival of the machine. But the Explorer in his struggle to remain detached from the ritual remains conscious of another ethic. The more he flees the role of judge, the more pronounced becomes his freedom to decide the fate of the ritual. He must either profess in favor of the ritual, or refuse to do so. His decision, whether actively or passively rendered, will determine its maintenance or cessation. At the moment he retains ultimate freedom, he is simultaneously in the throes of a horrible revelation—he cannot escape the freedom being forced upon him. He must either reject the ritual or sustain it. Either way he must pay the price of judgment, involving awareness, responsibility, and commitment. And he must be brought to the brink of an awareness that he offers nothing to fill the gaping responsibility created by his decision.

Ironically, he issues his decision on the basis of moral squeamishness, and in so doing he decides upon the irrelevant. The humane properties of the machine are not the issue, which is, quite simply, whether the ritual should continue to function. Asked about the essential, the machine and its function, he rules on the accident, the machine, and its method. Rendering judgment on the accident, he nonetheless dooms the essence, at the same time failing to provide any substitute. And in disposing of the ritual, he, in a characteristic note of Kafkaesque irony, sustains the inhumanity he speaks against.

The decline of the machine is due neither to enlightened perspective on penology, nor to humanitarian motives. The machine was created by human whim to satisfy the mind's need for deception. The imagination that conceived the ceremony was unmindful of the necessary agony and torture in the ritual. It was seeking to avert all suffering invoked by awareness of nothingness. The former popularity of the ritual attests to at least temporary success. Likewise, the new commandant, whose disinterest in the machine hastened its demise, has been guided not by principle, but by the same whims that bore the machine into existence. The infernal machine is destroyed by lust. The host of women with whom the new commandant carouses, and who by their cajoling dominate his resolutions, have been repelled by it. But their motives appear all the more repulsive, as they toy with the condemned, fattening him with delicacies, so that vomiting accompanies the instant of sacrifice.

In opposition to the new commandant's passive destruction, the Officer, the surviving disciple of the old commandant, and the sole remaining enthusiast, attempts to revive the ritual. Gaining an adherent could affirm the vitality of the machine, especially if the new believer would exercise his influence. In the delicately poised moment when the ritual is dying, but when its mechanical performance has not ceased; when the Officer's enthusiasm sustains while the new commandant's disinterest chills, the Explorer arrives. Here he encounters a situation where it is no longer possible to withstand the awareness that he must judge. He must either revive the ritual or destroy it, and even his efforts to escape determining the machine's fate will incur its destruction.

But since freedom and control constitute the ultimate dread, he still frantically strives to avoid pronouncing final doom. He shuns the moment of decision with greater fervor than he promotes his conviction concerning the morality of the machine. For to the Explorer, as for the Officer and the new commandant, morality comprises little more than personal whim, a bothersome and potentially dangerous revelation of their own freedom. The Officer and the commandant, however, have each discovered a means of avoiding the ultimate expression of freedom. The commandant's harem and the Officer's zeal provide commitments at other levels. Their commitments neutralize each other, and the Explorer, a fugitive from decision, finding security in being an outsider, now must break the stalemate. Freedom has pursued him even into the penal colony.

In a typically Kafkaesque dilemma, we have a graphically depicted terror that turns out to be only the symptom of a far greater one. The machine, the most compelling focus of the narrative, is discovered to be less important than the decision concerning it. The days of the machine are numbered, but the promptings that led to its creation remain vital. All that is terrible about the machine—the impersonal selection, the propagation of extended torments, the distorted notions of justice, apply equally to the Explorer, who would permit these terrors to endure rather than commit himself to a decision. So terrible is the freedom from which he attempts to escape that he will quickly concede his moral sentiments.

The predicament of the Explorer further parallels the horror by the ritual. In turning the wheel of fortune, he recalls the void of communion. In the moment of casting a choice, the individual sacrifices all that the ceremony provides. He is aware of his freedom, his ability to effect consequences. In the same instant he perceives that void that reveals the communion as both vitally necessary and hopelessly inadequate. His heightened awareness defrocks terror of protective chaos. The Officer firmly committed to a revealed order, doggedly maintains it for fear he, too, should come face to face with nothingness. But the Explorer through his life of meandering has never found a satisfactorily permanent escape. Forever poised on a brink of decision, he has frighteningly little to do except shun the occasion that would make judgment imperative. When avoidance is no longer possible, his only defense is some ill formed, hastily uttered moral clichés. To his dismay these verbal attempts to escape produce even greater awareness, and seal his fate as arbiter.

The machine enters its final performance, and the Officer, now a priest without a following, dies significantly by the malfunction of the instrument that was his life. His death, however, crystallizes the situation for the Explorer. With the accidents dispelled, the essence is clear and confusion is no longer possible. He cannot escape the awareness that he now controls circumstance, and that he must exercise his freedom.

The despair that concludes this tale of dreadful freedom derives not from the mutilated body of the Officer, nor from the overall bleakness of the colony, but rather from the hero's failure to remain uninvolved. And the tattered body of the Officer manifests the irradicable presence of a freedom he had hoped did not exist. (pp. 309-16)

Leonard R. Mendelsohn, "Kafka's 'In the Penal Colony' and the Paradox of Enforced Freedom," in Studies in Short Fiction, *Vol. VIII, No. 2, Spring, 1971, pp. 309-16.*

Paul J. Dolan (essay date 1976)

[*In the following excerpt, Dolan argues that the tyrannical model of authority and justice depicted in "In the Penal Colony" prefigures the totalitarian barbarity of nazism.*]

"In the Penal Colony" is Franz Kafka's artistic statement of his sense of self-torture and the fantasies of self-destruction with which he lived. The story is also a prophecy of the horrors of German National Socialism in Europe from 1933 to 1945. The two visions, personal and public, psychological and political are, in fact, one.

The two are united because Kafka attempted no prophecy. He wrote of his own nightmare feelings so completely and so honestly that he wrote the history of the future when others made those feelings of guilt and self-torture motives for public policy and the nightmare became everyday reality.

If nazism had not happened, the story would still have mattered because it deals uniquely with the sense of pain with which some people somehow manage to live on a day-to-day basis. Nazism, however, revealed how that sense of the world as a torture chamber could be externalized and all the self-hatred redirected at the scapegoats. Nazism was a harnessing of the madness within and that is why it worked. Kafka is the poet of the madness within. Like Dostoyevsky, whom he knew, and Conrad, whom he did not, he wrote of the "Underground"—the dark cellar of unexpressed emotion wherein are stored the savage impulses of our lives. The modern artist has taken great pains to remind us that no social or political amelioration has removed those dark places. Hitler, himself a kind of daemonic artist, was able to reach within and tap them in his audience.

A terrible discovery that came in the wake of twentieth-century tyranny is the way in which ordinary men cooperated with it. The whole horror of nazism is unthinkable without the picture of some solid citizen in a small town thrilled to act at the Führer's command. What Kafka knew and wrote about before it had happened was the action of that good burgher. He knew that actions came from the tyranny of madness present in almost all of us and that Hitler in his person and his party suddenly made the madness acceptable behavior and released the ordinary man to act out the idea of torture he carried within himself.

The experiments of Stanley Milgram, reported in his *Obedience to Authority,* demonstrated that a large percentage of "normal" people will act in a brutal manner in a "totalitarian" situation. These people will excuse themselves on the grounds that they are acting in accordance with orders and with the requirements of authority rather than with simple humanity. The people become, in effect, automata; trapped in their own instinctive fears, unable to respond in a human way, they become what Kafka's Czech contemporary, Karel Capek, called "robots."

The robot is potential within the "normal" person. Kafka, knowing this, created in the character of the officer the symbol for the modern political robot. The Officer of **"In the Penal Colony"** is the character with whom we identify and he haunts us when the story is over. In fact, when Kafka toyed with new endings for the story, he had the Officer appear as a ghost on the ship with the Explorer. The character grips us as he does because Kafka writes the story from his point of view. As the focus of the action, the Officer speaks what Kafka feels and he appeals to us, represented by the Explorer, to understand him.

A doctrinaire Marxist critic of Kafka thought he detected a proto-Fascist streak in the novelist. He was on the right track but reached the wrong conclusion. We do not identify with the Officer because Kafka is a proto-Fascist; we identify with his capacity for devotion to that which will destroy him and recognize with a shudder that we understand his appeal because we share his madness. In writing of his own fear, Kafka could not have known that the Old Commandant would return and reverse, if only temporarily, the process of the gradual evolution of a benevolent state.

I do not think **"In the Penal Colony"** is a consistent allegory of any kind nor that there is a key to its meaning. Without attempting a systematic allegorical reading, I want to trace some of the relationships of the private and the public, the psychological and the historical, in the story. I will begin with the story itself and its sources and analogues in Kafka's fears, dreams, visions, and fantasies. That is its private dimension. The public I will consider in terms of Albert Speer's remarkable book, *Inside the Third Reich*. This memoir shows that Kafka did not write exclusively of feelings unique to him, nor of concerns solely theological. He wrote of human attitudes, and Speer reveals with terrifying ingenuousness how those attitudes made the Nazi holocaust possible. Finally, I want to talk about the point at which the private vision and the public prophecy meet: the technocracy, the country of technology and bureaucracy which is the modern state. Kafka's daily life was that of a bureaucrat and, as Heinz Politzer points out, "the highly technical description of the execution machine owes many a turn of phrase to the professional work Kafka had to perform for the Workers' Accident Insurance Institute. Ironically, one of his special fields of study was the prevention of accidents." This man, a bureaucrat crushed and sustained by the bureaucracy, the artist of the apparatus, a Czech Jew writing in German, alienated from his family and unable to make one of his own, haunted always by nightmares of torture, destruction and punishment, wrote of his experience as the alien-citizen of the modern state.

. . . . .

"In the Penal Colony" opens with the Officer introducing the Explorer to the machine—a remarkable apparatus. The opening in the hot, sandy valley with the two characters and the mute chorus of soldier and condemned man seems to be that of a story about Dreyfus on Devil's Island and Kafka's awareness of the Jew in the world of the imperial military. Typical of Kafka, however, that expectation is set up in the reader only to be frustrated. The real thread of the narrative begins with the Explorer's indifference to the world and work of the Officer. It is clear that the Explorer has come only to be polite, and at the suggestion of the Commandant that he might wish to witness the execution of a soldier for disobedience and insulting behavior. Because the story is so elusive, I will retell it as simply as possible here.

The Officer is working very hard to interest the Explorer, and somehow his exertions, in his heavy uniform, in the heat, begin to disturb us. We are, at first, touched by the Officer's anxiety that nothing go wrong. The Officer says: "Things sometimes go wrong of course; I hope that nothing goes wrong today, but we have to allow for the possibility. The machinery should go on working continuously for twelve hours. But if anything does go wrong it will only be some small matter that can be set right at once." Only later do we begin to realize some of the meaning in the Officer's pettish remarks about the New Commandant—that he cannot disrupt the design of the Old Commandant for the colony. It is quickly evident that both apparatus and colony have fallen far from their original designs.

The Explorer begins to be impressed by the Officer's hard work in the heat. He, like the reader, begins to respond to the enthusiasm of the other, an enthusiasm which seems attractive in the atmosphere of decay and lassitude. Such is the beginning of moral confusion: one begins by admiring enthusiasm until it becomes fanaticism, and even after that if it promises relief from boredom or the self. Kafka has begun involving us in the fate of the madman. When the Officer then begins his dramatic monologue of justification, the Explorer is already half-caught in the procedure; he "felt a dawning interest in the apparatus."

The Officer seems upset that the New Commandant has not explained to the Explorer how the sentence is to be executed. Yet, even as he condemns this latest breach of protocol, the Officer is pleased to be able to show to the visitor the plans and drawings for the machine, the scriptures of the Old Commandant. To the Explorer's surprised question as to whether the Old Commandant did everything, the Officer, with a glassy look, replies simply, "Yes." These scriptures, the elaborate plans for the machine are, according to Heinz Politzer, very like Kafka's own manuscript writings. In this sense the story is a statement by Kafka of his feelings about himself as a writer. His offense is to feel and see as he does; his punishment is to write what he feels with his own blood.

The Officer explains to the Explorer that, as the machine works, whatever commandment the prisoner has disobeyed is written into his body. In this case the statement is, "Honor Thy Superiors!" When the Explorer asks if the condemned man knows his sentence, the Officer replies that he will learn it on his body. When the Explorer expresses his shock at this, the Officer impatiently replies, "Guilt is never to be doubted." The offense of which the man is guilty is sleeping on duty and insulting a superior. The condemned man was required to get up at every hour to salute the door of his captain; and when at two o'clock in the morning the captain found him asleep and whipped him across the face, the man grabbed his foot and threatened to eat him alive. Now he is in chains and will be punished.

The offense is obviously one which fascinates Kafka.

Among Karl Rossman's many misadventures in *Amerika* is his problem with the Head Porter who scolds him and judges him a troublemaker because Karl failed to greet him "properly" every time they met, no matter how many times, in the course of a day. The offense, in both works, seems an echo of some expected ritual acknowledgment of dependency within the family and the violation of the commandment to honor one's father and mother, but especially one's father.

The condemned man stands, therefore, in chains, waiting to be punished for his disobedience. The chains seem superfluous since we have already been told that he would probably not run away even if he were unchained. When Kafka wrote this story, it would seem logical to assume that readers would account for the passivity of the prisoner by his ignorance of his fate. History has made his attitude more ambiguous. He may be motivated by ignorance of his fate or he may be the victim who simply refuses to believe what is being done to him right up to the moment he is placed in the execution chamber. He may even, in his ignorance, blindness, hope, belief in the sanctity of his own life, guilt, or innocence, be a victim willing to be punished for whatever crime the authority says he has committed.

To the troubled Explorer, the Officer explains more of the details of the machine, pressing him to read the "script," the plan for punishment; but the Explorer cannot. Remarking that the calligraphy is not for school children, the Officer explains that the script is designed to be completed in twelve hours of writing. The implication of the remark about the calligraphy, coupled with the place of children at the grand executions in the old days, is that a child witnesses the torture of individuals in the world and then grows up to understand and to appreciate the elaborate mechanisms of torture humans have devised for themselves.

The Officer presses on with details of the machine's operation and speaks reverently of the sixth hour when the prisoner understands his sentence, "Enlightenment comes to the most dull-witted." This, says the Officer, was "a moment that might tempt one to get under the Harrow oneself." In the last six hours, relieved of the burden of doubt about his guilt, the prisoner grows in his understanding of his sentence until he dies.

Such, at least, is the plan of the Old Commandant and his disciple for bringing a citizen to awareness. The real operation is much less edifying. As the real prisoner is placed upon the machine, one of the wrist straps, which has rotted, breaks. The Explorer begins to question the whole operation but is not yet able to do anything. The Officer complains bitterly that the New Commandant is not supporting properly the execution machine. The Explorer, now concerned, wonders if he should intervene. He thinks it a ticklish matter for him, a visitor to the colony, not even a citizen of the mother country, and yet he wonders what he should do because, "The injustice of the procedure and the inhumanity of the execution were undeniable." The Explorer is, I think, giving the response of Cain. "Am I my brother's keeper?" is the first and the still unanswered political question.

The Explorer's uncomfortable thoughts are interrupted by the Officer's cry of rage. The condemned man vomited when forced to take the felt gag into his mouth. The Officer is furious because the machine is befouled. The New Commandant is at fault because he has not forced the prisoner to fast and his ladies have stuffed the prisoner with candy, "He has lived on stinking fish his whole life long and now he has to eat sugar candy!" The gag has not been replaced even though hundreds have chewed it and slobbered over it in their death agonies. The emotional logic of this disgusting scene seems to favor the Officer against the New Commandant. If the punishment is inevitable, if it is to be rammed down one's throat, then it is worse if it is sugar coated. I do not know if the Old and New Commandants correspond to the God of the Old and New Testaments, or, more personally, to Kafka's grandfather, the butcher, and father, the dealer in ladies' linens; but as the Officer himself later performs the ambiguous sexual gesture of accepting the gag into his mouth, he is accepting the reality of pain and guilt which handkerchiefs and candy cannot hide.

At this point the rhythm of the story changes; the Officer asks to speak to the Explorer in "confidence." "This procedure and method of execution, which you are now having the opportunity to admire, has at the moment no longer any open adherents in our colony. I am its sole advocate." The Officer has begun his direct appeal to the Explorer with a story of the way it was in the old days under the Old Commandant when hundreds turned out to witness the magnificent spectacle of justice being done and jockeyed for seats close enough to observe in detail the transformation at the sixth hour. The Old Commandant, in his wisdom, provided that the children should have the preferred places from which to observe the "look of transfiguration" so that, presumably, they would be prepared, in their turn, to administer and to accept such justice. The Officer regrets that things have declined to the point of no crowds and the filthy gag and that "it is impossible to make those days credible now."

As the Explorer looks away, the Officer mistakes his reaction for sympathy and asks if he does indeed realize the shame of things as they now are. The Officer says that the Explorer has been sent as a witness by the New Commandant so that he can discredit the whole procedure, but the Officer pleads for his understanding and support. The Explorer is pleased to know that he can be influential and says to the Officer, "I can neither help nor hinder you." Thinking that he can get away that easily is part of the Explorer's problem.

The Officer presses on, his mad paranoia becoming absolutely clear as he constructs a scenario for the next day's conference in which the Explorer can support him. The Officer is planning a coup, an insane political gesture, like Hitler's in 1923, and he is demanding the Explorer's support: "it will force him [the New Commandant] to his knees to make the acknowledgment: Old Commandant, I humble myself before you. That is my plan; will you help me to carry it out?" The Explorer, even though "fundamentally honorable and unafraid," hesitates for one breath, "No," he says, "I do not approve. . . . your sincere conviction has touched me, even though it cannot influence my judgment."

The Explorer hesitates because he is partially captured by the Officer's desperation. The Officer seems so pathetic, so human, so alive in the midst of the desolation, that we, the Explorer and the reader, have to respond to him. The Explorer is like Marlow and the Officer like Kurtz, the two conscious characters in the heart of darkness. In the midst of the banality around them, Marlow and the Explorer can understand and even be tempted by the nightmare vision of the man they find in the wilderness. The Explorer, the visitor to the penal colony, begins to feel the reality of guilt, and the barbarism always possible to man.

"So you did not find the procedure convincing," says the Officer, " . . . then the time has come." Because he has failed to convince the Explorer of the justice of his cause, the Officer is willing to sacrifice himself to that cause. As the condemned man is set free, the Officer presents another drawing to the Explorer and deciphers it for him when he cannot read the inscription: BE JUST. The soldier and condemned man cavort; the Officer wipes off the machine, strips naked, and throws his clothes into the pit. "The Explorer bit his lip and said nothing. He knew very well what was going to happen, but he had no right to obstruct the Officer in anything. If the judicial procedure which the Officer cherished were really so near its end—possibly as a result of his own intervention, as to which he felt himself pledged—then the Officer was doing the right thing; in his place the Explorer would not have acted otherwise." Confirmed in his policy of nonintervention, the Explorer assumes that self-destruction is not a form of injustice or inhumanity. Perhaps he feels that it is necessary to execute the primitive self, if the enlightened self is to rule unchallenged.

The reactions of the condemned man are less self-conscious. When the condemned man realizes that the Officer plans to submit himself to the machine, he is happy: "So this was revenge. Although he himself had not suffered to the end, he was to be revenged to the end. A broad, silent grin now appeared on his face and stayed there all the rest of the time."

The Officer places himself upon the machine and even is able to take the gag into his mouth. The condemned man and the soldier run up; the Officer allows himself to be strapped in; the machine starts itself and works very quietly.

Then, as the Explorer and the other two watch, the machine goes crazy and begins to vomit out its insides. "The explorer wanted to do something . . . to bring the whole machine to a standstill, for this was no exquisite torture such as the officer desired, this was plain murder." To the enlightened onlooker, the slow, exquisite torture of a life in pain is acceptable, but the violence of suicide is not. The Explorer pushes the corpse of the Officer off the machine into the pit. There is no change in the Officer's face, no sign of redemption, only the great iron spike, like that on top of a helmet, protruding through his forehead.

The story now becomes the story of the Explorer's reaction. With the other two witnesses, he rushes from the scene to the inhabited colony, to civilization. On the outskirts of the settlement he stops at the teahouse in which the Old Commandant is buried. The building is old, dark and cavernous, like a church, or a womb, or the dark places of the human heart, and in it the Explorer "felt the power of past days." The soldier tells him that the Old Commandant is buried here because the priest would not let him lie in the churchyard. The Explorer finds the grave against the back wall where the poor people, the dock workers, are gathered. On the grave is this inscription, "Here rests the Old Commandant. His adherents, who now must be nameless, have dug this grave and set up this stone. There is a prophecy that after a certain number of years the Commandant will rise again and lead his adherents from this house to recover the colony. Have faith and wait!" Like Frederick Barbarossa, he may return.

The inscription seems a prediction of the horrors to come because Kafka saw so clearly into one kind of human psyche that he understood how it might express itself in history. We can now read the story as if it were a retrospective study of nazism; as if Kafka had seen it all, the concentration camps in which his sisters died, the torture machines, the ordinary men become fanatics, and simply recorded it. History gives the story its peculiar quality of *deja vu* and makes the inscription on the tomb of the Old Commandant seem a parody of the epitaph of Arthur of Britain: *Rex quondam et futuris.* In Kafka's story, the Old Commandant lies underground, in the cellar, the rat hole in the floorboards of civilization first described by Dostoyevsky's man with the diseased liver [in *Notes from the Underground*].

The habitués of the teahouse reveal nothing. They seem to find the inscription "ridiculous." The Explorer gives them some coins and leaves for the harbor. He gets away in a small boat and, when the soldier and the condemned man rush to the dock to join him in his flight to freedom, he threatens them with a knotted rope and makes his escape without them. This representative of the advanced, civilized, and rational nations wants no further business with the inhabitants of the penal colony. The Explorer wants nothing more to do with the darkness and destruction to which his explorations have led him. He will, if necessary, resort to force to keep himself free from involvement with anyone connected with the hideous act. (pp. 125-35)

. . . . .

One of Kafka's most famous diary entries is that for August 2, 1914: "Germany has declared war on Russia.—Swimming in the afternoon." Just before this, in the entry for July 31 in which he mentions the General Mobilization, Kafka wrote: "But I will write in spite of everything, absolutely; it is my struggle for self-preservation." Dedicated to his writing and his private vision, Kafka seems to ignore the ordinary details of the outside world. What he does is to make his painful compositions stand for his sense of the realities of that world. Thus, **"The Great Wall of China"** is a parable of Kafka's vision of World War I and his status as a Czech, Jew, German in that war.

Kafka's political insight begins with his sense of himself as a victim of tyranny, the tyranny of his father: "For me you took on the enigmatic quality that all tyrants have whose rights are based on their person and not on reason. At least so it seemed to me" (**"Letter to His Father"**). He writes, later in the same letter, "My writing was all about you; all I did there, after all, was to bemoan what I could not bemoan upon your breast. It was an intentionally long-drawn-out leave-taking from you, yet, although it was enforced by you, it did take its course in the direction determined by me." Kafka, in that struggle, articulated his ambivalent feelings about that tyranny in such a way that the corpus of his work may be read as the statement of the individual as cooperative victim and willing prisoner in the process of destruction. The Officer makes clearer our responses to . . . Albert Speer, the Nazi armaments minister who seems completely a Kafka character. We do not sympathize with what the Officer represents; we simply understand better the mechanisms of madness in the individual which can become the mechanisms of madness in the state.

Kafka's personal writings are filled with analogues to the machinery and the punishments of **"In the Penal Colony."** His diary entry for July 21, 1913, reads: "This block and tackle of the inner being. A small lever is somewhere secretly released, one is hardly aware of it at first, and at once the whole apparatus is in motion. Subject to an incomprehensible power, as the watch seems subject to time, it creaks here and there, and all the chains clank down their prescribed path one after the other."

Later, on January 24, 1914, the year of the war and the story, Kafka made this entry in his diary: "Recently, when I got out of the elevator at my usual hour, it occurred to me that my life, whose days more and more repeat themselves down to the smallest detail, resembles that punishment in which each pupil must according to his offense write down the same meaningless (in repetition, at least) sentence ten times, a hundred times or even oftener; except that in my case the punishment is given me with only this limitation: 'as many times as you can stand it.' " (pp. 135-37)

The torture machine, the *Apparat* mentioned over and over again in the beginning of the story, is part of Kafka's perception of everyday reality. Kafka is not the Officer any more than Dostoyevsky is the Underground Man, but the character is some part of the creator, and the Explorer speaks for Kafka's sane self in recognizing the inevitable self-destruction of the mad self. Kafka was not a "proto-Fascist"; his prophecy of nazism came from the fact that he wrote so clearly, so honestly of his own inner sense of destructive madness. He could not know that he spoke for a world.

The story seems not to have relieved Kafka of his terrible anxiety. . . . [The] dream detailed below is recounted in the diary for January 1915, some months after the completion of the story.

> I had agreed to go picnicking Sunday with two
> friends, but quite unexpectedly slept past the
> hour when we were to meet. My friends, who
> knew how punctual I ordinarily am, were surprised, came to the house where I lived, waited

Cover of the first edition of "In the Penal Colony," *published by Kurt Wolff in 1919.*

outside awhile, then came upstairs and knocked on my door. I was very startled, jumped out of bed and thought only of getting ready as soon as I could. When I emerged fully dressed from my room, my friends fell back in manifest alarm. "What's that behind your head?" they cried. Since my awakening I had felt something preventing me from bending back my head, and I now groped for it with my hand. My friends, who had grown somewhat calmer, had just shouted "Be careful, don't hurt yourself!" when my hand closed behind my head on the hilt of a sword. My friends came closer, examined me, led me back to the mirror in my room and stripped me to the waist. A large, ancient knight's sword with a cross-shaped handle was buried to the hilt in my back, but the blade had been driven with such incredible precision between my skin and flesh that it had caused no injury. Nor was there a wound at the spot on my neck where the sword had penetrated; my friends assured me that there was an opening large enough to admit the blade, but dry and showing no trace of blood. And when my friends now stood on chairs and slowly, inch by inch, drew out the sword, I did not bleed, and the

opening on my neck closed until no mark was left save a scarcely discernible slit. "Here is your sword," laughed my friends, and gave it to me. I hefted it in my two hands; it was a splendid weapon, Crusaders might have used it.

Who tolerates this gadding about of ancient knights in dreams, irresponsibly brandishing their swords, stabbing innocent sleepers who are saved from serious injury only because the weapons in all likelihood glance off living bodies, and also because there are faithful friends knocking at the door, prepared to come to their assistance?

In August 1917, Kafka began to work on alternate endings for **"In the Penal Colony."** He had said of the story, after reading it aloud at Franz Werfel's, that he was "not entirely dissatisfied, except for its glaring and ineradicable faults." Whether or not the remark was simply ironic, Kafka did continue to think about the ending of the story. The diary entries for August 7, 8 and 9, 1917, have to do with changes in the story—changes that were never made. Most revealing in connection with these contemplated changes, however, is the entry for August 3, 1917, where Kafka records a dream in which he is one of his own characters: "Once more I screamed at the top of my voice into the world. Then they shoved a gag into my mouth, tied my hands and feet and blindfolded me. I was rolled back and forth a number of times, I was set upright and knocked down again, this too several times, they jerked at my legs so that I jumped with pain; they let me lie quietly for a moment, but then, taking me by surprise, stabbed deep into me with something sharp, here and there, at random." Having dreamed his story, Kafka toyed with endings in which the ghost of the Officer haunts the Explorer who thinks he can get away.

Kafka made the Officer so moving and so persuasive because he lived his fate. He wrote, as he said, as an act of self-preservation. Thanks to that we can understand better some of the madness of modern history.

. . . . .

A bureaucrat concerned with technology, driven to write his nightmares, is a possible description of Franz Kafka. **"In the Penal Colony"** is, among other things, a symbolic treatment of the two most important "facts" of modern political life: technology and bureaucracy. The two "facts," unideological and apolitical, shape the citizen's experience of the state. Apparatus and system are not the causes of the modern state, but its products. The connection between Kafka's story and nazism is that the Nazis made the nightmare real. The Nazis used the products of the modern state to bring about the rule of barbarism. One of the best commentaries on this dimension of **"In the Penal Colony"** is *Inside the Third Reich,* the memoirs of Albert Speer.

Speer was an architect who became, early in the 1930's, Hitler's personal architect and city planner. Always close to Hitler, hard-working and talented, he became in 1942 Minister of Armaments and War Production and devoted himself to organizing the German economy for the prosecution of the war. At Nuremberg he was sentenced to twenty years in prison and, while serving his sentence at

Spandau, wrote his reflections on Hitler, on himself, on the technocracy of evil he served so well. As he says, in his strange mixture of confession and defense, of denunciation and apologia, "Dazzled by the possibilities of technology, I devoted crucial years of my life to serving it." One can open Speer's memoirs at random and come upon passages that are eerily Kafkaesque. This, for example, is how the Minister of Armaments and War Production speaks of his accomplishments in the service of a regime he now knows to have been completely evil:

> Within half a year after my taking office we had significantly increased production in all the areas within our scope. Production in August 1942, according to the *Index Figures for German Armaments End-Products,* as compared with the February production, had increased by 27 percent for guns, by 25 percent for tanks, while ammunition production almost doubled, rising 97 percent. The total productivity in armaments increased by 59.6 percent. [footnote omitted] Obviously we had mobilized reserves that had hitherto lain fallow.

The prideful rhetoric seems familiar because it is the rhetoric of the Officer trying to convince the Explorer of the efficacy of the system and the apparatus.

In another passage, Speer includes, unknowingly, the guard and the prisoner. The only difference is that these are real people, prisoners of war:

> The prisoners themselves, as I sometimes had a chance to observe, also feared Himmler's growing economic ambitions. I recall a tour through the Linz steelworks in the summer of 1944 where prisoners were moving about freely among the other workers. They stood at the machines in the lofty workshops, served as helpers to trained workers, and talked unconstrainedly with the free workers. It was not the SS but army soldiers who were guarding them. When we came upon a group of twenty Russians, I had the interpreter ask them whether they were satisfied with their treatment. They made gestures of passionate assent. Their appearance confirmed what they said. In contrast to the people in the caves of the Central Works, who were obviously wasting away, these prisoners were well fed. And when I asked them, just to make conversation, whether they would prefer to return to the regular camp, they gave a start of fright. Their faces expressed purest horror.

> But I asked no further questions. Why should I have done so; their expressions told me everything. If I were to try today to probe the feelings that stirred me then, if across the span of a lifetime I attempt to analyze what I really felt—pity, irritation, embarrassment, or indignation—it seems to me that the desperate race with time, my obsessional fixation on production and output statistics, blurred all considerations and feelings of humanity. An American historian has said of me that I loved machines more than people. [footnote omitted] He is not wrong. I realize that the sight of suffering people influenced only my emotions, but not my conduct. On the plane of feelings only sentimentality emerged; in

the realm of decisions, on the other hand, I continued to be ruled by the principles of utility. In the Nuremberg Trial the indictment against me was based on the use of prisoners in the armaments factories.

> By the court's standard of judgment, which was purely numerical, my guilt would have been greater had I prevailed over Himmler and raised the number of prisoners in our labor force, thus increasing the chances of more people for survival. Paradoxically, I would feel better today if in this sense I had been guiltier. But what preys on my mind nowadays has little to do with the standards of Nuremberg nor the figures on lives I saved or might have saved. For in either case I was moving within the system. What disturbs me more is that I failed to read the physiognomy of the regime mirrored in the faces of those prisoners—the regime whose existence I was so obsessively trying to prolong during those weeks and months. I did not see any moral ground outside the system where I should have taken my stand. And sometimes I ask myself who this young man really was, this young man who has now become so alien to me, who walked through the workshops of the Linz steelworks or descended into the caverns of the Central Works twenty-five years ago.

A final quotation from Speer should make clear Kafka's political significance.

> In a sense my hopes had been realized. The judicial guilt had been concentrated to a large extent upon us, the defendants. But during that accursed era, a factor in addition to human depravity had entered history, the factor that distinguished our tyranny from all historical precedents, and a factor that would inevitably increase in importance in the future. As the top representative of a technocracy which had without compunction used all its know-how in an assault on humanity, [footnote omitted] I tried not only to confess but also to understand what had happened. In my final speech I said:

> Hitler's dictatorship was the first dictatorship of an industrial state in this age of modern technology, a dictatorship which employed to perfection the instruments of technology to dominate its own people. . . . By means of such instruments of technology as the radio and public-address systems, eighty million persons could be made subject to the will of one individual. Telephone, teletype, and radio made it possible to transmit the commands of the highest levels directly to the lowest organs where because of their high authority they were executed uncritically. Thus many offices and squads received their evil commands in this direct manner. The instruments of technology made it possible to maintain a close watch over all citizens and to keep criminal operations shrouded in a high degree of secrecy. To the outsider this state apparatus may look like the seemingly wild tangle of cables in a telephone exchange; but like such an exchange it could be directed by a single will. Dictatorships of the past needed assistants of high quality in the lower ranks of the leadership

also—men who could think and act independently. The authoritarian system in the age of technology can do without such men. The means of communication alone enable it to mechanize the work of the lower leadership. Thus the type of uncritical receiver of orders is created.

The **"Penal Colony"** and the *Third Reich* are the same place. Such is the power of Kafka's vision that he writes in 1914, not as if terrible potentialities will be realized, but as if they already had been.

In the penal colony the inhabitants are exiles and emigrés, the disenfranchised citizens, those in exile in the country of their birth. At the heart of the chronicle of this colony is the machine that renders justice. To have BE JUST tatooed into the body is a parody of the teaching of political virtue, a basic responsibility of the state. In *The Republic* Socrates tried to define justice by describing the just state and its citizens. Plato wrote of a state of which justice was the soul. Kafka envisioned a state in which the *Apparat* was the soul.

"In the Penal Colony" was written in 1914, the year of Armageddon, the beginning of the end of the modern era. Kafka wrote before the advent of the totalitarian state, but he wrote as one who had seen it and returned. Thirty years later, other, less visionary men travelled to that strange country. All subsequent statistics and reports tend to verify the accuracy of Kafka's preliminary sketch. (pp. 138-44)

> *Paul J. Dolan, "Kafka: The Political Machine," in his* Of War and War's Alarms: Fiction and Politics in the Modern World, *The Free Press, 1976, pp. 125-44.*

Arnold Weinstein   (essay date 1982)

[*In the following essay, Weinstein interprets "In the Penal Colony" as a commentary on language, self-knowledge, and spirituality.*]

Like all of Kafka's best stories, **"In the Penal Colony"** is maddeningly rife with multiple and contradictory interpretations. Some have made it announce Auschwitz and Dachau; others have seen in it a grim reminder of harsher Old Testament values, according to which our modern liberal world stands either condemned or threatened; the brief tale has been read psychologically, psychoanalytically, anthropologically, historically, paradoxically and parabolically. No matter how one reads it, however, the story's resolution, i.e. the explorer's response to the penal colony, appears so ambivalent that it becomes effectively impossible to do the very thing that is central here and happening everywhere in Kafka: pronounce judgment. My purpose, in proposing a new look at the story, is to centralize the notion of communication and language; in so doing, we begin to perceive the awesome coherence of Kafka's materials: the disturbing, echoing analogies between the narrative frame, the nature of the Machine, and the purposes of art.

"It's a remarkable [*eigentümlich*] piece of apparatus." Kafka's genius in mixing understatement and prophecy—

so often in evidence in the first lines of his stories—is fully displayed here. Just how *"eigentümlich, "* just how special the machine is, is something the explorer and, indeed, the reader must gradually come to understand. The entire story may, in fact, be seen as a gloss on these lines: how can the officer make the explorer adequately comprehend the machine? The critical debate concerning the story suggests that its readers have been equally perplexed, equally stymied in their grasp of these strange events. There is nothing contrived or redundant about Kafka's insistence on the process of understanding. The desperation and passion of the story lie precisely in the officer's efforts to reach the explorer, to bring the outsider over to his own point of view. One might even go so far as to say that the officer's project is more profoundly rhetorical than it is judgmental: to persuade the explorer counts ultimately more than punishing the prisoner. One even has the sense that the justice of the entire System (that of the Old Commander, to be sure) is strangely dependent on the explorer's verdict: to understand the special nature of the machine would restore Truth and Clarity to a world riddled with doubt and equivocation. This mutual drama of understanding is, as it were, the hidden script of the story, and Kafka shows, if I may extend his own metaphor, just how thick our skin is.

There was a time, we are told, when the validity of the machine did not require such special pleading. The spectacle of justice being done was an occasion of civic and spiritual celebration, a time of community. Crowds came from far and near, and children were given preferential treatment in seating arrangements. It is no wonder that children witnessed these events, since they seem to have possessed a rather extraordinary educational potential. There was not yet any uncertainty or confusion in matters of innocence and guilt: all parties—including the victim—experienced a collective revelation of truth. These were halcyon days, epistemologically as well as morally:

> " . . . often enough I would be squatting there with a small child in either arm. How we all absorbed the look of transfiguration on the face of the sufferer, how we bathed our cheeks in the radiance of that justice, achieved at last and fading so quickly! What times these were, my comrade!" The officer had obviously forgotten whom he was addressing; he had embraced the explorer and laid his head on his shoulder. The explorer was deeply embarrassed, impatiently he stared over the officer's head.

Notice how the moment of transparency is an irresistible moment of sharing and bonding. Moreover, the community spirit embodied in these public executions is again activated, communalized through narration; the officer embraces the explorer, as a natural extension of those brother days, but finds coolness, objectivity and embarrassment instead. The officer seeks, throughout the entire story, to "touch" the explorer; the explorer, man from another realm, keeps his distance. I am less interested in assessing the explorer's character than in underscoring his detachment, his quasi-professional sense of noninvolvement. Yet, as we shall see, distanced judgment counts for naught in Kafka; "understanding" something comes, sooner or later, to mean "entering" into it, and in this story such an entry will be literally enacted at the close. In Kafka's work, filled as it is with endless corridors, closed doors, secret chambers and labyrinthine passages, contact with the Other, sought, feared or enacted at every level of the narrative, is both the ultimate hunger and the ultimate taboo.

From our vantage point in the latter part of the 20th century, **"In the Penal Colony"** can hardly be viewed as anything other than a horror story, a torture story. The grotesque disproportion between crime and punishment, the radical assumption of guilt, the heinous nature of the sentence, the powerfully symbolic dysfunction of the machine, all this seems to constitute an irreversible indictment of the officer and his penal system. Finally, the machine itself appears to be on trial: technical know-how, mechanical expertise and scientific engineering have, as we know today better than Kafka can have known in 1914, a will and impetus of their own, determining rather than serving the human uses to which they are put. The machine may then be *"eigentümlich,"* in that it is the most seductive and potent agent of the story, the ultimate winner in the modernist game of rhetorical persuasion, the forerunner not only of Dachau and Auschwitz, but of all the technological nightmares of our own nuclear age.

And yet . . . Kafka's story refuses to fit this scenario. There is something great as well as something disturbing in Kafka's machine. Technical craft, fine-tuning and scientific precision must have a special (*eigentümlich*) appeal to any artist. Given what we know of Kafka's self-discipline as a writer, his torturous sense that what he had written would not quite do, we are compelled to feel that this complex, harmonious, (up-to-now) perfectly functioning machine—with its complete adequation of ends and means—cannot be simply dismissed as evil. Finally, our post-1914 history, with its well-known atrocities, has, it is true, enabled us to read Kafka's story in a grimly prescient manner; but it has also led us to *misread* Kafka's story, to see in it the precursor of concentration camps, but to miss the echoes of Flaubertian aesthetics, the Flaubertian mystique of a *mot juste* that would miraculously wed language to reality. The most painstaking and scrupulous of authors, Kafka knew all too well that words veil as well as disclose, that they can only name, never be; how can he not have yearned for that Edenic realm where language and substance are united, that *Heimat* whose uniform the officer still wears, in poignant contrast to the homelessness of the explorer who is afloat in the relativism of his age and is rooted nowhere. Finding a potent language is, then, the unifying thread of Kafka's story: in this light, the machine's special power perfectly images the drama of understanding and contact at the heart of the tale.

Understanding is the cornerstone of all community, and language has, since the beginning of human society, played a crucial bridgemaking role in the interactions between men and their gods, between men and themselves. Much of Kafka's work seems polarized by the two dominant modes of such relationships, the Old Law and the New Law, the injunctions of authority versus the openness of love. In this story, Kafka has introduced still another basic antithesis: the memory of a time when Truth was known and despotically enforced, versus our modern period of liberal relativism with its bureaucratic procedures. The written word, as Kafka well knew, has long been central to the transmission of Truth; the German word for "writing" is *"Schrift,"* and Kafka significantly noted that it also stands for "Scriptures," for holy books. A number of critics have been drawn to this connection, and they have sketched elaborate parallels between the religiously guarded, hieroglyphic instructions for the machine and the sacred books of the past; but, whether it be Old Testament or New, Torah or Talmud, this written document now fails to create its community of believers. The explorer cannot decipher it. But, let us not reduce the role of *"Schrift"* to the page of instructions for the machine; if we apply to it the more modern sense of "language," "discourse," or *"écriture,"* then we see the larger spectrum of communicative acts which make up the form and meaning of the tale. The old absolute code may be defunct, but the machine remains, and so, too, does human language. In the secular present, literature itself may be called on to regenerate the interactions between men and their gods, men and themselves. Written and spoken language are the last remaining agents of connection. They are civilization's vehicle for understanding, and if they can no longer preemptorily command assent, they can perhaps strive for a still nobler goal: to invite response, to incite love. Understanding and love enable mutuality in a world that contains only individuals. Understanding and love are modes of entry, promises of reciprocity. The writer, more than most, plays a role in this drama, because his is the medium that bonds and connects. In the old days, the machine made truth visible, and all understood, together. As a means of commonality, such understanding has nothing to do with logic or system; it is knowledge, in the biblical sense of experience, of entry into things. Without this kind of understanding, human beings are either logical robots or animals of instinct, achieving no knowledge worth having, whether of the self or of the other. **"In the Penal Colony"** is about the inadequacy of these extremes, and it is in the creation of his macabre but mesmerizing machine that we may find Kafka's strange remedy.

The distance maintained by the explorer has already been mentioned. Vaguely an emissary of "our" humanist society, he is perplexed by the conflict between judgment and action; he disapproves, but does not want to meddle. He leaves the island apparently unchanged in his views, preventing the soldier and the prisoner from following him. He threatens them with a heavy, knotted rope, as if they were subhuman. And they are. Kafka has described the prisoner as "a man with crude features and thick lips," whose passivity is "doglike and submissive"; his crime is strictly one of instinct: when whipped in the face by his superior, "instead of getting up and begging pardon, the man caught hold of his master's legs, shook him and cried, 'Throw that whip away or I'll eat you alive.'" The soldier and the prisoner, squatting in dirt and vomit, listen uncomprehendingly as the officer explains—in French no less, so that the opaqueness of our language is even more blatantly illustrated—the machine to the explorer. All we see is "the movement of his blubber lips, closely pressed together, [which] showed clearly that he [the prisoner] could not understand a word." Asking if the prisoner even knows what his crime is, the explorer dutifully demonstrates his allegiance to the humanist code; but that code, predicated on the possibility of self-knowledge and implemented through the use of spoken and written language, is shattered by the officer's answer, an answer that resonates throughout the story: "There would be no point in telling him. He'll learn it on his body." Whereas most critics have focused on the glaring injustice of such a procedure, the calm assuredness that guilt need hardly be "proven" since it is concomitant with existence, what has gone largely uncommented is Kafka's radical view of communication itself. For now we see the awesome mediation which the machine is to provide: spoken language, French in this case, but arguably all language, including potentially this story, the full exchange between the officer and the explorer, the reader and the text, fails to deliver its message, fails to penetrate one's being, to get through one's skin, to make an entry, to effect intercourse or discourse, to transform animals into men.

Kafka is dealing with the most elemental problem known to verbal creatures. Language cannot *be* what it says. And men's skins are thick. This story depicts a search for language that is immediate rather than mediated, and it comes up with a terrible solution: we must learn viscerally, not verbally; the script must be in us, not in front of us. As if he were a geneticist, aware that our very chemistry and molecules perform linguistic operations, Kafka seems to be saying that the verbal message can achieve a magic oneness with its referent, only if it is encoded in our flesh. Kafka's machine is a writing machine. It actualizes and vitalizes all our tired metaphors and proverbs for knowledge: "tief," "deep" awareness, to understand something "viscerally," to scratch the surface, to be penetrated by knowledge, to have an "inner" certainty. Thick-skinned, "thick-lipped" humans need no less. The machine provides deep knowledge; its prisoners achieve a visceral understanding of their crimes; its needles constantly furnish "a new deepening of the script." At the sixth hour, metamorphosis occurs, and the dual event happens: animals become men, and individuals become a community:

> Only about the sixth hour does the man lose all desire to eat. I usually kneel down here at that moment and observe what happens. The man rarely swallows his last mouthful, he only rolls it around his mouth and spits it out into the pit. . . . But how quiet he grows at just about the sixth hour! Enlightenment comes to the most dull-witted. It begins around the eyes. From there it radiates. A moment that might tempt one to get under the Harrow oneself. Nothing more happens than that the man begins to understand the inscription, he purses his mouth as if he were listening. You have seen how difficult it is to decipher the script with one's eyes; but our man deciphers it with his wounds.

Let there be no mistake about the double miracle at work here. It is a miracle of truth, but it is no less a miracle of art: transparency is at hand, and language is one with experience and knowledge.

Such knowledge and such language are fatal. Biologically, the individual is a closed system, but orifices and apertures play their role in our life. The animal body takes in and puts out food; the species cannot continue if the male does not enter the female. Safety is provided by enclosure, but the entries and exits of the body must have daily commerce if the organism is to survive. In Kafka's work, food and sex—the most basic modes of entry into the closed body—are portrayed in starkly ambivalent ways: K. and Frieda lick and nuzzle each other like dogs; Gregor Samsa starves to death, while sensing in the music and love of his sister that impossibly refined nourishment which he seeks; the hunger artist's rarefied art—his professional refusal of the body—is replaced by solid appetites of the panther. The prisoner, at the sixth hour, spits out the food so that he can attend to the new body language he is receiving. Kafka seems to feel horror at the body, but he reveres the human longing for sustenance and contact. This yearning is viscerally experienced by many of his characters, but gratification does not appear to be fully imaginable, much less achievable. His are the most searching, uncompleted characters in modern literature. Hence, he has bequeathed to us the most thorough embodiment of walled-in, bureaucratized, reified man that we have. Functionaries inhabit Kafka's world, because functions have replaced relationships; mutuality and reciprocity are cut off at every turn. Demarcation is everywhere, preserving distances, making character into cipher, defying intercourse. **"The Burrow"** is merely an extreme instance of the fear of contact and violation, of being broken and entered, which is everywhere operative in his work.

Art would seem, in Kafka's world, to promise a finer intercourse, an unthreatening commerce between selves, a penetration that gratifies but does not maim. If nourishment and love cannot come through the flesh, then perhaps the mind and its agency of language can provide them. Thus, we return to the notions of understanding and knowledge as openness to the Other. Language is doubtless the most privileged vehicle of figurative contact; it renders possible a very special type of exchange, wherein the self remains physically intact but nonetheless entered. The beauty and horror of Kafka's story lie in the creation of physical language, a material linguistics with a distinct cutting edge that guarantees immediacy and requires no translation. The enclosed nature of the self and the thickness of its heart, mind and skin can at last be cut through. **"In the Penal Colony"** presents a nightmarish version of the *open* self as the *opened* self, with the attendant horror of violation and mutilation fully enacted. The flesh itself must be rent, before understanding is achieved.

"In the Penal Colony" is ultimately a strange love story. It registers at all levels the failure of communication, the falling short of language, the unrelated and uncomprehending selves. The prisoner's ignorance of his "crime" is only one phase of the breakdown; the main thrust of the tale, informed by the narrative strategy and endowing the material with a muted urgency, lies in the officer's declaration; his efforts to "touch" the explorer, to explain what is special about the machine, to bring the past to life, are essentially an attempt at seduction. All fails. The prisoner is left untouched. The skeptical explorer does not respond to the officer's passion, the only real emotion in the story.

The pleas are received but unmet. The explorer leaves, perhaps to explore other places. Has he understood the machine? Has the reader understood the story?

In the end, as we know, the machine acts. When the explorer fatefully denies the officer his help, when the effort to explain the machine has been seen to fail, the exemplary, illuminating reversal finally takes place. The officer frees the prisoner and takes his place. The machine butchers him and self-destructs. Here, I think, we are at the heart of Kafka's world. Many critics have understandably focused on the behavior of the machine, suggesting either that it is a travesty of justice (the officer is not "saved"), or that it is proper poetic justice (the officer gets his just deserts). But the most eloquent act of the tale is not that of the machine; it is the *geste* of the officer. For he enacts the major transformation of the work: *the officer becomes the prisoner*. His mission is no longer to supervise or explain; he will encounter the machine himself, but from the inside, this time.

No more lessons. Explanations and instruction—whether deriving from holy books or as the modus operandi of modern life—are no more than a futile kind of verbal ping-pong, a doomed mode of knowledge. There is only one way to understand the machine: that is to become the prisoner. In becoming the prisoner, the officer breaks out of his role in the hierarchy and achieves, briefly, the experience of the Other. The machine breaks down because, in some profound way, its work has already been done, achieved by the officer's *geste*. The potent language offered by the machine is only one element of communication; response is the other. The officer is butchered, I think, because he has never been concerned with what truth or justice look like—from the other side. He has courted and pleaded with the explorer; yet he has regarded the prisoner as subhuman. Even though there is no sign of redemption on his face, there is no sign of torture either; the officer's act has granted him a bodily—rather than verbal—experience of justice, the fateful "inside" view that is required if one is to understand or judge others.

We know that Kafka remained dissatisfied with the last pages of the story, those that depict the explorer's visit to the tea house and final departure. The fragments that he wrote in 1917 suggest that the explorer was ultimately more implicated, more drawn in, than appears at first glance. In particular, he feels bonded to the officer, even to the extent of seeing the dead man in his imagination, with a spike protruding from his forehead. Asked if his appearance is magic, the ghost officer replies, "A mistake on your part; I was executed on your command." I think it is fair to say that this fragment of a finale completes the communicative act; moreover, it restates the story's central truth: to understand the other is to become the other, to be intimately involved with his life and death.

In becoming the prisoner, the officer undergoes the fundamental Kafkaesque metamorphosis, the one that haunts his best work. To become another is the recurring structural drama of Kafka's stories: its twin faces are love and metamorphosis, understanding and trauma, transcendence of the flesh and rending of the flesh. The officer becomes the prisoner no less than Gregor Samsa becomes a bug. Kafka's country doctor experiences the same elemental upheaval: he projects, easily enough, onto the boy's wound the sexual drama at home; but he is made to lie, naked, on the bed with the boy, thereby revealing his manifold impotence, showing his own malady, becoming the patient. The officer, placing himself within the machine, illuminates Kafka's classic procedure: rational discourse and logical explanation are doomed to futility. Knowledge comes only through personal transformation, and it must be *"am eigenen Leibe erfahren,"* experienced in the flesh.

Thick-skinned humans come to knowledge of Others by an act of violent metamorphosis. *In* Kafka's stories, this transformation is frequently literal and monstrous, for the language bridge does not hold, and discourse remains sterile, short of undertanding. But, *through* Kafka's stories, even that metamorphosis may be a figurative one of great beauty; through art, and perhaps only through art, we are able, without being dismembered or metamorphosed, to become another, to extend our first person onto the lives and events we read about. Kafka's painstaking narrative art, perhaps more than that of any other twentieth century writer, demands that extension of us, requiring that we experience, vicariously, the limits and sensations of a bug, the yearning of the hunger artist, the powerlessness of the doctor, the maze-like quandaries of K. and Joseph K., the fascination of the machine. Kafka's very narrative techniques, his skillful control of point-of-view, his intensely myopic realism, his courage to be literal—all these are features of his craft, his own writing machine, which are intended to *open* us to the world of the Other.

Many find **"In the Penal Colony"** a grisly, brutal story. Like the story of the exodus from the Garden, it is about the cost of knowledge. We are so accustomed to defining knowledge as information, so habituated to language as explanatory, that the high stakes and cruel outcome of Kafka's parable seem melodramatic or Gothic. But his story depicts, with rare power, the drama of human understanding. In Borges' fine essay, "Kafka and his Precursors," he suggests that great art creates new constellations, that we see, as critics, both backwards and forwards in our efforts to discern intellectual kinship between authors. Kafka's metamorphic view of relationship and knowledge may serve as a model for literature's claim to tell us about Others. Using Borges as precedent, I would like to suggest two particular texts which leave us with the same dark knowledge. Melville's tortured tale, "Benito Cereno," depends entirely on point-of-view narrative, thereby showing that the perfectly innocent mind cannot see evil. But the underside of Melville's story is the unwritten narrative, the experience of Cereno himself which the reader begins to understand only when the tale is over. Masquerading as a white man in control, Cereno has in fact been forced to obey his Black "slaves" at every turn; the reader has seen the innocent version of events, but Cereno has experienced *from the inside,* the collapse of his role, the reality of the Blacks. And he dies. In somewhat similar manner, Faulkner's *Absalom, Absalom!* dramatizes the cost of knowledge: in this case, the two college boys, Quentin and Shreve, must somehow go beyond the data of history if they are to understand the past; in extremely elaborate ways, they achieve what Faulkner calls an "overpass to love," as they "become" the protagonists of the Civil War and experience, again from the inside, the human feelings that make up history, in this case, a bloody history of fratricide, both personal and national. Yet, here too, Faulkner does not minimize the cost of such an "overpass," and the book closes on a note of futility and exhaustion, a keen sense that we can become the Other only momentarily, and even then at the cost of our own integrity. The Melville and Faulkner examples are not properly metamorphic, but they have the same cardinal truth at their heart: knowledge of the other entails eclipse of the self, and can lead to death as well as to love.

Beyond even the metamorphosis, however, there is the machine. Kafka's writing machine is a mad figure for the role of art and understanding in a world filled exclusively with signs and flesh. How can signs and flesh be connected, the thickness of matter be penetrated by the logos of spirit? The Word of the past, the Word that spoke Truth and commanded Assent, is gone. But the writer remains. Kafka's machine depicts the need that every writer has felt for a language so potent, that it would become the reality whereof it speaks. The writing machine bespeaks and, *à sa façon,* remedies the absence of understanding in a degraded world: the animal body has no access to its soul; the individuals attain no contact with each other. The machine is indeed intolerable in its flagrant violation of the body, but it functions as a sublime symbol of Kafka's—and all artists'—aspirations: to read his work is to be penetrated by it; his words are inscribed in our flesh; our understanding of the story, of the Other, is to be both visceral and transcendent. The text is the machine: the metamorphosis is in us. (pp. 21-31)

Arnold Weinstein, "Kafka's Writing Machine: Metamorphosis in the Penal Colony," in Studies in Twentieth Century Literature, *Vol. 7, No. 1, Fall, 1982, pp. 21-33.*

With regard to the "Penal Colony," there may have been a misunderstanding here. I have never been really wholehearted in my desire to have this story published. There are two or three pages shortly before the end that are contrived, and their presence points to a deeper defect; somewhere a worm is at work, devouring the very substance of the story.

—*Franz Kafka, in* I Am a Memory Come Alive: Autobiographical Writings by Franz Kafka, *1974.*

Clayton Koelb (essay date 1982)

[*An American critic and educator, Koelb's publications include* Inventions of Reading: Rhetoric and the Literary Imagination *(1988) and* Kafka's Rhetoric: The

Passion of Reading *(1989). In the following essay, he offers a deconstructive analysis of "In the Penal Colony," interpreting the execution machine as an allegory of reading, writing, and the transmission of authority.*]

The fabulous execution machine that is the center of attention in Kafka's **"In der Strafkolonie"** stands "in [einem] tiefen, sandigen, von kahlen Abhängen ringsum abgeschlossenen Tal." At the time represented by the narration, this natural theater is almost empty: no one is there except the principal performers themselves, the officer, the traveller, the condemned prisoner, and the soldier in charge of the prisoner. But such performances as the one about to take place did not always attract so small an audience, the officer explains to the traveller: "Wie war die Exekution anders in früherer Zeit! Schon einen Tag vor der Hinrichtung war das Tal von Menschen überfüllt; alle kamen nur zu sehen . . . Vor hunderten Augen—alle Zuschauer standen auf den Fußspitzen bis dort zu den Anhöhen—wurde der Verurteilte vom Kommandanten selbst unter die Egge gelegt." The theatrical character of the proceeding is clearly stressed, and the "Zuschauer" are clearly represented as the audience of a kind of performance in which the death of the chief performer is the climactic—though not central—action. The central action of a proper execution as described by the officer in **"In der Strafkolonie"** is an act of reading.

My reader may protest here that I am surely mistaken; that what is involved in Kafka's story is clearly an act of *writing,* and that the attention of the story's reader is focused on the mechanism whereby the machine *writes* upon the body of the condemned prisoner. There is some justice to this objection, for the process of inscription gets more verbal space than the process of decipherment. But I will try to show that this inscription is simply the reproduction of an act of writing that had taken place long before the time of the narration and that as such it is the embodiment of the intellectual re-production which we ordinarily call 'reading.'

My reader may also protest at my reformulation of Jacques Derrida's famous title. The comparison implied by my borrowing is not, I want to stress, between my essay and Derrida's but between Kafka's myth and Derrida's. The object of attention in both Kafka's story and Derrida's essay is a machine involved in the process of writing and reading. In "Freud and the Scene of Writing" Derrida is particularly interested in an analogy Freud had drawn between the operation of the perceptual apparatus and a device called the Mystic Writing-Pad, familiar to American children as a toy marketed under the name of "Magic Slate." Near the end of the "Note on the Mystic Writing-Pad," Freud noted: "If we imagine one hand writing upon the surface of the Mystic Writing-Pad while another periodically raises its covering sheet from the wax slab, we shall have a concrete representation of the perceptual apparatus of our mind." Freud seems to have assumed that the 'writing machine' needs external assistance to run. "That the machine does not run by itself means . . . a mechanism without its own energy," comments Derrida. "The machine is dead. It is death. . . . A pure representation, a machine, never runs by itself." A machine that *did* run by itself—what would that be? No longer a pure representation, it would deconstruct the very notion of a "machine." A machine running by itself, especially a writing / reading machine, would deconstruct itself. Perhaps it would also self-destruct.

Derrida is also interested in the sexual terms of Freud's mechanical metaphors, especially since they are also terms of aggression and even rape. He speaks of "metaphors of path, trace, breach, of the march treading down a track which was opened by effraction through neurone, light or wax, wood or resin, in order violently to inscribe itself in nature, matter, or matrix," and he quotes Freud's own descriptions of *Bahnung,* "pathbreaking," mentioning particularly Freud's equation of "all complicated machinery" with the male genitals and of writing with a forbidden sexual act.

The sexual aspect of Kafka's execution machine is far more overt than that of Freud's metaphor of psychic writing (as Derrida reads it). The device is designed in such a way as to make the process of execution an unmistakable travesty of copulation. The condemned prisoner is laid out, naked, on a platform covered with a layer of cotton and named "the Bed," while the Harrow, a mechanism shaped exactly like a human body, is placed in contact with him. In this copulation of man and machine, however, the male sexual role is reserved entirely to the machine. Not only is it covered with hundreds of penetrating and spraying organs, but it also performs a grotesque parody of sexual excitement ("strafft sich sofort dieses Stahlseil zu einer Stange"). This "Straffheit" of the machine, which is really just a reflection of the "Straffheit" of the old Commandant and his ethic, an ideal of "straffe Zucht," rigid discipline, is thus both sexual and authoritarian.

Kafka's machine and Derrida's conception of Freud's machine are comparable, then, in a number of ways. To point this out seems to me to be a proper starting-point for this inquiry, not because I imagine Kafka to have been influenced by Freud's "Note on the Mystic Writing-Pad" or Derrida to have been influenced by Kafka's story, but because all three represent treatments of the theme of inscription. Just as Derrida sees in Freud's metaphors of writing an approach to the problematic of writing that lies at the heart of our philosophical tradition, so do I wish to examine Kafka's story, particularly its central metaphor, as a direct confrontation with the issue of the relation between a text and the soul upon which it seeks to inscribe itself.

There is good evidence that Kafka was concerned with this issue, in these or analogous terms, from sources other than **"In der Strafkolonie."** What we find over and over again in his writings—the diaries provide many examples—is an attitude toward the act of reading in which eagerness is mixed with a high level of anxiety, in which the reader is viewed as one who suffers something to be done to him. Such a mixture of fear and anticipation is evident in his description of his reading of Dickens in a diary entry of August, 1911:

> Ist es so schwer und kann es ein Außenstehender begreifen, daß man eine Geschichte von ihrem Anfang an in sich erlebt, vom fernen Punkt bis zu der heranfahrenden Lokomotive aus Stahl,

Kohle und Dampf, sie aber auch jetzt noch nicht verläßt, sondern von ihr gejagt sein will und Zeit dazu hat, also von ihr gejagt wird und aus eigenem Schwung vor ihr läuft, wohin sie nur stößt und wohin man sie lockt.

Even here we see the beginnings of an imagery of reading in which the reader is pursued by a powerful machine which is the text he reads. The text is bigger and stronger than the reader, and it is frightening, even though one may *want* to "run before it."

The powerful text *penetrates* the reader. Kafka describes his reading of Schäfer's *Karl Stauffers Lebensgang* this way: "[Ich] bin von diesem großen, in mein nur in Augenblicken erhorchtes Innere dringenden Einbruch so befangen und festgehalten. . . . " Later he says of the same work, "Wenn man über einem Buch . . . gleichgültig von was für einem Menschen . . . still hält, nicht aus eigener Kraft ihn in sich zieht . . . sondern hingegeben—wer nur nicht Widerstand leistet, dem geschieht es bald—von dem gesammelten fremden Menschen sich wegziehen und zu seinem Verwandten sich machen läßt, dann ist es nichts Besonderes mehr, wenn man . . . sich in seinem neu erkannten . . . eigenen Wesen wieder wohler fühlt." There is a theory of reading implied here wherein the reader does not act upon the text, but rather the text takes the initiative and acts upon the reader. The reader *submits,* and this submission is the only thing he need do. The book then takes charge and both picks up the reader and forces its way inside him. The text writes upon the reader and even makes him into a kind of copy of itself.

Kafka's scene of writing, then, is really just as much a scene of reading. There is, in fact, not much distinction to be made between writing and reading in this mythology, wherein reading is understood to be a passive reception of an aggressive and powerful text. Writing is the creation of a template that directs an act of inscription, and reading is the suffering of that inscription upon the reader's psyche. Obviously, what is needed is a mechanism to mediate, to bring the writer's template-text into contact with the reader's psychic matrix. The function of Kafka's machine is just this. It does not *record* the words of the old Commandant; rather it makes those words, previously recorded on paper, sensible to the condemned prisoner. The officer possesses the autograph manuscript of what represents to him the most sacred scripture: " 'Ich verwende noch die Zeichnungen des früheren Kommandanten. Hier sind sie,'—er zog einige Blätter aus der Ledermappe—'ich kann sie Ihnen leider nicht in die Hand geben, sie sind das Teuerste, was ich habe.' " The task of the machine is not simply to write the commandments of paternal authority—the old Commandant has in fact already written them, all of them, and given them over to the officer—but to make that writing legible to the victim. Kafka is careful to make clear that, as marks on paper, the writing of the old Commandant is not legible at all:

> Der Reisende hätte gerne etwas Anerkennendes gesagt, aber er sah nur labyrinthartige, einander vielfach kreuzende Linien, die so dicht das Papier bedeckten, daß man nur mit Mühe die weißen Zwischenräume erkannte. "Lesen Sie," sagte der Offizier. "Ich kann nicht," sagte der

Reisende. "Es ist doch deutlich," sagte der Offizier.

This scripture, then, already exists in the documents preserved by the officer. It has already been written. The function of the machine is to make the scripture comprehensible to the prisoner. In other words, its chief job is to serve as the means by which one may *read* what is written. And this reading takes time. *Man muß lange darin lesen.* The machine insures that the condemned man will spend an average of twelve hours in continuous study, at the end of which time he will be dead.

This is not to say that understanding itself is necessarily deadly in Kafka's view. It seems rather that the process of the painful opening up of the self—a process, that is, of reading—is inevitably destructive. If understanding could be achieved directly by some less complicated means, it would not be painful or destructive at all, but glorious and thrilling. Kafka creates a myth of the loss of the possibility of such direct and happy access to understanding and its replacement by reading in the well-known little story **"Der neue Advokat."** The impossibly great distance between Macedonia and India is the distance between the psyche and the truth, between man and God, between the present and the absent. In Kafka's mythology there exists a former time, a golden age now past, in which that distance was smaller and could be bridged by heroic but nonetheless conceivable efforts. Now, today, not even those like Bucephalus who once achieved the impossible, crossed the infinite gap, can do so again.

It is of particular significance that what is presented as the best (*faute de mieux*) alternative to the conquest of India is reading. Bucephalus' study of the old law books is not, as one might easily suppose, a sign of having given up utterly on the quest which Alexander represented. There would have been many, far easier ways to abandon the search for the gates of India than by transforming oneself from war-horse to human student of law. No, the metamorphosed battle-charger is still engaged in the same activity as before, but he must now work through a less direct and, certainly, less satisfactory means. What was easy as Alexander's horse is difficult, perhaps even impossible as a human reader, but there is no better alternative. It means a loss of selfhood for Bucephalus, who must deny his nature as horse, animal, *alogon,* in order to pursue this special activity which is the particular province of humankind. All that is left to him of his old self is his high-stepping gait, a characteristic that is admirable in a horse but not a little grotesque in a man. Reading, then, is a costly and perhaps hopeless compromise whose goal is to attain what would otherwise be unattainable.

Alexander's method for attaining the gates of India and thereby abolishing the otherwise infinite distance between the mind and the truth is an act of violence and rebellion against paternal authority. The story stresses the fact that Alexander had cursed his father, Philip. That in itself is not enough to make India attainable, as the story makes clear, but it was an important element in Alexander's success. Alexander had usurped paternal authority so that he might possess authority himself, a usurpation Kafka knew to be essential to establishing personal independence. Alexander had succeeded in making himself a paternal power, a rider of horses and wielder of riding whips. Bucephalus had achieved the same thing Alexander had achieved—he had reached the gates of India—but by an opposite strategy. He had acquiesced fully and gladly to the role of adjunct and subject subservient to the riding whip which Alexander had, in a very real sense, taken over from Philip.

The turn to reading in **"Der neue Advokat"** thus represents not so great a change as might seem. The prisoner about to be executed in **"In der Strafkolonie"** has been condemned for having failed to perform his duty "bei jedem Stundenschlag aufzustehen und vor der Tür des Hauptmanns zu salutieren. Gewiß keine schwere Pflicht und eine notwendige . . ." As one might expect, the prisoner had been unable to stay awake and was discovered sleeping by the captain, who lashes the man across the face with his riding whip. "Statt nun aufzustehen und um Verzeihung zu bitten, faßte der Mann seinen Herrn bei den Beinen, schüttelte ihn und rief: 'Wirf die Peitsche weg, oder ich fresse dich." By using the whip, the captain tries to place the prisoner in the role of the ridden animal. The prisoner rebels, but the role is now to be forced upon him by the execution machine, which not only rides him but even penetrates his flesh, makes him even less than animal, makes him an object upon which to inscribe commandments, a matrix upon which is to be impressed the stamp of rigid authority. The imagery of reading in **"In der Strafkolonie"** thus connects the rule of reader with the role of servant and animal and even suggests the comparison between reader and horse through the riding whip of the captain and the way in which the victim is *ridden* by the Harrow. Bucephalus' transformation from horse to reader is, in terms of such imagery, a transformation only from the literal to the figurative position of beast of burden, of "ridden" thing.

The goal of reading, the abolition of the distance between the human mind and what Wilhelm Emrich has termed "absolute completeness," is at once a thing impossible of attainment *and* the only thing worth pursuing. Since it is "no longer" possible (since the end of the golden age of Alexander) actually to cross this distance, we are compelled to the alternative of crossing it figuratively, by means of traces. Kafka has provided a striking parable on this theme in **"Zur Frage unserer Gesetze,"** wherein it is disclosed that there is a substantial doubt about the existence of the text whose reading is the central activity of the culture depicted:

> Übrigens können auch diese Scheingesetze eigentlich nur vermutet werden. Es ist eine Tradition, daß sie bestehen und dem Adel als Geheimnis anvertraut sind, aber mehr als alte und durch Alter glaubwürdige Tradition ist es nicht und kann es nicht sein, denn der Charakter dieser Gesetze verlangt auch das Geheimhalten ihres Bestandes. Wenn wir als Volk aber seit ältesten Zeiten die Handlungen des Adels aufmerksam verfolgen, Aufschreibungen unserer Voreltern darüber besitzen, sie gewissenhaft fortgesetzt haben und in den zahllosen Tatsachen gewisse Richtlinien zu erkennen glauben, die auf diese oder jene geschichtliche Bestimmung schließen

lassen, und wenn wir nach diesen sorgfältigst gesiebten und geordneten Schlußfolgerungen uns für die Gegenwart und Zukunft ein wenig einzurichten suchen—so ist das alles unsicher und vielleicht nur ein Spiel des Verstandes, denn vielleicht bestehen diese Gesetze, die wir hier zu erraten suchen, überhaupt nicht.

The people of the story have only interpretations of the laws, and interpretations of those interpretations, regressing forever in a perfect *mise en abîme* toward a text which may not exist. But in a manner that is typical of Kafka's fiction, the narrator and his people do not find this a cause for despair or for abandonment of belief in the laws. To be sure, there is a party "die nachzuweisen sucht, daß wenn ein Gesetz besteht, es nur lauten kann: Was der Adel tut, ist Gesetz," but this group is a small minority. The people look forward to a time when the law will belong to them and even indulge in self-hatred because they do not feel themselves "des Gesetzes gewürdigt." The narrator sums up the issue with this closing comment:

> Man kann es eigentlich nur in einer Art Widerspruch ausdrücken: Eine Partei, die neben dem Glauben und die Gesetze auch den Adel verwerfen würde, hätte sofort das ganze Volk hinter sich, aber eine solche Partei kann nicht entstehen, weil den Adel niemand zu verwerfen wagt. Auf dieses Messers Schneide leben wir. Ein Schriftsteller hat das einmal so zusammengefaßt: Das einzige, sichtbare, zweifellose Gesetz, das uns auferlegt ist, ist der Adel und um dieses einzige Gesetz sollten wir uns selbst bringen wollen?

Alexander may have been able to both curse the father, Philip, and still attain direct access to "absolute completeness"; but the people of the problematic laws cannot do so, since the authority of the paternal(istic) nobility is the only tangible link they possess to the absent text of the absolute Law. They continue to believe in the nobility because they want to believe in the law.

The traveller in **"In der Strafkolonie"** finds himself in the position of being able (or, from another point of view, being required) to repudiate all belief in the laws as they are explained to him by the officer. The central issue in the story is that belief, and the climax occurs when the traveller's disbelief causes the officer to review his course of action:

> "Das Verfahren hat Sie also nicht überzeugt," sagte er für sich und lächelte, wie ein Alter über den Unsinn eines Kindes lächelt und hinter dem Lächeln sein eigenes wirkliches Nachdenken behält.
>
> "Dann ist es also Zeit," sagte er schließlich. . . .
>
> "Du bist frei," sagte der Offizier zum Verurteilten in dessen Sprache. Dieser glaubte es zuerst nicht.

The explorer's disbelief in the system of reading advocated by the old Commandant and the officer has the immediate effect of freeing the prisoner from the deadly obligation of reading. The prisoner escapes the fate of being the medium of inscription through which, by a deadly act of violence, the world would be forced into conformity with the word. The prisoner's momentary disbelief in his own good fortune reflects the fact that he has not had the slightest idea what has been happening to him, except of course that it has been bad. The entire conversation between the traveller and the officer has been conducted in French, "und französisch verstand gewiß weder der Soldat noch der Verurteilte." Understanding was meant to come to him only as a result of the inscription on his body.

The prisoner is to be initiated into the mysteries of the officer's system of belief by the process of his execution. As Heinz Politzer has noted, the officer's ability to read the labyrinthine script of the old Commandant is a sign of his participation in a system of belief: "For the outsider it remains unintelligible, unreadable, and thoroughly confusing. The officer experiences as reality what for the Explorer is at best a successful artifice. In other words, the officer still belongs to a system of belief—whatever the merits of this system and the creed of this belief may be."

One of the cornerstones of that creed is certainly the injunction intended for the body of the prisoner: "Ehre deinen Vorgesetzten!" The act of reading demanded by the old Commandant's system is an act of obedience, of honor to one's superior, for it is an act that acknowledges the absolute authority of the "superior" text and its author. Honoring superiors is equivalent to honoring the laws which those superiors promulgate. Indeed, just as in **"Zur Frage unserer Gesetze"** it is impossible to distinguish between the Laws themselves and the nobility who interpret and administer them, so too here it is impossible to distinguish personal, human, paternal authority from the injunctions of that authority. The old Commandant exists now only as the inscription of his laws.

The prime function of the Vorgesetzter, one of the "superiors," is the administration of the law. When he carries out this function properly he may be called just. If the principal injunction for subjects is "Ehre deinen Vorgesetzten," then surely the first commandment for "Vorgesetzte" is "Sei gerecht." Indeed, there is no reason to believe that any other commandments than these are necessary to regulate a society based upon the reading of the Law, and it may well be that the officer has no other inscriptions than these in his leather wallet. In this system, both subject and superior have a certain absolute authority over the other: the superior has absolute power to interpret the law and to pass judgment, even according to such a principle as the officer's "Die Schuld ist immer zweifellos," and the subject has absolute authority over the legitimacy of the superior's power, over his claim to being just. As is clear from **"Zur Frage unserer Gesetze,"** the "small group of nobles" who rule retain power only because the subject people continue to believe in them.

The situation in **"In der Strafkolonie"** reflects a social order in which the belief in the justice of the "superiors" has all but died out. The scene of reading which once attracted huge audiences now takes place in a nearly empty theater: "Als der alte Kommandant lebte, war die Kolonie von seinen Anhängern voll; die Überzeugungskraft des alten Kommandanten habe ich zum Teil, aber seine

Macht fehlt mir ganz; infolgedessen haben sich die Anhänger verkrochen, es gibt noch viele, aber keiner gesteht es ein." A key concept here is that of "Überzeugung" (conviction, belief), something which the officer has in abundance and which he wishes to convey to others, particularly the explorer, who represents the officer's last hope of perpetuating his claim to legitimacy as judge in the colony. "Überzeugunskraft" is "persuasive power," the virtue most prized by the orator, the practitioner of rhetoric. It is something which the old Commandant was especially known for and which he has preserved as much by his machine as by the officer. Torture apparatus has ever been found an effective way of exercising persuasive power, but here that power is apotheosized into a means of effecting both transfiguration (Verklärung) and salvation (Erlösung). The persuasive power of the old Commandant is not matched by the officer, however. He is able to generate no conviction in the new ruling elite or in the traveller himself. "Das Verfahren hat Sie also nicht überzeugt" are the officer's climactic words. It is the procedure's central function to be convincing, to enforce belief. If it cannot do it, "then the time has come."

The officer tells the traveller of former successful scenes of reading, but the story offers no evidence that the "transfiguration" he speaks of testifies to anything more than his own faith in the system. *He* detected signs of the prisoner's dawning understanding at the sixth hour of torture, but did the prisoner really experience such understanding? By the very nature of the deadly process of reading, it is impossible to interrogate the prisoner to find out.

Even though the officer accepts the traveller's disbelief in his system of justice as a condemnation of the entire procedure and as a death sentence for himself and that system, his conviction is unaffected. The officer cannot escape, as the condemned prisoner has, through the traveller's disbelief, for *his* belief is unshaken. Indeed, it is precisely in terms of the principles of his system that he sentences himself, for only such a notion as "Guilt is never to be doubted" could justify taking one man's doubt as the occasion for self-execution. The fact that the explorer is unconvinced represents an accusation, but by the rules under which the officer and old Commandant judged others, such an accusation is always enough to produce a verdict of "guilty." Since the traveller has in effect accused the officer of failing to obey the central injunction given to the "Vorgesetzten," he cannot fail to sentence himself to suffer "Sei gerecht" to be written on him by his own machine.

The officer's act of self-execution is, therefore, as much an act of defiance of the explorer's opinion as it is an acceptance of his judgment. The officer asserts thereby the authority of the Law and of the Law's injunctions as the trace of the absent father. If he has failed to convince others, if he has been lacking in the power of persuasion, he must get in touch with the source of all power, which is embodied in the text. He must read the Law. And to do so, he must first do to himself what other condemned prisoners have had done to them: he must renounce his male role of authority and power to become a female matrix upon which the father may write. It is for this reason that he engages in an elaborate act of divestiture and symbolic self-emasculation: After taking off all his clothes, his uniform with its braid and tassles, he breaks his sword and throws the pieces, along with the rest of his things, into the pit. Now the officer is ready to receive the inscription, and it soon becomes clear that the machine is itself somehow ready to take him as its last victim.

I would like to pause here and look back a moment to the relation that has been tentatively established between the narration of **"In the Penal Colony"** and its readers. Up to this point, the events represented have been bizarre, to be sure, but nothing has happened to disturb the notion that what is related here is *convincing* in the Aristotelian sense of *eikos*. We do not suppose that these events have happened or that we would be very likely to hear of them happening, but they are not so outrageous that we are prevented from thinking that they could happen. The technology of the machine is uncertain and comes close to the bounds of credibility, but it does not cross those bounds. The narration itself, in other words, has not solicited the reader's disbelief. Once the officer begins the process of his own execution, however, the nature of the narration changes: the events reported pass over from the realm of the merely bizarre into *atopia*, the land of the outlandish. The machine suddenly begins to act like a living creature:

> Der Offizier aber hatte sich der Maschine zugewendet. Wenn es schon früher deutlich gewesen war, daß er die Maschine gut verstand, so konnte es jetzt einen fast bestürzt machen, wie er mit ihr umging und wie sie gehorchte. Er hatte die Hand der Egge nur genähert, und sie hob und senkte sich mehrmals, bis sie die richtige Lage erreicht hatte um ihn zu empfangen; er faßte das Bett nur am Rande, und es fing schon zu zittern an; der Filzstumpf kam seinem Mund entgegen, man sah, wie der Offizier ihn eigentlich nicht haben wollte, aber das Zögern dauerte nur einen Augenblick, gleich fügte er sich und nahm ihn auf. Alles war bereit . . . kaum waren die Riemen angebracht, fing auch schon die Maschine zu arbeiten an; das Bett zitterte, die Nadeln tanzten auf der Haut, die Egge schwebte auf und ab. Der Reisende hatte schon eine Weile hingestarrt, ehe er sich erinnerte, daß ein Rad im Zeichner hätte kreischen sollen; aber alles war still, nicht das geringste Surren war zu hören.

The explorer's disbelief, having set the prisoner free from the obligation of reading the deadly script—writing *en tei psuchei*—seems simultaneously to liberate the narration from the obligation of verisimilitude and the machine from the dead world of the mechanical. Up to this point the machine, like Freud's Mystic Pad, could not run by itself; now it begins to develop or manifest its own volition, its own *animus*. It does so only now because the system of writing and reading in which it was a crucial figure could not allow a machine that runs by itself or a narration in which the word and the world diverge. Now that that system is no longer credited, the machine may act on its own—though that act must needs be one of self-destruction.

The machine, liberated by the explorer's disbelief, destroys itself by rebelling against the condition of its existence, which insists that such a machine may not run by itself. The apparatus transcends its own nature by its act of self-destruction, for in doing so it ceases to be simply the representative of the system of reading and writing the Law. The officer, on the other hand, remains up to his death—and even beyond—the representative (Vertreter) he claimed he was of the "heritage of the old Commandant." His face in death "war, wie es im Leben gewesen war; (kein Zeichen der versprochenen Erlösung war zu entdecken;) was alle anderen in der Maschine gefunden hatten, der Offizier fand es nicht; die Lippen waren fest zusammengedrückt, die Augen waren offen, hatten den Ausdruck des Lebens, der Blick war ruhig und überzeugt, durch die Stirn ging die Spitze des großen eisernen Stachels." The dead officer's face thus testifies both to the inefficacy of the system he championed and his absolute faith in its efficacy. Even as a corpse he retains his "Überzeugung."

In the play that is acted out upon this scene of reading, the principal figures are indeed "representations" of others: the machine stands for the procedure of administering justice in which it plays such a prominent role; the officer represents, as best he can, the old Commandant and his tradition; and the explorer, the traveller from the West, finds himself in the role of sole and final judge of the procedure he witnesses. The officer feels honored by his role, though he admits to his shortcomings when compared to the old Commandant himself. The traveller evidently feels uncomfortable with the role thrust upon him, realizing as he must that by making his opinion known the officer will understand him to be taking over the officer's role. The machine, when it comes time for it to perform, throws away the script and behaves in a manner completely different from that assigned to it by the old Commandant's system. It neither delivers the promised transfiguration to the officer nor behaves like a proper machine.

The bulk of the narrative of **"In der Strafkolonie"** is taken up with the officer's scenarios. The principal scenario, of course, is the process of execution of inscription, the telling of which takes up much of the text, but another, the description of the triumph of the old Commandant's system by way of its defense by the explorer before the new Commandant, is also elaborated at some length and in several variants. The officer is forever writing scripts—though even in this he is only a representation of that *arche*-script-writer, the old Commandant. But the actors available to him regularly fail to follow the text given them: the explorer is unwilling to participate in the defense of the old Commandant's system and offers an alternative scenario which the officer rejects by ignoring it; and of course the machine itself fails to perform the rule assigned to it in the great play conceived by the old Commandant. The system of reading, which is both reading-the-Law and reading-the-script, has broken down utterly.

The theatrical metaphor proposed at the opening of the story by the theater-like setting of the scene of action is centrally relevant to the issue of reading which is at stake in Kafka's tale. The drama as we have understood it since classical times is a form of action which is impossible without an authoritative text to which all the actors adhere scrupulously. *Ad libbing* (that is, free speaking and free acting) must be held to a very small minimum. The performance of a play is a kind of communal act of reading, and if the play is well known the audience will inevitably make judgments about the adequacy and appropriateness of the reading which the performance has given. We talk quite intelligibly and correctly of an actor's "reading" of a part, even though he has memorized his lines and does no actual reading on the stage. The acting out of a drama is thus a way of making the world—a small part of the world, that is, and an artificially controlled part at that—conform to the word of the script. The actor, like the subject, must obey his superior. Acting in a play and being a citizen in a society ruled by the Law are two forms of essentially the same activity.

It is not only the condemned prisoner who escapes from the torture of reading: both the traveller and the machine escape by refusing to play the roles assigned to them by the officer's scripts. It must be acknowledged, though, that in spite of the *ad libitum* behavior of both the traveller and the machine, in spite of their spoiling the scenario, both end up to some extent playing the very roles they have refused. The explorer finds himself being the very judge he has condemned, for his refusal to defend the system is perceived as a verdict against it and the sentence of its death. The machine *does* execute that sentence, destroying both itself and the officer, and thereby apparently the system of reading devised by the old Commandant.

The play, however, is not quite over. After the principal scene of reading there is, as a sort of epilogue, a second. There is yet another inscription, another scenario, left behind in the name of the old Commandant. After the death of the officer and the destruction of the machine, the traveller returns with the soldier and the prisoner to the town and to the teahouse where the old Commandant's grave had been placed. Near the back of the building, underneath one of the tables, is a gravestone upon which is an inscription foretelling the return of the Old Commandant. The demise of the system of reading which the explorer has precipitated and which the reader has witnessed is alleged by this inscription to be only temporary. This scenario calls for the resurrection of the old Commandant and the reimposition of his system. All that is necessary, in the meantime, is patience and faith: "Glaubet und wartet!" Belief, as we have seen, is the core of the system, so that all that is needed for the revival of the old Commandant is a sufficiency of belief.

The reading of the gravestone has been a performance before an audience, and this audience expects the explorer to make a judgment about what he has read, just as the officer had expected him to judge the local system of justice. But where the officer has expected a favorable decision, the patrons of the teahouse expect an unfavorable one. They expect him to share their disbelief, or so it seems to him. But apparently the explorer's disbelief is not so strong as to allow him to dismiss the inscription as ridiculous. Although nothing is said about the explorer's feelings, he is apparently frightened: he wants to leave the island as soon as possible. He goes directly to the harbor to engage a boat to take him out to his steamer and manages to escape just quickly enough to prevent the soldier and prisoner, he thinks, from trying to escape with him.

The traveller cannot dismiss the inscription on the gravestone even though he was firm in his disapproval of the machine and its method of dispensing justice, for he is not prepared to (in the words of **"Zur Frage unserer Gesetze"**) "repudiate the nobility." In spite of his aversion for the brutality of the old Commandant's methods, the explorer is a believer in respect for authority. He is prepared to let the unfortunate prisoner be executed for failure to salute the door of his superior and only prevents it from happening, as it were, in spite of himself: "Er war weder Bürger der Strafkolonie, noch Bürger des Staates, dem sie angehörte. Wenn er diese Exekution verurteilen oder gar hintertreiben wollte, konnte man ihm sagen: Du bist ein Fremder, sei still." He even feels himself "schon ein wenig für den Apparat gewonnen," and he admires the officer: "Ihre ehrliche Überzeugung geht mir nahe," he tells him, almost apologizing for his own lack of conviction.

The explorer is threatened by the gravestone, the scenario it proposes, and the injunction it proclaims, because there is something in him which is unable to find the promised resurrection ridiculous. He belongs to and believes in an order which values respect for superiors and adherence to the scenarios authorized by society. He has more human understanding for the officer, who does his duty and has the courage of his convictions, than for the condemned prisoner, who is not serious and plays like a child with the soldier after his release and shows childlike curiosity about the machine. This annoys the traveller: "Er war entschlossen, hier bis zum Ende zu bleiben, aber den Anblick der Zwei hätte er nicht lange ertragen. 'Geht nach Hause,' sagte er." Actually, the prisoner is behaving precisely as the officer has said viewers of executions used to do in the old days, showing great and animated interest in the operation of the machine. But it annoys the traveller because the prisoner cannot possibly fully understand what is happening, cannot know what the machine is really supposed to do. He is just playing in the same sort of half joking way he has wrestled with the soldier and reclothed himself in his filthy and cut-up garments. He doesn't take it seriously enough. The officer, though the defender of a barbarous system, was serious, and that the explorer could understand and sympathize with: "Er hatte das Gefühl, als müsse er sich jetzt des Offiziers annehmen, da dieser nicht mehr für sich selbst sorgen konnte."

Though he rejects the "straffe Zucht" of the old Commandant, the explorer is not prepared to accept the uninhibited playfulness of the condemned man, who indeed shows only the most perfunctory respect for his superiors. His disbelief in the old Commandant's system is really directed only at the machine itself and the executions it carries out, not at the assumptions that underlie the system. The old Commandant and the officer have ruthlessly pursued the notion of reading as writing "in the soul" to its ultimate consequence, something neither the traveller of Kafka's story nor the Freud of Derrida's essay wishes to do. Derrida's Freud wants to conceive of the human psyche as a scene of writing, but he does not want to acknowl-

edge the element of the mechanical—that is, of death—which his analogy would ascribe to the living soul. Kafka's traveller wants to banish death from the scene of reading, but not thereby banish also respect for authority, duty, seriousness. He wants the old Commandant's principles, but he does not want them applied with the old Commandant's rigor. And given that ambivalence, he might feel that the resurrection of the old Commandant was not something to be dismissed as ridiculous after all. The only course of action he can follow is to flee the scene altogether, to thus escape the choice between the deadly seriousness of "straffe Zucht" and the childish playfulness of those who do not read.

"In der Strafkolonie" is thus a story of escape, particularly of escape from the deadly rigors of one sort of reading by means of the timely application of disbelief. While it is true that the explorer's disbelief is not as rigorous as the system against which it is applied, it is at least temporarily effective. The explorer is able to escape from the problematic choice put to him by the scenario of the gravestone only by the usually unavailable strategy of departing for another world. Kafka's heroes do not ordinarily have this option, or at least do not recognize themselves as having it. It does not occur to Joseph K. that he might simply ignore the court that has put him on trial, nor does Landsurveyor K. seriously consider leaving the castle village. The reader recognizes these possibilities, to be sure, but the characters do not, or at least do not act upon such recognition. The Reisender, however, precisely because he is a traveller, can move, if this place does not suit him, to another place where the out-of-place (*to atopon*) will not be such a commonplace.

If the story has ended in the realm of *atopia* with the incredible self-destruction of the machine, it has begun unquestionably with the *topos,* the verbal commonplace. As Günter Anders was probably the first to point out, it is Kafka's common procedure to take a linguistic commonplace, a piece of what has been called *endoxal* knowledge, and develop a story out of a literal reading of the *topos.* Anders points to the metaphor of "reading with one's wounds" as an example: " 'Am eignen Leibe etwas erfahren,' sagt die Sprache, wenn sie der Wirklichkeit der Erfahrung Ausdruck geben will: Dies die Basis für Kafkas **'Strafkolonie,'** in der dem Verbrecher die Strafe nicht mündlich mitgeteilt, sondern mit einer Nadel in den Leib geritzt wird." Heinz Politzer points to another *topos* as a possible starting point for the tale: "A popular German adage says: 'He who refuses to hear must feel,' feel the pain of punishment. Moreover, there exists an etymological connection between 'hearing,' 'listening,' and 'obeying' (*hören, horchen,* and *gehorchen*) so that Kafka could rely on his German readers to understand intuitively the meaning of his machine: he who disobeyed was bound to feel the consequence on his own body. Translating a proverb into an image, Kafka followed an old convention related to the technique of the fable." More recently, Ruth V. Gross has demonstrated the extensive role of *topoi,* particularly proverbs, in "Eine alltägliche Verwirrung," arguing for the primacy of language over all other elements in the story: "The proverb seems to contain the weight of human experience in the form of a commonplace; it resides in the language at that level. Kafka . . . has created a one-page wordplay with 'Eine alltägliche Verwirrung,' and it is precisely a play on Kafkan language—*gemeine Sprache.*"

The entire narrative structure of **"In der Strafkolonie"** can also be seen as an elaboration and gloss on a certain *topos* or set of *topoi.* The proverbial "Am eignen Leibe etwas erfahren" becomes a text to be read, a scenario to be acted out in the fictional narrative. Considered from this point of view, the story **"In der Strafkolonie"** itself represents an act of reading, but reading precisely in the terms set forth by the old Commandant's system. It is reading which brings action into conformity with injunction, the world into conformity with the word, the story into conformity with the proverb, and (ultimately) the *endoxa* into deadly contact with its opposite, paradox. Kafka's procedure and the old Commandant's both are based on respect for the authority of the text to be read and on the necessity of making the reader behave in the manner prescribed by the text. Kafka's reading of the *topoi* of "feeling on your body" and "writing in the soul" are as rigorously consequential as the old Commandant could wish. He takes these metaphors seriously.

It is a curious fact, however, that the rigorous reading of *topoi* leads to *atopia,* that taking endoxal statements seriously leads to paradox. Paradox, as Ruth V. Gross has pointed out, is the opposite of proverbial opinion, indeed its "antidote": "a certain conflict is set up between what is 'contrary to opinion,' the figure of paradox, and the verbal vehicle of opinion, the commonplace or proverb—endoxal knowledge . . . the commonplace is the 'already-there' of language. Its antidote is paradox." The imagery of the antidote is noteworthy and entirely proper. Kafka participates completely in the tradition which understands language as both poison and antidote, both sense and nonsense, both A and not-A.

Commonplaces taken seriously, their metaphors pursued conscientiously in all their implications, turn into the very agents most effective in neutralizing commonplaces. *Topoi* are the antidote to *topoi.* Just as the officer must follow even to his own death the paradoxical requirements of his system, a system that commands officers to be just and at the same time assumes that guilt is never to be doubted, so does Kafka follow the requirements of an analogous system in which language must be taken seriously, even though to do so turns inevitably into a kind of play—wordplay. Kafka's narration, like that narration's central figure, the machine, participates in a silent but thorough act of self-de(con)struction. (pp. 511-25)

> *Clayton Koelb, " 'In der Strafkolonie': Kafka and the Scene of Reading," in* The German Quarterly, *Vol. LV, No. 4, November, 1982, pp. 511-25.*

E. R. Davey (essay date 1984)

[*In the following essay, Davey emphasizes the function of the execution machine in "In the Penal Colony" and its implications for an allegorical interpretation of Kafka's story.*]

It is an oddity of critical commentary on Kafka's **"In der Strafkolonie"** that the machine is regarded as an instrument whose functions, although variously described, have from the moment of its first planning and construction, been clearly predictable. It is assumed that it has been constructed in order to execute and to bring about understanding and redemption. Thus, if it should fail in any of these respects (as eventually it does), it must be considered to have "broken down" like any other piece of machinery. It can then be thrown away and forgotten, which is clearly what the New Commandant hopes for.

Of course, this point of view could not have become standard were there not evidence enough to support it. The whole of the Officer's explanation of his machine seems to leave no room for doubt about what it is expected to do: in the process of execution it brings enlightenment and redemption. These appear to be as certain to him as any of the other, lesser functions—such as swilling away the blood or discarding the corpse into the pit.

However, I shall claim in this article that the assumption, fundamental to current discussion of the **"Strafkolonie"** (namely, that the machine's functions are determined and predictable) is mistaken. It is a mistake which leads to a number of oversights, false conclusions and problems of interpretation which have, from time to time, beleaguered criticism of the work. Not the least of these is the question of why the "Forschungsreisende" ("the Explorer") abandons the colony with such undignified haste, why the Officer puts himself into the machine, or how it was that an execution could once have been so significant a festival occasion.

In my view, these questions have not been answered entirely satisfactorily because the most basic of all questions has not been properly attended to: Why should the Old Commandant design and construct his machine in the first place?

Consider the critical position as it presently stands. The machine, as a reflection and product of an absolutist regime, or a reflection of beliefs about life and death, brings its victim to the point of understanding what he is accused of, and accepting the justice of that accusation. As "reward" (or consequence) he receives redemption at the point of death.

Now, is it really sufficient to assume that it was built simply for this purpose, or, as Nagel says, to demonstrate "ad oculos" "die zweifelsfreie Richtigkeit des geltenden Prinzips" ("the unquestionable justice of the prevailing principle"—a dual, not an alternative function)? In a weak sense, it obviously is. In a stronger sense, it is not, and it is this which interests me.

Let us suppose, as so many critics have done over the years, that the Old Commandant really believed that human life, its unavoidable afflictions and final end were justified only on the grounds that all men are guilty. Suppose, further, that he believed death brought enlightenment, and that enlightenment entailed redemption. Suppose, if you will, that he believed all this beyond doubt. Why should he set about building a machine which merely duplicated a natural system—even if he knew how to do it? Arrogance? Curiosity about the extent of his powers . . . ? If so, then the existence of the machine is actually superfluous. It achieves nothing, according to the religious conviction we have ascribed to the Old Commandant, which could not be achieved without it.

What this means is simple enough: given a man as gifted and intelligent as the Old Commandant seems to have been, it is exceedingly difficult to work out why he would have gone to the trouble of building his "eigentümlichen Apparat" ("strange apparatus"), and why it should have formed so important a part of a people's (religious?) life, if the only reasons we can think of are the ones generally accepted today. They are not only uncharacteristic of the Old Commandant as portrayed to us by his achievement, they are so hopelessly inadequate as to put their validity in question. Not to explain satisfactorily the very existence of the machine is to fail to explain satisfactorily the story. After all, the description of the machine's history, its construction and final operation take up almost three quarters of the text: **"In der Strafkolonie"** is a story *about* a remarkable machine.

What can save the Old Commandant and his machine from this accusation, respectively, of arrogance and superfluousness? It can be done if we take the machine, as I believe we must, to be an *experimental* machine; not, that is to say, a machine having, *from the start,* predictable results. It is built to find out *if,* through a process of suffering, man could be brought to recognize an existential guilt and thereby experience redemption ("Erlösung").

Imagine, for a moment, that in his search for a perfect model several prototypes failed, what conclusions could the Old Commandant draw? There are essentially two. First, the machine is "wrong" (i.e. technically inadequate); second, there can be no such thing as a "correct machine" because the premise itself, "die Schuld ist zweifellos" ("guilt is beyond doubt"), is wrong. It is immediately apparent that there is no way of deciding which is the case, nor any way that the last possibility can be excluded as a cause of failure. The very building and operation of the machine places the maxim "die Schuld ist zweifellos" in question. Furthermore, because no operation with a fresh "victim" can be considered a copy of the previous one, and because failure must always include the possibility that guilt might *not* be existential, the metaphysical assertion can never get beyond merely statistical probability. Even the successful machine cannot do more than prove the individual case. But, inasmuch as it does, so the machine "answers" the question implicitly raised by its latest operation: "is guilt existential?" The "answer" is not a categorical "yes", but a conditional one: "yes, in this case".

Since the universality of guilt cannot be proved, the dependent question of redemption is also in doubt. The Old Commandant could claim, when guilt is accepted, that redemption follows (if his interpretation of the victim's facial expression is correct—and *much* depends on this interpretation), because the machine has never failed to show it. But if the acceptance, or the reality, of existential guilt is a precondition of redemption, then failure there will result in failure of the effect—redemption will not be attained. In this case, too, the Old Commandant would have to entertain the possibility that the "fault" lies in the victim, not in the technical apparatus. A "failure" in the midst of a series of successes would be particularly significant because it would strongly suggest that the exception is to be attributed to the only variable: the victim himself. This is a state of affairs which will always remain true of the execution machine and its operation.

The consequences of this interpretation are considerable.

To begin with, it puts the Officer's naïveté and enthusiasm in a different light. Not exactly the insidious, deceitful monster envisaged by Pascal, he becomes an advocate for a theological interpretation of human existence. True, he overlooks the cruelty. The tremendous significance of the Old Commandant's "discoveries" make him incapable of concern for the individual's sufferings except insofar as they form part of the "experiment". Some mitigation may be found in his actual circumstances. He is fighting the extinction of a belief about human life which he feels is immensely important. There is no time, even if there ever was any, for "misplaced squeamishness". He is aware of it—"vielleicht sind Sie ein grundsätzlicher Gegner . . . einer derartigen maschinellen Hinrichtung" ("you are perhaps a fundamental opponent . . . of such a mechanical execution")—but there are so much more important matters to be dealt with. Will everything the Old Commandant worked for be lost through misunderstanding, ignorance, and failure in moral courage? Will the truth, and the means of affirming it (for it needs exhaustive reaffirmation), be discarded for what he (and not only he, because so many readers have joined him) regards as a weak and degenerate civilization under the New Commandant? The "Forschungsreisende" is his last hope; time is limited; he must work as quickly as possible if his case is to be won. Therefore, a great deal is left implicit.

Implicit, too, is something which actually diminishes the apparently tyrannical and authoritarian nature of the machine, something uniformly overlooked by commentators on the story.

It is generally, and correctly, assumed that the Old Commandant's belief about suffering, death and redemption entails the belief that guilt must be existential. But this is not precisely an assertion; it is a logical consequence of the Old Commandant's "discovery", and it is worth nothing that the Officer makes this clear. He does not simply assert: "die Schuld ist immer zweifellos." He says: "der Grundsatz, nachdem ich entscheide, ist . . ." ("the premise on which I work is . . ."), which lends the premise a more human, less absolute dimension. The successful working of the machine makes this assumption more and more likely as time goes on. Not to get too involved, it could be said that what the machine does is to make both victim and audience (although the latter in a different way) realize that, however innocent we may feel ourselves to be, we have all breached some law or other. It does not matter whether we know at the time the law we have breached, or not. It is sufficient that it is written, and that we finally learn how we have acted contrary to it. The machine vastly exceeds normal legal process inasmuch as it brings the victim to a true recognition of his guilt—for, without this, there could be no redemption. This means, in fact, that the victim is brought to the point of condemning himself. Man becomes the judge of himself and, like the judge, must condemn on evidence of guilt. In consequence of this acknowledged guilt, the victim becomes his own executioner. He is led to accede to his own execution. There is no further resistance to death, either in the sense of a powerful, blind urge to go on living, or in the sense of doubt as to the justice of his end. So there is no need of courts and advocates, nor all the clumsy apparatus of legal process.

It is a state of affairs, we might remark in passing, closely related to the plight of Joseph K in *Der Prozess.* Joseph K's search for a higher authority to determine the question of his guilt or innocence can be taken as an attempt to escape his own verdict on himself by dramatizing (which is what he does) an accusing body. The dissolution of the "Courts" in *Der Prozess,* and thus Joseph K's "freedom", depends uniquely on his willingness to accept his own judgement on himself as final and beyond appeal. For as long as he refuses to do this (his reasons may be good ones), and for as long as he searches for a sanctioning authority, he will never escape the labyrinth of his own inventions—except by death.

Unlike Joseph K, the victims of the execution machine go willingly, even joyfully, to their death. If they could, they would take the knife and plunge it into their own breasts uttering, at the same time, their last word: guilty! In its ability to reconcile man to his death, the machine is to be considered oddly humane; in its seeming ability to reward the victim with redemption, it is greater than any other instrument on earth!

All this might help account for the Officer's enthusiasm, even for his oversights and omissions. To some extent, it accounts also for his anxiousness, but not entirely. He is anxious that the magnitude of the Old Commandant's "discoveries" may be lost for ever, so much is clear. However, he is anxious, too, because the "Forschungsreisende" represents a test which takes them both back to the origins of the machine and its conception, therefore to the residual doubts and difficulties which lie beneath his confidence and which cannot be expunged without turning the machine and its operation into a wilful—too wilful—deceit.

There is, for instance, no means of telling whether the final look on the victim's face is one of redemption, and therefore proof of a Being capable of forgiving what man has condemned in himself and in others, or whether it can be explained as a moment, like that recorded by Dostoevskii's Prince Mishkin immediately prior to an epileptic fit, of perfect joy at the dissolution of all desire (save the desire to die, perhaps)—i.e. "Erlösung" in a way that the English word "redemption" makes almost impossible to envisage. In this last case, there is no question of redemption; there is need only of irrefutable knowledge of one's guilt, even though "guilt" might finally entail the existence of God, a set of absolute laws, and the freedom to obey them. Like the machine's incapacity to prove the universality of guilt, this is just another thing that the Officer will have to leave the "Forschungsreisende" to understand for himself.

There is, however, a special sense in which the machine has never been tried at all, in which its potential as an "experimental apparatus" remains hidden as much from the Officer as from the "Forschungsreisende", and even from the Old Commandant. This is a matter of a rather different order, and cannot be left implicit any longer because, while it is not the final test of the machine, it is, nevertheless, one that is of supreme significance at this moment, one which may even have the effect of replacing the Officer with the "Forschungsreisende" as the New Executioner!

So far the machine has only been operated on guilty men, those who have committed a known offence against the regulations. To be sure, the prisoner in the story has not been told what his offence is, nor that he has been condemned to death for it. But he must know that he has done *something* wrong—he overslept, at least, and he was rude to his senior officer. In the Old Commandant's time, the mere fact that he was brought to the machine must have made it perfectly clear that he was about to die. What this means is that the machine may have been assisted by a predisposition in the "victim" to recognize his guilt.

How important is this predisposition? Neither the Old Commandant nor the Officer could possibly know. It might be quite unimportant. If their belief that guilt is always beyond doubt *is* true for all, then it would make no difference who was placed in the machine. For as long as it "worked properly", its success could be guaranteed.

But the phrase, "die Schuld ist immer zweifellos", contains a subtle ambiguity. It could refer to the unimpeachable honesty and good judgement of the authorities: no person will be delivered into the machine unless his guilt is beyond doubt. Suppose that the Officer takes this for granted, then he can be easy in his mind that he was never given "the wrong person". But here we have at once to assume that a distinction *is* (or can be) made between him who is "guilty" and him who is—at least legally—"not guilty". Legally, it would be possible to send "the wrong man". This is not to say that the legal distinction between guilt and innocence can be upheld absolutely; it most certainly does mean that there will be people who *feel* themselves "innocent" and can prove themselves innocent, given the chance, in a way envisaged by the New Commandant—legal innocence established through the courts. The question is, how far can that feeling of innocence go?

Given a set of regulations, it might go very far indeed. To cut short an otherwise tricky discussion, let us simply assert that there could be one who was (rightly or wrongly) fully convinced of his innocence, moreover in an absolute sense: "ich bin unschuldig" ("I am innocent"), as Joseph K claims, in full knowledge of that statement's amplitude. He could mean this in the sense that he had broken no laws, or that the laws were "wrong", and he could also mean it, if necessary, in the sense that he could not help being what he is, and therefore doing what he has done. Actually, it matters little, or not at all, how he substantiates his claim to innocence; it is sufficient that he should be fully convinced of it, and that no normal court should be able to prove an offence against him. With this kind [of] person, it would seem, the machine has had no dealings.

Now, perhaps we could say that to expand an individual experience of guilt into an experience of a general, underlying guilt is one thing. To awaken a sense of existential guilt in a person wholly convinced of his innocence is another. It could mean creating something which did not previously exist. If it cannot do it, either the machine must be considered to have "gone wrong", to have fallen short of its maker's specifications, or—more interestingly—to have shown *the impossibility of the task* because guilt is not existential, and innocence is a reality. Should the machine fail in this respect, and yet go on to execute the innocent victim, then it has committed a crime. As a system, it is itself immediately and irrevocably "guilty", its own moral cleanliness is sullied, and its subsequent right to execute even the most guilty of men is extinguished. It is no better than he, and is actually indifferent to his guilt or innocence: it will kill either way.

Can there be much doubt that the machine's pristine cleanliness, which was for so long the Officer's pride, its coherence as a piece of machinery in perfect working order, was an expression of the (moral) difference between it and its victim, even though that victim became an integral part of it? Remember the filthiness of the prisoner, his vomit, his animal-like demeanour. At the end, sometime about the twelfth hour, there would no longer be any moral difference. The guiltless machine and the guiltless spirit are, for an instant, one. The wretched body is cast down into the blood-soaked earth, where it belongs.

But *is* the machine guiltless? The "Forschungsreisende" is inwardly convinced of the opposite—"die Ungerechtigkeit des Verfahrens und die Unmenschlichkeit der Exekution war zweifellos" ("the injustice of the procedure and the inhumanity of the execution were beyond doubt"—which is also a negation of "die Schuld ist zweifellos" stylistically emphasized)—and the Officer later shows himself to be aware of this, as we have already seen. Since the Officer cannot be sure that the Explorer is wrong, and since he puts great store on the Explorer's ability to resuscitate interest and faith in the machine (does not the resurrection of the Old Commandant depend, largely, on this man's reaction to it?), there is nothing left but to put his machine to the ultimate test: it must prove itself in the face of "innocence". This is the test it has never been subjected to, but which the Old Commandant must have foreseen as necessary and inevitable.

It has sometimes been asked why the Officer should substitute himself for the prisoner. I suppose, while it is clear that the prisoner must be set free, if it is just a question of finding an "innocent" man, why not put in the guard? He is "technically" innocent, at least, and would no doubt kick up a fuss if he found himself where his prisoner was supposed to be! He would offer a more difficult test for the machine. Would he be the final test, though? The Officer cannot be sure—and that is enough. The Officer must be *absolutely certain* that the substitute is fully convinced of his own innocence. No person can be sure of another's feelings: at best, one can be sure only of one's own.

But can it be said that the Officer is convinced absolutely of his own innocence? I believe it can. There is no point in running the machine if it is merely to show that it works

as the Officer has described. This is why he removes the prisoner. It would have no influence on the "Forschungsreisende". To demonstrate, on the other hand, that there is no such thing as innocence, no such thing as "the wrong person", and, at the same time, that death is to be regarded as condign punishment for a guilt finally revealed even to him who had been perfectly convinced of his innocence, is an immense accomplishment. Nothing could more greatly redound to the Old Commandant's honour; nothing could better show the Officer's integrity, and nothing could better justify his death. He must take the risk that the "Forschungsreisende" will not believe him, of course, but that risk is slight. They understand one another now—"der Offizier [handelte] vollständig richtig; der Reisende hätte an seiner Stelle nicht anders gehandelt" ("the Officer behaved absolutely correctly; the explorer would have done the same in his place"). For sure, the Officer knew that he would have to put the machine to the ultimate test—"dann ist es also Zeit" ("then it is time therefore") alludes, perhaps, to the long put off decision—and, as if somehow aware of it, and impatient to accept the challenge, the machine adopts of its own accord the right position for his body, and sets itself in motion once he has programmed the "Zeichner" ("the programmer") and laid himself on the "Bett" ("the bed").

Here we might note two things.

First, the substitution involves at least one other problem for the Officer. What "crime" is to be fed into the "Zeichner"? In all previous cases, the crime is defined by the prisoner's deed—"ehre deinen Vorgesetzten" ("honour your superior"), for example. While it was not the machine's task simply to announce the specific crime to the prisoner, but to show the crime as a manifestation of a deeper-lying sinfulness (and guilt), the choice of "Schrift" ("text") was settled. However, if the Officer is innocent (despite his assertion of existential guilt), there is no "portal" through which he can be led to an understanding of the "law" by which all men are judged guilty. He is "outside", "beyond", "different from". Is then the choice of "Schrift" arbitrary, or a gamble? "Sei gerecht" ("Be just"). But "sei gerecht", and the complicated hieroglyph which is its character (and therefore its unique functioning) supposes disobedience; it is, primitively, the index of a breach. The Officer's gamble is that in not exposing himself to the machine earlier, perhaps he has sinned, and that somehow this offence will be his "portal" to the law. However, even if he has been guilty in this regard he cannot feel his guilt. Otherwise he would know his crime, and the machine would not be asked to do anything it has not done countless times before. Inasmuch as he remains convinced of his innocence, so the choice of "Schrift" is arbitrary. He could as well toss them all into the air and choose the one to land nearest him—if there were not considerations of purity.

Second, it should be noted that "sei gerecht" pertains as much to the machine as it does to the Officer, and possibly more so. It implies that the machine should dispense justice to all men. But its punishment can only be just if all the victims are guilty. To the machine, "sei gerecht" is a stipulation: you may treat this man as you have treated all others only if he is guilty. Whether or not the machine is capable of acting in any other way than the way it has been designed is extremely doubtful. Built on the premise of existential guilt, it may not be able to entertain the possibility of innocence.

But by "machine" we are not talking only of the inorganic parts; we are obliged to include the organic and spiritual parts constituted by the "victim". Once the "victim" is laid on the "Bett", he becomes an integral part of the apparatus. This can be seen in the machine's structure. It unites, and at the same time distinguishes between, two parts: the upper part ("Egge", "harrow"; "Zeichner"), and the lower part ("Bett"). Each is powered by a different battery, which endorses their independence. Their point of contact is the human body. It physically bridges the gap between "upper" and "lower", and has the peculiar distinction of belonging wholly to neither, while at the same time being the indispensable bond through which unity is reached. Looked upon merely as "material" for processing, the presence of the "victim" is no more interesting than meat in a canning factory. When it is remembered, on the other hand, that this "victim" regulates the process, introduces chance into an apparently determined mechanical system—for redemption (and death) only take *on average* ("durchschnittlich") twelve hours—and that through him the process itself is translated from the material back into the intellectual sphere, and that this constitutes the machine's final justification for existence, then the "victim" as "part of the machinery" is undeniably important. Intellect and suffering are the spiritual wheels which complete the machine. Consequently, every new "victim" slightly, but crucially, alters the machine's composition, and each operation is a new beginning. It is always possible that, even if the inorganic machinery functions properly, the desired result will not be achieved.

Thus because it is a machine sensitive to spiritual states, it is not impossible that, faced with innocence, or stubborn refusal to admit guilt, it will perform quite differently. To be just, it *must*. It could, for example, confront stubbornness with stubbornness—go on writing indefinitely. It could refuse to write at all. Either of these might be considered a "proper functioning", verifiable by trying it out again on another victim. Or it could fall to pieces, as any other sensitive apparatus might if put to a task for which it was not constructed.

Is this what happens? Is it that the machine does not stand up to the ultimate challenge: to prove to an innocent man his real guilt? Or has long use and longer neglect simply brought the machine into such a state of disrepair that it would have broken down regardless of the victim? Shall we say that its failure then is a meaningless accident? It tells us nothing? It really is just so much scrap metal, and the New Commandant can heave a sigh of relief?

In the first place, it does not fail to kill its victim; all the machinery of torture works, although its working is now uncontrolled, uncoordinated and overhasty. The only operation that actually sticks is the final ejection of the corpse into the grave. But once the body is pulled off the "Egge", the machine is ready for use once more—"die Egge wollte schon in ihre alte Lage zurückkehren" ("the harrow tried to return to its original position"). But it has

become exclusively an instrument of torture and execution, "just an engine", because the "Zeichner", whose function was to deploy mechanical processes to a spiritual end, has fallen to pieces. Why?

Let us imagine that the machine lived up to its designer's highest possible expectations: not only was it a model *intended* as (or devoutly hoped to be) a truthful paradigm of the universal system, but it was *in fact* "true", or "true" to a phase in that archetype. Death brought revelation; human life was designed such that each moment contributed towards a specific spiritual end. Our lives were a kind of writing; death the final disclosure of the meaning of that script—for that was the last word of the sentence, and the one most deeply written. However, the usefulness of models lies both in their capacity to demonstrate how, on the one hand, a system might work, and, on the other, how it might fail. So, if the Old Commandant's creation was "true" to a system working correctly, who is to say that, in its collapse, the machine does not "tell the truth" also? Moreover, not just "true" in that it has broken down; "true" (more importantly) in the cause of, and possibly the time of, its breakdown: the Officer's self-sacrifice.

Allusions to the crucifixion, often remarked upon, carry considerable force now. Obviously, the father-son relation obtains, emblematically at least, between the Old Commandant and the Officer. The Old Commandant is the author of the "Schriften"—treated with the same reverence as the Jews treat Holy Scripture. He was extraordinarily gifted ("Soldat, Richter, Konstrukteur, Chemiker, Zeichner"—"Soldier, Judge, engineer, chemist, draftsman"). It is said that he will return—"es besteht die Prophezeiung, dass der Kommandant . . . auferstehen [wird] . . . " ("there is the prophecy that the Commandant will be resurrected")—which suggests that he has transcended death, that he is eternal in some way. This will be false, of course, folklore, myth. But it does not matter because it sets the Old Commandant up as a model, like his machine: he "stands for". So, therefore, does the "son", or Officer. It can be no accident that the Officer's death bears some resemblance to that of Christ. It is undergone with similar motives: all else to one side, each hopes that his death will win him adherents by demonstrating, to all doubting Thomases, that what has hitherto been only belief is *true*. The flowing blood, and, if one has in mind Byzantine and Romanesque depictions of the crucifixion, the impassive face, showing no sign of the violence to which the body has been subjected, as also the iron spike which recalls the spear and the crown of thorns, is each witness to this resemblance.

Then, naturally, one conclusion might be that such a "machine" cannot cope with innocence. The final look of conviction on the Officer's face ("der Blick war ruhig und überzeugt"—"his expression was calm and firm") can be taken either as a sign of his conviction that he is right about the need for self-sacrifice and the machine's ability to perform its task even on an "innocent" man, or that the Officer *is innocent,* and has maintained it throughout. This conviction resists the purpose of the "Zeichner". Instead of the "Schrift" conquering the Officer's will, the Officer's will withstands the "Schrift". The mediating apparatus between "Schrift" and man—the "Zeichner"—is thus squeezed out, as between two opposing, and equally powerful forces, and the machine falls into a disorder from which it will never recover.

And yet this is by no means the only conclusion to be drawn. It might also be said that it makes little difference to this catastrophe if the cause of the break-down is mechanical wear and tear, if the "Zeichner" would have fallen to pieces no matter who was placed on the "Bett". In this case, the model reveals a structural imperfection, or Divine negligence, and an identifiable time at which that imperfection showed itself. It represents, anyway, the collapse of a teleology, a rationale of suffering and death, and leaves in their place a different, much inferior engine accidentally, irreversibly, and quite unconsciously (therefore blamelessly) reduced to torture and execution. Nothing from "above" now reaches that which is "below". The "Schriften" remain, of course; the intention that they should guide and control the machine of material creation also remains, but the contact between the two spheres is lost because that which translated the spiritual into the physical has disintegrated. The spiritual is thus stripped both of power and utility, and the physical performs as best it can on its worn, ever more worn, cogs, springs, ratchets and flywheels.

Thus, by a miraculous coincidence, a machine might be seen as performing the rupture between God and man, between the Idea and its realization in space and time, and, without knowing it, the New Commandant has the machine which best symbolizes his "humanitarian" principles (if that is what they are)! But the machine's state of disrepair is as significant as its earlier state of "good order". It can only be forgotten at our peril. Certainly, it is "scrap", but it is "scrap" charged with meaning.

Whichever way we look at the machine's break-down, its message is equally grim. Is it not this from which the "Forschungsreisende" flees? If so, then we should not believe that the "Forschungsreisende" flees the "Strafkolonie" for a better world. There isn't one. He simply flees. He flees himself as grotesquely imaged by the island and the islanders he went to inspect with such a feeling of superiority. He flees anywhere, but always around in circles, and the most he can hope for is that the boat will sink with all hands—but especially his. (pp. 271-82)

> *E. R. Davey, "The Broken Engine: A Study of Franz Kafka's 'In der Strafkolonie',"* in Journal of European Studies, *Vol. 14, No. 56, December, 1984, pp. 271-83.*

FURTHER READING

Criticism

Burns, Wayne. "Kafka and Alex Comfort: The Penal Colony Revisited." *Arizona Quarterly* 8, No. 2 (Summer 1952): 101-20.

Illustrates the thematic similarities between Kafka's story and Alex Comfort's novel *On This Side Nothing,* which depicts an imaginary fascist regime's oppression of a Jewish ghetto in Northern Africa.

———. " 'In the Penal Colony': Variations on a Theme by Octave Mirbeau." *Accent* XVII, No. 1 (Winter 1957): 45-51.

Demonstrates how Kafka adopts the sensationalistic depictions of colonial brutality and exploitation in Mirbeau's novel *Le jardin des supplices,* and transforms them into an allegory of the human condition.

Dodd, W. J. "Dostoyevskian Elements in Kafka's Penal Colony." *German Life and Letters* XXXVII, No. 1 (October 1983): 11-23.

Contends that Dostoyevsky's portraits of submissive waifs and authoritarian despots influenced Kafka's rendering of his own characters in "In the Penal Colony."

Globus, Gordon G., and Pillard, Richard C. "Tausk's 'Influencing Machine' and Kafka's 'In the Penal Colony.' " *American Imago* 23, No. 3 (Fall 1966): 191-207.

Interprets Kafka's story as a Freudian allegory about narcissistic regression in schizophrenics.

Jayne, Richard. "Kafka's 'In der Strafkolonie' and the Aporias of Textual Interpretation." *Deutsche Vierteljahrs Schrift Für Literaturwissenschaft Und Geistesgeschichte* 66, No. 1 (March 1992): 94-128.

Analyzes "In the Penal Colony" from a structuralist perspective, contending that Kafka subverts traditional notions of power and justice through irony and "semiotic codes which structure the text as an open complex of reference."

Kirchberger, Lida. " 'In the Penal Colony' or The Machinery of the Law." In her *Franz Kafka's Use of Law in Fiction: A New Interpretation of 'In der Strafkolonie,'* Der Prozess, *and* Das Schloss, pp. 13-42. New York: Peter Lang Publishing, 1986.

Asserts that the execution machine is a literal expression of the metaphor of "the machinery of the law."

Loeb, Ernst. "Kafka's 'In the Penal Colony' as a Reflection of Classical and Romantic Religious Views." In *Franz Kafka (1883-1983): His Craft and Thought,* edited by Roman Struc and J. C. Yardley, pp. 89-99. Waterloo, Ontario: Wilfrid Laurier University Press, 1986.

Interprets Kafka's story as a religious allegory contrasting Judaism and Christianity.

Norris, Margot. "Sadism and Masochism in Two Kafka Stories: 'In der Strafkolonie' and 'Ein Hungerkünstler.' " *Modern Language Notes* 93, No. 3 (April 1978): 430-47.

Citing the influence of sadomasochism on Kafka's imagination, Norris argues that allegorical readings of Kafka's stories overemphasize their religious dimension and miss the irony in his sometimes erotic depictions of ascetic suffering.

Pascal, Roy. "Officer Versus Traveller: 'In the Penal Colony.' " In his *Kafka's Narrators: A Study of His Stories and Sketches,* pp. 60-89. New York: Cambridge University Press, 1982.

Analyzes the function of the anonymous third-person narrator in Kafka's story.

Politzer, Heinz. " 'A Country Doctor' and 'In the Penal Colony.' " In his *Franz Kafka: Parable and Paradox,* pp. 83-115. Ithaca, N.Y.: Cornell University Press, 1962.

Asserts that Kafka's narrative technique transforms the didactic function of parables into modernist irony and paradox.

Sacharoff, Mark. "Pathological, Comic, and Tragic Elements in Kafka's 'In the Penal Colony.' " *Genre* IV, No. 4 (December 1971): 392-411.

Assesses Kafka's portrait of the officer, concluding that its mixture of comic and tragic elements underscores the ambivalent blend of sympathy and revulsion which his personality elicits from the explorer.

Steinberg, Erwin R. "The Judgment in Kafka's 'In the Penal Colony.' " *Journal of Modern Literature* 5, No. 3 (September 1976): 492-514.

Examines Kafka's conflicting attitudes towards Judaism and Christianity, as symbolized by the two commandants in "In the Penal Colony."

Street, James B. "Kafka through Freud: Totems and Taboos in 'In der Strafkolonie.' " *Modern Australian Literature* 6, Nos. 3-4 (1973): 93-106.

Analyzes "In the Penal Colony" using Freudian concepts of patricide and ritual sacrifice.

Thiher, Allen. "In the Penal Colony." In his *Franz Kafka: A Study of the Short Fiction,* pp. 51-67. Boston: Twayne Publishers, 1990.

Interprets Kafka's story as a symbolic examination of the relationship between writing and the law.

Thomas, J. D. "The Dark at the End of the Tunnel: Kafka's 'In the Penal Colony.' " *Studies in Short Fiction* IV, No. 1 (Fall 1966): 12-8.

Argues that what the author sees as Kafka's essentially Jewish pessimism and sense of guilt is a more useful framework than Christian allegory for interpreting "In the Penal Colony."

Warren, Austin. "An Exegetical Note on 'The Penal Colony.' " *The Southern Review* 7, No. 2 (Autumn 1941): 363–65.

An influential essay that explains the story's significance in terms of religious allegory.

F. W. Murnau

1888-1931

(Full name Friedrich Wilhelm Murnau; pseudonym of Friedrich Wilhelm Plumpe) German film director.

INTRODUCTION

One of Germany's leading silent film directors, Murnau is best remembered for *Nosferatu, eine Symphonie des Grauens,* (*Nosferatu the Vampire*), the first full-length film adaptation of Bram Stoker's novel *Dracula* (1897). Directing during the early part of the twentieth century, Murnau's work was highly influenced by the artistic movement known as German Expressionism, which emphasized "intensity of feeling," subjectivity, and self-expression. Murnau's films are noted for their inventive use of space and light; their simplistic but evocative sense of atmosphere, utilizing—unlike many German Expressionist films—natural landscapes rather than studio sets; and their use of the *entfesselte Kamera,* or "unchained," mobile camera.

Of Swedish origin, Murnau was born in Bielefield, Westphalia. He first developed an interest in theater as a child when his sister began to stage plays in the attic of their home. Murnau studied art history and literature at the University of Heidelberg, and his knowledge of these subjects is evident in the lyrical quality and fantastic sets of his films. Acting in amateur theater companies in Heidelberg, Murnau was invited by director Max Reinhardt to join his Deutsches Theater Company. He adopted the stage name Murnau, after a town in Bavaria, in order to avoid identification by his father, who disapproved of Murnau's desire to act. During World War I Murnau served in the German air force as a pilot until 1917 when his plane was forced to land in Switzerland. He was interned there and began directing propaganda films for the German Embassy in Bern. In 1919 he founded a film-producing company, the Murnau Veidt Filmgesellschaft, with former members of the Reinhardt school. With the success of his 1924 film *Der letzte Mann* (*The Last Laugh*), American film producer William Fox of Fox Studios in Hollywood, California, contracted Murnau to direct four films, including *Sunrise: A Story of Two Humans,* in the United States. After a falling out with Fox, Murnau left the company and began working with the famous documentarist Robert Flaherty. Murnau died in a car accident near Santa Barbara in March 1931, shortly before the release of *Tabu,* which he co-directed with Flaherty.

Murnau's popularity over the years has fluctuated along with critical reassessments of his most important works. Critics argue whether *Nosferatu, The Last Laugh,* or *Sunrise* is his greatest film. *Nosferatu* established Murnau's reputation in Germany as a major director. Written by Henrick Galeen and starring Max Schreck, Murnau's ver-

sion differs from Stoker's novel on several points: Murnau changed the setting from England to Germany, modified the characters' names and their roles, and changed the premise of the original plot. Some scholars note that in Murnau's adaptation, the story reflects the political milieu of the Weimar Republic rather than that of Victorian society. Critics have lauded the film for its rich symbolism, its innovative technical aspects, and its uniquely Expressionistic attributes. *Nosferatu* is considered Expressionistic—not for its "distortion of reality" as is typical of other films of this genre—but as Robin Wood comments, for its evocation of an "atmosphere and an ethos" and its display of the horrors of the natural world. Filmed on location rather than in the studio, Murnau adhered to his belief in the supremacy of simplicity, using special effects sparingly and relying instead on camera angles and long shots lingering over vast empty spaces to convey a sense of horror and alienation.

The Last Laugh, written by Carl Mayer and starring Emil Jannings, was popular with audiences and influential on other filmmakers. A political satire of German society and its identification of self-worth with social status, the film concerns the doorman of an elegant hotel who loses his dignity with his demotion to men's room attendant. *The Last Laugh* is often considered to have been inspired by *Kammerspiel*, a genre of German theatre designated by small audiences and intimate situations depicting daily life in which gestures and emotions are subdued rather than exaggerated. Many critics, however, have noted that Emil Jannings's expressions are anything but subdued, challenging an absolute definition of the film. The film was shot exclusively in the studio, without intertitles, and depended heavily on special effects. Many critics note that Murnau's use of a mobile camera and point-of-view shots revolutionized the way directors approached the representation of dramatic action.

Sunrise, Murnau's first American production, won several Academy Awards: Janet Gaynor was named best actress, and Charles Rosher and Karl Struss were honored for their cinematography. The film also inspired the creation of a special award for Artistic Quality of Production. Based on a piece of short fiction by German playwright and novelist Hermann Sudermann, the film was hailed by critics as pictorially one of the most beautiful films ever created. The sequence of a peasant couple traveling on a trolley to the city is one of the most frequently discussed scenes in film criticism.

Murnau is additionally known for cinematic adaptations of Goethe's drama *Faust* (1808; *Faust*) and Molière's *Le Tartuffe* (1664; *Tartuffe*). His last film, *Tabu*, concerns the "metaphysical and tragic" forces which threaten the social order of a South Pacific society with the encroachment of modern civilization. Despite Murnau's lack of success at American box offices and the fact that several of his films have been lost or destroyed, his work has been extremely influential on succeeding film directors. His use of the moving camera, creation of mood and atmosphere through light and shadow, and concentration on dark and tragic themes were inspirations for Orson Welles's stylistic approach in *Citizen Kane* (1941) and influenced the development of the cinematic genre known as film noir. In assessing his career, many scholars note the wide scope of Murnau's talent and the relationship between his film and his personal temperament. Lotte Eisner has stated: "All his films bear the impress of his own inner complexity, of the struggle he waged within himself against a world in which he remained despairingly alien."

PRINCIPAL WORKS

Der Knabe in Blau (film) 1919
　[The Boy in Blue]
Der Januskopf (film) 1920
　[Janus-Faced]
Satanas (film) 1920
Der Gang in die Nacht (film) 1921
Schloß Vogelöd (film) 1921
　[Haunted Castle]
Der brennende Acker (film) 1922
　[Burning Soil]
Marizza, genannt die Schmugglermadonna (film) 1922

Nosferatu, eine Symphonie des Grauens (film) 1922
　[Nosferatu the Vampire]
Phantom (film) 1922
Die Austreibung (film) 1923
　[Driven from Home]
Der letzte Mann (film) 1924
　[The Last Laugh]
Faust (film) 1926
Tartüff (film) 1926
　[Tartuffe]
Sunrise: A Story of Two Humans (film) 1927
†*Four Devils* (film) 1928
†*City Girl* (film) 1930
‡*Die zwölfte Stunde: Eine Nacht des Grauens* (film) 1930
　[Nosferatu the Vampire]
†*Tabu* [with Robert Flaherty] (film) 1931

*These titles were given to these films upon their release in the United States.

†These films have soundtracks.

‡This is a revised edition of Murnau's *Nosferatu* with a soundtrack.

CRITICISM

Kenneth White (essay date 1931)

[*In the essay below, which was written in the months after Murnau's death, White discusses Murnau's innovative film techniques and contributions to American cinema.*]

A week or so before the opening of *Tabu*, an automobile speeding along a California highway plunged over an embankment and carried F. W. Murnau to his death. The loss his death brought has been variously estimated; but, definitely, it has made a gap in the small circle of directors whose work, principally in the silent movie, had distinction. Death removed the chance of further collaboration between two men, Flaherty and Murnau, whose work together on *Tabu* produced as fine results as that other noteworthy collaboration between Eisenstein and Alexandrov produced in *Old and New* and *Ten Days That Shook the World*.

When the German-made *Last Laugh* was released in this country for the first time, in the twenties, a definite movie method could be seen working toward a definite end. Murnau had done what a number of people had been hoping for a long time could be done: the movie camera was made to do things other than simply elaborate subtitles. Charlie Chaplin had, of course, taken a confessedly banal idea in *A Woman of Paris* and cut out all the pictorial and subtitle verbiage thick in previous pictures. Murnau had taken a fairly complex idea and found adequate camera devices to express it. The pantomime everyone had thought to be the derived art of the movies was not discoverable in *The Last Laugh.* The doorman got drunk, but not in the way a pantomimic actor with subordinate properties got drunk; the camera did it for him. *The Last Laugh,* in fact, stated and solved a series of problems in movie technique: continuity of idea and time, so that time is not a lapse, a space between actions, but a development of action; the relation between the actor and the objects about him, and the convincing establishment of this relation as a real and moving one for the spectator; the possibilities of distortion and of abstraction. A hotel livery glittered before the adoring eyes of a whole community. Time passed in the lives of the people on the screen, not by means of words, not even by direct gestures of the actors; instead, windows were opened on a courtyard, bedding was hung out to air, the sun moved so much further across a dark wall. Time passed visibly and actually. Events that stirred people crashed immediately before the eyes of the spectator, as they did before the eyes of the persons touched: doors flashed in elongations, a trunk toppled down, carrying with it prestige, in a series of light waves and buttons on a uniform assumed enormous proportions.

It is interesting to note that an attempt was made by Josef von Sternberg, in the recent *Dishonored,* to establish some continuity between idea and time by superimposing the progress of one scene on another whose progress had not yet been completed. And it is interesting to note that only once or twice was von Sternberg's cloudy method successful, when the foregoing scene lingered like a memory-image in the action of the following one. Otherwise the problems stated in *The Last Laugh* receive attention only from a few directors like Lubitsch and Eisenstein.

Sometime after the success of *The Last Laugh,* Murnau came to America to work for Fox. When *Sunrise* was completed, the marvels of news reels with actual sounds were only just bursting on a public eager for imitation. George Bernard Shaw was seen and heard to be cute and Fascist soldiers on horseback deployed and shouted and clomped-clomped-clomped endlessly over paving stones for very attentive and astonished eyes, before *Sunrise* was shown. For forty-five minutes thereafter *Sunrise* was unexcelled among movies. The next forty-five minutes of *Sunrise* displayed the heaviness of German humor.

Sunrise may not appear in retrospect as important as *The Last Laugh. Sunrise* was less obviously experimental and more complete. The manner and method of *Sunrise* was so individual, so self-contained that any attempt to accept the precise statement of problems it contained would have to result in a mere imitation of the solution to these problems. The relation of sound to gestures and motions of the actors was explored; the cry of a horn, for instance, identified, without imitating, the cry of a woman through her cupped hands to searchers after a drowned body. The sound-meaning was immediate, not associative as previous musical accompaniments, like "hurry music" or "Yankee Doodle" assisting Revolutionary soldiers to fight the British, had been. A trolley car bumping through a countryside, with two distraught, unhappy, frightened people and the placid motorman, into a city was not just a scenic event like the covered wagons that had spread out over plains under cottonwhite clouds in numerous movie "epics." The trolley car was a vehicle of emotion, not simply a means of getting from one scene to another in the picture.

There was much to be admired in *Sunrise* apart from its total effect: the composition of the shots, the dramatic pace of events, papers blown with people before a rain-filled wind; but *Sunrise* bored audiences who were not bored with the manoeuvres of Fascist soldiers. And *Four Devils* came in the horrible period when movies starting out as silent had talking sequences jammed into them.

Murnau went to the South Seas with Robert Flaherty, who had made *Moana* and *Nanook of the North.* The company backing them failed; Murnau himself financed the expedition. *Tabu* was shown for the first time on March 18th [1931].

Whether Flaherty had learned his lesson when *Moana* was butchered to program length and accordingly insisted upon presenting Paramount with a completed film to release, is a question idle beside the fact that the editing in *Tabu* is simply amazing. Events seem to take their impetus from the same source that flings the sudden spear into the fish in the opening sequences, from the water-chutes down which the bathers so precipitantly ride. The idyllic mood is established and never lost. Not a shot is displayed which does not concern and accentuate the story and the mood. There is no lingering over beautiful landscapes. The landscape folds into the mood of the picture, just as the islanders appear to live with equal grace in and out of water, or as the drowning lover finally merges with the broadening sight of the sea. In comparison, *Moana* seems a trifle wordy with camera pictures even in the cut version, until one remembers that *Moana* was a record of South Sea Island life and that comparison between the two arises only through the accident of like locales.

The manners of white civilization impinge directly upon the two lovers' flight from the tabu's bane; but not in the form of brutal traders and plutocrats blind to simplicity. The festive dancing only is different, the payment of bills prevents the lovers' further flight. The white touch is sure and firm and hampering but it plays the subordinate part the landscape plays. The idyll is flawless.

In *Tabu,* the camera under Murnau's direction played again the sensitive inclusive eye. A milieu was created, events shaped in it their enlarged proportions: clapping hands increase their tensity as the movements of the dancers rise to a pitch of exaltation which is broken instantaneously, ominously, by the flinging of a wreath; a knife in the hands of the priest cuts a rope and as intense a climax as the films have ever presented is remembered. The brain keeps the image of the swimmer's hands on a rope taut, then slashed in two over the edge of a boat.

What is unfortunate about a good movie is its ephemeral quality. A director who wishes to study a predecessor cannot seek out, as a painter can, a museum where the predecessor is always on view. He has to be contented with what he can get immediately from the screen, and he gets usually the gross effects rather than the mechanism by which the effects are obtained. The value which Murnau's work might have for a student director, if it were accessible over a long period of time, is inestimable. For the problems which Murnau stated in all of his pictures are problems persistent in the making of good movies. New solutions may be accumulated and a different order of problems arise, but the problems of editing, continuity in idea and time, of distortions, abstraction and the development of movies beyond the mere imitation of nature or the stage, remain constant. (pp. 581-84)

Kenneth White, "F. W. Murnau," in The Hound & Horn, *Summer, 1931, pp. 581-84.*

C. A. Lejeune (essay date 1931)

[*In the following essay, Lejeune praises Murnau's creative camera work in* The Last Laugh.]

Of all the films that the late F. W. Murnau ever made, *The Last Laugh* is probably the least sensational and certainly the most important. Murnau had all the instincts of a showman, and his other films, with the possible exception of *City Girl,* carried a marked sense of the desire to shock and grip and stimulate an audience. *Dracula* [which is more commonly known as *Nosferatu*] was a frank thriller, cunningly and almost pedantically designed, even in its early age a better thriller than the screen is in the habit of producing to-day; *Tartuffe,* within its limits of formalism, gave a deliberate affront to sensibility; *Faust,* beautiful and imaginative as it was in many sequences, had all the tinsel and bombast of a world-circus; *Sunrise* and *The Four Devils* made a straight bid for sensation, and achieved it with an exciting use of lit and photographed movement that came strangely to America from the east; *Tabu* has Flaherty's hand on the reins. Only *The Last Laugh* is unambitious. It deals with simple people and everyday emotions. It carries no legend of the fantastic; does nothing oddly, calls no attention to itself. But somehow it penetrates, with unhurried pace, into a cinema that the other films have left largely untouched—a cinema of logical unfolding, in which the camera visions and makes visual as it goes.

The Last Laugh was an important film for Murnau who made it, for [Emil] Jannings who played in it, for Germany, for the European screen. But it was above all an important film for the camera. It gave the camera a new dominion, a new freedom. It gave the camera prestige, and all the concessions that prestige brings. It influenced the future of motion picture photography, not only in the country that produced it, but in studios all over the world, and without suggesting any revolution in method, without storming critical opinion as *Caligari* had done, it turned technical attention towards experiment, and stimulated the better brains on the production side of the cinema towards a new kind of camera-thinking with a definite narrative end.

All his working life Murnau was in love with his cameras. Even in the early days of *Dracula,* he pampered them, and pandered to them, and of all the technical resources that the studios of Hollywood had to offer him in later days, it was the enhancements to photography that pleased him most. He never lost a kind of childish excitement in the sense of flying and hovering over a film with a camera; he loved to peer down from heights; to swing giddily above a flattened and minuscule world; he leapt, eagerly, at the elevation of Mephisto's viewpoint in *Faust* and sought the circus roof with *The Four Devils.* But in *The Last Laugh* he flattered the cameras with the hardest job of all; he gave them the story to tell, he trusted them with the continuity.

I have yet to find a really satisfying definition of the much-abused word "continuity." Paul Rotha describes it in his book as "the development of the thematic-narrative from point to point during the showing of a film," or alternatively "the psychological guidance of the spectator," but both these definitions seem to me to miss the curiously heterogeneous components of the narrative medium. The very essence of continuity is its arrangement of mosaic bits of celluloid, pictures and titles, words and faces, long-shots and close-ups, in such a way as to produce a continuous unity of narrative, or drama, or mood.

The Last Laugh was, I think, the first film with a definite camera continuity, and although it was not the last, it still remains the best. Murnau, when he came to the job of giving film form to his story of the old hotel janitor, was faced with an assemblage of continuity methods, none of which seemed to suit his very simple and very deliberate needs. All the early devices for continuity had been shaped for a cinema that rioted in sensation, suspense and pace. From the early straightforward shooting of a film along its dramatic highlights, sign-posted with explanatory captions, a system of parallel plots had been developed by D. W. Griffith on a Dickens model: suspense scenes worked a stranglehold on the audience with their alternating shots; interest was snapped at its highest point, concentration on character was divided in an attempt to increase the dramatic impetus; and directors vied with one another in their enthusiasm to tell a film story unusually, backwards, sideways, in jerks, spots or flashes, or in any other direction but the simple one which leads from the beginning through the middle to the end.

Into a cinema which was trying, mainly, to build up continuity from disintegration, came Murnau with his scenario-writer, [Carl] Mayer, and his cameraman, [Karl] Freund. They had to produce a film from a story which depended entirely on its straightforward trajectory, a story of sequential development, held together by the single figure of one bewildered old man. And, casting round for a new continuity which would leave the story free to develop, without investing their film with any literary flavour, they hit on the idea of letting the camera do the whole job.

There are no titles in *The Last Laugh* to confuse the issue with verbal associations; photography titles for us, comments and reveals. The story is unfolded in forward and logical stages; the camera, as it were, moves onwards with it, and we behind the camera. No startling angle breaks the rhythm. We are never confronted with the sudden close-up. the broken dramatic sequence, the flashing transition from face to face. There is no juggling with distances. If we must approach a man from far off, we do it, not in one gigantic flea-hop, but through all the intervening stages, and in the same way we leave him again. We are conscious of the camera just ahead of us, like a vast super-human eye. It fixes its beam upon some inanimate object, a door, a window, a staircase, and presently that door, window or staircase becomes animate, a living actor in the drama. The camera hatches out life wherever its eye rests. In every picture lies the fruition of the last, the promise of the next, and the audience, carried along with half-divinations from scene to scene, find themselves always a little right, never wholly justified, with thought thrown forward, gripped in the plot.

Through this equipment of continuity, Murnau gives to his story of the fall and rise of a hotel porter, the semblance of some universal truth. He puts the porter's story, as it were, into the heart of a vaster continuity, in which there is no finality, no isolation of action or of thought. The swinging doors of the hotel have acquired, of late, a popular literary symbolism, but when Murnau used them to indicate the endless revolution of fortune, the callous passage of pomposity, their significance was still unworn. They are the chorus of his picture, commenting on it and giving it unity. Through, within, and across the story, there are swing-doors turning, the ripple of their circles spreading out to touch many lives; swing-doors still vibrant with the atmosphere of the last comer, disturbed, personal, chafing in pause. Watching them we feel, as Murnau meant us to feel with every advance and withdrawal of his cameras, how the events of life move in a causal rhythm, how helpless we are to scatter or reorder them.

It is fine to read, with the crowd of hotel guests, the final news of the porter's millionaire inheritance; to watch him, superb and smiling, above the minion waiters, to follow him, now one of the mighty, down the stairs and corridors of his shame, to bow him out to happiness from the doorway that he used to serve. But we do not really believe either in the finality or the happiness. It was Murnau's achievement in *The Last Laugh,* that his cameras denied finality. The whole object of his film was to assert the sense of continuity and passage—continuity through passage—and the distinction of his film that it did this for the first time with the undisputed, unaided materials of the screen. (pp. 118-24)

> C. A. Lejeune, "Murnau and 'The Last Laugh'," in her Cinema, *Alexander Maclehose & Co., 1931, pp. 118-24.*

Dorothy B. Jones   (essay date 1954)

[*In the essay below, Jones, an author and film critic, provides a stylistic and thematic analysis of* Sunrise.]

Among the works of the German-born director F. W. Murnau, *Sunrise* (1927) remains today a film which is still enjoyed and appreciated by discriminating cinema audiences, as well as by many average movie-goers when they are given the opportunity to see it. Despite the fact that *Sunrise* is a silent film, the average person enjoys it as a fascinating story told with honesty and sincerity. Others with more finely developed capacities for discrimination find additional pleasure in the profound understanding of human nature—implicit in all of Murnau's best

work—and also admire and appreciate the subtle artistry with which he fashioned this picture.

Yet, strangely enough, *Sunrise* is a film which has rarely been given serious consideration by film critics. Although all have not expressed the scorn which Paul Rotha recorded in [his 1949] *The Film Till Now,* most critics have either ignored it completely in their discussion of Murnau's work or passed over it lightly as an unfortunate, Hollywood-influenced production unworthy of its talented director. A quarter of a century, although possibly not an appreciable length of time for a film to live, may perhaps give us the perspective necessary to reëvaluate *Sunrise* and to understand why it has thus far stood the test of time.

Based on the short story "A Trip to Tilsit" by Hermann Sudermann, *Sunrise* tells of a young peasant whom a city woman seduces to drown his wife. He takes his wife across the lake to the city but cannot carry through the plan. The young couple rediscover their love for one another and spend a happy day in the city. On the trip home however, a storm blows up, the boat is capsized, and the wife is lost. The city woman, assuming that her plan has succeeded, goes to the house of the man who is nearly insane with grief and anger. He is choking her to death when word comes that his wife is safe. The city woman leaves and the man and wife continue their life together.

A motion picture telling such a story is bound to be a psychological melodrama. But in the hands of Fred W. Murnau, this story is told with such striking simplicity that it has the universal appeal of a fable. The film has a lyric quality which has rarely been achieved in moving images. And the camera which focuses almost exclusively on the young peasant and his wife is less concerned with the objective events of the story than with the meaning of the events to these two human beings.

A high tribute to the artistry of this film is the pervading naturalness and simplicity. For, although Murnau deliberately created a simple folk tale, he simultaneously has shown us the tremendously complicated human motivations and the subtle moods which lie behind the actions of even the most simple people. The postures and movements of the actors, the varying pace as the story unfolds, the lighting, the camera movement, and, above all else, the relationship of the central characters to the ever-moving backgrounds in which they are pictured have all been employed as means for helping us to share and understand the human emotions which are dramatized in this film.

Thus, Murnau was not content to characterize the peasant (as Sudermann did) as a boorish, overbearing and somewhat cunning man whom one can readily imagine capable of murdering his wife. Instead, the peasant in the film is pictured as an essentially simple, hard-working young man who loves his wife and child. By so doing, Murnau has given his central character greater universality; but, at the same time, he has raised the interesting psychological question of how it is possible for such a man to agree to murder his wife. In the opening sequences, Murnau sets out to provide the answer by detailing with remarkable cinematic skill and artistry the nature of the man's relationship to the city woman.

Under a low full moon, the man is seen moving slowly through the mists of the dark meadows to a rendezvous with the city woman. The camera slowly follows him, then moves on past him to a clump of willows, and finally on through the willow branches to reveal a clearing where waits the city woman, dressed in a tightfitting black gown, sophisticated, bored, twirling a flower in her hand. As she hears the man approaching, she hurriedly powders her nose; then she looks expectantly toward the camera as he comes toward her, and they embrace and kiss fiercely.

In the scene which follows, the city woman suggests that the man murder his wife. He is horrified, grabs her by the throat, and almost strangles her. As he gets up to leave, she comes after him. He tries to fight her off, but she holds him by the neck and then by the hair as she finally succeeds in kissing him passionately on the face, and then on the mouth. They drop to the ground; and bending over him with more kisses, she tells him, "Leave all this behind—come to the city." In large type, the words are repeated: "COME TO THE CITY."

Crucial to an understanding of the entire story is the rising emotional climax of the man's seduction by the city woman; and this is reproduced by the succession of carefully selected and combined background images, as well as by the actions of the players themselves. The sequence begins with what Lewis Jacobs has well described [in his *The Rise of the American Film* (1939)] as a mood of "quiet sensuality. . . . [in which] The overhanging mists, the dew, the full moon, the sinuous and constant movement of the camera—all combined to create a dark, somnolent mood." But this mood prevails only in the first part of the sequence. When the siren whispers in his ear that he should murder his wife, the scene becomes one of violent anger; and this mood, in turn, is transformed by the city woman into one of violent sexuality.

This last mood is accomplished, in part, when she forces him to submit to her kisses and is carried further up a rising scale of sexual excitement by the images (presumably of her creation) on the screen which suggest the excitement of city life. As the meadow behind them dissolves into a travel shot of a large city square at night filled with moving traffic, the couple appear to move into the center of the square, and eventually fade from sight as the whole screen pictures a succession of rapid travel shots. Whereas in the opening of the sequence the camera moves slowly and sensuously, now it moves rapidly and with abandonment in long breath-taking and dizzying strokes, peering down glittering streets and finally climbing recklessly up the side of tall buildings to take in the sky line of the metropolis alive with moving searchlights. The sexual significance of the dance-band and dance-hall images which follow is implicit: the dance-band leader with his back to the camera dominates the screen (the man who calls the tune and sets the pace for the dancers) while to his right, the screen features the dance floor with its scattered dancers; and this entire image moves in a circular fashion toward him as if gyrating to the wild music of his band.

But the movements of the dance-band images which next fill the entire screen are at an even higher pitch of excitement and are still more clearly sexual in their kinesthetic meaning. All of the musicians rise up and down in unison on the stressed beat; and, in the interim, they sway in unison from side to side. The sexual significance of this rhythmic pattern is once more related to the man and city woman when they reappear on the lower half of the screen where the woman is revealed on her knees doing a wild orgiastic dance to the music of the band. As the band fades from view, the city woman has obviously aroused the man into taking an active role as her sex partner. There immediately follows a blurry long shot of the village as seen from over the lake, with the full moon just beginning to pass behind a cloud. By means of its total imagery, this shot suggests the exquisite sensation of intense sexual pleasure (which, as suggested by this diffuse long shot, blurs awareness of objective reality); and, at the same time, it symbolically suggests the imminent climax of passion (as the moon starts to pass behind a cloud). But even more telling is the contrast between the hazy beauty of this long shot of the village and the dark ugliness of the following close-up which shows the matted bulrushes to reveal where the pair have lain together. Further, as the camera pans slowly a little to the left, the deep mud close by is revealed; and the camera follows their footprints through the mire until her high-heeled, patent-leather shoes come into view. Then, the camera tilts up to take in her black figure gathering together the rushes with which he is to save himself after drowning his wife. In these two successive shots, Murnau has contrasted the pure beauty of intense sexual feeling with the dark cold ugliness of the return to realities which follow when, passion spent, the man is left to face the meaning of his act.

This seduction sequence makes possible our understanding how such an essentially simple and boyish person could agree to murder his wife. The nature of the man's relationship to the city woman is clearly suggested by visual analogy in the early part of the sequence—before the murder of the wife has been proposed. From a view of the lovers, the film cuts to show the young wife seeking solace at the bedside of her child whom she holds on her arm and kisses. In the succeeding image, the city woman is holding the man on her arm as she kisses his face and neck, while he (in a comparable position to the child in the previous picture) lies back smiling. By this association of images, the relationship between the city woman and the man is defined: she, the worldly-wise woman, is as the mother; and he, as the child.

Also from the seduction sequence, we learn that this woman is sexually the active aggressor rather than a mere temptress. She has just suggested that he murder his wife, yet he allows himself to be seduced and thus commits himself to her and to her plan for murder. They have lain together on the rushes in the mud, the picture tells us; and he has become as cruel as she, for he has accepted her and is wedded to her and what she stands for. He feels guilt toward his wife, but he is bound by an even greater guilt to the city woman—the shared guilt of a sex act which has committed him to murder—which is made clear when we see him for the first time following his seduction. Gathering the rushes, the city woman turns to him and says, "After the boat has capsized, save yourself with these bulrushes. The rushes will hold you up—scatter them before you reach the shore and tell everyone she drowned by accident." (Throughout this scene, the man stands passive, his hands thrust into his pockets, his back to the camera, his shoulders hunched over in the depressed and somehow bestial posture, which remains characteristic of him until later when his resolution breaks, and he finds himself unable to carry through the city woman's plans.) The rushes are now symbolic both of the death plan for the wife and of the act of infidelity, two secrets which the man shares with the city woman.

Bearing the bundle of rushes, the man returns home and stealthily enters the barn. About to hide the rushes, the man is nosed by the horse and is so greatly startled that we become aware of how acute is his feeling of guilt. As he covers the bundle carefully with canvas, pressing it down out of sight with both hands, something in his manner and gesture suggests that in his own mind he is already hiding the dead body of his wife.

That the man's guilt centers upon this bundle of rushes is brilliantly suggested in his manner of awakening the next morning. In sleep, he moves slightly and turns his face toward the camera. Then his eyes abruptly open, and in sudden panic he sits bolt upright on the edge of the bed, his eyes wide with terror. There is a quick cut to a shot in which the camera moves in very quickly toward the bundle of rushes, now half-revealed as they lie under the canvas, and brings them into sharp focus in a close-up. Again we see his startled face, as he throws back the comforter and peers more closely. Realizing he has been dreaming, the man relaxes, puts his head down on his hands, and covers his eyes.

The camera's rapid truck in on the bulrushes, bringing them from a blurry to a clear focus, reproduces the startled sensation of awakening and carrying the fearful vision of a dream over into reality; and the man's reactions indicate the weakening sensation of relief which follows. More than this, we realize fully the man's great guilt as he awakens in horror to the thought that the rushes have been uncovered.

But Murnau uses still other means to show the man's acceptance of the city woman's plan to murder his wife. The very image of the murder which the man carries in his mind is the one originally supplied by the city woman. During their rendezvous in the field, the woman had first asked, "Couldn't she get drowned?"; and the caption dissolved into a picture of the husband standing in the boat and pushing his wife into the water. This image makes specific the woman's plan as her words urge him, "Then overturn the boat, it will look like an accident." Later when the man thinks of the plan to which he has become partner, this same image reappears and makes plain that *her* thought is dominating him.

Even more explicitly, the following morning the man weeps with remorse as he looks out through the doorway at his young wife feeding the chickens; and the ghost image of the city woman appears behind him, her hands

going around him as she presses him close and kisses him. He averts his face, and her image dissolves, but now again, she appears below him, smiling, her lips lifted to his, inviting a kiss. At the same time, a large close-up of her, kissing his hair, appears behind him. The size of this close-up, a ghost image which takes up almost a third of the screen, suggests the overpowering influence of her presence. He presses his clenched fists against his temples, and the images slowly fade.

Throughout the entire first portion of the film, we see a man in deep conflict. This is perhaps most vividly summarized in a single close-up shortly after he has asked his wife to go across the lake with him to the city. She gaily makes preparations for the journey, obviously convinced that this is a gesture of reconciliation. Then there is a close-up of the man's hands as they move down slowly and deliberately around the bundle of rushes, like hands around the neck of a victim who is about to be strangled. His hands lift the bundle up slowly, and the camera tilts up to reveal his face, taut and glassy-eyed. The grim gesture in relation to the symbolic bundle of rushes makes clear that although he feels impelled to go through with the murder of his wife, he feels deep rage toward the city woman; and it is she, rather than his wife, whom he would really like to murder (for when the city woman first suggested the murder, he attempted to choke her; and later, at the close of the film, when he believes his wife to be lost, he does in fact almost murder her in this fashion). Yet there appears to be no way out, no way to resolve the conflict. The depth of his resultant depression is suggested by his stooped posture, his sluggish walk, his unshaven and generally unkempt appearance, his dark brooding countenance, and his complete self-absorption which sets him apart from all that goes on around him.

In all of this, Murnau demonstrates an intuitive understanding of the dynamics of personality. But *Sunrise* raises and convincingly answers the even more amazing psychological question of how a woman can accept and forgive her husband after he has planned to murder her. To begin with, the man and wife are shown to be simple peasant people, and their life together has been a good one. We catch a glimpse of this early in the film when the servant tells of what their life was like before the coming of the city woman: "They used to be like children . . . carefree . . . happy. . . ." And in a brief flashback, we see the man plowing the field while the wife and child sit under a tree close by; then he stops his work to play with the child. Clearly, this young couple loved one another and enjoyed life together prior to the arrival of the city woman.

But the real answer to the question is to be found in the characterization of the wife as a gentle, loving, and genuinely happy woman. Above all else, her womanly qualities of tenderness and compassion are repeatedly emphasized—as she weeps and fondles the baby after her husband has left her to meet the city woman, as she lovingly covers her sleeping husband and gently strokes his brow the following morning, and as she tenderly stoops to feed the baby chicks and shows kindness toward the dog.

Actually in the wife, Murnau has created an image of pure goodness, just as in the city woman his creation is one of evil. Never for one moment is there a shadow of jealousy, anger, or even resentment in this woman whose husband has not only been unfaithful, but has planned her murder. Yet so great is Murnau's skill and understanding as a master of character that we do not resent this perfection in the wife; in fact, we are scarcely aware of it. For he has succeeded in making this image of human perfection completely real and understandable by combining mature serenity and compassionate understanding with childlike innocence and simplicity. There is no trace of righteousness in this woman; indeed, her goodness appears like the innate goodness of an essentially happy child. Although she is pictured as a mother, the wife appears to rely upon the servant who cares for the child. Indeed, the wife herself often seems to be like a child; for example, her appearance on the night of her husband's seduction: she is sleeping in the moonlight, and the long shot of the bedroom makes her seem small and childlike.

The wife's complete trust and reliance upon her husband is the key which makes her behavior appear believable. To her husband's infidelity and his attempt to kill her, she responds like a child whose trust in an adult has been broken; when he leaves her for another woman, she is heartbroken; when he attempts to murder her, her first reaction is one of fear and withdrawal, then of grief. These are the reactions of a child who feels his security completely bound up in an adult and who feels hopelessly incapable of doing anything to free himself from the relationship. Yet in the process of reconciliation, the wife shows a maturity and understanding which do not appear in the least inconsistent with what has gone before.

As the man and wife set out on their journey across the lake, an incident occurs which foreshadows the events to come. The dog, barking loudly, wants to follow them. (Perhaps the animal has sensed something wrong in the man's dark mood.) He breaks his chain, jumps the fence, and swims toward the boat. The wife wants to turn back at once; but the husband, with his hard and distant mood, turns a deaf ear to her pleas. (What is the suffering of a dog to a man who is about to drown his wife?) Only after the wife helps the animal into the boat does the husband turn back, unwillingly. As he walks the dog up the little hill back toward the kennel, the wife looks after him with troubled eyes. Now fully aware of his dark mood, she starts to rise as if to get out but soon relaxes, smiling a little at her own doubts; then sitting there with the rippling water filling the screen behind her, she begins to look genuinely frightened and again starts to rise. But the man comes down the path; and the wife, looking small and alone, sits back again in the stern of the boat. A moment later, they are pulling away from the shore—his body crouched over the oars, his dark face lowered, his thoughts centered within himself.

When they reach the center of the lake, the man rows more and more slowly and finally stops altogether. The wife leans forward toward him, her eyes wide with fear. He puts first one then the other oar into the boat and moves toward her, his hands hanging apelike by his sides, his face cruel, hard, and determined. The wife draws back in terror, then, as his figure looms over her, pleads for

mercy. A close-up of his two hands outstretched as if about to throw her overboard is followed by a pan shot of his arms thrown in a sudden gesture across his face; the awful moment has come and gone, and his resolution is broken. Quickly he steps back and frantically rows toward the shore, as she sits in the stern, her face covered with her hands. A rapid series of brief shots spell out the empty moments as, head down, he rows desperately with increasing speed, and as numbly she sits with her hands covering her face. Neither looks at the other, but as the boat hits the shore, he moves toward her and makes a gesture to help her out of the boat. Suddenly activated by fear of her husband, she rushes past him, jumps onto the shore, and runs away while he, calling and pleading, follows her.

The sequence of the trolley ride into the city with its series of long unbroken shots is one of the most volubly expressive passages of the entire picture. The interminable agony of these two human beings huddled on the platform of the trolley—she numb and remote, drawn as far away from him as possible, he mute and miserable beside her—is more acutely felt because of the landscape which flows endlessly past the windows. Following its winding track, the trolley carries them along the edge of the lake (where, as if in mute reference to what has gone before, a lone boat is seen out on the water), through the woods, into the outskirts, and finally into the very center of the city itself. Despite the gradually increasing activity around them, they remain unseeing until the trolley comes to a stop at the end of the line in the middle of a wide city square.

In the city, the camera follows the couple as each moment brings them a little closer to that moment of understanding which is the rebirth of their love for one another. The simplicity, the subtle beauty with which this is achieved on the screen is difficult to describe in words. The dangers of moving traffic, the impersonality of the crowds, the strangeness of the city places—all help to draw them together as he protects and guides her through the streets. Filled with remorse, he tries to reassure her of his love; but though she accepts the food and flowers which he offers her, his kindness only makes her weep the more. Finally they go into a church where a wedding is taking place. Seated in one of the rear pews, they listen together as the wedding vows are taken. "Keep her and protect her from all harm," the minister tells the groom, and the husband too is finally able to weep. "Wilt thou love her?" the minister asks; the groom nods solemnly. And the husband, tears falling, gropes blindly for his wife's hand and puts his head down on her lap, as she caresses and strokes his head. Now she guides him (as he guided her when she wept) out of the pew to the side aisle. In the corridor of the church, they are shown standing together, her arms about him, his face hidden on her shoulder. He drops to his knees, hiding his face against her. A close-up shows her stroking his hair, and he raises his face to ask, "Forgive me." In answer, she kisses his brow. There follows a close-up of two bells in the church tower, swinging in alternate directions, yet tolling together. The man is weeping now in relief, and she kisses his cheek. He smiles, and she, smiling also, gently turns his face toward her (out of shadow and into light) and kisses him tenderly on the mouth. There follows now a huge close-up of the two bells tolling in unison, ringing out the joy of new love and the harmony of human under-standing.

The reconciliation of this husband and wife is one of the most moving stories ever told on the screen, and it is told almost entirely visually. (There are only half a dozen titles in this entire portion of the film—from the time when the man sees he cannot go through with the murder until the scene just described.) So well are these two human beings portrayed that at no moment is there any doubt as to what they are feeling. Their emotions are expressed not only in their carriage, movements, and facial expressions, but by the telling way in which they are pictured in relation to the scene around them. In addition to the examples already given, we have them leaving the church and walking out into the square, unaware of the traffic around them. The background itself dissolves to express their subjective attitude toward reality, for they are seen to be walking dreamily through a meadow full of flowers which indicates that they have returned once more to the country scenes in which they first fell in love. But it is of supreme importance that each successive stage of the reconciliation is pictured at considerable length. We do not sense briefly, but instead observe over a period of time and in some detail the full expression of each feeling and attitude; and thus, we ourselves become fully steeped in the subtly changing moods of these two people. Furthermore, this slowness of pace allows time for us to absorb the deeper meanings implicit in the physical posture and movements of the actors. For example, early in the reconciliation sequence, the wife looks into her husband's face as she accepts the flowers which he offers her and then weeps into them. We cannot help but be aware (though perhaps unconsciously) that the wife is holding these flowers exactly as a mother cradles a baby in her arms. By his direction, Murnau time and again subtly suggests the thought behind even the simplest act and gesture.

Naturally for a contemporary movie audience, *Sunrise* moves at a much slower pace than today's sound films. But if the observer adjusts himself to this pace at the beginning of the picture, he will be rewarded except possibly for a few individual scenes in which the actors' motions have been slowed down to the point of tedium, to detract from rather than add to the sense of reality. However, the artistry of this film is so great that even in such scenes, Murnau's intention may well have been to create deliberately a partial sense of unreality. For example, in the tense moments when the husband walks toward the wife in the stern of the boat, his actions are so slow that they appear almost as slow-motion photography; and his posture and movements are therefore exaggerated so that they become strange and unnatural. A sense of the unbelievable actually happening before our eyes was undoubtedly exactly what Murnau was aiming for to make this moment appear like some strange nightmare. Today, however, the sense of the unbelievable goes beyond what Murnau intended; therefore, the effect he desired is not wholly achieved, possibly because the contrast in pace intended in this scene has been heightened further by the conditioning our eyes have been given during the intervening years through a much faster tempo of movement on the screen.

Perhaps the most remarkable thing about this motion picture is the fluidity of its images, which flow freely from objective to subjective realities and back without any break in continuity. For example, after the man leaves the city woman and returns home, he is shown lying on his bed and looking toward his wife (and toward the camera) who is sleeping nearby. He continues staring in horror toward her, and slowly water begins to appear on the lower rim of the screen, gradually flooding it completely and obliterating all else but his outstretched figure. He appears to be completely surrounded by the rippling water, while his eyes remain open in the same fixed expression of horror. Then gradually his figure is obliterated by the water; and, as the morning sun catches the ripples, the camera pans up to reveal the shore line of the town shrouded in the morning mist; and this is followed by a picture of his wife, standing in the morning light, looking down on him as he sleeps.

In addition to the complete fluidity of images, this segment also illustrates another characteristic of the entire motion picture—the richness of meaning inherent in the images. The image of the man staring in horror toward his wife is seen sufficiently long for us to grasp what he is thinking. Then, as the water begins to appear at the bottom of the frame, we feel from the image itself how this thought (of the drowning) slowly hems him in and finally surrounds him until he loses consciousness in sleep (as suggested by the obliteration of his figure beneath the water itself). The image has symbolic meaning also, for we see it is he (rather than his wife) who is drowning—he is being lost because of his acceptance of the city woman's plan for murder, just as he was lost once he submitted to her sexual advances. Indeed in this image, Murnau again links the murder plan and the seduction, for the image of the man's outstretched figure being gradually surrounded and finally submerged by the rippling water is also symbolic of the sex act which sealed his acceptance of the murder plan. And this same image may be interpreted as having future reference as well, for the waters which, in this scene, shut off his sight of his wife, are, we are told, the waters of the lake near the village—the same waters into which he will peer hopelessly, after hours of search, believing that she is forever lost to him.

Murnau's method of cinematic expression in much of the film is unique. As in the seduction sequence and others, the walk of the married couple into the center of the square outside the church conveys its meaning not by relating one completely fresh image to the next, but by retaining an image of the person (or people) and by slowly dissolving the background so as to make it expressive of the thought or mood of the person being shown. In some instances, the image of the person also dissolves into a mood picture which occupies the entire screen. Here, the step back to objective reality is taken by a brief intermediate one of the reappearance of the individual whose thought is being portrayed. This figure appears before the mood background disappears and before the original scene is reaffirmed. Thus both the objective situation and the emotions or thoughts of the person being shown are visually interpreted, and continuity between them is unbroken. So, Murnau's film moves with ease from the act

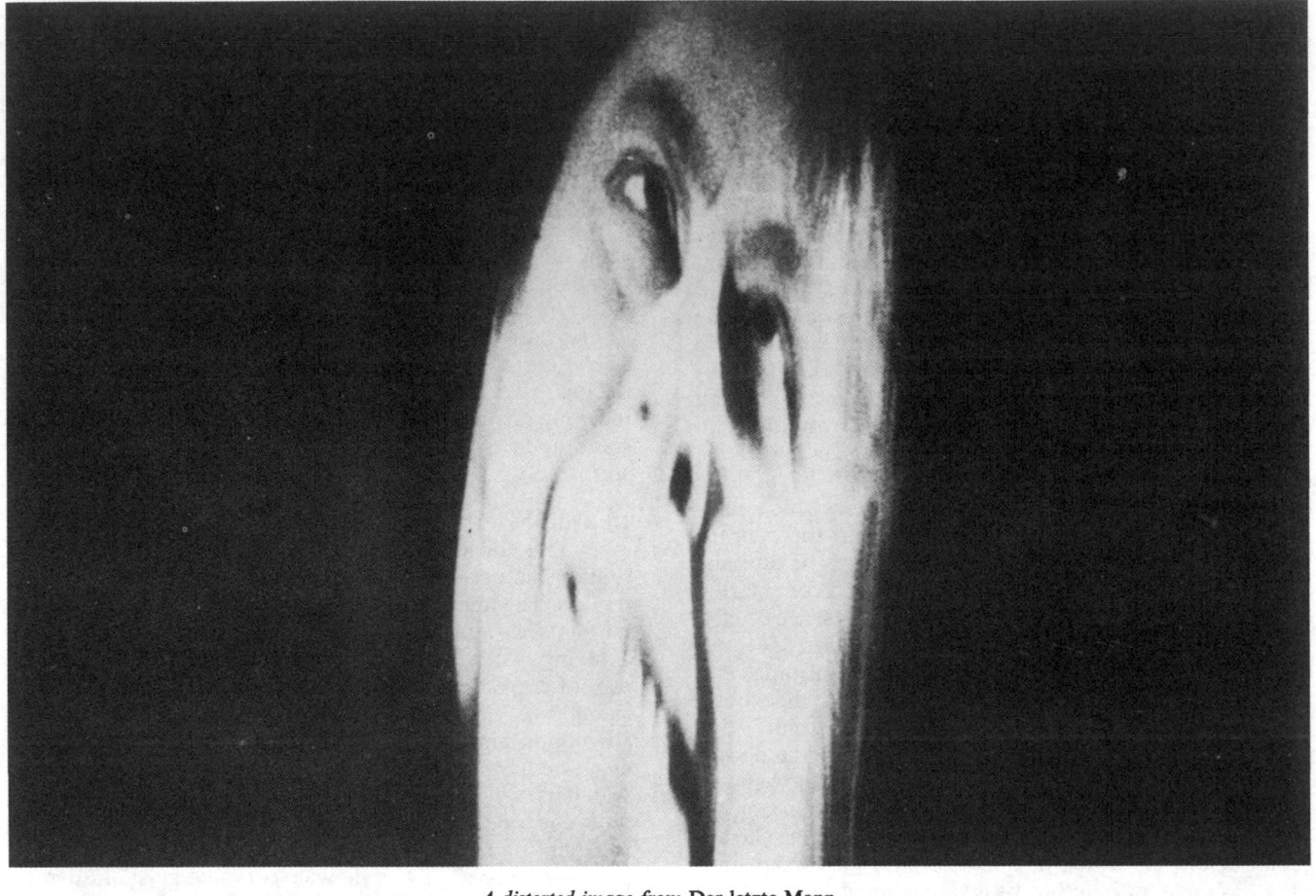

A distorted image from Der letzte Mann.

itself to the unconscious idea behind it, from the reality in which a character finds himself to his concurrent fantasy, and back once more to reality with complete freedom—all of which suggests again and again the depths which lie beneath the surface of human behavior.

Murnau uses other cinematic means for communicating the thoughts of his characters. For example, when a character speaks of a past or anticipated event, Murnau pictures it, and always in such a way that he distinguishes it from the immediate events of the story itself. For example, to represent a remembered scene (as when the servant recalls the happy days of the young couple), he slightly blurs the focus in order to contrast the vague quality of recollection with the more precise vision of reality. Or to picture a plan of action which is told by one person to another (as when the city woman outlines her plan of murder to the man), Murnau records the action in slow-motion which helps show that the act is one of passion rather than careful design. One of the remarkable things about all of these devices is that they are natural to the style of *Sunrise* and are consequently accepted without conscious realization that they are in any way unusual.

In this connection, and purely from a pictorial standpoint *Sunrise* is one of the most beautiful motion pictures ever made. Close study reveals that the composition of each shot in relation to the motion to be photographed within

it must have been planned in advance and executed with great care. Unforgettable for their sheer beauty in composition and expressive motion are such pictures as that of the wife, framed in the doorway. As she makes the simple gesture of stooping down to feed the baby chicks gathered around her, a feeling of womanly tenderness is captured in an image of lasting beauty. Another memorable moving image is the city woman's view of the village street from her bedroom window, as the peasants with their lanterns begin to gather for the night search on the lake.

Fred W. Murnau was a true motion-picture artist. Perspective, composition, action, balance of motion within the frame, and lighting were all fully conceived in advance and were carefully worked out on the set before anything was recorded on film. All of the sets for *Sunrise* were built with the perspective of the camera in mind. For example, the ceilings of the interiors slanted downward, walls converged slightly toward the back of the set, and floors slanted slightly. Yet, as seen through the eyes of the camera, the interiors appear only to have unusual depth. Those who worked with Murnau state that he was an artist who knew always exactly what he wanted and tirelessly aimed to achieve it.

Murnau expresses meaning frequently by means of subtle symbolism. The reeds which symbolize the man's act of infidelity as well as his acceptance of the city woman's plan for murder play a particularly ironic role in the closing portion of the film. After their reconciliation, the young couple spend a happy day in the city, sharing many small adventures. They sail home by moonlight, deeply content in their new love. But as they near home a sudden severe storm blows up. The man remembers the bulrushes which he had surreptitiously hidden in the prow of the boat and with which he had intended to save himself. Now he manages to tie the rushes with a rope to his wife's back as she clings to him in helpless terror. A moment later the mountainous waves sweep over them both, and the boat is capsized. The man is washed ashore, but the wife is lost.

During the search which follows, the bundle of rushes plays an important and pictorially dramatic part. Summoned from their beds by the husband, the men of the village leave in their small boats to search the lake. We see a long shot of the dark water as from the top right corner of the frame the body of the wife, supported by the bundle of bulrushes, floats on the tide downward to the lower left of the frame. The search continues, and the husband leans far out over the prow of one of the boats, his lantern almost dipping into the dark water, as he calls her name repeatedly into the night. Again, we see the wife's body move silently through the water across the frame. But this time a trail of rushes marks her path for one bundle has scattered, and her head is slowly being submerged. This trail of rushes comes into the light of the husband's lantern, and we see his horror-struck face. There is a beautiful and dramatic close-up of his lantern held over the dark water as a bunch of the rushes which support her wet shawl move into its light, followed by another bunch containing the rope. Again, we see a close-up of his horror-struck face, then, a shot of the old man at the oars who, after looking toward the husband at the prow, silently removes his hat and bows his head. Now the husband collapses, and one of the men comes to help and comfort him.

Thus, to the end, the rushes remain symbolic of the man's betrayal of his wife. The outcome—or what appears to be the outcome when the search is abandoned—is exactly as the man and the city woman had planned: he has been saved, the wife has been drowned, and the villagers accept it as an accident. But the meaning of these events to the man himself has now been completely altered by intervening happenings: whereas before he wished his wife dead so that he could go away with the city woman, now he wants his wife alive; whereas before he desired the city woman, now he is certain that he loves only his wife. He must suffer not only the anguish of her death, but the horrible guilt of knowing that only a few hours ago he had wished for it.

There are innumerable other instances of the use of symbolism throughout this film. For example, the flowers offered by the man to the wife after they leave the restaurant have a double meaning: flowers are an expression of love not only for the living, but for the dead. Symbolically they are an appropriate offering: they remind us (and her) that he had wished her to be dead; and, at the same time, they express his present feelings of love toward her. Also the two bells in the church tower ringing out together are expressive of the harmony and joy that the man and wife are feeling together; they are the wedding bells which mark their reconsecration to one another.

Meaning in *Sunrise* is also frequently communicated by establishing significant contrasts, either within a given image or by contrasting a mood or circumstance to an earlier one which occurred in the same setting. For an example of contrasting a character and his background in a given image in order to heighten our awareness about the mood of the character we see the husband, his head lowered over the oars in dark brooding, against the lake which glitters brightly in the sunlight. Similarly, the city woman, with her sophisticated clothes, her affected manner of walking, etc., appears in striking contrast among the simple peasant folk. This latter contrast is seen in reverse in the barbershop and ballroom scenes when the man and wife with their quaint country dress and manners mingle with city people. For contrast of mood in the same setting, we have the gay mood of the young couple as they board the trolley to return home, for this cannot be seen without recalling the agony which marked their trolley ride into the city. Nor can the husband's grief as he enters the bedroom and passes his wife's empty bed be seen without recalling his earlier entrance after his seduction by the city woman. These contrasts in mood are strongly felt not only because they occur with the same people in the same setting, but also because the camera records the scene from exactly the same angle to intensify our unconscious awareness.

In any discussion of contrasting moods in *Sunrise,* the striking difference in feeling between the first and second portions of the film must be noted. Lewis Jacobs has written,

> . . . the first half was characteristically Murnau. . . . This half had a lyrical quality and was removed from the real world . . . . The second half, obviously suffering from Hollywood interference, was completely different. Its mood was realistic; the lyricism was dissipated by comic relief; the universality was destroyed by melodrama.

The same contrast in the handling of the first and second portions of the film has been noted by many other critics, and most of them have similarly assumed that the shift was due to interference with Murnau's original purposes.

Actually, however, when we grasp the underlying theme of this film, no such interference is apparent. The mood which Murnau created in the first part of the film does indeed remove it from the real world, and this is exactly as Murnau had intended. He was picturing a situation of conflict which drew the man into a world where his real values and his normal perspective on his life had, through his infatuation with the city woman, been completely altered. A man obsessed, he moved in a strange and unreal world. This mood continues unbroken until the man finds himself unable to go through with the city woman's plan for murder, and at this moment the spell is broken. The period of reconciliation forms the transition to the second portion of the film, which Lewis Jacobs has correctly described as realistic. Now the man is no longer being driven by emotions which run counter to the main current of his life and remove him from reality into a strange and unreal world. From a man living in torment, he becomes once more himself, a simple peasant who is in love with his pretty wife. Consequently the entire mood and treatment become realistic. Notably, humor begins the moment the reconciliation has been completed: outside the church, people line the walks awaiting the appearance of the bride and groom; but the peasant and his wife come out of the church, their arms entwined, oblivious of all around them, and make their way through the aisle of curious and amused onlookers. And as the pair, imagining themselves in a flowering meadow, walk out into the square, our smiles turn to laughter, especially when they find themselves embracing amid the confusion and hubbub of stalled traffic. Finally, reaching the curb in safety, they, themselves, laugh heartily—not only at the incident but in relief at being at long last in the fresh air of normalcy. Here, the realistic mood and treatment, with accompanying strains of humor and gaiety, begin and continue unbroken until the tragedy of the storm when the man is once more thrown back into the world of nightmare. And now reality itself appears to have taken on the shape of that nightmare. The return to the earlier mood is tremendously effective, since it reminds us that reality often does confront us with circumstances which seem to reflect and stir up our deepest conflicts, throwing us into a torment which mocks the normalcy of our more healthy emotions.

Thus, not only are the changes of mood from unrealistic to realistic and back again completely in keeping with Murnau's purpose, but they come about gradually and understandably in terms of what is happening to the characters. With truly remarkable insight, Murnau has used the peasant's familiar background of the village to heighten the sense of nightmare and the unfamiliar scenes of the city as a background for the naturalness and genuine feeling between the husband and wife. And, with the three central characters themselves, the contrast also in a sense becomes one between the simplicity and naturalness of country life on the one hand and the complexity and synthetic qualities of city living on the other. (This contrast is humorously underscored, for example, in the series of alternating shots which place the natural grace and simplicity of the man and wife in counterpoint to the pseudo-sophisticated manner of a city couple who are among the onlookers during the peasant dance in the ballroom.) Although the realistic scenes of the city may not have the same lyricism of the earlier and final sequences of the film, they have a charm and warmth and reflect Murnau's sensitivity and understanding of people. Instead of detracting from the universality of the film, the sequences in the city add to it; for the two dominant moods of the picture, though in complete contrast, complement each other. They are "the bitter and the sweet" which Murnau refers to in his line of preface; they are what the modern psychiatrist might more accurately describe as the sharp difference of feeling which exists when we are dominated on the one hand by unconscious (socially unacceptable) drives, or on the other by conscious (socially acceptable) ones. That this contrast was Murnau's intent, rather than the result of interference from Hollywood, is borne out by the fact that Charles Rosher, Karl Struss, Frank Powolny, and others who worked with him on this picture all assert that Murnau worked entirely without studio interference of any kind and that the picture was, in every sense, one of his own making.

The happy ending of *Sunrise* has also been marked by some critics as a Hollywood imposition. Some, among them the noted British critic Paul Rotha, apparently feel that the picture should have ended in tragedy, that the wife should have been drowned in the storm, leaving the man to face the bleakness of life without her. Such a point of view is in a way understandable since, except for the happy ending, *Sunrise* almost perfectly fulfills the definitions of tragedy outlined by Aristotle in his *Poetics*. To begin with, the man fits Aristotle's definition of a tragic hero, for he is "neither eminently virtuous or just, nor yet involved in misfortune by deliberate vice or villainy, but by some error of human frailty." Such a man is by far the best hero of a tragedy, Aristotle tells us, "for our pity is excited by misfortunes undeservedly suffered, and our terror, by some resemblance between the sufferers and ourselves." In this respect the man in *Sunrise* is an ideal hero, for his weakness, as dramatized in the film, is a universal one, existing in every human being to a greater or lesser degree. Actually, the man's weakness is inherent in his passive tendencies, his unconscious desire—existent in all of us to some degree—to be led, controlled, possessed, and perhaps even violated by someone stronger than himself. These tendencies are activated in his relationship to the aggressive and dominating city woman, and because of them she is able to seduce him into the idea of murdering his wife.

Tragedy in its highest form must also involve "discovery," according to Aristotle, "a change from unknown to known, happening between those characters whose happiness or unhappiness forms the catastrophe of the drama, and terminating in friendship or enmity." In the Greek tragedies, this meant the discovery of blood ties between two persons, either one or both of whom were unaware of the relationship. In a modern drama, it is appropriate that the revelation should be one of a psychological rather than purely physical sort. Thus does the man in *Sunrise* discover that his wife, whom he has agreed to do away with, is actually the woman he loves. This "discovery" by the man of an already existing fact (which one feels is understood and fully accepted by the wife from the beginning of the story) is beautifully and subtly dramatized in the early city sequences, and culminates in their reconsecration to one another in the church.

Another primary element of tragedy as defined by Aristotle is "revolution" which he describes as "a change. . . . into the reverse of what is expected from the circumstances of the action." This, indeed, is what occurs in *Sunrise* in the latter portion of the film. After a happy day in the city, the young pair plan to sail home by moonlight—"a second honeymoon." All is well between them, and one expects that they will return happily to their home and that the city woman will be sent on her way. Just as on the trip across the lake to the city, we had a sense of impending danger, now by the very contrasting circumstances of the homeward journey, we are assured of a happy and safe return. But the reverse of what is expected happens. Thus the climax of the story involves "revolution" in the Aristotelian sense.

But inevitably in evaluating *Sunrise* in these terms, we come to the crucial matter of the happy ending itself. Now the modern idea of tragedy rests primarily on the question of whether the ending is happy or unhappy. This factor was not so important in the judgment of Aristotle who applied the term "tragedy" to many plays of high seriousness which ended happily (for example, Sophocles' *Philoctetes*). In defining what he regards as the "perfect" plot for tragedy, however, Aristotle does specify that "the change of fortune should not be from adverse to prosperous, but the reverse . . . " And it might be argued that had the wife been drowned *Sunrise* would have been in form almost a perfect Aristotelian tragedy. Such a fateful ending would even have met Aristotle's requirement of implied design, for the man in the end was forced to suffer by chance that which he had originally intended should happen. Since the artistry of this film is so great, and since it has been substantiated that Murnau completed his picture without interference of any kind, the question then arises as to why Murnau rejected an unhappy ending.

Before answering this question it may be well to point out that the short story on which the film is based did have a tragic ending. In the story, however, the man is drowned while his wife survives: he could have saved himself, but instead, in his efforts to save her life, he loses his own. This tragic ending appears to be completely correct for the story as it is developed by Hermann Sudermann, for in it the man is shown to be far more villainous than in the picture. Also in the short story, the man schemes over a long period of time with the woman (the servant in the household of the young peasant couple) and cold-bloodedly plans his wife's murder. Sudermann has the man redeem himself at the end by dying in the act of saving his gentle wife. Through such an ending, good triumphs over evil: the good wife survives, the evil woman fails in her murder plan and loses the man, and the man proves himself essentially good through his act of sacrifice. Thus, Murnau had two possible tragic endings from which to choose. On the one hand, had the wife been drowned, the film could have provided the emotional catharsis found in the highest form of Aristotelian tragedy. On the other hand, had Murnau followed the original story more closely, the picture could have been a tragedy in the modern sense of the word, carrying with it a sense of finality, of heroic grandeur, of exaltation.

Actually, neither of these endings would have provided a convincing or satisfying conclusion for the motion picture which Murnau made, for his entire development of the story makes the ending which he chose the only possible one for this picture. Murnau rejected both these tragic endings because either one of them would have negated the film's underlying mood and theme and destroyed the remarkable unity of his work. For Murnau did not want to make us feel either purged of emotion (in the Aristotelian sense) or exalted (in the manner of the more modern tragedy). From his film in its entirety, he wanted above all else simply to make us feel the wonder of human relationships—the complex motivations which govern the lives of human beings (even the lives of a simple peasant and his wife), the nuances as well as the quiet depths of understanding which exist between a man and a woman who love one another, the subtle moods which color the days of our lives. *For the theme of the picture is that not events themselves, but their meaning to human beings and the use to which we put them is what matters.* This theme is inherent in the development of the story which writer Carl Mayer and director Murnau worked out together, and it accounts for the unusual cinematic techniques which Murnau used throughout in telling this story—techniques which, as we have already shown, made it possible for him to place primary emphasis throughout on the *meaning* of events to his central characters. This theme is likewise borne out by the film's ending. Murnau shows how the man's affair with the city woman, even his attempt to carry through the city woman's plan for murder, brings the man and wife to a new awareness of their love for one another, thus enriching their lives. And, significantly, it is the bundle of reeds (symbolic of the man's infidelity and the murder plan) which the man uses to save his wife. By the end then, the reeds become the very means by which these two people are able to continue their life together.

Thus in *Sunrise,* Murnau tells us that good and evil are both part of living, that our mistakes and our suffering need not ruin us, but that what these events mean to us and what we do with them is what matters, for they may indeed become the very means by which our tomorrow may prove to be a better day. Life goes on, Murnau tells us, and bitter or sweet is essentially good, for there is always the promise of the sunrise and another day. (pp. 238-62)

> *Dorothy B. Jones, " 'Sunrise': A Murnau Masterpiece," in* The Quarterly of Film, Radio and Television, *Vol. IX, No. 2, Winter, 1954, pp. 238-62.*

Art—authentic art—is simple. But simplicity demands the maximum of artistry. The camera is the director's pencil. It should have the greatest possible mobility in order to record the most fleeting harmony of atmosphere. It is important that the mechanical factor should not stand between the spectator and the film.

—F. W. Murnau, quoted in Lotte H. Eisner's The Haunted Screen, 1952.

Lotte H. Eisner   (essay date 1965)

[*A German-born film critic, book reviewer, and journalist, Eisner wrote for Germany's* Film Kurier, *regularly contributed to film periodicals, and authored full-length studies on Murnau and Fritz Lang. The excerpt below was taken from the 1969 English translation of the 1965 revised edition of her* L'ecran demoniaque: Influence de Max Reinhardt et de l'expressionisme, *which was originally published in 1952. In the first part of the following excerpt, she analyzes camera effects in* The Last Laugh *and examines the film's place in the tradition of German Expressionism. In the second half of the excerpt, Eisner discusses Murnau's use of light, shadow, and other visual effects in* Faust.]

[In **The Last Laugh** scriptwriter Carl Mayer and director F. W. Murnau] tackle the tragi-comedy inherent in the destiny of a hotel doorman, proud of his braided livery, admired by his family and neighbours, the general of his own back yard. Having grown too old to carry the heavy luggage, he is retired and put in charge of the gentlemen's lavatories where he has to exchange his dress uniform for a simple white jacket. His family feel dishonoured and he becomes the laughing-stock of the neighbours, who in this way take their revenge for the adulation they have previously lavished on him. This is pre-eminently a German tragedy, and can only be understood in a country where uniform is King, not to say God. A non-German mind will have difficulty in comprehending all its tragic implications.

Murnau's imaginative power overlaps the framework of the *Kammerspielfilm* [which is an intimate genre of theatre, comprised of a small audience, dimly lighted sets where gestures and voice projection are subdued rather than exaggerated], and this is not solely because **The Last Laugh** contains more characters than is usual in the genre. Apart from the protagonist, who was to have been played by Lupu Pick himself and is played here by Jannings with an appropriate pompous aplomb, the other characters display a singular lack of depth: they only seem to be there at all to give this pathetic hotel doorman his cue. This is perhaps a remnant of the Expressionist doctrine that denies a personal life to all the characters with whom the hero is in conflict. A contemporary dramatic critic, referring to [Walter] Hasenclever's Expressionist drama *Der Sohn,* called such characters 'die Ausstrahlungen seiner Innerlichkeit', the radiations of the hero's inner essence. Vague puppets like the anonymous guests at the hotel, the neighbours of 'the last of men', exist only in the way they react to the hero, and only come to life when he appears. Once he has gone up to his room they can turn out the gaslights on the stairs. And when all the inhabitants of this microcosm busy themselves at their windows and on their balconies every morning, airing sheets and beating eiderdowns, their gestures seem to serve no other purpose but that of a modest, quasi-mechanical accompaniment to the main action, the brushing of the sacred uniform.

Murnau deliberately emphasizes this effect: the doorman going off to work in his gold-braided splendour is filmed in such a way that he seems much taller than the people he meets; during the wedding scene he appears at the centre of the image with more depth, sharpness and height than the guests around him, who remain blurred.

Nevertheless Expressionist techniques have but little place in this film. If Murnau uses them for the dream passages, it is only because this style has a capacity for fantasy which he can draw upon for the effects he judges necessary at this point. Of course, having, like all his compatriots, a weakness for symbols, he never tires—and Carl Mayer eggs him on—of bringing out, as soon as the opportunity arises, the 'metaphysical' meaning of an object. The porter's umbrella becomes as it were his sceptre, and he only gives it up to one of the hotel pages on rare occasions, with a heavily underlined magnanimity. The button torn from the doorman's livery as he is stripped of his uniform is filmed in its fall, a detail which makes the stripping the equivalent of a military degradation. Yet symbol in a work by Murnau never has the false profundity beneath which so many Germans conceal a solemn void. In the hands of Murnau and Mayer symbols relate to the action; the absence of this button, for example, constrains the doorman to remember, despite himself, the humiliation which preceded his dream of triumph. At the same time, the symbol takes on the implacable character of Destiny: when the doorman goes down towards the lavatory, it is the descent into Hell, and inexorably the leaves of the door swing to behind him. Lubitsch, whose taste for vaudeville delights in artificial double meanings, also uses incessantly opening and closing doors, but they are far from assuming the significance they take on in Murnau. In *Nosferatu* the closing of the gate by invisible hands emphasizes the fact that the young man will from now on be incapable of freeing himself from the doom which is about to overtake an entire town.

The merry-go-round of the revolving door, whose movements the doorman is so proud of controlling, becomes the whirlpool of life itself. Once again the inorganic world, the object absolutely necessary to the action, is invested with a transcendental meaning which is solemnly insisted upon in the German manner. But Murnau, unlike Pick, who easily lapses into an arid symbolism, succeeds in bringing his revolving door to life.

Objects can also determine or accelerate the peripetias of the tragedy: the movement of the door leading to the lavatory betrays the doorman's downfall to a women neighbour. The door swings again when the rich client, outraged at not being attended to immediately, sweeps past in search of the manager; the camera seizes upon this movement, which alternately reveals and conceals the slumped form of 'the last of men'. And the obstinate swinging of this door recalls the swinging of the light cast by the invisible lamp in the deserted cabin of the phantom ship in *Nosferatu.*

Murnau elaborates and counterpoints his symbols in the slow manner of his compatriots, and it is in this field that the influence of Carl Mayer is most felt. In the cloakroom the well-to-do client twirls his proud moustache, brushes his hair around a brilliantined parting, and performs exactly the same fatuous gestures as the doorman in his days of glory. Or the tension in the atmosphere corresponds once again to a state of mind: the despairing doorman goes home to his empty room in which the objects convey all the desolation of a morning after the night before, windows ajar with their meagre curtains fluttering, overturned chairs and dirty glasses littering the disorder, leftovers from the feast which are but the visible reflection of his spiritual despair. (pp. 207-11)

Murnau gives dimension to his symbols by varying the shooting angles. The doorman, resplendent in his uniform and puffed up with fatuity, is filmed from below, flaunting his belly, an enormous, ridiculous and cumbersome mass, like a Tsarist general or a capitalist in a Soviet film. After his disgrace, however, in the lavatory he is filmed from above, crushed by his downfall.

Karl Freund's camera tirelessly details the doorman's mortifications, going everywhere with him, rushing with him down the hotel corridors, playing with the beams of the nightwatchman's torch, which moves forward, flashes around, then moves forward again. German film-makers were always fond of the effects of light slipping along walls, giving depth to two-dimensional space. (pp. 211-12)

Under Murnau, the moving camera is never used merely decoratively or symbolically. Consequently every movement, even when his joy at having 'unchained' the camera is apparent, has a precise, clearly-defined aim. Thus, in *Tabu,* he showed each of the native canoes dashing out to meet a sailing ship; the camera shots are varied and inventive, and he cuts rapidly between the different canoes, making them cross each other and even sending the hero back to the shore to fetch his little brother, who has arrived too late; Murnau takes every opportunity to play on the ebb and flow of the narrow canoes slipping swiftly through the limpid water.

The success of the admirable opening of *The Last Laugh* is entirely due to the handling of the camera. Through the windows of the lift as it goes down we see at a single glance the entire hall of the hotel and the revolving door beyond, and we perceive the particular atmosphere created by the uninterrupted flow of visitors entering and leaving beneath the vibrant lights; in a series of breathtaking jumps outlines break and immediately reform.

Murnau's camera exploits all possible visual resources. It bares—slowly, skillfully, by degrees—the pitiful state of the doorman whom we could still see, a few moments before, safe and sound in the sumptuous security of his heavy livery: it pitilessly reveals the crumpled neck of a shabby jacket, the worn patches on a woollen cardigan, and moves steadily—for nothing must escape us—along his legs huddled in a pair of baggy wrinkled trousers.

Murnau likes to join mobile camera effects to the effects of shots through a pane of glass, just as at the opening he filmed the hall of the hotel from the lift. The scene of the turning-point—the manager informing the doorman of his appointment to a more modest function—is seen from a distance through a glass panel. The mobile camera moves in and focuses on the doorman's dismay and the manager's indifferent back. Through another glass wall we see the housekeeper charged with leading Jannings to his new post moving towards him with all the rigidity of Inexorable Fate, while the lost uniform glows in symbolic splendour from the wardrobe. (pp. 213-14)

The smooth surfaces of windows, which in German films so frequently replace that other smooth surface, the mir-ror, give Murnau special pleasure. His camera delights in opalescent surfaces streaming with reflections, rain, or light: car windows, the glazed leaves of the revolving door reflecting the silhouette of the doorman dressed in a gleaming black waterproof, the dark mass of houses with lighted windows, wet pavements and shimmering puddles. It is an almost Impressionistic way of evoking atmosphere: his camera captures the filtered half-light falling from the street-lamps, rays which the movement of the camera transforms into pulsing grooves of light; it seizes the reflections of toilet articles seen in the lavatory mirrors, and the slanting shadow of street railings through the basement window.

The doorman's drunken dream is the direct result of all the impressions he has received in the course of his conscious life. The leaves of the revolving door, now gigantic and Expressionistically distorted, collide with the sleeping man's brain and split it in two: a precise image of the schizoid nature of all dreams. The outline of the leaves is accentuated in proportion as their real form becomes indistinct: soon there is only the wooden frame left, then suddenly nothing but the corners whirling round and round. Are these corners the graphic representation of the ideal revolving door? Or are they intended to mean the flapping door of the cloakroom, which is at times superimposed on the spinning of the revolving door? Murnau's artistry shuffles, blends and overlaps the ingredient impressions of an entire destiny, just as, in the hotel hall of the dream, he uses hazy superimposed images—the ghostly lift going up and down—to condense impressions of haste, impersonality, incessant change and transitoriness. The meaning of the blurred anonymity of the extras around the doorman, who is presented in relief, finally appears to us in all its clarity: his tragedy is shown to us as it occurs within himself.

Murnau had shown the doorman in the manager's office, at a critical moment, failing to haul an excessively heavy valise on to his shoulders, and the swift cut had enabled us to perceive almost simultaneously the lively new doorman casually manoeuvring a huge trunk. Now, in his *Wunschtraum* (compensatory dream), a rejuvenated Jannings juggles triumphantly with an enormous trunk which a whole team of flunkeys have failed to lift. The Expressionist character of all this is obvious. The circle of hotel servants, larvae with identical livid expressions and shaved heads, who flock round the trunk which they are too puny to cope with, comes closer to the aim of 'the most expressive expression' than many thoroughbred Expressionist creations.

The 'unchained' camera totally dominates this drunken dream: movement and vision unite into a single dramatic factor giving driving force to the action which, outside the dream, remains static. In the passage which indicates the beginning of the doorman's drunkenness, when he can no longer tell whether the chair he is sitting on has suddenly whirled into space or whether it is the room that has started turning around him, the counterpoint of movements is composed in a masterly manner: the camera follows the stunning slide of the chair and films the distortion of objects as the doorman sees them. It is true that all Murnau's films exploit the possibilities of panning, tracking, and high-angle shots to the full, but here the 'subjective' camera becomes the point of departure for an extraordinary vortex of visions without the composition of the image ever suffering from it in the least. He dovetails his shots, leaves one direction for another in his montage, juggles with proportions until the hero's vertigo takes hold of us in our turn and we find ourselves being swept away in the movement. Never has the unconscious been evoked with such constructive violence. (pp. 214-17)

Murnau had already attempted to capture what Balázs calls 'the reality submerged by the dream' in his film **Phantom**: in a chaos of objects, a table starts turning, streets pass 'in a staggering daylight', swept along in a fantastic maelstrom, steps go up and down beneath feet which, even when they do not move, seem to be unstable.

Certain passages in the film other than in the dream bear the trace of an evolved Expressionism. Murnau's audiences were still used to the trances and frenzies of the ecstatic theatre; to make them understand the despair of 'the last of men' he shows him about to run away with his livery, momentarily petrified, listing to one side like a sinking ship. His tragic silhouette slants across the screen, against the wall he used to pass in front of every day in his puffed-up, uniformed complacency.

The Expressionists had already exploited this oblique body-attitude to emphasize exalted dynamism and its associated frenzy of gesture. It was thus that Wiene showed his diabolical doctor, full of excited emotion at the book revealing the secret of hypnosis: a trick shot makes the now gigantic Caligari rear up obliquely, petrified in the kind of paroxysm frequently found in the acting of stage-actors directed by Karl Heinz Martin, Jürgen Fehling, or even Piscator. Nosferatu is also shown in this attitude at the moment of giving up his last breath. We recall Kurtz's statement that the diagonal, with its expressive violence, sets up an unexpected reaction in the spectator's soul; Hans Richter also claims that a diagonal can in itself express extreme degrees of emotion.

Another Expressionistic device is the effect of gargantuan laughter—enormous gaping mouths, immense black cavities twisted in infernal mirth—which seems to engulf the 'last of men's' back yard. The scene, after the dream, of a woman neighbour's face anamorphosed in a distorting mirror, is another Expressionistic effect, and was adopted by Metzner for his *Überfall*. In the laughter-scene in the back yard the misogynistic Murnau spares no detail of the frightful bosomy women. Ufa did not miss the implications of this mass mirth; they were to use its effects with many variations, down to showing, on a single image, a dozen people telephoning at the same time. In *Metropolis* the covetousness of the spectators watching the robot's dance is expressed by a row of lustful eyes.

These days people criticize **The Last Laugh** for its slowness of pace. But Murnau's fondness for developing each detail, amplifying the least gesture or suggesting his hero's every changing expression with excessive minuteness, is due, all allowance made for Janning's over-acting, to the fact that the *Stimmung* [or the creation of mood or atmo-

sphere] of the *Kammerspielfilm* requires proper pauses. It is also due—however contradictory this may seem—to the fact that the use of the mobile camera, conferring greater fluidity on the title-free narrative, permits him to explore characters and objects at length. What is more, the narrative itself—a trivial anecdote of human vanity, a banal event deeply rooted in a Germanic world—demands this ponderous rhythm, this weighty immobility which can alone give it meaning. (pp. 217-21)

. . . . .

[Murnau's **Faust**] starts with the most remarkable and poignant images the German chiaroscuro ever created. The chaotic density of the opening shots, the light dawning in the mists, the rays beaming through the opaque air, and the visual fugue which diapasons round the heavens, are breathtaking.

The highlighted, slightly puzzling figure of an archangel is contrasted with the demon, whose contours, in spite of the darkness, have a grandiose relief. Jannings, as the demon, temporarily renounces his over-acting and for once is out-acted by his role; the demon appears really primordial, a creature from the first age of the world. (Though this was not to stop Jannings from flaunting his usual fatuity once the demon descends to earth, and exasperating the non-German spectator as much as ever.)

No other director, not even [Fritz] Lang, ever succeeded in conjuring up the supernatural as masterfully as this. The entire town seems to be covered by the vast folds of a demon's cloak (or is it a gigantic, lowering cloud?) as the demoniac forces of darkness prepare to devour the powers of light.

Carl Hoffmann's camera gives the terrestrial part of this film extraordinary modelling and has the power of impregnating everything, down to the cloth of a garment, with diabolism. Before transforming his Mephisto into a Spanish caballero, wearing elaborate silks, Murnau subtly confronts him, dressed in a puckered smock like some medieval villein, with the wealthy burgher Faust, in his rich, sweeping, velvet cloak. At times Mephisto's smock is gnawed by the shadows into depriving him of all resemblance to a human being. Like Scapinelli in *The Student of Prague* this little peasant suddenly appears to be a creature of Hell.

Murnau has Paul Wegener's and Arthur von Gerlach's gift for lighting costumes (though one may except the instance of the rejuvenated Faust, overdressed and a trifle androgynous, and that obsequious caballero Jannings at the fancy-dress ball).

In Faust's study the nebulous wavering light of the opening scenes persists. There are none of the arbitrary contrasts, over-accentuated contours, or artificially serrated shadows found in so many German films. The forms come through the misty light gently, opalescent. If Murnau is recalling the light-quality in Rembrandt's Faust etching, he interprets its function in his own fashion. Here the imprecise contours take up the supernatural theme of the opening, its resonance developing as if controlled by the pedals of an invisible pianist. In the auditorium the aged

Faust rears up, immense, in front of the semicircle of disciples: here the masses and values balance each other in a perpetual shifting of tonality, as forms shade out, a beard crossed by trembling rays of light turns into moss, and the alchemical retorts shimmer in the *sfumato*.

Even the movement of a cheerless fair is merely blocked out in its main masses of flattened tone. Not a ray of sunlight filters through the fairground booths, and the capers and somersaults of the sideshow performer are purely mechanical. Everything exists merely as the prelude to the imminent disaster. Suddenly panic breaks out: the plague sweeps away all these people and the storm overturns scaffoldings and rips apart the wretched booths. The huddled corpse of the juggler slants across the field of vision parallel to a shred of canvas straining against the tempest. Murnau's particular rhythm so dominates the film that the elaboration of this composition avoids the heaviness found, for example, in the scene with the young woman in [Hans Kobe's] *Torgus*. This is still more apparent in the passage where the monk attempts to halt the stream of revellers lusting after their last pleasures, and falls down. Decorative arabesque is replaced by incident, the dynamic of which increases the intensity of the action.

Throughout the film we meet with the richly subtle modelling deriving from Murnau's peculiar fascination with visual effects: e.g. the vision of plague-victims' corpses, the dead mother's pathetic marble features, or the monk standing waving his cross in front of the revelling mob. In the group surrounding Gretchen's pillory it is impossible to forget the heavy features of a slowly chewing rustic or the expressions of the choirboys, open-mouthed, innocent, unaware, like the beautiful ambiguous angels in Botticelli; Dreyer, close to Murnau in many respects, recalled these images in his *Vredens Dag (Day of Wrath)*. Contrasting with this circle of faces in high relief is that of Gretchen, strangely empty, stung by the snow, and this image recalls Lillian Gish, more moving, however, in *Way Down East*.

The light can waver over faces (the fleeing shadows of the unseen mob cast across the features of the dying monk) or stream in from all sides (Faust burning dusty tomes, Mephisto's blackened phantom conjuring the flames). The two effects are combined at the misty crossroads where Faust invokes the demon: a rising chain of circles of light casts a wavering glow over his face. Fiery letters flame across the screen, promising Faust—as Dr. Caligari before him—power and greatness. From inside a church waves of gentle light rising towards the vaulted roof with the hymn-singing spill out through the open door and condense into a kind of wall with which the creatures of darkness collide. These subtleties of lighting participate in the action, like the torchglow weaving through the town at night when the enlarged form of the once more demoniac Mephisto rears up crying murder, or like Gretchen on the pyre when she recognizes Faust beneath his aged features and leans towards him imploringly; the flames leap towards the sky and a globe of light hangs there as the symbol of eternal grace, the apotheosis of a fulfilled redemption.

The movement of the mobile camera is less easy to follow than in *The Last Laugh*. In the two-year interval Murnau had learned to gauge the depth of his tracking shots and the range of his pans, and to subordinate his enthusiasm to the rhythm of the film as a whole. The hilly terrain of his medieval town particularly lends itself to high-angle shots, but he contrives not to use them too often. If Carl Hoffmann's camera exploits the deep gash of a sharply-inclined stepped street it is because Gretchen's tragic destiny, embodied in her lover and his counsellor the devil, will stem from between these sharp-eaved roofs. Though Murnau obviously takes great visual pleasure in the famous panoramic shot during Faust's journey, this trip through the air does have a precise aim. But we may prefer the tracking shot of superimposed hills and valleys representing an anguished cry from Gretchen's open mouth—a cry thrown at Faust from the depths of her misery.

Histories of the cinema never tire of telling us that Dupont was the only director capable of filming a scene as seen by the actor, quoting the instance of the scenes filmed over an actor's shoulder in *Variety*. But Murnau had nothing to learn from Dupont. In *Nosferatu* the camera (the spectator) sees the small forms gesticulating in the alleyway through the eyes of the madman clinging to the roof. In *Faust* Murnau's technique is wrapped in such discretion that it almost passes unnoticed; nevertheless an American critic has singled out the scene in which the perspective of Faust pursuing Gretchen is centred on Mephisto who, by the mere fact of being invisible, manifests the sarcasm with which he greets these first steps towards her downfall.

The movement of images is complemented by counterpoints of rhythm: the pale-toned procession of children slowly climbing the steps towards the cathedral, holding taper-like white lilies, contrasts with the crowd of pikemen bristling with staves and flags as they advance towards the doorway. [The critic adds in a footnote: "The technique is the same as for the meeting of Tartuffe and Orgon. In another sequence the device is used to show the opposition between the mob and the monk trying to halt it."]

Murnau varies the shots of the stepped streets with great artistry: hooded men carry up coffins through the evil night, crowds bring up those stricken with the plague. If we watch this incessant fluctuation of masses attentively, we immediately realize to what an extent Lubitsch mechanized his crowd movements; here the massed bodies are given a tirelessly regular, pulsing *organic* movement towards the figure of Faust, healer by the grace of Satan.

The steeply-pitched roofs ornamented with tiles seem to be the only remaining elements of a semi-abstract architecture created for Murnau by Herlth and Röhrig, the designers of *Destiny*. This architecture is at a far remove from the authentic town we see in *Nosferatu* and closer, despite the precision of the line, to the setting Poelzig designed for *The Golem*. If the steeply-pitched roofs leading to Gretchen's house suggest many an instance of Expressionist architecture, the evolution it has undergone is shown by the duel scene in the little square, where the impression of enclosed space is reinforced by the corbelled upper storey jutting into the night. Here nothing is excessive, neither the shadows gnawing at the façade nor the doorway, which seems to become the entrance to some mysterious cavern; however slow Murnau's rhythm may be, the fascinating fluidity that he obtains from the camera cancels out any static ornamental heaviness the settings might have had. (pp. 285-93)

> *Lotte H. Eisner, "Murnau and the 'Kammerspielfilm'" and "The Climax of the Chiaroscuro," in her* The Haunted Screen: Expressionism in the German Cinema and the Influence of Max Reinhardt, *translated by Roger Greaves, Thames & Hudson, 1969, pp. 207-21, 285-93.*

Gilberto Perez Guillermo   (essay date 1967)

[*In the following analysis of* Nosferatu, *Guillermo discusses the film's setting and Murnau's manipulation of light, shadow, and action, arguing that "the natural world is the true protagonist" of the film.*]

Made in Germany in 1922, during the heyday of expressionist fantasy, F. W. Murnau's *Nosferatu* manifestly indulges the period taste for the horrific: the story is adapted (albeit freely) from *Dracula;* the vampire is monstrously conceived as the thin, repulsively bald Nosferatu, somehow suggestive of both a human skeleton and a rat. Yet, contrary to expressionist practice, the context is not of oppressively murky artificial sets. The settings are chiefly authentic: the ferocious landscape of the Carpathian mountains, the narrow streets and closely packed houses of a small town of the Baltic. The photography is limpid, almost naturalistic, free for the most part of elaborate lighting effects. Even the much-mentioned trick photography (which is in fact rather less prominent than film historians would have us believe) is of an elementary purity: self-opening doors and jerkily fast-moving carriages appear not amidst hazy shadows, but against a real, three-dimensional world brought into clear focus.

In retrospect, it is only too clear that a conventionally expressionistic film could scarcely have been expected of Murnau; that he could not have succumbed to elaborate fantasy in *Nosferatu* any more than, ten years later in *Tabu,* he succumbed to [Robert] Flaherty's dogged naturalism. The natural and the fantastic are but elements of an overall design, sometimes separate and distinguishable, sometimes inextricably mingled. Neither can be said to dominate the film.

The use of natural settings may at first glance seem simply a trick, a decoration designed to render the fantastic narrative more plausible and effective. In Dreyer's *Vampyr,* for instance, the deliberately blurred natural settings remain simply a stylistic device, brilliant but not indispensable: *Vampyr* probably would not be basically changed if shot in, say, an appropriate Old Dark House. *Nosferatu,* on the other hand, is unimaginable except in natural settings. To think of it as a more or less effective rendering of a given narrative is to miss its greatest riches: its strange, impassioned poetry; its sense of mystery, of the opaqueness inherent in a world seemingly fully revealed before our eyes; its view of the world as inescapably oppressive and sinister, however natural and commonplace

it may seem. Far from a decoration on the *Dracula* story, the natural world is the true protagonist of *Nosferatu.*

Cinema, like painting, can concentrate on the rendering of solid objects, each having a specific importance and each perceived from a specifically suitable point of view; or it can take the opposite course and impose a single viewpoint on the entire visual field, the privileged object of perception being, effectively, empty space. (Most films, of course, combine the two approaches.) These two different modes may be characterised, respectively, as the cinema of close-ups (Dreyer, Dovzhenko, Eisenstein) and the cinema of long shots (Murnau, Mizoguchi, Antonioni), although these techniques are not strictly necessary for the accomplishment of one or the other purpose.

Close-ups are the means by which, in Eisenstein's films, an object is isolated from its surroundings and perceived, from successively different angles, as possessing palpable bulk and a definite shape. Conversely, the unity of the visual field in Mizoguchi's films rests largely on his use of long shots. Yet, persistently as Dreyer brings the faces of his characters into privileged attention, only in *Jeanne d'Arc* does he actually rely extensively on close-ups. And Murnau can use a close-up—recall that exquisite shot in *Tabu* of Reri hiding behind Matahi's back as they confront the police officer—without for a moment losing sight of the rest of the visual field. It is, then, less a matter of an actual use of close-ups or long shots than of the impression created. An object, one might say, is effectively in close-up if it draws attention to itself, to a peculiar quality and meaning all its own; effectively in long shot if it becomes virtually meaningless when disengaged from the rest of the visual field.

Expressionist cinema is a cinema of objects and mists and obtrusive sets, of space obsessively filled. Murnau's cinema, on the other hand, is primarily a cinema of empty space. Signs of expressionism which appear in Murnau's films are for the most part (an exception is *Faust*) only superficial; and his best work (*Nosferatu, Tabu,* parts of *Sunrise* and *Tartuffe*) rather avoids them. In these films, as in [Diego Rodríguez de Silva] Velázquez's *Ladies in Waiting* and *The Spinners,* space becomes the central object: the space traversed during the trolley ride in *Sunrise,* immeasurably more expressive than any of the individual objects passed; the space surrounding the lovers' hut in *Tabu,* charged with the menace of a hostile world. Even the revolving door in *The Last Laugh,* often cited in the textbooks as an example of the use of symbolic objects in silent German cinema, is less prominent in itself than as a pivotal point in the space around it.

Like Velázquez, Murnau looks past the foreground and into the background; deep-focus photography, to judge from the evidence in Lotte Eisner's recent book, was employed from quite early in his career. Attention is not restricted to a sharply delimited object standing in the foreground, or even to a number of significant objects strategically placed within the frame. It is dispersed throughout the whole, throughout space; and space, fluid in nature and not likely to be contained within sharp limits, palpably extends all around the frame of the film. Murnau's compositions, his shots of details, have a certain imbalance, a deliberate incompleteness which relates them inextricably to the world around them.

With Murnau a shot is fundamentally unstable, its structure constantly threatened, from all directions, by an encroaching outside world. The charged and restless quality of his images stems, in part, from the sense they convey both of the immediacy of that outside world and of its ineffable strangeness. The slow entrance of a ship into frame, interrupting the dance of celebration of Reri and Matahi in *Tabu,* physically marks the beginning of a sustained assault on the world within the frame, on the lovers' private world into which the world outside forces them to retreat further and further. This differs not only from the static and self-enclosed images of a Dovzhenko, but also from a director technically much closer to Murnau, [Jean] Renoir, where the sense of a world existing all around the frame, far from causing instability and unrest, comes about perfectly casually. It is, perhaps, a matter of a simple difference in basic attitudes: Renoir warmly accepts the world, while Murnau finds himself hopelessly at odds with it.

Despite their obvious differences in story and setting, *Nosferatu* and *Tabu* are in some respects remarkably alike. Of Murnau's surviving films, they are the only ones set chiefly in natural surroundings, the only ones to have been produced outside the major German and American studios. Among the films of the high silent period—when ostentatious technique was the order of the day—they are both admirably restrained. Furthermore, they are surprisingly similar in structure. Excluding the prelude in the Baltic town in *Nosferatu,* both films begin in settings far removed from ordinary experience—in one case the spectral landscape surrounding Nosferatu's castle, in the other an impossibly idyllic island of the South Seas. These remote worlds, immensely dissimilar as they are, both contain a menace. It is a menace which at first seems specifically associated with the setting, but which in fact, we come to realise, is far more fundamental. In both cases the menace expands—in both cases transported by means of a ship—to a more immediate, ordinary world. There, despite what, in *Nosferatu,* may seem like a happy ending, the menace prevails.

Yet to compare the two films in this way is to neglect not only the obvious, but also rather more significant differences. In *Tabu,* as in *Sunrise,* a fundamental polarity exists between the leading characters and their environment, a polarity in terms of which both the environment and the characters are virtually defined. In *Nosferatu,* on the other hand, the physical world almost invariably stands at the centre, an intensely charged pole lacking a balancing counterpart. The vampire himself, prominent and impressive as he is, is generally photographed from a distance—across an archway in his castle or amidst deserted streets in the quietly sleeping Baltic town—so that he appears, disturbingly, as somehow merged with the physical environment. There is, to be sure, an obvious analogy between the young married couple of *Nosferatu* and the leading characters of *Sunrise* and *Tabu.* Yet in the earlier film the couple is much less conspicuous a physical presence, the acting is of a coarse—and viewed today somewhat risi-

ble—expressionistic variety. Furthermore, in *Nosferatu,* despite various attempts (of considerable historical significance), the subjective point of view of the leading couple is never quite successfully established. The characters, then, prominently as they may figure in the original narrative, come across rather weakly in the completed film; and all the more so in contrast with the fiercely portrayed, the disrupted and oppressive world that surrounds them. Of such a world, toward which Murnau's imagination always gravitated, one finds in *Nosferatu* the undiluted essence.

If, in a film like *Tabu,* one were to respond directly to the physical environment, the result would probably be close to the paradisiacal calm of Flaherty's *Moana.* It is the peculiar poignancy of Murnau's film that, from the point of view of the lovers, nature's beauty acquires somehow a sinister quality; a quality so incongruous with what one would naturally expect that it evokes a sense of betrayal. Reri and Matahi, at the same time that they hope to attain a happiness, a harmony with nature, that never seems quite out of reach, come to feel a freezing indifference, almost an overt hostility, from the natural world.

In *Nosferatu* there is no such ambivalence. Despite its density, the earlier film has none of the dissonances of *Tabu*; its effect is of an unequivocal, an almost unrelieved blackness. The long and perfectly composed line of coffins that we see in *Nosferatu* through the young wife's window is in itself, without reference to the wife's point of view which we are supposed to share, a definitive image. We respond directly to the regularity of those patterns of death, to the quiet fierceness of that image. What concerns us here is not, as in the later films, the characters' alienation and their attempts to resist the encroachments of the world outside; it is rather the absolute barrenness, the inescapable hostility of that outside world.

Nosferatu begins with a somewhat perfunctory prelude set in the Baltic town. A real-estate agent, obviously insane, acting under the long-range influence of Nosferatu, assigns his young and only recently married clerk to transact some business in Nosferatu's distant castle. Rather surprisingly, since the trip will for months take him away from his young wife, the clerk seems very happy to go. It is then that *Nosferatu* properly starts; almost at once we are immersed in the weird Carpathian landscape. The part of the film that follows—the sequence around the vampire's castle—perhaps comes closest to the conventional horror film. The world is remote, fragmented, invested with a sinister atmosphere by very deliberate means—often by the use of trick photography and of expressionist angle shots. This part of the film, in fact, is fashioned, like the original story, after the classic nightmare plot (of which the whole of Dreyer's *Vampyr* is another version), in which a succession of bizarre and seemingly unconnected events is seen from the point of view of a journeying young man.

Where Murnau yet differs from the Dreyer of *Vampyr,* and from most other exponents of the horrific, is in the clarity of his technique, in the perfect simplicity with which he presents what are usually rather self-conscious and elaborate effects. The camera tricks in *Nosferatu* have often been criticised for their crudity. An obvious criti-

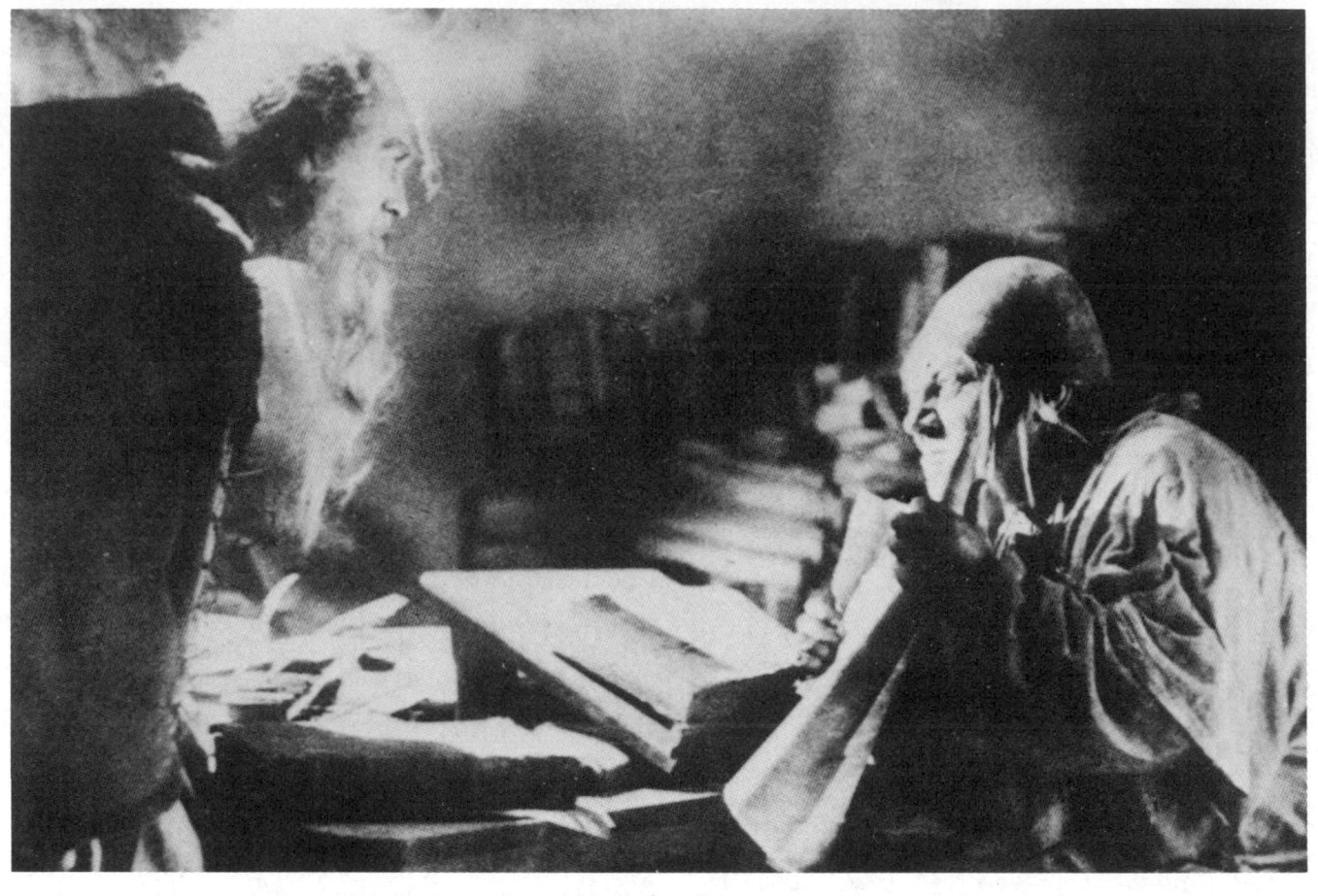

A scene from Faust.

cism, one might say, since the technical resources of **Nos-feratu** are manifestly very limited; and yet it overlooks what seems to be a quite conscious refusal on Murnau's part to bridge the gap between the natural and the fantastic, to blend more acceptably the jerky motions of doors and carriages with their natural surroundings. The trick photography simply and defiantly unsettles a context of reality. The result is bewildering; and—as in the scene in which the clerk watches, from a window of the castle, the incredibly rapid loading of a carriage with earth-filled coffins—often quite effective.

The trick photography, like the odd camera angles, Murnau uses deliberately as an endistancing device. As such it becomes less and less prominent as the film moves from the remoteness of the Carpathian castle to the greater immediacy of the Baltic town. The clerk, having (literally) miraculously survived the encounter with Nosferatu, sets for home. Parallel to him, and with the same destination, a ship advances carrying Nosferatu and the earth-filled coffins. The two parallel motions, as well as various details from the Baltic town, are bound together in an intricate cross-cut structure (no doubt influenced by Griffith); a structure dominated by the recurring, massive ship; and culminating, with accumulated force, in the highly charged image of the ship's arrival in town. The clerk's journey plays only a secondary role; significantly, even as

his wife awaits his return she instinctively turns toward the sea, the sea that brings Nosferatu and the coffins. The cross-cutting builds up an impressive rhythm; sometimes, one feels, at a sacrifice of meaning. Some of the details included do not seem relevant, and one especially regrets the presence of a biology class studying examples of natural vampirism. Yet it is in the context of this rhythm that Murnau succeeds in investing some perfectly familiar objects—the ship, the wind, the waves—with a quality of the supernatural; thus setting the ground for the town sequence with its indissoluble fusion of the quotidian and the uncanny.

Aboard the ship the vampire has exterminated the entire crew. It is the plague, the townspeople believe as they inspect the phantom ship that has arrived at their docks; and the plague spreads all across town. With the plague scenes the film attains, at the same time as its dramatic climax, the climax of directness toward which, from the deliberate remoteness of the early passages, it has been steadily moving. The streets and arches, the Nordic houses and pointed roofs, are unblinkingly photographed in deep focus and natural light. The small-town milieu is vividly and effortlessly captured; in a few shots a sense is conveyed both of the greyness and boredom of the town's past and of the bleakness and horror of its present. Yet, for all the increased directness, all the unyielding photographic naturalism of these scenes, something, one senses, remains elusively beyond what the camera can capture. The physical world, placed almost tangibly before our eyes, is still somehow distant, inscrutable, ghostly.

For Murnau has shot these scenes almost exclusively in long shots; long shots which at first glance would seem to reveal everything, yet leave everything imprecise; which refuse to give a clue, to isolate an especially meaningful detail, and gradually make us aware that isolated details would in any case have no meaning; which in attempting to show us the whole, show us only that the whole is outside our grasp. The devastation of the little bourgeois town, horrible as it is in itself, seems only the reflection of some horror outside our grasp—a *supernatural* horror, to be sure, and yet one which seems not extraneous but ingrained amidst the natural surroundings.

The tone is set, from the start, with the simple yet resonantly weird scene of Nosferatu's arrival in town—at night, supposedly, though as shot the scene actually conveys the impression of early morning. Tiptoeing across deserted streets, Nosferatu, who has shown himself capable of propelling ships and carriages at fantastic speeds, now politely relinquishes his powers in order not to disturb the town's sleep. The supernatural, it seems, has snugly adapted itself to the town's rhythm of living. The monstrous figure of the vampire, photographed from a distance, appears, in the greyness of early morning, uncannily to blend with the natural surroundings. Indeed, since Nosferatu does not appear, after that scene, until the end of the film, it seems as though he had dissolved into the texture of those cheerless façades.

The ensuing plague, supposedly caused by the vampire's direct intervention, seems actually, to judge by all appearances, a perfectly natural phenomenon. We may be told that the familiar mark of the vampire is found in all victims of the plague, but, except for an earlier shot of the dead ship captain, we see no direct evidence of this; and the vampire himself is nowhere to be seen. Furthermore, the townspeople, it sometimes appears, are not aware of the presence of anything exceptionally sinister in their midst. Death is received with suitable solemnity, not uncontrollable panic; coffins are carried in orderly procession; a town official calmly goes marking with a cross the houses of the dead.

And yet an unshakeable strangeness pervades those quiet and composed funeral patterns. Just as the arriving vampire yielded to the tone and quality of the small-town milieu, so now this entire milieu subtly reflects the special circumstances of Nosferatu's arrival. The coffin that Nosferatu carried with him finds a repeated echo in the coffins of victims of the plague; the town streets are still quite as deserted, quite as silent and sombre as they were on the night of Nosferatu's arrival. It is as if, almost imperceptibly, the town's sleep had turned into death. And so the town's quietness and solemnity come to appear as a sign not so much of the townspeople's composure and control over the situation as of the intangible, strangulating grip of the supernatural. Horror and solemnity overlap, at times seem almost to coincide. One cannot speak of the supernatural as a hidden presence amidst the commonplace,

but of its becoming in some degree identified with the commonplace, with the very conventions and outward manifestations of bourgeois life. As always with Murnau, the surface, the visible image, unable to encompass the whole, is yet bound intimately to it. Appearances are not deceptive, they are simply opaque, inherently incomplete; and precisely by our sense of their opaqueness and their incompleteness they make us aware of the whole, aware of the invisible.

Just as the physical world, and not any of the human characters, is the true protagonist of *Nosferatu,* so death, and not the monstrous eponymous vampire, is its true subject. Some say that the vampire symbolises death: if so, how can the film end, in abrupt and arbitrary reversal of its steady linear development, with the death of the vampire, the death of death? In fact, *Nosferatu* ends, as one would expect it to end, with the irreducible triumph of death. This is only reaffirmed by the death of the vampire—and, at the same time, by the death of the young wife who in giving herself to him causes his death. Without the film's closing sequences Nosferatu's relation to the death he supposedly brings about would remain unclear; for what strikes us most in the plague scenes is the utter impersonality, the inability to associate disaster with an individual agent.

In the splendid, underrated *Tartuffe* that Murnau did with Emil Jannings the true character of Tartuffe is not fully revealed, in his sinisterness and his vulnerability, until the scene in which he glides down the stairs to meet Elmire in her room. In much the same way (and in circumstances similar to those of Tartuffe's undoing), the true nature of the vampire is revealed fully only in the last sequence of *Nosferatu.* The vampire, as he is shown heading toward the wife's bedroom, abruptly coming out of the large dilapidated house that faces the young couple's house, is not only frightening but also, at the same time, aching, vulnerable. And upstairs, in the wife's bedroom, he becomes for the first time a mere phantom disconnected from the physical world, an impotent shadow struggling to possess the young woman's body, lecherously staying by her side until after sunrise. Daylight, which has done nothing to dispel the strangeness and horror that cover the town streets, now, through the window, kills the vampire.

A title then states that after his death the sick no longer died, and happiness was regained; yet it would be impossible for the camera to return to those streets and show them as happy again. The wife's sacrifice has been to no avail. What has vanished into thin air is merely a shadow; the substance of a hostile world is left intact. (pp. 150-53, 159)

Gilberto Perez Guillermo, "Shadow and Substance: Murnau's 'Nosferatu'," in Sight and Sound, *Vol. 36, No. 3, Summer, 1967, pp. 150-53, 159.*

John D. Barlow   (essay date 1982)

[*Barlow is an American educator specializing in German, film studies, and women's studies. In the excerpt below, he offers a stylistic and thematic analysis of* Nosferatu.]

F. W. Murnau's *Nosferatu, eine Symphonie des Grauens* [*Nosferatu, a Symphony of Horror,* 1922], the first and still the most remarkable of all vampire films, presents a host of problems to anyone interested in studying it. The original negative of the film is lost; all existing versions are copies. None seems to be complete. Enno Patalas is supposed to have "unearthed several scenes unavailable in other versions" of *Nosferatu*. There are further complications caused by a film released in 1930 with the title *Die zwölfte Stunde—Eine Nacht des Grauens* [*The Twelfth Hour—A Night of Horror*], an "artistic adaptation" of *Nosferatu* made by a Dr. Waldemar Roger, in which scenes have been rearranged and added, many of them obviously not the work of Murnau. Fortunately, the original shooting script of Murnau's film exists, along with his own emendations. There also is a difference in the names and intertitles used in the different prints of the film. Most prints available in the United States refer to Count Dracula or Nosferatu, Renfield, Jonathon Harker, Nina, and so on. This is also true of the screenplay published by Roger Manville, presumably a shot-by-shot protocol of a print in Great Britain. But the shooting script refers to an entirely different cast of characters, as follows:

> Count Orlok, the Nosferatu [Dracula]
> Thomas Hutter [Jonathan Harker]
> Ellen, his wife [Nina; also Lucy]
> (Lord) Harding, a shipbuilder [Westenra]
> Anny, his sister (Ellen's friend) [Ruth]
> Professor Sievers, municipal physician [the town doctor]
> Knock, a house agent (Hutter's employer) [Renfield]
> Professor Bulwer, a Paracelsian [the professor; also Dr. von Helsing]

The story, freely adapted from Bram Stoker's novel *Dracula,* is presented as a diary chronicling a plague in the fictitious city of Wisborg in 1843. In many prints of the film the plague takes place in Bremen in 1838. Murnau's shooting script frequently refers to Wismar, where much of the film was actually shot. One John Cavallius, the diarist, claims to have studied the Great Death in Wisborg and tells the story of the vampire Nosferatu as an explanation of its cause. The idea that epidemics of the plague were actually the work of vampires is an old superstition that survived into the nineteenth century.

Thomas Hutter (Jonathon Harker), a happily married young man, receives an assignment from his eccentric and obviously diabolical employer Knock (Renfield), a real-estate agent, to travel to Transylvania to arrange for a Count Orlok (Count Dracula) to buy a sinister old deserted building in Wisborg (Bremen). Hutter leaves his wife, Ellen (Nina), with her friend Anny (Ruth) and Anny's brother, the shipbuilder Harding (Westenra). He travels into the mountains. While dining at an inn, Hutter remarks that he must hurry on to Count Orlok's castle, causing immediate alarm among the peasants at the inn. That night in his bedchamber Hutter discovers a book about vampires. He reads in it a little, then contemptuously sets it aside and falls asleep.

The next day, after a full day's journey, the coach hastily leaves Hutter by a bridge crossing to a barren landscape.

The terrified driver refuses to go farther, claiming that the other side of the pass is haunted. Thomas crosses the bridge and is met by a strange coach that jerks at supernatural speed along the road. This coach takes him on a journey through an eerie and forbidding forest to Count Orlok's castle. The coach drives away, leaving him alone. There are no servants. The huge doors of the dilapidated castle open by themselves. Within the courtyard stands Count Orlok himself, who tells Hutter that all the servants are asleep. He invites his guest to have something to eat. When Hutter accidentally cuts himself, the Count becomes strangely excited at the sight of the young man's blood.

Hutter falls asleep and awakens the next morning to discover two dots on his neck. At twilight Count Orlok appears again, this time becoming obsessed with Hutter's picture of Ellen. Back in his room Thomas discovers the book of vampires that he had been reading earlier at the inn and that apparently had been accidentally packed with his luggage. This time he reads it intensely. Then the Count, looking more horrifying than ever, comes after him. Back in Wisborg, Ellen, having nightmares, cries out, calling his name, as if trying to warn him.

Back at Orlok's castle, Thomas has awakened in despair. He discovers a coffin with Count Orlok's ghoulish face staring up through the rotting boards. Later he watches as the Count has a wagon loaded with coffins at great speed. Orlok climbs into the last, the lid covers it, and the driverless wagon moves off.

Here there is a long parallel-montage sequence in which we see the stages of Count Orlok's journey in his coffin to Wisborg, Hutter's recovery in a hospital and journey back home, Knock's insanity and incarceration in an asylum, Ellen waiting for her husband's return, and Prof. Bulwer's (Dr. von Helsing) experiments with carnivorous plants and polyps. Count Orlok, as Nosferatu the vampire, kills everyone aboard the ship transporting the coffins. The sequence rises to a rapid montage climax in which the ship's ghostly arrival, Hutter's reunion with Ellen, and Knock's escape from the asylum all coincide.

At this point the plague is raging in Wisborg. Count Orlok has established himself in his new home, conveniently with a view of Ellen's room. Ellen finds the book of vampires, the one her husband had been reading in Transylvania, and learns that only a chaste woman who keeps the vampire by her side till dawn can break the spell. Against her husband's orders, she opens her window when she goes to bed at night. Orlok comes to her and spends the night with her, sucking her blood. At dawn he is annihilated in the light and disappears in a feeble puff of smoke. We see Knock, back in his cell in despair, slump over, then Ellen dying in Hutter's arms. A shot of Count Orlok's castle in Transylvania in ruins signifies the defeat of the vampire's power.

The artistry of *Nosferatu* is not always immediately evident on first viewing. This is particularly true when the film is seen on television. Although most of it takes place at night, none of it was shot at night. Originally, tinting was used to convey the darkness of night. In the untinted prints currently available the viewer can easily be put off by the daytime appearance of what is known to be a night-time event. Viewers need to remind themselves, for example, that Nosferatu carries his coffin through the city at night when the streets are deserted, otherwise he would have to be lying in his coffin. Also, the acting of the supporting characters is unimpressive. Only Max Schreck as Count Orlok and Alexander Granach as Knock seem to bring anything uniquely personal to their characters. Schreck, who did not otherwise distinguish himself as an actor, is probably the most remarkable vampire ever screened, not only visually in his rodentlike appearance and movements, but in actually creating [what Siegfried Kracaver terms in his 1947 study *From Caligari to Hitler*] a "tragically ambiguous" count, a conception elaborated by Werner Herzog in his 1979 remake of the same title.

The use of outdoor photography and filming on location, both for the scenes in the town of "Wisborg" and those in Transylvania, was unusual in German film at this time. [Fritz] Lang, for example, had a huge artificial forest built in filming *Siegfried* (1924), a practice Leni Riefenstahl was to continue in working on *Tiefland* (released 1954) in the early 1940s. Furthermore, as we have seen, the expressionistic conception of films like *Caligari* and *Raskolnikow* depended primarily on studio architecture. Nevertheless, even with all the outdoor, naturalistic photography, it is impossible to think of *Nosferatu* without taking into account the expressionistic milieu of its origin and the expressionistic spirit in its conception.

Natural images of waves, clouds, trees and forests, blades of grass, leaves driven in the wind, mountains, and animals, both domestic and wild, abound in *Nosferatu.* They are always beautifully filmed, often at twilight or from compelling camera angles. Most importantly, they are edited into the action with great sensitivity, never appearing on the screen too long to become tedious or too short to become ornamental. Murnau's steadfast rejection of ornamentation makes these images significant. There are no gratuitous images. Every shot counts. Nothing is wasted and nothing is used as a vague attempt to create atmosphere. Murnau well understood that the viewers of a horror film are looking for terror and that precise suggestion, rather than elaboration and shock effects, is the best method of frightening them, since it encourages them to participate by using their imagination. They invest images with terror, particularly the animal images, like the running horses and the hyenalike animals edited into Hutter's confrontation with the people in the country inn at dusk as he travels to Count Orlok's castle. The use of animals in *Nosferatu,* both in this way and in the emphasis on Orlok's rodentlike appearance, is an implicit expressionistic gesture. Theodor Däubler wrote in 1919, "The return to the animal through art is our decision for expressionism." He was probably thinking of Franz Marc's paintings of animals, Kafka's animal stories, and the animal symbolism of much expressionistic poetry.

These images help to create the notion of an alien world. The environment of horror films is nearly always such a world, inhabited by strange beasts and customs. In this different world a Western European individual very easily seems clumsy and out of touch. Hutter's status as a foreigner is later mirrored by Count Orlok's alienation in northern Germany. As with the Gothic horror in the 1933 *King Kong* and Jacques Tourneur's *I Walked with a Zombie* (1943), we are dealing here with a confrontation of two civilizations. Hutter becomes regenerated later as he returns home, while the ultimate foreigner, the vampire count, unable to die and unable to live as a human being, brings the plague and its rats with him wherever he goes. *Nosferatu* is, to some extent, an exercise in xenophobia.

Once the alien world is established through suggestion, Murnau uses a little trick photography, stop action and negative film, to adumbrate the weirdness of the strange world. The stop action, meant to convey the ghostly progress of Count Orlok's coach, causes it to move along by swift jerks. The experiment does not work. The effect is more comic than horrifying. But the use of negative film to show an uncanny and forbidding forest, with the coach moving through it at normal speed, is brilliant and remains one of the most striking images of film expressionism, especially since it is brief and occurs only once. The smoke or mist that rises in the foreground only adds to the image's power. This negative shot is a perfect sign of a threatening, alien world, being as it is a totally opposite distortion of the real world. Count Orlok's world is the other side, the negation of the one Thomas Hutter comes from, and therefore its complement.

A few other tricks are used. Stop action is used again to show Nosferatu piling the coffins on the wagon, getting into one of them, and then being driven off at breakneck speed by a driverless wagon. Later, the Count materializes in a double exposure sitting on a pile of coffins in the ship's hold, while a sick man lies in the hammock in the foreground. When the ship's mate smashes his axe into the coffin later on, Nosferatu rises up in front of him, stiff as a board and pivoting up from the feet. At the end of the movie the vampire fades away in a double exposure. Most of these tricks are unobtrusive. The stop action is a blunder, as it was in depicting the ghostly speed of the coach earlier. Nosferatu's popping up from the coffin as if on a spring has a fascinating grotesqueness about it, while the double-exposure appearance and disappearance are stock-in-trade representations of ghostliness.

Fritz Arno Wagner's camera angles are contrived to emphasize a sinister and threatening aspect of things, as in views of Count Orlok's castle and some of the shots taken in the city, particularly the glimpses of the crowd chasing Knock through the narrow streets. These angular visions are often subjective shots, representing the character's frightened or distorted sense of reality. But they also reveal something about the objects perceived. This is particularly true in two views of the crowd pursuing Knock after his escape from the asylum. The first is from the roof of a building where he is seen looking down at the crowd in the narrow street below. The crowd is secure and safe in the civically defined space of the narrow street, throwing stones at Knock on his precarious perch of expulsion. While Knock may be mad, these righteous citizens are more coldly brutal than he. Once again the vampire world is established as just the other side of the collectively vicious bourgeois world. The second view is the one of the crowd tearing up the scarecrow it had mistaken for Knock, shot from his point of view very close to the ground. The frenzy of this mob of normal people as it rips a human effigy to shreds is in this instance more arbitrarily vicious than the obsession of the man it is chasing or even of Nosferatu.

One of the most impressive uses of camera angles is in the shots of the spectral ship sailing to Wisborg with its cargo of coffins infested with rats. The ship is always shown without any signs of life aboard, even before Nosferatu has done away with the entire crew. One particular shot of only the sails, in gray tones, taken at an oblique angle looking upward, leaves even the motion of the ship to the imagination. The sails are filled with wind, but nothing flutters. The viewer has the sense of total silence and lifelessness, of a death ship moved by an uncanny power. Eisner has pointed out how the ship moving across the entire screen, both at sea with all sails set and eerily and ominously entering the harbor at night, creates a chilling phantom effect. The sails and the ship's rigging are prominent in the spectacular low-angle shot of Nosferatu from the ship's hold as he moves menacingly toward the captain.

Eisner also mentions Murnau's sense of depth of focus and how effectively he creates an atmosphere of horror by simply having the actor move steadily toward the camera, a device similar to the depictions of Homunculus. This is particularly evident in the scene in Hutter's room at the castle where Count Orlok, with a hideous expression on his face, moves toward Hutter—we see it all from Hutter's viewpoint—and into his room through a door that opens and closes by itself. The steady, unspectacular movement of this grotesque creature toward the camera, with only occasional cuts to Hutter to emphasize the subjectivity, is far more chilling by virtue of its relentlessness than a fussy mixing of different shots would be. Although the vampire is costumed and made up to be frightening, it is the simple cinematic procedure used by Murnau that gives the scene its great intensity.

This high degree of intensity is found also in the anxiety and tension conveyed by two other devices discussed by Eisner: Murnau's use of rapid montage when Hutter returns home and Nosferatu arrives with his coffins and the framing of the funeral procession through Wisborg's narrow streets. The latter is viewed from a high window with a bar right across the image. The crossbar frames the scene, contrasting with the verticals of the buildings along the street. The effect is one of entrapment and confinement, underscoring the helplessness of the viewers—both the people looking out the window and the actual viewers of the movie—to do anything about the plague and the death in the city at that time. Another terrifying framing shot, this one supported by dark shadows, is the first meeting between Hutter and Count Orlok at the castle. Hutter has just entered through an enormous door which has opened by itself. He sees the Count emerge from the darkness, walking nimbly in his direction. The next shot is from behind Orlok, who stands there tall, his shoulders slightly hunched, his arms crossed in front of him. In the distance, a silhouette in the archway, the small figure of Hutter pauses, as if startled—a perfect abstraction of a fiend watching an innocent enter his lair.

Nosferatu is famous for its attention to inanimate objects and the significance they play in its narrative. A number of these have already been mentioned, but it is still important to call attention to their expressionistic characteristics. First of all, Knock's letter from Count Orlok: an unbelievable hodgepodge of scribblings from various alphabets and magic sign systems, projecting the other-worldly madness of the Count into Hutter's apparently safe bourgeois world. The building Knock suggests as Orlok's home is ideal for a vampire. Rotting, dilapidated, almost a ruin, it is the perfect abode for the living dead. In the beginning, when Hutter, having returned home to prepare for his trip to Transylvania, runs into his room to pack, we can see Orlok's future house through Hutter's window. It is a remarkable shot: Ellen is at the side of the door, facing the camera in great distress, while Hutter rummages around in the other room. Behind him, the building is ominously visible in the window as if mocking Ellen's concern, a sign of the destiny waiting for both of them. Another inanimate mocking observer is the skeleton clock that watches over Count Orlok and Hutter during the latter's first few hours in the castle. In fact, this scene, filmed in the studio, reveals an ingenious medley of objects. The tiled floor, with its suggestion of Byzantine splendor and tyranny, and the high-backed chairs, elongated like Count Orlok himself, provide the scene with a suggestion of that linear and angular dynamism so familiar in *Caligari*. Not only does the ship which brings Nosferatu to Wisborg have ghostly properties, but the small boat that carries him across a still body of water to his new home has them as well. The boat moves with its own power as the vampire stands in it holding his coffin. There is a slight resemblance to Böcklin's painting *Isle of the Dead*.

Murnau combines the contorted faces of his two demonic actors—Max Schreck as Nosferatu and Alexander Granach as Knock—with decaying natural objects to create images of horror. Hutter's discovery of Nosferatu's staring face looking up through the rotting planks of his coffin is one such image. Toward the end of the movie Knock hides from the pursuing crowd behind an old stump. The camera first focuses on the stump, then Knock appears from behind it, his bald pate slowly coming into view, at first scarcely recognizable. Then we see his face, grinning with insane glee, before he bounds off. In both cases, rotting wood, combined with faces of an unearthly madness, becomes an index of the vampire's mode of existence: neither living nor inorganic, but "undead" (the name *Nosferatu* comes from a Rumanian word meaning "undead").

Nosferatu's terminal visit to Ellen is filmed in a remarkable shadow sequence. The vampire has been waiting at the window, desperate for a sign from Ellen. As he waits at the window a helpless victim of his own passion, the pathos of his character is clear. This is no ordinary monster, so familiar to us in the countless vampire films from Tod Browning's 1931 *Dracula* on, but an expelled and alienated figure, incapable of anything except the pursuit of precisely that from which he is alienated. One has to wait until Werner Herzog's *Nosferatu* to find again a vampire capable of arousing such sympathy. It is just this capacity for generating sympathy that makes Murnau's vampire so much more terrifying than most of his more inhuman counterparts. He gives his vampire human dimensions by not indulging in any obligatory blood-letting or trick transformations like the growing of fangs. The only transformation is gradual: Nosferatu's fingernails seem to have grown to an excessive length in many of the later sequences, usually when he is on a rampage. But we never see them grow. There is no significant physical difference between Count Orlok and Nosferatu.

When Ellen opens her window, Nosferatu moves away from his window with the subdued frenzy of a lecher suddenly to be granted his deepest longing. We see him leave his Wisborg home in stiff, cadaverous excitement. But inside Ellen's home, going up the stairs and opening her door, he is a shadow, almost spiderlike in the way he moves along the wall. This well-known shadow sequence is virtually a primer for the expressionistic shadow. Any shadow is an abstraction, a two-dimensional, colorless outline, without detail, of an individual. After the intense pathos of the shots of Nosferatu at the window and leaving his home, it would not have been possible to show the heightened intensity of his meeting with Ellen in photographic detail without falling into a mawkish anticlimax. The vampire's shadow had already been used in the same way during his attack on Hutter at the castle. There the horror of his approach could not have been surmounted by the actual attack, so we only see the shadow covering the terrified Hutter. Here, outside Ellen's bedroom, the shadow, in itself an image of doom, becomes the ultimate abstraction of the vampire's stealth, lust, and demonic possession, a shadow slanted on the wall, distorted out of shape in proportions larger than life, the clutching fingers exaggerated into claws. The viewer's imagination, already stimulated and programmed by what has preceded this scene, has to provide the details. The same is true in the following bloodsucking scene: the viewer gets a glimpse of the vampire's rodentlike face bending over Ellen, then, in the shadows, his bald pate and the forms of their two bodies. Jack Kerouac, in a note written for the New York Film Society, found this to be a "horribly perverted love scene unequalled for its pathetic sudden revelation of the vampire's essential helplessness."

Murnau's film is the story of an outsider. We never hear anything of Count Orlok's past. There is no attempt to explain or even partly justify his obsession as in most other vampire films, including Herzog's. This point is even more significant when we realize that it is the first of its genre. Murnau was not taking his audience's knowledge of vampire lore for granted, but he assumed that the audience would recognize the tragic dimension in Count Orlok's alienation from humanity without belaboring the background or personal history. Furthermore, as is the case with many expressionist heroes, Count Orlok has no woman and is denied the comforts of home. Murnau's vampire longs for human contact but must destroy the human beings he comes into contact with and ends being destroyed himself by the one human being who gives her-

self totally to him. Obsessed by a destructive desire, he is destroyed by it in the end. (pp. 81-91)

> *John D. Barlow, "Light and Shadow," in his* German Expressionist Film, *Twayne Publishers, 1982, pp. 64-98.*

Dudley Andrew   (essay date 1984)

[*Andrew is an American educator and critic who frequently writes about film. In the excerpt below, which was printed in a slightly different form in the August 1977 issue of* Quarterly Review of Film Studies, *he provides a thematic and stylistic examination of* Sunrise, *claiming that the film succeeds as a dialectic between the characters on the screen and the audience.*]

The fullest criticism of a film like **Sunrise** is a never ending one, a dialogue with the film that demands several "critical passes," each one qualifying its predecessor. We may well begin with a view of its relation to Murnau's themes and styles or with its particular evocation of the pastoral, the melodrama, or the medieval fable, but we will be forced to return to it again to go beyond these initial positionings of the film in an *oeuvre* and in a genre. These successive readings, suspicious or synthetic, develop a history of experience and of understanding so that the term "artwork" might better be thought of actively, as that which is done and changed, rather than passively, as an object to be weighed, measured, and catalogued.

The primary and overwhelming subject of **Sunrise** is self-consciously announced in the film's first titles: the bitter and the sweet, mixed in every life, are hailed as the timeless strains of a song celebrating the life of two humans. In a first passage through the film, **Sunrise** promises to deliver to us a concept, and observe for us the achievement, of humanity. The film's drama chronicles the movement toward this goal as a movement toward the bond of the couple.

This is a song of *two* humans and this two-ness is essential to the possibility of both song and humanness. Since the plot involves three characters, since Margaret Livingston received star billing along with Janet Gaynor and George O'Brien, this can only mean that she, the cat woman and vamp, is nonhuman, inhuman.

Just as this most natural of worlds refuses a song of three, so also is a solo inconceivable. The world of **Sunrise** is erotic at its base. Man needs woman and she him. Together they produce the song. The energy of the unattached human as it searches for or neglects its mate is capable of wreaking inhuman suffering. The film traverses that suffering and promotes a discovery of the song of humanity as a ritual in which the free sexuality of the individual is anchored by another human. The naturalness of the sun beaming down its approval on the couple at the end is not available to the individual. When light floods the wife feeding her chickens earlier in the film, its sanctifying glow is qualified by the mise-en-scène which divides the outside from the inside, the left from the right, making us recall the pathetic distance between her bed and that of her husband; she is no Beatrice. Her achievement comes only in relation to her husband as she is transformed from the wounded bird of the café to the mothering bird of the church.

It is in the church that the couple is furthest from home, yet it is here that they reachieve their union and validate the family and community life behind them. Before they begin their voyage home (stepping out of the church to the approval of a city community and marching toward and within a rear-projected Edenic landscape), a beam of light delicately mottled by an ornate window grid fixes itself upon them. The film will end when another such beam can transfigure them and their home, but only after the man expiates the offense that has driven them to the city and extirpates its cause. In the church they bow before a higher law and are illuminated; in the finale they become that law, become the sun, and illuminate the entire community. In John Donne's terms we witness their "canonization": this is the community's song about a pitiable couple who are not merely returned to the welcoming community but whose return validates that community. From the outset, then, *Sunrise* is a purgatorial community ritual flowing from the screen to the spectator, who is invited by the song into the ritual and into the community. The first viewing of *Sunrise* is a complicit and integrating one.

What is it that gnaws at the achievement of this canonization, that makes us view this film askance? Surely it is the suspicion that the community of 1927 America has cleverly designed this "miracle" for its own aggrandizement and perpetuation. The song of two humans becomes the song of nature, and both not only are domesticated at the end but decree the law under which domestication becomes a value. In this sleight of hand the ideology of the average spectator undergoes a glorification achieved by the very characters (the potentially universal Man and Woman) whose problems brought that ideology into question. Since their capitulation to the laws of society (the laws of family) is pictured as the triumph of love (eros and agape ringing out from the church bell tower) they bring back from the church not only their determination to live within the law, but a renewed grace, love, which is the source of the law.

Thus, through experience innocence is regained, not only the personal innocence conferred by forgiveness but a communal innocence that celebrates the origin of the laws of the family and validates a posteriori the drama that questioned those laws. As Mary Ann Doane has so forcefully shown [in her "Desire in *Sunrise*," *Film Reader* 2, 1977], the image of the sun serves to mask the contradictions in this solution.

> The Man, in the beginning of the film, is tempted to test and transgress this law, but the law is re-invoked as supreme by the closure of the film. Furthermore, the man reassumes the place of the father within the family unit. The sun here serves to sanction and naturalize the Symbolic Order and the symbolic activity of the text. . . . Yet, the final signature of the text is not that sun which is the most natural thing in nature but an artificial stylized sun.
>
> The natural originary presence (of the sun),

sanctioning the textual work and its symbolic activity, is always already metaphorical—and everything, including nature, becomes Text.

Our suspicion before *Sunrise* is certainly triggered and sustained by the inordinately powerful effect of the antisocial elements which a first complicit viewing thinks to have suppressed. No doubt the marsh scene and the two frightening water journeys receive extraordinary elaboration precisely to increase the confidence of the community when they are dissolved like morning fog; but they also seem to have their own attraction. Here, of course, we are in the midst of the aesthetic of the horror tale, the mystery novel, the gothic romance. And here *Sunrise* could be, and has been, justly compared to Murnau's earlier work (especially *Nosferatu* and *Faust* but *Phantom* and *Schloss Vögelod* as well) and to filmmaking practice in the twenties generally. Indeed, it invites full-blown genre comparisons and those comparisons in turn demand an analysis of the social and psychological impulses behind this kind of story.

But rather than pursue investigations into such determining forces as William Fox's position in Hollywood, Hollywood's position in U. S. culture, Murnau's homosexuality, the decline of German Expressionism, the function of the pastoral within recently urbanized societies, the problem of Christianity in a capitalist order and so on, all of which naturally arise here, I would like to emphasize the particular achievements of *Sunrise* in aestheticizing its problematic. While *Sunrise* is certainly another song validating the chaste life of the family while brutally banishing the sexual visions it couldn't help but entertain, while it is another compulsive version of a general myth, a symptom of a lasting psychosocial scene, the film continues to haunt us in its particularity. In our next return to the film we must not neglect its claims to universality which stem from its ideological work as allegory, but we must attend to the "progress" of this film in relation to its themes. For Murnau has reimagined this theme in a way that is new. While his problematic can be thought of as banal, powerful, ideologically complicit, eternal, or whatever, his film, as a visual meditation and interpretation of that problematic, permits us to make a gain, achieve a perspective, on its dark psychosocial origins, origins that will continue to fascinate us as they fascinated Murnau, who returned to this problem again and again.

The surplus of meaning which overruns the banks of *Sunrise*'s traditional narrative is first of all a visual surplus. The precision of the compositions suggests a second text and a second context for meaning. And it suggests this immediately, for following the title cards announcing the narrative and thematic concerns of the film is a series of four autonomous shots grouped under the heading "Summertime—Vacation Time." Under the aegis of this title and attributable to no source, these shots are able to establish a "look of the world" before that world becomes implicated in narrative. Thematically vacation time promises to test the values of a leisured class, but it suggests as well a visual variety based on free movement, free activities, and the boundlessness of a bright outdoors.

Narratively Murnau's four shots denote, in succession,

"Good-bye to the City," "Vertiginous flight toward pleasure," "Relaxation," and "Welcome to the calmness of a new environment." But visually they form a much more pointed dialogue, a dialogue that continues through the remainder of the film. The first shot, a stylized painting of a train station, suddenly breaks into action as one train and then another pulls out of the screen. Shot 2 superimposes these trains on opposing diagonals in Eisensteinian conflict. Shot 3 is a split-screen vision of a stately ocean liner on the left which inherits the travel motif from the frantic trains, while on the right a woman in a bathing suit leans on a pier. From the bottom of the screen a man surfaces, nearly pulling himself up on the woman's legs. The final shot (actually three related shots) is classically composed by a camera that is inside a vacation boat as it nears a village shore. Two thin masts trisect the screen. Small sailboats run laterally across the top. Following an insert of the shore, the movement of the camera becomes autonomous as it cranes up for a full look at the village before descending toward the dock where onlookers are gathered to welcome it.

The shots establish four different graphic paradigms, and each of these paradigms will play a key role in the film's visual drama. The final shot of the prologue, with its intricate movement and perfect composition, might well be considered the most "typically Murnau" and it is with this that we begin.

A. Let us call its effect "classical," since it is in itself harmonious and geometrically proportional and because its simplicity allows us to read into it allusions to established graphic traditions. The passengers are arranged on the boat as in some early nineteenth-century French painting: the two thin masts trisect the screen like pillars in a quattrocento Annunciation. The natural lines of movement in this composition are accentuated and complicated by two gentle motions: a sailboat breezily traverses the top of the frame right to left, and the camera lazily slides forward with the progress of the boat. Far from disrupting the composition, this movement seeks to rebalance the screen or to create a symmetry in time. In this case the camera gently leaps from the people on the boat, and, after surveying the village in its tame flight, comes to land on waiting onlookers and a waiting dock. Thus the moving camera independently seeks out the ideal (classical) point of rest, locking within the shot the energy that motivated it.

Much has been made of Murnau's virtuosity with camera movements, and those in *Sunrise* are breathtaking. Their power, however, largely stems from the spareness with which he employed this technique—only fourteen of over six hundred shots. Several of these are follow-shots in which the stationary camera decides to pursue the character in view. More accurately, the camera is pulled in the wake of a drama receding from it. The vamp early in the film walks by the panning camera and threatens to go completely out of view, but soon we are implicated in the cadence of her plan. Later, the man, back to us, wanders toward the marsh, and the camera, full of our desire, initiates one of the most complex and thrilling movements in all of cinema. It crosses the fence at its own spot, turns on the man who in his stupor passes by it and makes for the vamp. But the camera finds its own, more direct path, pushing past bushes until she is revealed in the moonlight. When the man reenters screen left we are doubly startled, having forgotten that we had abandoned him. Indeed, we are perhaps ashamed to have reached the vamp before him in our driving impatience. This shame is intensified at the end of the sequence when the camera, nose in mud, sniffs after the retreating sinners. It is a daring, highly unconventional shot, and it delivers its image of guilt not only by its content (high-heel shoes oozing with mud, while the marsh refuses to give up the imprint of the shoe), but by making us feel guilty as we literally track the couple down.

For the most part these tracking movements serve to animate and prolong classical compositions rather than manufacture drama. While it is true that most of the tracking shots, notably the trolley ride, open up new acting spaces for the marital drama, the very stateliness of the duration of these shots moves our attention from the drama to focus on the very design of the image. Indeed, the moving camera allows us to watch the shot in the process of being designed. This graphic rather than dramatic use of tracking contributes to the persistant view of Murnau as an "aesthetic," high-art director, a view reinforced by biographical attention placed on Murnau's study of art history and on the pictorialism of his earlier films, especially *Faust.* Scrutinized with the eyes of an art critic, *Sunrise* becomes an endless series of citations. Robin Wood catalogues many of these [in "Murnau II, *Sunrise*," *Film Comment*, May-June, 1976]: the still lifes of wooden bowls and bread on a table that is raked à la Van Gogh; the second honeymoon voyage in which the vertical moonstreak and small sailboat on the dark lake recall paintings of the *Brucke* group; the scene of the search for the lost wife with its frontal image of bobbing lanterns, suggesting impressionism; the inserts of the village itself, seen always mistily or at night with the steeple and full moon prominent above the clustered houses, which draw on a frequent *topos* in late nineteenth-century painting. I leave it to others to establish the sources for such "pictorially aware" compositions as those given us in the amusement park, café, or church.

Wood goes on to suggest that the stylization of certain gestures is an even more important aspect of the heritage of painting in this film. The baby reaching to touch its mother's face; the wife feeding her chickens; the insert of the "holy" family under a fruit tree and beside the ox-drawn plow—one could multiply such scenes which suggest, which cry out for references. Frequently the drama itself is rendered as a conflict of pictorial styles. The delicately curved neck of the wife, whose head is consistently surrounded by a horizonless field of water, is juxtaposed with a frontal view of the man whose gesture of rowing thrusts him aggressively toward us. Indeed, the film as a whole has been seen as a conflict between Expressionism and Naturalism, Germany and America.

As in any fable, the story proceeds between two distinctly segregated poles: the vamp and the wife, the city and the country, land and water, night and morning. While the alternation of these elements produces a dramatic energy which is intensified by sequences of conflicting pictorial styles, the same energy can also be released within a single shot through the use of diagonal compositions, to which I now turn.

B. Conflict is explicit in the paradigm announced by the film's second shot—a locomotive screaming diagonally across the screen, crossed by another to form an X. In the body of the film itself such energy is not so self-contained, for diagonals appear only one at a time and point to a space and a time beyond them.

Murnau saves this composition for a particular moment in the film, giving us a strong clue to the rhetorical strategy at work in his storyboard. After the wife has agreed to the journey and has said goodbye to her baby, we see the boat, the death ship, tied to the dock. Its diagonal composition is marked by the entrance of the man who draws the line with his heavy feet. There follows a sequence of some twenty-two shots before he and his wife are alone on the lake. Nearly all of these shots are self-consciously diagonal, a fact that gives unity to the sequence and allows for a silent drama between man, woman, boat, and dog. Murnau would never allow such compositions to achieve their own resolution but he does let them build the growing tension. For instance, the direct energy of the man is countered by that of the dog pulling frantically at his chain to form an even purer diagonal. After ten shots elaborating this graphic drama, Murnau shows us the boat leaving the shore and, instead of cutting to the charging dog, he allows the dog to enter the scene from the center, leap off the dock, and swim out to the boat.

A number of diagonals recur in the following sequences until the boat reaches the farther shore. In the city itself they are essentially absent. That they represent and contain a driving and perverse energy is attested to by their use in conjunction with the vamp. Particularly at the film's end she is shown walking downscreen along roads or fence lines whose diagonal composition leads her to the bottom corner of the frame. Unforgettable is the scene in which she is driven by the man diagonally to screen left and then rolled to the bottom front of the screen by force of a fence which has cued the direction of the action all along. Indeed, the vamp's final exit from the village drops her diagonally away from us to the upper left-hand corner of the screen, leaving the glistening lake restored. Murnau emphasizes the defeat of the diagonal when the shot following her exit displays the crossed bodies of the reunited couple. The diagonal is a figure of absence as well as of passion; it is an image of a lack as well as of the drive to fill that lack. In *Sunrise* it is overcome by the presence of the cross which brings all energy back to a center and holds it there.

The interplay between squarely composed images and unbalanced or diagonal ones, between the crossing trains and the pleasure boat, dramatizes the narrative in a traditionally pictorial manner. Murnau's achievement here lies in his ability to make this interplay deeply conflicting without resorting to conventional montage, and it is this for which we normally salute him. Each shot has an integrity that makes it valuable in itself. Placed in sequences these shots resonate even more fully because of the dramatic context in which they participate.

But such pictorial interplay is not unique to *Sunrise.* One finds it surely in Murnau's other works and in early German film generally. Moreover, Murnau isn't at all faithful in *Sunrise* to this strategy. The barbershop sequence, for instance, is a traditional Hollywood set piece complete with establishing shot and an elaboration of fragments. At one point eleven straight glances stitch the comic scene together, culminating in close-up inserts of the masher's shoe being stepped on and the husband's pocketknife slowly opening. What could have been a suspenseful scene is lightened in the overarticulation of its presentation. By rendering it via comic-strip montage, Murnau sets this fake drama off against the more primitive and powerful dangers which flank it and which he delivers to us intact, as if in awe of their permanence and seriousness.

The great moments of *Sunrise* certainly could not exist in montage. The evil and grace which this film imagines for us cannot be given fragmentarily nor could they be grouped and held within such logical and essentially human boundaries. The intelligence of the stylistic oppositions labeled here classical and dynamic is not congruent with these more supernatural aspects of the film. Through its occasional montage and through its consistently tasteful stylistic deployment *Sunrise* will always be recognized as a model film; but it is despite this taste and intelligence that *Sunrise* makes us return to it once more seeking the source of its more primitive attraction for us.

C. The first and third shots of the prologue provide entrees to another type of experience that *Sunrise* dares to envisage. If the frame and all its potentials for repose and dynamism can be seen as cultural modes of organizing conflict, these two shots suggest the film's openness to noncultural forces, to chaos and the preternatural.

Initially the third shot appears conventional enough, the two forces in the frame, an advancing ocean liner and a resting female bather, cut off from one another in split screen. This shot in fact is the transition to the purely reposeful classical composition of the final prologue shot discussed above. It tames the dynamism of the crossing trains and, while maintaining the explicit conflict between two entities, it gives each entity an autonomous space within which to relax. Thus far the shot is interesting, even logical, but certainly not remarkable.

Suddenly a form disturbs this interplay. A figure rises from the bottom of the screen, a man pulling himself up to be with the woman. While his motion might be seen to counterbalance the descent of the ocean liner from the top left of the frame, something eerie far outweighs this formal explanation: we learn in this, the film's third shot, that *the frame is not sovereign.* We recognize that throughout the film it may be framing the wrong things or ignoring something hovering on its edges. Similarly the frame can drop elements once their dramatic importance is exhausted, exiling them from the play of light on the screen. The vamp suffers this fate when she is being strangled by the man. His murderous intention is interrupted by the close-up of the nurse calling him back to the miracle of the rebirth of his wife and his hope. He lets go of the vamp who literally falls out of the frame, descending, we might imagine, to some other world. This is the opposite of the prologue shot where from the bottom of the frame emerged a sudden male presence. The vamp, we might further imagine, would have preferred strangulation. After all, he had tried to strangle her on the marsh before she was able to transform that passion into eroticism. But she is denied passion because she is, in the end, denied framing. She is lost to the world of the film and drops from it as though censored. She will, of course, be officially dispensed with in the film's coda in the shot already described as a diagonal leave-taking, but it is this moment of graphic rejection, this refusal of the screen to give her space, that is her true demise. For what lies beyond the frame? It is this question which *Sunrise* continually poses and which upsets all purely pictorial accounts of its power.

The power of the unseen and the unframed is attested to by every audience. The most startling moment of the film is invariably the sudden intrusion of a horse's head into the shot of the man hiding the bulrushes. This scene raises tension not because it is exceptionally dramatic, though it does bear with it the specter of the marsh scene, but because the sovereignty of the frame is shattered. If we are frightened with the man, for an instant our fear persists beyond his. For the fact is that we can no longer trust the framing of any shot. We must constantly run our eyes around the perimeter of the screen in search of the unknown.

Murnau first discovered this structure in *Nosferatu* when the mystery ship glides into the pretty harbor, disrupting its peaceful sleep and infesting it with plague. He returns to this very image on smaller scale in *Sunrise*. At the beginning and end of the murder voyage occur shots in which we see at first only a dock or a mooring post. Silently into the frame slips the shadow, then the prow of the rowboat. While the framing of these last shots is in part motivated by the function of a harbor, a dock, a mooring post, all of which exist to wait upon the arrival of a vessel, Murnau nonetheless could conceivably keep us waiting interminably in expectation of that which we cannot see. This sense of the interminable lies behind the most effective use of this compositional structure, the scenes of the search for the wife.

Lanterns bobbing from the prows of a huddle of rowboats create an effect Robin Wood termed "impressionist." Like some Monet painting the function of the edges of the frame is very problematic. This scene with its complex molecular movement, its indecipherable composition, and its context of a black surrounding lake seems aimless. These boats go nowhere. These searching light beams cannot penetrate the lake below. The pathetic husband tests all perimeters. Once he even calls out along the frontal axis directly at us, the spectators. Is there any space that will yield up his wife? At the end of the sequence, in what is surely the film's most pathetic moment, his boat drifts and bobs completely out of frame. This moment of despair is achieved by the failure of cinematic framing, by the dispersal of the filmed elements in search of an absent center.

In the midst of these directionless shots Murnau inserts a privileged narrator's view of the wife floating unconscious. This miraculous vision which no one sees begins on solid black. For four full seconds we are asked to stare at the imperturbable lake, an image of the husband's despair. Then a form grows in the upper right and begins slipping down the diagonal. The camera doesn't budge. It can't frame or even locate her. When she has completely disappeared bottom left we realize we are without bearings and that this inhuman accident of sight is over. The husband recovers a piece of lace, a trace of this passing, but the lake is black again. What we have been given here is a glance at grace. Its possibility has been affirmed as it has passed through our view, but its absence from the man and his drama has also been marked. Grace is as unframable as death. We glimpse only its trace.

It is in this same transcendental space, this time conjured up in flashback by the rescuer, that we view the miracle of the wife's recovery. Once again a pitch black lake covers the screen, an undifferentiated chaos within which composition is meaningless. Then the rescue boat nudges in from bottom right and constructs the diagonal along which the wife begins to descend. The space of nothingness has been graced, yet remains imaginary, to be called to mind in memory or in story.

D. I have saved for last the first shot of the prologue, indeed of the film; for in its obvious internal mutation (from static drawing to live action), it introduces both the simplest and the most important paradigm of shots.

To begin with the simple, this shot announces a drama between Expressionism and Naturalism. The stylized flat of the train station with its latticework lines is animated without warning, great billows of smoke rising in the middle of the picture. As one train and then another moves out of the station, our eyes scan the screen for the realistic detail we had at first ignored in attending to the extraordinary design of the scene. One can hardly help watching for this kind of interplay throughout the film. Contemporary critics were alert to the contradictions Murnau's relocation in Hollywood was certain to elicit. George O'Brien's heavy, hunched saunter plays against a sweet and airy Janet Gaynor, natural in the American way except for the East European wig all her fans bemoaned. More subtly, the peasant house which the vamp inhabits is European in decor and in presentation (the curiously raked table), whereas the final scene of the peasants is shot straight on in American style. One is tempted to label all the dark scenes (marsh and both lake journeys) as German in their style, while the sunny sequences, particularly the middle portion of the film in the city, might be termed American. But this formula is too pat and fails to account for the graphics of the Luna Park and the café sequence. Nevertheless it may be true, as has been suggested, that this film is Murnau's final death struggle with the expressionism of his early films. The expulsion of the vamp is then a clear victory for Janet Gaynor (her hair now luxuriously undone) and the American way.

Much more important than this obvious mixture of styles, the first shot of the film undergoes internal transmutation and it is this above all that characterizes Murnau's approach to action. Here a static design is magically animated. Later superimpositions will invade an image from within and corrupt or save it. Think of the lake bubbling over the face of George O'Brien, or the three faces of the

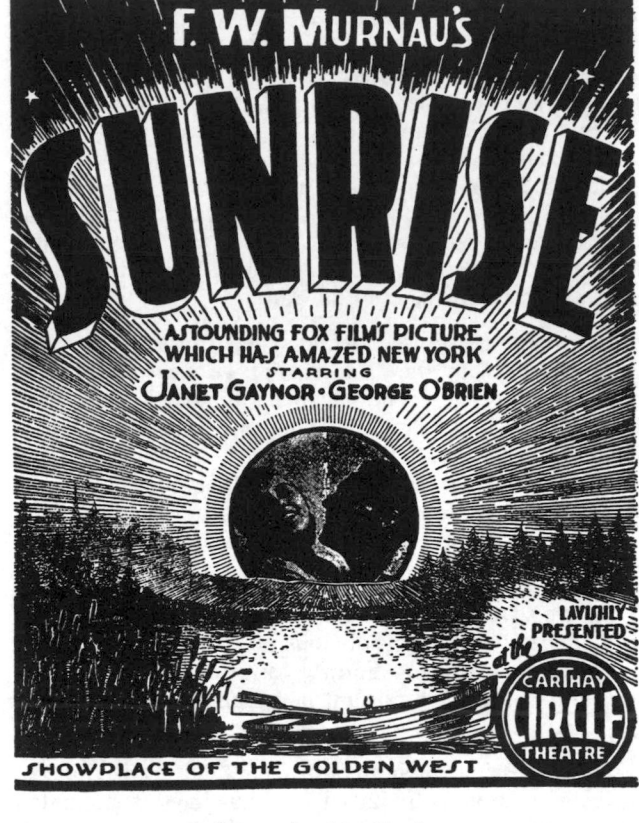

Poster advertising Sunrise.

vamp fading in from the space around O'Brien to tempt him on.

Referring to the darker German films of Murnau, Alexandre Astruc discussed the power of this method [in his "Fire and Ice," in *Cahiers du Cinéma in English*, No. 1, January, 1966]:

> What will the image become? The meeting place for a certain number of lines of force whose placement will directly recall Velasquez and Caravaggio. Yet each image demands to be annihilated by the next tragedy which is installed right in the heart of the seemingly indifferent. Watch how corruption is born out of tranquility. Murnau operates slyly. The key to all Murnau's work is a fatality hidden behind the most harmless elements of the frame.
>
> Each image is an unstable equilibrium, better still the distraction of a stable equilibrium brought about by its own elan.

A perfectly framed and static view of the man's home is undone by a single movement, his shadow appearing in the window signaling the vamp; or later in nearly the same situation, the shadow of his head by a small window preceding the sudden swinging open of the door. These shots have something of the demonic about them as the composition disintegrates into a threatening action, threatening primarily because the mutation originates in the center of the frame.

Murnau carefully blocks his scenes to achieve this kind of effect. The crucial scene of the husband's return to his bedroom, sick with evil passion spent and with the onus of more evil deeds still to do, is given as an intrusion into the sanctuary of his wife's resting place. Small and unaware, she lies bathed in moonlight while from a downstage center doorway first his shadow and then his hulk looms up and covers her. Like the superimpositions of the vamp that finally urge him to take the awful step, to ask his wife to boat with him, there is no forewarning. In the center of a marital bedroom the specter appears. In the midst of life, temptation unaccountably wells up. Evil in the world of *Sunrise* cannot be warded off by vigilance. There are no boundaries to protect. It arises and corrupts from within.

So many shots reinforce this vision. Smoke and fog rise up from the center of dozens of seemingly static compositions. Murnau even used this structure in his intertitles when the graphics of "couldn't she get drowned?" become liquid and slide iconically to the bottom of the screen, dissolving into a pictograph of the wife falling from a boat and in slow motion descending to the bottom of the lake and of the frame. Indeed the final image of the film is the resurrection of these graphics, "Finis" rises (as from the lake) to center screen and to a solidity that it has been the film's job to achieve.

Surely the most powerful use of this structure and one that speaks to us with an innate strength the years cannot diminish are the performances of the principals at those moments when we see an emotion or idea crossing their faces. Janet Gaynor stands before George O'Brien and his request that she come with him across the lake; she hesitates, her lips quivering, and then explodes into an unforgettable smile, certain that the long night of her husband's inner struggle is over. Characteristically, Murnau refuses to cut away from her to the reverse shot of O'Brien, for the drama must develop within the scene and in its own "rural" time.

Other privileged moments occur at the café as the man passes her the plate of cakes and her face disintegrates in tears. In the church it is O'Brien's turn to crumble and be restored in front of his partner. And of course at the film's end these two human faces beam together in transfigured joy only to demand further transcendental mutation: all within the immutable stillness of a perfectly composed frame these faces dissolve into and become the glorious superimposed sunrise. The energy of their love cannot push the film forward in time; instead it accumulates in the frame until it literally radiates its final image.

The parabolic origin of *Sunrise* is unmistakable. The characters are nameless, their drama timeless. Its impact applies "wherever the sun rises, whether in city or country."

Who is presenting us this parable? Images, and paradigms of images, exist only as they are presented and become present to someone. Just as stories are more than a sequence of events, so images are more than an array of pictorial elements. What narration is to story, so framing is to images. Indeed the very term "to frame" is ambiguous enough to refer to representation and narration alike. We frame a picture and we frame a story. In motion pictures we frame both. And so, who is presenting us the parable of *Sunrise*? Early in the film we are shown. As the man leaves his home to pursue temptation in the marsh, we are given a sudden unaccountable explanatory insert. Two village women recall how "they used to be like children but now he ruins himself; moneylenders take their farm." These women conjure up the appropriate images to support their gossip and then one of them, whom we shall later recognize as the nurse, says, "while she sits alone." Her glance curiously seeks our own and for an instant we can be certain that the entire film is a community parable told by its citizens to us, an extension of that community. Thus the framing of the flashback to explain the story shows the visible presence of the storyteller and lets us infer the framing of the film as parable. In the film's final sequence the community once more explains to itself, and to us, the miracle of the rescue, taking credit for the happy end.

Between these two blatant interventions of community there exist many moments and types of framing, all of which put the images of the film to use. Think of the explicit dreams conjured up by one character for another: the image of the wife falling from the boat inserted by the vamp into the mind of the man so forcefully that it recurs even when he is alone; the pastoral garden in which the "remarried" couple takes their promenade; the angels with violins they dream up at the carnival; and so on.

This ability of characters in the film to situate or frame a scene leads to another graphic paradigm not mentioned above: *repoussoir*. When a character in foreground is silhouetted by the light stemming from a background scene, that character's thickness is lost but his or her control over the background scene is established. This paradigm is inaugurated in the film's first sequence when the vamp slips into the dining room of the home where she lodges. The peasants in the foreground literally frame her entrance. The next sequence opens with a more dramatic instance of this effect. Two more peasants, so sharply silhouetted as to be featureless, stand up against the camera and to the right. The vamp's exit from the house throws the deepest plane of the frame into brightness and focus so that we observe her, through these nameless peasants, slink up the street. These two shots in fact prepare us for the villagers' flashbacks to come. The drama of the film is seen by and through the eyes of the village.

Other uses of *repoussoir* include the vision of the city seen through the backs of the couple viewing it; the trolley trip to the city in which the driver is flattened and darkened against the bright landscape developing before him. The most complicated uses of this shot are reserved for the last third of the film: the wife in a glance-object format eyes a couple dancing at the amusement park. This couple is shot to look like paper dolls pushed up against the dance-hall window. Behind them the sparkling room appears full of other dancers and the band. Since the camera begins to track in on this view we are in the position of the wife framing a heavenly couple who in turn sense the paradise behind them. Even more complicated is the search for the adrift wife. Here the vamp frames the townspeople, first through her window and then catlike from the tree branch

above them while they in turn are silhouetted against a further scene, the arena of the search itself.

These remarkable shots which explicitly pose the question of seeing and conjuring are only the exposed side of a structure that never ceases to operate in the film. *Sunrise* is an elaborate interplay of viewers viewing and willful characters striving to frame their desires. Nor are we as spectators aloof from this interplay. We too have our desires and strive to frame this parable for ourselves. When the vamp slinks down the street she passes the village observers. They lose interest, yet we pan with her, we truck behind her, caught up in her lure and in the mystery of her project. She stops to peer in the window of a home where a man is having his hair cut. We have voyeuristically caught her in her own voyeurism. Guilty already, we track on to the fence of another house. She whistles at the little square of a window in front of her. The power of her whistle is part of her encompassing glance. Inside the man at his table decenters the classic composition by leaning nearly off-screen in response. When she whistles again he stands in the middle of the screen against a post. To his left is the kitchen with his off-screen wife. To his right the off-screen source of the alluring whistle. He is caught. It is enough for Murnau to show us from the vamp's viewing spot the shadow of a hand motioning in the window. The vamp has made her conquest by commanding the field without being seen.

In the famous tracking shot which discovers her under the moonlight she prepares to be seen, but only as a necessary tactic in her larger plan. She wants not to be taken but to take. In the scene which follows it is she who controls the frame from its center. She grasps his head and glares at us defiantly. She proposes the murder and keeps the man from recoiling out of the frame. Right up against the edge he leans, lifting his hands in horror. But he does not leave. And when he throws the vamp to the ground she knows she will win. Her final strategy is to point to the glories of the city. Sitting before us, exactly replicating our own viewing situation, the couple looks on at the marvelous vision unrolling before them, a vision that inspires the vamp's voluptuous dance and the man's aroused passion. It is "a movie" that has seduced him. He gives himself to her. The actual moment of sexual intercourse is signaled by a long shot of the moon beside the village steeple.

The erotic iconography of this piece of censorship is unmistakable, but the shot serves to return the story to more distant hands. The vamp who has controlled each frame to this moment is relieved of the image in her frenzy. This is why we must follow her tracks and locate her once more in the succeeding shots. The steeple image has implicated the cosmos itself in the sin and has allowed the vamp to step out of the frame without losing her control over the man. Alone, he is seen groping his way amidst the shadows of fishnets and branches, still caught in his sin. It is only in sleep that her spell is loosed, the water bubbling through his consciousness like the river of Lethe, like the water into which he must send his wife.

The flowing dissolves carrying this water culminate in a tableau of the village at dawn stretched out along the lake. Murnau here has taken narrative authority from the man, expressing thereby that relaxation of conscience the guilty seek in unconsciousness. This momentary and illusory relief persists into the next shot as we reenter the room to find the wife hovering solicitously over him, encompassing him in her selfless gaze. The peacefulness of this transition is shortlived, however, broken by the mad eyes of the waking man which in delirium have mercilessly brought back in hallucination the bundle of bulrushes he had so carefully shoved out of view.

This startling return of the film to his eyes is a burden on the viewer who had only been too glad to be under the domestic care of his wife. Worse, the man turns his horror-laden eyes on the wife herself and frames her as she feeds the chickens. It seems at first that the power of her benevolence richly described in this classically composed shot will be sufficient to thwart his intentions. But as he looks at her, and as he hesitates between the goodness he sees and the evil in his eyes' intent, the lure of the vamp materializes in three superimpositions that hem him in. Abruptly he stands and walks into the image containing his wife, corrupting its purity. In this glance-object pattern we have been left holding the glance while the viewer (the man) has entered the field he had earlier framed. Thus we are made complicit.

The attempted murder can also be understood as the interplay between conflicting "views." The conflict is established when first the man and then his wife sits alone in the boat waiting for one another. A look of doubt crosses her eyes which now seek to hold on to the shore. Yet that shore rotates and recedes from her. The man is in control of the boat and of the horizon. She is under his view and looks frantically about at the shore she is no longer allowed to possess. As the crescendo nears she is continually framed against a solidly aquatic background that she can't escape. She looks left and right. A flock of birds flies away. There is nothing solid to hold her eyes. She slips under his power, cowering over the edge of the boat, falling into that background, until her hands reaching out in supplication break through the trance of his intention. He falls back and rows to the shore. At this point Murnau once more relieves his couple of the drama. Neither character can look at the other. Both relinquish the scene. Murnau cuts freely around the boat, letting the energy of the oars and the thrusting prow carry the film to the shore.

The second movement of the film, the reconciliation in the city, absolutely alters the direction of the first. Where before we had an interplay of wills, now we have a convergence of wills. Where before we participated in the flight of desire, now we participate in the desire for stasis.

The entire city section is cushioned in protective brackets that insure its harmony. The trolley, which leads the disconsolate couple in, later takes them happily away. Twice the wife is protected from the treacherous traffic: once blinded by despair, once by euphoria. Twice the couple find themselves in restaurants, once unable to eat or look at one another, they must leave; later they eat and look so much that they fly away in imagination. Between all this narrative protection and framing lie the great images of reconciliation for which the film is well known, the scenes in the church and in the photographer's studio.

The reconciliation in the church, after the failure of flowers and cakes, is attributable no doubt to God and his visible presence in the lighting of the mise-en-scène. But more powerfully, it is a product of art, of a mediated experience that allows both parties to mingle their feelings at a protective distance. The spectacle of the wedding depersonalizes the power of love so that it can bypass the horrendous breach of promise represented in the film's first movement. Where personal love failed (cake and flowers), institutional love succeeds. The unworthy find worth beneath the umbrella of the church's blessing, a blessing general enough to extend beyond the sanctuary and into the congregation.

In positioning themselves before this ritual the couple asks anonymously for the blessing. They view in order to be renewed. By reason of their anonymity the couple here implicates the audience once and for all. The gaze of the spectator in the back row is bound up in the gaze of the man at the ritual before him. His identification with the groom and its power to bring him to his knees keys our own identification with the man. The film here signals the mode of response it demands from us, signals itself as a ritual, the very observing of which has the power to liberate the viewer. Having looked at this spectacle the man no longer needs to look at his wife. He buries his head in her lap and she bends her neck in protection. This pietistic moment closes the distance between them so that their glances no longer need to meet or avert themselves. They look now together at a future that opens up before them, thanks to the mediation of a spectacle engrossing enough to command both their views, meaningful enough to unite them.

If the sequence in the church places the spectator within the process of narration, the photographer catches that same spectator in the act of imaging. The couple themselves demand a final framing in which the world looks at them, in which they lose their sight and become sighted. Their kiss, inverted in the lens, captured and held on the photographic plate, is the culmination of their reconciliation. It is this physical object, this icon, which rests cushioned between the frames and brackets of the city section.

The pleasure the photographer takes in framing them, a pleasure multiplied by all those who watch their country dance at the carnival, is of course entirely too facile. The anarchic impulse of adultery is not so easily tamed. The dance and the photograph embody a social solution (an artistic solution) to a problem society only pretends to control. The photograph and the dance, like Murnau's classical compositions, pretend to hold and objectify a social value, but these values themselves can be seen within a larger, nonsocial context. This shifting of contexts produces the film's most beautiful moment. As they sail home under a benevolent honeyed moon, the couple in foreground "images" a barge of dancing peasants floating across the top of the frame. This scene brings into nature the dance of the amusement park, and it explicitly rhymes with the vision of the city framed earlier by the vamp. Like that earlier vision and like the wedding spectacle viewed in the church, the image of the barge produces immediate consequences for the viewers. The couple reaches together in their one explicit moment of mutual sexual interest. But the barge floats off the screen, and its irridescent bonfire gives way to the surrounding blackness of the lake. The family unit is blessed by society in the photograph and in the serenading barge; but both blessings are suddenly nothing more than little squares within a larger more forbidding frame.

In this context, the wind preceding the storm is unframed and unframable. Driving the city dwellers out of their artificial pleasures, it leaves the floating couple without social support. Nature's passion, indiscriminately unleashed in this storm, threatens the simple reconciliation of the city. Passion and the vamp demand to be heard.

The fairy-tale quality of this cosmic justice is supported by the shift of the film to the view once more of the vamp. Bare skin gleaming in the intermittent light, she glares at the townspeople first through her window and then from her tree. At the height of the drama we are presented with the film's most complicated visual moments. We frame the vamp who in glance-object format frames the townspeople on the shore; they themselves are staring into the darkness of the lake at little rescue boats. The men aboard those boats look in despair at the forlorn husband whose eyes frame the blackness of the water. At the center of this intricately embedded structure is the wife's absence. At the outside stand we, the film spectators who, with the vamp, observe the pathetic impotence of society in the face of this absence.

The final drama to be played pits the dominant gaze of the demonic vamp against that of the man. Having looked into the nothingness of the water, he returns to the sanctuary of his marital bedroom and kneels before the empty tabernacle of his wife's bed. He ought, it seems, to give up sight and life right here, but he is awakened from his emptiness by the whistle of the vamp come back to envelop him. Her error is to enter the space she has framed. Whereas before he had gone to her, now she goes to him, invading the sanctity of the house.

Murnau achieves an enormously satisfying shift of power by letting us watch, from her imperious post behind the fence, the foolish audacity of the vamp. Instead of commanding the scene from that post, this time she inserts herself into the scene. The terror of the storm, the night, and the dark side of passion are condensed in her small form which hesitates outside the house. In chasing her down and brutally burying her beneath the frame, the husband clears the way for refilling the house. The all-seeing vamp has been seen; passion has been recognized and dealt with. Domestic life can now be sanctified by nature itself: the entire family, seen all together for the first time since the pastoral flashback, arranges itself on the wife's bed. The cross of her window frame, instead of throwing its portentous shadow, is now wreathed with flowers. This unmistakable Easter icon is motivated only by the resurrection of a wholesome love through the near death of the innocent wife, who suffered to redeem the sinful husband thereby casting Satan back to hell.

This ending satisfies the on-screen community. Outside the couple's room they recount the rescue. And then, as if to laugh at the fate just overcome, they reenact comically the origin of the story: the rescuer accepts a kiss, two kisses from the nurse, and his wife tweaks him by the ear. This little flirtation once more traces the cracks in the social structure, cracks it was the work of this film to caulk. It recalls other "light" moments like the man's attack on the barbershop masher, like the comic flirtation of the vamplike manicurist, and like the sudden violence of the woman with the falling shoulder straps. Together these jokes dismiss with laughter the paradox of sexuality as the basis for marriage as well as for adultery. The community's solution to this paradox was to freeze the couple in a second wedding ceremony, in a picture, and in a dance. Yet these social solutions are put in jeopardy not only by the storm but by every antisocial gesture society tries to cover with laughter.

And so the unenlightened community retires with their laughter and leaves us alone with the couple. As we have seen, the diagonals generated by the drama here at last cross themselves in stasis. Here the easy "look" captured by the photographer and tested by the desperate "looking" in the night is transformed into the source of all seeing, the sun. And here finally the framing of people and desires which has propelled the film from image to image can end: for we are confronted with a tableau that looks back at us and holds us prisoner beneath it. When the projection bulb goes out and the houselights fade in, we sit staring at a screen that has lost its glow. The almighty sun, able to hold the very image of love, was itself a prisoner of the screen. And as we look about, the film becomes once more a parable, a snapshot of love, at sea in a more pervasive darkness. We are ushered out of the theater like the community from the couple's home.

Like all great art *Sunrise* has given us an impossible image, the timeless satisfaction of our yearnings, a limitless "looking become look," a "conscious sun." The recognition of the impossibility of this yearning is the final achievement of the film or, more properly, of the experience of the film. The couple has escaped the rising and setting of the sun by becoming the sun. We mortals must watch it pass out of sight aware of our distance from it and from them. The experience of *Sunrise*, then, is an exercise of our sense of distance and of light, of framing a world and yet being at the mercy of that which is beyond the frame.

Visual life is an oscillation between searching and being positioned. In *Sunrise* this oscillation is explicit, and we have used the dialectic "framing—being framed" to describe it, but we might as easily have talked about surfaces and depths. For to hold an object or a person in view is to pin it to the screen and to treat it two-dimensionally. Whereas, to be at the mercy of an unstable frame or of a scene (the wife adrift) that resists framing is to experience the solidity of that which we seek.

This opposition between framing and being framed is at the heart of cinema. In its determination to create good stories and beautiful tableaux, cinema tries to hold the world in its power. In its failure to do this, in the nonnarrative, unpainterly aspects which form the grain of every film and become foregrounded in some, cinema is at the mercy of what it strives to perceive. This opposition of surfaces and depths speaks explicitly to the viewer of the film, for it marks a tension in the movie theater. On the one hand the spectator joins the community and "uses" the example of the story to recover and reinvest a commitment to culture. The film is like a mural painting on which the viewer can see the couple, the community, the locales of danger, and even himself, and across which a world view is reframed. On the other hand this same spectator has paid an admission fee to leave social positioning behind and to dream alone in the theater whatever dreams the film might evoke. A voyeur concealed before a fascinating spectacle he does not control, that spectator wants in part to be caught out, framed suddenly by a turning of the light on him.

The very phenomenon of cinema, it seems, feeds these conflicting impulses. As social critics insist, movies are the plaything of the dominant ideology. They are, even in their pretenses at social comment (pretenses *Sunrise* at least has the good taste to ignore), thoroughly institutional products supporting an institutionalized way of life. Yet movies are also considered dream material capable of appealing to and unleashing our most nonsocial fantasies.

It is *Sunrise*'s feat to have paid tribute to both these impulses in its narrative structure, in the interplay of its graphics and, most stunningly, in its implication of the viewer within its flow. Watching it, we are led to agree with the nurse that there is a moral order in the universe and that it has generated our culture. But we can also sense the mystery of events beyond the nurse, beyond the community. The primordial chaos of the vamp and the inhuman beauty of the apotheosis of the couple let us imagine a life beyond social health and prosperity. And in our imagining the film repositions us, decentering us from our social selves. It is no doubt this tension between the positioning we perform on the story and that other positioning it performs on us that makes us return to this film again and again.

The experience of *Sunrise* is in the mode of the experience of any masterwork. Its story is as conventional and ideological as renaissance *topoi* like the Nativity or the Flight to Egypt. Its craftsmanship, like the flawless form of a fifteenth-century classic, seems unquestioned and unquestionable. It puts the eye and the mind to rest. But as classic, *Sunrise* assumes the aura of the institutions with which it is complicit; it is after all a product made under the patronage of William Fox. Fox bought Murnau and his German expressionist team explicitly to construct for him a piece of high art. This mogul of the "low-class film" commanded the creation of an artwork to rise loftily like a dirigible over his studio as advertisement and as example.

No doubt the Medicis had better taste than William Fox, but they served in their day a similar function: to foster work that would at once advance the art and uphold the culture, drawing special attention to its patron. Such works deserve their homes in the Uffizi at Florence or the Venetian Accademia, or the National Gallery in Washington, D. C., places whose location and architecture assure our proper respect.

The thousands of viewers who file up to such works, like those thousands in our classes and film societies who are placed before *Sunrise,* are placed before a cultural monument. The stability and "correctness" of the story and the form assure their respect and perhaps their admiration. The very structure of these works likewise insists on a certain positioning of the spectator called for by the use of perspective and, in *Sunrise,* by the narrative. Hence the spectator not only fixes a world but is fixed in relation to that world. This is the hidden and insidious task of every classic: under the guise of greatness and even of freedom, supported by a philanthropic patron, artists advance the institution of art for the glory of culture. The artist's product becomes an artifact of prestige and of the market, capable of being owned, sold, used as collateral. And collateral it genuinely is, for it guarantees the social order that produced it! Moreover, as a classic it is displayed pedagogically to instruct all members of a culture in the rightness of that culture and in the reposeful attitude they should assume before an order that is both vast and natural.

But *Sunrise* is more than a classic, and it is on this surplus that we must end. When Giotto shaped his *Flight to Egypt* he did not disturb the story nor did he disrupt its visual form, creating as he did a much-imitated composition. This is Giotto's classicism; but his faces go beyond such good taste and sense. They have mystified and disturbed for centuries and they will continue to do so. They mark a dimension of his painting which cannot be accommodated to an institution and which cannot be easily "placed" by a spectator. Indeed, they unsettle the spectator in a depositioning that requires a reappraisal of the work, if only to permit that befuddled viewer to regain balance. Similarly Piero de Cosimi's Medici-sponsored allegories disorient us by the distention of his figures and Filippino Lippi's by the strange radiance of his colors. This radiance doesn't *serve* the monumental aspect of his painting; it *disturbs* it, haunting the spectator in the process.

In the same way *Sunrise* can disturb and disorient even while it recounts a myth, even while its form puts us at ease. In the eerie, unpredictable power of the frame, and in the even less predictable transference of the work of framing, *Sunrise* continues to unsettle. We admire its surface to be startled by its depth.

If this is the potential of all cinema, it is the realization of a very few works indeed. And if we sense something beyond respect and admiration for this film we must find a new word for our experience: awe. *Sunrise* partakes of the awesome. And it insists that we return to it, not in blind obsessive reenactment but in a deepening comprehension of both work and self-insured by the oscillation of positioning and unbalance we undergo. If this film is a masterwork, its mastery is something that changes hands. Ultimately we master this film only to find ourselves mastered in return. (pp. 30-58)

Dudley Andrew, "The Turn and Return of 'Sunrise'," in his Film in the Aura of Art, *Princeton University Press, 1984, pp. 28-58.*

Bert Cardullo (essay date 1985)

[*In the essay below, Cardullo identifies* Nosferatu *as an Expressionist drama and a sociopolitical commentary on the Weimar Republic.*]

Critics have discussed certain Expressionist features of F. W. Murnau's *Nosferatu* (1922, based on Bram Stoker's novel *Dracula* [1897]), but none has conceived of it as a fully Expressionist work. One reason for this is that most critics' understanding of the Expressionist movement, in drama as well as in film, is superficial. For them a film such as *The Cabinet of Dr. Caligari* (1920) is Expressionistic less for what it means than for how it looks with its "oppressively murky artificial sets" [Gilberto Perez Guillermo, "Murnau's *Nosferatu*," *Sight and Sound* 36, Summer 1967]. And for Robin Wood, a discussion of Expressionism in *Nosferatu* need only be limited to a catalogue of its stylistic manifestations in the film, in other words to how the film looks:

> The first shot of the vampire's castle jutting up from the rock, the strange geometrical patterning of arch-forms out of which Nosferatu emerges to meet [Hutter], the use of "unnatural" camera angles as in the shot from the hold of the ship, the trick effects [the speeded-up coach; the shots in negative], the huge shadow as Nosferatu ascends the stairs to [Ellen's] room, the shadow of his fingers clenching into a fist upon her heart. ["Murnau's Midnight and *Sunrise*," *Film Comment* 12, May-June 1976]

Expressionism is primarily a drama of the mind, however, whether on stage or on screen. It is concerned with the essence, not the surface, of reality; therefore it, more than other styles, must be defined, not by its own surface characteristics but by the essence they seek to embody. [In their 1971 *The German Cinema*] Roger Manvell and Heinrich Fraenkel describe Expressionism as "essentially a movement designed to get away from actuality and to satisfy the desire to probe seemingly fundamental truths of human nature and society by presenting them through fantasy and dramatized mysticism." Expressionism gets away from actuality through a retreat into the mind and at the same time, paradoxically, through a projection of that mind onto the world. Expressionism externalizes, "expresses," what is inside the mind, it makes "outer" what is "inner." If Impressionism could be said to be the subjective rendering of the visible world, Expressionism is the subjective expression of an inner world, a vision. Many Expressionist plays, dating back to Strindberg's *To Damascus* (1898), a progenitor of the movement, have been called "Ich-dramas," dramas of the "I," the self, on a journey through the mind's inner reaches and the world's outer ones. Many Expressionist works are either explicitly or implicitly political: they react against the social tyranny of the bourgeoisie, on the one hand, and the political tyranny of demagogues, on the other.

Nosferatu's Expressionism has been overlooked, I believe, largely because of its natural, rather than fantastic, settings: the landscape of the Carpathian mountains, the narrow streets and closely packed houses of a small town on the Baltic Sea (where Murnau shot what we are to take as

Bremen, Germany, in 1838, a significant time as will later be shown). But the film may be regarded as Hutter's (Jonathan Harker in Stoker's *Dracula*) "Ich-drama"; and the two other main characters, Ellen, his wife (Nina in the novel), and Nosferatu (Dracula in the novel), may be seen as aspects of Hutter's self. Hutter is no conscious, active rebel against society, as are many Expressionist heroes, themselves often extensions of their creators. He is, rather, a passive instrument of Murnau's mythic design; himself no rebel, Murnau doesn't make a rebel of his alter ego Hutter. A witness to or observer of the German sociopolitical scene, Murnau makes Hutter a witness to or observer of the relationship between Ellen and Nosferatu. Hutter himself is "narrated" by a fictitious contemporary of his who serves as a surrogate for Murnau, by a *historian* whose diary provides the story of Hutter's trip to Transylvania and Nosferatu's descent on Bremen. Professor Van Helsing is Dracula's nemesis in Stoker's novel; Van Helsing plays only a small part in Murnau's film (he's renamed Professor Bulwer). He is obviously not Nosferatu's antagonist: both Annie (Lucy in the novel) and Ellen ask that the Professor be called, once Nosferatu has made his presence felt in Bremen, but the Professor does not go to them and in fact can do nothing to stop Nosferatu. Murnau reduces Van Helsing's role significantly so that Ellen can become simultaneously Nosferatu's destroyer and his victim.

Hutter is clearly linked to Ellen, as an aspect of himself, through marriage. They have recently been married, seem happy—the film begins with Hutter picking flowers for his wife—and together symbolize the bourgeois "correctness" of the Weimar Republic, during which *Nosferatu* was made. He is a clerk in a real estate office in their home town of Bremen. His boss, Knock (Renfield in the novel), asks him to close a property deal—for a house directly opposite his and Ellen's—with Graf Orlok, known as Nosferatu, of Transylvania. Surprisingly, Hutter is more than happy to go, even though the trip will take him away for months from his bride. He seems exultant when he tells Ellen that she cannot travel with him, that she must not risk the danger of crossing the Carpathian mountains. This is the first indication we get, on a mythic or symbolic level (not a psychological one), of Hutter's attraction-repulsion, love-hate, for his wife, for his own bourgeois existence. In place of this humdrum, stifling existence, he gets to travel on horseback to a remote and different place and to do business with a count. His journey will become less a journey away from Bremen than into himself and as much a linking up with Nosferatu as a leave-taking from Ellen.

Hutter is linked to Nosferatu, as an aspect of himself, through business. Hutter works for Knock, who is obviously demented and acts under the long-range influence of Nosferatu; ostensibly, Hutter volunteers to make the long trip to Graf Orlok's castle in order to improve his own position in the real estate office at the same time that he earns his commission. Nosferatu symbolizes the tyrant, about whose depiction in a group of German films from 1920-1924 Siegfried Kracauer has written [in his 1947 *From Caligari to Hitler: A Psychological History of the German Film*]:

In this film type, the Germans of the time—a people still unbalanced, still free to choose its regime—nursed no illusions about the possible consequences of tyranny; on the contrary, they indulged in detailing its crimes and [the] sufferings it inflicted. Was their imagination kindled by the fear of bolshevism? Or did they call upon these frightful visions to exorcise lusts which, they sensed, were their own and now threatened to possess them? (It is, at any rate, a strange coincidence that, hardly more than a decade later, Nazi Germany was to put into practice that very mixture of physical and mental tortures which the German screen then pictured.)

In 1921–1922, when *Nosferatu* was made, Germany was going through a period of great instability, the result of its defeat in World War I and the overthrow of its traditional monarchy. The new German government was an attempt at democracy, but many officials of the Weimar Republic had rightist political leanings. At the same time, Bolshevism was taking root in Germany. The country was thrown into economic and social plight after the collapse of the currency: bread lines began forming and riots broke out everywhere. Kracauer comments, "The Germans obviously held [at this point] that they had no choice other than the cataclysm of anarchy or a tyrannical regime."

If Bram Stoker's *Dracula* was a novel of Victorian sexual repression, Murnau's *Nosferatu* is a film of Weimar-Republic autocratic repression. At one end, in Bremen, there is Ellen, a pallid, emaciated figure who stands for the weakness, the shakiness, of German democracy in the early 1920s and whose recent marriage to Hutter represents their attempt to fall into line with the surface order of bourgeois life in Bremen, with its closely packed houses, carefully charted streets, tightly knit families, and fastidiously kept living quarters. At the other end, in Transylvania, there is Nosferatu, himself a pallid, emaciated figure who, in his shadowiness, stands for the subterranean impulse in the German people of the time toward autocracy: he represents their skeleton in the closet, as it were, ready to emerge and declare itself at any moment. Nosferatu lives alone in his huge castle; it is as if, in his will to absolute power, he has become the sole inhabitant of his realm: he rules all, he *is* all. Appropriately, Nosferatu emerges only at night, sleeping by day in an earth-filled coffin located in a crypt beneath his castle—he also sleeps in such a coffin in the hold of the ship that carries him to Bremen.

Robin Wood has noted that the arch is a visual leitmotif in the film, that it is used by Murnau "particularly to characterize the vampire as a repressed force who is always emerging from under arches or archshapes that seem to be trying unsuccessfully to press down upon him, often forming a background of darkness." (Wood sees Nosferatu, however, as a symbol of repressed sexuality rather than repressed tyranny.) The arch is also used to link Nosferatu with Hutter. There is an arch over the bed in which Hutter sleeps at the inn, just before he enters the vampire's domain. When he enters Nosferatu's castle, Hutter passes under a large arch, just as, when Nosferatu enters Bremen after disembarking from the ship *Demeter,* he walks beneath a large arch. When they meet for the first time, Nosferatu emerges from one arch, Hutter from another; they face each other under yet another arch. Nosferatu's crypt is arched, and when Hutter descends into it to find the vampire's coffin, he passes under a huge, oppressive overhang of rock. There are some other scenes in which arches connect Nosferatu with Hutter. At the end of the dinner scene, for example, when Nosferatu is excited by the blood from Hutter's finger (which he cut while trying to slice some bread), the arch in the background strongly resembles the one from which he first emerged. When Hutter awakens the next day at sunrise, he is still beneath an arch of sorts—the arched ceiling of his room. He eats breakfast in front of an arch, goes outdoors through an arched doorway, passes under a dark arch that takes up the entire foreground of the image, then sits down to write a letter to Ellen under the arches of a small pavilion. He is even standing under an arch when he calls to the postman (on horseback) to come pick up his letter. Hutter's daytime movement through this series of arches is later mirrored by Nosferatu's nighttime passage under several arches on his way to suck the sleeping Hutter's blood.

In between the "democracy" of Ellen/Bremen and the "demagogy" of Nosferatu/Transylvania, or beyond them both, lies anarchy, symbolized by the rough terrain, raw or uncontrolled nature, over which Hutter must travel in order to reach Nosferatu's castle. Along the way, he will ride up and down hills, across woods, and through mists and rushing water; he will encounter "spooked" horses (pursued by a jackal), wolves, and eerie birds. The choice for Murnau's Expressionist hero is between a fragile, yet suffocating democracy on the one hand and a steady, yet equally oppressive tyranny on the other hand, with anarchy the route between these two poles. Ellen and Bremen are his projection, his "mindscreen," just as are Nosferatu and Transylvania. As for the trick photography (the speeded-up coach, the incredibly rapid loading of a carriage with earth-filled coffins), the shots in negative, the odd camera angles, the "supernaturally" opening doors in the castle, and the "supernaturally" propelled ship that takes Nosferatu to Bremen (or rather, "supernaturally" manned sailing ship, the entire crew of which Nosferatu has destroyed), one explanation is that not only are these "endistancing devices" separating the vampire's world from that of the German town, as Gilberto Perez Guillermo believes, but also that these devices are the work of Murnau's/the Expressionist hero's consciousness. To underline this point, Murnau has Hutter insist in a letter to Ellen from Transylvania that, even though the frightening things happening to him seem real, they are all part of a dream. The hero's consciousness projects onto the tyrant's world the extraordinary power that it *imagines* this world to have. Low-angle shots, for instance, make Nosferatu loom up in the frame, and shots in negative suggest that this despot has the ability, not only to speed up motion, but also to reverse the usual positions of light and shadow on objects. That Murnau filmed *Nosferatu* "in the world," on location and not in the studio, lends the scenes of trick photography and "supernatural" motion a reality, a convincingness, that they would otherwise not have: these scenes seem to be not merely the products of someone's febrile mind, as they would seem had they been shot within the confines of a studio, but the products of an entire world at the mercy of an omnipotent, nearly godly, tyrant.

Returning to the subject of Hutter's symbolic attraction-repulsion or love-hate toward his wife, toward both his own tidy bourgeois existence and the precarious democratic structure that supports it, it should be noted that, unlike the Expressionist dramatists, who wrote more or less for a coterie audience, Murnau set his story, not in the present, but in what Lane Roth calls "the safety of the past" [in "Dracula Meets the 'Zeitgeist': *Nosferatu,* (1922) as Film Adaptation," *Literature/Film Quarterly* 7, 1979], where the more "democratic" or popular audience could, if it chose, ignore the film's contemporary sociopolitical implications. Thus, whenever this paper mentions Bremen, Germany, in 1838, one should transpose its social and political order to the Bremen of 1922. For example, Hutter runs from Ellen to Nosferatu, and thus to the promise of financial gain and career advancement. This move makes sense, given the seriously troubled German economy in 1922; Germany as a whole was similarly to run over to Hitler's side ten years later when he artificially stimulated the country's economy with his war machine. Hutter has the same love-hate toward Nosferatu, however, that he has toward his wife. Even though he discovers that the count is a vampire and has in fact assaulted him, Hutter does not try to destroy him (as the count was destroyed in the novel by being beheaded and having a stake driven through his heart). When Hutter sees Nosferatu lying asleep in his coffin during the day, he can only draw back in horror—the same reaction he has when, near the end of the film, Ellen tells him of the vampire's designs on her. Despite the fact that Nosferatu would suck the life out of Hutter and his wife, just as a tyrant would suck the life out of his people, Hutter can do nothing to oppose him. Hutter seems repulsed by yet drawn to an aspect of himself that he sees in Nosferatu. He hates the bourgeois in himself, he is suspicious of the capitalistic democracy that would promote the middle class, but he races back to Ellen from Transylvania. He hates the tyrant in himself, he is suspicious of the "benevolent" dictator who promises to make life better for all the people, yet he does not kill Nosferatu; in effect, he allows the count to make the voyage by ship to Bremen.

It is as if Hutter has deliberately sought out the tyrant Nosferatu, so as to make him aware of Ellen's existence. Nosferatu wants her the instant Hutter shows him her miniature, and Ellen seems to want him. Two incidents suggest this. Hutter returns to Bremen the same way he arrived in Transylvania—by land; the vampire travels to Bremen by sea. When we get a shot of Ellen awaiting her husband's return, however, she is looking out to sea. At one point we see her sleepwalking on her balcony; suddenly she collapses, declaring as she does so, "He's coming, I must go to meet him." Murnau implies that she means Nosferatu, because he cuts to her, not from a shot of Hutter on horseback, but from one of the ship with the vampire aboard it. Ellen seems attracted to Nosferatu at the same time that she is repulsed by him. She allows him to ravish her, to suck her blood, and to destroy himself in the process: she intentionally keeps him at her side until dawn, at which moment the rays of the sun cause him to dissolve into nothingness. Nosferatu is similarly attracted to Ellen at the same time that he is repulsed by her. All the while he is making love to her in his way, is sucking her blood,

he is draining her of life. She dies, and he vanishes into the air.

Nosferatu has taken with him many of the burghers of Bremen, who have died of the plague spread by rats that have made the journey from Transylvania with him. He is repeatedly associated with these rats—they swarm from his earth-filled coffins in the hold of the ship. Indeed, he himself looks like a rat with his long and pointed, hairy ears, his claws, and his fangs; and he moves like one, especially along the streets of Bremen, skulking and sidling in his fear of being set upon by the citizens. In the Expressionist hero Hutter's mind, the tyrant is both a bloodsucker—a parasite—and a spreader of infectious disease, of a political philosophy that is at once deadly and contagious. Thus Hutter projects Nosferatu as a vampire who looks and moves like a rat and who in effect leads a large pack of rats, his "army," the extension of his will. At least two critics have written of the supposed ambiguous nature of the plague in this film: it is spread by rats, yet the vampire's marks are on the victims' necks, as if Nosferatu had visited each one personally. I am arguing that the "ambiguity" is intentional on Murnau's/Hutter's part, that Nosferatu is meant to appear as both rat and vampire, infector and bloodsucker.

Only Hutter seems to have knowledge of the presence of Nosferatu in town, although the tyrant has been afraid that both Hutter and the townspeople would discover him. Yet Hutter, the generator of the apocalyptic vision, stands passively by as Nosferatu decimates much of the population of bourgeois Bremen. The tyrant destroys them, then one of them—Ellen—sacrifices herself to destroy him. Hutter has watched the bourgeois in himself cancel out, and be cancelled out by, the autocrat in himself. He has pitted social tyranny—the bourgeoisie in its conformity and hegemony—against political tyranny—the tyrant in his isolation and omnipotence. The frightened bourgeoisie, on whose fears any tyrant feeds in a time of economic and social unrest (as Hitler was to feed on the fears of the German middle class), itself helps to pull the tyrant down in the end, to take the life out of him. The Expressionist hero Hutter has witnessed the destruction of the two aspects of himself, each of which he both loves and hates: the democratic bourgeois that he is and the "benevolent" dictator that he would be; his will to equality and his will to power.

Hutter is the Expressionist hero as passive bourgeois, not as active intellectual or artist; as a representative of the people, not as their antagonist. He stands, not apart from society, but as a part of it. There is no escape for him into visionary ecstasy, as there might be for the Expressionist rebel, or into art, as there was for the Expressionist creators themselves. He makes no pronouncements concerning the creation of the "New Man," nor does he offer a prescriptive aesthetics. He is left at the end to mourn the loss of himself, the Nosferatu who is gone (along with his agent and Hutter's boss, Knock, who expires back in jail the moment he senses that Nosferatu has perished), and the Ellen who is dead. A title declares that there were no more deaths from the plague and that happiness was regained, but the camera does not return to the streets of

Bremen. We are left with the overwhelming impression of destruction, of loss; a shot of Hutter mourning over Ellen's body is followed by the last shot of the film, which appears to be the product of Hutter's memory: an image of Nosferatu's now vacant castle jutting up into the sky.

The title of Murnau's next film, *Der letzte Mann* (*The Last Man,* 1924, incorrectly translated as *The Last Laugh* in America), could as well be the title of *Nosferatu.* The later work contains Expressionistic elements, but they are fused to a realistic base. We have gone from Hutter's nightmare vision in *Nosferatu* to Emil Jannings' nightmares in *Der letzte Mann,* from the tragic division of one character to the pathetic oneness of another, from the end of the world to a happy ending. Murnau's escape, as Expressionist filmmaker, from the potential artistic dead end of *Nosferatu* was to re-create the everyday world in *Der letzte Mann* and put into it a *character* in a dead end, from which he would be rescued by a dream-come-true: the inheritance, from an American, of a large sum of money. For Murnau, the antidote to Expressionistic nightmare was the opposite extreme: realistic fantasy. (pp. 25-32)

> Bert Cardullo, "Expressionism and 'Nosferatu'," in San Jose Studies, *Vol. 11, No. 3, Fall, 1985, pp. 25-33.*

Robert C. Allen on *Sunrise*:

To the film historian few films are more conspicuously extraordinary than *Sunrise.* Its synchronous musical and sound effects track make it a curious technological hybrid. It incorporates the efforts of, respectively, the most famous writer, director, and designer of the German "Golden Age," yet was made in Hollywood. Produced within the studio system, the *Sunrise* project was nevertheless given attention and freedom which, if not unique, were certainly highly unusual. Indeed, it is tempting to consider *Sunrise* that most fortunate of accidents, one of the few of many Hollywood extravagances which, more through happenstance than foresight, turned out to be a work of lasting cinematic art.

Robert C. Allen in his "William Fox Presents 'Sunrise'," in Quarterly Review of Film Studies, August, 1977.

Janet Bergstrom   (essay date 1986)

[*In the following essay, Bergstrom examines elements of sexuality, spectatorship, and abstraction in Murnau's films. Arguing that Murnau's handling of these elements reflects the cinema and theater traditions of the Weimar Republic, Bergstrom also discusses how these elements affected Murnau's reception in America.*]

F. W. Murnau was a prestige director in the Weimar cinema, both by industry standards and in the eyes of the public, when he accepted William Fox's offer in 1925 to work in Hollywood. The contract was signed soon after *Der Letzte Mann* (*The Last Laugh*) had its spectacular world premiere in Berlin; by the time Murnau arrived in the United States about a year later, American critics were describing *The Last Laugh* as the greatest achievement of film as an art form the world had ever seen. Meanwhile, Murnau had increased his own reputation as an artist-director with the release of two more [Universum Film Aktien Gesellschaft (UFA)] super-productions, *Tartuffe* and *Faust.* Fox organized a fairly massive publicity campaign around signing the "German genius," promoting as "the world's greatest film artist" a director he was willing to pay a high price to import. As a commodity negotiated from one national cinema to its most important competitor, Dr. Murnau or F. W. Murnau, Ph.D., as he was often deferentially referred to by every level of the critical establishment, conformed to a highly desirable image at this time in the United States—the cultured European artist-intellectual. That William Fox would bring in such a unique talent was meant to indicate to the press, and thereby to the public, that Fox Films was committed to making quality motion pictures, like the larger studios it was aiming to catch up with in another arena—the marketplace.

In order to help achieve Fox's goal, Murnau was given control that became legendary over his first American film, *Sunrise.* Time and expense were unimportant so long as the desired effect was achieved. Consequently, time and cost over-runs were fabulous. William Fox, as far as can be determined, stayed out of the production almost entirely.

Sunrise, released in 1927, received even more critical applause than *The Last Laugh.* Although not all reviewers were happy with the simplicity of the plot or the stylized acting, everyone seemed overwhelmed by its visual beauty. Both cinematographers, Charles Rosher and Karl Struss, received an Academy Award. Murnau had made the camera the star of the picture, to paraphrase an opening-night review. However, *Sunrise* was not a popular film; it was very expensive and it did not make money. William K. Everson, eminent historian of the American silent cinema, claims [in his *American Silent Film,* 1978] that "the enormous critical success of *Sunrise,* however, caused it to be the single most influential picture of the period . . . ," and that "the impact of *Sunrise* as a film, and of Murnau as a new artistic leader, was enormous, especially at Fox."

But Murnau's career with Fox was to last for only two more films, and in neither case was he able to maintain anything like the control he had had over *Sunrise.* William Fox was apparently no longer willing or able to finance prestige at a loss. This law of the marketplace was typical of the American way, which would sooner or later be felt by all the émigrés invited to Hollywood. Murnau made only one more film, *Tabu* (1929), an independent production shot in the South Seas with the documentary filmmaker, Robert Flaherty. A few days before *Tabu* opened, Murnau was killed in a freak car accident on his way to Santa Barbara, California.

Murnau's decision to leave the German film industry for Hollywood meant, among other things, that he would undertake to make films for a different audience and within the context of a somewhat different set of formal and narrative conventions. The consensus after his death seemed to be that Dr. Murnau was a misfit in the American studio system, unlike, for example, Ernst Lubitsch, who had left a very successful and much-publicized career in Germany about five years before Murnau, but who had made the transition look easy by establishing himself almost immediately as a major Hollywood director. What might have rendered Murnau "unfit" for Hollywood? In responding to this question, I am particularly interested in seeing how conventions relating to sexual identity, the spectator, and modes of abstraction do or do not carry over from one highly conventionalized national cinema to another, namely, from Weimar to Hollywood. These are, I feel, the key issues in Murnau's case.

The emphasis here is different from that found in most discussions of "the Germans" coming to Hollywood. It is misleading to talk about the German émigrés as if one were describing a single, homogeneous group. In fact there were wide differences in times and circumstances of arrival, as well as differences in individual personality and approaches to filmmaking. Second, my essay relies on an understanding of conventions in cinema at a given point in their development, not on personalities. Although personal idiosyncrasy plays a part in how conventions may be used, disregarded, or adapted, it is a secondary consideration. For example, the "fact" that Lubitsch fit into the Hollywood social/business world with delight and ease, while the "cultured" Murnau remained "aloof," has limited explanatory power when it comes to the reception of their films in the United States. Lubitsch was one of the first of a long line of Weimar directors to become successful in Hollywood, even if their successes were far from identical, while Murnau stands out as a major exception. I would suggest that the ways in which Murnau treated conventional aspects of cinematic representation—in particular his formulation of sexual identity and of a mode of looking virtually required of the spectator—were among the most important reasons both for his success in Germany and for his lack of acceptance as an "American" director.

On the one hand, I am interested in Murnau as an example of a Weimar director who, like Lubitsch and others later with their own configuration of personal and professional circumstances, difficulties, and successes, attempted to enter another highly conventionalized cinema. On the other hand, I want to explore Murnau's particular contribution to the cinematic conventions of his day, and the extent to which the experimentation he was engaged in could carry over to the American cinema. A comparison between the Weimar and Hollywood cinemas need not, of course, be formulated in terms of directors; Murnau is meant to be seen here as a director in the context of the conventions of his day—his audience(s), his possibilities, his limitations. Examples from Murnau's films will come from *Nosferatu* (1922), *Faust* (1926), and *Sunrise* (1927). References to his other films are absent only because of lack of space, as all his films relate, in different ways, to the issues at hand.

Among the many newspaper obituaries of Murnau that have been preserved, I came upon one that contains an un-

usually interesting appraisal of Murnau's reception in the United States:

> Then came Murnau's version of the Faust legends, which was certainly one of the most beautiful motion pictures ever made. As a matter of fact, it was so superior in its pictorial loveliness that, in some curious manner, a number of distinguished observers were frightened by it. Suddenly they developed an inordinate interest in virility, and announced sadly that the exquisite visual qualities of *Faust* gave it an effete touch which was out of keeping with the stark, grim manliness that was inherent in films. . . . Then, too, there was that weakness of the director in handling women. Both in *The Four Devils* and *Sunrise* [Janet] Gaynor was unnecessarily handicapped, in the former by a role which the director neglected; in the latter by a clumsy blonde head-dress. In both pictures the character of the villainess . . . was overstressed in the early Theda Bara manner. [Richard Watts, Jr., in his "Sight and Sound," *New York Herald Tribune,* March 18, 1931]

It is noteworthy that this columnist connects the element most generally admired in Murnau's films, pictorial beauty, with the aspects most widely criticized by American reviewers at the time of the films' release and by later commentators, namely the lack of virility in male protagonists (especially the young Faust) and the unrealistic representation of female characters. Extreme pictorial loveliness of an almost abstract nature is juxtaposed with a lack of virility; their proximity is enough to inspire fear. I would like to suggest that, unlike the American cinema, the Weimar cinema's tendency to abstraction allowed for modes of viewing more commonly associated with the fine arts, specifically with looking at paintings, to cast a kind of aesthetic veil over images of feminized male figures as well as one-dimensional female characters. This mode of viewing itself was made possible by the circulation of the films within a cultural tradition that put a high value on the arts. It could be assumed that in Weimar Germany Murnau had an audience with an art historical awareness, even if only in a very generalized sense; beyond that, for a more restricted group, references could be made to particular genres and styles of painting.

If women were one-dimensional in Murnau's films, that dimension was not physical or sensual, unless it corresponded to the notion of sensuality in death, familiar from the Romantic tradition in literature, or the morbid fascination with the female body in Symbolist and Pre-Raphaelite painting, realized by artists such as Puvis de Chavannes, Millais, Munch, Moreau, Redon, and Fuselli. In this regard, a number of images from Murnau's films come to mind: the final shots of Gretchen in *Faust,* of Nina in *Nosferatu* (both of whom die), and of the wife in *Sunrise* floating in the water as if drowned and then laid out on her bed surrounded by her long, wavy hair as if she were dead, the severe braids finally undone.

In Murnau's films, the woman's body becomes an abstraction. Compared to its conventional representation in commercial narrative films, the woman's body is at a loss, both metaphorically and literally. As Raymond Bellour has shown in great detail [in his 1979 *L'Analyse du film*], the classical Hollywood cinema, consistent with a system of representations characteristic of the 19th century, came progressively to locate its representation of sexuality, and the symbolic significance of sexual difference in establishing identity, in the body of the woman. Laura Mulvey, from an explicitly feminist perspective, extended a similar claim to narrative cinema in general [in her "Visual Pleasure and Narrative Cinema," *Screen* 16, 1975]. This was also often true of the Weimar cinema, although unlike the American cinema, class identity is usually as strongly marked in both iconographic and narrative terms as sexual identity, and the two are almost always won or lost in the same moment. Typing by social class was so important to Weimar narratives that it often obscured the significance of sexual definition. In Murnau's films, however, the reverse seems to be true: sexual identity is emphasized over class identity. Furthermore, femininity, insofar as it can be associated with eroticism or sexuality, has been displaced from the woman's body to several kinds of substitutes. The woman's body is at a loss literally in that it has a reduced physical presence, lacking a sexual dimension; metaphorically, the symbolic function of the woman's body in establishing sexual difference is greatly diminished. The few exceptions to this pattern serve only to reinforce it: the City Woman in **Sunrise** is exclusively sexual, but exactly for that reason her symbolic connotations are as one-dimensional as the desexualized, ethereal type of female character which predominates in Murnau's films. Substitutes to make up for this loss can be located in Murnau's films at the level of story and characters, and can also be seen in the mode of apprehension of the film by the spectator.

To say that the woman's body becomes an abstraction is to assert something more than the general reliance on abstracted situations and characters in the Weimar cinema. In order to understand the significance of this statement, the investigation of Murnau's use of conventions to represent the woman's body and sexuality more generally will have to be deferred temporarily, as his particular use of conventions—that is, his reworking or displacement of certain internalized "rules" of the Weimar cinema—cannot be understood without first establishing what these conventions were.

Certainly abstraction was more obvious in the Weimar cinema than in Hollywood films. Abstraction was already accessible, acceptable, and familiar because of the tradition of Expressionist theater, by the twenties no longer an avant-garde movement but part of mainstream theatrical productions. Most noticeably, one finds types clearly designated as such: characters often do not have names, but are meant to denote a position, generally within a family and/or class structure. Thus the credits may list "the mother," "the son," "the prostitute," "the countess," "the boss," etc. However, within the films there is often no need for even these labels because the symbolic function of characters is readily apparent, conventionally related to problems of both class and sexual identity, and because an elaborate iconography of costume, makeup, and acting stylization, largely derived from Expressionist theater, had been developed to grant the spectator an immediate

visual identification with the various types who would enter into the narrative.

What is not immediately apparent, however, is that this cinema used a *popular* acceptance of abstraction through a limited repertoire of character types (very uncharacteristic of the American cinema, for example) in stories that are often highly ambiguous. Moreover, the structural ambiguity of many Weimar plots (such as the myriad variations on the theme of the double) was made increasingly convincing *as ambiguous* by means of stylistic or formal devices that seemed to be the area of greatest experimentation within this cinema. Formal innovation came to function stylistically, and according to industry voices "artistically," so as to render fundamentally *unstable* the foundation for the types which were so readily identifiable. Power as it relates to class and sexual definition is not comprehensible in this cinema aside from the concept of instability. [In his 1947 *From Caligari to Hitler*] Siegfried Kracauer is correct in observing the endless attempts at class rise that end in failure and impotence, or a fall out of class altogether into prostitution, anonymity, madness, or death. In these typical stories of unstable symbolic identities, stylistic conventions are continually reworked both to increase abstraction and to underscore the idea of ambiguity.

The use of space, an important example, is markedly different here from the way it developed in the Hollywood cinema. The 180-degree rule, for example, is one of the fundamentals of the classical American continuity style. The camera is supposed to remain on one side of an imaginary line in the different positions it may occupy to film a scene. Although it is an oversimplification, one could think of the spatial arrangement of a traditional theater and its audience. The purpose of the rule is to help the viewer maintain spatial orientation with respect to the scene—to help build the illusion that it is a real space (and a real story) before one's eyes. The more general principle that applies is the "rule" of invisible editing (by no means reducible to any set of formulas): the spectator should follow story and characters, and should not notice style, particularly editing or camera as such.

However much the phrase occurs in the critical literature, it does not make sense to talk about violations of the 180-degree rule in the context of the Weimar cinema, because either one would have to say that it is routinely violated, or one would have to observe that it is not a convention of editing in Weimar films. In general, the use of space is flexible to the point of extreme disorientation with respect to the relative place of elements within what one might expect to be a coherent space. Great use is made of point of view shots which may or may not be attributed later to an unexpected character, glance/object set-ups where it may or may not be clear who is looking and thus what the significance of the object is, and alternation that joins highly disparate spaces which may or may not be explained in terms of story.

This last variant might consist of simple chase-type crosscutting or complex alternation that includes many elements and highly imaginative uses of ellipsis and associational montage. For example, the opening scene of Fritz

Shadow of the vampire, from Nosferatu.

Lang's *M* (1931), which has frequently been analyzed as an accomplished example of Weimar experimentation, is built on an extremely subtle and complicated system of alternations. The intended meaning, in one sense, is absolutely clear: through alternation on both sound and image tracks, and through variations of presence and absence of the little girl, her mother, and the anticipated murderer, we know Elsie's mother's worry as it becomes fear, and we know Elsie moves from danger to death. But the point, formally, is that Lang can present this in highly elliptical fashion, so that we feel we can make assumptions based on what we in fact have not seen. In his films, this technique often works against the spectator as a trap, but precisely a trap made possible by a highly conventionalized system of elliptical editing.

Ambiguity in editing could also be related to the other area of pride in Weimar cinematic specialization: camera style and lighting. Instability of class, sexual identity, and space is often correlated with the manipulation of vision, with what the characters and/or audience are allowed to see. This directed and thematic use of light, within a system that generally favored low light levels compared to Hollywood or pre-Weimar German films, was also inspired by the theater of Max Reinhardt and others, but was transformed with great inventiveness by film directors and their cinematographers.

Murnau's reworking of these conventions relating to abstraction and ambiguity is evident in at least two important areas: his use of the familiar device of the double, and, on a level that pertains to the spectator's mode of viewing, his self-conscious use of the Weimar cinema's highly promoted and successful image as art cinema.

Murnau's own media image as a film artist, not just a director, clearly fit into the larger picture of his industry and its desire to build and maintain an audience. The German film industry took pride in characterizing itself as superior to other national cinemas artistically, and had developed a commercial appeal for its films based on a "high art" self-identification. There are constant references to film as art in the trade and popular film journals of the twenties in Germany. This became a selling point both in competing for domestic audiences, primarily with American films, and in building up a healthy and widely-reviewed export business. From the perspective of American trade journals, where the success of this campaign could be seen indirectly, the corner on artistry that German films seemed to be consolidating in the eyes of influential American critics was undeserved, unwelcome, and contested.

The theme of the double was popular from the 19th century Romantic tradition of German literature; Lotte Eisner, in *The Haunted Screen,* frequently refers to this tradition when describing typical plots of Weimar films. Among her examples are the story of the man who loses his shadow or mirror image and gains an evil twin (*The Student of Prague* syndrome); stories of split personalities, greatly varied; and the representation of mental or psychological derangement, accomplished through an exaggerated, stylized shift in acting in which, typically, the character slows drastically in pace, stares fixedly but no longer sees the external world, sometimes sees apparitions, often gropes along a wall, and almost invariably puts hand to head.

To turn from this general discussion to Murnau's specific contribution, I believe that although the kinds of conventions outlined here are limited in number, it is reasonable to assume that the contemporary audience for Weimar cinema was already accustomed to types, to a conceptual cinema that was in certain regards highly conventionalized. It can be argued, further, that this "popularizing" of abstraction and ambiguity allowed Murnau to represent sexuality in a displaced and abstracted fashion—that is to say (with the foregoing discussion in mind) that he was able to reshape or modify conventions in a way that could still be seen as falling within the norms of his audience and industry.

For example, Murnau's use of the double in *Nosferatu* and *Sunrise* has been linked by Robin Wood [in "Murnau," *Film Comment* 12, 1976] to the repression of sexuality. According to Wood's argument, Nosferatu, the vampire, represents sexuality itself, and as such must be eliminated from the world of the narrative. His double is Jonathan, who shares none of Nosferatu's characteristics, lacking in particular both power and sexuality. Nosferatu's antagonist is not Jonathan, but his wife, Nina, who sacrifices her own life for her husband. In a highly ambiguous gesture, where she seems both to need and to repudiate sexuality/Nosferatu, she attracts and keeps the vampire with her until the cock crows at dawn. Nosferatu then disintegrates into vapor, and Nina dies. Wood draws a convincing parallel between Nosferatu and the City Woman in *Sunrise,* both creatures of the night, the unnatural, and sexuality. The City Woman clearly represents evil, and a threat to nature, the family, and civilization. (One might add that visually, as well as functionally, she is very close to Mephisto in *Faust,* dressed in black satiny materials, and is, like him, the character with the greatest physical presence in the film.) Her failure to entice the man from the country to murder his wife, sell his farm, and go away with her to the city is viewed by Wood as analogous to the necessary destruction of the vampire at the end of *Nosferatu.* This victory over sexuality, however, is not only won by default—the man remains passive throughout—but it has its price.

> As with *Nosferatu* . . . the sharp division remains between "pure" love and eroticism. The wife of *Sunrise* quite lacks the blanched and angular quality of Nina, the appearance of a female Christ-on-the-Cross, but, although very feminine, she strikes the spectator as decidedly unsensual (an impression to which her tightly knotted hair contributes a great deal). And sensuality, again, is depicted unequivocally as evil and destructive (Wood 1976).

The chief double Wood sees in *Sunrise* is the husband,

who is alternately a "monster" and "normal," depending on whether or not he is under the sway of the City Woman. The entire second half of the film is devoted to repudiating (more or less successfully) the monster in him, ending with the departure of the City Woman.

It seems to me important for Murnau's representation of sexuality that the system of the double, which is emphasized by Wood, is brought into another old and accepted system, much-analyzed in other contexts: a system of triangulation where the one desiring and the love object are connected indirectly through a mediator. It is partly this overlay of conventional systems which masks the indirect sexual substitutions that make narratively unacceptable representations of desire possible on another level. In Murnau's case, this systematic complication of the way sexuality is represented allows for sexual investment in semi-conventional terms, with aesthetic references used as the basis for the presentation of images that might or might not be called homoerotic. A system of relays, delays, and necessarily deferred gratification is built up out of a series of basically static views of compositions that recall paintings, and that call upon the viewer to look at the image on the screen as if he or she were looking at a work of art. There is a culturally sanctioned precedent for appreciating the sensuality of young men's bodies, for example, in the history of art. For if one asks what position is assigned to the woman in Murnau's films, one quickly realizes that this question is subordinate to a more insistent one: where is the location of the feminine? Although the representation of the feminine is not necessarily stable, many important examples can be found of a clearly-coded feminine displaced onto the body of an aestheticized male-gendered character.

Such, for example, is the image of the young Faust that gave American critics pause—too feminine, not only in face, expression, and body (revealed by his velvety costumes), but also in the postures he habitually adopts. How do we first see him? Through the mediation of Mephisto, we see with the aged and despairing Faust the beautiful face of a young man, like a portrait, shimmering in a bowl of liquid poison he intends to drink to end his life. "Is it death?" asks Faust. "It is your youth," replies Mephisto. A few moments later, Mephisto holds out Faust's youth to him again as an image in a mirror, and with this image, seduces him into signing the pact that gives him one trial day to experience Mephisto's services. Throughout the film, Mephisto is the figure who mediates, suggests, and defines Faust's desire until the climactic moment of Gretchen's call for help. And although Faust ultimately establishes his identity through his relationship to Gretchen—sin and redemption—throughout the film we are able to treasure his youth as a sensuous, artistic wonder, much as the old Faust is taken with the image of the young Faust.

Because the young man is said to represent his own youth, Faust's desire is designated by the narrative as natural, rather than as the result of a sexualized seduction. Desire for the young Faust is represented as being even more indirect by the fact that Mephisto, the mediator, is necessary to Faust's temptation. That the temptation is sexual is made clear by the first act Mephisto performs after endowing Faust with the young man's body: he presents a diaphanous vision of a woman, almost naked in transparent veils, as the pleasure Faust's youth is entitled to. The young man eagerly accepts. Thus, the woman's body is presented (very briefly) as sexuality, and in a way that directs our narrative interest away from the sight of the young Faust himself. Her sexuality is presented as the work of the devil, as entrapment, for Faust will sign his soul away a few scenes later to avoid interrupting this first gratification of his sexual appetite. Given all this narrative and stylistic machinery, the viewer is left to enjoy the beauty of the young Faust without thinking twice. Moving or still, his image *as* image welcomes the gaze. In the film, there is no image of a woman that can compete with it, except for Gretchen. But she represents, almost exactly like the wife in *Sunrise* and not unlike Nina in *Nosferatu,* the asexual madonna, with a powerful and different sort of attraction.

The shifting of doubles into triangular patterns is equally pronounced in *Nosferatu*; the displacement of sexuality is also evident, although it is not so dazzling or obviously aestheticized as in *Faust.* The film can be read, as Robin Wood sees it, as the story of Nosferatu's desire for Nina and her reciprocal desire (albeit unwilling) for him, i.e., for sexuality. However, we can also read it as the seduction of Jonathan by Nosferatu, and Jonathan's compliance, mediated by the figure of Nina, whom the narrative presents simply as the wife trying to save her husband. Two scenes soon after Jonathan's arrival at the remote castle make the triangular connection between Nina, Jonathan, and Nosferatu quite clear. Jonathan is offered dinner at a long table set only for one. Nosferatu sits with him, studying a letter that describes in weird hieroglyphics the house Jonathan has been sent to sell him. He peers over the top of the letter to stare at Jonathan as he eats. Jonathan uneasily slices a piece of bread, the clock strikes midnight, he cuts his thumb, and Nosferatu approaches rapidly to suck the wound: "You've hurt yourself. Your precious blood." Jonathan backs slowly away from him, stumbling on the low tier of stairs behind him, then falling back into a chair, eyes wide. Nosferatu sits down next to him. It is in the same position, almost reclining, that Jonathan awakens the next morning. He examines his neck with a mirror, interpreting the vampire's mark as insect bites. After a brief scene where we see Jonathan writing to Nina, a title tells us that evening has come. Now Jonathan is again with Nosferatu, at a table looking at the letter Jonathan has brought. A cameo portrait of Nina that has fallen out of Jonathan's satchel catches Nosferatu's eye. He picks it up, oblivious to Jonathan and his papers. "What a beautiful neck your wife has." He then announces: "I am buying the house . . . the beautiful, deserted house that faces yours. . . . "

Nosferatu's desire for Jonathan is always mediated by Nina, just as his desire for Nina is mediated by Jonathan. The meaning of this apparent interchangeability, however, is altered by the different ways in which we are given each body as an image. While Nina has certain feminine attributes—she is ethereal, unphysical, progressively more fragile and ill—Jonathan has others. The unnatural kiss that the vampire finally gives Nina, that kills both of them

(not all that different from the scene at the stake at the end of *Faust*) is, initially, given to Jonathan, who serves as a substitute. Unlike Nina's rigidity, his body offers no resistance, even in his fright when the vampire enters his bedroom. Jonathan's acquiescence (no matter how unknowing or unwilling in narrative terms) nourishes the vampire, and like the young Faust, the attitudes his body repeatedly adopts could be termed feminine. As in the example just cited, he is frequently made to step slowly backwards, and then drape himself across a chair, a bed, or some other piece of the decor. Because Jonathan's body is always softened by his costumes, particularly the folds of his frock coats, he often appears simply as a male figure arranged for us to see.

In narrative terms, Jonathan represents the passive, impotent male so common in the Weimar cinema, as Kracauer has observed. Iconographically, his image as the immobilized male character, literally and symbolically deflated, also fits Kracauer's description, but Kracauer's explanation of how this iconographic convention is linked to the displacement of power need not follow, or at any rate, need not be exclusive. Through an overlay of conventions, Murnau at the same time evokes a different kind of looking by the way he positions Jonathan in the image, one that is both non-narrative and non-judgemental. For once in the Weimar cinema, the passive, masochistic male is seen sympathetically, not as an object of pity. His posture can be interpreted as feminine, but not—or not only—according to the typical scenario of symbolic defeat. It may be translated as a quotation from the highly valued tradition of painting. The moment of loss of power, as Robin Wood points out even about Nosferatu, is poignant. In other words, the emphasis is displaced from class and from sexual identity (which is *apparently* preserved as normal) to an erotics of looking. Conventions of narrative cinema which, in these films, center on heterosexual relationships and never introduce a non-heterosexual character (unlike many other Weimar films) are overlaid by the conventions of a less goal-oriented way of looking.

The displacement of desire from the woman's body to the man's, and, importantly, to other, more generalized substitutes, works because Murnau can call on a different sort of spectator convention than is operative in most narrative films—as if another system of reading were superimposed over the classical mode. This is only possible because abstraction and ambiguity are already strongly established, and in fact overdetermined, in Weimar cinema. Unlike the American continuity system, where the ideal is for everything to serve a purpose, here not everything need fit into an explicable narrative economy. The acceptance of ambiguity implies a kind of tolerance, a willingness to forego certainty.

Looking at paintings is not the same as looking at films, and I would like to suggest that the kinds of paintings Murnau is recalling in his visual themes and compositions, such as the portraits of Rembrandt or Vermeer, or the landscape paintings of Caspar David Friedrich or Altdorfer (as Eric Rohmer . . . has studied in the case of *Faust* [in his *L'organisation de l'espace dans le "Faust" de Murnau,* 1977]), are intended to elicit a contemplative look. In the contours and postures of the young Faust it is difficult to avoid thinking of the Endymion reproduced by Barthes in *S/Z*. One might speculate that this look is analogous to that special kind of looking Laura Mulvey described as characteristic of Sternberg's use of Marlene Dietrich—a visual spectacle that, unlike what is supposed to happen in American, action-oriented films, functions to stop the narrative. In Mulvey's analysis, this out-of-time look is always tied to the woman's body; in fact, her entire discussion of pleasure in looking at narrative film centers on characters who will claim attention within the visual field. Pleasure derived from looking at the woman's body is only possible through two processes for the spectator: voyeurism or fetishism. These processes correspond, according to a Freudian schema, to two modes of pleasure in looking (scopophilia): active and passive. Mulvey implies, through omission of any discussion of the female spectator, that the woman experiences narrativized visual pleasure in the same way that the male spectator does. Mulvey's argument, the most provocative to have appeared on the subject of the woman's body in film, has served to highlight the following question: what about the female spectator? Why should one assume that her relationship to the woman on the screen is the same as a man's? This problem has led to a theoretical impasse; the problem appears to be locked into an inadequate conceptualization of feminine sexuality within psychoanalytic theory.

But it seems to me that this is the wrong question to begin with, unless one is interested in the female spectator only from historical and sociological perspectives. Setting up viewer identification in terms that oppose the "male spectator" to the "female spectator" impoverishes the psychoanalytic description of sexual identity. Likewise, assigning fictional characters fixed sexual identities that correspond to gender is often unhelpful in understanding the movement of desire in particular films. Perhaps there is another avenue available within a psychoanalytic framework which leads toward a non-reductive description of sexual orientation and pleasure, less dependent on gender-defined objects, or simply less object-oriented.

In his early and enduring work, *Three Essays on the Theory of Sexuality* (1905), Freud proposed a conceptual framework for a model of sexual identity that is much more flexible than Mulvey's polemic would lead one to believe. He makes an extremely important distinction between sexual object and sexual aim. This allows Freud to differentiate between inversion and perversion, and among a number of perversions (including voyeurism and fetishism). The individual's adult sexual identity is defined not only by the choice of love object (male/female), but also by the preference of sexual aim (active/passive). In fact, each category (object and aim) describes a spectrum of real or imaginary choices. Object choice, therefore, is not the sole determinant of sexual identity. Another important thing to notice is that Freud essentially redefines the meaning of "choice" by maintaining that sexual desire is characteristically unstable, both in object and in aim. Most fundamentally, because Freud argues for a predisposition to bisexuality, the field of choice of both sexual object and sexual aim is defined as a continuum where the

end points (male/female and active/passive) are ideal, or theoretical. Freud's theory of bisexuality means neither "either/or" (heterosexual or homosexual) nor "both" (if that means two fixed choices).

While Mulvey makes use of the distinction between object choice and aim, she uses them as if they were both gender-specific in narrative cinema; woman is object, man is subject of the gaze: "the image of woman as (passive) raw material for the (active) gaze of man." The contemplative look that seems central to erotic pleasure in Murnau's films might be conceptualized in terms of a passive sexual aim, unlike Mulvey's "(active) gaze of man," and libidinal investment need not be tied to any single or gendered object. I am proposing that the erotics of looking, specifically in Murnau's case but more generally as well, could be freed from the exercise of lining up spectators or characters according to a male/female dichotomy. This is not to deny the importance of identification or classification based on gender; on the contrary, it allows gender identification to be interpreted as part of a more complex picture. If we can tentatively say that the desire in looking at paintings has a passive aim, we can see how pleasurable variations in imagining sexual identification and orientation can become acceptable to a large audience—which would probably not be possible if translated into object choice.

The description of narrative cinema offered by Mulvey, among others, is character-centered and accounts for visual pleasure strictly in terms of the way figures are viewed within a setting (decor or action). While in Murnau's films there are figures that attract our visual attention, even if their narrative function and their visual pleasure function are not aligned exactly as in the classical American cinema, Murnau also gives an important place to images of landscapes (or compositions that recall genre paintings of the sea, country people, or even the city) which invite the same kind of contemplative look. I believe that this look is continuous with figure-oriented images in Murnau's films, and that both are invested with a generalized, non-object-oriented sexuality.

On the one hand, there are memorable images of landscapes which are clearly associated through montage or superimposition with sexuality, and which are connected, with more or less abstraction, to a character's imaginary point of view. The City Woman and the man she is seducing conjure up sexualized landscapes together—or possibly he has visions that she evokes for him. The landscape composition of the marsh lit by the moon, visible at first as the backdrop for their sexual meeting, is transformed into a highly sexualized image of the city, with fan-like montages of jazz musicians, dancers, the amusement park; and then is brought back to the marsh through the City Woman's erotically-charged dance. Two shots from *Faust* bracket the film and associate the faces that mean negative and positive sexuality for Faust: first, the huge face of Mephisto fills the screen, superimposed over the city, breathing out the plague; near the end of the film, an immense close-up of Gretchen is superimposed over the landscape as she calls out to Faust for help. On the other hand, there are many landscape compositions elsewhere in *Sunrise* and abundantly in *Faust* and *Nosferatu* that are reminiscent of the lonely, quasi-religious genre paintings of the German Romantic tradition. They correspond to a very generalized sexuality which is not made explicit in the narrative; it is aestheticized directly for the spectator and for the fulfillment, in the slow pace of the images, of visual pleasure.

Through Murnau's displacement of sexual investment in the image from its narrative position as melodrama (the drama of the heterosexual couple as centerpiece for narrative and symbolic conflict), sexuality as a denoted presence is, in a sense, lost to abstraction. But by the same techniques or strategies, sexuality is gained in a more general and all-pervasive sense for the spectator. For not only is the spectator encouraged to feast his or her eyes on all the carefully composed sequences of images, which are loosely organized as an alternation of landscape and figure, but the spectator is also encouraged to relax rigid demarcations of gender identification and sexual orientation.

The "problem" of *Sunrise* in the United States lay in the fact that the American public was presented with a film made according to the conventions of another cinema that were significantly different from its own. The success of Murnau's reworking of conventions—overlaying narrative and stylistic conventions from the Weimar cinema with pictorial conventions from another tradition—was dependent on an audience willing to look at a film with the pace and attention required in looking at paintings. This meant, for the Weimar cinema, an audience that recognized and valued art and was also accustomed to cinematic conventions of abstraction and ambiguity. The American audience, on the other hand, was in the midst of a cinema that was perfecting conventions of narrative and visual action and economy of detail. The failure of *Sunrise* as a popular film could have been predicted. However, the experimentation that can be seen in Murnau's films—the alternation in attention between narrative and non-narrative elements used to displace sexual identification—is not only of historical interest. The attempt to understand Murnau's use of convention and innovation can help us see new possibilities for the cinematic representation of sexual identity. (pp. 243-60)

> *Janet Bergstrom, "Sexuality at a Loss: The Films of F. W. Murnau," in* The Female Body *in Western Culture: Contemporary Perspectives, edited by Susan Rubin Suleiman, Cambridge, Mass.: Harvard University Press, 1986, pp. 243-61.*

Judith Mayne   (essay date 1986)

[*Mayne is a critic and educator who specializes in film, feminist, and literary studies. In the following essay, she compares* Nosferatu *to Bram Stoker's novel* Dracula *(1897).*]

Were it not for the actual acknowledgment of Bram Stoker's 1897 novel *Dracula* in the credits, it might be easy to forget that F. W. Murnau's film *Nosferatu* has any direct connection to a literary source. Stoker's novel has been the most influential literary version of the vampire legend, but because that legend is so well-known, one tends to dis-

count the importance of this particular novel for the first screen version of Dracula's tale.

Is anything to be gained from an analysis of *Nosferatu* as an *adaptation* of the Stoker novel? Some of the temptation to dismiss a comparison between the two texts has less to do with this particular novel and this particular film than with the limitations of adaptation analysis itself. Critics of film adaptations of literary works may no longer insist, again and again, that "the novel (or play) was better," but the very notion of source (sacred or otherwise) and adaptation (faithful or not) is problematic. Many film adaptations have been little more than illustrated comic-book versions of the classics. But even more complex and sophisticated adaptations are evaluated more often than not according to how certain scenes and techniques were "translated" into film language. It is as if literature provides the unquestioned master code for which cinematic equivalents must be found.

That literature has a central place in the history of the cinema, and of the classical cinema in particular, is certain. But it is precisely the historical perspective which is so often lacking in the study of adaptations. By "historical perspective" I mean some obvious questions—why certain kinds of works were adapted at certain periods in film history, for example, or how the turn to literary sources was often an attempt to attract middle-class audiences to movie theaters, thus giving the cinema a certain legitimacy. An historical perspective on the relationship between literature and film also suggests that the relationship between two texts, one literary and one cinematic, is a dynamic encounter rather than a static rendering of a story line from one medium to another.

It could be argued that the acknowledgment of Stoker in Henrik Galeen's screenplay is more strategic than substantial. The acknowledgment might well be a gesture of legitimation, an identification with a literary source so as to validate Murnau's own contribution to the development of an art cinema. The problem with such a view, however, is that Bram Stoker is not an author one immediately associates with such validation. When an American producer like David O. Selznick turns to an author like Charles Dickens, the validative strategy is clear. Stoker, however, is more of an anomaly in nineteenth-century fiction, and many of the features of *Dracula*—its Gothic themes, its epistolary form—are characteristic of earlier periods of literary history. Praise of the novel as a literary gem seems to require a certain defensiveness. [In his 1981 *The Living Dead: A Study of the Vampire in Romantic Literature* James B. Twitchell] describes this anomalous status of *Dracula*: "The book appeared in 1897, at the height of literary Realism and Naturalism. Had it been written in 1820, I suspect that it would have been hailed, as *Frankenstein* is, as a Romantic milestone." Perhaps Stoker was less a romantic cast out in a sea of realists and naturalists than he was symptomatic of changes taking place in the very scope and function of narrative. The sheer number of film versions of *Dracula* do not necessarily attest to some fundamental affinity between Stoker's handling of the vampire legend and the nature and appeal of the cinema. Yet that *Dracula* was published in 1897, during the very years that the cinema was emerging, may well be, as the saying goes, "no coincidence." Stoker provides Murnau not only with a source for the film version of *Dracula,* but also with a set of reflections and meditations on the very nature of story-telling itself. There are numerous suggestions, in Murnau's film, that the vampire story as it is plotted in Stoker's novel is not just being transformed, but commented upon as well.

Dracula may be divided into three major parts, each focusing on Dracula's relationship to a victim. In the first section, Jonathan Harker has traveled from England to Transylvania to make a real-estate transaction with the Count. His experiences in the bizarre castle are described in his journal and in his correspondence with his fiancée Mina. Jonathan is attacked by the vampire, and in addition he encounters three female vampires, part of the Count's "family," who are anxious to make Jonathan their victim as well. The second part of the novel takes place in England where the Count has now purchased his house. Here the major voices of the novel are Mina, her friend Lucy, and Dr Seward, a rejected suitor of Lucy, who is director of an insane asylum. Lucy becomes Dracula's next victim. Dr Van Helsing is brought in to assist the group of men—including Jonathan, Dr Seward, and Lucy's fiance—in destroying the vampire. Lucy herself becomes a vampire and preys on children.

The Count's attacks on Jonathan and Lucy presage what is to come in the final section of the novel, in which Mina becomes his next intended victim. Van Helsing and the group of men now involved in the case successfully destroy the vampire and save Mina. Mina returns to her normal way of life, and Jonathan, by this time Mina's husband, informs us in an epilogue that the couple had a son and lived happily ever after.

These three sections of the novel correspond to the progressive stages of the central conflict of *Dracula,* which is not between Dracula and his victims, but rather between Dracula and Van Helsing. The struggle is between two different cultures and two different orders: between good and evil, between the forces of civilization and the forces of nature, between reason and passion. And the contested terrain, on every count, is the body of the woman, Mina. The structure of *Dracula* is a striking illustration of what is commonly referred to as classical narrative. Order is restored by the victory of the good patriarchal figure. The object of struggle, the woman's body, returns to its "normal" functions of marriage and child-bearing, while the husband Jonathan implicitly assumes the patriarchal role of Van Helsing (even though he does so in a way that is nondescript).

The manner in which Stoker and Murnau plot and resolve their material is quite different, but both work within a similar field of oppositions. Attention is drawn in both the novel and the film to the excessive contrasts which construct these fictional universes. In the opening pages of the novel, the opposition between east and west establishes a geography, as it were, for the oppositions which will develop in the course of the novel: good versus evil, science versus mysticism, and so on. So too does the beginning of Murnau's film suggest a field of oppositions, with Jona-

than and Nina (Mina becomes Nina in the American print of Murnau's film) first seen within a tranquil context of domesticated nature denoted by flowers and kittens, soon contrasted with the wild and barbaric nature associated with Nosferatu.

Now *Dracula* and **Nosferatu** can hardly be singled out for their reliance on a set of binary oppositions—these are, after all, rather classic oppositions in western literature and film. What does seem particular to these texts, however, and perhaps to the art of horror in general, is the obsession not only with oppositions, but with the hypothetical area between opposing terms. In the opening pages of *Dracula,* for instance, Jonathan speaks of the twilight, and of the "great masses of greyness" characteristic of Transylvania. The fascination which Count Dracula holds might have less to do with his incarnation of evil than with the impossibility of categorizing him according to dualistic categories of thought. Central to both *Dracula* and **Nosferatu,** then, is a dangerous territory where opposing terms are not so easily distinguishable.

The basic material of Stoker's novel is present in Murnau's film, if plotted differently. We begin in Germany (rather than England) where Jonathan's employer Renfield (a conflation of the realtor and the madman in the novel) sends him away to arrange for Nosferatu's purchase of a house. Jonathan's trip is represented in the film, and after a brief stay in the castle (where he also becomes the vampire's victim), his return to Germany is shown at some length, alongside of the Count's simultaneous journey on board a ship where all of the crew members are killed, one by one. With the arrival of the Count in Germany, a plague erupts. Jonathan's wife Nina puts an end to the plague by sacrificing herself. Having read in *The Book of the Vampires* that the vampire will perish if a pure woman spends the night with him, she does so. At the conclusion of the film, Nosferatu vanishes into thin air, and Nina dies. Much more so than the novel, the film is concerned with that hypothetical area between west and east, between the land of reason and the land of passion, between self and other. The sheer amount of screen time devoted to passage, to voyage, suggests precisely the central function of the space "between" in the film. Whereas the novel, by its conclusion, dispels any possibility of an identity between opposing terms, the film remains, almost resolutely, in that twilight.

Murnau's stress on that twilight area emerges from a rereading of Stoker's novel. To speak of **Nosferatu** simply as an adaptation does not do justice to this process of rereading. More suggestive are the terms proposed by the Russian formalist Boris Eikhenbaum in a 1926 essay on the relationship between film and literature:

> Cinema is not simply a moving picture, but a special photographic language. This language, in all its "naturalism," does not materialise literature as theatre does. What results, rather, is something analogous to a dream: a person approaches; now you see only the eyes, now the hands—then everything disappears—another person—a window—a street, and so on. Just as if, having read a novel, you saw it in a dream. ["Literature and Cinema," in *Russian Formal-*

ism, edited by Stephen Bann and John E. Bowlt, 1973]

That there are important analogies between film and dreams has been argued in film theory and criticism, and perhaps certain transformations of literary sources are particularly well described through the language of the dream work. Specifically, the changes which most set *Nosferatu* apart from Stoker's novel appear to be the result of a process of displacement, not unlike that dream mechanism whereby disturbing associations are stripped of their intensity.

Two such displacements occur in *Nosferatu.* First, Van Helsing is in no way the protagonist of the film. Instead of a conflict between two patriarchal figures, we have an encounter between a man and a woman. The vampire is destroyed, but so is the woman—there is no happy ending here. Yet Van Helsing is not eliminated from the film. His role is, rather, purely metaphoric: he is shown giving a lecture on carnivorous plants. Second, any trace of female vampirism is erased from the film. In Stoker's novel, the presence of female vampires—the three women at Dracula's castle, Lucy after her initiation, and even Mina for a brief time—allows the opposition between good and evil to take the specifically female form of a conflict between chastity and sexuality. It is through vampirism that female sexuality is represented in the novel. Here, for instance, is how Jonathan describes the approach of one of the female vampires:

> The girl went on her knees, and bent over me, simply gloating. There was a deliberate voluptuousness which was both thrilling and repulsive, and as she arched her neck she actually licked her lips like an animal, till I could see in the moonlight the moisture shining on the scarlet lips and on the red tongue as it lapped the white sharp teeth. Lower and lower went her head as the lips went below the range of my mouth and chin and seemed to fasten on my throat.

At first sight, the erasure—or censorship—of female vampirism with its attendant implications seems much more absolute than what happens to Van Helsing. However, there is an ambivalence in the representation of Nina.

In a famous scene which occurs early in the film, images of Jonathan being attacked by Nosferatu alternate with images of Nina, at home in her bedroom, suddenly awake. A title informs us that Nina sensed the danger to her husband. Yet in this alternation between the vampire's castle and the Harker home, an eyeline match between the vampire and Nina suggests not only Nosferatu's attraction to Nina, but her own arousal as well. In Stoker's novel, the poles of attraction and repulsion are confused in Jonathan's reaction to the three women vampires. In *Nosferatu* the poles are also confused, albeit more subtly, in Nina's reaction to the vampire. The ambivalence is more pronounced later in the film, when Jonathan (and Nosferatu) are about to return. Robin Wood describes the scene as follows [in "Burying the Undead: the Use and Obsolescence of Count Dracula," *Mosaic* 16, Winter-Spring, 1983]:

The two men are exactly paralleled as Nina's two husbands; Nina sits by the shore . . . looking out to sea, ostensibly for Jonathan, whose mode of travel is by land; in the sleepwalking scene she exclaims "He is coming! I must go to meet him!" after a shot, not of Jonathan, but of the vampire's ship.

These two key elements, Van Helsing and female vampirism, are not simply "left out" of the film version of the novel—there are many elements which are omitted, for whatever reasons. These are elements which are, rather, displaced, and hence reworked in such a way as to be enormously significant for the film as a whole. That Van Helsing appears at all in Murnau's film, and in such a purely metaphoric way, suggests that the forces of science, reason, and civilization can no longer successfully wage battles against the Draculas of the world, but exist only to give illustrated lectures. In the novel *Dracula,* narrative closure can still be achieved through the positive force of a figure like Van Helsing. However, the fact that such a colorless and drab figure as Jonathan Harker is designated as Van Helsing's successor could be read easily as a weakness within that narrative coherence. Murnau seizes upon that weakness in his rereading of *Dracula* as an encounter between male and female.

What then happens to the representation of woman in this encounter? The disappearance of female vampirism suggests that the dichotomy which characterizes the representation of female sexuality in the novel is replaced, in the film, by a profound ambivalence—stressing, again, the "twilight" which characterizes *Nosferatu* as a whole. As is the case of the function of Van Helsing, female vampirism can be read as a weak link in the novel. As Robin Wood points out: "It is the woman that the work is really about." In the second half of the novel, it is Mina who is central, with Dracula appearing very rarely.

Whenever we speak of binary oppositions, we refer above all to a separation between the self and the other, and it is precisely that separation which is closed in Murnau's rendering of the novel. This is ultimately a reading against the grain of the novel, attentive to those symptoms that reveal "otherness" as not so easily separable after all. One might ask then what perspective informs this reading against the grain. Here we encounter another problem, peculiar not to adaptation analysis but to many German films of the 1920s. Siegfried Kracauer's reading of German cinema in *From Caligari to Hitler* has so overdetermined reception of a film like *Nosferatu* that it has become almost *too* simple to understand the guiding perspective of Murnau's reading of Stoker. If Van Helsing is reduced to pure decoration, and if sexual dichotomy becomes sexual ambivalence, the rationale must be the obsession with tyrants and evil that—according to Kracauer—so possessed the German imagination. Thus Murnau takes the conventions of an essentially Victorian novel and turns them upside down to portray a world obsessed with dark, omnipotent forces which form an integral part of our so-called rational universe. It would appear from this vantage point that Murnau's adaptation of *Dracula* amounts to so much superstructure built upon the base of German angst.

A critique of Kracauer's notion of film as a barometer of

collective fears and fantasies is beyond the scope of this essay. In any case, one could argue for a Kracaueresque reading of *Nosferatu,* particularly if one's inquiry is defined by reflection theory—however simple or sophisticated. To address historically the relationship between film and literature does not mean simply re-creating the dominant panorama of given ages. Such an engagement requires, in the case of *Nosferatu,* exploration not only of how Dracula is so easily shaped by the context of Weimar Germany, but also of how the very substance of a novel like Stoker's responds so directly to our very conception of the cinema.

Along these lines of inquiry, Eikhenbaum's suggestion that in a filmic adaptation we see a novel as if in a dream, is again useful. Central to the dream analogy is the relationship between a subject and discourse—between, that is, the organizing intelligence of a text and the modes through which it is revealed, such as point of view and perspective. In other words, the issue of *narration* is crucial in the transformation of *Dracula* into a film. Here the characteristic of *Dracula* which is most striking is its epistolary structure. The use of journals and letters to create multiple points of view is unique in Stoker's novel, for this predominantly eighteenth-century literary form is coupled with a nineteenth-century technological imagination. Both Jonathan and Mina keep their journals in shorthand, and write to each other in shorthand as well. They share a secret code, suggesting intimacy, but it is a curiously efficient and machine-like form of intimacy. When Mina writes in her journal, "I am anxious, and it soothes me to express myself here: it is like whispering to one's self and listening at the same time," we can easily imagine ourselves in the company of many an eighteenth-century heroine who has retired to the closet. But Mina then continues: "And there is also something about the shorthand symbols that makes it different from writing." *Different* from writing: Mina describes a tension in language, between self-expression and imposition of a code, which parallels the overall tension in the novel between opposing terms.

Surely the most unusual voice in the novel is that of Dr Seward, director of the insane asylum. For Seward's journal is kept on phonograph records! On the one hand, the function of the phonograph is to give a certain naturalism to the voice of the doctor. But more important, the phonograph suggests, even more strongly than the shorthand used by Jonathan and Mina, a technological arsenal at the disposal of this narrator. Herein lies one of the supreme ironies of the novel. No matter how refined and complex the technological means might be, they fail to elucidate the enigma of Dracula.

There is, in *Dracula,* a problem of narration. For all their obsessive recording and interpretation of what is going on around them, these narrators cannot put the pieces together. The differing points of view on the Count's invasion are first presented in the novel in a relatively isolated way, but as the plot thickens, the characters read each other's diaries in their attempt to decipher the phenomenon of Dracula. The final showdown with the Count is prepared by piecing together all the diaries, as well as a variety of documents, concerning, for example, the sale of the house. Dr Seward observes that the goal of such a collation is the emergence of a "whole connected narrative." The assumption is that a story must be told, that the various fragments must connect, that a narrative structure and coherence must be achieved before any direct battle with the vampire can be initiated. Narrative is, then, the supreme form of understanding in the novel.

The emergence of the "whole connected narrative" is also riddled with ironies. The men decide that it will be better for all concerned if Mina does not participate in their plans. What they do not realize at first is that Mina is quickly becoming Dracula's next victim. Mina travels, let us say, the distance separating the world of these men from the world of Dracula. As a result, she has more of a finely tuned narrative intelligence, and is able to interpret more successfully the facts which the men have compiled about their enemy.

The epistolary technique of *Dracula* assures that the vampire remains the object of knowledge, even if an elusive one. Hence the distinction between subject and object remains fixed and absolute. The distinction is also one of speech and writing. For the narrators of *Dracula,* with their shorthand and their phonographs, all seek to make their writing as direct an imitation as possible of direct speech. Of Dracula, however, it is pointed out very early in the novel that his knowledge of the English language— the speech of the text—comes only from books. Yet that Mina, who is a bridge between the two poles of the novel, should emerge as the most clever of story-tellers is a sign that even the distance between subject and object is not as great as the triumphant conclusion of the novel would lead us to believe.

It seems to me a mistake, however, to conclude that Mina therefore emerges as the central narrator within the novel, as the authoritative narrative voice. There is, rather, a single *technique* which allows Mina and the men to solve the mystery. That technique is hypnosis. When Van Helsing hypnotizes Mina, she reveals information about her seduction by the Count which later, in a conscious state and with the assistance of Van Helsing, she interprets. The argument could thus be made that it is Van Helsing, as hypnotist, who is the supreme narrative authority in the novel. More important, it seems to me, is that a process beyond the realm of discursive language is required to complete the story, to solve the problem of narration that is posed in the novel.

The assemblage of first-person narrations in *Dracula* means that there are several narrators, yet one—Van Helsing—emerges as the most authoritative. Thus the narrating intelligence of the novel is, if not reducible or identical to the point of view of Van Helsing, then at least aligned with it. A fundamental difference between narrative in film and the novel concerns just this relationship between narrator and narrating intelligence. In film, narration need not be—indeed, most often is not—identified with any particular narrator. Now at first glance, *Nosferatu* seems to simplify the epistolary structure of the novel by maintaining the device of a narrational journal, but from only one person's point of view. Titles at the beginning of the film are ostensible reproductions of the journal of the city scribe, Johann Cavallius: "From the diary of Johann Cavallius, able historian of his native city of Bremen: NOSFERATU! That name alone can chill the blood! NOSFERATU! Was it he who brought the plague to Bremen in 1838?" This narrator is more or less the equivalent of an omniscient point of view, since he is not a character within the film, and supposedly recounts the story of Nosferatu with all the salient details intact. This narration appears only in written titles along with snippets of dialogue. There is not really a visual point of view which can be called that of the narrator, unless it be the high-angle long shot of the city which opens the film. The role of this narrator is defined, then, primarily in terms of language.

Now there is nothing particularly striking about the function of this narration; indeed, it is quite conventional. The narrator's interventions are more than conventional, however; they are so literal as to be uninsightful. The kind of information he provides—informing us why the vampire always travelled with coffins of earth, for instance—is not exactly useless, but not particularly pertinent either. The narrator almost always intervenes in those passages of the film where cross-cutting creates strong thematic and visual associations. We have discussed the scene, early in the film, where images of Jonathan being approached by the vampire in his castle alternate with images of Nina, awakened suddenly in the night. There is a moment of intense identification between Nina and the vampire. But the narrator comments only on the literal significance of the scene—that Nina was aware of a threat to her husband's well-being.

The narrator intervenes in a similar way when Dr Van Helsing is introduced. Given the purely metaphoric function of Van Helsing, this is perhaps the only moment in the film where some kind of introduction is necessary to assure narrative coherence. An alternation occurs between Van Helsing lecturing, and Renfield catching flies in his cell at the asylum. The narrator may be said to introduce the analogy between vampirism in the plant world and in the human world. But as in the previous scene, he fails to comment on any of the more subtle analogies. For each scene contains point-of-view shots from the perspective of the scientist as well as the madman. Hence an affinity is implied between the scientist and the madman in terms of the looks they bring to bear on their objects of study, and passion, respectively. That affinity, that identification, is not unlike the pull between Nosferatu and Nina suggested, also by cross-cutting, in the previous scene.

Something happens on screen, then, that eludes the written commentary of the narrator. The figure of the narrator is pulled in two directions. He represents narration, of course; and he also represents written language. There is, in *Nosferatu* as well as in *Dracula,* a problem of narration. Here, the problem of narration is also a failure of language. Within the fictional universe of the film, language is as limited as it is in the narrator's commentary. Jonathan sees the marks of the vampire on his throat when he looks at himself in a mirror, but neither *The Book of the Vampires* nor the letter he writes to Nina can decipher them. Officials turn to the log of the ship to seek some ex-

planation of the similar marks on the neck of the ship's captain, but the mystery of Nosferatu still eludes them. Language is limited, that is, until Nina reads *The Book of the Vampires.* Suddenly the language of books, of the written text, has become endowed with narrative potency. How, then, has this problem of narration been resolved?

In silent film, written titles represent one possible form of narration, among many others. Narration is understood most often in film in visual terms, for obvious reasons. We often equate, in fact, point of view as a narrative device with the camera eye. If the first image following the titles of *Nosferatu*—the high-angle long shot of the city— suggests that definition of narration, with the eye of the camera imitating somehow the omniscient text of the narrator, the images which follow trace another conception of narration in the cinema. Nina and Jonathan are presented in turn—from the very start, one notes that cross-cutting, here in a more restrained spatial environment than later in the film, is the primary narrative mode of the film. Cross-cutting only becomes narration when a specific relationship is articulated. That relationship is defined in terms of differing perceptions of the screen surface. We first see Jonathan in front of a mirror, a window at his side. We first see Nina through a window, as she plays with a kitten. The frames of these images will be significant as the film progresses. Jonathan will gaze into a mirror as he attempts to comprehend the bite marks on his neck. He cannot comprehend them, indicating, as does the mirror, a failure of recognition in general. Indeed, the mirror is a dominant motif throughout *Nosferatu,* and is a form taken by the theme of the double underscored by Lotte Eisner in her discussion of this and other films of the period [in her *The Haunted Screen,* 1969].

In virtually all of the scenes involving cross-cutting, a mirror effect is established. For the identification between Nina and the vampire, between Van Helsing and Renfield, is a mirror effect; and, more important, is a form of narration in which *surface* is key: the screen as mirror surface, the film as projection. Nosferatu indeed functions as a mirror for all of the characters in the film. In this sense he is a narrating presence within the film. Only Renfield and Nina recognize themselves in the mirror of Nosferatu. Thus, prior to the conclusion of the film, cross-cutting links the demise of Renfield, escaped from the asylum and caught by the townspeople, with Nina's decision, after reading *The Book of the Vampires,* to sacrifice herself. Nina crosses a threshold; she goes through the looking-glass. In narrational terms, the screen surface has become both mirror and passageway. That passage is marked by her beckoning to Nosferatu through the window, from which the vampire's house has been visible in the Harkers' bedroom. The cinema screen becomes, then, mirror and window simultaneously.

The problem of narration in *Nosferatu* is the disjuncture between narrator and screen, and that problem is resolved by the development of film narration as surface and projection. Whereas *Dracula* resolves its problem of narration through hypnosis in order to produce a classical (if somewhat weak) resolution, *Nosferatu* affirms, rather, the fragility and the tenuousness of narrative. This is narrative which embraces ambiguity, by positing the film screen as both mirror and passageway. Theorized conversely as a window open onto the world, or as a mirror in which we see and project idealized images of ourselves, the film screen in *Nosferatu* is both. German angst notwithstanding, *Nosferatu* designates the cinema as a form perfectly suited to the embrace of that ambiguity, to the lure of the twilight which in Stoker's novel is dispelled. Between the novel *Dracula* and the film *Nosferatu* a dialogue takes place, one on the nature of the narrative experience.

There remains a missing link in the common narrative concerns of *Dracula* and *Nosferatu.* An imagination informs both works, an imagination that it is altogether appropriate to describe as a narrative imagination in its own right. This is psychoanalysis. That hypnosis should have such a strategic role in the novel indicates one correspondence between psychoanalysis and questions of narrative. But hypnosis is only one of the symptoms of the psychoanalytic influence. *Dracula* has been read as a variation on a number of Freudian themes, from the group killing of the father (elaborated in *Totem and Taboo*) to the Oedipus complex, from Van Helsing as ego and Dracula as id to sexual symbolism. What is striking about the novel is not that psychoanalytic readings "apply," but that they are so embedded, almost to excess, within the text. One could note, of course, that *Dracula* is a text contemporary with Freud's writings. More important, the novel is the fictional construction of the fascination of psychoanalysis.

The fiction of psychoanalysis thus presented in *Dracula* invites speculation on the cinema. Here, for instance, is a scene, early in the novel, where Jonathan writes of the vampires:

> Something made me start up, a low, piteous howling of dogs somewhere far below in the valley, which was hidden from my sight. Louder it seemed to ring in my ears, and the floating motes of dust to take new shape to the sound as they danced in the moonlight. I felt myself struggling to awake to some call of my instincts; nay, my very soul was struggling, and my half-remembered sensibilities were striving to answer the call. I was becoming hypnotised! Quicker and quicker danced the dust; the moonbeams seemed to quiver as they went by me into the mass of gloom beyond. More and more they gathered till they seemed to take dim phantom shapes. And then I started, broad awake and in full possession of my senses, and ran screaming from the place. The phantom shapes, which were becoming gradually materialised from the moonbeams, where those of the three ghostly women to whom I was doomed. I fled, and felt somewhat safer in my own room, where there was no moonlight and where the lamp was burning brightly.

If it seems excessive to suggest that Jonathan might well be describing the cinema, compare the passage to Maxim Gorky's famous and much-quoted reflection on the early Lumière film, *L'Arrivée d'un train en gare* [as cited in Richard Taylor's *The Politics of Soviet Cinema 1917-1929,* 1979].

> Yesterday I was in the kingdom of the shadows.

> If only you knew how strange it was to be there. There are no sounds, no colours. There, everything—the earth, the trees, the people, the water, the air—is tinted in the single tone of grey: in a grey sky there are grey rays of sunlight; in grey faces, grey eyes, and the leaves of the trees are grey like ashes. This is not life but the shadow of life, and this is not movement but the soundless shadow of movement.

> . . . A railway train appears on the screen. It darts like an arrow straight towards you—look out! It seems as if it is about to rush into the darkness in which you are sitting and reduce you to a mangled sack of skin, full of crumpled flesh and shattered bones, and destroy this hall and this building, so full of wine, women, music and vice, and transform it into fragments and into dust.

The point here is not that "becoming hypnotized" in *Dracula* somehow anticipates the cinema, but rather that narrative takes shape as the posing of certain questions which will be taken up by the cinema—at, as the Gorky citation suggests, a kind of founding mythic moment.

I have kept psychoanalysis waiting in the wings, saved it as the punchline, as it were, to the dialogue between *Dracula* and *Nosferatu.* This might be read as a somewhat coy gesture. For psychoanalysis is as omnipresent in contemporary film studies as it is in Stoker's novel. That the basic elements of the cinema—the screen, image projections, dream analogies—interlock with the language of psychoanalysis has become a given in film theory. Murnau's film may not evoke psychoanalytic themes in quite the explicit fashion of *Dracula,* but in its meditation on a Victorian novel, *Nosferatu* suggests how questions of narrative and questions of psychoanalysis intertwine. If narrative is the supreme form of knowledge in *Dracula,* it is a form of knowledge served by hypnosis. Put another way, the function of hypnosis is to harness the unconscious to the desire for narrative resolution. But narrative in *Nosferatu* is not so well-served by the insights of psychoanalysis. For *Nosferatu* explores the other side of the connection between narrative and psychoanalysis, where the disruption of that supreme form of knowledge is acknowledged. Between *Dracula* and *Nosferatu,* then, between the novel and the cinema, between voice and screen, between the desire for resolution and the embrace of ambiguity, is that "kingdom of the shadows" where phantom shapes have become the reigning figures of narrative. (pp. 25-38)

Judith Mayne, "Dracula in the Twilight: Murnau's 'Nosferatu' (1922)," in German Film & Literature: Adaptations and Transformations, *edited by Eric Rentschler, Methuen, 1986, pp. 25-39.*

FURTHER READING

Criticism

Allen, Robert C. "William Fox Presents *Sunrise.*" *Quarterly Review of Film Studies* 2, No. 3 (August 1977): 327-38.

Relates role of William Fox, head of Fox Film Corporation, in the release and production of *Sunrise.*

Enckell, Mikael. "A Study in Scarlet: Film and Psychoanalysis (II)." In *Eisenstein Revisited: A Collection of Essays,* edited by Lars Kleberg and Håkan Lövgren, pp. 113-31. Stockholm: Almqvist & Wiksell International, 1987.

Discusses Murnau's *Nosferatu,* the vampire theme, and mythical associations of vampirism from a psychoanalytic viewpoint.

Guillermo, Gilberto Perez. "F. W. Murnau: An Introduction." *Film Comment* 7, No. 2 (Summer 1971): 13-15.

Claims that *Nosferatu* is Murnau's most important film and discusses the filmmaker's manipulation of space and subjectivity in this work.

Henderson, Brian. "The Long Take." In *Movies and Methods: An Anthology,* edited by Bill Nichols, pp. 314-24. Berkeley: University of California Press, 1976.

Stylistic analysis of *mise-en-scène* techniques used by Murnau, Max Ophüls, and Orson Welles. Henderson examines how the works of these directors contribute to and reflect classic film theory.

Lipkin, Steven N. "*Sunrise*: A Film Meets Its Public." *Quarterly Review of Film Studies* 2, No. 3 (August 1977): 329-55.

Historical overview of the release of and critical reaction to *Sunrise.*

Luhr, William. "*Nosferatu* and Postwar German Film." *Michigan Academician* XIV, No. 4 (Spring 1982): 453-58.

Examines and compares Murnau's *Nosferatu* and Werner Herzog's 1979 remake in terms of their social, political, and historical contexts.

Roth, Lane. "Film, Society and Ideas: *Nosferatu* and *Horror of Dracula.*" In *Planks of Reason: Essays on the Horror Film,* edited by Barry Keith Grant, pp. 245-54. Metuchen, N.J.: Scarecrow Press, 1984.

Compares and contrasts the 1958 British film *Horror of Dracula* and Murnau's *Nosferatu.*

Wood, Robin. "Murnau's Midnight and *Sunrise.*" *Film Comment* 12, No. 3 (May-June 1976): 4-10.

Explores Murnau's treatment of identity and the conflict between human and animal nature in *Nosferatu.*

———. "Murnau II: *Sunrise.*" *Film Comment* 12, No. 3 (May-June 1976): 11-19.

Stylistic analysis of *Sunrise,* discussing the film's affinity with painting, music, poetry, and the German Expressionistic school. Wood notes that the film's framing, composition, and use of juxtapositions and contrasts represent attempts to exaggerate the film's emotional content.

———. "Burying the Undead: The Use and Obsolescence of Count Dracula." *Mosaic* XVI, Nos. 1-2 (Winter-Spring 1983): 175-87.

Discusses Bram Stoker's novel *Dracula,* Murnau's film version, and the 1979 film adaptation by John Badham.

Additional coverage of Murnau's life and career is contained in the following source published by Gale Research: *Contemporary Authors,* Vol. 112.

Arthur Quiller-Couch

1863-1944

(Full name Arthur Thomas Quiller-Couch; also wrote under the pseudonym Q) English critic, anthologist, novelist, short story writer, and poet.

INTRODUCTION

Quiller-Couch was best known to late nineteenth and early twentieth century readers by the pseudonym "Q," under which he wrote novels, short stories, poetry, and literary criticism. He achieved commercial success as a journalist and writer of popular fiction, and, through his lectures on literature at Cambridge University, became one of the most respected academic figures of his time. In addition, critics suggest that Quiller-Couch's numerous anthologies, most notably *The Oxford Book of English Verse,* significantly influenced the literary taste of three generations of English readers.

Quiller-Couch was born in Bodmin, Cornwall. Educated at Trinity College, Oxford, he went to London in 1887 to work as a writer and editor for the liberal newspaper *The Speaker.* After he returned to Cornwall in 1892, he continued to write for this publication until 1899. From his seaside home in Fowey, Cornwall, Quiller-Couch wrote and published numerous novels, short stories, poems, parodies and critical essays, and was active in local politics and education. In 1900 he became the editor of the influential annual anthology *The Oxford Book of English Verse,* a position he retained until 1939. In 1910 he was knighted by the Liberal Government for exemplary civic service to England, in part for helping to establish a comprehensive system of secondary-level public schools throughout Cornwall. Following his appointment in 1912 to the position of King Edward VII Professor of English Literature at Cambridge University, he became a popular and well-respected lecturer who presented literature as a living art to be enjoyed by ordinary people. Throughout his thirty-two years at Cambridge, Quiller-Couch maintained his family home on the coast of Cornwall, travelling between Cambridge and Fowey several times each year in order to preserve both his public life as "a Cambridge man" and his private world as husband, father, and Cornish yachtsman. Two months after he was injured in an automobile accident, Quiller-Couch died in Fowey at the age of eighty.

Quiller-Couch's novels and stories were popular with critics and the reading public for their unpretentious humor, authentic historical detail, and affectionate portrayal of Cornish life and folklore. Critics of his early fiction, noting its sense of adventure and sharply defined characters, compared his style to that of Robert Louis Stevenson, whose unfinished novel *St. Ives* Quiller-Couch completed in 1897, three years after Stevenson's death. As a literary

critic and literature professor, Quiller-Couch's devotion to the classics upon which his traditional Victorian education had been based led him to prize clarity of thought and mastery of style in his own writing and in that of his pupils and contemporaries. While some critics characterize Quiller-Couch as a "sentimental popularizer of literature," others have praised his synthesis of scholarship and humanism, suggesting that Quiller-Couch's greatest literary achievement has its source in his passionate portrayal of literature as an important part of human experience. In his introduction to a posthumously-published anthology of Quiller-Couch's works, F. Brittain wrote that Quiller-Couch's "chief contribution to English letters was his style, in which there lives again the chivalrous, hospitable 'Q' who loved bright colors, dressed with care, was accurate but not pedantic, and refused ever to be hurried."

PRINCIPAL WORKS

Dead Man's Rock (novel) 1887
The Astonishing History of Troy Town (novel) 1888

Noughts and Crosses (short stories) 1891
The Delectable Duchy (short stories) 1893
Green Bays (poetry) 1893
Wandering Heath (short stories) 1895
Adventures in Criticism (essays) 1896
Poems and Ballads (poetry) 1896
*St. Ives (novel) 1898
The Ship of Stars (novel) 1899
Old Fires and Profitable Ghosts (short stories) 1900
The Oxford Book of English Verse, 1250-1900 [editor]
    (poetry) 1900
Two Sides of the Face (short stories) 1903
Shining Ferry (novel) 1905
From a Cornish Window (essays) 1906
The Mayor of Troy (novel) 1906
Sir John Constantine (novel) 1906
The Oxford Book of Victorian Verse [editor] (poetry)
    1912
The Vigil of Venus, and Other Poems (poetry) 1912
News from the Duchy (short stories) 1913
Poetry (essays) 1914
On the Art of Writing (essays) 1916
Shakespeare's Workmanship (essays) 1918
Studies in Literature. 3 vols. (essays) 1918-29
On the Art of Reading (essays) 1920
The Oxford Book of English Prose [editor] (prose)
    1925
A Lecture on Lectures (essay) 1927
The Duchy Edition of Tales and Romances by Q. 30 vols.
    (novels and short stories) 1928-29
The Poet as Citizen, and Other Papers (essays) 1934
The Oxford Book of English Verse, 1250-1918 [editor]
    (poetry) 1939
Memories and Opinions (unfinished autobiography)
    1944
Q Anthology (poetry, short stories, essays, lectures, and
    letters) 1949

*This work is an unfinished novel by Robert Louis Stevenson that
was completed by Quiller-Couch.

CRITICISM

Punch (essay date 1887)

[*The following is a review of Quiller-Couch's first book,
the novel* Dead Man's Rock, *which was published under
the pseudonym* "Q".]

Have Messrs. Louis Stevenson and Rider Haggard combined under the signature of "Q." to write at all events the
first part of the weird and exciting Romance entitled
Deadman's Rock? If not let those two authors look to their
laurels. There is much in this book to remind the reader
of *Treasure Island,* especially the fiendish Sailor's uncouth
chaunt, "Sing hey for the deadman's eyes, my lads," which,
however, is not a patch upon Mr. Stevenson's "Ho!

Ho! Ho! and a bottle of rum," in *Treasure Island*. Then
there is one line in "Q.'s" story, "And here a strange thing
happened," which must call to mind Mr. Rider Haggard's
patent of "and now a strange thing happened." "Q"—
rious coincidence, isn't it? But a "coincidence" is not likely to annoy Mr. Haggard.

In the first part the most impatient reader will find that
he cannot afford to skip a couple of lines without detriment to the narrative, but in the second part he may skip
handfuls, as the lovemaking is common-place, and time is
wasted over the tragedy which is written by one of the heroes, and over the description of their life in London. But
on the other hand the scene in the gambling-house is exciting and artistically worked up,—and coming immediately
after this, the lovemaking is uncommonly tame,—and the
scene at the Theatre is also very good, but after this there
is a lull in the excitement until the end approaches, when
there is one very strong situation. But the actual finish is
weak. So the summing up is that the first part is first-rate,
and the second part is, on the whole, second-rate. But who
is "Q."? That is the Q. and what is the A.? *Deadman's
Rock* is not a good book for very nervous persons or children: for the latter *Almond Rock* would be far preferable.

A review of "Deadman's Rock," in Punch,
*Vol. XCIII, No. 2415, October 22, 1887, p.
192.*

The Athenaeum (essay date 1893)

[*In the following review of* Green Bays, *the critic affirms
Quiller-Couch's skill as a verse writer, while concluding
that he does not demonstrate a gift for writing serious
poetry.*]

Q's verses [in **Green Bays: Verses and Parodies**] are distinctly clever, they are touched with genuine humour, but
they have rarely that distinction in fun which was the secret of C. S. Calverley. The piece called **"Retrospec-
tion"**—avowedly after C. S. C.—will show the difference
in the quality of fooling. Q's actual parodies are, as a rule,
better than his more generally humorous verse; and nothing in the book is better than the Wordsworthian **"Anecdote for Fathers,"** of which we give a few stanzas:—

I have a boy, not six years old,
A sprite of birth and lineage high:
His birth I did myself behold,
His caste is in his eye.

And oh! his limbs are full of grace,
His boyish beauty past compare:
His mother's joy to wash his face,
And mine to brush his hair!

One morn we strolled on our short walk,
With four goloshes on our shoes,
And held the customary talk
That parents love to use.

(And oft I turn it into verse,

And write it down upon a page,
Which, being sold, supplies my purse
And ministers to age.)

So as we faced the curving High,
To view the sights of Oxford town,
We raised our feet (like Nelly Bly),
And then we put them down.

Not less admirable is the parody of **"Caliban upon Setebos,"** and the example of Whitmanese in **"Behold! I am not one that goes to lectures."** It is, of course, easy to make fun of Whitman, but better fun of the kind has never been made than this utterance of "Me Imperturbe! Me Prononcé!" Yet, clever and amusing as are these exercises in verse, they are after all only the best kind of undergraduate wit, more appropriate to the *Oxford Magazine* than to a volume which reaches after any sort of bays. The more serious pieces are not so good as those which admit themselves to be frivolous; they have even more the air of being poetical exercises, and with less assumption of spontaneity. For instance:—

> Trust in thyself,—then spur amain:
> So shall Charybdis wear a grace,
> Grim Ætna laugh, the Libyan plain
> Take roses to her shrivelled face.
> This orb—this round
> Of sight and sound—
> Count it the lists that God hath built
> For haughty hearts to ride a-tilt.

Is there not here a curious stiffness and formality, a certain lifelessness, as if the thought in the writer's mind had failed to quicken itself into the activity of verse? A seventeenth century conceit **"Upon Graciosa, Walking and Talking,"** has, in its quaint formality, a certain charm; but the most ingenious and acceptable of the comparatively serious things in the volume is the poem called **"The White Moth,"** which is worth quoting in its entirety:—

> "If a leaf rustled, she would start:
> And yet she died, a year ago.
> How had so frail a thing the heart
> To journey where she trembled so
> And do they turn and turn in fright,
> Those little feet in so much night?"

> The light above the poet's head
> Streamed on the page and on the cloth,
> And twice and thrice there buffeted
> On the black pane a white-wing'd moth:
> 'Twas Annie's soul that beat outside
> And "Open, open, open!" cried.

> "I could not find the way to God;
> There were too many flaming suns
> For signposts, and the fearful road
> Led over wastes where millions
> Of tangled comets hissed and burned—
> I was bewildered and I turned.

> "O, it was easy then! I knew
> Your window and no star beside.
> Look up, and take me back to you!"
> —He rose and thrust the window wide.
> 'Twas but because his brain was hot
> With rhyming; for he heard her not.

> But poets polishing a phrase
> Show anger over trivial things;
> And as she blundered in the blaze
> Towards him, on ecstatic wings,
> He raised a hand and smote her dead;
> Then wrote "That I had died instead!"

There is a sort of tragic comedy about this piece—something of the tone which we find in that wonderful little poem of James Thomson, "In the Room"—that gives evidence of higher possibilities than any of the merely comic or merely serious pieces in the volume. But it is alone among a crowd of clever futilities, and it is not in itself enough to justify a very confident assurance of hope for the future. (pp. 694-95)

> *A review of "Green Bays: Verses and Parodies," in* The Athenaeum, *No. 3423, June 3, 1893, pp. 694-95.*

William Archer   (essay date 1901)

[*Archer was a Scottish literary critic, journalist, playwright and author. In the following excerpt from his book* Poets of the Younger Generation, *he discusses the merits and shortcomings of Quiller-Couch's poetry.*]

Mr. Quiller Couch was a poet before he left Clifton College. One of his school poems, **"Athens,"** was privately printed at Bodmin in 1881, and is treasured in the British Museum. It is not miraculous—not a "Blessed Damozel"—but it is remarkable work for a schoolboy. At Oxford he distinguished himself by the ingenious and spirited parodies collected (with other verses) under the title of **Green Bays** (1893). Up to this point, however, his verse denoted general literary capacity rather than specially poetic endowment. It is on his single volume of **Poems and Ballads** (1896) that his position as a poet is based, and based, I think, very firmly.

The journalist in Mr. Couch has done some injustice to the poet. It is much to be regretted that a man who can write such admirable verse should write so little. But the time that he gives to prose is not all a dead loss to poetry; for several of his short stories in **Noughts and Crosses, The Delectable Duchy,** and **Wandering Heath,** are as true poems as any in the language. My present business, however, is not with prose poems. Whatever the compensations, one cannot but regret that Mr. Couch's verse should be so scant in quantity, for in quality it is individual and often delightful. Poetry is an art which demands more leisure and a less pre-occupied mind than Mr. Couch, I suspect, is in a position to bring to it. The poet must be able to lie in wait for his ideas and imprison them as they arise, not in mere notebook jottings, but in poetic form. When a great poem knocks at the doors of Being, it is not to be put off till a more convenient season. "Now or never" it wails, as it is reabsorbed into the vasty deep from whence it sprang. The poet who cultivates the Muse only in his leisure moments may do good work, but scarcely great. In a word, if Mr. Couch wrote more verse he would write it still better. But for what we have received I, for my part, am truly thankful.

Along with his many qualities, Mr. Couch has two limitations. The first is a lack of metrical impulse, manifesting itself in a preference for short, staccato measures, often very cunningly woven, but lacking in swing and sonority. The second limitation is an odd one in so excellent a story-teller—several of his poems do not tell their own story, or tell it but obscurely. Here is a piece, for example, which ought to be very impressive—which *is* impressive in its very vagueness—but would certainly have been none the worse for a little definition of outline:

"Shadows"

As I walked out on Hallows' E'en,
I saw the moon swing thin and green;
I saw beside, in Fiddler's Wynd,
Two hands that moved upon a blind.

As I walked out on Martin's Feast,
I heard a woman say to a priest—
"His grave is digged, his shroud is sewn;
And the child shall pass for his very own."

But whiles they stood beside his tomb,
I heard the babe laugh out in her womb—
"My hair will be black as his was red,
And I have a mole where his heart bled."

There is a touch of the Border Ballad—"Clerk Saunders" or "The Twa Corbies"—in this, as in a good many others of Mr. Couch's pieces; and their spirit is seized with excellent skill and sympathy. But the significance of the "Two hands that moved upon the blind" somehow escapes me. If Mr. Couch had hit upon a more speaking trait for this couplet, the poem would not have been less impressive for being less enigmatic. The shadow pantomime is not enough. Tennyson objected to Wordsworth's "Thorn" that there was too much "hammering to set a scene for so small a drama." Here Mr. Couch has fallen into the opposite error. After much wrestling with **"Sabina"** (the second poem in the book) I think I have fathomed its mystery. It is the allegory of a mother's pain on surrendering her son to the love of another woman:

The stair was steep; the Tower was tall;
Sabina's strength was gone:
She leaned a hand against the wall
And let her boy run on.
. . . . .
"Child! Child!" she called, and "Wait for me!"
But ever the boy's feet ran;
And up through the Whisp'ring Gallery
Came the voice of her dead man—
. . . . .
The dead man said, "He will not wait.
High in a naked room
A maiden listens, strong as fate,
And selfish as the tomb.

"Her sisters, as they cross the floor,
Throw glances at the clock;
Her father fumbles with the door,
He knows he may not look:

"Her mother pins the bridal crown,
And pricks her trembling thumbs:
But the bride has laid her mirror down,
Her small foot drums and drums.

"A minute—hark! Ah joy, ah joy!

The helpless door falls wide,
The harp of God and the laugh of a boy
Sing aubade to the bride.

"The bride she rises from her chair—
Now never stretch your hands!
The harp, the voice, the climbing stair—
Naught else she understands."

The idea comes out pretty clearly in these stanzas (how fine the third of them is, by the way!); but they are only seven out of eighteen, and the remaining verses, as it seems to me, only obscure, or, at the very least, overburden, the allegory. As for **"Doom Ferry"** and **"Dolor Oogo"** (a very strong piece of work, I imagine, if only one could grasp the situation), as for **"The Comrade"** and **"The Gentle Savage,"** I have given them up in despair. To a more strenuous spirit, no doubt, they might yield up their secret; but I submit that, in the first two at any rate, there ought to be no need for fumbling after a clue. **"The Comrade"** and **"The Gentle Savage"** are symbolical or spiritual songs, and perhaps I lack the spiritual instinct or experience which should enable me to interpret them. But **"Doom Ferry"** and **"Dolor Oogo"** are simply ballads; and a ballad which does not tell its own story is like a clock with no hands. Be the workmanship never so perfect, the thing does not serve its primary purpose.

The longest of these *Poems and Ballads* is a blank-verse monologue entitled "Columbus at Seville." It is a strong and even masterly piece of work. It would not be out of place among Browning's *Dramatis Personæ,* only that the blank verse has not Browning's spasmodic vigour, but rather the smooth polish of Matthew Arnold. (pp. 94-7)

Mr. Couch always writes well in grave and classic measures. Here, for instance, is a strong and beautiful stanza from a description of the gods of old sleeping their long sleep on a green lawn beside a stilly lake:

There the long grasses topped a banquet spread
—For that the turf had been their only table—
With cates and fruit and delicate white bread,
Roses afloat in craters carved with fable.
There droop'd a wreath from each relaxèd head,
And there on garland and on god were shed
The coverlet of years innumerable.

Keats would have loved and envied the line "Roses afloat in craters carved with fable." Mr. Couch's most characteristic note, however, is not that of culture-poetry, but of primitive Keltic imagination, expressing itself in simple ballad measure. To my thinking, the most indubitably inspired of his poems is that weird transcript of a legend with which he has also dealt in prose, **"The Masquer in the Street."** . . . Equally characteristic, if not equally haunting, is **"The Planted Heel,"** a poem instinct with a very peculiar quality of imagination. The same may be said of **"The Least of These"** and the Carols: they are as Cornish as saffron cakes or tamarisk hedges.

One can also trace in Mr. Couch the influence of the sixteenth-and seventeenth-century lyrists. It was a genuine affinity that made him the editor of that delightful anthology, *The Golden Pomp, a Procession of English Lyrics from Surrey to Shirley.* Take, for example, this tender and exquisite little song, a trait direct from love's psychology:

"The Kerchief"

When I 'gan to know thee, dear,
Thy faults I did espy;
And "Sure this is a blemish here,
And that's a blot," said I.

But from that hour I did resign
My judgment to my fate,
Thou art no more than only mine
To love and vindicate.

The kerchief that thou gav'st I wear
Upon mine eyelids bound,
And every man I meet I dare
To find the faults I found.

This might quite well be signed by the best of the Cavalier Poets. For the form of his poem on the loss of the *Victoria* Mr. Couch has gone still further back and has adapted the stanza of Drayton's "Agincourt." Making all allowance for deliberate quaintness of form, one has to admit that there are one or two unfortunate prosaisms in these spirited verses; notably the conclusion of this stanza:

But She, the stricken hull,
The doomed, the beautiful,
Proudly to fate abased
Her brow Titanic.
Praise now her multitude
Who, nursed in fortitude,
Fell in on deck and faced
Death without panic.

The final verses, on the other hand, are memorably noble:

Now for the seamen whom
Thy not degenerate womb
Gave thus to die for thee,
England, be tearless:
Rise, and with front serene
Answer, thou Spartan queen,
"Still God is good to me:
My sons are fearless."

Back to the flags that fly
Half-mast at Tripoli,
Back on the sullen drum
Mourning *Victoria,*
Loud, ay, and jubilant,
Hurl thine imperial chant—
In morte talium
Stat Matris gloria!

With a few amendments of detail, this poem would be worthy a place of honour in every *Lyra Heroica* of the future. (pp. 99-101)

> William Archer, "A. T. Quiller Couch," in his
> Poets of the Younger Generation, *John Lane,*
> *The Bodley Head, 1901, pp. 94-104.*

The Athenaeum   (essay date 1916)

[*In the following review of* On the Art of Writing, *the critic praises Quiller-Couch's good taste and common sense while questioning the practice of publishing academic lectures verbatim.*]

Sir Arthur Quiller-Couch no one would expect to write professorially, though he holds the dignity of King Edward VII Professor of English Literature at Cambridge. In truth, . . . "Q" not only writes but also lectures as a novelist, and is full of good stories of a post-prandial, but never inapposite-kind, like that of Defoe's religious old lady who illustrated the danger of language too ornate for its content when, "seeing a bottle of over-ripe beer explode, and cork and froth fly up to the ceiling, she cried out, 'O, the wonders of Omnipotent Power!' " We do not doubt that "Q's" audience had a pleasant time, and trust that they were no less edified.

We regret, however, that he did not further revise his lectures *On the Art of Writing* before reprinting them. In spite of the distinction he draws between oratory and writing, a lecture is not rhetoric, and, as a rule, wants but a little pruning away of formal allocutions and the like to make it a good essay. "Q" would have shown the same respect for his readers as he showed for "Mr. Vice-Chancellor and Gentlemen," had he made a few appropriate modifications. As it is, we get a verbatim report, with now and then in one paragraph a reference to some newspaper comment on the preceding paragraph, which strikes one as more curious than if he had left in the "applause" and "laughter" with which, no doubt, he was freely interrupted.

These lectures may well be appraised as a capital example of the wisdom of letting a practical writer, who is also a critic, discuss and expound the principles on which he has himself attained success in his art. The Chair he holds was founded to promote "the study of English Literature from the age of Chaucer onwards," and the occupant was enjoined to treat the subject "on literary and critical rather than on philological and linguistic lines." "Q" obeyed these directions by lecturing on the art of writing, and treating this as "a living business," just as the Greeks treated the branches of culture dedicated to the Muses as necessary exercises in the training of a gentleman.

> Literature [he remarks] is not an abstract Science, to which exact definitions can be applied. It is an Art rather, the success of which depends on personal persuasiveness, on the author's skill to give as on ours to receive.

(p. 176)

"Q" has two lectures on **"The Capital Difficulty of Verse"** and **"The Capital Difficulty of Prose."** In verse, the difficulty is to annihilate the flat passages, to sustain interest in the monotonous parts between the dramatic incidents. In prose, it is to deal adequately with the "high moments of philosophizing," to express emotion impregnated with thought. Here and in two lectures on **"The Lineage of English Literature,"** and two others on **"English Literature in our Universities,"** he handles literary history with refreshing freedom and unabashed common sense, disdaining academic conventions. He has no patience with those who extol Elizabethan prose for virtues it never possessed or even aimed at. Enough that the Authorized Version made the path straight for the development of prose, and offers a standard of excellence that is strangely neglected by professors and other teachers of English literature. He [traces] . . . the lineage of English literature not to Beowulf and Sleswick, but to the Mediterranean peoples and the inspiration of Greece and Rome. He repeats an oft-told tale when he follows the direct and indirect reactions of the classics from the age of the trouvères to that of Keats, Tennyson, and Browning; but it is a tale that can be told anew with profit so long as its lessons are applied aptly. "Q" carries his scholarship lightly. He is not weighed down with the special erudition of the average professor, though he indulges occasionally in the elaborate rhetoric which belongs specially to Oxford. He shows good taste, sanity, and a clear sense of what principles mean to the expert who has to apply them.

The final lecture is on **"Style."** "Style in writing is much the same thing as good manners in other human intercourse."

> Literature being an Art, do you not see how personal a thing it is—how can it escape being personal? No two men (unless they talk Jargon) say the same thing in the same way. As is a man's imagination, as is his character, as is the harmony in himself, as is his ear, as is his skill, so and not otherwise than they can respond to that imagination, that character, that order of his intellect, that harmony of his soul, his hearers will hear him.

Thus, not in one of his best sentences, "Q" enforces a double lesson—that style is worth cultivating for its own sake, as well as for its value as a touchstone for the appreciation of literature.

The mention of **"Jargon"** refers to an intercalary lecture where this topic is considered at length. Jargon is "that infirmity of speech—that flux, that determination of words to the mouth, or to the pen"—which is familiar in Parliamentary debates, newspapers, and Bluebooks, committees, Official Reports, and such-like. It was treated more fully, but not perhaps more effectively, by the authors of *The King's English.* "Q" produces many examples in which abstract words like "case," "instance," "character," "nature," "condition," and "degree" are used to disguise vagueness of meaning. He brands clumsy or useless phrases like "in connexion with," "relative to," and "associated with," and in some diverting comparisons and parodies shows the flabbiness of abstract writing that avoids saying anything in a direct and concrete way. The morning after we had read this chapter, we picked up *The Times,* and found that a whole anthology of the jargon satirized by "Q" could easily be compiled from that single issue. In one letter we found the phrase "having regard to" three times, varied with the still more hideous "regard being had to."

> Surely [said the correspondent] now is the time when the future of the land should be considered dispassionately with a view to lifting our most important industry out of the rut of party politics so as to enable the best use to be made out of the land, thus protecting our food supply, a

necessity which is brought nearer home to us daily by the submarine menace.

"Q" would have been delighted to underline at least half-a-dozen phrases of that. He could also have culled several flowers of jargon from the leading articles, and many garlands from the paragraphs of news.

> The German press campaign against Cardinal Mercier is evidently designed to poison public opinion in neutral countries so that when the step of arresting the Cardinal is taken neutrals may think that some reason existed for Germany's action.
>
> In the present state of military operations, it is considered out of the question that Cardinal Mercier will be shot.

The first sentence might read,

> The campaign against Cardinal Mercier in the German press is evidently designed to make neutral countries believe that there is justification for arresting him.

The next probably means,

> Since Germany is not prospering at the front, it is not likely that Cardinal Mercier will be shot.

(pp. 176-77)

"Q" regards style, manner of expression, or, to put it more accurately, execution, as all-important. If words are the material of literature, then the art of writing is a principal division of the art of literature. This must be so, whether words are taken as units of sound and sense in verses, sentences, and paragraphs, or whether the chief stress is laid on the scheme of thought which they express. (p. 177)

> *"The Pursuit of English and the Study of Literature," in* The Athenaeum, *No. 4604, April, 1916, pp. 176-78.*

George Saintsbury   (essay date 1918)

[*Saintsbury has been called the most influential English literary historian and critic of the late nineteenth and early twentieth centuries. In the following excerpt from his review of* Studies in Literature, *he argues that formal lectures on literature should focus on writers whose work may be observed in "the firm perspective of the past," rather than on living writers.*]

At p. 68 [of ***Studies in Literature***] Sir Arthur justifies the programme of his Chair, which was, it seems, expressly "to open the study of English down to our own times." He does not in fact in this book deal with any living writer except Mr. Hardy, who is a classic already; but he seems rather anxious about the principle, though he frolics round its opponents as "fixing upon a date upon which English literature took to its bed and expired." Of course nobody does anything of the sort and the remark, like others, is a harmless joke. But perhaps it may be permitted to one who has thought (and had practical occasion to think) the subject out rather seriously—and who, with all due respect to Sir Arthur and the University of Cambridge, does not agree with them—to state his reasons for disagreement. Why did I (there can be no harm in the *ego* here, for it makes the matter more practical) deliberately abstain twenty years ago from lecturing on Francis Thompson and John Davidson—for the first of whom I had some, and for the second great admiration? And why should I, if I held a chair at the present moment, decline to lecture on those living writers whom Sir Arthur suggests?

The reasons are too numerous to exhaust here: but some of the chief of them may be given.

The first and most obvious, though by no means the strongest, is the difficulty of "speaking out," and the probable unfairness of such speaking when it is done *ex cathedra* and not as the scribes. The second objection is stronger. About the writers of the past there is a certain *corpus* of more or less settled judgment. The professor himself need not and should not merely spoon this into his students' ears; he may and should comment, contest, vary, fill in, and so forth, as his wits and his knowledge allow him to do. But there is always the general judgment remaining: and unless he is a silly paradoxer he will respect it and refer if not defer to it. And with it to qualify, steady and correct his own estimates, his pupils will have a body of literary doctrine on which to form their own mind and taste. The things are set and seen in "the firm perspective of the past" and will so abide.

Contemporary writers are in a wholly different case. Their work is usually not done; and work in that condition is always unsatisfactory to judge. There is between them and the contemporary student a distracting atmosphere of mist and dust and dazzle and all manner of illusion; while (almost worst of all) the atmosphere, though existing in both cases, is not the same between the professor and the object on the one hand, and the student and the object on the other.

But the strongest argument, though perhaps it may be the most unexpected, is the last. Is it not a mistake—almost a crime—to thrust in the personality of schoolmaster and professor between student and contemporary poet? It was not the least sensible and respectable action of the life of Mr. Arthur Pendennis that he did not insist on walking home that night with Mr. Philip Firmin and Miss Charlotte Baynes [in W. M. Thackeray's *The Adventures of Philip*]. And there is a real analogy between the relation of young readers to young poets and that of man and maid. The schoolmaster and the professor may prepare—should doubtless have prepared—the youthful reader to judge new poetry by what they have taught him about older; they may and should have guarded him against going a-flirting with the Tuppers and following after the Lewis Morrises of his own day. But this done, the commerce of new writer and young reader should be—at any rate had best be—undisturbed. The harm done to literature by making it the subject of teaching has, I think, been exaggerated, and affects some people hardly at all; but it exists, and does affect a good many others. Out of which last fact a humorist might perhaps extract a Gilbertian argument on Sir Arthur's side, and urge that if professors begin to lecture on Mr. Abercromby or Mr. Masefield, the

students will be driven by natural recalcitrance to prefer Tennyson and Browning, Coleridge and Shelley, and so on backwards. But in seriousness there can be, I think, no better motto than "Laissez la verdure." I never myself had any difficulty in liking Æschylus or Lucretius because I learnt them at school or was lectured to on them at college. But I *do* thank the goodness and the grace which spared me lectures and classes on Tennyson and Swinburne. (pp. 14-16)

> *George Saintsbury, "Studies in English Literature," in* The Bookman, *London, Vol. LV, No. 325, October, 1918, pp. 14, 16.*

Quiller-Couch's attitude toward female students:

Q's invariable practice of addressing his audience as 'Gentlemen', even though it always included women and even though the women were often in a majority, gave rise to the legend that he objected to their presence at his lectures. If it had been so, he could have refused admission to all women other than the members of Girton and Newnham Colleges, but he did nothing of the kind. On the contrary, he admitted everyone who cared to attend, whether they were men or women, and he frequently did this against the wishes of the administrative staff of the University, whose duty it was to see that outsiders did not attend lectures without special permission. He also admitted women as freely as men to his informal evening discussions, from which (as he was not compelled to hold them) he could have excluded even the members of the two women's colleges if he had wished. He addressed his audiences as 'Gentlemen' because he believed in being strictly correct on formal occasions, as he showed by the very dress he wore. In theory, he was lecturing to members of the University only; and, since the women's colleges were not legally included in the University, he maintained that it would be incorrect for him to include them in his form of address.

> *F. Brittain, in his* Arthur Quiller-Couch: A Biographical Study of Q, *1947.*

J. C. Squire   (essay date 1920)

[*Squire was a prolific British poet and critic who founded and edited the* London Mercury. *His criticism, like his poetry, is considered traditional and good-natured. In the following excerpt from the American version of his* Life and Letters: Essays, *he praises Shakespeare's Workmanship.*]

What a pleasure it is to get a book on Shakespeare and know before you open it that it will be fresh, frank, and sensible, free at once from old fustian and from new fantasies, and certain to send you back to read your author with increased understanding and enjoyment! Sir Arthur Quiller-Couch's *Shakespeare's Workmanship* has all the merits of his previous works and the additional attraction of the greatest subject a literary critic can write about.

Sir Arthur treats Shakespeare as a human artist, though the greatest: a man capable of indolence, wilful caprice, and occasional ineptitude: an artist working, like others, under limitations, unwilling (as great artists are) to repeat old triumphs, always attacking new difficulties, and sometimes (as in that last group of plays which cover long periods of time and deal with slow spiritual processes) failing to surmount them. With so full a book before him the reviewer can do no more than quote and criticise a few things at random. Sir Arthur throws light on every play and on the principles of art in general; the study of "workmanship" gives him a very wide reference with limits difficult to determine. He is extraordinarily good on *Hamlet,* in which he says, after all the wiseacres have dowered Shakespeare with all their philosophies and pathologies, there is no "mystery" whatever—except the slight unsolved and usually unnoticed mystery as to why the murdered king was succeeded by his brother, and not by his son. He notes in the *Merchant of Venice* how Shakespeare was handicapped by his ready-made and preposterous plots about the pound of flesh and the casket. They gave him little room for the natural development of character, he had to concentrate on Shylock or Portia. There ought, says Sir Arthur, "to be a close time" for the discussion of the Trial Scene.

Discussing criticisms made against the weaknesses and complexities of *Cymbeline,* he says, justly, that what Shakespeare did in that play was to create Imogen, the loveliest and noblest heroine in all literature; and that since he did so rare a thing we may assume that that is what he was chiefly trying to do. *As You Like It* elicits the remark that it is "arguable of the greatest creative artists that, however they learn and improve, they are always trading on the stored memories of childhood."

There is one play about which, exercising a reader's right with the utmost deference and diffidence, I dare to differ from Sir Arthur and from the majority of critics. I do not think *Macbeth* entirely comes off. Sir Arthur remarks, and this indisputable truth has been disastrously forgotten by many modern playwrights, that whatever a "hero" is, does, or suffers, it is essential that he should command the sympathies of the audience. He sets forth all the case against Macbeth, and adds that the great poetry which is put into his mouth "drapes him with the illusion of greatness," but that this is not enough, and that he is only saved by being represented as a victim of some fatal hallucination of undefined strength imposed on him by evil supernatural powers. I thoroughly agree with Sir Arthur's attack on those who under-estimate the importance of the supernatural element in the play, and who fail to understand the spell that a story like that of the witches on the blasted heath must exercise on all imaginative minds. I agree with his diagnosis of Shakespeare's problem here and of the means he adopted to solve it. Where I differ from him is in holding, unlike him, that Shakespeare failed. There was, I think, a double failure. Easy though Shakespeare found it to write great speeches and impute them to any character, it was not so easy to convince us that that character really spoke them. The great imaginative passages spoken by Hamlet, by Prospero, and by the raving Lear, we can accept not as Shakespeare's, but as theirs: they spring directly from their intellects and emotions as we know them; they are more intense than their contexts, but all of a piece with them. These men have no

need to be "draped" with the illusion of greatness, for they *are* great. With Macbeth it is different. When he says things like

> And all our yesterdays have lighted fools
> The way to dusty death

the great language *is* a "drapery." It hangs loosely and awkwardly upon him; it does not belong to him; the greatness is Shakespeare's, and not his; the illusion is not produced. Macbeth is not made great by the mere loan of a poet's imagery, and he is not made sympathetic, however adequately his crime may be explained and palliated, by being the victim of a hallucination. We might feel very deeply with such a victim had he won our affection or admiration previous to his hallucination or were he, outside that, a fine fellow; but this man has never attracted us at all; and though any weak doomed man must arouse some measure of pity, our interest in Macbeth is nothing compared with that which we feel in Hamlet and Othello and Lear, and even less than that which is stirred by his inexcusable and unhallucinated, but tigerishly resolute, lady.

The principal character in *Macbeth,* in fact, is dull; he makes no appeal; we do not greatly mind what happens to him; and the play, in spite of sublime scenes and poetry, is an illustration and a warning to artists who deny, or forget, that no powers of execution and no subordinate achievement can compensate for a central figure who is "unsympathetic," and that it is better for a "hero" to provoke active fear or hate than indifference or half-contemptuous pity. It is no use having a hero who makes people feel, from first to last, that he wants a good shaking. The mistake was not one that Shakespeare usually made; but his plot beat him. The emotional hold of the play would have been immeasurably greater had he set Macbeth against an equally prominent but lovable character: given him, say, an innocent, horror-stricken wife instead of a fellow-murderer who is not only as incapable as he of drawing our affection, but who incidentally throws him into the shade as a criminal.

The end of *Othello*—on which Sir Arthur barely touches—is a subtler matter; whether one thinks the workmanship fails depends upon whether one believes that the most noble and generous Othello, even though a Moor, and deceived, and mad with jealousy, really could have—did, in fact—kill his wife. Men in such situations, no doubt, have killed guiltless wives, and some of these men have possibly been strong and lovable people. But I, at least, experience when I come to that death, not those feelings which one has when a tragedy works to its inevitable and natural climax, but, mingled with sickening horror for poor little Desdemona, anger and irritation not against Othello, but against Shakespeare, who is directing him. Sir Arthur, in his brief parenthesis on the play, quotes a lady as having shouted to Othello from the auditorium: "You great black fool; can't you *see?*" What I feel like saying, and I can't think my impressions are unique, is not that, but: "Look here, Shakespeare, you'd no right to do this merely because, before you started, you decided that this was the way the story should go. You know better. You're monkeying with human nature, and you've no excuse."

Sir Arthur's readers must hope that he will supplement

this volume with another covering—with whatever central theme—those plays which are not studied in this volume. There is one, I think, which really should have been here, the main characteristics of Shakespeare's technical aims and achievements being the subject. That play is *Troilus and Cressida.* Too little attention has always been given to it; and those critics who have, at length, written about it have concentrated too much upon the love-story—drawing, incidentally, from this quite convincing picture of a fickle girl and an embittered lover unjustifiable deductions about Shakespeare's frame of mind when he wrote it.

The chief interest of the play, and certainly its chief interest as a piece of "workmanship," seems to me to lie in its vividness as a panorama, as a series of suddenly illuminated scenes in which many characters, Greek and Trojan, live and move, each with his distinct face and opinions and temper. It resembles one of those bright and crowded "compartment" pictures that the early Flemings painted. If both Troilus and Cressida were left out, the siege of Troy, in sections, would remain; and I cannot think (and I am sure Sir Arthur would not think) that in making that great tapestry Shakespeare did not know what he was doing, and know that, in drama, it was a novel and difficult thing. (pp. 161-68)

> *J. C. Squire, "Four Papers on Shakespeare,"
> in his* Life and Letters: Essays, *George
> H. Doran Company, 1921, pp. 161-88.*

C. Lewis Hind   (essay date 1921)

[*In the following excerpt from his book* Authors and I, *Hind proposes that Quiller-Couch's skill as a writer is best revealed in his literary criticism.*]

I permit myself to think of him as "Q." So he signed in *The Speaker* during the early nineties. This signature appeared, week by week, at the foot of an essay story—racy, humorous, pointed, brief. I thought them fine at the time: these swift studies in characterisation seemed to promise that one day "Q" would become a foremost novelist, a sort of second Robert Louis Stevenson.

He did not. He tarries. As a novelist he has not conquered. Others have passed him, and I fancy that, since *True Tilda* issued about ten years ago, he has gradually eased away from the fiction market. Many novels stand to his name. I remember reading, with rather an effort, *The Splendid Spur, Hetty Wesley,* and *Shining Ferry,* and I studied with much care his conclusion of *St. Ives,* which Stevenson left unfinished. It was a deft piece of work, the mechanics faultless, but it was not Stevenson. He is not a great romancer: he lacks Stevenson's lilt and background; and his childlike joy is metallic: it does not ooze out in the way of his master. As a romancer I submit "Q" has not found his centre.

Is he a poet, is poetry his true centre? I think not. He has written some charming and pretty poetry, he has made some neat and witty parodies (some think that they are better than Owen Seaman's), but his heartiest admirers would not label him a great poet.

Let us look at the man himself and see if we can discover what is "Q's" line in literature. He is a stay-at-home. For a few years he tried London, but in 1891 he returned to Cornwall where he has lived ever since. The first book he published after his return to Cornwall was *I Saw Three Ships.*

Ships he can see from his windows at the Haven, Fowey, Cornwall, adventuring out from Plymouth, or Plymouth bound. Ships are his companions; he is a great yachtsman, and his club is the Royal Fowey Yacht Club. Are we then to suppose that his centre is yachting? Hardly. Yachting is his recreation.

When I made a walking tour through Cornwall and reached Fowey early on a spring evening my first employment, after a bite of supper, was to call upon "Q." We sat in his library and I wondered mildly at the number of books owned by this tall, slight, blonde, athletic-looking writer who, in spite of his tan breeziness, and Yo, Heave Ho air, spoke like a scholar. Fleet Street has left little impression upon him. Oxford has. Scholarship might have tamed and tied him, as it tames and ties so many; his learned honours are numerous: M.A. Oxford, M.A. Cambridge, Litt.D. Bristol, but like G. W. Steevens, academic honours have been powerless to stultify the essential "Q." He is of the Stevenson school—gay, original, with flashes of insight, wearing his learning lightly and bending it to bright use in the give and take of the day's work. While we sat talking in his library above the Cornish sea, hearing his rapid comments on books and thought, I said to myself: "You are a born writer, and you could write decently and daringly on anything; you could turn out a lyric or an epic, a paragraph or a novel of a couple of hundred thousand words, but at heart you are a creative critic, a stimulating guide and brotherly friend to all who would shape their thought and lives from a study of the best literature. Yes, you are a creative critic. That is your literary centre." If anyone wants to be convinced of this let him read Quiller-Couch's *On the Art of Writing* and particularly *Studies in Literature.*

Since 1918 when it was published by the Cambridge University Press, *Studies in Literature* has been my chief bedside book. Dip into it where I will, a page here, a page there, I always find it tonic. Some of the essays were delivered to his class at Cambridge. Fortunate undergraduates! Your fathers, by Cam and Isis, heard Ruskin and Matthew Arnold: you have heard one who is worthy, as lecturer, to rank with them. Who that heard it can forget his indignation that anybody should call a "sloppy sentence good enough"; and who, having heard it, can forget his illustration and comment: "I desire that among us we make it impossible to do again what our Admiralty did with the battle of Jutland, to win a victory at sea and lose it in a despatch."

And the Rhymer, the budding Cambridge poet, hearing the following—would he not hurry home, with quick feet, to re-fashion his verses?

> Gentlemen—as your noun is but a name and
> your adjective but an adjunct to a name, while
> along your verb runs the nerve of life; so, if you

Quiller-Couch's home overlooking the harbor at Fowey.

would write melodiously, throughout vowels must the melody run.

And this about those pedagogues who classify poets into the Classic and the Romantic School—is it not final?

> "The play's the thing." *Hamlet, Lycidas,* or *The Cenci* is the thing. Shakespeare, Milton, Shelley did not write "classicism" or "romanticism." They wrote *Hamlet, Lycidas, The Cenci.*

And would not this burst of praise, no qualifications here, send a literary undergraduate, with eager eyes and rising pulse, to "the great Donne, the real Donne"—

> . . . his Sermons, which contain (as I hold) the most magnificent prose ever uttered from an English pulpit, if not the most magnificent prose ever spoken in our tongue.

This appears in the essay on "Some Seventeenth Century Poets." The thoughts of youth are long, long thoughts, and I can well imagine an undergraduate who heard this lecture never losing, throughout his life time, the memory of how Donne, Herbert, Vaughan, Traherne, Crashaw, and others swung our noble tongue, soaring as they shaped it. It is like drinking from a deep well.

And if the reader, having read some of "Q's" novels, and knowing how alert and lively is his fancy, desires something more than creative criticism of the best of the past, let him absorb the essay called **"The Commerce of Thought,"** wherein "Q" lets his imagination play over the old trade routes.

> You will see, as this little planet revolves back out of the shadow of night to meet the day, little threads pushing out over its black spaces— dotted ships on wide seas, crawling trains of emigrant waggons, pioneers, tribes on the trek, olive-gatherers, desert caravans, dahabeeyahs pushing up the Nile . . . the trade routes.

So he worms into this fascinating subject till he comes to his main thesis—the wanderings, alightings, and fertilising of man's thought.

As my eyes roam these pages they fall upon a footnote— just a footnote, and you know what footnotes usually are. What do you think of this footnote? Does it not set the imagination stirring?

> It is observable how many of the great books of the world—the *Odyssey,* the *Æneid, The Canterbury Tales, Don Quixote, The Pilgrim's Progress,*

Gil Blas, Pickwick, and *The Cloister and the Hearth*—are books of wayfaring.

I repeat: it is in creative criticism that "Q" has found his centre. Let others busy themselves with the novel. It is his destiny to deal creatively with the higher branch, with poetry, and the literature that is safe beyond the phases and fashions of our day. He makes us long to read the best; he makes us lament that we pretend we have no time for that great adventure. (pp. 246-51)

> Charles Lewis Hind, "A. T. Quiller-Couch," in his Authors and I, *John Lane Company, 1921, pp. 246-51.*

Robert Lynd   (essay date 1922)

[*Lynd, an Irish journalist and author, served as literary editor of the* London News Chronicle *and contributed regularly to the* New Statesman and Nation *under the pseudonym "Y. Y." In the following review of* Studies in Literature (Second Series), *he observes that Quiller-Couch's reprinted lectures clearly reflect his speaking style.*]

"Q" is an evangelist of literature to the University of Cambridge. His aim, it is clear, is not to criticise, but to make converts. He addresses not the "saved" but those who may still be hesitating. Hence he does not dispute subtly as among the doctors: he knows that the rousing address has its place in the propaganda of literature as well as of religion. Like many evangelists, he also knows how to mingle fervour with playfulness. His jests are not the least effective weapon of his piety. He is, indeed, determinedly familiar and human. He embraces his hearers, not with that personal intimacy which is the secret of so many good writers, but with that general intimacy which is the secret of so many good speakers.

Whether, when reprinting his lectures, he would not have done well to recast them and rid them of their platform manner is a question on both sides of which there is something to be said. There is abundant precedent for the republication of speeches, and there have been no better speeches on literature in our time than "Q.'s." Apart from this, it would be almost impossible to edit them into the form of literary essays without rewriting them. Their present form—its very looseness, digressiveness and deliberate reiteration—is essentially the form of the spoken word, not of the written. Take, for example, the passage [in *Studies in Literature,* second series] on the coming of Milton's blindness while his epic was still unwritten:

> Blindness—total blindness: and upon that, in 1660, loss of place, exile, persecution, hiding. . . . Think of it all!

> Ah, but what of the great work that we see him—so long ago and after so long a preparation—on the eve of writing. Almost twenty years have passed: Milton has now turned fifty: and not a line of it is written. "Is that also lost, then? . . ."

> No, for see! This man—sans light, sans friends, sans hope, sans everything . . . ; this indomita-

ble man seats himself in his shabby leathern chair as in a throne, throws a leg over its arm in the old negligent boyish attitude, and begins to speak our great English epic.

It is very unlikely that if "Q" had been writing a book or an essay on Milton, he would have used this particular kind of emphasis—"Think of it all!" "Ah, but what . . .?" "No; for see!"—so frequently on a single page. For a writer these things would be irritating. In a professor inciting young men and women to the love of literature they are legitimate and probably even effective.

"Q" in several of his lectures has shown us a good example by giving the "devil's advocate" a fair hearing against the famous men he praises—Byron and Shelley among them. The "devil's advocate," I think, has to be heard against "Q" himself if we are to realise how good these studies of his are for their purpose. There are several literary critics who equal—perhaps surpass—"Q" in intellectual and imaginative curiosity. He seldom opens a new door to the understanding of a great writer. On the other hand, there is no literary critic except "Q" who could preach the gospel of good literature to youth with just this attractiveness and passion. It is as though "Q" himself had renewed his youth in the company of youth. He has the ardour touched with persiflage of the best sort of undergraduate. He speaks like a man at the beginning of a new age. He has gone back to the heresies of twenty, and believes with Shelley in the return of the golden years. He still feels the rage of youth against Matthew Arnold for his deathless phrase about Shelley—"a beautiful and ineffectual angel, beating in the void his luminous wings in vain." He even pauses, in the course of his discussion on Arnold's criticism, to throw in the indignant jibe:

> Have you ever sat in a drawing-room and listened to a middle-aged lady taking away a servant girl's character? She talks just like that.

This is all very lively, but it is surely possible to love Shelley and yet to see that, if Lamb disliked him and Matthew Arnold underestimated him, they were repelled by a striking imperfection in his genius. He was a doctrinaire, and the artist, like the statesman, is usually suspicious of doctrine that is not in harmony with human experience. Shelley was in revolt against human experience—in revolt against it on behalf of something nobler. He was in revolt against it in a sense in which Christ was not in revolt against it. Christ always foresaw consequences, whereas Shelley did not. That is probably what one means by a doctrinaire—a man with a theory of which he does not foresee the consequences. "Q," it is only fair to say, after he has made hay with Matthew Arnold, faces those facts about Shelley that made Matthew Arnold censorious. He brushes aside the theory of free love with the smiling quotation from Dr. Johnson: "If (said he) I had no duties, and no reference to futurity, I would spend my life in driving briskly in a post-chaise with a pretty woman." But, when experience has said its word on Shelley, it has spoken not the last word, but only the preface to the first word of real importance. Shelley's spirit is greater than any of his dogmas. His very excesses are excesses of hope, and with him hope was imaginative, creative. "Shelley," writes "Q," "has much to teach us yet. If he can teach us the root of the matter—that human society will never be reformed but on some law of love and understanding—he will come in time to an even greater kingdom than he yet inherits." "Q" also assures his hearers that Shelley "means to-day—or should mean to us if we have any sense in our heads—something more momentous, more imperative, than he meant to us a few years ago, when we worshipped such things as 'The Skylark' or 'When the Lamp is Shattered' for their mere beauty." It is always his aim to show great authors, not only in relation to life, but to the life of our own time.

In his attitude to Byron as to Shelley, "Q" enthusiastically takes side with the estimate of youth. He thrills in youthful sympathy with Byron as the arch-rebel defying the Almighty Himself:

> You may smile at any man—small, bi-forked creature that he is standing up, questioning; arraigning, denouncing the higher powers; but you must acknowledge the right of the challenge. If God created man in His image, man has a right (shall we not even say, a duty?) to erect himself to the fullest inch of that image and ask questions. Does it not, at any rate, argue a certain nobility of mind (if exorbitant) in one betrayed by his fellow creatures, that he walks straight up and has it out with the Creator Himself?

As a matter of fact, Byron would have been but a mortal and passing poet if he had challenged no one but the Creator. He aimed his keenest shafts at more human powers, and what he thought about God matters less to us to-day than what he thought about George III or the Duke of Wellington. It is his raging thoughts about the great figures of his own age that keep *Don Juan* alive, even for many who care little for the greater part of his poetry. "I believe," "Q" declares in his enthusiasm, "*Don Juan* will some day be recognised for one of the world's few greatest epics." We may quarrel with this view of it, believing that it is not the epical but the comical parts of *Don Juan* that make it surer of immortality than anything else that Byron wrote. But this is the kind of reasonable exaggeration that tempts people to read. Exaggeration that is not a mere bogus imitation of excitement but itself springs from profound excitement plays a legitimate part in literary criticism. And "Q" is as profoundly excited by Byron as any Continental critic. To him Byron is still "a mind that had some measure of the Titanic."

If much of "Q's" work shows signs of the responsive enthusiasm of youth, however, there is also always in the background a strong sense of experience and a middle-aged respect for the achievements even of the day before yesterday. His is a catholic appreciation, and, though he likes to see young men in revolt against their time, he does not apparently like to see them in revolt against their fathers' time, with its quite considerable gods. In the last chapter of his book, "The Victorian Age," he takes Mr. Strachey to task for laughing at Queen Victoria's emotions at the time of the opening of the Great Exhibition, and protests: "Hang it all, sir! If the 1st May, 1851, *was* a day of ecstasy to her, she was a woman, a little more than thirty, and she was in love, and it is long ago." And to the disparagers of the Victorian Age in general he says pertinently enough:

> Now, I ask you to consider this. If, in the second year of the reign of Queen Victoria, one of her Judges of Assize, Lord Denman, at Launceston sentenced a boy of thirteen to penal servitude for life for stealing three gallons of potatoes; and if by the close of the reign such a sentence had become not merely illegal but unthinkable, so that, at the least, it had changed places with the offence and, if anyone, then the judge rather than the criminal, should have gone to penal servitude for life—who were—who can have been—the wizards that wrought this topsy-turvy on the national conscience?

"Q," I fancy, is a lecturer who loves controversy, and he brings into criticism the excitement of an argument—an argument, if possible, for the defence, while vigorously attacking the attack. He is a man of humour as well as a controversialist, however, with the same lucky results with which he combines the parts of moralist and heretic. These things alone would not make him an ideal professor of literature. But they help to make the talk of a man of letters interesting. It is because of these, perhaps, that "Q" is most interesting of all when he is discussing, not an author, but a question, as he did in *The Art of Writing.* (pp. 361-62)

Robert Lynd, "The Evangelism of 'Q'," in New Statesman, *Vol. XIX, No. 481, July 1, 1922, pp. 361-62.*

Quiller-Couch's adherence to daily routine:

At the age of eighty Q still began every day at Cambridge with a tepid bath in an icy bathroom. Having finished his bath he dressed for the morning—without hurrying; for dressing was to him, like everything he did, a ceremony that had to be carried out properly. No one ever succeeded in making him rush through anything unnecessarily, though if speed was essential he would be as quick as anyone. Always the best-dressed man in Cambridge, he was so still. If he was to deliver a formal lecture during the morning he put on correct morning dress. Otherwise he put on either a tweed suit of brighter colours than most men dared to wear or a bright brown jacket and shooting breeches, with stockings and high spats. Whatever else he wore, he would have a silk handkerchief (of a colour to match his suit) in his breast pocket and would wear a stiff double collar, and a blue or brown bow tie sown with fairly large white roundels. The corners of his jackets were always cut square, never rounded off.

The next ceremony was breakfast, which he took at the side table in his keeping room. Although he was always very particular about the selection, the cooking and the serving of food, he ate remarkably little at this or any other meal. After breakfast he wrote a letter home: throughout fifty-four years of married life he had written home every day whenever he was away.

F. Brittain, in his Arthur Quiller-Couch: A Biographical Study of Q., *1947.*

Richard Eberhart   (essay date 1940)

[*Eberhart is an American poet and critic. In the following review of the 1939 edition of* The Oxford Book of English Verse 1200-1918, *he examines Quiller-Couch's criteria for including poems in this anthology.*]

Q used to come late to his class in Aristotle's Poetics which met once a week in the evening across from St. John's. It was the only official meeting in Cambridge at which one was allowed the liberty of abandoning formal dress. The dozen students waited expectantly in the large room at one end of which burned a great fire in the old English fireplace which went up to the ceiling. At a pleasant lateness Q's man would appear, a dutiful vanguard in butler's togs, holding aloft a silver tray bearing port and cigars. He would place his burden on a long rectangular table which dominated the room. About ten paces behind would come Q, in a sort of toddle, mellow from dinner, dressed in evening clothes. He suffused a certain geniality. He was amiable, old, a bit crotchety, but obviously a man of telling charm. "Good evening, gentlemen," and he would wave his pupils to the silver altar. They would help themselves, or be served, while Q was fussing about getting ready to sit down, his back to the fire, at the head of the long table. Then in the most leisurely fashion, he would begin talking about the Poetics. It is notable that he only discussed one paragraph during each weekly meeting; it is unforgettable that his digressions constituted the main part of the discourse, these beginning soon, and usually straying far from Aristotle—in fact, the course was an ambulatory one in Q's diverting personality. That was a decade ago. I am told the course is still given.

Memories induce a certain relaxation when one begins to discuss Sir Arthur's new edition of *The Oxford Book of English Verse.* The heart may accept what the mind rejects. Critical perception demands a harsh dealing with this book; memory pays tribute to a kindly scholar and a pleasant gentleman.

The first and famous *Oxford Book* was fairly just. This volume is less just, and exposes painful errors of taste. The pain is greater the more seriously you consider that this book, like its predecessor, may determine the taste of great numbers of readers for years to come, and fix in their minds the reputation and rank of the writers. What excuse can one concoct for a "famous" editor who leaves out D. H. Lawrence entirely, but includes W. H. Davies? I feel this omission and cannot condone it. Surely Lawrence wrote at least one worthy poem? I do not hold that he wrote many, but I do not agree with his excision. Upon careful study of the later part of the volume, one would like to make laconic remarks to any young poet beginning his career. Don't follow knowledge like a sinking star (or anything else) beyond the utmost bounds of human thought; don't for Heaven's sake "die, or faint, or fail," be a "scorner of the ground," or seek "harmonious madness"; or strive "to find the uncreated light"; or espouse the prose formulation of poetry; or make it new by returning to vocal folk myth. No. Your strategy should lie elsewhere. Be a middle-minded man, be a center of the road

singer, be smooth and dare not, be obvious, and above all be middle-Christian, and you will make Q's grade, were he to be spared a quarter of a century to build a later book. Thus, if you are Emily Dickinson, you will get one little poem; but if you are Oliver St. John Gogarty, you will get two. You could not afford to be Hopkins, with four poems, lacking "The Windhover" or "Carrion Comfort"; or Housman, your best poems unrepresented, even if you could not vent your spleen on the anthologist; or Hardy, flattened and thinned, without a balanced picture of your art and scope; and as unfortunate would it be to be the later Yeats, for you would not be represented at all.

Q is faulty as definitive editor of the best poetry since 1900. In addition, most readers will probably regret his admitted insecurity of judgment among the poetical works since 1918. One wishes he had cared to cope with Eliot and Pound at least, unless, unkind, one supposes his choices there would be as questionable as those in Hardy, Hopkins, and Yeats. It is only fair, however, to accept roughly a term of twenty years beyond which critical estimation should not be attempted. Was he unaware of Isaac Rosenberg, who died in 1918, but published two books in 1915? Could he not have chosen more than one poem by Owen, who died in 1918, but was not published until 1921? For the book is heavy with minor poets showing one poem each (Edward Thomas is accorded two). Harold Monro might have rated one; T. E. Hulme (even), and Herbert Read, and Richard Aldington might have rated one, where such sympathy is shown to one-poem poets of the nineteenth century; perhaps Graves more than one. This is not to exhaust the list of possibilities before 1918.

Q has resurrected notable anonymous pieces; he has corrected mistakes, as in the restoration of the severed "Ecstasy," by Donne, and in crediting to Thomas Osbert Mordaunt (1730-1809) "The Call," which he formerly gave to Sir Walter Scott. He has added poets of former times, such as Lord Herbert of Cherbury and Charles Wesley; he has added light pieces, such as the four-page addition to Prior of "Jinny the Just," and "The Ballad of Bouillabaisse," by Thackeray. He has banned minor poets to oblivion, and raised up others from the shades: a collation of such editing makes a nice pleasure. He has juggled the entries of a good many poets, adding or subtracting, according to a critical estimation some may call whim. Clare has still only one poem; one Praed is substituted for another; a third is added to a minor like Mangan. Beddoes is cut from three to two: all cases of injustice. But a charming, delightful thing Q has done is to insert several two- or four-line poems, dug from one wonders where. May I quote No. 395, anonymous, which endears Q to the reader:

ON ELEANOR FREEMAN

who died 1650, aged 21

Let not Death boast his conquering power,
She'll rise a star that fell a flower.

And there is a long stretch of the book, from Herrick

through Milton and Marvell, to Vaughan, over a hundred pages, left without change. Shakespeare is not touched.

My main disappointment, for purposes of this review, is in Q's maladministration of Hopkins, Housman, Hardy, and Yeats. Hardy's five entries are insufficient, not composite. The editor would have had to add the poem on Meredith and "Channel Firing," at least. A. E. Housman receives but three poems, suffering misfortune at the hands of an editor living almost across the street. Hopkins's utmost peculiarities and values are not exhibited. Q relaxes to add a tenth to Bridges (Hopkins has four), but in this case the sentimentality of "On a Dead Child" is lost in "Elegy: on a Lady, Whom Grief for the death of her Betrothed killed," of stately formal song. Something stronger than concern is called out against the editor, however, because of his feeble treatment of Yeats. Only two pieces are added to the earlier three, "Down by the Salley Garden," and "Aedh wishes for the Cloths of Heaven," a total and ignominious disregard of the author of "The Tower" and all later works.

I conclude with a question: Would English literature be shown to greater advantage if all, or most of the one-poem poets were left out, only the major figures showing, and these with more poems? Q has obviously paid a good deal of attention to minor poets, in the earlier part switching one for another, in the latter part discovering a considerable number for inclusion. My conclusion is that the Muse has not appeared only to her greatest servants throughout the centuries in England; that many single poems of minor writers deserve preservation; and that this whole corpus of work definitely shows to the glory (if not to the highest glory) of English poetry. One poet with one good poem preserved for centuries may be about as well off as some writer more famous in his time, dwindled to a few period poems. It is a tribute to English poetry that not all its excellent poems are written by the major figures. It is a tribute to Q that he is aware of this.

But now the class is over. "Good evening, gentlemen," and Q toddles back into the inner room. (pp. 263-67)

Richard Eberhart, "Q's Revisions," in The Kenyon Critics: Studies in Modern Literature from The Kenyon Review, *edited by John Crowe Ransom, The World Publishing Company, 1951, pp. 263-67.*

Robert J. Geist   (essay date 1951)

[*Geist is an American critic who has written and co-authored numerous composition and grammar texts. In the following essay, he discusses* "Interlude: On Jargon."]

As a freshman I frequently wrote awkward sentences in my themes, sentences I knew to be awkward before the instructor scrawled a huge "Awkward" or "Clumsy" across them. Completely baffled in my attempts to revise them, I found Sir Arthur Quiller-Couch's **"Interlude: On Jargon"** a revelation; at last I could get hold of something definite in those sentences, something that was a key to the needed revision. Six years later, full of enthusiasm for the

essay, I first set out to teach it to a freshman class—in fact, four freshman classes. My enthusiasm so far exceeded my understanding that, when those four classes finished with me, I could find nothing wrong with the word *case* except that it sounded like the German word for cheese.

Conversations with other instructors have convinced me that I was not and am not alone in finding Quiller-Couch's essay full of pitfalls for the unwary instructor. A distinguished Oxford professor finds his reputation and the lecture platform sufficient guaranty against objections from his audience; an undistinguished American instructor has no such safeguard from his handful of unselected listeners. Convinced that **"Jargon"** is the greatest single essay on the art of writing, I would like to point out some of the objections.

In general, most students, if they react at all, react antagonistically; and for this antagonism Quiller-Couch is at least in part responsible. He is not, of course, responsible for the natural antagonism many students feel toward criticism of so essential a part of their makeup as style; they sometimes feel too strongly that the style is the man, and hence the man is being criticized; but Quiller-Couch is responsible for the antagonism wrought by one who is too positive in his statements, one who does not practice what he preaches, one who loses track of his real point in order to be humorous. Of *with regard to* and *in respect of,* Quiller-Couch says, "I say it is not enough to avoid them nine times out of ten, or ninety-nine times out of a hundred. You should never use them." The average freshman is likely to resent this unyielding condemnation of some of his favorite locutions. Furthermore, when the freshman reads that elegant variation is a favorite trick of jargon, he wonders just what he has hold of when Quiller-Couch says, "Here again is a string, a concatenation—say, rather, a tiara of gems of purest ray serene from the dark unfathomed caves of a Scottish newspaper." Thomas Gray means little enough to the student; for him Quiller-Couch is merely indulging in a flux of words to the pen. Again, the student reads that jargon "dallies with Latinity," only to find, a few pages later, that Quiller-Couch suggests closing "our *florilegium.*" Nor is Latinity all. *Logos,* in Greek characters, leaves the student cold, or infuriated at this professor who has constantly used the jargon of his profession—poetical quotation and foreign words. Most antagonizing of all perhaps is Quiller-Couch's obscuring the real point in order to be humorous. The second vice of jargon, we are told, is the use of "vague woolly abstract nouns"—like *case, instance, character, nature, condition, persuasion, degree.* It is essential for the student to keep in mind that these words are objectionable because they are vague woolly abstract nouns, but Quiller-Couch immediately leads the reader away from vagueness and woolliness by saying, or implying, that *case,* jargon's dearest child, is objectionable because its Latin ancestor did not mean what vague woolly abstract *case* does mean—*situation, circumstance, instance.* Obviously, the ancestral meaning of a word is not the criterion by which we judge its present meaning, but, by inaccurately supposing that *case* can only mean *container,* Quiller-Couch achieves the mildly amusing: "then try how, with a little trouble, you can extricate yourself from that case," and the hilarious: "Poor

Mr. Cox! left gasping in his aquarium." I do not object to the undeniable humor in the gasping Mr. Cox, though students frequently fail tó find it funny; but it is essential to recognize that the humor is actually beside the point and detracts from the idea that *case* is objectionable because it is a vague woolly abstract noun. The person who wrote "in the case of Mr. Harold Cox" did not mean or say that Mr. Cox was in a container; and the reader does not interpret that Mr. Cox was in one, aquarium or otherwise. The writer did say that Mr. Cox was in a case, a situation—which in effect says nothing and leaves the reader to interpret whether Mr. Cox did not weep or was not wept for. I should certainly not wish to delete Sir Arthur's antagonizing sins from the essay; they give the essay flavor. I believe, however, that these sins should be written large for the student; in fact, I happily agree with the students in finding fault with Quiller-Couch and make our agreement a means to understand his essential point.

The instructor must, of course, seek to counteract the student's antagonism whenever it interferes with the essential point. Thus upon reading, "The first [vice of jargon] is that it uses circumlocution rather than *short straight* speech," some antagonized student inevitably doesn't want to use short, straight, simple speech all the time; it's childish. Well, what is the difference between the simplicity of childhood and the simplicity of maturity, the simplicity of writing like Swift's? Like Quiller-Couch, we fall back on illustration. A first-class jargoneer once wrote in a theme on modern methods of teaching:

> Now let us ask what the effects of the emphasis
> upon the influence of environment are.

About one in fifty freshmen fathoms the meaning of the sentence; yet the writer had a definite idea, and each word adds meaning. The sentence very clearly has the simplicity of childhood—and the incomprehensibility. The verbs *let, ask,* and especially *are* could hardly be simpler; and the series of prepositional phrases has the simplicity of a chain—perhaps a concatenation. The revised sentence reads:

> Now let us ask how emphasizing the influence
> of environment affects modern teaching.

The sentence is immediately clear—short, straight, simple—but the grammatical simplicity of the childish sentence has given way to grammatical complexity. Since a gerund (*emphasizing*) used as subject and taking an object is in the language, not to be analyzed by grammarians, but to express more precisely the logical relation between sentence elements, the grammatical complexity of the revised sentence creates a simplicity and directness not found in the original sentence, the simplicity and directness of the mature writer.

Regarding the second vice of jargon—the use of the already-mentioned vague woolly abstract nouns—we can avoid trouble with Quiller-Couch's illustrations only if we keep clearly in mind that *case* and the others are objectionable as general abstract nouns that cover the intended meaning without stating it precisely. We have already cited the misleading reference to Latin *casus;* Quiller-

Couch's second example is also somewhat beside the point:

> [From a cigar-merchant.] In any case, let us send
> you a case on approval.

Slight analysis is sufficient to make clear that the fault lies in the repetition of a word in two entirely different meanings. Here the word repeated happens to be *case;* but repetition, not meaning, is at fault. Even Quiller-Couch would not object to the second *case,* a container for cigars. The first *case* is obviously the vague woolly abstract *case,* but it is precisely what the writer wants. He wishes to be as vague, broad, and general as possible in order that you will let him send you cigars on approval. If one tries to avoid this *case,* one can only resort to synonymous expressions: *under any circumstances, in any event, no matter what, whatever the situation.* One may prefer these synonyms, but one must recognize that whenever a writer wishes to be general or vague, he may legitimately use a vague woolly abstract noun. It seems to me essential that this legitimate use of *case* be pointed out.

Perhaps a word of caution is in order regarding Quiller-Couch's suggested correction for his fourth illustration:

> Even in the purely Celtic areas only in two or
> three cases do the Bishops bear Celtic names.
>
> For "cases" read "dioceses."

This correction, fitting enough in the sentence, suggests the hunt for synonyms, but a vague woolly abstract noun like *case* rarely lends itself to so concrete a synonym as *diocese.* Rather, as Fowler points out:

> There is some danger that, as writers become
> aware of the suspicions to which they lay themselves
> open by perpetually using *case,* they may
> take refuge with *instance,* not realizing that most
> instances in which *case* would have damned
> them are also cases in which *instance* will damn
> them.

Hunting synonymns for vague woolly abstract nouns, then, is dangerous, and I rather suspect that when the writer of this fourth example wrote *cases* he did not intend or mean *dioceses.* He pretty clearly meant two or three bishops. "Even in the purely Celtic areas only two or three Bishops bear Celtic names." This use of general abstract nouns as mere padding without necessarily destroying meaning is, of course, extremely common. "In most cases working students get help from home," to take a recent freshman example. Quiller-Couch's next example: "In most instances the players were below their form," probably illustrates the same point.

Students often object to the censure cast upon the amusing sentence: "He was conveyed to his place of residence in an intoxicated condition." One will do well to recognize that this expansiveness does lend itself to humor, but, to carry a straightforward message, "He was carried home drunk." In order to be humorous, moreover, an expansive passage is best set off against a simple direct background, as Quiller-Couch's concatenation—say, rather, a tiara—itself illustrates.

The essay ends fittingly with a forceful idea forcefully expressed—but marred in the freshman mind by *perpend* and *logos*. Let me end with the reminder that I criticize Quiller-Couch's essay only because I consider it invaluable to the student who understands it. (pp. 150-53)

> *Robert J. Geist, "On 'On Jargon'," in* Toward Liberal Education, *Louis G. Locke, William M. Gibson, George Arms, eds., revised edition, Rinehart & Company, 1952, pp. 150-53.*

R. J. Schork   (essay date 1990)

[*In the following essay, Schork suggests a solution to the word-puzzle in Quiller-Couch's story* "The Roll-Call on the Reef."]

Sir Arthur Quiller-Couch's 1895 ghost story, **"The Roll-Call on the Reef,"** uses a familiar technique to achieve both narrative immediacy and authenticating distance: the tale within the tale. In this case, a quarryman host tells his anonymous guest a tale he had heard from his father about the eerie events following a terrible coastal storm. The father had witnessed two British transports founder on the rocks "in the night o' the twenty-first of the year 'nine." The HMS *Despatch,* homeward bound from Corunna with a detachment of the 7th Hussars, went down with a terrible loss of life. Only a very few troopers survived—including the master trumpeter whose calls, especially a final "God Save the King," buoyed the spirits of the doomed men. The HMS *Primrose,* outward bound from Portsmouth, lost all hands except for a small drummer-boy.

These latter two survivors recuperated in the coastal village and became comrades. "Nothing delighted the pair more than to borrow a boat off my father and pull to the rocks" where the ships had gone down. There they played their tattoos and calls. Eventually the drummer was recalled to active service with the Marines, but the badly injured trumpeter stayed in the village and lived in the cottage of the narrator's father. Before they parted, however, the survivor-friends hung their instruments on a hook by the chimney-piece and secured them with a padlock that opened only when the six brass rings spelled a secret word.

Quite a bit later, "about three o'clock in the morning, April fourteenth of the year 'fourteen," the drummer reappears at the cottage. "His scarlet jacket had a red hole by the breastbone, and blood was welling there." The trumpeter opens the lock; they both take their instruments and row out for a final visit to the rocks where their comrades had died. Then the pair goes to Gunner's Meadow where the drowned Marines and Hussars were buried. The trumpeter calls the roll. Each of the dead troopers answers, and ends his report with "God Save the King." The drummer joins them.

When the trumpeter returns to the cottage, he hangs the two instruments by the chimney again—and resets the half-dozen brass rings of the padlock. The new word is "Bayonne," where the drummer had been killed. Just as "Corunna" had to lose an "n" to conform to the six rings, so too must "Bayonne" drop one of its "n's." Three days

later the master trumpeter of the Queen's Own 7th Hussars is himself dead and laid in Gunner's Field.

The narrator's father "held his tongue" about the apparition of the mortally wounded drummer, until he felt obliged to tell the entire story to Parson Kendall. The Parson tested the validity of the tale by spelling out "B-A-Y-O-N-E" on the rings. The lock, of course, snapped open. The Parson advised silence, since "a miracle's wasted on a set of fools." At the father's request, however, he reset the lock and linked the trumpet and drum once more, "dead nor alive." The word chosen, we are told, was a "holy word." In fact, at the start of the tale the narrator tells his guest that no one will ever guess the Parson's word, which "locked down a couple o' ghosts in their graves with it."

Despite this disclaimer, Sir Arthur certainly intended his readers to attempt to guess the word. If Parson Kendall were some dour chapel-preacher likely to condemn as diabolical an apparition from the otherworld, I would venture that his word might have been "GEHEN[N]A," the abode of the dead. On the other hand, I suspect that by accepting the responsibility for insuring the union of the Hussar's and the Marine's instruments, Parson Kendall endorsed and glorified their eternal bond, in this world and the next. Thus, I would wager that his holy word was "HOSAN[N]A." (pp. 603-04)

> *R. J. Schork, "The Holy Word," in* Studies in Short Fiction, *Vol. 27, No. 4, Fall, 1990, pp. 603-04.*

FURTHER READING

Biography

Brittain, F. *Arthur Quiller-Couch: A Biographical Study of Q.* New York: The Macmillan Company, 1947, 174 p.
  Anecdotal account of Quiller-Couch's life that includes illustrations and a comprehensive bibliography of his published works.

Davies, Hugh Sykes. " 'Q': Myth, Man, and Memory." *The Listener* XLIX, No. 1264 (21 May 1953): 847-48.
  Review of F. Brittain's *Arthur Quiller-Couch* written by a former Cambridge University student who describes his memories of Quiller-Couch.

Rowse, A. L. "Q as Cornishman." *The Spectator* 172, No. 6047 (19 May 1944): 448-49.
  Describes Quiller-Couch as "the best-loved Cornishman of his time."

Criticism

Bolton, W. F. "Sources and Non-sources: Politics and the English Language." *College Literature* XI, No. 1 (Winter 1984): 71-7.
  Traces similarities of phrasing and theme in the writing of George Orwell and Arthur Quiller-Couch.

Mais, S. P. B. " 'Q' As Critic." In his *Books and Their Writers,* pp. 200-30. London: Grant Richards, 1920, 343 p.
> Reprinted review of Quiller-Couch's *Studies in Literature* and *Shakespeare's Workmanship.*

Putt, S. Gorley. "Technique and Culture: Three Cambridge Portraits." In *Essays and Studies 1961,* edited by Derek Hudson, pp. 17-34. London: Cox and Wyman, 1961, 114 p.
> Comparison of Putt's three mentors at Cambridge University: Quiller-Couch, Charles Snow, and F. R. Leavis.

Ransom, John Crowe. "The Cathartic Principle." *The American Review* V, No. 3 (Summer 1935): 287-300.
> Ransom treats Quiller-Couch's *The Poet as Citizen* as a "twentieth-century Victorian" view of Aristotle's concept of art as catharsis.

Sheppard, Alfred Tresidder. " 'Q': The Romance of Sir A. T. Quiller-Couch." *The Bookman (London)* LXXIV, No. 440 (May 1928): 101-4.
> Review of the *Duchy Edition of the Tales and Romances of Sir Arthur Quiller-Couch* that focuses on lesser-known works.

Willey, Basil. *The "Q" Tradition.* Cambridge: University Press, 1946. 35 p.
> Inaugural address by Basil Willey, Quiller-Couch's successor as King Edward VII Professor of English at Cambridge.

Additional coverage of Quiller-Couch's life and career is contained in the following source published by Gale Research: *Contemporary Authors,* **Vol. 118.**

Eugene Manlove Rhodes

1869-1934

American novelist, essayist, and short story writer.

INTRODUCTION

Rhodes is best known for his fiction set in the American Southwest. These novels are distinctive in the western genre for their assiduous attention to verisimilitude in time and place and Rhodes's depiction of the cowboy as noble and intelligent. Although some critics fault his novels for implausible plots, most commentators claim that Rhodes's realistic portrayal of the cowboy milieu in the late-nineteenth century secures his position among notable authors of western fiction.

Rhodes was born in Tecumseh, Nebraska. In 1881 his family settled in the Tularosa basin in New Mexico, and this region later became the setting for many of his novels and stories. In 1888 Rhodes enrolled at the University of the Pacific at Stockton, California, but returned to New Mexico after two years because of financial hardship. For several years he worked as a miner, horse wrangler, schoolteacher, and cattle rancher. Rhodes married in 1899, and in 1906 moved to Apalachin, New York. His first novel, *Good Men and True,* was serialized in the *Saturday Evening Post* in 1910. In 1919 Rhodes, in failing health, moved to Los Angeles and sold the motion picture rights to six of his novels. After three years in Los Angeles Rhodes returned to New York, but for health reasons moved to Sante Fe and finally Palm Beach, California in 1931. He died of a heart attack in 1934.

Rhodes is praised by critics for his accurate account of late-nineteenth-century New Mexico in his fiction, and he often incorporated such real-life characters as the legendary sheriff Pat Garrett and the outlaw Bill Doolin in his stories. In his first novel, *Good Men and True,* a dissolute politician plots the downfall of an innocent Texas Ranger. Eventually, the politician is foiled by the protagonist, a cowboy named Jeff Bransford, a character taken directly from Rhodes's past. In addition to depictions of genuine characters, Rhodes painstakingly described details of cattle ranching and Southwestern culture. Although critics credit his authentic re-creation of time and place, they fault the weak structure of his novels. As commentator Edwin W. Gaston Jr. asserted, Rhodes "works with materials inherently realistic but builds naively romantic plot structure," and in Rhodes's novels, the storylines rely on the premise that those in power positions, like bankers or sheriffs, are corrupt, while outlaws and cowboys are intelligent and decent. Rhodes's most critically acclaimed novel, *Pasó por Aquí,* chronicles the adventures of a fleeing bank robber and his encounter with a Mexican family stricken by diphtheria. The thief stops to nurse the ailing family and earns the respect of the local sheriff, who, at

the novel's conclusion, aids the protagonist's escape without the robber learning that his benefactor originally intended to arrest him.

Although Rhodes was a popular author of western novels, his fiction has generally not received the serious critical attention that his champions believe he deserves. These commentators urge a reevaluation of his oeuvre, for according to Bernard DeVoto, "his work was true to the life of the cattle kingdom, he was an artist in prose, and he portrayed both the reality and the romance of that brief era with a fidelity that only a few have ever tried to maintain and only he succeeded in maintaining."

PRINCIPAL WORKS

Good Men and True (novel) 1910
Bransford in Arcadia; or, The Little Eohippus (novel) 1914
The Desire of the Moth (novel) 1916
West Is West (novel) 1917

CRITICISM

The New York Times Book Review (essay date 1914)

[*In the following essay, the reviewer gives a positive assessment of Rhodes's novel* Bransford in Arcadia; or, The Little Eohippus.]

If Columbus had "beached his shallops on the sundown side of this continent" would the salmon now be our national bird, would Arizona have become our "mother of Presidents," and would all the prizefights now "be pulled off in Boston"?

These are some of the questions which Jeff Bransford and his fellow cowboys discuss around the campfire at the Sinks of Lost River in the first chapter of Mr. Rhodes's new novel [**Bransford in Arcadia; or, The Little Eohippus**]. The book is an enlargement of his story, **The Little Eohippus,** which had serial publication last year, whose action he has changed enough to make it take its entire course along the Mexican border, mainly in southern New Mexico. His hero, Jeff Bransford, will be an old acquaintance to the readers of Mr. Rhodes's former novel, **Good Men and True,** and they will be glad to meet him again and to find his whimsicalities, his engaging pretense of ingenuousness, and his virile and sophisticated reality almost constantly in the limelight.

Mr. Rhodes knows range life in the Southwest and he knows the cowboy very thoroughly, even though he does choose, for the sake of better effect, to embroider interesting patterns upon his everyday clothing. But Mr. Rhodes's novels have one quality which distinguishes them from most Southwestern stories, and that is their truthfulness to the various sides of modern Southwestern life. Time was when the range and the roundup, the camp and the headquarters, summed up pretty nearly the whole of life in that region. And, because it was a picturesque life and novels about it found a ready audience, the cattle ranch and the cowboy became a stock, conventionalized theme and novels based upon it were multiplied and continued to multiply until, conditions having changed, they became utterly false to the region they pretended to portray. Mr. Rhodes has lived recently in the Southwest and knows the new developments that have changed entirely the former conditions. He knows the irrigation projects, the mining schemes, the health resorts, the new towns, and the very different life they have brought to the old-time desert and cattle range. His stories do not deal with this new life in its up-to-date development. They go back a few years, when the changes were taking on headway and the cowboy was still an important person. But they take account of the new face these changes were putting upon the Southwest, and they give a faithful picture of many of its phases. His knowledge and his willingness to use it in thus breaking away from time-honored custom in the writing of Southwestern fiction give to his stories freshness, truth, and individuality.

The chapters of his new novel are held together by some slender strands of plot, which the reader will care very little about. He will be much more interested in the personality of Jeff Bransford and that interesting person's exploits. He will want to know, indeed, how Jeff is going to come out with his love affair and what will happen to him in consequence of his interference with Uncle Sam's mails when he strove to enable Old Man Taylor to hold down the Butterbowl homestead. But, for the most part, Jeff and his Little Eohippus are quite interesting enough without any plot. Wherever Jeff happens to be he can always say

---

Characteristics of Rhodes's fiction:

Of primary importance is the *setting,* the backdrop of desert and mountains that Rhodes adored. His land is southern New Mexico, from Belen in the north to El Paso and from Silver City beyond the Rio Grande to Roswell on the Pecos, a domain he made his own even as Harvey Fergusson did the landscape of northern New Mexico.

And the *characters.* Although drawn in the flat, their actions are real, for they were taken from the people Rhodes knew and often gave their true names. They talk the lingo of the range as heard by a writer with an ear for the cadence and nuance of living speech.

Harder to isolate is the *flavor* of the writer himself, his charm that he magically infused into his prose. His was a personal way of writing that led him at times to pepper his narratives with utterances quite unlike the usual *Post* style.

Still another Rhodes hallmark is his *literary allusiveness,* the flowery talk of the waddies which echoed his own reading. Many are the legends of "the locoed cowboy" who read as he rode.

Finally, there is also present throughout his work the shock of *reversed values* which came from Rhodes having been the underdog at outs with the law. His good guys are the bad guys and vice versa. His villains are the bankers, lawyers, landowners, law officers, his heroes the loners running for their lives. Rhodes perceived that a man in adversity sometimes rises to his best and becomes a Robin Hood, a Cyrano de Bergerac, a Musketeer.

Lawrence Clark Powell, in his Southwest Classics: The Creative Literature of the Arid Lands, Essays on the Books and Their Writers, *1974.*

something entertaining and he can be trusted to do something that will set things moving. And then there is Pringle, who knows some Latin and likes to quote it, who wrote home to his friends from the Denver carnival the story of his journey in three words: "Hic—hock—hike."

Mr. Rhodes's cowboys are highly entertaining, much more entertaining, indeed, than they would have been had he drawn them without accentuating their peculiarities or without giving them credit for keener wit and quicker intelligence than can be claimed by most of their tribe. Sometimes he goes a little too far with this injection of individuality into the cowboy's character—gets him out of drawing and injures the illusion. But even then he is entertaining.

The narrative is charged with the fascination of the Southwest. The author evidently has felt it himself, and he has enough of the poet in his pen to make the reader feel the charm of desert and mountain and wonderful sky, just as he has also the capacity to make one feel the sense of fuller and freer life that tingles in the veins of those who breathe the air of the plateau region.

> *"Range Life in Mexico and New Mexico," in* The New York Times Book Review, *February 1, 1914, p. 49.*

Walter Van Tilburg Clark   (essay date 1949)

[*Clark was an American educator and author. In the following essay, he discusses the defining qualities of Rhodes's fiction.*]

To all devotees of the Western, and to the many old followers of Rhodes in particular, the first sizable collection of the work of the Nebraska-born novelist of the cattle country to appear since his death in 1934 is an important event.

There are no fewer than thirteen pieces included, among them the novels, **The Trusty Knaves** and **Good Men and True;** the novelettes, **The Desire of the Moth** and **Hit the Line Hard;** four short stories; an historical narrative, **"Penalosa,"** about the early Spaniards in Rhodes' New Mexico and Texas; an essay in which Rhodes amusingly ridicules a pseudo-English tradition of speech as against the natural vernacular; and that best-known of his poems, **"The Hired Man on Horseback."**

The tales are the meat of the collection, and in them the initiated will meet again many old friends of the mesa and river-canyon country. In all the stories is the old Rhodes' abundance of action and humorous word-play. . . .

To those less given to Westerns, and not yet won by Rhodes, one reservation—well, one and a half—must be confessed. With two or three exceptions, the tales are so similarly contrived as to confuse the memory. Always there is some one climactic event, involving political skullduggery, murder or robbery, and always the snarl is unsnarled by the cowboy hero and his associates; the villains are bankers, politicians, law officers or professional crooks, and the promising tenderfoot appears as a foil to his more knowing comrades, so that after a time their

mere office to the machinery of the stories begins to create an impression of stereotyped figures.

This impression is the more unfortunate because actually Rhodes' characters, down to the least male figure, are highly and believably individualized. Only his young women, his heroines—and they are few and relatively unimportant—are sometimes hard to believe. It has been so with others who wrote about an essentially masculine life—Melville, London, even Conrad. Despite having been an observer of unusual keenness and sympathy, Rhodes, the Indian agent, cowboy, and scout for the Government during the Geronimo uprising, seldom broke the bounds of the traditional Western formula.

In fairness to him, however, it must be remembered that he was among the first tellers of the Western story, and so more followed than a follower. Moreover, considered singly, his tales are always lively and clever, with a flavor quite distinct from others of their kind, so that actually we might more justly say that they suffer from Rhodes' being too much like Rhodes.

Rhodes is the peer of Owen Wister in portraying the cowboy in his code, and often, though briefly and incidentally, the equal of such factual narrators as Andy Adams and Will James in presenting the mode of his working life. In variety and scope he is the best of the four. None of his tales is without many amusing and characteristic incidents. And constantly there are the enormous landscapes—all so lovingly done that no other purveyor of the Western can even touch them.

Rhodes himself is never intrusive but ever present—easygoing, genial, understanding beyond his time and region, yet profoundly fond of that region, of the men of that time,

---

Rhodes and his writing:

Save one or two of his intimate friends, no one will ever know how he suffered when some slight, excusable error appeared in one of his stories. Upon such infrequent occasions I have known him to walk the floor for hours, condemning himself in choice and pungent language, puffing at his pipe until the room was like a locomotive roundhouse, subsiding only when he was completely exhausted. He was always generous in regard to the mistakes of others. Seldom if ever did he "take his pen in hand" to criticize anything other than an absolute and flagrant misstatement. For one so vigorous in his likes and dislikes, he was exceedingly tenderhearted toward writers, especially novices, who not infrequently asked him to read their stories. "So-and-so can't write—never will," he would say (confidentially, of course), "but I didn't have the heart to tell him so. It would sound too uppity." What he suffered when actually engaged in writing a story, no one, save those nearest him, can even imagine. He spent enough time in preparation alone, or what he termed preparation, to have written twice as much as he finally accomplished.

Henry Herbert Knibbs, in his introduction to The Proud Sheriff, *1968.*

---

of the life they made together and the code that arose from the union. "The rattlesnake's code—no better," he says of it. But then he adds slyly, a typical Rhodes addition: "It is worthy of note that no better standard has ever been kept with such faith."

Walter Van Tilburg Clark, "Chronicler of Cowboys," in The New York Times Book Review, November 20, 1949, p. 7.

W. H. Hutchinson   (essay date 1957)

[In the following excerpt from his introduction to The Rhodes Reader, Hutchinson delineates how Rhodes's fiction differed from "formula" westerns.]

Insofar as the public and the critics generally were concerned in his lifetime, Rhodes wrote "westerns." There was one exception to this critical dismissal and a most notable one, Bernard DeVoto, who had known the cowpuncher world as a youth and then had let his cultivated mind play upon that world, upon all the facets of the land he loved, with the genius of gusto given to but few. His regard for Rhodes, as man and man of letters, abided with him for many, many years. Since DeVoto possessed another rare quality—the capacity for rounded maturity—his published appraisals of Rhodes gain added weight.

In 1938 [in his "The Novelist of the Cattle Kingdom," in The Hired Man on Horseback] he termed Rhodes' stories: ". . . the only embodiment on the level of art of one segment of American experience. They are the only body of fiction devoted to the cattle kingdom which is both true to it and written by an artist in prose."

In 1954, he said again [in Harper's, December 1955]: "Back in 1938 I pointed out that only Gene Rhodes had succeeded in making first-rate fiction out of the cattle business. The statement still stands but the argument would be tighter if Mr. Walter Van Tilburg Clark had not meanwhile published an excellent novel called The Oxbow Incident. . . . But Mr. Clark's subject is the mob spirit that leads to a lynching. So his scene might be almost anywhere and though he uses a few stage properties from horse opera, he uses none of its sentiments or traditions." In this same piece, he says of the "western": ". . . it was turned into the path that has led to its present solemnity by its one novelist, Rhodes, and by the fabulists Harold Bell Wright and Zane Grey."

In 1955, in one of the last pieces turned out before his death, DeVoto devoted himself to a discussion of Owen Wister, his literary origins and the resultant birth of the "western." Speaking herein of The Virginian, he summed up his case for Gene Rhodes: "The cowboy story has seldom produced anything as good; apart from Gene Rhodes, it has not even tried to do anything different."

It is comforting to have such a buttress as Bernard DeVoto for purely personal opinions, comforting because it is Rhodes as a precursor of, and practitioner concurrent with, the virgins-villains-varmints school who requires detailed examination.

In the women in his stories, and the best of them have no women whatsoever, Rhodes is at his worst, and that is worse than any other man of stature in the "western" field. If his women are young women, they are passionately and infrangibly virginal, and his heroes move like marionettes in their presence. It is extremely hard to find even the suspicion of a *bad* woman in all his writings; he had known them, *seguro que si!*, but they had no place in his fiction. Occasionally, an older woman appears fleetingly in his stories after years of frontier abrasion have made her road-weary. Only when this happens is Rhodes' feminine cast at all credible.

In portraying his villains, Rhodes veered wildly from the formula. *Imprimis,* he never cast his villains by the color of their skin. If he has the Hispanic New Mexican in a villainous role, it is because his prototype was that in life. Rhodes' Anglo villains are both *heavy* and *sneaky,* . . . but they are that because they were that in life, and whatever category they fit makes but a part of Rhodes' villainous whole—the sons of Mary. His true villains are always those who did not work with their hands—bankers, merchants, lawyers, *políticos*—and who profited, grew swollen and fat, on the lives of those who did work with their hands for daily bread and conquered the frontier while doing it. It would have been easier by far to two-dimensionalize these characters, but Rhodes went to infinite pains in his story construction to show how these villains of his were parasites at the breasts of the country that had nurtured him. He did this because it was true to his experience, true to his country and his people. In doing it, he limned in fiction the salient truth about the west-that-was—a truth unrecognized, overlooked, and neglected for many years by the serious scholars—the truth that the West was the captive, exploited province of the financial, political, and industrial East.

It is only when Rhodes has his villain a proper Easterner that said villain becomes incredible. This is not due to the characterization of motivation of that villain but to the affected mannerisms given him and to his speech.

Indeed, it is the speech he gives to his characters from Western life—a speech far removed from the idiom of the "western"—that has led many critics, and not a few true Rhodesians, to feel that Gene Rhodes' fictional cowboys all talked like Gene Rhodes. There is some truth to this feeling. Rhodes recognized his tendency when he used pages 65–67 of *Bransford in Arcadia* to explain the availability of classical literature to his cow persons through the medium of Bull Durham coupons that were negotiable for volumes in Munro's Library of Popular Novels. Rhodes was a reader, an omnivorous reader, all of his life, devouring everything that came his way even unto The Congressional Record. The brave-talking heroes of Sir Walter Scott's fiction almost ruined him. He revered Shakespeare and Conrad, and he felt that Stevenson and Kipling had used the English language more skillfully than any others. So his cowboys' speech is pricked with allusions and larded with classical quotations. Yet, he had real-life examples in Bill Barbee, the Texan who revelled in *Richard III,* in Aloys Priesser, the Bavarian chemist of Engle, in Henri Touissant, the *Jornada* pioneer whose library contained the world's classics. There were others, but these three will do to point this premise: if T. S. Eliot in his plays has made his country, or country-bred, English families oversubtle in their appreciation of English literature, so much and no more can be charged against Gene Rhodes and his riders of the stars. He gave an idealized depiction, in fine prose, of men who had the language within themselves but who lacked the idiom of their readers to say it themselves, in life, in such wise.

When it comes to the varmints in his stories, Rhodes again veered wildly from the formula under discussion. You have only to compare the horses in his yarns—Wisenose, Brown Jug, Buck, Cry Baby, and Abou Ben Adam—with the horseflesh in other "westerns" to prove the point. The flora and fauna of his chosen country are integral parts of his fiction, as they were of the very lives of the characters he took from life. His people are what they are, do what they do, because of their country, its needs, demands, and conditionings.

It is the vasty land itself, shimmering in the heat or shrouded in infrequent mists, eroded, dusty, sun-drenched, as implacable and as compelling as the sea, that makes Rhodes' canvas for his portraits of the West-That-Was. Only Walter Van Tilburg Clark can equal the evocative richness of Rhodes' landscapes and both men share the inability to enrich certain of their human types.

It is these major differences, both of accomplishment and shortcoming, from the formula "western," past and present, that give Rhodes his place. There is a reason for these differences, for this place; reason quite apart from the mechanics of prose construction.

No other writer of "westerns," Andy Adams included, encompassed so much living in the trans-Mississippi West they all purported, still purport, to record as did Rhodes. He had had twelve years of prairie and sky in Nebraska and Kansas—wind, grass, drought, blizzards, cyclones, grasshoppers, and green buds swelling in the creek bottoms when spring came—before he came to New Mexico with his father in 1881, "the year that Billy the Kid was killed."

Thereafter, for twenty-five years, he was horse-wrangler, bronc rider, cowboy, miner, wagon freighter, school teacher, road-builder, dishwasher, homesteader, carpenter, water-mason, blacksmith, and rancher who went broke in the losing battle against drought, cow-country interest, and from an uneconomic passion for raising horses in a land where the feral bands were a nuisance.

It is not necessary to live as did Rhodes to write stories about the West, or even "western" stories, as a number of currently prominent practitioners will be happy to tell anyone who cares to write them on the matter. It is the fact that Rhodes *did* live it, that the totality of the free range experience was summated in his personal life, that makes his writings come from the "inside-out," from a deep wellspring of personal experience that was the abiding strength of his life. There is yet another factor in Rhodes' writings that is lacking from those, like this, written wherever the typewriter is handy.

Rhodes wrote his stories, almost all of them that are worth while, far removed from the country and the life he loved; the country and the life he left because his personal code demanded it. His knowledge was sharpened by the expatriate's longing, deepened by distance, enhanced by the frustrations of his exile. His land and his people came out on paper as the remembered mellow haze of a coal-oil lamp seen shining through the cabin window when the man and his world were young. Yet upon what he wrote, you may, as an archaeologist, depend. The people and the land of six New Mexico counties, Socorro, Sierra, Doña Ana, Lincoln, Otero, and Grant, are preserved for all time in the clear amber of his joyous, dancing, illuminated prose.

If the "western" had not burgeoned as it did, only to wither literarily as the inevitable result of incest, Rhodes might have gained in his lifetime the stature which some now feel is his. Certainly, at the time he started his real career, the competition was tough. Stevenson, Kipling, Conrad, London, Stephen Crane, Rex Beach, Stewart Edward White, all were working the outdoor-action-adventure field on a higher level, of pay and merit, than the dime novel or the emergent forerunners of the pulps. Admittedly, these writers did not specialize in the so-called "western" for which Wister, Hough, Adams, Lewis, and Phillips had made the first rough castings. But, and this is the point to be remembered, everything they did write competed in the editorial market places with Rhodes' fiction. He hit his stride, with his own style and tone and pace, against such competition, and he maintained his place until both his productivity and his critical acclaim were inundated by the tidal wave of "westerns" that crested in the twenties behind Zane Grey's first breaking on the pleasant literary beach staked off by the cognoscenti as their own.

In the rise of "regional" writing in those same twenties, following the blazes of Turner and the steps of Paxson, Rhodes did not seem to qualify, even though New Mexico so claims him today. Certainly, his people, places, and incidents are regional to a degree of being provincial, often happily parochial, while being at the same time universal—meaning anywhere west of the one hundredth meridian and north of a given point. But they were accepted, typed, and dismissed as "westerns." A suitable example comes from the *New York Times Book Review,* November 19, 1933, where **The Trusty Knaves** got mentioned under the section-heading, "Western Loot," while Kenneth Roberts' *Rabble in Arms* got the full treatment under a banner head, "An Epic Tale of the American Revolution." Not to disparage Kenneth Roberts, but to make a point, it can be said that *Rabble* contained no more valid history, no more authentic Americana, no more good writing and reading, than did **Knaves.** It did, however, possess one singular advantage. It was laid in a setting that had no built-in connotations to the critical mind.

There is another factor in Rhodes' critical dismissal. His work in the twenties and thirties ran exactly counter to the mainstream of literary acclaim. Implicit in everything Rhodes wrote are the best traditions, values, customs, and morals—the basic philosophy—of the American physical frontier. This sorted poorly with F. Scott Fitzgerald, Mencken, Nathan, Sherwood Anderson, *et al.,* and, most certainly, had little in common with *The Plastic Age, Little*

Caesar, Black Oxen, Three Soldiers, A Farewell to Arms, or Judge Ben Lindsey's theories about companionating. For final and conclusive critical damnation, he wrote for the *Saturday Evening Post.*

Rhodes, himself, contributed to his own neglect. He was dismissed by the literati because he allegedly wrote "westerns," but, while his stories gave great satisfaction to *Satevepost* readers, the great reader market for "westerns" never cottoned to them as books. Rhodes was a poet-cowboy, not a cowboy-poet nor even a cowboy-writer, in his love of words and their uses. Only a writer for radio can appreciate exactly how Rhodes, remembering the tales he had heard in his youth, wrote to fire his readers' minds through their ears and not their eyes. He was a conscious and deliberate prose stylist, an anomaly in his genre, and his plots were incredibly intricate. The humor in his yarns subtly combined the humor of words with a scene sense of the comic situation he had learned from Henry Wallace Phillips. The "western" fan picking up a Rhodes story was apt to react like a pup with his first porcupine and to learn the lesson of abstention with but one experience.

Rhodes' other and greatest contribution to his own neglect was his productivity. He was a slow worker by nature and a spasmodic one, writing not alone for his market but, also, taking inordinate pains that every word would stand up in the minds of those in New Mexico who had known Gene Rhodes as well as Rhodes had known them and their joint country. In adding up the corpus of his life's work, he, himself, could arrive at but 1,200,000 words which is a mere bagatelle alongside the output of Grey, Mulford, Raine, Seltzer, Drago, Tuttle, Cunningham, or a score of others, past and present. Lack of output, ordinarily, is an acceptable yardstick for critical acclaim, but it was not so with Rhodes. More important, practically speaking, is the fact that five-year gaps between books are worse than two-year gaps between major periodical appearances when it comes to keeping an author in his public's mind. And, certainly, such gaps give a book publisher no reason to waste time, money, and effort in promoting the sale of such infrequencies.

Despite Rhodes' lack of productivity, it is interesting to note that he did achieve a very high degree of utilization of what he did write. More interesting is the fact that his work continues to find a niche in the current market place—anthologies, reprints, television, and films—and this despite Frank Dobie's latest feeling [in his *Guide to Life and Literature of the Southwest*] that "His fiction becomes increasingly dated."

What Don Pancho says, in part, is absolutely true. Rhodes' style, technique, and tone, all are hopelessly archaic in most of his stories. His very early stories are an emetic and, as has been noted, so are his characterizations of women and of Eastern society, people, and manners. But—

The best of his yarns about his own country and his own people retain the nourishing, essential juices of true literature. Coming upon them today, when the expanse of the "western-story" is a vast reach of sheer craftsmanship speckled with great cloud-patches of slipshod writing and escapist plots, Rhodes' stories have the startling impact of an antelope's rump seen shining across long, arid, sun-drenched leagues where no living thing was thought to be.

There is only one obstacle in the way of those who would seek to read Rhodes today, to hone these opinions against the stone of personal experience. Barring one paperback reprint, **Sunset Land,** Eugene Manlove Rhodes is out of print. His published books have been pursued for years by what DeVoto terms "a coterie as select and discriminating as any that ever boosted a tenth-rate English poet into a first-rate reputation." If his books, or his stories in frayed copies of old magazines, can be found today they will ring like a shod hoof on *malpaís* in the mind and heart of any purchaser who knows the West-That-Was. They will make, also, a severe dent in the purse. It is this scarcity and price that give solid substance to the partisan literary summation of Gene Rhodes that first was made of De Maupassant: "He was almost irreproachable in a genre which was not." (pp. xix-xxvi)

> W. H. Hutchinson, "Virgins, Villains, and Varmints," in The Rhodes Reader: Stories of Virgins, Villains, and Varmints by Eugene Manlove Rhodes, edited by W. H. Hutchinson, University of Oklahoma Press, 1957, pp. vii-xxvi.

James K. Folsom   (essay date 1966)

[*In the following excerpt from his* The American Western Novel, *Folsom evaluates the strengths and weaknesses in Rhodes's fiction, as well as prominent themes in* Good Men and True, Páso por aqúi, *and the short story "No Mean City."*]

The ability to assess facts in such a way as to understand their underlying significance is . . . at the heart of the many portrayals of Western heroes by Eugene Manlove Rhodes, without question one of the best writers in the Western tradition. Himself a cowboy, Rhodes is one of the few Western authors who is both qualified at first hand to write about the "West-that-was" and who has the literary ability to transcend the often pointless anecdotalism of such writing. He is the only Western author to have received the scholarly accolades of republication in two full-length reprints and of a careful and thorough bibliography. Though his *aficionados* are often somewhat extravagant in their praise, their general point is well taken; for Rhodes's work is immeasurably superior to the generality of slick Western fiction, even though Rhodes himself was a writer for the slick magazines.

All this is not an attempt to explain away the manifest faults which spoil much of Rhodes's work. At times, when his adherence to the conventions of "slick" writing trips him up, he can be one of the most maddening of writers. His stories are marred by an annoying coincidental quality, in which someone invariably happens along just at the right moment to hear the villains plotting their crimes, which they do explicitly and at great length. On occasion his overexplicitness destroys an otherwise profoundly moving fictional moment; as in **"Loved I Not Honor**

More," where the story—based on an incident of Rhodes's own biography—of a rancher who will not sell his spare horses to the British cavalry for remounts because he does not want to support the British war against the Boers is spoiled by a sentimental ending in which the rancher and the English major who has come to buy the horses first box with one another and afterwards shake hands to prove there are no hard feelings. Even his often beautifully conceived dialogue deteriorates far too much into the tedious smartness which passes for wit among the devotees of the slick magazines. When Rhodes is at his best, however, these faults are only those of detail, which may mar but do not destroy the real quality of his fiction.

Rhodes's greatest strength as a Western writer is to be found in his presentation of the Western hero, with the explication of whose character he concerns himself in most of his novels and stories. One of the more interesting, though certainly not the best, of these is *Good Men and True* (1910). This novel tells of a rancher, Jeff Bransford (who, like many of Rhodes's heroes, appears in several works), who is involved in a shooting scrape and is captured by a local politician and former State Senator named Judge Thorpe. Thorpe had engineered the assassination of one Captain Charles Tillotson of the Texas Rangers, which Bransford's coincidental arrival on the scene had frustrated. Thorpe, however, being a resourceful man, had kidnapped the wounded Bransford so that Tillotson would be accused of murder, one of the assassins having been killed in the gunfight and Bransford being the only witness. Thorpe's plan is to hold Bransford incommunicado until Tillotson is convicted of murder and duly executed, after which he will be released. Bransford, who before his kidnapping had been teaching himself to type, agrees to keep quiet in his captivity if Thorpe will get him a typewriter, and asks as well for permission to write to his wife. Thorpe agrees to both of these proposals, providing Bransford submit the letter to his censorship. Bransford accordingly writes a long and involved letter recounting his adventures in Old Mexico which passes Thorpe's censorship and is duly posted. The letter is mailed to Bransford's wife, but his friends get it, for Bransford is not married—a detail he had neglected to mention to Judge Thorpe. This clever ruse alerts Bransford's friends, who manage to deduce from the clues contained in the apparently innocuous letter that Bransford is held captive in a certain area of Juarez and on the basis of this deduction begin a search for him, letting him know their plans by means of enigmatic notices placed in the personal columns of the local newspaper with which Judge Thorpe has considerately provided Bransford. The rest of the novel tells of the progress of the search and ends with Bransford's rescue, after which Judge Thorpe is captured and turned over to justice and Captain Tillotson is vindicated.

As this summary should have emphasized, *Good Men and True* bears a very close resemblance to one typical kind of detective story, the tale of ratiocination in which the detective ponders the meaning behind some baffling clue. Most significant in terms of our discussion of the cowboy hero is the enigmatic letter which Bransford sends to his friends and which they successfully decipher. Both Bransford and his friends are able to communicate by means of

language which they understand but which their opponents do not, and in their correspondence they convey information by a language of allusion of which their adversaries are unaware. The metaphorical structure of the novel is summed up in the scene where Judge Thorpe reads the letter which Bransford has so carefully constructed. Thorpe can see nothing beneath the surface meaning of the letter and assumes that it has been written according to his instructions, while in fact the entire document is a cleverly reasoned exercise in code.

Rhodes's stories generally have a distinct detective-story flavor. Usually, however, as in this novel, Rhodes's preoccupations go beyond the mere discovery of the "truth" behind a particular event. Bransford's friends not only decipher the letter but act upon their information in order to set Bransford free. In this regard they are typical of another related aspect of the character of the Western hero, the fact that he is conceived as basically an *active* person. His insight beneath the surfaces of the world around him does not lead him to a position of philosophical despair. He sees what must be done and then does it, knowing that what he does is justifiable because he understands more of the facts than does anyone else.

The fact that the cowboy hero is both insightful and active gives him a certain distrust of the forms by which less gifted mortals operate; for he believes that he is better able to resolve problems on his own than by means of the conventional methods used by ordinary men. It is significant that none of Bransford's friends thinks of calling in the police, or for that matter any outsider. They would only gum things up. Bransford's friends, impatient of restrictions, work outside the law, and here is precisely the point; for if one knows, through a deeper perception into the heart of things, what the right course of action is, one should act on this knowledge despite the forms of legality or of conventional opinion. (pp. 116-18)

Perhaps the most successful combination of the typical cowboy hero with the ever present *ubi sunt* may be found in Eugene Manlove Rhodes's magnificent novelette *Pasó por Aquí* (1926). This story tells of a man named Ross McEwen, who has robbed a store and made a successful getaway into the wilderness. He has only managed to make his escape, however, by abandoning his stolen money to the pursuing posse. When almost trapped, he had thrown the money away "lak a man to feed the hen een hees yard," as Monte, the Spanish-American narrator of part of the story puts it, and when the posse had dismounted to chase the blowing currency McEwen had successfully eluded them. His pursuers have no intention of giving up the chase because of this temporary setback; they know he must make a break for the Mexican border and they also know that they will catch him sooner or later if they merely stake out the water holes, to which he must come for water before making the long, dry trip across the desert. McEwen's attempts to elude the posse become consistently both more cunning and more desperate, and the conflict between the two parties turns into a battle of wits similar to those we have seen between the cowboy hero and his adversaries in other stories. McEwen has all the odds against him, and he loses his only great advantage when the posse declines to chase him but decides instead to wait at the water holes until he is driven out of the hills by thirst. McEwen must abandon his first horse, and he steals a second one, choosing an unshod mount which will be harder for the pursuit to track. This horse too fails him and as his next mount he takes a steer, which will leave no distinguishable tracks. Finally—afoot—he manages to arrive at a well which the posse has left unguarded, only to discover that the Mexican inhabitants of the little ranch for which this well supplies the water are all stricken with diphtheria. Though McEwen could now escape, he elects to stay and to nurse the Mexican family. "I am here to help you," he says.

So far the story of *Pasó por Aquí* is a reasonably conventional one of romantic peril and escape, but Rhodes is not content to leave it that way. When McEwen is finally run down, the leader of the pursuers is Pat Garrett, the sheriff who had killed Billy the Kid. McEwen does not know him by sight, and Garrett preserves his incognito. After the Mexican family has been restored to health, Garrett and McEwen ride off to Tularosa, where McEwen, still unaware of Garrett's real identity, will take the train and get safely away.

In this story we see another approach to the theme of law and justice. . . . Garrett, convinced that, as Monte says, McEwen "ees tek eshame for thees bad life," decides to take the law into his own hands and see justice done by turning McEwen loose rather than by turning him over to the legal machinery of New Mexico. As in many another Western story a dude is present who, until the course of action is explained, cannot understand it. She, a nurse from the East, remarks that Garrett could legally be impeached and thrown out of office for dereliction of duty; but, as Monte significantly says in the lines which conclude the story, "Who will tell? . . . We are all decent people."

It is obvious on the surface that one preoccupation of *Pasó por Aquí* is precisely this familiar discussion of how justice can best be done outside the law. McEwen has atoned for his misdeed of robbing the store by his later moral action of helping the stricken Mexican family; and since no harm has been done to anyone—the money had all been recovered when McEwen had scattered it in front of the posse and no one else had been injured by McEwen—Garrett feels that the whole incident is best forgotten.

Combined with this preoccupation is a completely different theme, however, a lament for the passing of the old order. McEwen and Garrett are both presented as the last men of their particular types. Garrett, the man who shot Billy the Kid, is the last of the old-time sheriffs, at home in Tularosa with the "old-timers," rather than in Alamogordo with the "new peoples." To Tularosa, where he is known, he takes McEwen who will be accepted at the train as one of Garrett's friends. Similarly McEwen is the last of the old-time bad men, and his renunciation of his free and easy ways at the end of the story symbolically represents the passing of the wild freedom of the old times.

On another level, then, the story is a lament for the old days, and this theme is beautifully developed in the world

Rhodes as cowboy, riding for the Bar Cross ranch in New Mexico, c. 1894.

of the tale, in which the great symbolic fact of life is the fact that the world has changed. McEwen, who has not been in the country for many years, is no longer at home there, for the face of the country is different from the way it had been on his last visit. New Mexico is no longer the wilderness he had remembered, but is now filled with the windmills of the "new peoples" who prevent his escape. It is at one of these new ranches that he is finally symbolically "trapped" by civilization, when he stops to help the family crippled by diphtheria, a disease unknown to the older time. The same symbolic defeat by civilization which keeps him from successfully escaping his pursuers is reinforced by the moral change which he undergoes at the ranch. When he discovers that there is no longer any room for the old-style bad man his final escape becomes ironic; for though he is set free he is at the same time banished. There is no room for Ross McEwen in the new country.

The basic theme of the story, then, is mirrored in its title *Pasó por Aquí*—"passed by here"—and to the nurse whose Eastern perceptions represent the inability to understand what is happening beneath the surface of the world around her Monte explains the meaning of the story's action. His explanation is itself a metaphor from the history of New Mexico, for he tells her of the famous landmark, Inscription Rock. Long ago, he says, when his Spanish ancestors first settled the Southwest, they were in the habit of writing on this rock as they passed by it, *pasó por aquí,* with their names and the date. All of these men, as Monte tells the story, had thought to themselves "What lar-rge weelderness ees thees! And me, I go now eento thees beeg lonesome, and perhaps I shall not to r-return!", and had made for themselves a gravestone on Inscription Rock. McEwen is the last man to "pass by here," and at the end of the story the last sheriff and the last bad man ride away from the country of the new peoples, never to return.

Pasó por Aquí, which begins as a particular examination of the relationship between law and justice in a world of permanence, ends as a metaphor of the course of history in a world of change. The conflict between McEwen and Pat Garrett is strongly reminiscent of the similar conflict between Scratchy Wilson and Jack Potter in "The Bride Comes to Yellow Sky." In both stories the course of history renders the conflict itself irrelevant, and the bad man has ultimately no choice but that of laying aside his gun. He can no longer stand against the course of history, but must acquiesce in the passing of the wild and free world he had loved. The inscription he leaves behind him, carved into solid rock, ironically symbolizes only his own impermanence. (pp. 137-40)

. . . . .

Even Eugene Manlove Rhodes on occasion writes stories in which the course of history is interpreted in positive terms. Although, as was suggested above, Rhodes habitually imputes virtue and happiness to an older society which is gradually being replaced, he now and again affirms the course of history itself rather than any particular stage within it. Such a story is **"No Mean City"** (1919), in plot a melodramatic spy thriller about a World War I German attempt to blow up the strategic Engle Dam, near Engle, New Mexico. The story's interest, however, does not inhere in the plot, which is predictable and commonplace; inevitably the German saboteurs are frustrated and the good men and true of Engle come out victorious. The interest in the story lies rather in Rhodes's brilliant development of the theme of the community, presented through the little town of Engle and its townsmen, which he develops so that it comes to stand as a metaphor for America. The men who frustrate the saboteurs are an old settler, Teagardner, the last survivor of the original band which had surveyed the site of Engle for the Santa Fe Railroad, and a younger one, Cady, the first boy born in Engle. The plot of the story takes Teagardner and Cady on a series of nostalgic pilgrimages into the community's past. Teagardner, starting from the town of Engle, goes first to the mine where he had prospected when he was young; then to another mine, now almost forgotten, where he and his best friend, now dead, had worked together many years before; and finally, in the best scene in the story, he and Cady together row a boat over the old Gonzales ranch, which they can see beneath them under one hundred feet of water, and where both had worked before the dam was built.

This nostalgic pilgrimage does not add up, however—as it does in *Pasó por Aquí*—to a lament for the old times. The historical process in **"No Mean City"** is seen not as a disaster but as an explanation of the loyal affection which the inhabitants of Engle feel for even such an unpromising place as this desolate New Mexican town. It is, as the title says, "no mean city," and it stands at once for the particular love of man for a place where he has roots and for the general love of Americans for their country. The love of man for his home is not limited in the story to one group of people—be they cattlemen, nesters, pioneers, or whoever—who allegedly have more understanding of and hence affection for their home than others.

Rather this love is presented as a universal fact of history; the implication is clear that as long as Engle exists someone will love it enough to fight for it, and even if it is abandoned to progress as was the old Gonzales ranch, there will still be those who remember it.

In **"No Mean City"** Rhodes affirms a deeply held ideal which he often presents in a more peripheral way, the idea of "community." As Rhodes usually defines the idea of community, it refers to a particular social group, isolated in time, who band together against hostile outsiders. The league of sympathy between Pat Garrett and McEwen against the "new peoples" in *Pasó por Aquí* comes to mind, as does the union of cattlemen against intruders in many of his other stories. Occasionally, however, as in **"No Mean City,"** Rhodes perceives that a community may be defined in terms of continuity through time as well as in terms of identity of present interests. In such cases, the bond of communal relations must be that of similar perceptions into the significance of history. Those to whom Engle is dear are not limited to one time or to one social group, for to them the community is a symbol not of a particular time but of hope in the historic process. (pp. 193-95)

> *James K. Folsom, "Good Men and True" and "Growing Up with the Country," in his* The American Western Novel, *College & University Press, 1966, pp. 99-140, 177-203.*

Edwin W. Gaston, Jr.   (essay date 1967)

[*Gaston is an American educator and critic. In the following excerpt, he provides an overview of Rhodes's essays, poetry, and fiction.*]

To the paradoxes of place and literature in the Southwest may be added the seeming contradiction that was Eugene Manlove Rhodes. A native of Nebraska and a resident of New York for a third of his life, Rhodes confined his interests almost solely to the New Mexico of his young manhood and declining years. He looked fondly upon the old days, but never became misanthropic. Little educated formally, he tediously cultivated a keen mind through self-instruction and fashioned a literary career unmatched in many respects among Southwestern writers. Most of his fiction sold to the well-paying *Saturday Evening Post,* and his novels appeared in book form after their serialization in the *Post.* Not a few of his works sold to motion pictures. Nevertheless, from the cradle to the grave, Rhodes experienced almost constant financial distress. Intellectually, a classicist, he produced romance. Philosophically, a Humanistic democrat, he championed (like Dickens) the underdog against the forces of corruption and privilege; but he also defended Albert B. Fall of the "Teapot Dome" scandal. To Rhodes, the villain frequently was the law enforcement officer and such other "respectables" as the banker, lawyer, and merchant: the hero often was the bank robber and the rustler. A cowboy and miner before taking up the pen, Rhodes depicted occupation and place as few could hope to succeed; but he failed to portray convincingly even those characters borrowed from real life. (pp. 3-4)

Eugene Manlove Rhodes's literary reputation finally rests on his fiction, the stories and novels he wrote about the West being both more plentiful than, and superior in art and content to, the other things he wrote. Yet his essays and letters provide insights into certain facets of the author's life and thought to be found nowhere else, and his poetry serves as his first medium of publication. Any analysis of Rhodes's writing, then, not only must take into account these works inferior to his fiction, but indeed can profit by starting with them.

Five essays that Rhodes published over a period of twenty-three years provide a representative view of his work in this genre. In content, they reveal the writer's interests to be catholic, ranging from contemporary event to history. In theme, they show Rhodes's inherent democracy and humanity, his distaste for credulity and affectation, and his opposition to the main currents of American literary thought of his day.

Of the five essays considered here, four constitute responses to contemporary event; although two of them are historical in content. **"The Barred Door,"** published in the May 6, 1911, issue of the *Saturday Evening Post,* concerns New Mexico's long-thwarted bid for statehood. What actually occasioned it was a dinner October 15, 1909, in Albuquerque for President William Howard Taft. Planned as one means of winning Taft's and the Republican Party's support for statehood, the gathering took an unforeseen turn that dissipated the good intentions and, it was feared, permanently spoiled the Territory's chances for admittance to the Union. After three speakers had mixed praise for Taft with pleas for statehood, a fourth—Albert B. Fall—assailed both the President and his Party (the GOP) for dangling New Mexico since 1846. At his New York residence, Rhodes heard about the *faux pas* and kept his eye on Congress, which from 1909 to 1911, as for half a century before, barred the door to his Southwestern home. His essay, although rebuking his friend Fall for credulity, directs most of its attack upon Congress for broken promises. It satirically asks not for statehood, but for Congressional refraining from making any more promises. Whether because or in spite of Rhodes's attack, Congress responded by admitting New Mexico to the Union in 1912.

Also rooted in history, but resulting from current event is Rhodes's essay, **"In Defense of Pat Garrett,"** first published in the September, 1927, issue of *Sunset.* Pat F. Garrett had been sheriff of Lincoln County, New Mexico, on July 14, 1881, when he shot and killed William H. Bonney (Billy the Kid). His action had produced mixed reaction, but possibly nothing like the criticism it received in 1926 with the publication of Walter Noble Burns's fictionized *The Saga of Billy the Kid.* In portraying the Kid as a Western Robin Hood, Burns sullied the character of the sheriff. And although Garrett and Rhodes had often been at odds, as in the case of Rhodes's friend's (Oliver Milton Lee's) arrest in the disappearance of Colonel Albert Fountain, the attack upon Garrett provoked Rhodes. The essay sought to set the record straight.

Earlier, in **"The West That Was,"** published in the September, 1922, issue of *Photodramatist,* Rhodes had trained his sights on other writing that he felt betrayed the West.

His immediate purpose had been to separate the fact from the fiction for the benefit of Hollywood scenarists and related writers. He praised Hamlin Garland, William Allen White, and Willa Cather for ably portraying the Midwest and lamented the failure of the West to be so well understood in spite of efforts by Andy Adams, Owen Wister, Emerson Hough, and others to present credible canvasses. In analyzing the ignorance about the West, Rhodes attacked H. L. Mencken and others for disdaining Western writing. A similar attack he had launched earlier in a digression in his novel, *Stepsons of Light* (1920). In this essay, then, was another blast in a long series of volleys against the main currents of American literary thought, which Rhodes characterized as "brilliance with indecency," "dullness with indecency," and "dullness without indecency." "Half of us," charged Rhodes, "have huddled along the eastern coast, ankle deep in the Atlantic, our backs to the West, peering across at Europe."

Rhodes's battle with the "Eastern Literary Establishment" set an example that is at once a cause and an effect of Western literary ills. Actually, it had been anticipated by his essay, **"Say Now Shibboleth,"** published a year before **"The West That Was."** **"Say Now Shibboleth"** registers opposition to intellectual and social snobbery as reflected in strict adherence to dictional niceties. "Anything is 'provincial,' " objects Rhodes, "that does not conform to New England usage." And in following this charge with others in **"The West That Was"** and still later works, Rhodes established a pattern to be followed to the present by other Western writers. The Texas historian Walter Prescott Webb, for example, attacked not only Eastern literary attitudes, but (in *Divided We Stand*) the economic supremacy of the North over the West. His friend, J. Frank Dobie, like Webb an intimate of Rhodes, likewise and frequently berated the East. Even Conrad Richter, himself an Easterner but also a Southwestern resident for a quarter of a century, objected to Mencken and company for what he considered to be their betrayal not only of the West but of Americanism in general. And in an address delivered in October, 1966, to the Western Literature Association meeting in Salt Lake City, novelist Vardis Fisher, of Idaho, singled out T. S. Eliot as symbolic of the Eastern writers who have rendered their country's literature (including the West's) great disservice.

The reaction of Rhodes and his followers, as previously suggested, is a cause as well as an effect of Western literary shortcomings. Its self-consciousness is quite evident in the pledge that Rhodes's biographer W. H. Hutchinson and others have made to improve the "literary caliber" of Western writing and thus to secure its acceptance on "the same plane as other forms of native writing." What is wrong here is not the resolution to produce better literature, but to produce better Western literature. As Longfellow pointed out long ago in *Kavanagh* (1849) literature either is great or it is not. Neither nationality nor regionalism has any bearing finally on the outcome. When Webb says that Rhodes failed of recognition because he portrayed the West as it was and not as "Easterners" thought it ought to be, he reflects more than his economic prejudice. He reveals a conviction that, in order to be great, Western literature must be minutely faithful to place.

Such fierce pride of community that makes Rhodes and company promote actuality above all other literary virtue has blinded many defenders of Rhodes (and the "western") to a basic fallacy: one who has experienced occupation and place to the extent that Rhodes lived ranching and mining in New Mexico has difficulty transcending the actualities—the minutiae—and rising to the level of art. After all, art is not life. It orders life and transcends it. It fails when it achieves merely photographic rendition.

One other essay by Rhodes, **"Penalosa,"** derives from history, but does not constitute a response—as does, say, **"In Defense of Pat Garrett"**—to contemporary event. Originally included in the "Barnaby Bright" section of the novel, *West Is West* (1917), **"Penalosa"** was published individually in 1934 in Santa Fe. It praises Don Diego Dionisio Penalosa, who had incurred the wrath of the Spanish Inquisition by defending the Apaches in New Mexico against the oppression of the Spanish Church and State. To Rhodes, revealing his own democracy and humanity, Penalosa was the "first in America to strike a blow for freedom."

His letters, including those that have been collected and published by May Davison Rhodes in *The Hired Man on Horseback* and W. H. Hutchinson in *A Bar Cross Man,* are interesting for the personal qualities they reveal about Eugene Manlove Rhodes. Those to his brother-in-law George Davison, for example, bear the stamp of an independent spirit reluctant to seek aid in borrowing money or in marketing a manuscript, but also of a cheerful soul that can stare economic adversity in the face and still laugh. The letters to the Southwestern writer Agnes Morley Cleaveland, who had admired his stories in the obscure publication *Out West* and had told him so, show the naivete of one with a compulsion to write but without knowledge of what to do with the finished product. Mrs. Cleaveland got Robert Hobart Davis of the Munsey publications to help. Davis had been the first editor to publish Conrad Richter's works; and although he did not actually publish any of Rhodes's works, he offered sound advice.

Letters Rhodes addressed to countless admirers and not a few critics demonstrate the sense of obligation, not to mention the awe, of one suddenly projected into the national spotlight and self-conscious of the glare. So strong was his sense of obligation to his reading public that Rhodes spent hours painstakingly answering in longhand almost every letter he received. When the burden became impossibly heavy, he devised an intricate and humorous form letter which allowed him to check the options appropriate to a given situation.

Again, Rhodes's letters reinforce the insistence of his other writing upon fidelity to fact about the West. To Paul Eldridge of the University of Oklahoma, he wrote that William French's tedious but authentic *Recollections of a Western Rancher, 1883–1899* was the best Western book he had read. Here is Rhodes the writer turned critical reader. As critical reader, his March 11, 1925, letter to Walter P. Webb further shows, Rhodes could conclude that Andy Adams' works were "fiction, not true stories"; whereas Charlie Siringo's autobiography was "straight goods and not a work of fiction."

Additional letters to Webb and others provide insight into Rhodes's theories and practices of literary art. "The way to write," Rhodes wrote Webb in 1924, "is to do so. When you have something to say, and say it in your own way, you are getting somewhere." From the great writers, Rhodes insisted elsewhere, ideas (content), but not style might be obtained by an aspiring writer. The only way one can say something worthwhile is in his "own way." Saying something, moreover, took a long time—at least for Rhodes. First, he experienced the gestation period, writing a work over a period of months or even years in his "head." Then, he committed the work to paper in longhand. Once at work on a story, Rhodes lived it. On the walls of his study were maps of the country he told about. Tacked on walls or doors would be great sheets of paper several feet in length upon which were penciled scenes, incidents, phrases, quotations, bits of conversation, and notes. Finally, Rhodes pored over the typescript, revising up to a dozen times. Even once in galley a work was unsafe from Rhodes's insatiable urge to revision. Changes—not corrections, but changes—to the galleys of *Copper Streak Trail* are said by W. H. Hutchinson to have cost Rhodes twenty percent of the cost of setting the entire manuscript. As Henry H. Knibbs stresses, Rhodes was a slow writer not because he was lazy or because he distrusted his own ability to write, but because he was so extremely critical of his work.

But perhaps more than anything, Rhodes's letters reveal his resentment of writing for a living. As early as 1914, prior to the mid-way point of his literary career, Rhodes wrote that he would cease writing for a living at the earliest possible moment. He would, he said, "go West" and write "when he felt like it."

Stylistically, Rhodes's essays and letters promote the same freshness of diction that characterizes his fiction. In the case of the essays, however, the figurative approach frequently obscures the point he is attempting to make. In the essays, too, digressions detract from coherence and unity. The overall impression is something of a rambling Addisonianism, but definitely more rambling than Addisonian.

Quantitatively and qualitatively, poetry rests on the middle rung of the ladder of Eugene Manlove Rhodes's works, greater in number and worth than the essays but inferior in both ways to the fiction. Yet poetry is the first and almost the last medium in which Rhodes worked and published. His **"Charlie Graham,"** which appeared in 1896 in *Land of Sunshine,* antedated his first story, **"The Hour and the Man,"** by six years. And his **"Einstein's Universe,"** published in the April 18, 1931, issue of the *Saturday Evening Post,* was one of the last pieces he wrote. Nevertheless, during the intervening thirty-five years between **"Charlie Graham"** and **"Einstein's Universe,"** Rhodes produced only thirty-two known poems.

For brief analysis, Rhodes's poems may be classified as elegies, nature, democratic or protest, humorous-satiric-whimsical, love, religious, and nostalgic. Collectively, however, they promote essentially the same themes found in his fiction, so that the variety of their categories is more indicative of topical breadth than of intellectual growth.

The first of two elegiac poems that may be considered as representative of the classification, **"Charlie Graham"** memorializes an oldtimer for whom Rhodes once worked. In the winter of 1899, while writing at night on his first story, Rhodes worked during the day, digging a well for Graham. It was an experience reminiscent of Faulkner's writing *As I Lay Dying* on an upturned wheelbarrow while working for a power company in Oxford. Although genuinely sympathetic, **"Charlie Graham"** suffers from sentimentality. **"The Last L'Envoi"** is Rhodes's personal epitaph and hence something of a private elegy. It partakes in form and spirit of a similar work by one of Rhodes's models, Rudyard Kipling.

Less discernible in Rhodes than in other elegiac poets, certain American characteristics peculiar to the genre still evidence themselves. The American elegy, as opposed to the foreign, has tended to transcend the immediate and deal with the general. That is to say that, instead of conveying merely the poet's individual sense of loss, the elegy expands to comprehend the entire nation's. Witness Whitman's "When Lilacs Last in the Dooryard Bloom'd." So, too, with **"Charlie Graham."** From the poet's grief at the death of a friend, the poem expands to suggest something of a regional loss in the death of a man symbolic of an older way of life now gone or nearly past.

The nature poems Rhodes composed early in his career. Confined to the Southwest of his young manhood, they celebrate such regional endowments as flowers—the yucca (**"A Blossom of Barren Lands,"** 1899) and the primrose (**"With an Evening Primrose,"** 1902); the landscape (**"A Ballade of Gray Hills,"** 1900); and bees (**"A Ballade of Wild Bees,"** 1902). Neither of these poems whose title includes "Ballade," however, is a ballad, but a lyric. And that about bees is strongly derivative of a poem on the same subject by Whittier, one of Rhodes's favorite poets. **"A Ballade of Gray Hills"** sees the hills and stars as symbols of peace.

That Rhodes ceased to focus upon nature for poetic subject once he had moved to the East suggests that he could not establish empathy with an alien scene. But a more likely explanation is that, responding increasingly to national events that would have been remote to his semi-isolated New Mexico, he concerned himself more with people than with place as the years unfolded.

Such a concern with events and people are found in Rhodes's democratic or protest poems. *"Te Deum Laudamus"* (1901) opposes American imperialism in the Philippines. **"Pegasus at the Plow"** (1929) laments the taming by civilization of the free spirit. **"Nineteen Thirty-One"** (1931), a parody of Kipling's "Danny Deever," criticizes the high interest rates charged farmers and registers opposition to the Volstead Act. It is remotely reminiscent of Wordsworth's "London, 1802." **"The Little People"** (1932) pays tribute to the common man all over the world and in all times. **"The Hired Man on Horseback,"** considered by many to be Rhodes's finest poem, attacks newspaper columnists and others who have written disparagingly of the cowboy. Rhodes's model for the hired man is thought to have been Fred Crosby, superintendent of

stock at the Mescalero Reservation and formerly foreman of the Bar Cross.

These protest poems seethe with righteous indignation that is relieved only occasionally and then insufficiently by humor to redeem them. And **"The Hired Man on Horseback,"** despite Dobie's claim of being the finest range poem yet written, allows sentimentality to intrude to the extent that the work becomes melodramatic.

Invariably lighter in tone and ordinarily less serious in content but still the better for both, the humorous-satiric-whimsical poems may finally be Rhodes's best. They deal with a variety of subjects. **"As Is the Needle to the Pole"** (1901) pokes gentle fun at girls. A companion piece, **"Relativity for Ladies"** (1931) facetiously insists that woman's age does not change like man's. The whimsical vignette of a small girl, **"Little Next Door"** (1916), dwells on the innocence of childhood. Similarly concerning childhood is **"The Prairie Farmer,"** which stresses that the magazine of the same name that Rhodes read as a boy can afford delight to a child in an isolated land. Much more temperate than the later protest poem **"Nineteen Thirty-One," "My Banker"** (1930) nevertheless carries a pointed thrust. **"Advice"** (1931), which suggests that the dentist's best counsel is "Close!," is an exercise in fun akin to **"The Ballad of East and West"** (1931), which burlesques newspaper bridge game lessons. Although nonetheless humorous, three other poems concern more serious topics. **"Important—Einstein's Universe"** (1930) takes up the scientist's revisions of his own opinions of the universe. **"Personal Liberty"** (1931) examines the abuse of personal liberty. And **"Fire Song"** (1932), a tribute to Benjamin Franklin, debunks the debunkers of Franklin and other Founding Fathers.

Rhodes's love poems include **"White Fingers"** (1910), which envisions love as hands playing upon a mandolin; **"Lyn Dyer's Dream"** from the novel, *Stepsons of Light* (1920); and **"Recognition"** (1926). These contribute little to the content or form of the corpus of the world's love poems.

"A Song of Harvest" (1923), constituting a prayer to accept "my row," or life as it has been, contributes little other than vernacular to the world's religious poetry. But **"The Immortals"** is of somewhat more significance in that it links Rhodes with Mark Twain. It is a poem about a soldier who breaks his spear and gives it to Joan of Arc for a cross. Like Twain who devoted a novel to the subject, Rhodes rises to the defense of the historic maiden and also exposes the hypocrisy of the religion that condemned her to death. In this respect, **"The Immortals"** invites comparison with Rhodes's prose work, **"Penalosa,"** which defends Don Diego Dionisio Penalosa against the Inquisition that resented his humanity toward the Apache Indians.

Finally, two of Rhodes's nostalgic poems may be considered. Both were written near the end of his life after he had finally returned from the East to New Mexico but actually too late to enjoy the homecoming. **"Engle Ferry"** (1929) deals wistfully with a ferry at Engle Ford now gone.

"Night Message" (1930), imitative of a telegram in form, expresses longing for the West "that was."

In structure, Rhodes's poetry follows traditional stanzaic patterns and such conventional forms as the lyric and ballad. They reveal no experimental impulse, as works by many of Rhodes's contemporaries do. The images, for example, are more abstract than concrete. Then, mostly end rimed, Rhodes's poems often suffer from irregularity of meter that obviously is not calculated and which certainly contributes no unique effects. When these flaws are coupled with the dearth of original idea, the evaluation of Rhodes's verse would be dire indeed were it not for the spirit of the poet that somehow comes through and saves the works from complete failure. At best Rhodes is no Frost, whom he admired and who, in turn, admired Rhodes's prose. But at worst Rhodes is a decided cut above Edgar Guest, a popular contemporary of his, and of Eugene Field, to whom Rhodes alludes in his novel, *The Proud Sheriff,* and whom by implication Rhodes admired.

Fiction finally is Eugene Manlove Rhodes's forte. By far, the bulk of his work consists of novels and stories, and the prestige of his labor rests on them. As a fictionist, however, Rhodes did not excel at story-telling; nor, if dialogue is excluded, in creating memorable characters; nor in coming to grips with significantly universal themes. What he did with distinction was to describe Western landscapes and to explicate the Western occupations of mining and ranching. Many of the stories eventually found their way into the novels. And those that did not contribute little but detail to an understanding of Rhodes's fiction. For these reasons, only the novels are treated in the following analysis of theme, plot, place, character, and dialogue.

As well as a homogeneity of subject and point of view, Rhodes's fiction features a persistence of themes. Perhaps the best way of generalizing about them is to say that Rhodes accepted the elementary Christian and democratic virtues. But to thus speak is not to imply that the author accepted Christianity without reservation. Rhodes's son Alan said that his father rejected the belief in Jesus Christ as the son of God. What Eugene Rhodes accepted were Christ's teachings, which he called "the best we have." Also, the idea of Hell was inconsistent to Rhodes with the concept of a "loving God." At any rate, Rhodes's themes persist, but still evidence little intellectual growth. What occurs mostly instead is the repetition of idea or at best the development of corollaries. Such thematic tendencies may be observed in the survey that follows.

Good Men and True, Rhodes's first novel, revolves around the theme of corruption in high place. S. S. Thorpe, a sinister El Paso politician, is seeking to discredit and even murder Texas Ranger Captain Charles Tillotson, who is investigating Thorpe's activities. Unaware of the intrigue, Jeff Bransford arrives in the city to report to his employer, an attorney named Simon Hibler, on whose New Mexico ranch Bransford is foreman. While waiting to see Hibler, Bransford is shown how to operate a typewriter by Hibler's law clerk, who types the familiar expression, "Now is the time for all good men and true to come to the aid of their party." Later, Bransford becomes accidentally involved in an attempted midnight assassination.

Knocked unconscious, he comes to in a Juarez hideout to which Thorpe's men have taken him, and learns that he has killed Oily Broderick, a professional killer Thorpe has retained to assassinate the ranger Tillotson. Ironically, as Bransford further learns, Tillotson has been charged with Broderick's death and is to stand trial. Bransford is given the choice of death at the hands of Thorpe's men or, if he cooperates, life and reward by Thorpe. Cooperation means that Bransford would remain a willing prisoner of Thorpe until Tillotson had been tried and convicted. Thereafter the captive cowboy would be freed and rewarded. Bransford pretends to accept the compromise, and manages to smuggle to friends a coded message containing the expression, "Now is the time for all good men and true to come to the aid of their party." The "good men and true" are Bransford's fellow cowboys, John Wesley Pringle, William Beebe, and Leo Ballinger. Realizing that Bransford is in danger because of his reference in the coded message to a wife who does not exist, they storm the hideout, effect Bransford's release, and thwart Thorpe's scheme.

Jeff Bransford also functions as the hero of Rhodes's second novel, *The Little Eohippus* (1912). Likewise appearing in this work are Pringle, Beebe, and Ballinger. *The Little Eohippus* derives its title from the primitive four-toed horse, except that Bransford's is a tiny turquoise that he carries in his pocket. Turning on the theme of corruption in high place, it finds Bransford thwarting the plot of a banker, Stephen Walter Lake of Arcadia, to burglarize his own bank. Bransford meets Ellinor Hoffman, Lake's house guest, on a horseback ride and accepts her invitation to attend a masquerade party at the banker's home. A bitter enemy of Lake, Bransford attends the ball only because he can come disguised as a football player with a nose guard. During the ball, the bank is burglarized and the town night watchman critically shot. Bransford's nose guard is found on the scene. Apprehended, Bransford flees the legal hearing rather than admit he was with Ellinor Hoffman at the time of the burglary and thus bring suspicion upon her character. Coming to Bransford's rescue this time are Johnny Dines and Billy White, who prove that Lake burglarized his own bank to cover stock market losses. Pringle, Beebe, and Ballinger—merely peripheral figures in this novel—remain all the while back at the ranch.

A lawyer is employed in *Hit the Line Hard* (1915) to illustrate the theme of corruption in high place. Octaviano Baca, in fact, is the political boss, as well as the leading attorney, of Saragossa. He, a storekeeper and banker named Martin Bennett, the gamblers Beck and Scanlon, and a fifth accomplice named Owen Quinliven—all have taken money from the estate of Quinliven's late ranching partner Roger Drake. The dead man's nephew and heir—Roger Olcott Drake, II, an Eastern college graduate—and a perceptive cowboy, Neighbor Jones, set about to recover the money. Although Drake is the college man (the title derives from his football expression, "Don't flinch; don't foul; hit the line hard"), Jones serves as quarterback. Jones turns members of the gang on one another. Having sown the seeds of suspicion, he waits until Beck steals money from both Bennett's bank and his partner's (Scanlon's) safe. Then, he steals the money from Beck. The gang is powerless to act in that any sort of reprisal would reveal how it had obtained the money in the first place.

Rhodes's fourth novel, *The Desire of the Moth* (1916), continues the theme of corruption in high place but shifts from politician and banker to law enforcement officer. Matthew Lisner, Dona Ana County sheriff, is the villain. He is plotting to discredit a young rancher named Kit Foy, who is opposing Lisner's bid for re-election. Foy is engaged to marry Stella Vorhis. Fearful of what will happen to Foy, Stella turns to the same John Wesley Pringle who had played minor roles in Rhodes's first two novels. A former employee of Stella's father, Pringle is enroute to his ranch at Rainbow Mountain when he meets Stella in Las Uvas and agrees to help Foy. Lisner, Stella tells Pringle, is attempting to stir anew a feud between Foy and another young rancher named Dick Marr. Pringle first thwarts an attempt by Lisner's men to kill Foy in a barroom brawl. Then, when Dick Marr is killed by Lisner's man Jose Espalin and when Foy is blamed, Pringle saves the rancher's life by "arresting" him before the sheriff can. In the process, Pringle proves that Lisner, not Foy, is the villain. Anastacio, Lisner's own political lieutenant, and Nueces River, chief of police in Dona Ana, assist Pringle in revealing Lisner's plot because they will not tolerate Lisner's corruption. Lisner's career thus is ruined when he is arrested for complicity in the death of Dick Marr.

West Is West (1917) is a sort of potpourri of Western Americana. Among its themes are corruption in high place, the nobility of the outlaw, and the manly response to danger. Such an abundance of themes, with supporting events and characters, would preclude the work's being a unified novel were it not for the presence of a few central figures who keep turning up throughout. Of these central figures, Emil James is perhaps foremost, even though he functions more as observer than actual participant. Before James appears on the scene, however, a "prologue" has related how Miss Bennie May Morgan has almost lost her virginity to her father's ranching rival Clay Mundy. Mundy and Bennie May have been meeting clandestinely, and she has fallen in love with him. Pretending love, Mundy arranges for an imposter dressed as a minister to perform a mock wedding. But before the ruse can be perpetrated, Mundy's range hand, Sandy MacGregor, accosts his employer and dies with him in a shootout. Although a refugee from the law himself, MacGregor treasures Bennie May's honor more than his own life. His example illustrates the theme of the nobility of the outlaw. Following the "prologue," the scene shifts to the Golden Fleece mine that has just experienced an explosion. Eight men from the day shift are trapped but are rescued by the superhuman efforts of such miners as Caradoc Hughes. The heroic act illustrates the theme of the manly response to danger. At this point Emil James rides onto the scene. He meets John Sayles Waterson, Jr., an Eastern college man. As observers and occasional participants, James and Waterson are on hand for a spate of action: (1) a cattlemen's-sheepherders' rivalry between Bennie May Morgan's father and the Fuentes clan; (2) a runaway freight car laden with dynamite that is stopped by the heroic efforts of Nate Logan, who thus atones for an earlier act of cowardice and

wins the community's respect again; (3) Steve "Wildcat" Thompson's outwitting corrupt officials and settling without payment a tax lien against his property; (4) the murder and robbery by Walter Keough, manager of the telephone company, of miserly old Gibson; (5) the murder by Bill Tait of Jim Van Atta, a mine operator; (6) the rescue by the gambler Crooknose Evans of Katie Quinn, a virtuous girl tricked into a brothel, with the rescue's being effected before Katie's virtue has been despoiled; and (7) the thwarting by Dick Rainbolt of Mendenhall, Gray, and Spencer's plot to sabotage and later steal the mine they operate for J. C. Armstrong. At the end, Waterson returns to Baltimore, leaving Emil James in the admiring hands of Bennie May Morgan. Keough and Tait have been apprehended for their murders; Katie Quinn reunited with Billy Murphy; Dick Rainbolt taken in hand by Armstrong's niece Judith Elliott; and Crooknose Evans lured away by Helen Fuentes.

Copper Streak Trail (1917) returns to the lawyer as the example of corruption in high place. And this time the villain has the added dimension of being an Easterner, not a Westerner. Oscar Mitchell is a rival of his cousin, Stanley (Kid) Mitchell, for the wealth of their aging Uncle McClintock. Both Oscar and the uncle reside in Vesper, New York, the home Stanley left after an argument with his uncle over his engagement to Annie Selden. To cement his relationship with Uncle McClintock, Oscar Mitchell conspires with the sinister Mayer Zurich, an Arizona strongman, to ruin the mining operation of Stanley Mitchell and Pete Johnson. Zurich succeeds in framing Stanley with a holdup charge, but fails to foil Johnson who goes to New York and enlists the support of Annie Selden and, more importantly, Uncle McClintock. Returning to Arizona, Johnson beats Zurich's accomplice at poker and forces him to admit that he, not Stanley Mitchell, committed the robbery. Stanley is released and joins Johnson in a race with Zurich and his men to make safe their mining claim. They are diverted from their purpose by the disappearance of the young son of a friend, and thus lose the race to Zurich. Revealing a decent side of his nature and supporting the subordinate theme of the nobility of the outlaw, however, Zurich leaves Stanley and Johnson most of the claim after learning why they were late in arriving. Oscar Mitchell, meanwhile, is discredited by the Westerners and disinherited by his Eastern Uncle McClintock, who forgives both Stanley and Annie Selden.

Stepsons of Light (1920), like *The Desire of the Moth,* focuses upon a corrupt law enforcement officer to illustrate the theme of deviation in high place. Ed Caney, deputy sheriff of Dona Ana County, is the villain. He shoots to death Adam Forbes, who has staked a mining claim; and with his accomplices, Weir and Hales, he places the blame on the cowboy Johnny Dines. Caney's story, however, fails to convince Pete Harkey, Charlie See, and others. When Dines is arrested, his accusers attempt to stir up a lynch mob. Charlie See thwarts the mob in a saloon brawl by throwing pool balls in much the same fashion that Eugene Manlove Rhodes himself once did in a fight in a California barroom. During the examining trial of Dines, See reveals Carney's guilt and then shoots the deputy sheriff to death in the courtroom.

Once in the Saddle (1925) the final novel revolving around the theme of corruption in high place, features a mine operator named Malloch. He fails to provide decent housing for his miners and also forces them to shop at his company store at Salamanca. The real villain of the piece, however, is Malloch's strongman, John C. Calhoun (Cal) Pelly. When Pliny Mullins and Tommy Garrett start digging a well to provide water for a competing housing project Mullins is planning for Malloch's miners, the well is almost sabotaged by a dynamite explosion. Mullins and Garrett confront Malloch, and are warned by Pelly to settle elsewhere. Mullins suspects that Pelly and Malloch are planning to jump Pinky Ford's claim to a ranch that contains plenty of water. The claim, he suspects, is faulty because of muddled surveyor's markings on the cornerstone. Mullins warns Ford, who nevertheless is killed in a fall from his horse while enroute with Pelly to fight sheepherders. Pelly hides Ford's body, fearful that he will be accused of murder. Then he robs a paymaster and leaves evidence that would cast suspicion on the missing Ford. Pelly even hides the money in Ford's cabin. His crime, however, is exposed by Mullins.

Pasó Por Aquí (1926) is one of two novels by Rhodes that promotes the primary theme of the nobility of the outlaw. Its protagonist, Ross McEwen, robs the bank at Belden and flees a posse headed by Sheriff Pat Garrett, of Lincoln County. In flight, he encounters a Mexican family stricken with diphtheria: old Florencio Telles; his late son's widow, Estefania; and her two small sons, Felix and Demetrio. McEwen's basic humanity dictates that he ignore his own safety and instead remain with the family until help arrives. First on the scene, Garrett sends to Alamogordo for a doctor and nurses, one of whom is Miss Jay Hollister, who previously has been hostile to the Western country in which Ben Griggs wants her to remain. So impressed is Miss Hollister with the outlaw's selflessness and with Garrett's charity (the sheriff allows McEwen to escape) that her views of the region change for the better. Here she has seen unfolded a morality play in which thief, sheriff, and peasant appear equal—all with bedrock human virtue. The title of the story derives from Inscription Rock on which for ages men have carved their names beneath the expression: *Pasó Por Aquí* (passed this way). In this case, the reference is an understatement of McEwen's service and of the nobility of the outlaw.

The nobility of the outlaw also informs Rhodes's novel, *The Trusty Knaves* (1931). Using the alias Bill Hawkins, the real-life outlaw Bill Doolin appears in Target about the same time that George Carmody is passing through with his cattle herd. The country has been wracked by drought, and Carmody is seeking grass and water for his livestock. Charlie Bird is accompanying Carmody. Also around are Elmer (Slim) Farr, a rancher; and Johnny Pardee, foreman of another cattle outfit. Farr and Pardee become suspicious that Ernie Patterson is behind a series of robberies in the area. Their suspicions are confirmed when Patterson approaches Hawkins about a plot to cast suspicion for a planned robbery on Carmody. What the plotters do not tell Hawkins is that they plan to implicate him as well. Hawkins and others, however, turn the tables, making Hawkins (or Doolin) a "trusty knave."

The Proud Sheriff (1932), Rhodes's last novel, is one of his few works to employ the theme of decency in high place. Its hero is Sheriff Spinal Maginnas of Sierra County. As the story opens, Dad Wilson and his youthful partner Otey Beech are working a small gold claim. Beech goes to Hillsboro, seat of Sierra County, which has not—thanks to Maginnas—had a murder in ten years. Short of funds, Otey receives largesse from Sam Travis, who, along with the merchant Gus Krumm, is murdered. Suspicion points to Beech. The youth is jailed, but his innocence is believed by Maginnas and a coroner's jury that refuses to indict Beech. Later, when confronted by Maginnas, Spencer Allen attempts to shoot the sheriff and is instead killed himself. Allen and Laura Krumm, the murdered merchant's wife, have been having a love affair. Krumm discovered the two and was shot by Allen, who then shot the unsuspecting Sam Travis as he happened upon the scene.

Philosophically, the themes promoted by Eugene Manlove Rhodes further illustrate the paradox of the author. At once they contain seemingly contradictory elements of humanism and skepticism. For example, to Rhodes, man possesses almost unlimited possibility. In *The Desire of the Moth,* John Wesley Pringle (speaking for the author) tells the corrupt Sheriff Matthew Lisner: "A good many people lay their fine-drawn plans, but they mostly don't come off! Men are but dust, they tell us. Magnificent dust! This nice little old world of ours, in the long run, is going right." On the other hand, to Rhodes, man is fraught with limitations. In *Copper Streak Trail,* the author observes that man fails "to see the obvious; to think upon the thing seen; to judge between our own resultant and conflicting thoughts, with no furtive finger of desire to tip the balance; and to act upon that judgment without flinching." Or, as Bill Hawkins tells Pres Lewis in *The Trusty Knaves*: "When you ride up to that [Carmody's] camp, you ride a-whistlin' real loud and pleasant. That Charlie Bird, he's half Cherokee and half white, and them's two bad breeds."

These seemingly contradictory views of man become reconciled, however, when one considers that both are necessary for Rhodes to demonstrate a fundamental ambiguity of life: man is at once good and evil. As H. H. Knibbs has pointed out, Rhodes is never blind to man's limitations; but he also knows from personal experience that merely to survive in his day called for courage, loyalty, perseverance, and a broad tolerance.

Similarly, the seemingly contradictory views of the outlaw and the lawman that Rhodes reveals become harmonized. As Walter Campbell and others have demonstrated, the criminal in both Indian and white frontier communities was not, unless mentally disturbed, antisocial or intentionally destructive of community mores. Moreover, the Eastern laws imposed upon Western conditions did not always fit. This is what Rhodes's character "Wildcat" Thompson has in mind when he says a man that "keeps a foolish law is only a fool—but a man who doesn't break a wicked law is a knave and a coward, or both, and fool besides." When Rhodes thus makes the outlaw noble and the law enforcement officer unjust, he is not being contradictory but merely faithful to fact.

As the earlier synoptic analysis of Rhodes's themes perhaps suggested, plots provide merely a loose framework from which the author can dangle his descriptions of occupation, people, and place. They also constitute a platform from which he can expound his views not only of the West, but of life in general. Some critics have insisted that the plots are "incredibly intricate." But they are confusing intricacy for lack of selectivity and unity. What Rhodes really does well is the individual episode, once he has introduced his characters and provided a frame for their action. What he does not do well is introduce the characters and provide a frame smoothly enough to unify the episodes into a single work.

Part of the problem with plot is that Rhodes allows the actual history upon which he is drawing for story material to get out of hand. For example, Chapter III of **The Desire of the Moth** provides a history of the great Chihuahuan desert, the *Jornado del Muerto.* While interesting, the discussion actually constitutes digression, contributing really nothing to the plot line. Another digression, in **West Is West,** details the Range War Code: (1) never fight while enjoying the enemy's hospitality; (2) never fight on neutral ground; (3) never fight without fresh offense; (4) never smile and then shoot; (5) never ambush an enemy unless he is in pursuit; to ambush an unsuspecting (that is, non-pursuing enemy) is "bushwhacking;" and (6) employ the rattlesnake's ethics: warn before striking. But, again, the information intrudes upon the story. Rhodes employed the archaeology of the cattle kingdom just as Dreiser sifted court records, and with some of the same adverse results.

Like Faulkner's, Rhodes's fictional settings correspond to those in actual life; and his characters at least superficially are indigenous to place. Here, however, the similarity ends. Rhodes seldom bothers to alter the names either of places or people; and the practice underscores his failure to transcend the level of actuality. With place, the failure is not so crucial as with characters. Like Sinclair Lewis, Rhodes employs characters promiscuously, assigning a name (often the real-life) to every person appearing on the range or the streets. The practice detracts from the major characters. But first the settings.

Rhodes's world may be divided, as W. H. Hutchinson has done it, into three areas of Southern New Mexico: (1) the Western, extending eastward from the Black Range crest to the Rio Grande at Elephant Butte, including mining camps; (2) the Central, between the Rio Grande and the San Andres-Organ crest, including the *Jornado del Muerto;* and (3) the Eastern, between the San Andres-Organ chain and the Sacramento-Sierra Blanca ranges, including the shifting gypsum dunes called the White Sands. This is the territory comprising Grant, Sierra, Luna, Socorro, Dona Ana, Otero, and Lincoln Counties. It extends from Silver City (the fictional "Argentine") in the West to El Paso, Texas, in the South, and from Roswell in the East to Belen in the North. Included are such other towns as Alamogordo (which Rhodes sometimes calls "Arcadia"), Deming ("Target"), Dona Ana ("Tripoli"), Las Cruces ("Las Uvas" or "San Lucas"), La Luz ("Rainbow's End"), Socorro ("Saragossa"), Tularosa ("Oasis"), and White Oaks ("Heart's Desire").

In portraying his world, Rhodes proves superior to any

Rhodes two weeks before his death, 1934.

New Mexican writer (save possibly Conrad Richter) from the standpoint of evoking the richness of the landscape. The key to his descriptive ability is his power of observation. No detail is too unimportant; no sound or action too insignificant; no quality of nature too trivial. Witness the following richly evocative passage from **The Desire of the Moth**:

> Organ Mountain flung up a fantasy of spires, needle-sharp and bare and golden. The long straight range—saw-toothed limestone save for this twenty-mile sheer upheaval of the Organ— stretched away to north and south against the unclouded sky, till distance turned the barren gray to blue-black, to blue, to misty haze; till the sharp, square-angled masses rounded to hillocks—to a blur—a wavy line—nothing.

As De Maupassant insisted a writer must do, Rhodes sees something unique in the commonplace; and as Ford Madox Ford said of Hemingway, Rhodes uses ordinary words in an extraordinary way to express his vision. The truly remarkable quality about Rhodes's landscapes is that he painted most of them from memory while residing in faraway New York and often as many as twenty years after he had experienced what he describes.

If Rhodes proves capable of brilliant landscapes, he fails badly in portraying the characters with which he peoples his world. Part of his problem here, as previously suggested, is that he draws too heavily upon actual life. Many of his characters appear under their actual names or are thinly disguised. Jefferson C. Bransford, of **Good Men and True** and **The Little Eohippus,** for example, is an actual name. According to W. H. Hutchinson, Bransford was the son of an Oglala Sioux (reputedly the niece of Red Cloud) and a Virginian mountain man (William A. Bransford) associated with the brothers Bent. Then, Emil James, twice sheriff of Socorro County in actual life, appears under his own name in **West Is West** and some of the short stories. So do Sheriff Pat Garrett, of Lincoln County, in **Pasó Por Aquí**; and Deputy Sheriff Anastacio Barela in the short story, **"Charming Fellow, Anastacio."**

Artistically, the tendency to draw heavily upon actual persons leads Rhodes into a trap. Because he knows the people so well he leaves too much to the imagination of the reader by minimizing detail in characterization and by omitting essential background material. In other words, Rhodes fails to see that the reader can not know an actual person as well as he—a friend and associate.

Rhodes's best works have no women, or at least none in prominent roles. This underscores his inability to depict credible women unless they have reached middle age. And when the weakness is coupled with Rhodes's aversion to the tainted woman, the result is that all his young heroines are hopelessly romantic. Yet Rhodes perhaps should not be scored too heavily here: for all of its raw reality, the West essentially was romantic to those who lived there. Witness such notions as the early Spanish vision of *Cibola* (the cities of gold) and the much later chivalric code that dominated the life of Rhodes's youth. At any rate, no unselfconscious women appear in Rhodes's works: no prostitutes; only one threatened virginity; and only one tarnished virtue.

An even harder time than with women characters Rhodes has with his villains. His primary villains, like his model Shakespeare's Iago, are conscious of their villainy and thus have little humanity or credibility. Mayer Zurich of **Copper Streak Trail** is one of the few exceptions. The secondary villains are cowmen who have gone wrong and hence, Rhodes seems to say, are to be somewhat excused.

Finally, Rhodes's heroes are little better. They include the quick, tough young cowboy or miner; the slightly older and hence less physically quick but yet more sharp-witted cowboy or miner; the garrulous, shrewd old Southwesterner whose abundant speech contains rich veins of wisdom; the young newcomer to the Southwest, eager companion of the oldtimer, who proves himself a man; and the loyal friend who risks fortune or life to do a favor.

In short, as Eugene Cunningham has said, Rhodes could not create people; he could only "photograph color, record in faintest intonation, real people he knew."

Next to landscape canvasses, Rhodes's dialogue emerges as the finest example of his art. Bernard DeVoto insists that in this performance Rhodes rivals Twain, and he is just about right. The talk is characterized by earthy naturalness, salty freshness of the cowboy vernacular with its unusual figures of speech and understatement, and spirited humor.

Such, then, have been three paradoxes: the American Southwest as an ethnic and geographic region; the early fiction of the Southwest and its contemporary offspring, the "western"; and that son of the Southwest, the cowboy chronicler, Eugene Manlove Rhodes. There remains for consideration only a fourth paradox that has been the criticism of Rhodes's literary works. That some have praised Rhodes and others damned him creates no seeming contradiction. The paradox arises from the blend of praise and criticism and particularly from the conclusion to which the mixture leads: Rhodes was a successful failure.

Among the praise heaped upon Rhodes has been that of Lawrence Clark Powell, distinguished critic and librarian. Powell has called Rhodes "the most literary and humanistic cowboy-writer of them all." Rhodes's books, says Powell, are to the Southern Rio Grande Valley of New Mexico what Harvey Fergusson's are to the North—"an essential expression of the land and its lore, wind and weather." Like Joseph Conrad, insists another admirer, Conrad Richter, "there is only one Eugene Manlove Rhodes and no one remotely resembling him," his "raciness," his "wit," and his "sardonic humor." Rhodes's work, says DeVoto, is "the only body of fiction devoted to the cattle kingdom which is both true to it and written by an artist in prose." J. Frank Dobie, the late dean of Southwestern letters, says Rhodes has the "right tune"; that, more than most Western writers, he is "conscious of art"; and that he is "a writer for writing men." Nevertheless, concedes Dobie, "he cannot be classed as great because his grasp" is "too often disproportionately short of the long reach."

The unique fiction of Eugene Manlove Rhodes:

A newspaper article about Eugene Manlove Rhodes by a very thoughtful historian of the West characterizes him as "a bold, gallant, card-playing, pool-playing, cowpunching natural son of the American West." It is this philistine conception of what constitutes natural sons that makes the civilized pursuit of art and ideas so difficult everywhere in America and especially in the Southwest. The passionate few are not passionate in their regard for Eugene Manlove Rhodes because he was a card-playing cowpuncher; they are passionate towards him because of the way his cultivated mind played upon the cowpuncher world. One part of him was a part of this world, but the "immortal residue" of him was beyond it—the part that justified Bernard De Voto in calling his fiction the only fiction of the cattle country "that reaches a level which it is intelligent to call art." Being a good hand on horseback did not make Gene Rhodes a good writer, though pride and vitality are common denominators of both.

True art always transcends the provincial. Gene Rhodes loved his waddie land and its people passionately. He made that land more interesting, gave it significance, added something of the spirit to its expanses. We dwellers upon it must feel an abiding gratitude to him.

J. Frank Dobie, in his introduction to The Best Novels and Stories of Eugene Manlove Rhodes, *edited by Frank V. Dearing, 1949.*

Of the evaluations, Dobie's more nearly rings true. Rhodes is good, yes, very good at depicting place and occupation. And his buoyant spirit redeems still other aspects of his art. But finally he is not great beyond the confines of regionalism. Still, within the region that is the American Southwest, Rhodes deserves a place beside Dobie, Paul Horgan, Richter, and Frank Waters. Or, to employ Rhodes's own phrase, in such a company, "he'll do to take along." (pp. 14-39)

> *Edwin W. Gaston, Jr., in his* Eugene Manlove Rhodes: Cowboy Chronicler, *Steck-Vaughn Company, 1967, 44 p.*

Jon Tuska　(essay date 1976)

[*Tuska is an American editor, writer, and producer with a special interest in cinema history. In the following excerpt, he analyzes Rhodes's romanticized treatment of biographical elements and historical events in his fiction.*]

> If I envied the favored few
> That lightly loitered their light lives through,
> I said no word as I watched them go,
> But I set my teeth, and I hoed my row.
> —Eugene Manlove Rhodes

The parents of Eugene Manlove Rhodes—Hinman Rhodes and Julia Mae Manlove—first met in Schuyler County, Illinois. Julia was a vivacious, energetic woman with a reputation for being an excellent rider. As befitted the daughter of a prosperous family, she attended Lombard College at Galesburg, Illinois. In July, 1866, brevetted with the rank of colonel, Hinman Rhodes joined the influx of other Union Army veterans entering Nebraska Territory. He purchased numerous town lots at Tecumseh and became a partner in a general mercantile business, Rhodes & Tingle. He and Julia were married on March 5, 1868. Eugene was born in a double log cabin at Tecumseh on January 7, 1869. It was two weeks after his mother's twenty-sixth birthday. Nebraska had become a state and Hinman was away from home at the time serving his first term in the newly formed state legislature.

In 1871, during the elder Rhodes' second term in the legislature, the firm of Rhodes & Tingle failed. Rather than dodge the debts of the defunct partnership, the colonel's attitude was summed up in a homily of that day, "I pay for what I break." It took Hinman Rhodes years to pay out what was owed. His son was profoundly impressed by this attitude and it became his own standard for measuring himself and for distinguishing friends and enemies alike. It also made him something of an anachronism among Americans in this century. (p. 227)

[In his essay "Novelist of the Cattle Kingdom"] Bernard DeVoto commented . . . on Rhodes' inability to draw young female characters from life. His heroines, when he did include one, are in DeVoto's words "incredible, and the attitude in which they are approached, the lush and trepidant veneration, the tropical breathlessness in the presence of mysterious, mysteriously fine, and infrangibly virginal female flesh makes one wonder why an artist who could differentiate the colors of grasses under a five-miles-distant wind never bothered to observe what a woman looks like. They are distillations of sweetness and exist merely to stimulate the hero to precariously gallant behavior, usually on occasions when good sense in a woman would have made it impossible, and to reward him when the complications have been worked out." Rhodes himself confessed in a letter to historian Walter Prescott Webb that "there was no 'star' system on the range. Also, few women and vague in my stories—because they are just so in my memories." In a subsequent letter to Webb, Rhodes observed that "Sir Walter Scott's novels . . . just about ruined me." Combined with his idealization of his father, Rhodes no doubt derived from Scott much of his idea of a hero, but with this idealization of a father-hero went inevitably the idealization of womanhood. He preferred—to place the matter in the context of the contrast between women which Scott used in *Waverly* (1814)—a Rose Bradwardine to a Flora Mac-Ivor. "It is," DeVoto concluded about Rhodes' fictional females, "only when they have reached middle age, when he can read from their hands and faces what life in the desert had cost them, that they are human or even credible."

It was possibly for reasons of health that Hinman Rhodes decided to move to New Mexico. The colonel, now fifty-four, went first, taking only Gene with him. The year was 1881. "I came to New Mexico the year that Billy the Kid was killed," Gene Rhodes later remarked.

During his early years in New Mexico, Hinman Rhodes worked as a miner. On one occasion he accepted a temporary job in Old Mexico, leaving Gene in charge of the family which had taken residence in an adobe house in Engle. At times Gene would accompany his father on local jobs; at other times he would work by himself for such prospectors as "Uncle Ben" Teagarten, a man in his high seventies, and Preston G. Lewis, a Virginian who bore a striking resemblance to graven images of Jove. Later, in his fiction, Gene's father came to serve as the model for the character, John Wesley Pringle; Teagarten as Ben Teagardner and Pres Lewis, called by his right name, appeared as themselves. Gene also worked as a swamper for a freight rig and he saw a herd of cattle watered at gun point at the Rincon railroad pens. These experiences he incorporated decades later in what I regard as his finest novel, *The Trusty Knaves* (1934). Notwithstanding his various jobs, Gene worked mostly for the Bar Cross, although his employment by the spread was scarcely sequential, and it was this outfit in his subsequent fiction which came to represent the best he had known of the final days of the free range in a lonesome land.

Hinman Rhodes was granted a monthly pension of $12.50 for his Civil War disability. He filed on an eighty-acre homestead at the head of Cottonwood Canyon in the San Andrés Mountains. Gene was seventeen by now and he helped his father erect a two-room cabin with a rock fireplace. The colonel embarked on a career as a stockman, although on a small scale. To help meet expenses Gene worked for the Bar Cross as a wrangler. He smoked cigarettes rolled from Blackwell's Genuine Bull Durham Tobacco. Each four ounce sack contained two coupons; four coupons bought any paperback title in Munro's Library of Popular Novels. The list included, among others, titles by Conan Doyle, Wilkie Collins, Alexandre Dumas, Robert Louis Stevenson, Jules Verne, and Anthony Trollope. It was probably at this time that Rhodes first discovered Stevenson's fiction, an author for whom he would always retain a special attachment.

The Santa Fe "Ring," a group headed by attorney Thomas B. Catron, had conspired to gain economic and political control of New Mexico Territory. W. G. Ritch, a "Ring" member, had been appointed acting governor under Lew Wallace during the final phase of the Lincoln County War. It was Ritch who had refused to pay Pat Garrett, then sheriff of Lincoln County, a $500 reward for capturing Billy the Kid and he tried to avoid payment again after the Kid broke jail and Garrett ambushed him at the Maxwell home at Fort Sumner. In 1887 Ritch filed a contest of Hinman Rhodes' homestead which precipitated a lengthy legal battle.

In 1888 the colonel's pension was raised to $25 a month and it was then that Gene approached him to borrow $50 so he might enter the University of the Pacific, a Methodist institution in San Jose, California. Just what influence the fact that Rhodes' family was Methodist may have had on Gene's selection of this school cannot be said with certitude, but he did attend for almost two years, earning the remainder of his expenses himself and confined, during the school year, to a diet consisting almost exclusively of oatmeal. His course work included Latin, Greek, geography, mathematics, mythology, and ancient history. Later when this became blended with his desultory reading over the years and was combined with his customary setting of New Mexico peopled by the men he had known there, the style of his fiction emerged, an aggregate so peculiar to him, a Westerner writing about the West in prose informed by classical references, snatches of poetry and homespun doggerel, a profound familiarity with the Bible and its splendid, fabulous imagery. Rhodes' first literary efforts occurred while he was an underclassman and were published in the school's newspaper. His earliest predilection was for poetry. In an autobiographical non-Western story, **"The Torch,"** published in 1908 in *Out West,* Rhodes had one of the characters express what must have been his own feelings about his college years. " 'I was there two years, the happiest of my life. Not one care, not one unhappy moment. I had attained my majority at thirteen. At least, I have done a man's work ever since. I had never known any boys. Just rough men. I had my youth in one deep, priceless draught.' "

Hinman Rhodes in 1889 entered his application for the position of agent at the Mescalero Indian reservation. This agency had been a central pawn in the Lincoln County War and the victors of that struggle, Catron, John H. Riley, and Colonel William L. Rynerson among them, had retained political control of valuable government subsidies such as the Mescalero beef contract. Catron, Riley, and Rynerson owned the Tularosa ranch adjacent to the agency and had customarily filled the beef contracts with inferior livestock. They opposed Hinman Rhodes' appointment and, once he had secured it and tried to institute

honest business practices at the agency, they sought his removal. In 1890 Hinman Rhodes lost his homestead contest with W. H. Ritch and in August, 1891, he lost his position at the agency. Gene, who had now returned from school, was so infuriated by this contretemps that he aligned his political sympathies with the Democratic machine which stood in opposition to the Republican "Ring." The leaders of the Democratic machine were Albert Bacon Fall and Oliver Milton Lee. Gene had first met the latter in 1885 when he had worked briefly for the Bar W near Carrizozo. When New Mexico achieved statehood in 1912, Fall changed parties, becoming a Republican so he could join Thomas B. Catron in the U.S. Senate. Fall later resigned his Senate seat to become Secretary of the Interior in the Harding Administration only to find himself embroiled in the Teapot Dome and Elk Hill scandals. He was accused, convicted, and finally sentenced to prison for accepting a bribe of $100,000 from the Sinclair Oil Company to allow clandestine oil exploration on federal and Indian lands. Despite all the evidence to the contrary, Gene remained convinced of Fall's innocence and "sided" him until the end.

Gene himself in late 1892 filed on a homestead, about six miles north of what had been his father's homestead, located in the bottom lands of what became known as Rhodes' Canyon. Here he built a two-room *jacal* and set up a large horse corral. There was a spring on this eighty acres and control of it, along with some illegal fencing, gave Gene possession of fifty sections of the Public Domain. He took care of the cattle owned by his parents and he worked at odd jobs to supplement his income, including bronc busting. Then he turned around and leased his ranch to the Bar Cross, three years while Cole Railston was ramrod, two while Carroll McCombs had the job. "Gene never claimed to be a top-hand," Railston said of him years afterward, "but he was an all-around good hand. I never knew him to carry a pistol. Next to cowboying and reading, he liked poker and a fight. He was not a trouble-maker, far from it, but no one stepped on his toes or rode his pet horse. I never knew a man to throw Gene in a wrestling match. He was a real good bronc rider."

In April, 1895, Bill Doolin entered New Mexico and the bad man hid out at Rhodes' ranch. He also managed to save Rhodes' life when Rhodes was in danger of being stomped to death by a wild horse. This episode inspired the basic plot of *The Trusty Knaves.*

The Rhodes family moved to Mesilla where Gene's brother, Clarence, walked three miles a day to the state college located at Las Cruces. Clarence earned $12.50 a month doing janitorial work at the college while attending classes in mining engineering. Gene, when he was in town, audited courses in English and history, but most of his time was spent in poker games, often with card sharps and they ended as frequently as not in bouts of fisticuffs.

Colonel Albert J. Fountain was a Santa Fe "Ring" Republican. He had been appointed Billy the Kid's defense attorney at his trial at Mesilla. Since the "Ring" wanted the Kid dead, the trial concluded with predictable results. In 1896, with A. B. Fall and Thomas B. Catron locked in a political contest to dominate the Territory, Oliver Milton

Lee and William McNew, two Fall cronies, were indicted for brand changing and cattle stealing. Fountain attended the court session at which these indictments were handed down. A. B. Fall ostensibly feared Fountain's political power. Shortly after the trial, Colonel Fountain and his nine-year-old son Henry disappeared in the area around White Sands. Lee was widely suspected of having been behind their murders. Governor W. T. Thornton, Catron's law partner during the time of the Lincoln County War, hired Pat Garrett to hunt down and capture Lee. Garrett's *modus operandi* in his manhunt for Billy the Kid had been to shoot from ambush and by this means he dispatched not only the Kid but also Tom O'Folliard and Charlie Bowdre who rode with the Kid. Chances were rather good that Lee would never be brought to trial. However, the case dragged on for two years and despite having had Garrett installed as sheriff of Doña Ana County in order to make any killing from ambush Garrett might do official and legal it seemed as if nothing was going to happen. McNew, to escape assassination, surrendered himself and was safely in custody at Las Cruces, outside Garrett's jurisdiction. In July, 1898, Garrett led a posse to ambush Lee and James Gililland. The latter had by now also been charged with the Fountain murders although no bodies had ever been found. Garrett and the posse opened fire on the building in which the fugitives were presumably asleep. But Lee and Gililland were able to turn the tables. Deputy Sheriff Kent Kearney was mortally wounded and Garret and the others, to their humiliation, were compelled to walk away with their hands held high in the air. Lee and Gililland then kept on the prod, seeking shelter occasionally at Rhodes' secluded ranch. Rhodes bunked with them much of the time except when he worked sporadically for Charles J. Graham whose ranch served as a listening post for Garrett's pursuit activities.

Clarence in the meantime graduated from college and secured employment as a mining engineer working in Old Mexico. The family sold the Mesilia home. Gene's mother and sister moved to Pasadena. Colonel Rhodes remained in New Mexico for another two years, living with friends and intermittantly with Gene at his ranch before he, too, went to California. In 1896 Gene had his first poem published in a commercial magazine, *Land of Sunshine* edited by C. F. Lummis. Henceforth, Gene continued to submit poems and Lummis continued to publish them.

The Lee and Gililland case persisted for another two and a half years before Rhodes negotiated their voluntary surrender to George Curry, then sheriff of Otero County. The county was named after Miguel A. Otero who had succeeded Thornton as territorial governor. Otero was at loggerheads with Catron and the "Ring" and it seemed an auspicious time to end the matter if Lee and Gililland could only avoid Garrett. During the Lincoln County War, Curry had backed Garrett's election as sheriff of Lincoln County. Billy the Kid had even spent a night at Curry's place without Curry's knowing who he was until after he had left. Later, Curry would join the Rough Riders. As would be the case with A. B. Fall, Curry switched parties from Democrat to Republican. This move permitted President Theodore Roosevelt to appoint Curry governor in 1907. It was from Curry a year later that Garrett,

down on his luck, would borrow $50 and he still had the check on his person when he was murdered from ambush. The surrender of Lee and Gililland proved a success even though Garret was himself on the same train as Rhodes and the two fugitives and recognized none of them.

Oliver Milton Lee was an expert cowman and a man who loved horses. He was fastidious in his dress and in his person; and he was wont to read the Greek and Latin classics in their original languages. Rhodes used him as the model for Kit Foy, a character in his short novel *The Desire of the Moth* (1920). In the novel Kit Foy is engaged to marry Stella Vorhis. However, Foy is framed for a murder by Matthew Lisner, a sheriff running for re-election. John Wesley Pringle, who had made his debut in Rhodes' first novel, *Good Men and True* (1910), saves the day by effectively scheming to have the sheriff exposed by his own men. When Kit and Stella are reunited at the end, Pringle, an old man, "bent and kissed her hands—lest, looking into his eyes, she should read in the book of his life one long, long chapter—that bore her name." *The Desire of the Moth* was serialized in *The Saturday Evening Post* in 1916 and it was filmed by Universal in 1917 with Monroe Salsbury cast as Kit Foy. Lest one might think that the crooked sheriff in the story was based on Pat Garrett, it must be noted that Rhodes made a hero of Garret, and by name, in a subsequent book, *Pasó por Aquí* (1927), which ran serially in the *Post* in 1926. And he went even further. In 1927 in response to the appearance of Walter Nobel Burns' *The Saga of Billy the Kid* (1926), Rhodes published an article in *Sunset* magazine titled **"In Defense of Pat Garrett."** In it he repeated the common belief that the Kid and Garrett had been on friendly terms during the Kid's rustling days and that the Kid never should have been sentenced to hang, "not unless they hanged several others at the same time." "I wonder if you can believe," he added, with regard to the Kid, "that my deepest feeling for him is pity for his hard fate?"

Billie Wilson was a young desperado who had been captured with Billy the Kid when Garrett and his posse ambushed the Kid at Stinking Springs, killing the unarmed Charlie Bowdre in the process. Wilson and the Kid were taken in shackles to the prison at Santa Fe. Wilson later escaped, making his way eventually to Texas where he married under an assumed name, started a family, and became a customs inspector near Langtry. When Garrett learned of Wilson's reform, he notified him that he would use his influence to gain for him a presidential pardon. Installed as sheriff of Doña Ana County during the Lee case, Garrett managed to entice Governor Thornton and other prominent New Mexicans to join him in securing a pardon which was granted by President Grover Cleveland.

Charles A. Siringo, a range detective who retired to write rather successfully about the Old West, became friends with Rhodes in later years. Rhodes even encouraged his publisher Houghton Mifflin to publish one of Siringo's books. Siringo happened to be in New Mexico at the time of Garrett's pursuit of the Kid and he included a highly imaginative account of the Kid's life and escapades in his early book, *A Texas Cowboy* (1885). For most of the details about the Kid, Siringo cribbed from the book Ash

Upson ghosted for Pat Garrett about the Kid's early years and his capture, escape, and death. Upson was an itinerant journalist and one of Garrett's cronies. However, Siringo did include one apocryphal anecdote about the Kid the origin of which seems to lie with him exclusively. "A man," he wrote, "now a highly respected citizen of White Oaks, was lying at the point of death in Fort Sumner, without friends or money, and a stranger, when the Kid, who had just come into town from one of his raids, went to his rescue, on hearing of his helpless condition; the sick man had been placed in an old out-house on a pile of sheep skins. The Kid hired a team and hauled him to Las Vegas, a distance of over a hundred miles, himself, where he could receive care and medical aid. He also paid the doctor and board bills for a month, besides putting a few dollars in money in the sick man's hand as he bid him good bye."

I do not believe there is a word of truth in this anecdote; but it is the kind of incident that particularly appealed to Rhodes' romantic sense of the Old West which had vanished, as did Garrett's action on behalf of Billie Wilson. Rhodes may have opposed Garrett in the Lee case, but he would never judge a man all of a piece. *Pasó por Aquí* is commonly considered to be Rhodes' finest Western story. In this judgment I cannot concur. For me, the principal charm of the story lies in the two long soliloquies given to the Mexican-American, Monte, whose border English would serve to inspire numerous other Western writers, not least of all Clarence E. Mulford who had created the Bar-20 saga and in his character El Toro in a different series of books was the most obvious in his imitation. For the basic plot of *Pasó por Aquí* Rhodes appears to have combined Siringo's anecdote about the Kid with the true incident of Billie Wilson's pardon. Ross McEwen, in Rhodes' story, holds up a bank in rather daring fashion and is pursued by a posse. He throws away the paper money rather than face capture. After changing horses, he finally is compelled to ride a steer for several miles before the steer, too, plays out. McEwen comes upon a Mexican-American family suffering from diphtheria and nurses it through the illness, even though this activity exposes him to arrest. Pat Garrett is among those who are on McEwen's trail and he is sufficiently impressed with what McEwen has done—he finds the Mexican-American family's rancho by means of McEwen's signal fire—that, although cognizant of McEwen's real identity, he manages to provide him with a safe-conduct out of the Territory.

I think James K. Folsom is correct in *The American Western Novel* (1966) when he views much of Rhodes' fiction, and *Pasó por Aquí* in particular, as nostalgia, "a lament for the old times." There is no conventional romance in this story, as there isn't in much that Rhodes wrote, but Rhodes did introduce an Eastern nurse into *Pasó por Aquí*, Jay Hollister, who works at the hospital at Alamogordo and who hates the West. She is not made to change her mind, neither through love for a cowboy nor because her Eastern values are found to be ineffectual. Instead, her values remain unassailable in the face of the Western values illustrated by McEwen, Garrett, and Monte. It is Monte's second soliloquy to the nurse which closes the story. " 'And thees fellow, too, thees redhead,' " he says of McEwen, " 'he pass this way, "pasó por aquí" . . . and

he mek here good and not weeked. But, before that—I am not God!' " " 'And him the sheriff !' " Nurse Hollister objects, realizing that Garrett has let a wanted man escape. " 'Why they could impeach him for that. They could throw him out of office.' " " 'But who weel tell?' " Monte responds. " 'We are all decent people.' "

Folsom in his critique of Rhodes recognized that Rhodes' *aficionados* have at times been too extravagant in their praise of his fiction, that there are manifest flaws which spoil much of his work. "At times," Folsom wrote, "when his adherence to the conventions of 'slick' writing trips him up, he can be one of the most maddening of writers. His stories are marred by an annoying coincidental quality in which someone invariably happens along just at the right moment to hear the villains plotting their crimes, which they do explicitly and at great length. . . . Even his often beautifully conceived dialogue deteriorates far too much into the tedious smartness which passes for wit among the devotees of the slick magazines. When Rhodes is at his best, however, these faults are only those of detail, which may mar but do not destroy the real quality of his fiction." Folsom saw, aptly, that Rhodes' major contribution to Western fiction was in his presentation of a cowboy hero, a man who "is both insightful and active" and with "a certain distrust of the forms by which less gifted mortals operate; for he believes that he is better able to resolve problems on his own than by the conventional methods used by ordinary men." *Pasó por Aquí* was not brought to the screen until almost two decades after Rhodes' death, titled *Four Faces West* (United Artists, 1948). It was produced by Harry Sherman, the man who had brought Clarence E. Mulford's Hopalong Cassidy to the screen portrayed by William Boyd. The formula of the cinematic Western had been too simplified by that time for a story of the subtle tensions between supposed Eastern and Western values to hold much interest for the audience. In fact, Sherman himself had once described his successful formula for Westerns in these terms: open big, forget the middle, and come to a furious finish. No story by Rhodes could be reshaped to embody that philosophy and *Pasó por Aquí,* as written, is ultimately unfilmable. (pp. 229-37)

In January, 1902, Rhodes had published his first short story in *Out West* magazine. Spurred on by financial desperation and encouraged by [his wife] May's unwavering belief in his ability as a storyteller, Rhodes published eight more stories in *Out West* that year and in 1903. These stories brought him to the attention of Henry Wallace Phillips whose Western stories featuring such characters as Red Saunders and Agamemnon Jones appeared regularly in such major magazines as *McClure's* and *The Saturday Evening Post.* Somehow Phillips was able to persuade Rhodes to send him raw material for plots, scenes, and characters and then Phillips would work the elements into stories which he would publish under his name and for which Rhodes received neither credit nor remuneration. Eventually, however, Phillips did agree to give Rhodes a co-author credit on several short stories published in *The Saturday Evening Post.* The collaboration may have taught Rhodes something about commercial writing for the slick magazines. It certainly did make his name familiar to the editors at the *Post* which was to remain the principal outlet for his fiction throughout his literary career.

Emerson Hough, who had once practiced law at White Oaks before returning East to write, hired Pat Garrett in 1904 to take him on a tour of various areas in New Mexico so he could gather material for a book he was working on, *The Story of the Outlaw* (1907). The two encountered Rhodes and Hough encouraged Gene to continue writing. Rhodes at the time would write out his stories in a scarcely legible longhand and then send them East for May to type. George Davison, his brother-in-law, would try to place the stories with a number of magazines. In a letter Rhodes wrote to George Davison in 1905, he told of having met Agnes Morley Cleaveland for the first time. She was already an established writer and her fiction was bringing her two cents a word. Rhodes expressed the hope that he might do as well. (pp. 239-40)

Rhodes' writing habits had become even more preposterous than had been those of Balzac. He first sketched out each story in his head, complete as to characters and sequence of incidents. Then, after this gestation period which might require months or even years, he began to write down the story, usually under the impetus of financial need, revising his longhand script repeatedly, until finally May would type it. Then he would revise the typescript going through as many as eleven drafts. Once the story was published, he would rewrite it again before moving on to a new story. The occurrence of a death in the family could incapacitate him for months, as happened in the case of his father and of Barbara [his daughter], but it might also happen after the death of even a casual acquaintance. During the day, Rhodes would both work his own farm and help out May's father on his farm. At night, he would write. As early as December, 1907, Rhodes reported to George Davison that he had earned $1,747 from writing stories that year and that he had spent all of it. "And again—to write stories one needs some ease—and *rest* when you are worn out. Otherwise," he lamented, "I can see my finish. . . . Tonight for instance, I am very tired. Can hardly write legibly. But I must write at night or not at all."

Agnes Morley Cleaveland had read some of Rhodes' stories in *Out West* magazine and it had been she who recommended him to her editor at *Munsey's,* Bob Davis. Davis liked Rhodes' fiction but he objected to what he felt—correctly—to be an essayist quality in much of it. Mrs. Cleaveland stopped to visit with Gene and his family on a trip East. She had not seen her own son, who was Alan's age, for the last six months. She perplexed May Rhodes upon leaving by saying, " 'My children will venerate me as one of the pioneer mothers.' "

Wayne Brazel shot Pat Garrett in the back on a lonely road in New Mexico in 1908 while Garrett was relieving himself. A. B. Fall assisted in Brazel's defense. Although Garrett had scarcely been in a position to threaten any one, Brazel was acquitted on the grounds of self-defense! Thanks to his new prominence as a consequence of his stories in the *Post,* many New Mexicans wrote to Rhodes, including Fall who commented in a letter that everyone had

been afraid that Garrett "was going to kill someone and a sigh of relief went up when he was finally killed."

As late as 1934, and despite *Pasó por Aquí* and his article in Garrett's defense Rhodes summed up his attitude toward the sometime lawman: "It is only fair to say that Garrett was a better man in Billy the Kid's time than in my day. Being made sheriff with the definite object of killing a man—for big pay—is not good for character. Neither is unlimited legend. He disintegrates."

In August, 1910, *Good Men and True* was published in a cloth edition by Henry Holt & Company. In October of that year, after reading the book himself, Holt sent Rhodes a personal letter. "You overflow with ideas to a very enviable extent," he observed, "and put more of them into your conversations than almost any human being but yourself would be able to do. Now what I want to take the liberty of doing, is to call your attention to the old saw— and there was never a sounder one—that *Art is selection,* which in your case of course would involve selecting the people from whom your wit and ideas should flow, and selecting from the ideas themselves only the best. You are to be envied and congratulated on your power in producing these good things, but if you give only the best, the total effect will be better than if you gave with great freedom, and your reputation of course will then be gauged by your best and not by your average." I do not think that Rhodes ever benefitted from this advice. He was convinced in his viscera that every Westerner was a complete individual, totally unlike another, except that his heroes were united by the code he projected into them. Easterners, by contrast, were conformists and tended to be too much alike to be interesting. Rhodes was also intent on making his villains engaging conversationalists. If there was one plot mechanism which most appealed to him, it was that of the detective story, and, although the reader might know the identity of the villain before most of the characters, much of the emphasis is on how the villain is discovered and his schemes exposed.

In 1913, May's father died and her mother moved in with them. This could not have been altogether pleasant for Gene. When the war broke out in Europe, Rhodes did not see the conflict as endangering the United States in any way and he had deep reservations about the colonial policies of both Germany and Great Britain. Once the *Lusitania* was sunk, however, . . . Gene lost his impartiality. He threw himself into farming with monomaniacal diligence, convinced that this, more than anything else he might do, would help achieve final victory. He wrote only one propaganda piece, for the Binghampton *Press,* and otherwise nothing at all. Even his letter writing diminished.

Gene was strickened with influenza in 1919. It was the first major organic illness of his fifty years. His heart became enlarged and his condition would continue to plague him for the rest of his life, finally bringing on his death. His asthma worsened. In November of that year, *The Saturday Evening Post* purchased the serial he had been at work on, *Stepsons of Light,* published as a book first in 1921. Dedicated to May Davison Rhodes, Gene felt this story to be his favorite. In a little Prologue to the cloth edition, Rhodes reflected that "today we dimly perceive that

the history of America is the story of the pioneer. . . .
They went West for food. What they did there was to
work; if you require a monument—take a good look." All
of Rhodes' optimism and his romantic attachment to his
vision of the West had at last found a voice. Basically,
Stepsons of Light is the story of how three greedy men kill
Adam Forbes to gain his gold claim and try to blame it
on Johnny Dines and how Johnny, triumphantly, through
the informality of a frontier court is able to prove his innocence and their guilt. The story is somewhat marred by the
interpolation of a long essay on realism and pessimism in
literature with Rhodes' position being made clear. "It is
the business of the realist to preach how man is mastered
by circumstances; it is the business of a man to prove that
he will be damned first." This sermon was unnecessary. It
is articulated by the action of the plot. Aunt Peg, a character in the story, feels that " 'the people who care for other
things more than they do for money are slowly crowded
out by the people who care more for money than for anything else.' " Rhodes' plot, however, contradicts this. It
demonstrates the moral superiority of the West in that
those who care most for money do *not* succeed. Yet, he
could not withhold an occasional critical observation
which was informed by that very realism which he condemned. "In Doña Ana County taxes were high and life
was cheap. Since the Civil War, Doña Ana had been be-
deviled by the rule of professional politicians."

Johnny Dines is no less chivalrous—or, perhaps, just plain
stupid is the word—than is Jeff Bransford in *The Little
Eohippus* (1912). Bransford breaks jail and escapes, pursued by a posse, rather than allow the heroine to soil herself by appearing in court and establishing his innocence.
Dines would rather lose his life than involve a woman in
his struggle. Such was Rhodes' romanticism. Even the victim, however, is given a eulogy. " 'He did many things
amiss,' " old Pete Harkey says of Adam Forbes; " 'he took
wrong turnings. But he was never too proud to turn back,
to admit a mistake, or to right his wrongdoing. He paid
for what he broke.' " The villains in *Stepsons of Light*
make the same mistake the villain Lake makes in *The Little Eohippus,* "of failing to reckon with the masterless
men, who dwell without the wall." Johnny Dines had
come to Jeff Bransford's aid in *The Little Eohippus.* Charlie See comes to Johnny's aid in *Stepsons of Light,* but, as
John Wesley Pringle before him, he must ride off at the
end, leaving Johnny and the heroine behind, "for at the
world's edge some must fare alone; through all their
dreams one unforgotten face—laughing, and dear, and
lost."

It would be a mistake, however, to think that most of
Rhodes' magazine serials ended with the heroine and the
hero embracing. Nothing could be further from the truth,
although Rhodes had it to his credit to be the first to publish a ranch romance in a slick magazine. Owen Wister
began the tradition of the ranch romance, this most formulary ingredient of what was to become the formulary
Western, in *The Virginian* (1902), but only the novel ends
in marriage; the parts of this novel which Wister published
first in magazines as short stories do not contain the romance. In Rhodes' first *Post* serial, *Good Men and True,*
Jeff Bransford is taken prisoner by the villain and there is
no heroine in the story. It wasn't until **"The Line of Least
Resistance"** was serialized in the *Post* in 1910 that Rhodes
introduced a romance as a unifying plot ingredient. **"The
Line of Least Resistance"** was never published in book
form, *The Desire of the Moth* continues the tradition, as
do *The Little Eohippus,* published in cloth in 1914 by
Henry Holt & Company under the title *Bransford in Arcadia, or The Little Eohippus,* and *Stepsons of Light.* But
in his best longer fiction, from *Pasó por Aquí* through *The
Trusty Knaves,* Rhodes eschews romance completely. Far
more important in all of his longer fictions, including even
the ranch romances, is the role played by friendship. **"The
Line of Least Resistance,"** for example, has the obligatory—for that time—"savage redskins" as its menace, but
what is enduring about it is neither the romance nor the
battle with the Indians, rather the friendship between Don
Kennedy and Hiram Yoast which brings the story to life
and sustains its interest. As Bret Harte and Owen Wister
before him, Rhodes used many of the same characters in
a number of stories of varying lengths. This applies not
only to major characters, such as Jeff Bransford and John
Wesley Pringle, but even minor ones, such as Spinal
Maginnis and Travis the dwarf who appear in *Stepsons of
Light* and return in *The Proud Sheriff* (1935) or the minor
villain, MacGregor, one of Bransford's jailers in *Good
Men and True,* who is the central character in the first of
the four long short stories which Rhodes rather ineptly
tried to weave together into a novel he titled *West Is West*
(1917).

The money which Rhodes realized from his sale of *Stepsons of Light* to the *Post* enabled him to purchase a train
ticket to Los Angeles where he hoped to spend Christmas
with his mother whom he had not seen since 1911. . . .
It had been Rhodes' original intention to spend six months
in California and then return to New Mexico for a visit
in preparation for writing another magazine serial. It was
not to be. His stay in California stretched out to three
years during which time he wrote virtually nothing, although he did sell several properties to motion picture
producing companies. As early as 1914 Universal had purchased *The Little Eohippus* and **"The Line of Least Resistance"** and had filmed them as two-reelers. I have already
mentioned that *The Desire of the Moth* was filmed in
1917. Now, with Rhodes in Hollywood, remake rights
were negotiated as well as new contracts. *Bransford in Arcadia; or, The Little Eohippus* (Universal-Eclair, 1914)
was remade as a feature film titled *Sure Fire* (Universal,
1921) directed by John Ford and starring Hoot Gibson.
The Desire of the Moth was remade as *The Wallop* (Universal, 1921) directed by John Ford with Harry Carey in
the lead, cast as John Wesley Pringle. Carey also starred
in *West Is West* (Universal, 1920) directed by Val Paul.
When Carey's contract with Universal expired, he signed
a new one with Robertson-Cole Productions and starred
in *Good Men and True* (Robertson-Cole, 1922) directed
by Val Paul who had followed him from Universal. The
same company also filmed *Stepsons of Light* under the
title *The Mysterious Witness* (Robertson-Cole, 1923) starring Robert Gordon with his character name changed
from Johnny Dines to Johnny Brant. (pp. 241-46)

[The mid-1920s] must have been particularly anguished

ones for Rhodes. In what he did write, he seems to have
been driven more than ever to protect his idealized view
of Westerners. He might have scraps of paper all over his
desk with notes scrawled on them, bits of story, incidents,
snatches of dialogue; he might have extremely detailed
maps of New Mexico which he could consult constantly
when describing topography in his fiction; but what
glowed inside of him was no longer mere memories of
what had been and the people he had known. Instead, his
fiction was now the product of a vision, of a way of life—
however much of it might in reality be imaginary—that
he desperately preferred to the life he was living and the
way of life with which he was surrounded.

As early as *The Little Eohippus,* Rhodes had included two
chapters in which Jeff Bransford, disguised as Tom West,
goes East to New York to continue his courtship of Ellinor
Hoffman. In *Copper Streak Trail* (1922) Pete Johnson, in
order to get to the bottom of the villainy which has resulted in his partner Stanley Mitchell's being imprisoned on
a fraudulent charge, has got to go East, to New York state,
where he encounters Mitchell's crooked cousin, a lawyer
named Oscar, Stanley's fiancée, the local schoolteacher,
and Stanley's rich Uncle McClintock who has disinherited
Stanley because he wants to marry the schoolteacher,
Mary Selden. In Arizona, Pete and Stanley have discovered a rich copper deposit, but it will need capital before
it can be worked effectively. C. Mayer Zurich, the rich and
unscrupulous storekeeper in Cobre, Arizona intends to
jump the claim. He has been in the employ of Oscar
Mitchell, making life difficult for Stanley, but Zurich is a
Western villain; the true polecats are the Easterners,
Oscar and his assistant, Joe Pelman. " 'Necessity doesn't
make me a crook,' " Pelman confesses to Oscar. " 'I'm
crooked by nature. I like crookedness. . . . That's why
I'm with you.' " Once matters have been settled in the
East, Johnson returns to Arizona. Stanley is released.
Joined by two loyal friends, Pete and Stanley head out to
protect their claim. Zurich and his men are in pursuit, intent on jumping it as soon as they are led to the spot by
the rightful owners. However, fate intervenes. Young
Bobby Carr, the ten-year-old son of the freighter working
for Pete and Stanley, has been lost while searching for
some horses and the four set out to find him. This leaves
the claim unattended, but, when they return, with Bobby
safe, all they find at the claim is a note insisting that it be
called the "Bobby Carr Mine" and in which Zurich and
his men inform Pete: "We did not know about the boy, or
we would have helped, of course. Only for him you had
beat us. So this squares that up!" Once Oscar tries to grab
the mine for himself, he is foiled by Zurich. Westerners
may be villains, but they are still decent human beings.
Rhodes' negative attitude toward the East is to be found
in his characters and what happens to them; in words, the
worst he permitted himself to say was that in Apalachin
"there are no traditions—and no ballads." In *Once in the
Saddle,* one of Rhodes' most poorly constructed stories,
Pliny Mullins wants to found a township in New Mexico
away from the unfair dealings of a capitalistic mine-owner
and human exploiter so that " 'them little kids I seen will
have homes and a white man's chance.' " When Malloch,
the mine-owner, questions Pliny about his motives, he
jeers: " 'Just principle? The square deal, the great tradi-

tion—all that sort of rot? High-minded redresser of
wrong, dispenser of justice?' " " 'Just that kind of rot exactly,' " Pliny tells him.

At this time Rhodes began corresponding with Walter
Prescott Webb. "Yes," Rhodes admitted in a letter to
Webb, "what you say about making my books hard to
read is probably quite true and, next to the fact that there
are few women in the yarns, explains why they don't sell."
He also insisted that, "while denounced as a weird romance, my yarns are founded solidly upon remembered
facts—not the action, often imaginary, but the people,
codes, traditions." His highest esteem he reserved for
Andy Adams, but he added to his list of truthtellers Will
James, Owen Wister, Peter B. Kyne, and even William
MacLeod Raine and Jackson Gregory, while he condemned Zane Grey, Charles Alden Seltzer, and Mulford
as the three worst writers of Western fiction.

More and more the ideas of code and tradition came to
preoccupy Rhodes. In a letter to Vincent Starrett he confessed that "I took real men for my models, yes, and by
heck I did a good job in showing them as they were. But
I *did not* write about other *real men within my knowledge*
whose lives were disgusting and shameful. I like a good
horse better than a balky horse or a runaway horse or a
man-killing horse—or a horse with the botts or blind stag-
gers. And I like a man who works and jokes and lends better than I do one who cheats at cards. To make it brief—
the best men I know are the most interesting to me—the
men who pay their debts—and they are the ones I write
about. Most people nowadays prefer to write about boot-
leggers and bootlickers." It is probably for this reason
that, given Rhodes' ambivalent attitude toward the real
Pat Garrett, when he made him a character in his short
novel it was an idealized image. The tone of Rhodes' letters during the last decade of his life, particularly those in
which he addressed Western fiction, indicates that increasingly for him the West, as he viewed it, constituted an alternative to the present reality. It was a preferable way of
life. "We knew only too many who were without charm
or interest," he observed. "But the silly ephemeral fashion
of the day gives acclaim only to stories about Minus People. Most of our successful novels are case histories of sick
souls—neither more nor less. I like Plus People." Western
fiction, for Rhodes, had become a refuge, a retreat, a philosophical and moral statement, even an *ideological* statement which is why his work was never able to rise above
the level of the historical romance. He was not interested
in the total reality embodied in a true historical reconstruction. (pp. 249-52)

Harrison Leusler, a field editor for Houghton Mifflin, persuaded Rhodes to write a book in collaboration with
Clement Hightower about the old days and the old timers
in New Mexico. Rhodes worked on and off on this book
until his death, at which time it was far from complete. In
fact, what little of it was publishable May incorporated in
her biography of her husband. Rhodes wrote a short story
for *The Saturday Evening Post,* **"Maid Most Dear,"** the
first fiction the magazine had published of his since 1926.
He also wrote five sets of verses. Included in the latter was
his long poem, **"The Hired Man on Horseback."** J. Frank

Dobie later commented on the poem in his *Guide to Life and Literature of the Southwest* (1952) that it is imbued with a "passionate fidelity to his own decent kind of men, with power to ennoble the reader, and with the form necessary to all beautiful composition. This is the sole and solitary piece of poetry to be found in all the myriads of rhymes classed as 'cowboy poetry.' " The serial on which Rhodes was at work was *The Trusty Knaves* and he persisted working and reworking, writing and rewriting from July, 1930 until February, 1931. The *Post* bought it for $7,500. Gene and May could now afford to move to California.

H. H. Knibbs had never really been a Westerner. Much of what he felt to be true about the West, he had learned from Rhodes. In *Partners of Chance,* he remarked that "in direct and effectual kindliness, without obviously expressed sympathy, the Westerner is peculiarly supreme." Now *son maître* expressed the same sentiment in *The Trusty Knaves,* only far more eloquently. "A thousand handsomely printed books have said, not casually, but shrieking and beating their breasts, that life in the Western half of the United States has been all sodden misery, drab and coarse and low. . . . If these books tell the truth, then any and all my stories are shameless lies. What I remember is generosity, laughter, courage, and kindness. Kindness most of all; kindness from evil men and worthless men, as well as from good men." At the center of this novel is the town of Target, rather obviously a surrogate for Engle. The Establishment, consisting of a lawyer, a judge, a sheriff, a town marshal, and an unsuccessful rancher and his men decide to rob the bank. Bill Hawkins, who is actually the outlaw Bill Doolin, has staked out the bank for himself; but, when he learns of the plan of the town's leading citizens to rob it, he sets about to thwart the attempt. There is no violence in the story. It can almost be called a comedy with dramatic overtones, a comedy of Western manners. Rhodes deplored the apathy of really good men who " 'never do much of anything—not when it's risky. . . . Always fussing about the rules, stopping for Sunday and advice of counsel. Then, they foster a brutal prejudice against guessing, good men do. Worst of all, they wonder does it pay. That's fatal—that last.' " Rhodes obviously agreed with Jumbo Wilkins, a character in William MacLeod Raine's *Oh, You Tex* (1920), who believes that in the West a man makes his own luck. " 'Some folks are born with two strikes against them. . . . That's nonsense,' " one of Rhodes' characters reflects in *The Trusty Knaves.* " 'That's doin' the baby act. It's not luck; it's the man. Every time.' " Perhaps what I personally like so much about Rhodes' fiction are his sentiments. During his lifetime, among a select coterie of readers and critics, Rhodes was regarded as the doyen of authors of Western fiction. Yet, why was he not commercially more successful? Ira Kent of Houghton Mifflin put the matter rather succinctly in a letter written in 1927. "You have been urgent with us in the matter of getting your work to market," he told Rhodes. "Now I propose to be a little urgent with you about that part of the work that must precede sales, namely, the writing of books. A fairly even flow of production is one of the greatest aids in building up the market for an author. Your books have come too infrequently and at too long intervals."

California, as Rhodes saw it, was only to be a respite from the winds and dust of New Mexico. He intended to live part of the year in California and part in New Mexico. The home in Palm Beach, between La Jolla and San Diego, was gray in color with a eucalyptus tree spread over it and a western exposure to the rolling surf. It was purchased on a Trust Deed, with no money down and monthly installments of $18.53, including interest. What Rhodes did there was to work; he worked harder and, I think, more concentratedly than he had at any time in his life. He wrote letters and he wrote on the old timers book and he wrote fiction. *Beyond the Desert* (1934) and *The Proud Sheriff* came out of these years, albeit the latter was too short to be published as a book until H. H. Knibbs agreed to write a long introduction to flesh it out to the required length.

Rhodes continued to spend money easily. Although the country was in the grip of the Depression, Rhodes at least earned enough to get by; but as always he was improvident. When he sent *Beyond the Desert* off to the *Post* and the *Post* rejected it, regarding it as overwritten and the pace too leisurely, Rhodes wired back that the editors could revamp the story any way that was wanted, only he had to have money. The *Post* sent him a hundred dollars. The story was cut by a fourth before the *Post* would publish it. *The Proud Sheriff* encountered similar editorial obstacles and is also thinly plotted. In it, young Otey Beach is framed for a murder he did not commit and Sheriff Spinal Maginnis sets about to find the true culprit. *Beyond the Desert* is the story of three conspirators who want to seize Bud Copeland's ranch because it has the only useable water on it that the railroad needs in order to build a spur line. The villains prove no match for the imposing good and decent men who join with Bud to save his spread. Sam Travis, Rhodes' good-hearted dwarf is probably the most memorable character in *The Proud Sheriff.* In *Beyond the Desert* that distinction goes to Lithpin Tham, a man of questionable past who joins with the decent men and about whom it is remarked that "fanciful fellows, one or two, had been troubled, once or twice, with an uneasy guess that but for this ludicrous handicap of speech, better folk might have been kinder to Sam Clark, and that life as Sam Clark might have been different, and easier, than life as Lithpin Tham." It was an imperfection about which Rhodes could write from first-hand knowledge. Notwithstanding, this was not the way Western fiction was currently being written for the slick magazines where the emphasis was increasingly on violence and action.

"I would have you note that no man is killed in *The Trusty Knaves,*" Rhodes wrote to Bernard DeVoto in 1933. "I lived like that for twenty-five years—among folks who would shoot if forced to, but who would rather laugh." Rhodes went so far as to refuse an opportunity to review Eugene Cunningham's *Buckaroo* (1933), a copy of which was sent to him by Houghton Mifflin which was also Cunningham's publisher. Rhodes claimed his reason for demurring was that he was not paid for writing reviews. In 1934 he even wrote in a letter to Cunningham that he could not really judge his novel. I suspect the real reason for Rhodes' reticence was that Cunningham was one of the originators of the *Blut und Boden* school of Western fiction—300 characters are killed off in the course of *Buckaroo*—and this, doubtless, offended Rhodes' sensibility at the same time as it reminded him of how out of joint he had become with the times. (pp. 253-56)

"While the incidents of Gene Rhodes' life were as vividly realistic as those of any modern novel," H. H. Knibbs said of him [introduction to *The Proud Sheriff*] "intellectually and at heart he was a romantic." Rhodes usually chose for his villains the kinds of men who, historically, did exploit the West, in Bernard DeVoto's words "the speculators, the bankers and manipulators, the mortgagees and monopolists, all the operators of the machinery by which the East systematically plundered its captive province . . . " ["The Novelist of the Cattle Kingdom," in *The Hired Man on Horseback*]. Rhodes' heroines may be impossible and his heroes often too good to be true and his plots too contrived; yet he did portray outlawry accurately as disorganized class struggle, men in their confusion trying to survive among all the land-grabbers and Eastern capitalists preying upon them. This was the very soul of his literary vision, this and those unforgettable characters with a snatch of doggerel or poetry on their lips, men who laugh a lot. He wrote romantic Western fiction for an ideological reason: he wanted to prove something to his readers. In the end, all an author can give you is himself. With Rhodes, as with his characters, you either like him at once, or you do not. There does not seem to be a middle path. (pp. 256-57)

> *Jon Tuska, "Eugene Manlove Rhodes: An Appreciation," in his* A Variable Harvest: Essays and Reviews of Film and Literature, *McFarland & Company, Inc., Publishers, 1990, pp. 227-57.*

FURTHER READING

Criticism

Busby, Mark. "Eugene Manlove Rhodes: Ken Kesey Passed by Here." *Western American Literature* XV, No. 2 (Summer 1980): 83-92.
> Examines the influence of Rhodes's *Pasó por Aquí* on Ken Kesey's *One Flew over the Cuckoo's Nest.*

DeVoto, Bernard. "Introduction: The Novelist of the Cattle Kingdom." In *The Hired Man on Horseback: My Story of Eugene Manlove Rhodes,* by May Davison Rhodes, pp. xix-xliv. Boston: Houghton Mifflin, 1938.
> Praises Rhodes's storytelling ability.

———. "Costume Piece: Horizon Land." In his *Minority Report,* pp. 284-87. Boston: Little, Brown, 1940.
> Urges reevaluation of Rhodes's fiction, asserting that "his work was true to the life of the cattle kingdom, he was an artist in prose, and he portrayed both the reality and the romance of that brief era with a fidelity that only a few have ever tried to maintain and only he succeeded in maintaining."

Dobie, J. Frank. "A Salute to Gene Rhodes." In *The Best Novels and Stories of Eugene Manlove Rhodes,* edited by Frank V. Dearing, pp. xi-xxii. Boston: Houghton Mifflin, 1949.
> Anecdotal sketch of Rhodes with brief critical information on his fiction.

Fife, Jim L. "Two Views of the American West." *Western American Literature* I, No. 1 (Spring 1966): 34-43.
> Compares the disparate depictions of the American West by Rhodes and Sinclair Lewis.

Hutchinson, W. H. "I Pay for What I Break." *Western American Literature* I, No. 2 (Summer 1966): 91-6.
> Surveys biographical elements in Rhodes's fiction.

———. "The West of Eugene Manlove Rhodes." *Arizona and the West* 9, No. 3 (Autumn 1967): 211-18.
> Praises verisimilitude in Rhodes's fiction.

Keleher, William A. "Writing Men." In his *The Fabulous Frontier: Twelve New Mexico Items,* pp. 119-54. Santa Fe, N. Mex.: Rydal Press, 1945.
> Biographical information regarding Rhodes's life in New Mexico.

Knibbs, Henry Herbert. Introduction to *The Proud Sheriff,* by Eugene Manlove Rhodes, pp. xxi-lvi. Norman: University of Oklahoma Press, 1968.
> Anecdotal introduction to novel. Knibbs discusses Rhodes's approach to fiction.

Powell, Lawrence Clark. "Pasó por Aquí: Eugene Manlove Rhodes." In his *Southwest Classics: The Creative Literature of the Arid Lands, Essays on the Books and Their Writers,* pp. 161-74. Los Angeles: Ward Ritchie Press, 1974.
> Biographical and critical essay on Rhodes.

Rabindranath Tagore

1861-1941

(Pseudonym of Sir Ravīndranāth Thākura; also transliterated as Ravīndranátha, Rabindra Nath) Indian poet, playwright, novelist, short story writer, essayist, and philosopher.

INTRODUCTION

Tagore is one of modern India's most famous and highly regarded authors. Astonishingly prolific in a variety of genres, he achieved his greatest renown as a lyric poet. His poetry is imbued with a deeply spiritual and devotional quality bordering on mysticism, while in his novels, plays, short stories, and essays, his social and moral concerns predominate.

Tagore was born into an upper-caste Hindu family and raised on their estate in Calcutta. He began his education at the age of five under private tutors, and started writing poetry when he was eight years old. In 1878 Tagore made his first trip to England to attend schools and universities in Brighton and London. During this period he read extensively in English and European literature. In 1890 Tagore was placed in charge of the family estates, and daily contact with peasants and farmers aroused his empathy for the misery and squalor of India's poor. During the ensuing decades Tagore remained a conscientious and vocal proponent of agricultural and educational reform. In 1901 Tagore founded a school at his retreat at Santiniketan. He devoted this institution to the intellectual freedom of the individual and modeled it after the *tapovana,* or "forest schools" of ancient India. Santiniketan later developed into an international university called Visva-Bharati ("Universal Wisdom").

In 1912 Tagore embarked on a tour of England and the United States, making the acquaintance of Ezra Pound, W. B. Yeats, George Bernard Shaw, and other artists and intellectuals. The publication in English of *Gitanjali* in 1912, with an adulatory preface by Yeats, made Tagore famous in Europe and America, and the following year he was awarded the Nobel Prize for literature. After the First World War, Tagore joined Shaw, Bertrand Russell, and other advocates of pacifism in denouncing the destructive nationalism practiced by many of Europe's leaders. With the rise of fascism in the 1920s and 1930s and the continuing struggle in India against British control, Tagore remained a frequent and outspoken champion of individual freedom, democracy, and internationalism. He died in 1941.

Many critics consider Tagore's artistic maturity to date from the early 1880s. *Prabhat sangit,* published in 1883, reflects Tagore's discovery of the wellsprings of his lyricism in a mystical encounter with God and nature. In the

years leading up to the First World War, his poetry became increasingly mystical, religious, and philosophical in its concerns. Tagore's expression of a personal communion with a supreme deity who inspires his praise and devotion culminated in *Gitanjali* (*Song Offerings*). In the poetry of Tagore's final years, he gave rein to formal experimentation, producing prose poems and terse lyrics on predominately religious and philosophical themes.

Tagore's novels include *Naukhadubi* (*The Wreck*), *Gora,* and *Ghare-bhaire* (*The Home and the World*). While they are mostly conventional in style and plotting, dealing frequently with crossed romances and improbable coincidences of fate, his novels are considered effective in dramatizing the moral conflicts between tradition and modernity in colonial India. Tagore's short stories similarly rely on conspicuous plotting devices for their effect, and often depict supernatural events from a psychological perspective, heightening the tension between fantastic and realistic modes of perception.

Critics of Tagore's works are nearly unanimous in designating him as one of the preeminent lyric poets of the twentieth century. An assiduous student of classical Sanskrit, Bengali, and European literatures, Tagore passionately affirmed his Indian heritage and identity, yet repudiated nationalism and asserted his devotion to a universal divinity. While some critics feel that Tagore's prodigious output is uneven in its artistic value, his very prolificacy is often considered a measure of his creative achievement.

PRINCIPAL WORKS

Kavi-kahini (poetry) 1878
Sandhya sangit (poetry) 1882
Prabhat sangit (poetry) 1883
Kari o komal (poetry) 1886
Manasi (poetry) 1890
Sonar tari (poetry) 1894
Chitra (poetry) 1896
Naivedya (poetry) 1901
Kheya (poetry) 1906
Naukhadubi (novel) 1906
  [*The Wreck,* 1923]
Gitanjali (poetry) 1910
  [*Song Offerings,* 1912]
Gora (novel) 1910
  [*Gora,* 1924]
Raja (drama) 1910
  [*The King of the Dark Chamber,* 1914]
Dakghar (drama) 1912
  [*The Post Office,* 1914]
The Crescent Moon (poetry) 1913
Balaka (poetry) 1916
  [*A Flight of Swans* (partial translation), 1955]
Fruit-Gathering (poetry) 1916
Ghare-baire (novel) 1916
  [*The Home and the World,* 1919]
The Hungry Stones, and Other Stories (short stories) 1916
Sacrifice, and Other Plays (dramas) 1917
"Lover's Gift" and "Crossing" (poetry) 1918
Mashi, and Other Stories (short stories) 1918
Palataka (poetry) 1918
The Fugitive, and Other Poems (poetry) 1919
Lipika (prose poems, allegories, and short stories) 1922
  [*Lipika,* 1969]
Broken Ties, and Other Stories (short stories) 1925
Puravi (poetry) 1925
  [*Poems from "Puravi"* (partial translation), 1960]
Fireflies (poetry) 1928
Mahua (poetry) 1929
  [*The Herald of Spring* (partial translation), 1957]
Sesher kavita (novel) 1929
  [*Farewell, My Friend,* 1949]
The Child (poetry) 1931
The Golden Boat (poetry, prose poems, allegories, and short stories) 1932
Punascha (poetry) 1932
Char adhyaya (novel) 1934
  [*Four Chapters,* 1950]

Patraput (poetry) 1935
Shesh saptak (poetry) 1935
**Prantik* (poetry) 1938
**Arogya* (poetry) 1940
**Rogashajyaya* (poetry) 1940
Janmadine (poetry) 1941
**Sesh lekha* (poetry) 1941
  [*Tagore's Last Poems,* 1972]
The Parrot's Training, and Other Stories (satire and short stories) 1944
The Runaway, and Other Stories (short stories) 1959
Rabindra-racanabali. 27 vols. (poetry, dramas, novels, short stories, and essays) 1964-66

*These works were translated and published as *Wings of Death* in 1966.

CRITICISM

Buddhadeva Bose   (essay date 1948)

[*An Indian critic and educator, Bose was associated early in his career with the authors of the* kallol *movement, who attacked the traditionalist tendencies of Bengali literature. He was the editor of the influential poetry review* Kavita *from 1935 to 1961. In the following essay, Bose praises Tagore's works.*]

Rabindranath Tagore is a phenomenon. If Nature, manifest in the even light of the sun, forsook the forms of fields and hills and trees, and flowered in words, that, indeed, were he. There has not been a greater literary force, or a greater force, a force like Nature's, expressing itself in literature.

This sounds fantastic, but is true. I do not mean that he is the greatest writer or poet in my experience, or even the greatest modern. If I had not read Shakespeare, I would not have known to what extreme heights (and depths) the spirit of man can travel. If I had not read Yeats, I would have been left with only an imperfect notion of the capacity of the lyric: knowing him, I have known the uttermost meaning that a poem of twenty words may contain. What I am thinking of as Rabindranath's unique merit is his quantity, his immense range, his fabulous variety. It would be trite to call him versatile; to call him prolific very nearly funny. The point is not that his writings run into a hundred thousand pages of print, covering every form and aspect of literature, though this matters: he is a source, a waterfall, flowing out in a hundred streams, a hundred rhythms, incessantly. Yet in his boyhood or youth he displayed no prodigious talents, no revolutionary fire; he obeyed conventions and followed his elders; he was rather slow, rather dim and timid. If he had died at Keats's age, he would have been a minor poet of the anthologies, taking his turn with twenty others; at Shelley's, a fascinating figure whom poets and scholars would be constantly 'discovering'; if his life had closed at fifty, or seventy even, he would not have meant to us as much as he does. His death, at eighty, has been premature, for he was still changing, still growing. Throughout his life, he has grown like some great tree, slowly, imperceptibly, with gentle passivity. A tree meant to live for centuries; tangled, interwoven, deep-rooted, drinking the life of the earth and the sun; complicated in details, but totally simple. Destiny had planned his life well: unlike Wordsworth, or even Browning or Tennyson, he grew greater with each furrow on his face: it was necessary for him, as for Yeats, to live long. If Yeats had not lived to be seventy-five, or Rabindranath to be eighty, some of the most beautiful poetry of our epoch would have remained unwritten, and two of its greatest poets unfulfilled.

Rabindranath is our Chaucer and Shakespeare, our Dryden, and our equivalent of the English translators of the Bible. To describe him in terms of English literature, one must name quite a number of authors, for he compresses in one man's lifetime the development of several centuries. He has created language, both prose and verse. The range of his verse technique will carry us from Wyatt and Surrey, across Spenser, Marlowe, Dryden, Shelley and Swinburne, right up to the early Ezra Pound. He is possessed by the lyric; but among his momentous works are narrative verse and verse dramas; his ballads excel Scott's; his child poems, more abundant than Blake's, blend Blake's innocence with an almost sophisticated humour. Sly, shy, like Chaucer's, this humour runs through his work in an arterial flow; this and his great lyric gift are the two moulders of his prose. His extent of development in prose is even greater than in verse: from Bankimchandra's stiff formalism to the diamond depths of Rabindranath's later prose—the way is so long and so hard that we never cease to marvel he could traverse it all. In the last phase, his verse became like prose, not in Byron's sense, but T. S. Eliot's; and his prose became the same as poetry. He is the only instance where the greatest poet of a country is thought by some greater in prose. He has brought us the short story when it was hardly known in England, and introduced the psychological novel; his two prose comedies, early-Shakespearean in temper, are yet without a third; his criticism is profuse and fundamental, his satire occasional and brilliant. His sermons are prose poems, his controversy is Marvell's garden where we must tread on flowers; his travel-diaries are rich in both observation and contemplation. He has created a new form of the prose play; has written on philosophy, education, politics, science; on prosody, music and the peasantry; on every question of the day. Among his best works are his autobiographies and certain collections of letters; he is the author of the best Bengali Primer. This list is long, but not without omissions. He has done all, all that can be done with the written word. And all these are parts of, and contribute to, an inner harmony which his variety or his abundance never disturbs. His verse and prose, his fiction, drama and song, his poetry and his humour are mutually linked and dependent; one is beautiful with the other's aid; his greatness is the greatness of the whole. In many of these different branches, perhaps, and certainly in some, others have surpassed him; but he has no equal in this immense process of ramification and unification, this vastness, this vast

completeness. Rabindranath is the world's most complete writer.

I am aware that all this may seem confusing to those readers of the East and West who know him by the English *Gitanjali*. *Gitanjali* has been rightly praised by the world: it is the quintessence of Rabindranath and a miracle of translation. The miracle is not that so much has survived; but the poems are re-born in the process, the flowers bloom anew on a foreign soil. Denuded of the sensuous metrical arrangements of the original and the more than Swinburnian rhymes, they are more quiet in the English, more docile, the surrender more utter. The Song Offerings are more of song in the original and more of an offering in the English. We in Bengal find in the English a strange freshness, a beauty not as ours; we, who are steeped in the Bengali, are newly moved by certain passages, as if the original did not exist. There are moments when the translation surpasses the original, such as the passage Ezra Pound thought 'like some pure Hellenic':

> There comes the morning with the golden basket
> in her right hand bearing the wreath of beauty,
> silently to crown the earth.

In Bengali this is:

> Shéthā ushā dān hāté dhori shvarna-thālā
> Niyé āshé ekkhāni mādhuryer mālā
> Nirabé parāyé dité dharār lalāté.

I shall attempt a literal translation to show the difference:

> There dawn, holding a golden plate in her right
> hand, brings a garland of sweetness, silently to
> place it on the forehead of the earth.

The advantages of the English are obvious. 'Basket' is a better visual image than the 'garland on the plate' of Hindu ritual; 'right hand' sounds better than 'dān hāt', and the compression of the English is admirable. The original is loose-knit, weakened by 'poetic diction'; it has never struck a Bengali reader as remarkable.

There is another, a converse, and a more severe test. I have felt that 'minor' poems translate well; but great poetry is obstinate. One of the great lines quoted by Arnold, Dante's 'in His will lies our peace', does not, in the English, correspond to Arnold's estimation of it. A good many pages of the *Oxford Book of Greek Verse in Translation* are dull. We have not yet in Bengali (a sorry thing to say) any adequate translation of Kalidasa; and Satyendranath Datta, one of our ablest craftsmen in verse, himself turned 'The Indian Serenade' and 'La Belle Dame Sans Merci' into childish babble. We have, however, very good translations from Heine, Hugo, Stevenson, D. H. Lawrence, from Noguchi and the Chinese Anthology. Our poet-translators have persuaded even the difficult Eliot, but discreetly left alone the crystal clearness of Yeats. It is said that Sister Nivedita tried for three days to translate a single line from Rabindranath—'Nishidin bharshā rākhish, oré mon habei habé'—and gave up the job in despair; that a similar despair came to Rabindranath with Chandidasa's famous line—'Chālé neel shāri ningāri ningāri parāna shahita mor'. How, then, did it go with his own great lines? A poem we all think one of his most beautiful, how has it fared in English?

> Aji srāvana-ghana gahana-mohé
> Gopana taba charana phélé,
> Nishār mato nirab, ohé,
> Shabār dithi erāye élé.
> Prabhāt āji mudéchhé ānkhi,
> Bātāsh brithā jétéchhé dāki,
> Nilāj neel ākāsh dhāki
> Nibir megh ké dilo mélé.
>
> Kujanaheen kānanabhumi
> Duār deoyā shakal gharé,
> Ekélā kon pathik tumi
> Pathikheen pathér paré.
> Hé akā shakhā, hé priyatama,
> Royéchhé kholā é ghar mama,
> Shamukh diyé shvapana-shama
> Jéyo nā moré halāy thélé.

A little poem of two stanzas, four parts, corresponding to the four divisions of our music; haunting in metre, rhyme and alliteration; a perfect lyric. We should have thought it untranslatable, like Shakespeare's songs; but here is the English:

> In the deep shadows of the rainy July, with secret steps, thou walkest, silent as night, eluding all watchers.
> Today the morning has closed its eyes, heedless of the insistent calls of the loud east wind, and a thick evil has been drawn over the ever-wakeful blue sky.
> The woodlands have hushed their songs, and doors are all shut at every house. Thou art the solitary wayfarer in this deserted street. Oh my only friend, my best beloved, the gates are open in my house—do not pass by like a dream.

The translation is almost literal. Only, 'sravāna-ghana gahana-mohé'—'in the deep dark enchantment of July'—is suitably simplified; 'the futile calls of the wind' becomes 'the insistent calls of the loud east wind', the 'immodest blue sky' becomes 'ever-wakeful' (for the associations of our 'modesty'—'lajjā'—can be conveyed by no English word); and the 'spreading heavy clouds' change to 'a thick veil', for 'cloud' begets quite different images in Bengal and England. (Which poet, thinking of the magnificent rain of a Bengal July, would write 'I wandered lonely as a cloud' or even 'I bring fresh showers for thirsting flowers'!) Deviations from the original are small, as if the poem never suffered the grill of translation, but came straight from the poet's heart. My mind hums with the Bengali, and yet, as I copy out the English words, I tremble to their subtler rhythm. *Gitanjali* is more than a great work in English; it is the work of a great English poet.

Rabindranath, when he started translating from his own work to beguile a convalescence, had published at least fifty volumes in verse and prose. Was it by accident or design that he chose the poems he did? Did he review his entire work before making up his mind, or was he simply guided by the fact that those songs were then his latest? We have no means to ascertain. The choice was far from easy, but, whether deliberate or haphazard, wise. The *Gitanjali* group of poems are such as would translate beautifully or not at all. Being, in the main, songs, they are short, simple and as much disembodied as written words can be. The language is plain; the terms universal; nothing 'local' stands in the way. These, if one can judge by the translations themselves, are also the qualities of the classical poetry of China; at any rate, it seems more fresh, more free in translation than the poetry of any other country. *Gitanjali,* over and above these intrinsic advantages, had the great and rare luck of the translator's being the author himself, an author who had already worked in words for well over thirty years. It was destined to a miraculous transformation.

Similar felicity attended **The Crescent Moon, The Post Office** and one or two others. After a time, however, the translations did not seem to go so well. Perhaps, in the poems, the lack of metre, of technical variety, began to tell at last; I think the situation was somewhat like Whitman's, where the sameness of the prose rhythm makes the poems look repetitive. And his prose fiction definitely palled. The anti-climax to Yeats's Introduction came from E. M. Forster who, with a somewhat youthful iconoclasm, summed up **The Home and the World** as 'a boarding-house flirtation that masks itself in mystic or patriotic talk', Sandip 'a West Kensingtonian Babu', 'amorous and amoral', and the action leading 'to the death of another Babu, who was chivalrous and young'. Finally, Forster found in the book a 'strain of vulgarity'; and we rather wonder whether, while writing this review, he had allowed himself to be infected.

But we should not be as hasty in blaming Forster as he was in his remarks. Rabindranath's fiction suffers terribly in English. He did not translate himself, and there were no Garnetts for him. Selection was often wrong. In particular, it is hard to conceive **Ghare-Baire** attractive in English, and **The Home and the World,** such as it is, need not have appeared. It is luxuriant even in Bengali, and even for Rabindranath. It has 'that lusciousness, that over-profusion' of 'South Oriental work' from which Pound was happy to find **Gitanjali** free. Bengali can bear this to a great extent; a little of it will suffocate English. We have to remember that Rabindranath is the most metaphorical writer in a highly metaphorical language. He thinks in metaphors; he argues in similes. Bengali is partial to this habit of thought; but English, in spite of Shelley and Swinburne, is different; it is a level language, moving in logical sequences; *Gitanjali* itself had to be modified and modulated to suit its character. Rabindranath's fiction, needing much more of this 'treatment', has been left untended. We hold him great in fiction, specially the short story, and a certain quantity of it, properly presented, could make friends everywhere in the world. But wrong books, wrongly served, have eclipsed him.

Edward Thompson, so far the only reliable European writer on Bengali literature, was, in his last years, sadly conscious of Rabindranath's decline in the West. In a letter quoted by William Rothenstein in his autobiography, Thompson, melancholy and apologetic, tries to explain the situation: 'Tagore has been unlucky in this—so far as the *English* influence on his work goes he belongs to the

Tennysonian age, but he has the misfortune to come up for judgment by the age of T. S. Eliot and Aldous Huxley. He won't get justice now—nothing could get him justice. . . . A literature in which every poet was like T. S. Eliot and every novelist like E. M. Forster would be fairly arid. We do need less narrow canons of criticism.' Thompson's words are not as well chosen as well meaning. A writer of one age *must* come up for judgment by another, and take his chance with the changes in the literary atmosphere. Shakespeare must be judged by Dryden, Donne by Johnson, Swinburne by Eliot. And it is good, indeed necessary, that it is so; for the criticism of each age is a kind of renewal for old authors. We do not look upon a writer as belonging to a single age, and that his own; he must have something valid for all times, if he is valid at all. There is a certain unavoidable repulsion for our immediate predecessors; our ancestors are more interesting than our parents, two centuries easier to cross than fifty years. The aversion to Rabindranath which, at the moment, we notice also in Bengal, is merely a symptom of the times. But the times flow incessantly, and Time never stops, so that a symptom will begin to disappear almost as soon as we discern it. Thompson's 'age of Eliot and Huxley' is already a thing of the past; he was thinking of *The Waste Land* and perhaps *Antic Hay,* whereas now we are faced with *Four Quartets* and *The Perennial Philosophy.* The time seems to be approaching when Rabindranath will finally take his place in the literature of the world. He will certainly begin to be re-read; possibly he will be translated anew. Perhaps he will meet his Garnetts, after all.

Rabindranath cannot be appraised except in the whole. To see him as he is, all he is and means, his great range, his unequalled variety, one must read at least one prose comedy, one verse drama, certain essays and travel-books, two or three symbolical plays, some twenty tales and short novels and five hundred poems or so. I say this with an eye on those who cannot read him except in translation, and hope this introduction will stimulate some of them to learn his tongue so as to read him in the original, more of him and more in him.

The selection, to be only barely representative, should include much that has not yet appeared in English, or appeared in a defective form. As Shakespeare cannot be measured only by *As You Like It,* or *Hamlet,* or the *Sonnets,* though his essence is in all three, so Rabindranath cannot be gauged only by *Gitanjali* or *The Post Office* or *The Religion of Man.* He can be judged by these, or any of these, for in India we say that the drop contains the ocean; judged, but not gauged. In Bengal we have no special place for *Gitanjali;* to us it is in no sense his best or most significant work; it is a great book, one of his great books, one of the fifty, perhaps, we are for ever reading. We hold our breath as we follow his amazing development; book after book, at times five or six in a year, each distinct from its predecessor, new in form and content. One manner, one mood, one kind of music has not held him long; none of his successes has enthralled him; he has been outgrowing himself every day of his life. Repetition there must be in one whose quantity is so vast, repetition on the surface and down in the depths: he turns a story to a play, a verse tale to a dance drama; he writes the same story twice, the same

poem in verse and in prose, composes the same song four or five times, and these at uncertain intervals, now of hours, now of years. But 'same' is hardly the word here, for each repetition is a revision, and each revision a rebirth, for each wears a new beauty. He has repeated himself as all great writers do, realizing a vision in work after work, revealing what Henry James called 'the figure in the carpet', a pattern of continuous thought already existing in the mind, but not seen till the end. We say about him what in the **'Tajmahal'** poem he says of Shah-Jahan: ever he left behind his deeds, being greater than all of them. The cry of *Balaka,* the 'lightning cry' of 'storm-drunk' wings in dark deodar forests, that, really, is the cry of his own soul:

> Héthā nay, héthā nay, anya kothā, anyā konkhāné.
> Not here, not here, but elsewhere, somewhere else.

Europe has seen him in *Gitanjali:* a mystic, almost a saint. The entire non-Bengali world shares this view, and even a certain section of Bengal. 'He is the first among our saints who has not refused to live,' says Yeats's Bengali doctor. This is very possibly true, but ultimately misleading, for our conception of a saint is different from that of Christendom. I am not sure that this reputation has served our poet well. It has diverted attention from his 'professional' excellence in literature to his 'amateur' interest in philosophy—I hope the two words will offend none. Many of the books on him, both in Bengali and English, seek to show his connection with Bergson, the Upanishadas and our medieval saints rather than to present him as a writer. This, indeed, is the source of the dangerous and persistent rumour that he is always talking about 'God and all that'. It is true he is godly, not, however, in Yeats's sense of 'godly and grave', but simply in the sense of good. We who speak his language go to him for his sweet warmth, for that harmony in which power becomes peace, the peace and power of the sun after whom he is so rightly named. His benediction is our life: he teaches us speech and song, love and courtesy. *Gitanjali* does not suffice us: we must have his songs of the seasons, of youth and love, his orchestral odes, and those dramatic poems where, recreating our epics, he brings us a new, a more Western humanism. He it is who has made the rich red blood of young Europe flow through the veins of our literature, through our life and thought, and our ancient strifeless world. It is owing to him that we feel quite at home in Western literature, as if Bengal were no other than a part of Europe. He has made us, for the first time since our classical age, citizens of the world. Historically, he is our Elizabethan Renaissance rather than our Romantic storm or Tennysonian calm; he discovers Europe for us and becomes, in the process, Pound's 'new Greece'. In comedies he is a sophisticated man of the world; in stories, of a tenderness so pure that it melts into humour; in song an Ariel, more ethereal than Shakespeare's, and a Prospero in intellect, a Prospero inspired not by any revenge, but by the desire to serve. This Elizabethan multiplicity is unified by what we must call, in the deepest sense, his inherent religious feeling. He 'knows life'; in truth, he knows it well enough to know that knowledge is useless, and writes plays like *The Post*

Office where, instead of the definite and limited world of realistic drama, we have the eternal flow. He is learned, so learned that his learning never shows, and in his essays and criticism, thought and feeling become one and the same. The work of his very last phase, of the last two years of his life, is again a new beginning; he calls the first of this series *Navajatak,* (*The New Born*)—having exhausted such titles as *The End, Postscript, The Last Septet*—a new beginning ending in the old man's endless humility Eliot speaks of. And to have him, we must have all these, not the one or the other, not the earlier or the later sequence, but all, but all.

The only defect Pound notices in him is that his poetry is 'pious'. This is natural, for in Europe poetry and religion separated long ago; since the Renaissance mystical writing has had no place in accredited literature. In India, this divorce has taken place only recently; it is still a common notion with us that the poet is a religious man; and to us Rabindranath's 'piety' is, by itself, nothing remarkable, deserving neither praise nor blame. The Vaishnavas and our medieval mystics are still sung throughout the country; and to this day God is not only a hackneyed subject in our literature, it is a subject so natural that we are neither amused, nor shocked, nor pleased by the fact of its presence. We take it for granted, and then look for the poetry. A certain amount (a small amount in proportion to the whole) of Rabindranath's poetry is truly mystical; he is the greatest religious poet in a country where, for centuries, all great poets have been religious; but he is much more than that, much else, for he gives us both heaven and earth, or heaven in earth. The usual order is reversed in him: the older he grows, the more 'secular' he becomes. He writes in old age some of his most passionate love songs, love poems, love stories; he writes of the Santhal maiden working to build her clay cottage and the lover she will meet as soon as the day's work is done, and of the low-born girl, riding a pony like a gipsy and followed by village dogs. His love overflows; his pity is abounding; we live in him the whole of our life. 'Sweet is this earth, and sweet the dust of the earth,' is his message at parting. Yet he is not sad to leave it; he is prepared for the journey, waiting for the boat without impatience. 'And because I love this life,' had he not said long ago, 'I know I shall love death as well.'

Heaven and earth he has, both life and death, but no death-in-life, no purgatory, no hell. This, if anything, this is what we miss in him, we who know the literature of the West. His vision comprehends suffering, earthly coils and earthly toils, jealousy, despair, greed, but not Eliot's 'horror and boredom'. Shakespeare, Baudelaire, Eliot himself reach out to worlds which Rabindranath never writes about, though he seems to glimpse them in his strange, at times weird paintings. . . . But at least he is like Shakespeare in this that he seems never to have experienced boredom.

Bengal has changed much since Yeats heard, 'perhaps for the first time in literature, our voice as in a dream'. He was happy to discover a land where writing poetry did not seem 'strange, unnatural, or in need of defence'. 'In my own country,' he said, 'four-fifths of our energy is spent in the quarrel with bad taste.' What he admired most in Rabindranath was his spontaneity; a simplicity and an innocence which, after Blake, had faded from English writing, and Yeats himself was out to recapture. Today, Bengal is much like Yeats' Ireland. The poet's occupation is no longer thought natural; he is fallen on the thorns of political cacophony. We have to fight not only bad taste, but also parrot-politics, of this colour and the other, demanding that art must serve their ends. We have to waste our time in propaganda so that propaganda may not enlist the whole of literature. Spontaneity is gone; simplicity and innocence are lost; nothing remains for us but hard work, the discipline of self-consciousness, and an incorruptible pride in the rôle of the poet. (pp. 1-13)

> *Buddhadeva Bose, "Rabindranath," in his* An Acre of Green Grass: A Review of Modern Bengali Literature, *Orient Longmans Ltd., 1948, pp. 1-13.*

In the work of Mr. Tagore the source of the charm is in the subtle underflow. It is nothing else than his "sense of life."

—*Ezra Pound, in his "Rabindranath Tagore," *The Fortnightly Review, *March 1913.*

Mary M. Lago   (essay date 1976)

[*An American critic and educator, Lago has published numerous articles on late Victorian and Edwardian literature. In addition to translating short stories and poems by Tagore, she is the editor of* Imperfect Encounter: Letters of William Rothenstein and Rabindranath Tagore, 1911-1941. *In the following excerpt, she provides an overview of Tagore's lyric poetry.*]

The reader of Tagore's poems, in Bengali or in English, receives an overwhelming impression of a great variety of metaphysical overtones. This is true even when the content of the poems is not explicitly religious. . . . [The] influence of the *bhakti* movement in India, and of Bengali Vaishnavism in particular, permeates Bengali culture and was notably resurgent during Tagore's formative years. It helped to shape his view of himself and of the world. Being a poet, he easily and naturally thought, wrote, and spoke metaphorically, even when he dealt with prosaic subjects. The metaphors that came naturally to mind were the Vaishnava and related metaphors, in all their variations upon the theme of the intimate personal relation between God and the human soul. This philosophy of an everlasting search for unity logically attracted a sensitive young man raised in a family whose members saw the world as a set of interlocking units and invariably advocated synthesis as the means of keeping the units from breaking apart. This view was inclusive: it was not limited to political and social problems but extended to philosophical consideration of questions of existence itself. "All organic beings live like a flame, a long way beyond themselves," Rabindranath wrote in 1919. "They have thus a smaller and a larger body. The former is visible to the eye; it can be touched, captured and bound. The latter is indefinite; it has no fixed boundaries, but is widespread both in space and time." He was referring to the idea of a university, but so unified was his thought on all subjects that one does not violate the original context of his statement by adapting it to his views on man's relationship with God. The vast majority of his poems, and especially of those translated into English, deal, directly or indirectly, with the smaller and larger, or inner and outer, aspects of reality. Nature is the touchstone, again and again, and it is a rare poem by Tagore that does not reflect in some way the skies, rivers, and landscape of Bengal.

In Vaishnava lyrics it is sometimes the human soul and sometimes God—that is, sometimes Radha, and sometimes Krishna—who is the seeker. Radha goes out into the stormy night, wrapped in a blue cloak and with the sounds of her jewelry muffled, to search for Krishna. At other times, Krishna comes to search for her, and she is awakened from sleep only by the sound of his departing footsteps. Now and again they meet, but only briefly; one or the other slips away, their separations symbolizing the fleeting nature of man's glimpses of the nature of God.

Because man is less than omniscient, he is the partner fated to be eternally baffled by the complexities of this partnership. He is the suppliant, and this is the posture that Tagore, in his poems upon this Vaishnava model, assigns to his poetic persona. His supplications are neither abject nor petulant; although they are sometimes outbursts of irritation or frustration, the steady note throughout is a note of loving, wistful longing. These poems are in the mode of Professor Godbole's dance and song that open the third part of E. M. Forster's *A Passage to India*. To the uninitiated Westerner, Godbole appears rather lovable but also slightly silly, and the ceremony seems, in Lionel Trilling's phrase, a "glorification of mess and relaxation." But Godbole's invocatory dance and song are a more colloquial expression of the theme that Tagore affirms with his lines: "I am here to sing thee songs. In this hall of thine I have a corner seat." To the Western eye, accustomed to certain standards of ecclesiastical decorum, Godbole's "braying banging crooning" accompaniment, his lopsided pince-nez, the jumble of objects on the altar, and especially the misspelled motto "God si Love," speak only of undignified mess and inappropriate relaxation. But in the contexts attaching to Vaishnava faith and worship, external mess is irrelevant, and appearances are deceptive. Behind these is the unyielding tension that characterizes every relation between man and God. Tagore's poems, of the type best known to Western readers, are constructed upon a parallel line of tension (reinforced in the Bengali poems by rhyme and meter that were unfortunately sacrificed to the English versions) between the suppliant person's disappointments in the struggle for union with the Divine Being and his iron-willed dedication to the search. Readers seeking a parallel among the English poets may refer to the poems of George Herbert. Tagore's poetic conceits do not show such careful attention to structural de-

tail as do Herbert's, but the motif of unremitting search is at the core of every poem.

This search goes on in the natural, not the supernatural world. The poems are filled with sounds and suggestions of Nature close at hand, and this is equally strong in Tagore's less explicitly metaphysical poems. They suggest daily life lived much out of doors, and an intimate acquaintance with the cycle of the seasons. This sense of an ongoing cycle is more imperative in Tagore's poems than in those of most of the West's recognized nature poets, for the pattern of Indian seasons is more clear-cut and the principal annual change, from dry season to monsoon, is more dramatic than in the temperate zones. Against this natural setting Tagore designs vignettes and miniature dramas: a young woman turning her head with a swift backward glance as she steps into a carriage, a child whose lamp has gone out on a dark staircase, a newly wedded husband receiving the first letter from his wife, an empty house, a neglected street. The details are supplied by indirection and suggestion, and also present by suggestion is a metaphor of the individual as symbol for something much larger than himself. Unfortunately, many readers in the West failed to note these larger connotations and rested content with whatever they found attractively exotic: jingling ankle-bells, flower garlands, and incense drifting from a temple at sundown.

Unfortunately for both the West and for Tagore, many of his readers never knew—still do not know—that so many of his poems were written as words for music, with musical and verbal imagery and rhythms designed to support and enhance each other. The volume *Gitabitān* (*Song-Collection*) contains words for 2,265 *Rabindrasangit*, in addition to the libretti for several of his dance-dramas or dramatic song-cycles. This is a prodigious achievement (Schubert wrote 614 songs), and the songs are an important demonstration of Tagore's belief in the efficacy of cultural synthesis. He used all the musical materials that came to hand: the classical ragas, the boat songs of Bengal, Vaishnava *kīrtan* and *Bāul* devotional songs, village songs of festival and of mourning, even Western tunes picked up during his travels and subtly adapted to his own uses.

Rabindranath was roundly criticized for including the classical ragas in his experiments. His defense was that music that is not responded to, which does not arouse some answering excitement in the listener, is not fully alive. In 1921 he wrote the essay **"Sonār Kāthi"** (**"The Golden Wand"**). The wand of the title belongs to a Prince who will use it to awaken a Princess who has slept for hundreds of years inside a fortified palace. She is surrounded by riches and watched by fierce guards. The Prince represents the living, moving world of the arts—specifically, the new influences from the West. The Princess is the spirit of Indian classical music. The riches that surround her are the great achievements of musical artists through the ages, and the jealous attendants are named "Expertise." They stay awake night and day, so that no one, least of all the Prince with the golden wand of experimentation, may get in and awaken the Princess.

"We can clearly see," Tagore wrote, "that in our country music is not on the move. The experts are saying, music is not a thing that is meant to move, it will stay seated in the drawing-room and all of you must come to it and energetically applaud the performances; but the difficulty is that the age of the drawing-room is gone. Now the place where we stop to rest is the wayside inn. We cannot remain static because we want to pay respect to that which is static. The river on which we are rowing is moving; if the boat does not move, even though it be very valuable, we shall have to abandon it." Indian music, he believed, and Indian literature as well, had nothing to fear from the spirit of exploration and experimentation. The arts of India were not so frail that the touch of new influences could kill them. Bengalis had already rediscovered the Bāul and Vaishnava songs. The Prince, in other words, had already evaded the guards. If the Princess would not awaken, ordinary people would respond to his invitation and, if forced to choose, would follow him and leave the Princess sound asleep among her riches.

In Bengali poetry, also, Tagore assumed the role of the Prince. This was an area in which experimentation was equally unwelcome to the conservative. Serious Bengali poetry in the nineteenth century was still dominated by the rules and aesthetic of Sanskrit poetics. The Bengali word *kabi*—poet—and its Sanskrit root—*kavi*—meant originally "seer," and in Bengali tradition all the serious responsibility attaching to preternatural insight attaches also to the poet's calling. The Sanskrit rhetoricians and aestheticians had painstakingly defined and prescribed the successive stages by which a poem leads to an experience of *rasa,* a term most simply translated as meaning a state of aesthetic enjoyment.

Tagore viewed poetry both seriously and reverently, but for him this did not rule out experimentation. Poetry, like music, had to be kept in touch with the moving stream of life. He tried forms and meters new to Bengali poetry. He combined one of the oldest of Bengali meters, the *payār* (two lines of fourteen syllables each), with subject-matter drawn from the most commonplace details of daily living. He substituted the personal, intimate tone of the lyric for the grandeur and the austerity of the epic modes. Most important, he initiated a rhetorical revolution in modern Bengali poetry by using language that orthodox literary pundits considered unsuited to serious poetry: he used the simpler colloquial diction and verb forms of the vernacular instead of the highly Sanskritized, more formal and sonorous diction of literary Bengali. This important change occurred, appropriately enough, at the turn of the century, marked by Tagore's volume called *Kshanikā.* The title refers to matters that are fleeting, momentary, ephemeral. The impact of these sixty-two poems, written during two summer months, was, however, anything but ephemeral. Bengali critics were shocked and disapproving, and Tagore was reprimanded, then and later, as if he were a cultural renegade. However, he not only made it easier for other Bengali poets to experiment in their own manner, but, at a time when wider international contacts and opportunities were becoming available, he made it possible for them to meet on more equal terms with poets who were leading other national literary traditions away from formality and toward flexibility.

Tagore himself did more than any other Bengali of modern times to widen Bengali writers' international contacts and opportunities. The pivotal event was, of course, his winning the Nobel Prize for Literature in 1913. Inextricably bound up with this great event was the problem of translation, a problem always central to international literary exchange; it becomes especially thorny when, as in the case of Rabindranath's poems, the form is changed from rhymed metrical verse to free verse, when the editors neither know the language of the original poems nor enlist as consultant any one who does, and the general public has neither information about other poetry in the Bengali language nor access to instruction in that language. The curious complex of circumstances and happenstances that brought this about has been documented in detail. What has received less attention is the separation between what Tagore wrote in the first instance, and what eventually became established in the minds of Western readers as Tagore's characteristic poetic idiom. The separation is best explained by a specific example; a similar process of poetic metamorphosis was repeated for all of the poems in all of the major collections published in the West during his lifetime.

The poem that appears as Number 54 in *Fruit-Gathering* (1916) is the Bengali poem, Number 65 in *Gitāli* (*Songs;* i.e., lyric poems) (1914); it is in a section on worship in *Gitabitān.* If one examines these in reverse order, that is, working from the English version back to the Bengali, one begins to see what elements were lost or sacrificed along the way.

The English version is very slight, and its slightness is part of its appeal. The poem sketches the eternal verities in terms of intangibles, like night, pain, or love, or in terms of the earth, a material object much too large for the human grasp. Each idea is neatly contained in a sentence, as if to say that nothing is too abstract or too large to be outside the province of the poet.

> The Cloud said to me, "I vanish"; the Night said,
> "I plunge into the fiery dawn."
> The Pain said, "I remain in deep silence as his footprint."
> "I die into the fulness," said my life to me.
> The Earth said, "My lights kiss your thoughts every moment."
> "The days pass," Love said, "but I wait for you."
> Death said, "I ply the boat of your life across the sea."

The concrete and the abstract, tangible and intangible speak to the poet. Each states its unique contribution to his existence. Each sets limits to its responsibility. The poet whom they address answers not a word, and this silence implies acceptance of his human condition and his covenant with the Maker of Life.

What of the same poem in Bengali? Even for readers who do not know the language, the transliterated text conveys some idea of the meter and the rhyme:

> *Megh boleche jābo, jābo, rāt boleche jāi,*
> *Sāgar bole, kul mileche, āmi to ār nāi,*

Dukkha bole, "Rainu cupe, tāhār pāer china-
rupe,"
Āmi bole, "Milāi āmi ār kichu nā cāi."
Bhuban bole, "Tomār tore āche baranmālā,"
Gagana bole, "Tomār tore laksha pradip jālā."
Prem bole je "juge juge tomār lāgi āchi jege,"
Maranh bole, "Āmi tomār jibantori bāi."

Translated literally, and with no attempt to keep the rhyme that is readily apparent in the transliteration, the text is this:

> The cloud said, "I'll go, I'll go"; the night said, "I go."
> The ocean says, "I have reached the shore, I am no more."
> Sorrow says, "[I] keep silent, like the mark of His footprint."
> The self says, "Merging into that, I want nothing more."
>
> Earth says, "For you is the garland of invocation."
> Sky says, "For you, a million lamps are alight."
> Love says [that] "age after age I wake for you."
> Death says, "I row your boat of life."

Most striking, between the Bengali poem and the English version in *Fruit-Gathering*, is a difference in dramatic situation. In the English poem the self makes no response; in the Bengali poem the self makes a very significant reply: "The self says, 'Merging into that, I want nothing more.'" This is both a reply and a commitment and thus radically alters both the tone and the situation of the poem, which turns upon this fourth line as upon a pivot. Up to this point the attitudes expressed have been negative or noncommittal. The cloud and the night speak of departure; the ocean speaks of self-effacement; Sorrow speaks of silence. But the silent sorrow is also sign and substance of something that endures. As soon as the self states willingness to accept all of these as conditions of life, it becomes the motivator instead of passive subject or recipient. Now earth, sky, love, and death not only recognize the place of the self in the scheme of things but acknowledge it as their own reason for being. Thus the theme of the poem is brought home: by demanding nothing, the self gains everything. Not even Love, which links the self to the cosmos, waits passively; it awakens again and again because of the self's acceptance of all that Sorrow represents. Thus even Death must become the servant of the selfless self.

When the music is added to these Bengali words, the musical imagery states the theme even more explicitly, for the first line becomes a refrain after each stanza, with the additional repetition of the second line in the final refrain. The song thus follows the *aba* form common in Western music. The melody is perfectly intelligible to the Western listener; there is nothing esoteric in its tonality. It is a Romantic song serving as vehicle for a statement about the nature of life and of the universe.

Both the English and the Bengali versions end with the idea of Death as servant. But the musical imagery does not end there. It returns by means of the refrain to the first line and its suggestions of departure and conclusion, but the musical line rounds as if to suggest a circle that is not quite closed. Thus the song ends on a note that suggests a ques-

tion asked and an answer requested. Every line of the song has this inconclusive rounded shape that parallels the philosophy suggested by the words: the fundamental questions must be repeated as long as one lives, and there is no fully satisfying answer to any of the puzzles of the human condition.

Could Tagore have translated the Bengali more literally? He could have, and it may be claimed that he should have done so. All one can say now with certainty is that he chose not to do so, and that had he elected further to reproduce the rhyme and the meter in English, he would have confronted an entirely new set of equally difficult questions.

Certain volumes and poems are landmarks among the volumes of Bengali poetry. The first of these to be generally recognized as a new departure in the tradition was *Sandhyā Sangit (Evening Songs)* (1882). These were the product of a dreary stretch in the summer of 1881, after Tagore's false start to England. His brother Jyotirindranath and his wife, Rabindranath's principal mentors at that time, were away from the city; some members of the family were plainly disgruntled by his earlier failure to finish his studies in England; and he settled disconsolately into a room at the top of the Calcutta house and began to write poems on a slate, which he found less intimidating than bound manuscript books he had used for earlier work. The result was a series of poems with titles and, in large part, with content morbidly and mawkishly Romantic, but notable for their disregard of traditional metrics. He had discarded the three-beat meter to which he had become accustomed and had turned to a meter based on multiples of two beats. "I felt like rising from a dream of bondage to find myself unshackled," he recalled. "I cut extraordinary capers just to make sure I was free to move." The collection is cherished today chiefly for Rabindranath's recollections of the historical novelist, Bankimchandra Chatterji, whom Bengalis like to call the "Walter Scott of Bengal." Rabindranath arrived at a wedding just as Bankimchandra, also a guest, was receiving a garland. He placed it around Rabindranath's neck, saying to the host, " 'The wreath to him, Ramesh; have you not read his *Evening Songs*?' "

The host had not read *Evening Songs*, and they survive as an indicative early effort. In **"Ahabānsangit"** (**"Song of Summons"**), the first poem of *Prabhāt Sangit (Morning Songs)* (1883), Tagore scolded himself vigorously for the twilight vaporings of the earlier book, and between the two is assuredly the difference between night and day. *Morning Songs* is all sparkle and sunlight, motion and metamorphosis. The most important metamorphosis is that of the poet himself. In a morning moment of epiphany he had had a sunburst glimpse of relations between, on the one hand, the natural world, in its most trivial details, and, on the other hand, his own potential powers as poet and his role as observer and interpreter. He never forgot this experience, which he described both in *My Reminiscences* and in his 1930 Hibbert Lecture at Oxford. His exhilaration was recorded at once in **"Nirjharer Shapnabhāngā"** (**"The Awakening of the Waterfall"**), the most important poem in the group, not only for its personal connotations, but, as Edward Thompson has noted, for its use of a river as a central metaphor. In **"The Awakening of the Waterfall"** a ray of sunlight enters a frozen cave and melts the accumulated ice, which grows from separate drops into a rivulet, and finally into a leaping stream. Thompson calls it a "Himalayan picture," and the description of the growing river, flowing from the hills through the countryside to the sea, is a poetic topography of India.

Bhanusingha Thākurer Padavali (*Poems of Bhanu Singh*) (1884) belongs with his juvenilia, as these poems first began to appear in a Calcutta periodical in 1877. They cannot be compared with *Morning Songs,* published the preceding year, but they are of interest because they are Rabindranath's early efforts at imitating the Vaishnava lyrics. He copied their device of the *bhanitā,* or signature line, a concluding couplet in which the poet, using his own name, inserts a third-person comment on the action or theme of the poem. As a gentle hoax, Rabindranath allowed these to be published as by a fifteenth-century (but entirely fictitious) Vaishnava lyricist named Bhanu Singh. (There is a further play on his own name, since *"Bhānu"* is a synonym for *Rabi,* which means "sun.") Rabindranath recalled with glee how a Bengali scholar abroad received a doctorate in Germany for a thesis on this newly rediscovered Vaishnava poet. But Thompson records a conversation in which Tagore speaks with great seriousness about his debt to the Vaishnava poets, and about his good luck in having encountered them at so early an age.

Sonār Tori (*The Golden Boat*) (1894) belongs to the East Bengal period of Tagore's writings, which saw such steady output of fine short fiction. The poems were written between 1891 and 1893, and they mark the emergence of a concept central to Tagore's personal and poetic life: the *jibandebatā,* or (to borrow Thompson's translation of the term), the Life-Deity. He quotes Prasanta Mahalanobis, who defined it as "the presiding deity of the poet's life— not quite that even—it is the poet himself—the Inner Self of the poet, who is more than his earthly incarnation." This concept, like the memory of the morning vision, became an integral part of Tagore's view of all creative activity. In diction, rhyme scheme, meter, and stanza structure, the title poem, **"The Golden Boat,"** is far simpler than **"The Awakening of the Waterfall"**; consonantal resonances flow without hindrance from line to line. The poem is allegorical: a farmer whose harvest has been interrupted by the rains sits alone on the riverbank beside his cut grain. A boat arrives and takes his harvest, which has been so plentiful that there is no place for him in the boat, and he is left, beneath the lowering clouds.

There was a spate of critical argument about this allegory, and Tagore had to explain that the boat is the boat of life—the *jibantori*—steered by the Muse and floating on the stream of time, that comes to collect all our works and takes them away to be added to the sum of man's achievements, leaving us behind. Literal explanation of the allegory is heavy-handed beside the rapid flow and the beautiful sound combinations of the Bengali in **"The Golden Boat."** The important point about the poem is that, like the poems of *Morning Songs,* it was another highly influential experiment in Bengali prosody, and it introduced a metaphor that became a touchstone of Tagore's work: the boat of life, metaphoric ancestor of the *jibantori* rowed by Death in the last line of Number 54 of *Fruit-Gathering.* Unlike *Morning Songs, The Golden Boat* moves away from hot-house Romanticism toward the clean, spare lines that came to be called "modern." It is an autumnal collection, in which Tagore, whom Bengalis like to call the "Shelley of Bengal," echoes Shelley's "there is a harmony / In autumn, and a lustre in its sky, / Which thro' the summer is not heard or seen, / As if it could not be, as if it had not been!" In **"Niruddesh Jātrā"** (**"Journey to an Unknown Destination"**), the last poem of *The Golden Boat,* the cultivator has been taken into the boat. He asks repeatedly where he is going, but the boatman only points toward the horizon.

In the seven years from 1893 through 1900, Tagore produced seven volumes of poems, culminating with the wonderful *Kshanikā* which serves also as introduction to his fully mature work: Thompson rightly calls this book a watershed. Tagore no longer felt obliged to "cut extraordinary capers just to make sure I was free to move." He had discarded the Romantic extravagances of *Morning Songs* and was increasingly comfortable with the informality and succinctness that characterized *The Golden Boat.* In *Kshanikā* he carried these to a new extreme, not only using the simpler colloquial verb forms, but also the *hasanta,* a linguistic device that silences the final vowel of a word and adds greater terseness. This of course played hob with the classical rules for prosody and raised howls of anguish among the pandits: *Kshanikā* began their long feud with Tagore. Thompson relates how a suggested appointment as a Matriculation examiner in Bengali at Calcutta University was protested on the grounds that Tagore wrote bad Bengali; how examination passages from his works were assigned to be rewritten in "chaste" (literary) Bengali; and how the University Senate objected to his receiving an honorary degree, since " 'he was not a Bengali scholar.' " It took the Nobel Prize in 1913 to bring the doctorate in its wake.

The *Kshanikā* poems are secular, personal in the best Romantic manner. Thompson discusses the volume at some length and gives a fair sampling of its themes. These are set forth with the wit and wisdom that friends like William Rothenstein valued so highly in Tagore, the submerging of which in self-conscious solemnity they so deplored. Each poem creates its own atmosphere by a few quick, concise images; by a surprising use of rhyme and assonance; and by lines that vary in length and weight, often bringing the reader up short by means of unexpected variations. Irony is deft and very lightly laid on; amusement at the small foibles of gentle people is benign and affectionate; there is some delightful fooling of the kind that Thompson calls "*pandit*-baiting"; love poems strike a note of wistful rather than wrenching loneliness; and the poet meditates pensively upon the minor slings and arrows of fortune. *Kshanikā* is Rabindranath relaxed. The reader of Bengali compares these poems with the later English prose versions and will not be comforted.

Kshanikā was followed by *Naibedya* (*Offerings*) (1901), one hundred poems written at the rate of nearly one a day.

Where *Kshanikā* was lighthearted, *Naibedya* is portentous and somber. Tagore was deeply disturbed by the Boer War, which he saw as a sign of worse to come in relations among the Western powers, with inevitable repercussions upon India. Nor was all going well within India. Lord Curzon had become Viceroy in 1898, and his zeal for reorganizing the governmental bureaucracy was well known. This spread alarm and uncertainty among educated Bengalis, who, like most English-educated Indians, looked to the government for jobs commensurate with their new learning. As the ranks of English-educated Indians grew, competition for government jobs sharpened. Inflation was on the increase, and Bengalis began to feel threatened both culturally and economically. Resentment and anxiety fostered political radicalism, just in time for a vehement response to Curzon's publication, in October 1903, of his plan to partition Bengal. All of this is in the background of *Naibedya.* It contains poems on religious and patriotic themes; these find common ground in Rabindranath's pleas, both implicit and explicit in the poems, for India to hold fast, no matter what might happen, to dignity, self-respect, and faith.

The Bengali *Gitānjali* (*Song-Offering*) is only one of ten volumes of Tagore's Bengali lyrics from which the poems for the English *Gitanjali: Song-Offerings* were selected for translation. Many Bengali critics consider it oversensuous, so much given to musings and digressions about beauty that it falls short of the standard of his best work. It seems to lack the tension that gives such shape and strength to the best of his lyrics, and to the Vaishnava lyrics. Tagore himself was aware of this. He told Edward Thompson that at the time of writing these poems he was very restless, with many undefined longings to know more about the rest of the world: " 'My restlessness became intolerable. I wrote *Dākghar* [*The Post-Office,* a play] in three or four days. About the same time I wrote *Gitānjali*. . . . I did not intend to publish [the poems]. I knew people would be disappointed, and would say that after *Sonār Tori* they were very poor. But I knew they were very intimately my own.' "

Whatever their limitations, the *Gitānjali* poems are an integral part of Tagore's total poetic canon. Their wistfulness, which, if one were to read all 159 poems at a sitting, would become very wearisome, echoes a dominant mood of *Kshanikā.* The devotional theme in *Gitānjali* is a gentler modulation from the religious strain in *Naibedya,* separated from the contexts of patriotic urgency. In *Gitānjali* both the wistfulness and the devotional attitude are colored by Tagore's restlessness in 1910, in his semi-seclusion at Santiniketan.

The Bengali *Gitānjali* is important for still another reason: it introduced a period of intensive song-writing that is now called Tagore's Gitanjali period, a reference not so much to the Nobel Prize won by the English volume, as to this period of resurgent song-writing. It was as if the malaise that led him abroad in 1912 and the tremendous events that followed also led him back to his particular lyric muse and stirred up a series of fervent responses to her. This had been foreshadowed by an earlier collection, *Kheyā* (*The Ferry;* or, *Crossing*) (1906), in which Vaishnava mysti-

cism and metaphors play a dominant but somewhat lugubrious part: Thompson finds this collection of poems "one long wail," and Buddhadeva Bose identifies it with what he calls Tagore's "dark period." The poems abound with exclamation marks, refrains, static rhyme patterns, and references to the singer who sits sadly alone. Yet *Kheyā* leads directly, in both theme and manner, to the poems that frame 1912, the pivotal year: *Gitānjali, Gitimālya* (*Song Garland*) (1914), and *Gitāli* (*Songs*) (1914). These volumes are less self-centered than *Kheyā* and have more of the detachment of *Kshanikā,* together with its simplicity. They fairly cry out to be set to music. Nature is present in nearly every poem of these three volumes, but it is Nature simplified, needing no exclamation marks to dramatize the poet-singer's awareness of the scenes that he observes. A number of the poems in *Gitimālya* were written and dated from London, Urbana, Gloucestershire, and the S. S. *Lahore,* which brought Rabindranath home in 1913; they are evidence of his conscious efforts during his wanderings not to lose sight of his cultural origins and his Muse.

Balākā (*A Flight of Cranes*) (1916) was written between 1914 and 1916, so that it followed immediately upon *Gitimālya* and *Gitāli.* The poems of *Balākā* reflect a time of account-taking and of Tagore's reactions to the turbulence of the past four years: the excitement surrounding the Nobel award and the knighthood that followed in 1915, the premonitions of political disaster, and the anxieties of the World War. These did not render him artistically incapable. On the contrary, they seemed to galvanize him into new resolutions. "Strangely enough I had a strong sense of the presence of death this time in the hills," he wrote to Rothenstein in June 1914, "which gave me a clearer perspective of things enabling me to come away with a realisation of freedom I seldom had before. I have a strong hope that henceforth my works will be truer and my dedication of self more complete." *Balākā* reflects that new sense of freedom and that dedication to a new effort at finding his best form of poetic expression. In the old Bengali fourteen-syllable *payār* and in radical departures from it, he presents a review and reprise of motifs and themes that had marked major turnings in his work: the migratory bird—in this instance, the wild crane; the river life and the figures in the landscape of riverine Bengal; pilgrims and other travelers on the open road; human love merging into divine love; and expectations of eventual union with the Beloved. The tone of *Balākā* is peaceful, but it is not at all supine, joyful but not raucous. Its tone is set throughout by rhetoric that can only be described as social: the rhetoric of apostrophe. It is as if the poet, who has now seen more of the world outside of India than he has ever seen before, wishes to particularize and personalize his audience, even to compel its attention. This audience is infinitely varied: it comprises the world, youth, the premature spring flowers, a photograph of a long-dead sister-in-law, the wild cranes, even the Taj Mahal, and even Shakespeare. There are no incongruities in this list. Forward motion, symbolized by the flight of the wild cranes, is the essence of Tagore's mood at the time. Everything in the world, the tangible and the intangible, was in a state of flux; the momentum of his identification with this forward motion seemed to sweep him past the old restrictions and the injunctions of pandits and pedants. *Balākā* evidences the sheer delight in experimentation with sounds and rhythms that makes *Kshanikā* a watershed, and the great variety of *Balākā* makes it equally difficult to translate. Kripalani warns everyone, including the author, away from the attempt: "The author's own attempt was suicidal; ours can only be murderous."

The chronology of Tagore's international travels and the record of his extra-poetic activities readily explain why, between 1916 and 1932, no single volume is as adventuresome as *Balākā.* The poet's energies and powers of concentration were too much diverted into other channels, and he was too worried by this diversion to write the kind of poetry that flows from an unencumbered mind. What he had seen of the West during his travels filled him with foreboding, and he poured his energies, as well as his money, into the effort to make Visva-Bharati, his new international university at Santiniketan, an example to the world, of how humanism and humanitarianism might resist and neutralize materialism and worship of the machine. In 1922 he wrote to Rothenstein:

> Since science has taken place of religion, Man has been cultivating his faith in the brute and arming himself for the struggle for existence which is the process of the natural selection for the survival of the brute. All the same the fact is that man is man and we must keep him reminding [*sic*] of it by constantly appealing to his humanity. I have taken that task in my country though the time is unfavourable the minds of the people being overcast with storm clouds of resentment. I have occasional doubts in my mind as to whether I have not strayed away from my own true vocation; if that be so I have come too far off my track to be able to retrace my steps. I must jog on to the end of my days even though I feel weary and homesick for the solitude where my dreams had their early nest.

By 1932, although he had in the intervening years produced a great many poems, he had convinced himself that his career as a poet had ended. He published the set of contemplative poems called *Parisesh* (*The End*) (1932). But it was not the end. As if to contravene his verdict on himself, he rushed at once into a spate of experimentation. The result was *Punascha* (*Postscript*) (1932), the first of four volumes in this style. Bengali critics refer to these as prose-poems, and in his preface to *Punascha* Tagore himself speaks of the prose form of the English *Gitanjali* and confesses that he has long wished to experiment in Bengali with this form but had been deterred by timidity. The poems are, however, not prose-poems in the form of the English *Gitanjali,* in which the Bengali lines are cast into solid blocks of prose, or are knocked down into sentences with the self-sufficiency of aphorism rather than the euphonious linkage from line to line found in lyrics that are rhymed and strictly metrical. The poems of *Punascha* are actually free verse, and the lines, if not measured and rhymed, have a poetic progression. The very nature of the Bengali language, with its clear-cut vowel sounds and consonantal verb endings, its repetitive devices for conveying emphasis and onomatopoeia, builds into the poems the assonance, internal rhythm, and liquid sounds that make it easy for free verse to flow musically from one line to the next.

These free-verse or prose poems are lyric in tone, but they are less compact, more leisurely than the early lyrics. This is in part a result of the more diffuse form, but it is related also to their subject-matter. In the affectionate use of such details as endow daily living with both dignity and wonder, and sometimes in elliptical method and compactness, the best poems of *Punascha* recall *Kshanikā.* In the most successful poems of *Punascha,* Tagore is again the observer, but—the reader cannot but be influenced by the knowledge that this is now the elderly Tagore, his international travels all but over, who observes—he is more detached, much less involved in the action or scene of the poem, and content to be so.

One poem that sums up these best qualities and is at the same time deeply moving is "Ekjan Lok" ("A Man"). It is a self-portrait of the poet, lethargic and uncomfortable after an airless, sleepless night, and an account of how the passing of an anonymous up-country man stirs his imagination into functioning once again as a poet's imagination should. The farmer's appearance is quickly sketched in: he is lean, with shaven, shrunken cheeks; he wears patched country-made shoes and a short tunic of printed chintz; he carries a prosaic umbrella on his shoulder and a bamboo stick under his arm. His passing registers on no more than the farthest horizon of the poet's consciousness, and the event, or rather non-event, is described in lazy, loping phrases, like the gait of the tall, lean countryman himself; the very words *"ekjan lok,"* which appear in this part of the poem, have a long-drawn loping quality; it is simply impossible to snap out or to snap off these Bengali words when reading them aloud. But in the next line the poet's imagination leaps into action: he sees himself as he must have appeared to the countryman, that is, on an equally remote verge of the imagination. And then at once we have the countryman suddenly brought into focus. He has at home a cow in its stall, a parrot in a cage, a wife with bangles on her arms—the reader hears the bangles jingle as she grinds wheat for the day's meal. The washerman lives next door, the grocer across the lane, and there is a debt to a moneylender from Afghanistan. In the mind of the countryman, the poet is *"ekjan lok"*—just a man.

A number of equally memorable personalities are sketched in *Punascha* and in the other volumes from this period. Nature, also, acquires personality, even personification. It is less a setting for the poem, as in the early lyrics, than it is a character. One of the best-known poems of *Punascha* is "Kopāi," which is the name of a tiny river near Santiniketan. The poet's mind idly follows the course of the river, which gradually becomes a personality contrasted with that of the majestic, all-consuming Brahmaputra. The Kopai is undistinguished, friendly with its neighbors, slim and graceful of shape, speaking the language of those who live along its banks. It is a graceful poem, reflecting the modest grace of its subject. The serenity of both the river and the poem reflect the serenity of the poet, a serenity doubly welcome after the confusions and turmoil of his international career.

Tagore's last years saw the publication of poems that are

much more self-centered than those of the *Punascha* group. Even to the non-reader of Bengali, the mere appearance of the poems suggests tenseness, for they are tightly drawn up on the page, and for the most part the poet himself—specifically, the approaching end of his life—is their subject. He was spurred to composition by illness, or by recovery from illness. In this group are *Prāntik* (*The Borderland*) (1938); *Rogashajyāya* (*From the Sickbed*) (1940); *Arogya* (*Recovery*) (1941); *Janmadine* (*On the Birthday*) (1941); and *Sesh Lekhā* (*Last Writings*) (1941), published posthumously.

Sisir Kumar Ghose, in *The Later Poems of Tagore*, makes these poems the occasion for an examination of ambivalences in Tagore's view of the past, of fame, of his acceptance of life itself, and of the necessity for leaving it. Lyrical declamations on the necessity for departing this world were far easier, Ghose suggests, when the poet was younger and that necessity was not imminent; in *Prāntik* Tagore renounces desires for worldly recognition and returns, but very quickly he takes up the idea that the sense of having lived life to the full is its own reward. All this, Ghose says, is put in terms of the past and is therefore in a mode of pathos, and these ambivalences rob the poems of their effect because the tension is unrelenting, transitions are lacking, and contact with the reader is soon lost. The poet has in fact gone out of his way to disassociate himself from contemporary events, a disassociation that in itself represents a personal crisis for the poet. It represents as well, Ghose says, a lack of saving cathartic tension in his poems.

It seems unfair to blame a man, at the end of a life of eighty years, for not being in his last poems what he has never tried to be. Tagore's actions, his polemical writings, and especially his letters show that ambivalence had always been a characteristic strain in his temperament. His moods tended to swing like a pendulum, and he often made hasty judgments, as Leonard Elmhirst noted early in his stay at Santiniketan: "Early on, only a day or two after my arrival in November [1921] I had realized that Tagore sometimes made snap judgments on first acquaintance, that his enthusiasm quickly aroused could as quickly evaporate, and that until others, in whom he had confidence, members of his family or staff, had reported back to him of what was afoot, he could be deeply sceptical." Yet these hasty judgments, which sometimes had deplorable results, were related to an important part of his temperamental equipment as a poet: his pervasive curiosity, which even in the last of his poems, never flagged. He had always felt that he must see, feel, and experience, vicariously or directly, as much as possible of the range of human experience. In this he was remarkably consistent. When Mussolini invited him to visit Italy in 1926, then proceeded to make propaganda capital of Tagore's visit, Tagore gave a personal, poetic justification for what was assuredly a blunder in public relations: a poet must know as much as he possibly can about everything, and therefore he had to know about Mussolini. Elmhirst wrote: "Tagore's letter to the *Manchester Guardian* about his visit to Mussolini [repudiating Mussolini's statements about his approval of Italian policies] would have informed all English readers of what had happened but of course Tagore himself was both sad at

having been misled in Italy and proud of having at last made his contact with a real Dictator." One appreciates Tagore as a poet who has taken the trouble to display for one's benefit every facet of a lovely gem; one does not complain because looking at all the facets takes up so much of one's time and energy. (pp. 38-57)

Mary M. Lago, in her Rabindranath Tagore, *Twayne Publishers, 1976, 176 p.*

If Mr. Tagore had been born in Brooklyn, he would never be a fashionable poet. There is a quaint exotic aroma about his poems, like sandal-wood or stale cigarettes or the back room of a Chinese laundry.

—*Joyce Kilmer, in his "Rabindranath Tagore," America, 17 July 1915.*

Melvin D. Palmer   (essay date 1981)

[*In the following essay, Palmer examines the contradictions underlying the critical adulation of Tagore following the publication of* Gitanjali *in 1912, and offers his own assessment of Tagore's English-language poetry.*]

Some literary problems never seem to go away. In spite of various attempts to look at Tagore's English translations critically, there persists a certain blindness to the possibility that his early poems in English did not uniformly merit the great attention they received. For example, after taking note of some critics who said that Tagore's poems were "too thin and ethereal" and that they "lacked in intensity and passion," Humayun Kabir ignored and begged the question by concluding, "Tagore's standing as a poet is so unquestioned that it is not necessary even to discuss these aspersions of his critics." Accordingly, this essay will take another look at Tagore's earliest appearance in England and America in an attempt to urge a realistic view of these poems and to plead for an expert and sensitive translation of carefully selected poems—his best work—into English. I believe that he deserves better than he has received at the hands of his critics, at the hands of his English and American enthusiasts, and even at his own hands in his own translations.

Is it fair to judge his English versions by an aesthetic not his own and by the poems of writers whose native language is English? Perhaps not entirely, but they appeared as poems in English and are therefore fair game. Nothing I say, however, is intended to detract from the great achievement of Tagore in Bengali nor to preclude the possibility that his best poems may yet appear in suitable English dress. On the contrary, the time is overdue for such an appearance.

As everyone knows, it was *Gitanjali* that launched his great reputation in the 1910's. The manuscript of this book got Tagore the attention of William Butler Yeats, who wrote an introduction to it and praised it highly, and the attention of Sturge Moore, who immediately nominated Tagore to the selection committee for the Nobel Prize in Literature. It was *Gitanjali* that catapulted his receiving the prize in 1913. It was this book that excited Ezra Pound, who sent selections from it to Harriet Monroe for publication in an early issue of *Poetry* magazine, the most influential of the little magazines in the renaissance of America poetry during the 1910's. It was the poetry of this book that critics considered equal or superior to everything in the West from the Songs of David, the writings of the Christian mystics, and Dante, on down to Milton, Wordsworth and Shelley. Things had moved very fast. All of this attention came within a year and nine months of his translating the poems. The year 1913 saw not only the first London and New York trade editions of *Gitanjali,* but also the first editions of *Crescent Moon* and *The Gardener,* both translated by Tagore and revised slightly by Yeats. These appeared in other editions in the same decade, together with first editions of a number of other books by Tagore. Tagore was indeed one of the sensations of the time.

Whether he had wanted it or not, and whether his poetry merited the adulation it received or not, Tagore was caught up in a whirlwind of others' devising. He neither expected nor encouraged the adulation. In fact, he seemed baffled and embarrassed by all the attention he was getting. To William Rothenstein, his friend and literary intermediary, he wrote, "I never could have dreamt that my translations were worth anything, and up to the last moment was fearful lest you should be mistaken in your estimation of them." Further, he indicated to Rothenstein a very modest aim in the translation: "to make them simple with just a suggestion of rhythm to give them a touch of the lyric, avoiding all archaisms and poetical conventions." That such comments were more than mere courtesy and humility is evidenced by other letters, for example this one to Indira Devi:

> You have alluded to the English translation of *Gitanjali.* To this day I have not been able to imagine how I came to do it and how people came to like it so much. That I cannot write English is such a patent fact, that I never had even the vanity to feel ashamed of it.

In view of this attitude, one cannot help feeling sorry for this humble, modest writer when one makes or reads unflattering observations on his poetry. For little more than an exercise, he had translated some of his poems into English and then passed them on as a courtesy to his newly acquired friend, Rothenstein, who then set the whirlwind in motion. Nevertheless, one must unsentimentally judge a poet by his poems and not by his intention, nor by the strength and sincerity of his feelings when he wrote the poems.

Even during the 1910's Tagore's poems were far from universally admired. In a letter to Harriet Monroe, the poet Alice Meynell responded to Tagore's appearance in *Poetry* by admitting that she was "trying to meet Mr. Tagore half-way." Much more bluntly, John Butler Yeats, the painter and father of the poet, wrote thus to his son about the content and style of Tagore's poetry:

> His ideas are vapourously philanthropic . . . Out of vapour you can make a background or an atmosphere, not the body of the poetry, the feelings it excites [are] too tepid, and who indulges himself in that kind of speculation weakens his power in its very source.

The simple truth of the matter is that the early English versions of Tagore's poetry do not conform well with the demands of the new poetry emerging in England and especially America, nor actually to the demands of earlier English poetry either. These poems, as poetry, do not in fact merit the adulation they received. As poetry, they do justify Tagore's own hesitations and the hesitations and complaints of intellectuals like Alice Meynell and John Butler Yeats. (pp. 78-81)

Among the most influential poets of the English-speaking world, it was Yeats and Pound who did more than anyone else to establish Tagore's reputation in England and America, yet both in time lost patience with Tagore. Any analysis of Tagore's reputation and his poems in English must take into account the attitudes and motivations of these two writers. As professional men of letters and humanitarians, both were interested in the literature of the

As a painter, Tagore exhibited affinities with European expressionists. This example is entitled "Mother and Child."

non-English speaking world: therefore, Yeats and Pound would naturally encourage this new and different voice from the East. It was their job to do so; nevertheless, one must observe that they went overboard in their enthusiasm. The introduction Yeats wrote to *Gitanjali* was called "hyperbolical" and "impetuous," and one review seemed to contain a sarcastic, veiled reference to Yeats as an aesthete and Pound as an iconoclast when it reported that Tagore's poetry has "the familiar humanitarianism that appeals so piquantly alike to the delicate aesthete and the prosperous iconoclast."

It is easier to defend Yeats, however, than Pound. Yeats tried hard to work with Tagore and the Macmillan Company over revisions of Tagore's poetry but gave the job up after three books. The work frustrated him, for he knew that his revisions of Tagore were only cosmetic, as a letter of 1917 indicates:

> I merely make ordinary press revisions for there is nothing between that and exhaustive revising of all phrases and rhythms that "have lost their soul" or have never had souls. Tagore's English has grown better, this is to say more simple and more correct, but it is still often very flat.

By the 1930's his tone had become even more impatient. To Rothenstein he wrote:

> Damn Tagore. We got out three good books, Sturge Moore and I, and then, because he thought it more important to see and know English than to be a great poet, he brought out sentimental rubbish and wrecked his reputation.

Yeats had apparently never had anything but limited appreciation for Tagore anyway. In an earlier, 1912, letter to Edmund Gosse, he admitted that *Gitanjali* "is unequal and there are dull pages," but he also said, "you will not read far in it without coming to great beauty."

Why, then, in addition to a sense of professional duty as a man of letters and those passages of "great beauty," did Yeats support Tagore? Some reasons may have little to do with the worth of Tagore's poetry, as such. In the same letter to Gosse referred to above, Yeats said that Tagore's election to a particular group in England would be a piece of "wise imperialism" and that honouring Tagore would "honour India also." Perhaps these motives were also close to the surface in the encouragement Yeats gave Tagore as a poet. In addition, Mary Lago has argued that the qualities Yeats found most attractive in Tagore— "innocence, simplicity, spontaneity, and the sense of a mythic tradition, dim, undefined, but certainly reaching back to the unrecorded past"—were the very "attributes that Yeats was determined to reconstruct for Irish literature." Similar to this observation but written sarcastically was the comment of a contemporary reviewer who said that Tagore's poems were "lauded by Yeats for the good reason that they somehow belong to the same trailing end of the romantic movement as do his own sweet mysticisms." Yeats no doubt did find Tagore a kindred spirit for his own early romantic and mystical inclinations, but Yeats was rapidly leaving romanticism behind; and his mysticism, though comparable at times to Eastern mysticism, was maturing poetically to the point that it would

find expression in such lines as the concluding passage of "Among School Children." Here he starts with the images of blossoming and dancing, one image each from nature and art:

> Labour is blossoming or dancing where
> The body is not bruised to pleasure soul,
> Nor beauty born out of its own despair,
> Nor blear-eyed wisdom out of midnight oil.

And then the culmination comes:

> O chestnut-tree, great-rooted blossomer,
> Are you the leaf, the blossom or the bole?
> O body swayed to music, O brightening glance,
> How can we know the dancer from the dance?

In their tightness and texture, these lines make *Gitanjali*'s poems look loose, tepid, pale, like the pseudo-mystical and pseudo-poetic lines of Kahlil Gibran's *Prophet.* I can find nothing in Tagore's English translation to match, as pure poetry, these lines by Yeats.

Though Yeats was accused of impetuosity in his promotion of Tagore, Pound's response to Tagore was more clearly impetuous. In letters to Harriet Monroe, he revealed for Tagore an interest that bordered on pure, uncritical, literary politics. He wrote, "I'll try to get some of the poems of the very great Bengali poet Rabindranath Tagore. They are going to be *the* sensation of the winter . . . " A month later he had come up with *"The Scoop"* that he had acquired some poems for *Poetry* and that *"we're* to hold down the American copyright . . . we—*Poetry*—have got six poems at the least; and nobody else will have *any."* One gets the impression that Pound was more interested in the scoop than in the poetry.

When Pound responded to poetry whose texture excited him, he was quite clear and coherent, as in this comment on the poetry of "H. D." (again to Monroe):

> I am sending you some *modern* stuff by an American, I say modern, for it is in the laconic speech of the Imagists, even the subject matter is classic . . . This is the sort of American stuff I can show here and in Paris without its being ridiculed. Objective—no slither; direct—no excessive use of adjectives, no metaphors that won't permit examination. It's straight talk, straight as the Greek.

Pound could not have written that enthusiastically about Tagore's style. By contrast, he had to struggle and practically admit failure in his comments on Tagore. He does say that the "precision of his language remains" in translation and that his poetry contains "occasional brilliant passages," but such comments are few and vague, and they are overshadowed by other observations that express a lack of confidence. After calling the appearance of Tagore's poems "very important," Pound admits that "I am by no means sure . . . I can convince the reader of this importance." Later, he says, "there is in him the stillness of nature . . . He is at one with nature, and finds no contradictions." His poems illustrate a "balance and correction," but "I cannot prove it." Finally, after some of the vaguest comments in all of his criticism, Pound seems to throw his arms in the air and admit, "I do not think I have ever undertaken so difficult a problem of criticism" and that "When criticism fails one can do no more than go, personally, security for the value of the work one is announcing."

After these youthful outbursts, Pound, like Yeats, collected himself and spoke more realistically (to Monroe once again):

> God knows *I* didn't ask for the job of correcting Tagore. He asked me to. Also it will be very difficult for his defenders in London if he takes to printing anything except his best work. As a religious teacher he is superfluous . . . And his philosophy hasn't much in it for a man who has "felt the pangs" or been pestered with Western civilization . . . In his original Bengali he has the novelty of rime and rhythm and expression, but in a prose translation it is just "more theosophy." Of course if he wants to set a lower level than that which I am trying to set in my translations of Kabir, I can't help it. It's his own affair.

Pound, like Yeats a major advocate of Tagore, could not in all honesty find Tagore's English versions very remarkable.

Yeats and Pound helped create the image of Tagore as an exotic Hindu mystic whose calm wisdom counterpoints and shames our Western hustle and bustle. Part of their attraction to Tagore was no doubt a nostalgia for Tagore's simpler, less complicated attachment to life than the Western world could claim, caught up as it was in materialism and technology; and standing, as it was, on the brink of world war. It was a nostalgia for unity—a dream. Pound said in his review of Tagore in *Poetry* magazine, "The Bengali brings us the pledge of calm which we need overmuch in an age of steel and mechanics. It brings a quiet proclamation of the fellowship between man and the gods, between man and nature." We find this theme echoed over and over. On Tagore's presence in America and his lectures there, Harriet Monroe observed, "Something in his quiet dignity made our overactivity seem absurd." A reviewer in the *Athenaeum* similarly remarked that "His verse has a serenity which is one of the lessons most needed by the restless peoples of the West." Indeed, it was largely for this that Tagore was lionized and sentimentalized, in spite of fears by Rothenstein that "Tagore's saintly looks, and the mystical element in his poetry should attract . . . the sentimentalists who abound in England and America."

In short, it was largely for his tone and content that Tagore was given such immediate adulation, and not for the texture of his poetry. The moderns had rejected Romantic and Victorian poetry, together with conventional diction and forms. And even though Tagore's simple style and his choice of prose poetry coincided to a degree with the interests of the new poets, the kinship was simply not strong enough to sustain much interest for very long. While poets like Pound were busily refining the new poetry into existence, Tagore's own translations did not show enough freshness to command continued attention. A review in the *Athenaeum* put its finger on Tagore's major weakness as a poet in English when it described his poems' "negation of movement and colour, and the deliberate flavour-lessness of their simplicity . . . " This "negation" and "flavourlessness" was in direct contradiction to the aims of poetry as practiced and advocated by Yeats and Pound.

In fact, while poets in England and America were turning their backs on older styles and sentiments, Tagore clung to them. He took modern poetry to task. The major Western influences on Tagore were Romantic: Goethe in Germany; Wordsworth, Keats, and Shelley in England; Whitman and Emerson in America. He refers to these poets time after time, nor is the attraction surprising. Most of these poets had themselves been influenced by Indian thought and literature. The pantheism and transcendentalism of European and American Romantics had been derived in large part from the rapid transmission of Indian writings in the West during the late eighteenth and early nineteenth centuries. What Tagore liked in the romantics was essentially what they had gotten from India—their mystical insistence on the closeness, indeed, the unity of the divine, the human, and the natural world in general. Tagore had little interest in the kind of sensibility that came to be called existential. In fact, his aesthetic was diametrically opposed to it: "Poetry and the arts cherish in them the profound faith of man in the unity of his being with all existence."

In the 1910's the Romantic temperament and the Romantic concepts that had for a time in the nineteenth century linked East and West were rapidly falling away. Tagore maintained his ways, and they were the ways of Romanticism. From its beginnings, Indian literature had been Romantic. The lyrical lushness of the *Ramayana,* for example, and its delineation of the close kinship between human, divine, and natural are not found in ancient Western saga. The delicate fairyland motifs of the *Ramayana* are not found in the same way in early Western literature. The story of Rama and Sita themselves, with all the mystical and romantic overtones concerning the unity of the masculine and feminine, the unity of adored and adorer—these ideas are not found in ancient Western literature. It was not until medieval times in the West that male-female pairs and tones of romance coloured our literature. Then after the Middle Ages, the Romantic sensibility went underground again until the late eighteenth century, when poets like Goethe and Wordsworth revived and refined Romanticism. Indian literature has always been romantic; Western literature has not. Romanticism was in retreat in the West when Tagore made his appearance there. A contemporary reviewer called Tagore's poetry in English "a true flower of the autumn of romance." Tagore would not have understood that. Romanticism was for him perennial. The irony is that he appeared during the autumn of romance in the West. (pp. 82-9)

An objective view of Tagore's poetry and his reputation reveals that those English and American readers who admired him did so for reasons other than the excellence of his poetry as poetry. They found occasional passages worthy of being called good poetry, but they were struck, by and large, by his sentiments and his tone. Tagore wrote some 3,000 poems and songs. I know of no English or American poet who wrote as much. He penned some 100,000 lines of poetry. This quantity astonishes those who realize that a great writer like John Milton wrote only about 18,000 lines of poetry. Was Tagore able to plug into some cosmic field of creativity and produce poetry at will without much need for polish and revision? Or did he spin out his lyrics all too easily, producing only slight variations on a few simple themes, achieving excellence only every now and then? These are difficult questions for readers of English and American poetry to answer. We have seen only a portion of his poetry and have reasons to suspect the quality of the translations of much of what we have seen.

The translations of Amiya Chakravarty and Aurobindo Bose, especially, have gone a long way to fill our lack, but most readers of Tagore's poetry in the last quarter-century have had basically the same translations that came out in the 1910's. After not having been published in America since the 1910's, for example, *The Gardener* and *Crescent Moon* reappeared in 1956 and 1957, respectively. *Gitanjali,* after having appeared as a book in America only once since 1920, appeared again in 1957. *Fruit Gathering,* published originally in 1916, came out again in America in 1957. It is true that these were contained in the *Collected Poems and Plays,* first published in America in 1936, but the translations were the same, and this book saw new editions in 1956, 1961, and 1962. *The Tagore Reader,* first published in 1961, did have some new translations, but it also reprinted some of the old ones.

What we see in all of this publishing activity is a revitalized interest in Tagore. His reputation went down after 1920, and even though there were some editions of his work in the thirties and forties, the period after 1956 saw a remarkable increase in publishing activity in America. Part of this renewed interest had to do with the Tagore birth centenary in 1961, but it also coincided with a larger turning to the East that swept America in the sixties and still shows some signs of life. Though Tagore was not read by American youth to the same degree that Hesse and others were, this second big period of Tagore's popularity may nevertheless be part of a larger vogue for the spiritual meaning of the East. As a vogue, it should remind us of the fears of Rothenstein, expressed in the 1910's, that "the mystical element in his [Tagore's] poetry should attract the sentimentalists who abound in England and America." I believe that an objective evaluation of Tagore's poetry would be the best corrective to such sentimentality and that a good edition of his best poems would give Tagore a perennial reputation, and not one that ebbs and flows with changing vogues.

I once heard a teacher-poet-critic characterize the success of poems according to the degree to which they satisfied his hunger for poetry. (His taste was educated.) Only rarely do I find lines in Tagore that satisfy my hunger. One such is this, from *Gitanjali,* 60: "On the seashore of endless worlds is the great meeting of children". Another, from *Lover's Gift,* is this: "There is a looker-on who sits behind my eyes." Yet another—from a later poem, "The Child"—is this: "The darkness of the valley stares like the dead eye-sockets of a giant." Even more rarely do I find a complete poem that satisfies my hunger. One such is this

beautifully simple statement (in which I find none of the faults mentioned above):

> On the bank of Rup-Narain
> I awake:
> This world
> Is not a dream.
> In words of blood I saw
> My being.
> I knew myself
> Through hurts
> And pain.
> Truth is hard
> And never deceives.
> I loved that hardness,
> Death-long *tapasya* of suffering
> To win truth's terrible value
> And to pay all debts
> In death.

The poetic truth of this poem is hard and doesn't deceive, and therein lies its beauty.

When there are poems like this available, why must we be swamped with Tagore's less-than-good poetry? In recent years, some of our outstanding poets have turned increasingly to translation. John Ciardi, for example, combined the duties of poet and scholar in order to render Dante into excellent English poetry. Robert Bly and Denise Levertov have turned to the East. What we need now is a gifted poet to select from Tagore's voluminous writings a good hundred or so lyrics, like **"On the Bank of Rup-Narain,"** and transform them into the kind of excellent English poetry that is capable of bearing the large heart, mind, and soul of this sincere, kindly, wise, and, I am convinced, incompletely appreciated poet. (pp. 94-7)

Melvin D. Palmer, "Tagore's Poetry in English: A Candid View," in Rabindranath Tagore: American Interpretations, *edited by Ira G. Zepp, Jr., A Writers Workshop Publication, 1981, pp. 78-98.*

Tagore's 1916 visit to the United States:

In Southern California Tagore was delighted by the harmony of man and nature, and especially by the beauty of the women, of whom he remarked, "It is a pleasure simply to watch them." The fragrant groves of orange trees so intoxicated him that one day he spent hours just sitting in meditation among them. "This is a beautiful country," he told the reporters who were always dogging his heels. "I believe it has a great future." His mood was decidedly optimistic. "America is unhampered and free to experiment for the progress of humanity," he declared. "Of course she will make mistakes, but out of these series of mistakes she will come to some higher synthesis of truth and be able to hold up the banner of Civilization. She is the best exponent of Western ideals of humanity."

Stephen Hay in Rabindranath Tagore: American Interpretations, *1981.*

Kristine M. Rogers   (essay date 1989)

[*In the following excerpt, Rogers discusses Tagore's innovative use of metric patterns from folk songs to loosen the stylistic constraints of traditional Bengali prosody.*]

Written Bengali in the nineteenth century was a special kind of literary language, called *sādhubhāsā* or 'pure speech'. It was a well-defined, universally-accepted literary style, based on the Middle Bengali of the sixteenth century, which was very different from the spoken Bengali of Tagore's day. The *sādhubhāsā* drew heavily on ancient Sanskrit for vocabulary and syntax. It used many compound words of the Sanskrit types as well as the older and heavier pronominal and verbal forms of Middle Bengali. It was a good vehicle for the traditional Bengali metre called *payār*. Despite Tagore's experimentations which began in 1887, this literary language continued as the norm well into the twentieth century.

There has been no equivalent phenomenon in English literature. One has to imagine it. What if the sole and absolute way of writing English down through the centuries had been the English in *Beowulf,* or the English of Chaucer, or even the English of Shakespeare? This written norm would have applied to everything—books, journals, newspaper articles, even personal correspondence. Not only the archaic vocabulary would have been required, but also the style of rhymed couplets in iambic pentameter, for example. Imagine living in Britain or the United States at the turn of this century and reading about events of the day—Wilbur and Orville Wright's Kitty Hawk flight in 1903, for instance—in Chaucerian English in iambic pentameter! A situation not unlike this hypothetical one existed in Bengal at that time. The written language had been the same for centuries while the spoken language, of course, had changed constantly. While it is true that Bengali prose had reached a measure of respectability by the mid-nineteenth century, still it was required also to follow the *sādhubhāsā* rules about grammar and syntax even as it struggled to free itself from the metric rules.

Imagine further. What if, while the vocabulary, syntax, rhyme, and metre of Chaucer remained the norm for written English in subsequent centuries, various regions of people of Anglo-Saxon heritage began developing a folk literature which changed and developed as everyday speech changed and developed? These folk traditions actually did develop in English and were allowed in time to transform both written and spoken English. In Bengal, however, the interaction between the folk and literary traditions did not take place. They were two separate worlds until Tagore slowly but surely dissolved the barriers between them and made them one.

If such was the state of the Bengali language, what then was the nature of Tagore's Bengali audience? The people who would have listened to and/or read Tagore's poetry were definitely upper-class Bengalis like Tagore himself, members of the *bhadralok,* the wealthy and cultured élite of Calcutta. They were well and widely read (though not well and widely enough to suit Tagore sometimes). The upper-class Bengalis were analytical, given to reflecting upon a work of art and how it affected them. They were articulate. They saw themselves as possessors of great artistic sensibility (*sahridayas,* to use the Sanskrit term). Many of these upper-class Bengalis wrote poetry themselves and published it in the many private newspapers and journals which kept the Calcutta *bhadralok* buzzing with literary feeling and controversy. Evening poetry readings and musical recitals, in which these people presented their own compositions, were the major form of entertainment.

One might conclude from the above that there was a very active critical tradition in Bengal in the nineteenth century. Such was not the case, however: literary and artistic criticism did not occur in any organised kind of way. Tagore often lamented the fact that there were no worthy literary standards against which to judge poetry, plays, and novels. He felt that each person criticised a poem or play according to his/her own likes and dislikes rather than according to some identifiable and accepted criteria, and he was quite right in this perception of his countrymen's judgements. They could articulate how they felt about a poem or play, but they could not say whether it was inherently good or bad. But then neither could Tagore. What he was unaware of, because he himself was part of it, was the influence of certain unconscious criteria underpinning his own aesthetic judgements as well as those of his fellow Bengalis. These criteria had a great deal to do with the role of the audience in a work of art on the Indian subcontinent.

Bengalis in the late nineteenth century were not critics; they were first and foremost an audience. Deeply grounded in the traditions of Sanskrit poetics, they expected to be filled with *rasa,* or literary relish, by a poem or play. They expected to be lifted up into a kind of transcendental state. In such a state they became one with the poet, with the poem or play, and with Eternal Truth and Beauty. Any rational, organised critical tradition, as we know it in the West, would have militated against this 'communion'—this state of union between poet and audience, between a poem and Eternal Truth. To be a critic, one must resist identification; one must maintain a substantial distance; one must remain an observer and not become a participant. The Bengali audience was at all times a total participant in the aesthetic experience. Those Bengalis who were artists and writers themselves also expected 'communion' to result when their own works were presented. That communion was the affirmation and reward they sought.

Tagore too had these assumptions about the audience, the work of art, and the artist. He, as poet and playwright and novelist, expected communion, an appreciative oneness, in response to his creations. . . . [He] achieved this communion with the members of his extended family. They understood his genius and were willing to follow him, unquestioningly, wherever this genius would take him. He was, after all, one of their own, steeped in the family tradition of producing something extraordinary and unprecedented through a combination of the new and the old. But the Bengali literati at large were not steeped in such a tradition, did not give Tagore the benefit of the doubt, and so could not follow him in his development, particularly as a poet. As he pursued his own inner lights, Tagore began to innovate, to change the norms through which he wanted that oneness between poet and audience to be achieved. The more he innovated, the less his late nineteenth-century Bengali *bhadralok* audience could commune with him because they were not aware of his new assumptions. Over the years he followed fewer and fewer of the traditional rules, so more and more of his audience fell by the wayside, using the lame (to Tagore) excuse: 'I didn't like it.' What that statement really meant was, 'I didn't understand it. You aren't doing any of the things I have learned to respond to.' The extremely sensitive Bengali audience, deprived of its communion, was vicious in its censure of its greatest poet during his lifetime.

Tagore had a very thin skin. He suffered greatly from this negative response, perceiving it as unjust. Time and time again in his letters and essays, he lashed out at his 'critics,' saying they were good for nothing and that he had no use for them. A good poem stands by itself, he believed, and does not need analysis; that is, a good poem generates the desired communion of itself. A bad poem does not deserve to be read, much less analysed; that is, it does not generate communion and should be ignored. Not even Tagore, so maligned as he felt, could articulate precisely what made a poem good or bad. Some interior sense of identification and oneness was still the only standard, even for him.

Tagore's genius continued to alienate him from his audience throughout his eighty-year life. The innovations he made early in his poetic career became the norms for Bengali poetry later in his life. But by then he had moved on to other innovations, thus violating the very norms he himself had set earlier. Small wonder that he so often despaired of his audience and they of him.

Of course, over the years Tagore and his poetic art were not the only things that changed. His audience was changing as well. He sought out and found other listeners, outside the narrow circle of the Calcutta *bhadralok*. He felt called to speak for all of Bengal, for the poor, for India, for universal humankind. Through changes in subject matter, metre and rhyme schemes, and philosophical attitudes, he both courted and attracted other audiences. The locus of the communion changed. He seemed to reach out in ever-widening circles to encompass the universe.

For a brief period in the second decade of the twentieth century, Tagore achieved 'communion' with Western Europe. Certain poets and artists in England, among them William Butler Yeats and William Rothenstein, found comfort against the menacing portents of the First World War in Tagore's translations of some of his religious poetry. This communion with Europe was short-lived because the critical tradition in the West is *too* strong. Western readers are sons and daughters of Aristotle; they are not *sahridayas*. After that initial excitement in Europe that brought Tagore the Nobel Prize for Literature in 1913, a decision that still generates controversy today, his popularity faded drastically. He remained known only to those who were already Indophiles. Such is the case today.

It is crucially important to understand the background to the state of the Bengali language and the nature of Tagore's nineteenth-century audience if we wish to appreciate any of Tagore's major achievements. For those who do not read Bengali, the task is probably impossible. What follows is an attempt to describe several of Tagore's innovations in terms of some parallels in English literature.

What did the Bengali *bhadralok* between 1880 and 1900 expect to hear from Tagore the poet? By and large, that audience expected to hear the Bengali version of Sanskrit *mahākāvya*. It expected 'great poems' dealing with great themes: gods and goddesses, heroes and heroines, engaged in divine and semi-divine activities throughout the three worlds. The audience expected these poems to be written in the traditional Bengali metre, called *payār,* with its rhymed couplets with fourteen syllables to a line. There was usually a pause after the first eight syllables, and again at the end of the line:

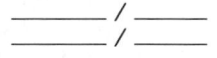

The overall effect in Bengali would have been not unlike the overall effect of the speech in English blank verse from Act 4, Scene 1 of *The Merchant of Venice,* which begins: 'The quality of mercy is not strain'd; / It droppeth as the gentle rain from heaven / Upon the place beneath.' These are high and noble sentiments proclaimed in high and noble verse. A more contemporary example in English of what the Bengali audience expected to hear from Tagore is the sonnet by Elizabeth Barrett Browning, which begins: 'How do I love thee? Let me count the ways.' Again, Browning's sonnet is measured and rhythmic speech, enshrining some of the most glorious of human emotions. These two examples were chosen in particular because each has become a cliché in our everyday English language. The tendency to quote these passages has occurred, in large part, because of the verbal music of the lines. Too bad our memories are so short! The verbal music is sustained throughout both passages. If we could remember more, we could recite the whole thing as we walk down the street or attend to our daily work, just as the Bengalis even today recite Tagore's poems and sing his songs.

If the above passages indicate what Tagore's audience might have expected, what did they actually hear? They heard many, many things but not anything they had come to expect. One English parallel of what his audience heard is the following:

> Humpty-Dumpty sat on a wall.
> Humpty-Dumpty had a great fall.
> All the King's horses and all the King's men
> Couldn't put Humpty together again.
> (Children's Nursery Rhyme)

And this:

> It's a gift to be simple, it's a gift to be free.
> It's a gift to come down where you ought to be.
> And when you find yourself in the place just right,
> Then you'll be in the valley of love and delight.
> (American Shaker Song)

Tagore took his audience totally by surprise. He presented them with metric patterns they identified as appropriate to nursery rhymes, to a school child's recitation of the multiplication tables. In some ways even more confounding was his use of the boat songs and folk ballads, particularly of East Bengal—rhythms and imagery until that time beyond the pale of serious literature—as models for his own songs and poems.

It is fascinating to track the path of Tagore's experiments with metre, rhyme and theme in poetry. One can do so by reading the poems he wrote between 1890 and 1900 particularly, and his essays in Bengali metre (*chanda*), most of the latter written after 1900. Initially, Tagore experimented with the traditional *payār* metre: breaking up the lines, varying the place of the caesura, enjambing the lines, lengthening them from fourteen to eighteen syllables, deliberately choosing words which had only consonant-vowel-consonant-vowel patterns, then just as deliberately choosing words with consonant clusters (or conjuncts as they are called in Bengali). This last series of experiments brought the great breakthrough: the rhythm natural to Bengali is not so much a function of long and short vowels (as it is in Sanskrit) but rather a function of the frequency of the consonant clusters. Tagore 'discovered' or 'invented' a new metre which reckoned the rhythm on the basis of consonants, not vowels. This metre was later called *mātrābritta* metre. Tagore's first book of poems in *mātrābritta* metre was **Mānasi (Imaginary Woman)**, published in 1890.

Once a tiny crack gave way within the wall of the traditional patterns, it was a small matter to make the whole edifice crumble. Tagore turned to his collection of folk ballads and nursery rhymes (assisted in this collection process by his nieces and nephews . . .) and began to use those rhythms for the first time in serious poetry. His first book of poetry in *svarabritta* or folk metre was **Kshanikā (Fleeting Moments)** published in 1900. That book, like **Mānasi**, was another turning point.

From 1900 on, Tagore played constantly with all three of these basic metric styles. Poetry seemed above all else to be *lilā* (creative play) for him, and he never seemed to tire of spinning out form after form after form. In his last years Tagore wrote what he called *gadya chanda* or prose verse, something comparable to what we call free verse in English but also different. It was as though the two separate lines of his experimentation—the line of poetic innovation and the line of prose development . . .—converged finally, and something newer and more wonderful than either was born.

As he experimented with metre, Tagore also innovated in other ways: he used fewer and fewer of the pronominal and verbal forms of the *sādhubhāsā*, choosing instead the shorter spoken forms. He also indicated (by means of a special diacritical mark) that all the words were to be pronounced the way they were in normal speech. And finally, as noted earlier, he turned from gods and goddesses as the subject of his poems, to ordinary, everyday people and their lives, and then to his own inner emotions and state of mind. (pp. 35-41)

[The] years Tagore spent on the rivers of East Bengal supervising the family estates profoundly affected his political, social and poetic consciousness. During this time the endless experimentation with metre and the continuing compilation of ballads, East Bengali boat songs and other

formulations from the folk tradition perfected the technical side of Tagore's poetic art. These changes culminated in the publication in 1900 of **Kshanikā (Fleeting Moments)**, the pivotal book in Tagore's poetic career. Most of these poems were written during the months of *Jyaistha* and *Ashār* (mid-May to mid-July) in 1900, when Tagore was living at Shelidah on one of the *zamindāris*. Beside the fact that these poems were written within the same few months, they have two other noteworthy characteristics in common. First, forty-nine of the sixty-two poems are written in *svarabritta* metre, the Bengali metre used in folk ballads and nursery rhymes. It was the first time this metre was used in serious poetry by an established poet. Second, there is a special relationship in almost every instance between the *svarabritta* metre and the content of the poem. These forty-nine poems are different from the remaining thirteen, which are written in *mātrābritta* metre, Tagore's earlier innovation. The metre became half the message.

Tagore broke new ground in the language of **Fleeting Moments.** It is bare, unornamented and simple. It is the language of conversation, filled with the same ease, effortlessness and vitality of a person speaking his or her mother tongue in an everyday situation. Many years after the book was published, Tagore wrote in an essay entitled **'Bhāsār Kathā'** published in *Sabujpatra* (*Caitra*, 1917):

> In **Kshanikā** I first used in a continuous manner natural Bengali language and natural Bengali meter. At that time, the energy, force, and beauty of that language became clear. I saw that this language is not a vehicle just for rural matters like a horse or a rustic pony; its power of movement and power to convey are much greater than the artificial language of books.

The poet realised that the ancient Bengali folk metre (using colloquial forms of pronouns, verbs and participles) was a vehicle worthy of carrying more important things than lays and ballads of the countryside. In fact, he found that the metre natural to Bengali had more expressive power than the *sādhubhāsā* which up to his time, as indicated earlier, had been the norm for the written word.

The poems in **Fleeting Moments** celebrate the meaning of the title: the transitoriness of the individual moment. The root of the Bengali word *kshanikā* is *ksan* or 'moment' which Sukumar Sen, one of Tagore's most sensitive critics, rightly interprets in the context of the book as both 'moment' (*muhurta*) and 'celebration' (*utsab*). Life is a series of moments, each of which must be snatched up and relished with gusto. There is a spirit of restlessness, impatience and freedom in these poems. This sense of freedom brings forth two responses in the poet, says Sen: (a) a joy that has no cause; and (b) an hostility to every kind of bond. Sen divides the poems in the book into those categories. Upendranath Bhattacharya, another reliable Tagore scholar, in his more extensive discussion, organises the poems into three categories: (1) celebrating the present moment; (2) poking fun at the traditional ascetic values; and (3) bidding a peaceful and restrained farewell to the life of enjoyment and pleasure. However one divides the themes, it is immediately apparent that the poet is saying very serious things despite his lighthearted, restless manner:

Not having the courage to make known deep matters in a solemn voice, the poet stealthily expresses very deep things in these easy poems in a casual voice. Rabindranath's thought, by reaching for the limits of form, has entered into the domain of the formless.

In *Fleeting Moments,* the poet presents a kaleidoscope of personal emotion, beautiful but ephemeral. The realisation of the transitory character of the individual moment fills the poet with terror as well as joy, anxiety as well as freedom, and he longs to be irresponsible as well as unencumbered. Sometimes his mood is playful and happy, sometimes nostalgic, sometimes irreverent and a little sarcastic, sometimes serious and foreboding. In some poems he gently reproves a beloved whose expectations he feels are too demanding. In other poems, he assumes the role of a traveller-lover who tenderly addresses his house-dwelling beloved. In some poems he takes issue with accepted norms of behaviour, vowing that he will never conform to the outmoded aspects of his society. In still others he admits the fear, sadness and misgivings he feels when he realises that his youth is over. The interplay between these various themes and emotional tones and the bouncing rhythm of the folk metre adds a deeper dimension to each poem's import. In the playful and irreverent poems the metre reinforces the emotional tone; in the more serious ones the metre undercuts the meaning, apparently in a valiant attempt to hide the true depths of the poet's feelings, thereby making them appear all the more genuine. In every case, each beat of the metre is the tap of time as it rushes headlong into Eternity.

One example from *Fleeting Moments* is 'The Drunkard' ('Mātāl'):

You smash the door to smithereens
and revel rashly here and there.
You squander your savings overnight,
dissolve your future into air.
Setting out with an ominous star,
you ridicule the norms and rules.
The wrong route at the wrong time—
you're only up to mischief. Fools!
You'll cut the rudder with your own two hands,
then a stormy gale will swell.
Still my friends, I'll take your vow:
to dash dead-drunk toward hell!

I've wasted my days with pious folk,
before their wisdom I've been meek.
Learning much my hair turned grey;
seeing more, my eyes grow weak.
The fact of birth has made me steward
of immortal good and ill;
the burden of such dissipation
clearly stupifies my will.
Your stormy gale grinds all to dust
and scatters it about pell-mell.
Now I know the joy of joys:
to dash dead-drunk toward hell!

Let a demon seize me by the hair,
let my fortunes flee in disarray.
The straight shall now divide and bend,
and I, befuddled, lose my way.
Men with families fill the world;
men of skill, the marketplace.

There is no dearth of famous folks,
too many folks of lesser grace.
So let them oil the world's great wheels
while I pursue the maelstrom. Too well
I know the work of works, my friends:
to dash dead-drunk toward hell!

My intellect, my prudent judgement
this day I do renounce in full.
I cast aside all knowledge, wisdom;
the gatherings of scholars no longer pull.
My flask of memories I knock to the floor,
spilling the wealth of this life's tears.
I plunge into the brimming wine,
its froth anoints my laughing sneers.
A raving wind rips off the emblem
of my former rank and weal.
I vow to take the high, broad road:
to dash dead-drunk toward hell!

(Translation by Kristine M. Rogers)

This poem, one among several in the book which poke fun at the norms and conventions of society, has another dimension. It is the celebration of reversals, the glorification of chaos, the renunciation of ordinary common sense and good judgement for the sake of another order of reality. The principal image is inebriation, an especially noxious vice in the Hindu society, which condemns all drinking of alcohol. The behaviour described in this poem would make the practitioner truly an outcaste. In choosing this image as a protest against the conventions of society, Tagore is both affirming an aspect of the literary and cultural tradition he inherited as well as changing it, giving it his own unique psychological and emotional twist.

In the first verse, the poet repeats society's conventional condemnation of the drunkard. In the second, he admits that a virtuous life, again according to societal standards, has got the poet himself exactly nowhere. In the third, he decides there are enough ordinary, conformist folks to keep the world going; his efforts are not necessary. In the final verse, he renounces all his intellectual faculties, his place in society, his well-being and security in order to 'plunge into the brimming wine' flowing from a 'flask of memories' containing the entire 'wealth of this life's tears.' He vows to take the 'high, broad road' and 'dash dead-drunk toward hell.' In four verses, Tagore has moved from conventional society, to counterculture, to the sorrow in the depths of his own heart and at the core of the universe.

The poet desires to be free of the proscriptions of conventional wisdom, the expectations of elders and learned men, the social obligations of the cultural élite. All these are only a 'fact of birth,' a chance occurrence. He now wants to make a choice; he wills to live by another set of standards. Intoxicated and destitute, he will cast prudence and responsibility to the wind: '. . . a stormy gale will swell'; 'Your stormy gale grinds all to dust . . . '; 'while I pursue the maelstrom . . . '; and 'A raving wind rips off the emblem . . . '. The wild abandon of this joyous revelry has a definite connection with the wind. And this image of the wind holds the key to the cultural encoding of the poem.

The words in the original Bengali describing the wind are: stormy (*jhoro*), uncommon (*sristichārā*), and raving (*ma-*

donmatta). In ancient times one of the words in Sanskrit which referred to madness was *vātula* (or *vātul*) which initially means 'inflated with wind or affected by the wind disease,' and then 'mad or insane, entirely devoted to or bent upon' as well as 'whirlwind, gale or hurricane'. Another word, *vyākula* (*byākul* in Bengali), means 'entirely filled with, intently engaged in, eager and impatient'. These two words have been given as the origin of the word 'Bāul'.

The Bāuls have been for centuries a deviant religious group in Bengal. They follow the *ulta* path, a path 'turned upside down,' because they believe they must proceed against the current of traditional Hindu social and ethical norms in order to advance spiritually. They gather truths from all religious perspectives but subscribe totally to none. Some of the Bāuls participate in esoteric tantric practices, secret rites of which wine is a main component. Many others are simply itinerant singing beggars. All of them have renounced the conventions of acceptable society. In using such phrases as the 'wrong path,' and 'stormy gale,' and 'raving wind', Tagore is alluding to this counter-culture religious movement. Drunkenness and revelry are the signs of the divine intoxication of the Bāuls. The *ulta* path is *not* the way to eternal damnation as conventional ethics would have it. Rather, the *ulta* path is a genuine means to liberation, an avenue to a deeper sobriety and a greater freedom, the 'joy among joys' and the 'work among works'.

Tagore, possibly the greatest Bāul of them all, chooses a special kind of wine for his singular kind of inebriation. In his state of frenzied revelry, he knocks over a 'flask of memories', spilling the 'wealth of this life's tears'. His memories and his tears are the 'brimming wine' into which he will plunge, its froth accentuating facial expressions of disgust, derision, and . . . agony! This is Tagore's *ulta* path: to inebriate himself with sorrow; to catch the froth of pain and bitterness on his beard; to consent, however unclearly, to being the cause of his own undoing. As he does in this poem, so he did throughout his life. His genius was to master and perfect his tradition and then to move beyond it. He was never satisfied with what he had achieved, so he constantly innovated; and thus he was always at odds with the past and the present.

The folk metre in the poem magnifies its complexities. The lilting, sing-song rhythm is an attempt to make light of and possibly to anesthetise the bitterness and pain. The metre is also a way to hold the hostility and disillusionment in check, coating them with a veneer of humour. We are initially engaged by this humour; soon we become uncomfortable at the deepening condemnation of society; finally, we are aghast to realise that the poet is neither joking nor derisive. He is weeping, pretending not to care at all because in reality he cares too much. The renunciation is in actual fact a commitment to follow his path to its end, whatever the cost. (pp. 41-7)

> *Kristine M. Rogers, "Rabindranath Tagore: Inheritor and Creator of Traditions," in* Rabindranath Tagore: Perspectives in Time, *edited by Mary Lago and Ronald Warwick, The Macmillan Press Ltd., 1989, pp. 26-49.*

France Bhattacharya   (essay date 1989)

[*In the following essay, Bhattacharya identifies the supernatural elements in Tagore's short stories and considers his use of both fantasy and realism as a fiction writer.*]

Tagore's short fiction presents abundant evidence of his genius as a story-teller, which his fame as a poet slightly overshadows. He was virtually the first writer in Bengali to take up the cultivation of this modern literary genre. Between 1884 and 1925 he wrote more than eighty short stories, all very different one from the other. Omitting the last three, published together fifteen years later, we shall consider those gathered in 1959 as the single volume, **Galpa Guccha.** Some ten of these may be labelled as 'supernatural' stories (*récits fantastiques*).

The supernatural in literature has been variously defined. For example, 'The supernatural . . . is characterised . . . by a brutal intrusion of mystery in the frame of real life' Or, 'The supernatural, as a whole, is a break with the accepted order, it is the eruption of the unacceptable in the midst of the inalterable daily rule of law.'

To these two definitions let us add another, from the pen of one of the masters of the short story, Maupassant. In 'La Peur' he wrote that the supernatural serves 'in the semi-darkness of a strange tale, to allow a glimpse of a whole world of disquieting things, uncertain, threatening.' More recently, Tzvetan Todorov, in his *Introduction à la littérature fantastique,* has given a far more precise definition of supernatural literature as a sub-genre of fiction. According to him, three conditions are necessary: 'Firstly, the text must force the reader to consider the world of the characters as a world of living persons and to hesitate between a natural and a supernatural explanation of the events described. Besides, this hesitation can also be felt by a character; thus the role of the reader is, so to say, entrusted to a character of the story and at the same time the reader's hesitation finds itself represented, it becomes one of the themes of the work. . . . Lastly, it is necessary that the reader adopt a certain attitude with regard to the text. He has to reject an allegorical interpretation as well as a poetical interpretation. These three requirements are not of the same value. The first and the third constitute, truly, the genre; the second may remain unfulfilled.'

We shall consider ten of Tagore's short stories in the light of these definitions, not following the chronological order of composition—literary history not being our concern in the present instance—but going from the general to the particular, analysing first the stories that can be called 'supernatural' under the widest possible definition, and ending with those that correspond exactly to Todorov's definition. The narrative technique is our principal focus. The author tells the story as third-person narrator, or it is told by what Todorov calls a represented narrator, that is, a protagonist who is a first-person narrator. The choice is important. In both cases a second narrator may intervene whose discourse is relayed by the first: a narrative within a narrative. In this case the represented narrator becomes the first person, so to speak, reacting to the story that he has heard and is now repeating. The represented narrator's views influence the ordinary reader's views.

'Ghāter Kathā' ('The Landing-Steps' Tale') has a first-person narrator: the *ghāt* itself, the stone steps leading to the river. Their role introduces, at the outset, a factor that is logically unexplainable, but this does not really disturb the reader, who sees it as an element more poetical than supernatural. Indeed, the descriptive opening of the story brings it close to being a kind of prose-poem. Obviously the *ghāt*, as narrator, is spokesman for an environment. It has more longevity than man has; yet, unlike Nature, it is not capable of cyclical renewal. Between the river, which is eternal, and the ephemeral inhabitants of its banks, the *ghāt* personifies the memory of generations. Whether allegorical or poetic, the narrative technique that makes the *ghāt* the speaker is never to be taken at its face value.

The supernatural, in its widest sense, that is, the bestower of a sense of mystery, exists also in the enigmatic personality of the 'renouncer,' the *sannyāsin*, who one day enters the life of Kusum, a young widow. Could he be her husband believed dead in a faraway land? Married when the girl was still a child, the couple had only glimpsed each other during the ceremony, then had been separated until the wife reached puberty. The question about the identity of the renouncer remains until the end. Had this man fled the cares and worries of the world, thus embracing the monastic way of life? In strict religious terms, sins are considered living-dead, and mystery accompanies the renouncer wherever he goes. Thus we have an example of the 'social-supernatural', dealing here with customs and creeds peculiar to India.

'Durāsā' ('Hope for the Unattainable') inhabits the border between the supernatural and the mysterious without allowing the supernatural totally to penetrate reality. Again there is a first-person narrator, an astonished witness of what he sees and hears. According to Todorov's formulation, this narrator is the privileged reader of the story. At every moment he questions the veracity of the story he has heard and which he now tells us. We are never allowed to forget the exceptional dimension of the narrated events, which border on the incredible. We identify ourselves with the city-bred, blasé, and sophisticated witness. Here the hesitation of the represented narrator defines the supernatural, while he listens to a story in which the circumstances of its narration and the identity of the teller are as strange as the narrated events. A narration within a narration is very useful in this kind of supernatural tale, as it helps the ordinary readers, ourselves, to react in the desired manner.

The first-represented narrator, who initiates the story, is a Bengali tourist visiting the Himalayan resort of Darjeeling. He walks alone in the rain and thick mist. He is self-assured, his view of life slightly ironical. The misty setting already suggests an atmosphere conducive to the supernatural. The tourist hears the sobs of a woman; she is a *sannyāsini*, an ochre-clad knotted-haired renouncer. A woman's cry in the street is surprising, but much more surprising are the sobs of one who, having conquered the senses, should ignore suffering. The tourist is not in the habit of mixing with wandering holy persons. Yet want of occupation, his solitude, and the unusual surroundings induce him to hear the woman's tale. The *sannyāsini* speaks Urdu, a language that the Bengali speaks rather poorly; this distancing introduces an additional element of strangeness. The woman's story begins in 1857, during the Mutiny, and the historical framework lends credence to the narrated events. In fact, the protagonist has been a Muslim princess in love with a Brahmin, the General-in-Chief of her father's army. Thirty-eight years have passed since she left her father's palace to search north India for the General, who had rejected her out of caste pride. She has tried to transform herself in body and soul to become a Hindu. The day Tagore's story begins, she has found the man she loves, but he is now old and fallen, an ordinary family man married to a casteless hill woman. The princess realises that she has wasted her life searching for an orthodox Brahmin who no longer exists.

The Bengali gentleman hesitates to believe this unlikely tale. Such social barriers are no less formidable than those between us and the dead. Tagore, in this story as in 'Ghāter Kathā,' insists on the significance of social transgression. As Todorov notes, the advent of the supernatural is closely linked to some transgression: 'Be it within the limit of social life or of the narration, the advent of the supernatural element always constitutes a break in the system of pre-established rules, and finds there its justification.' At the end the tourist no longer questions the likelihood of the narrated events but now questions the very existence of the woman narrator. The *sannyāsini* disappears, suddenly lost in the thick fog. When he comes to his senses the sun is shining, and the tourists, numerous now, stare at the *bābu* seated alone on a road-side stone. He does not rule out the possibility of a perceptional error. His hesitation calls into question the distance between the real and the imaginary; their contours blur.

Like the two preceding tales, 'Mahāmāyā' has a strong element of mystery; but there is no supernatural in the strict sense of the term. Tagore here takes up his recurrent theme of the living-dead. The central action of 'Mahāmāyā' occurs in its first part; the second offers explanations and a conclusion, but this destroys the sense of the supernatural, which arises from the reader's hesitation over the various strange happenings. A third-person non-represented narrator describes events without making them absolutely clear. Mahamaya—which means 'the great cosmic illusion'—is the name of a high-class Brahmin girl, a *Kulin*, for whom the lack of money makes marriage impossible. In a dilapidated temple she meets Rajiv, a Brahmin of an inferior rank. He loves her, wants to marry her and wants to take her away from the village. She will not disgrace her family but promises to meet Rajiv before his departure. That same night her elder brother marries her off on the cremation ground to a dying old man of her caste. By the next day she is a widow, to be burned to death on her husband's funeral pyre. Before this can happen, she goes in the night to Rajiv's house, makes him promise never to look at her face again, and leaves with him.

Here are all the ingredients of a supernatural tale: the ominous settings; the grim disposition of the protagonists, who express very little of their feelings; and the doubt as to whether Mahamaya is now a ghost. Although a third-person omniscient narrator tells the story, nothing is inserted to enlighten the reader as to whether Mahamaya has actually been on the pyre and has now risen as a ghost. Suddenly, however, there *are* explanations. Mahamaya did not die on the pyre but was burned and disfigured. A violent rain had extinguished the fire. Alone in the world, she had come for refuge to her lover. So straightforward an explanation is fatal to the supernatural. And yet the feeling of mystery remains, for the reader identifies himself with Rajiv, who does not know whether this Mahamaya is really the person who fled the pyre. But her presence is enough for him until, one day, unable to control his curiosity, he removes the veil that, like death, hangs between them. The matter is no longer in doubt. Mahamaya, the same and yet another, leaves, never to come back. The reader's surprise springs principally from the short story's social content. One shudders at the thought of marriage customs so revolting as the union of a young girl with a dying old man, the absolute power of a brother over his younger sister, and a widow's dying on her husband's funeral pyre. Mahamaya, who has gone through the ordeal by fire, belongs to death even though she is still alive. This woman is, truly, a kind of ghost. The supernatural reappears here at a deeper level of the story, along with the strong note of social protest.

One of the most powerful stories on this living-dead theme—a major category in the thematic analysis of the supernatural story—is **'Jivita o Mrita'** (**'Living and Dead'**), written at the beginning of Tagore's career as a short-story writer. Although divided into five chapters, it is nevertheless rather short. A childless widow lives in the family of a *zamindār,* her brother-in-law. The sole object of her affection is her small nephew. One day in the rainy season her heart suddenly stops beating, and she is declared dead. To keep the police from asking questions, the *zamindār* orders her body taken to the cremation ground at night. During the vigil, while the Brahmins who accompanied her wait for fuel, the corpse moves. The Brahmins, terrified, flee for help; when they return, they find only footprints on a muddy path. They think it wiser to tell the *zamindār* that the body has been cremated according to the rules.

Here also the narration is in the third person, and the omniscient narrator explains that the woman had fallen into a sort of coma and later regained consciousness. The supernatural element vanishes, since there is no longer any possibility for hesitation between the natural and the supernatural. The widow was never dead because she did not really die, but now her relatives consider her dead and are happy to be rid of her; she is a living woman whom society treats as one dead. Behind that assumption is a firmly entrenched superstition that anyone brought to the cremation ground as dead—or even taken to the Ganges to die there—belongs indisputedly to Death. The victim in our story considers *herself* dead to society. Not for a moment does she think of coming home; she knows she would bring there the 'evil eye'. 'I am my ghost', she says. The great irony is that she who was compelled to follow a high-caste Hindu widow's restricted ascetic life is now totally free for the first time. She enjoys, for a while, the pleasure

of independence, but soon fear overtakes her. She is ill at ease in the world of the living, since she absorbs the feeling of awe she produces in others. Free from rules of social conduct, but lacking any social role, she behaves differently from women of her caste and condition. She scandalises and frightens people. When, unable to resist her affection for her nephew, she goes home to catch a glimpse of him, she jumps into the pond and drowns in order to prove by her death that she had been alive.

The story describes a psychological case that is a result of social pressure. Only incidentally does it analyse the feeling of dread in witnesses of these—for them—unexplainable events. Once again the supernatural, as defined by Todorov, is absent. Once again Tagore is primarily concerned with criticism of social behaviour, which he condemns without didacticism but also without complacency. Woman, in Tagore's short stories, is most often a living-dead, a non-person whom society deprives of independence. At first subjected to her father, then to her husband, and at last to her son, if she is blessed with one, she can live only by proxy.

Two further stories differ thematically from those already discussed: mystery in both is linked to the acquisition and conservation of riches. Women play no part in their plots. The early story **'Sampatti-Samarpan'** (**'Riches in Custody'**) is about an old miser who knowingly buries with his riches in a temple cellar his only descendant, in the hope that the boy, becoming a *yaksa,* will look after his gold. The *yaksa* is a mystical guardian of treasures, an assistant of the god Kubera. But the old man hears day and night the cries of the dying boy. The story is based on a superstitious belief, but there is nothing here of the supernatural. Neither the omniscient narrator—the story is told in the third person—nor the reader believes for one moment in the boy's metamorphosis. No one doubts that remorse and eventual madness cause the constant shouts and sobs that the old man hears unceasingly—his own.

'Guptadhān' (**'Hidden Riches'**) is a later and longer story. It too is written in the third person. A man tries to decipher an enigma that will locate a treasure. At last he finds it, with the help of a mysterious *sannyāsin,* but he chooses to leave the riches untouched, for he is at last aware that the gold is of little value in comparison to freedom and life. This story is actually an allegorical tale. Its message is clear: cupidity is a suffocating prison. The lesson is more important than the fiction. As so often in allegory, there is no attempt at maintaining a high degree of verisimilitude. The *sannyāsin,* for instance, hidden but ever-present, waits days and nights near the opening of a labyrinth, expecting the hero to ask his help. Nor is there an explanation of the presence in a forest of such a quantity of gold.

On the other hand, the explanation given when the enigma is unravelled eliminates the supernatural. We learn that there is no real mystery, that everything is a matter of cleverness and luck. Thus the reader's hesitation between the 'marvellous' and the 'real' leads to allegory, not to the supernatural. Tagore was not averse to allegory, but in **'Guptadhān'** the numerous and lengthy digressions on the contrast between the beauty of Nature and the sterility of gold sound somewhat too moralistic.

Another group of short stories have as their theme, central or peripheral, the presence of the dead on earth. At first glance, these would seem to belong to the supernatural genre, but certain distinctions must be made. **'Kankāl'** (**'The Skeleton'**) belongs to Tagore's first series of stories. The first-person narrator is a young man who in childhood has learned anatomy with the help of a human skeleton kept in his study. A few years later, he spends a sleepless night in this room. In the dark, he sees the skeleton and hears it breathe. Linguistic devices introduce the dead's arrival on the scene. There are speech modalisations that modify the relation between the narrator and his discourse; for instance: 'it seemed to me that,' or 'it was as if'. The narrator proclaims that he is quite aware that his feeling of another's presence in the room is nothing but the product of his feverish brain, and the beatings he hears are nowhere but in his head. Still, he is afraid, and to control himself he engages the invisible being in conversation. The ghost says that he has come to see his own skeleton! Fear vanishes. The dialogue begins on a humorous note, and the skeleton, which is that of a woman, not a man, tells its life story. She was a child-widow, very proud of her beauty, who poisoned the doctor with whom she was in love, to punish him for marrying another. She then had killed herself, hoping to recover in the other world both her beloved and her beauty. But she finds herself a skeleton in a classroom. The story ends with the first croakings of the morning raven.

The reader feels fully justified in seeing this narrator as a day-dreamer who tries to give himself a fright, then allows himself some sensuous musings. Indeed the child-widow expresses herself with unusual frankness. Very rarely do Tagore's characters speak so candidly about love. The reader associates this kind of language with the narrator, a bold and mischievous young man, rather than with a high-caste woman, even though she is a ghost. Humour and laughter have driven away the supernatural, and **'Kankāl'** is a pleasant parody of the 'supernatural' short story.

'Māstārmasāy' (**'The Tutor'**) offers an example of the supernatural unaccompanied by comical or satirical overtone. On the contrary, pathos is the major note of this long story divided into a prologue and eleven short chapters. The prologue sets the scene; the remainder comprises a flashback. A third-person narrator introduces a young man named Majumdar, just come back to Calcutta from England, who takes a hired cab to return home after a dinner and numerous glasses of wine. Despite his drowsiness, he senses that the horses only go round and round in the open Maidan. Later he feels that someone sits by his side, but he sees no one. He shrinks aside, to allow more space for the invisible occupant whose bulk continuously increases. Then a pair of eyes that seem to peer at him in the dark remind him of someone. But of whom? When the cabman can control his horses, Majumdar reaches home. 'But during the night he did not sleep well. He kept asking himself: whose stare was this?'

The story tries to answer this question. First we learn of the affectionate relationship between a rich boy and his private tutor. When the pupil grows up, the teacher finds a responsible job in a British commercial firm. But because he is unable to repay several thousand rupees of the firm's money, stolen from his house by his spoilt ex-student, the teacher, his reputation in ruins, dies suddenly in a cab—of a stroke, one presumes.

The name Majumdar, mentioned once in the prologue, has suggested the link between the young man in the cab and the selfish and unscrupulous pupil responsible for his teacher's downfall. The other common factor is the journey to England. Otherwise, the text never says that they are one and the same. This time, the non-represented omniscient narrator does not let the reader believe for one moment the objective reality of a ghost's presence in the cab. The young man is drowsy, tipsy and sleepy. Psychologically, he is no longer watchful and may be unable to ward off the remorse that troubles him when, back in Calcutta, he thinks about his old teacher.

The impression of the supernatural is stronger for the phenomenon of the cab with its two maddened horses careering round and round. But even this can be taken for a simple nightmare resulting from indigestion, until one reads the last words of the cabman: 'Sir, it may not be only a dream. Three years ago, on this day, something happened in my cab.' Two explanations are possible, but there is some hesitation about each. The first supposes the intervention of the supernatural, as suggested by the cabman. The second takes into consideration only physical and material phenomena, in this case indigestion leading to a nightmare. The sophisticated reader may attempt a psychological explanation based on the guilty feelings of the cab passenger. The story, however, does not suggest such a reading. The chapters following the prologue give no place to the supernatural. They tell a very cruel story about the callousness of the rich. Strangely enough, the supernatural element, with its unresolved question introduced at the beginning, somewhat lightens the grimness of the social picture and lessens the sentimentality of the plot. A rational reader reacts to the supernatural in fiction in a way that stimulates an intellectual approach: he takes it as a clever game organised for his pleasure; he tries to see how he is almost made to believe in it. The reader is prompted to try finding as many explanations as possible for the strange event in the cab. Thus he is less aware of the sentimental overload of the story. In a story, based on the use of the supernatural, such as Maupassant's 'Le Horla', the reader is carried away by irrational fear of the unknown. This is a rare achievement on the part of the author.

'Nisithe' (**'In the Night'**) also suggests three types of explanation for strange happenings: the natural, the supernatural, both explicitly mentioned; and a psychological explanation. The first-person narrator is a country doctor, one of whose patients is the *zamindār* of the area. This eminent person calls on the doctor late at night; he cannot sleep; the medicines do not work. The *zamindār* rejects the doctor's suggestion that he has drunk too much wine. Hesitating, he begins his life story. (I prefer to use the term 'first-represented narrator' rather than primary narrator, because one should not forget that, even in stories told by a third person, there is a narrator—non-represented—not to be identified with the author.) The first-represented narrator, the physician, has in this case a double function. First, he reacts to the narrated events before we, the readers, can do so. Thus he influences our own interpretation. Second, as a medical man, he is ever ready to offer a natural explanation, if not a scientific one, of the phenomenon his patient describes. The *zamindār's* first wife, while nursing him back to health when he was near death, lost the child she was bearing. For a time, he had nursed her devotedly. He took her away for a change of air. Nothing helped. Realising that she would never recover, she urged him to take a second wife. The husband swore that he could never love anyone else. The sick woman laughed mockingly, but when the *zamindār* fell in love with a young girl, the wife poisoned herself in order to set him free. Thereafter, each time the man kissed his young wife he heard peals of laughter. The question *'Se ke?'* ('Who is she?') resounded in the darkness. When the *zamindār* ends his story, it is dawn. He recovers his assurance and wants to reassert his authority over the doctor to whom he has just shown his weakness. But the following night, 'again there was a knock on my door. "Doctor! Doctor!" '

This story, more basically than **'Māstārmasāy'**, employs the supernatural, and yet the *'fantastique'* never can appear. The physician, with whom the ordinary reader identifies himself, does not believe in the reality of the calls from beyond that trouble the landowner. For him, excessive drinking is the explanation. The doctor offers no other comment. Nor does the modern reader believe that the *zamindār* hears voices from the nether world. Without refuting the doctor's words, one inclines toward a psychological explanation: the events are outer manifestations, in a neurotic form, of a man's guilty feelings.

As in **'Māstārmasāy'** the object of a loving soul's perfect dedication suffers from a guilt complex that takes the form of a deep anguish accompanied by sensory hallucinations. Young Majumdar is suddenly oppressed by the remembrance of his past behaviour. He will likely quell his remorse and forget his old teacher completely, but one feels sure, as the text itself suggests, that the *zamindār* will never be cured. The more he responds to the charm of his younger wife, the more his trouble will increase, until he goes mad. The strong moral undertones of short stories like these confirm Tagore's interest in deep-level psychology.

'Manihārā' (**'The Lost Jewels'**) and **'Kshudhita Pāshān'** (**'Hungry Stones'**) present the supernatural undiluted. **'Manihārā'**'s first-person narrator is a trader who moors his boat near the dilapidated steps of a *ghāt* dominated by a vast deserted house. It is evening. A thin and sickly man, the village school-teacher, describes for the trader the strange events at the old mansion fifteen years earlier. He himself came to the village only five years later.

The protagonist of the school-master's story is Phani Bhusan, another trader, who has inherited a large fortune and a successful business. He settles in the big house with his beautiful young wife, who is childless. She is more interested in her jewel collection, his gift to her, than in her husband's love. When one day he asks for her ornaments, to tide over a business crisis, she refuses and leaves hurriedly for her parents' home. Accompanied by a distant cousin and covered from head to foot with jewels hidden under a veil, she boards a small boat from this *ghāt* on a rainy night. When the husband returns, his business again in good shape, he learns that she has never reached her destination. His searches are fruitless. Days pass. One night, he hears footsteps and the clinking of jewels, from the *ghāt* to the closed gate of the house. But it is locked from the outside, and his vain efforts to open it waken him: he has been sleepwalking.

The next night he leaves the gate open. The footsteps come to the bedroom door. He shouts his wife's name, 'Mani!' and wakes up. The third night, the footsteps approach him, and he faces a skeleton covered with ornaments. The eyes shine in their sockets. He follows it down the steps to the river and enters the water. He wakes then but lets himself be carried away by the current, never to waken again. Here ends the school-master's tale.

The bare facts of the narration seem easily explained by the husband's love for his wife and his desire to see her again, and we note that her very name, 'Mani,' means 'jewel'. It seems natural that his love should persist as dreams. The story insists on his auto-conditioning, his auto-suggestion, his hope of seeing her in the other world.

Strangely enough, it is the beginning of the story, as told by the trader-narrator, that introduces ambiguity. The initial description prepares the reader for mysterious happenings. The trader himself confesses to a strange emotion. The reader, who usually trusts the first-represented narrator implicitly, is surprised when that narrator declines to reveal his real name to the schoolmaster. Why not? This unexplained secrecy makes possible the final dramatic revelation that the newcomer's name is like that of the unfortunate husband, Phani Bhusan. Schoolmaster and reader are surprised that the trader has come to this place for a change of air; the climate of Ranchi, from which he says he comes, is healthier than Gangetic Bengal. It is further strange that the first-represented narrator knows the other's innermost thoughts. And how can the schoolmaster know every detail of these people's lives and feelings? Is this evidence of the author's lack of skill? In Tagore's case, surely not. This violence to verisimilitude is deliberate. It puts the whole story, with its two successive narrators, under the seal of the 'strange'.

The schoolmaster is described as 'ghostlike': he is emaciated, ageless, with abnormally bright, shining eyes. The trader, who paints this portrait for us, actually thinks of Coleridge's Ancient Mariner. He seems to belong to another age, when one considers his judgement of Phani Bhusan and his wife and their relationship. The end of the story is particularly interesting because it stimulates new questions. The trader too is named Phani Bhusan: the schoolmaster's story then seems to be a fabrication: the man did not drown, and his wife's name is not Manimalika. But then this Phani Bhusan mentions his wife's real name, Nrityakali. It is the name of the terrible goddess who haunts cremation grounds, accompanied by imps and ghosts: a very unlikely name for a girl. A joke? A way of saying that Phani Bhusan's wife is identified with the goddess dancing among the funeral pyres? Is Phani

Bhusan himself a ghost? Is every word of the story true? That the reader hesitates and asks himself these questions points to the presence of the supernatural in a perfect form.

'Kshudhita Pāshān', which dates from approximately the same period, is, in a different way, a model of the genre. A man on holiday with his family is the first-person narrator. He meets a Bengali *bābu* in Muslim dress. This gentleman has a surprising depth and range of knowledge. As they all await the same train at a country junction, the *bābu* tells them of a long-ago event, when he was tax-collector for the Nizam and lived in an ancient marble palace on the bank of a river. The tax-collector, though warned never to spend the night there, ignored the advice. First the palace provoked fear, then began to bewitch him. Late on a summer afternoon he sits on the *ghāt*-steps and hears footsteps, as of invisible women going to the river to bathe. He hears laughter, the splashing of water. The wind rises, and everything disappears. Thinking he is the victim of poetical delirium, and rejecting supernatural happenings, he decides to eat more substantially.

The next evening the palace attracts irresistibly. He hears footsteps, musical instruments, fountains. The arrival of his servant restores normality. When he sleeps in the mansion he is made to follow an invisible woman, an 'Arab', to a door guarded by a sleeping eunuch. Another night he feels the presence of a woman, hears sobs, sees blood streaming down her face. At dawn, the collector fears that he is going mad. His old assistant then tells him about the unfulfilled desires of the previous inhabitants of this palace. All this remains a prisoner of these stones. If he stays three nights in this place, madness is the best of what can happen to him. 'Is there no salvation?—there is only one way of escape, but a very different one. I will let you know . . . but, first I must tell you the story of the Iranian slave . . .'

The travellers' train comes, and the ex-collector has no time to end his story. The first-represented narrator thinks they have been told a lie. His theosophist friend, on the contrary, believes in the reality of the collector's experiences. This story contains two conflicting viewpoints. The reader must make his own judgement.

Literature is important in this story. We know that the tax-collector recites in Sanskrit, English and Persian. This is one of the very few things we know about him. He quotes Shakespeare, and his tale abounds in direct or indirect allusions to the *Arabian Nights*. 'It seemed to me', he says, 'that a young woman from the *Arabian Nights* had taken flight from the world of fiction.' The end of the story is typical of *Arabian Nights* narrative technique, which leaves one tale unconcluded before taking up another. In this study, for the first time, we find ourselves facing writing that is pure play. The referential aspect of language is less important than its semantic value. The world evoked all through the collector's narrative is made of words, not of things. It is made and unmade by twists and turns of sentences.

If the writing were bereft of all representativeness, we would have to deal with a poetical text, and in that case the supernatural as such would have disappeared. The narrator himself is repeatedly aware of this danger. The language quickly renews its work of elaborating sensory images that return 'reality' to the discourse. Then the supernatural reappears. Fascinated, the reader participates in the narrative's progression, which by turns builds and destroys a house of words—a work of such sophistication that it appears akin to the art of an illusionist. Let us examine some of the author's methods. To enable his 'visions' to retain their illusory nature, while describing them the narrator says that he hears but does not see anything. Immediately he takes himself to be a victim of sensory illusion, but having said that he again hears footsteps, 'as if a lot of people were running down the steps.' With an 'as if ', he makes it clear that he sees no image, but he adds that he seems clearly to see young women coming down to bathe. Again, 'Though there had been no sound whatsoever . . . I heard, all the same . . . '. Once again: 'The river was calm as before, but it seemed obvious to me that the wave had been raised by some hands . . . '.

The second supernatural experience begins solely with the single 'It seemed to me' that starts the narrative, followed later by a single 'as if '. As always, the narrator sees nothing, but it is 'as if ' he smelled some perfumes of bygone times. Then he hears, without qualification, noises of different kinds: gongs, clinking of chandeliers and of jewels, the melody of a *sitar*. Only that world now seems true to him, a world that he nevertheless knows is immaterial, inaccessible, untouchable.

During the third experience, the narrator falls asleep, then wakes up. He does not see anyone, yet it seems clear that someone is pushing him. That 'someone'—the Bengali word is *yena*—signs with fingers adorned with invisible rings, asking him to follow her: 'Although I could not see this invisible messenger with my eyes, her image was not invisible to my mind.' Later he feels himself in danger; he seems to confront a eunuch who is armed but somnolent. The sentence admits of no modalisation, so the reader is led to believe in the reality of the vision. But precisely then a cry wakens the narrator, who finds himself lying on his camp bed!

Then everything begins again: smells and sounds first, then fragmentary and fleeting visions of the young woman. Touch is not absent. The reader participates in a festival of sensations. The narrator, taking the reader with him, is carried away in a sensual delirium born of language that has no reality except in the words. In some other stories, like 'Nisithe,' or even 'Manihārā', one could search for psychological reasons to justify the presence of a character's hallucinatory visions or auditions. Such an exercise would be meaningless here. It matters little whether the collector's musing is phantasms bordering on eroticism. The tortured and laughing slave girl; the recumbent eunuch, sword in hand; the bathing women: all this world of figures seems to emerge from an exotic fiction. We are reminded of Alain Robbe-Grillet's later novels where 'oriental' or 'American' settings are but the pretext for a discourse that develops and defines at every moment its sets of rules, organises its own coherence. Such a *rapprochement* is not a blasphemy; on the contrary, it is an homage to the extraordinary modernity of the Bengali poet. **'Kshudhita Pāshān'** is one story from which Tagore's famous humanism is absent. The supernatural that transgresses the limits of the real and the unreal survives today more in science-fiction than in stories. It has found a new existence also among authors who make their fiction an exploration of the expressible (*le dicible*), whereas their nineteenth-century ancestors were concerned above all with giving, by means of language, an account of the reality of their times.

In his short stories Tagore repeatedly described a social reality that then and there allotted a large place to the supernatural. His moral preoccupations weighed heavily in the balance and prevented his exploiting to the full the possible outcome of the confrontation between the real and the unreal. He resisted the temptation to play with the supernatural, to write a straightforward ghost story— *bhuter galpa*—perhaps because of his humanitarianism and concern for truth. One cannot blame him for that. Nevertheless he did once free himself, to write for pleasure texts whose constant oscillation between the real and the supernatural, between the imaginary and the illusionary, takes the power of language to its highest point. (pp. 67-81)

> France Bhattacharya, "The Supernatural in Tagore's Short Stories," in Rabindranath Tagore: Perspectives in Time, *edited by Mary Lago and Ronald Warwick, The Macmillan Press Ltd., 1989, pp. 67-82.*

FURTHER READING

Bibliography

Henn, Katherine. *Rabindranath Tagore: A Bibliography.* London: Scarecrow Press, 1985, 330 p.
  Comprehensive bibliography of English-language criticism and translations of Tagore's books.

Biography

Kripalani, Krishna. *Rabindranath Tagore: A Biography.* London: Oxford University Press, 1962, 417 p.
  Critical biography.

Lago, Mary M. *Rabindranath Tagore.* Boston: Twayne Publishers, 1976, 176 p.
  Biographical and critical study.

Thompson, Edward. *Rabindranath Tagore: His Life and Work.* 1928. Reprint. New York: Haskell House Publishers, 1974, 105 p.
  Considers Tagore's life separately from his work and emphasizes the variety of his pursuits and activities.

Criticism

Aronson, A. *Rabindranath through Western Eyes.* Allahabad, India: Kitabistan, 1943, 160 p.
  Examines Tagore's reception in Europe and the United States after he was awarded the Nobel Prize for literature in 1913.

Bhattacharya, Vivek Ranjan. *Tagore's Vision of a Global Family.* New Delhi, India: Enkay Publishers, 1987, 226 p.
  Biographical and critical overview which focuses on the internationalism of Tagore's themes.

Bose, Abinash Chandra. *Three Mystic Poets: A Study of W. B. Yeats, A. E. and Rabindranath Tagore.* Kolhapur, India: School & College Bookstall, 1945, 160 p.
  Ranks Tagore among the greatest lyrical poets in world literature and praises his poetry for its mystical fervor and wisdom.

Bose, Nemai Sadhan, ed. *Rabindranath Tagore in Perspective.* Calcutta, India: Visva-Bharati, 1989, 225 p.
  Critically examines Tagore's aesthetics, politics, poetry, short stories, plays, and paintings, among other facets of his creative personality.

Chakrabarti, Mohit. *Rabindranath Tagore: Diverse Dimensions.* New Delhi, India: Atlantic Publishers & Distributors, 1990, 191 p.
  Offers close analysis of Tagore's poems and songs, with an emphasis on the diversity of his creative endeavors.

Chatterjee, Kalyan K. "Renaissance and Modernity: Tagore in Perspective." *Review of National Literatures,* no. 10 (1979): 35-43.
  Discusses Tagore's poetry in the context of European modernism and the renaissance in Indian literature during the early twentieth century.

Dimock, Edward C. "Rabindranath Tagore—'The Greatest of the Bauls of Bengal'." *The Journal of Asian Studies* XIX, No. 1 (November 1959): 33-51.
  Discusses Tagore's identification with the Baul tradition of minstrel poetry which flourished in medieval Bengal.

Ghose, Sisirkumar. *The Later Poems of Tagore.* Westport, Conn.: Greenwood Press, 1961, 310 p.
  Offers close analysis of the poetry Tagore wrote during the final ten years of his life, when he experimented with free verse and prose poems.

Gokak, Vinayaka Krishna. "A New World-Perspective for Readers of Tagore's Poetry." *Indian Literature* XXIX, No. 4 (July-August 1986): 9-20.
  Assesses Tagore's stature as a poet, comparing his artistic and spiritual development with that of W. B. Yeats and other modern poets.

Iyengar, K. R. Srinivasa. "Rabindranath Tagore." In his *Indian Writing in English.* New Delhi, India: Sterling Publishers, 1963, 830 p.
  Offers an overview of Tagore's poetry and prose, with an emphasis on his knowledge of English and his coalescence of Eastern and Western styles of thought.

Kabir, Humayun. "Advent of Tagore." In his *Studies in Bengali Poetry.* Bombay, India: Bharatiya Vidya Bhavan, 1962, 125 p.
  Considers the extent of Tagore's influence on Bengali literature and the impact of his international fame on Indian politics.

Mukerji, Dhurjati Prasad. *Tagore: A Study.* Calcutta, India: Manisha Press, 1943, 125 p.
  Assesses Tagore's stature and influence. In each chapter,

Mukerji focuses on a distinct facet of Tagore's creative activity.

Mukerji, Nirmal. "The Poetry of Rabindranath Tagore: The Last Phase." In *Aspects of Indian Writing in English,* edited by M. K. Naik. Madras, India: The Macmillan Company of India, 1979, 319 p.

Considers the poetry that Tagore wrote in the last five years of his life.

Naravane, Vishwanath S. *An Introduction to Rabindranath Tagore.* Madras, India: The Macmillan Company of India, 1977, 180 p.

Critical survey of Tagore's career, divided into chapters on his life, philosophy, poetry, drama, fiction, art, and pedagogy.

Radhakrishnan, S., et al., eds. *Rabindranath Tagore: A Centenary Volume, 1861-1961.* New Delhi, India: Sahitya Akademi, 1961, 525 p.

Appreciations of Tagore's life, art, and influence, featuring commentators from Asia, Europe, and the United States.

Ray, Sitansu. "Tagore Songs: An Aesthetic Approach." *Indian Horizons* XXXV, Nos. 1-2 (1986): 23-35.

Assesses Tagore's songwriting, emphasizing his eclectic use of both traditional and contemporary sources.

Roy, Basanta Koomar. *Rabindranath Tagore: The Man and His Poetry.* New York: Dodd, Mead & Co., 1916, 225 p.

Offers an overview of Tagore's career as a poet, educator, philosopher, and feminist.

Shahane, V. A. "Rabindranath Tagore: A Study in Romanticism." *Studies in Romanticism* III, No. 1 (Autumn 1963): 53-64.

Examines Tagore's affinities with the English Romantic poets and such Modernists as T. S. Eliot and W. B. Yeats.

Sykes, Marjorie. *Rabindranath Tagore.* Bombay, India: Longmans, Green and Co., 1943, 130 p.

Overview of Tagore's career intended as a general introduction for students and nonspecialists.

Thompson, Edward. *Rabindranath Tagore: Poet and Dramatist.* London: Oxford University Press, 1926, 315 p.

A study of Tagore's poetry and drama that seeks to redress the limitations of his stereotypical reputation as an "oriental mystic."

Additional coverage of Tagore's life and career is contained in the following sources published by Gale Research: *Contemporary Authors,* Vols. 104 and 120; *Twentieth-Century Literary Criticism,* Vol. 3; and *Major 20th-Century Writers.*

The Age of Innocence

Edith Wharton

(Full name Edith Newbold Jones Wharton) American novelist, short story writer, critic, autobiographer, and poet.

The following entry presents criticism of Wharton's novel *The Age of Innocence,* published in 1920. For a discussion of Wharton's complete career, see *TCLC,* Volumes 3 and 9. For criticism of Wharton's novel *Ethan Frome,* see *TCLC,* Volume 27.

INTRODUCTION

The Age of Innocence, regarded by many critics as Wharton's best novel, won the Pulitzer Prize for fiction in 1921. Set in New York in the 1870s, the novel focuses on the influence of societal values and mores on representative members of the city's upper class during the nineteenth century. The novel, which has been described as both a nostalgic and a somewhat cynical depiction of the New York of Wharton's childhood, has enjoyed both popular acclaim and critical recognition throughout the twentieth century.

From her perspective as one born into the nineteenth century social elite of "old New York," Wharton observed the shift of power and wealth from established society families to the nouveau riche of the Industrial Revolution, and she utilized this background in much of her fiction, including *The Age of Innocence.* Wharton seemed to embrace the conventions of her society, traveling widely in Europe with her husband and maintaining fashionable homes in New York and Newport. By the turn of the century, however, the role of society matron and hostess gave way to her growing reputation as a successful author with the publication of *The Decoration of Houses* and numerous short stories and poems. In 1913, after twenty-eight years of marriage, Wharton divorced her husband, who shared neither her intellectual nor her artistic abilities and interests. Critics have suggested that the moral, social, and intellectual dilemmas which confront central characters Newland Archer and Ellen Olenska in *The Age of Innocence* mirror those Wharton experienced in her personal and professional lives.

Wharton herself described *The Age of Innocence* as a "simple" story of two people trying to live up to their deeply felt values. The novel explores issues of hypocrisy and fidelity, centering on the conflict between personal desire and social obligation. Newland Archer is a socially prominent young lawyer engaged to be married to pretty, respectable May Welland. Shortly after the engagement is formally announced, Archer falls in love with Countess Ellen Olenska, Welland's cousin, who has left her unfaithful Polish husband and returned as an outsider to the old

New York society into which she was born. Her European sophistication and apparent self-assurance are at once attractive and threatening to Archer. He is torn between the predictable life of propriety, tradition, and social responsibility to which he and his fiancee belong, and the realm of intellectual and moral freedom and personal fulfillment he imagines he could enjoy with Ellen Olenska. Unable or unwilling to break his own moral code and flout the standards of his society, Archer chooses to marry Welland. Then, despairing of the monotony he foresees for his life, he once again turns to the Countess, believing his bride is too much a product of their society to understand his desire for something more than their prescribed lives can offer. As Archer and Olenska appear to be on the threshold of establishing a more intimate relationship, they are confronted, individually, with his wife's announcement of her pregnancy. Ellen Olenska returns to Europe, and Newland Archer stays behind, resigned to life as a faithful husband, loving father, and upstanding citizen. *The Age of Innocence* reaches its conclusion as Archer, now widowed and traveling in Europe with his grown son years later, realizes that he finally has the social freedom and the ready opportunity to engage in a relationship with the woman he had always loved. Complicating matters, however, he also learns from an unexpected source that his wife had been aware of his feelings for her cousin all along. As the novel ends, Archer, having made his decision not to pursue a reality which might not live up to a lifetime of dreams, sits on a bench outside Countess Olenska's Paris apartment, reflecting on the ironies of his life.

Criticism of *The Age of Innocence* often focuses on the autobiographical aspects of the novel. Alluding to the unconventional artistic and intellectual pursuits of Wharton's youth—she was far better educated in languages and literature than most women of her social circle—some critics draw a parallel between the author and the character of Ellen Olenska. Others consider Newland Archer's divided loyalties to be reflective of Wharton's own desire to transcend her marital and societal boundaries. While the work has been described as Wharton's confrontation with the world of her childhood, it is also considered an affirmation of the social order of duty, honor, and commitment Wharton believed in: to act outside the social ethic was to threaten the stability—indeed, the very existence—of the moral order.

Some critics, including Stuart P. Sherman and Robert Morss Lovett, who sat on the committee that awarded her the Pulitzer Prize in 1921, faulted the novel for its apparent lack of contemporary relevance in the aftermath of World War I. Other commentators, though generally agreeing that Wharton's depiction of the 1870s New York social scene was accurate in detail and manner, suggest that the novel was essentially her nostalgic attempt to ignore postwar realities. Jeanne Boydston characterizes *The Age of Innocence* as rooted in nostalgia and a romanticized perception of the role of woman in society, and sees the book as the harbinger of Wharton's romanticization of woman in her later fiction. In contrast, Mary E. Papke considers the novel a further exploration of the social criticism Wharton introduced in her earlier works, and describes *The Age of Innocence* as an attempt by Wharton to reconcile the contradictions of past and present generations. In general, Wharton's contemporaries applauded her ability to depict the social complexities of the world into which she was born, and later critics agree that *The Age of Innocence* serves as a reliable guide to understanding a world which no longer exists. Commenting on Wharton's novel, Margaret B. McDowell has asserted that: "it would be hard to find a book in which the problems of a group of people at a certain time are more carefully perceived, their manners and conventions more meticulously documented and criticized . . . and the conflicts between tradition and change more memorably dramatized."

CRITICISM

William Lyon Phelps　(essay date 1920)

[*An American critic and educator, Phelps was for over forty years a lecturer on English literature at Yale. In the following review, he praises* The Age of Innocence, *commending it as Wharton's best work.*]

In this present year of emancipation it is pleasant to record that in the front rank of American living novelists we find four women, who shall be named in alphabetical order— the only order that makes the world safe for democracy; much appreciated by opera impresarios, managers of stock companies and other great diplomats. The big four are Dorothy Canfield, Zona Gale, Anne Sedgwick, Edith Wharton. From the first we have thus far had no new novel in 1920; but the year must be counted as a notable one in the history of American prose fiction when it has seen the appearance of three works of the distinction of *Miss Lulu Bett, The Third Window* and *The Age of Innocence.* Any modern British novelist might be proud to sign his name to each and all of these books.

Mrs. Wharton's admirable career is a progression from the external to the internal; she began as a decorator and is now an analyst. She has always been an expert in gardens and in furniture. Her first book was called *Decoration of Houses,* written in 1897 in collaboration with O. Codman, and in 1904 she produced a work on Italian villas and their gardens. These studies of interior decorating and landscape gardening are much in evidence in her novels; I do not remember when I have read a work of fiction that gives the reader so vivid an idea of the furnishing and illuminating of rooms in fashionable houses as one will find in *The Age of Innocence.*

Those who are interested in good dinners—and who is not?—will find much to admire in these brilliant pages. Many years ago when reading about prehistoric banquets in Dickens, I determined that some day I would write an essay on novelists from the culinary point of view. I have never "got around to it"; but this story would loom large in such a disquisition. The formal and elaborate dinner parties in New York in the seventies are described here with a gusto that the steady undercurrent of irony quite fails to conceal; there were epicures in those days who sallied from their Fifth Avenue mausoleums not to talk, but to dine. They were professional diners-out, who noticed details—why does she allow her butler to cut the cucumbers with a steel knife?

It was *The House of Mirth* (1905), that gave Mrs. Wharton an international reputation; if one wishes to see how far her art has advanced since that popular book, one has merely to compare it with *The Age of Innocence.* By the side of the absolute mastery of plot, character and style displayed in her latest novel, *The House of Mirth* seems almost crude. That austere masterpiece, *Ethan Frome,* stands in a room all by itself; it is an illustration, however, of the fact that our novelist, who knows Paris and Continental urban scenes so well, was equally at home in a barren American village.

I was not at all impressed by *The Custom of the Country* (1918); the satire became burlesque, and the writer's habitual irony—most impressive when most subdued—fell into cascades of feminine shrieks. Like her idol and master, Henry James, she is forever comparing America with Europe, to the latter's advantage. I have no quarrel with her on this score, for, after all, it is simply a matter of taste, so far as questions of art are concerned; but it is only occasionally in this latest book that the direct comparison is made. Describing a hot day in Boston:

> Archer found a cab and drove to the Somerset Club for breakfast. Even the fashionable quarters had the air of untidy domesticity to which no excess of heat ever degrades the European cities.

It is a matter of no importance, but I do not believe that statement to be true. I should not like to compare my knowledge of Europe with hers; Mrs. Wharton has either missed city scenes in Europe in the dog days, or has shut her eyes.

The two previous novels in her career which most clearly foreshadow the power and technique displayed in *The Age of Innocence* are *Madame de Treymes* (1907) and *The Reef* (1912). I think, with the exception of the novel now before us, *The Reef* is her finest full-length story. In one of the many intimate letters written to her by Henry James, and now published in the already famous two volumes, we find the following admirable remarks on *The Reef,* and if one will read them immediately after finishing *The Age of Innocence,* one will see how perfectly they apply to Mrs. Wharton's style at its best:

> In the key of this, with all your reality, you have yet kept the whole thing, and, to deepen the harmony and accentuate the literary pitch, have never surpassed yourself for certain exquisite *moments,* certain images, analogies, metaphors, certain silver correspondences in your *façon de dire,* examples of which I could pluck out and numerically almost confound you with, were I not stammering in this in so handicapped a way. There used to be little notes in you that were like fine, benevolent finger marks of the good George Eliot—the echo of much reading of that excellent woman, here and there, that is, sounding through. But now you are like a lost and recovered "ancient" which *she* might have got a reading of (especially were he a Greek), and of whom in *her* texture some weaker reflection were to show. For, dearest Edith, you are stronger and firmer and finer than all of them put together; you go further and you say *mieuk,* and your only drawback is not having the homeliness and the inevitability and the happy limitation and the affluent poverty of a Country of your Own (*comme moi, par exemple!*).

The style of *The Age of Innocence* is filled with the "silver correspondences" spoken of by Henry James; and the book would be a solid satisfaction, as it is an exquisite delight, had the writer only possessed the homeliness, the rugged simplicity that is lost under the enamel of finished sophistication. The English critic, R. H. Hutton, said that Goethe was the wisest man of modern times that ever lacked the wisdom of a little child—this particular kind of wisdom is not to be found in the works of Mrs. Wharton, though we find everything but that.

Yet I am in no mood to complain. Edith Wharton is a writer who brings glory on the name America, and this is her best book. After reading so many slipshod diaries called "novels," what a pleasure it is to turn the pages of this consummate work of art. The common method today of writing a novel is to begin with the birth of the hero, shove in all experiences that the author can remember of his own childhood, most of which are of no interest to any one but himself, take him to school, throw in more experiences, introduce him to the heroine, more experiences, quit when the book seems long enough, and write the whole biography in colloquial jargon.

Here is a novel whose basis is a story. It begins on a night at the opera. The characters are introduced naturally—every action and every conversation advance the plot. The style is a thing of beauty from first page to last. One dwells with pleasure on the "exquisite moments" of passion and tragedy, and on the "silver correspondences" that rise from the style like the moon on a cloudless night.

New York society and customs in the seventies are described with an accuracy that is almost uncanny; to read these pages is to live again. The absolute imprisonment in which her characters stagnate, their artificial and false standards, the desperate monotony of trivial routine, the slow petrifaction of generous ardours, the paralysis of emotion, the accumulation of ice around the heart, the total loss of life in upholstered existence—are depicted with a high excellence that never falters. And in the last few pages the younger generation comes in like fresh air. Mrs. Wharton is all for the new and against the old; here, at all events, her sympathies are warm. She would never, like Solness, fear youth knocking at the door.

The two young women of the story are contrasted in a manner that is of the essence of drama without being in the least artificial. The radiantly beautiful young wife might have had her way without a shadow on it, were it not for the appearance of the Countess Olenska, who is, what the other women are not, a personality. Newland Archer, between these two women, and loved by both, is not at all to be envied. The love scenes between him and Ellen are wonderful in their terrible, inarticulate passion; it is curious how much more real they are than the unrestrained detailed descriptions thought by so many writers to be "realism." Here is where Mrs. Wharton resembles Joseph Conrad and Henry James, for the love scenes in this book are fully worthy of those two men of genius. So little is said, so little is done, yet one feels the infinite passion in the finite hearts that burn. I wonder what old Browning would have thought of this frustration; for the story is not altogether unlike "The Statue and the Bust."

I do not believe I shall ever forget three scenes between Archer and Ellen—the "outing" at Boston, the night carriage drive from the ferry in New York, and the interview in the corner of the Museum of Art, with its setting of relics. These are scenes of passion that Conrad, or Henry James, yes, that Turgenev might have written.

I wonder if the horrible moment when Newland Archer, looking at his incomparably lovely and devoted young wife, suddenly has the diabolical wish that she were dead, is a reminiscence of Mrs. Wharton's early studies of Sudermann. In a powerful story by that writer, "The

Wish," not only is that momentary impulse the root of the tragedy, but it is analyzed with such skill that no one is likely to forget it. It comes into this novel like a sudden chill—and is inexpressibly tragic. You remember what the doctor said in Sudermann's tale?

The harmony of Mrs. Wharton's management of English sentences is so seldom marred that I wish she would change this phrase, the only discord I found in the book: "varied by an occasional dance at the primitive inn when a man-of-war came in."

And is not Guy de Maupassant out of place in the early seventies? Archer is unpacking some new books; "a new volume of Herbert Spencer, another collection of Guy de Maupassant's incomparable tales, and a novel called 'Middlemarch,' as to which there had lately been interesting things said in the reviews." I suppose Mrs. Wharton knows her Maupassant thoroughly; but unless I am quite at fault, it was not in the early seventies, but in the early eighties, that his tales began to appear.

But these are flecks. The appearance of such a book as *The Age of Innocence* by an American is a matter for public rejoicing. It is one of the best novels of the twentieth century and looks like a permanent addition to literature. (pp. 1, 11)

William Lyon Phelps, "As Mrs. Wharton Sees Us," in The New York Times Book Review, *October 17, 1920, pp. 1, 11.*

Joseph Warren Beach (essay date 1932)

[*Beach was an American critic and educator who specialized in American literature and English literature of the Romantic and Victorian eras. In the following excerpt, he discusses structure, plot, dialogue, and characterization in* The Age of Innocence.]

[*The Age of Innocence*] is a historical novel in the sense that, published in 1920, it is laid in the New York of the 1870's, the "age of innocence," and that much is made, in a deft and unobtrusive way, of the physical aspect of old New York, the cultural interests, and, above all, the social and moral tone, of the four hundred of the time. Much is made, again, of the quaint exclusiveness of the few families who are acknowledged to be paramount. As for the moral tone, alluded to in the title, the great thing is the disposition of good society of the seventies to ignore the existence of anything "unpleasant," to convey delicate meanings, if they must be conveyed, by implication without the use of words, never frankly to face realities that do not conform to the prevailing ideal, and inexorably to purge society of any person who has offended against the conventional code.

It is this social ideal which is represented by May Welland. There is in the end something impressive in the quiet, selfish cruelty with which she holds her fiancé and husband to his obligations, even using her prospective motherhood (of which she is not even certain) to "hold up" him and the woman he loves. It is not to her own happiness so much as to a kind of idol, a jealous god of respectability, that she compels their sacrifice. And since they do sacri-

fice to this god, they thereby acknowledge his authority, and a kind of rightness in his ideal. On this point, indeed, the irony, the satire breaks down, since the author has an air of subscribing, herself, to the moral code in question.

The story is very simple. The Countess Ellen Olenska, an American woman who has married abroad unhappily and run away from a dreadful husband, has now returned to New York and wishes to be taken back into the fold. In spite of a certain ambiguity in her history and status, she is backed by the right people among her connections, and arouses the interest of Newland Archer, a young lawyer engaged to marry her cousin May Welland. He is deputed by the family to persuade her not to sully their name by suing for divorce. In this mission he succeeds, and meantime falls in love with her. But when he declares his love it is already too late, for he has won her over so completely to his idea of decency that she cannot conceive of finding her happiness at May's expense. And so Newland marries May and sees nothing more of Ellen for a long time.

But now it becomes a question of her going back to her unspeakable husband—a solution greatly to the taste of the New York relatives. Newland opposes this; their love flames up again; and it is a question whether they may flout the idol to which they have sacrificed. But this is prevented by May's confiding to Ellen that she is pregnant, and the family have the satisfaction of packing Ellen off again to Europe. Such is the story, except for an epilogue chapter reviewing Newland's life of good works over many years, and ending with the visit of his son Dallas to Madame Olenska in her Paris apartment.

The book is remarkable for unity and simplicity of action. There are, of course, other characters than these mentioned, and other tenuous threads of plot, but no loose threads—everything is skilfully woven in and pertinent to the main action. Each chapter, almost without exception, makes one discriminated occasion, the French ideal of a scene of drama. Leaving out of account the epilogue, the entire action covers about two years' time. But most of this time falls between chapters, near the beginning of the second book, and the drama proper occupies two periods of several months each, with a close-knit, continuous thread of limited issues.

What more than anything else contributes to the unity and compactness of the drama is that Newland Archer is present in every scene, and that everything is shown from his point of view. The author may begin a chapter with what seems like an objective account of a scene or of certain circumstances necessary to our understanding it, but invariably, in such a case, within a page or two she reminds us that what she has described or chronicled is what was seen by Archer or known to him: "As he mused on these things"; "these things passed through Newland Archer's mind as he watched the Countess Olenska"; "Newland Archer, standing on the verandah of the house, looked curiously down upon this scene." And much more commonly the chapter begins with him directly.

Quite as remarkable as the consistent point of view is the consistency with which this view is directed upon a particular object or issue. Three persons are presented—one the person seeing, and the others the two persons seen, and the limitation helps Ellen Olenska and May Welland as much as it does the man observing them.

In particular, the limitation of what we know and think of Ellen to what Newland thinks and knows gives her reality, artistic distinctness, and intensity. And at the same time it provides the story, as the author controls what new information she shall release from point to point, and keeps our curiosity and concern at the same white heat as Newland's.

This is most striking of all in the first book, in which the "exposition" is carried forward step by step with the story. The great question here is as to the actual character and status of Ellen, from the moment when, in their box at the opera, Newland heard the remark of old Sillerton Jackson on the public recognition given the countess by the Mingotts, "I didn't think the Mingotts would have tried it on." In the following chapter Newland is made to wonder at the Countess's disrespectful way of referring to New York; later, at her inviting him to call—an act so unconventional—what did *that* mean? The gossip of dinner tables makes him speculate on the exact circumstances of her leaving her husband and what degree of reprobation attached to her behavior. This ambiguity is intensified by her relations to the dreadful Mrs. Struthers, whose home is the meeting-place of amusing and talented bohemians, and to Julius Beaufort, the banker of notorious reputation. When Newland urges her, in the common interest, not to divorce her husband, there lurk in the background certain vague charges which her husband has made against her. He cannot get her to make a specific statement as to the nature of these charges; he wonders if she has it in mind to marry her lover who helped her away, and in just what sense he was her lover.

All these questions come to a head in the final chapter of Book I, the *scene-à-faire* of this drama. Here, in true James manner, the two persons are like players in some dark game; with each new play, with each new revelation of fact or motive, the situation takes a new turn; and the scene moves forward from surprise to surprise. Newland, fearing that he has not strength to hold out long, has been urging May to hasten the date of their marriage, and she has become aware that he is interested in some other woman, and has offered to set him free. When now he tells Ellen of May's offer, she wants to know about the "other" woman—does she love Newland? When he reveals that *she* is the other woman, she replies that *he* is the one who has made their love impossible by persuading her not to divorce Olenski. . . . It next appears that it is not her husband that she has feared or anything that he has "on" her; she has merely wished to avoid bringing scandal upon him and May. . . . And now Newland is determined that he will not marry May, that he must have Ellen. . . . Ah, but that is impossible, and it is he himself who has made it impossible. Ellen has come to realize that she cannot rightly love Newland unless she gives him up; she cannot be happy unless she remains true to the ideals which he has taught her. . . . But even then, we feel, she might have yielded to the urgency of Newland; she is, we suspect, on the point of yielding, when a telegram arrives

from May announcing that she has consented to advance the date of the marriage as Newland had wished. And this chapter and this book end with Newland's announcement to his sister that he is to be married in a month.

If Edith Wharton shows her expertness more in one thing than another, it is in her dialogue. But it is the dramatic continuity of issue that gives its point to the dialogue and determines that it shall have structural, functional value as well as interest for itself alone. In *The Age of Innocence,* certainly, she does not indulge herself with talk which is merely entertaining, which is devised for setting forth certain pet opinions of the author or for displaying the humors and eccentricities of the characters. Some aspects of New York society tone are amusingly hit off in certain passages of dialogue, but she manages to subordinate this interest strictly to that of her theme and make it serve the major issue. Her dialogue has some of the point of Thackeray's, but it is more dramatically knit together.

It is in general pointed and crisp from pruning and selection and from concentration on an issue. She is very deft in the springing of new items of information, carefully prepared, the timing of curtains, the isolation of significant bits. There are no long fat speeches of explanation, as so often in Hugh Walpole, for example; it is all broken up into half-utterances, challenges, questions, meanings developed through the give-and-take of dialogue. The chapters are short, and the chapter-divisions serve to set in provocative relief the culminating lines, like Sillerton Jackson's remark at the end of the first chapter, "I didn't think the Mingotts would have tried it on."

Very fine is the breathlessly awaited pronouncement of old Mr. Van der Luyden in Chapter VII. The Van der Luydens are the acknowledged arbiters of taste in the four hundred; upon their reaction depends the reception given Ellen by every one that counts. It seems that the Leffertses—influential, but not omnipotent—have pronounced against her. And now Newland and his mother have come to appeal to the higher court. The preliminary conversation with Mrs. Van der Luyden is not detailed, nor the Archers' presentation of Ellen's case. A word or two is recorded of solemn remark on Mr. Van der Luyden's daily custom of reading the *Times* in the afternoon. Emphasis is laid by the Archers on the fact that he ought to know of what is going on in Ellen's case. Everything is centered on the Archers' suggestion that this is all a dodge on the part of Lawrence Lefferts.

> "The *Leffertses!*—" said Mrs. van der Luyden.
>
> "The *Leffertses!*—" echoed Mrs. Archer. "What would Uncle Egmont have said of Lawrence Lefferts's pronouncing on anybody's social position? It shows what Society has come to."
>
> "We'll hope it has not quite come to that," said Mr. van der Luyden firmly.

And so we know that Ellen's case is won.

It is above all the thing not said that counts in the dialogue of Edith Wharton, and the full implications of the little said. Everything said by Ellen is telling because of our concern to know what lies beneath it, and everything said about her—especially by May—is exciting because of our feeling of a latent hostility, our uncertainty how much is known and thought. The effect of wit is produced by clipped and weighted remarks left full of hidden implications. There is a passage in which Newland is discussing Ellen with his mother and his sister Janey:

> "I hope you like her, Mother."
>
> Mrs. Archer drew her lips together. "She certainly lays herself out to please, even when she is calling on an old lady." [She is referring to herself.]
>
> "Mother doesn't think her simple," Janey interjected, her eyes screwed upon her brother's face.
>
> "It's just my old-fashioned feeling; dear May is my ideal," said Mrs. Archer.
>
> "Ah," said her son, "they're not alike."

And so the thing is left, without comment, to make its own effect.

The dialogue of Edith Wharton often reminds one of James's in its way of linking speech to speech, one character catching up the phrase or point of the other's remark by way of challenge, question, matching of the idea and carrying it farther:

> "I want," she went on, "to be perfectly honest with you—and with myself. For a long time I've hoped this chance would come: that I might tell you how you've helped me, *what you've made of me*"
>
> Archer sat staring beneath frowning brows. He interrupted her with a laugh. "And *what do you make out that you've made of me?*"
>
> She paled a little. "*Of you?*"
>
> "Yes: for *I'm of your making* much more than you ever were of mine. I'm the man who married one woman because another told him to."
>
> Her paleness turned to a fugitive flush. "I thought—you promised—you were not to say such things today."
>
> "Ah—how like a woman! None of you will ever see *a bad business* through!"
>
> She lowered her voice. "*Is* it *a bad business*—for May?"

And so the interchange continues through the next three pages.

The trick is James's. But then one thinks at once of the great difference in the way it is turned. The dialogue of Edith Wharton is so much slighter, brighter, smarter, wittier than that of James. The issues are so much more obvious; the story moves forward so much more swift and sparkling. One does not have in her the feeling of threading a long and arduous labyrinth. The development of situation in James is carried out with all the fullness and relentlessness of Ibsen. In Wharton one thinks rather of something in French comedy.

There are many other superficial reminders of James in

The Age of Innocence. We cannot forget that Archer is the family name of the heroine in *The Portrait of a Lady*. And as for Newland, we remember that Christopher Newman is the hero of *The American* and Chad Newsome that of *The Ambassadors*. The Countess Olenska reminds us of Eugenia Young, morganatic wife of the Prince of Silberstadt-Schneckenstein, who, in *The Europeans,* comes back to the bosom of her Boston family under circumstances so similar; she reminds us also of Madame Merle in *The Portrait of a Lady*. And if, in the end, she turns out capable of a spiritual fineness which is not like anything in the character of Madame Merle or Eugenia Young, this very spiritual fineness is again in the formula of many another James heroine. When she says to Archer, "Then you'll help me?" we are reminded of the similar appeal of Madame de Vionnet to Lambert Strether. When Archer nearly gets her to agree to "come to him" once, it is a repetition of the situation between Merton Densher and Kate Croy in *The Wings of the Dove*. When at the end, Newland Archer sends up his son Dallas to see the Countess Olenska, and, seated on a bench in the park below, reflects, "It's more real to me here than if I went up," we have a situation and a reflection that might be found in any one of a dozen stories of James.

And yet, in Edith Wharton, as in Anne Douglas Sedgwick or in Ethel Sidgwick, we have a follower of James as different from him as she is like him. Even in her handling of the point of view—perhaps most of all in her handling of this very problem—we find the difference. In *The Age of Innocence* and many other stories she is as strict as James in the observance of the limited point of view, but the effect is not the same. Everything is rendered through the consciousness of Newland Archer, but nothing is made of his consciousness.

Newland Archer is one of the palest and least individualized characters ever offered to the public by a distinguished writer of fiction. He is hardly more than a device for projecting a situation and characters much more real than himself. We do not dwell with him in the narrow prison of his predicament as we dwell with Fleda Vetch or Maggie Verver; we do not puzzle out with him the strange writing on the wall as we do with Merton Densher and Lambert Strether. The limited point of view is here a compositional device of great value; it serves to focus the attention upon the simple issues. It gives sharpness and precision. But it does not serve as in James for enrichment and deepening of the effect. It is not a means of steeping us imaginatively in the special and rare solution which is the essence of a unique personality.

For this very reason Mrs. Wharton is a more popular writer than her master. There is so much less weight of the "subjective" to make the story drag. And if she has adopted the "dramatic" device of the limited point of view, she has avoided that over-emphasis on the conscious process which makes it bad "theater." So that here again, as in Miss Sedgwick, it is an attenuated version of Henry James which best illustrates the ideal of the well-made novel. (pp. 294-303)

Joseph Warren Beach, "The Well-Made Novel: Sedgwick, Wharton," in his The Twentieth Century Novel: Studies in Technique, *Appleton-Century-Crofts, Inc., 1932, pp. 287-303.*

Louis O. Coxe   (essay date 1955)

[*In the following excerpt, Coxe commends Wharton's portrayal of the subtleties of nineteenth-century New York society.*]

How to get the reader to go back to *The Age of Innocence* convinced of pleasure and profit to come? Times and readers change but this novel, written at the height of Edith Wharton's powers, retains a power the gradual release of which one becomes aware of with time, with acquaintance, with a more delicate attuning of the ear and the sensibility to the things Edith Wharton was writing about. And it seems to me one of the graces and delights of the *Age of Innocence* lies exactly in the multifariousness of its thematic material, in its refusal to tie itself down to "meaning," the while that it glitters with a density, a hardness of surface that only a truly novelistic eye could have seen and an informing mind recreate.

The seeing is the thing. What does Conrad say? "It is above all to make you *see* . . . and it is everything." I know of no other American novelist with Edith Wharton's power (in this book, at any rate) of simple vision, of showing us who was there and in what grouping, what juxtapositions. The very opening moment of the novel serves as an example: the scene at the opera. Newland Archer and his beautifully dressed, languidly self-assured companions, the tenor and the soprano on the ornate stage, May Welland all in white and pink. Then the entrance into the Mingott box of the Countess Olenska, the dark lady of this plot! Nowhere does Edith Wharton's grip relax; her hold on actuality is everywhere firm. She has been there—she knows. From the smallest flower in the Beaufort conservatory to the styling of dresses by Worth in the seventies—she knows it all and she knows how to put it before us in all its appeal of the rare, the far-off, the perhaps absurd. And in so doing, she does not patronize either her readers or her characters and their world; in fact, the irony cuts several ways at once, with the result that those of us who succumb to the temptation of contempt for fashionable New York society in the seventies get our comeuppance; she does not flatter us with the delusion that we have progressed or found a new freedom. We have simply changed masters.

The scenes that strike us so vividly throughout the novel are of different sorts, and not one seems there for its own sake. The wonderfully vivid tableau of May, the still glowing, Dianaesque matron on the lawn at Newport, bow at shoulder, while the rosy girls watch her marksmanship and the idle gentlemen assess the ladies and their quality—surely no delight in mere grouping and bric a brac, though such delight is legitimate on the author's part and ours, but a lively sense of surface and attitude, without which no deeper probing is possible. And the probing takes us deep enough for comfort, down to the quick of a society, a world, a whole history of the American sensibility.

That indeed seems to emerge as the finest quality of Edith

Wharton's theme in *The Age of Innocence,* the whole question of the old and the new, of passion and duty, of the life of the feelings and that of the senses. For us, reading the book some thirty-five years after its publication, the complexities of meaning alone make the novel seem far richer than many another more highly touted. And again, here is no apparatus composed of symbols, near-allegory and didacticism, but a tissue of objects, places, attitudes and desires.

If one can plump for a single "meaning" that the book may hold for us today, it may well be that of the lost life of feeling, the kind of life, the kinds of feeling, that Newland Archer's son seems utterly incapable of understanding or knowing. At the very end, when Newland Archer, for the last time, retreats from Ellen Olenska and from the sort of experience his son Dallas is only too glad to meet, we feel the fullness of the irony. Archer, with his insecurity, his sensitivity and his passion has obeyed the moral imperatives of his class and time and has given up Ellen and love for the furtherance of the shallow-seeming aims, all amorphous as they are, of his world. He has stuck to May and to his New York, giving up another world.

What has he got in return? Another writer would perhaps say, quite simply, "Nothing" and indict the time and himself along with it, but of course to Edith Wharton "everything is true in a different sense." What Newland has lost is not Ellen, but May, whom he never took pains to know or to love, May who knew all along the extent and the fullness of her husband's "sacrifice." That the first inkling Archer gains of this should come from the casual, almost flippant, remarks of his son Dallas adds another twist to the ironic knot. What does Dallas know of the life of the feelings and passions, he who has always known who he is, what he wants, where he is going? He has only to ask and it is straightaway made clear to him: "What's the use of making mysteries?" says Dallas, "It only makes people want to nose 'em out." And we quite agree, knowing with our unerring hindsight that the best that can be said for Dallas' world is that he and his fellows knew not what mysteries they made, whereas Archer and his contemporaries most certainly did. For Dallas it would have been so simple: run away with Ellen Olenska and hang what people will say. It is no longer necessary for him to run and scandalize in order that he may enjoy Fanny Beaufort. Times have changed, and in this simpler and freer world of Dallas' young manhood, there are no occasions to exercise the feelings nor nourish passion. Like every son who ever was, he can see in the married life of his parents only the grim, the incommunicable, the faintly ludicrous:

> ". . . you date, you see, dear old boy. But mother said. . . . "

> "Your mother?"

> "Yes: the day before she died. It was when she sent for me alone—you remember? She said she knew we were safe with you and always would be, because once, when she asked you to, you'd given up the thing you most wanted."

> Archer received this communication in silence. . . . At length he said in a low voice: "She never asked me."

> "No. I forgot. You never did ask each other any-
> thing, did you? And you never told each other
> anything. You just sat and watched each other,
> and guessed at what was going on underneath.
> A deaf-and-dumb asylum, in fact! Well, I back
> your generation for knowing more about each
> other's private thoughts than we ever have time
> to find out about our own.—I say, Dad," Dallas
> broke off, "you're not angry with me? If you are,
> let's make it up and go and lunch at Henri's. I've
> got to rush out to Versailles afterward."

For Dallas, it is just that simple—and what a knot of irony
has tightened in this brief passage! Can Dallas or anyone
like him begin to understand the meaning of the kind of
feelings Archer has known? Have they the time? the imagination? the passion? What can the notion of a buried life
mean to one who can conceive only of surface? As Archer
himself puts it to himself . . . "the thing one's so certain
of in advance: can it ever make one's heart beat wildly?"

Newland Archer does not say this to his son. Times have
changed and the steady cultivation of the affections, of nuances of feeling which only an ordered society allows
seems to the new generation "a deaf and dumb asylum."
Dallas and his contemporaries have a kindly contempt for
such old-fashioned, illiberal notions, would throw down
all the canons by which a rigid society governed its members. Archer, who sees that "there [is] good in the new
order too" still asks:

> What was left of the little world he had grown
> up in, and whose standards had bent and bound
> him?

And again:

> "That's it: they (Dallas' generation) feel equal to
> things—they know their way about," he mused,
> thinking of his son as the spokesman of the new
> generation which had swept away all the old
> landmarks, and with them the sign-posts and the
> danger-signals."

And the danger signal! The innocence of Newland Archer,
to think that the society of which he was a part could set
and keep the life it sought—could hold it, make it last by,
by occasional raids on dissenters and backsliders by the
van der Luydens, come down in all their minatory splendor from Skuytercliff—to keep offenders in line! All dreadfully amusing—and yet. . . . And yet the innocence of
Dallas to propose remaking the world and human nature—to think that to cast off one form of bondage means
freedom.

Here (one hesitates on the threshold of sociology) we are
back at the Americanism of our novel and the old saw of
American innocence, the curious underside of it that the
novelists (the best of them) alone can show us. What have
we here in Newland Archer but Lambert Strether seen
from another point of view—and from both points he figures as American. My lost youth. Lost, all lost. The discovery, too late, that what one had known as final is all
too patently, seen from here and now, no such matter. If
James would in some sort show us that America is too
simple, too unknowing, Edith Wharton seems to be saying
that only if America can evolve a society which feels deep-

ly and can say what it feels can it do more than shift from
generation to generation, without a sense of the past, without depth, without blessing. What to feel with and about,
we wonder, contemplating the prospect. *The Age of Innocence* makes this clear enough, I think, to us in 1955 who
have rather more sense of what the Dallases of the twentieth century have got us into, all innocent as they were. The
total commitment of May to her world and to Newland
Archer: is there nothing admirable in this? Nothing of the
heroic? For I believe that if any character in this novel partakes of the heroic nature, it is indeed May Welland, she
of the pink and white surface and the candid glance, whose
capacity for passion and sacrifice her husband never knew.
And—irony again—her son Dallas sees it all so clearly,
but it is to him "prehistoric," "dated." The innocence of
May Welland, so perfectly adjusted to her society, so
much a product of "race, moment, milieu," takes on at
least a kind of grandeur which, if we put any stock at all
these days in the uncommon, approaches the tragic.

Edith Wharton is very clear about all of this: she opposes
Archer, the near-rebel, with May, the total conformist.
Here a lesser novelist would have been content to rest, in
the mere showing of the processes by which an American
with separatist tendencies is broken to harness and curb.
That she does not leave it at this adds dimension to the
book and to the novelist's vision. The emphasis here rests
finally upon the ways in which an individual, in more or
less settled times, can come to identify his illusions with
those of his world. The rightness or wrongness of such
identification we may determine if we can, though for my
part I would say that the triumph of Edith Wharton's realism strikes one as most sweeping in just her very refusal
to draw any such line: she seems merely to say, that is the
way things were for these people. Had you done differently, it would have been a different time, place and cast.

If this novel is not quite a retelling of *Bérénice* there is in
it some, at least, of Racine's sense of fatality and of the
course of duty as a form of fate to be defied at one's peril.
As Archer quite clearly sees, to follow one's simple duty
means that one must in some sense lose one's life. Yet this
is not really the tragedy for Archer; it comes at last, as we
have seen, to his final inability to see that if he cannot—
must not—have Ellen and the rich life of "Europe," he
still has May. But having once had a vision of Ellen Olenska and her passion, May, the white and conventional
counterpart of Ellen, must figure to him as the embodiment of the society that denies the vision's fulfillment. It
is not so, of course. With his careful, lifelong cultivation
of the sensibilities and the passions, Newland Archer has
unfitted himself for passionate, devoted action. May has
the last word. How rich in its suffering and incommunicable love must have been her buried life! And that very capacity to feel and to suffer serves as a cousinly and female
bond between the fair lady and the dark—between May
and Ellen. Archer, the object of two such loves, has never
been able to take the risk of either.

What a waste! Is that what one says on finishing the book?
Perhaps. All that wasted motion, feeling, suffering. All
that Past blotted out by change and the nice detergent of
the new generation. In a sense, America *is* waste, as Edith

Wharton very well knew—wasteful of its past, that greatest of resources. Yet we today, who have perhaps a nostalgia for such past times as that Edith Wharton dwells on, would do well to realize how supremely well she makes us heirs and possessors of that long-ago world. If the backward longing for the twenties Fitzgerald provoked and could not satisfy came to nothing, it may be that another novelist shall one day possess it for us, as Hawthorne possessed for us the New England of our inescapable origins. Bit by bit they will piece our American grand tour together, the novelists. We may very well not like what we find. But when we do find it—not complete but moving—we shall give Edith Wharton more of her due than she has yet received. Beyond that, and there really are things and places beyond America, we can do honor to one of the fine novels of our century. We can try to read it. (pp. 16-18)

Louis O. Coxe, "What Edith Wharton Saw in Innocence," in The New Republic, *Vol. 132, No. 26, June 27, 1955, pp. 16-18.*

Viola Hopkins (essay date 1958)

[*In the following essay, Hopkins analyzes Wharton's use of language in* The Age of Innocence, *calling the novel an example of Wharton's style at its best.*]

That Edith Wharton's style has received little critical attention could mean merely that it is undistinguished or that in comparison with the main interest of her work—her rich social observation informed with her well-developed ethical sense—it is unimportant. More likely, however, it has not been given its due because it lacks the eccentricities usually associated with an individual style, for example the suspensions of the Jamesian parenthesis or the startling dislocations of syntax typical of Faulkner's prose. And indeed her writing shows little evidence of her having wrestled with language to make it do more than it apparently can: her diction and syntax more than meet the requirements of clarity and precision prescribed by English I textbooks, but do not call attention to themselves. Even her imagery is conventional in that, unlike Proust, Woolf, and the later James in whose writings metaphor and symbol largely replace straightforward description, Mrs. Wharton follows the traditional novelist's method of describing characters, action, and setting. Nevertheless, though her writing does not lend itself to parody—the sure sign of a mannered style—it is both distinctive in itself and effective as an instrument for conveying the complexities of the cultural values embodied in her novels. Because *The Age of Innocence* illustrates her style at its best, an examination of how language—syntax, diction, and imagery—works in this novel will throw into relief the qualities peculiar to her style and its contribution to the over-all meaning of the novel.

"Order the beauty even of Beauty is," the epigraph of Mrs. Wharton's *The Writing of Fiction,* can also serve as a motto for an analysis of her style and of her moral sense. For her fiction shows her deep and essential commitment morally to a traditional, aristocratic society, structurally to the controlled and perfectly formed work of art, and stylistically to the balanced, chiseled, polished sentence.

But if this reverence for order sometimes degenerates into mere fastidiousness, at the same time she carefully distinguishes between arid conventions, on one hand, which wither the feelings and imagination or close the mind to all but the trivial and, on the other hand, a code of behavior that allows for the cultivation of mind and heart. Thus, reviewing his life, Newland Archer at the age of fifty-seven both "honoured" and "mourned" for his past. "After all, there was good in the old ways." But he had missed the "flower of life" in doing his "duty," for "the worst of doing one's duty was that it apparently unfitted one for doing anything else." Though he had been a responsible father, a public benefactor, and a friend of Theodore Roosevelt, he is a mere shade of a man, like Marcher in "The Beast in the Jungle," one "to whom nothing whatever was to happen." The price of morality and social conformity, Mrs. Wharton makes us feel, is high; for Archer, no less than his very selfhood. Yet undoubtedly she would have us believe that of the two evils, the disintegration of the social order is worse than the death of the spirit.

Order, then, is the clue to Mrs. Wharton's aesthetic and cultural ideals, but it is arrived at dialectically through a dramatized conflict between individual self-fulfilment, identified with reality, and social responsibility. Responsibility to society is of course a real obligation, but society itself rests on false appearances. This discrepancy between what is and what is professed or assumed to be is revealed through irony in expression and incident. Irony, which only an additional twist would make tragic absurdity, underlies the central relationships. Ellen renounces Newland, thus forcing him to marry May, on the very grounds that he had used earlier when trying to dissuade her from divorcing her husband: "The individual, in such cases, is nearly always sacrificed to what is supposed to be the collective interest: people cling to any convention that keeps the family together—protects the children, if there are any." When May announces that she is to have a child, the door of escape for Newland is irrevocably locked; his earlier words are flung back at him with a double intensity. Furthermore, Newland first realizes at the farewell dinner given by his wife for Ellen that everyone assumes he has been having a love affair with Ellen, though in fact their love was not consummated. Finally, Newland's remaining faithful to May patches the rent in the social fabric, but, as becomes clear when it is revealed in the last chapter that his son is engaged to Beaufort's "bastard," Fanny, the fabric itself has disintegrated.

But that irony is a condition of Edith Wharton's intelligence, and an expression of the tensions in her vision of moral and aesthetic order is nowhere better demonstrated than in her style. We need look no further than the intricately developed opening passage for an illustration of style as a reflection of her dedication to order and as a finely forged weapon in her attack on the weaknesses of New York society.

On a January evening of the early seventies, Christine Nilsson was singing Faust at the Academy of Music in New York.

Though there was already talk of the erection, in the remote metropolitan distances "above the

Forties," of a new Opera House which should compete in costliness and splendour with those of the great European capitals, the world of fashion was still content to reassemble every winter in the shabby red and gold boxes of the sociable old Academy. Conservatives cherished it for being small and inconvenient, and thus keeping out the "new people" whom New York was beginning to dread and yet be drawn to; and the sentimental clung to it for its historic associations, and the musical for its excellent acoustics, always so problematic a quality in halls built for the hearing of music.

Here, where the intention is to make ironic definitions and discriminations, the highly ordered, balanced sentence is the chief instrument. Though paragraph organization is important, especially in the achievement of climax or anticlimax, the balancing of parallel elements or, more exactly, the varying and modifying of co-ordinates within each sentence, serves to make fine distinctions and to mask subtly sharp thrusts without blunting them.

The pattern of the third sentence illustrates the way in which balanced sentence structure helps to create ironical effects. The "world of fashion" is neatly and authoritatively divided into three groups: the "conservatives," the "sentimental," and the "musical." The importance of this exact arrangement and parallelism can be judged if the sentence is rewritten to contain exactly the same information with changes only in connectives and word order.

> The sentimental clung to it for its historical associations, and the musical for its excellent acoustics, always so problematic a quality in halls built for the hearing of music, and because of its being small and inconvenient and thus keeping out the "new people" whom New York was beginning to dread and yet be drawn to, the conservatives cherished it.

When embedded in the middle of the sentence, the pleasant paradox that halls built for music may not have good acoustics becomes blurred, and the crispness of the distinctions among the classes is lost when a periodic sentence order is introduced and the specific order of the co-ordinate clauses is re-arranged. (That the music lovers should be placed last is in itself a satirical comment.) Serving a purpose similar to that of the varied refrain in a poem or song, the formal arrangement calls attention to the variations of thought within each parallel group; the parallelism itself creates a rhythmical pattern analogous to the metrical pattern of poetry. Excessive formality is avoided and a conversational tone maintained by skilful variations in structure. "For being small and inconvenient" is balanced with "thus keeping out the 'new people,'" but "whom New York was beginning" introduces an irregularity: with the concluding antithesis "to dread and yet be drawn to," order is restored. The brevity of the next clause, "the sentimental clung to it for its historical associations," changes the pace and gives emphasis to the last classification, the "musical." Its satirical intention thinly veiled in the guise of an appositive to "acoustics," the phrase "always so problematic a quality in halls built for the hearing of music," with a mellifluence arising from the repetition of *l*'s, rounds off the sentence and paragraph.

Another example of the ironic final phrase is:

> [If Archer] had probed to the bottom of his vanity (as he sometimes nearly did) he would have found there the wish that his wife should be as worldly-wise and as eager to please as the married lady whose charms had held his fancy through two mildly agitated years; without, of course, any hint of the frailty which had so nearly marred that unhappy being's life, and had disarranged his own plans for a whole winter.

The bite of the phrase owes a great deal to the exact parallel arrangement of the two clauses, "life" contrasting with "plans for a whole winter"; the shock value of "for a whole winter" would be lost if, for example, it were placed before "had disarranged."

Not all of Mrs. Wharton's flashing ironies are traceable to a "last line" device. For example:

> People had always been told that the house at Skuytercliff was an Italian villa. *Those who had never been to Italy believed it; so did some who had.* The house had been built by Mr. van der Luyden in his youth, on his return from the "grand tour," and in anticipation of his approaching marriage with Miss Louisa Dagonet. (My Italics.)

Here, the wry, epigrammatic judgment is embodied in the middle of the paragraph, an illustration of the casualness of her wit. Though the epigram is the hallmark of her style in satirical passages, she does not use the novel as a showcase to display her cleverness: the witticisms spring naturally from the situation, and though they sometimes have a general applicability, usually they are at the expense of the characters and mores of the society depicted in the novel. Her ridicule of the absurd in human, and specifically American, nature is understated, offhand, and enmeshed in the context.

So far we have seen how sentence structure and ordering of sentences within paragraphs produce a style of flashing thrust and unperturbed recovery; of formality and regularity tempered with easiness and studied disorder, a felicitous style for exposure of pretentiousness and complacency. But diction also contributes to the highly written but conversational quality of her writing. (Of course, only for the purposes of analysis are diction and syntax considered as two separate aspects of style.)

Thus, the method of contrast is not always dependent on parallel sentence structure, as we can see by returning to the first passage quoted. The new Opera House (which we recognize as the present Metropolitan Opera House) is contrasted with the old academy. Abstract and slightly pejorative, "costliness" and "splendour," characterizing the Opera House to be built in the unsought future, are opposed to the concrete "shabby red and gold boxes," which evoke a sense of substance and immediacy, an image of tarnished gilt and worn velvet. The academy is valued for its very decay of splendor, for its insularity, even provincialism; the old academy is "sociable," of course, only if one is a member of the "world of fashion."

Mrs. Wharton's ironical evaluation of the social world,

moreover, is expressed not only through the epigrammatic sentence but also through overstatement. Thus, Mrs. Mingott's having her reception rooms upstairs and her bedroom on the ground floor is in "flagrant violation of all the New York proprieties." While "flagrant violation" conveys Mrs. Mingott's daring as judged by her peers, its excessiveness in referring to "proprieties" slyly mocks the social legalism and timidity of this society. Similarly, in the following paragraph, the hyperbolic "honourable" is used instead of a more neutral phrase such as "socially acceptable"; less frought with satirical implications, the advantage for departure of taking a Brown coupé is "immense"; and "masterly intuitions" appears where a heavier hand might have inserted "shrewd guesses":

> It was Madame Nilsson's first appearance that winter, and what the daily press had already learned to describe as "an exceptionally brilliant audience" had gathered to hear her, transported through the slippery, snowy streets in private broughams, in the spacious family landau, or in the humbler but more convenient "Brown *coupé*." To come to the Opera in a Brown *coupé* was almost as honourable a way of arriving as in one's own carriage; and departure by the same means had the immense advantage of enabling one (with a playful allusion to democratic principles) to scramble into the first Brown conveyance in the line, instead of waiting till the cold-and-gin congested nose of one's own coachman gleamed under the portico of the Academy. It was one of the great livery-stableman's most masterly intuitions to have discovered that Americans want to get away from amusement even more quickly than they want to get to it.

To create a double vision—that of the author's in conjunction with the character's—the serious word is used for trivialities, the word with moral overtones for conventions. Two specimens of this device are: to use "two silver-backed brushes with his monogram in blue enamel to part his hair" is Newland's "duty" and "this undoubted superiority [having a ballroom] was felt to compensate for whatever was regrettable in the Beaufort past."

Her satirical strokes are in some instances very light, but nevertheless telling. Members of the *monde* "scramble" into public carriages. Others wait for the gleam of the "cold-and-gin congested noses" of their coachmen. And while the frequent shortening of "New York society" to "New York" may have been simply a habit of speech with Mrs. Wharton, the abbreviation flickers with mild irony. As far as the New York elite are concerned, why, they are New York.

Clichés are used occasionally, especially in expository and descriptive passages, to render the flavor of the social milieu. Of special significance are the habits of setting off with quotation marks such phrases as "above the Forties," "new people," "Brown coupé," and of parenthesizing others as, for example, "with a playful allusion to democratic principles" in the passage above. The very frequency of this practice suggests that the author intends more than merely to apologize to the reader for employing well-worn phrases. And, indeed, words so emphasized usually stand for accepted attitudes and fashions or customs of the

1870's which were no longer current in 1920, the publication date of the novel. Sometimes, as when the voice of the present comments on the past, the quotation marks become a factual intrusion into a fictional world, especially if they merely point up the quaintness of old New York. But in most cases the device is used skilfully to project the voice of the society of which Newland Archer is both a reflection and a reflector.

The voice we hear in general is that of a knowing, sympathetic but critical, spectator-member of that society. The writing never seems slangy or racily colloquial, in spite of clichés, because though the style is conversational, the conversations providing the norm would be overheard in the drawing rooms of New York, not in the parlors of Sauk Center, Minnesota. Therefore, a glance at the "cold-and-gin congested nose" suffices; the graphic details of a naturalistic close-up would be in bad taste and, besides, irrelevant. Moreover, the winding elusiveness of a Proustian sentence or the free-floating imagery of James's later novels would be as out of place as naturalistic detail because the point of view is always from the outside *in,* rather than from the inside *out.* That Mrs. Wharton was personally both an insider and an outsider—a New York expatriate in France—is reflected in the point of view and stylistic devices. The point of view is mainly Newland Archer's, but the novel is not narrated through his consciousness. His mind and perceptions are not the filter, as Lambert Strether's are in *The Ambassadors,* through which the "action" is strained. We are not allowed free entry into his mind; we are told what he feels and thinks, even though, remaining well behind the scene, the author never intrudes or visibly dangles the proverbial puppet-characters. From first to last we are aware of her controlled, well-bred voice and of her thoughts about Archer's thoughts.

Thus, since it is through the eyes of a spectator, detached but intimately familiar with it, that the world is seen, it is primarily the outside world, the visible gestures and habits, which is bodied forth. The "real" world is in fact so completely furnished that we cannot escape visualizing and feeling its three dimensional solidity. For example, we first see Newland Archer entering the opera house fashionably late:

> There was no reason why the young man should not have come earlier, for he had dined at seven, alone with his mother and sister, and lingered afterward over a cigar in the Gothic library with glazed black-walnut bookcases and finial topped chairs which was the only room in the house where Mrs. Archer allowed smoking. But in the first place, New York was a metropolis, and perfectly aware that in metropolises it was "not the thing" to arrive early at the opera; and what was or was not "the thing" played a part as important in Newland Archer's New York as the inscrutable totem terrors that ruled the destinies of his forefathers thousands of years ago.

And Ellen Olenska's first appearance, also at the opera, is in a gown revealing "a little more shoulder and bosom than New York was accustomed to seeing."

This introduction to these two characters illustrates Mrs. Wharton's practice throughout the book. Her rationale for creating detailed background was that "the bounds of

Edith Wharton, early 1920s.

a personality are not reproducible by a sharp black line, but . . . each of us flows imperceptibly into adjacent people and things." And certainly her use of detail never degenerates into mere reporting or local color. Their library characterizes the Archers; Ellen's *décolletage* as well as the reactions to it at the opera "places" for us dramatically both Ellen and New York society and reveals important shades of differences in taste and custom that presage further conflict and complications. Like the fabrics and household objects in Dutch paintings, the interiors and details of dress of Mrs. Wharton's New Yorkers are richly suggestive of the inner life of their owners.

The descriptive detail, moreover, constitutes in itself a kind of imagery; for example, May's wedding dress is first of all a costume of blue-white satin and old lace. The fact that, like the other women of her set, she wears her wedding dress for the first year or two of marriage is a concrete detail adding to our picture of this frugal, essentially bourgeois upper class. Finally, May's torn and mud-stained wedding dress becomes symbolic of the stains on her marriage made by Archer's passion for Ellen.

The actual verbal imagery also reflects the New York

world and mode of speech. Mrs. Wharton's writing is not studded with striking, extended, or violent metaphors. Sometimes her writing even suffers from excessive reliance on faded or tired metaphors and similes such as are not uncommon in conversation: a word falls "like a bombshell"; bandages are taken off eyes; Newland did not have a "blank page to offer his bride in exchange for the unblemished one she was to give him"; if he had been as sheltered as she had been "they would have been no more fit to find their way about than the Babes in the Wood"; Catherine "slept like a baby"; Ellen's words "fell into his breast like burning lead." More neatly finished but no less conventional is the comparison of marriage to a haven: "Marriage was not the safe anchorage he had been taught to think, but a voyage on uncharted seas." As one would expect of a traditionally educated person, the well-known classical myths are alluded to casually. Jane "hovered Cassandra-like"; Ellen's actions followed her emotions with "Olympian speed"; May is frequently referred to as "Diana-like." More specific literary allusions usually have a source in Newland's reading or in plays he has seen. For example, he makes the connection between van der Luyden's determined protection of Ellen and the zeal of the main character in *Le Voyage de M. Perrichon* in clinging to the young man he had rescued.

While some of the imagery is so neutral as to be unnoticeable, several types of recurring images mostly governed by Newland's point of view call into question the values of the world which he had heretofore taken for granted. The "anthropological" image, for example, drawn from recent books Newland has been reading, appears on the second page and permeates the novel. "What was or was not 'the thing' played a part as important in Newland Archer's New York as the inscrutable totem terrors that had ruled the destinies of his forefathers thousands of years ago." New York families are constantly referred to as "tribes" or "clans." The New York wedding was "a rite that seemed to belong to the dawn of history." "Concealment of the spot in which the bridal night was to be spent [was] one of the most sacred taboos of the prehistoric ritual." "He saw in a flash that if the family had ceased to consult him it was because some deep tribal instinct warned them that he was no longer on their side." May's dinner for Ellen was "the tribal rally around a kinswoman about to be eliminated from the tribe." This pervasive "tribal" imagery is one means by which Newland's little world is seen in perspective, its ethnocentrism exposed, and its "civilization" shown to be unflatteringly primitive.

Another important group of images by which this world is judged clusters around the van der Luydens, the Pharaohs of the pyramidal New York social structure. Mr. van der Luyden seats himself "with the simplicity of a reigning sovereign" and speaks "with a sovereign gentleness"; Mrs. van der Luyden considers his "least gesture as having an almost sacerdotal importance" and beams on Mrs. Archer "with the smile of Esther interceding with Ahasuerus." Dining with the van der Luydens when their cousin the Duke was their guest had "almost a religious solemnity." Though ludicrously self-conscious of their "sovereignty," the van der Luydens are good, kind, gentle—and dead. "She always, indeed, struck Newland Archer as having been rather gruesomely preserved in the airless atmosphere of a perfectly irreproachable existence, as bodies caught in glaciers keep for years a life-in-death." Van der Luyden's eyes have a "look of frozen gentleness"; the life-in-death image echoes in the words "cold," "chilly," "frozen," "icy," which crop up almost always in conjunction with this august name. And there are still other "death" images: their "large shrouded room" was to Archer "so complete an image of its owners." The tinkle of the door bell at Skuytercliff "seemed to echo through a mausoleum; and the surprise of the butler who at length responded to the call was as great as though he had been summoned from his final sleep."

Neither the death nor religious imagery is confined to the van der Luydens, though the sovereign-priestly combination is. The elevation of good taste to a biblical commandment is briskly mocked: "Few things seemed to Newland Archer more awful than an offence against 'Taste,' that far-off divinity of whom 'Form' was the mere visible representative and viceregent." "Etiquette required that she should wait, immovable as an idol." "On the far side of the ribbon, Lawrence Lefferts's sleekly brushed head seemed to mount guard over the invisible deity of 'good Form' who presided at the ceremony." Sometimes the religious imagery conveys appreciation for the sacredness of the old values: the first few hours of engagement "had in them something grave and sacramental." May "became the tutelary divinity of all of his [Newland's] old traditions and reverences."

While Mrs. Wharton was hardly a true romantic and "of the devil's party without knowing it," Ellen Olenska thinks New York is "heaven," which "struck Newland Archer as . . . [a] disrespectful way of describing New York society." It is heaven indeed, for it is a world in which no one has any need to cry, or any of the needs of flesh and blood, "any more than the blessed in heaven." "Does anything ever happen in heaven?" Ellen asks; and other images support this view of New York as a deadly, "heavenly" place. Newland feels he is "being buried alive under his future." "The silence that followed lay on them with the weight of things final and irrevocable. It seemed to Archer to be crushing him down like his own gravestone." The sight of "busy animated people on the Beaufort lawn shocked him as if they had been children playing in a grave-yard." When Newland heard the talk disposing of the Beauforts after their financial ruin, "a deathly sense of the superiority of implication and analogy over direct action, and of silence over rash words, closed in on him like the doors of the family vault."

If New York is like heaven to Ellen, what she left behind was a "hell" with traditional connotations. When May remarks that Ellen might after all be happier with her husband, Newland rebukes her—he had called her his "dear and great angel" when they were first betrothed—

> "I don't think I ever heard you say a cruel thing before."
>
> "Cruel?"
>
> "Well—watching the contortions of the damned is supposed to be a favourite sport of the angels; but I believe even they don't think people happier in hell."

We have seen how the social data create the solidity and tangibility of Newland's world of appearances and how some types of images tend to qualify and evaluate this world. But all of the imagery is not on the side of individual self-fulfilment. One type which must be mentioned speaks in this debate between self and society for stability of the clan, for "duty." Frequently, the precariousness of Newland's position in relation to the social world is rendered through images of falling, sinking, and drifting. "He felt as though he had been struggling for hours up the face of a steep precipice, and now, just as he had fought his way to the top, his hold had given way and he was pitching down headlong into darkness." During the wedding ceremony, Newland "became aware of having been adrift far off in the unknown." " 'Darling!' Archer said [to his bride]—and suddenly the same black abyss yawned before him and he felt himself sinking into it, deeper and deeper." Listening to the Count's emissary reporting on the efforts of the Mingotts to force Ellen's return, Archer had "the sense of clinging to the edge of a sliding precipice." In Boston to see Ellen, "he had such a queer sense of having slipped through the meshes of time and space," and in his interview with her, "his imagination spun about the hand [Ellen's] as about the edge of a vortex."

This imagery of precipice, abyss, and vortex seems a psychologically crude method of expressing an emotional state, but it does effectively suggest the dangers of Newland's alienation from the social world. To step out of the established order, to seek reality in a relationship outside its pale, is to step into the void, the dark abyss. The social framework which provides control, form, and order in the lives of those whom it supports may be based on conventions and outworn ideals, but the person dispensing with the framework runs the risk of self-extinction; what one is depends to some extent on one's real and recognized relationships with others.

Thus, the tension between the rebel and the traditionalist is heightened both by the imagery and by the epigrammatic sentence. On the one hand, images sustain the criticism of convention developed through the traditional fictional means of incident and characterization, and on the other hand, they underscore the dangers of lawless self-gratification. The finely balanced, neatly turned sentences lash with a whip the insanities of the social order while reflecting in their very firmness, polish, and economy the amenities and uprightness of that vanished world. Edith Wharton's style, compared to Hemingway's or Meredith's, is unmannered, but as this analysis of patterns of syntax, diction, and imagery has tried to show, her prose is not only marked by her personal stamp but admirably suited to her satiric yet tender view of *The Age of Innocence.* (pp. 345-57)

> *Viola Hopkins, "The Ordering Style of 'The Age of Innocence',"* in American Literature, *Vol. XXX, No. 3, November, 1958, pp. 345-57.*

Edwin M. Moseley   (essay date 1959)

[*Moseley is an American educator and critic. In the following essay, he examines Wharton's use of names and literary and classical allusions as character development devices.*]

In *The Age of Innocence* (1920), Edith Wharton plays with the names of her three main characters obviously and subtly, positively and ironically. When May Welland appears at the opera, pink-faced and fair-haired, dressed in white tulle caught modestly at her breasts with a gardenia, and holding a bouquet of lilies of the valley, one immediately associates her name with youth and virginity. When she makes her second formal entry at the van der Luydens' dinner party, Wharton belabors the point: "In her dress of white and silver, with a wreath of silver blossoms in her hair, the tall girl looked like a Diana just alight from the chase." This is the first of several explicit equations of May and Diana, but as one proceeds further into the book, the connotations of innocence, chastity, and wholesomeness give way to the overlapping ones of conformity, sterility, and even masculinity. Newland Archer, Wharton's protagonist, to whom May is engaged, has followed his fiancée to St. Augustine: he walks beside her in the Florida

sun, and her blown hair glitters "like silver wire," her eyes are "almost pale in their youthful limpidity," and "her face wore the vacant serenity of a young marble athlete."

In the movement of the novel, although Newland has followed May from New York to St. Augustine to urge an earlier marriage than convention approves, his pursuit of her is much less the positive action of the eager hero desiring to be with the lovely heroine than the negative one of protecting himself from the fascinations of a beautiful temptress. Ellen Olenska serves this function as the dramatic foil of her cousin May. Appearing like May at the opening scene of the opera, Ellen is described as

> a slim young woman, a little less tall than May Welland, with brown hair growing in close curls about her temples and held in place by a narrow band of diamonds . . . which gave her what was then called "a Josephine look," . . . carried out in the cut of the dark blue velvet gown rather theatrically caught up under her bosom by a girdle with a large old-fashioned clasp.

Ellen, momentarily separated from her husband, a Polish count, is everything that May is not. She has just come from the ancient society of Europe into the nouveau society of New York in the 1870's, and Newland, ever the amateur sociologist, psychologist, and anthropologist, conjectures:

> Rich and idle and ornamental societies must produce many more such situations . . . in which a woman naturally sensitive and aloof would yet, from the force of circumstances, from sheer defenselessness and loneliness, be drawn into a tie inexcusable by conventional standards.

There is the paradox of Ellen's grace, her femininity, her exquisite taste, and a suspected taint of corruption. Newland cannot shake the sense of this taint from his mind, and in a typically Jamesian manner, Wharton continually teases the reader without ever clarifying the actual situation. Newland is torn between May, dressed in white, but with whalebone in the proper places, and Ellen, dressed always in dark colors (she even wore black at her coming-out party!), but in clothes that are flowing and supple. Ellen is a kind of Aphrodite in contrast to May's Diana; indeed, it is highly probable that Wharton gave her the name Ellen consciously as a variation of Helen, the Greek protegée of Aphrodite and herself a prototype of beauty and passion. We shall see that several patterns point to such a pun on Wharton's part.

The novel opens with a production of Gounod's *Faust* at the old New York Academy. The prima donna is singing *"M'ama . . . non m'ama . . . M'ama!"*—Margaret's "artless" song of "love triumphant." A few pages later, looking at the white-clad May sitting in her opera box, Newland assures himself that May does not even know what the scene of Faust's seductive wooing of Margaret is all about. "He contemplated her absorbed young face with a thrill of possessorship in which pride in his own masculine initiation was mingled with a tender reverence for her abysmal purity." "We'll read Faust together . . . by the Italian lakes," he thinks to himself as he imagines their projected European honeymoon. Newland seems repeatedly to see himself as a kind of Faust who will initiate May into the realities of life, but Wharton's tone of course suggests not a seduction of May but a freeing of her from conformity. The supreme irony is, as in the case of Eliot's Prufrock, that although Newland can ask the overwhelming questions and perhaps even articulate the answers, he has no strength to "force the moment to its crisis." He has a Faustian thirst for knowledge; he reads all the new books on anthropology, which enable him to see his own society in its proper perspective of time, but there is no faculty for translating his relativistic attitudes into action. He becomes increasingly pathetic in that with his new learning, he cannot undo the trap of his society. At best he is a mock Faust in that rather than initiating May, our Margaret, it is she who tightens the hold of society on him. She sends a telegram saying that she will wed him soon, this at the end of Part I just when he first reaches out to touch Ellen, and she refuses to see Europe through his eyes. Without saying a word, this innocent employs strategies to keep him forever with her in her narrow and proper environment. He marries her in a society wedding that he is sophisticated enough to describe as a tribal rite, but he soon has a sense of drowning in her world, of stifling in her drawing room, of sitting beside her in the pony carriage as *she* handles the reins. Somehow our Margaret, maintaining the outward appearance of complete innocence, has managed to emasculate our Faust!

In a chapter in which Newland, returned from his honeymoon, expresses surprise that "life should be going on in the old way when his own reactions to it had so completely changed," May wins an archery contest at a lawn-fête given by the rake Beaufort. "Gad," says Lawrence Lefferts of her literal skill, "not one of the lot holds the bow as she does." "Yes," replies Beaufort, "but that's the only kind of target she'll ever hit." May, however, is satisfied at winning diamond-tipped arrows in recognition of her athletic prowess. It is Newland, whose name after all *is* Archer, whose never hitting any other kind of a target is a pathetic miss. Wharton is hardly the kind of writer who would consciously make Newland's ineffectual arrow a sexual image, but the sad fact of his recurrent misses is nevertheless in the novel and not unrelated to his being an emasculate Faust in his lack of true strength. He has intellectual curiosity, he seeks passion, he wants to develop his aesthetic sense, but he has none of the Faustian tragic intensity that would enable him to experience either the grand damnation of the classical Faust or the grand redemption of Goethe's protagonist.

I am about to suggest, of course, that Ellen is a half-mock version of Goethe's second heroine, Helen of Troy. One general interpretation of Goethe's Helen is that she is aesthetic beauty in a classical sense and that Faust through his union with her—that is, through the appreciation of the classical aesthetic which she represents—approaches the attainment of ideal beauty. Although he ultimately loses her in Goethe's dramatic poem, Faust nevertheless produces by her Euphorion, who symbolizes the spirit of poetry created by the joining of the romantic and the classical, and is himself ennobled by his relationship with her. Wharton goes to great lengths to associate Ellen with intellectual freedom, with a sure artistic taste, with a sense

of feeling at home with painters and musicians. As he becomes more drawn to her, Newland imagines an almost bohemian utopia where he and Ellen can enjoy free expression, personally, intellectually, artistically. He cannot even get May to be impressed by the Louvre when they visit Paris, but to him Ellen *is* taste, sensitivity, creativity, and consequently a woman with whom he would like to flee to a world "where we shall be simply two human beings who love each other, who are the whole of life to each other; and nothing else on earth will matter." "Oh, my dear—" she answers, "where is that country? Have you ever been there?" I have, she says, and there "I've had to look at the Gorgon," who although she may not blind one, "dries up one's tears." Newland's choice, then, is between drowning with May and being turned into stone with Ellen. In the evolution of the book, he is forced to do the former, which is after all the proper and less dramatic kind of death.

In the next-to-last chapter, where Wharton really rings down her curtain before a summarizing epilogue, Ellen is sacrificed to the preservation of society, of which May has become the custodian and which Newland must endure. May's family sends Ellen back to Europe in what Wharton describes as a rite in which the tribe devours its scapegoat. May ironically uses the announcement of her pregnancy to keep Newland from following Ellen to Europe.

While we are mentioning Newland's futile pursuit of Ellen, we might point out that Wharton builds her structure on a scene from *The Shaughraun,* a popular play of 1874 by Dion Boucicault. The scene which she describes and keeps before us as a paradigm in pantomime has the hero kissing a ribbon falling down the back of the heroine's flowing, Ellen-like dress and then leaving the room "without her hearing him or changing her attitude." In Part I of *The Age of Innocence* Wharton meticulously establishes Newland's dilemma by vacillating between scenes of Newland-pursuing-May and Newland-thrown-with-Ellen; Newland's movement is ostensibly toward May, but implicitly toward Ellen. At the end of Part I he kisses Ellen's shoe, but she makes it clear that no consummation of their affection is possible—just when May's telegram agreeing to marriage arrives. In Part II, after he is actually married to May, the movement is literally toward Ellen. He stands on a hill and looks down at her on a wharf, but she does not turn around and he does not call out to her. He follows her to the Blenkers' summer place and kisses what he believes to be her dainty umbrella beside the garden pavilion, only to discover that she is away and that the umbrella belongs to the absent sister of a silly girl who discovers him there. (This scene is watched over by a crippled wooden Cupid on the top of the garden house just as the previous one has in its background the cupids on Mrs. Mingott's ceiling.) Newland follows Ellen to Boston, where he does go up the river with her to a private dining room, but at first their rendezvous is against the background of chattering old-maid schoolteachers and the entire meeting has over it the cloud of the arrival of Monsieur Rivière, the secretary with whom Ellen is rumored to have run away in Europe. A plan to meet her in Washington, D.C., is thwarted by the illness of Mrs. Mingott. And a final promise of Ellen to "come to him once," given against the background of unidentified cultural implements from Ilium displayed in a case in a tomb-like museum room, is never fulfilled; Ellen leaves, and Newland remains. A recurrent emphasis of the novel is "near and yet far," applied both to Newland's cold relationship with his wife May and to his warm feeling for Ellen despite the apparent impossibility of his ever actually being with her. Newland is able to move neither from one position nor toward another—except, say, by going half of the distance each time, which will never get him there.

Newland Archer's first name is too obvious a pun to define, but it should be pointed out that his name, like his dilemma, is highly reminiscent of that of Christopher Newman in James's *The American*. As James's men inevitably find, the European women of beauty, grace, and taste always have about them some taint of corruption—at least by the provincial American standards from which somehow the emasculate protagonists are unable to free themselves. One might even pursue the idea that Archer, the last name of Wharton's protagonist, is borrowed from Isabel Archer, the heroine of *The Portrait of a Lady*, who is torn in manifold ways between the milieus of America and Europe. Isabel has been said to be an *arch*, a bridge between American and European values; actually, she can be compared in innumerable ways to both Ellen, who marries a European, and to Newland, who would like to do so under the illusion that freedom, love, and art can be found abroad. The experienced Isabel could tell him otherwise, but she could also tell him that unless he is brave enough to take a step, he will never really know and perhaps never really develop from facing reality, the only effective teacher.

Actually, Wharton does not seem to include the tragic elevation of character through suffering in her scheme of things. At one point in her novel, she has Newland Archer's spinster sister wonder why Ellen had not changed her name to Elaine, a more cosmopolitan name, as it were. Wharton may not be using Tennyson's Elaine as a correlative, but one cannot help but think of a point that Tennyson makes in both "The Lady of Shalott" and "Lancelot and Elaine." As long as one looks at life through a mirror, or vicariously through the medium of art, it is colorful and fanciful, but when one faces it directly, he meets only the awful reality of hurt, of aloneness, of death itself. That Perseus could kill the Medusa only by looking at her through the mirror of his shield has received an endless number of allegorical interpretations. Ellen keeps warning Newland that a look at the Gorgon's head freezes emotion—almost as if she *is* an Elaine who has learned from the bitter experience of immersing herself fully in life.

One final suggestion about the American Archer's last name. Wharton forces attention to it through her constant identification of May with Diana, the archer goddess who in this case never hits a real target, never involves herself passionately in anything. Is Newland, despite his Faustian illusions about his "advanced" ideas, really an inverted Apollo, the mock archer-god and brother to May's sterile Diana? Is he incapable, like May, of true involvement—and even in a more pathetic way than she in that he knows

the truth about the world but has no strength to "murder or create." Apollo did both with his arrow-rays, often rashly, but nevertheless compulsively, strongly, warmly. Even in the final chapter, the epilogue to Wharton's drama, when May in turn has been sacrificed to let the society relax its mores and move into a new stage, Newland is kept within the old society's bounds. He goes at last to Europe with his son, who is about to marry a girl because he likes her and not because she belongs, a girl who incidentally is a protegée of Ellen. His son enters the door of Ellen's apartment and climbs the stairs to—what will he find there? Newland, literally free, dares not enter for "fear lest that last shadow of reality should lose its edge." He watches a servant come out on the balcony and close the shutters; then he walks back "alone" to his hotel. One thinks of James's Strether in *The Ambassadors* standing before the balcony of his ward's French apartment. However cautiously, Strether did enter and was drawn further and further into the mysteries of European life. Was this life natural and free? Was it an abomination? Which way lies the abyss: in American repression or in French expression of the true self? What ordinary man can choose between fire and ice? (pp. 156-60)

Edwin M. Moseley, " 'The Age of Innocence': Edith Wharton's Weak Faust," in College English, *Vol. 21, No. 2, December, 1959, pp. 156-60.*

James W. Gargano   (essay date 1970)

[*In the following essay, Gargano disputes popular interpretations of* The Age of Innocence *as either a praiseworthy novel of manners or a clever work of questionable social value, and suggests that the novel is fundamentally flawed in plot, character development, and structural integrity.*]

Since its appearance in 1920, Edith Wharton's *The Age of Innocence* has been praised as a technically proficient and vivacious novel of manners and belittled as a clever but not very meaningful experiment in social taxidermy. While conceding that it is "not Mrs. Wharton's strongest novel," Blake Nevius, for example, considers it a brilliant work of art: "It is a triumph of style, of the perfect adaptation of means to a conception fully grasped from the outset." Irving Howe, too, admires its remarkable stylistic versatility and finish: "Simply as a piece of writing *The Age of Innocence* is Mrs. Wharton's masterpiece, for it is difficult to think of many American novels written in a prose so polished and supple." Yet, as early as 1921, Vernon L. Parrington dismissed the book as having little or no relevance to the major issues of American life; he pronounced it thin, formal, and essentially concerned with the trivial existences of "rich nobodies." In spite of her responsiveness to Edith Wharton's artistry, Katherine Mansfield found no warmth or "wildness" in the novel. She complained that the book's emotional "temperature is so sparklingly cool" and that the characters are "arranged for exhibition purposes, framed, glazed, and hung in the perfect light." Even Edmund Wilson, in "Justice to Edith Wharton," concluded that "*The Age of Innocence* is already rather faded."

The unfavorable critics acknowledge, predictably enough, that *The Age of Innocence* possesses elegance, wit, and lively portraiture or caricature. Nevertheless, they all object that these excellences are invested in a bloodless form and an empty charm of manner; Mrs. Wharton is thus accused of failing to animate her characters with vital humanity, with pertinence to man's serious and permanent concerns. Parrington, indeed, is so patronizing as to declare "that it doesn't make the slightest difference whether one reads the book or not, unless one is a literary epicure who lives for the savor of things." And Miss Mansfield's entreaty for "a little wildness" voices her conviction that the novel is after all a brittle *jeu d'esprit.* Such disparagement echoes Robert Herrick's judgment, as early as 1915, that Mrs. Wharton's pictures of American society have a "marvelous thinness—tinniness rather."

It is my opinion that the adverse criticism of *The Age of Innocence* cannot be wished away by more-or-less unexamined encomiums on the book's finesse and finely barbed satire. For, if the novel suffers from anaemia, it cannot be a masterpiece of form and style; form, in the best sense, is not crafty concoction, and style is not to be mistaken for modish and elegant mannerisms. Both form and style are, simultaneously, the dynamic and ordered expression of actions, emotions, and ideas instinct with life; if what James calls the "felt life" of a novel ebbs into inconsequence, we can be sure that the vitality of its form and style will also be dissipated. The major questions about *The Age of Innocence,* then, are whether or not its incidents accumulate relationship and meaning in their progress toward a resolution, and whether or not the characters develop, in coherent dramatic terms, from given psychological potentialities to self-fulfillment.

I believe that *The Age of Innocence* has more surface than depth, that it possesses a specious tidiness and an ingrained structural disorder. The stylization of the settings and incidents extends, with unfortunate result, to the account of human nature, in which everything that does not fit the prefabricated design is clipped away. Essentially, the novel suffers from three crippling faults: its style, often slipping into slick-magazine levity and even "cuteness," ends by burlesquing the characters and action; it fails, because of weaknesses in characterization and structural logic, to focus properly on its main theme; and since it does not searchingly explore the problem of freedom, with which it purportedly deals, it does not earn its rather righteous and insipid resolution. These flaws drain the novel of its energy and seriousness, contributing to that curious sense of smartness and vapidity condemned by some of Mrs. Wharton's critics.

The most immediate attraction of *The Age of Innocence* is in the irresistible flow of its wit, playful malice, and caricature. From top to bottom, from the dried-out van der Luydens to Mrs. Struther, New York society is fixed and formulated in satirical phrases. Mrs. van der Luyden gives the impression of someone "rather gruesomely preserved in the airless atmosphere of a perfectly irreproachable existence, as bodies caught in the glaciers keep for years a rosy life-in-death." Old Catherine Mingott has turned, in her later years, into "something as vast and august as a

natural phenomenon," Mrs. Archer's "serene unimaginativeness rested easily in the accepted and familiar," and May Archer's face wore "the vacant serenity of a young marble athlete." Equally sparkling characterizations "define" Lawrence Lefferts, New York's arbiter of "form," and Sillerton Jackson, the authority on "family." Archer's sister and Mr. Welland, too, are favorite objects of Mrs. Wharton's well-turned satirical thrusts.

The neat strokes and civilized sparkle of authorial commentary, unsupported by the sense of hidden depths, finally give the novel an effect of superficiality and artifice. Mrs. Wharton's insistent laugh at the expense of her characters ultimately turns against her; when she requires them to act as human beings they reveal themselves to be merely oddities, postures, and puppets. She seems to forget that they make up the society for whose benefit Archer must renounce his love for Ellen. Their gossip, frivolity, and self-important inanities hardly merit any sacrifice for them. In the course of the novel, they perform as the author's satirical mood of the moment requires, but they almost never behave from inner compulsion.

Clearly, Mrs. Wharton is trying to have it both ways: society is inane, self-centered, and fatuous; yet Archer's moral sense demands that he give up his love in order to preserve society's "sound" arrangements. The novel cannot stand the strain of this lapse in logic. The terms in which Archer's problem is presented do not permit society to show the reasonableness of its rights and exactions. Consequently, since the novel does not afford its protagonist significant alternatives, his final acquiescence in his fate appears absurd and his suffering gratuitously punitive and meaningless. To measure Mrs. Wharton's failure, one need only compare Newland Archer's empty sacrifice with Isabel Archer's achievement of responsible freedom in her parting from Caspar Goodwood in *The Portrait of a Lady.*

Strictly speaking, the first part of *The Age of Innocence* seems to focus, not on Archer's conflict with a repressive society, but more narrowly on his relations with two women who never become truly representative. Clearly, May, his betrothed and later his wife, does not effectively symbolize social restraints; it is she who, correctly diagnosing his lessening affection for her, offers to free him from his engagement. Although she does not know of Archer's attachment to Ellen, she candidly enjoins him to follow his heart even if he must repudiate a formal commitment. When Archer responds to May's generosity with frightened and false assurances of love for her, it is difficult to blame society for his dissimulation. In short, Archer refuses liberty when it is thrust upon him only to hunger for it when he has trapped himself. His behavior may be pathetically "human," but it illustrates his own psychological immaturity rather than the machinations of a perverse and closed society. Under the circumstances, neither fictive nor any other kind of logic can prove May to be anything but the victim of Archer's internal confusion and timidity; for she has finally to learn that she has been married under false pretenses to a man in love with another woman.

I believe that Mrs. Wharton lost control of the direction her novel should have taken. Because of May's magnanimity and Archer's dishonesty, his obsessive feeling of marital and social imprisonment never seems quite real. Yet, strangely enough, Edith Wharton remains unaware of the irony of May's fate as she traces Archer's search for exits from his claustral lot. I feel that Louis O. Coxe's reading of *The Age of Innocence* shows how completely the author has failed in her intention. "What Newland has lost," says Coxe, "is not Ellen but May whom he never took pains to know or to love, May who knew all along the extent and fullness of her husband's 'sacrifice.' " Unfortunately, the novel's point of view, far from supporting Coxe's interpretation, reduces the radiant May to a virginal nonentity, a *tabula rasa*. The potentialities which she reveals early in the book cannot be realized—not because of her husband—but because they do not suit Mrs. Wharton's convenience. She is stunted because the novel's thesis demands that she be. In spite of Coxe's contention that of all the characters of *The Age of Innocence* "May partakes of the heroic nature," the action reaches its climax in Archer's recognition that he must renounce Ellen and live a sterile life. It is an irony neither Archer nor Mrs. Wharton appears to understand that May praises his self-sacrifice on her deathbed; then, when informed of his wife's awareness of his love for Ellen, he feels relieved "that, after all, someone had guessed and pitied." In short, Archer has been transformed into a victim-hero because he deceived his fiancee and did not abandon his wife during her pregnancy. I am convinced that Mrs. Wharton cannot be very sure of the implications her novel has set in motion. For, if one is sensitive to the dramatic line of the novel, Archer, as Werner Berthoff declares, "sooner or later becomes a perfect parody of leisure-class bloodlessness and deviousness."

Mrs. Wharton's delineation of Ellen Olenska provides another example of multiple inconsistencies and confusions. Certainly, neither the author nor Newland Archer ever face up to the nature of Ellen's motives in encouraging his private visits to her after his engagement to May has been announced. Is the countess naive, lonely, or merely uninhibited by the social rigors imposed by New York's puritan mentality? Has she taken a fancy to Archer and decided to compete with her cousin for him? Old Mrs. Mingott suggests that Ellen possesses an endearing spice of wickedness in her, and Archer's mother laments that the countess is not "simple." Yet, Archer, from whose point of view she is consistently observed, only once questions the purport of what appear to be her audacious intentions. At the end of the "betrothal visit" to Mrs. Mingott, Ellen invites him to "come and see me some day"; he is surprised enough to consider that "she ought to know that a man who's just engaged doesn't spend his time calling on married women."

Although Blake Nevius asserts that "Nothing . . . is more subtly expressed than the changes which Archer's affair with Ellen work in his perceptions," Mrs. Wharton never quite clarifies the "logic" or emotion which underlies Ellen's early actions. At the van der Luydens' reception for the Duke of St. Austrey, for example, she touches "his knee with her plumed fan" in a way that "thrilled him like a caress"; in addition, she almost peremptorily tells him, " 'Tomorrow, then, after five—I shall expect you?' "

Later, at the theatre, she asks Archer "in a low voice" whether the lover in the play will send his beloved "a bunch of yellow roses"; she thus suggestively identifies him as the anonymous sender of the yellow roses she has twice received. Moreover, her "colour rose" when he sentimentally remarks that he is leaving the theatre "to take away with me" the romantic picture of the stage lovers. She even goes so far as to inquire, " 'What do you do while May is away?' " Among her other freedoms, she writes to Archer from Skuytercliff, implying that she has run away from trouble and closing with a quiet lure, "I wish that you were with us." Since she has by this time read his amatory temperature, her letter cannot be altogether "innocent." In fact, when he follows her to Skuytercliff, she says "with a just perceptible chill in her voice, 'May asked you to take care of me.' " In frankly confessing that she cannot feel unhappy in his presence, she must be aware of the stimulation her words work in him. Even after Beaufort's fortuitous coming to Skuytercliff nips her growing intimacy with Archer, she pursues him with another missive: "Come late tomorrow; I must explain to you." (Incidentally, Archer's retreat, at this point, from Ellen to May seems to imply that he is more intimidated by sex than by society.)

All this "evidence" (more might be easily added) requires the reader to question the motives of the early Ellen Olenska. Though she believes or pretends to believe that Archer loves May, she plays upon his susceptibilities with either practiced skill or self-indulgent recklessness. Perhaps, it may be argued that she, like Archer, never quite understands what she is doing, that they both drift involuntarily toward danger. Still, she charges with apparent conviction that his failure to countenance her decision to divorce Count Olenski made their marriage impossible. If her words mean anything, they assure the reader that the countess was ready, after a few meetings with Archer, to disregard May's formal "claims" on him. This undoubtedly represents more "wildness" than Miss Mansfield could find in *The Age of Innocence* and undoubtedly more wildness than Edith Wharton intended to introduce into it. To put it most unkindly, I do not believe that what I regard as Ellen's maneuvers are designed to characterize her at all; they exist merely to forward the plot and to bring about Archer's dilemma in the second part of the novel.

If I am mistaken and the early Ellen is intended to be either calculating or wild, then her "conversion" seems more than a little extraordinary. Her discovery of Archer's effort to save her from social ostracism transforms her into an almost conventional, self-sacrificing heroine, a spokesman for the order she had once facilely ignored. Because of the point of view of the novel, this transformation is accomplished off stage; in a sense, it is achieved without ever dramatically happening. It thus becomes another in the series of ironic and fortuitous events "produced" by the author to keep Archer in his social straightjacket. It takes its place with Beaufort's well-timed appearance at Skuytercliff at the moment when the lovers might have come to an understanding; with the opportune arrival of May's telegram when Archer proposes to Ellen; with the contrived materialization of Riviere when he is needed; and with May's convenient pregnancy when her husband has determined to leave her. Ellen's conversion, then, provides another well-staged irony which, though carried off with a certain adroit brilliance, has no source in her character; she merely, as I see it, becomes a different person in order to further Edith Wharton's purposes. In short, society must be saved no matter what happens to the novel.

For all its gloss and stylistic wit, *The Age of Innocence* is a great contrivance rather than a great work of art. Indeed, the skill with which it is fabricated almost disguises its failure to deal seriously with the problem of individual freedom and social responsibility. In spite of Archer's delusive opportunities, no possibilities for freedom really exist, no honorable route out of his stifling world is really open to him. A look at those persons who rebel against or try to liberalize New York's social norms reveals that Mrs. Wharton conceives of "deviation" as ludicrous, immoral, or downright vulgar. For example, Medora Manson's emancipation has led her to dress clamorously, to run through a number of husbands, and to impoverish herself; of course, she is slightly insane. Old Catherine Mingott pleasantly jibes at conformity and behaves with a certain safe bravura, but then no one really takes her seriously; besides, her trust in the unorthodox Beaufort nearly causes her death. A cynical hypocrisy enables Lawrence Lefferts to carry on furtive affairs of the heart while posing as society's "informer" and high priest of form; even in his own clandestine adventures Archer never forgets that Lefferts is a cad. As for Beaufort, his open disregard for New York's ladylike circumspection is always associated with incivility, arrogance, and dishonesty. In other words, there is no generous or decent spokesman for freedom, except May in her one "great moment"; otherwise she is the formidable representative of innocuous and submissive innocence. Certainly, Mrs. Wharton labors to compile a mass of social evidence against freedom, but it is a moral case built flimsily of straw. As much as the people she so coolly satirizes, she wants above all to avoid unpleasantness; she is desperately scared that society may revolt against her moral provincialism.

In the epiloguelike last chapter of *The Age of Innocence,* Archer accepts his tamed condition with bowed head, a desolate mind, and a reverence for the "old ways." Somehow, in spite of his sacrifice, the spirit of Beaufort infects the land; Lawrence Lefferts' prophecy that "our children will be marrying Beaufort's bastards" has become a reality. Although Archer grants that there is "good in the new order, too," he convicts the new generation, represented by his son Dallas, of an inability to sense the existence of those moral niceties that save the world. Dallas, one feels, will neither suffer nor "grow"; his adolescent verve, broadly caricatured in his breezy bluntness of expression, his humorous incredulity at his father's parochial codes, will immunize him against disaster and knowledge. As for Archer, he remains to the end an "old-fashioned" dilettante caressing his romantic faith in the utility of renunciation. Yet, Mrs. Wharton implies, his life has been a confrontation with the fates, a discovery of the inevitable limits inherent in the nature of things. Consequently, he appears to be alienated from his son by a certain aristocratic privilege of making moral discriminations, suffering for

his ideals in a well-upholstered library, and maintaining a dignified reticence about his renunciations. But, the reader may justifiably ask, hasn't Mrs. Wharton reduced the work and purpose of the Fates to obstructionist meddling in behalf of a genteel subculture of New York?

So, *The Age of Innocence* ends with a facile formulation. The future looms as a time of ethical disintegration, for the "new generation" has swept away all the old landmarks, and with them the "sign-posts and the danger signal." In other words, the ways of Archer's society are finally justified by his arid adhesion to "totem terrors" and taboos which keep life within traditional and monotonous grooves. The harvest of wisdom is contained in a tired epigram, "The worst of doing one's duty was that it apparently unfitted one for doing anything else." Though such a *bon mot* is wrapped in protective irony it seems to contain the burden of the whole novel. In unconsciously reversing Thoreau's famous denunciation of his era, Mrs. Wharton appears to believe that it is an aristocratic responsibility to live a life of "quiet desperation." (pp. 22-8)

> *James W. Gargano, " 'The Age of Innocence':*
> *Art or Artifice?" in* Research Studies, *Vol. 38,*
> *No. 1, March, 1970, pp. 22-8.*

Irving Jacobson (essay date 1973)

[*In the following excerpt, Jacobson examines verbal and nonverbal communication in* The Age of Innocence.]

Newland Archer . . . is a man who finds himself trapped between shifting generations, standards, and values. In quasi-anthropological terms, one might say that *The Age of Innocence* is about an Outsider, Ellen Olenska, who cannot be accepted into the Tribe—New York society—and an Insider, Newland Archer, who cannot break out. The Tribe itself is a short-lived island of genteel traditionalism, founded upon money earned through mercantile commercialism and destroyed—or, made irrelevant—by the new money and freedoms made possible by industrial capitalism. The narrowness of that Tribe's field of vision is illustrated in a brief passage from the novel: "The next morning, when Archer got out of the Fall River train, he emerged upon a steaming midsummer Boston. The streets near the station were full of the smell of beer and decaying fruit, and a shirt-sleeved populace moved through them with the intimate abandon of boarders going down the passage to the bathroom." The "shirt-sleeved populace" filling the city around him, in Boston or New York, is much further from Newland Archer's consciousness than the fantasy founded figures of the European intelligensia. When Ned Winset suggests the two alternatives open to the dissatisfied man of action in America—emigration and getting into the "muck" of politics, Newland Archer, as a "gentleman," is able to accept neither, nor is he able to find a viable alternative between those extremes.

By the end of the novel, he is at the doorway of a new, more activist culture, on the brink of the twenties. Signalling the changed world, there is a new communications medium, the telephone. According to Marshall McLuhan, "Media, by altering the environment, evoke in us unique ratios of sense perceptions. The extensions of any one sense alters the way we think and act—the way we perceive the world. When these ratios change, man changes." If anything, the telephone signals an end to the genteel system of hieroglyphic communication by encouraging, indeed requiring, direct and explicit verbal exchange. Thus the new era is mirrored in the conversational style of Newland's son, Dallas Archer: open, uninhibited, and direct. If he has lost some of the old sensitivities, he has gained in awareness, self-confidence, and the ability to express himself and develop his talents freely. But just as Ellen Olenska is left suspended between the commitment of marriage and the freedom of divorce, Newland Archer is left suspended in time, between the past and the future. Dissatisfied with the past and unable to face a new future, he is left with only "the packed regrets and stifled memories of an inarticulate lifetime." Trapped in a cultural gap between America and Europe and between two disparate generations of Americans, his situation is similar to that of Mrs. Lidcote in Edith Wharton's short story, **"Autres Temps . . . ,"** who was "overwhelmed at the senseless waste of her own adventure, and wrung with the irony of perceiving that the success or failure of the deepest human experiences may hang on a matter of chronology."

Innocence as a theme in *The Age of Innocence* and as a *modus vivendi* for its inhabitants can been seen to have several aspects, or corollaries, which contribute in interrelated ways toward stifling the natural human processes of perception, communication, and growth. This is not to say, however, that innocence is entirely without positive qualities. On a personal level, it confers a certain amount of grace and charm upon its embodiment in the novel, May Welland. She is introduced in the first chapter, at the opera, with all the accoutrements of maidenly poise: white dress, fair braids, "warm pink" blush, modest tulle tucker, gardenia, lilies-of-the-valley, white-gloved fingertips, and downcast eyes. Detail for detail, the description forms a distinct antithesis with that of the more experienced, and socially threatening, Countess Olenska. May Welland is compared, at several points in the novel, to the virgin moon goddess, Diana, and she is said to have "a classic grace" and "nymph-like ease," a simplicity of carriage and a serenity of manner which charm and delight those around her.

And, indeed the rigorous maintenance of social innocence confers a certain amount of safety and security upon the accepted members of New York society. This is emphasized in a dialogue between Mrs. Archer and her son, Newland:

> "New York is neither Paris nor London."
>
> "Oh, no, it's not!" her son groaned.
>
> "You mean, I suppose, that society here is not as brilliant? You're right, I daresay; but we belong here, and people should respect our ways when they come among us, Ellen Olenska especially: she came back to get away from the kind of life people lead in brilliant societies."

Mrs. Archer's assertion, for all its partiality, does not go unsubstantiated in the novel. Ellen Olenska affirms the value of social innocence when she says, "I want to do

what you all do—I want to feel cared for and safe." And there is another valuable aspect of innocence presented as an integral part of New York society, that of absolute business integrity: "unblemished honesty was the noblesse oblige of old financial New York."

But the negative consequences of New York's innocence—those of boredom, loneliness, ignorance, evasion, and hypocrisy—are factors whose collective oppression clearly outweighs, in total effect, the more pristine attributes of innocence. Hypocrisy is a strategy of evasion by which the ignorance of other people can be sustained. It is best illustrated in the person of Lawrence Lefferts, "the foremost authority on 'forms' in New York, and it is synecdochically operant in chapter thirty-three. There, for social consumption, Lefferts presents a performance extolling the value of public morality: "Never had Lefferts so abounded in the sentiments that adorn Christian manhood and exalt the sanctity of the home." According to Erving Goffman, when someone makes an implicit or explicit claim to be a particular kind of person, he automatically exerts a moral pressure upon others, obliging them to treat him in certain prescribed ways—in this case, with approval and support, but the transparency of Lefferts' performance becomes evident in several ways. First, he overplays his role and makes a crude and extreme statement which violates the sensibilities of several gentlemen in his audience. Also, to borrow Goffman's terminology, Lefferts can be described as having failed "to segregate his audiences so that the individuals who witness him in one of his roles will not be the individuals who witness him in another of his roles." Thus it is possible for Sillerton Jackson to confidentially remark to Newland Archer, "Queer, those fellows who are always wanting to set things right. The people who have the worst cooks are always telling you they're poisoned when they dine out." And thus it is possible for Wharton to achieve a moment of high irony in the novel. For at the precise moment in time when Newland Archer is ceremonially separated by society from the woman he loves—and to whom he has not made love— Lefferts has the symptomatic audacity to ask Archer to cover for him so that he can visit his own mistress of the moment.

"I say, old chap; do you mind just letting it be understood that I'm dining with you at the club tomorrow night? Thanks so much, you old buck! Good night." The flip tone of this request suggests the casual nature of Lefferts' sexual adventures as well as a casual attitude toward the self-righteous performance he had staged for the benefit of a genteel audience. In a dramaturgical sense, this is a glimpse of the actor backstage; and if he seems to move with too much facility from one role to another, from one reality to another, one can only question the wisdom of a society which not only sanctions but requires his doing so. But one must also recognize the degree to which Newland Archer gives consent to Lefferts' maneuvers, allowing the young hypocrite to form, with him, a "team," in Goffman's sense: a "set of individuals who co-operate in staging a single routine," that "routine" being the deception of Lefferts' wife. Innocence can be maintained only by deliberate effort.

There are other forms of dishonesty pervading *The Age of Innocence* as people force themselves to mould their lives and responses to the forms of conventional cultural expectations. For example, while May Welland is announcing her engagement, her mother, Mrs. Welland, is described as having "affected the air of parental reluctance considered suitable to the occasion." Again, when Catherine Mingott suggests May and Newland marry sooner than they'd planned, Mrs. Welland "interposed with the proper affectation of reluctance," to which Catherine replies with her own characteristic, and unusual, spontaneity: "Fiddlesticks." But even the spontaneity of the older woman is absorbed into the societal ballet, as her comments are received with "the proper expressions" of amusement, incredulity, and gratitude. On another level, Julius Beaufort sets up elaborate fronts to establish a convincing facade of successful respectability. For example, when rumors of his shady financial speculations spread rampantly through New York, Beaufort parades his wife at the opera wearing a new emerald necklace to assure the relevant public that his position will continue to be maintained. In general, one might say that hypocrisy, affectation, presenting a false front, and evasion are forms of miscommunication. It would be naive to suppose that they cannot be found in any society and at any time, but they pervade the texture of social relationships in *The Age of Innocence* so thoroughly that they become habitual and thereby permeate personal relationships as well, making a real, an honest marriage or friendship impossible.

Early in the novel, Newland Archer notes that "Nothing about his betrothed pleased him more than her resolute determination to carry to its utmost limit that ritual of ignoring the 'unpleasant' in which they had both been brought up." This is one of the main unifying elements in the culture as described by Edith Wharton, and it has at its roots a refusal to communicate—or even to perceive—the nature of reality in a social, personal, or economic sense. Culture as defined by Edward T. Hall is both "learned and shared behavior" and a system of communications, a kind of silent language, and one can see that a great deal of the psychic expenditure in genteel New York culture is concerned with establishing what may and may not be allowably communicated. At one point in the novel, Archer thinks of Mr. Letterblair as a "selfish, well-fed, and supremely indifferent old man" whose voice was "the Pharisaic voice of a society wholly absorbed in barricading itself against the unpleasant," the issue being that of Ellen Olenska's desire for a divorce. The use of the verb "barricade" forms a link with the subcurrents of medieval and anthropological metaphors running throughout the novel, portraying New York society as a "tight little citadel" or as a "tribe." It tends to emphasize the primitive, defensive, and self-protective nature of Newland Archer's world, the degree to which it will exclude those elements which might cause discomfort, disturb the *status quo,* or stimulate change and growth. Also, the use of an active verb suggests the degree to which innocence is the result of an enforced *activity,* rather than a kind of blank-minded unawareness, although that activity is as often as not an automatic one and although blank-minded unawareness is sometimes its consequence.

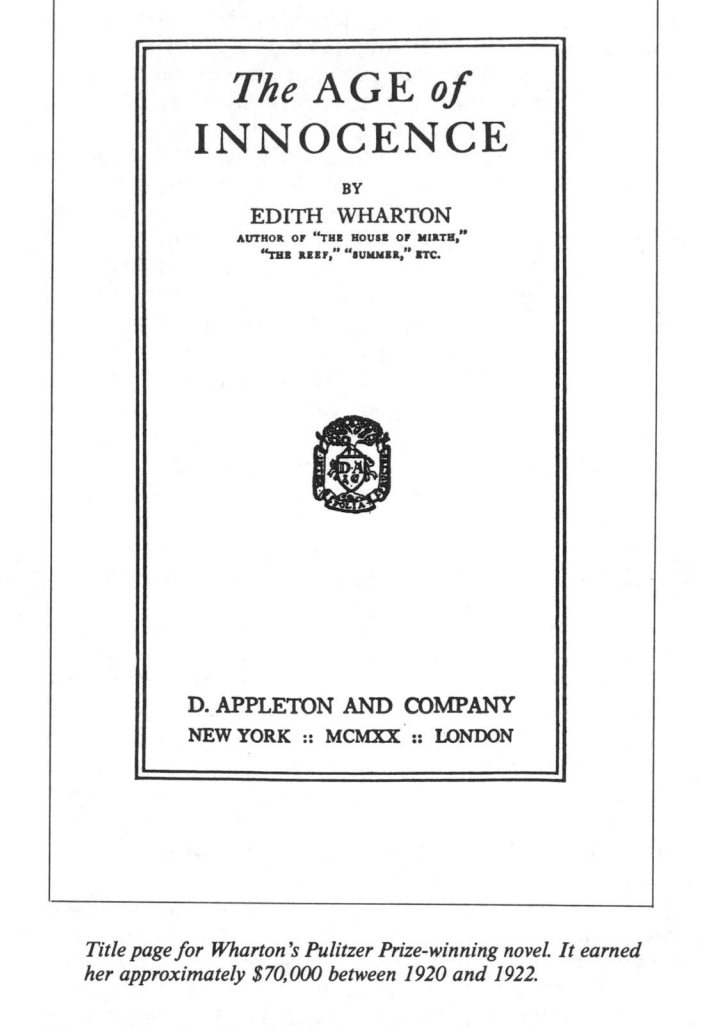

Title page for Wharton's Pulitzer Prize-winning novel. It earned her approximately $70,000 between 1920 and 1922.

The media for this kind of education in evasion are both verbal and nonverbal: silence, often accompanied by a blush, or verbal distraction, as by changing the subject. Edith Wharton makes her most dramatic use of the silent communicative blush in **"Autres Temps . . . ,"** where it becomes the only way Franklin Ide and Leila can communicate a sense of reality to Mrs. Lidcote. But what their deep crimson blushes also communicate might be verbalized thus: I do not want to acknowledge the truth of your situation, nor do I want you to do so. And I certainly don't want you to articulate that truth. The technique of changing the subject is illustrated, in *The Age of Innocence,* by a conversation between Sillerton Jackson and Mrs. Archer witnessed by Jane Archer. On the brink of mentioning an apparently scandalous situation in which Mrs. Lemuel Struthers had lived, Jackson "glanced at Janey, whose eyes began to bulge from under her prominent lids" and promptly altered the course of his conversation.

When Newland Archer suggests that Ellen Olenska seek the aid and comfort of the older women in her circle of acquaintance, he says, "They like and admire you—they want to help you." "Oh, I know—I know!" she responds, "but on condition that they don't hear anything unpleasant. Aunt Welland put it in those very words when I tried. . . . Does no one want to know the truth here, Mr. Archer? The real loneliness is living among all these kind people who only ask one to pretend!" The isolation of someone like Ellen Olenska, whose experiences have carried her beyond the acceptable borderlines of her family's cultural standards, is a natural consequence of their ignoring the unpleasant. On a similar level, one can imagine the more helpless loneliness of a less imaginative woman like Regina Beaufort, excluded from the only society she's known because of the financial indiscretions of her husband.

Since the "unpleasant"—no matter how it is defined—is always an integral part of the reality of life, to ignore it is to condemn oneself to a partiality of vision, to cultivate within oneself a perceptual insensitivity and a view of life based upon partial truths and convenient falsehoods. Thus, not ever having listened to Ellen Olenska, New York society finds it quite easy to misconstrue Count Olenski's motivations for inviting her back to Europe. As M. Rivière comments, "they seem to regard her husband's wish to have her back as proof of an irresistible longing for domestic life. . . . Whereas it's far from being as simple as that." Seeing her husband's actions in their own cultural terms—because it is easiest to do so—they are able to justify a sustained insensitivity toward someone of their own class, making it easy for them to condemn, ostracize, and eventually expel her from the "tight little citadel."

Ignoring the unpleasant makes it impossible for people to understand it, and this, of course, results in an inability to cope with it, to work what few changes human beings are capable of imposing upon reality so that it might become less "unpleasant." For example, the cultivated innocence of Gertrude Lefferts renders her so perceptually impotent that: "in the most conspicuous moments of (her husband's) frequent love affairs with other men's wives, she went about in smiling unconsciousness, saying that 'Lawrence was so frightfully strict'; and had been known to blush indignantly, and avert her gaze, when someone alluded in her presence of the fact that Julius Beaufort (as became a 'foreigner' of doubtful origin) had what was known in New York as 'another establishment.' Newland Archer's wife is more capable of perceiving that he is involved in another relationship—perhaps because the nature of that relationship is more engaging and dynamically significant than those in which Lawrence Lefferts indulges—and she proves herself capable of short-circuiting the situation with some amount of cunning. But the real problem, having to do with her husband's fundamental needs, goes unperceived and unresolved. As a perceptual and experiential antithesis to these women, Ellen Olenska appears to Newland Archer as the most honest woman he'd ever met. "You look at things as they are," he asserts, and she replies, "Ah—I've had to. I've had to look at the Gorgon." The use of this metaphor places her sense of reality and experience beyond the reach of Archer, who's known only the glib, formal pleasantries of an insulated environment. The effects of facing the Gorgon, of looking at not only the "unpleasant" but also the dismally tragic aspects of life, are dual: "she dries up one's tears" and "she fastens (one's) eyelids open, so that they're never again in

the blessed darkness." Thus it becomes impossible for Ellen Olenska to succumb to the distraught and guiltily passionate romanticism of Newland Archer and engage in a love affair which would violate their obligations to the people who care for them—obligations which, ironically, had been impressed upon her early in the novel by Newland Archer himself.

Writing about Henry James, Leslie Fiedler asserted that, "Representing innocence and experience, the Pale Maiden and Dark Lady also stand in James' personal mythology for the American and the European, or more precisely, the American girl who has remained true to her essential Niceness and the American lady who has fallen to the level of European cynicism and moral improvisation." Later Fiedler comments that, "There are ambiguous undertones in all of James' renderings of the conflict of Dark Lady and White Maiden; for though he never doubts the moral superiority of the ethos projected by the Nice American Girl, he yearns for the grace and cultured ease of the European lifestyle." Thus it is significant that Newland Archer *does* come to doubt the value of innocence, indeed, that he comes to regard it as a kind of life-in-death in which he has become fatally trapped. "Something he knew he had missed: the flower of life," he recognizes at the end of the novel, and he had substituted for that "flower of life" a sense of respectability, a modest involvement in reform movements, an overriding concern for what Nick Carraway, in *The Great Gatsby,* speaks of as the "fundamental decencies of life."

It is therefore significant that Edith Wharton constantly alludes to May Welland as a kind of Diana figure, for on an archetypal level one finds here a synthesis of innocence and death. The arrows of Diana brought sudden death to those whom they struck. She represented and exercised qualities that were antagonistic to one another, curing the ailments and solving the problems of mortals, and also imposing evil and suffering upon them. The virgin goddess of the chase, she never married, never experienced either the joys or the sorrows of love. Themes converge when May Welland is described thus: "Perhaps that faculty of unawareness was what gave her eyes their transparency and her face the look of representing a type rather than a person, as if she might have been chosen to pose for a Civic Virtue or a Greek goddess. The blood that ran so close to her fair skin might have been a preserving fluid rather than a ravaging element; yet her look of indestructible youthfulness made her seem neither hard nor dull, but only primitive and pure."

The "unawareness" refers specifically to the fact that she has just been married and seems not to anticipate the fact that marriage will call for behavioral and emotional adjustments and changes. Her upbringing has rendered her not only incapable of imagining these factors in advance but also incapable of actually responding to them or changing in consequence of them:

> May was still, in look and tone, the simple girl
> of yesterday, eager to compare notes with him
> as to the incidents of the wedding, and discussing them as impartially as a bridesmaid talking
> it all over with an usher. At first Archer had fan-

cied that this detachment was the disguise of an inward tremor, but her clear eyes revealed only the most tranquil unawareness. She was alone for the first time with her husband, but her husband was only the charming comrade of yesterday. There was no one whom she liked as much, no one whom she trusted as completely, and the culminating "lark" of the whole delightful adventure of engagement and marriage was to be off with him alone on a journey, like a grown-up person, like a "married woman," in fact.

To suggest that she might have posed for a statue of Civic Virtue implies to what extent she is a product, a model, a paradigm of what her culture expects, and, indeed, requires of her. She is at once representative and superlative, succeeding in ways that someone like Janey Archer fails. To suggest that her blood was more like a "preserving fluid" than a "ravaging element" implies to what extent she is incapable of passion, emotionally sterile, and sexually unresponsive. But her composure is the opposite of Ellen Olenska's, for it does not stem from having lived life, from having absorbed life experiences and having grown to maturity as a result of them, but rather from having remained impervious to them. In two words, her composure is "cool" and "boyish." Incapable of being ravaged by the passion of blood, she can at best remain "preserved," embalmed in an "indestructible youthfulness." The currents of life and death merge in Edith Wharton's use of language, so that one can sense the irony of May's being most deathlike at a time when she should be most alive. Her youthfulness is "indestructible" because she is incapable of growing up, because she was raised and married and maintained as the frozen and consequently frigid image of the Young American Girl. No one—not even Newland Archer—really *wants* her to grow up. Even when she ceases to *be* innocent, the illusion of her innocence is rigorously maintained. As Leslie Fiedler explains (still writing about Henry James), "The American Girl is innocent by definition, *mythically* innocent; and . . . her purity, therefore, depends upon nothing she does or says."

Her naiveté provides a kind of stimulus for Newland Archer, as he formulates fantasy-plans to educate and sophisticate her. At *Faust* he thinks it "darling" that she has no idea what the opera is about, and he looks forward to revealing the masterpieces of literature to his bride on their honeymoon. Yet the presence of Ellen Olenska is the decisive factor precipitating his premarital anxieties; an outsider, a Europeanized Dark Lady, if you will, she makes him conscious of just how much he would have to do battle with in order to turn the girl, May, into a womanly companion. It is important for his masculine ego that his wife be ignorant and yet seem capable of growth, seem to have "a glow of feeling that it would be a joy to waken." But "he felt himself oppressed by this creation of factitious purity, so cunningly manufactured by a conspiracy of mothers and aunts and grandmothers and long-dead ancestresses, because it was supposed to be what he wanted, what he had a right to, in order that he might exercise his lordly pleasure in smashing it like an image made of snow." The violent sexual metaphor ascribes to him an illusory power beyond that of literal defloration, as though May's initiation into sexuality could change her in any

meaningful way. Thus there is not only fear and resentment but also a sense of impotence, later in the novel, when he thinks: "What if 'niceness' carried to that extreme degree were only a negation, the curtain dropped before an emptiness? As he looked at May . . . he had the feeling that he had never yet lifted that curtain."

One must note how deeply entrenched Newland Archer is within his own culture, how the pattern of his marriage and even of his love affair closely follows those of Lawrence Lefferts and Julius Beaufort. That is, he gives up any real sense of responsibility for the sexual, intellectual, and emotional growth of his wife and seeks elsewhere for the richness of heterosexual experiences. There is never any emotional confrontation between Archer and May, not when she asks him whether there might be another woman in his life, or when she is unable to see the value of further conversations with M. Rivière. Their marriage falls deathly into place on their honeymoon, when Archer decides that "It was less trouble to conform with the tradition and treat May exactly as all his friends treated their wives than to try to put into practice the theories with which his untrammelled bachelorhood had dallied." Thus at the point much later in their marriage when May ceases to be innocent—when she exercises her primitive cunning and guile by telling Ellen Olenska that she is pregnant, although she is not—an action marked symbolically by her falling in the mud and ruining her wedding dress—Archer is incapable of perceiving the significance of the action. He goes on to treat her, throughout an entire marriage, as mythically innocent. She is allowed to die, "generous, faithful, unwearied; but so lacking in imagination, so incapable of growth, that the world of her youth had fallen into pieces and rebuilt itself without her ever being conscious of the change." May Welland lives and dies unperceiving, her mind sealed against imagination and her heart sealed against experience, in an illusory, protective world of acceptable forms.

It is a conservative world, one in which, as Thorstein Veblen wrote, "Innovation is bad form." Alfred Kazin described the society in which Edith Wharton grew up as a "lifeless class, rigidly and bitterly conservative, filling its days with the desire to keep hold, to keep away from innovation and scandal and restless minds. There was nothing in it to elevate an intellectual spirit; even its pleasures had become ceremonial. To judge it in the light of the new world of industrial capitalism was to discriminate against it, for it offered no possibilities of growth." One can hardly say that Edith Wharton judged by capitalist standards, but it is clear that some of Newland Archer's dissatisfaction stems from his not having any meaningful work to perform. His leisure class standards require that he maintain, at best, an amorphous position in a law firm where he is required to do practically nothing. Indeed, there is one moment in the novel when, arriving late at the office, he "perceived that his doing so made no difference whatever to anyone, and was filled with sudden exasperation at the elaborate futility of his life," sounding a little like Lt. Henry in *A Farewell to Arms*: "It evidently made no difference whether I was there to look after things or not."

According to Alfred Kazin, "Edith Wharton became a

writer not because she revolted against her native society, but because she was bored with it." But the dynamics of boredom suggest a more integral kind of analysis is necessary. For boredom occurs when attention is deliberately paid to something lacking interest, when excitement accumulates not toward the "chosen" or "proper" object of attention but in a struggle over some "distraction" which might really stimulate one's interest. Life in New York society is presented as so full of "Thou shalts" and "Thou shalt nots" that one can easily imagine a sensibility like Wharton's being both resentful and bored. Indeed, *The Age of Innocence* is, in many ways, an act of aggression—hardly a polemical diatribe, but nevertheless a dramatic statement of why it was impossible for an artist to develop in America. The verbal and nonverbal strictures placed upon perception, communication, and growth were an essential part of that impossibility.

The humanities, as Newland Archer notes, were "meanly housed" in New York, compressed in neighborhoods where artists, musicians, and "people who wrote" somehow managed to sustain themselves, totally out of the perceptual ranges of the upper classes. People like Catherine Mingott or Julius Beaufort, who in other times or places might have been patrons, have no use for artists or intellectuals. The alternatives provided by American Bohemianism, as represented by Ned Winsett, Emerson Sillerton, Medora Manson, Dr. Carver, and the Blenkers, are made to seem rather seedy and unacceptable. There is nothing tolerable, much less romantic, about living in poverty in America. As Wharton wrote in *False Dawn,* a great poet like Poe could die in New York, unrecognized and unaided, and the sensitive owner of Pre-Raphaelite paintings might never find "the man who understands" them. Conventionally acceptable art is represented by the noncommunicative pastiche that begins the novel: a German text of a French opera sung by a Swedish artist and translated into Italian for an English-speaking audience. But even that is largely ignored, the opera being a place for conversation and the public presentation of self.

The importance of a sustaining milieu that encourages rather than discourages personal development is best illustrated by the comparison and contrast of two minor characters, Ned Winsett and M. Rivière. Both men are unsuccessful, financially and artistically. But Rivière lives in a world in which "no one who loved ideas need hunger mentally," whereas Winsett lives in intellectual and aesthetic as well as financial poverty. Thus it is sadly humorous to hear M. Rivière express a wish to come to New York for a combination of financial rewards and intellectual excitement. It is on the same level of irony that one finds Ellen Olenska remark that she had thought she was conforming with American notions of freedom when she'd initiated divorce proceedings. Finally she has to go to France to find a sense of freedom and "the incessant stir of ideas, curiosities, images and associations thrown out by an intensely social race in a setting of immemorial manners." So did Edith Wharton.

The culture in which Newland Archer is so deeply embedded is described as a kind of hieroglyphic world, "where the real thing was never said or done or even thought, but only represented by a set of arbitrary signs." This provides a certain commonality of experience—or, sometimes, inexperience—a nonverbal communications system by which everyone can know, in terms of New York's cultural semantics, that when Mrs. Beaufort leaves her box at the opera at the end of the third act, her ball will begin as scheduled, a half hour later. As Edward T. Hall explains, in *The Silent Language,* "Spatial changes give a tone to a communication, accent it, and at times even override the spoken word. The flow and shift of distance between people as they interact with each other is part and parcel of the communication process." Thus when Countess Olenska, at a dinner party, leaves the Duke of St. Austrey and crosses a room to sit by Newland Archer, she offers him a glimpse of a wholly foreign life style. For "It was not the custom in New York drawing rooms for a lady to get up and walk away from one gentleman in order to seek the company of another." In doing so, and in remaining "at perfect ease" about it, she communicates a sense of naturalness and candor which is reinforced verbally, in her conversations with Archer.

The hieroglyphic system can provide an opportunity for people of common background to communicate silently and thus experience a special kind of emotional closeness. Early in the novel, when May and Newland confront a problem situation together, he becomes aware that "The persons of their world lived in an atmosphere of faint implications and pale delicacies, and the fact that he and she understood each other without a word seemed to the young man to bring them nearer than any explanation would have done." But the system makes it possible for society to radically misinterpret the perceptual signals it receives, as when Archer realizes he and Ellen are considered to be "lovers in the extreme sense peculiar to 'foreign' vocabularies." And it renders its adherents awkward and inarticulate when confronting unusual situations. Approaching the issue of Ellen Olenska's proposed divorce, Archer felt "as awkward and embarrassed as a boy." Unable to find an adequate verbal rendition of his emotional response to her, he leaves her house, at one point, "bursting with the belated eloquence of the inarticulate." Thus it is unsurprising that his last gesture toward her is negative and inarticulate, albeit symbolic. Sending his son to Ellen Olenska with only the cryptic message that he is "old-fashioned," he reinforces the refusals of his lifetime to break out of the limitations of time, place, and experience imposed upon him by an already moribund culture. Poised between nostalgia and despair, he accepts paralysis and yields the future to those courageous enough to seize upon it. (pp. 69-81)

Irving Jacobson, "Perception, Communication, and Growth as Correlative Themes in Edith Wharton's 'The Age of Innocence'," in Agora, *Vol. 2, No. 2, Fall, 1973, pp. 68-82.*

Joseph Candido   (essay date 1978)

[*In the following essay, Candido discusses the significance he finds in Wharton's final revisions of* The Age of Innocence.]

> **As an adult, Edith Wharton was obsessed by the need to be able to talk to sympathetic and understanding friends. "I have no one to *talk* to" is the lament that characterizes her most despondent moments.**
>
> —*Cynthia Griffin Wolff, in her* A Feast of Words: The Triumph of Edith Wharton, *1977.*

The Age of Innocence, published in 1920, comes approximately at the midpoint of Edith Wharton's career: seven years after her divorce of Edward Wharton and four years after the death of her close friend Henry James. Yet in addition to the lingering emotional strains undoubtedly caused by these two events, she was also, at the time of the novel's composition, embroiled in an arduous love affair with Walter Berry (substantially cooler on his part than on hers), and witness to the slow and painful death of her "beloved" Howard Sturgis, made all the more "poignant" by the fact that "it was impossible for [her] to go to him." Moreover, when one adds to this succession of misfortune the deaths of her cousin and three "dear friends" during World War I, it seems remarkable indeed that in the years immediately following the war Edith Wharton was able to return to her fiction with enthusiasm, apparently unperturbed in her professional life by what she herself called the "battalions" of sorrows in her personal one.

Perhaps the most unequivocal statement regarding Wharton's unique ability to put aside personal problems while concentrating on her writing comes from Percy Lubbock. He says of her that

> I never heard of her deranged in her work by troublesome moods, or left high and dry, between page and page, by any distemperature of the brain; the lissomness of her mind, the head and push of her fancy, she seemed able to count upon these without question.

Here, in Lubbock's own terms, is the "serious and practical craftsman," the consummate artist about whom Grace Kellogg could say "she wrote exactly what she wanted to write, and by it was fulfilled." Indeed, there was little about Edith Wharton in those emotionally trying years after the war which did not, externally at least, indicate her extraordinary self-discipline and artistic control. Madame Saint-René Taillandier, one of her many French acquaintances, recalls with admiration this salient feature of the author's personality:

> Shall I make a confession? The perfection of her taste, extending to everything, even to the smallest details of her establishment, the arrangement of the flower-beds, the symmetry of the hedges, the neat ranks of the trees in the orchard—sometimes, when I was too conscious of it all, it chilled me. . . . With Mrs. Wharton I was intimidated by the esthetic perfection of everything about her; I felt that if I had made any

sort of mistake in my appearance that clear eye would observe it. . . .

It is in large part with the observations of this "clear eye" that the serious student of Edith Wharton's fiction must concern himself, for there is every indication that its acute perceptions were not confined to gardens and furniture alone. Edith Wharton was as meticulous in the writing of fiction as in the choice of drawing-room appointments, as "chilling" and relentless in the pursuit of artistic perfection as in the discovery of "mistakes" in personal appearance. The fact that she was able to write as accomplished a work as *The Age of Innocence* while in the midst of personal dilemmas attests to her artistic discipline; and the interested scholar need look no further than the galleys of the novel to see the remarkable acuteness of her "clear eye" at work.

Both the galley and page-proofs of *The Age of Innocence* are extant and part of the collection of the Lilly Library at Indiana University, Bloomington. Since the page-proofs do not bear any markings, other than corrections by its two proofreaders of errors in punctuation, spelling, or typesetting, it is to the galleys that one must turn to find the author's final substantive alterations of the text. The galleys consist of ninety-one sheets (7½" x 24"), numbered consecutively, with the following heading on each of the first eleven leaves: "21095—The AGE OF INNOCENCE—Galley [sheet number in arabic numeral]." From sheets twelve to ninety-one the heading changes slightly as the word "Galley" is omitted; but aside from this minor alteration it corresponds exactly to the heading on sheets one to eleven.

The galleys of *The Age of Innocence* bear two distinct kinds of markings: the notations of the proofreader from the Appleton-Century Company (in green ink), whose remarks are largely confined to the demarcation of pages, correction of obvious mistakes in typesetting, and questions addressed to the author on matters of form such as punctuation or italicization; and the last-minute alterations of the text (in black ink) made by Edith Wharton herself. It is possible to determine with some degree of accuracy the length of time that Wharton spent in making these final changes, for the proofreader dates the galleys in his own hand, "7/23/20," and a letter from Rutger B. Jewett at Appleton-Century to the author reveals that these same galleys were mailed back to the company from France with her corrections on August 12 of the same year. Thus Wharton had completed her final changes of the galleys merely twenty days after it can be documented that they were still in the hands of her proofreader at Appleton-Century, a fact that underscores further Lubbock's characterization of her as a "serious and practical craftsman."

Although her revisions of the galleys are diverse, ranging from the simple correction of spelling and punctuation to the rewriting of whole sentences, there is a general tendency on Wharton's part when she makes substantive changes to delete words and phrases rather than add them. For purposes of discussion it is convenient to divide these various kinds of deletion into three basic groups: the removal of adjectives, the removal of descriptive phrases, and the removal of references to concrete objects and places. Clearly such categories are arbitrary and overlapping, perhaps even reductive, yet they do nonetheless provide an orderly means for examining the precise artistic effects for which the author strives as she puts the finishing touches on her novel.

Edith Wharton's tendency to remove adjectives from the narrative as she makes her last-minute changes should come as no surprise to the literary critic who is familiar with the author's stated artistic preferences. In *The Writing of Fiction* she says in reference to "M. Maeterlinck's book on the bee" that

> I was first dazzled, then oppressed, by the number and the choice of his adjectives and analogies. Every touch was effective, every comparison striking; but when I had assimilated them all, and remade out of them the ideal BEE, that animal had become a winged elephant. The lesson was salutary for a novelist.

This tendency on her part to shun overstatement, to maintain that an author can sometimes render his subject more persuasively by withholding details rather than by using an "oppressive" number of adjectives, is reflected clearly in the emendations Wharton makes on the galleys of *The Age of Innocence.* Early in Chapter VI, for instance, when Archer for the first time experiences misgivings about his forthcoming marriage to May Welland, he imagines his future with her as "a voyage on uncharted seas." Surely this description provides the reader with the information necessary to understand Archer's exact feelings at this moment; but only when one compares this statement to its earlier version in the galleys does the precise effect that the author hopes to achieve by altering it become apparent. The unrevised passage refers to Archer's projected marriage as "a problematic voyage on the open seas." By changing "open" to "uncharted" and simply eliminating the adjective "problematic," Wharton creates as more suggestive, less explicit statement of Archer's marital future, and in the process imbues it with a mysterious and unprescribed quality that it lacked when it was more specifically rendered. A problematic voyage on the open seas is simply that; but a voyage on "uncharted" seas (perhaps merely "problematic," perhaps far worse) made all the more terrifying by the fact that the seas are unexplored, suggests an enigmatic vastness to Archer's future that the more concrete description of it does not. Thus by simply excising one adjective and making another less specific, the author renders more forcefully the sense of emotional disorientation that Archer feels as he contemplates the most important event of his life.

This propensity for understatement manifests itself repeatedly in other changes that Wharton makes on the galleys. Mr. van der Luyden's "large lifeless shrouded room" becomes "the large shrouded room"; "the frozen trees" and "the dry snow" that serve as part of the backdrop for Archer's meeting with Ellen at Skuytercliff are changed simply to "the trees" and "the snow"; and "the velvet portieres" in Mrs. Mingott's drawing room as well as the "loosely-tied crimson roses" of Ellen's "little low-studded drawing-room" are all rendered more simply as "the por-

tieres," the "crimson roses," and "the low-studded drawing-room."

Alterations such as these are obviously significant as part of a clearly distinguishable pattern involving the deletion of adjectives, but they command even greater attention when Wharton uses them to refashion character. There is a general tendency in these instances to blur deliberately the bold outlines of personality, to depict in less detail the external actions or features of a character in order to draw him more subtly. Thus, instead of "Mr. van der Luyden's imposing figure," the revised version has "Mr. van der Luyden's figure," old Medora Manson's "much knuckled hand" is changed simply to "her hand," "Nastasia's rapid step" to "Nastasia's step," "the perspiring travellers" to "the travellers," and "May's sudden blush" to "May's blush." There are, of course, many other examples of such alterations throughout the galleys; yet in these five instances one can see evidence enough of Wharton's determination to achieve the subtlest of effects, to draw character in delicate and suggestive lines rather than in broad, obvious strokes. The author invites the reader to see her characters clearly and distinctly, yet not to see so much of them or so deeply into them that they lose all trace of ambiguity. It is apparent only that Mr. van der Luyden has a "figure," Nastasia a "step," and May a "blush." The precise qualities or motives behind these outward characteristics remain for the reader to infer from the narrative context; for the characters become not merely objectivities embellished by description, but rather clear and perceptible forms upon which one's imaginative capabilities are invited to work. Indeed, the "lesson" Wharton claims to have learned from M. Maeterlinck's unsuccessful description of the bee is one she rigorously applies in making her final revisions of *The Age of Innocence.*

Similar effects such as those produced by the deletion of adjectives occur also when Wharton chooses to remove descriptive phrases from the narrative. One instance is in the scene in which Archer first discusses with Ellen the social implications of divorce in Old New York. The episode is marked by a strenuous verbal and emotional restraint, intended obviously to reflect not only the latent and repressed feelings of love in each character but also the difficulty they have in speaking openly with one another about Ellen's "unpleasant" past in a stifling atmosphere of propriety and convention. At the moment when Archer finally suggests to Ellen that her proposed divorce from Olenski might create more problems than it solves, the scene (in the galleys) continues as follows:

> "He can say things—things that might be unpl—might be disagreeable to you: say them publicly, so that they would get about, and harm you even if—"
>
> "If—?" she questioned, just above her breath.
>
> "I mean: no matter how unfounded they were."

The published version of the scene is identical to this one except for the fact that Ellen's reply to Archer is shortened simply to "If—". Considered from a purely narrative point of view, of course, this change has absolutely no effect on the actual outcome of the scene; but it does alter considerably the reader's attitude toward Ellen. The alternatives in characterization between which the author chooses at this moment are clear: she can either create a woman who responds tentatively and with some anxiety to the evocation of a regrettable past, or depict a composed and impenetrable personality who faces truth or falsehood (at this point one doesn't know which) with stoic equanimity. The fact that she chooses the latter makes the reader's response to Ellen substantially more complex; for it is necessary to react to her inscrutable "If" without the aid of explanatory action. She becomes the enigma to the reader that she does to Archer. In fact, even later in the scene, when Archer is just on the verge of winning his point, the author makes another change that also depicts Ellen in a less self-revealing fashion than in the galley version. The earlier version says that at the conclusion of Archer's conversation with her, "Madame Olenska rose with a sigh," but the published text states merely that "Madame Olenska rose." Again by excising a descriptive phrase which reveals an emotional response on Ellen's part, Wharton makes it more difficult to understand her character's precise state of mind. One senses, as Archer does, that in any attempt to assess Ellen's feelings, the best that can be hoped for is only "the belated eloquence of the inarticulate."

Perhaps the most curious emendations that Wharton makes on her novel in preparing it for the press are her deliberate attempts to make the reader's awareness of place less concrete. One striking illustration of this technique occurs just before the comically ironic episode in which Archer mistakes the "lumbering" Miss Blenker's parasol for Ellen's. As Archer approaches the shabby Blenker home he notices "a ghostly summer-house of trellis-work that had once been white, surmounted by a wooden Cupid who had lost his bow and arrow but continued to take ineffectual aim." The detail here is superb; for the scene juxtaposes two separate "archers," each in his own way incapable of effecting romantic success. But only when one compares this final version of the scene to its earlier form in the galleys does the remarkable deftness of the author's touch become apparent. The earlier version of the scene reads "a ghostly summer-house of trellis-work that had once been white, surmounted by a wooden Cupid who had lost his bow and arrow but continued to take ineffectual aim *at the gate*" (italics added). Although the only change that Wharton makes in revising this passage is to delete the phrase "at the gate," an awareness of this minor emendation allows the reader to see a complexity in the scene that he might otherwise have missed. By having the dilapidated Cupid aim "at the gate" the author at least suggests a perceptible direction to his unavailing attempts to arouse love; but when she deletes even this detail, the effect is to depict his love-making powers (and Archer's by analogy) as completely without a clear objective. Indeed, this is precisely the idea that Archer's *dénouement* with Miss Blenker seems to underscore, for he enters the box-garden drawn by the parasol "like a magnet"; yet as subsequent events reveal, his euphoric romantic instincts are completely misguided. His own "ineffectual aim," as directionless and unspecified as that of the Cupid on the summer-house, reduces him to little more than a vivified parody of the figure above him.

It should be noted that not all of Wharton's attempts to restrict the reader's awareness of concrete objects and places lend themselves to detailed analysis, but taken as a whole they do reflect the same tendency to blur the sharp contours of reality as those emendations involving the removal of adjectives and descriptive phrases. Thus, during Archer's first private meeting with Ellen, when Nastasia enters the room carrying teacups and dishes, she does not place the tray "on a low table in front of [Ellen]" as she does in the earlier version, but instead "on a low table." Similarly, Ned Winsett's "general nod from the threshold" as he leaves Madame Olenska's parlor becomes simply a "general nod"; the members of the Newport Archery Club assembled at the Beauforts' do not stand "near the tent" but "on the lawn"; and Archer, pacing nervously about his room, moves not "out of the radius of the lamp on his table," but "out of the radius of the lamp." Although none of these emendations changes significantly the tonal or thematic impact of the scenes in which they occur, they do illustrate the author's determination to strike precisely the right artistic chord, to create what one critic has so aptly called her "economy of style, economy of incident, economy of emotion."

Perhaps the most engaging scene in *The Age of Innocence,* from the standpoint of sheer emotional tension, is the episode in which Archer and Ellen reveal their love for one another. This meeting, like so many of those involving the romantically frustrated couple, is marked by such inordinate verbal and behavioral restraint on their part that they enfeeble the passions they try to express. The reader sees before him two people desperately in love, yet imprisoned by a code of propriety that sacrifices feeling for "right" behavior, impulse for control. In fact, even at the moment that they are actually able to profess their mutual love, they are paradoxically separated by this very expression, "divided by the distance [Ellen's] words had created." The scene is one of the most memorable in the book and, judging from the number of last-minute changes that the author makes on it in the galleys, perhaps one of the most thoughtfully conceived.

Wharton's emendations of the scene have the effect of underscoring the tension between the polished, non-resistant surface of life and the powerful emotions that beat helplessly beneath it. For instance, the moment Archer informs Madame Olenska that May is in no hurry to marry him, Ellen merely "look[s] up at him." In the earlier version, however, Ellen registers much more interest in this unexpected news by "look[ing] up quickly." A knowledge of both the early and later versions here allows the reader to see a significance in Ellen's apparent casualness that would otherwise have gone unnoticed. Ellen is a woman in love, and it seems only logical that with her first awareness of Archer's possible availability she would betray some emotion. Yet by excising the one detail that reveals Ellen's real interest in Archer's statement, Wharton makes her behavior fully consistent with that of a "lady" in her particular social and personal circumstance. She is, after all, a married woman and the cousin of the girl to whom Archer is engaged. In this situation the canons of social taste, even for a spirit as liberal as Ellen's, must take precedence over the impulse to respond emotionally. In fact, there are several other instances throughout the scene when Wharton makes changes that produce the same effect as this one. For example, just after Archer asks Ellen, "do you see me marrying May after this?" (their mutual expression of love), Ellen's reaction (in the earlier version) is " 'I don't see you,' she said at length, painfully, putting that question to May. 'Do you?' " In the published version of the scene, however, Wharton deletes the adverb "painfully," thus bringing Ellen's behavior once more within the limits of the strictest social propriety. As before, she removes an emotional response on Ellen's part (when it seems only logical that Ellen should have one) in order to underscore the struggle within her between natural passion and affected restraint. The reader is meant to feel, perhaps, since he does not actually know the earlier version, only partially to feel, that again Ellen sacrifices genuine emotion to the god of respectability.

It is interesting to note that Wharton does not confine emendations of this nature solely to those passages in the scene which involve Ellen. Archer's behavior, too, comes under her careful scrutiny as she puts the finishing touches on her text. So it is that in the earlier version when Archer tells Ellen that "May guessed the truth" about his love for another woman, he says it "abruptly"; yet in the published text the line reads simply: " 'May guessed the truth,' he said." And later in the scene after Ellen explains to him that it is "too late to do anything" about their situation, the text in the galleys continues with " 'Ah, I don't understand you!' he cried." In the published version, however, Archer's exclamation is diminished in intensity to merely "Ah, I don't understand you!" The author tries in these instances to imbue Archer's actions and speech with the same sense of emotional restriction that characterizes Ellen's. In fact, this notion that both characters fall victim to an identical dilemma involving the conflict between an ingrained restraint and natural affection seems at the heart of still another revealing change that Wharton makes in the scene. At the moment when Archer and Ellen join in their first and only embrace, the earlier version of the narrative says of Ellen that "she gave him back all his kisses." In final form, however, this line is changed slightly, yet significantly, to "she gave him back all his kiss." There could be no more revealing example than this of Wharton's attempt to strike a tenuous balance between emotion and restraint, for just at the moment that the couple share their love most intimately, the author sees fit to restrict the nature of its very expression. They kiss but once, and this for the last time in the book. The "barrier of words" that inevitably drops between them cannot be surmounted by such tentative professions of love; and it is precisely this juxtaposition of passion with the inadequate means for expressing it that Wharton's careful alterations of the scene are designed to underscore.

It should be noted in conclusion that not all the changes that Wharton makes on the earlier version of the text involve deletions of adjectives, descriptive phrases, and references to objects and places. The text as it exists in the galleys reveals, in addition to the emendations already mentioned, several other changes which show the author striving for a precise artistic effect. One notices, for instance, her sharp irony in the making as she draws in detail the character of Sillerton Jackson. This high priest of taste, whose sole function is to pass judgment on others' adherence to the canons of form and propriety, pontificates regularly on the behavior of Old New York:

> When one was related to the Mansons and the Rushworths one had a "*Droit de cite*" (as Mr. Sillerton Jackson called it) in New York society.

This passage from the version in the galleys shows persuasively enough how informed Jackson's pronouncements are; but the author qualifies the nature of his opinions by making only a slight change in the text when she casts it in final form: " . . . (as Mr. Sillerton Jackson, who had frequented the Tuileries, called it). . . ." By inserting this single clause (contrary to her usual method of revision) Wharton forces the reader to regard Jackson's use of the French expression in a somewhat different light from what he would have had she retained the earlier version. His pronouncements regarding "taste" and "form" now seem to come not from an oracular arbiter of societal mores, but from a man whose behavior is as foppishly derivative as those he seeks to criticize. There are times, too, when Wharton makes alterations to produce a subtle change in tone. Such is the case when during Archer's meeting with Ellen in the old house at Skuytercliff he throws "a log upon the embers" rather than a "shovelful of coal into the grate" as he does in the earlier version. This same propensity for more suggestive phraseology seems also to be at work when she changes Archer's statement to May during their honeymoon in London, perhaps ironically, from " 'Look here—the rain's stopping' " to " 'Look here—the fog's lifting' "; and it also manifests itself later when the older and more reflective Archer, looking back on his accomplishments, numbers among them "starting the first school for crippled children" rather than "the first training-school for nurses" as the earlier version states.

Surely it would be a mistake to overemphasize changes such as these by lavishing critical interpretation on them, for their effect does little more than evoke a slightly different mood rather than actually change meaning. Yet whatever the impetus behind these or any other alterations that Wharton makes, there can be little doubt that at all times during the period of final emendation she showed the artistic discipline and love for nuance that characterized the other aspects of her life. Indeed, *The Age of Innocence* bears so completely the marks of finely wrought craftsmanship that Blake Nevius, approaching the novel from a purely critical perspective, can say that

> *The Age of Innocence* is not Mrs. Wharton's strongest novel, but, along with *Ethan Frome,* it is the one in which she is most thoroughly the artist. It is a triumph of style, of the perfect adaptation of means to a conception fully grasped from the outset. It would be difficult to say that she faltered or overreached at any point.

The fact that the sensitive critic can respond so readily to the novel's sheer technical brilliance gives evidence enough of the deftness with which Wharton used her "clear eye" as she prepared her manuscript for the press. (pp. 21-30)

Joseph Candido, "Edith Wharton's Final Alterations of 'The Age of Innocence'," in Studies in American Fiction, *Vol. 6, No. 1, Spring, 1978, pp. 21-31.*

David A. Godfrey (essay date 1988)

[*In the following essay, Godfrey focuses on Wharton's portrayal of the relationship between language usage and social conduct in* The Age of Innocence.]

"A standard; the word perhaps gives me my clue. When I said, in my resentful youth, that I had been taught only languages and manners, I did not know how closely, in my parents' minds, the two were related," wrote Edith Wharton in her autobiography, *A Backward Glance*. Because the two were intimately linked in her own mind as well, language plays a crucial role in relating the self to its society throughout her canon. What she terms a "standard" is of course an ideal or cultural norm, an index of the way things ought to be rather than a description of the way they are. Stating explicitly in **"The Great American Novel"** that "As she [America] has reduced the English language to a mere instrument of utility . . . so she has reduced relations between human beings to a dead level of vapid benevolence," Wharton repeatedly associates a failure of language with a failure of relationships. In particular she is concerned with the debilitating effects of a language of cowardice upon the relationships her Old New Yorkers are able to form and sustain. Since *The Age of Innocence* is her fullest and most subtle exploration of the subject, I focus on it here.

In Wharton's depiction of Old New York, the community as a whole is more important than the individual. Unlike the nouveaux riches, who see society as a cluster of atomic and absolute individuals, each having primacy over the social group, Old New Yorkers see their society as an organic entity. The purpose of their controlling norms, as Wharton repeatedly emphasizes, is to perpetuate the community and its types of interaction: "The first duty of such a class was to maintain a strict standard of uprightness in affairs. . . . Their value lay in upholding two standards of importance in any community, that of education and good manners, and of scrupulous probity in business and private affairs." Language, the principal instrument of socialization and an integral part of social behavior, plays an important role in the realization of those ideals: "Usage, in my childhood, was as authoritative an element in speaking English as tradition was in social conduct." In her fictive New York, social conduct and English usage are similarly indivisible, thus providing a means of evaluating the effects of language on the Old New Yorkers. Like their historical prototypes, Wharton's fictive Old New Yorkers desire a stable, humane, and united society founded upon traditional values. All too often, however, their cowardly use of language undercuts their ability to "live up" to "long established standards of honour and conduct."

Despite their articulateness, her Old New Yorkers simply refuse to discuss subjects of consequence. For instance, they refuse to recognize divorce as well as marriage as a legitimate means of gaining wealth and social position.

Considering the subject too vulgar for discussion, they wish primarily to avoid the "nasty talk" associated with Ralph and Undine Marvell's divorce in *The Custom of the Country* and the possible "beastly" or "unpleasant talk" should Ellen Olenska pursue her plans for divorce in *The Age of Innocence.* To avoid such subjects the old upper class has developed what Ralph Marvell comes to see as the "full and elaborate vocabulary of evasion." Learning, sometime after their divorce, that Undine wishes to sell him their son so that she can pay the Pope to annul their marriage,

> he recalled all the old family catch-words, the full and elaborate vocabulary of evasion: "delicacy," "pride," "personal dignity," "preferring not to know about such things"; Mrs. Marvell's: "All I ask is that you won't mention the subject to your grandfather," Mr. Dagonet's: "Spare your mother, Ralph, whatever happens," and even Laura's terrified: "Of course for Paul's sake, there must be no scandal."

That the old upper class, like Ralph's mother, should find "the idea of talking over the situation . . . positively frightening" is a severe indictment of its cowardice. The "full and elaborate vocabulary of evasion," another manifestation of language as a "deadly drug," is what Wharton terms "turns of speech," cliches that avoid "what are evasively called the 'facts of life'."

The Old New Yorkers' failure to use language for its root purpose of expression is pernicious, stunting individual development and subverting the social order. "Preferring not to know about such things," they don't. Consequently they have become in effect dead concerning a number of vital subjects—the making and dissolving of families and homes, the making and disposing of wealth, and, especially, the sustaining and creating of viable cultural values. In short, the old upper class can be so readily conquered by the "invaders" largely because it deigns to recognize that it is fighting for survival. Yet as Wharton writes in *French Ways and Their Meaning,*

> Things are not always and everywhere well with the world, and each man has to find it out as he grows up. It is the finding out that makes him grow, and until he has faced the fact and digested the lesson he is not grown up—he is still in the nursery. The same is true of countries and peoples. The "sheltered life," whether of the individual or the nation, must either have a violent and tragic awakening—or never wake up at all.

Her fictive Old New Yorkers, it is clear, never woke up at all—and, what is worse, did not want to. Although they have developed their vocabulary of evasion to help them preserve the social order, it ironically contributes largely to the society's demise by legitimizing a sheltered way of life.

By doing so, the language of cowardice negates one of language's most essential functions, that of providing members of a social group with a specific stock of social knowledge. Because language explains and justifies the social order, it is fundamental to a society's coherence, as Peter L. Berger and Thomas Luckmann point out in *The*

Social Construction of Reality. Through the process of socialization the members of a social order come to see their "social world as a consistent whole," one that is literally coherent since it all "hangs together." Moreover, socialization produces a distinct type of person, one whose life takes on meaning and makes sense only in terms of the social knowledge as shaped and transmitted by language: "the primary knowledge of the institutional order is the sum total of 'what everybody knows' about a social world, an assemblage of maxims, morals, proverbial nuggets of wisdom, values and beliefs, myths, and so forth."

In *The Age of Innocence,* "the tight little citadel of New York" is still a consistent world that "hangs together," although it is beginning to lose its coherence. Its socialization produces the Old New Yorker, that distinct type of person necessary for the preservation and propagation of the social organism. Moreover, its rhetoric certainly explains and justifies the social order, but it fails to provide a body of knowledge that helps individuals deal with difficult social problems, especially those related to subjects they "prefer not to know" about.

This becomes abundantly apparent in *The Age of Innocence* when Newland Archer attempts to deal with Ellen Olenska's marital problems:

> "Now we're coming to hard facts," he thought, conscious in himself of the same instinctive recoil that he had so often criticised in his mother and her contemporaries. How little practice he had in dealing with unusual situations! Their vocabulary was unfamiliar to him, and seemed to belong to fiction and the stage. In face of what was coming he felt as awkward and embarrassed as a boy.

The epitome of the Old New Yorker, Newland Archer has been "successfully" socialized. In learning and mastering Old New York's world view, he has learned its explanations and justifications as objective reality and internalized them as subjective truth, as his reverence for the "dictates of Taste" and "the god of Form" indicate. Yet as William Barrett observes, "I wake each day into the words that are waiting for me. I exist, I am what I am, within the world that language lays open to me." The words Archer wakes into clearly close rather than open his world, one reason he has so much difficulty coping with the "case" of Ellen Olenska.

Like his fellow New Yorkers, Archer suffers from stunted development and a bad case of cowardice. From his nearly religious faith in what is or is not "the thing" he moves toward a vague and impossible ideal that he calls late in the novel "that other vision in my mind." When the novel opens he is so fully of his world that he is only marginally capable of thought—and of free speech as well. Thus when he recognizes the Mingott strategy behind their "flaunting" of Ellen at the opera, all he can do is repeat helplessly the cliches with which he has been conditioned to respond. His first response is egocentric as well as automatic: "To receive the Countess Olenska in the family circle was a different thing from producing her in public, at the opera of all places, and in the very box with the young girl whose engagement to him, Newland Archer, was to be an-

nounced within a few weeks." Noticeably, his response is nearly identical to that made by Lawrence Lefferts, Old New York's "foremost authority on 'form,' " who gives voice not only to Archer's thoughts but to all the men's in the box: "This parading her at the opera is another thing!" In his conclusions all Archer can do is repeat helplessly after Old New York's "great authority on 'family' ": "No, he felt as old Sillerton Jackson felt; he did not think the Mingotts would have tried it on!" Archer thinks himself superior to the other men in the box, but as his formulaic responses make clear, he is virtually their clone. Hence he is content to hold his view on women "without analysing it, since he knew it was that of all the carefully brushed, white-waist-coated, buttonhole-flowered gentlemen who succeeded each other in the club box" and to accept their "doctrine on all the issues called moral." Not to do so would be "troublesome—and rather bad form."

In his unconscious conformity to his social group, Archer has simply failed to mature. Again, several of William Barrett's observations help explain Archer's relationship to his society when he says that in our ordinary, everyday world

> none of us is a private Self confronting a world of external objects. None of us yet even a Self. We are each simply one among many; a name among the names of our schoolfellows, our fellow citizens, our community. This everyday public quality of our existence Heidegger calls "the One." The one is the impersonal and public creature whom each of us is even before he is an I, a real I. One has such and such a position in life, one is expected to behave in such-and-such a manner, one does this, one does not do that, etc., etc. We exist thus in a state of "fallenness" . . . in the sense that we are as yet below the level of experience to which it is possible for us to rise. So long as we remain in the womb of this externalized and public existence, we are spared the terror and the dignity of becoming a Self.

When the novel opens, Archer is clearly a public, externalized "One" among many, although he very quickly rebels against some of the conventions of his class, especially those "verbal generosities" that are in fact a "humbugging disguise" that "tied things together and bound people down to the old pattern." Yet despite his rebellion, Archer never fully matures, not because he is entrapped in a particular socio-economic class or, as he mistakenly believes, in a marriage to the wrong woman, but because he does not have an adequate or workable vision of an ideal culture and because he is incapable of free speech. But free speech can only be the result of training, discipline, education—something the Old New Yorkers' determination to avoid "unpleasantness" and their consequent vocabulary of evasion work against.

Since language provides the individual with one's cognitive approach to the world, Archer's language indicates his woefully inadequate conceptualization of experience. Too cowardly to deal literally with Ellen's "case," he repeatedly chooses a vocabulary that seems indeed to belong to fiction and stage. For instance, he thinks of her European society as a place where "the Countess Olenska had lived and suffered, and also—perhaps—tasted mysterious joys," and he sees the pitiable Medora Manson, Ellen's aunt, as a "messenger of Satan" who has come "straight out of the hell from which Ellen Olenska had just escaped." In his immaturity and cowardice Archer is sometimes comically naive: "She said the words 'my husband' as if no sinister associations were connected with them." Whatever the details of Ellen's vague past, she is not a "dark lady" from some Gothic thriller or scrofulous French novel. Archer's attempt to view her as if she were derives not only from his inexperience and his growing sexual attraction to her, but his presupposition that she is "naturally" guilty of some "vague charge" by her husband.

Because of that erroneous presupposition, Archer deliberately resorts to the automatic, unthinking responses he has been conditioned to make. To avoid his own thoughts about Ellen's past and to prevent her from saying anything about it he argues the family line, even though he *fully intends* to oppose his family and help Ellen get a divorce. Acting out of sheer cowardice, then, he makes the most crucial statement of his life, one that in its literal meaning becomes the central passage of the novel:

> "The individual, in such cases, is nearly always sacrificed to what is supposed to be the collective interest; people cling to any convention that keeps the family together—protects the children, if there are any," he rambled on, pouring out all the stock phrases that rose to his lips in his intense desire to cover over the ugly reality which her silence seemed to have laid bare. Since she would not or could not say the one word that would have cleared the air, his wish was not to let her feel that he was trying to probe into her secret. Better to keep on the surface in the prudent old New York way, than risk uncovering a wound he could not heal. "It's my business, you know," he went on, "to help you see these things as the people who are fondest of you see them."

Reciting these "stock phrases" ostensibly to help her understand her plight and therefore to avoid embarrassing or harming herself in what he romantically pictures to himself as her "mad plunges against fate," Archer simply lacks the courage to face the facts, whatever they may be. Significantly, despite his inability to address Ellen's problems, he leaves her "bursting with the belated eloquence of the inarticulate."

Since Archer never develops an adequate vocabulary for dealing with life's exigencies, never experiences what Wharton terms elsewhere "the releasing power of language," he never matures into what she considers genuine adulthood, never develops "the courage to look at things as they are," her "first test of mental maturity." Because Archer does not mature, he quite rightly sees himself at one point as "the prisoner of this hackneyed vocabulary." Thus it is entirely appropriate that in the novel's epilogue he attempts "to deal all at once with the stocked regrets and stifled memories of an inarticulate lifetime."

As part of its cognitive function language typifies behavior, allowing individuals to deal with their experiences as part of a general and recognized class rather than as unique phenomena. Despite his attempt to see an affair with Ellen as unique or exceptional, and therefore as justifiable, Archer finally recognizes what is tautologically true: he can have an affair with Ellen only by having an affair with Ellen. But that means using the same dodges and expedients that Lawrence Lefferts uses to continue his philandering, including the language (hence the "hackneyed vocabulary") that legitimizes such behavior. In the Old New York code, the "game" of deceiving one's wife is thus called "protecting a woman's honour," but as Archer admits to himself, the act is "despicable." A transgression against the wife and the entire community, it diminishes "all the old decencies that he and his people had always believed in." Wharton's comment, nearly twenty years earlier, that in George Eliot's fiction "one does not gain one's pleasure at the cost of the social organism" is an apt description of her own work.

All societies are necessarily founded upon illusions having the ontological status of fact. Archer, for instance, originally sees May's innocence as "abysmal," but later realizes that it is a "factitious purity"—literally a fiction treated as fact. His discovery that Old New York's "elaborate system of mystification" is based on illusion is a prerequisite for adulthood: only children live in *the* world; adults live in *a* world. Refusing to come to terms with his insight, Archer characteristically attempts to evade its consequences.

Part of his problem is that with the possible exceptions of old Mrs. Manson Mingott and Julius Beaufort, Ellen Olenska is the only genuinely mature adult Archer knows. Ellen readjusts his vision so that the world he wants to live in is no longer identical to the world he has to live in, as it is at the beginning of the novel. At least partially as a result of that disorientation, he comes to want statements to be absolutely true, regardless of the consequences. Moreover, despite his own incapacity for free speech, he refuses to acknowledge the necessary social or public use of language to preserve the social coherence. Thus he becomes somewhat bored and irritated when statements are made with "the proper affectation of reluctance" and received with "the proper expressions of amusement, incredulity, and gratitude." He thinks himself superior to such conventions, but the novel repeatedly demonstrates how deeply dependent on them he is. He apparently never realizes that all conventions are arbitrary, that all societies must have them in order to maintain their coherence.

As Wharton makes quite clear, usage is a central aspect of "the thing," and as Northrop Frye points out in his discussion of free speech and its relationship to the "public" or "rhetorical" use of language, "In this conception of the 'right thing,' there are two factors involved, one moral and one aesthetic. They are inseparable and equally important. . . . [There is] a social standard beyond the merely intellectual standards of truth and falsehood, which has the power of final veto." But since Archer never realizes that the moral and aesthetic ("Form") aspects of "the thing" are equally important and inseparable, his discovery that the world he has to live in (the real culture) is not identical to the world he wants to live in (an ideal culture) leads not to adulthood but to disillusionment and discontent.

To become a genuine adult capable of living freely in a society necessarily founded upon illusion, Newland Archer must develop the ability to choose what is most valuable from the entirety of his cultural heritage, and then let the rest go. Above all, he must develop the power to choose and select, so that he neither believes everything literally—as he does at the beginning of the novel—nor rejects everything—as he attempts to do later. Because he is incapable of such selectivity, he never develops an adequate vision of an ideal culture. Instead, he wishes to flee his *milieu* and escape from society altogether. His vision of what he would like life to be like is patently escapist and infantile. Thus he tells Ellen, "I can sit perfectly still beside you, like this, with that other vision in my mind, just quietly trusting to it to come true." But as Ellen probes this statement to find out what Archer has in mind, it becomes clear that he can articulate no realistic vision of a life with her:

> "Is it your idea, then, that I should live with you as your mistress—since I can't be your wife?" she asked.
>
> The crudeness of the question startled him: the word was one that women of his class fought shy of, even when their talk flitted closest about the topic. He noticed that Madame Olenska pronounced it as if it had a recognized place in her vocabulary, and he wondered if it has been used familiarly in her presence in the horrible life she had fled from. Her question pulled him up with a jerk, and he floundered.
>
> "I want—I want somehow to get away with you into a world where words like that—categories like that—won't exist. Where we shall be simply two human beings who love each other, who are the whole of life to each other, and nothing else on earth will matter."

Archer's vision of an ideal world bears a curious resemblance to Lawrence Selden's vision of a "republic of the spirit" in *The House of Mirth* where one could supposedly be free "from everything." Both are equally impossible, cowardly visions of escape from reality. Noticeably, Ellen immediately takes full measure of Archer's fantasy and rejects it outright, seeing that in real terms his vision means merely a squalid affair in some "miserable little country." Her rejection of his fantasy and her admonition that he look at realities rather than visions characteristically leaves him "dazed with inarticulate pain."

Unlike Newland Archer, Ellen Olenska has not been debilitated by a vocabulary of evasion. A genuine adult, she looks the "Gorgon," life, in the face. In sharp contrast to Archer, Ellen is capable of assimilating what is most valuable in her cultural heritage into a workable and realistic ideal in which personal and societal needs are balanced and largely identical. The central paradox of the novel is that her vision of relationships is founded upon the "stock phrases" Archer had recited to her in order to evade dealing with her divorce. Thus her "resigned acceptance" is of something quite different than what he thinks. Contrary to what he believes, she understands perfectly the un-

voiced assumptions behind his pathetic presentation. Later, in one of the novel's most crucial scenes, Ellen makes clear how seriously she had taken his statement, as well as how thoroughly she had understood it:

> "Isn't it you who made me give up divorcing—give it up because you showed me how selfish and wicked it was, how one must sacrifice one's self to preserve the dignity of marriage . . . and to spare one's family the publicity, the scandal? And because my family was going to be your family—for May's sake and for yours—I did what you told me, what you proved to me I ought to do. Ah," she broke out in a sudden laugh, "I've made no secret of having done it for you!"

Along these same lines, she has also tested Archer's view of his relationship to May. When he tells her that May is willing to give him up if he is in love with someone else, Archer again fails to understand Ellen's response:

> "That *is* noble," she said with a slight break in her voice.
>
> "Yes. But it's ridiculous."
>
> "Ridiculous? Because you don't care for anyone else?"
>
> "Because I don't mean to marry anyone else."
>
> "Ah."
>
> There was another long interval.

Once Ellen has taken Archer's measure, she holds him to his argument against divorce, making him live what he says, not as a bundle of evasive cliches but as positive moral and social values.

Ellen, then, does not represent an escape from that "sense of unreality in which he felt himself imprisoned." In fact, she represents the same values and the same way of life May does. Both women stand for solidarity, continuity, and the family, three of the most important elements in Wharton's ideal of a "real relation to life." In May's most important statement she tells Archer that "I couldn't have my happiness made out of a wrong—an unfairness—to somebody else." While not given the same emphasis or elaboration as Ellen's various statements, her comment is virtually identical to what Ellen repeatedly tells Archer: "You hated happiness bought by disloyalty and cruelty and indifference. That was what I'd never known before—and it's better than anything I've known." And when Ellen laughs at Archer's vision of their life together she tells him quite simply, "But there's no us in that sense! We're near each other only if we stay far from each other. Then we can be ourselves. Otherwise we're only Newland Archer, the husband of Ellen Olenska's cousin, and Ellen Olenska, the cousin of Newland Archer's wife, trying to be happy behind the back of the people who trust them." Because of her passionate dedication to the family, she is able to force Archer to adhere to the same values: "It was the perfect balance she had held between their loyalty to others and their honesty to themselves that had so stirred and tranquilized him."

A drawing of Wharton by Kate Rogers Nowell, 1906.

Furthermore, once Ellen has assimilated the values lying behind Archer's bundle of "stock phrases," she practices what she believes, treating her entire family the same way she does May and Newland. Thus when Beaufort's "smash" disgraces his wife, another member of the Mingott clan, Ellen sticks by her for familial as well as personal reasons. As old Mrs. Mingott tells Archer:

> "The day after she got here she put on her best bonnet and told me, as cool as a cucumber, that she was going to call on Regina Beaufort. 'I don't know her; who is she?' says I. 'She's your grandniece, and a most unhappy woman,' she says. 'She's the wife of a soundrel,' I answered. 'Well,' she says, 'and so am I, and yet all my family want me to go back to him.' Well, that floored me, and I let her go; and finally one day she said it was raining too hard to go out on foot, and she wanted me to lend her my carriage. 'What for?' I asked her; and she said, 'To go and see Cousin Regina'—*cousin!* Now, my dear, I looked out the window and saw it wasn't raining a drop; but I understood her, and I let her have the carriage. . . . I've always liked courage above everything."

But Ellen directs her energy specifically to the preserving of May and Newland's relationship, and, once they are married, their marriage. She does this consistently from her first statement, "I want you to talk to me about May," through her various testing of his purposes, to her willing

participation in the Old New York ritual of banishment. This latter point deserves some elaboration. Old New York sees itself as eliminating Ellen from the tribe, but Ellen has already willingly decided to return to Europe, not for the reasons her family believes, but because the obtuse and persistent Archer has made her continued stay in New York an impossibility. As Archer realizes, "She would go only if she felt herself becoming a temptation to Archer, a temptation to fall away from the standard they had both set up. Her choice would be to stay near him as long as he did not ask her to come near; and it depended upon himself to keep her just there, safe but secluded." Ironically, she returns to Europe not because she is Archer's lover but so she will not be.

The undependable Archer cannot resist temptation, and finally he gives in to the urge to sleep with her just once. But Ellen makes their proposed liaison conditional: "Shall I—once come to you, and then go home?" By "home," she means Europe, and Archer despairingly accepts her terms. May's announcement of her pregnancy to Ellen later the same day in no way changes Ellen's resolve: she has already decided to leave America. Ellen, then, willingly submits to the ritual banishment so as not to destroy the social illusion, solidarity, and coherence that result from its enactment. This element of illusion and disillusionment is again central, for Ellen has remained in America largely to prevent the social illusions from failing. As she pointedly tells Archer, "If it's not worthwhile to have given up, to have missed things, so that others may be saved from disillusionment and misery—then everything I came home for, everything that made my other life seem by contrast so bare and so poor because no one there took account of them—all these things are a sham or a dream." In particular, the one person Ellen wants to save from disillusionment is May, and even when she tells Archer so specifically he fails to understand:

> "Ah—how like a woman! None of you will ever see a bad business through!"
>
> She lowered her voice. "Is it a bad business—for May? . . . For that's the thing we've always got to think of—haven't we—by our own showing?" she insisted.

"My own showing?" he echoed, his blank eyes on the sea. Yet if the central paradox of the novel is Ellen's transformation of a bundle of cliches into the controlling values of the novel and a workable social standard, the central irony is that Archer himself really believes in these values. He talks May into announcing their engagement early, wishing that "the necessity of their action had been represented by some ideal reason and not simply by poor Ellen Olenska." But since he and May agree in one of their mute "duologues" that "we're doing this because it's right," he clearly does act in accordance with some social standard involving family solidarity and social coherence. Later, in what I read as the turning point of the novel, he realizes that he is just like Lawrence Lefferts, different in degree but not in kind. He is not unique and he knows it. Moreover, he knows that to have an affair with Ellen is to violate a social standard he really believes in. As he tells Ellen, such an affair is "detestable." Even so, he cannot resist temptation, but the terms of his putative success indicate how appalling the deed really is to him:

> He sat there without conscious thoughts, without sense of the lapse of time, in a deep and grave amazement that seemed to suspend life rather than quicken it. "This was what had to be, then . . . this was what had to be," he kept repeating to himself, as if he hung in the clutch of doom. What he had dreamed of had been so different that there was a mortal chill in his rapture.

Archer remains a visionary to the end, never coming fully alive, never fully maturing. Central to his stunted development is his inarticulateness, his inability to conceive or articulate adult relationships. His condition is not unique, and Wharton repeatedly points out that he is representative of his class as a whole.

Since language retains and accumulates historical and biographical information, it provides individuals the means of evaluating and interpreting experience. All societies are necessarily selective in what they retain, and their very vocabularies largely determine what is and is not accumulated. Old New York's "full and elaborate vocabulary of evasion" restricts the society's body of knowledge, preventing Old New Yorkers from dealing adequately with everyday situations and further reducing the social stock of knowledge transmitted to the next generation.

Yet I find it quite interesting that the values controlling *The Age of Innocence* are precisely those controlling Wharton's first novel, *The Valley of Decision* (1902). There Wharton states in her own voice that the "domestic virtues" should be based upon "faithfulness to the family sanctities, reverence for the marriage tie, courage to sacrifice the loftiest passion to the most plodding duty"; that social stability depends upon the constant winning of "the battle of the spiritual and the sensual, of conscience against appetite"; that "personal relation[s]" should be subordinated, "unflinchingly, to the ideal of those larger relations that link the individual to the group"; and that a society's "standard of conduct" should be "regulated by the needs of the race rather than by individual passion, a conception of each existence as a link in the great chain of human endeavor."

In *The Age of Innocence,* for the most part, these values have become incorporated into the language of cowardice. As such they have become part of Old New York's systematic rationale for evading "unpleasantness," a means of reassuring its members that all is well with the world. Yet in the character of Ellen Olenska, Wharton shows how the "vocabulary of evasion" can become deeply significant. As in *The Valley of Decision,* the key lies in Wharton's statement that "through the set mask of language the living thoughts looked forth, old indeed as the world, but renewed with the life of every heart that bore them." Ellen has—and demonstrates—the courage to bear them. (pp. 27-44)

> David A. Godfrey, " 'The Full and Elaborate Vocabulary of Evasion': The Language of Cowardice in Edith Wharton's Old New

York," in The Midwest Quarterly, *Vol. XXX, No. 1, Autumn, 1988, pp. 27-44.*

Wharton's perceptiveness:

We drove about in a taxi-cab, the oldest and dirtiest and most ramshackle cab in Rome, with a driver whose black coat had turned greenish with age. Even my not very violent national pride rebelled against this, and I asked Edith whether she would not like me to procure a car a little more in keeping with her station in life. She said no, she would stick to this man and engage him again, because he looked as if he would be kind to her little dog while we were inside a church. It was quite true: he was very tender with the little creature, and it gave me an insight into the quickness of her perceptions. She noticed details of expression and subtle nuances of mood in a flash, while apparently rather bored or otherwise preoccupied.

Nicky Mariano, quoted in Percy Lubbock, Portrait of Edith Wharton, *D. Appleton-Century, 1947.*

Jeanne Boydston   (essay date 1988)

[*In the following excerpt, the critic suggests that Wharton's depiction of New York society in* The Age of Innocence *is rooted in nostalgia and a romanticized perception of family life.*]

The Age of Innocence represents Wharton's attempt to move back through the history of her own culture to discover an alternative model of social life. The "new people" loom distinctly on the horizon of Newland Archer's world, to be sure, ready at a moment either to buy up or simply to rebuild old New York's most cherished symbols of community. But the novel is not about the invaders *per se.* It is, instead, about the people whose lives they would later invade—an extended meditation (through the vehicle of Newland Archer's life) on the nature of human relations *before* Fifth Avenue became a mere social equivalent for industrial wealth.

Perhaps because of its more singular focus, *The Age of Innocence* has a beguiling sense of unity; from Archer's first introduction to the Countess Olenska to his final farewell, the novel develops with a flawlessness of tone that characterizes neither *The House of Mirth* nor *The Custom of the Country.* Nonetheless, *The Age of Innocence* is an unsettled work which finally achieves reconciliation only in an affecting but telling recourse to the mysticism of an idealized vision of the home.

The lessons Newland Archer learns by the end of this novel are, like those of *Little Women* and *The Wide, Wide World,* the lessons of the home: to renounce personal well-being for the good of others, to nurture familial bonds, to value the refuge of the family above the pleasures of the world, and, at all costs, to protect the home from the corruption of "public" life. This is what Ellen Olenska, who has experienced life without a home, knows; as much as May's pregnancy, it is why she leaves: " . . . happiness bought by disloyalty and cruelty and indifference" is always got at too dear a price. Over the course of his engagement and marriage, Archer slowly comes to agree. At the end of the novel, he has not only given Ellen up, but, in a type of "innocent family hypocrisy," he has never even spoken of her. Rather, through the years he has devoted himself to the world of his family: to parenting, to work in the civic arena, and to the preservation of his home. Indeed, after May's death, Archer himself becomes an emblem of motherhood, combining affectionate single-parenting and a public career of benevolent reform with a civilizing role reminiscent of the eternal "feminine": if, as he recognizes, he has in some respects missed "the flower of life," he concludes that "it did not so much matter if marriage was dull duty, as long as it kept the dignity of a duty: lapsing from that, it became a mere battle of ugly appetites."

A dull duty, however, is hardly an engaging alternative to the ugly appetites of industrial wealth. Indeed, the domestic life to which Archer submits himself is both arid and silent. Communications are constantly flawed; whatever he may think, Archer never accurately assesses May's thoughts—even less those of Ellen Olenska. Family allegiance, moreover, is in fact little more than habit and a respect for social forms. Archer's sudden insight that his wedding is virtually indistinguishable from "a first night at the opera" echoes throughout the novel and raises unanswered questions about how the protocol of his world is finally to be differentiated from the shallow spectacle of Lily Bart's or Undine Spragg's. Wanting to discover homes bound together by "grave endearing traditions," Wharton found only the deep malaise of a dilettante's way of life.

Nonetheless, Newland Archer is, by the end of the novel, a clearly sympathetic and victorious character. Few scenes in Wharton's fiction are more gently rendered than Archer's final leave-taking as he sits alone on a bench, five floors below Ellen's home. A decade and a half after the publication of *The Age of Innocence,* Wharton would remember Archer's as a "mild and leisurely" world which, whatever its other failings, held always to "scrupulous probity in business and private affairs." They were values she thought worth preserving. It was for herself as well as for the character Newland Archer that Wharton wrote, at the end of *The Age of Innocence,* "he honored his own past, and he mourned for it."

Undoubtedly, Wharton's nostalgia resulted, in part, from the personal and public losses of her middle and later years. But the origins of this tone lie as well in the polarities that had always characterized her analysis of industrial society. Perhaps precisely because in her lifetime the ravages of capitalism grew so glaring, Wharton clung to the belief that industrialism was a phenomenon of the "public" world, and that its opposite still existed in the home. Early in her career she began to formulate the home, not simply as a symbol, but as an objectively different set of conditions. From there, the plunge into a fully romanticized celebration of motherhood, such as characterized her later works, was but a matter of degree. (pp. 37-8)

Jeanne Boydston, " 'Grave Endearing Tradi-

tion': Edith Wharton and the Domestic Novel," in Faith of a (Woman) Writer, *edited by Alice Kessler-Harris and William McBrien, Greenwood Press, 1988, pp. 31-40.*

Katie Trumpener and James M. Nyce (essay date 1988)

[*In the following essay, the critics discuss Wharton's use, in* The Age of Innocence, *of archaeological and anthropological concepts, perspectives, and metaphors to portray a society that no longer exists.*]

> It is remarkable the difference that even one foreigner can make in a community when he is not yet accustomed to its ways. The way he can isolate its customs and hold them up for your inspection. Things that had been natural to you as bread suddenly need to be explained and the really maddening thing is that you can't explain them. After a while you begin to wonder if they're real at all.
>
> Frank O'Connor,
> *The Custom of the Country*

> My whole outlook upon social life is determined by the question: how can we recognize the shackles that tradition has laid upon us? For when we recognize them, we are also able to break them . . . I consider it the duty of those who are devoted to the study of social problems to become clear in regard to these questions and to see to it that through their influence the intellectual chains in which tradition holds us are gradually broken.
>
> Franz Boas, *I Believe*

Edith Wharton's 1920 *The Age of Innocence,* set in the period and place in which she herself grew up, is a novel which uses concepts, perspectives and metaphors from archaeology and what was then a new discipline—anthropology—as a way of structuring the story. As well, the novel itself serves as an exemplum of the difficulties encountered when the methods of the social sciences are applied to the author's own culture.

At the first glance, the novel appears to be a Jamesian novel of manners which uses the advent of a foreigner, Ellen Olenska, into a closed social circle to catalyse the story's events and to change Newland Archer's perception of the culture to which he belongs. In short, Ellen acts as a foil against which this society can be evaluated and seen for what it is. Wharton however complicates every factor of this experimental mixing of cultures. Ellen Olenska is not only raised abroad but New York born, so that she is neither totally estranged from nor wholly part of New York society.

From the beginning of the novel, Wharton places the reader at two removes from the story: the remove of time and the objective remove of the social sciences. The principal story takes place some thirty years before the time in which the epilogue is set and fifty years before the book was written. The story proper is thus a retrospective study of a New York subculture, now extinct, an ethnography of a distinctive set of customs and a way of life which no longer exists save in sentiment and memory 'as bodies caught in glaciers keep for years a rosy life-in-death'.

The past then is being presented from the perspective of the present, and the story is clearly dated for the reader by the use of extensive period detail. In the course of the story, to give but one example, Newland reads recent anthropological and scientific studies as well as literature. Among these are 'a new volume of Herbert Spencer, another collection of the prolific Alphonse Daudet's brilliant tales and a novel called *Middlemarch,* as to which there had been lately interesting things said in the reviews'. And we learn that 'Old-fashioned New York dined at seven'. . . .

The books of the hour, 'a wonderful new volume called *The Renaissance* by Walter Pater', the faddish pastimes of every age group and the current fashions in female dress are mentioned not just in passing or merely to flesh out the setting of the novel. Rather these details are brought deliberately to the reader's attention as cultural artifacts of the Old New York. These are the 'recovered fragments' of a lost world, fixed forever in their specific time and place as clearly as the potshards preserved at Pompeii by 'a flood of lava on a doomed city' or as the Cesnola antiquities mouldering in the glass cases of the Metropolitan Museum, those 'small broken objects—hardly recognizable domestic utensils, ornaments and personal trifles—made of glass, of clay, of discolored bronze and other time-blurred substances'.

Although the passage of time made the 1870's appear to the 1920's a distinctive age, one of stability and of innocence, Wharton is careful to show us that the perspective of the past about itself was quite different than that of the period which came after it. The denizens of Old New York, far from seeing their world as stable, perceived it as being in a state of flux; indeed they are continually 'talking against time', as Wharton puts it, anticipating the future and the changes it will bring as well as the havoc it will wreak upon life as they know it. Newland's mother, like others, senses the gradual erosion of those very customs which she feels define her culture and hence herself. She therefore is almost obsessive about the need to keep things the same.

Nor is the age a particularly innocent one. What appears to be simplicity proves in fact to be in May, Newland's fiancée, a refusal to see what she does not wish to see and a provinciality that 'seals the mind against imagination and the heart against experience'; or in characters like Lawrence Lefferts, a facade behind which vice is hidden. A mask of innocence hides the hypocrisy, then, 'of a society wholly absorbed in barricading itself against the unpleasant'.

If the book's title refers, ironically, to the nostalgia Americans of the 1920's felt for the recent past, it also refers to Old New York's ideal of womanhood. This 'innocence' is the first standard of his society that Newland questions. May, like a character in a morality play, is assigned this role. Her 'innocence', as Newland comes to recognize, is one of only feigned stupidity but nevertheless the ignorance she cultivates enables her, ultimately, to keep her

husband. The effects of social training are even more evident in the other women of Newland's circle.

Gertrude Lefferts, bound by Old New York's conception of marriage, has to endure her husband's many infidelities. Newland's sister Janey, since she never marries, is even in middle age stuck rather grotesquely playing the role of a virgin. Newland is perceptive enough to realize that the women of his age and set are not all they have the potential to be.

> No doubt she [May] simply echoed what was said for her; but she was nearing her twenty-second birthday, and he wondered at what age 'nice' women began to speak for themselves. . . . It would presently be his task to take the bandage from this young woman's eyes and bid her look forth on the world, but how many generations of the women who had gone to her making had descended bandaged to the family vault? He shivered a little, remembering some of the new ideas in his scientific books and the much-cited instance of the Kentucky cave-fish, which had ceased to develop eyes because they had no use for them. . . . She was making the answers that instinct and tradition had taught her to make—even to the point of calling him original.
>
> 'Original! We're all as like each other as those dolls cut out of the same folded paper. We're like patterns stenciled on a wall'.

It is in fact his increasing frustration with the New York courtship and marriage mores which leads him to find parallels between the supposedly civilized customs of his own society and the 'savage' rites of primitive tribes. In both, there is the same blind reverence for custom and social forms. 'In reality' Newland realizes, all men live 'in a kind of hieroglyphic world, where the real thing was never said or done or even thought, but only represented by a set of arbitrary signs'.

Wharton's second remove for her story is decidedly an anthropological one. Anthropological metaphors are used throughout the novel and Wharton often depicts New York society in these terms. There is much discussion for example of this society's rites, rituals, taboos, idols and tribal discipline. All this forces the reader to examine the book's characters from the perspective of an ethnographer while at the same time attending to the drama of their story. The reader, like Wharton herself, applies 'to the investigation of his friends' affairs the patience of a collector and the science of the naturalist'. But where Wharton and the reader manage, while recognizing the flaws and limitations of the cultural structure, still to accept this society on its own terms, Newland seems unable to tolerate New York once he sees through it. The more objectively he is able to examine it, the more alienated he feels. The study of anthropology has revealed to Newland a new way of seeing social interaction but has jolted him so far out of his own society that he is, for a time, unable to re-enter it. Like Ellen Olenska, he feels a stranger in his own land, able to perceive his own age with the detachment of a natural historian or an anthropologist, and views it objectively but as it were 'through the wrong end of a telescope'.

New York (and America, by extension) seems to be a kind of frontier outpost that either attempts to keep up outdated European standards or, as Newland's friend Winsett puts it, is left with 'just a few little local patches of culture, dying out here and there for lack of—well, hoeing and cross-fertilizing: the last remnants of the Old European tradition that your forebears brought with them'. Old New York is as well a culture that denies its obvious similarities, particularly in its adherence to social form, with less complex cultures. May has succeeded Pocahantas as the model American woman. Just as her attitudes epitomize, for Newland, the narrowness of New York values, her parochialism ('his wife's way of showing herself at ease with foreigners was to become more uncompromisingly local in her references') symbolizes America's difficulty in seeing beyond itself.

The New York Newland now sees so horrifies him that he dreams of fleeing America altogether with Ellen, who has come to symbolize, for him, a freedom from social rules. But one's culture cannot be escaped that easily; and as Ellen points out, to leave one's own tribe is to become an exile. If one cannot live by the conventions of one's own culture, one is doomed to even greater alienation in another. Newland seems tragically unable to compromise, although there are, as the lives of several incidental characters make quite clear, alternatives available to him other than exile.

The artists of New York, for example, apparently live undisturbed by the social rules which govern New York society.

> Beyond the small and slippery pyramid which composed Mrs. Archer's world lay the almost unmapped quarter inhabited by artists, musicians and 'people who wrote.' These scattered fragments of humanity had never shown any desire to be amalgamated with the social structure.

Perhaps the role Edith Wharton would like to have the reader take in the story is that of the archeologist Emerson Sillerton. Unlike Sillerton Jackson, his cousin, a known busybody and observer of the New York social scene, Emerson is a more scientific, more objective observer. Presumably it is his full-time devotion to the social sciences and to the excavation of past cultures which gives him a detached perspective on New York life and the strength to distance himself from it. Although he married into one of New York's leading families, he and his wife do not take up their expected place, but instead fulfill their social engagements each year with a single garden party. Having thus discharged their social obligations, they live the rest of the year relatively undisturbed and 'when he traveled, [he] took her to explore tombs in Yucatan instead of going to Paris or Italy'. Such leeway, then, is possible in New York for those who dare to be Bohemian.

Newland then is trapped as much by his fear of social pressure as by the society's actual force. When Ellen, inevitably, is lured away from him by May's 'innocent' scheming, he will not defy peer opinion and go after her. Instead he allows May and the clan to re-assimilate him and he spends the rest of his marriage either play-acting or sleep-walking his way through his social obligations.

In the last chapter of the book, twenty-six years have gone by and many of the traditional ways which seemed endangered during Mrs. Archer's lifetime have now vanished completely. The new society, Wharton tells us, apparently without irony, is one of few conventions and little pretense, but this, she believes, has its negative as well as positive aspects. There are no conventions because there are almost no social ties or obligations any more. New York, for Wharton, has moved from one extreme to the other. Central American archaeology and the pre-Revolutionary architecture of America are now, when they can no longer be useful, studied enthusiastically by the young. The Cesnola antiquities, and all the lessons to be learned from them, were ignored in the Old Museum in favour of the heroic portraiture of the Wolfe collection. What was once neglected is modish now that it can no longer be critically applied to American life.

The study of culture can no longer aid in the understanding of American society since, in Wharton's view, neither American society nor any of its values have remained intact. Individuals in America have become as a result 'social atoms spinning . . . in the huge kaleidoscope'. The present interest in history is depicted as an egocentric and distorted one, since nobody's past is of any account any more and the previous generation is already sentimentalized and misunderstood.

Newland Archer, who once almost defied his age has now, grown old and old fashioned, come to represent it. Although he does welcome some of the changes the years have brought, he fears them more; and the social structure which he once saw as imprisoning he now remembers as benevolent. The final chapter shows Newland to be a tragic figure, aware that his culture has warped him as much as it did May and that he allowed it to do so. In his youth, he had known 'moments when a man's imagination, so easily subdued to what it lives in, suddenly rises above its daily level and surveys the long windings of destiny'— moments in which he saw beyond New York's model of the universe and had a 'sense of other lives outside his own, other cities beyond New York and a whole world beyond his world'. Newland understood at some level that no one culture, no one set of values, is intrinsically better than another. But ultimately he was unable to accept the full consequences of a 'Copernican' social universe, for it would have destroyed the sense and the order of his life.

Wharton herself apparently could not fully accept her own conclusions. Hence the epilogue is not successful in sustaining the critical perspective taken in the body of the novel. There, Edith Wharton seems to argue that there are principles common to all cultures that both hold the culture together and imprison members of the culture within it. In the epilogue, however, contemporary American society is depicted as being almost completely without the principles that maintain social order and conformity—a portrayal of society that is not only at odds with the rest of the book but one seemingly designed to soften its ominous message. The relativism of anthropology is suddenly replaced by a nostalgia which has caused critics such as James Tuttleton, who have recognized the anthropological perspective of the work, to misunderstand the book. He writes:

> [Her method] was to demonstrate the importance for men of the web of culture, meanings and mores which enclose them and to warn of the disaster in store for those who become culturally deracinated or alienated and for those who destroy the delicate web in a radical obsession to reform it.

—but, because of the epilogue, Tuttleton argues in the end that Wharton not only portrays but upholds a conservative model of social order.

Historical novels (from *Vanity Fair* and *Middlemarch,* to Willa Cather's *A Lost Lady*) that cover the author's own lifetime tend to portray their culture as undergoing radical changes between the years of the author's childhood and the years in which the chronicle is written down. Like these authors, Wharton interweaves personal experience with historical truth. In doing so, however, she abandons the objectivity the rest of the work has so carefully established and which makes it as much an ethnography of Old New York as a novel.

Much of the effectiveness of her portrayal of this New York society comes from the thoroughness with which Wharton established that it no longer exists. In order to examine his own culture, the reader must be allowed to distance himself from it. This remove may be the product of history or of critical theory. How important it is the examples of Newland and Edith Wharton herself make clear. They have difficulties in applying observations made about other cultures, as outsiders, to their own; and this demonstrates the problems anthropologists have in understanding and living with their own discoveries.

Wharton's failure is the more disappointing because the critical perspective of the rest of the book is complex, subtle and almost modernist, a fact not noticed by those critics who have approached Wharton with preconceived notions about her political and artistic conservatism. Wharton managed not only to incorporate into a novel of manners principles coming out of the then emerging discipline of anthropology, but in her treatments of the conflicts between the individual, culture and history, she anticipated later developments in the field. Among these, implicit in the body of the book, is the manner in which she compared cultures and dealt with social order and deviance. As well, her portrayal of culture as a system of hieroglyphs that need to be decoded points toward poststructural analyses of culture. The book's organizing principle is revealed in Edith Wharton's metaphor of society as a museum without walls. For Newland and the reader, Old New York becomes a study gallery where American society can be observed and understood. For Newland (and Ellen) this occurred when they 'were staring silently at the glass cabinets [of the Cesnola antiquities] which contained the recovered fragments of Illium'.

The irony and pathos of the novel come from the fact that Wharton is able, on the whole, to erect this almost invisible museum glass of time, distance and perspective between the events of the novel and herself so that the reader is able to laugh at the self-importance and pomposity of the characters and to regret that they and all they had valued has passed away.

In the Cesnola wing of the Metropolitan Museum, in the pivotal scene of the novel, Newland has eyes for nothing but Ellen, imagining her as the new centre for his life and that their love is a way to transcend the limitations and the impermanence of human society. It is Ellen, the permanent exile, who realizes that Archer, despite his resolve and his understanding of his own culture, will never be able to free himself from it. As well, with the insight of one who lives between two cultures, she knows how little all the artifacts and conventions of culture will mean in the end.

> 'It seems cruel,' she said, 'that after a while nothing matters . . . any more than these little things, that used to be necessary and important to forgotten people, and now have to be guessed at under a magnifying glass and labeled: 'Use unknown'.

(pp. 161-68)

Katie Trumpener and James M. Nyce, "The Recovered Fragments: Archeological and Anthropological Perspectives in Edith Wharton's 'The Age of Innocence'," in Literary Anthropology: A New Interdisciplinary Approach to People, Signs and Literature, *edited by Fernando Poyatos, John Benjamins Publishing Company, 1988, pp. 161-69.*

I once pleased her by telling her that she was the only person I knew who seemed to understand with equal fulness both the protestant and the catholic mentality. She then told me that it had always been her ambition to write a novel of which the centre should be the conflict of these two impulses.

—Kenneth Clark, quoted in Percy Lubbook, Portrait of Edith Wharton, 1947.

Ada Van Gastel   (essay date 1990)

[*In the following excerpt, Van Gastel traces the influence of Wharton's extensive knowledge and lifelong interest in architecture and interior decoration on* The Age of Innocence.]

Edmund Wilson was one of the first critics to perceive that, when Wharton took up fiction writing, she carried over her extensive knowledge of architecture and interior decoration to the realm of literature. "The poet of interior decoration", he called her. Many critics after Wilson have recognized the importance of houses in Wharton's fiction, but most studies focus either on Wharton's skill in evoking scenes—her "visualizing power" in the words of Blake Nevius—or on Wharton's use of "place" in its geographical sense—on, for instance, her use of New York, New England towns such as Starkville and North Dormer, or foreign countries such as France. As yet, no study exists of the way in which Wharton employs both the location and decoration of houses as signs to convey information about the *dramatis personae* in one of her greatest novels, *The Age of Innocence.* (p. 139)

In *The Age of Innocence,* Wharton is able to use the location and decoration of houses as signs about characters because the close-knit society of New York in the 1870s possessed a fixed scale of values and operated as much by way of signs as by way of words. "In reality they all lived in a hieroglyphic world, where the real thing was never said or done or even thought, but only represented by a set of arbitrary signs", Wharton writes. Thus the van der Luyden's barouche delivering a large square envelope to Mrs Mingott's door "means" that countess Ellen Olenska is accepted by the van der Luydens, which in turn "means" that she will soon be accepted by the whole of New York society. The locations and the decorations of houses in *The Age of Innocence* similarly function as "signs" in this "hieroglyphic world".

The house of Mr and Mrs Henry van der Luyden, for example, is located in the fashionable section of Madison Avenue in the center of New York, reflecting the van der Luyden's position at the centre of New York society. Being "direct descendants of the first Dutch governor of Manhattan, and related by pre-Revolutionary marriage to several members of the French and British aristocracy", the van der Luydens represent old, aristocratic New York. The size of the house ("large"), the height of the rooms ("high-ceilinged"), the materials employed in the interior decoration (marble, ormulu, brocade) as well as the colour scheme (white and various pale shades) all connote a stately, solemn formality. So far does this solemn formality extend that most traces of life are removed from the interior. Upon entering the drawing room, Newland Archer notices that the chairs are "obviously uncovered for the occasion", while the gauze is "still veiling" the mantel ornaments and the Gainsborough painting. Newland even feels a "chill" descend upon him. Others privileged to enter this mansion similarly "shivered there". The dinner parties at the van der Luydens possess an aura of "religious solemnity" (the forthright Ellen Olenska calls them "gloomy"). When Newland rings the doorbell at the van der Luydens's house at Skuytercliff, the sound echoes "as through a mausoleum", while the butler takes so long to respond that it is as though he has to be summoned "from his final sleep".

These mansions—grand but bereft of life—reflect the personalities of Mr and Mrs Henry van der Luyden. With their tall, spare frames, faded hair, pale eyes, and look of "frozen gentleness", the couple is majestic and imposing—but also pallid and aloof to the point of coldness. Newland never fails to be struck with the likeness of Mrs van der Luyden to a portrait of her painted twenty years earlier, for she appears to have "rather gruesomely preserved in the airless atmosphere of a perfectly irreproach-able existence, as bodies caught in glaciers keep for years a rosy life-in-death". Indeed, just as the van der Luydens attempt to protect their revered *objects d'art* by covering them with cloths and using them as little they can, they try to preserve their venerated selves by doing as little as possible: Mrs van der Luyden never goes out in public, the couple rarely comes to New York, and the two very seldom invite people to their home. Even in their daily conduct they exert themselves little, both being "shy and retiring" in their bearing.

However, there is more to the van der Luydens than this frosting of formality: deep down, buried below many layers of aloof irreproachability, the couple harbours feelings of warmth and love. It is Ellen Olenska—the outsider who catalyzes so many emotions—who brings these submerged feelings to the surface. It is for Ellen that the van der Luydens decide to break their semi-seclusion in order to arrange a select dinner party to ostentatiously welcome her to New York. Mr van der Luyden afterwards goes in person to visit Ellen in her townhouse. He also sends her on various occasions carnations from his orangeries. The couple even invites Ellen for a fortnight to their estate to visit Skuytercliff on the Hudson—a place where prior to that moment "a chilly weekend" was the most ever offered to some privileged few. Especially for Ellen do they open up the small ancient house of the original seventeenth-century patroon. With its low squat walls, tiled hearth, rows of Delft plate, panels, brasses, rush-bottomed chairs, and iron pot hanging from an ancient crane in the kitchen chimney, the Patroon's house calls up scenes of friendly domesticity as depicted in old Dutch paintings (e.g. works of Johannes Vermeer, Pieter de Hooch, and Jan Steen). The house seems to be "magically created" as an idyllic place where Ellen and Newland can at last be alone. For a few brief but ideal moments they are alone. Ellen declares:

> "I can't feel unhappy when you're here".
>
> "I shan't be here long", he rejoined, his lips stiffening with the effort to say just so much and no more.
>
> "No; I know. But I'm improvident: I live in the moment when I'm happy".

As esteemed vestiges of the past, the van der Luyden houses do not contain a single piece of modern furniture—which subtly reminds us that the couple has no modern scion in the form of offspring. Engrossed in fending off the emergence of new orders, the van der Luydens are unable to produce anything new: they can only guard salvages from the past; they can only keep the embers smouldering of a tradition that was once living, but which is now all but dead. Like their Delftware, Sevres, George II plate, Lowestoft, and Crown Derby, the van der Luydens are antiques—fragile, valuable relics of a previous era.

In contrast to the van der Luydens, Julius Beaufort is very much a parvenu. Having only recently entered society, he still resides on the periphery; his house is located at the end of Fifth Avenue. The lower end, to be precise, just as Beaufort has risen from the lower classes: "the Beauforts were not exactly common; some people said they were even worse". Beaufort has besieged the bastion of society with the power of money. He has purchased an impressive mansion which

> was one of the few [houses] in New York that possessed a ballroom . . . This undoubted superiority was felt to be compensable for whatever was regrettable in Beaufort's past.

This archetypal self-made man refuses to use anything that has been touched by any one else: instead of renting the accoutrements for his annual ball (as all others do), Beaufort has bought his own chairs, his own awning, and his own red velvet carpet to be rolled down the steps by his own silk-stockinged footmen. Beaufort's actions vividly demonstrate that it is not enough for the *nouveau riche* to have money—he must display it as well. The more conspicuous the consumption, the better, to use Thornstein Veblen's famous phrase. Conspicuous consumption, is evident in the very layout of Beaufort's house:

> The house had been boldly planned with a ballroom, so that . . . one marched solemny down a vista of enfiladed drawing rooms (the seagreen, the crimson and the *bouton d'or*), seeing from afar the many candled lusters reflected in the polished parquetry, and beyond that the depths of a conservatory where camillias and tree ferns arched their costly foliage over seats of black and gold bamboo.

Furthermore, by hosting the annual meeting of the Newport Archery club, Beaufort acquires the chance to show off his seaside resort—an immaculately kept mansion.

Conspicuous consumption necessarily demands an audience—one needs to be in the public's eye in order to use it as an inroad into the citadel of society. What better way to stay in the public's eye than by spurring talk? A well-proven method is shown by a passage from Wharton's autobiographical *A Backward Glance,* a passage in which she relates that in the New York of her youth, "Art and music and literature were rather timorously avoided (unless Trollope's last novel were touched upon, or a discrete allusion made to Mr. William Astor's audacious acquisition of a Bouguerean Venus)". Partly in order to spur talk, Beaufort (who, according to R. W. B. Lewis, is a composite of William Astor and several other historical figures) has acquired the painting "Love Victorious", "the much-discussed nude of Bourguereau". But this nude serves another function as well for it also alludes to a temperament trait of its owner: Beaufort likes the ladies a bit too much. He is "always in quest of amorous adventures". He has taken up with Mrs Lemuel Struthers (widow of the shoe-polish king); is more than interested in Ellen Olenska; and, after his financial downfall, rumour has it that "he hasn't spent all his money on Regina [his wife]".

As it is, it does not suffice to conspicuously display acquired wealth on some special occasions during the year. The Spanish-leather chairs in Beaufort's library, the heavy lusters, the blooming camelias, and the luscious ferns—these all demand continual upkeep. Even so, though Beaufort uses his wealth as an inroad into the citadel of New York society, once inside, he must pay continual homage to New York's financial code, to its code of "unblemished

honesty". A passage from Wharton's *A Backward Glance* illuminates this financial code:

> New York has always been a commercial community, and in my infancy the merits and defects of its citizens were those of a mercantile middle class. The first duty of such a class was to maintain a strict standard of uprightness in affairs; and the gentlemen of my father's day did maintain it, whether in law, in banking, shipping or wholesale commercial enterprises. I well remembered the horror excited by any irregularity in affairs, and the relentless social ostracism inflicted on the families of those who lapsed from professional or business integrity.

Beaufort's violation of this code of scrupulous honesty results in a prompt expulsion from society—which in turn means that he has to give up his Fifth Avenue mansion.

While Beaufort's house dominates one end of Fifth Avenue, the other end is presided over by Mrs Manson Mingott's mansion. Catherine Mingott has situated herself on the periphery of the city, the upper end of Fifth Avenue, reflecting the fact that she haughtily looks down upon the New York society. Having travelled abroad in her youth, "Catherine the Great" (as she is nicknamed) now finds New York too confining, too narrow for her taste. She likes to defy its conventions, and, for example, delights in having married her two daughters to foreigners (an Italian Marquis and an English banker). She also enjoys associating familiarly with *personae non gratae,* such as Papists, and Opera singers. But, she put "the crowning touch to her audacities by building a large house of pale cream-colored stone (when brown sandstone seemed as much the only wear as a frockcoat in the afternoon) in an inaccessible wilderness near the Central Park". So crucial is this architectural sign that Wharton reiterates it a moment later: "The cream-colored house (supposed to be modelled on the private hotels of the Parisian aristocracy) was there as a visible proof of her moral courage". This Matriarch of the Mingott line refuses to fit in the straight-jacket of convention. This is brought out most clearly by her decision to establish herself on the ground floor—"in flagrant violation of all New York proprieties"—in order not to have to ascend the stairs with her voluminous mounds of flesh. Since she likes to display her different views publicly, she does not attempt to cover up her idiosyncratic living arrangement with screens or closed doors. Instead, she always leaves open the door between her sittingroom and bedroom. Her visitors can thus see her huge, low bed (upholstered like a sofa) and her toilet table with "frivolous lance flow and a gilt framed mirror". The "foreignness" of this vista both "startled and frustrated" her visitors, recalling to them,

> scenes in French fiction, and architectural incentives to immortality such as the simple American had never dreamed of. That was how women with lovers lived in the wicked old societies, in apartments with all the rooms on one floor, and all the indecent propinquities that their novels described.

Having travelled abroad and seen more of the world, Mrs Mingott is one of the few who combines the foreign with the domestic, the old with the new. As the high and mighty Matriarch of the line, she resolutely advocates traditional family values such as solidarity; but she also declares (apropos the new setting of May Welland's engagement ring) "I like all the novelties". In her house, she has "*mingled* with the Mingott heirlooms the frivolous upholstery of the Second Empire" (my italics). She similarly has *interspersed* American-made objects with "souvenirs of the Tuileries of Louis Napoleon". The wide range and strong individuality of the interior of Mrs Mingott's house foreshadows that it is she who will become the most "devoted champion" of Ellen Olenska.

"There's no one of my own children that takes after me but my little Ellen", Mrs Mingott declares. Indeed, Ellen Olenska has emulated her grandmother's foreign taste by marrying a Polish nobleman and settling abroad. Furthermore, she has emulated her grandmother's defiance of conventions by openly deserting her husband when her marriage did not work out and by now coming back to New York. However, when she left America some ten years earlier, she forfeited her "place" in New York— "place" in the literal sense of a house to live in as well as in the figurative sense of a position in New York's hierarchical society. As to the latter, Mrs Mingott and the van der Luydens take it upon themselves to marshal her back into the élite. In regard to the former, Ellen Olenska shows her independence by only temporarily accepting the shelter of relatives, and by then renting a house of her own. The house she takes is situated on West Twenty-third Street in a neighbourhood which is euphemistically labelled as "des quartiers excentriques". The location of Countess Olenska's house thus reflects the fact that she is in the eyes of New York "eccentric". Ellen is surrounded by "small dressmakers, bird-stuffers and 'people who wrote' ". The circumlocutory phrase here as well as the quotations marks around the verb in "people who 'wrote' " well convey the snivel of snobbish New York which (as Wharton reports in *A Backward Glance*) grudgingly pronounced Washington Irving a gentleman "in spite of the disturbing fact that he 'wrote'."

The neighbourhood where Ellen Olenska settles has another function since it also points to her affinity with the arts and her own artistic talents. Varying the phrase she has used earlier, Wharton later describes the neighbourhood as inhabited by "artists, musicians and 'people who wrote' ". Ellen likes to meet artists, "dramatic artists, singers, actors, and musicians", and tells Newland she misses not seeing these in New York. Moreover, she herself possesses much artistic talent. Not a single one of her visitors fails to see this. "She has a real gift for arranging flowers", Henry van der Luyden declares. The English Duke of St Austrey is impressed with how "cleverly" she has arranged her drawing room. And Newland, when he is let into her house, is struck with "the way in which Medora Manson's shabby hired house, with its blighted background of pampas grass and Rogers statuettes, had, by a turn of the hand, and the skillful use of a few properties, been transformed into something intimate, "foreign", subtly suggestive of old romantic scenes and sentiments". Wondering how Ellen Olenska has accomplished this, Newland "tried to analyze the trick, to find a clue to it in

the way the chairs and tables were grouped, in the fact that only two Jacqueminot roses (of which nobody ever bought less than a dozen) had been placed in the slender vase at his elbow, and in the vague pervading perfume that was not what one put on handkerchiefs, but rather like the scent of some far-off bazaar, a smell made up of Turkish coffee and ambergris and dried roses".

As all true works of art, Ellen's interior decorating in last instance defies analysis. However, it is noteworthy that in his attempt to describe it, Newland appeals to more than one sense organ: his visual sense is stimulated by the grouping of the chairs and tables as well as the arrangement of the flowers, and his olfactory as well as gustory senses are animated by the "perfume" of "dried roses" and "Turkish coffee". With its Italian paintings, Greek bronzes, Japanese cups, French novels by Bourget, Huysmans, and the Goncourt brothers, and with the brief appearance of a "Sicilian-looking maid" who only speaks Italian, Ellen's room is as cultured and cosmopolitan as its mistress. It is "unlike any other room" Newland has seen before. This is, among other reasons, because of the books: in the view of old New York the drawing room is a part of the house in which books are considered "out of place"—to say nothing of books being "scattered about", as they are in Ellen's room. As for this latter point, old New York is personified in Lucretia Jones's criticism of her twelve-year old daughter's first attempt to write realistic fiction. Upon reading the opening lines of Edith Wharton's first story—" 'Oh, how do you do, Mrs Brown?' said Mrs Tomkins. 'If only I had known you were going to call I should have tidied up the drawing-room'."—Mrs Jones coldly observed: "Drawing rooms are always tidy".

Since it is so "unlike any other room" he knows, Newland labels the room "foreign". And—just as the New Yorkers visiting Mrs Mingott's house—he associates it with "romantic scenes and sentiments", with "something intimate". Indeed, Newland is "virtually seduced" by the room. While the room arouses all of Archer's senses, he fails to grasp it rationally: not only does Ellen's decorative talent defy his analytic powers, the Italian paintings on the walls also do not figure in the books he has read, the studies of John Ruskin, John Addington Symonds, Vernon Lee, P. G. Hamerton, and Walter Pater. Archer is therefore unable to respond verbally to the room; he can only respond by sending the decorator of the room a bouquet of yellow roses, roses which likewise exceed the verbal realm as they are "too rich, too strong, in their fiery beauty". Unable to find words for his feelings, Newland does not attach a card to the roses. This passage thus foreshadows the climactic carriage scene in which Newland exclaims: "I want—I want somehow to get away with you into *a world where words* like that—categories like that— *won't exist*. Where we shall be simply two human beings who love each other".

So overpowering is the foreign and intimate atmosphere of Ellen's room that Newland cannot help but be drawn into it. The result is that New York seems very far away, as though seen "through the wrong end of a telescope". Newland thus can no longer get himself to tell his cousin that New York believes that it is improper for her to be seen driving about the streets in Beaufort's carriage. The simile in which he expresses this to himself again evinces that it is Ellen's room which has effected this change:

> to give advice of that sort would have been like telling someone who was bargaining for attar-of-roses in Samarkand that one should always be provided with arctics for a New York winter. New York seemed much farther off than Samarkand.

The "attar-of-roses" with its olfactory appeal, the foreignness of Samarkand, and the notion of sensuality presiding over rationality, all point to Ellen.

While waiting for the arrival of Ellen, Newland's thoughts turn to the architectural style of the house which his prospective father-in-law, Mr Welland, has selected, and he thinks about the manner in which his fiancee will decorate this house. This "transition" in Archer's thoughts has puzzled critics such as Cynthia Griffin Wolff and Gary Lindberg. However, if we assume that architecture and interior decoration function as signs conveying information about characters, there no longer is anything "curious" about this transition. Throughout the novel, Newland cannot help but compare Ellen to May, the dark lady to the blond lady. The foreignness and intimacy of Ellen's room, of Ellen, are all the more exciting to Newland when contrasted to the prim, proper, predictable life he can expect with May: "The young man felt that his fate was sealed: for the rest of his life he would go up every evening between the cast-iron railings of that greenish-yellow doorstep, and pass through a Pompeian vestibule into a hall with a wainscoting of varnished yellow wood". The cast-iron railings connote severe restriction (the railings even conjure up prison bars). This image of confinement strikingly contrasts with the freedom and natural beauty suggested by the "giant wisteria" which adorns the facade of Ellen's house. Freedom is crucial to Ellen: "I had to be free", she declares. She is appalled when Newland suggests that she go back to her husband to avoid "a lot of beastly talk": "But my freedom—is that nothing?" The wisteria also stands for Ellen's natural sense of beauty. Unlike Archer, Ellen does not need critical studies to guide her taste. Hers is a natural talent. She herself determines what she likes, what she does not like. To Newland's grim remark that she has located herself in a neighborhood that is considered "not fashionable", she astonishedly replies: "Fashionable! Do you all think so much of that? Why not make one's own fashion?".

Musing about the interior of his future home, Newland momentarily realizes that he is unable to fancy how May precisely will decorate the drawing room—only to reassure himself:

> she submitted cheerfully to the purple satin and yellow tuftings of the Welland drawing room, to its sham buhl tables and gilt vitrines full of modern Saxe. He saw no reason to suppose that she would want anything different in her own house.

The Welland's home on Bellevue Avenue is a house "in which one always knew exactly what [was] happening at a given hour". Even an outsider always knows what is going on since the curtains are never closed at night. The "perpetually reminding clicks of the disciplined clocks" suit Mr Welland, a man "with no opinions but with many habits". The "perpetually renewed stacks of cards and invitations on the hall table" agree with Mrs Welland, a woman whose chief concern in life is that every hour be always "provided for". This overregulated existence which buries itself in "tyrannical trifles" has the same effect on Newland as the Wellands' heavy carpets and voluminous cushions: it stultifies him as a narcotic does.

Interestingly enough, the reader later discovers that May does *not* decorate her drawing room in the style of her parents. Instead, she opts for sofas and armchairs of pale brocade; for little plush tables bedecked with silver toys, knobby vases, porcelain animals and efflorescent photograph frames; for tall rosy-shaded lamps which "sho[o]t up like tropical flowers among the palms"; and for "a gift bamboo *jardiniere*" with primulas and cinerarias. Nature is brought indoors and, in the process, is tamed. May tames everything, from her waist which she squeezes into a twenty-inch girdle to Newland's secret passion for Ellen which she converts into overt family concern (she explicitly asks him to pay his respects to her cousin). The discrepancy between the picture Newland initially conjures up of May's drawing room and the way in which we later see her decorate it makes clear that Newland is slightly mistaken in May. Indeed, he never fully comes to know his wife. He is astounded when his son tells him after her death that, while he had always assumed May ignorant of his feelings for Ellen, in fact, she "knew all along".

Newland's early thoughts on interior decoration provide yet more clues to personalities. Surrounded by the foreign atmosphere and books in Ellen's drawing room, Newland consoles himself for the way he erroneously expects his future home to look with the thought that May "would probably let him arrange his library as he pleases—which would be, of course, with "sincere" Eastlake furniture, and the plain new bookcase without glass doors". In her excellent *Felicitous Space*, Judith Fryer has called Newland's preference for Eastlake furniture a "devastating criticism". According to Fryer, it indicates that "he is a man of "taste" rather than a man of principles". Fryer here alludes to Wharton's distinction in *The Decoration of Houses* between persons of "taste"—people who divorce the aesthetic dimension from all other dimension—and persons of "principle"—people who recognize that styles relate to a whole complete of social factors. We have seen above that Wharton believed that decoration should be a branch of architecture, that there should be a harmonious balance between every element in the house and the overall structure. Wharton thus objected to the fact that Charles Eastlake merely looked at furniture as ornament; that he failed to take into account the architectural design of the building. What Fryer does not mention, but what our analysis shows, is that Newland's preference for Eastlake suggests that he can only see parts of larger wholes—Newland only sees a part of the whole May, a part of the whole Ellen.

Newland's vision of his library with Eastlake furniture and bookcases reveals yet more of his personality. Eastlake's furniture being a vogue among the younger generations in the last quarter of the nineteenth century, Newland's intoxication with it signifies that he is not as rebellious, as independent of his surroundings, as he considers himself to be. Indeed, the choice of Eastlake foreshadows the fact that on the surface he will conform to New York and marry the New York May rather than the "foreign" Ellen. Moreover, Newland's longing to have the library as his own room, and in particular his interest in bookcases, foreshadows two additional things. While on the outside Newland will conform to New York, on the inside he will not do this but will instead create a private sanctuary for his innermost thoughts. In this private place, not the conventional May but the nonconformist Ellen will reign. In the course of the novel, Newland will retreat more and more often to his library to be alone with his dreams of Ellen:

> he had built up within himself a kind of sanctuary in which she [Ellen] throned among his secret thoughts and longings. Little by little it had become the scene of his real life, of his rational activities; thither he brought the books he read, the ideas and feelings which nourished him, his judgments and visions.

Ellen, indeed, is connected in Newland's mind with books. Newland's first daydreams about Ellen were prompted by her drawing room with all its scattered books; his first dreams of her at night were induced by a volume of poetry which he had ordered because the title had attracted him. The volume significantly is entitled, *The House of Life.* Later he no longer needs such a catalyst. With the passing of time, Newland even comes to think of Ellen "abstractly, serenely, as one might think of some imaginary beloved in a book or picture". Moreover, as seen in the quotation above, to Newland his mental life with Ellen becomes more "real" than his real life. This process of reversal—induced by the interior of Ellen's drawing room which made Samarkand seem closer than New York—gains momentum in the course of the novel until it culminates in the epilogue.

The epilogue takes place some thirty years later. Wharton indicates the passage of time by describing the changes in architectural and decorative taste. The pre-Revolutionary and Georgian styles have become fashionable again, while the Colonial style has fallen out of favour and is now only coveted by "the millionaire grocers of the suburbs" (the last phrase is a good example of Wharton's "trickle-down" theory of taste). Newland's own room has been "done over" by his son Dallas with "English mezzotints, Chippendale cabinets, bits of chosen blue-and-white and pleasantly shaded electric lamps". But, significantly, Newland has not been willing to give up his old Eastlake writing-table; he likewise has retained, and (will be seen to refuse to surrender) memories of three decades earlier. The location of Newland's house is again as telling as the interior decoration. While in the course of three decades others have moved away, Newland still resides in the small townhouse selected by Mr Welland at the time of his engagement, suggesting that Newland resists change. Furthermore, it also shows—especially in combination with the place where Archer spends his summers, the Wel-

lands' house in Newport—that he lacks the courage to break away from his father-in-law.

In imagining Ellen's life in Paris, Newland uses images he has come to associate with her on account of her New York house—that is, a foreign setting (the Italian paintings, Greek bronze, Japanese cups, and French novels), sensual natural vegetation (the giant wisteria outside and jacqueminot roses inside), and intellectual stimulation (the new Huysmans novels and other books). Accordingly, Newland pictures Ellen in the City of Light with all its unique, Parisian landmarks (the "majestic river", the public gardens with statues) amidst "the radiant outbreak of spring", blooming horse-chestnuts, an abundance of flowers, and "whiffs of lilacs from the flower-carts". The life he conjures up is full of "art and study and pleasure that filled each mighty artery to bursting". Once he has arrived in Paris, he further discovers that Ellen lives close to the lively Champs-Elysees, the flowery Tuileries Gardens, and the cultural mecca of the Louvre.

How this location contrasts with the place Newland Archer has selected for his stay in Paris—the quiet stillness of the Place Vendôme (a place which was nearly deserted with the coming of the new century). As this location suggests, Newland has become a quiet, withdrawn, conservative man. Paris makes him realize this. When confronted with Ellen's many-windowed apartment above the flowering horse-chestnuts, near the golden splendour of the Manart drome, Newland decides not to go up to meet her. Why? Because he would be forced to re-adjust his mental picture of her, an image he has relished for nearly thirty years. By staying outside, Newland can keep his mental picture of Ellen intact. "It's more real to me here than if I went up," he announces. Archer thus completes the process of reversal of imagined life and real life instigated by Ellen's drawing room on Twenty-third Street (where "New York seemed much farther off than Samarkand". Now Archer only wants his imagined life, only wants his imagined, mental picture of Ellen in the drawing room of her Paris apartment, "with azaleas banked behind her on a table". (pp. 140-53)

Ada Van Gastel, "The Location and Decoration of Houses in 'The Age of Innocence'," in Dutch Quarterly Review of Anglo-American Letters, Vol. 20, No. 2, 1990, pp. 138-53.

Mary E. Papke   (essay date 1990)

[*In the following excerpt, the critic focuses on* The Age of Innocence *as a vehicle for social criticism.*]

In 1920, Wharton produced what most critics believe to be her great American novel, *The Age of Innocence,* which spans several generations and various social worlds. Here, Wharton explores fully the transformations introduced in her earlier works and painfully attempts to reconcile the good from the past with the positive of the present modern world, imagining briefly an unchaotic future of individual and collective fulfillment and security. (p. 106)

The Age of Innocence . . . presents Old New York in its

heyday and a brief glimpse at the modern society of the late 1910s. This most famous of her works elaborates upon the social criticism presented in her earlier novels in that it offers both a realistic reevaluation of her own genteel culture and a tentatively optimistic view of a new American society and modern world. It is, as Wharton wrote to Bernard Berenson, "a 'simple & grave' story of two people trying to live up to something that was still 'felt in the blood' at that time."

The Age of Innocence is also simply the story of a conventional man torn between his love for a social rebel and his relationship with his ideological mate. Wharton had previously utilized this love-triangle plot device in her historical epic, *The Valley of Decision* (1902), and in her social reform novel, *The Fruit of the Tree* (1907). In each case, unconventional love—Odo's for Fulvia, Amherst's for Bessy and Justine—was compromised by the man's inability to surrender fully his traditional world view. Similarly, in *The Age of Innocence,* Newland Archer can never fulfill his love for Ellen Olenska precisely because he cannot pull himself out of "the rage of conformity." In all three novels, compromise arises, for both men and women, because of their conscious acceptance but incomplete comprehension of hegemonic ideology and its power. *The Age of Innocence* offers a harsher social critique than do the other two texts, however, in that it sets up the ideology of separate spheres, the foundation of male supremacist ideology, only to explode it. Further, Wharton shows her readers that the price of conformity is as exacting for some men as it is for some women; in Newland Archer she offers the reader her most sympathetic male figure.

As Josephine Donovan writes, "the ironic title refers to a prelapsarian age; the novel is set in New York in the 1870s, but the 'innocence' of the title is seen by Wharton to be fraudulent . . . . " Old New York is here portrayed as steeped in convention; genteel customs are still supreme despite the dim but visible Invaders on the social horizon. The ruling traditions appear to be private and public honesty, bourgeois morals and taste, collective cohesion. In reality, genteel manners are a mask disguising hypocrisy, immorality, gross materialism, and collective tyranny. It is again a society already advocating appearance over reality: "stylishness was what New York most valued." Further, it is a world in which actuality is manipulated in order to save appearances: "In reality they all lived in a kind of hieroglyphic world where the real thing was never said or done or even thought, but only represented by a set of arbitrary signs." Indeed, as one sees by the end, Newland's society is based on the symbolic sacrifice of too real individuals, the "taking life 'without effusion of blood'," if this be necessary for collective show and survival. The class motto of New York is succinctly put by Newland's mother: "if we don't all stand together, there'll be no such thing as Society left." This sacrificing of individuals to the tribal needs occurs most prominently at Ellen's casting-out dinner, but one also sees it in the maneuvering of Newland into a position of complicity, a sacrifice of himself in which he unconsciously assists.

Newland Archer, at the outset, is a socially secure "dilettante" and as fatuous a male ideologue as are Lawrence

Selden and George Darrow. He is engaged to May Welland who is, for her time, a perfect "product of the system." Newland's attitude toward her is equally perfect in its ideological purity; he sees her as his future possession ideally constructed of "abysmal purity," "whiteness, radiance, goodness," "truth . . . reality . . . the life that belonged to him," "peace, stability, comradeship and the steadying sense of an unescapable duty." This, of course, before the Fall: after meeting Ellen Olenska, a social outcast of good family lineage, these positive values become for Newland negative and sterile.

Newland does not then come to despise May herself, since he is incapable of seeing her individual self, but only the collective conspiracy which she embodies for him, that conspiracy necessarily born out of the genteel ideology exacting specific sexual/social roles for all individuals within separate spheres. Newland first faults May for being part of a matriarchal plot against male self-will:

> And he felt himself oppressed by this creature of factitious purity, so cunningly manufactured by a conspiracy of mothers and aunts and grandmothers and long-dead ancestresses, because it was supposed to be what he wanted, what he had a right to, in order that he might exercise his lordly pleasure in smashing it like an image made of snow.

Newland sees male power, in other words, as merely a female gift to men; his self-image is thus tainted by association with female will. Newland, of course, denies any personal complicity in this state of affairs, and even though he sometimes spouts liberation rhetoric, his sympathies at this point lie only with himself and the male world as he does battle with what he perceives as the repulsively feminine world embodied in May:

> It would presently be his task to take the bandage from this young woman's eyes, and bid her look forth on the world. But how many generations of the women who had gone to her making had descended bandaged to the family vault? He shivered a little, remembering some of the new ideas in his scientific books, and the much-cited instance of the Kentucky cave-fish, which had ceased to develop eyes because they had no use for them. What if when he had bidden May Welland to open hers, they could only look out blankly at blankness?

Newland both damns and supports, then, the ideology of separate spheres for women and men, an especially false construct in his case since both worlds are clearly inscribed within the same circle. Indeed, as is quickly made clear, Newland is less afraid of May's emptiness than of his own two-dimensional "character" which his relationship with her brings to light. Newland is repulsed by May because she reflects his own blindness and his particular "truth" and "reality," "the life that belonged to him." In short, he is terrorized by the realization that their supposedly separate worlds are one in which there is seemingly no space for individual desire or vision. In answer to her praise of his individualist stance, Newland exposes what it is in May and in himself which is irremediable: " 'Original! We're all as like each other as those dolls cut with the roses, and was vexed at having spoken of them. He wanted to say: "I called on your cousin yesterday," but hesitated. If Madame Olenska had not spoken of his visit it might seem awkward that he should. Yet not to do so gave the affair an air of mystery that he disliked. To shake off the question he began to talk of their own plans, their future, and Mrs.Welland's insistence on a long engagement.

"If you call it long! Isabel Chivers and Reggie were engaged for two years: Grace and Thorley for nearly a year and a half. Why aren't we very well off as we are?"

It was the traditional maidenly ~~interrogation~~ *interrogation*, and he felt ashamed of himself for finding it singularly childish. No doubt she simply echoed what was said for her; but she was nearing her twenty-second birthday, and he wondered at what age "nice" women began to speak for themselves.

"Never, if we won't let them, I suppose," he mused, and recalled his mad outburst to Mr.Sillerton Jackson: "Women ought to be as free as we are —"

It would presently be his task to take the bandage from this young woman's eyes, and bid her look forth on the world. But how many generations of the women who had gone to her making had descended bandaged to the family vault? He shivered a little, remembering some of the new ideas in his scientific books, and the much-cited instance of the Kentucky cavefish, which had ceased to develop eyes because they had no use for them. What if, when he had bidden May Welland to open hers, they could only look out blankly at blankness?

"We might be much better off. We might be altogether together — we might travel."

Her face lit up. That would be ~~lovely~~ *"lovely"*, she owned: she

The Age of Innocence, corrected typescript.

out of the same folded paper. We're like patterns stencilled on a wall'."

Newland is correct, however, in sensing a conspiracy against himself, but he is deluded in thinking women the sole perpetrators simply because they are the most visible actors in the plot to keep him within and useful to his society. He is himself an actor within that conspiracy, realizing too late his function in maintaining the society in which he is privileged enough to exist. As he comes to see, "In the rotation of crops there was a recognized season for wild oats; but they were not to be sown more than once" and that one time is to be in service to the reapers: his individual desire, his will to desire, must be subordinated to the tribal will to survive. His utter inability to affect that society in any way other than to surrender his seed for its "crops," his utter inability to effect self-realization, blinded as he has been and continues to be by his own limited consciousness, turns him both against and to woman, "the subject creature . . . versed in the arts of the enslaved." Only with women can Newland act out the fantasies of his subjugation or of his mastery.

In a perversely irresponsible act, Newland marries May, this despite his belief that their union is predicated on "a dull association of material and social interests held together by ignorance on the one side and hypocrisy on the other." Since he believes that May has been made for him but not by him, she is made to serve him both as his oppressor and as the scapegoat of his disillusionment. It comes as no surprise that Newland experiences his marriage as "the same black abyss yawned before him, and he felt himself sinking into it, deeper." His complicity through his marriage with the hegemony makes of his life an "endless emptiness." Newland, however, does not realize this fully until the end of his life; he only intuits in his youth that his way of being has made of him a walking corpse. As he tells May early on in their marriage: " 'I *am* dead—I've been dead for months and months'."

On the other hand, Ellen provokes his social self and finally revitalizes his individual self, if only for a short time. At first he responds to her as would any other genteel, chivalrous man. He is drawn into association with her by his relationship with May and at the outset of their friendship, counsels Ellen to fit herself, as he has done, to society or to be outcast again: " 'one can't make over society. . . . The individual, in such cases, is nearly always sacrificed to what is supposed to be the collective interest; people cling to any convention that keeps the family together'." Newland is not then totally aware of how firmly set he is within the larger family, society; neither is he conscious of the structures of power surrounding Ellen, those which she fully comprehends. With her, he does not come to understand the true separation of female and male worlds—that predicated upon desire—or her attempt to coexist peacefully on the edges of both spheres. Instead, he attempts to remake her in his image rather than finding himself through their relationship. For instance, he soon figures her simply as a helpless female who needs a knight such as he: "she stood before him as an exposed and pitiful figure, to be saved at all costs from farther wounding herself in her mad plunges against fate." That she is an or-

phan and an outcast fits beautifully into his fantasy. And so he places her on the pedestal of his affections, the one from which he has dethroned May. He then begins to play out the role of romantic lover, supposedly ceding to her his power and will, that which May stole from him, while in actuality he does battle against her defenses against him.

For example, in their first major love scene, Newland is spurned and then envisions himself as most despairing and desperate lovers do, as on the edge of nothingness: "He felt as though he had been struggling for hours up the face of a steep precipice, and now, just as he had fought his way to the top, his hold had given way and he was pitching down headlong into darkness." Even though Ellen has tried to teach him "the need of thinking himself into conditions incredibly different from any that he knew," Newland cannot even with her accept responsibility for his own acts or see beyond his romantic delusions and his limited consciousness. In a later assault on her sense of self and responsibility, and in a curious inversion of his criticism of May, he faults Ellen for destroying his secure world while denying him hers. He tells her, " 'You gave me my first glimpse of a real life, and at the same moment you asked me to go on with a sham one. It's beyond human enduring—that's all'."

In essence, Ellen awakens his dormant sense of selfhood achievable within an alternative reality beyond the confines of New York. Indeed, in her home, dress, manners, presentation of self—again, all matters of appearance—she comes to embody for him potential self fulfillment through "the actual business of living":

> for the first time Archer found himself face to face with the dread argument of the individual case. Ellen Olenska was like no other woman, he was like no other man: their situation, therefore, resembled no one else's, and they were answerable to no tribunal but that of their own judgment.

However, since he is incapable of matching action to realization, he then constructs a new fantasy, one as self-serving as the previous versions. After his marriage, Ellen is enshrined in Newland's particular republic of the spirit: "he had built up within himself a kind of sanctuary in which she throned among his secret thoughts and longings." It is clear by the end that Newland has not loved Ellen Olenska for her individuality but merely as another objectified ideal, for he can never truly comprehend that which is "like nothing that he was accustomed to look at (and therefore able to see)." Newland, in short, remains self-deceived on all accounts, and his inability to relinquish repressive idealism and romanticism for pragmatic action is made evident to the resisting reader through Wharton's straightforward yet complex presentation of Newland's two women. Their realities and experience first complement and then counteract Newland's oppressive world view.

Ellen, while admittedly in love with Newland, seeks only social security and not another chance at social revolt. She understands that the world of women, seen for example in the sphere of Catherine Mingott, is still necessarily aligned with the world of men so that it might survive. She is not, however, a totally passive object: she strives throughout the story to maintain her personal sense of integrity and self while simultaneously making over society in small ways so that she can in turn find a comfortable position in that world. To this effect, she is perfectly willing to sacrifice her desire: as she tells Newland, " 'I can't love you unless I give you up'." a statement of foresight and not evasion as was Robert Lebrun's to Edna Pontellier. She does so first by continuously reminding him of his reality, May and his position in society, and ultimately by abdicating her personal love and social security, returning to an outcast's life. Ellen both understands self-desire and responsibility to self and others whereas Newland only feels desire and a longing for self. She counters Newland's idealism with pragmatism and logic—" 'we'll look, not at visions, but at realities' "—and in responding to his romantic view of an illicit affair, finally lays the illusive and ill-used republic of the spirit to rest:

> [Newland says,] "I want—I want somehow to get away with you into a world where words like that—categories like that—won't exist. Where we shall be simply two human beings who love each other, who are the whole of life to each other; and nothing else on earth will matter." She drew a deep sigh that ended in another laugh. "Oh, my dear—where is that country?"

Ellen knows that such utopian or romantic dreams are socially futile since they cannot be actualized. She has been "beyond" Newland's world, and she realizes that one must live within one's society or be alienated, observe the amenities even if they be inanities or be without a *modus vivendi.* One must do so, that is, while one must also seek to transform one's society, albeit if only in small ways. Ellen's tragedy, though she would not call it that, results from her singularity: except for the aged and the eccentric, she has no community in which to position herself, no community with which she might effect social change. She remains throughout an orphan in search of family.

Similarly, May is motivated by a desire for community, and she is clearly not the helpless innocent Newland believes her to be; neither is she at all passive in her fulfillment of ideological prescription. Only at Ellen's casting-out farewell dinner given by May does Newland realize that May has understood him all along and that she has actively but not maliciously conspired against Ellen and him in order to protect her immediate and extended family, society. So too does Newland learn after May's death that she had comprehended his affections for both her and Ellen and that she, like Ellen, had done only what she believed to be right. Newland as well after the departure of Ellen does the right thing: he returns to the woman made for him, May, and fulfills the roles assigned him. He becomes Newland Archer, the good husband, father, social citizen. They all force themselves to live good lives. Each woman, as well as Newland, fulfills ideological roles: martyr, moral superior, beloved object, the ideal. They are all complicit, then, in maintaining the hegemonic world view, and each suffers accordingly. However, Ellen also comprehended and opposed strict ideological adherence, at the same time refusing to fall victim to the alienating experi-

ence of blind, unreflective passion. Instead, what was first shown to the reader as her self-eccentricity is in the end revealed as a hopeful self-realization effected by a willful woman secure in a new land. There she seems to have found a community, though it is one which remains invisible, not yet inscribable.

It is at the end, a generation later and after the Lily Barts and Undine Spraggs, that Newland assimilates and evaluates his life experiences. After Ellen, Newland had lived a good life with May and unlike the majority of Wharton's characters had worked toward social reform. His genteel world gives way to the new money society and the world of new woman. His final philosophical reading of social evolution is that "there was good in the old ways" but "good in the new order too." More important, however, is his realization that strict fulfillment of social duties had only served to establish him firmly in "a deep rut," the anonymity of conformity. His unthinking complicity with patriarchal ideology costs Newland self-fulfillment, resulting in "an inarticulate lifetime," Wharton's most pointed warning to men of the penalties of power. Newland comes to understand this not only through May but for himself: "Something he knew he had missed: the flower of life." Yet his struggle with consciousness, as well as that of May and Ellen, is not without fruition. In the nurturing of a less repressive and more dynamic social order—in Newland's own work and in his son Dallas' upbringing—there is the potential realization of a humanistic, socially responsive consciousness denied Newland in his own life, a consciousness that would obliterate individual self-effacement and effect the full articulation of both male and female experience.

Wharton does not offer Newland absolution for his complicity; she does, however, show that life is a continuum, a dynamic web of action and reaction, potentially a revolutionary process of transcendence. Even though Newland cannot climb up to Ellen's level at the end, Wharton gives the reader a glimpse of a new structure of feeling, a positive world in which woman's will and desire are central and no longer marginal, in which both men and women can indeed dare and defy and yet live. Thus does Wharton, by calling into question both the conventional and the transgressive, struggle with her form—her particular set of arbitrary signs—and content—the full inscription of human relations. In this her pivotal work, she . . . subtly traversed literary and ideological boundaries, revealed in sharp detail what she knew of the human condition, and called yet again for quiet revolution. *The Age of Innocence* does not celebrate some mythic prelapsarian way of being, does not invest all value in a looking backward. Instead, it raises very important questions about how one might live not only a good but a full life in a postlapsarian world. (pp. 147-55)

Mary E. Papke, "Edith Wharton's Social Fiction," in her Verging on the Abyss: The Social Fiction of Kate Chopin and Edith Wharton, *Greenwood Press, 1990, pp. 103-74.*

> **The Age of Innocence reveals a universal dimension as Edith Wharton comments upon the oppression of women by convention and their emancipation from it, the role of marriage and the family in determining the quality of a civilization, and, above all, the conflict between sexual passion and moral obligation.**
>
> —*Margaret B. McDowell in her* Edith Wharton, *1976.*

Kathy Miller Hadley (essay date 1991)

[*In the following essay, the critic describes the three story lines Wharton considered for* The Age of Innocence *and discusses the significance of the structure and perspective she eventually selected for the novel's final version.*]

In her 1920 *The Age of Innocence,* Edith Wharton presents a story which, on the surface, is a man's story, and which in many ways appears to be a conventional nineteenth-century romance. These things *appear* to be so because Wharton tells the story from Newland Archer's point of view, focusing on his consciousness and the way he deals with the potential love triangle in which he finds himself. But as Rachel Blau DuPlessis argues, while nineteenth-century authors made certain "that *Bildung* and romance could not coexist and be integrated for the heroine at the resolution," twentieth-century women writers are "writing beyond" such endings, breaking the narrative structure which says that women must ultimately sacrifice their questing to marriage, or die. In *The Age of Innocence,* Wharton writes beyond a traditional nineteenth-century ending by ironically undermining the structure of the novel and its focus on Newland Archer, a would-be American hero, and by drawing the reader's attention to the untold stories of Ellen Olenska and May Welland.

Wharton's careful structuring of *The Age of Innocence* is evidenced by the three different plans she outlined for the novel. In the first version, May and Archer break their engagement. Archer is shocked when Ellen responds to his proposal by suggesting that they spend a few weeks together to make sure of their feelings for each other. Ellen and Newland marry despite Archer's misgivings but eventually separate because Ellen's soul "recoils" from the prospect of an old New York marriage. Ellen returns to Europe, where "She is very poor, & very lonely, but she has a real life"; Archer returns to his mother's house. Apparently this version of the novel would have emphasized Ellen's ability to act and to cause extensive changes in the lives of others.

Wharton's second plan calls for a much more conventional novel: Archer marries May and has a brief affair with Ellen, who then returns to Europe. Discussing these plans, Alan Price concludes that Wharton shifted the focus from Ellen to Archer in the second version partly because: "she could not be confident [in her first plan] that her readers would share her sympathy for a woman who broke up the engagement of a nice girl, suggested a trial marriage, and then abandoned her husband because she thought New York's seasonal social life was dull."

The third plan again has Archer marrying May but having an affair with Ellen. Although everyone else surmises that Newland and Ellen are lovers, May "suspects nothing." As a Catholic, Ellen cannot divorce, so she could not marry Newland even if he left May. But Ellen again grows tired of New York and her affair with Archer and returns to "the freedom and variety of her European existence." The final dinner for Ellen in versions two and three is simply a good-bye, not the ritual of ostracism it becomes in the finished novel.

By the time she had completed *The Age of Innocence* in its published form, Wharton had made Ellen Olenska an ostensibly minor character, while Newland Archer became the novel's central figure. As Wharton's chosen center of consciousness, Newland appears to be a traditional American hero: the American male whose search for a new frontier, according to such critics as Henry Nash Smith and Richard Chase, makes this country's literature distinctly American. Discussing the way the myth of the American hero has displaced women writers from the canon and has trivialized women characters in fiction, Nina Baym says that the myth entails "the pure American self" confronting "the promise offered by the idea of America . . . that in this new land, untrammeled by history and social accident, a person will be able to achieve complete self-definition." Society becomes "something artificial and secondary to human nature" which "exerts an unmitigatedly destructive pressure on individuality." Because both society and landscape are "depicted in unmistakably feminine terms," the American hero is realized as the opposite of the feminine, and the myth becomes exclusively male.

The American hero's story becomes, in effect, a male *bildungsroman;* thus Archer, whose first name refers to the American hero's quest for a *new land,* struggles with his romantic triangle and his need for self-definition. Newland persistently fails to define himself, however. Married to May for a year, he contrasts his present life with his "vision of the past" and muses, "What am I? A son-in-law—." At the end of the novel, Newland reminisces about having "risen up at the call" to politics (dropping "thankfully" into obscurity when not re-elected), and of having been "a good citizen" and "what was called a faithful husband." To the end, Wharton emphasizes that Newland is defined by his social roles.

May is originally the frontier on which Newland plans to exercise his selfhood. She is to be a "miracle of fire and ice," both passion and purity, which he will create by his "enlightening companionship." But Newland relinquishes this goal after his wedding, concluding that "There was no use in trying to emancipate a wife who had not the dimmest notion that she was not free," an assumption based largely on the "most tranquil unawareness" Newland believes he sees in May's eyes.

Ellen is the promising landscape; for Newland, this quite *unfree* woman comes to represent the freedom of a world different from his own. Sitting beside Ellen in his wife's carriage, Newland tells her, "The only reality to me is this." When Ellen asks if he wants her to be his mistress, the flustered Newland replies:

> I want somehow to get away with you into a world where words like that—categories like that—won't exist. Where we shall be simply two human beings who love each other, who are the whole of life to each other; and nothing else on earth will matter.

This is the new-land of Archer's name. What he really wants is the ability to move between May's and Ellen's worlds without any cost to himself, and without deciding between the two worlds. That Newland seeks a dream world rather than an actual place is suggested by the fact that he had previously rejected the possibility of a physical quest. When Ned Winsett had spoken of emigrating, Newland had thought, "Emigrate! As if a gentleman could abandon his own country!" Ironically, one of the few physical journeys Newland does make is his flight from Ellen to Florida, where he begs May to hasten their wedding—with the result that Ellen can be, at most, his mistress. Ellen sees through his romanticized longing for another world and responds, "Oh, my dear—where is that country?"

Wharton undermines her own form throughout the novel, writing beyond the story about Newland Archer to convey a sense of the women characters that her attention to her audience and to acceptable forms removed from center stage. Beside Newland's *bildungsroman* is that of Ellen Olenska, whose search *is* manifested by a physical journey—"home" to New York, then back again to Europe. Wharton makes it clear that Ellen's return to New York is a type of quest. At the van der Luydens' dinner, Newland assures Ellen that she is "among friends." She answers, "Yes—I know. Wherever I go I have that feeling. *That's why I came home.* I want to forget everything else, to become a complete American again" (my emphasis).

Not that Ellen's journey to New York involves a whole-sale acceptance of its ways. She refuses to live with her grandmother because she "had to be free," and she moves away from the social center of New York to be surrounded by artists, as she was in France. When Archer tells her that her house is in an unfashionable quarter, she says, "Why not make one's own fashions? But," she concedes, "I suppose I've lived too independently; at any rate, I want to do what you all do—I want to feel cared for and safe." She continues, "Being here is like—like—being taken on a holiday when one has been a good little girl and done all one's lessons." She appeals to Newland for help with learning how to fit in: "But you'll explain these things to me—you'll tell me all I ought to know." Newland responds, "It's you who are telling me: opening my eyes to things I'd looked at so long that I'd ceased to see them." He has turned Ellen's appeal for help around, thus refocusing her energies, and the reader's, on *his* quest. Newland is unable to truly help Ellen because he is so self-absorbed.

Ellen's respect for the ways of old New York becomes increasingly tinged with skepticism. She soon begins to see New York differently: it is no longer a haven. Ellen's early ability to see through the van der Luydens' reclusiveness anticipates her increasing ability to make her own informed judgments about New York and to decide whether or not her quest should end there. Newland, trying to steer Ellen away from the influence of Julius Beaufort, assures her that the older women "want to help you." Ellen answers, "on condition that they don't hear anything unpleasant . . . Does no one want to know the truth here, Mr. Archer? The real loneliness is living among all these kind people who only ask one to pretend!" Ellen has already discovered that she must continue to be a "good little girl" if she is to get along in New York; her success there depends on behaving to please others, as children must do, and stifling her adult views and feelings. If she fails to do so, Ellen may, like a bad little girl, lose her allowance.

In a later scene, Newland (not yet married) confesses his love for Ellen and speaks of their freeing themselves for each other. But Ellen rejects Newland's plan because of the sense of loyalty he has made her feel: "you hated happiness bought by disloyalty and cruelty and indifference. That was what I'd never known before—and it's better than anything I've known." Ellen's words suggest that Wharton wants the reader to view Newland positively, as a champion of loyalty, kindness, and concern. But while Ellen sees his advice that she give up her divorce suit as evidence of Newland's strong moral character, Newland was simply representing the family's view when he gave her that advice. By speaking for the family and urging Ellen not to divorce, Newland has, in effect, sabotaged his own quest. Finding that they are now inconvenient to him, he is willing to overthrow the principles for which he had stood. Ellen, however, refuses to do so.

In this scene, Ellen also tells of Granny's revealing how New York sees her.

> I was perfectly unconscious at first that people here were shy of me—that they thought I was a dreadful sort of person . . . New York simply meant peace and freedom to me: it was coming home.

She tries to explain to Archer the way this realization has affected her: "I *was* lonely; I *was* afraid. But the emptiness and the darkness are gone; when I turn back into myself now I'm like a child going at night into a room where there's always a light." This is a critical stage in Ellen's quest. She has learned to find comfort and strength within herself, rather than seeking them in the external world. She is now able to leave New York (returning only when her grandmother has a stroke), so that she does not disrupt Newland's and May's wedding. But Archer responds, "I don't understand you!" He still assumes that a woman needs a man to sustain her; earlier in their confrontation, when she cried "I can't love you unless I give you up," he had retorted, "And Beaufort? Is he to replace me?" Newland, unable to comprehend Ellen's psychological self-reliance, continues to think that she is simply rejecting him in favor of another man.

Because she is seen through Newland's eyes and appears primarily as a factor in his quest, much of Ellen's story is untold. Discussing the politics of the untold story, Du-Plessis says:

> To compose a work is to negotiate with these questions: What stories can be told? How can plots be resolved? What is felt to be narratable by both literary and social conventions? Indeed, these are issues very acute to certain feminist critics and women writers, with their senses of the untold story, the other side of a well-known tale.

Wharton negotiates such questions by constantly *reminding* us that Ellen's is an untold story. She ironically invites the reader to speculate about Ellen's story by focusing on Newland's obsessive curiosity about it—a curiosity that is fed by Ellen's own willingness to leave her story untold. In this way, Newland's quest becomes largely a search for information about *Ellen's*.

In Ellen's legal file, Newland finds a letter from her husband which he tells himself contains "the vague charge of an angry blackguard"—that Ellen had had an affair with his secretary. Yet Newland wonders, "how much truth was behind it? Only Count Olenski's wife could tell." Many of Newland's subsequent conversations with Ellen involve attempts to answer this question. Initially, he gropes for a denial, but Ellen does not give one. When he asks what she thinks she can gain by divorcing her distant husband, Ellen says, "But my freedom—is that nothing?" Newland concludes that "the charge in the letter was true, and that she hoped to marry the partner of her guilt." For Newland, apparently, Ellen's freedom *does* mean nothing; he assumes that she would only want to be free from one man in order to marry (i.e., relinquish her freedom to) another.

Unsettled by Ellen's failure to deny having an affair, Newland "rambled on" in "his intense desire to cover over the ugly reality which her silence seemed to have laid bare." Newland needs to know whether or not Ellen has had an affair because for him it is important to keep women in categories: he remembers how young men make an "abysmal distinction between the women one loved and respected and those one enjoyed—and pitied." He tries to tell himself that in Europe, there might arise situations "in which a woman naturally sensitive and aloof would yet, from the force of circumstances . . . be drawn into a tie inexcusable by conventional standards." Newland is clearly uncomfortable with such a scenario, however; only when Ellen implicitly denies her husband's accusation, saying "I had nothing to fear from that letter," is Newland ready to commit himself to her.

Contrasted with Ellen's *bildungsroman* is May's seemingly conventional romance. But Wharton undermines May's romance plot, as well. One of the more obvious ways in which Wharton wrote beyond a traditional nineteenth-century novel ending was her handling of Newland's and May's wedding. Rather than concluding the novel with Archer's feelings for Ellen resolved beforehand, as it would have a conventional novel, the wedding begins Book II of *The Age of Innocence.* Structurally, placing the

wedding here suggests a new beginning, but in fact Newland's conflict continues—and intensifies—once he is married.

The wedding itself is an extremely ironic occasion. It takes place the Tuesday after Easter, a holiday that symbolizes regeneration, new life, hope; yet, as Virginia Blum notes, the service is "cast in funereal language." Newland compares his wedding with an Opera night and wonders if, "when the Last Trump sounded, Mrs. Selfridge Merry would be there with the same towering ostrich feathers in her bonnet, and Mrs. Beaufort with the same diamond earrings and the same smile—and whether suitable proscenium seats were already prepared for them in another world." With this imagery, Wharton juxtaposes the two traditional nineteenth-century novel endings: marriage and death become one. Newland cannot concentrate on the ceremony; he looks for Ellen, and misses half of the bridal procession.

Placing the wedding in the center of the novel suggests that *The Age of Innocence* will fit another pattern that developed early in the twentieth-century: novels "which either begin with [the heroine's] marriage or launch her rapidly into it, and concern a working out of her identity within or against the context of the marriage." Wharton does not work out May's identity, however; May's story, like Ellen's, remains untold. The difference is that, while Newland becomes obsessed with Ellen's story, he has almost no curiosity about his wife's. He prefers the potentially scandalous past of another woman even to the present of his own wife who, he assumes, has no past worth his notice.

Newland discounts May's experience because he perceives her as completely innocent. In fact, we see May only through his eyes; Newland projects his ideal of innocence onto May (just as he projects an aura of secrecy onto Ellen). May appears to be the innocent of the novel's title, but she is not, and Newland must misinterpret his interactions with May in order to continue viewing her as innocent. When May questions his reason for wanting to hasten their wedding, Newland recognizes her insight. But when she "flushed with joy" at his assurance that "There is no pledge—no obligation whatever—of the kind you think," May "seemed to have descended from her womanly eminence to helpless and timorous girlhood." Ironically, he is disappointed with May for believing that he is telling the truth.

This scene also indicates May's "potential for growth and change." This potential is what Archer does not see. One of the few times in the novel that he really looks at his wife is near the end, when he "was struck by something languid and inelastic in her attitude" and briefly "wondered if the deadly monotony of their lives had laid its weight on her also." He does not consider that she may suspect his feelings for Ellen, much less that she may be pregnant. Newland then trivializes what he sees by attributing May's languid demeanor to the fact that he had forgotten to meet her at her grandmother's that day.

Only in the novel's penultimate chapter, at the dinner for Ellen, does Archer realize how much his wife has suspected and how often she has acted. "And then it came over him, in a vast flash made up of many broken gleams, that to all of them he and Madame Olenska were lovers . . . he understood that, by means as yet unknown to him, the separation between himself and the partner of his guilt had been achieved, and that now the whole tribe had rallied about his wife on the tacit assumption that nobody knew anything." The "means" had culminated in May's telling Ellen she was pregnant, before she knew for certain; and in telling this lie, May was "acting with the knowledge and approval of the family," as Judith Fryer notes. Fryer says that *"Because of the way we are used to reading novels,* the romance of Newland and Ellen at first obscures the force of the countersubject: the inexorableness of the offensive launched by the women" against Ellen (my emphasis). Wharton gives us what appears to be a traditional novel and then surprises us with this most powerful glimpse of May's untold story. In fact, it has been Newland's lack of attention to May's story that has enabled her to destroy his hope of "escape": while he fell asleep exhausted after arranging for Ellen to come to him once, May was having the "really good talk" with Ellen that causes her to finally decide to return to Europe.

May's careful, knowing control of her situation—contrasted with Newland's ignorance—makes the title of **The Age of Innocence** especially ironic. Wharton appears to have intended this effect. Her working title for this novel was *Old New York.* In both of the plans in which Newland and May marry, Newland has an affair with Ellen which his wife never suspects. Only in the final version, when she changed the title to **The Age of Innocence,** did Wharton invert the relationship between suspicion and truth, changing May into a woman who assumes that her husband has had an affair when he has not.

Also ironic is the way Wharton treats May as domesticator. This role, like that of May's innocence, is largely projected onto her by Newland. Early in the novel, Newland had "thanked heaven that he was a New Yorker, and about to ally himself with one of his own kind." But as he becomes enamored with Ellen, "there were moments when he felt as if he were being buried alive under his future." His response is to rush to May, to encourage her, in effect, to seal his future before he risks involvement with Ellen. Much later, at the dinner which is "the tribal rally around a kinswoman about to be eliminated from the tribe," Newland "felt like a prisoner in the center of an armed camp." These and other references to Newland's feeling trapped are juxtaposed with the fact that he begged that his wedding be hastened, and that May offered to break their engagement when she sensed that he loved another woman.

As Wharton takes care to describe it, May's house represents all the negative aspects of domesticity; here Newland also feels trapped, as the following scene indicates. One winter evening in his library, watching May as she sews, Newland opens the window because "The room is stifling: I want a little air." Leaning out the window, "The mere fact of not looking at May, seated beside his table, under his lamp, the fact of seeing other houses, roofs, chimneys, of getting the sense of other lives outside his own, other

cities beyond New York, and a whole world beyond his world, cleared his brain and made it easier to breathe." May is infringing on Newland's space; this is *his* table, *his* lamp, *his* library—the only room in the house he has decorated as he likes. He looks out the window to "a whole world beyond," much as the traditional American hero looks to the landscape and the frontier for escape from a domesticated world.

But Wharton undermines Newland's perception in two ways. In this scene, Newland is frustrated because Ellen has just refused to become his mistress. And Newland's sense of May as entrapper is ironic because he has considerably misunderstood her character. Before opening the window, "he said to himself with a secret dismay that he would always know the thoughts behind [her clear brow], that never, in all the years to come, would she surprise him by an unexpected mood, by a new idea, a weakness, a cruelty or an emotion." Yet Wharton makes it clear that Archer does *not* know May's thoughts; he not only hasn't realized that she suspects his feelings for Ellen, he does not yet know that May and the rest of the family have determined to exclude him from their discussions of Ellen. When May says, "Do shut the window. You'll catch your death," he wants to tell her, "I am dead—I've been dead for months and months." But any sympathy we may feel for him wanes when he thinks, "What if it were *she* who was dead! . . . [May] might die, and set him suddenly free." Having failed to take control of his own life, Newland now passively hopes for a catastrophe to change his life for him.

If May represents domesticity and her house, that domesticating force, Ellen's house represents escape for Newland. Ellen's drawing room is "unlike any room he had known"; it contains pictures that "bewildered him, for they were like nothing that he was accustomed to look at (and therefore able to see) when he travelled in Italy." In the same way, Newland is "unable to see" Ellen herself; she will remain, for him, wrapped in an aura of European mystique. Newland had contrasted Ellen's drawing room, with its "vague pervading perfume . . . like the scent of some far-off bazaar," with the stuffy, conventional house that awaited him after his conventional honeymoon with May. As Fryer notes, Ellen "offers the possibilities of individual freedom and experience, instinct and variety, cultural and sexual richness . . . [so] Newland sends her not lilies-of-the-valley, but yellow roses."

Unlike the typical nineteenth-century woman's *bildungsroman,* Ellen's story ends in neither death nor marriage. Her quest has not been sacrificed to romance, as far as we know; she rejects the novel's two major romance possibilities: an affair with Newland and return to her husband. At the end of the novel, twenty-six years after Ellen is banished from New York, Newland has an opportunity to see her again. May has died, and Newland, in Paris with his son Dallas, has received an invitation to Ellen's. But upon reaching her apartment building, Newland decides not to go in. Critics have offered several convincing reasons for this ending: Newland may be afraid to take the risk of a real relationship, or that Ellen will have changed too much; or, he may be so struck with Dallas' revelation that

May had understood what it meant for him to give up Ellen, that he does not want to disturb his memory of May, who had "guessed and pitied."

However we choose to interpret Newland's declining to see Ellen at the end, the fact is that with this ending, Wharton leaves the resolution of Ellen's *bildungsroman* open, and once again invites us to speculate about her untold story. Like Newland, we can only imagine whether or not quest and romance coexist for Ellen, just as we can only imagine what it was like for May to live at the center of "a kind of innocent family hypocrisy" in which her husband and children treated her as one "so lacking in imagination, so incapable of growth" that she saw nothing that happened around her. Wharton does invite us to imagine the best for Ellen, however, by suggesting that she has kept herself free all these years.

So the novel ends with the bittersweet denouement of Newland Archer's quest in which, because his son touches on what he and May had never spoken of, "He had to deal all at once with the packed regrets and stifled memories of an inarticulate lifetime," a life which "had been too starved." And in the same city where his quest comes to an end is Ellen, who so far as we can tell, enjoys the "freedom and variety of her European existence" on the same street in Paris where the divorced Wharton lived for many years, surrounding herself with "a quiet harvest of friendship." (pp. 262-70)

> *Kathy Miller Hadley, "Ironic Structure and Untold Stories in 'The Age of Innocence',"* in Studies in the Novel, *Vol. XXIII, No. 2, Summer, 1991, pp. 262-72.*

Evelyn E. Fracasso   (essay date 1991)

[*In the following essay, Fracasso outlines Wharton's use of physical traits to reveal the character of May Welland.*]

May Welland, beautiful virginal fiancee of Newland Archer, eligible attorney and man-about-town, and product of 1870 New York's beau monde, is the subject of much of the criticism written about Edith Wharton's *The Age of Innocence,* and there are widely divergent views as to her role and significance in the novel. Is she, as Elizabeth Ammons contends, "still in the nursery . . . a precious human burden . . . her class's ideal of helpless humanity . . . a lovely human doll whose uselessness aggrandizes her owner's social standing," or is she, as Margaret B. McDowell maintains, "a woman of considerable strength" with "a toughness and a tenacity of purpose which show that she is more than the clinging, helpless woman so much cherished as the New York aristocrats' ideal?" Is she "staid and already completely predictable . . . the tribal member par excellence . . . trained to go to any lengths to ignore the unpleasant" (Lawson), or is she "not the cardboard stereotype that Archer perceives" but one with "the potential for growth and change . . . a person of greater depth than he thought" (Wershoven)?

Frances Theresa Russell helps answer this critical dilemma by pointing out that "Mrs. Wharton belongs to the class of romantico-realistic novelists whose main object is to present characters by means of situations, employing for this purpose the straight literal method, vivified and illumined by occasional imaginative illustrations." She adds that "anything and everything is subject to this symbolic treatment" and "beginning with physique, she [Wharton] is particularly interested in eyes." A close textual analysis of May Welland's physical characteristics with particular attention to her eyes, therefore, provides sufficient evidence that she is neither "her class's ideal of helpless humanity" nor "a cardboard stereotype," but instead, she is a perceptive, strong-willed, and determined woman who develops into "a person of greater depth" than Newland Archer could ever have imagined.

The novel opens at the opera, at a performance of *Faust,* where May is introduced as "a young girl in white" with "warm pink" cheeks and dropped eyes, touching her bouquet of lilies-of-the-valley with "white-gloved finger-tips." This detailed description of May's physical features coupled with her fiance's rather boastful observation that "she doesn't even guess what it's [Faust] all about" provides the reader with a clear picture of an ingenuous and demure young girl whom Archer hopes to shape into the worldly-wise mold of the married woman with whom he has recently had a two-year-long affair. This initial impression of May is reinforced when Archer asks her permission to announce their engagement at Mrs. Julius Beaufort's annual after-the-opera ball, and she gazes up at him, her face "rosy as the dawn," her dropped eyes "radiant."

At the ball later that evening, May is portrayed as still clutching her lilies-of-the-valley, although her face is now pale and her candid eyes are burning with excitement, the epitome of helpless feminity. However, when Archer whisks her away to the strains of the "Blue Danube" after announcing their engagement, Wharton intimates, through a direct reference to May's eyes, that there may be more depth and more complexity to this young girl than the whiteness, radiance, and goodness that Archer is holding in his arms suggests: "Her lips trembled into a smile, but the eyes remained distant and serious, as if bent on some ineffable vision."

Nonetheless, Archer sees nothing profound in May's eyes and persists in a narrow view of his betrothed. Even when he studies a photograph of "the frank forehead, serious eyes and gay innocent mouth of the young creature whose soul's custodian he was to be," he perceives her only as a young woman who knows nothing of the world. Musing about the fresh new ideas, interests, and feelings that he hopes to awaken in May, he concludes that it will be up to him "to take the bandage from this young woman's eyes and bid her look forth on the world." At the same time, however, he fears that his fiancee's eyes may never see anything new and different if she remains ensconced in her stagnant and predictable conventional world.

Certainly Wharton's description of May's eyes—filled with "a bright unclouded admiration"—when Archer talks of their future together seems to support his view that nothing problematic will ever obscure her childlike vision. Nonetheless, when he proposes that they break from convention and elope, May is unaccustomedly assertive as she terms the idea "vulgar" and arbitrarily changes the subject.

Similarly, a short time later, when Archer visits May at St. Augustine where she is staying with her parents for the winter, he observes only that her eyes appear to him "almost pale in their youthful limipidity" and that her face seems to possess "the vacant serenity of a young marble athlete." However, she is obviously disturbed by the intensity of the kiss with which he greets her. Fully aware that there is an urgency in her fiance that was not evident before, May blushes and deliberately draws away from him. For his part, Archer attempts to alleviate her embarrassed response by encouraging her to talk of "familiar and simple things." Now that he has met and is attracted to her charming worldly-wise cousin, Ellen, (the pariah of the family, who is presently seeking a divorce from her husband, a ne'er-do-well Polish count), he does not want May doomed to an innocence "that seals the mind against imagination and the heart against experience!"

But May is not as naive as Archer believes. When, at their next meeting, he suggests that they advance the date of their wedding, May's hitherto blank, unclouded, limpid eyes suddenly become "eyes of such despairing clearness." She asks if his request is occasioned by a change in his feelings for her—whether he still cares for her, or if, in fact, there is another woman. Perceptive enough to realize that their relationship has become less intense since their engagement, she does not wish to make a mistake by advancing the date of their wedding. No longer the trembling-lipped ingenue at her engagement ball, May is now portrayed with "resolutely steadied lips" speaking out with strength and determination:

> One hears and one notices—one has one's own feelings and ideas. . . . I couldn't have my happiness made out of a wrong—an unfairness—to somebody else. And I want to believe that it would be the same with you. What sort of a life could we build on such foundations?

Her painful discourse continues as she urges her fiance to return to his former paramour if that is what he wishes to do. Archer is startled and dizzied by her "quiet lucidity" and protests that there is no other woman in his life. With his pronouncement, May flushes with joy, and her eyes become "full of happy tears." Sadly, Archer erroneously assumes that the new May, who had just displayed such unexpected boldness and insight, has suddenly faded away and been replaced by the "helpless and timorous" girl he had previously judged her to be. Consequently, he becomes dejected by "the vanishing of the new being who had cast that one deep look at him from her transparent eyes."

Although Wharton has described May's eyes thus far as "bright," "light," "limpid," "too-clear," and only once as "distant and serious," now for the first time, she categorizes them as "transparent," a designation alerting the reader to heed the deep-seated strength and "tenacity of purpose" that will be more openly demonstrated by May and reflected in her most prominent physical feature.

Certainly May seems uncharacteristically manipulative in the months that follow. Fearful of her fiance's growing attachment to her cousin, Ellen, she deliberately moves up her wedding date. Unknown to her, however, by the time Archer receives her letter requesting this change, he has already declared his love to Ellen. Nonetheless, as a man of honor and tradition (a tradition he had previously urged May to reject), Archer proceeds with the wedding on the date May requests.

Nonetheless, Ellen remains a formidable presence, and just the mention of her name, even after the wedding, causes May's eyes to react, her color to rise. When Ellen's name is introduced into the conversation at her mother-in-law's Thanksgiving Day dinner, for example, a "sudden blush" appears on May's face that "surprised her husband as much as the other guests about the table." Wharton describes the blush as "permanently vivid" and notes its significance. Archer terms it "menacing" but chooses to ignore the reason for its appearance.

Again, later that evening, he seems oblivious to his wife's reaction to his announcement that he must travel to Washington, where Ellen is presently staying. May's face pales as she questions whether he is going on business, yet she looks him "straight in the eyes with her cloudless smile" and even suggests that he visit Ellen while he is there. Her smile may be "cloudless," but her mind is neither cloud-free, nor "still in the nursery." May is fully aware of her husband's feelings for Ellen, yet she wisely neither accuses nor objects to his trip.

Instead, she exploits the "slight stroke" her grandmother suffers to delay and perhaps even cancel his departure. After requesting that her husband go "straight to Granny's," May's face is pale but "smiling." When Ellen is also summoned to New York because of Granny's illness, Archer lies to his wife that his case has been postponed, and May, aware of his deceit, looks directly at her husband once more and courageously suggests that he meet Ellen when she arrives at the train station. Her eyes are again prominent in this scene, only on this occasion Wharton describes them for the first time in yet another dimension—their color—to mirror May's mood as she bids her husband goodbye: " 'Goodbye, dearest,' she said, her eyes so blue that he wondered afterward if they had shone on him through tears."

The following evening, May's physical appearance continues to reflect her inner spirit—her face remains wan and pallid, and her eyes, still damp, "kept the blue dazzle of the day before." Her husband is aware of her sad and listless state, but because he is annoyed with her for not openly discussing her feelings with him (although he feels no need to reveal his to her), he irritatingly presumes that she, too, is wearied by their monotonous and passionless lives. Settling back with a volume of history, he broods over her lack of interest in literature and erroneously concludes, as he is wont to do, that he would always know his wife's thoughts and that "never, in all the years to come, would she surprise him by an unexpected mood, by a new idea, a weakness, a cruelty or an emotion."

But May's mood is quite changed a week later when she

returns home after having a long talk with her cousin Ellen. Unpredictably, she caresses her husband as she enters, and he is astonished. He notices that she is sparkling and animated. She blushes, and a rosy glow brightens her face, not unlike that which shone forth at St. Augustine when she questioned him about the reason for advancing their wedding date. On that occasion, her eyes were filled with happy tears when he reassured her there was no other woman in his life. Now, her eyes are "the same swimming blue" as they were on the day Archer went to pick up Ellen at the train station, yet he also perceives in them that same profound insight that surfaced for only a moment in Florida when she reached "beyond the usual range of her vision." And the blush Archer termed "menacing" at the Thanksgiving Day dinner has reappeared.

Wharton's description suggests that the unclouded radiance in May's eyes that was evident during her naive, unsophisticated girlhood days has been replaced by an "unnatural vividness" resulting from her husband's obvious fascination with her beautiful and charming cousin. Unfortunately, because Archer has already become deeply involved with Ellen, he does not notice the physical manifestations signalling the changes that have taken place in his wife since their marriage. As Carol Wershoven points out:

> He is too concerned with his own situation, and thus, even after marriage, will not make the best of what he considers a bad bargain. Even when Archer recognizes in his wife "the same reaching towards something beyond the usual range of her vision" that he had seen in his fiancée, and remembers "the passionate generosity latent under that incurious calm," he ignores it. . . . "he had long given up trying to disengage her real self from the shape into which tradition and training had moulded her."

On the following night, May surprises her husband again at a performance of *Faust*, the opera performed on the night their engagement was announced. Her eyes are shining once more, and she is dressed in her white satin and lace wedding dress, a dress that she has seldom worn during the two years of their marriage. Archer is reminded of their wedding, which is precisely May's intention, but he also recalls her courageous declaration in Florida that she would not want to marry him if she knew he loved another woman. He decides, therefore, that he must finally be honest with his wife and tell her of his love for Ellen. Feigning a headache, he requests that they leave the opera at once. May pales, obviously aware of his intention, but her face, in spite of its pallor, has "a curious tranquillity of expression that seem[s] drawn from some secret inner source."

At home, as Archer begins to blurt out Ellen's name, his wife interrupts him with the news that her cousin is returning to Europe. All the while, she looks directly at him with her resolute transparent eyes, a designation given them when she demonstrated in Florida an uncharacteristic boldness and assertiveness. Now she lowers her expressive eyes, but a "fugitive flush" passes over her face. After showing him Ellen's letter, she tells him of her warm friendly visit with her cousin the previous day, but she purposefully omits a crucial detail of their conversation.

May, here as elsewhere, seems a strategist of the sharpest kind as Archer's declaration to her is checked.

And May continues to display a toughness and tenacity of purpose in the days that follow. At Ellen's farewell dinner—which May planned—even Archer catches "the glitter of victory in his wife's eyes." Nonetheless, after the guests have departed, he once more attempts to tell her that he must get away from everything and ultimately join Ellen. May, "all dew and roses," interrupts him before he can proceed. Demurely hiding her face, she tells him that she is pregnant. Then, with "blood flushing up to her forehead," she also discloses that she revealed her condition to Ellen during their long conversation two weeks before. When her husband questions her further, she admits to not having been certain at that time, but with "blue eyes wet with victory," she exclaims that now she knows she was correct.

Consequently, Archer, a man of honor and tradition, displays the same steadfast character of two years before when May advanced the wedding date. He remains with his wife and forsakes the woman he loves.

Ironically, years later, long after May's death giving birth to their third child, he discovers that his wife had told her eldest son the day before she died that once, at her request, his father had given up the thing he most wanted. Archer is stunned by this new insight into May's character, for throughout their marriage, he had persisted in his judgment that she was incapable of an unexpected mood or a new idea or emotion, that in fact, she lacked imagination and was "incapable of growth." As Margaret B. McDowell points out:

> His egocentric temperament, which limits his imagination, prevents him from seeing May as a woman instead of a stereotype. He never sees that what he calls "her abysmal purity" is a myth largely of his own formulation—one that underestimates her intelligence and the extent of her worldly knowledge.

Had he reflected carefully on the circumstances of his hasty wedding ceremony as well as on the details leading to his final parting with Ellen, perhaps Archer would have seen evidence of his wife's "potential for growth and change" while she was still alive. Certainly May's ingenuity was not lacking in that final scene with her son when she told him that it was at her request that his father had given up what he had wanted most.

Wharton's intention and meaning as to May's role and significance in the novel, therefore, seem clear. The toughness and tenacity, the depth of feeling and strength of character were always present in May, and Wharton provides clear evidence of these characteristics in her symbolic treatment of May's expressive eyes. (pp. 43-8)

Evelyn E. Fracasso, "The Transparent Eyes of May Welland in Wharton's 'The Age of Innocence'," in Modern Language Studies, *Vol. 21, No. 4, Fall, 1991, pp. 43-8.*

FURTHER READING

Criticism

Auchincloss, Louis. "Edith Wharton and Her New Yorks." *Partisan Review* XVIII, No. 4 (July-August 1951): 411-19.

> Discusses Wharton's portrayal of New York throughout her career. Auchincloss suggests that Wharton herself felt that her depiction of New York society became unduly negative during the course of her career and that *The Age of Innocence* reflects her acknowledgment of the value of certain aspects of the social order she had earlier satirized.

Blackall, Jean Frantz. "The Intrusive Voice: Telegrams in *The House of Mirth* and *The Age of Innocence.*" *Women's Studies Quarterly* 20, No. 2 (1991): 163-68.

> Discussion and comparison of Wharton's use of inter-character correspondence in two of her novels.

Chandler, Marilyn R. "*The Age of Innocence:* Tribal Rites in the Urban Village." In her *Dwelling in the Text: Houses in American Fiction,* pp. 149-79. Los Angeles: University of California Press, 1991.

> In-depth examination of architectural and interior design details and their role as metaphors for "pretentious elaboration of class structures and rituals" in *The Age of Innocence.*

Dooley, R. B. "A Footnote to Edith Wharton." *American Literature* 26 (March 1954): 78-85.

> Description of members of New York's nineteenth-century upper-class society who are thought to have been models for Wharton's characters in *The Age of Innocence.*

Lawson, Richard H. "*The Age of Innocence.*" In his *Edith Wharton,* pp. 15-28. New York: Frederick Ungar Publishing, 1977.

Examination of *The Age of Innocence* and its significance in the course of Wharton's career.

Lubbock, Percy. *Portrait of Edith Wharton.* New York: D. Appleton-Century, 1947, 249 p.

> A profile of Wharton consisting of reminiscences by her friends and excerpts from letters.

McDowell, Margaret B. "*The Age of Innocence.*" In her *Edith Wharton,* pp. 92-104. Boston: Twayne Publishers, 1976.

> Critical analysis of the structure, social context, and symbolism of *The Age of Innocence.*

McWilliams, Jim. "Wharton's *The Age of Innocence.*" *The Explicator* 48, No. 4 (Summer 1990): 268-70.

> Focuses on Wharton's portrayal of Ellen Olenska's hands as a symbol of freedom.

Mizener, Arthur. "*The Age of Innocence.*" In his *Twelve Great American Novels,* pp. 68-86. New York: New American Library, 1967.

> Assessment of *The Age of Innocence* in the context of Wharton's life and career.

Strout, Cushing. "Complementary Novels of Manners by James, Wharton, Howells, and Cahan." In his *Making American Tradition: Visions and Revisions from Ben Franklin to Alice Walker,* pp. 52-71. New Brunswick: Rutgers University Press, 1990.

> Comparative discussion of *The Age of Innocence* and Henry James's novel *The Portrait of a Lady,* published in 1881.

Wolff, Cynthia Griffin. "Studies of Salamanders: The Fiction, 1912-1920." In her *A Feast of Words: The Triumph of Edith Wharton,* pp. 189-334. New York: Oxford University Press, 1977.

> Critical analysis of *The Age of Innocence* in a biographical and critical study of Wharton's life and works.

Additional coverage of Wharton's life and career is contained in the following sources published by Gale Research: *Concise Dictionary of American Literary Biography,* 1865-1917; *Contemporary Authors,* Vols. 104, 132; *Dictionary of Literary Biography,* Vols. 4, 9, 12, 78; *DISCovering Authors; Major 20th-Century Writers; Short Story Criticism,* Vol. 6; *Twentieth-Century Literary Criticism,* Vols. 3, 9, 27; and *World Literature Criticism.*

Twentieth-Century Literary Criticism

Cumulative Indexes
Volumes 1-53

How to Use This Index

The main references

```
Calvino, Italo
    1923-1985.....CLC 5, 8, 11, 22, 33, 39,
                                73; SSC 3
```

list all author entries in the following Gale Literary Criticism series:

BLC = *Black Literature Criticism*
CLC = *Contemporary Literary Criticism*
CLR = *Children's Literature Review*
CMLC = *Classical and Medieval Literature Criticism*
DA = *DISCovering Authors*
DC = *Drama Criticism*
HLC = *Hispanic Literature Criticism*
LC = *Literature Criticism from 1400 to 1800*
NCLC = *Nineteenth-Century Literature Criticism*
PC = *Poetry Criticism*
SSC = *Short Story Criticism*
TCLC = *Twentieth-Century Literary Criticism*
WLC = *World Literature Criticism, 1500 to the Present*

The cross-references

```
See also CANR 23; CA 85-88;
    obituary CA 116
```

list all author entries in the following Gale biographical and literary sources:

AAYA = *Authors & Artists for Young Adults*
AITN = *Authors in the News*
BEST = *Bestsellers*
BW = *Black Writers*
CA = *Contemporary Authors*
CAAS = *Contemporary Authors Autobiography Series*
CABS = *Contemporary Authors Bibliographical Series*
CANR = *Contemporary Authors New Revision Series*
CAP = *Contemporary Authors Permanent Series*
CDALB = *Concise Dictionary of American Literary Biography*
CDBLB = *Concise Dictionary of British Literary Biography*
DLB = *Dictionary of Literary Biography*
DLBD = *Dictionary of Literary Biography Documentary Series*
DLBY = *Dictionary of Literary Biography Yearbook*
HW = *Hispanic Writers*
JRDA = *Junior DISCovering Authors*
MAICYA = *Major Authors and Illustrators for Children and Young Adults*
MTCW = *Major 20th-Century Writers*
SAAS = *Something about the Author Autobiography Series*
SATA = *Something about the Author*
YABC = *Yesterday's Authors of Books for Children*

Literary Criticism Series
Cumulative Author Index

A.
See Arnold, Matthew

A. E. . . . . TCLC 3, 10
See also Russell, George William
See also DLB 19

A. M.
See Megged, Aharon

A. R. P-C
See Galsworthy, John

Abasiyanik, Sait Faik   1906-1954
See Sait Faik
See also CA 123

Abbey, Edward   1927-1989 . . . . . . CLC 36, 59
See also CA 45-48; 128; CANR 2, 41

Abbott, Lee K(ittredge)   1947- . . . . . . CLC 48
See also CA 124; DLB 130

Abe, Kobo   1924-1993 . . . . . CLC 8, 22, 53, 81
See also CA 65-68; 140; CANR 24; MTCW

Abelard, Peter   c. 1079-c. 1142 . . . CMLC 11
See also DLB 115

Abell, Kjeld   1901-1961 . . . . CLC 15
See also CA 111

Abish, Walter   1931- . . . . CLC 22
See also CA 101; CANR 37; DLB 130

Abrahams, Peter (Henry)   1919- . . . . . CLC 4
See also BW; CA 57-60; CANR 26;
DLB 117; MTCW

Abrams, M(eyer) H(oward)   1912- . . . CLC 24
See also CA 57-60; CANR 13, 33; DLB 67

Abse, Dannie   1923- . . . . CLC 7, 29
See also CA 53-56; CAAS 1; CANR 4;
DLB 27

Achebe, (Albert) Chinua(lumogu)
1930- . . . . . CLC 1, 3, 5, 7, 11, 26, 51, 75;
BLC 1; DA; WLC
See also BW; CA 1-4R; CANR 6, 26;
CLR 20; DLB 117; MAICYA; MTCW;
SATA 38, 40

Acker, Kathy   1948- . . . . CLC 45
See also CA 117; 122

Ackroyd, Peter   1949- . . . . CLC 34, 52
See also CA 123; 127

Acorn, Milton   1923- . . . . CLC 15
See also CA 103; DLB 53

Adamov, Arthur   1908-1970 . . . . . . CLC 4, 25
See also CA 17-18; 25-28R; CAP 2; MTCW

Adams, Alice (Boyd)   1926- . . . CLC 6, 13, 46
See also CA 81-84; CANR 26; DLBY 86;
MTCW

Adams, Douglas (Noel)   1952- . . . CLC 27, 60
See also AAYA 4; BEST 89:3; CA 106;
CANR 34; DLBY 83; JRDA

Adams, Francis   1862-1893 . . . . NCLC 33

Adams, Henry (Brooks)
1838-1918 . . . . TCLC 4, 52; DA
See also CA 104; 133; DLB 12, 47

Adams, Richard (George)
1920- . . . . CLC 4, 5, 18
See also AITN 1, 2; CA 49-52; CANR 3,
35; CLR 20; JRDA; MAICYA; MTCW;
SATA 7, 69

Adamson, Joy(-Friederike Victoria)
1910-1980 . . . . CLC 17
See also CA 69-72; 93-96; CANR 22;
MTCW; SATA 11, 22

Adcock, Fleur   1934- . . . . CLC 41
See also CA 25-28R; CANR 11, 34;
DLB 40

Addams, Charles (Samuel)
1912-1988 . . . . CLC 30
See also CA 61-64; 126; CANR 12

Addison, Joseph   1672-1719 . . . . LC 18
See also CDBLB 1660-1789; DLB 101

Adler, C(arole) S(chwerdtfeger)
1932- . . . . CLC 35
See also AAYA 4; CA 89-92; CANR 19,
40; JRDA; MAICYA; SAAS 15;
SATA 26, 63

Adler, Renata   1938- . . . . CLC 8, 31
See also CA 49-52; CANR 5, 22; MTCW

Ady, Endre   1877-1919 . . . . TCLC 11
See also CA 107

Aeschylus
525B.C.-456B.C. . . . . CMLC 11; DA

Afton, Effie
See Harper, Frances Ellen Watkins

Agapida, Fray Antonio
See Irving, Washington

Agee, James (Rufus)
1909-1955 . . . . TCLC 1, 19
See also AITN 1; CA 108;
CDALB 1941-1968; DLB 2, 26

Aghill, Gordon
See Silverberg, Robert

Agnon, S(hmuel) Y(osef Halevi)
1888-1970 . . . . CLC 4, 8, 14
See also CA 17-18; 25-28R; CAP 2; MTCW

Aherne, Owen
See Cassill, R(onald) V(erlin)

Ai   1947- . . . . CLC 4, 14, 69
See also CA 85-88; CAAS 13; DLB 120

Aickman, Robert (Fordyce)
1914-1981 . . . . CLC 57
See also CA 5-8R; CANR 3

Aiken, Conrad (Potter)
1889-1973 . . . CLC 1, 3, 5, 10, 52; SSC 9
See also CA 5-8R; 45-48; CANR 4;
CDALB 1929-1941; DLB 9, 45, 102;
MTCW; SATA 3, 30

Aiken, Joan (Delano)   1924- . . . . CLC 35
See also AAYA 1; CA 9-12R; CANR 4, 23,
34; CLR 1, 19; JRDA; MAICYA;
MTCW; SAAS 1; SATA 2, 30, 73

Ainsworth, William Harrison
1805-1882 . . . . NCLC 13
See also DLB 21; SATA 24

Aitmatov, Chingiz (Torekulovich)
1928- . . . . CLC 71
See also CA 103; CANR 38; MTCW;
SATA 56

Akers, Floyd
See Baum, L(yman) Frank

Akhmadulina, Bella Akhatovna
1937- . . . . CLC 53
See also CA 65-68

Akhmatova, Anna
1888-1966 . . . . CLC 11, 25, 64; PC 2
See also CA 19-20; 25-28R; CANR 35;
CAP 1; MTCW

Aksakov, Sergei Timofeyvich
1791-1859 . . . . NCLC 2

Aksenov, Vassily . . . . CLC 22
See also Aksyonov, Vassily (Pavlovich)

Aksyonov, Vassily (Pavlovich)
1932- . . . . CLC 37
See also Aksenov, Vassily
See also CA 53-56; CANR 12

Akutagawa Ryunosuke
1892-1927 . . . . TCLC 16
See also CA 117

Alain   1868-1951 . . . . TCLC 41

Alain-Fournier . . . . TCLC 6
See also Fournier, Henri Alban
See also DLB 65

Alarcon, Pedro Antonio de
1833-1891 . . . . NCLC 1

Alas (y Urena), Leopoldo (Enrique Garcia)
1852-1901 . . . . TCLC 29
See also CA 113; 131; HW

Albee, Edward (Franklin III)
1928- . . . . . . CLC 1, 2, 3, 5, 9, 11, 13, 25,
53; DA; WLC
See also AITN 1; CA 5-8R; CABS 3;
CANR 8; CDALB 1941-1968; DLB 7;
MTCW

Alberti, Rafael   1902- . . . . CLC 7
See also CA 85-88; DLB 108

Alcala-Galiano, Juan Valera y
See Valera y Alcala-Galiano, Juan

Alcott, Amos Bronson   1799-1888 . . NCLC 1
See also DLB 1

Alcott, Louisa May
1832-1888 . . . . NCLC 6; DA; WLC
See also CDALB 1865-1917; CLR 1;
DLB 1, 42, 79; JRDA; MAICYA;
YABC 1

Aldanov, M. A.
See Aldanov, Mark (Alexandrovich)

Aldanov, Mark (Alexandrovich)
1886(?)-1957 . . . . TCLC 23
See also CA 118

Aldington, Richard 1892-1962...... **CLC 49**
See also CA 85-88; DLB 20, 36, 100

Aldiss, Brian W(ilson)
1925-................. **CLC 5, 14, 40**
See also CA 5-8R; CAAS 2; CANR 5, 28;
DLB 14; MTCW; SATA 34

Alegria, Claribel 1924-............ **CLC 75**
See also CA 131; CAAS 15; HW

Alegria, Fernando 1918-........... **CLC 57**
See also CA 9-12R; CANR 5, 32; HW

Aleichem, Sholom .... **TCLC 1, 35**
See also Rabinovitch, Sholem

Aleixandre, Vicente 1898-1984 ... **CLC 9, 36**
See also CA 85-88; 114; CANR 26;
DLB 108; HW; MTCW

Alepoudelis, Odysseus
See Elytis, Odysseus

Aleshkovsky, Joseph 1929-
See Aleshkovsky, Yuz
See also CA 121; 128

Aleshkovsky, Yuz .... **CLC 44**
See also Aleshkovsky, Joseph

Alexander, Lloyd (Chudley) 1924- .. **CLC 35**
See also AAYA 1; CA 1-4R; CANR 1, 24,
38; CLR 1, 5; DLB 52; JRDA; MAICYA;
MTCW; SATA 3, 49

Alfau, Felipe 1902-............... **CLC 66**
See also CA 137

Alger, Horatio, Jr. 1832-1899..... **NCLC 8**
See also DLB 42; SATA 16

Algren, Nelson 1909-1981 .... **CLC 4, 10, 33**
See also CA 13-16R; 103; CANR 20;
CDALB 1941-1968; DLB 9; DLBY 81,
82; MTCW

Ali, Ahmed 1910-................ **CLC 69**
See also CA 25-28R; CANR 15, 34

Alighieri, Dante 1265-1321 .... **CMLC 3**

Allan, John B.
See Westlake, Donald E(dwin)

Allen, Edward 1948-.............. **CLC 59**

Allen, Roland
See Ayckbourn, Alan

Allen, Sarah A.
See Hopkins, Pauline Elizabeth

Allen, Woody 1935-........... **CLC 16, 52**
See also AAYA 10; CA 33-36R; CANR 27,
38; DLB 44; MTCW

Allende, Isabel 1942- ... **CLC 39, 57; HLC 1**
See also CA 125; 130; HW; MTCW

Alleyn, Ellen
See Rossetti, Christina (Georgina)

Allingham, Margery (Louise)
1904-1966 .... **CLC 19**
See also CA 5-8R; 25-28R; CANR 4;
DLB 77; MTCW

Allingham, William 1824-1889 ... **NCLC 25**
See also DLB 35

Allison, Dorothy E. 1949- .... **CLC 78**
See also CA 140

Allston, Washington 1779-1843.... **NCLC 2**
See also DLB 1

Almedingen, E. M. .... **CLC 12**
See also Almedingen, Martha Edith von
See also SATA 3

Almedingen, Martha Edith von 1898-1971
See Almedingen, E. M.
See also CA 1-4R; CANR 1

Almqvist, Carl Jonas Love
1793-1866 .... **NCLC 42**

Alonso, Damaso 1898-1990 .... **CLC 14**
See also CA 110; 131; 130; DLB 108; HW

Alov
See Gogol, Nikolai (Vasilyevich)

Alta 1942-...................... **CLC 19**
See also CA 57-60

Alter, Robert B(ernard) 1935-...... **CLC 34**
See also CA 49-52; CANR 1

Alther, Lisa 1944-.............. **CLC 7, 41**
See also CA 65-68; CANR 12, 30; MTCW

Altman, Robert 1925-............. **CLC 16**
See also CA 73-76; CANR 43

Alvarez, A(lfred) 1929-........... **CLC 5, 13**
See also CA 1-4R; CANR 3, 33; DLB 14,
40

Alvarez, Alejandro Rodriguez 1903-1965
See Casona, Alejandro
See also CA 131; 93-96; HW

Amado, Jorge 1912-.... **CLC 13, 40; HLC 1**
See also CA 77-80; CANR 35; DLB 113;
MTCW

Ambler, Eric 1909-........... **CLC 4, 6, 9**
See also CA 9-12R; CANR 7, 38; DLB 77;
MTCW

Amichai, Yehuda 1924- ...... **CLC 9, 22, 57**
See also CA 85-88; MTCW

Amiel, Henri Frederic 1821-1881 .. **NCLC 4**

Amis, Kingsley (William)
1922- ... **CLC 1, 2, 3, 5, 8, 13, 40, 44; DA**
See also AITN 2; CA 9-12R; CANR 8, 28;
CDBLB 1945-1960; DLB 15, 27, 100;
MTCW

Amis, Martin (Louis)
1949- .... **CLC 4, 9, 38, 62**
See also BEST 90:3; CA 65-68; CANR 8,
27; DLB 14

Ammons, A(rchie) R(andolph)
1926- .... **CLC 2, 3, 5, 8, 9, 25, 57**
See also AITN 1; CA 9-12R; CANR 6, 36;
DLB 5; MTCW

Amo, Tauraatua i
See Adams, Henry (Brooks)

Anand, Mulk Raj 1905-........... **CLC 23**
See also CA 65-68; CANR 32; MTCW

Anatol
See Schnitzler, Arthur

Anaya, Rudolfo A(lfonso)
1937- .... **CLC 23; HLC 1**
See also CA 45-48; CAAS 4; CANR 1, 32;
DLB 82; HW 1; MTCW

Andersen, Hans Christian
1805-1875 .. **NCLC 7; DA; SSC 6; WLC**
See also CLR 6; MAICYA; YABC 1

Anderson, C. Farley
See Mencken, H(enry) L(ouis); Nathan,
George Jean

Anderson, Jessica (Margaret) Queale
.... **CLC 37**
See also CA 9-12R; CANR 4

Anderson, Jon (Victor) 1940- .... **CLC 9**
See also CA 25-28R; CANR 20

Anderson, Lindsay (Gordon)
1923-...................... **CLC 20**
See also CA 125; 128

Anderson, Maxwell 1888-1959 ..... **TCLC 2**
See also CA 105; DLB 7

Anderson, Poul (William) 1926- .... **CLC 15**
See also AAYA 5; CA 1-4R; CAAS 2;
CANR 2, 15, 34; DLB 8; MTCW;
SATA 39

Anderson, Robert (Woodruff)
1917-...................... **CLC 23**
See also AITN 1; CA 21-24R; CANR 32;
DLB 7

Anderson, Sherwood
1876-1941 .... **TCLC 1, 10, 24; DA;
SSC 1; WLC**
See also CA 104; 121; CDALB 1917-1929;
DLB 4, 9, 86; DLBD 1; MTCW

Andouard
See Giraudoux, (Hippolyte) Jean

Andrade, Carlos Drummond de ...... **CLC 18**
See also Drummond de Andrade, Carlos

Andrade, Mario de 1893-1945..... **TCLC 43**

Andrewes, Lancelot 1555-1626 .... **LC 5**

Andrews, Cicily Fairfield
See West, Rebecca

Andrews, Elton V.
See Pohl, Frederik

Andreyev, Leonid (Nikolaevich)
1871-1919 .... **TCLC 3**
See also CA 104

Andric, Ivo 1892-1975 .... **CLC 8**
See also CA 81-84; 57-60; CANR 43;
MTCW

Angelique, Pierre
See Bataille, Georges

Angell, Roger 1920-.............. **CLC 26**
See also CA 57-60; CANR 13

Angelou, Maya
1928- ... **CLC 12, 35, 64, 77; BLC 1; DA**
See also AAYA 7; BW; CA 65-68;
CANR 19, 42; DLB 38; MTCW;
SATA 49

Annensky, Innokenty Fyodorovich
1856-1909 .... **TCLC 14**
See also CA 110

Anon, Charles Robert
See Pessoa, Fernando (Antonio Nogueira)

Anouilh, Jean (Marie Lucien Pierre)
1910-1987 ...... **CLC 1, 3, 8, 13, 40, 50**
See also CA 17-20R; 123; CANR 32;
MTCW

Anthony, Florence
See Ai

Anthony, John
See Ciardi, John (Anthony)

Anthony, Peter
See Shaffer, Anthony (Joshua); Shaffer,
Peter (Levin)

Anthony, Piers 1934-.............. **CLC 35**
See also CA 21-24R; CANR 28; DLB 8;
MTCW

Antoine, Marc
See Proust, (Valentin-Louis-George-Eugene-) Marcel

Antoninus, Brother
See Everson, William (Oliver)

Antonioni, Michelangelo 1912-..... **CLC 20**
See also CA 73-76

Antschel, Paul 1920-1970...... **CLC 10, 19**
See also Celan, Paul
See also CA 85-88; CANR 33; MTCW

Anwar, Chairil 1922-1949 .... **TCLC 22**
See also CA 121

Apollinaire, Guillaume .. **TCLC 3, 8, 51; PC 7**
See also Kostrowitzki, Wilhelm Apollinaris de

Appelfeld, Aharon 1932-....... **CLC 23, 47**
See also CA 112; 133

Apple, Max (Isaac) 1941-........ **CLC 9, 33**
See also CA 81-84; CANR 19; DLB 130

Appleman, Philip (Dean) 1926-..... **CLC 51**
See also CA 13-16R; CAAS 18; CANR 6, 29

Appleton, Lawrence
See Lovecraft, H(oward) P(hillips)

Apteryx
See Eliot, T(homas) S(tearns)

Apuleius, (Lucius Madaurensis)
125(?)-175(?) .... **CMLC 1**

Aquin, Hubert 1929-1977......... **CLC 15**
See also CA 105; DLB 53

Aragon, Louis 1897-1982........ **CLC 3, 22**
See also CA 69-72; 108; CANR 28; DLB 72; MTCW

Arany, Janos 1817-1882........ **NCLC 34**

Arbuthnot, John 1667-1735.......... **LC 1**
See also DLB 101

Archer, Herbert Winslow
See Mencken, H(enry) L(ouis)

Archer, Jeffrey (Howard) 1940-.... **CLC 28**
See also BEST 89:3; CA 77-80; CANR 22

Archer, Jules 1915- .... **CLC 12**
See also CA 9-12R; CANR 6; SAAS 5; SATA 4

Archer, Lee
See Ellison, Harlan

Arden, John 1930- .... **CLC 6, 13, 15**
See also CA 13-16R; CAAS 4; CANR 31; DLB 13; MTCW

Arenas, Reinaldo
1943-1990 .... **CLC 41; HLC 1**
See also CA 124; 128; 133; HW

Arendt, Hannah 1906-1975 .... **CLC 66**
See also CA 17-20R; 61-64; CANR 26; MTCW

Aretino, Pietro 1492-1556 .... **LC 12**

Arghezi, Tudor................... **CLC 80**
See also Theodorescu, Ion N.

Arguedas, Jose Maria
1911-1969 .... **CLC 10, 18**
See also CA 89-92; DLB 113; HW

Argueta, Manlio 1936-............ **CLC 31**
See also CA 131; HW

Ariosto, Ludovico 1474-1533........ **LC 6**

Aristides
See Epstein, Joseph

Aristophanes
450B.C.-385B.C.... **CMLC 4; DA; DC 2**

Arlt, Roberto (Godofredo Christophersen)
1900-1942 .... **TCLC 29; HLC 1**
See also CA 123; 131; HW

Armah, Ayi Kwei 1939-.. **CLC 5, 33; BLC 1**
See also BW; CA 61-64; CANR 21; DLB 117; MTCW

Armatrading, Joan 1950-......... **CLC 17**
See also CA 114

Arnette, Robert
See Silverberg, Robert

Arnim, Achim von (Ludwig Joachim von Arnim) 1781-1831 .... **NCLC 5**
See also DLB 90

Arnim, Bettina von 1785-1859.... **NCLC 38**
See also DLB 90

Arnold, Matthew
1822-1888 ..... **NCLC 6, 29; DA; PC 5; WLC**
See also CDBLB 1832-1890; DLB 32, 57

Arnold, Thomas 1795-1842 ...... **NCLC 18**
See also DLB 55

Arnow, Harriette (Louisa) Simpson
1908-1986 .... **CLC 2, 7, 18**
See also CA 9-12R; 118; CANR 14; DLB 6; MTCW; SATA 42, 47

Arp, Hans
See Arp, Jean

Arp, Jean 1887-1966............... **CLC 5**
See also CA 81-84; 25-28R; CANR 42

Arrabal
See Arrabal, Fernando

Arrabal, Fernando 1932-... **CLC 2, 9, 18, 58**
See also CA 9-12R; CANR 15

Arrick, Fran..................... **CLC 30**

Artaud, Antonin 1896-1948 ..... **TCLC 3, 36**
See also CA 104

Arthur, Ruth M(abel) 1905-1979.... **CLC 12**
See also CA 9-12R; 85-88; CANR 4; SATA 7, 26

Artsybashev, Mikhail (Potrovich)
1878-1927 .... **TCLC 31**

Arundel, Honor (Morfydd)
1919-1973 .... **CLC 17**
See also CA 21-22; 41-44R; CAP 2; SATA 4, 24

Asch, Sholem 1880-1957 .... **TCLC 3**
See also CA 105

Ash, Shalom
See Asch, Sholem

Ashbery, John (Lawrence)
1927-...... **CLC 2, 3, 4, 6, 9, 13, 15, 25, 41, 77**
See also CA 5-8R; CANR 9, 37; DLB 5; DLBY 81; MTCW

Ashdown, Clifford
See Freeman, R(ichard) Austin

Ashe, Gordon
See Creasey, John

Ashton-Warner, Sylvia (Constance)
1908-1984 .... **CLC 19**
See also CA 69-72; 112; CANR 29; MTCW

Asimov, Isaac
1920-1992 ...... **CLC 1, 3, 9, 19, 26, 76**
See also BEST 90:2; CA 1-4R; 137; CANR 2, 19, 36; CLR 12; DLB 8; DLBY 92; JRDA; MAICYA; MTCW; SATA 1, 26, 74

Astley, Thea (Beatrice May)
1925-..................... **CLC 41**
See also CA 65-68; CANR 11, 43

Aston, James
See White, T(erence) H(anbury)

Asturias, Miguel Angel
1899-1974 .... **CLC 3, 8, 13; HLC 1**
See also CA 25-28; 49-52; CANR 32; CAP 2; DLB 113; HW; MTCW

Atares, Carlos Saura
See Saura (Atares), Carlos

Atheling, William
See Pound, Ezra (Weston Loomis)

Atheling, William, Jr.
See Blish, James (Benjamin)

Atherton, Gertrude (Franklin Horn)
1857-1948 .... **TCLC 2**
See also CA 104; DLB 9, 78

Atherton, Lucius
See Masters, Edgar Lee

Atkins, Jack
See Harris, Mark

Atticus
See Fleming, Ian (Lancaster)

Atwood, Margaret (Eleanor)
1939-..... **CLC 2, 3, 4, 8, 13, 15, 25, 44; DA; PC 8; SSC 2; WLC**
See also BEST 89:2; CA 49-52; CANR 3, 24, 33; DLB 53; MTCW; SATA 50

Aubigny, Pierre d'
See Mencken, H(enry) L(ouis)

Aubin, Penelope 1685-1731(?)........ **LC 9**
See also DLB 39

Auchincloss, Louis (Stanton)
1917-.............. **CLC 4, 6, 9, 18, 45**
See also CA 1-4R; CANR 6, 29; DLB 2; DLBY 80; MTCW

Auden, W(ystan) H(ugh)
1907-1973 ...... **CLC 1, 2, 3, 4, 6, 9, 11, 14, 43; DA; PC 1; WLC**
See also CA 9-12R; 45-48; CANR 5; CDBLB 1914-1945; DLB 10, 20; MTCW

Audiberti, Jacques 1900-1965 ...... **CLC 38**
See also CA 25-28R

Auel, Jean M(arie) 1936-.......... **CLC 31**
See also AAYA 7; BEST 90:4; CA 103; CANR 21

Auerbach, Erich 1892-1957 .... **TCLC 43**
See also CA 118

Augier, Emile 1820-1889 .... **NCLC 31**

August, John
See De Voto, Bernard (Augustine)

Augustine, St. 354-430 .... **CMLC 6**

Aurelius
See Bourne, Randolph S(illiman)

Baroja (y Nessi), Pio
1872-1956 . . . . **TCLC 8; HLC 1**
See also CA 104

Baron, David
See Pinter, Harold

Baron Corvo
See Rolfe, Frederick (William Serafino
Austin Lewis Mary)

Barondess, Sue K(aufman)
1926-1977 . . . . **CLC 8**
See also Kaufman, Sue
See also CA 1-4R; 69-72; CANR 1

Baron de Teive
See Pessoa, Fernando (Antonio Nogueira)

Barres, Maurice 1862-1923 . . . . **TCLC 47**
See also DLB 123

Barreto, Afonso Henrique de Lima
See Lima Barreto, Afonso Henrique de

Barrett, (Roger) Syd 1946- . . . . **CLC 35**
See also Pink Floyd

Barrett, William (Christopher)
1913-1992 . . . . **CLC 27**
See also CA 13-16R; 139; CANR 11

Barrie, J(ames) M(atthew)
1860-1937 . . . . **TCLC 2**
See also CA 104; 136; CDBLB 1890-1914;
CLR 16; DLB 10; MAICYA; YABC 1

Barrington, Michael
See Moorcock, Michael (John)

Barrol, Grady
See Bograd, Larry

Barry, Mike
See Malzberg, Barry N(athaniel)

Barry, Philip 1896-1949 . . . . **TCLC 11**
See also CA 109; DLB 7

Bart, Andre Schwarz
See Schwarz-Bart, Andre

Barth, John (Simmons)
1930- . . . . . . **CLC 1, 2, 3, 5, 7, 9, 10, 14,
27, 51; SSC 10**
See also AITN 1, 2; CA 1-4R; CABS 1;
CANR 5, 23; DLB 2; MTCW

Barthelme, Donald
1931-1989 . . . . . . **CLC 1, 2, 3, 5, 6, 8, 13,
23, 46, 59; SSC 2**
See also CA 21-24R, 129, CANR 20,
DLB 2; DLBY 80, 89; MTCW; SATA 7,
62

Barthelme, Frederick 1943- . . . . **CLC 36**
See also CA 114; 122; DLBY 85

Barthes, Roland (Gerard)
1915-1980 . . . . **CLC 24**
See also CA 130; 97-100; MTCW

Barzun, Jacques (Martin) 1907- . . . . **CLC 51**
See also CA 61-64; CANR 22

Bashevis, Isaac
See Singer, Isaac Bashevis

Bashkirtseff, Marie 1859-1884 . . . **NCLC 27**

Basho
See Matsuo Basho

Bass, Kingsley B., Jr.
See Bullins, Ed

Bass, Rick 1958- . . . . **CLC 79**
See also CA 126

Bassani, Giorgio 1916- . . . . **CLC 9**
See also CA 65-68; CANR 33; DLB 128;
MTCW

Bastos, Augusto (Antonio) Roa
See Roa Bastos, Augusto (Antonio)

Bataille, Georges 1897-1962 . . . . . . **CLC 29**
See also CA 101; 89-92

Bates, H(erbert) E(rnest)
1905-1974 . . . . **CLC 46; SSC 10**
See also CA 93-96; 45-48; CANR 34;
MTCW

Bauchart
See Camus, Albert

Baudelaire, Charles
1821-1867 . . . . . **NCLC 6, 29; DA; PC 1;
WLC**

Baudrillard, Jean 1929- . . . . **CLC 60**

Baum, L(yman) Frank 1856-1919 . . . **TCLC 7**
See also CA 108; 133; CLR 15; DLB 22;
JRDA; MAICYA; MTCW; SATA 18

Baum, Louis F.
See Baum, L(yman) Frank

Baumbach, Jonathan 1933- . . . . . . **CLC 6, 23**
See also CA 13-16R; CAAS 5; CANR 12;
DLBY 80; MTCW

Bausch, Richard (Carl) 1945- . . . . . . **CLC 51**
See also CA 101; CAAS 14; CANR 43;
DLB 130

Baxter, Charles 1947- . . . . **CLC 45, 78**
See also CA 57-60; CANR 40; DLB 130

Baxter, George Owen
See Faust, Frederick (Schiller)

Baxter, James K(eir) 1926-1972 . . . . **CLC 14**
See also CA 77-80

Baxter, John
See Hunt, E(verette) Howard, Jr.

Bayer, Sylvia
See Glassco, John

Beagle, Peter S(oyer) 1939- . . . . **CLC 7**
See also CA 9-12R; CANR 4; DLBY 80;
SATA 60

Bean, Normal
See Burroughs, Edgar Rice

Beard, Charles A(ustin)
1874-1948 . . . . **TCLC 15**
See also CA 115; DLB 17; SATA 18

Beardsley, Aubrey 1872-1898 . . . . . **NCLC 6**

Beattie, Ann
1947- . . . . **CLC 8, 13, 18, 40, 63; SSC 11**
See also BEST 90:2; CA 81-84; DLBY 82;
MTCW

Beattie, James 1735-1803 . . . . **NCLC 25**
See also DLB 109

Beauchamp, Kathleen Mansfield 1888-1923
See Mansfield, Katherine
See also CA 104; 134; DA

Beaumarchais, Pierre-Augustin Caron de
1732-1799 . . . . **DC 4**

**Beauvoir, Simone (Lucie Ernestine Marie
Bertrand) de**
1908-1986 . . . . **CLC 1, 2, 4, 8, 14, 31, 44,
50, 71; DA; WLC**
See also CA 9-12R; 118; CANR 28;
DLB 72; DLBY 86; MTCW

Becker, Jurek 1937- . . . . **CLC 7, 19**
See also CA 85-88; DLB 75

Becker, Walter 1950- . . . . **CLC 26**

Beckett, Samuel (Barclay)
1906-1989 . . . . . . **CLC 1, 2, 3, 4, 6, 9, 10,
11, 14, 18, 29, 57, 59; DA; WLC**
See also CA 5-8R; 130; CANR 33;
CDBLB 1945-1960; DLB 13, 15;
DLBY 90; MTCW

Beckford, William 1760-1844 . . . . **NCLC 16**
See also DLB 39

Beckman, Gunnel 1910- . . . . **CLC 26**
See also CA 33-36R; CANR 15; CLR 25;
MAICYA; SAAS 9; SATA 6

Becque, Henri 1837-1899 . . . . **NCLC 3**

Beddoes, Thomas Lovell
1803-1849 . . . . **NCLC 3**
See also DLB 96

Bedford, Donald F.
See Fearing, Kenneth (Flexner)

Beecher, Catharine Esther
1800-1878 . . . . **NCLC 30**
See also DLB 1

Beecher, John 1904-1980 . . . . **CLC 6**
See also AITN 1; CA 5-8R; 105; CANR 8

Beer, Johann 1655-1700 . . . . **LC 5**

Beer, Patricia 1924- . . . . **CLC 58**
See also CA 61-64; CANR 13; DLB 40

Beerbohm, Henry Maximilian
1872-1956 . . . . **TCLC 1, 24**
See also CA 104; DLB 34, 100

Begiebing, Robert J(ohn) 1946- . . . . . **CLC 70**
See also CA 122; CANR 40

Behan, Brendan
1923-1964 . . . . **CLC 1, 8, 11, 15, 79**
See also CA 73-76; CANR 33;
CDBLB 1945-1960; DLB 13; MTCW

Behn, Aphra
1640(?)-1689 . . . . **LC 1; DA; DC 4; WLC**
See also DLB 39, 80, 131

Behrman, S(amuel) N(athaniel)
1893-1973 . . . . **CLC 40**
See also CA 13-16; 45-48; CAP 1; DLB 7,
44

Belasco, David 1853-1931 . . . . **TCLC 3**
See also CA 104; DLB 7

Belcheva, Elisaveta 1893- . . . . **CLC 10**

Beldone, Phil "Cheech"
See Ellison, Harlan

Beleno
See Azuela, Mariano

Belinski, Vissarion Grigoryevich
1811-1848 . . . . **NCLC 5**

Belitt, Ben 1911- . . . . **CLC 22**
See also CA 13-16R; CAAS 4; CANR 7;
DLB 5

Bell, James Madison
1826-1902 . . . . **TCLC 43; BLC 1**
See also BW; CA 122; 124; DLB 50

Bell, Madison (Smartt) 1957- . . . . . . **CLC 41**
See also CA 111; CANR 28

Bell, Marvin (Hartley) 1937- . . . . . **CLC 8, 31**
See also CA 21-24R; CAAS 14; DLB 5;
MTCW

Bell, W. L. D.
See Mencken, H(enry) L(ouis)

Bellamy, Atwood C.
See Mencken, H(enry) L(ouis)

Bellamy, Edward 1850-1898 ...... NCLC 4
See also DLB 12

Bellin, Edward J.
See Kuttner, Henry

Belloc, (Joseph) Hilaire (Pierre)
1870-1953 .... TCLC 7, 18
See also CA 106; DLB 19, 100; YABC 1

Belloc, Joseph Peter Rene Hilaire
See Belloc, (Joseph) Hilaire (Pierre)

Belloc, Joseph Pierre Hilaire
See Belloc, (Joseph) Hilaire (Pierre)

Belloc, M. A.
See Lowndes, Marie Adelaide (Belloc)

Bellow, Saul
1915- ...... CLC 1, 2, 3, 6, 8, 10, 13, 15,
25, 33, 34, 63, 79; DA; SSC 14; WLC
See also AITN 2; BEST 89:3; CA 5-8R;
CABS 1; CANR 29; CDALB 1941-1968;
DLB 2, 28; DLBD 3; DLBY 82; MTCW

Belser, Reimond Karel Maria de
1929- .... CLC 14

Bely, Andrey .... TCLC 7
See also Bugayev, Boris Nikolayevich

Benary, Margot
See Benary-Isbert, Margot

Benary-Isbert, Margot 1889-1979 ... CLC 12
See also CA 5-8R; 89-92; CANR 4;
CLR 12; MAICYA; SATA 2, 21

Benavente (y Martinez), Jacinto
1866-1954 .... TCLC 3
See also CA 106; 131; HW; MTCW

Benchley, Peter (Bradford)
1940- .... CLC 4, 8
See also AITN 2; CA 17-20R; CANR 12,
35; MTCW; SATA 3

Benchley, Robert (Charles)
1889-1945 .... TCLC 1
See also CA 105; DLB 11

Benedikt, Michael 1935- .... CLC 4, 14
See also CA 13-16R; CANR 7; DLB 5

Benet, Juan 1927- .... CLC 28

Benet, Stephen Vincent
1898-1943 .... TCLC 7; SSC 10
See also CA 104; DLB 4, 48, 102; YABC 1

Benet, William Rose 1886-1950 ... TCLC 28
See also CA 118; DLB 45

Benford, Gregory (Albert) 1941- .... CLC 52
See also CA 69-72; CANR 12, 24;
DLBY 82

Bengtsson, Frans (Gunnar)
1894-1954 .... TCLC 48

Benjamin, David
See Slavitt, David R(ytman)

Benjamin, Lois
See Gould, Lois

Benjamin, Walter 1892-1940 ..... TCLC 39

Benn, Gottfried 1886-1956........ TCLC 3
See also CA 106; DLB 56

Bennett, Alan 1934- .... CLC 45, 77
See also CA 103; CANR 35; MTCW

Bennett, (Enoch) Arnold
1867-1931 .... TCLC 5, 20
See also CA 106; CDBLB 1890-1914;
DLB 10, 34, 98

Bennett, Elizabeth
See Mitchell, Margaret (Munnerlyn)

Bennett, George Harold 1930-
See Bennett, Hal
See also BW; CA 97-100

Bennett, Hal .... CLC 5
See also Bennett, George Harold
See also DLB 33

Bennett, Jay 1912- .... CLC 35
See also AAYA 10; CA 69-72; CANR 11,
42; JRDA; SAAS 4; SATA 27, 41

Bennett, Louise (Simone)
1919- .... CLC 28; BLC 1
See also DLB 117

Benson, E(dward) F(rederic)
1867-1940 .... TCLC 27
See also CA 114; DLB 135

Benson, Jackson J. 1930- .... CLC 34
See also CA 25-28R; DLB 111

Benson, Sally 1900-1972 .... CLC 17
See also CA 19-20; 37-40R; CAP 1;
SATA 1, 27, 35

Benson, Stella 1892-1933........ TCLC 17
See also CA 117; DLB 36

Bentham, Jeremy 1748-1832 ..... NCLC 38
See also DLB 107

Bentley, E(dmund) C(lerihew)
1875-1956 .... TCLC 12
See also CA 108; DLB 70

Bentley, Eric (Russell) 1916-...... CLC 24
See also CA 5-8R; CANR 6

Beranger, Pierre Jean de
1780-1857 .... NCLC 34

Berger, Colonel
See Malraux, (Georges-)Andre

Berger, John (Peter) 1926- .... CLC 2, 19
See also CA 81-84; DLB 14

Berger, Melvin H. 1927- .... CLC 12
See also CA 5-8R; CANR 4; CLR 32;
SAAS 2; SATA 5

Berger, Thomas (Louis)
1924- .... CLC 3, 5, 8, 11, 18, 38
See also CA 1-4R; CANR 5, 28; DLB 2;
DLBY 80; MTCW

Bergman, (Ernst) Ingmar
1918- .... CLC 16, 72
See also CA 81-84; CANR 33

Bergson, Henri 1859-1941....... TCLC 32

Bergstein, Eleanor 1938- .... CLC 4
See also CA 53-56; CANR 5

Berkoff, Steven 1937-............. CLC 56
See also CA 104

Bermant, Chaim (Icyk) 1929- ...... CLC 40
See also CA 57-60; CANR 6, 31

Bern, Victoria
See Fisher, M(ary) F(rances) K(ennedy)

Bernanos, (Paul Louis) Georges
1888-1948 .... TCLC 3
See also CA 104; 130; DLB 72

Bernard, April 1956- .... CLC 59
See also CA 131

Bernhard, Thomas
1931-1989 .... CLC 3, 32, 61
See also CA 85-88; 127; CANR 32;
DLB 85, 124; MTCW

Berrigan, Daniel 1921-............. CLC 4
See also CA 33-36R; CAAS 1; CANR 11,
43; DLB 5

Berrigan, Edmund Joseph Michael, Jr.
1934-1983
See Berrigan, Ted
See also CA 61-64; 110; CANR 14

Berrigan, Ted..................... CLC 37
See also Berrigan, Edmund Joseph Michael,
Jr.
See also DLB 5

Berry, Charles Edward Anderson 1931-
See Berry, Chuck
See also CA 115

Berry, Chuck .... CLC 17
See also Berry, Charles Edward Anderson

Berry, Jonas
See Ashbery, John (Lawrence)

Berry, Wendell (Erdman)
1934- .... CLC 4, 6, 8, 27, 46
See also AITN 1; CA 73-76; DLB 5, 6

Berryman, John
1914-1972 ...... CLC 1, 2, 3, 4, 6, 8, 10,
13, 25, 62
See also CA 13-16; 33-36R; CABS 2;
CANR 35; CAP 1; CDALB 1941-1968;
DLB 48; MTCW

Bertolucci, Bernardo 1940- .... CLC 16
See also CA 106

Bertrand, Aloysius 1807-1841 .... NCLC 31

Bertran de Born c. 1140-1215..... CMLC 5

Besant, Annie (Wood) 1847-1933 ... TCLC 9
See also CA 105

Bessie, Alvah 1904-1985.......... CLC 23
See also CA 5-8R; 116; CANR 2; DLB 26

Bethlen, T. D.
See Silverberg, Robert

Beti, Mongo.............. CLC 27; BLC 1
See also Biyidi, Alexandre

Betjeman, John
1906-1984 .... CLC 2, 6, 10, 34, 43
See also CA 9-12R; 112; CANR 33;
CDBLB 1945-1960; DLB 20; DLBY 84;
MTCW

Bettelheim, Bruno 1903-1990 ...... CLC 79
See also CA 81-84; 131; CANR 23; MTCW

Betti, Ugo 1892-1953............. TCLC 5
See also CA 104

Betts, Doris (Waugh) 1932-.... CLC 3, 6, 28
See also CA 13-16R; CANR 9; DLBY 82

Bevan, Alistair
See Roberts, Keith (John Kingston)

Beynon, John
See Harris, John (Wyndham Parkes Lucas)
Beynon

Bialik, Chaim Nachman
1873-1934 .... TCLC 25

Bickerstaff, Isaac
See Swift, Jonathan

Bidart, Frank 1939- . . . . CLC 33
See also CA 140

Bienek, Horst 1930- . . . . CLC 7, 11
See also CA 73-76; DLB 75

Bierce, Ambrose (Gwinett)
1842-1914(?) . . . . TCLC 1, 7, 44; DA;
SSC 9; WLC
See also CA 104; 139; CDALB 1865-1917;
DLB 11, 12, 23, 71, 74

Billings, Josh
See Shaw, Henry Wheeler

Billington, Rachel 1942- . . . . CLC 43
See also AITN 2; CA 33-36R

Binyon, T(imothy) J(ohn) 1936- . . . . CLC 34
See also CA 111; CANR 28

Bioy Casares, Adolfo
1914- . . . . CLC 4, 8, 13; HLC 1
See also CA 29-32R; CANR 19, 43;
DLB 113; HW; MTCW

Bird, C.
See Ellison, Harlan

Bird, Cordwainer
See Ellison, Harlan

Bird, Robert Montgomery
1806-1854 . . . . NCLC 1

Birney, (Alfred) Earle
1904- . . . . CLC 1, 4, 6, 11
See also CA 1-4R; CANR 5, 20; DLB 88;
MTCW

Bishop, Elizabeth
1911-1979 . . . . . . CLC 1, 4, 9, 13, 15, 32;
DA; PC 3
See also CA 5-8R; 89-92; CABS 2;
CANR 26; CDALB 1968-1988; DLB 5;
MTCW; SATA 24

Bishop, John 1935- . . . . CLC 10
See also CA 105

Bissett, Bill 1939- . . . . CLC 18
See also CA 69-72; CANR 15; DLB 53;
MTCW

Bitov, Andrei (Georgievich) 1937- . . . CLC 57
See also CA 142

Biyidi, Alexandre 1932-
See Beti, Mongo
See also BW; CA 114; 124; MTCW

Bjarme, Brynjolf
See Ibsen, Henrik (Johan)

Bjornson, Bjornstjerne (Martinius)
1832-1910 . . . . TCLC 7, 37
See also CA 104

Black, Robert
See Holdstock, Robert P.

Blackburn, Paul 1926-1971 . . . . . . CLC 9, 43
See also CA 81-84; 33-36R; CANR 34;
DLB 16; DLBY 81

Black Elk 1863-1950 . . . . TCLC 33

Black Hobart
See Sanders, (James) Ed(ward)

Blacklin, Malcolm
See Chambers, Aidan

Blackmore, R(ichard) D(oddridge)
1825-1900 . . . . TCLC 27
See also CA 120; DLB 18

Blackmur, R(ichard) P(almer)
1904-1965 . . . . CLC 2, 24
See also CA 11-12; 25-28R; CAP 1; DLB 63

Black Tarantula, The
See Acker, Kathy

Blackwood, Algernon (Henry)
1869-1951 . . . . TCLC 5
See also CA 105

Blackwood, Caroline 1931- . . . . CLC 6, 9
See also CA 85-88; CANR 32; DLB 14;
MTCW

Blade, Alexander
See Hamilton, Edmond; Silverberg, Robert

Blaga, Lucian 1895-1961 . . . . CLC 75

Blair, Eric (Arthur) 1903-1950
See Orwell, George
See also CA 104; 132; DA; MTCW;
SATA 29

Blais, Marie-Claire
1939- . . . . CLC 2, 4, 6, 13, 22
See also CA 21-24R; CAAS 4; CANR 38;
DLB 53; MTCW

Blaise, Clark 1940- . . . . CLC 29
See also AITN 2; CA 53-56; CAAS 3;
CANR 5, DLB 53

Blake, Nicholas
See Day Lewis, C(ecil)
See also DLB 77

Blake, William
1757-1827 . . . . . NCLC 13, 37; DA; WLC
See also CDBLB 1789-1832; DLB 93;
MAICYA; SATA 30

Blasco Ibanez, Vicente
1867-1928 . . . . TCLC 12
See also CA 110; 131; HW; MTCW

Blatty, William Peter 1928- . . . . CLC 2
See also CA 5-8R; CANR 9

Bleeck, Oliver
See Thomas, Ross (Elmore)

Blessing, Lee 1949- . . . . CLC 54

Blish, James (Benjamin)
1921-1975 . . . . CLC 14
See also CA 1-4R; 57-60; CANR 3; DLB 8;
MTCW; SATA 66

Bliss, Reginald
See Wells, H(erbert) G(eorge)

Blixen, Karen (Christentze Dinesen)
1885-1962
See Dinesen, Isak
See also CA 25-28; CANR 22; CAP 2;
MTCW; SATA 44

Bloch, Robert (Albert) 1917- . . . . CLC 33
See also CA 5-8R; CANR 5; DLB 44;
SATA 12

Blok, Alexander (Alexandrovich)
1880-1921 . . . . TCLC 5
See also CA 104

Blom, Jan
See Breytenbach, Breyten

Bloom, Harold 1930- . . . . CLC 24
See also CA 13-16R; CANR 39; DLB 67

Bloomfield, Aurelius
See Bourne, Randolph S(illiman)

Blount, Roy (Alton), Jr. 1941- . . . . . CLC 38
See also CA 53-56; CANR 10, 28; MTCW

Bloy, Leon 1846-1917. . . . . TCLC 22
See also CA 121; DLB 123

Blume, Judy (Sussman) 1938- . . . CLC 12, 30
See also AAYA 3; CA 29-32R; CANR 13,
37; CLR 2, 15; DLB 52; JRDA;
MAICYA; MTCW; SATA 2, 31

Blunden, Edmund (Charles)
1896-1974 . . . . CLC 2, 56
See also CA 17-18; 45-48; CAP 2; DLB 20,
100; MTCW

Bly, Robert (Elwood)
1926- . . . . CLC 1, 2, 5, 10, 15, 38
See also CA 5-8R; CANR 41; DLB 5;
MTCW

Bobette
See Simenon, Georges (Jacques Christian)

Boccaccio, Giovanni 1313-1375
See also SSC 10

Bochco, Steven 1943- . . . . CLC 35
See also CA 124; 138

Bodenheim, Maxwell 1892-1954 . . . TCLC 44
See also CA 110; DLB 9, 45

Bodker, Cecil 1927- . . . . CLC 21
See also CA 73-76; CANR 13; CLR 23;
MAICYA; SATA 14

Boell, Heinrich (Theodor) 1917-1985
See Boll, Heinrich (Theodor)
See also CA 21-24R; 116; CANR 24; DA;
DLB 69; DLBY 85; MTCW

Boerne, Alfred
See Doeblin, Alfred

Bogan, Louise 1897-1970 . . . . . CLC 4, 39, 46
See also CA 73-76; 25-28R; CANR 33;
DLB 45; MTCW

Bogarde, Dirk . . . . CLC 19
See also Van Den Bogarde, Derek Jules
Gaspard Ulric Niven
See also DLB 14

Bogosian, Eric 1953- . . . . CLC 45
See also CA 138

Bograd, Larry 1953- . . . . CLC 35
See also CA 93-96; SATA 33

Boiardo, Matteo Maria 1441-1494 . . . . LC 6

Boileau-Despreaux, Nicolas
1636-1711 . . . . LC 3

Boland, Eavan 1944- . . . . CLC 40, 67
See also DLB 40

Boll, Heinrich (Theodor)
1917-1985 . . . . CLC 2, 3, 6, 9, 11, 15, 27,
39, 72; WLC
See also Boell, Heinrich (Theodor)
See also DLB 69; DLBY 85

Bolt, Lee
See Faust, Frederick (Schiller)

Bolt, Robert (Oxton) 1924- . . . . CLC 14
See also CA 17-20R; CANR 35; DLB 13;
MTCW

Bomkauf
See Kaufman, Bob (Garnell)

Bresson, Robert 1907- . . . . **CLC 16**
See also CA 110

Breton, Andre 1896-1966. . . **CLC 2, 9, 15, 54**
See also CA 19-20; 25-28R; CANR 40;
CAP 2; DLB 65; MTCW

Breytenbach, Breyten 1939(?)- . . **CLC 23, 37**
See also CA 113; 129

Bridgers, Sue Ellen 1942- . . . . **CLC 26**
See also AAYA 8; CA 65-68; CANR 11,
36; CLR 18; DLB 52; JRDA; MAICYA;
SAAS 1, SATA 22

Bridges, Robert (Seymour)
1844-1930 . . . . **TCLC 1**
See also CA 104; CDBLB 1890-1914;
DLB 19, 98

Bridie, James. . . . . **TCLC 3**
See also Mavor, Osborne Henry
See also DLB 10

Brin, David 1950- . . . . **CLC 34**
See also CA 102; CANR 24; SATA 65

Brink, Andre (Philippus)
1935- . . . . **CLC 18, 36**
See also CA 104; CANR 39; MTCW

Brinsmead, H(esba) F(ay) 1922- . . . . **CLC 21**
See also CA 21-24R; CANR 10; MAICYA;
SAAS 5; SATA 18

Brittain, Vera (Mary)
1893(?)-1970 . . . . **CLC 23**
See also CA 13-16; 25-28R; CAP 1; MTCW

Broch, Hermann 1886-1951. . . . . . . **TCLC 20**
See also CA 117; DLB 85, 124

Brock, Rose
See Hansen, Joseph

Brodkey, Harold 1930-. . . . . **CLC 56**
See also CA 111; DLB 130

Brodsky, Iosif Alexandrovich 1940-
See Brodsky, Joseph
See also AITN 1; CA 41-44R; CANR 37;
MTCW

Brodsky, Joseph . . . . **CLC 4, 6, 13, 36, 50**
See also Brodsky, Iosif Alexandrovich

Brodsky, Michael Mark 1948- . . . . . **CLC 19**
See also CA 102; CANR 18, 41

Bromell, Henry 1947-. . . . . **CLC 5**
See also CA 53-56; CANR 9

Bromfield, Louis (Brucker)
1896-1956 . . . . **TCLC 11**
See also CA 107; DLB 4, 9, 86

Broner, E(sther) M(asserman)
1930- . . . . **CLC 19**
See also CA 17-20R; CANR 8, 25; DLB 28

Bronk, William 1918-. . . . . **CLC 10**
See also CA 89-92; CANR 23

Bronstein, Lev Davidovich
See Trotsky, Leon

Bronte, Anne 1820-1849. . . . . **NCLC 4**
See also DLB 21

Bronte, Charlotte
1816-1855 . . . **NCLC 3, 8, 33; DA; WLC**
See also CDBLB 1832-1890; DLB 21

Bronte, (Jane) Emily
1818-1848 . . . . **NCLC 16, 35; DA; PC 8;
WLC**
See also CDBLB 1832-1890; DLB 21, 32

Brooke, Frances 1724-1789 . . . . **LC 6**
See also DLB 39, 99

Brooke, Henry 1703(?)-1783 . . . . **LC 1**
See also DLB 39

Brooke, Rupert (Chawner)
1887-1915 . . . . **TCLC 2, 7; DA; WLC**
See also CA 104; 132; CDBLB 1914-1945;
DLB 19; MTCW

Brooke-Haven, P.
See Wodehouse, P(elham) G(renville)

Brooke-Rose, Christine 1926- . . . . . . **CLC 40**
See also CA 13-16R; DLB 14

Brookner, Anita 1928- . . . . . . **CLC 32, 34, 51**
See also CA 114; 120; CANR 37; DLBY 87;
MTCW

Brooks, Cleanth 1906- . . . . **CLC 24**
See also CA 17-20R; CANR 33, 35;
DLB 63; MTCW

Brooks, George
See Baum, L(yman) Frank

Brooks, Gwendolyn
1917- . . . . **CLC 1, 2, 4, 5, 15, 49; BLC 1;
DA; PC 7; WLC**
See also AITN 1; BW; CA 1-4R; CANR 1,
27; CDALB 1941-1968; CLR 27; DLB 5,
76; MTCW; SATA 6

Brooks, Mel. . . . . **CLC 12**
See also Kaminsky, Melvin
See also DLB 26

Brooks, Peter 1938- . . . . **CLC 34**
See also CA 45-48; CANR 1

Brooks, Van Wyck 1886-1963. . . . . . **CLC 29**
See also CA 1-4R; CANR 6; DLB 45, 63,
103

Brophy, Brigid (Antonia)
1929- . . . . **CLC 6, 11, 29**
See also CA 5-8R; CAAS 4; CANR 25;
DLB 14; MTCW

Brosman, Catharine Savage 1934-. . . . **CLC 9**
See also CA 61-64; CANR 21

Brother Antoninus
See Everson, William (Oliver)

Broughton, T(homas) Alan 1936- . . . **CLC 19**
See also CA 45-48; CANR 2, 23

Broumas, Olga 1949-. . . . . **CLC 10, 73**
See also CA 85-88; CANR 20

Brown, Charles Brockden
1771-1810 . . . . **NCLC 22**
See also CDALB 1640-1865; DLB 37, 59,
73

Brown, Christy 1932-1981. . . . . **CLC 63**
See also CA 105; 104; DLB 14

Brown, Claude 1937- . . . . . . **CLC 30; BLC 1**
See also AAYA 7; BW; CA 73-76

Brown, Dee (Alexander) 1908- . . **CLC 18, 47**
See also CA 13-16R; CAAS 6; CANR 11;
DLBY 80; MTCW; SATA 5

Brown, George
See Wertmueller, Lina

Brown, George Douglas
1869-1902 . . . . **TCLC 28**

Brown, George Mackay 1921-. . . . **CLC 5, 48**
See also CA 21-24R; CAAS 6; CANR 12,
37; DLB 14, 27; MTCW; SATA 35

Brown, (William) Larry 1951-. . . . . . **CLC 73**
See also CA 130; 134

Brown, Moses
See Barrett, William (Christopher)

Brown, Rita Mae 1944- . . . . . **CLC 18, 43, 79**
See also CA 45-48; CANR 2, 11, 35;
MTCW

Brown, Roderick (Langmere) Haig-
See Haig-Brown, Roderick (Langmere)

Brown, Rosellen 1939-. . . . . **CLC 32**
See also CA 77-80; CAAS 10; CANR 14

Brown, Sterling Allen
1901-1989 . . . . **CLC 1, 23, 59; BLC 1**
See also BW; CA 85-88; 127; CANR 26;
DLB 48, 51, 63; MTCW

Brown, Will
See Ainsworth, William Harrison

Brown, William Wells
1813-1884 . . . . **NCLC 2; BLC 1; DC 1**
See also DLB 3, 50

Browne, (Clyde) Jackson 1948(?)-. . . **CLC 21**
See also CA 120

Browning, Elizabeth Barrett
1806-1861 . . . . . **NCLC 1, 16; DA; PC 6;
WLC**
See also CDBLB 1832-1890; DLB 32

Browning, Robert
1812-1889 . . . . **NCLC 19; DA; PC 2**
See also CDBLB 1832-1890; DLB 32;
YABC 1

Browning, Tod 1882-1962 . . . . **CLC 16**
See also CA 141; 117

Bruccoli, Matthew J(oseph) 1931- . . **CLC 34**
See also CA 9-12R; CANR 7; DLB 103

Bruce, Lenny. . . . . **CLC 21**
See also Schneider, Leonard Alfred

Bruin, John
See Brutus, Dennis

Brulls, Christian
See Simenon, Georges (Jacques Christian)

Brunner, John (Kilian Houston)
1934-. . . . . **CLC 8, 10**
See also CA 1-4R; CAAS 8; CANR 2, 37;
MTCW

Brutus, Dennis 1924- . . . . . . **CLC 43; BLC 1**
See also BW; CA 49-52; CAAS 14;
CANR 2, 27, 42; DLB 117

Bryan, C(ourtlandt) D(ixon) B(arnes)
1936-. . . . . **CLC 29**
See also CA 73-76; CANR 13

Bryan, Michael
See Moore, Brian

Bryant, William Cullen
1794-1878 . . . . **NCLC 6; DA**
See also CDALB 1640-1865; DLB 3, 43, 59

Bryusov, Valery Yakovlevich
1873-1924 . . . . **TCLC 10**
See also CA 107

Buchan, John 1875-1940 . . . . **TCLC 41**
See also CA 108; DLB 34, 70; YABC 2

Buchanan, George 1506-1582 . . . . **LC 4**

Buchheim, Lothar-Guenther 1918- . . . **CLC 6**
See also CA 85-88

Calhoun, John Caldwell
1782-1850 .... **NCLC 15**
See also DLB 3

Calisher, Hortense 1911- .... **CLC 2, 4, 8, 38**
See also CA 1-4R; CANR 1, 22; DLB 2;
MTCW

Callaghan, Morley Edward
1903-1990 .... **CLC 3, 14, 41, 65**
See also CA 9-12R; 132; CANR 33;
DLB 68; MTCW

Calvino, Italo
1923-1985 ..... **CLC 5, 8, 11, 22, 33, 39,
73; SSC 3**
See also CA 85-88; 116; CANR 23; MTCW

Cameron, Carey 1952- .... **CLC 59**
See also CA 135

Cameron, Peter 1959- .... **CLC 44**
See also CA 125

Campana, Dino 1885-1932 .... **TCLC 20**
See also CA 117; DLB 114

Campbell, John W(ood, Jr.)
1910-1971 .... **CLC 32**
See also CA 21-22; 29-32R; CANR 34;
CAP 2; DLB 8; MTCW

Campbell, Joseph 1904-1987 ...... **CLC 69**
See also AAYA 3; BEST 89:2; CA 1-4R;
124; CANR 3, 28; MTCW

Campbell, (John) Ramsey 1946- .... **CLC 42**
See also CA 57-60; CANR 7

Campbell, (Ignatius) Roy (Dunnachie)
1901-1957 .... **TCLC 5**
See also CA 104; DLB 20

Campbell, Thomas 1777-1844 .... **NCLC 19**
See also DLB 93

Campbell, Wilfred .... **TCLC 9**
See also Campbell, William

Campbell, William 1858(?)-1918
See Campbell, Wilfred
See also CA 106; DLB 92

Campos, Alvaro de
See Pessoa, Fernando (Antonio Nogueira)

Camus, Albert
1913-1960 .... **CLC 1, 2, 4, 9, 11, 14, 32,
63, 69; DA; DC 2; SSC 9; WLC**
See also CA 89-92; DLB 72; MTCW

Canby, Vincent 1924- .... **CLC 13**
See also CA 81-84

Cancale
See Desnos, Robert

Canetti, Elias 1905- ...... **CLC 3, 14, 25, 75**
See also CA 21-24R; CANR 23; DLB 85,
124; MTCW

Canin, Ethan 1960- .... **CLC 55**
See also CA 131; 135

Cannon, Curt
See Hunter, Evan

Cape, Judith
See Page, P(atricia) K(athleen)

Capek, Karel
1890-1938 ..... **TCLC 6, 37; DA; DC 1;
WLC**
See also CA 104; 140

Capote, Truman
1924-1984 ...... **CLC 1, 3, 8, 13, 19, 34,
38, 58; DA; SSC 2; WLC**
See also CA 5-8R; 113; CANR 18;
CDALB 1941-1968; DLB 2; DLBY 80,
84; MTCW

Capra, Frank 1897-1991 .... **CLC 16**
See also CA 61-64; 135

Caputo, Philip 1941- .... **CLC 32**
See also CA 73-76; CANR 40

Card, Orson Scott 1951- .... **CLC 44, 47, 50**
See also CA 102; CANR 27; MTCW

Cardenal (Martinez), Ernesto
1925- .... **CLC 31; HLC 1**
See also CA 49-52; CANR 2, 32; HW;
MTCW

Carducci, Giosue 1835-1907 ...... **TCLC 32**

Carew, Thomas 1595(?)-1640 .... **LC 13**
See also DLB 126

Carey, Ernestine Gilbreth 1908- .... **CLC 17**
See also CA 5-8R; SATA 2

Carey, Peter 1943- .... **CLC 40, 55**
See also CA 123; 127; MTCW

Carleton, William 1794-1869 ...... **NCLC 3**

Carlisle, Henry (Coffin) 1926- ..... **CLC 33**
See also CA 13-16R; CANR 15

Carlsen, Chris
See Holdstock, Robert P.

Carlson, Ron(ald F.) 1947- .... **CLC 54**
See also CA 105; CANR 27

Carlyle, Thomas 1795-1881 .. **NCLC 22; DA**
See also CDBLB 1789-1832; DLB 55

Carman, (William) Bliss
1861-1929 .... **TCLC 7**
See also CA 104; DLB 92

Carnegie, Dale 1888-1955 .... **TCLC 53**

Carossa, Hans 1878-1956 .... **TCLC 48**
See also DLB 66

Carpenter, Don(ald Richard)
1931- .... **CLC 41**
See also CA 45-48; CANR 1

Carpentier (y Valmont), Alejo
1904-1980 .... **CLC 8, 11, 38; HLC 1**
See also CA 65-68; 97-100; CANR 11;
DLB 113; HW

Carr, Emily 1871-1945 .... **TCLC 32**
See also DLB 68

Carr, John Dickson 1906-1977 ...... **CLC 3**
See also CA 49-52; 69-72; CANR 3, 33;
MTCW

Carr, Philippa
See Hibbert, Eleanor Alice Burford

Carr, Virginia Spencer 1929- .... **CLC 34**
See also CA 61-64; DLB 111

Carrier, Roch 1937- .... **CLC 13, 78**
See also CA 130; DLB 53

Carroll, James P. 1943(?)- .... **CLC 38**
See also CA 81-84

Carroll, Jim 1951- .... **CLC 35**
See also CA 45-48; CANR 42

Carroll, Lewis .... **NCLC 2; WLC**
See also Dodgson, Charles Lutwidge
See also CDBLB 1832-1890; CLR 2, 18;
DLB 18; JRDA

Carroll, Paul Vincent 1900-1968 .... **CLC 10**
See also CA 9-12R; 25-28R; DLB 10

Carruth, Hayden 1921- .... **CLC 4, 7, 10, 18**
See also CA 9-12R; CANR 4, 38; DLB 5;
MTCW; SATA 47

Carson, Rachel Louise 1907-1964 ... **CLC 71**
See also CA 77-80; CANR 35; MTCW;
SATA 23

Carter, Angela (Olive)
1940-1992 ...... **CLC 5, 41, 76; SSC 13**
See also CA 53-56; 136; CANR 12, 36;
DLB 14; MTCW; SATA 66;
SATA-Obit 70

Carter, Nick
See Smith, Martin Cruz

Carver, Raymond
1938-1988 ... **CLC 22, 36, 53, 55; SSC 8**
See also CA 33-36R; 126; CANR 17, 34;
DLB 130; DLBY 84, 88; MTCW

Cary, (Arthur) Joyce (Lunel)
1888-1957 .... **TCLC 1, 29**
See also CA 104; CDBLB 1914-1945;
DLB 15, 100

Casanova de Seingalt, Giovanni Jacopo
1725-1798 .... **LC 13**

Casares, Adolfo Bioy
See Bioy Casares, Adolfo

Casely-Hayford, J(oseph) E(phraim)
1866-1930 .... **TCLC 24; BLC 1**
See also CA 123

Casey, John (Dudley) 1939- .... **CLC 59**
See also BEST 90:2; CA 69-72; CANR 23

Casey, Michael 1947- .... **CLC 2**
See also CA 65-68; DLB 5

Casey, Patrick
See Thurman, Wallace (Henry)

Casey, Warren (Peter) 1935-1988 ... **CLC 12**
See also CA 101; 127

Casona, Alejandro .... **CLC 49**
See also Alvarez, Alejandro Rodriguez

Cassavetes, John 1929-1989 .... **CLC 20**
See also CA 85-88; 127

Cassill, R(onald) V(erlin) 1919- ... **CLC 4, 23**
See also CA 9-12R; CAAS 1; CANR 7;
DLB 6

Cassity, (Allen) Turner 1929- .... **CLC 6, 42**
See also CA 17-20R; CAAS 8; CANR 11;
DLB 105

Castaneda, Carlos 1931(?)- .... **CLC 12**
See also CA 25-28R; CANR 32; HW;
MTCW

Castedo, Elena 1937- .... **CLC 65**
See also CA 132

Castedo-Ellerman, Elena
See Castedo, Elena

Castellanos, Rosario
1925-1974 .... **CLC 66; HLC 1**
See also CA 131; 53-56; DLB 113; HW

Castelvetro, Lodovico 1505-1571 ..... **LC 12**

Castiglione, Baldassare 1478-1529 ... **LC 12**

Castle, Robert
See Hamilton, Edmond

Castro, Guillen de 1569-1631 .... **LC 19**

Castro, Rosalia de 1837-1885 ..... **NCLC 3**

Cather, Willa
    See Cather, Willa Sibert

Cather, Willa Sibert
    1873-1947 .... TCLC 1, 11, 31; DA;
                                    SSC 2; WLC
    See also CA 104; 128; CDALB 1865-1917;
    DLB 9, 54, 78; DLBD 1; MTCW;
    SATA 30

Catton, (Charles) Bruce
    1899-1978 .... CLC 35
    See also AITN 1; CA 5-8R; 81-84;
    CANR 7; DLB 17; SATA 2, 24

Cauldwell, Frank
    See King, Francis (Henry)

Caunitz, William J. 1933- .... CLC 34
    See also BEST 89:3; CA 125; 130

Causley, Charles (Stanley) 1917-..... CLC 7
    See also CA 9-12R; CANR 5, 35; CLR 30;
    DLB 27; MTCW; SATA 3, 66

Caute, David 1936-............... CLC 29
    See also CA 1-4R; CAAS 4; CANR 1, 33;
    DLB 14

Cavafy, C(onstantine) P(eter)...... TCLC 2, 7
    See also Kavafis, Konstantinos Petrou

Cavallo, Evelyn
    See Spark, Muriel (Sarah)

Cavanna, Betty .... CLC 12
    See also Harrison, Elizabeth Cavanna
    See also JRDA; MAICYA; SAAS 4;
    SATA 1, 30

Caxton, William 1421(?)-1491(?)..... LC 17

Cayrol, Jean 1911-................ CLC 11
    See also CA 89-92; DLB 83

Cela, Camilo Jose
    1916- .... CLC 4, 13, 59; HLC 1
    See also BEST 90:2; CA 21-24R; CAAS 10;
    CANR 21, 32; DLBY 89; HW; MTCW

Celan, Paul .... CLC 53
    See also Antschel, Paul
    See also DLB 69

Celine, Louis-Ferdinand
    .... CLC 1, 3, 4, 7, 9, 15, 47
    See also Destouches, Louis-Ferdinand
    See also DLB 72

Cellini, Benvenuto 1500-1571 .... LC 7

Cendrars, Blaise
    See Sauser-Hall, Frederic

Cernuda (y Bidon), Luis
    1902-1963 .... CLC 54
    See also CA 131; 89-92; DLB 134; HW

Cervantes (Saavedra), Miguel de
    1547-1616 ..... LC 6, 23; DA; SSC 12;
                                            WLC

Cesaire, Aime (Fernand)
    1913- .... CLC 19, 32; BLC 1
    See also BW; CA 65-68; CANR 24, 43;
    MTCW

Chabon, Michael 1965(?)- .... CLC 55
    See also CA 139

Chabrol, Claude 1930-............ CLC 16
    See also CA 110

Challans, Mary 1905-1983
    See Renault, Mary
    See also CA 81-84; 111; SATA 23, 36

Challis, George
    See Faust, Frederick (Schiller)

Chambers, Aidan 1934- .... CLC 35
    See also CA 25-28R; CANR 12, 31; JRDA;
    MAICYA; SAAS 12; SATA 1, 69

Chambers, James 1948-
    See Cliff, Jimmy
    See also CA 124

Chambers, Jessie
    See Lawrence, D(avid) H(erbert Richards)

Chambers, Robert W. 1865-1933... TCLC 41

Chandler, Raymond (Thornton)
    1888-1959 .... TCLC 1, 7
    See also CA 104; 129; CDALB 1929-1941;
    DLBD 6; MTCW

Chang, Jung 1952-................ CLC 71
    See also CA 142

Channing, William Ellery
    1780-1842 .... NCLC 17
    See also DLB 1, 59

Chaplin, Charles Spencer
    1889-1977 .... CLC 16
    See also Chaplin, Charlie
    See also CA 81-84; 73-76

Chaplin, Charlie
    See Chaplin, Charles Spencer
    See also DLB 44

Chapman, George 1559(?)-1634...... LC 22
    See also DLB 62, 121

Chapman, Graham 1941-1989 ...... CLC 21
    See also Monty Python
    See also CA 116; 129; CANR 35

Chapman, John Jay 1862-1933 ..... TCLC 7
    See also CA 104

Chapman, Walker
    See Silverberg, Robert

Chappell, Fred (Davis) 1936-.... CLC 40, 78
    See also CA 5-8R; CAAS 4; CANR 8, 33;
    DLB 6, 105

Char, Rene(-Emile)
    1907-1988 .... CLC 9, 11, 14, 55
    See also CA 13-16R; 124; CANR 32;
    MTCW

Charby, Jay
    See Ellison, Harlan

Chardin, Pierre Teilhard de
    See Teilhard de Chardin, (Marie Joseph)
    Pierre

Charles I 1600-1649............... LC 13

Charyn, Jerome 1937- .... CLC 5, 8, 18
    See also CA 5-8R; CAAS 1; CANR 7;
    DLBY 83; MTCW

Chase, Mary (Coyle) 1907-1981 ...... DC 1
    See also CA 77-80; 105; SATA 17, 29

Chase, Mary Ellen 1887-1973 .... CLC 2
    See also CA 13-16; 41-44R; CAP 1;
    SATA 10

Chase, Nicholas
    See Hyde, Anthony

Chateaubriand, Francois Rene de
    1768-1848 .... NCLC 3
    See also DLB 119

Chatterje, Sarat Chandra 1876-1936(?)
    See Chatterji, Saratchandra
    See also CA 109

Chatterji, Bankim Chandra
    1838-1894 .... NCLC 19

Chatterji, Saratchandra .... TCLC 13
    See also Chatterje, Sarat Chandra

Chatterton, Thomas 1752-1770 ...... LC 3
    See also DLB 109

Chatwin, (Charles) Bruce
    1940-1989 .... CLC 28, 57, 59
    See also AAYA 4; BEST 90:1; CA 85-88;
    127

Chaucer, Daniel
    See Ford, Ford Madox

Chaucer, Geoffrey
    1340(?)-1400 .... LC 17; DA
    See also CDBLB Before 1660

Chaviaras, Strates 1935-
    See Haviaras, Stratis
    See also CA 105

Chayefsky, Paddy .... CLC 23
    See also Chayefsky, Sidney
    See also DLB 7, 44; DLBY 81

Chayefsky, Sidney 1923-1981
    See Chayefsky, Paddy
    See also CA 9-12R; 104; CANR 18

Chedid, Andree 1920-............. CLC 47

Cheever, John
    1912-1982 ...... CLC 3, 7, 8, 11, 15, 25,
                                    64; DA; SSC 1; WLC
    See also CA 5-8R; 106; CABS 1; CANR 5,
    27; CDALB 1941-1968; DLB 2, 102;
    DLBY 80, 82; MTCW

Cheever, Susan 1943-.......... CLC 18, 48
    See also CA 103; CANR 27; DLBY 82

Chekhonte, Antosha
    See Chekhov, Anton (Pavlovich)

Chekhov, Anton (Pavlovich)
    1860-1904 .... TCLC 3, 10, 31; DA;
                                    SSC 2; WLC
    See also CA 104; 124

Chernyshevsky, Nikolay Gavrilovich
    1828-1889 .... NCLC 1

Cherry, Carolyn Janice 1942-
    See Cherryh, C. J.
    See also CA 65-68; CANR 10

Cherryh, C. J..................... CLC 35
    See also Cherry, Carolyn Janice
    See also DLBY 80

Chesnutt, Charles W(addell)
    1858-1932 .. TCLC 5, 39; BLC 1; SSC 7
    See also BW; CA 106; 125; DLB 12, 50, 78;
    MTCW

Chester, Alfred 1929(?)-1971....... CLC 49
    See also CA 33-36R; DLB 130

Chesterton, G(ilbert) K(eith)
    1874-1936 .... TCLC 1, 6; SSC 1
    See also CA 104; 132; CDBLB 1914-1945;
    DLB 10, 19, 34, 70, 98; MTCW;
    SATA 27

Chiang Pin-chin 1904-1986
    See Ding Ling
    See also CA 118

Couch, Arthur Thomas Quiller
    See Quiller-Couch, Arthur Thomas

Coulton, James
    See Hansen, Joseph

Couperus, Louis (Marie Anne)
    1863-1923 .... TCLC 15
    See also CA 115

Court, Wesli
    See Turco, Lewis (Putnam)

Courtenay, Bryce   1933- .... CLC 59
    See also CA 138

Courtney, Robert
    See Ellison, Harlan

Cousteau, Jacques-Yves   1910-...... CLC 30
    See also CA 65-68; CANR 15; MTCW;
    SATA 38

Coward, Noel (Peirce)
    1899-1973 .... CLC 1, 9, 29, 51
    See also AITN 1; CA 17-18; 41-44R;
    CANR 35; CAP 2; CDBLB 1914-1945;
    DLB 10; MTCW

Cowley, Malcolm   1898-1989 .... CLC 39
    See also CA 5-8R; 128; CANR 3; DLB 4,
    48; DLBY 81, 89; MTCW

Cowper, William   1731-1800....... NCLC 8
    See also DLB 104, 109

Cox, William Trevor   1928- ... CLC 9, 14, 71
    See also Trevor, William
    See also CA 9-12R; CANR 4, 37; DLB 14;
    MTCW

Cozzens, James Gould
    1903-1978 .... CLC 1, 4, 11
    See also CA 9-12R; 81-84; CANR 19,
    CDALB 1941-1968; DLB 9; DLBD 2;
    DLBY 84; MTCW

Crabbe, George   1754-1832....... NCLC 26
    See also DLB 93

Craig, A. A.
    See Anderson, Poul (William)

Craik, Dinah Maria (Mulock)
    1826-1887 .... NCLC 38
    See also DLB 35; MAICYA; SATA 34

Cram, Ralph Adams   1863-1942.... TCLC 45

Crane, (Harold) Hart
    1899-1932 .... TCLC 2, 5; DA; PC 3;
                                              WLC
    See also CA 104; 127; CDALB 1917-1929;
    DLB 4, 48; MTCW

Crane, R(onald) S(almon)
    1886-1967 .... CLC 27
    See also CA 85-88; DLB 63

Crane, Stephen (Townley)
    1871-1900 .... TCLC 11, 17, 32; DA;
                                         SSC 7; WLC
    See also CA 109; 140; CDALB 1865-1917;
    DLB 12, 54, 78; YABC 2

Crase, Douglas   1944- .... CLC 58
    See also CA 106

Crashaw, Richard   1612(?)-1649...... LC 24
    See also DLB 126

Craven, Margaret   1901-1980....... CLC 17
    See also CA 103

Crawford, F(rancis) Marion
    1854-1909 .... TCLC 10
    See also CA 107; DLB 71

Crawford, Isabella Valancy
    1850-1887 .... NCLC 12
    See also DLB 92

Crayon, Geoffrey
    See Irving, Washington

Creasey, John   1908-1973......... CLC 11
    See also CA 5-8R; 41-44R; CANR 8;
    DLB 77; MTCW

Crebillon, Claude Prosper Jolyot de (fils)
    1707-1777 .... LC 1

Credo
    See Creasey, John

Creeley, Robert (White)
    1926- ..... CLC 1, 2, 4, 8, 11, 15, 36, 78
    See also CA 1-4R; CAAS 10; CANR 23, 43;
    DLB 5, 16; MTCW

Crews, Harry (Eugene)
    1935- .... CLC 6, 23, 49
    See also AITN 1; CA 25-28R; CANR 20;
    DLB 6; MTCW

Crichton, (John) Michael
    1942- .... CLC 2, 6, 54
    See also AAYA 10; AITN 2; CA 25-28R;
    CANR 13, 40; DLB 81; JRDA;
    MTCW; SATA 9

Crispin, Edmund .... CLC 22
    See also Montgomery, (Robert) Bruce
    See also DLB 87

Cristofer, Michael   1945(?)- .... CLC 28
    See also CA 110; DLB 7

Croce, Benedetto   1866-1952 ...... TCLC 37
    See also CA 120

Crockett, David   1786-1836 .... NCLC 8
    See also DLB 3, 11

Crockett, Davy
    See Crockett, David

Croker, John Wilson   1780-1857 .. NCLC 10
    See also DLB 110

Crommelynck, Fernand   1885-1970 .. CLC 75
    See also CA 89-92

Cronin, A(rchibald) J(oseph)
    1896-1981 .... CLC 32
    See also CA 1-4R; 102; CANR 5; SATA 25,
    47

Cross, Amanda
    See Heilbrun, Carolyn G(old)

Crothers, Rachel   1878(?)-1958..... TCLC 19
    See also CA 113; DLB 7

Croves, Hal
    See Traven, B.

Crowfield, Christopher
    See Stowe, Harriet (Elizabeth) Beecher

Crowley, Aleister.................. TCLC 7
    See also Crowley, Edward Alexander

Crowley, Edward Alexander   1875-1947
    See Crowley, Aleister
    See also CA 104

Crowley, John   1942-.............. CLC 57
    See also CA 61-64; CANR 43; DLBY 82;
    SATA 65

Crud
    See Crumb, R(obert)

Crumarums
    See Crumb, R(obert)

Crumb, R(obert)   1943- .... CLC 17
    See also CA 106

Crumbum
    See Crumb, R(obert)

Crumski
    See Crumb, R(obert)

Crum the Bum
    See Crumb, R(obert)

Crunk
    See Crumb, R(obert)

Crustt
    See Crumb, R(obert)

Cryer, Gretchen (Kiger)   1935-...... CLC 21
    See also CA 114; 123

Csath, Geza   1887-1919.......... TCLC 13
    See also CA 111

Cudlip, David   1933- .... CLC 34

Cullen, Countee
    1903-1946 ..... TCLC 4, 37; BLC 1; DA
    See also BW; CA 108; 124;
    CDALB 1917-1929; DLB 4, 48, 51;
    MTCW; SATA 18

Cum, R.
    See Crumb, R(obert)

Cummings, Bruce F(rederick)   1889-1919
    See Barbellion, W. N. P.
    See also CA 123

Cummings, E(dward) E(stlin)
    1894-1962 ...... CLC 1, 3, 8, 12, 15, 68;
                                      DA; PC 5; WLC 2
    See also CA 73-76; CANR 31;
    CDALB 1929-1941; DLB 4, 48; MTCW

Cunha, Euclides (Rodrigues Pimenta) da
    1866-1909 .... TCLC 24
    See also CA 123

Cunningham, E. V.
    See Fast, Howard (Melvin)

Cunningham, J(ames) V(incent)
    1911-1985 .... CLC 3, 31
    See also CA 1-4R; 115; CANR 1; DLB 5

Cunningham, Julia (Woolfolk)
    1916- .... CLC 12
    See also CA 9-12R; CANR 4, 19, 36;
    JRDA; MAICYA; SAAS 2; SATA 1, 26

Cunningham, Michael   1952- .... CLC 34
    See also CA 136

Cunninghame Graham, R(obert) B(ontine)
    1852-1936 .... TCLC 19
    See also Graham, R(obert) B(ontine)
    Cunninghame
    See also CA 119; DLB 98

Currie, Ellen   19(?)-.............. CLC 44

Curtin, Philip
    See Lowndes, Marie Adelaide (Belloc)

Curtis, Price
    See Ellison, Harlan

Cutrate, Joe
    See Spiegelman, Art

Czaczkes, Shmuel Yosef
    See Agnon, S(hmuel) Y(osef Halevi)

D. P.
    See Wells, H(erbert) G(eorge)

Dabrowska, Maria (Szumska)
1889-1965 . . . . CLC 15
See also CA 106

Dabydeen, David 1955- . . . . CLC 34
See also BW; CA 125

Dacey, Philip 1939- . . . . CLC 51
See also CA 37-40R; CAAS 17; CANR 14,
32; DLB 105

Dagerman, Stig (Halvard)
1923-1954 . . . . TCLC 17
See also CA 117

Dahl, Roald 1916-1990 . . . . . CLC 1, 6, 18, 79
See also CA 1-4R; 133; CANR 6, 32, 37;
CLR 1, 7; JRDA; MAICYA; MTCW;
SATA 1, 26, 73; SATA-Obit 65

Dahlberg, Edward 1900-1977 . . . CLC 1, 7, 14
See also CA 9-12R; 69-72; CANR 31;
DLB 48; MTCW

Dale, Colin . . . . TCLC 18
See also Lawrence, T(homas) E(dward)

Dale, George E.
See Asimov, Isaac

Daly, Elizabeth 1878-1967 . . . . CLC 52
See also CA 23-24; 25-28R; CAP 2

Daly, Maureen 1921- . . . . CLC 17
See also AAYA 5; CANR 37; JRDA;
MAICYA; SAAS 1; SATA 2

Daniel, Samuel 1562(?)-1619 . . . . LC 24
See also DLB 62

Daniels, Brett
See Adler, Renata

Dannay, Frederic 1905-1982 . . . . CLC 11
See also Queen, Ellery
See also CA 1-4R; 107; CANR 1, 39;
MTCW

D'Annunzio, Gabriele
1863-1938 . . . . TCLC 6, 40
See also CA 104

d'Antibes, Germain
See Simenon, Georges (Jacques Christian)

Danvers, Dennis 1947- . . . . CLC 70

Danziger, Paula 1944- . . . . CLC 21
See also AAYA 4; CA 112; 115; CANR 37;
CLR 20; JRDA; MAICYA; SATA 30,
36, 63

Dario, Ruben 1867-1916 . . . TCLC 4; HLC 1
See also CA 131; HW; MTCW

Darley, George 1795-1846 . . . . NCLC 2
See also DLB 96

Daryush, Elizabeth 1887-1977 . . . . CLC 6, 19
See also CA 49-52; CANR 3; DLB 20

Daudet, (Louis Marie) Alphonse
1840-1897 . . . . NCLC 1
See also DLB 123

Daumal, Rene 1908-1944 . . . . TCLC 14
See also CA 114

Davenport, Guy (Mattison, Jr.)
1927- . . . . CLC 6, 14, 38
See also CA 33-36R; CANR 23; DLB 130

Davidson, Avram 1923-
See Queen, Ellery
See also CA 101; CANR 26; DLB 8

Davidson, Donald (Grady)
1893-1968 . . . . CLC 2, 13, 19
See also CA 5-8R; 25-28R; CANR 4;
DLB 45

Davidson, Hugh
See Hamilton, Edmond

Davidson, John 1857-1909 . . . . TCLC 24
See also CA 118; DLB 19

Davidson, Sara 1943- . . . . CLC 9
See also CA 81-84

Davie, Donald (Alfred)
1922- . . . . CLC 5, 8, 10, 31
See also CA 1-4R; CAAS 3; CANR 1;
DLB 27; MTCW

Davies, Ray(mond Douglas) 1944- . . CLC 21
See also CA 116

Davies, Rhys 1903-1978 . . . . CLC 23
See also CA 9-12R; 81-84; CANR 4

Davies, (William) Robertson
1913- . . . . . CLC 2, 7, 13, 25, 42, 75; DA;
WLC
See also BEST 89:2; CA 33-36R; CANR 17,
42; DLB 68; MTCW

Davies, W(illiam) H(enry)
1871-1940 . . . . TCLC 5
See also CA 104; DLB 19

Davies, Walter C.
See Kornbluth, C(yril) M.

Davis, Angela (Yvonne) 1944- . . . . . . CLC 77
See also BW; CA 57-60; CANR 10

Davis, B. Lynch
See Bioy Casares, Adolfo; Borges, Jorge
Luis

Davis, Gordon
See Hunt, E(verette) Howard, Jr.

Davis, Harold Lenoir 1896-1960 . . . . CLC 49
See also CA 89-92; DLB 9

Davis, Rebecca (Blaine) Harding
1831-1910 . . . . TCLC 6
See also CA 104; DLB 74

Davis, Richard Harding
1864-1916 . . . . TCLC 24
See also CA 114; DLB 12, 23, 78, 79

Davison, Frank Dalby 1893-1970 . . . CLC 15
See also CA 116

Davison, Lawrence H.
See Lawrence, D(avid) H(erbert Richards)

Davison, Peter (Hubert) 1928- . . . . . CLC 28
See also CA 9-12R; CAAS 4; CANR 3, 43;
DLB 5

Davys, Mary 1674-1732 . . . . LC 1
See also DLB 39

Dawson, Fielding 1930- . . . . CLC 6
See also CA 85-88; DLB 130

Dawson, Peter
See Faust, Frederick (Schiller)

Day, Clarence (Shepard, Jr.)
1874-1935 . . . . TCLC 25
See also CA 108; DLB 11

Day, Thomas 1748-1789 . . . . LC 1
See also DLB 39; YABC 1

Day Lewis, C(ecil)
1904-1972 . . . . CLC 1, 6, 10
See also Blake, Nicholas
See also CA 13-16; 33-36R; CANR 34;
CAP 1; DLB 15, 20; MTCW

Dazai, Osamu . . . . TCLC 11
See also Tsushima, Shuji

de Andrade, Carlos Drummond
See Drummond de Andrade, Carlos

Deane, Norman
See Creasey, John

de Beauvoir, Simone (Lucie Ernestine Marie Bertrand)
See Beauvoir, Simone (Lucie Ernestine
Marie Bertrand) de

de Brissac, Malcolm
See Dickinson, Peter (Malcolm)

de Chardin, Pierre Teilhard
See Teilhard de Chardin, (Marie Joseph)
Pierre

Dee, John 1527-1608 . . . . LC 20

Deer, Sandra 1940- . . . . CLC 45

De Ferrari, Gabriella . . . . CLC 65

Defoe, Daniel
1660(?)-1731 . . . . LC 1; DA; WLC
See also CDBLB 1660-1789; DLB 39, 95,
101; JRDA; MAICYA; SATA 22

de Gourmont, Remy
See Gourmont, Remy de

de Hartog, Jan 1914- . . . . CLC 19
See also CA 1-4R; CANR 1

de Hostos, E. M.
See Hostos (y Bonilla), Eugenio Maria de

de Hostos, Eugenio M.
See Hostos (y Bonilla), Eugenio Maria de

Deighton, Len . . . . CLC 4, 7, 22, 46
See also Deighton, Leonard Cyril
See also AAYA 6; BEST 89:2;
CDBLB 1960 to Present; DLB 87

Deighton, Leonard Cyril 1929-
See Deighton, Len
See also CA 9-12R; CANR 19, 33; MTCW

Dekker, Thomas 1572(?)-1632 . . . . LC 22
See also CDBLB Before 1660; DLB 62

de la Mare, Walter (John)
1873-1956 . . TCLC 4, 53; SSC 14; WLC
See also CDBLB 1914-1945; CLR 23;
DLB 19; SATA 16

Delaney, Franey
See O'Hara, John (Henry)

Delaney, Shelagh 1939- . . . . CLC 29
See also CA 17-20R; CANR 30;
CDBLB 1960 to Present; DLB 13;
MTCW

Delany, Mary (Granville Pendarves)
1700-1788 . . . . LC 12

Delany, Samuel R(ay, Jr.)
1942- . . . . CLC 8, 14, 38; BLC 1
See also BW; CA 81-84; CANR 27, 43;
DLB 8, 33; MTCW

De La Ramee, (Marie) Louise 1839-1908
See Ouida
See also SATA 20

de la Roche, Mazo 1879-1961 . . . . . . **CLC 14**
See also CA 85-88; CANR 30; DLB 68;
SATA 64

Delbanco, Nicholas (Franklin)
1942- . . . . **CLC 6, 13**
See also CA 17-20R; CAAS 2; CANR 29;
DLB 6

del Castillo, Michel 1933- . . . . **CLC 38**
See also CA 109

Deledda, Grazia (Cosima)
1875(?)-1936 . . . . **TCLC 23**
See also CA 123

Delibes, Miguel . . . . **CLC 8, 18**
See also Delibes Setien, Miguel

Delibes Setien, Miguel 1920-
See Delibes, Miguel
See also CA 45-48; CANR 1, 32; HW;
MTCW

DeLillo, Don
1936- . . . . . **CLC 8, 10, 13, 27, 39, 54, 76**
See also BEST 89:1; CA 81-84; CANR 21;
DLB 6; MTCW

de Lisser, H. G.
See De Lisser, Herbert George
See also DLB 117

De Lisser, Herbert George
1878-1944 . . . . **TCLC 12**
See also de Lisser, H. G.
See also CA 109

Deloria, Vine (Victor), Jr. 1933- . . . . **CLC 21**
See also CA 53-56; CANR 5, 20; MTCW;
SATA 21

Del Vecchio, John M(ichael)
1947- . . . . **CLC 29**
See also CA 110; DLBD 9

de Man, Paul (Adolph Michel)
1919-1983 . . . . **CLC 55**
See also CA 128; 111; DLB 67; MTCW

De Marinis, Rick 1934- . . . . **CLC 54**
See also CA 57-60; CANR 9, 25

Demby, William 1922- . . . . . **CLC 53; BLC 1**
See also BW; CA 81-84; DLB 33

Demijohn, Thom
See Disch, Thomas M(ichael)

de Montherlant, Henry (Milon)
See Montherlant, Henry (Milon) de

de Natale, Francine
See Malzberg, Barry N(athaniel)

Denby, Edwin (Orr) 1903-1983 . . . . . **CLC 48**
See also CA 138; 110

Denis, Julio
See Cortazar, Julio

Denmark, Harrison
See Zelazny, Roger (Joseph)

Dennis, John 1658-1734 . . . . **LC 11**
See also DLB 101

Dennis, Nigel (Forbes) 1912-1989 . . . . **CLC 8**
See also CA 25-28R; 129; DLB 13, 15;
MTCW

De Palma, Brian (Russell) 1940- . . . . **CLC 20**
See also CA 109

De Quincey, Thomas 1785-1859 . . . **NCLC 4**
See also CDBLB 1789-1832; DLB 110

Deren, Eleanora 1908(?)-1961
See Deren, Maya
See also CA 111

Deren, Maya . . . . **CLC 16**
See also Deren, Eleanora

Derleth, August (William)
1909-1971 . . . . **CLC 31**
See also CA 1-4R; 29-32R; CANR 4;
DLB 9; SATA 5

de Routisie, Albert
See Aragon, Louis

Derrida, Jacques 1930- . . . . **CLC 24**
See also CA 124; 127

Derry Down Derry
See Lear, Edward

Dersonnes, Jacques
See Simenon, Georges (Jacques Christian)

Desai, Anita 1937- . . . . **CLC 19, 37**
See also CA 81-84; CANR 33; MTCW;
SATA 63

de Saint-Luc, Jean
See Glassco, John

de Saint Roman, Arnaud
See Aragon, Louis

Descartes, Rene 1596-1650 . . . . **LC 20**

De Sica, Vittorio 1901(?)-1974 . . . . . **CLC 20**
See also CA 117

Desnos, Robert 1900-1945 . . . . **TCLC 22**
See also CA 121

Destouches, Louis Ferdinand
1894-1961 . . . . **CLC 9, 15**
See also Celine, Louis-Ferdinand
See also CA 85-88; CANR 28; MTCW

Deutsch, Babette 1895-1982 . . . . **CLC 18**
See also CA 1-4R; 108; CANR 4; DLB 45;
SATA 1, 33

Devenant, William 1606-1649 . . . . **LC 13**

Devkota, Laxmiprasad
1909-1959 . . . . **TCLC 23**
See also CA 123

De Voto, Bernard (Augustine)
1897-1955 . . . . **TCLC 29**
See also CA 113; DLB 9

De Vries, Peter
1910-1993 . . . . **CLC 1, 2, 3, 7, 10, 28, 46**
See also CA 17-20R; 142; CANR 41;
DLB 6; DLBY 82; MTCW

Dexter, Martin
See Faust, Frederick (Schiller)

Dexter, Pete 1943- . . . . **CLC 34, 55**
See also BEST 89:2; CA 127; 131; MTCW

Diamano, Silmang
See Senghor, Leopold Sedar

Diamond, Neil 1941- . . . . **CLC 30**
See also CA 108

di Bassetto, Corno
See Shaw, George Bernard

Dick, Philip K(indred)
1928-1982 . . . . **CLC 10, 30, 72**
See also CA 49-52; 106; CANR 2, 16;
DLB 8; MTCW

Dickens, Charles (John Huffam)
1812-1870 . . . . . . **NCLC 3, 8, 18, 26; DA**
See also CDBLB 1832-1890; DLB 21, 55,
70; JRDA; MAICYA; SATA 15

Dickey, James (Lafayette)
1923- . . . . **CLC 1, 2, 4, 7, 10, 15, 47**
See also AITN 1, 2; CA 9-12R; CABS 2;
CANR 10; CDALB 1968-1988; DLB 5;
DLBD 7; DLBY 82; MTCW

Dickey, William 1928- . . . . **CLC 3, 28**
See also CA 9-12R; CANR 24; DLB 5

Dickinson, Charles 1951- . . . . **CLC 49**
See also CA 128

Dickinson, Emily (Elizabeth)
1830-1886 . . **NCLC 21; DA; PC 1; WLC**
See also CDALB 1865-1917; DLB 1;
SATA 29

Dickinson, Peter (Malcolm)
1927- . . . . **CLC 12, 35**
See also AAYA 9; CA 41-44R; CANR 31;
CLR 29; DLB 87; JRDA; MAICYA;
SATA 5, 62

Dickson, Carr
See Carr, John Dickson

Dickson, Carter
See Carr, John Dickson

Didion, Joan 1934- . . . . . **CLC 1, 3, 8, 14, 32**
See also AITN 1; CA 5-8R; CANR 14;
CDALB 1968-1988; DLB 2; DLBY 81,
86; MTCW

Dietrich, Robert
See Hunt, E(verette) Howard, Jr.

Dillard, Annie 1945- . . . . **CLC 9, 60**
See also AAYA 6; CA 49-52; CANR 3, 43;
DLBY 80; MTCW; SATA 10

Dillard, R(ichard) H(enry) W(ilde)
1937- . . . . **CLC 5**
See also CA 21-24R; CAAS 7; CANR 10;
DLB 5

Dillon, Eilis 1920- . . . . **CLC 17**
See also CA 9-12R; CAAS 3; CANR 4, 38;
CLR 26; MAICYA; SATA 2, 74

Dimont, Penelope
See Mortimer, Penelope (Ruth)

Dinesen, Isak . . . . **CLC 10, 29; SSC 7**
See also Blixen, Karen (Christentze
Dinesen)

Ding Ling . . . . **CLC 68**
See also Chiang Pin-chin

Disch, Thomas M(ichael) 1940- . . . **CLC 7, 36**
See also CA 21-24R; CAAS 4; CANR 17,
36; CLR 18; DLB 8; MAICYA; MTCW;
SAAS 15; SATA 54

Disch, Tom
See Disch, Thomas M(ichael)

d'Isly, Georges
See Simenon, Georges (Jacques Christian)

Disraeli, Benjamin 1804-1881 . . **NCLC 2, 39**
See also DLB 21, 55

Ditcum, Steve
See Crumb, R(obert)

Dixon, Paige
See Corcoran, Barbara

Dixon, Stephen 1936- . . . . **CLC 52**
See also CA 89-92; CANR 17, 40; DLB 130

Dobell, Sydney Thompson
1824-1874 .... NCLC **43**
See also DLB 32

Doblin, Alfred .... TCLC **13**
See also Doeblin, Alfred

Dobrolyubov, Nikolai Alexandrovich
1836-1861 .... NCLC **5**

Dobyns, Stephen 1941- .... CLC **37**
See also CA 45-48; CANR 2, 18

Doctorow, E(dgar) L(aurence)
1931- ..... CLC **6, 11, 15, 18, 37, 44, 65**
See also AITN 2; BEST 89:3; CA 45-48;
CANR 2, 33; CDALB 1968-1988; DLB 2,
28; DLBY 80; MTCW

Dodgson, Charles Lutwidge 1832-1898
See Carroll, Lewis
See also CLR 2; DA; MAICYA; YABC 2

Dodson, Owen (Vincent)
1914-1983 .... CLC **79; BLC 1**
See also BW; CA 65-68; 110; CANR 24;
DLB 76

Doeblin, Alfred 1878-1957 .... TCLC **13**
See also Doblin, Alfred
See also CA 110; 141; DLB 66

Doerr, Harriet 1910- .... CLC **34**
See also CA 117; 122

Domecq, H(onorio) Bustos
See Bioy Casares, Adolfo; Borges, Jorge
Luis

Domini, Rey
See Lorde, Audre (Geraldine)

Dominique
See Proust, (Valentin-Louis-George-Eugene-)
Marcel

Don, A
See Stephen, Leslie

Donaldson, Stephen R. 1947- .... CLC **46**
See also CA 89-92; CANR 13

Donleavy, J(ames) P(atrick)
1926- .... CLC **1, 4, 6, 10, 45**
See also AITN 2; CA 9-12R; CANR 24;
DLB 6; MTCW

Donne, John
1572-1631 .... LC **10, 24; DA; PC 1**
See also CDBLB Before 1660; DLB 121

Donnell, David 1939(?)- .... CLC **34**

Donoso (Yanez), Jose
1924- .... CLC **4, 8, 11, 32; HLC 1**
See also CA 81-84; CANR 32; DLB 113;
HW; MTCW

Donovan, John 1928-1992 .... CLC **35**
See also CA 97-100; 137; CLR 3;
MAICYA; SATA 29

Don Roberto
See Cunninghame Graham, R(obert)
B(ontine)

Doolittle, Hilda
1886-1961 ..... CLC **3, 8, 14, 31, 34, 73;**
DA; PC 5; WLC
See also H. D.
See also CA 97-100; CANR 35; DLB 4, 45;
MTCW

Dorfman, Ariel 1942- ... CLC **48, 77; HLC 1**
See also CA 124; 130; HW

Dorn, Edward (Merton) 1929- ... CLC **10, 18**
See also CA 93-96; CANR 42; DLB 5

Dorsan, Luc
See Simenon, Georges (Jacques Christian)

Dorsange, Jean
See Simenon, Georges (Jacques Christian)

Dos Passos, John (Roderigo)
1896-1970 ...... CLC **1, 4, 8, 11, 15, 25,**
34; DA; WLC
See also CA 1-4R; 29-32R; CANR 3;
CDALB 1929-1941; DLB 4, 9; DLBD 1;
MTCW

Dossage, Jean
See Simenon, Georges (Jacques Christian)

Dostoevsky, Fedor Mikhailovich
1821-1881 ...... NCLC **2, 7, 21, 33, 43;**
DA; SSC 2; WLC

Doughty, Charles M(ontagu)
1843-1926 .... TCLC **27**
See also CA 115; DLB 19, 57

Douglas, Ellen
See Haxton, Josephine Ayres

Douglas, Gavin 1475(?)-1522 .... LC **20**

Douglas, Keith 1920-1944 .... TCLC **40**
See also DLB 27

Douglas, Leonard
See Bradbury, Ray (Douglas)

Douglas, Michael
See Crichton, (John) Michael

Douglass, Frederick
1817(?)-1895 ..... NCLC **7; BLC 1; DA;**
WLC
See also CDALB 1640-1865; DLB 1, 43, 50,
79; SATA 29

Dourado, (Waldomiro Freitas) Autran
1926- .... CLC **23, 60**
See also CA 25-28R; CANR 34

Dourado, Waldomiro Autran
See Dourado, (Waldomiro Freitas) Autran

Dove, Rita (Frances)
1952- .... CLC **50, 81; PC 6**
See also BW; CA 109; CANR 27, 42;
DLB 120

Dowell, Coleman 1925-1985 .... CLC **60**
See also CA 25-28R; 117; CANR 10;
DLB 130

Dowson, Ernest Christopher
1867-1900 .... TCLC **4**
See also CA 105; DLB 19, 135

Doyle, A. Conan
See Doyle, Arthur Conan

Doyle, Arthur Conan
1859-1930 .... TCLC **7; DA; SSC 12;**
WLC
See also CA 104; 122; CDBLB 1890-1914;
DLB 18, 70; MTCW; SATA 24

Doyle, Conan 1859-1930
See Doyle, Arthur Conan

Doyle, John
See Graves, Robert (von Ranke)

Doyle, Roddy 1958(?)- .... CLC **81**

Doyle, Sir A. Conan
See Doyle, Arthur Conan

Doyle, Sir Arthur Conan
See Doyle, Arthur Conan

Dr. A
See Asimov, Isaac; Silverstein, Alvin

Drabble, Margaret
1939- .... CLC **2, 3, 5, 8, 10, 22, 53**
See also CA 13-16R; CANR 18, 35;
CDBLB 1960 to Present; DLB 14;
MTCW; SATA 48

Drapier, M. B.
See Swift, Jonathan

Drayham, James
See Mencken, H(enry) L(ouis)

Drayton, Michael 1563-1631 .... LC **8**

Dreadstone, Carl
See Campbell, (John) Ramsey

Dreiser, Theodore (Herman Albert)
1871-1945 .... TCLC **10, 18, 35; DA;**
WLC
See also CA 106; 132; CDALB 1865-1917;
DLB 9, 12, 102; DLBD 1; MTCW

Drexler, Rosalyn 1926- .... CLC **2, 6**
See also CA 81-84

Dreyer, Carl Theodor 1889-1968.... CLC **16**
See also CA 116

Drieu la Rochelle, Pierre(-Eugene)
1893-1945 .... TCLC **21**
See also CA 117; DLB 72

Drop Shot
See Cable, George Washington

Droste-Hulshoff, Annette Freiin von
1797-1848 .... NCLC **3**
See also DLB 133

Drummond, Walter
See Silverberg, Robert

Drummond, William Henry
1854-1907 .... TCLC **25**
See also DLB 92

Drummond de Andrade, Carlos
1902-1987 .... CLC **18**
See also Andrade, Carlos Drummond de
See also CA 132; 123

Drury, Allen (Stuart) 1918- .... CLC **37**
See also CA 57-60; CANR 18

Dryden, John
1631-1700 ... LC **3, 21; DA; DC 3; WLC**
See also CDBLB 1660-1789; DLB 80, 101,
131

Duberman, Martin 1930- .... CLC **8**
See also CA 1-4R; CANR 2

Dubie, Norman (Evans) 1945- ...... CLC **36**
See also CA 69-72; CANR 12; DLB 120

Du Bois, W(illiam) E(dward) B(urghardt)
1868-1963 .... CLC **1, 2, 13, 64; BLC 1;**
DA; WLC
See also BW; CA 85-88; CANR 34;
CDALB 1865-1917; DLB 47, 50, 91;
MTCW; SATA 42

Dubus, Andre 1936- .... CLC **13, 36**
See also CA 21-24R; CANR 17; DLB 130

Duca Minimo
See D'Annunzio, Gabriele

Ducharme, Rejean 1941- .... CLC **74**
See also DLB 60

Duclos, Charles Pinot 1704-1772 . . . . . **LC 1**

Dudek, Louis 1918- . . . . **CLC 11, 19**
See also CA 45-48; CAAS 14; CANR 1;
DLB 88

Duerrenmatt, Friedrich
. . . . **CLC 1, 4, 8, 11, 15, 43**
See also Duerrenmatt, Friedrich
See also DLB 69, 124

Duerrenmatt, Friedrich
1921-1990 . . . . . . **CLC 1, 4, 8, 11, 15, 43**
See also Duerrenmatt, Friedrich
See also CA 17-20R; CANR 33; DLB 69,
124; MTCW

Duffy, Bruce (?)- . . . . **CLC 50**

Duffy, Maureen 1933- . . . . **CLC 37**
See also CA 25-28R; CANR 33; DLB 14;
MTCW

Dugan, Alan 1923- . . . . **CLC 2, 6**
See also CA 81-84; DLB 5

du Gard, Roger Martin
See Martin du Gard, Roger

Duhamel, Georges 1884-1966 . . . . **CLC 8**
See also CA 81-84; 25-28R; CANR 35;
DLB 65; MTCW

Dujardin, Edouard (Emile Louis)
1861-1949 . . . . **TCLC 13**
See also CA 109; DLB 123

Dumas, Alexandre (Davy de la Pailleterie)
1802-1870 . . . . **NCLC 11; DA; WLC**
See also DLB 119; SATA 18

Dumas, Alexandre
1824-1895 . . . . **NCLC 9; DC 1**

Dumas, Claudine
See Malzberg, Barry N(athaniel)

Dumas, Henry L. 1934-1968 . . . . . **CLC 6, 62**
See also BW; CA 85-88; DLB 41

du Maurier, Daphne
1907-1989 . . . . **CLC 6, 11, 59**
See also CA 5-8R; 128; CANR 6; MTCW;
SATA 27, 60

Dunbar, Paul Laurence
1872-1906 . . . . **TCLC 2, 12; BLC 1; DA;**
　　　　　　　　　　　PC 5; SSC 8; WLC
See also BW; CA 104; 124;
CDALB 1865-1917; DLB 50, 54, 78;
SATA 34

Dunbar, William 1460(?)-1530(?) . . . . **LC 20**

Duncan, Lois 1934- . . . . **CLC 26**
See also AAYA 4; CA 1-4R; CANR 2, 23,
36; CLR 29; JRDA; MAICYA; SAAS 2;
SATA 1, 36, 75

Duncan, Robert (Edward)
1919-1988 . . . . **CLC 1, 2, 4, 7, 15, 41, 55;**
　　　　　　　　　　　　　　　　　　　　PC 2
See also CA 9-12R; 124; CANR 28; DLB 5,
16; MTCW

Dunlap, William 1766-1839 . . . . **NCLC 2**
See also DLB 30, 37, 59

Dunn, Douglas (Eaglesham)
1942- . . . . **CLC 6, 40**
See also CA 45-48; CANR 2, 33; DLB 40;
MTCW

Dunn, Katherine (Karen) 1945- . . . . . **CLC 71**
See also CA 33-36R

Dunn, Stephen 1939- . . . . **CLC 36**
See also CA 33-36R; CANR 12; DLB 105

Dunne, Finley Peter 1867-1936 . . . . **TCLC 28**
See also CA 108; DLB 11, 23

Dunne, John Gregory 1932- . . . . **CLC 28**
See also CA 25-28R; CANR 14; DLBY 80

Dunsany, Edward John Moreton Drax
Plunkett 1878-1957
See Dunsany, Lord; Lord Dunsany
See also CA 104; DLB 10

Dunsany, Lord . . . . **TCLC 2**
See also Dunsany, Edward John Moreton
Drax Plunkett
See also DLB 77

du Perry, Jean
See Simenon, Georges (Jacques Christian)

Durang, Christopher (Ferdinand)
1949- . . . . **CLC 27, 38**
See also CA 105

Duras, Marguerite
1914- . . . . . . **CLC 3, 6, 11, 20, 34, 40, 68**
See also CA 25-28R; DLB 83; MTCW

Durban, (Rosa) Pam 1947- . . . . **CLC 39**
See also CA 123

Durcan, Paul 1944- . . . . **CLC 43, 70**
See also CA 134

Durrell, Lawrence (George)
1912-1990 . . . . **CLC 1, 4, 6, 8, 13, 27, 41**
See also CA 9-12R; 132; CANR 40;
CDBLB 1945-1960; DLB 15, 27;
DLBY 90; MTCW

Dutt, Toru 1856-1877 . . . . **NCLC 29**

Dwight, Timothy 1752-1817 . . . . . . **NCLC 13**
See also DLB 37

Dworkin, Andrea 1946- . . . . **CLC 43**
See also CA 77-80; CANR 16, 39; MTCW

Dwyer, Deanna
See Koontz, Dean R(ay)

Dwyer, K. R.
See Koontz, Dean R(ay)

Dylan, Bob 1941- . . . . . . **CLC 3, 4, 6, 12, 77**
See also CA 41-44R; DLB 16

Eagleton, Terence (Francis) 1943-
See Eagleton, Terry
See also CA 57-60; CANR 7, 23; MTCW

Eagleton, Terry . . . . **CLC 63**
See also Eagleton, Terence (Francis)

Early, Jack
See Scoppettone, Sandra

East, Michael
See West, Morris L(anglo)

Eastaway, Edward
See Thomas, (Philip) Edward

Eastlake, William (Derry) 1917- . . . . . **CLC 8**
See also CA 5-8R; CAAS 1; CANR 5;
DLB 6

Eberhart, Richard (Ghormley)
1904- . . . . **CLC 3, 11, 19, 56**
See also CA 1-4R; CANR 2;
CDALB 1941-1968; DLB 48; MTCW

Eberstadt, Fernanda 1960- . . . . **CLC 39**
See also CA 136

Echegaray (y Eizaguirre), Jose (Maria Waldo)
1832-1916 . . . . **TCLC 4**
See also CA 104; CANR 32; HW; MTCW

Echeverria, (Jose) Esteban (Antonino)
1805-1851 . . . . **NCLC 18**

Echo
See Proust, (Valentin-Louis-George-Eugene-)
Marcel

Eckert, Allan W. 1931- . . . . **CLC 17**
See also CA 13-16R; CANR 14; SATA 27,
29

Eckhart, Meister 1260(?)-1328(?) . . **CMLC 9**
See also DLB 115

Eckmar, F. R.
See de Hartog, Jan

Eco, Umberto 1932- . . . . **CLC 28, 60**
See also BEST 90:1; CA 77-80; CANR 12,
33; MTCW

Eddison, E(ric) R(ucker)
1882-1945 . . . . **TCLC 15**
See also CA 109

Edel, (Joseph) Leon 1907- . . . . . . **CLC 29, 34**
See also CA 1-4R; CANR 1, 22; DLB 103

Eden, Emily 1797-1869 . . . . **NCLC 10**

Edgar, David 1948- . . . . **CLC 42**
See also CA 57-60; CANR 12; DLB 13;
MTCW

Edgerton, Clyde (Carlyle) 1944- . . . . **CLC 39**
See also CA 118; 134

Edgeworth, Maria 1767-1849 . . . . . . **NCLC 1**
See also DLB 116; SATA 21

Edmonds, Paul
See Kuttner, Henry

Edmonds, Walter D(umaux) 1903- . . **CLC 35**
See also CA 5-8R; CANR 2; DLB 9;
MAICYA; SAAS 4; SATA 1, 27

Edmondson, Wallace
See Ellison, Harlan

Edson, Russell . . . . **CLC 13**
See also CA 33-36R

Edwards, G(erald) B(asil)
1899-1976 . . . . **CLC 25**
See also CA 110

Edwards, Gus 1939- . . . . **CLC 43**
See also CA 108

Edwards, Jonathan 1703-1758 . . . . **LC 7; DA**
See also DLB 24

Efron, Marina Ivanovna Tsvetaeva
See Tsvetaeva (Efron), Marina (Ivanovna)

Ehle, John (Marsden, Jr.) 1925- . . . . **CLC 27**
See also CA 9-12R

Ehrenbourg, Ilya (Grigoryevich)
See Ehrenburg, Ilya (Grigoryevich)

Ehrenburg, Ilya (Grigoryevich)
1891-1967 . . . . **CLC 18, 34, 62**
See also CA 102; 25-28R

Ehrenburg, Ilyo (Grigoryevich)
See Ehrenburg, Ilya (Grigoryevich)

Eich, Guenter 1907-1972 . . . . **CLC 15**
See also CA 111; 93-96; DLB 69, 124

Eichendorff, Joseph Freiherr von
1788-1857 . . . . **NCLC 8**
See also DLB 90

Evan, Evin
　　See Faust, Frederick (Schiller)

Evans, Evan
　　See Faust, Frederick (Schiller)

Evans, Marian
　　See Eliot, George

Evans, Mary Ann
　　See Eliot, George

Evarts, Esther
　　See Benson, Sally

Everett, Percival
　　See Everett, Percival L.

Everett, Percival L.　1956-......... **CLC 57**
　　See also CA 129

Everson, R(onald) G(ilmour)
　　1903-...................... **CLC 27**
　　See also CA 17-20R; DLB 88

Everson, William (Oliver)
　　1912-................... **CLC 1, 5, 14**
　　See also CA 9-12R; CANR 20; DLB 5, 16;
　　MTCW

Evtushenko, Evgenii Aleksandrovich
　　See Yevtushenko, Yevgeny (Alexandrovich)

Ewart, Gavin (Buchanan)
　　1916-.................... **CLC 13, 46**
　　See also CA 89-92; CANR 17; DLB 40;
　　MTCW

Ewers, Hanns Heinz　1871-1943 ... **TCLC 12**
　　See also CA 109

Ewing, Frederick R.
　　See Sturgeon, Theodore (Hamilton)

Exley, Frederick (Earl)
　　1929-1992 .... **CLC 6, 11**
　　See also AITN 2; CA 81-84; 138; DLBY 81

Eynhardt, Guillermo
　　See Quiroga, Horacio (Sylvestre)

Ezekiel, Nissim　1924-............. **CLC 61**
　　See also CA 61-64

Ezekiel, Tish O'Dowd　1943-....... **CLC 34**
　　See also CA 129

Fadeyev, A.
　　See Bulgya, Alexander Alexandrovich

Fadeyev, Alexander.............. **TCLC 53**
　　See also Bulgya, Alexander Alexandrovich

Fagen, Donald　1948-............. **CLC 26**

Fainzilberg, Ilya Arnoldovich　1897-1937
　　See Ilf, Ilya
　　See also CA 120

Fair, Ronald L.　1932-............. **CLC 18**
　　See also BW; CA 69-72; CANR 25; DLB 33

Fairbairns, Zoe (Ann)　1948- .... **CLC 32**
　　See also CA 103; CANR 21

Falco, Gian
　　See Papini, Giovanni

Falconer, James
　　See Kirkup, James

Falconer, Kenneth
　　See Kornbluth, C(yril) M.

Falkland, Samuel
　　See Heijermans, Herman

Fallaci, Oriana　1930-............. **CLC 11**
　　See also CA 77-80; CANR 15; MTCW

Faludy, George　1913-............. **CLC 42**
　　See also CA 21-24R

Faludy, Gyoergy
　　See Faludy, George

Fanon, Frantz　1925-1961... **CLC 74; BLC 2**
　　See also BW; CA 116; 89-92

Fanshawe, Ann .... **LC 11**

Fante, John (Thomas)　1911-1983 ... **CLC 60**
　　See also CA 69-72; 109; CANR 23;
　　DLB 130; DLBY 83

Farah, Nuruddin　1945-..... **CLC 53; BLC 2**
　　See also CA 106; DLB 125

Fargue, Leon-Paul　1876(?)-1947 ... **TCLC 11**
　　See also CA 109

Farigoule, Louis
　　See Romains, Jules

Farina, Richard　1936(?)-1966 .... **CLC 9**
　　See also CA 81-84; 25-28R

Farley, Walter (Lorimer)
　　1915-1989 .... **CLC 17**
　　See also CA 17-20R; CANR 8, 29; DLB 22;
　　JRDA; MAICYA; SATA 2, 43

Farmer, Philip Jose　1918-....... **CLC 1, 19**
　　See also CA 1-4R; CANR 4, 35; DLB 8;
　　MTCW

Farquhar, George　1677-1707 .... **LC 21**
　　See also DLB 84

Farrell, J(ames) G(ordon)
　　1935-1979 .... **CLC 6**
　　See also CA 73-76; 89-92; CANR 36;
　　DLB 14; MTCW

Farrell, James T(homas)
　　1904-1979 ...... **CLC 1, 4, 8, 11, 66**
　　See also CA 5-8R; 89-92; CANR 9; DLB 4,
　　9, 86; DLBD 2; MTCW

Farren, Richard J.
　　See Betjeman, John

Farren, Richard M.
　　See Betjeman, John

Fassbinder, Rainer Werner
　　1946-1982 .... **CLC 20**
　　See also CA 93-96; 106; CANR 31

Fast, Howard (Melvin)　1914- ...... **CLC 23**
　　See also CA 1-4R; CAAS 18; CANR 1, 33;
　　DLB 9; SATA 7

Faulcon, Robert
　　See Holdstock, Robert P.

Faulkner, William (Cuthbert)
　　1897-1962 ..... **CLC 1, 3, 6, 8, 9, 11, 14,
　　18, 28, 52, 68; DA; SSC 1; WLC**
　　See also AAYA 7; CA 81-84; CANR 33;
　　CDALB 1929-1941; DLB 9, 11, 44, 102;
　　DLBD 2; DLBY 86; MTCW

Fauset, Jessie Redmon
　　1884(?)-1961 ...... **CLC 19, 54; BLC 2**
　　See also BW; CA 109; DLB 51

Faust, Frederick (Schiller)
　　1892-1944(?) .... **TCLC 49**
　　See also CA 108

Faust, Irvin　1924-................. **CLC 8**
　　See also CA 33-36R; CANR 28; DLB 2, 28;
　　DLBY 80

Fawkes, Guy
　　See Benchley, Robert (Charles)

Fearing, Kenneth (Flexner)
　　1902-1961 .... **CLC 51**
　　See also CA 93-96; DLB 9

Fecamps, Elise
　　See Creasey, John

Federman, Raymond　1928- ...... **CLC 6, 47**
　　See also CA 17-20R; CAAS 8; CANR 10,
　　43; DLBY 80

Federspiel, J(uerg) F.　1931-........ **CLC 42**

Feiffer, Jules (Ralph)　1929-.... **CLC 2, 8, 64**
　　See also AAYA 3; CA 17-20R; CANR 30;
　　DLB 7, 44; MTCW; SATA 8, 61

Feige, Hermann Albert Otto Maximilian
　　See Traven, B.

Fei-Kan, Li
　　See Li Fei-kan

Feinberg, David B.　1956-.......... **CLC 59**
　　See also CA 135

Feinstein, Elaine　1930-............ **CLC 36**
　　See also CA 69-72; CAAS 1; CANR 31;
　　DLB 14, 40; MTCW

Feldman, Irving (Mordecai)　1928-.... **CLC 7**
　　See also CA 1-4R; CANR 1

Fellini, Federico　1920-1993 ..... **CLC 16, 81**
　　See also CA 65-68; CANR 33

Felsen, Henry Gregor　1916- .... **CLC 17**
　　See also CA 1-4R; CANR 1; SAAS 2;
　　SATA 1

Fenton, James Martin　1949- .... **CLC 32**
　　See also CA 102; DLB 40

Ferber, Edna　1887-1968............. **CLC 18**
　　See also AITN 1; CA 5-8R; 25-28R; DLB 9,
　　28, 86; MTCW; SATA 7

Ferguson, Helen
　　See Kavan, Anna

Ferguson, Samuel　1810-1886..... **NCLC 33**
　　See also DLB 32

Ferling, Lawrence
　　See Ferlinghetti, Lawrence (Monsanto)

Ferlinghetti, Lawrence (Monsanto)
　　1919(?)-........ **CLC 2, 6, 10, 27; PC 1**
　　See also CA 5-8R; CANR 3, 41;
　　CDALB 1941-1968; DLB 5, 16; MTCW

Fernandez, Vicente Garcia Huidobro
　　See Huidobro Fernandez, Vicente Garcia

Ferrer, Gabriel (Francisco Victor) Miro
　　See Miro (Ferrer), Gabriel (Francisco
　　Victor)

Ferrier, Susan (Edmonstone)
　　1782-1854 .... **NCLC 8**
　　See also DLB 116

Ferrigno, Robert　1948(?)-......... **CLC 65**
　　See also CA 140

Feuchtwanger, Lion　1884-1958 ..... **TCLC 3**
　　See also CA 104; DLB 66

Feydeau, Georges (Leon Jules Marie)
　　1862-1921 .... **TCLC 22**
　　See also CA 113

Ficino, Marsilio　1433-1499 .... **LC 12**

Fiedeler, Hans
　　See Doeblin, Alfred

Fiedler, Leslie A(aron)
1917- . . . . CLC 4, 13, 24
See also CA 9-12R; CANR 7; DLB 28, 67;
MTCW

Field, Andrew   1938- . . . . CLC 44
See also CA 97-100; CANR 25

Field, Eugene   1850-1895 . . . . NCLC 3
See also DLB 23, 42; MAICYA; SATA 16

Field, Gans T.
See Wellman, Manly Wade

Field, Michael . . . . TCLC 43

Field, Peter
See Hobson, Laura Z(ametkin)

Fielding, Henry
1707-1754 . . . . LC 1; DA; WLC
See also CDBLB 1660-1789; DLB 39, 84,
101

Fielding, Sarah   1710-1768 . . . . LC 1
See also DLB 39

Fierstein, Harvey (Forbes)   1954- . . . CLC 33
See also CA 123; 129

Figes, Eva   1932- . . . . CLC 31
See also CA 53-56; CANR 4; DLB 14

Finch, Robert (Duer Claydon)
1900- . . . . CLC 18
See also CA 57-60; CANR 9, 24; DLB 88

Findley, Timothy   1930- . . . . CLC 27
See also CA 25-28R; CANR 12, 42;
DLB 53

Fink, William
See Mencken, H(enry) L(ouis)

Firbank, Louis   1942-
See Reed, Lou
See also CA 117

Firbank, (Arthur Annesley) Ronald
1886-1926 . . . . TCLC 1
See also CA 104; DLB 36

Fisher, M(ary) F(rances) K(ennedy)
1908-1992 . . . . CLC 76
See also CA 77-80; 138

Fisher, Roy   1930- . . . . CLC 25
See also CA 81-84; CAAS 10; CANR 16;
DLB 40

Fisher, Rudolph
1897-1934 . . . . TCLC 11; BLC 2
See also BW; CA 107; 124; DLB 51, 102

Fisher, Vardis (Alvero)   1895-1968. . . . CLC 7
See also CA 5-8R; 25-28R; DLB 9

Fiske, Tarleton
See Bloch, Robert (Albert)

Fitch, Clarke
See Sinclair, Upton (Beall)

Fitch, John IV
See Cormier, Robert (Edmund)

Fitgerald, Penelope   1916- . . . . CLC 61

Fitzgerald, Captain Hugh
See Baum, L(yman) Frank

FitzGerald, Edward   1809-1883 . . . . NCLC 9
See also DLB 32

Fitzgerald, F(rancis) Scott (Key)
1896-1940 . . . . . TCLC 1, 6, 14, 28; DA;
SSC 6; WLC
See also AITN 1; CA 110; 123;
CDALB 1917-1929; DLB 4, 9, 86;
DLBD 1; DLBY 81; MTCW

Fitzgerald, Penelope   1916- . . . . . . CLC 19, 51
See also CA 85-88; CAAS 10; DLB 14

Fitzgerald, Robert (Stuart)
1910-1985 . . . . CLC 39
See also CA 1-4R; 114; CANR 1; DLBY 80

FitzGerald, Robert D(avid)
1902-1987 . . . . CLC 19
See also CA 17-20R

Fitzgerald, Zelda (Sayre)
1900-1948 . . . . TCLC 52
See also CA 117; 126; DLBY 84

Flanagan, Thomas (James Bonner)
1923- . . . . CLC 25, 52
See also CA 108; DLBY 80; MTCW

Flaubert, Gustave
1821-1880 . . . . NCLC 2, 10, 19; DA;
SSC 11; WLC
See also DLB 119

Flecker, (Herman) James Elroy
1884-1915 . . . . TCLC 43
See also CA 109; DLB 10, 19

Fleming, Ian (Lancaster)
1908-1964 . . . . CLC 3, 30
See also CA 5-8R; CDBLB 1945-1960;
DLB 87; MTCW; SATA 9

Fleming, Thomas (James)   1927- . . . . CLC 37
See also CA 5-8R; CANR 10; SATA 8

Fletcher, John Gould   1886-1950 . . . TCLC 35
See also CA 107; DLB 4, 45

Fleur, Paul
See Pohl, Frederik

Flooglebuckle, Al
See Spiegelman, Art

Flying Officer X
See Bates, H(erbert) E(rnest)

Fo, Dario   1926- . . . . CLC 32
See also CA 116; 128; MTCW

Fogarty, Jonathan Titulescu Esq.
See Farrell, James T(homas)

Folke, Will
See Bloch, Robert (Albert)

Follett, Ken(neth Martin)   1949- . . . . CLC 18
See also AAYA 6; BEST 89:4; CA 81-84;
CANR 13, 33; DLB 87; DLBY 81;
MTCW

Fontane, Theodor   1819-1898 . . . . . NCLC 26
See also DLB 129

Foote, Horton   1916- . . . . CLC 51
See also CA 73-76; CANR 34; DLB 26

Foote, Shelby   1916- . . . . CLC 75
See also CA 5-8R; CANR 3; DLB 2, 17

Forbes, Esther   1891-1967. . . . . CLC 12
See also CA 13-14; 25-28R; CAP 1;
CLR 27; DLB 22; JRDA; MAICYA;
SATA 2

Forche, Carolyn (Louise)   1950- . . . . . CLC 25
See also CA 109; 117; DLB 5

Ford, Elbur
See Hibbert, Eleanor Alice Burford

Ford, Ford Madox
1873-1939 . . . . TCLC 1, 15, 39
See also CA 104; 132; CDBLB 1914-1945;
DLB 34, 98; MTCW

Ford, John   1895-1973. . . . . CLC 16
See also CA 45-48

Ford, Richard   1944- . . . . CLC 46
See also CA 69-72; CANR 11

Ford, Webster
See Masters, Edgar Lee

Foreman, Richard   1937- . . . . CLC 50
See also CA 65-68; CANR 32

Forester, C(ecil) S(cott)
1899-1966 . . . . CLC 35
See also CA 73-76; 25-28R; SATA 13

Forez
See Mauriac, Francois (Charles)

Forman, James Douglas   1932- . . . . . . CLC 21
See also CA 9-12R; CANR 4, 19, 42;
JRDA; MAICYA; SATA 8, 70

Fornes, Maria Irene   1930- . . . . . . CLC 39, 61
See also CA 25-28R; CANR 28; DLB 7;
HW; MTCW

Forrest, Leon   1937- . . . . CLC 4
See also BW; CA 89-92; CAAS 7;
CANR 25; DLB 33

Forster, E(dward) M(organ)
1879-1970 . . . . . CLC 1, 2, 3, 4, 9, 10, 13,
15, 22, 45, 77; DA; WLC
See also AAYA 2; CA 13-14; 25-28R;
CAP 1; CDBLB 1914-1945; DLB 34, 98;
DLBD 10; MTCW; SATA 57

Forster, John   1812-1876 . . . . NCLC 11

Forsyth, Frederick   1938- . . . . . . CLC 2, 5, 36
See also BEST 89:4; CA 85-88; CANR 38;
DLB 87; MTCW

Forten, Charlotte L. . . . . TCLC 16; BLC 2
See also Grimke, Charlotte L(ottie) Forten
See also DLB 50

Foscolo, Ugo   1778-1827. . . . . NCLC 8

Fosse, Bob . . . . CLC 20
See also Fosse, Robert Louis

Fosse, Robert Louis   1927-1987
See Fosse, Bob
See also CA 110; 123

Foster, Stephen Collins
1826-1864 . . . . NCLC 26

Foucault, Michel
1926-1984 . . . . CLC 31, 34, 69
See also CA 105; 113; CANR 34; MTCW

Fouque, Friedrich (Heinrich Karl) de la Motte
1777-1843 . . . . NCLC 2
See also DLB 90

Fournier, Henri Alban   1886-1914
See Alain-Fournier
See also CA 104

Fournier, Pierre   1916- . . . . CLC 11
See also Gascar, Pierre
See also CA 89-92; CANR 16, 40

Fowles, John
1926- . . . . CLC 1, 2, 3, 4, 6, 9, 10, 15, 33
See also CA 5-8R; CANR 25; CDBLB 1960
to Present; DLB 14; MTCW; SATA 22

Gallico, Paul (William) 1897-1976 ... **CLC 2**
See also AITN 1; CA 5-8R; 69-72;
CANR 23; DLB 9; MAICYA; SATA 13

Gallup, Ralph
See Whitemore, Hugh (John)

Galsworthy, John
1867-1933 .... **TCLC 1, 45; DA; WLC 2**
See also CA 104; 141; CDBLB 1890-1914;
DLB 10, 34, 98

Galt, John 1779-1839 .... **NCLC 1**
See also DLB 99, 116

Galvin, James 1951- .... **CLC 38**
See also CA 108; CANR 26

Gamboa, Federico 1864-1939 ..... **TCLC 36**

Gann, Ernest Kellogg 1910-1991 .... **CLC 23**
See also AITN 1; CA 1-4R; 136; CANR 1

Garcia, Cristina 1958- .... **CLC 76**
See also CA 141

Garcia Lorca, Federico
1898-1936 .... **TCLC 1, 7, 49; DA;
DC 2; HLC 2; PC 3; WLC**
See also CA 104; 131; DLB 108; HW;
MTCW

Garcia Marquez, Gabriel (Jose)
1928- .... **CLC 2, 3, 8, 10, 15, 27, 47, 55;
DA; HLC 1; SSC 8; WLC**
See also Marquez, Gabriel (Jose) Garcia
See also AAYA 3; BEST 89:1, 90:4;
CA 33-36R; CANR 10, 28; DLB 113;
HW; MTCW

Gard, Janice
See Latham, Jean Lee

Gard, Roger Martin du
See Martin du Gard, Roger

Gardam, Jane 1928- .... **CLC 43**
See also CA 49-52; CANR 2, 18, 33;
CLR 12; DLB 14; MAICYA; MTCW;
SAAS 9; SATA 28, 39

Gardner, Herb .... **CLC 44**

Gardner, John (Champlin), Jr.
1933-1982 ..... **CLC 2, 3, 5, 7, 8, 10, 18,
28, 34; SSC 7**
See also AITN 1; CA 65-68; 107;
CANR 33; DLB 2; DLBY 82; MTCW;
SATA 31, 40

Gardner, John (Edmund) 1926- ..... **CLC 30**
See also CA 103; CANR 15; MTCW

Gardner, Noel
See Kuttner, Henry

Gardons, S. S.
See Snodgrass, W(illiam) D(e Witt)

Garfield, Leon 1921- .... **CLC 12**
See also AAYA 8; CA 17-20R; CANR 38,
41; CLR 21; JRDA; MAICYA; SATA 1,
32

Garland, (Hannibal) Hamlin
1860-1940 .... **TCLC 3**
See also CA 104; DLB 12, 71, 78

Garneau, (Hector de) Saint-Denys
1912-1943 .... **TCLC 13**
See also CA 111; DLB 88

Garner, Alan 1934- .... **CLC 17**
See also CA 73-76; CANR 15; CLR 20;
MAICYA; MTCW; SATA 18, 69

Garner, Hugh 1913-1979 .... **CLC 13**
See also CA 69-72; CANR 31; DLB 68

Garnett, David 1892-1981 .... **CLC 3**
See also CA 5-8R; 103; CANR 17; DLB 34

Garos, Stephanie
See Katz, Steve

Garrett, George (Palmer)
1929- .... **CLC 3, 11, 51**
See also CA 1-4R; CAAS 5; CANR 1, 42;
DLB 2, 5, 130; DLBY 83

Garrick, David 1717-1779 .... **LC 15**
See also DLB 84

Garrigue, Jean 1914-1972 .... **CLC 2, 8**
See also CA 5-8R; 37-40R; CANR 20

Garrison, Frederick
See Sinclair, Upton (Beall)

Garth, Will
See Hamilton, Edmond; Kuttner, Henry

Garvey, Marcus (Moziah, Jr.)
1887-1940 .... **TCLC 41; BLC 2**
See also BW; CA 120; 124

Gary, Romain .... **CLC 25**
See also Kacew, Romain
See also DLB 83

Gascar, Pierre .... **CLC 11**
See also Fournier, Pierre

Gascoyne, David (Emery) 1916- .... **CLC 45**
See also CA 65-68; CANR 10, 28; DLB 20;
MTCW

Gaskell, Elizabeth Cleghorn
1810-1865 .... **NCLC 5**
See also CDBLB 1832-1890; DLB 21

Gass, William H(oward)
1924- ... **CLC 1, 2, 8, 11, 15, 39; SSC 12**
See also CA 17-20R; CANR 30; DLB 2;
MTCW

Gasset, Jose Ortega y
See Ortega y Gasset, Jose

Gautier, Theophile 1811-1872 ..... **NCLC 1**
See also DLB 119

Gawsworth, John
See Bates, H(erbert) E(rnest)

Gaye, Marvin (Penze) 1939-1984 ... **CLC 26**
See also CA 112

Gebler, Carlo (Ernest) 1954- .... **CLC 39**
See also CA 119; 133

Gee, Maggie (Mary) 1948- .... **CLC 57**
See also CA 130

Gee, Maurice (Gough) 1931- .... **CLC 29**
See also CA 97-100; SATA 46

Gelbart, Larry (Simon) 1923- ... **CLC 21, 61**
See also CA 73-76

Gelber, Jack 1932- .... **CLC 1, 6, 14, 79**
See also CA 1-4R; CANR 2; DLB 7

Gellhorn, Martha Ellis 1908- ... **CLC 14, 60**
See also CA 77-80; DLBY 82

Genet, Jean
1910-1986 ... **CLC 1, 2, 5, 10, 14, 44, 46**
See also CA 13-16R; CANR 18; DLB 72;
DLBY 86; MTCW

Gent, Peter 1942- .... **CLC 29**
See also AITN 1; CA 89-92; DLBY 82

Gentlewoman in New England, A
See Bradstreet, Anne

Gentlewoman in Those Parts, A
See Bradstreet, Anne

George, Jean Craighead 1919- ...... **CLC 35**
See also AAYA 8; CA 5-8R; CANR 25;
CLR 1; DLB 52; JRDA; MAICYA;
SATA 2, 68

George, Stefan (Anton)
1868-1933 .... **TCLC 2, 14**
See also CA 104

Georges, Georges Martin
See Simenon, Georges (Jacques Christian)

Gerhardi, William Alexander
See Gerhardie, William Alexander

Gerhardie, William Alexander
1895-1977 .... **CLC 5**
See also CA 25-28R; 73-76; CANR 18;
DLB 36

Gerstler, Amy 1956- .... **CLC 70**

Gertler, T. .... **CLC 34**
See also CA 116; 121

Ghalib 1797-1869 .... **NCLC 39**

Ghelderode, Michel de
1898-1962 .... **CLC 6, 11**
See also CA 85-88; CANR 40

Ghiselin, Brewster 1903- .... **CLC 23**
See also CA 13-16R; CAAS 10; CANR 13

Ghose, Zulfikar 1935- .... **CLC 42**
See also CA 65-68

Ghosh, Amitav 1956- .... **CLC 44**

Giacosa, Giuseppe 1847-1906 ...... **TCLC 7**
See also CA 104

Gibb, Lee
See Waterhouse, Keith (Spencer)

Gibbon, Lewis Grassic .... **TCLC 4**
See also Mitchell, James Leslie

Gibbons, Kaye 1960- .... **CLC 50**

Gibran, Kahlil 1883-1931 .... **TCLC 1, 9**
See also CA 104

Gibson, William 1914- .... **CLC 23; DA**
See also CA 9-12R; CANR 9, 42; DLB 7;
SATA 66

Gibson, William (Ford) 1948- ... **CLC 39, 63**
See also CA 126; 133

Gide, Andre (Paul Guillaume)
1869-1951 .... **TCLC 5, 12, 36; DA;
SSC 13; WLC**
See also CA 104; 124; DLB 65; MTCW

Gifford, Barry (Colby) 1946- .... **CLC 34**
See also CA 65-68; CANR 9, 30, 40

Gilbert, W(illiam) S(chwenck)
1836-1911 .... **TCLC 3**
See also CA 104; SATA 36

Gilbreth, Frank B., Jr. 1911- ...... **CLC 17**
See also CA 9-12R; SATA 2

Gilchrist, Ellen 1935- .. **CLC 34, 48; SSC 14**
See also CA 113; 116; CANR 41; DLB 130;
MTCW

Giles, Molly 1942- .... **CLC 39**
See also CA 126

Gill, Patrick
See Creasey, John

Gilliam, Terry (Vance) 1940-....... CLC 21
    See also Monty Python
    See also CA 108; 113; CANR 35

Gillian, Jerry
    See Gilliam, Terry (Vance)

Gilliatt, Penelope (Ann Douglass)
    1932-1993 .... CLC 2, 10, 13, 53
    See also AITN 2; CA 13-16R; 141; DLB 14

Gilman, Charlotte (Anna) Perkins (Stetson)
    1860-1935 .... TCLC 9, 37; SSC 13
    See also CA 106

Gilmour, David 1949-............. CLC 35
    See also Pink Floyd
    See also CA 138

Gilpin, William 1724-1804....... NCLC 30

Gilray, J. D.
    See Mencken, H(enry) L(ouis)

Gilroy, Frank D(aniel) 1925-........ CLC 2
    See also CA 81-84; CANR 32; DLB 7

Ginsberg, Allen
    1926- ...... CLC 1, 2, 3, 4, 6, 13, 36, 69;
                                DA; PC 4; WLC 3
    See also AITN 1; CA 1-4R; CANR 2, 41;
    CDALB 1941-1968; DLB 5, 16; MTCW

Ginzburg, Natalia
    1916-1991 .... CLC 5, 11, 54, 70
    See also CA 85-88; 135; CANR 33; MTCW

Giono, Jean 1895-1970....... CLC 4, 11
    See also CA 45-48; 29-32R; CANR 2, 35;
    DLB 72; MTCW

Giovanni, Nikki
    1943 ... CLC 2, 4, 19, 64; BLC 2; DA
    See also AITN 1; BW; CA 29-32R;
    CAAS 6; CANR 18, 41; CLR 6; DLB 5,
    41; MAICYA; MTCW; SATA 24

Giovene, Andrea 1904-............. CLC 7
    See also CA 85-88

Gippius, Zinaida (Nikolayevna) 1869-1945
    See Hippius, Zinaida
    See also CA 106

Giraudoux, (Hippolyte) Jean
    1882-1944 .... TCLC 2, 7
    See also CA 104; DLB 65

Gironella, Jose Maria 1917- .... CLC 11
    See also CA 101

Gissing, George (Robert)
    1857-1903 .... TCLC 3, 24, 47
    See also CA 105; DLB 18, 135

Giurlani, Aldo
    See Palazzeschi, Aldo

Gladkov, Fyodor (Vasilyevich)
    1883-1958 .... TCLC 27

Glanville, Brian (Lester) 1931-...... CLC 6
    See also CA 5-8R; CAAS 9; CANR 3;
    DLB 15; SATA 42

Glasgow, Ellen (Anderson Gholson)
    1873(?)-1945 .... TCLC 2, 7
    See also CA 104; DLB 9, 12

Glassco, John 1909-1981 .... CLC 9
    See also CA 13-16R; 102; CANR 15;
    DLB 68

Glasscock, Amnesia
    See Steinbeck, John (Ernst)

Glasser, Ronald J. 1940(?)-........ CLC 37

Glassman, Joyce
    See Johnson, Joyce

Glendinning, Victoria 1937-........ CLC 50
    See also CA 120; 127

Glissant, Edouard 1928-....... CLC 10, 68

Gloag, Julian 1930- .... CLC 40
    See also AITN 1; CA 65-68; CANR 10

Gluck, Louise (Elisabeth)
    1943- .... CLC 7, 22, 44, 81
    See also Glueck, Louise
    See also CA 33-36R; CANR 40; DLB 5

Glueck, Louise.................. CLC 7, 22
    See also Gluck, Louise (Elisabeth)
    See also DLB 5

Gobineau, Joseph Arthur (Comte) de
    1816-1882 .... NCLC 17
    See also DLB 123

Godard, Jean-Luc 1930-.......... CLC 20
    See also CA 93-96

Godden, (Margaret) Rumer 1907-... CLC 53
    See also AAYA 6; CA 5-8R; CANR 4, 27,
    36; CLR 20; MAICYA; SAAS 12;
    SATA 3, 36

Godoy Alcayaga, Lucila 1889-1957
    See Mistral, Gabriela
    See also CA 104; 131; HW; MTCW

Godwin, Gail (Kathleen)
    1937- .... CLC 5, 8, 22, 31, 69
    See also CA 29-32R; CANR 15, 43; DLB 6;
    MTCW

Godwin, William 1756-1836...... NCLC 14
    See also CDBLB 1789-1832; DLB 39, 104

Goethe, Johann Wolfgang von
    1749-1832 .... NCLC 4, 22, 34; DA;
                                PC 5; WLC 3
    See also DLB 94

Gogarty, Oliver St. John
    1878-1957 .... TCLC 15
    See also CA 109; DLB 15, 19

Gogol, Nikolai (Vasilyevich)
    1809-1852 .... NCLC 5, 15, 31; DA;
                                DC 1; SSC 4; WLC

Goines, Donald
    1937(?)-1974 .... CLC 80; BLC 2
    See also AITN 1; BW; CA 124; 114;
    DLB 33

Gold, Herbert 1924-....... CLC 4, 7, 14, 42
    See also CA 9-12R; CANR 17; DLB 2;
    DLBY 81

Goldbarth, Albert 1948-........ CLC 5, 38
    See also CA 53-56; CANR 6, 40; DLB 120

Goldberg, Anatol 1910-1982 .... CLC 34
    See also CA 131; 117

Goldemberg, Isaac 1945- .... CLC 52
    See also CA 69-72; CAAS 12; CANR 11,
    32; HW

Golden Silver
    See Storm, Hyemeyohsts

Golding, William (Gerald)
    1911-1993 .... CLC 1, 2, 3, 8, 10, 17, 27,
                                58, 81; DA; WLC
    See also AAYA 5; CA 5-8R; 141;
    CANR 13, 33; CDBLB 1945-1960;
    DLB 15, 100; MTCW

Goldman, Emma 1869-1940...... TCLC 13
    See also CA 110

Goldman, Francisco 1955-......... CLC 76

Goldman, William (W.) 1931-.... CLC 1, 48
    See also CA 9-12R; CANR 29; DLB 44

Goldmann, Lucien 1913-1970 ...... CLC 24
    See also CA 25-28; CAP 2

Goldoni, Carlo 1707-1793 .... LC 4

Goldsberry, Steven 1949-.......... CLC 34
    See also CA 131

Goldsmith, Oliver
    1728-1774 .... LC 2; DA; WLC
    See also CDBLB 1660-1789; DLB 39, 89,
    104, 109; SATA 26

Goldsmith, Peter
    See Priestley, J(ohn) B(oynton)

Gombrowicz, Witold
    1904-1969 .... CLC 4, 7, 11, 49
    See also CA 19-20; 25-28R; CAP 2

Gomez de la Serna, Ramon
    1888-1963 .... CLC 9
    See also CA 116; HW

Goncharov, Ivan Alexandrovich
    1812-1891 .... NCLC 1

Goncourt, Edmond (Louis Antoine Huot) de
    1822-1896 .... NCLC 7
    See also DLB 123

Goncourt, Jules (Alfred Huot) de
    1830-1870 .... NCLC 7
    See also DLB 123

Gontier, Fernande 19(?)- .... CLC 50

Goodman, Paul 1911-1972.... CLC 1, 2, 4, 7
    See also CA 19-20; 37-40R; CANR 34;
    CAP 2; DLB 130; MTCW

Gordimer, Nadine
    1923- .... CLC 3, 5, 7, 10, 18, 33, 51, 70;
                                DA
    See also CA 5-8R; CANR 3, 28; MTCW

Gordon, Adam Lindsay
    1833-1870 .... NCLC 21

Gordon, Caroline
    1895-1981 .... CLC 6, 13, 29
    See also CA 11-12; 103; CANR 36; CAP 1;
    DLB 4, 9, 102; DLBY 81; MTCW

Gordon, Charles William 1860-1937
    See Connor, Ralph
    See also CA 109

Gordon, Mary (Catherine)
    1949- .... CLC 13, 22
    See also CA 102; DLB 6; DLBY 81;
    MTCW

Gordon, Sol 1923-................ CLC 26
    See also CA 53-56; CANR 4; SATA 11

Gordone, Charles 1925-.......... CLC 1, 4
    See also BW; CA 93-96; DLB 7; MTCW

Gorenko, Anna Andreevna
    See Akhmatova, Anna

Gorky, Maxim............. TCLC 8; WLC
    See also Peshkov, Alexei Maximovich

Goryan, Sirak
    See Saroyan, William

Gosse, Edmund (William)
    1849-1928 .... TCLC 28
    See also CA 117; DLB 57

Gotlieb, Phyllis Fay (Bloom)
1926- .... CLC **18**
See also CA 13-16R; CANR 7; DLB 88

Gottesman, S. D.
See Kornbluth, C(yril) M.; Pohl, Frederik

Gottfried von Strassburg
fl. c. 1210- .... CMLC **10**

Gould, Lois .... CLC **4, 10**
See also CA 77-80; CANR 29; MTCW

Gourmont, Remy de 1858-1915.... TCLC **17**
See also CA 109

Govier, Katherine 1948- .... CLC **51**
See also CA 101; CANR 18, 40

Goyen, (Charles) William
1915-1983 .... CLC **5, 8, 14, 40**
See also AITN 2; CA 5-8R; 110; CANR 6;
DLB 2; DLBY 83

Goytisolo, Juan
1931- .... CLC **5, 10, 23**; HLC **1**
See also CA 85-88; CANR 32; HW; MTCW

Gozzi, (Conte) Carlo 1720-1806 .. NCLC **23**

Grabbe, Christian Dietrich
1801-1836 .... NCLC **2**
See also DLB 133

Grace, Patricia 1937- .... CLC **56**

Gracian y Morales, Baltasar
1601-1658 .... LC **15**

Gracq, Julien .... CLC **11, 48**
See also Poirier, Louis
See also DLB 83

Grade, Chaim 1910-1982 .... CLC **10**
See also CA 93-96; 107

Graduate of Oxford, A
See Ruskin, John

Graham, John
See Phillips, David Graham

Graham, Jorie 1951- .... CLC **48**
See also CA 111; DLB 120

Graham, R(obert) B(ontine) Cunninghame
See Cunninghame Graham, R(obert)
B(ontine)
See also DLB 98, 135

Graham, Robert
See Haldeman, Joe (William)

Graham, Tom
See Lewis, (Harry) Sinclair

Graham, W(illiam) S(ydney)
1918-1986 .... CLC **29**
See also CA 73-76; 118; DLB 20

Graham, Winston (Mawdsley)
1910- .... CLC **23**
See also CA 49-52; CANR 2, 22; DLB 77

Grant, Skeeter
See Spiegelman, Art

Granville-Barker, Harley
1877-1946 .... TCLC **2**
See also Barker, Harley Granville
See also CA 104

Grass, Guenter (Wilhelm)
1927- ..... CLC **1, 2, 4, 6, 11, 15, 22, 32,
49**; DA; WLC
See also CA 13-16R; CANR 20; DLB 75,
124; MTCW

Gratton, Thomas
See Hulme, T(homas) E(rnest)

Grau, Shirley Ann 1929- .... CLC **4, 9**
See also CA 89-92; CANR 22; DLB 2;
MTCW

Gravel, Fern
See Hall, James Norman

Graver, Elizabeth 1964- .... CLC **70**
See also CA 135

Graves, Richard Perceval 1945- .... CLC **44**
See also CA 65-68; CANR 9, 26

Graves, Robert (von Ranke)
1895-1985 ...... CLC **1, 2, 6, 11, 39, 44,
45**; PC **6**
See also CA 5-8R; 117; CANR 5, 36;
CDBLB 1914-1945; DLB 20, 100;
DLBY 85; MTCW; SATA 45

Gray, Alasdair 1934- .... CLC **41**
See also CA 126; MTCW

Gray, Amlin 1946- .... CLC **29**
See also CA 138

Gray, Francine du Plessix 1930-.... CLC **22**
See also BEST 90:3; CA 61-64; CAAS 2;
CANR 11, 33; MTCW

Gray, John (Henry) 1866-1934 .... TCLC **19**
See also CA 119

Gray, Simon (James Holliday)
1936- .... CLC **9, 14, 36**
See also AITN 1; CA 21-24R; CAAS 3;
CANR 32; DLB 13; MTCW

Gray, Spalding 1941- .... CLC **49**
See also CA 128

Gray, Thomas
1716-1771 ...... LC **4**; DA; PC **2**; WLC
See also CDBLB 1660-1789; DLB 109

Grayson, David
See Baker, Ray Stannard

Grayson, Richard (A.) 1951- .... CLC **38**
See also CA 85-88; CANR 14, 31

Greeley, Andrew M(oran) 1928- .... CLC **28**
See also CA 5-8R; CAAS 7; CANR 7, 43;
MTCW

Green, Brian
See Card, Orson Scott

Green, Hannah
See Greenberg, Joanne (Goldenberg)

Green, Hannah .... CLC **3**
See also CA 73-76

Green, Henry .... CLC **2, 13**
See also Yorke, Henry Vincent
See also DLB 15

Green, Julian (Hartridge) 1900-
See Green, Julien
See also CA 21-24R; CANR 33; DLB 4, 72;
MTCW

Green, Julien .... CLC **3, 11, 77**
See also Green, Julian (Hartridge)

Green, Paul (Eliot) 1894-1981...... CLC **25**
See also AITN 1; CA 5-8R; 103; CANR 3;
DLB 7, 9; DLBY 81

Greenberg, Ivan 1908-1973
See Rahv, Philip
See also CA 85-88

Greenberg, Joanne (Goldenberg)
1932- .... CLC **7, 30**
See also CA 5-8R; CANR 14, 32; SATA 25

Greenberg, Richard 1959(?)- .... CLC **57**
See also CA 138

Greene, Bette 1934- .... CLC **30**
See also AAYA 7; CA 53-56; CANR 4;
CLR 2; JRDA; MAICYA; SAAS 16;
SATA 8

Greene, Gael .... CLC **8**
See also CA 13-16R; CANR 10

Greene, Graham
1904-1991 .... CLC **1, 3, 6, 9, 14, 18, 27,
37, 70, 72**; DA; WLC
See also AITN 2; CA 13-16R; 133;
CANR 35; CDBLB 1945-1960; DLB 13,
15, 77, 100; DLBY 91; MTCW; SATA 20

Greer, Richard
See Silverberg, Robert

Greer, Richard
See Silverberg, Robert

Gregor, Arthur 1923- .... CLC **9**
See also CA 25-28R; CAAS 10; CANR 11;
SATA 36

Gregor, Lee
See Pohl, Frederik

Gregory, Isabella Augusta (Persse)
1852-1932 .... TCLC **1**
See also CA 104; DLB 10

Gregory, J. Dennis
See Williams, John A(lfred)

Grendon, Stephen
See Derleth, August (William)

Grenville, Kate 1950- .... CLC **61**
See also CA 118

Grenville, Pelham
See Wodehouse, P(elham) G(renville)

Greve, Felix Paul (Berthold Friedrich)
1879-1948
See Grove, Frederick Philip
See also CA 104; 141

Grey, Zane 1872-1939 .... TCLC **6**
See also CA 104; 132; DLB 9; MTCW

Grieg, (Johan) Nordahl (Brun)
1902-1943 .... TCLC **10**
See also CA 107

Grieve, C(hristopher) M(urray)
1892-1978 .... CLC **11, 19**
See also MacDiarmid, Hugh
See also CA 5-8R; 85-88; CANR 33;
MTCW

Griffin, Gerald 1803-1840 .... NCLC **7**

Griffin, John Howard 1920-1980.... CLC **68**
See also AITN 1; CA 1-4R; 101; CANR 2

Griffin, Peter .... CLC **39**

Griffiths, Trevor 1935- .... CLC **13, 52**
See also CA 97-100; DLB 13

Grigson, Geoffrey (Edward Harvey)
1905-1985 .... CLC **7, 39**
See also CA 25-28R; 118; CANR 20, 33;
DLB 27; MTCW

Grillparzer, Franz 1791-1872...... NCLC **1**
See also DLB 133

Grimble, Reverend Charles James
See Eliot, T(homas) S(tearns)

Grimke, Charlotte L(ottie) Forten
1837(?)-1914
See Forten, Charlotte L.
See also BW; CA 117; 124

Grimm, Jacob Ludwig Karl
1785-1863 .... **NCLC 3**
See also DLB 90; MAICYA; SATA 22

Grimm, Wilhelm Karl 1786-1859 .. **NCLC 3**
See also DLB 90; MAICYA; SATA 22

Grimmelshausen, Johann Jakob Christoffel
von 1621-1676 .... **LC 6**

Grindel, Eugene 1895-1952
See Eluard, Paul
See also CA 104

Grossman, David 1954- .... **CLC 67**
See also CA 138

Grossman, Vasily (Semenovich)
1905-1964 .... **CLC 41**
See also CA 124; 130; MTCW

Grove, Frederick Philip .... **TCLC 4**
See also Greve, Felix Paul (Berthold
Friedrich)
See also DLB 92

Grubb
See Crumb, R(obert)

Grumbach, Doris (Isaac)
1918- .... **CLC 13, 22, 64**
See also CA 5-8R; CAAS 2; CANR 9, 42

Grundtvig, Nicolai Frederik Severin
1783-1872 .... **NCLC 1**

Grunge
See Crumb, R(obert)

Grunwald, Lisa 1959- .... **CLC 44**
See also CA 120

Guare, John 1938- .... **CLC 8, 14, 29, 67**
See also CA 73-76; CANR 21; DLB 7;
MTCW

Gudjonsson, Halldor Kiljan 1902-
See Laxness, Halldor
See also CA 103

Guenter, Erich
See Eich, Guenter

Guest, Barbara 1920- .... **CLC 34**
See also CA 25-28R; CANR 11; DLB 5

Guest, Judith (Ann) 1936- .... **CLC 8, 30**
See also AAYA 7; CA 77-80; CANR 15;
MTCW

Guild, Nicholas M. 1944- .... **CLC 33**
See also CA 93-96

Guillemin, Jacques
See Sartre, Jean-Paul

Guillen, Jorge 1893-1984 .... **CLC 11**
See also CA 89-92; 112; DLB 108; HW

Guillen (y Batista), Nicolas (Cristobal)
1902-1989 .. **CLC 48, 79; BLC 2; HLC 1**
See also BW; CA 116; 125; 129; HW

Guillevic, (Eugene) 1907- .... **CLC 33**
See also CA 93-96

Guillois
See Desnos, Robert

Guiney, Louise Imogen
1861-1920 .... **TCLC 41**
See also DLB 54

Guiraldes, Ricardo (Guillermo)
1886-1927 .... **TCLC 39**
See also CA 131; HW; MTCW

Gunn, Bill .... **CLC 5**
See also Gunn, William Harrison
See also DLB 38

Gunn, Thom(son William)
1929- .... **CLC 3, 6, 18, 32, 81**
See also CA 17-20R; CANR 9, 33;
CDBLB 1960 to Present; DLB 27;
MTCW

Gunn, William Harrison 1934(?)-1989
See Gunn, Bill
See also AITN 1; BW; CA 13-16R; 128;
CANR 12, 25

Gunnars, Kristjana 1948- .... **CLC 69**
See also CA 113; DLB 60

Gurganus, Allan 1947- .... **CLC 70**
See also BEST 90:1; CA 135

Gurney, A(lbert) R(amsdell), Jr.
1930- .... **CLC 32, 50, 54**
See also CA 77-80; CANR 32

Gurney, Ivor (Bertie) 1890-1937 ... **TCLC 33**

Gurney, Peter
See Gurney, A(lbert) R(amsdell), Jr.

Gustafson, Ralph (Barker) 1909- .... **CLC 36**
See also CA 21-24R; CANR 8; DLB 88

Gut, Gom
See Simenon, Georges (Jacques Christian)

Guthrie, A(lfred) B(ertram), Jr.
1901-1991 .... **CLC 23**
See also CA 57-60; 134; CANR 24; DLB 6;
SATA 62; SATA-Obit 67

Guthrie, Isobel
See Grieve, C(hristopher) M(urray)

Guthrie, Woodrow Wilson 1912-1967
See Guthrie, Woody
See also CA 113; 93-96

Guthrie, Woody .... **CLC 35**
See also Guthrie, Woodrow Wilson

Guy, Rosa (Cuthbert) 1928- .... **CLC 26**
See also AAYA 4; BW; CA 17-20R;
CANR 14, 34; CLR 13; DLB 33; JRDA;
MAICYA; SATA 14, 62

Gwendolyn
See Bennett, (Enoch) Arnold

H. D. .... **CLC 3, 8, 14, 31, 34, 73; PC 5**
See also Doolittle, Hilda

Haavikko, Paavo Juhani
1931- .... **CLC 18, 34**
See also CA 106

Habbema, Koos
See Heijermans, Herman

Hacker, Marilyn 1942- .... **CLC 5, 9, 23, 72**
See also CA 77-80; DLB 120

Haggard, H(enry) Rider
1856-1925 .... **TCLC 11**
See also CA 108; DLB 70; SATA 16

Haig, Fenil
See Ford, Ford Madox

Haig-Brown, Roderick (Langmere)
1908-1976 .... **CLC 21**
See also CA 5-8R; 69-72; CANR 4, 38;
CLR 31; DLB 88; MAICYA; SATA 12

Hailey, Arthur 1920- .... **CLC 5**
See also AITN 2; BEST 90:3; CA 1-4R;
CANR 2, 36; DLB 88; DLBY 82; MTCW

Hailey, Elizabeth Forsythe 1938-... **CLC 40**
See also CA 93-96; CAAS 1; CANR 15

Haines, John (Meade) 1924- .... **CLC 58**
See also CA 17-20R; CANR 13, 34; DLB 5

Haldeman, Joe (William) 1943-..... **CLC 61**
See also CA 53-56; CANR 6; DLB 8

Haley, Alex(ander Murray Palmer)
1921-1992 ... **CLC 8, 12, 76; BLC 2; DA**
See also BW; CA 77-80; 136; DLB 38;
MTCW

Haliburton, Thomas Chandler
1796-1865 .... **NCLC 15**
See also DLB 11, 99

Hall, Donald (Andrew, Jr.)
1928- .... **CLC 1, 13, 37, 59**
See also CA 5-8R; CAAS 7; CANR 2;
DLB 5; SATA 23

Hall, Frederic Sauser
See Sauser-Hall, Frederic

Hall, James
See Kuttner, Henry

Hall, James Norman 1887-1951 ... **TCLC 23**
See also CA 123; SATA 21

Hall, (Marguerite) Radclyffe
1886(?)-1943 .... **TCLC 12**
See also CA 110

Hall, Rodney 1935- .... **CLC 51**
See also CA 109

Halliday, Michael
See Creasey, John

Halpern, Daniel 1945- .... **CLC 14**
See also CA 33-36R

Hamburger, Michael (Peter Leopold)
1924- .... **CLC 5, 14**
See also CA 5-8R; CAAS 4; CANR 2;
DLB 27

Hamill, Pete 1935- .... **CLC 10**
See also CA 25-28R; CANR 18

Hamilton, Clive
See Lewis, C(live) S(taples)

Hamilton, Edmond 1904-1977....... **CLC 1**
See also CA 1-4R; CANR 3; DLB 8

Hamilton, Eugene (Jacob) Lee
See Lee-Hamilton, Eugene (Jacob)

Hamilton, Franklin
See Silverberg, Robert

Hamilton, Gail
See Corcoran, Barbara

Hamilton, Mollie
See Kaye, M(ary) M(argaret)

Hamilton, (Anthony Walter) Patrick
1904-1962 .... **CLC 51**
See also CA 113; DLB 10

Hamilton, Virginia 1936- .... **CLC 26**
See also AAYA 2; BW; CA 25-28R;
CANR 20, 37; CLR 1, 11; DLB 33, 52;
JRDA; MAICYA; MTCW; SATA 4, 56

Hammett, (Samuel) Dashiell
1894-1961 . . . . **CLC 3, 5, 10, 19, 47**
See also AITN 1; CA 81-84; CANR 42;
CDALB 1929-1941; DLBD 6; MTCW

Hammon, Jupiter
1711(?)-1800(?) . . . . **NCLC 5; BLC 2**
See also DLB 31, 50

Hammond, Keith
See Kuttner, Henry

Hamner, Earl (Henry), Jr. 1923- . . . **CLC 12**
See also AITN 2; CA 73-76; DLB 6

Hampton, Christopher (James)
1946- . . . . **CLC 4**
See also CA 25-28R; DLB 13; MTCW

Hamsun, Knut . . . . **TCLC 2, 14, 49**
See also Pedersen, Knut

Handke, Peter 1942- . . **CLC 5, 8, 10, 15, 38**
See also CA 77-80; CANR 33; DLB 85,
124; MTCW

Hanley, James 1901-1985 . . . **CLC 3, 5, 8, 13**
See also CA 73-76; 117; CANR 36; MTCW

Hannah, Barry 1942- . . . . **CLC 23, 38**
See also CA 108; 110; CANR 43; DLB 6;
MTCW

Hannon, Ezra
See Hunter, Evan

Hansberry, Lorraine (Vivian)
1930-1965 . . . . **CLC 17, 62; BLC 2; DA;
DC 2**
See also BW; CA 109; 25-28R; CABS 3;
CDALB 1941-1968; DLB 7, 38; MTCW

Hansen, Joseph 1923- . . . . **CLC 38**
See also CA 29-32R; CAAS 17; CANR 16

Hansen, Martin A. 1909-1955 . . . . . **TCLC 32**

Hanson, Kenneth O(stlin) 1922- . . . . **CLC 13**
See also CA 53-56; CANR 7

Hardwick, Elizabeth 1916- . . . . **CLC 13**
See also CA 5-8R; CANR 3, 32; DLB 6;
MTCW

Hardy, Thomas
1840-1928 . . . . . . **TCLC 4, 10, 18, 32, 48,
53; DA; PC 8; SSC 2; WLC**
See also CA 104; 123; CDBLB 1890-1914;
DLB 18, 19, 135; MTCW

Hare, David 1947- . . . . **CLC 29, 58**
See also CA 97-100; CANR 39; DLB 13;
MTCW

Harford, Henry
See Hudson, W(illiam) H(enry)

Hargrave, Leonie
See Disch, Thomas M(ichael)

Harlan, Louis R(udolph) 1922- . . . . . **CLC 34**
See also CA 21-24R; CANR 25

Harling, Robert 1951(?)- . . . . **CLC 53**

Harmon, William (Ruth) 1938- . . . . . **CLC 38**
See also CA 33-36R; CANR 14, 32, 35;
SATA 65

Harper, F. E. W.
See Harper, Frances Ellen Watkins

Harper, Frances E. W.
See Harper, Frances Ellen Watkins

Harper, Frances E. Watkins
See Harper, Frances Ellen Watkins

Harper, Frances Ellen
See Harper, Frances Ellen Watkins

Harper, Frances Ellen Watkins
1825-1911 . . . . **TCLC 14; BLC 2**
See also BW; CA 111; 125; DLB 50

Harper, Michael S(teven) 1938- . . **CLC 7, 22**
See also BW; CA 33-36R; CANR 24;
DLB 41

Harper, Mrs. F. E. W.
See Harper, Frances Ellen Watkins

Harris, Christie (Lucy) Irwin
1907- . . . . **CLC 12**
See also CA 5-8R; CANR 6; DLB 88;
JRDA; MAICYA; SAAS 10; SATA 6, 74

Harris, Frank 1856(?)-1931 . . . . . . **TCLC 24**
See also CA 109

Harris, George Washington
1814-1869 . . . . **NCLC 23**
See also DLB 3, 11

Harris, Joel Chandler 1848-1908 . . . **TCLC 2**
See also CA 104; 137; DLB 11, 23, 42, 78,
91; MAICYA; YABC 1

**Harris, John (Wyndham Parkes Lucas)
Beynon** 1903-1969 . . . . **CLC 19**
See also CA 102; 89-92

Harris, MacDonald
See Heiney, Donald (William)

Harris, Mark 1922- . . . . **CLC 19**
See also CA 5-8R; CAAS 3; CANR 2;
DLB 2; DLBY 80

Harris, (Theodore) Wilson 1921- . . . . **CLC 25**
See also BW; CA 65-68; CAAS 16;
CANR 11, 27; DLB 117; MTCW

Harrison, Elizabeth Cavanna 1909-
See Cavanna, Betty
See also CA 9-12R; CANR 6, 27

Harrison, Harry (Max) 1925- . . . . . . **CLC 42**
See also CA 1-4R; CANR 5, 21; DLB 8;
SATA 4

Harrison, James (Thomas)
1937- . . . . **CLC 6, 14, 33, 66**
See also CA 13-16R; CANR 8; DLBY 82

Harrison, Kathryn 1961- . . . . **CLC 70**

Harrison, Tony 1937- . . . . **CLC 43**
See also CA 65-68; DLB 40; MTCW

Harriss, Will(ard Irvin) 1922- . . . . . . **CLC 34**
See also CA 111

Harson, Sley
See Ellison, Harlan

Hart, Ellis
See Ellison, Harlan

Hart, Josephine 1942(?)- . . . . **CLC 70**
See also CA 138

Hart, Moss 1904-1961 . . . . **CLC 66**
See also CA 109; 89-92; DLB 7

Harte, (Francis) Bret(t)
1836(?)-1902 . . . . **TCLC 1, 25; DA;
SSC 8; WLC**
See also CA 104; 140; CDALB 1865-1917;
DLB 12, 64, 74, 79; SATA 26

Hartley, L(eslie) P(oles)
1895-1972 . . . . **CLC 2, 22**
See also CA 45-48; 37-40R; CANR 33;
DLB 15; MTCW

Hartman, Geoffrey H. 1929- . . . . **CLC 27**
See also CA 117; 125; DLB 67

Haruf, Kent 19(?)- . . . . **CLC 34**

Harwood, Ronald 1934- . . . . **CLC 32**
See also CA 1-4R; CANR 4; DLB 13

Hasek, Jaroslav (Matej Frantisek)
1883-1923 . . . . **TCLC 4**
See also CA 104; 129; MTCW

Hass, Robert 1941- . . . . **CLC 18, 39**
See also CA 111; CANR 30; DLB 105

Hastings, Hudson
See Kuttner, Henry

Hastings, Selina . . . . **CLC 44**

Hatteras, Amelia
See Mencken, H(enry) L(ouis)

Hatteras, Owen . . . . **TCLC 18**
See also Mencken, H(enry) L(ouis); Nathan,
George Jean

Hauptmann, Gerhart (Johann Robert)
1862-1946 . . . . **TCLC 4**
See also CA 104; DLB 66, 118

Havel, Vaclav 1936- . . . . **CLC 25, 58, 65**
See also CA 104; CANR 36; MTCW

Haviaras, Stratis . . . . **CLC 33**
See also Chaviaras, Strates

Hawes, Stephen 1475(?)-1523(?) . . . . . **LC 17**

Hawkes, John (Clendennin Burne, Jr.)
1925- . . . . . . **CLC 1, 2, 3, 4, 7, 9, 14, 15,
27, 49**
See also CA 1-4R; CANR 2; DLB 2, 7;
DLBY 80; MTCW

Hawking, S. W.
See Hawking, Stephen W(illiam)

Hawking, Stephen W(illiam)
1942- . . . . **CLC 63**
See also BEST 89:1; CA 126; 129

Hawthorne, Julian 1846-1934 . . . . . **TCLC 25**

Hawthorne, Nathaniel
1804-1864 . . . . . . **NCLC 39; DA; SSC 3;
WLC**
See also CDALB 1640-1865; DLB 1, 74;
YABC 2

Haxton, Josephine Ayres 1921- . . . . **CLC 73**
See also CA 115; CANR 41

Hayaseca y Eizaguirre, Jorge
See Echegaray (y Eizaguirre), Jose (Maria
Waldo)

Hayashi Fumiko 1904-1951 . . . . . . **TCLC 27**

Haycraft, Anna
See Ellis, Alice Thomas
See also CA 122

Hayden, Robert E(arl)
1913-1980 . . . . **CLC 5, 9, 14, 37; BLC 2;
DA; PC 6**
See also BW; CA 69-72; 97-100; CABS 2;
CANR 24; CDALB 1941-1968; DLB 5,
76; MTCW; SATA 19, 26

Hayford, J(oseph) E(phraim) Casely
See Casely-Hayford, J(oseph) E(phraim)

Hayman, Ronald 1932- . . . . **CLC 44**
See also CA 25-28R; CANR 18

Haywood, Eliza (Fowler)
1693(?)-1756 . . . . **LC 1**

Hazlitt, William 1778-1830 . . . . . **NCLC 29**
See also DLB 110

Hazzard, Shirley 1931- . . . . **CLC 18**
See also CA 9-12R; CANR 4; DLBY 82;
MTCW

Head, Bessie
1937-1986 . . . . **CLC 25, 67; BLC 2**
See also BW; CA 29-32R; 119; CANR 25;
DLB 117; MTCW

Headon, (Nicky) Topper 1956(?)- . . . **CLC 30**
See also Clash, The

Heaney, Seamus (Justin)
1939- . . . . **CLC 5, 7, 14, 25, 37, 74**
See also CA 85-88; CANR 25;
CDBLB 1960 to Present; DLB 40;
MTCW

Hearn, (Patricio) Lafcadio (Tessima Carlos)
1850-1904 . . . . **TCLC 9**
See also CA 105; DLB 12, 78

Hearne, Vicki 1946- . . . . **CLC 56**
See also CA 139

Hearon, Shelby 1931- . . . . **CLC 63**
See also AITN 2; CA 25-28R; CANR 18

Heat-Moon, William Least . . . . **CLC 29**
See also Trogdon, William (Lewis)
See also AAYA 9

Hebbel, Friedrich 1813-1863 . . . . . **NCLC 43**
See also DLB 129

Hebert, Anne 1916- . . . . **CLC 4, 13, 29**
See also CA 85-88; DLB 68; MTCW

Hecht, Anthony (Evan)
1923- . . . . **CLC 8, 13, 19**
See also CA 9-12R; CANR 6; DLB 5

Hecht, Ben 1894-1964 . . . . **CLC 8**
See also CA 85-88; DLB 7, 9, 25, 26, 28, 86

Hedayat, Sadeq 1903-1951 . . . . **TCLC 21**
See also CA 120

Heidegger, Martin 1889-1976 . . . . . . **CLC 24**
See also CA 81-84; 65-68; CANR 34;
MTCW

Heidenstam, (Carl Gustaf) Verner von
1859-1940 . . . . **TCLC 5**
See also CA 104

Heifner, Jack 1946- . . . . **CLC 11**
See also CA 105

Heijermans, Herman 1864-1924 . . . **TCLC 24**
See also CA 123

Heilbrun, Carolyn G(old) 1926- . . . . . **CLC 25**
See also CA 45-48; CANR 1, 28

Heine, Heinrich 1797-1856 . . . . **NCLC 4**
See also DLB 90

Heinemann, Larry (Curtiss) 1944- . . **CLC 50**
See also CA 110; CANR 31; DLBD 9

Heiney, Donald (William)
1921-1993 . . . . **CLC 9**
See also CA 1-4R; 142; CANR 3

Heinlein, Robert A(nson)
1907-1988 . . . . . . **CLC 1, 3, 8, 14, 26, 55**
See also CA 1-4R; 125; CANR 1, 20;
DLB 8; JRDA; MAICYA; MTCW;
SATA 9, 56, 69

Helforth, John
See Doolittle, Hilda

Hellenhofferu, Vojtech Kapristian z
See Hasek, Jaroslav (Matej Frantisek)

Heller, Joseph
1923- . . . . **CLC 1, 3, 5, 8, 11, 36, 63; DA;**
WLC
See also AITN 1; CA 5-8R; CABS 1;
CANR 8, 42; DLB 2, 28; DLBY 80;
MTCW

Hellman, Lillian (Florence)
1906-1984 . . . . . . **CLC 2, 4, 8, 14, 18, 34,**
44, 52; DC 1
See also AITN 1, 2; CA 13-16R; 112;
CANR 33; DLB 7; DLBY 84; MTCW

Helprin, Mark 1947- . . . . . **CLC 7, 10, 22, 32**
See also CA 81-84; DLBY 85; MTCW

Helyar, Jane Penelope Josephine 1933-
See Poole, Josephine
See also CA 21-24R; CANR 10, 26

Hemans, Felicia 1793-1835 . . . . . . **NCLC 29**
See also DLB 96

Hemingway, Ernest (Miller)
1899-1961 . . . . **CLC 1, 3, 6, 8, 10, 13, 19,**
30, 34, 39, 41, 44, 50, 61, 80; DA; SSC 1;
WLC
See also CA 77-80; CANR 34;
CDALB 1917-1929; DLB 4, 9, 102;
DLBD 1; DLBY 81, 87; MTCW

Hempel, Amy 1951- . . . . **CLC 39**
See also CA 118; 137

Henderson, F. C.
See Mencken, H(enry) L(ouis)

Henderson, Sylvia
See Ashton-Warner, Sylvia (Constance)

Henley, Beth . . . . **CLC 23**
See also Henley, Elizabeth Becker
See also CABS 3; DLBY 86

Henley, Elizabeth Becker 1952-
See Henley, Beth
See also CA 107; CANR 32; MTCW

Henley, William Ernest
1849-1903 . . . . **TCLC 8**
See also CA 105; DLB 19

Hennissart, Martha
See Lathen, Emma
See also CA 85-88

Henry, O. . . . . **TCLC 1, 19; SSC 5; WLC**
See also Porter, William Sydney

Henryson, Robert 1430(?)-1506(?) . . . . **LC 20**

Henry VIII 1491-1547 . . . . **LC 10**

Henschke, Alfred
See Klabund

Hentoff, Nat(han Irving) 1925- . . . . . **CLC 26**
See also AAYA 4; CA 1-4R; CAAS 6;
CANR 5, 25; CLR 1; JRDA; MAICYA;
SATA 27, 42, 69

Heppenstall, (John) Rayner
1911-1981 . . . . **CLC 10**
See also CA 1-4R; 103; CANR 29

Herbert, Frank (Patrick)
1920-1986 . . . . **CLC 12, 23, 35, 44**
See also CA 53-56; 118; CANR 5, 43;
DLB 8; MTCW; SATA 9, 37, 47

Herbert, George 1593-1633 . . . . **LC 24; PC 4**
See also CDBLB Before 1660; DLB 126

Herbert, Zbigniew 1924- . . . . **CLC 9, 43**
See also CA 89-92; CANR 36; MTCW

Herbst, Josephine (Frey)
1897-1969 . . . . **CLC 34**
See also CA 5-8R; 25-28R; DLB 9

Hergesheimer, Joseph
1880-1954 . . . . **TCLC 11**
See also CA 109; DLB 102, 9

Herlihy, James Leo 1927- . . . . **CLC 6**
See also CA 1-4R; CANR 2

Hermogenes fl. c. 175- . . . . **CMLC 6**

Hernandez, Jose 1834-1886 . . . . . . **NCLC 17**

Herrick, Robert 1591-1674 . . . . . **LC 13; DA**
See also DLB 126

Herring, Guilles
See Somerville, Edith

Herriot, James 1916- . . . . **CLC 12**
See also Wight, James Alfred
See also AAYA 1; CANR 40

Herrmann, Dorothy 1941- . . . . **CLC 44**
See also CA 107

Herrmann, Taffy
See Herrmann, Dorothy

Hersey, John (Richard)
1914-1993 . . . . **CLC 1, 2, 7, 9, 40, 81**
See also CA 17-20R; 140; CANR 33;
DLB 6; MTCW; SATA 25

Herzen, Aleksandr Ivanovich
1812-1870 . . . . **NCLC 10**

Herzl, Theodor 1860-1904 . . . . **TCLC 36**

Herzog, Werner 1942- . . . . **CLC 16**
See also CA 89-92

Hesiod c. 8th cent. B.C.- . . . . **CMLC 5**

Hesse, Hermann
1877-1962 . . . . **CLC 1, 2, 3, 6, 11, 17, 25,**
69; DA; SSC 9; WLC
See also CA 17-18; CAP 2; DLB 66;
MTCW; SATA 50

Hewes, Cady
See De Voto, Bernard (Augustine)

Heyen, William 1940- . . . . **CLC 13, 18**
See also CA 33-36R; CAAS 9; DLB 5

Heyerdahl, Thor 1914- . . . . **CLC 26**
See also CA 5-8R; CANR 5, 22; MTCW;
SATA 2, 52

Heym, Georg (Theodor Franz Arthur)
1887-1912 . . . . **TCLC 9**
See also CA 106

Heym, Stefan 1913- . . . . **CLC 41**
See also CA 9-12R; CANR 4; DLB 69

Heyse, Paul (Johann Ludwig von)
1830-1914 . . . . **TCLC 8**
See also CA 104; DLB 129

Hibbert, Eleanor Alice Burford
1906-1993 . . . . **CLC 7**
See also BEST 90:4; CA 17-20R; 140;
CANR 9, 28; SATA 2; SATA-Obit 74

Higgins, George V(incent)
1939- . . . . **CLC 4, 7, 10, 18**
See also CA 77-80; CAAS 5; CANR 17;
DLB 2; DLBY 81; MTCW

Higginson, Thomas Wentworth
1823-1911 . . . . **TCLC 36**
See also DLB 1, 64

Highet, Helen
See MacInnes, Helen (Clark)

Highsmith, (Mary) Patricia
1921- . . . . CLC 2, 4, 14, 42
See also CA 1-4R; CANR 1, 20; MTCW

Highwater, Jamake (Mamake)
1942(?)- . . . . CLC 12
See also AAYA 7; CA 65-68; CAAS 7;
CANR 10, 34; CLR 17; DLB 52;
DLBY 85; JRDA; MAICYA; SATA 30,
32, 69

Hijuelos, Oscar 1951- . . . . . CLC 65; HLC 1
See also BEST 90:1; CA 123; HW

Hikmet, Nazim 1902(?)-1963 . . . . . . CLC 40
See also CA 141; 93-96

Hildesheimer, Wolfgang
1916-1991 . . . . CLC 49
See also CA 101; 135; DLB 69, 124

Hill, Geoffrey (William)
1932- . . . . CLC 5, 8, 18, 45
See also CA 81-84; CANR 21;
CDBLB 1960 to Present; DLB 40;
MTCW

Hill, George Roy 1921- . . . . CLC 26
See also CA 110; 122

Hill, John
See Koontz, Dean R(ay)

Hill, Susan (Elizabeth) 1942- . . . . CLC 4
See also CA 33-36R; CANR 29; DLB 14;
MTCW

Hillerman, Tony 1925- . . . . CLC 62
See also AAYA 6; BEST 89:1; CA 29-32R;
CANR 21, 42; SATA 6

Hillesum, Etty 1914-1943 . . . . TCLC 49
See also CA 137

Hilliard, Noel (Harvey) 1929- . . . . . . CLC 15
See also CA 9-12R; CANR 7

Hillis, Rick 1956- . . . . CLC 66
See also CA 134

Hilton, James 1900-1954 . . . . TCLC 21
See also CA 108; DLB 34, 77; SATA 34

Himes, Chester (Bomar)
1909-1984 . . . CLC 2, 4, 7, 18, 58; BLC 2
See also BW; CA 25-28R; 114; CANR 22;
DLB 2, 76; MTCW

Hinde, Thomas . . . . CLC 6, 11
See also Chitty, Thomas Willes

Hindin, Nathan
See Bloch, Robert (Albert)

Hine, (William) Daryl 1936- . . . . CLC 15
See also CA 1-4R; CAAS 15; CANR 1, 20;
DLB 60

Hinkson, Katharine Tynan
See Tynan, Katharine

Hinton, S(usan) E(loise)
1950- . . . . CLC 30; DA
See also AAYA 2; CA 81-84; CANR 32;
CLR 3, 23; JRDA; MAICYA; MTCW;
SATA 19, 58

Hippius, Zinaida . . . . TCLC 9
See also Gippius, Zinaida (Nikolayevna)

Hiraoka, Kimitake 1925-1970
See Mishima, Yukio
See also CA 97-100; 29-32R; MTCW

Hirsch, E(ric) D(onald), Jr. 1928- . . . CLC 79
See also CA 25-28R; CANR 27; DLB 67;
MTCW

Hirsch, Edward 1950- . . . . CLC 31, 50
See also CA 104; CANR 20, 42; DLB 120

Hitchcock, Alfred (Joseph)
1899-1980 . . . . CLC 16
See also CA 97-100; SATA 24, 27

Hitler, Adolf 1889-1945 . . . . TCLC 53
See also CA 117

Hoagland, Edward 1932- . . . . CLC 28
See also CA 1-4R; CANR 2, 31; DLB 6;
SATA 51

Hoban, Russell (Conwell) 1925- . . CLC 7, 25
See also CA 5-8R; CANR 23, 37; CLR 3;
DLB 52; MAICYA; MTCW; SATA 1, 40

Hobbs, Perry
See Blackmur, R(ichard) P(almer)

Hobson, Laura Z(ametkin)
1900-1986 . . . . CLC 7, 25
See also CA 17-20R; 118; DLB 28;
SATA 52

Hochhuth, Rolf 1931- . . . . CLC 4, 11, 18
See also CA 5-8R; CANR 33; DLB 124;
MTCW

Hochman, Sandra 1936- . . . . CLC 3, 8
See also CA 5-8R; DLB 5

Hochwaelder, Fritz 1911-1986 . . . . . . CLC 36
See also CA 29-32R; 120; CANR 42;
MTCW

Hochwalder, Fritz
See Hochwaelder, Fritz

Hocking, Mary (Eunice) 1921- . . . . . CLC 13
See also CA 101; CANR 18, 40

Hodgins, Jack 1938- . . . . CLC 23
See also CA 93-96; DLB 60

Hodgson, William Hope
1877(?)-1918 . . . . TCLC 13
See also CA 111; DLB 70

Hoffman, Alice 1952- . . . . CLC 51
See also CA 77-80; CANR 34; MTCW

Hoffman, Daniel (Gerard)
1923- . . . . CLC 6, 13, 23
See also CA 1-4R; CANR 4; DLB 5

Hoffman, Stanley 1944- . . . . CLC 5
See also CA 77-80

Hoffman, William M(oses) 1939- . . . CLC 40
See also CA 57-60; CANR 11

Hoffmann, E(rnst) T(heodor) A(madeus)
1776-1822 . . . . NCLC 2; SSC 13
See also DLB 90; SATA 27

Hofmann, Gert 1931- . . . . CLC 54
See also CA 128

Hofmannsthal, Hugo von
1874-1929 . . . . TCLC 11; DC 4
See also CA 106; DLB 81, 118

Hogan, Linda 1947- . . . . CLC 73
See also CA 120

Hogarth, Charles
See Creasey, John

Hogg, James 1770-1835 . . . . NCLC 4
See also DLB 93, 116

Holbach, Paul Henri Thiry Baron
1723-1789 . . . . LC 14

Holberg, Ludvig 1684-1754 . . . . LC 6

Holden, Ursula 1921- . . . . CLC 18
See also CA 101; CAAS 8; CANR 22

Holderlin, (Johann Christian) Friedrich
1770-1843 . . . . NCLC 16; PC 4

Holdstock, Robert
See Holdstock, Robert P.

Holdstock, Robert P. 1948- . . . . CLC 39
See also CA 131

Holland, Isabelle 1920- . . . . CLC 21
See also CA 21-24R; CANR 10, 25; JRDA;
MAICYA; SATA 8, 70

Holland, Marcus
See Caldwell, (Janet Miriam) Taylor
(Holland)

Hollander, John 1929- . . . . . . CLC 2, 5, 8, 14
See also CA 1-4R; CANR 1; DLB 5;
SATA 13

Hollander, Paul
See Silverberg, Robert

Holleran, Andrew 1943(?)- . . . . CLC 38

Hollinghurst, Alan 1954- . . . . CLC 55
See also CA 114

Hollis, Jim
See Summers, Hollis (Spurgeon, Jr.)

Holmes, John
See Souster, (Holmes) Raymond

Holmes, John Clellon 1926-1988 . . . . CLC 56
See also CA 9-12R; 125; CANR 4; DLB 16

Holmes, Oliver Wendell
1809-1894 . . . . NCLC 14
See also CDALB 1640-1865; DLB 1;
SATA 34

Holmes, Raymond
See Souster, (Holmes) Raymond

Holt, Victoria
See Hibbert, Eleanor Alice Burford

Holub, Miroslav 1923- . . . . CLC 4
See also CA 21-24R; CANR 10

Homer c. 8th cent. B.C.- . . . . . CMLC 1; DA

Honig, Edwin 1919- . . . . CLC 33
See also CA 5-8R; CAAS 8; CANR 4;
DLB 5

Hood, Hugh (John Blagdon)
1928- . . . . CLC 15, 28
See also CA 49-52; CAAS 17; CANR 1, 33;
DLB 53

Hood, Thomas 1799-1845 . . . . NCLC 16
See also DLB 96

Hooker, (Peter) Jeremy 1941- . . . . . . CLC 43
See also CA 77-80; CANR 22; DLB 40

Hope, A(lec) D(erwent) 1907- . . . . CLC 3, 51
See also CA 21-24R; CANR 33; MTCW

Hope, Brian
See Creasey, John

Hope, Christopher (David Tully)
1944- . . . . CLC 52
See also CA 106; SATA 62

Hopkins, Gerard Manley
1844-1889 . . . . NCLC 17; DA; WLC
See also CDBLB 1890-1914; DLB 35, 57

Hopkins, John (Richard) 1931- . . . . . . CLC 4
See also CA 85-88

Jeffers, (John) Robinson
1887-1962 .... **CLC 2, 3, 11, 15, 54; DA;**
WLC
See also CA 85-88; CANR 35;
CDALB 1917-1929; DLB 45; MTCW

Jefferson, Janet
See Mencken, H(enry) L(ouis)

Jefferson, Thomas 1743-1826 .... **NCLC 11**
See also CDALB 1640-1865; DLB 31

Jeffrey, Francis 1773-1850....... **NCLC 33**
See also DLB 107

Jelakowitch, Ivan
See Heijermans, Herman

Jellicoe, (Patricia) Ann 1927-...... **CLC 27**
See also CA 85-88; DLB 13

Jen, Gish .... **CLC 70**
See also Jen, Lillian

Jen, Lillian 1956(?)-
See Jen, Gish
See also CA 135

Jenkins, (John) Robin 1912-....... **CLC 52**
See also CA 1-4R; CANR 1; DLB 14

Jennings, Elizabeth (Joan)
1926-..................... **CLC 5, 14**
See also CA 61-64; CAAS 5; CANR 8, 39;
DLB 27; MTCW; SATA 66

Jennings, Waylon 1937-.......... **CLC 21**

Jensen, Johannes V. 1873-1950.... **TCLC 41**

Jensen, Laura (Linnea) 1948-...... **CLC 37**
See also CA 103

Jerome, Jerome K(lapka)
1859-1927 .... **TCLC 23**
See also CA 119; DLB 10, 34, 135

Jerrold, Douglas William
1803-1857 .... **NCLC 2**

Jewett, (Theodora) Sarah Orne
1849-1909 .... **TCLC 1, 22; SSC 6**
See also CA 108; 127; DLB 12, 74;
SATA 15

Jewsbury, Geraldine (Endsor)
1812-1880 .... **NCLC 22**
See also DLB 21

Jhabvala, Ruth Prawer
1927-.................. **CLC 4, 8, 29**
See also CA 1-4R; CANR 2, 29; MTCW

Jiles, Paulette 1943-.......... **CLC 13, 58**
See also CA 101

Jimenez (Mantecon), Juan Ramon
1881-1958 ...... **TCLC 4; HLC 1; PC 7**
See also CA 104; 131; DLB 134; HW;
MTCW

Jimenez, Ramon
See Jimenez (Mantecon), Juan Ramon

Jimenez Mantecon, Juan
See Jimenez (Mantecon), Juan Ramon

Joel, Billy .... **CLC 26**
See also Joel, William Martin

Joel, William Martin 1949-
See Joel, Billy
See also CA 108

John of the Cross, St. 1542-1591 .... **LC 18**

Johnson, B(ryan) S(tanley William)
1933-1973 .... **CLC 6, 9**
See also CA 9-12R; 53-56; CANR 9;
DLB 14, 40

Johnson, Benj. F. of Boo
See Riley, James Whitcomb

Johnson, Benjamin F. of Boo
See Riley, James Whitcomb

Johnson, Charles (Richard)
1948- .... **CLC 7, 51, 65; BLC 2**
See also BW; CA 116; CAAS 18;
CANR 42; DLB 33

Johnson, Denis 1949-............. **CLC 52**
See also CA 117; 121; DLB 120

Johnson, Diane 1934-........ **CLC 5, 13, 48**
See also CA 41-44R; CANR 17, 40;
DLBY 80; MTCW

Johnson, Eyvind (Olof Verner)
1900-1976 .... **CLC 14**
See also CA 73-76; 69-72; CANR 34

Johnson, J. R.
See James, C(yril) L(ionel) R(obert)

Johnson, James Weldon
1871-1938 .... **TCLC 3, 19; BLC 2**
See also BW; CA 104; 125;
CDALB 1917-1929; CLR 32; DLB 51;
MTCW; SATA 31

Johnson, Joyce 1935-............ **CLC 58**
See also CA 125; 129

Johnson, Lionel (Pigot)
1867-1902 .... **TCLC 19**
See also CA 117; DLB 19

Johnson, Mel
See Malzberg, Barry N(athaniel)

Johnson, Pamela Hansford
1912-1981 .... **CLC 1, 7, 27**
See also CA 1-4R; 104; CANR 2, 28;
DLB 15; MTCW

Johnson, Samuel
1709-1784 .... **LC 15; DA; WLC**
See also CDBLB 1660-1789; DLB 39, 95,
104

Johnson, Uwe
1934-1984 .... **CLC 5, 10, 15, 40**
See also CA 1-4R; 112; CANR 1, 39;
DLB 75; MTCW

Johnston, George (Benson) 1913-... **CLC 51**
See also CA 1-4R; CANR 5, 20; DLB 88

Johnston, Jennifer 1930-........... **CLC 7**
See also CA 85-88; DLB 14

Jolley, (Monica) Elizabeth 1923-... **CLC 46**
See also CA 127; CAAS 13

Jones, Arthur Llewellyn 1863-1947
See Machen, Arthur
See also CA 104

Jones, D(ouglas) G(ordon) 1929-.... **CLC 10**
See also CA 29-32R; CANR 13; DLB 53

Jones, David (Michael)
1895-1974 .... **CLC 2, 4, 7, 13, 42**
See also CA 9-12R; 53-56; CANR 28;
CDBLB 1945-1960; DLB 20, 100; MTCW

Jones, David Robert 1947-
See Bowie, David
See also CA 103

Jones, Diana Wynne 1934- .... **CLC 26**
See also CA 49-52; CANR 4, 26; CLR 23;
JRDA; MAICYA; SAAS 7; SATA 9, 70

Jones, Edward P. 1950-.......... **CLC 76**
See also CA 142

Jones, Gayl 1949-........ **CLC 6, 9; BLC 2**
See also BW; CA 77-80; CANR 27;
DLB 33; MTCW

Jones, James 1921-1977.... **CLC 1, 3, 10, 39**
See also AITN 1, 2; CA 1-4R; 69-72;
CANR 6; DLB 2; MTCW

Jones, John J.
See Lovecraft, H(oward) P(hillips)

Jones, LeRoi .... **CLC 1, 2, 3, 5, 10, 14**
See also Baraka, Amiri

Jones, Louis B. .... **CLC 65**
See also CA 141

Jones, Madison (Percy, Jr.) 1925-... **CLC 4**
See also CA 13-16R; CAAS 11; CANR 7

Jones, Mervyn 1922-.......... **CLC 10, 52**
See also CA 45-48; CAAS 5; CANR 1;
MTCW

Jones, Mick 1956(?)-............. **CLC 30**
See also Clash, The

Jones, Nettie (Pearl) 1941-........ **CLC 34**
See also CA 137

Jones, Preston 1936-1979 .... **CLC 10**
See also CA 73-76; 89-92; DLB 7

Jones, Robert F(rancis) 1934-....... **CLC 7**
See also CA 49-52; CANR 2

Jones, Rod 1953- .... **CLC 50**
See also CA 128

Jones, Terence Graham Parry
1942- .... **CLC 21**
See also Jones, Terry; Monty Python
See also CA 112; 116; CANR 35; SATA 51

Jones, Terry
See Jones, Terence Graham Parry
See also SATA 67

Jones, Thom 1945(?)-............. **CLC 81**

Jong, Erica 1942-.......... **CLC 4, 6, 8, 18**
See also AITN 1; BEST 90:2; CA 73-76;
CANR 26; DLB 2, 5, 28; MTCW

Jonson, Ben(jamin)
1572(?)-1637 .... **LC 6; DA; DC 4; WLC**
See also CDBLB Before 1660; DLB 62, 121

Jordan, June 1936-, ... **CLC 5, 11, 23**
See also AAYA 2; BW; CA 33-36R;
CANR 25; CLR 10; DLB 38; MAICYA;
MTCW; SATA 4

Jordan, Pat(rick M.) 1941-........ **CLC 37**
See also CA 33-36R

Jorgensen, Ivar
See Ellison, Harlan

Jorgenson, Ivar
See Silverberg, Robert

Josipovici, Gabriel 1940-........ **CLC 6, 43**
See also CA 37-40R; CAAS 8; DLB 14

Joubert, Joseph 1754-1824 .... **NCLC 9**

Jouve, Pierre Jean 1887-1976 ...... **CLC 47**
See also CA 65-68

Joyce, James (Augustine Aloysius)
    1882-1941 . . . . . TCLC 3, 8, 16, 35; DA;
                                SSC 3; WLC
    See also CA 104; 126; CDBLB 1914-1945;
    DLB 10, 19, 36; MTCW

Jozsef, Attila 1905-1937. . . . . TCLC 22
    See also CA 116

Juana Ines de la Cruz 1651(?)-1695 . . . LC 5

Judd, Cyril
    See Kornbluth, C(yril) M.; Pohl, Frederik

Julian of Norwich 1342(?)-1416(?) . . . . LC 6

Just, Ward (Swift) 1935- . . . . CLC 4, 27
    See also CA 25-28R; CANR 32

Justice, Donald (Rodney) 1925- . . CLC 6, 19
    See also CA 5-8R; CANR 26; DLBY 83

Juvenal c. 55-c. 127 . . . . CMLC 8

Juvenis
    See Bourne, Randolph S(illiman)

Kacew, Romain 1914-1980
    See Gary, Romain
    See also CA 108; 102

Kadare, Ismail 1936- . . . . CLC 52

Kadohata, Cynthia. . . . . CLC 59
    See also CA 140

Kafka, Franz
    1883-1924 . . . . TCLC 2, 6, 13, 29, 47, 53;
                                DA; SSC 5; WLC
    See also CA 105; 126; DLB 81; MTCW

Kahn, Roger 1927- . . . . CLC 30
    See also CA 25-28R; SATA 37

Kain, Saul
    See Sassoon, Siegfried (Lorraine)

Kaiser, Georg 1878-1945 . . . . TCLC 9
    See also CA 106; DLB 124

Kaletski, Alexander 1946- . . . . CLC 39
    See also CA 118

Kalidasa fl. c. 400- . . . . CMLC 9

Kallman, Chester (Simon)
    1921-1975 . . . . CLC 2
    See also CA 45-48; 53-56; CANR 3

Kaminsky, Melvin 1926-
    See Brooks, Mel
    See also CA 65-68; CANR 16

Kaminsky, Stuart M(elvin) 1934- . . . CLC 59
    See also CA 73-76; CANR 29

Kane, Paul
    See Simon, Paul

Kane, Wilson
    See Bloch, Robert (Albert)

Kanin, Garson 1912- . . . . CLC 22
    See also AITN 1; CA 5-8R; CANR 7;
    DLB 7

Kaniuk, Yoram 1930- . . . . CLC 19
    See also CA 134

Kant, Immanuel 1724-1804 . . . . . . NCLC 27
    See also DLB 94

Kantor, MacKinlay 1904-1977 . . . . . CLC 7
    See also CA 61-64; 73-76; DLB 9, 102

Kaplan, David Michael 1946- . . . . . . CLC 50

Kaplan, James 1951- . . . . CLC 59
    See also CA 135

Karageorge, Michael
    See Anderson, Poul (William)

Karamzin, Nikolai Mikhailovich
    1766-1826 . . . . NCLC 3

Karapanou, Margarita 1946- . . . . CLC 13
    See also CA 101

Karinthy, Frigyes 1887-1938 . . . . . TCLC 47

Karl, Frederick R(obert) 1927- . . . . CLC 34
    See also CA 5-8R; CANR 3

Kastel, Warren
    See Silverberg, Robert

Kataev, Evgeny Petrovich 1903-1942
    See Petrov, Evgeny
    See also CA 120

Kataphusin
    See Ruskin, John

Katz, Steve 1935- . . . . CLC 47
    See also CA 25-28R; CAAS 14; CANR 12;
    DLBY 83

Kauffman, Janet 1945- . . . . CLC 42
    See also CA 117; CANR 43; DLBY 86

Kaufman, Bob (Garnell)
    1925-1986 . . . . CLC 49
    See also BW; CA 41-44R; 118; CANR 22;
    DLB 16, 41

Kaufman, George S. 1889-1961 . . . . . CLC 38
    See also CA 108; 93-96; DLB 7

Kaufman, Sue . . . . CLC 3, 8
    See also Barondess, Sue K(aufman)

Kavafis, Konstantinos Petrou 1863-1933
    See Cavafy, C(onstantine) P(eter)
    See also CA 104

Kavan, Anna 1901-1968 . . . . CLC 5, 13
    See also CA 5-8R; CANR 6; MTCW

Kavanagh, Dan
    See Barnes, Julian

Kavanagh, Patrick (Joseph)
    1904-1967 . . . . CLC 22
    See also CA 123; 25-28R; DLB 15, 20;
    MTCW

Kawabata, Yasunari
    1899-1972 . . . . CLC 2, 5, 9, 18
    See also CA 93-96; 33-36R

Kaye, M(ary) M(argaret) 1909- . . . . . CLC 28
    See also CA 89-92; CANR 24; MTCW;
    SATA 62

Kaye, Mollie
    See Kaye, M(ary) M(argaret)

Kaye-Smith, Sheila 1887-1956 . . . . . TCLC 20
    See also CA 118; DLB 36

Kaymor, Patrice Maguilene
    See Senghor, Leopold Sedar

Kazan, Elia 1909- . . . . CLC 6, 16, 63
    See also CA 21-24R; CANR 32

Kazantzakis, Nikos
    1883(?)-1957 . . . . TCLC 2, 5, 33
    See also CA 105; 132; MTCW

Kazin, Alfred 1915- . . . . CLC 34, 38
    See also CA 1-4R; CAAS 7; CANR 1;
    DLB 67

Keane, Mary Nesta (Skrine) 1904-
    See Keane, Molly
    See also CA 108; 114

Keane, Molly. CLC 31
    See also Keane, Mary Nesta (Skrine)

Keates, Jonathan 19(?)- . . . . CLC 34

Keaton, Buster 1895-1966 . . . . CLC 20

Keats, John
    1795-1821 . . . NCLC 8; DA; PC 1; WLC
    See also CDBLB 1789-1832; DLB 96, 110

Keene, Donald 1922- . . . . CLC 34
    See also CA 1-4R; CANR 5

Keillor, Garrison . . . . CLC 40
    See also Keillor, Gary (Edward)
    See also AAYA 2; BEST 89:3; DLBY 87;
    SATA 58

Keillor, Gary (Edward) 1942-
    See Keillor, Garrison
    See also CA 111; 117; CANR 36; MTCW

Keith, Michael
    See Hubbard, L(afayette) Ron(ald)

Keller, Gottfried 1819-1890 . . . . . . NCLC 2
    See also DLB 129

Kellerman, Jonathan 1949- . . . . CLC 44
    See also BEST 90:1; CA 106; CANR 29

Kelley, William Melvin 1937- . . . . . . CLC 22
    See also BW; CA 77-80; CANR 27; DLB 33

Kellogg, Marjorie 1922- . . . . CLC 2
    See also CA 81-84

Kellow, Kathleen
    See Hibbert, Eleanor Alice Burford

Kelly, M(ilton) T(erry) 1947- . . . . CLC 55
    See also CA 97-100; CANR 19, 43

Kelman, James 1946- . . . . CLC 58

Kemal, Yashar 1923- . . . . CLC 14, 29
    See also CA 89-92

Kemble, Fanny 1809-1893 . . . . NCLC 18
    See also DLB 32

Kemelman, Harry 1908- . . . . CLC 2
    See also AITN 1; CA 9-12R; CANR 6;
    DLB 28

Kempe, Margery 1373(?)-1440(?) . . . . . LC 6

Kempis, Thomas a 1380-1471 . . . . LC 11

Kendall, Henry 1839-1882 . . . . NCLC 12

Keneally, Thomas (Michael)
    1935- . . . . . . CLC 5, 8, 10, 14, 19, 27, 43
    See also CA 85-88; CANR 10; MTCW

Kennedy, Adrienne (Lita)
    1931- . . . . CLC 66; BLC 2
    See also BW; CA 103; CABS 3; CANR 26;
    DLB 38

Kennedy, John Pendleton
    1795-1870 . . . . NCLC 2
    See also DLB 3

Kennedy, Joseph Charles 1929- . . . . . CLC 8
    See also Kennedy, X. J.
    See also CA 1-4R; CANR 4, 30, 40;
    SATA 14

Kennedy, William 1928- . . . CLC 6, 28, 34, 53
    See also AAYA 1; CA 85-88; CANR 14,
    31; DLBY 85; MTCW; SATA 57

Kennedy, X. J. CLC 42
    See also Kennedy, Joseph Charles
    See also CAAS 9; CLR 27; DLB 5

Kent, Kelvin
    See Kuttner, Henry

Kenton, Maxwell
    See Southern, Terry

Kenyon, Robert O.
See Kuttner, Henry

Kerouac, Jack ..... **CLC 1, 2, 3, 5, 14, 29, 61**
See also Kerouac, Jean-Louis Lebris de
See also CDALB 1941-1968; DLB 2, 16;
DLBD 3

Kerouac, Jean-Louis Lebris de 1922-1969
See Kerouac, Jack
See also AITN 1; CA 5-8R; 25-28R;
CANR 26; DA; MTCW; WLC

Kerr, Jean 1923- .... **CLC 22**
See also CA 5-8R; CANR 7

Kerr, M. E. .... **CLC 12, 35**
See also Meaker, Marijane (Agnes)
See also AAYA 2; CLR 29; SAAS 1

Kerr, Robert .... **CLC 55**

Kerrigan, (Thomas) Anthony
1918- .... **CLC 4, 6**
See also CA 49-52; CAAS 11; CANR 4

Kerry, Lois
See Duncan, Lois

Kesey, Ken (Elton)
1935- ...... **CLC 1, 3, 6, 11, 46, 64; DA;**
WLC
See also CA 1-4R; CANR 22, 38;
CDALB 1968-1988; DLB 2, 16; MTCW;
SATA 66

Kesselring, Joseph (Otto)
1902-1967 .... **CLC 45**

Kessler, Jascha (Frederick) 1929- .... **CLC 4**
See also CA 17-20R; CANR 8

Kettelkamp, Larry (Dale) 1933- .... **CLC 12**
See also CA 29-32R; CANR 16, SAAS 3;
SATA 2

Keyber, Conny
See Fielding, Henry

Keyes, Daniel 1927- .... **CLC 80; DA**
See also CA 17-20R; CANR 10, 26;
SATA 37

Khayyam, Omar
1048-1131 .... **CMLC 11; PC 8**

Kherdian, David 1931- .... **CLC 6, 9**
See also CA 21-24R; CAAS 2; CANR 39;
CLR 24; JRDA; MAICYA; SATA 16, 74

Khlebnikov, Velimir .... **TCLC 20**
See also Khlebnikov, Viktor Vladimirovich

Khlebnikov, Viktor Vladimirovich 1885-1922
See Khlebnikov, Velimir
See also CA 117

Khodasevich, Vladislav (Felitsianovich)
1886-1939 .... **TCLC 15**
See also CA 115

Kielland, Alexander Lange
1849-1906 .... **TCLC 5**
See also CA 104

Kiely, Benedict 1919- .... **CLC 23, 43**
See also CA 1-4R; CANR 2; DLB 15

Kienzle, William X(avier) 1928- .... **CLC 25**
See also CA 93-96; CAAS 1; CANR 9, 31;
MTCW

Kierkegaard, Soren 1813-1855.... **NCLC 34**

Killens, John Oliver 1916-1987..... **CLC 10**
See also BW; CA 77-80; 123; CAAS 2;
CANR 26; DLB 33

Killigrew, Anne 1660-1685.......... **LC 4**
See also DLB 131

Kim
See Simenon, Georges (Jacques Christian)

Kincaid, Jamaica
1949- .... **CLC 43, 68; BLC 2**
See also BW; CA 125

King, Francis (Henry) 1923- ..... **CLC 8, 53**
See also CA 1-4R; CANR 1, 33; DLB 15;
MTCW

King, Stephen (Edwin)
1947- .... **CLC 12, 26, 37, 61**
See also AAYA 1; BEST 90:1; CA 61-64;
CANR 1, 30; DLBY 80; JRDA; MTCW;
SATA 9, 55

King, Steve
See King, Stephen (Edwin)

Kingman, Lee.................... **CLC 17**
See also Natti, (Mary) Lee
See also SAAS 3; SATA 1, 67

Kingsley, Charles 1819-1875..... **NCLC 35**
See also DLB 21, 32; YABC 2

Kingsley, Sidney 1906-............ **CLC 44**
See also CA 85-88; DLB 7

Kingsolver, Barbara 1955-...... **CLC 55, 81**
See also CA 129; 134

Kingston, Maxine (Ting Ting) Hong
1940- .... **CLC 12, 19, 58**
See also AAYA 8; CA 69-72; CANR 13,
38; DLBY 80; MTCW; SATA 53

Kinnell, Galway
1927- .... **CLC 1, 2, 3, 5, 13, 29**
See also CA 9-12R; CANR 10, 34; DLB 5;
DLBY 87; MTCW

Kinsella, Thomas 1928- .... **CLC 4, 19**
See also CA 17-20R; CANR 15; DLB 27;
MTCW

Kinsella, W(illiam) P(atrick)
1935- .... **CLC 27, 43**
See also AAYA 7; CA 97-100; CAAS 7;
CANR 21, 35; MTCW

Kipling, (Joseph) Rudyard
1865-1936 ...... **TCLC 8, 17; DA; PC 3;**
SSC 5; WLC
See also CA 105; 120; CANR 33;
CDBLB 1890-1914; DLB 19, 34;
MAICYA; MTCW; YABC 2

Kirkup, James 1918- .... **CLC 1**
See also CA 1-4R; CAAS 4; CANR 2;
DLB 27; SATA 12

Kirkwood, James 1930(?)-1989 ...... **CLC 9**
See also AITN 2; CA 1-4R; 128; CANR 6,
40

Kis, Danilo 1935-1989 .... **CLC 57**
See also CA 109; 118; 129; MTCW

Kivi, Aleksis 1834-1872 .... **NCLC 30**

Kizer, Carolyn (Ashley)
1925- .... **CLC 15, 39, 80**
See also CA 65-68; CAAS 5; CANR 24;
DLB 5

Klabund 1890-1928.............. **TCLC 44**
See also DLB 66

Klappert, Peter 1942-............ **CLC 57**
See also CA 33-36R; DLB 5

Klein, A(braham) M(oses)
1909-1972 .... **CLC 19**
See also CA 101; 37-40R; DLB 68

Klein, Norma 1938-1989 .... **CLC 30**
See also AAYA 2; CA 41-44R; 128;
CANR 15, 37; CLR 2, 19; JRDA;
MAICYA; SAAS 1; SATA 7, 57

Klein, T(heodore) E(ibon) D(onald)
1947- .... **CLC 34**
See also CA 119

Kleist, Heinrich von 1777-1811.... **NCLC 2**
See also DLB 90

Klima, Ivan 1931-................ **CLC 56**
See also CA 25-28R; CANR 17

Klimentov, Andrei Platonovich 1899-1951
See Platonov, Andrei
See also CA 108

Klinger, Friedrich Maximilian von
1752-1831 .... **NCLC 1**
See also DLB 94

Klopstock, Friedrich Gottlieb
1724-1803 .... **NCLC 11**
See also DLB 97

Knebel, Fletcher 1911-1993........ **CLC 14**
See also AITN 1; CA 1-4R; 140; CAAS 3;
CANR 1, 36; SATA 36; SATA-Obit 75

Knickerbocker, Diedrich
See Irving, Washington

Knight, Etheridge
1931-1991 .... **CLC 40; BLC 2**
See also BW; CA 21-24R; 133; CANR 23;
DLB 41

Knight, Sarah Kemble 1666-1727 ..... **LC 7**
See also DLB 24

Knowles, John
1926- .... **CLC 1, 4, 10, 26; DA**
See also AAYA 10; CA 17-20R; CANR 40;
CDALB 1968-1988; DLB 6; MTCW;
SATA 8

Knox, Calvin M.
See Silverberg, Robert

Knye, Cassandra
See Disch, Thomas M(ichael)

Koch, C(hristopher) J(ohn) 1932- ... **CLC 42**
See also CA 127

Koch, Christopher
See Koch, C(hristopher) J(ohn)

Koch, Kenneth 1925- .... **CLC 5, 8, 44**
See also CA 1-4R; CANR 6, 36; DLB 5;
SATA 65

Kochanowski, Jan 1530-1584....... **LC 10**

Kock, Charles Paul de
1794-1871 .... **NCLC 16**

Koda Shigeyuki 1867-1947
See Rohan, Koda
See also CA 121

Koestler, Arthur
1905-1983 .... **CLC 1, 3, 6, 8, 15, 33**
See also CA 1-4R; 109; CANR 1, 33;
CDBLB 1945-1960; DLBY 83; MTCW

Kogawa, Joy Nozomi 1935-........ **CLC 78**
See also CA 101; CANR 19

Kohout, Pavel 1928-.............. **CLC 13**
See also CA 45-48; CANR 3

Koizumi, Yakumo
   See Hearn, (Patricio) Lafcadio (Tessima
   Carlos)

Kolmar, Gertrud   1894-1943...... **TCLC 40**

Konrad, George
   See Konrad, Gyoergy

Konrad, Gyoergy   1933- ...... **CLC 4, 10, 73**
   See also CA 85-88

Konwicki, Tadeusz   1926-..... **CLC 8, 28, 54**
   See also CA 101; CAAS 9; CANR 39;
   MTCW

Koontz, Dean R(ay)   1945-......... **CLC 78**
   See also AAYA 9; BEST 89:3, 90:2;
   CA 108; CANR 19, 36; MTCW

Kopit, Arthur (Lee)   1937- .... **CLC 1, 18, 33**
   See also AITN 1; CA 81-84; CABS 3;
   DLB 7; MTCW

Kops, Bernard   1926-.............. **CLC 4**
   See also CA 5-8R; DLB 13

Kornbluth, C(yril) M.   1923-1958.... **TCLC 8**
   See also CA 105; DLB 8

Korolenko, V. G.
   See Korolenko, Vladimir Galaktionovich

Korolenko, Vladimir
   See Korolenko, Vladimir Galaktionovich

Korolenko, Vladimir G.
   See Korolenko, Vladimir Galaktionovich

Korolenko, Vladimir Galaktionovich
   1853-1921.................. **TCLC 22**
   See also CA 121

Kosinski, Jerzy (Nikodem)
   1933-1991.... **CLC 1, 2, 3, 6, 10, 15, 53,
   70**
   See also CA 17-20R; 134; CANR 9; DLB 2;
   DLBY 82; MTCW

Kostelanetz, Richard (Cory)   1940- .. **CLC 28**
   See also CA 13-16R; CAAS 8; CANR 38

Kostrowitzki, Wilhelm Apollinaris de
   1880-1918
   See Apollinaire, Guillaume
   See also CA 104

Kotlowitz, Robert   1924-........... **CLC 4**
   See also CA 33-36R; CANR 36

Kotzebue, August (Friedrich Ferdinand) von
   1761-1819.................. **NCLC 25**
   See also DLB 94

Kotzwinkle, William   1938- .. **CLC 5, 14, 35**
   See also CA 45-48; CANR 3; CLR 6;
   MAICYA; SATA 24, 70

Kozol, Jonathan   1936-........... **CLC 17**
   See also CA 61-64; CANR 16

Kozoll, Michael   1940(?)- .... **CLC 35**

Kramer, Kathryn   19(?)- .... **CLC 34**

Kramer, Larry   1935- .... **CLC 42**
   See also CA 124; 126

Krasicki, Ignacy   1735-1801....... **NCLC 8**

Krasinski, Zygmunt   1812-1859 .... **NCLC 4**

Kraus, Karl   1874-1936........... **TCLC 5**
   See also CA 104; DLB 118

Kreve (Mickevicius), Vincas
   1882-1954.................. **TCLC 27**

Kristeva, Julia   1941- .... **CLC 77**

Kristofferson, Kris   1936-......... **CLC 26**
   See also CA 104

Krizanc, John   1956-............. **CLC 57**

Krleza, Miroslav   1893-1981........ **CLC 8**
   See also CA 97-100; 105

Kroetsch, Robert   1927- ...... **CLC 5, 23, 57**
   See also CA 17-20R; CANR 8, 38; DLB 53;
   MTCW

Kroetz, Franz
   See Kroetz, Franz Xaver

Kroetz, Franz Xaver   1946- .... **CLC 41**
   See also CA 130

Kroker, Arthur   1945-............. **CLC 77**

Kropotkin, Peter (Aleksieevich)
   1842-1921.................. **TCLC 36**
   See also CA 119

Krotkov, Yuri   1917-............. **CLC 19**
   See also CA 102

Krumb
   See Crumb, R(obert)

Krumgold, Joseph (Quincy)
   1908-1980.................. **CLC 12**
   See also CA 9-12R; 101; CANR 7;
   MAICYA; SATA 1, 23, 48

Krumwitz
   See Crumb, R(obert)

Krutch, Joseph Wood   1893-1970.... **CLC 24**
   See also CA 1-4R; 25-28R; CANR 4;
   DLB 63

Krutzch, Gus
   See Eliot, T(homas) S(tearns)

Krylov, Ivan Andreevich
   1768(?)-1844 .... **NCLC 1**

Kubin, Alfred   1877-1959 .... **TCLC 23**
   See also CA 112; DLB 81

Kubrick, Stanley   1928-............ **CLC 16**
   See also CA 81-84; CANR 33; DLB 26

Kumin, Maxine (Winokur)
   1925-.................. **CLC 5, 13, 28**
   See also AITN 2; CA 1-4R; CAAS 8;
   CANR 1, 21; DLB 5; MTCW; SATA 12

Kundera, Milan
   1929-............ **CLC 4, 9, 19, 32, 68**
   See also AAYA 2; CA 85-88; CANR 19;
   MTCW

Kunitz, Stanley (Jasspon)
   1905-.................. **CLC 6, 11, 14**
   See also CA 41-44R; CANR 26; DLB 48;
   MTCW

Kunze, Reiner   1933-............. **CLC 10**
   See also CA 93-96; DLB 75

Kuprin, Aleksandr Ivanovich
   1870-1938 .... **TCLC 5**
   See also CA 104

Kureishi, Hanif   1954(?)-........... **CLC 64**
   See also CA 139

Kurosawa, Akira   1910-............ **CLC 16**
   See also CA 101

Kushner, Tony   1957(?)- .... **CLC 81**

Kuttner, Henry   1915-1958....... **TCLC 10**
   See also CA 107; DLB 8

Kuzma, Greg   1944-............... **CLC 7**
   See also CA 33-36R

Kuzmin, Mikhail   1872(?)-1936 .... **TCLC 40**

Kyd, Thomas   1558-1594...... **LC 22; DC 3**
   See also DLB 62

Kyprianos, Iossif
   See Samarakis, Antonis

La Bruyere, Jean de   1645-1696...... **LC 17**

Lacan, Jacques (Marie Emile)
   1901-1981 .... **CLC 75**
   See also CA 121; 104

Laclos, Pierre Ambroise Francois Choderlos
   de   1741-1803 .... **NCLC 4**

Lacolere, Francois
   See Aragon, Louis

La Colere, Francois
   See Aragon, Louis

La Deshabilleuse
   See Simenon, Georges (Jacques Christian)

Lady Gregory
   See Gregory, Isabella Augusta (Persse)

Lady of Quality, A
   See Bagnold, Enid

La Fayette, Marie (Madelaine Pioche de la
   Vergne Comtes   1634-1693...... **LC 2**

Lafayette, Rene
   See Hubbard, L(afayette) Ron(ald)

Laforgue, Jules   1860-1887........ **NCLC 5**

Lagerkvist, Paer (Fabian)
   1891-1974 .... **CLC 7, 10, 13, 54**
   See also Lagerkvist, Par
   See also CA 85-88; 49-52; MTCW

Lagerkvist, Par
   See Lagerkvist, Paer (Fabian)
   See also SSC 12

Lagerloef, Selma (Ottiliana Lovisa)
   1858-1940 .... **TCLC 4, 36**
   See also Lagerlof, Selma (Ottiliana Lovisa)
   See also CA 108; CLR 7; SATA 15

Lagerlof, Selma (Ottiliana Lovisa)
   See Lagerloef, Selma (Ottiliana Lovisa)
   See also CLR 7; SATA 15

La Guma, (Justin) Alex(ander)
   1925-1985 .... **CLC 19**
   See also BW; CA 49-52; 118; CANR 25;
   DLB 117; MTCW

Laidlaw, A. K.
   See Grieve, C(hristopher) M(urray)

Lainez, Manuel Mujica
   See Mujica Lainez, Manuel
   See also HW

Lamartine, Alphonse (Marie Louis Prat) de
   1790-1869 .... **NCLC 11**

Lamb, Charles
   1775-1834 .... **NCLC 10; DA; WLC**
   See also CDBLB 1789-1832; DLB 93, 107;
   SATA 17

Lamb, Lady Caroline   1785-1828.. **NCLC 38**
   See also DLB 116

Lamming, George (William)
   1927-............ **CLC 2, 4, 66; BLC 2**
   See also BW; CA 85-88; CANR 26;
   DLB 125; MTCW

L'Amour, Louis (Dearborn)
    1908-1988 .... **CLC 25, 55**
    See also AITN 2; BEST 89:2; CA 1-4R;
    125; CANR 3, 25, 40; DLBY 80; MTCW

Lampedusa, Giuseppe (Tomasi) di ... **TCLC 13**
    See also Tomasi di Lampedusa, Giuseppe

Lampman, Archibald 1861-1899 .. **NCLC 25**
    See also DLB 92

Lancaster, Bruce 1896-1963........ **CLC 36**
    See also CA 9-10; CAP 1; SATA 9

Landau, Mark Alexandrovich
    See Aldanov, Mark (Alexandrovich)

Landau-Aldanov, Mark Alexandrovich
    See Aldanov, Mark (Alexandrovich)

Landis, John 1950- .... **CLC 26**
    See also CA 112; 122

Landolfi, Tommaso 1908-1979... **CLC 11, 49**
    See also CA 127; 117

Landon, Letitia Elizabeth
    1802-1838 .... **NCLC 15**
    See also DLB 96

Landor, Walter Savage
    1775-1864 .... **NCLC 14**
    See also DLB 93, 107

Landwirth, Heinz 1927-
    See Lind, Jakov
    See also CA 9-12R; CANR 7

Lane, Patrick 1939- .... **CLC 25**
    See also CA 97-100; DLB 53

Lang, Andrew 1844-1912........ **TCLC 16**
    See also CA 114; 137; DLB 98; MAICYA;
    SATA 16

Lang, Fritz 1890-1976 .... **CLC 20**
    See also CA 77-80; 69-72; CANR 30

Lange, John
    See Crichton, (John) Michael

Langer, Elinor 1939- .... **CLC 34**
    See also CA 121

Langland, William
    1330(?)-1400(?) .... **LC 19; DA**

Langstaff, Launcelot
    See Irving, Washington

Lanier, Sidney 1842-1881 .... **NCLC 6**
    See also DLB 64; MAICYA; SATA 18

Lanyer, Aemilia 1569-1645 ,....... **LC 10**

Lao Tzu .... **CMLC 7**

Lapine, James (Elliot) 1949- .... **CLC 39**
    See also CA 123; 130

Larbaud, Valery (Nicolas)
    1881-1957 .... **TCLC 9**
    See also CA 106

Lardner, Ring
    See Lardner, Ring(gold) W(ilmer)

Lardner, Ring W., Jr.
    See Lardner, Ring(gold) W(ilmer)

Lardner, Ring(gold) W(ilmer)
    1885-1933 .... **TCLC 2, 14**
    See also CA 104; 131; CDALB 1917-1929;
    DLB 11, 25, 86; MTCW

Laredo, Betty
    See Codrescu, Andrei

Larkin, Maia
    See Wojciechowska, Maia (Teresa)

Larkin, Philip (Arthur)
    1922-1985 .... **CLC 3, 5, 8, 9, 13, 18, 33,**
                                       39, 64
    See also CA 5-8R; 117; CANR 24;
    CDBLB 1960 to Present; DLB 27;
    MTCW

Larra (y Sanchez de Castro), Mariano Jose de
    1809-1837 .... **NCLC 17**

Larsen, Eric 1941- .... **CLC 55**
    See also CA 132

Larsen, Nella 1891-1964 ... **CLC 37; BLC 2**
    See also BW; CA 125; DLB 51

Larson, Charles R(aymond) 1938-... **CLC 31**
    See also CA 53-56; CANR 4

Latham, Jean Lee 1902-........ **CLC 12**
    See also AITN 1; CA 5-8R; CANR 7;
    MAICYA; SATA 2, 68

Latham, Mavis
    See Clark, Mavis Thorpe

Lathen, Emma .... **CLC 2**
    See also Hennissart, Martha; Latsis, Mary
    J(ane)

Lathrop, Francis
    See Leiber, Fritz (Reuter, Jr.)

Latsis, Mary J(ane)
    See Lathen, Emma
    See also CA 85-88

Lattimore, Richmond (Alexander)
    1906-1984 .... **CLC 3**
    See also CA 1-4R; 112; CANR 1

Laughlin, James 1914-........... **CLC 49**
    See also CA 21-24R; CANR 9; DLB 48

Laurence, (Jean) Margaret (Wemyss)
    1926-1987 .. **CLC 3, 6, 13, 50, 62; SSC 7**
    See also CA 5-8R; 121; CANR 33; DLB 53;
    MTCW; SATA 50

Laurent, Antoine 1952- .... **CLC 50**

Lauscher, Hermann
    See Hesse, Hermann

Lautreamont, Comte de
    1846-1870 .... **NCLC 12; SSC 14**

Laverty, Donald
    See Blish, James (Benjamin)

Lavin, Mary 1912-...... **CLC 4, 18; SSC 4**
    See also CA 9-12R; CANR 33; DLB 15;
    MTCW

Lavond, Paul Dennis
    See Kornbluth, C(yril) M.; Pohl, Frederik

Lawler, Raymond Evenor 1922- .... **CLC 58**
    See also CA 103

Lawrence, D(avid) H(erbert Richards)
    1885-1930 .... **TCLC 2, 9, 16, 33, 48;**
                              DA; SSC 4; WLC
    See also CA 104; 121; CDBLB 1914-1945;
    DLB 10, 19, 36, 98; MTCW

Lawrence, T(homas) E(dward)
    1888-1935 .... **TCLC 18**
    See also Dale, Colin
    See also CA 115

Lawrence of Arabia
    See Lawrence, T(homas) E(dward)

Lawson, Henry (Archibald Hertzberg)
    1867-1922 .... **TCLC 27**
    See also CA 120

Lawton, Dennis
    See Faust, Frederick (Schiller)

Laxness, Halldor .... **CLC 25**
    See also Gudjonsson, Halldor Kiljan

Layamon fl. c. 1200-............ **CMLC 10**

Laye, Camara
    1928-1980 .... **CLC 4, 38; BLC 2**
    See also BW; CA 85-88; 97-100; CANR 25;
    MTCW

Layton, Irving (Peter) 1912-...... **CLC 2, 15**
    See also CA 1-4R; CANR 2, 33, 43;
    DLB 88; MTCW

Lazarus, Emma 1849-1887........ **NCLC 8**

Lazarus, Felix
    See Cable, George Washington

Lazarus, Henry
    See Slavitt, David R(ytman)

Lea, Joan
    See Neufeld, John (Arthur)

Leacock, Stephen (Butler)
    1869-1944 .... **TCLC 2**
    See also CA 104; 141; DLB 92

Lear, Edward 1812-1888 .... **NCLC 3**
    See also CLR 1; DLB 32; MAICYA;
    SATA 18

Lear, Norman (Milton) 1922- ...... **CLC 12**
    See also CA 73-76

Leavis, F(rank) R(aymond)
    1895-1978 .... **CLC 24**
    See also CA 21-24R; 77-80; MTCW

Leavitt, David 1961-............. **CLC 34**
    See also CA 116; 122; DLB 130

Leblanc, Maurice (Marie Emile)
    1864-1941 .... **TCLC 49**
    See also CA 110

Lebowitz, Fran(ces Ann)
    1951(?)- .... **CLC 11, 36**
    See also CA 81-84; CANR 14; MTCW

le Carre, John .... **CLC 3, 5, 9, 15, 28**
    See also Cornwell, David (John Moore)
    See also BEST 89:4; CDBLB 1960 to
    Present; DLB 87

Le Clezio, J(ean) M(arie) G(ustave)
    1940- .... **CLC 31**
    See also CA 116; 128; DLB 83

Leconte de Lisle, Charles-Marie-Rene
    1818-1894 .... **NCLC 29**

Le Coq, Monsieur
    See Simenon, Georges (Jacques Christian)

Leduc, Violette 1907-1972........ **CLC 22**
    See also CA 13-14; 33-36R; CAP 1

Ledwidge, Francis 1887(?)-1917 ... **TCLC 23**
    See also CA 123; DLB 20

Lee, Andrea 1953- .... **CLC 36; BLC 2**
    See also BW; CA 125

Lee, Andrew
    See Auchincloss, Louis (Stanton)

Lee, Don L. .... **CLC 2**
    See also Madhubuti, Haki R.

Lee, George W(ashington)
    1894-1976 .... **CLC 52; BLC 2**
    See also BW; CA 125; DLB 51

Lee, (Nelle) Harper
1926- .... **CLC 12, 60; DA; WLC**
See also CA 13-16R; CDALB 1941-1968;
DLB 6; MTCW; SATA 11

Lee, Julian
See Latham, Jean Lee

Lee, Larry
See Lee, Lawrence

Lee, Lawrence 1941-1990......... **CLC 34**
See also CA 131; CANR 43

Lee, Manfred B(ennington)
1905-1971 .... **CLC 11**
See also Queen, Ellery
See also CA 1-4R; 29-32R; CANR 2

Lee, Stan 1922- .... **CLC 17**
See also AAYA 5; CA 108; 111

Lee, Tanith 1947- .... **CLC 46**
See also CA 37-40R; SATA 8

Lee, Vernon .... **TCLC 5**
See also Paget, Violet
See also DLB 57

Lee, William
See Burroughs, William S(eward)

Lee, Willy
See Burroughs, William S(eward)

Lee-Hamilton, Eugene (Jacob)
1845-1907 .... **TCLC 22**
See also CA 117

Leet, Judith 1935- .... **CLC 11**

Le Fanu, Joseph Sheridan
1814-1873 .... **NCLC 9; SSC 14**
See also DLB 21, 70

Leffland, Ella 1931- .... **CLC 19**
See also CA 29-32R; CANR 35; DLBY 84;
SATA 65

Leger, Alexis
See Leger, (Marie-Rene Auguste) Alexis
Saint-Leger

**Leger, (Marie-Rene Auguste) Alexis
Saint-Leger** 1887-1975........ **CLC 11**
See also Perse, St.-John
See also CA 13-16R; 61-64; CANR 43;
MTCW

Leger, Saintleger
See Leger, (Marie-Rene Auguste) Alexis
Saint-Leger

Le Guin, Ursula K(roeber)
1929- .... **CLC 8, 13, 22, 45, 71; SSC 12**
See also AAYA 9; AITN 1; CA 21-24R;
CANR 9, 32; CDALB 1968-1988; CLR 3,
28; DLB 8, 52; JRDA; MAICYA;
MTCW; SATA 4, 52

Lehmann, Rosamond (Nina)
1901-1990 .... **CLC 5**
See also CA 77-80; 131; CANR 8; DLB 15

Leiber, Fritz (Reuter, Jr.)
1910-1992 .... **CLC 25**
See also CA 45-48; 139; CANR 2, 40;
DLB 8; MTCW; SATA 45;
SATA-Obit 73

Leimbach, Martha 1963-
See Leimbach, Marti
See also CA 130

Leimbach, Marti .... **CLC 65**
See also Leimbach, Martha

Leino, Eino .... **TCLC 24**
See also Loennbohm, Armas Eino Leopold

Leiris, Michel (Julien) 1901-1990... **CLC 61**
See also CA 119; 128; 132

Leithauser, Brad 1953-............ **CLC 27**
See also CA 107; CANR 27; DLB 120

Lelchuk, Alan 1938-............... **CLC 5**
See also CA 45-48; CANR 1

Lem, Stanislaw 1921-......... **CLC 8, 15, 40**
See also CA 105; CAAS 1; CANR 32;
MTCW

Lemann, Nancy 1956-............. **CLC 39**
See also CA 118; 136

Lemonnier, (Antoine Louis) Camille
1844-1913 .... **TCLC 22**
See also CA 121

Lenau, Nikolaus 1802-1850...... **NCLC 16**

L'Engle, Madeleine (Camp Franklin)
1918- .... **CLC 12**
See also AAYA 1; AITN 2; CA 1-4R;
CANR 3, 21, 39; CLR 1, 14; DLB 52;
JRDA; MAICYA; MTCW; SAAS 15;
SATA 1, 27, 75

Lengyel, Jozsef 1896-1975.......... **CLC 7**
See also CA 85-88; 57-60

Lennon, John (Ono)
1940-1980 .... **CLC 12, 35**
See also CA 102

Lennox, Charlotte Ramsay
1729(?)-1804 .... **NCLC 23**
See also DLB 39

Lentricchia, Frank (Jr.) 1940-...... **CLC 34**
See also CA 25-28R; CANR 19

Lenz, Siegfried 1926-............. **CLC 27**
See also CA 89-92; DLB 75

Leonard, Elmore (John, Jr.)
1925- .... **CLC 28, 34, 71**
See also AITN 1; BEST 89:1, 90:4;
CA 81-84; CANR 12, 28; MTCW

Leonard, Hugh
See Byrne, John Keyes
See also DLB 13

**Leopardi, (Conte) Giacomo (Talegardo
Francesco di Sales Save**
1798-1837 .... **NCLC 22**

Le Reveler
See Artaud, Antonin

Lerman, Eleanor 1952-............ **CLC 9**
See also CA 85-88

Lerman, Rhoda 1936-............. **CLC 56**
See also CA 49-52

Lermontov, Mikhail Yuryevich
1814-1841 .... **NCLC 5**

Leroux, Gaston 1868-1927....... **TCLC 25**
See also CA 108; 136; SATA 65

Lesage, Alain-Rene 1668-1747....... **LC 2**

Leskov, Nikolai (Semyonovich)
1831-1895 .... **NCLC 25**

Lessing, Doris (May)
1919- ..... **CLC 1, 2, 3, 6, 10, 15, 22, 40;
DA; SSC 6**
See also CA 9-12R; CAAS 14; CANR 33;
CDBLB 1960 to Present; DLB 15;
DLBY 85; MTCW

Lessing, Gotthold Ephraim
1729-1781 .... **LC 8**
See also DLB 97

Lester, Richard 1932-............. **CLC 20**

Lever, Charles (James)
1806-1872 .... **NCLC 23**
See also DLB 21

Leverson, Ada 1865(?)-1936(?) .... **TCLC 18**
See also Elaine
See also CA 117

Levertov, Denise
1923- ...... **CLC 1, 2, 3, 5, 8, 15, 28, 66**
See also CA 1-4R; CANR 3, 29; DLB 5;
MTCW

Levi, Jonathan .... **CLC 76**

Levi, Peter (Chad Tigar) 1931-..... **CLC 41**
See also CA 5-8R; CANR 34; DLB 40

Levi, Primo
1919-1987 .... **CLC 37, 50; SSC 12**
See also CA 13-16R; 122; CANR 12, 33;
MTCW

Levin, Ira 1929- .... **CLC 3, 6**
See also CA 21-24R; CANR 17; MTCW;
SATA 66

Levin, Meyer 1905-1981 .... **CLC 7**
See also AITN 1; CA 9-12R; 104;
CANR 15; DLB 9, 28; DLBY 81;
SATA 21, 27

Levine, Norman 1924-............. **CLC 54**
See also CA 73-76; CANR 14; DLB 88

Levine, Philip 1928-... **CLC 2, 4, 5, 9, 14, 33**
See also CA 9-12R; CANR 9, 37; DLB 5

Levinson, Deirdre 1931-........... **CLC 49**
See also CA 73-76

Levi-Strauss, Claude 1908- .... **CLC 38**
See also CA 1-4R; CANR 6, 32; MTCW

Levitin, Sonia (Wolff) 1934- .... **CLC 17**
See also CA 29-32R; CANR 14, 32; JRDA;
MAICYA; SAAS 2; SATA 4, 68

Levon, O. U.
See Kesey, Ken (Elton)

Lewes, George Henry
1817-1878 .... **NCLC 25**
See also DLB 55

Lewis, Alun 1915-1944............ **TCLC 3**
See also CA 104; DLB 20

Lewis, C. Day
See Day Lewis, C(ecil)

Lewis, C(live) S(taples)
1898-1963 ..... **CLC 1, 3, 6, 14, 27; DA;
WLC**
See also AAYA 3; CA 81-84; CANR 33;
CDBLB 1945-1960; CLR 3, 27; DLB 15,
100; JRDA; MAICYA; MTCW;
SATA 13

Lewis, Janet 1899-............... **CLC 41**
See also Winters, Janet Lewis
See also CA 9-12R; CANR 29; CAP 1;
DLBY 87

Lewis, Matthew Gregory
1775-1818 .... **NCLC 11**
See also DLB 39

Lewis, (Harry) Sinclair
1885-1951 ..... **TCLC 4, 13, 23, 39; DA;**
WLC
See also CA 104; 133; CDALB 1917-1929;
DLB 9, 102; DLBD 1; MTCW

Lewis, (Percy) Wyndham
1884(?)-1957 .... **TCLC 2, 9**
See also CA 104; DLB 15

Lewisohn, Ludwig 1883-1955...... **TCLC 19**
See also CA 107; DLB 4, 9, 28, 102

Lezama Lima, Jose 1910-1976 ... **CLC 4, 10**
See also CA 77-80; DLB 113; HW

L'Heureux, John (Clarke) 1934-.... **CLC 52**
See also CA 13-16R; CANR 23

Liddell, C. H.
See Kuttner, Henry

Lie, Jonas (Lauritz Idemil)
1833-1908(?) .... **TCLC 5**
See also CA 115

Lieber, Joel 1937-1971............. **CLC 6**
See also CA 73-76; 29-32R

Lieber, Stanley Martin
See Lee, Stan

Lieberman, Laurence (James)
1935- .... **CLC 4, 36**
See also CA 17-20R; CANR 8, 36

Lieksman, Anders
See Haavikko, Paavo Juhani

Li Fei-kan 1904-................. **CLC 18**
See also CA 105

Lifton, Robert Jay 1926-.......... **CLC 67**
See also CA 17-20R; CANR 27; SATA 66

Lightfoot, Gordon 1938-.......... **CLC 26**
See also CA 109

Lightman, Alan P. 1948- .... **CLC 81**
See also CA 141

Ligotti, Thomas 1953- .... **CLC 44**
See also CA 123

Liliencron, (Friedrich Adolf Axel) Detlev von
1844-1909 .... **TCLC 18**
See also CA 117

Lima, Jose Lezama
See Lezama Lima, Jose

Lima Barreto, Afonso Henrique de
1881-1922 .... **TCLC 23**
See also CA 117

Limonov, Eduard.................. **CLC 67**

Lin, Frank
See Atherton, Gertrude (Franklin Horn)

Lincoln, Abraham 1809-1865..... **NCLC 18**

Lind, Jakov .... **CLC 1, 2, 4, 27**
See also Landwirth, Heinz
See also CAAS 4

Lindsay, David 1878-1945....... **TCLC 15**
See also CA 113

Lindsay, (Nicholas) Vachel
1879-1931 .... **TCLC 17; DA; WLC**
See also CA 114; 135; CDALB 1865-1917;
DLB 54; SATA 40

Linke-Poot
See Doeblin, Alfred

Linney, Romulus 1930- .... **CLC 51**
See also CA 1-4R; CANR 40

Linton, Eliza Lynn 1822-1898.... **NCLC 41**
See also DLB 18

Li Po 701-763 .... **CMLC 2**

Lipsius, Justus 1547-1606 .... **LC 16**

Lipsyte, Robert (Michael)
1938- .... **CLC 21; DA**
See also AAYA 7; CA 17-20R; CANR 8;
CLR 23; JRDA; MAICYA; SATA 5, 68

Lish, Gordon (Jay) 1934-.......... **CLC 45**
See also CA 113; 117; DLB 130

Lispector, Clarice 1925-1977....... **CLC 43**
See also CA 139; 116; DLB 113

Littell, Robert 1935(?)- .... **CLC 42**
See also CA 109; 112

Littlewit, Humphrey Gent.
See Lovecraft, H(oward) P(hillips)

Litwos
See Sienkiewicz, Henryk (Adam Alexander
Pius)

Liu E 1857-1909............... **TCLC 15**
See also CA 115

Lively, Penelope (Margaret)
1933- .... **CLC 32, 50**
See also CA 41-44R; CANR 29; CLR 7;
DLB 14; JRDA; MAICYA; MTCW;
SATA 7, 60

Livesay, Dorothy (Kathleen)
1909- .... **CLC 4, 15, 79**
See also AITN 2; CA 25-28R; CAAS 8;
CANR 36; DLB 68; MTCW

Livy c. 59B.C.-c. 17 .... **CMLC 11**

Lizardi, Jose Joaquin Fernandez de
1776-1827 .... **NCLC 30**

Llewellyn, Richard .... **CLC 7**
See also Llewellyn Lloyd, Richard Dafydd
Vivian
See also DLB 15

Llewellyn Lloyd, Richard Dafydd Vivian
1906-1983 .... **CLC 80**
See also Llewellyn, Richard
See also CA 53-56; 111; CANR 7;
SATA 11, 37

Llosa, (Jorge) Mario (Pedro) Vargas
See Vargas Llosa, (Jorge) Mario (Pedro)

Lloyd Webber, Andrew 1948-
See Webber, Andrew Lloyd
See also AAYA 1; CA 116; SATA 56

Llull, Ramon c. 1235-c. 1316..... **CMLC 12**

Locke, Alain (Le Roy)
1886-1954 .... **TCLC 43**
See also BW; CA 106; 124; DLB 51

Locke, John 1632-1704 .... **LC 7**
See also DLB 101

Locke-Elliott, Sumner
See Elliott, Sumner Locke

Lockhart, John Gibson
1794-1854 .... **NCLC 6**
See also DLB 110, 116

Lodge, David (John) 1935-......... **CLC 36**
See also BEST 90:1; CA 17-20R; CANR 19;
DLB 14; MTCW

Loennbohm, Armas Eino Leopold 1878-1926
See Leino, Eino
See also CA 123

Loewinsohn, Ron(ald William)
1937- .... **CLC 52**
See also CA 25-28R

Logan, Jake
See Smith, Martin Cruz

Logan, John (Burton) 1923-1987..... **CLC 5**
See also CA 77-80; 124; DLB 5

Lo Kuan-chung 1330(?)-1400(?)...... **LC 12**

Lombard, Nap
See Johnson, Pamela Hansford

London, Jack.. **TCLC 9, 15, 39; SSC 4; WLC**
See also London, John Griffith
See also AITN 2; CDALB 1865-1917;
DLB 8, 12, 78; SATA 18

London, John Griffith 1876-1916
See London, Jack
See also CA 110; 119; DA; JRDA;
MAICYA; MTCW

Long, Emmett
See Leonard, Elmore (John, Jr.)

Longbaugh, Harry
See Goldman, William (W.)

Longfellow, Henry Wadsworth
1807-1882 .... **NCLC 2; DA**
See also CDALB 1640-1865; DLB 1, 59;
SATA 19

Longley, Michael 1939-.......... **CLC 29**
See also CA 102; DLB 40

Longus fl. c. 2nd cent. - .... **CMLC 7**

Longway, A. Hugh
See Lang, Andrew

Lopate, Phillip 1943-............ **CLC 29**
See also CA 97-100; DLBY 80

Lopez Portillo (y Pacheco), Jose
1920- .... **CLC 46**
See also CA 129; HW

Lopez y Fuentes, Gregorio
1897(?)-1966 .... **CLC 32**
See also CA 131; HW

Lorca, Federico Garcia
See Garcia Lorca, Federico

Lord, Bette Bao 1938-............ **CLC 23**
See also BEST 90:3; CA 107; CANR 41;
SATA 58

Lord Auch
See Bataille, Georges

Lord Byron
See Byron, George Gordon (Noel)

Lord Dunsany .... **TCLC 2**
See also Dunsany, Edward John Moreton
Drax Plunkett

Lorde, Audre (Geraldine)
1934-1992 .... **CLC 18, 71; BLC 2**
See also BW; CA 25-28R; 142; CANR 16,
26; DLB 41; MTCW

Lord Jeffrey
See Jeffrey, Francis

Lorenzo, Heberto Padilla
See Padilla (Lorenzo), Heberto

Loris
See Hofmannsthal, Hugo von

Loti, Pierre .... **TCLC 11**
See also Viaud, (Louis Marie) Julien
See also DLB 123

Louie, David Wong   1954- . . . . CLC 70
See also CA 139

Louis, Father M.
See Merton, Thomas

Lovecraft, H(oward) P(hillips)
    1890-1937 . . . . TCLC 4, 22; SSC 3
See also CA 104; 133; MTCW

Lovelace, Earl   1935-. . . . . CLC 51
See also CA 77-80; CANR 41; DLB 125;
    MTCW

Lovelace, Richard   1618-1657. . . . . . . LC 24
See also DLB 131

Lowell, Amy   1874-1925 . . . . TCLC 1, 8
See also CA 104; DLB 54

Lowell, James Russell   1819-1891 . . NCLC 2
See also CDALB 1640-1865; DLB 1, 11, 64,
    79

Lowell, Robert (Traill Spence, Jr.)
    1917-1977 . . . CLC 1, 2, 3, 4, 5, 8, 9, 11,
                        15, 37; DA; PC 3; WLC
See also CA 9-12R; 73-76; CABS 2;
    CANR 26; DLB 5; MTCW

Lowndes, Marie Adelaide (Belloc)
    1868-1947 . . . . TCLC 12
See also CA 107; DLB 70

Lowry, (Clarence) Malcolm
    1909-1957 . . . . TCLC 6, 40
See also CA 105; 131; CDBLB 1945-1960;
    DLB 15; MTCW

Lowry, Mina Gertrude   1882-1966
See Loy, Mina
See also CA 113

Loxsmith, John
See Brunner, John (Kilian Houston)

Loy, Mina . . . . CLC 28
See also Lowry, Mina Gertrude
See also DLB 4, 54

Loyson-Bridet
See Schwob, (Mayer Andre) Marcel

Lucas, Craig   1951- . . . . CLC 64
See also CA 137

Lucas, George   1944-. . . . . CLC 16
See also AAYA 1; CA 77-80; CANR 30;
    SATA 56

Lucas, Hans
See Godard, Jean-Luc

Lucas, Victoria
See Plath, Sylvia

Ludlam, Charles   1943-1987 . . . . . CLC 46, 50
See also CA 85-88; 122

Ludlum, Robert   1927- . . . . CLC 22, 43
See also AAYA 10; BEST 89:1, 90:3;
    CA 33-36R; CANR 25, 41; DLBY 82;
    MTCW

Ludwig, Ken. . . . . CLC 60

Ludwig, Otto   1813-1865. . . . . NCLC 4
See also DLB 129

Lugones, Leopoldo   1874-1938 . . . . . TCLC 15
See also CA 116; 131; HW

Lu Hsun   1881-1936 . . . . TCLC 3

Lukacs, George . . . . CLC 24
See also Lukacs, Gyorgy (Szegeny von)

Lukacs, Gyorgy (Szegeny von)   1885-1971
See Lukacs, George
See also CA 101; 29-32R

Luke, Peter (Ambrose Cyprian)
    1919- . . . . CLC 38
See also CA 81-84; DLB 13

Lunar, Dennis
See Mungo, Raymond

Lurie, Alison   1926-. . . . . CLC 4, 5, 18, 39
See also CA 1-4R; CANR 2, 17; DLB 2;
    MTCW; SATA 46

Lustig, Arnost   1926-. . . . . CLC 56
See also AAYA 3; CA 69-72; SATA 56

Luther, Martin   1483-1546 . . . . LC 9

Luzi, Mario   1914-. . . . . CLC 13
See also CA 61-64; CANR 9; DLB 128

Lynch, B. Suarez
See Bioy Casares, Adolfo; Borges, Jorge
    Luis

Lynch, David (K.)   1946-. . . . . CLC 66
See also CA 124; 129

Lynch, James
See Andreyev, Leonid (Nikolaevich)

Lynch Davis, B.
See Bioy Casares, Adolfo; Borges, Jorge
    Luis

Lyndsay, SirDavid   1490-1555 . . . . LC 20

Lynn, Kenneth S(chuyler)   1923- . . . . CLC 50
See also CA 1-4R; CANR 3, 27

Lynx
See West, Rebecca

Lyons, Marcus
See Blish, James (Benjamin)

Lyre, Pinchbeck
See Sassoon, Siegfried (Lorraine)

Lytle, Andrew (Nelson)   1902- . . . . . . CLC 22
See also CA 9-12R; DLB 6

Lyttelton, George   1709-1773 . . . . LC 10

Maas, Peter   1929- . . . . CLC 29
See also CA 93-96

Macaulay, Rose   1881-1958 . . . . . TCLC 7, 44
See also CA 104; DLB 36

Macaulay, Thomas Babington
    1800-1859 . . . . NCLC 42
See also CDBLB 1832-1890; DLB 32, 55

MacBeth, George (Mann)
    1932-1992 . . . . CLC 2, 5, 9
See also CA 25-28R; 136; DLB 40; MTCW;
    SATA 4; SATA-Obit 70

MacCaig, Norman (Alexander)
    1910- . . . . CLC 36
See also CA 9-12R; CANR 3, 34; DLB 27

MacCarthy, (Sir Charles Otto) Desmond
    1877-1952 . . . . TCLC 36

MacDiarmid, Hugh. . . . . CLC 2, 4, 11, 19, 63
See also Grieve, C(hristopher) M(urray)
See also CDBLB 1945-1960; DLB 20

MacDonald, Anson
See Heinlein, Robert A(nson)

Macdonald, Cynthia   1928-. . . . . . CLC 13, 19
See also CA 49-52; CANR 4; DLB 105

MacDonald, George   1824-1905. . . . . TCLC 9
See also CA 106; 137; DLB 18; MAICYA;
    SATA 33

Macdonald, John
See Millar, Kenneth

MacDonald, John D(ann)
    1916-1986 . . . . CLC 3, 27, 44
See also CA 1-4R; 121; CANR 1, 19;
    DLB 8; DLBY 86; MTCW

Macdonald, John Ross
See Millar, Kenneth

Macdonald, Ross. . . . . CLC 1, 2, 3, 14, 34, 41
See also Millar, Kenneth
See also DLBD 6

MacDougal, John
See Blish, James (Benjamin)

MacEwen, Gwendolyn (Margaret)
    1941-1987 . . . . CLC 13, 55
See also CA 9-12R; 124; CANR 7, 22;
    DLB 53; SATA 50, 55

Machado (y Ruiz), Antonio
    1875-1939 . . . . TCLC 3
See also CA 104; DLB 108

Machado de Assis, Joaquim Maria
    1839-1908 . . . . TCLC 10; BLC 2
See also CA 107

Machen, Arthur. . . . . TCLC 4
See also Jones, Arthur Llewellyn
See also DLB 36

Machiavelli, Niccolo   1469-1527 . . LC 8; DA

MacInnes, Colin   1914-1976 . . . . . . CLC 4, 23
See also CA 69-72; 65-68; CANR 21;
    DLB 14; MTCW

MacInnes, Helen (Clark)
    1907-1985 . . . . CLC 27, 39
See also CA 1-4R; 117; CANR 1, 28;
    DLB 87; MTCW; SATA 22, 44

Mackay, Mary   1855-1924
See Corelli, Marie
See also CA 118

Mackenzie, Compton (Edward Montague)
    1883-1972 . . . . CLC 18
See also CA 21-22; 37-40R; CAP 2;
    DLB 34, 100

Mackenzie, Henry   1745-1831 . . . . . NCLC 41
See also DLB 39

Mackintosh, Elizabeth   1896(?)-1952
See Tey, Josephine
See also CA 110

MacLaren, James
See Grieve, C(hristopher) M(urray)

Mac Laverty, Bernard   1942-. . . . . . . CLC 31
See also CA 116; 118; CANR 43

MacLean, Alistair (Stuart)
    1922-1987 . . . . CLC 3, 13, 50, 63
See also CA 57-60; 121; CANR 28; MTCW;
    SATA 23, 50

Maclean, Norman (Fitzroy)
    1902-1990 . . . . CLC 78; SSC 13
See also CA 102; 132

MacLeish, Archibald
    1892-1982 . . . . CLC 3, 8, 14, 68
See also CA 9-12R; 106; CANR 33; DLB 4,
    7, 45; DLBY 82; MTCW

MacLennan, (John) Hugh
1907-1990 . . . . CLC 2, 14
See also CA 5-8R; 142; CANR 33; DLB 68;
MTCW

MacLeod, Alistair 1936- . . . . CLC 56
See also CA 123; DLB 60

MacNeice, (Frederick) Louis
1907-1963 . . . . CLC 1, 4, 10, 53
See also CA 85-88; DLB 10, 20; MTCW

MacNeill, Dand
See Fraser, George MacDonald

Macpherson, (Jean) Jay 1931- . . . . . . CLC 14
See also CA 5-8R; DLB 53

MacShane, Frank 1927- . . . . CLC 39
See also CA 9-12R; CANR 3, 33; DLB 111

Macumber, Mari
See Sandoz, Mari(e Susette)

Madach, Imre 1823-1864 . . . . NCLC 19

Madden, (Jerry) David 1933- . . . . CLC 5, 15
See also CA 1-4R; CAAS 3; CANR 4;
DLB 6; MTCW

Maddern, Al(an)
See Ellison, Harlan

Madhubuti, Haki R.
1942- . . . . CLC 6, 73; BLC 2; PC 5
See also Lee, Don L.
See also BW; CA 73-76; CANR 24; DLB 5,
41; DLBD 8

Madow, Pauline (Reichberg) . . . . CLC 1
See also CA 9-12R

Maepenn, Hugh
See Kuttner, Henry

Maepenn, K. H.
See Kuttner, Henry

Maeterlinck, Maurice 1862-1949 . . . TCLC 3
See also CA 104; 136; SATA 66

Maginn, William 1794-1842 . . . . . . NCLC 8
See also DLB 110

Mahapatra, Jayanta 1928- . . . . CLC 33
See also CA 73-76; CAAS 9; CANR 15, 33

Mahfouz, Naguib (Abdel Aziz Al-Sabilgi)
1911(?)-
See Mahfuz, Najib
See also BEST 89:2; CA 128; MTCW

Mahfuz, Najib . . . . CLC 52, 55
See also Mahfouz, Naguib (Abdel Aziz
Al-Sabilgi)
See also DLBY 88

Mahon, Derek 1941- . . . . CLC 27
See also CA 113; 128; DLB 40

Mailer, Norman
1923- . . . . . . CLC 1, 2, 3, 4, 5, 8, 11, 14,
28, 39, 74; DA
See also AITN 2; CA 9-12R; CABS 1;
CANR 28; CDALB 1968-1988; DLB 2,
16, 28; DLBD 3; DLBY 80, 83; MTCW

Maillet, Antonine 1929- . . . . CLC 54
See also CA 115; 120; DLB 60

Mais, Roger 1905-1955 . . . . TCLC 8
See also BW; CA 105; 124; DLB 125;
MTCW

Maitland, Sara (Louise) 1950- . . . . . . CLC 49
See also CA 69-72; CANR 13

Major, Clarence
1936- . . . . CLC 3, 19, 48; BLC 2
See also BW; CA 21-24R; CAAS 6;
CANR 13, 25; DLB 33

Major, Kevin (Gerald) 1949- . . . . CLC 26
See also CA 97-100; CANR 21, 38;
CLR 11; DLB 60; JRDA; MAICYA;
SATA 32

Maki, James
See Ozu, Yasujiro

Malabaila, Damiano
See Levi, Primo

Malamud, Bernard
1914-1986 . . . . . . CLC 1, 2, 3, 5, 8, 9, 11,
18, 27, 44, 78; DA; WLC
See also CA 5-8R; 118; CABS 1; CANR 28;
CDALB 1941-1968; DLB 2, 28;
DLBY 80, 86; MTCW

Malaparte, Curzio 1898-1957 . . . . . TCLC 52

Malcolm, Dan
See Silverberg, Robert

Malherbe, Francois de 1555-1628 . . . . . LC 5

Mallarme, Stephane
1842-1898 . . . . NCLC 4, 41; PC 4

Mallet-Joris, Francoise 1930- . . . . . . CLC 11
See also CA 65-68; CANR 17; DLB 83

Malley, Ern
See McAuley, James Phillip

Mallowan, Agatha Christie
See Christie, Agatha (Mary Clarissa)

Maloff, Saul 1922- . . . . CLC 5
See also CA 33-36R

Malone, Louis
See MacNeice, (Frederick) Louis

Malone, Michael (Christopher)
1942- . . . . CLC 43
See also CA 77-80; CANR 14, 32

Malory, (Sir) Thomas
1410(?)-1471(?) . . . . LC 11; DA
See also CDBLB Before 1660; SATA 33, 59

Malouf, (George Joseph) David
1934- . . . . CLC 28
See also CA 124

Malraux, (Georges-)Andre
1901-1976 . . . . . . CLC 1, 4, 9, 13, 15, 57
See also CA 21-22; 69-72; CANR 34;
CAP 2; DLB 72; MTCW

Malzberg, Barry N(athaniel) 1939- . . . CLC 7
See also CA 61-64; CAAS 4; CANR 16;
DLB 8

Mamet, David (Alan)
1947- . . . . CLC 9, 15, 34, 46; DC 4
See also AAYA 3; CA 81-84; CABS 3;
CANR 15, 41; DLB 7; MTCW

Mamoulian, Rouben (Zachary)
1897-1987 . . . . CLC 16
See also CA 25-28R; 124

Mandelstam, Osip (Emilievich)
1891(?)-1938(?) . . . . TCLC 2, 6
See also CA 104

Mander, (Mary) Jane 1877-1949 . . . TCLC 31

Mandiargues, Andre Pieyre de . . . . . . CLC 41
See also Pieyre de Mandiargues, Andre
See also DLB 83

Mandrake, Ethel Belle
See Thurman, Wallace (Henry)

Mangan, James Clarence
1803-1849 . . . . NCLC 27

Maniere, J.-E.
See Giraudoux, (Hippolyte) Jean

Manley, (Mary) Delariviere
1672(?)-1724 . . . . LC 1
See also DLB 39, 80

Mann, Abel
See Creasey, John

Mann, (Luiz) Heinrich 1871-1950 . . . TCLC 9
See also CA 106; DLB 66

Mann, (Paul) Thomas
1875-1955 . . . . TCLC 2, 8, 14, 21, 35, 44;
DA; SSC 5; WLC
See also CA 104; 128; DLB 66; MTCW

Manning, David
See Faust, Frederick (Schiller)

Manning, Frederic 1887(?)-1935 . . . TCLC 25
See also CA 124

Manning, Olivia 1915-1980 . . . . . . CLC 5, 19
See also CA 5-8R; 101; CANR 29; MTCW

Mano, D. Keith 1942- . . . . CLC 2, 10
See also CA 25-28R; CAAS 6; CANR 26;
DLB 6

Mansfield, Katherine
. . . . TCLC 2, 8, 39; SSC 9; WLC
See also Beauchamp, Kathleen Mansfield

Manso, Peter 1940- . . . . CLC 39
See also CA 29-32R

Mantecon, Juan Jimenez
See Jimenez (Mantecon), Juan Ramon

Manton, Peter
See Creasey, John

Man Without a Spleen, A
See Chekhov, Anton (Pavlovich)

Manzoni, Alessandro 1785-1873 . . NCLC 29

Mapu, Abraham (ben Jekutiel)
1808-1867 . . . . NCLC 18

Mara, Sally
See Queneau, Raymond

Marat, Jean Paul 1743-1793 . . . . LC 10

Marcel, Gabriel Honore
1889-1973 . . . . CLC 15
See also CA 102; 45-48; MTCW

Marchbanks, Samuel
See Davies, (William) Robertson

Marchi, Giacomo
See Bassani, Giorgio

Margulies, Donald . . . . CLC 76

Marie de France c. 12th cent. - . . . . CMLC 8

Marie de l'Incarnation 1599-1672 . . . . LC 10

Mariner, Scott
See Pohl, Frederik

Marinetti, Filippo Tommaso
1876-1944 . . . . TCLC 10
See also CA 107; DLB 114

Marivaux, Pierre Carlet de Chamblain de
1688-1763 . . . . LC 4

Markandaya, Kamala . . . . CLC 8, 38
See also Taylor, Kamala (Purnaiya)

Markfield, Wallace 1926-. . . . . CLC 8
See also CA 69-72; CAAS 3; DLB 2, 28

Markham, Edwin 1852-1940 . . . . . TCLC 47
See also DLB 54

Markham, Robert
See Amis, Kingsley (William)

Marks, J
See Highwater, Jamake (Mamake)

Marks-Highwater, J
See Highwater, Jamake (Mamake)

Markson, David M(errill) 1927- . . . . CLC 67
See also CA 49-52; CANR 1

Marley, Bob. . . . . CLC 17
See also Marley, Robert Nesta

Marley, Robert Nesta 1945-1981
See Marley, Bob
See also CA 107; 103

Marlowe, Christopher
1564-1593 . . . . . LC 22; DA; DC 1; WLC
See also CDBLB Before 1660; DLB 62

Marmontel, Jean-Francois
1723-1799 . . . . LC 2

Marquand, John P(hillips)
1893-1960 . . . . CLC 2, 10
See also CA 85-88; DLB 9, 102

Marquez, Gabriel (Jose) Garcia. . . . . . CLC 68
See also Garcia Marquez, Gabriel (Jose)

Marquis, Don(ald Robert Perry)
1878-1937 . . . . TCLC 7
See also CA 104; DLB 11, 25

Marric, J. J.
See Creasey, John

Marrow, Bernard
See Moore, Brian

Marryat, Frederick 1792-1848 . . . . NCLC 3
See also DLB 21

Marsden, James
See Creasey, John

Marsh, (Edith) Ngaio
1899-1982 . . . . CLC 7, 53
See also CA 9-12R; CANR 6; DLB 77;
MTCW

Marshall, Garry 1934- . . . . CLC 17
See also AAYA 3; CA 111; SATA 60

Marshall, Paule
1929- . . . . CLC 27, 72; BLC 3; SSC 3
See also BW; CA 77-80; CANR 25;
DLB 33; MTCW

Marsten, Richard
See Hunter, Evan

Martha, Henry
See Harris, Mark

Martin, Ken
See Hubbard, L(afayette) Ron(ald)

Martin, Richard
See Creasey, John

Martin, Steve 1945- . . . . CLC 30
See also CA 97-100; CANR 30; MTCW

Martin, Violet Florence
1862-1915 . . . . TCLC 51

Martin, Webber
See Silverberg, Robert

Martindale, Patrick Victor
See White, Patrick (Victor Martindale)

Martin du Gard, Roger
1881-1958 . . . . TCLC 24
See also CA 118; DLB 65

Martineau, Harriet 1802-1876. . . . NCLC 26
See also DLB 21, 55; YABC 2

Martines, Julia
See O'Faolain, Julia

Martinez, Jacinto Benavente y
See Benavente (y Martinez), Jacinto

Martinez Ruiz, Jose 1873-1967
See Azorin; Ruiz, Jose Martinez
See also CA 93-96; HW

Martinez Sierra, Gregorio
1881-1947 . . . . TCLC 6
See also CA 115

Martinez Sierra, Maria (de la O'LeJarraga)
1874-1974 . . . . TCLC 6
See also CA 115

Martinsen, Martin
See Follett, Ken(neth Martin)

Martinson, Harry (Edmund)
1904-1978 . . . . CLC 14
See also CA 77-80; CANR 34

Marut, Ret
See Traven, B.

Marut, Robert
See Traven, B.

Marvell, Andrew
1621-1678 . . . . LC 4; DA; WLC
See also CDBLB 1660-1789; DLB 131

Marx, Karl (Heinrich)
1818-1883 . . . . NCLC 17
See also DLB 129

Masaoka Shiki. . . . . TCLC 18
See also Masaoka Tsunenori

Masaoka Tsunenori 1867-1902
See Masaoka Shiki
See also CA 117

Masefield, John (Edward)
1878-1967 . . . . CLC 11, 47
See also CA 19-20; 25-28R; CANR 33;
CAP 2; CDBLB 1890-1914; DLB 10;
MTCW; SATA 19

Maso, Carole 19(?)- . . . . CLC 44

Mason, Bobbie Ann
1940- . . . . CLC 28, 43; SSC 4
See also AAYA 5; CA 53-56; CANR 11,
31; DLBY 87; MTCW

Mason, Ernst
See Pohl, Frederik

Mason, Lee W.
See Malzberg, Barry N(athaniel)

Mason, Nick 1945-. . . . . CLC 35
See also Pink Floyd

Mason, Tally
See Derleth, August (William)

Mass, William
See Gibson, William

Masters, Edgar Lee
1868-1950 . . . . . . TCLC 2, 25; DA; PC 1
See also CA 104; 133; CDALB 1865-1917;
DLB 54; MTCW

Masters, Hilary 1928- . . . . CLC 48
See also CA 25-28R; CANR 13

Mastrosimone, William 19(?)- . . . . . . CLC 36

Mathe, Albert
See Camus, Albert

Matheson, Richard Burton 1926- . . . CLC 37
See also CA 97-100; DLB 8, 44

Mathews, Harry 1930-. . . . . CLC 6, 52
See also CA 21-24R; CAAS 6; CANR 18,
40

Mathias, Roland (Glyn) 1915-. . . . . . CLC 45
See also CA 97-100; CANR 19, 41; DLB 27

Matsuo Basho 1644-1694. . . . . PC 3

Mattheson, Rodney
See Creasey, John

Matthews, Greg 1949- . . . . CLC 45
See also CA 135

Matthews, William 1942-. . . . . CLC 40
See also CA 29-32R; CAAS 18; CANR 12;
DLB 5

Matthias, John (Edward) 1941-. . . . . . CLC 9
See also CA 33-36R

Matthiessen, Peter
1927- . . . . CLC 5, 7, 11, 32, 64
See also AAYA 6; BEST 90:4; CA 9-12R;
CANR 21; DLB 6; MTCW; SATA 27

Maturin, Charles Robert
1780(?)-1824 . . . . NCLC 6

Matute (Ausejo), Ana Maria
1925- . . . . CLC 11
See also CA 89-92; MTCW

Maugham, W. S.
See Maugham, W(illiam) Somerset

Maugham, W(illiam) Somerset
1874-1965 . . . . . . CLC 1, 11, 15, 67; DA;
SSC 8; WLC
See also CA 5-8R; 25-28R; CANR 40;
CDBLB 1914-1945; DLB 10, 36, 77, 100;
MTCW; SATA 54

Maugham, William Somerset
See Maugham, W(illiam) Somerset

Maupassant, (Henri Rene Albert) Guy de
1850-1893 . . . . NCLC 1, 42; DA; SSC 1;
WLC
See also DLB 123

Maurhut, Richard
See Traven, B.

Mauriac, Claude 1914-. . . . . CLC 9
See also CA 89-92; DLB 83

Mauriac, Francois (Charles)
1885-1970 . . . . CLC 4, 9, 56
See also CA 25-28; CAP 2; DLB 65;
MTCW

Mavor, Osborne Henry 1888-1951
See Bridie, James
See also CA 104

Maxwell, William (Keepers, Jr.)
1908- . . . . CLC 19
See also CA 93-96; DLBY 80

May, Elaine 1932- . . . . CLC 16
See also CA 124; 142; DLB 44

Mayakovski, Vladimir (Vladimirovich)
1893-1930 . . . . TCLC 4, 18
See also CA 104

Mayhew, Henry   1812-1887 ...... NCLC 31
See also DLB 18, 55

Maynard, Joyce   1953- .... CLC 23
See also CA 111; 129

Mayne, William (James Carter)
    1928- .... CLC 12
See also CA 9-12R; CANR 37; CLR 25;
JRDA; MAICYA; SAAS 11; SATA 6, 68

Mayo, Jim
See L'Amour, Louis (Dearborn)

Maysles, Albert   1926- .... CLC 16
See also CA 29-32R

Maysles, David   1932- .... CLC 16

Mazer, Norma Fox   1931- .... CLC 26
See also AAYA 5; CA 69-72; CANR 12,
32; CLR 23; JRDA; MAICYA; SAAS 1;
SATA 24, 67

Mazzini, Guiseppe   1805-1872 .... NCLC 34

McAuley, James Phillip
    1917-1976 .... CLC 45
See also CA 97-100

McBain, Ed
See Hunter, Evan

McBrien, William Augustine
    1930- .... CLC 44
See also CA 107

McCaffrey, Anne (Inez)   1926- ...... CLC 17
See also AAYA 6; AITN 2; BEST 89:2;
CA 25-28R; CANR 15, 35; DLB 8;
JRDA; MAICYA; MTCW; SAAS 11;
SATA 8, 70

McCann, Arthur
See Campbell, John W(ood, Jr.)

McCann, Edson
See Pohl, Frederik

McCarthy, Cormac, Jr. .... CLC 4, 57
See also McCarthy, Charles, Jr.
See also DLB 6

McCarthy, Mary (Therese)
    1912-1989 ... CLC 1, 3, 5, 14, 24, 39, 59
See also CA 5-8R; 129; CANR 16; DLB 2;
DLBY 81; MTCW

McCartney, (James) Paul
    1942- .... CLC 12, 35

McCauley, Stephen (D.)   1955- ..... CLC 50
See also CA 141

McClure, Michael (Thomas)
    1932- .... CLC 6, 10
See also CA 21-24R; CANR 17; DLB 16

McCorkle, Jill (Collins)   1958- ...... CLC 51
See also CA 121; DLBY 87

McCourt, James   1941- .... CLC 5
See also CA 57-60

McCoy, Horace (Stanley)
    1897-1955 .... TCLC 28
See also CA 108; DLB 9

McCrae, John   1872-1918 .... TCLC 12
See also CA 109; DLB 92

McCreigh, James
See Pohl, Frederik

McCullers, (Lula) Carson (Smith)
    1917-1967 .... CLC 1, 4, 10, 12, 48; DA;
                  SSC 9; WLC
See also CA 5-8R; 25-28R; CABS 1, 3;
CANR 18; CDALB 1941-1968; DLB 2, 7;
MTCW; SATA 27

McCulloch, John Tyler
See Burroughs, Edgar Rice

McCullough, Colleen   1938(?)- ...... CLC 27
See also CA 81-84; CANR 17; MTCW

McElroy, Joseph   1930- .... CLC 5, 47
See also CA 17-20R

McEwan, Ian (Russell)   1948- ... CLC 13, 66
See also BEST 90:4; CA 61-64; CANR 14,
41; DLB 14; MTCW

McFadden, David   1940- .... CLC 48
See also CA 104; DLB 60

McFarland, Dennis   1950- .... CLC 65

McGahern, John   1934- .... CLC 5, 9, 48
See also CA 17-20R; CANR 29; DLB 14;
MTCW

McGinley, Patrick (Anthony)
    1937- .... CLC 41
See also CA 120; 127

McGinley, Phyllis   1905-1978 ...... CLC 14
See also CA 9-12R; 77-80; CANR 19;
DLB 11, 48; SATA 2, 24, 44

McGinniss, Joe   1942- .... CLC 32
See also AITN 2; BEST 89:2; CA 25-28R;
CANR 26

McGivern, Maureen Daly
See Daly, Maureen

McGrath, Patrick   1950- .... CLC 55
See also CA 136

McGrath, Thomas (Matthew)
    1916-1990 .... CLC 28, 59
See also CA 9-12R; 132; CANR 6, 33;
MTCW; SATA 41; SATA-Obit 66

McGuane, Thomas (Francis III)
    1939- .... CLC 3, 7, 18, 45
See also AITN 2; CA 49-52; CANR 5, 24;
DLB 2; DLBY 80; MTCW

McGuckian, Medbh   1950- .... CLC 48
See also DLB 40

McHale, Tom   1942(?)-1982 .... CLC 3, 5
See also AITN 1; CA 77-80; 106

McIlvanney, William   1936- .... CLC 42
See also CA 25-28R; DLB 14

McIlwraith, Maureen Mollie Hunter
See Hunter, Mollie
See also SATA 2

McInerney, Jay   1955- .... CLC 34
See also CA 116; 123

McIntyre, Vonda N(eel)   1948- ..... CLC 18
See also CA 81-84; CANR 17, 34; MTCW

McKay, Claude ... TCLC 7, 41; BLC 3; PC 2
See also McKay, Festus Claudius
See also DLB 4, 45, 51, 117

McKay, Festus Claudius   1889-1948
See McKay, Claude
See also BW; CA 104; 124; DA; MTCW;
WLC

McKuen, Rod   1933- .... CLC 1, 3
See also AITN 1; CA 41-44R; CANR 40

McLoughlin, R. B.
See Mencken, H(enry) L(ouis)

McLuhan, (Herbert) Marshall
    1911-1980 .... CLC 37
See also CA 9-12R; 102; CANR 12, 34;
DLB 88; MTCW

McMillan, Terry (L.)   1951- ..... CLC 50, 61
See also CA 140

McMurtry, Larry (Jeff)
    1936- .... CLC 2, 3, 7, 11, 27, 44
See also AITN 2; BEST 89:2; CA 5-8R;
CANR 19, 43; CDALB 1968-1988;
DLB 2; DLBY 80, 87; MTCW

McNally, Terrence   1939- ...... CLC 4, 7, 41
See also CA 45-48; CANR 2; DLB 7

McNamer, Deirdre   1950- .... CLC 70

McNeile, Herman Cyril   1888-1937
See Sapper
See also DLB 77

McPhee, John (Angus)   1931- ...... CLC 36
See also BEST 90:1; CA 65-68; CANR 20;
MTCW

McPherson, James Alan
    1943- .... CLC 19, 77
See also BW; CA 25-28R; CAAS 17;
CANR 24; DLB 38; MTCW

McPherson, William (Alexander)
    1933- .... CLC 34
See also CA 69-72; CANR 28

McSweeney, Kerry .... CLC 34

Mead, Margaret   1901-1978 .... CLC 37
See also AITN 1; CA 1-4R; 81-84;
CANR 4; MTCW; SATA 20

Meaker, Marijane (Agnes)   1927-
See Kerr, M. E.
See also CA 107; CANR 37; JRDA;
MAICYA; MTCW; SATA 20, 61

Medoff, Mark (Howard)   1940- ... CLC 6, 23
See also AITN 1; CA 53-56; CANR 5;
DLB 7

Meged, Aharon
See Megged, Aharon

Meged, Aron
See Megged, Aharon

Megged, Aharon   1920- .... CLC 9
See also CA 49-52; CAAS 13; CANR 1

Mehta, Ved (Parkash)   1934- .... CLC 37
See also CA 1-4R; CANR 2, 23; MTCW

Melanter
See Blackmore, R(ichard) D(oddridge)

Melikow, Loris
See Hofmannsthal, Hugo von

Melmoth, Sebastian
See Wilde, Oscar (Fingal O'Flahertie Wills)

Meltzer, Milton   1915- .... CLC 26
See also AAYA 8; CA 13-16R; CANR 38;
CLR 13; DLB 61; JRDA; MAICYA;
SAAS 1; SATA 1, 50

Melville, Herman
    1819-1891 .... NCLC 3, 12, 29; DA;
                 SSC 1; WLC
See also CDALB 1640-1865; DLB 3, 74;
SATA 59

Menander
    c. 342B.C.-c. 292B.C. .... CMLC 9; DC 3

Mencken, H(enry) L(ouis)
1880-1956 . . . . TCLC 13
See also CA 105; 125; CDALB 1917-1929;
DLB 11, 29, 63; MTCW

Mercer, David 1928-1980 . . . . CLC 5
See also CA 9-12R; 102; CANR 23;
DLB 13; MTCW

Merchant, Paul
See Ellison, Harlan

Meredith, George 1828-1909 . . . TCLC 17, 43
See also CA 117; CDBLB 1832-1890;
DLB 18, 35, 57

Meredith, William (Morris)
1919- . . . . CLC 4, 13, 22, 55
See also CA 9-12R; CAAS 14; CANR 6, 40;
DLB 5

Merezhkovsky, Dmitry Sergeyevich
1865-1941 . . . . TCLC 29

Merimee, Prosper
1803-1870 . . . . NCLC 6; SSC 7
See also DLB 119

Merkin, Daphne 1954- . . . . CLC 44
See also CA 123

Merlin, Arthur
See Blish, James (Benjamin)

Merrill, James (Ingram)
1926- . . . . CLC 2, 3, 6, 8, 13, 18, 34
See also CA 13-16R; CANR 10; DLB 5;
DLBY 85; MTCW

Merriman, Alex
See Silverberg, Robert

Merritt, E. B.
See Waddington, Miriam

Merton, Thomas
1915-1968 . . . . CLC 1, 3, 11, 34
See also CA 5-8R; 25-28R; CANR 22;
DLB 48; DLBY 81; MTCW

Merwin, W(illiam) S(tanley)
1927- . . . . . . CLC 1, 2, 3, 5, 8, 13, 18, 45
See also CA 13-16R; CANR 15; DLB 5;
MTCW

Metcalf, John 1938- . . . . CLC 37
See also CA 113; DLB 60

Metcalf, Suzanne
See Baum, L(yman) Frank

Mew, Charlotte (Mary)
1870-1928 . . . . TCLC 8
See also CA 105; DLB 19, 135

Mewshaw, Michael 1943- . . . . CLC 9
See also CA 53-56; CANR 7; DLBY 80

Meyer, June
See Jordan, June

Meyer, Lynn
See Slavitt, David R(ytman)

Meyer-Meyrink, Gustav 1868-1932
See Meyrink, Gustav
See also CA 117

Meyers, Jeffrey 1939- . . . . CLC 39
See also CA 73-76; DLB 111

Meynell, Alice (Christina Gertrude Thompson)
1847-1922 . . . . TCLC 6
See also CA 104; DLB 19, 98

Meyrink, Gustav . . . . TCLC 21
See also Meyer-Meyrink, Gustav
See also DLB 81

Michaels, Leonard 1933- . . . . CLC 6, 25
See also CA 61-64; CANR 21; DLB 130;
MTCW

Michaux, Henri 1899-1984 . . . . . . CLC 8, 19
See also CA 85-88; 114

Michelangelo 1475-1564 . . . . LC 12

Michelet, Jules 1798-1874 . . . . . . NCLC 31

Michener, James A(lbert)
1907(?)- . . . . CLC 1, 5, 11, 29, 60
See also AITN 1; BEST 90:1; CA 5-8R;
CANR 21; DLB 6; MTCW

Mickiewicz, Adam 1798-1855 . . . . . NCLC 3

Middleton, Christopher 1926- . . . . . . CLC 13
See also CA 13-16R; CANR 29; DLB 40

Middleton, Stanley 1919- . . . . CLC 7, 38
See also CA 25-28R; CANR 21; DLB 14

Migueis, Jose Rodrigues 1901- . . . . . CLC 10

Mikszath, Kalman 1847-1910 . . . . . TCLC 31

Miles, Josephine
1911-1985 . . . . CLC 1, 2, 14, 34, 39
See also CA 1-4R; 116; CANR 2; DLB 48

Militant
See Sandburg, Carl (August)

Mill, John Stuart 1806-1873 . . . . . NCLC 11
See also CDBLB 1832-1890; DLB 55

Millar, Kenneth 1915-1983 . . . . CLC 14
See also Macdonald, Ross
See also CA 9-12R; 110; CANR 16; DLB 2;
DLBD 6; DLBY 83; MTCW

Millay, E. Vincent
See Millay, Edna St. Vincent

Millay, Edna St. Vincent
1892-1950 . . . . . . TCLC 4, 49; DA; PC 6
See also CA 104; 130; CDALB 1917-1929;
DLB 45; MTCW

Miller, Arthur
1915- . . . . CLC 1, 2, 6, 10, 15, 26, 47, 78;
DA; DC 1; WLC
See also AITN 1; CA 1-4R; CABS 3;
CANR 2, 30; CDALB 1941-1968; DLB 7;
MTCW

Miller, Henry (Valentine)
1891-1980 . . . . . . CLC 1, 2, 4, 9, 14, 43;
DA; WLC
See also CA 9-12R; 97-100; CANR 33;
CDALB 1929-1941; DLB 4, 9; DLBY 80;
MTCW

Miller, Jason 1939(?)- . . . . CLC 2
See also AITN 1; CA 73-76; DLB 7

Miller, Sue 1943- . . . . CLC 44
See also BEST 90:3; CA 139

Miller, Walter M(ichael, Jr.)
1923- . . . . CLC 4, 30
See also CA 85-88; DLB 8

Millett, Kate 1934- . . . . CLC 67
See also AITN 1; CA 73-76; CANR 32;
MTCW

Millhauser, Steven 1943- . . . . CLC 21, 54
See also CA 110; 111; DLB 2

Millin, Sarah Gertrude 1889-1968 . . CLC 49
See also CA 102; 93-96

Milne, A(lan) A(lexander)
1882-1956 . . . . TCLC 6
See also CA 104; 133; CLR 1, 26; DLB 10,
77, 100; MAICYA; MTCW; YABC 1

Milner, Ron(ald) 1938- . . . . . CLC 56; BLC 3
See also AITN 1; BW; CA 73-76;
CANR 24; DLB 38; MTCW

Milosz, Czeslaw
1911- . . . . . . CLC 5, 11, 22, 31, 56; PC 8
See also CA 81-84; CANR 23; MTCW

Milton, John 1608-1674 . . . LC 9; DA; WLC
See also CDBLB 1660-1789; DLB 131

Minehaha, Cornelius
See Wedekind, (Benjamin) Frank(lin)

Miner, Valerie 1947- . . . . CLC 40
See also CA 97-100

Minimo, Duca
See D'Annunzio, Gabriele

Minot, Susan 1956- . . . . CLC 44
See also CA 134

Minus, Ed 1938- . . . . CLC 39

Miranda, Javier
See Bioy Casares, Adolfo

Miro (Ferrer), Gabriel (Francisco Victor)
1879-1930 . . . . TCLC 5
See also CA 104

Mishima, Yukio
. . . . CLC 2, 4, 6, 9, 27; DC 1; SSC 4
See also Hiraoka, Kimitake

Mistral, Frederic 1830-1914 . . . . . . TCLC 51
See also CA 122

Mistral, Gabriela . . . . TCLC 2; HLC 2
See also Godoy Alcayaga, Lucila

Mistry, Rohinton 1952- . . . . CLC 71
See also CA 141

Mitchell, Clyde
See Ellison, Harlan; Silverberg, Robert

Mitchell, James Leslie 1901-1935
See Gibbon, Lewis Grassic
See also CA 104; DLB 15

Mitchell, Joni 1943- . . . . CLC 12
See also CA 112

Mitchell, Margaret (Munnerlyn)
1900-1949 . . . . TCLC 11
See also CA 109; 125; DLB 9; MTCW

Mitchell, Peggy
See Mitchell, Margaret (Munnerlyn)

Mitchell, S(ilas) Weir 1829-1914 . . TCLC 36

Mitchell, W(illiam) O(rmond)
1914- . . . . CLC 25
See also CA 77-80; CANR 15, 43; DLB 88

Mitford, Mary Russell 1787-1855 . . NCLC 4
See also DLB 110, 116

Mitford, Nancy 1904-1973 . . . . CLC 44
See also CA 9-12R

Miyamoto, Yuriko 1899-1951 . . . . . TCLC 37

Mo, Timothy (Peter) 1950(?)- . . . . . . CLC 46
See also CA 117; MTCW

Modarressi, Taghi (M.) 1931- . . . . . . CLC 44
See also CA 121; 134

Modiano, Patrick (Jean) 1945- . . . . . CLC 18
See also CA 85-88; CANR 17, 40; DLB 83

Peregoy, George Weems
See Mencken, H(enry) L(ouis)

Perelman, S(idney) J(oseph)
1904-1979 ... **CLC 3, 5, 9, 15, 23, 44, 49**
See also AITN 1, 2; CA 73-76; 89-92;
CANR 18; DLB 11, 44; MTCW

Peret, Benjamin 1899-1959 .... **TCLC 20**
See also CA 117

Peretz, Isaac Loeb 1851(?)-1915 ... **TCLC 16**
See also CA 109

Peretz, Yitzkhok Leibush
See Peretz, Isaac Loeb

Perez Galdos, Benito 1843-1920 ... **TCLC 27**
See also CA 125; HW

Perrault, Charles 1628-1703 .... **LC 2**
See also MAICYA; SATA 25

Perry, Brighton
See Sherwood, Robert E(mmet)

Perse, St.-John .... **CLC 4, 11, 46**
See also Leger, (Marie-Rene Auguste) Alexis
Saint-Leger

Peseenz, Tulio F.
See Lopez y Fuentes, Gregorio

Pesetsky, Bette 1932- .... **CLC 28**
See also CA 133; DLB 130

Peshkov, Alexei Maximovich 1868-1936
See Gorky, Maxim
See also CA 105; 141; DA

Pessoa, Fernando (Antonio Nogueira)
1888-1935 .... **TCLC 27; HLC 2**
See also CA 125

Peterkin, Julia Mood 1880-1961 .... **CLC 31**
See also CA 102; DLB 9

Peters, Joan K. 1945- .... **CLC 39**

Peters, Robert L(ouis) 1924- .... **CLC 7**
See also CA 13-16R; CAAS 8; DLB 105

Petofi, Sandor 1823-1849 .... **NCLC 21**

Petrakis, Harry Mark 1923- .... **CLC 3**
See also CA 9-12R; CANR 4, 30

Petrarch 1304-1374 .... **PC 8**

Petrov, Evgeny .... **TCLC 21**
See also Kataev, Evgeny Petrovich

Petry, Ann (Lane) 1908- ...... **CLC 1, 7, 18**
See also BW; CA 5-8R; CAAS 6; CANR 4;
CLR 12; DLB 76; JRDA; MAICYA;
MTCW; SATA 5

Petursson, Halligrimur 1614-1674 .... **LC 8**

Philipson, Morris H. 1926- .... **CLC 53**
See also CA 1-4R; CANR 4

Phillips, David Graham
1867-1911 .... **TCLC 44**
See also CA 108; DLB 9, 12

Phillips, Jack
See Sandburg, Carl (August)

Phillips, Jayne Anne 1952- ..... **CLC 15, 33**
See also CA 101; CANR 24; DLBY 80;
MTCW

Phillips, Richard
See Dick, Philip K(indred)

Phillips, Robert (Schaeffer) 1938- ... **CLC 28**
See also CA 17-20R; CAAS 13; CANR 8;
DLB 105

Phillips, Ward
See Lovecraft, H(oward) P(hillips)

Piccolo, Lucio 1901-1969 .... **CLC 13**
See also CA 97-100; DLB 114

Pickthall, Marjorie L(owry) C(hristie)
1883-1922 .... **TCLC 21**
See also CA 107; DLB 92

Pico della Mirandola, Giovanni
1463-1494 .... **LC 15**

Piercy, Marge
1936- .... **CLC 3, 6, 14, 18, 27, 62**
See also CA 21-24R; CAAS 1; CANR 13,
43; DLB 120; MTCW

Piers, Robert
See Anthony, Piers

Pieyre de Mandiargues, Andre 1909-1991
See Mandiargues, Andre Pieyre de
See also CA 103; 136; CANR 22

Pilnyak, Boris .... **TCLC 23**
See also Vogau, Boris Andreyevich

Pincherle, Alberto 1907-1990 ... **CLC 11, 18**
See also Moravia, Alberto
See also CA 25-28R; 132; CANR 33;
MTCW

Pinckney, Darryl 1953- .... **CLC 76**

Pindar 518B.C.-446B.C. .... **CMLC 12**

Pineda, Cecile 1942- .... **CLC 39**
See also CA 118

Pinero, Arthur Wing 1855-1934 ... **TCLC 32**
See also CA 110; DLB 10

Pinero, Miguel (Antonio Gomez)
1946-1988 .... **CLC 4, 55**
See also CA 61-64; 125; CANR 29; HW

Pinget, Robert 1919- .... **CLC 7, 13, 37**
See also CA 85-88; DLB 83

Pink Floyd .... **CLC 35**
See also Barrett, (Roger) Syd; Gilmour,
David; Mason, Nick; Waters, Roger;
Wright, Rick

Pinkney, Edward 1802-1828 ..... **NCLC 31**

Pinkwater, Daniel Manus 1941- .... **CLC 35**
See also Pinkwater, Manus
See also AAYA 1; CA 29-32R; CANR 12,
38; CLR 4; JRDA; MAICYA; SAAS 3;
SATA 46

Pinkwater, Manus
See Pinkwater, Daniel Manus
See also SATA 8

Pinsky, Robert 1940- .... **CLC 9, 19, 38**
See also CA 29-32R; CAAS 4; DLBY 82

Pinta, Harold
See Pinter, Harold

Pinter, Harold
1930- ..... **CLC 1, 3, 6, 9, 11, 15, 27, 58,**
73; DA; WLC
See also CA 5-8R; CANR 33; CDBLB 1960
to Present; DLB 13; MTCW

Pirandello, Luigi
1867-1936 ...... **TCLC 4, 29; DA; WLC**
See also CA 104

Pirsig, Robert M(aynard)
1928- .... **CLC 4, 6, 73**
See also CA 53-56; CANR 42; MTCW;
SATA 39

Pisarev, Dmitry Ivanovich
1840-1868 .... **NCLC 25**

Pix, Mary (Griffith) 1666-1709 .... **LC 8**
See also DLB 80

Pixerecourt, Guilbert de
1773-1844 .... **NCLC 39**

Plaidy, Jean
See Hibbert, Eleanor Alice Burford

Planche, James Robinson
1796-1880 .... **NCLC 42**

Plant, Robert 1948- .... **CLC 12**

Plante, David (Robert)
1940- .... **CLC 7, 23, 38**
See also CA 37-40R; CANR 12, 36;
DLBY 83; MTCW

Plath, Sylvia
1932-1963 ..... **CLC 1, 2, 3, 5, 9, 11, 14,**
17, 50, 51, 62; DA; PC 1; WLC
See also CA 19-20; CANR 34; CAP 2;
CDALB 1941-1968; DLB 5, 6; MTCW

Plato 428(?)B.C.-348(?)B.C. ... **CMLC 8; DA**

Platonov, Andrei .... **TCLC 14**
See also Klimentov, Andrei Platonovich

Platt, Kin 1911- .... **CLC 26**
See also CA 17-20R; CANR 11; JRDA;
SAAS 17; SATA 21

Plick et Plock
See Simenon, Georges (Jacques Christian)

Plimpton, George (Ames) 1927- ..... **CLC 36**
See also AITN 1; CA 21-24R; CANR 32;
MTCW; SATA 10

Plomer, William Charles Franklin
1903-1973 .... **CLC 4, 8**
See also CA 21-22; CANR 34; CAP 2;
DLB 20; MTCW; SATA 24

Plowman, Piers
See Kavanagh, Patrick (Joseph)

Plum, J.
See Wodehouse, P(elham) G(renville)

Plumly, Stanley (Ross) 1939- ...... **CLC 33**
See also CA 108; 110; DLB 5

Plumpe, Friedrich Wilhelm
1888-1931 .... **TCLC 53**
See also CA 112

Poe, Edgar Allan
1809-1849 ..... **NCLC 1, 16; DA; PC 1;**
SSC 1; WLC
See also CDALB 1640-1865; DLB 3, 59, 73,
74; SATA 23

Poet of Titchfield Street, The
See Pound, Ezra (Weston Loomis)

Pohl, Frederik 1919- .... **CLC 18**
See also CA 61-64; CAAS 1; CANR 11, 37;
DLB 8; MTCW; SATA 24

Poirier, Louis 1910-
See Gracq, Julien
See also CA 122; 126

Poitier, Sidney 1927- .... **CLC 26**
See also BW; CA 117

Polanski, Roman 1933- .... **CLC 16**
See also CA 77-80

Poliakoff, Stephen 1952- .... **CLC 38**
See also CA 106; DLB 13

Pym, Barbara (Mary Crampton)
1913-1980 . . . . CLC **13, 19, 37**
See also CA 13-14; 97-100; CANR 13, 34;
CAP 1; DLB 14; DLBY 87; MTCW

Pynchon, Thomas (Ruggles, Jr.)
1937- . . . . . CLC **2, 3, 6, 9, 11, 18, 33, 62,
72; DA; SSC 14; WLC**
See also BEST 90:2; CA 17-20R; CANR 22;
DLB 2; MTCW

Q
See Quiller-Couch, Arthur Thomas

Qian Zhongshu
See Ch'ien Chung-shu

Qroll
See Dagerman, Stig (Halvard)

Quarrington, Paul (Lewis) 1953- . . . . CLC **65**
See also CA 129

Quasimodo, Salvatore 1901-1968 . . . CLC **10**
See also CA 13-16; 25-28R; CAP 1;
DLB 114; MTCW

Queen, Ellery . . . . CLC **3, 11**
See also Dannay, Frederic; Davidson,
Avram; Lee, Manfred B(ennington);
Sturgeon, Theodore (Hamilton); Vance,
John Holbrook

Queen, Ellery, Jr.
See Dannay, Frederic; Lee, Manfred
B(ennington)

Queneau, Raymond
1903-1976 . . . . CLC **2, 5, 10, 42**
See also CA 77-80; 69-72; CANR 32;
DLB 72; MTCW

Quevedo, Francisco de 1580-1645 . . . . LC **23**

Quiller-Couch, Arthur Thomas
1863-1944 . . . . TCLC **53**
See also CA 118; DLB 135

Quin, Ann (Marie) 1936-1973 . . . . CLC **6**
See also CA 9-12R; 45-48; DLB 14

Quinn, Martin
See Smith, Martin Cruz

Quinn, Simon
See Smith, Martin Cruz

Quiroga, Horacio (Sylvestre)
1878-1937 . . . . TCLC **20; HLC 2**
See also CA 117; 131; HW; MTCW

Quoirez, Francoise 1935- . . . . CLC **9**
See also Sagan, Francoise
See also CA 49-52; CANR 6, 39; MTCW

Raabe, Wilhelm 1831-1910 . . . . TCLC **45**
See also DLB 129

Rabe, David (William) 1940- . . . CLC **4, 8, 33**
See also CA 85-88; CABS 3; DLB 7

Rabelais, Francois
1483-1553 . . . . LC **5; DA; WLC**

Rabinovitch, Sholem 1859-1916
See Aleichem, Sholom
See also CA 104

Radcliffe, Ann (Ward) 1764-1823 . . NCLC **6**
See also DLB 39

Radiguet, Raymond 1903-1923 . . . . TCLC **29**
See also DLB 65

Radnoti, Miklos 1909-1944 . . . . TCLC **16**
See also CA 118

Rado, James 1939- . . . . CLC **17**
See also CA 105

Radvanyi, Netty 1900-1983
See Seghers, Anna
See also CA 85-88; 110

Raeburn, John (Hay) 1941- . . . . CLC **34**
See also CA 57-60

Ragni, Gerome 1942-1991 . . . . CLC **17**
See also CA 105; 134

Rahv, Philip . . . . CLC **24**
See also Greenberg, Ivan

Raine, Craig 1944- . . . . CLC **32**
See also CA 108; CANR 29; DLB 40

Raine, Kathleen (Jessie) 1908- . . . CLC **7, 45**
See also CA 85-88; DLB 20; MTCW

Rainis, Janis 1865-1929 . . . . TCLC **29**

Rakosi, Carl . . . . CLC **47**
See also Rawley, Callman
See also CAAS 5

Raleigh, Richard
See Lovecraft, H(oward) P(hillips)

Rallentando, H. P.
See Sayers, Dorothy L(eigh)

Ramal, Walter
See de la Mare, Walter (John)

Ramon, Juan
See Jimenez (Mantecon), Juan Ramon

Ramos, Graciliano 1892-1953 . . . . . TCLC **32**

Rampersad, Arnold 1941- . . . . CLC **44**
See also CA 127; 133; DLB 111

Rampling, Anne
See Rice, Anne

Ramuz, Charles-Ferdinand
1878-1947 . . . . TCLC **33**

Rand, Ayn
1905-1982 . . . . . . CLC **3, 30, 44, 79; DA;
WLC**
See also AAYA 10; CA 13-16R; 105;
CANR 27; MTCW

Randall, Dudley (Felker)
1914- . . . . CLC **1; BLC 3**
See also BW; CA 25-28R; CANR 23;
DLB 41

Randall, Robert
See Silverberg, Robert

Ranger, Ken
See Creasey, John

Ransom, John Crowe
1888-1974 . . . . CLC **2, 4, 5, 11, 24**
See also CA 5-8R; 49-52; CANR 6, 34;
DLB 45, 63; MTCW

Rao, Raja 1909- . . . . CLC **25, 56**
See also CA 73-76; MTCW

Raphael, Frederic (Michael)
1931- . . . . CLC **2, 14**
See also CA 1-4R; CANR 1; DLB 14

Ratcliffe, James P.
See Mencken, H(enry) L(ouis)

Rathbone, Julian 1935- . . . . CLC **41**
See also CA 101; CANR 34

Rattigan, Terence (Mervyn)
1911-1977 . . . . CLC **7**
See also CA 85-88; 73-76;
CDBLB 1945-1960; DLB 13; MTCW

Ratushinskaya, Irina 1954- . . . . CLC **54**
See also CA 129

Raven, Simon (Arthur Noel)
1927- . . . . CLC **14**
See also CA 81-84

Rawley, Callman 1903-
See Rakosi, Carl
See also CA 21-24R; CANR 12, 32

Rawlings, Marjorie Kinnan
1896-1953 . . . . TCLC **4**
See also CA 104; 137; DLB 9, 22, 102;
JRDA; MAICYA; YABC 1

Ray, Satyajit 1921-1992 . . . . CLC **16, 76**
See also CA 114; 137

Read, Herbert Edward 1893-1968 . . . . CLC **4**
See also CA 85-88; 25-28R; DLB 20

Read, Piers Paul 1941- . . . . . . CLC **4, 10, 25**
See also CA 21-24R; CANR 38; DLB 14;
SATA 21

Reade, Charles 1814-1884 . . . . NCLC **2**
See also DLB 21

Reade, Hamish
See Gray, Simon (James Holliday)

Reading, Peter 1946- . . . . CLC **47**
See also CA 103; DLB 40

Reaney, James 1926- . . . . CLC **13**
See also CA 41-44R; CAAS 15; CANR 42;
DLB 68; SATA 43

Rebreanu, Liviu 1885-1944 . . . . TCLC **28**

Rechy, John (Francisco)
1934- . . . . CLC **1, 7, 14, 18; HLC 2**
See also CA 5-8R; CAAS 4; CANR 6, 32;
DLB 122; DLBY 82; HW

Redcam, Tom 1870-1933 . . . . TCLC **25**

Reddin, Keith . . . . CLC **67**

Redgrove, Peter (William)
1932- . . . . CLC **6, 41**
See also CA 1-4R; CANR 3, 39; DLB 40

Redmon, Anne . . . . CLC **22**
See also Nightingale, Anne Redmon
See also DLBY 86

Reed, Eliot
See Ambler, Eric

Reed, Ishmael
1938- . . . . CLC **2, 3, 5, 6, 13, 32, 60;
BLC 3**
See also BW; CA 21-24R; CANR 25;
DLB 2, 5, 33; DLBD 8; MTCW

Reed, John (Silas) 1887-1920 . . . . . . TCLC **9**
See also CA 106

Reed, Lou . . . . CLC **21**
See also Firbank, Louis

Reeve, Clara 1729-1807 . . . . NCLC **19**
See also DLB 39

Reid, Christopher (John) 1949- . . . . . CLC **33**
See also CA 140; DLB 40

Reid, Desmond
See Moorcock, Michael (John)

Reid Banks, Lynne 1929-
See Banks, Lynne Reid
See also CA 1-4R; CANR 6, 22, 38;
CLR 24; JRDA; MAICYA; SATA 22, 75

Reilly, William K.
See Creasey, John

Reiner, Max
　　See Caldwell, (Janet Miriam) Taylor
　　(Holland)

Reis, Ricardo
　　See Pessoa, Fernando (Antonio Nogueira)

Remarque, Erich Maria
　　1898-1970 . . . . CLC 21; DA
　　See also CA 77-80; 29-32R; DLB 56;
　　MTCW

Remizov, A.
　　See Remizov, Aleksei (Mikhailovich)

Remizov, A. M.
　　See Remizov, Aleksei (Mikhailovich)

Remizov, Aleksei (Mikhailovich)
　　1877-1957 . . . . TCLC 27
　　See also CA 125; 133

Renan, Joseph Ernest
　　1823-1892 . . . . NCLC 26

Renard, Jules　1864-1910 . . . . TCLC 17
　　See also CA 117

Renault, Mary . . . . CLC 3, 11, 17
　　See also Challans, Mary
　　See also DLBY 83

Rendell, Ruth (Barbara)　1930- . . CLC 28, 48
　　See also Vine, Barbara
　　See also CA 109; CANR 32; DLB 87;
　　MTCW

Renoir, Jean　1894-1979 . . . . CLC 20
　　See also CA 129; 85-88

Resnais, Alain　1922- . . . . CLC 16

Reverdy, Pierre　1889-1960 . . . . CLC 53
　　See also CA 97-100; 89-92

Rexroth, Kenneth
　　1905-1982 . . . . . . CLC 1, 2, 6, 11, 22, 49
　　See also CA 5-8R; 107; CANR 14, 34;
　　CDALB 1941-1968; DLB 16, 48;
　　DLBY 82; MTCW

Reyes, Alfonso　1889-1959 . . . . TCLC 33
　　See also CA 131; HW

Reyes y Basoalto, Ricardo Eliecer Neftali
　　See Neruda, Pablo

Reymont, Wladyslaw (Stanislaw)
　　1868(?)-1925 . . . . TCLC 5
　　See also CA 104

Reynolds, Jonathan　1942- . . . . CLC 6, 38
　　See also CA 65-68; CANR 28

Reynolds, Joshua　1723-1792 . . . . LC 15
　　See also DLB 104

Reynolds, Michael Shane　1937- . . . . CLC 44
　　See also CA 65-68; CANR 9

Reznikoff, Charles　1894-1976 . . . . . . CLC 9
　　See also CA 33-36; 61-64; CAP 2; DLB 28,
　　45

Rezzori (d'Arezzo), Gregor von
　　1914- . . . . CLC 25
　　See also CA 122; 136

Rhine, Richard
　　See Silverstein, Alvin

Rhodes, Eugene Manlove
　　1869-1934 . . . . TCLC 53

R'hoone
　　See Balzac, Honore de

Rhys, Jean
　　1890(?)-1979 . . . . CLC 2, 4, 6, 14, 19, 51
　　See also CA 25-28R; 85-88; CANR 35;
　　CDBLB 1945-1960; DLB 36, 117; MTCW

Ribeiro, Darcy　1922- . . . . CLC 34
　　See also CA 33-36R

Ribeiro, Joao Ubaldo (Osorio Pimentel)
　　1941- . . . . CLC 10, 67
　　See also CA 81-84

Ribman, Ronald (Burt)　1932- . . . . CLC 7
　　See also CA 21-24R

Ricci, Nino　1959- . . . . CLC 70
　　See also CA 137

Rice, Anne　1941- . . . . CLC 41
　　See also AAYA 9; BEST 89:2; CA 65-68;
　　CANR 12, 36

Rice, Elmer (Leopold)
　　1892-1967 . . . . CLC 7, 49
　　See also CA 21-22; 25-28R; CAP 2; DLB 4,
　　7; MTCW

Rice, Tim　1944- . . . . CLC 21
　　See also CA 103

Rich, Adrienne (Cecile)
　　1929- . . . . CLC 3, 6, 7, 11, 18, 36, 73, 76;
　　　　　　　　　　　　　　　　　　　　　PC 5
　　See also CA 9-12R; CANR 20; DLB 5, 67;
　　MTCW

Rich, Barbara
　　See Graves, Robert (von Ranke)

Rich, Robert
　　See Trumbo, Dalton

Richards, David Adams　1950- . . . . . . CLC 59
　　See also CA 93-96; DLB 53

Richards, I(vor) A(rmstrong)
　　1893-1979 . . . . CLC 14, 24
　　See also CA 41-44R; 89-92; CANR 34;
　　DLB 27

Richardson, Anne
　　See Roiphe, Anne Richardson

Richardson, Dorothy Miller
　　1873-1957 . . . . TCLC 3
　　See also CA 104; DLB 36

Richardson, Ethel Florence (Lindesay)
　　1870-1946
　　See Richardson, Henry Handel
　　See also CA 105

Richardson, Henry Handel . . . . TCLC 4
　　See also Richardson, Ethel Florence
　　(Lindesay)

Richardson, Samuel
　　1689-1761 . . . . LC 1; DA; WLC
　　See also CDBLB 1660-1789; DLB 39

Richler, Mordecai
　　1931- . . . . CLC 3, 5, 9, 13, 18, 46, 70
　　See also AITN 1; CA 65-68; CANR 31;
　　CLR 17; DLB 53; MAICYA; MTCW;
　　SATA 27, 44

Richter, Conrad (Michael)
　　1890-1968 . . . . CLC 30
　　See also CA 5-8R; 25-28R; CANR 23;
　　DLB 9; MTCW; SATA 3

Riddell, J. H.　1832-1906 . . . . TCLC 40

Riding, Laura . . . . CLC 3, 7
　　See also Jackson, Laura (Riding)

Riefenstahl, Berta Helene Amalia　1902-
　　See Riefenstahl, Leni
　　See also CA 108

Riefenstahl, Leni . . . . CLC 16
　　See also Riefenstahl, Berta Helene Amalia

Riffe, Ernest
　　See Bergman, (Ernst) Ingmar

Riley, James Whitcomb
　　1849-1916 . . . . TCLC 51
　　See also CA 118; 137; MAICYA; SATA 17

Riley, Tex
　　See Creasey, John

Rilke, Rainer Maria
　　1875-1926 . . . . TCLC 1, 6, 19; PC 2
　　See also CA 104; 132; DLB 81; MTCW

Rimbaud, (Jean Nicolas) Arthur
　　1854-1891 . . . . . NCLC 4, 35; DA; PC 3;
　　　　　　　　　　　　　　　　　　　　WLC

Rinehart, Mary Roberts
　　1876-1958 . . . . TCLC 52
　　See also CA 108

Ringmaster, The
　　See Mencken, H(enry) L(ouis)

Ringwood, Gwen(dolyn Margaret) Pharis
　　1910-1984 . . . . CLC 48
　　See also CA 112; DLB 88

Rio, Michel　19(?)- . . . . CLC 43

Ritsos, Giannes
　　See Ritsos, Yannis

Ritsos, Yannis　1909-1990 . . . . . CLC 6, 13, 31
　　See also CA 77-80; 133; CANR 39; MTCW

Ritter, Erika　1948(?)- . . . . CLC 52

Rivera, Jose Eustasio　1889-1928 . . . TCLC 35
　　See also HW

Rivers, Conrad Kent　1933-1968 . . . . . . CLC 1
　　See also BW; CA 85-88; DLB 41

Rivers, Elfrida
　　See Bradley, Marion Zimmer

Riverside, John
　　See Heinlein, Robert A(nson)

Rizal, Jose　1861-1896 . . . . NCLC 27

Roa Bastos, Augusto (Antonio)
　　1917- . . . . CLC 45; HLC 2
　　See also CA 131; DLB 113; HW

Robbe-Grillet, Alain
　　1922- . . . . . . CLC 1, 2, 4, 6, 8, 10, 14, 43
　　See also CA 9-12R; CANR 33; DLB 83;
　　MTCW

Robbins, Harold　1916- . . . . CLC 5
　　See also CA 73-76; CANR 26; MTCW

Robbins, Thomas Eugene　1936-
　　See Robbins, Tom
　　See also CA 81-84; CANR 29; MTCW

Robbins, Tom . . . . CLC 9, 32, 64
　　See also Robbins, Thomas Eugene
　　See also BEST 90:3; DLBY 80

Robbins, Trina　1938- . . . . CLC 21
　　See also CA 128

Roberts, Charles G(eorge) D(ouglas)
　　1860-1943 . . . . TCLC 8
　　See also CA 105; DLB 92; SATA 29

Roberts, Kate　1891-1985 . . . . CLC 15
　　See also CA 107; 116

Roberts, Keith (John Kingston)
1935- .... CLC 14
See also CA 25-28R

Roberts, Kenneth (Lewis)
1885-1957 .... TCLC 23
See also CA 109; DLB 9

Roberts, Michele (B.) 1949- .... CLC 48
See also CA 115

Robertson, Ellis
See Ellison, Harlan; Silverberg, Robert

Robertson, Thomas William
1829-1871 .... NCLC 35

Robinson, Edwin Arlington
1869-1935 .... TCLC 5; DA; PC 1
See also CA 104; 133; CDALB 1865-1917;
DLB 54; MTCW

Robinson, Henry Crabb
1775-1867 .... NCLC 15
See also DLB 107

Robinson, Jill 1936- .... CLC 10
See also CA 102

Robinson, Kim Stanley 1952- ...... CLC 34
See also CA 126

Robinson, Lloyd
See Silverberg, Robert

Robinson, Marilynne 1944- .... CLC 25
See also CA 116

Robinson, Smokey .... CLC 21
See also Robinson, William, Jr.

Robinson, William, Jr. 1940-
See Robinson, Smokey
See also CA 116

Robison, Mary 1949- .... CLC 42
See also CA 113; 116; DLB 130

Rod, Edouard 1857-1910 .... TCLC 52

Roddenberry, Eugene Wesley 1921-1991
See Roddenberry, Gene
See also CA 110; 135; CANR 37; SATA 45

Roddenberry, Gene .... CLC 17
See also Roddenberry, Eugene Wesley
See also AAYA 5; SATA-Obit 69

Rodgers, Mary 1931- .... CLC 12
See also CA 49-52; CANR 8; CLR 20;
JRDA; MAICYA; SATA 8

Rodgers, W(illiam) R(obert)
1909-1969 .... CLC 7
See also CA 85-88; DLB 20

Rodman, Eric
See Silverberg, Robert

Rodman, Howard 1920(?)-1985 ..... CLC 65
See also CA 118

Rodman, Maia
See Wojciechowska, Maia (Teresa)

Rodriguez, Claudio 1934- .... CLC 10
See also DLB 134

Roelvaag, O(le) E(dvart)
1876-1931 .... TCLC 17
See also CA 117; DLB 9

Roethke, Theodore (Huebner)
1908-1963 ...... CLC 1, 3, 8, 11, 19, 46
See also CA 81-84; CABS 2;
CDALB 1941-1968; DLB 5; MTCW

Rogers, Thomas Hunton 1927- ..... CLC 57
See also CA 89-92

Rogers, Will(iam Penn Adair)
1879-1935 .... TCLC 8
See also CA 105; DLB 11

Rogin, Gilbert 1929- .... CLC 18
See also CA 65-68; CANR 15

Rohan, Koda .... TCLC 22
See also Koda Shigeyuki

Rohmer, Eric .... CLC 16
See also Scherer, Jean-Marie Maurice

Rohmer, Sax .... TCLC 28
See also Ward, Arthur Henry Sarsfield
See also DLB 70

Roiphe, Anne Richardson 1935- ... CLC 3, 9
See also CA 89-92; DLBY 80

Rojas, Fernando de 1465-1541 ..... LC 23

**Rolfe, Frederick (William Serafino Austin
Lewis Mary)** 1860-1913 ..... TCLC 12
See also CA 107; DLB 34

Rolland, Romain 1866-1944 ...... TCLC 23
See also CA 118; DLB 65

Rolvaag, O(le) E(dvart)
See Roelvaag, O(le) E(dvart)

Romain Arnaud, Saint
See Aragon, Louis

Romains, Jules 1885-1972 .... CLC 7
See also CA 85-88; CANR 34; DLB 65;
MTCW

Romero, Jose Ruben 1890-1952 ... TCLC 14
See also CA 114; 131; HW

Ronsard, Pierre de 1524-1585 .... LC 6

Rooke, Leon 1934- .... CLC 25, 34
See also CA 25-28R; CANR 23

Roper, William 1498-1578 .... LC 10

Roquelaure, A. N.
See Rice, Anne

Rosa, Joao Guimaraes 1908-1967 ... CLC 23
See also CA 89-92; DLB 113

Rosen, Richard (Dean) 1949- .... CLC 39
See also CA 77-80

Rosenberg, Isaac 1890-1918 ...... TCLC 12
See also CA 107; DLB 20

Rosenblatt, Joe .... CLC 15
See also Rosenblatt, Joseph

Rosenblatt, Joseph 1933-
See Rosenblatt, Joe
See also CA 89-92

Rosenfeld, Samuel 1896-1963
See Tzara, Tristan
See also CA 89-92

Rosenthal, M(acha) L(ouis) 1917- ... CLC 28
See also CA 1-4R; CAAS 6; CANR 4;
DLB 5; SATA 59

Ross, Barnaby
See Dannay, Frederic

Ross, Bernard L.
See Follett, Ken(neth Martin)

Ross, J. H.
See Lawrence, T(homas) E(dward)

Ross, Martin
See Martin, Violet Florence
See also DLB 135

Ross, (James) Sinclair 1908- .... CLC 13
See also CA 73-76; DLB 88

Rossetti, Christina (Georgina)
1830-1894 ... NCLC 2; DA; PC 7; WLC
See also DLB 35; MAICYA; SATA 20

Rossetti, Dante Gabriel
1828-1882 ...... NCLC 4; DA; WLC
See also CDBLB 1832-1890; DLB 35

Rossner, Judith (Perelman)
1935- .... CLC 6, 9, 29
See also AITN 2; BEST 90:3; CA 17-20R;
CANR 18; DLB 6; MTCW

Rostand, Edmond (Eugene Alexis)
1868-1918 .... TCLC 6, 37; DA
See also CA 104; 126; MTCW

Roth, Henry 1906- .... CLC 2, 6, 11
See also CA 11-12; CANR 38; CAP 1;
DLB 28; MTCW

Roth, Joseph 1894-1939 .... TCLC 33
See also DLB 85

Roth, Philip (Milton)
1933- ...... CLC 1, 2, 3, 4, 6, 9, 15, 22,
31, 47, 66; DA; WLC
See also BEST 90:3; CA 1-4R; CANR 1, 22,
36; CDALB 1968-1988; DLB 2, 28;
DLBY 82; MTCW

Rothenberg, Jerome 1931- .... CLC 6, 57
See also CA 45-48; CANR 1; DLB 5

Roumain, Jacques (Jean Baptiste)
1907-1944 .... TCLC 19; BLC 3
See also BW; CA 117; 125

Rourke, Constance (Mayfield)
1885-1941 .... TCLC 12
See also CA 107; YABC 1

Rousseau, Jean-Baptiste 1671-1741 ... LC 9

Rousseau, Jean-Jacques
1712-1778 .... LC 14; DA; WLC

Roussel, Raymond 1877-1933 ..... TCLC 20
See also CA 117

Rovit, Earl (Herbert) 1927- .... CLC 7
See also CA 5-8R; CANR 12

Rowe, Nicholas 1674-1718 .... LC 8
See also DLB 84

Rowley, Ames Dorrance
See Lovecraft, H(oward) P(hillips)

Rowson, Susanna Haswell
1762(?)-1824 .... NCLC 5
See also DLB 37

Roy, Gabrielle 1909-1983 ...... CLC 10, 14
See also CA 53-56; 110; CANR 5; DLB 68;
MTCW

Rozewicz, Tadeusz 1921- .... CLC 9, 23
See also CA 108; CANR 36; MTCW

Ruark, Gibbons 1941- .... CLC 3
See also CA 33-36R; CANR 14, 31;
DLB 120

Rubens, Bernice (Ruth) 1923- ... CLC 19, 31
See also CA 25-28R; CANR 33; DLB 14;
MTCW

Rudkin, (James) David 1936- ...... CLC 14
See also CA 89-92; DLB 13

Rudnik, Raphael 1933- .... CLC 7
See also CA 29-32R

Ruffian, M.
See Hasek, Jaroslav (Matej Frantisek)

Ruiz, Jose Martinez . . . . CLC 11
  See also Martinez Ruiz, Jose

Rukeyser, Muriel
  1913-1980 . . . . CLC 6, 10, 15, 27
  See also CA 5-8R; 93-96; CANR 26;
  DLB 48; MTCW; SATA 22

Rule, Jane (Vance) 1931- . . . . CLC 27
  See also CA 25-28R; CAAS 18; CANR 12;
  DLB 60

Rulfo, Juan 1918-1986 . . . CLC 8, 80; HLC 2
  See also CA 85-88; 118; CANR 26;
  DLB 113; HW; MTCW

Runeberg, Johan 1804-1877 . . . . . . NCLC 41

Runyon, (Alfred) Damon
  1884(?)-1946 . . . . TCLC 10
  See also CA 107; DLB 11, 86

Rush, Norman 1933- . . . . CLC 44
  See also CA 121; 126

Rushdie, (Ahmed) Salman
  1947- . . . . CLC 23, 31, 55
  See also BEST 89:3; CA 108; 111;
  CANR 33; MTCW

Rushforth, Peter (Scott) 1945- . . . . . CLC 19
  See also CA 101

Ruskin, John 1819-1900 . . . . TCLC 20
  See also CA 114; 129; CDBLB 1832-1890;
  DLB 55; SATA 24

Russ, Joanna 1937- . . . . CLC 15
  See also CA 25-28R; CANR 11, 31; DLB 8;
  MTCW

Russell, George William 1867-1935
  See A. E.
  See also CA 104; CDBLB 1890-1914

Russell, (Henry) Ken(neth Alfred)
  1927- . . . . CLC 16
  See also CA 105

Russell, Willy 1947- . . . . CLC 60

Rutherford, Mark . . . . TCLC 25
  See also White, William Hale
  See also DLB 18

Ruyslinck, Ward
  See Belser, Reimond Karel Maria de

Ryan, Cornelius (John) 1920-1974 . . . CLC 7
  See also CA 69-72; 53-56; CANR 38

Ryan, Michael 1946- . . . . CLC 65
  See also CA 49-52; DLBY 82

Rybakov, Anatoli (Naumovich)
  1911- . . . . CLC 23, 53
  See also CA 126; 135

Ryder, Jonathan
  See Ludlum, Robert

Ryga, George 1932-1987 . . . . CLC 14
  See also CA 101; 124; CANR 43; DLB 60

S. S.
  See Sassoon, Siegfried (Lorraine)

Saba, Umberto 1883-1957 . . . . TCLC 33
  See also DLB 114

Sabatini, Rafael 1875-1950 . . . . TCLC 47

Sabato, Ernesto (R.)
  1911- . . . . CLC 10, 23; HLC 2
  See also CA 97-100; CANR 32; HW;
  MTCW

Sacastru, Martin
  See Bioy Casares, Adolfo

Sacher-Masoch, Leopold von
  1836(?)-1895 . . . . NCLC 31

Sachs, Marilyn (Stickle) 1927- . . . . . CLC 35
  See also AAYA 2; CA 17-20R; CANR 13;
  CLR 2; JRDA; MAICYA; SAAS 2;
  SATA 3, 68

Sachs, Nelly 1891-1970 . . . . CLC 14
  See also CA 17-18; 25-28R; CAP 2

Sackler, Howard (Oliver)
  1929-1982 . . . . CLC 14
  See also CA 61-64; 108; CANR 30; DLB 7

Sacks, Oliver (Wolf) 1933- . . . . CLC 67
  See also CA 53-56; CANR 28; MTCW

Sade, Donatien Alphonse Francois Comte
  1740-1814 . . . . NCLC 3

Sadoff, Ira 1945- . . . . CLC 9
  See also CA 53-56; CANR 5, 21; DLB 120

Saetone
  See Camus, Albert

Safire, William 1929- . . . . CLC 10
  See also CA 17-20R; CANR 31

Sagan, Carl (Edward) 1934- . . . . CLC 30
  See also AAYA 2; CA 25-28R; CANR 11,
  36; MTCW; SATA 58

Sagan, Francoise . . . . CLC 3, 6, 9, 17, 36
  See also Quoirez, Francoise
  See also DLB 83

Sahgal, Nayantara (Pandit) 1927- . . . CLC 41
  See also CA 9-12R; CANR 11

Saint, H(arry) F. 1941- . . . . CLC 50
  See also CA 127

St. Aubin de Teran, Lisa 1953-
  See Teran, Lisa St. Aubin de
  See also CA 118; 126

Sainte-Beuve, Charles Augustin
  1804-1869 . . . . NCLC 5

Saint-Exupery, Antoine (Jean Baptiste Marie
  Roger) de 1900-1944 . . . TCLC 2; WLC
  See also CA 108; 132; CLR 10; DLB 72;
  MAICYA; MTCW; SATA 20

St. John, David
  See Hunt, E(verette) Howard, Jr.

Saint-John Perse
  See Leger, (Marie-Rene Auguste) Alexis
  Saint-Leger

Saintsbury, George (Edward Bateman)
  1845-1933 . . . . TCLC 31
  See also DLB 57

Sait Faik . . . . TCLC 23
  See also Abasiyanik, Sait Faik

Saki . . . . TCLC 3; SSC 12
  See also Munro, H(ector) H(ugh)

Salama, Hannu 1936- . . . . CLC 18

Salamanca, J(ack) R(ichard)
  1922- . . . . CLC 4, 15
  See also CA 25-28R

Sale, J. Kirkpatrick
  See Sale, Kirkpatrick

Sale, Kirkpatrick 1937- . . . . CLC 68
  See also CA 13-16R; CANR 10

Salinas (y Serrano), Pedro
  1891(?)-1951 . . . . TCLC 17
  See also CA 117; DLB 134

Salinger, J(erome) D(avid)
  1919- . . . . . . CLC 1, 3, 8, 12, 55, 56; DA;
  SSC 2; WLC
  See also AAYA 2; CA 5-8R; CANR 39;
  CDALB 1941-1968; CLR 18; DLB 2, 102;
  MAICYA; MTCW; SATA 67

Salisbury, John
  See Caute, David

Salter, James 1925- . . . . CLC 7, 52, 59
  See also CA 73-76; DLB 130

Saltus, Edgar (Everton)
  1855-1921 . . . . TCLC 8
  See also CA 105

Saltykov, Mikhail Evgrafovich
  1826-1889 . . . . NCLC 16

Samarakis, Antonis 1919- . . . . CLC 5
  See also CA 25-28R; CAAS 16; CANR 36

Sanchez, Florencio 1875-1910 . . . . . TCLC 37
  See also HW

Sanchez, Luis Rafael 1936- . . . . CLC 23
  See also CA 128; HW

Sanchez, Sonia 1934- . . . . CLC 5; BLC 3
  See also BW; CA 33-36R; CANR 24;
  CLR 18; DLB 41; DLBD 8; MAICYA;
  MTCW; SATA 22

Sand, George
  1804-1876 . . . . . . NCLC 2, 42; DA; WLC
  See also DLB 119

Sandburg, Carl (August)
  1878-1967 . . . . CLC 1, 4, 10, 15, 35; DA;
  PC 2; WLC
  See also CA 5-8R; 25-28R; CANR 35;
  CDALB 1865-1917; DLB 17, 54;
  MAICYA; MTCW; SATA 8

Sandburg, Charles
  See Sandburg, Carl (August)

Sandburg, Charles A.
  See Sandburg, Carl (August)

Sanders, (James) Ed(ward) 1939- . . . CLC 53
  See also CA 13-16R; CANR 13; DLB 16

Sanders, Lawrence 1920- . . . . CLC 41
  See also BEST 89:4; CA 81-84; CANR 33;
  MTCW

Sanders, Noah
  See Blount, Roy (Alton), Jr.

Sanders, Winston P.
  See Anderson, Poul (William)

Sandoz, Mari(e Susette)
  1896-1966 . . . . CLC 28
  See also CA 1-4R; 25-28R; CANR 17;
  DLB 9; MTCW; SATA 5

Saner, Reg(inald Anthony) 1931- . . . . CLC 9
  See also CA 65-68

Sannazaro, Jacopo 1456(?)-1530 . . . . . . LC 8

Sansom, William 1912-1976 . . . . . . CLC 2, 6
  See also CA 5-8R; 65-68; CANR 42;
  MTCW

Santayana, George 1863-1952 . . . . . TCLC 40
  See also CA 115; DLB 54, 71

Santiago, Danny . . . . CLC 33
  See also James, Daniel (Lewis); James,
  Daniel (Lewis)
  See also DLB 122

Santmyer, Helen Hoover
1895-1986 .... CLC 33
See also CA 1-4R; 118; CANR 15, 33;
DLBY 84; MTCW

Santos, Bienvenido N(uqui) 1911-... CLC 22
See also CA 101; CANR 19

Sapper .... TCLC 44
See also McNeile, Herman Cyril

Sappho fl. 6th cent. B.C.-.... CMLC 3; PC 5

Sarduy, Severo 1937-1993 .... CLC 6
See also CA 89-92; 142; DLB 113; HW

Sargeson, Frank 1903-1982 .... CLC 31
See also CA 25-28R; 106; CANR 38

Sarmiento, Felix Ruben Garcia
See Dario, Ruben

Saroyan, William
1908-1981 ..... CLC 1, 8, 10, 29, 34, 56;
DA; WLC
See also CA 5-8R; 103; CANR 30; DLB 7,
9, 86; DLBY 81; MTCW; SATA 23, 24

Sarraute, Nathalie
1900- .... CLC 1, 2, 4, 8, 10, 31, 80
See also CA 9-12R; CANR 23; DLB 83;
MTCW

Sarton, (Eleanor) May
1912- .... CLC 4, 14, 49
See also CA 1-4R; CANR 1, 34; DLB 48;
DLBY 81; MTCW; SATA 36

Sartre, Jean-Paul
1905-1980 .... CLC 1, 4, 7, 9, 13, 18, 24,
44, 50, 52; DA; DC 3; WLC
See also CA 9-12R; 97-100; CANR 21;
DLB 72; MTCW

Sassoon, Siegfried (Lorraine)
1886-1967 .... CLC 36
See also CA 104; 25-28R; CANR 36;
DLB 20; MTCW

Satterfield, Charles
See Pohl, Frederik

Saul, John (W. III) 1942- .... CLC 46
See also AAYA 10; BEST 90:4; CA 81-84;
CANR 16, 40

Saunders, Caleb
See Heinlein, Robert A(nson)

Saura (Atares), Carlos 1932-....... CLC 20
See also CA 114; 131; HW

Sauser-Hall, Frederic 1887-1961.... CLC 18
See also CA 102; 93-96; CANR 36; MTCW

Saussure, Ferdinand de
1857-1913 .... TCLC 49

Savage, Catharine
See Brosman, Catharine Savage

Savage, Thomas 1915- .... CLC 40
See also CA 126; 132; CAAS 15

Savan, Glenn .... CLC 50

Saven, Glenn 19(?)- .... CLC 50

Sayers, Dorothy L(eigh)
1893-1957 .... TCLC 2, 15
See also CA 104; 119; CDBLB 1914-1945;
DLB 10, 36, 77, 100; MTCW

Sayers, Valerie 1952-............. CLC 50
See also CA 134

Sayles, John (Thomas)
1950- .... CLC 7, 10, 14
See also CA 57-60; CANR 41; DLB 44

Scammell, Michael .... CLC 34

Scannell, Vernon 1922- .... CLC 49
See also CA 5-8R; CANR 8, 24; DLB 27;
SATA 59

Scarlett, Susan
See Streatfeild, (Mary) Noel

Schaeffer, Susan Fromberg
1941- .... CLC 6, 11, 22
See also CA 49-52; CANR 18; DLB 28;
MTCW; SATA 22

Schary, Jill
See Robinson, Jill

Schell, Jonathan 1943-............ CLC 35
See also CA 73-76; CANR 12

Schelling, Friedrich Wilhelm Joseph von
1775-1854 .... NCLC 30
See also DLB 90

Scherer, Jean-Marie Maurice 1920-
See Rohmer, Eric
See also CA 110

Schevill, James (Erwin) 1920-....... CLC 7
See also CA 5-8R; CAAS 12

Schiller, Friedrich 1759-1805 .... NCLC 39
See also DLB 94

Schisgal, Murray (Joseph) 1926-..... CLC 6
See also CA 21-24R

Schlee, Ann 1934-................ CLC 35
See also CA 101; CANR 29; SATA 36, 44

Schlegel, August Wilhelm von
1767-1845 .... NCLC 15
See also DLB 94

Schlegel, Johann Elias (von)
1719(?)-1749 .... LC 5

Schmidt, Arno (Otto) 1914-1979.... CLC 56
See also CA 128; 109; DLB 69

Schmitz, Aron Hector 1861-1928
See Svevo, Italo
See also CA 104; 122; MTCW

Schnackenberg, Gjertrud 1953-..... CLC 40
See also CA 116; DLB 120

Schneider, Leonard Alfred 1925-1966
See Bruce, Lenny
See also CA 89-92

Schnitzler, Arthur 1862-1931 ...... TCLC 4
See also CA 104; DLB 81, 118

Schor, Sandra (M.) 1932(?)-1990 ... CLC 65
See also CA 132

Schorer, Mark 1908-1977 .... CLC 9
See also CA 5-8R; 73-76; CANR 7;
DLB 103

Schrader, Paul (Joseph) 1946-...... CLC 26
See also CA 37-40R; CANR 41; DLB 44

Schreiner, Olive (Emilie Albertina)
1855-1920 .... TCLC 9
See also CA 105; DLB 18

Schulberg, Budd (Wilson)
1914- .... CLC 7, 48
See also CA 25-28R; CANR 19; DLB 6, 26,
28; DLBY 81

Schulz, Bruno
1892-1942 .... TCLC 5, 51; SSC 13
See also CA 115; 123

Schulz, Charles M(onroe) 1922- .... CLC 12
See also CA 9-12R; CANR 6; SATA 10

Schumacher, E(rnst) F(riedrich)
1911-1977 .... CLC 80
See also CA 81-84; 73-76; CANR 34

Schuyler, James Marcus
1923-1991 .... CLC 5, 23
See also CA 101; 134; DLB 5

Schwartz, Delmore (David)
1913-1966 ...... CLC 2, 4, 10, 45; PC 8
See also CA 17-18; 25-28R; CANR 35;
CAP 2; DLB 28, 48; MTCW

Schwartz, Ernst
See Ozu, Yasujiro

Schwartz, John Burnham 1965- .... CLC 59
See also CA 132

Schwartz, Lynne Sharon 1939-..... CLC 31
See also CA 103

Schwartz, Muriel A.
See Eliot, T(homas) S(tearns)

Schwarz-Bart, Andre 1928-....... CLC 2, 4
See also CA 89-92

Schwarz-Bart, Simone 1938-........ CLC 7
See also CA 97-100

Schwob, (Mayer Andre) Marcel
1867-1905 .... TCLC 20
See also CA 117; DLB 123

Sciascia, Leonardo
1921-1989 .... CLC 8, 9, 41
See also CA 85-88; 130; CANR 35; MTCW

Scoppettone, Sandra 1936-........ CLC 26
See also CA 5-8R; CANR 41; SATA 9

Scorsese, Martin 1942- .... CLC 20
See also CA 110; 114

Scotland, Jay
See Jakes, John (William)

Scott, Duncan Campbell
1862-1947 .... TCLC 6
See also CA 104; DLB 92

Scott, Evelyn 1893-1963........... CLC 43
See also CA 104; 112; DLB 9, 48

Scott, F(rancis) R(eginald)
1899-1985 .... CLC 22
See also CA 101; 114; DLB 88

Scott, Frank
See Scott, F(rancis) R(eginald)

Scott, Joanna 1960- .... CLC 50
See also CA 126

Scott, Paul (Mark) 1920-1978.... CLC 9, 60
See also CA 81-84; 77-80; CANR 33;
DLB 14; MTCW

Scott, Walter
1771-1832 .... NCLC 15; DA; WLC
See also CDBLB 1789-1832; DLB 93, 107,
116; YABC 2

Scribe, (Augustin) Eugene
1791-1861 .... NCLC 16

Scrum, R.
See Crumb, R(obert)

Scudery, Madeleine de 1607-1701..... LC 2

Scum
See Crumb, R(obert)

Scumbag, Little Bobby
See Crumb, R(obert)

Seabrook, John
See Hubbard, L(afayette) Ron(ald)

Sealy, I. Allan 1951- .... **CLC 55**

Search, Alexander
See Pessoa, Fernando (Antonio Nogueira)

Sebastian, Lee
See Silverberg, Robert

Sebastian Owl
See Thompson, Hunter S(tockton)

Sebestyen, Ouida 1924- .... **CLC 30**
See also AAYA 8; CA 107; CANR 40;
CLR 17; JRDA; MAICYA; SAAS 10;
SATA 39

Secundus, H. Scriblerus
See Fielding, Henry

Sedges, John
See Buck, Pearl S(ydenstricker)

Sedgwick, Catharine Maria
1789-1867 .... **NCLC 19**
See also DLB 1, 74

Seelye, John 1931- .... **CLC 7**

Seferiades, Giorgos Stylianou 1900-1971
See Seferis, George
See also CA 5-8R; 33-36R; CANR 5, 36;
MTCW

Seferis, George .... **CLC 5, 11**
See also Seferiades, Giorgos Stylianou

Segal, Erich (Wolf) 1937- .... **CLC 3, 10**
See also BEST 89:1; CA 25-28R; CANR 20,
36; DLBY 86; MTCW

Seger, Bob 1945- .... **CLC 35**

Seghers, Anna .... **CLC 7**
See also Radvanyi, Netty
See also DLB 69

Seidel, Frederick (Lewis) 1936- ..... **CLC 18**
See also CA 13-16R; CANR 8; DLBY 84

Seifert, Jaroslav 1901-1986 ..... **CLC 34, 44**
See also CA 127; MTCW

Sei Shonagon c. 966-1017(?) ...... **CMLC 6**

Selby, Hubert, Jr. 1928- ..... **CLC 1, 2, 4, 8**
See also CA 13-16R; CANR 33; DLB 2

Selzer, Richard 1928- .... **CLC 74**
See also CA 65-68; CANR 14

Sembene, Ousmane
See Ousmane, Sembene

Senancour, Etienne Pivert de
1770-1846 .... **NCLC 16**
See also DLB 119

Sender, Ramon (Jose)
1902-1982 .... **CLC 8; HLC 2**
See also CA 5-8R; 105; CANR 8; HW;
MTCW

Seneca, Lucius Annaeus
4B.C.-65. .... **CMLC 6**

Senghor, Leopold Sedar
1906- .... **CLC 54; BLC 3**
See also BW; CA 116; 125; MTCW

Serling, (Edward) Rod(man)
1924-1975 .... **CLC 30**
See also AITN 1; CA 65-68; 57-60; DLB 26

Serna, Ramon Gomez de la
See Gomez de la Serna, Ramon

Serpieres
See Guillevic, (Eugene)

Service, Robert
See Service, Robert W(illiam)
See also DLB 92

Service, Robert W(illiam)
1874(?)-1958 ...... **TCLC 15; DA; WLC**
See also Service, Robert
See also CA 115; 140; SATA 20

Seth, Vikram 1952-............... **CLC 43**
See also CA 121; 127; DLB 120

Seton, Cynthia Propper
1926-1982 .... **CLC 27**
See also CA 5-8R; 108; CANR 7

Seton, Ernest (Evan) Thompson
1860-1946 .... **TCLC 31**
See also CA 109; DLB 92; JRDA; SATA 18

Seton-Thompson, Ernest
See Seton, Ernest (Evan) Thompson

Settle, Mary Lee 1918- .... **CLC 19, 61**
See also CA 89-92; CAAS 1; DLB 6

Seuphor, Michel
See Arp, Jean

**Sevigne, Marie (de Rabutin-Chantal) Marquise
de** 1626-1696 .... **LC 11**

Sexton, Anne (Harvey)
1928-1974 .... **CLC 2, 4, 6, 8, 10, 15, 53;
DA; PC 2; WLC**
See also CA 1-4R; 53-56; CABS 2;
CANR 3, 36; CDALB 1941-1968; DLB 5;
MTCW; SATA 10

Shaara, Michael (Joseph Jr.)
1929-1988 .... **CLC 15**
See also AITN 1; CA 102; DLBY 83

Shackleton, C. C.
See Aldiss, Brian W(ilson)

Shacochis, Bob .... **CLC 39**
See also Shacochis, Robert G.

Shacochis, Robert G. 1951-
See Shacochis, Bob
See also CA 119; 124

Shaffer, Anthony (Joshua) 1926-.... **CLC 19**
See also CA 110; 116; DLB 13

Shaffer, Peter (Levin)
1926- .... **CLC 5, 14, 18, 37, 60**
See also CA 25-28R; CANR 25;
CDBLB 1960 to Present; DLB 13;
MTCW

Shakey, Bernard
See Young, Neil

Shalamov, Varlam (Tikhonovich)
1907(?)-1982 .... **CLC 18**
See also CA 129; 105

Shamlu, Ahmad 1925- .... **CLC 10**

Shammas, Anton 1951-........... **CLC 55**

Shange, Ntozake
1948- .. **CLC 8, 25, 38, 74; BLC 3; DC 3**
See also AAYA 9; BW; CA 85-88; CABS 3;
CANR 27; DLB 38; MTCW

Shanley, John Patrick 1950-....... **CLC 75**
See also CA 128; 133

Shapcott, Thomas William 1935- ... **CLC 38**
See also CA 69-72

Shapiro, Jane..................... **CLC 76**

Shapiro, Karl (Jay) 1913- .. **CLC 4, 8, 15, 53**
See also CA 1-4R; CAAS 6; CANR 1, 36;
DLB 48; MTCW

Sharp, William 1855-1905 .... **TCLC 39**

Sharpe, Thomas Ridley 1928-
See Sharpe, Tom
See also CA 114; 122

Sharpe, Tom..................... **CLC 36**
See also Sharpe, Thomas Ridley
See also DLB 14

Shaw, Bernard.................... **TCLC 45**
See also Shaw, George Bernard

Shaw, G. Bernard
See Shaw, George Bernard

Shaw, George Bernard
1856-1950 .... **TCLC 3, 9, 21; DA; WLC**
See also Shaw, Bernard
See also CA 104; 128; CDBLB 1914-1945;
DLB 10, 57; MTCW

Shaw, Henry Wheeler
1818-1885 .... **NCLC 15**
See also DLB 11

Shaw, Irwin 1913-1984....... **CLC 7, 23, 34**
See also AITN 1; CA 13-16R; 112;
CANR 21; CDALB 1941-1968; DLB 6,
102; DLBY 84; MTCW

Shaw, Robert 1927-1978 .... **CLC 5**
See also AITN 1; CA 1-4R; 81-84;
CANR 4; DLB 13, 14

Shaw, T. E.
See Lawrence, T(homas) E(dward)

Shawn, Wallace 1943- .... **CLC 41**
See also CA 112

Sheed, Wilfrid (John Joseph)
1930- .... **CLC 2, 4, 10, 53**
See also CA 65-68; CANR 30; DLB 6;
MTCW

Sheldon, Alice Hastings Bradley
1915(?)-1987
See Tiptree, James, Jr.
See also CA 108; 122; CANR 34; MTCW

Sheldon, John
See Bloch, Robert (Albert)

Shelley, Mary Wollstonecraft (Godwin)
1797-1831 ...... **NCLC 14; DA; WLC**
See also CDBLB 1789-1832; DLB 110, 116;
SATA 29

Shelley, Percy Bysshe
1792-1822 .... **NCLC 18; DA; WLC**
See also CDBLB 1789-1832; DLB 96, 110

Shepard, Jim 1956-............... **CLC 36**
See also CA 137

Shepard, Lucius 1947- .... **CLC 34**
See also CA 128; 141

Shepard, Sam
1943- .... **CLC 4, 6, 17, 34, 41, 44**
See also AAYA 1; CA 69-72; CABS 3;
CANR 22; DLB 7; MTCW

Shepherd, Michael
See Ludlum, Robert

Sissman, L(ouis) E(dward)
1928-1976 .... **CLC 9, 18**
See also CA 21-24R; 65-68; CANR 13;
DLB 5

Sisson, C(harles) H(ubert) 1914-..... **CLC 8**
See also CA 1-4R; CAAS 3; CANR 3;
DLB 27

Sitwell, Dame Edith
1887-1964 .... **CLC 2, 9, 67; PC 3**
See also CA 9-12R; CANR 35;
CDBLB 1945 1960; DLB 20; MTCW

Sjoewall, Maj 1935- .... **CLC 7**
See also CA 65-68

Sjowall, Maj
See Sjoewall, Maj

Skelton, Robin 1925- .... **CLC 13**
See also AITN 2; CA 5-8R; CAAS 5;
CANR 28; DLB 27, 53

Skolimowski, Jerzy 1938- .... **CLC 20**
See also CA 128

Skram, Amalie (Bertha)
1847-1905 .... **TCLC 25**

Skvorecky, Josef (Vaclav)
1924- .... **CLC 15, 39, 69**
See also CA 61-64; CAAS 1; CANR 10, 34;
MTCW

Slade, Bernard .... **CLC 11, 46**
See also Newbound, Bernard Slade
See also CAAS 9; DLB 53

Slaughter, Carolyn 1946- .... **CLC 56**
See also CA 85-88

Slaughter, Frank G(ill) 1908- ...... **CLC 29**
See also AITN 2; CA 5-8R; CANR 5

Slavitt, David R(ytman) 1935-.... **CLC 5, 14**
See also CA 21-24R; CAAS 3; CANR 41;
DLB 5, 6

Slesinger, Tess 1905-1945 .... **TCLC 10**
See also CA 107; DLB 102

Slessor, Kenneth 1901-1971 .... **CLC 14**
See also CA 102; 89-92

Slowacki, Juliusz 1809-1849 ..... **NCLC 15**

Smart, Christopher 1722-1771 .... **LC 3**
See also DLB 109

Smart, Elizabeth 1913-1986........ **CLC 54**
See also CA 81-84, 118; DLB 88

Smiley, Jane (Graves) 1949- .... **CLC 53, 76**
See also CA 104; CANR 30

Smith, A(rthur) J(ames) M(arshall)
1902-1980 .... **CLC 15**
See also CA 1-4R; 102; CANR 4; DLB 88

Smith, Betty (Wehner) 1896-1972... **CLC 19**
See also CA 5-8R; 33-36R; DLBY 82;
SATA 6

Smith, Charlotte (Turner)
1749-1806 .... **NCLC 23**
See also DLB 39, 109

Smith, Clark Ashton 1893-1961 .... **CLC 43**

Smith, Dave .... **CLC 22, 42**
See also Smith, David (Jeddie)
See also CAAS 7; DLB 5

Smith, David (Jeddie) 1942-
See Smith, Dave
See also CA 49-52; CANR 1

Smith, Florence Margaret
1902-1971 .... **CLC 8**
See also Smith, Stevie
See also CA 17-18; 29-32R; CANR 35;
CAP 2; MTCW

Smith, Iain Crichton 1928- .... **CLC 64**
See also CA 21-24R; DLB 40

Smith, John 1580(?)-1631 .... **LC 9**

Smith, Johnston
See Crane, Stephen (Townley)

Smith, Lee 1944-.............. **CLC 25, 73**
See also CA 114; 119; DLBY 83

Smith, Martin
See Smith, Martin Cruz

Smith, Martin Cruz 1942- .... **CLC 25**
See also BEST 89:4; CA 85-88; CANR 6,
23, 43

Smith, Mary-Ann Tirone 1944-..... **CLC 39**
See also CA 118; 136

Smith, Patti 1946- .... **CLC 12**
See also CA 93-96

Smith, Pauline (Urmson)
1882-1959 .... **TCLC 25**

Smith, Rosamond
See Oates, Joyce Carol

Smith, Sheila Kaye
See Kaye-Smith, Sheila

Smith, Stevie .... **CLC 3, 8, 25, 44**
See also Smith, Florence Margaret
See also DLB 20

Smith, Wilbur A(ddison) 1933- ..... **CLC 33**
See also CA 13-16R; CANR 7; MTCW

Smith, William Jay 1918- .... **CLC 6**
See also CA 5-8R; DLB 5; MAICYA;
SATA 2, 68

Smith, Woodrow Wilson
See Kuttner, Henry

Smolenskin, Peretz 1842-1885.... **NCLC 30**

Smollett, Tobias (George) 1721-1771 .. **LC 2**
See also CDBLB 1660-1789; DLB 39, 104

Snodgrass, W(illiam) D(e Witt)
1926- .... **CLC 2, 6, 10, 18, 68**
See also CA 1-4R; CANR 6, 36; DLB 5;
MTCW

Snow, C(harles) P(ercy)
1905-1980 .... **CLC 1, 4, 6, 9, 13, 19**
See also CA 5-8R; 101; CANR 28;
CDBLB 1945-1960; DLB 15, 77; MTCW

Snow, Frances Compton
See Adams, Henry (Brooks)

Snyder, Gary (Sherman)
1930- .... **CLC 1, 2, 5, 9, 32**
See also CA 17-20R; CANR 30; DLB 5, 16

Snyder, Zilpha Keatley 1927- ...... **CLC 17**
See also CA 9-12R; CANR 38; CLR 31;
JRDA; MAICYA; SAAS 2; SATA 1, 28,
75

Soares, Bernardo
See Pessoa, Fernando (Antonio Nogueira)

Sobh, A.
See Shamlu, Ahmad

Sobol, Joshua .... **CLC 60**

Soderberg, Hjalmar 1869-1941 .... **TCLC 39**

Sodergran, Edith (Irene)
See Soedergran, Edith (Irene)

Soedergran, Edith (Irene)
1892-1923 .... **TCLC 31**

Softly, Edgar
See Lovecraft, H(oward) P(hillips)

Softly, Edward
See Lovecraft, H(oward) P(hillips)

Sokolov, Raymond 1941-.......... **CLC 7**
See also CA 85-88

Solo, Jay
See Ellison, Harlan

Sologub, Fyodor .... **TCLC 9**
See also Teternikov, Fyodor Kuzmich

Solomons, Ikey Esquir
See Thackeray, William Makepeace

Solomos, Dionysios 1798-1857 ... **NCLC 15**

Solwoska, Mara
See French, Marilyn

Solzhenitsyn, Aleksandr I(sayevich)
1918- ...... **CLC 1, 2, 4, 7, 9, 10, 18, 26,
34, 78; DA; WLC**
See also AITN 1; CA 69-72; CANR 40;
MTCW

Somers, Jane
See Lessing, Doris (May)

Somerville, Edith 1858-1949 ...... **TCLC 51**
See also DLB 135

Somerville & Ross
See Martin, Violet Florence; Somerville,
Edith

Sommer, Scott 1951- .... **CLC 25**
See also CA 106

Sondheim, Stephen (Joshua)
1930- .... **CLC 30, 39**
See also CA 103

Sontag, Susan 1933-... **CLC 1, 2, 10, 13, 31**
See also CA 17-20R; CANR 25; DLB 2, 67;
MTCW

Sophocles
496(?)B.C.-406(?)B.C..... **CMLC 2; DA;
DC 1**

Sorel, Julia
See Drexler, Rosalyn

Sorrentino, Gilbert
1929- .... **CLC 3, 7, 14, 22, 40**
See also CA 77-80; CANR 14, 33; DLB 5;
DLBY 80

Soto, Gary 1952-....... **CLC 32, 80; HLC 2**
See also AAYA 10; CA 119; 125; DLB 82;
HW; JRDA

Soupault, Philippe 1897-1990 ...... **CLC 68**
See also CA 116; 131

Souster, (Holmes) Raymond
1921- .... **CLC 5, 14**
See also CA 13-16R; CAAS 14; CANR 13,
29; DLB 88; SATA 63

Southern, Terry 1926- .... **CLC 7**
See also CA 1-4R; CANR 1; DLB 2

Southey, Robert 1774-1843 .... **NCLC 8**
See also DLB 93, 107; SATA 54

Southworth, Emma Dorothy Eliza Nevitte
1819-1899 .... **NCLC 26**

Souza, Ernest
See Scott, Evelyn

Soyinka, Wole
1934- ..... **CLC 3, 5, 14, 36, 44; BLC 3; DA; DC 2; WLC**
See also BW; CA 13-16R; CANR 27, 39; DLB 125; MTCW

Spackman, W(illiam) M(ode)
1905-1990 .... **CLC 46**
See also CA 81-84; 132

Spacks, Barry 1931- .... **CLC 14**
See also CA 29-32R; CANR 33; DLB 105

Spanidou, Irini 1946- .... **CLC 44**

Spark, Muriel (Sarah)
1918- .... **CLC 2, 3, 5, 8, 13, 18, 40; SSC 10**
See also CA 5-8R; CANR 12, 36; CDBLB 1945-1960; DLB 15; MTCW

Spaulding, Douglas
See Bradbury, Ray (Douglas)

Spaulding, Leonard
See Bradbury, Ray (Douglas)

Spence, J. A. D.
See Eliot, T(homas) S(tearns)

Spencer, Elizabeth 1921- .... **CLC 22**
See also CA 13-16R; CANR 32; DLB 6; MTCW; SATA 14

Spencer, Leonard G.
See Silverberg, Robert

Spencer, Scott 1945- .... **CLC 30**
See also CA 113; DLBY 86

Spender, Stephen (Harold)
1909- .... **CLC 1, 2, 5, 10, 41**
See also CA 9-12R; CANR 31; CDBLB 1945-1960; DLB 20; MTCW

Spengler, Oswald (Arnold Gottfried)
1880-1936 .... **TCLC 25**
See also CA 118

Spenser, Edmund
1552(?)-1599 .... **LC 5; DA; PC 8; WLC**
See also CDBLB Before 1660

Spicer, Jack 1925-1965 ...... **CLC 8, 18, 72**
See also CA 85-88; DLB 5, 16

Spiegelman, Art 1948- .... **CLC 76**
See also AAYA 10; CA 125; CANR 41

Spielberg, Peter 1929- .... **CLC 6**
See also CA 5-8R; CANR 4; DLBY 81

Spielberg, Steven 1947- .... **CLC 20**
See also AAYA 8; CA 77-80; CANR 32; SATA 32

Spillane, Frank Morrison 1918-
See Spillane, Mickey
See also CA 25-28R; CANR 28; MTCW; SATA 66

Spillane, Mickey .... **CLC 3, 13**
See also Spillane, Frank Morrison

Spinoza, Benedictus de 1632-1677 .... **LC 9**

Spinrad, Norman (Richard) 1940-... **CLC 46**
See also CA 37-40R; CANR 20; DLB 8

Spitteler, Carl (Friedrich Georg)
1845-1924 .... **TCLC 12**
See also CA 109; DLB 129

Spivack, Kathleen (Romola Drucker)
1938- .... **CLC 6**
See also CA 49-52

Spoto, Donald 1941- .... **CLC 39**
See also CA 65-68; CANR 11

Springsteen, Bruce (F.) 1949- ...... **CLC 17**
See also CA 111

Spurling, Hilary 1940- .... **CLC 34**
See also CA 104; CANR 25

Squires, (James) Radcliffe
1917-1993 .... **CLC 51**
See also CA 1-4R; 140; CANR 6, 21

Srivastava, Dhanpat Rai 1880(?)-1936
See Premchand
See also CA 118

Stacy, Donald
See Pohl, Frederik

Stael, Germaine de
See Stael-Holstein, Anne Louise Germaine Necker Baronn
See also DLB 119

Stael-Holstein, Anne Louise Germaine Necker Baronn 1766-1817 ..... **NCLC 3**
See also Stael, Germaine de

Stafford, Jean 1915-1979 ... **CLC 4, 7, 19, 68**
See also CA 1-4R; 85-88; CANR 3; DLB 2; MTCW; SATA 22

Stafford, William (Edgar)
1914-1993 .... **CLC 4, 7, 29**
See also CA 5-8R; 142; CAAS 3; CANR 5, 22; DLB 5

Staines, Trevor
See Brunner, John (Kilian Houston)

Stairs, Gordon
See Austin, Mary (Hunter)

Stannard, Martin 1947- .... **CLC 44**
See also CA 142

Stanton, Maura 1946- .... **CLC 9**
See also CA 89-92; CANR 15; DLB 120

Stanton, Schuyler
See Baum, L(yman) Frank

Stapledon, (William) Olaf
1886-1950 .... **TCLC 22**
See also CA 111; DLB 15

Starbuck, George (Edwin) 1931-.... **CLC 53**
See also CA 21-24R; CANR 23

Stark, Richard
See Westlake, Donald E(dwin)

Staunton, Schuyler
See Baum, L(yman) Frank

Stead, Christina (Ellen)
1902-1983 .... **CLC 2, 5, 8, 32, 80**
See also CA 13-16R; 109; CANR 33, 40; MTCW

Stead, William Thomas
1849-1912 .... **TCLC 48**

Steele, Richard 1672-1729 .... **LC 18**
See also CDBLB 1660-1789; DLB 84, 101

Steele, Timothy (Reid) 1948-....... **CLC 45**
See also CA 93-96; CANR 16; DLB 120

Steffens, (Joseph) Lincoln
1866-1936 .... **TCLC 20**
See also CA 117

Stegner, Wallace (Earle)
1909-1993 .... **CLC 9, 49, 81**
See also AITN 1; BEST 90:3; CA 1-4R; 141; CAAS 9; CANR 1, 21; DLB 9; MTCW

Stein, Gertrude
1874-1946 ...... **TCLC 1, 6, 28, 48; DA; WLC**
See also CA 104; 132; CDALB 1917-1929; DLB 4, 54, 86; MTCW

Steinbeck, John (Ernst)
1902-1968 ...... **CLC 1, 5, 9, 13, 21, 34, 45, 75; DA; SSC 11; WLC**
See also CA 1-4R; 25-28R; CANR 1, 35; CDALB 1929-1941; DLB 7, 9; DLBD 2; MTCW; SATA 9

Steinem, Gloria 1934-............. **CLC 63**
See also CA 53-56; CANR 28; MTCW

Steiner, George 1929-............. **CLC 24**
See also CA 73-76; CANR 31; DLB 67; MTCW; SATA 62

Steiner, K. Leslie
See Delany, Samuel R(ay, Jr.)

Steiner, Rudolf 1861-1925........ **TCLC 13**
See also CA 107

Stendhal 1783-1842.... **NCLC 23; DA; WLC**
See also DLB 119

Stephen, Leslie 1832-1904 .... **TCLC 23**
See also CA 123; DLB 57

Stephen, Sir Leslie
See Stephen, Leslie

Stephen, Virginia
See Woolf, (Adeline) Virginia

Stephens, James 1882(?)-1950...... **TCLC 4**
See also CA 104; DLB 19

Stephens, Reed
See Donaldson, Stephen R.

Steptoe, Lydia
See Barnes, Djuna

Sterchi, Beat 1949-............... **CLC 65**

Sterling, Brett
See Bradbury, Ray (Douglas); Hamilton, Edmond

Sterling, Bruce 1954-............. **CLC 72**
See also CA 119

Sterling, George 1869-1926....... **TCLC 20**
See also CA 117; DLB 54

Stern, Gerald 1925- .... **CLC 40**
See also CA 81-84; CANR 28; DLB 105

Stern, Richard (Gustave) 1928-... **CLC 4, 39**
See also CA 1-4R; CANR 1, 25; DLBY 87

Sternberg, Josef von 1894-1969..... **CLC 20**
See also CA 81-84

Sterne, Laurence
1713-1768 .... **LC 2; DA; WLC**
See also CDBLB 1660-1789; DLB 39

Sternheim, (William Adolf) Carl
1878-1942 .... **TCLC 8**
See also CA 105; DLB 56, 118

Stevens, Mark 1951- .... **CLC 34**
See also CA 122

Stevens, Wallace
　　1879-1955 . . . . **TCLC 3, 12, 45; DA;**
　　　　　　　　　　　　　PC 6; WLC
　　See also CA 104; 124; CDALB 1929-1941;
　　DLB 54; MTCW

Stevenson, Anne (Katharine)
　　1933- . . . . **CLC 7, 33**
　　See also CA 17-20R; CAAS 9; CANR 9, 33;
　　DLB 40; MTCW

Stevenson, Robert Louis (Balfour)
　　1850-1894 . . . . **NCLC 5, 14; DA;**
　　　　　　　　　　　　　　SSC 11; WLC
　　See also CDBLB 1890-1914; CLR 10, 11;
　　DLB 18, 57; JRDA; MAICYA; YABC 2

Stewart, J(ohn) I(nnes) M(ackintosh)
　　1906- . . . . **CLC 7, 14, 32**
　　See also CA 85-88; CAAS 3; MTCW

Stewart, Mary (Florence Elinor)
　　1916- . . . . **CLC 7, 35**
　　See also CA 1-4R; CANR 1; SATA 12

Stewart, Mary Rainbow
　　See Stewart, Mary (Florence Elinor)

Stifter, Adalbert 1805-1868 . . . . . . **NCLC 41**
　　See also DLB 133

Still, James 1906- . . . . **CLC 49**
　　See also CA 65-68; CAAS 17; CANR 10,
　　26; DLB 9; SATA 29

Sting
　　See Sumner, Gordon Matthew

Stirling, Arthur
　　See Sinclair, Upton (Beall)

Stitt, Milan 1941- . . . . **CLC 29**
　　See also CA 69-72

Stockton, Francis Richard 1834-1902
　　See Stockton, Frank R.
　　See also CA 108; 137; MAICYA; SATA 44

Stockton, Frank R. . . . . **TCLC 47**
　　See also Stockton, Francis Richard
　　See also DLB 42, 74; SATA 32

Stoddard, Charles
　　See Kuttner, Henry

Stoker, Abraham 1847-1912
　　See Stoker, Bram
　　See also CA 105; DA; SATA 29

Stoker, Bram . . . . **TCLC 8; WLC**
　　See also Stoker, Abraham
　　See also CDBLB 1890-1914; DLB 36, 70

Stolz, Mary (Slattery) 1920- . . . . **CLC 12**
　　See also AAYA 8; AITN 1; CA 5-8R;
　　CANR 13, 41; JRDA; MAICYA;
　　SAAS 3; SATA 10, 71

Stone, Irving 1903-1989 . . . . **CLC 7**
　　See also AITN 1; CA 1-4R; 129; CAAS 3;
　　CANR 1, 23; MTCW; SATA 3;
　　SATA-Obit 64

Stone, Oliver 1946- . . . . **CLC 73**
　　See also CA 110

Stone, Robert (Anthony)
　　1937- . . . . **CLC 5, 23, 42**
　　See also CA 85-88; CANR 23; MTCW

Stone, Zachary
　　See Follett, Ken(neth Martin)

Stoppard, Tom
　　1937- . . . . . . **CLC 1, 3, 4, 5, 8, 15, 29, 34,**
　　　　　　　　　　　　　　63; DA; WLC
　　See also CA 81-84; CANR 39;
　　CDBLB 1960 to Present; DLB 13;
　　DLBY 85; MTCW

Storey, David (Malcolm)
　　1933- . . . . **CLC 2, 4, 5, 8**
　　See also CA 81-84; CANR 36; DLB 13, 14;
　　MTCW

Storm, Hyemeyohsts 1935- . . . . **CLC 3**
　　See also CA 81-84

Storm, (Hans) Theodor (Woldsen)
　　1817-1888 . . . . **NCLC 1**

Storni, Alfonsina
　　1892-1938 . . . . **TCLC 5; HLC 2**
　　See also CA 104; 131; HW

Stout, Rex (Todhunter) 1886-1975 . . . **CLC 3**
　　See also AITN 2; CA 61-64

Stow, (Julian) Randolph 1935- . . **CLC 23, 48**
　　See also CA 13-16R; CANR 33; MTCW

Stowe, Harriet (Elizabeth) Beecher
　　1811-1896 . . . . **NCLC 3; DA; WLC**
　　See also CDALB 1865-1917; DLB 1, 12, 42,
　　74; JRDA; MAICYA; YABC 1

Strachey, (Giles) Lytton
　　1880-1932 . . . . **TCLC 12**
　　See also CA 110; DLBD 10

Strand, Mark 1934- . . . . . . **CLC 6, 18, 41, 71**
　　See also CA 21-24R; CANR 40; DLB 5;
　　SATA 41

Straub, Peter (Francis) 1943- . . . . . . **CLC 28**
　　See also BEST 89:1; CA 85-88; CANR 28;
　　DLBY 84; MTCW

Strauss, Botho 1944- . . . . **CLC 22**
　　See also DLB 124

Streatfeild, (Mary) Noel
　　1895(?)-1986 . . . . **CLC 21**
　　See also CA 81-84; 120; CANR 31;
　　CLR 17; MAICYA; SATA 20, 48

Stribling, T(homas) S(igismund)
　　1881-1965 . . . . **CLC 23**
　　See also CA 107; DLB 9

Strindberg, (Johan) August
　　1849-1912 . . . . . . **TCLC 1, 8, 21, 47; DA;**
　　　　　　　　　　　　　　　　　　　WLC
　　See also CA 104; 135

Stringer, Arthur 1874-1950 . . . . . . **TCLC 37**
　　See also DLB 92

Stringer, David
　　See Roberts, Keith (John Kingston)

Strugatskii, Arkadii (Natanovich)
　　1925-1991 . . . . **CLC 27**
　　See also CA 106; 135

Strugatskii, Boris (Natanovich)
　　1933- . . . . **CLC 27**
　　See also CA 106

Strummer, Joe 1953(?)- . . . . **CLC 30**
　　See also Clash, The

Stuart, Don A.
　　See Campbell, John W(ood, Jr.)

Stuart, Ian
　　See MacLean, Alistair (Stuart)

Stuart, Jesse (Hilton)
　　1906-1984 . . . . **CLC 1, 8, 11, 14, 34**
　　See also CA 5-8R; 112; CANR 31; DLB 9,
　　48, 102; DLBY 84; SATA 2, 36

Sturgeon, Theodore (Hamilton)
　　1918-1985 . . . . **CLC 22, 39**
　　See also Queen, Ellery
　　See also CA 81-84; 116; CANR 32; DLB 8;
　　DLBY 85; MTCW

Sturges, Preston 1898-1959 . . . . . . **TCLC 48**
　　See also CA 114; DLB 26

Styron, William
　　1925- . . . . **CLC 1, 3, 5, 11, 15, 60**
　　See also BEST 90:4; CA 5-8R; CANR 6, 33;
　　CDALB 1968-1988; DLB 2, DLBY 80;
　　MTCW

Suarez Lynch, B.
　　See Bioy Casares, Adolfo; Borges, Jorge
　　Luis

Suarez Lynch, B.
　　See Borges, Jorge Luis

Su Chien 1884-1918
　　See Su Man-shu
　　See also CA 123

Sudermann, Hermann 1857-1928 . . **TCLC 15**
　　See also CA 107; DLB 118

Sue, Eugene 1804-1857 . . . . **NCLC 1**
　　See also DLB 119

Sueskind, Patrick 1949- . . . . **CLC 44**

Sukenick, Ronald 1932- . . . . . **CLC 3, 4, 6, 48**
　　See also CA 25-28R; CAAS 8; CANR 32;
　　DLBY 81

Suknaski, Andrew 1942- . . . . **CLC 19**
　　See also CA 101; DLB 53

Sullivan, Vernon
　　See Vian, Boris

Sully Prudhomme 1839-1907 . . . . . . **TCLC 31**

Su Man-shu . . . . **TCLC 24**
　　See also Su Chien

Summerforest, Ivy B.
　　See Kirkup, James

Summers, Andrew James 1942- . . . . . **CLC 26**
　　See also Police, The

Summers, Andy
　　See Summers, Andrew James

Summers, Hollis (Spurgeon, Jr.)
　　1916- . . . . **CLC 10**
　　See also CA 5-8R; CANR 3; DLB 6

Summers, (Alphonsus Joseph-Mary Augustus)
　　Montague 1880-1948 . . . . **TCLC 16**
　　See also CA 118

Sumner, Gordon Matthew 1951- . . . . **CLC 26**
　　See also Police, The

Surtees, Robert Smith
　　1803-1864 . . . . **NCLC 14**
　　See also DLB 21

Susann, Jacqueline 1921-1974 . . . . **CLC 3**
　　See also AITN 1; CA 65-68; 53-56; MTCW

Suskind, Patrick
　　See Sueskind, Patrick

Sutcliff, Rosemary 1920-1992 . . . . . . **CLC 26**
　　See also AAYA 10; CA 5-8R; 139;
　　CANR 37; CLR 1; JRDA; MAICYA;
　　SATA 6, 44; SATA-Obit 73

Sutro, Alfred 1863-1933.......... TCLC 6
See also CA 105; DLB 10

Sutton, Henry
See Slavitt, David R(ytman)

Svevo, Italo .... TCLC 2, 35
See also Schmitz, Aron Hector

Swados, Elizabeth 1951- .... CLC 12
See also CA 97-100

Swados, Harvey 1920-1972 .... CLC 5
See also CA 5-8R; 37-40R; CANR 6;
DLB 2

Swan, Gladys 1934- .... CLC 69
See also CA 101; CANR 17, 39

Swarthout, Glendon (Fred)
1918-1992 .... CLC 35
See also CA 1-4R; 139; CANR 1; SATA 26

Sweet, Sarah C.
See Jewett, (Theodora) Sarah Orne

Swenson, May
1919-1989 .... CLC 4, 14, 61; DA
See also CA 5-8R; 130; CANR 36; DLB 5;
MTCW; SATA 15

Swift, Augustus
See Lovecraft, H(oward) P(hillips)

Swift, Graham 1949- .... CLC 41
See also CA 117; 122

Swift, Jonathan
1667-1745 .... LC 1; DA; WLC
See also CDBLB 1660-1789; DLB 39, 95,
101; SATA 19

Swinburne, Algernon Charles
1837-1909 ...... TCLC 8, 36; DA; WLC
See also CA 105; 140; CDBLB 1832-1890;
DLB 35, 57

Swinfen, Ann..................... CLC 34

Swinnerton, Frank Arthur
1884-1982 .... CLC 31
See also CA 108; DLB 34

Swithen, John
See King, Stephen (Edwin)

Sylvia
See Ashton-Warner, Sylvia (Constance)

Symmes, Robert Edward
See Duncan, Robert (Edward)

Symonds, John Addington
1840-1893 .... NCLC 34
See also DLB 57

Symons, Arthur 1865-1945 .... TCLC 11
See also CA 107; DLB 19, 57

Symons, Julian (Gustave)
1912- .... CLC 2, 14, 32
See also CA 49-52; CAAS 3; CANR 3, 33;
DLB 87; DLBY 92; MTCW

Synge, (Edmund) J(ohn) M(illington)
1871-1909 .... TCLC 6, 37; DC 2
See also CA 104; 141; CDBLB 1890-1914;
DLB 10, 19

Syruc, J.
See Milosz, Czeslaw

Szirtes, George 1948-............. CLC 46
See also CA 109; CANR 27

Tabori, George 1914-............. CLC 19
See also CA 49-52; CANR 4

Tagore, Rabindranath
1861-1941 .... TCLC 3, 53; PC 8
See also CA 104; 120; MTCW

Taine, Hippolyte Adolphe
1828-1893 .... NCLC 15

Talese, Gay 1932-................. CLC 37
See also AITN 1; CA 1-4R; CANR 9;
MTCW

Tallent, Elizabeth (Ann) 1954- ..... CLC 45
See also CA 117; DLB 130

Tally, Ted 1952-.................. CLC 42
See also CA 120; 124

Tamayo y Baus, Manuel
1829-1898 .... NCLC 1

Tammsaare, A(nton) H(ansen)
1878-1940 .... TCLC 27

Tan, Amy 1952- .... CLC 59
See also AAYA 9; BEST 89:3; CA 136;
SATA 75

Tandem, Felix
See Spitteler, Carl (Friedrich Georg)

Tanizaki, Jun'ichiro
1886-1965 .... CLC 8, 14, 28
See also CA 93-96; 25-28R

Tanner, William
See Amis, Kingsley (William)

Tao Lao
See Storni, Alfonsina

Tarassoff, Lev
See Troyat, Henri

Tarbell, Ida M(inerva)
1857-1944 .... TCLC 40
See also CA 122; DLB 47

Tarkington, (Newton) Booth
1869-1946 .... TCLC 9
See also CA 110; DLB 9, 102; SATA 17

Tarkovsky, Andrei (Arsenyevich)
1932-1986 .... CLC 75
See also CA 127

Tartt, Donna 1964(?)-............. CLC 76
See also CA 142

Tasso, Torquato 1544-1595 .... LC 5

Tate, (John Orley) Allen
1899-1979 .... CLC 2, 4, 6, 9, 11, 14, 24
See also CA 5-8R; 85-88; CANR 32;
DLB 4, 45, 63; MTCW

Tate, Ellalice
See Hibbert, Eleanor Alice Burford

Tate, James (Vincent) 1943- ... CLC 2, 6, 25
See also CA 21-24R; CANR 29; DLB 5

Tavel, Ronald 1940-............... CLC 6
See also CA 21-24R; CANR 33

Taylor, Cecil Philip 1929-1981 ..... CLC 27
See also CA 25-28R; 105

Taylor, Edward 1642(?)-1729.... LC 11; DA
See also DLB 24

Taylor, Eleanor Ross 1920-......... CLC 5
See also CA 81-84

Taylor, Elizabeth 1912-1975 ... CLC 2, 4, 29
See also CA 13-16R; CANR 9; MTCW;
SATA 13

Taylor, Henry (Splawn) 1942-...... CLC 44
See also CA 33-36R; CAAS 7; CANR 31;
DLB 5

Taylor, Kamala (Purnaiya) 1924-
See Markandaya, Kamala
See also CA 77-80

Taylor, Mildred D.................. CLC 21
See also AAYA 10; BW; CA 85-88;
CANR 25; CLR 9; DLB 52; JRDA;
MAICYA; SAAS; SATA 15, 70

Taylor, Peter (Hillsman)
1917- ...... CLC 1, 4, 18, 37, 44, 50, 71;
SSC 10
See also CA 13-16R; CANR 9; DLBY 81;
MTCW

Taylor, Robert Lewis 1912-........ CLC 14
See also CA 1-4R; CANR 3; SATA 10

Tchekhov, Anton
See Chekhov, Anton (Pavlovich)

Teasdale, Sara 1884-1933.......... TCLC 4
See also CA 104; DLB 45; SATA 32

Tegner, Esaias 1782-1846........ NCLC 2

Teilhard de Chardin, (Marie Joseph) Pierre
1881-1955 .... TCLC 9
See also CA 105

Temple, Ann
See Mortimer, Penelope (Ruth)

Tennant, Emma (Christina)
1937- .... CLC 13, 52
See also CA 65-68; CAAS 9; CANR 10, 38;
DLB 14

Tenneshaw, S. M.
See Silverberg, Robert

Tennyson, Alfred
1809-1892 .. NCLC 30; DA; PC 6; WLC
See also CDBLB 1832-1890; DLB 32

Teran, Lisa St. Aubin de .... CLC 36
See also St. Aubin de Teran, Lisa

Teresa de Jesus, St. 1515-1582 ...... LC 18

Terkel, Louis 1912-
See Terkel, Studs
See also CA 57-60; CANR 18; MTCW

Terkel, Studs..................... CLC 38
See also Terkel, Louis
See also AITN 1

Terry, C. V.
See Slaughter, Frank G(ill)

Terry, Megan 1932-............... CLC 19
See also CA 77-80; CABS 3; CANR 43;
DLB 7

Tertz, Abram
See Sinyavsky, Andrei (Donatevich)

Tesich, Steve 1943(?)-.......... CLC 40, 69
See also CA 105; DLBY 83

Teternikov, Fyodor Kuzmich 1863-1927
See Sologub, Fyodor
See also CA 104

Tevis, Walter 1928-1984 .... CLC 42
See also CA 113

Tey, Josephine.................... TCLC 14
See also Mackintosh, Elizabeth
See also DLB 77

Thackeray, William Makepeace
1811-1863 .... NCLC 5, 14, 22, 43; DA;
WLC
See also CDBLB 1832-1890; DLB 21, 55;
SATA 23

Thakura, Ravindranatha
See Tagore, Rabindranath

Tharoor, Shashi 1956- . . . . **CLC 70**
See also CA 141

Thelwell, Michael Miles 1939- . . . . . **CLC 22**
See also CA 101

Theobald, Lewis, Jr.
See Lovecraft, H(oward) P(hillips)

Theodorescu, Ion N. 1880-1967
See Arghezi, Tudor
See also CA 116

The Prophet
See Dreiser, Theodore (Herman Albert)

Theriault, Yves 1915-1983 . . . . **CLC 79**
See also CA 102; DLB 88

Theroux, Alexander (Louis)
1939- . . . . **CLC 2, 25**
See also CA 85-88; CANR 20

Theroux, Paul (Edward)
1941- . . . . **CLC 5, 8, 11, 15, 28, 46**
See also BEST 89:4; CA 33-36R; CANR 20;
DLB 2; MTCW; SATA 44

Thesen, Sharon 1946- . . . . **CLC 56**

Thevenin, Denis
See Duhamel, Georges

Thibault, Jacques Anatole Francois
1844-1924
See France, Anatole
See also CA 106; 127; MTCW

Thiele, Colin (Milton) 1920- . . . . **CLC 17**
See also CA 29-32R; CANR 12, 28;
CLR 27; MAICYA; SAAS 2; SATA 14,
72

Thomas, Audrey (Callahan)
1935- . . . . **CLC 7, 13, 37**
See also AITN 2; CA 21-24R; CANR 36;
DLB 60; MTCW

Thomas, D(onald) M(ichael)
1935- . . . . **CLC 13, 22, 31**
See also CA 61-64; CAAS 11; CANR 17;
CDBLB 1960 to Present; DLB 40;
MTCW

Thomas, Dylan (Marlais)
1914-1953 . . . **TCLC 1, 8, 45; DA; PC 2;
SSC 3; WLC**
See also CA 104; 120; CDBLB 1945-1960;
DLB 13, 20; MTCW; SATA 60

Thomas, (Philip) Edward
1878-1917 . . . . **TCLC 10**
See also CA 106; DLB 19

Thomas, Joyce Carol 1938- . . . . **CLC 35**
See also BW; CA 113; 116; CLR 19;
DLB 33; JRDA; MAICYA; MTCW;
SAAS 7; SATA 40

Thomas, Lewis 1913- . . . . **CLC 35**
See also CA 85-88; CANR 38; MTCW

Thomas, Paul
See Mann, (Paul) Thomas

Thomas, Piri 1928- . . . . **CLC 17**
See also CA 73-76; HW

Thomas, R(onald) S(tuart)
1913- . . . . **CLC 6, 13, 48**
See also CA 89-92; CAAS 4; CANR 30;
CDBLB 1960 to Present; DLB 27;
MTCW

Thomas, Ross (Elmore) 1926- . . . . . . **CLC 39**
See also CA 33-36R; CANR 22

Thompson, Francis Clegg
See Mencken, H(enry) L(ouis)

Thompson, Francis Joseph
1859-1907 . . . . **TCLC 4**
See also CA 104; CDBLB 1890-1914;
DLB 19

Thompson, Hunter S(tockton)
1939- . . . . **CLC 9, 17, 40**
See also BEST 89:1; CA 17-20R; CANR 23;
MTCW

Thompson, James Myers
See Thompson, Jim (Myers)

Thompson, Jim (Myers)
1906-1977(?) . . . . **CLC 69**
See also CA 140

Thompson, Judith . . . . **CLC 39**

Thomson, James 1700-1748 . . . . **LC 16**

Thomson, James 1834-1882 . . . . . . **NCLC 18**

Thoreau, Henry David
1817-1862 . . . . . . **NCLC 7, 21; DA; WLC**
See also CDALB 1640-1865; DLB 1

Thornton, Hall
See Silverberg, Robert

Thurber, James (Grover)
1894-1961 . . . **CLC 5, 11, 25; DA; SSC 1**
See also CA 73-76; CANR 17, 39;
CDALB 1929-1941; DLB 4, 11, 22, 102;
MAICYA; MTCW; SATA 13

Thurman, Wallace (Henry)
1902-1934 . . . . **TCLC 6; BLC 3**
See also BW; CA 104; 124; DLB 51

Ticheburn, Cheviot
See Ainsworth, William Harrison

Tieck, (Johann) Ludwig
1773-1853 . . . . **NCLC 5**
See also DLB 90

Tiger, Derry
See Ellison, Harlan

Tilghman, Christopher 1948(?)- . . . . . **CLC 65**

Tillinghast, Richard (Willlford)
1940- . . . . **CLC 29**
See also CA 29-32R; CANR 26

Timrod, Henry 1828-1867 . . . . **NCLC 25**
See also DLB 3

Tindall, Gillian 1938- . . . . **CLC 7**
See also CA 21-24R; CANR 11

Tiptree, James, Jr. . . . . **CLC 48, 50**
See also Sheldon, Alice Hastings Bradley
See also DLB 8

Titmarsh, Michael Angelo
See Thackeray, William Makepeace

**Tocqueville, Alexis (Charles Henri Maurice
Clerel Comte)** 1805-1859 . . . . . **NCLC 7**

Tolkien, J(ohn) R(onald) R(euel)
1892-1973 . . . . . . **CLC 1, 2, 3, 8, 12, 38;
DA; WLC**
See also AAYA 10; AITN 1; CA 17-18;
45-48; CANR 36; CAP 2;
CDBLB 1914-1945; DLB 15; JRDA;
MAICYA; MTCW; SATA 2, 24, 32

Toller, Ernst 1893-1939 . . . . **TCLC 10**
See also CA 107; DLB 124

Tolson, M. B.
See Tolson, Melvin B(eaunorus)

Tolson, Melvin B(eaunorus)
1898(?)-1966 . . . . **CLC 36; BLC 3**
See also BW; CA 124; 89-92; DLB 48, 76

Tolstoi, Aleksei Nikolaevich
See Tolstoy, Alexey Nikolaevich

Tolstoy, Alexey Nikolaevich
1882-1945 . . . . **TCLC 18**
See also CA 107

Tolstoy, Count Leo
See Tolstoy, Leo (Nikolaevich)

Tolstoy, Leo (Nikolaevich)
1828-1910 . . . . . . **TCLC 4, 11, 17, 28, 44;
DA; SSC 9; WLC**
See also CA 104; 123; SATA 26

Tomasi di Lampedusa, Giuseppe 1896-1957
See Lampedusa, Giuseppe (Tomasi) di
See also CA 111

Tomlin, Lily . . . . **CLC 17**
See also Tomlin, Mary Jean

Tomlin, Mary Jean 1939(?)-
See Tomlin, Lily
See also CA 117

Tomlinson, (Alfred) Charles
1927- . . . . **CLC 2, 4, 6, 13, 45**
See also CA 5-8R; CANR 33; DLB 40

Tonson, Jacob
See Bennett, (Enoch) Arnold

Toole, John Kennedy
1937-1969 . . . . **CLC 19, 64**
See also CA 104; DLBY 81

Toomer, Jean
1894-1967 . . . . **CLC 1, 4, 13, 22; BLC 3;
PC 7; SSC 1**
See also BW; CA 85-88;
CDALB 1917-1929; DLB 45, 51; MTCW

Torley, Luke
See Blish, James (Benjamin)

Tornimparte, Alessandra
See Ginzburg, Natalia

Torre, Raoul della
See Mencken, H(enry) L(ouis)

Torrey, E(dwin) Fuller 1937- . . . . **CLC 34**
See also CA 119

Torsvan, Ben Traven
See Traven, B.

Torsvan, Benno Traven
See Traven, B.

Torsvan, Berick Traven
See Traven, B.

Torsvan, Berwick Traven
See Traven, B.

Torsvan, Bruno Traven
See Traven, B.

Torsvan, Traven
See Traven, B.

Tournier, Michel (Edouard)
1924- . . . . **CLC 6, 23, 36**
See also CA 49-52; CANR 3, 36; DLB 83;
MTCW; SATA 23

Tournimparte, Alessandra
See Ginzburg, Natalia

Vaculik, Ludvik 1926- .... CLC 7
See also CA 53-56

Valenzuela, Luisa 1938-... CLC 31; SSC 14
See also CA 101; CANR 32; DLB 113; HW

Valera y Alcala-Galiano, Juan
1824-1905 .... TCLC 10
See also CA 106

Valery, (Ambroise) Paul (Toussaint Jules)
1871-1945 .... TCLC 4, 15
See also CA 104; 122; MTCW

Valle-Inclan, Ramon (Maria) del
1866-1936 .... TCLC 5; HLC 2
See also CA 106; DLB 134

Vallejo, Antonio Buero
See Buero Vallejo, Antonio

Vallejo, Cesar (Abraham)
1892-1938 .... TCLC 3; HLC 2
See also CA 105; HW

Valle Y Pena, Ramon del
See Valle-Inclan, Ramon (Maria) del

Van Ash, Cay 1918- .... CLC 34

Vanbrugh, Sir John 1664-1726 ...... LC 21
See also DLB 80

Van Campen, Karl
See Campbell, John W(ood, Jr.)

Vance, Gerald
See Silverberg, Robert

Vance, Jack .... CLC 35
See also Vance, John Holbrook
See also DLB 8

Vance, John Holbrook 1916-
See Queen, Ellery; Vance, Jack
See also CA 29-32R; CANR 17; MTCW

Van Den Bogarde, Derek Jules Gaspard Ulric
Niven 1921-
See Bogarde, Dirk
See also CA 77-80

Vandenburgh, Jane .... CLC 59

Vanderhaeghe, Guy 1951- .... CLC 41
See also CA 113

van der Post, Laurens (Jan) 1906-... CLC 5
See also CA 5-8R; CANR 35

van de Wetering, Janwillem 1931-.. CLC 47
See also CA 49-52; CANR 4

Van Dine, S. S. .... TCLC 23
See also Wright, Willard Huntington

Van Doren, Carl (Clinton)
1885-1950 .... TCLC 18
See also CA 111

Van Doren, Mark 1894-1972..... CLC 6, 10
See also CA 1-4R; 37-40R; CANR 3;
DLB 45; MTCW

Van Druten, John (William)
1901-1957 .... TCLC 2
See also CA 104; DLB 10

Van Duyn, Mona (Jane)
1921- .... CLC 3, 7, 63
See also CA 9-12R; CANR 7, 38; DLB 5

Van Dyne, Edith
See Baum, L(yman) Frank

van Itallie, Jean-Claude 1936-....... CLC 3
See also CA 45-48; CAAS 2; CANR 1;
DLB 7

van Ostaijen, Paul 1896-1928 ..... TCLC 33

Van Peebles, Melvin 1932- ...... CLC 2, 20
See also BW; CA 85-88; CANR 27

Vansittart, Peter 1920-............ CLC 42
See also CA 1-4R; CANR 3

Van Vechten, Carl 1880-1964 ...... CLC 33
See also CA 89-92; DLB 4, 9, 51

Van Vogt, A(lfred) E(lton) 1912-..... CLC 1
See also CA 21-24R; CANR 28; DLB 8;
SATA 14

Varda, Agnes 1928- .... CLC 16
See also CA 116; 122

Vargas Llosa, (Jorge) Mario (Pedro)
1936- ...... CLC 3, 6, 9, 10, 15, 31, 42;
DA; HLC 2
See also CA 73-76; CANR 18, 32, 42; HW;
MTCW

Vasiliu, Gheorghe 1881-1957
See Bacovia, George
See also CA 123

Vassa, Gustavus
See Equiano, Olaudah

Vassilikos, Vassilis 1933-......... CLC 4, 8
See also CA 81-84

Vaughn, Stephanie .... CLC 62

Vazov, Ivan (Minchov)
1850-1921 .... TCLC 25
See also CA 121

Veblen, Thorstein (Bunde)
1857-1929 .... TCLC 31
See also CA 115

Vega, Lope de 1562-1635 .... LC 23

Venison, Alfred
See Pound, Ezra (Weston Loomis)

Verdi, Marie de
See Mencken, H(enry) L(ouis)

Verdu, Matilde
See Cela, Camilo Jose

Verga, Giovanni (Carmelo)
1840-1922 .... TCLC 3
See also CA 104; 123

Vergil 70B.C.-19B.C. .... CMLC 9; DA

Verhaeren, Emile (Adolphe Gustave)
1855-1916 .... TCLC 12
See also CA 109

Verlaine, Paul (Marie)
1844-1896 .... NCLC 2; PC 2

Verne, Jules (Gabriel)
1828-1905 .... TCLC 6, 52
See also CA 110; 131; DLB 123; JRDA;
MAICYA; SATA 21

Very, Jones 1813-1880 .... NCLC 9
See also DLB 1

Vesaas, Tarjei 1897-1970......... CLC 48
See also CA 29-32R

Vialis, Gaston
See Simenon, Georges (Jacques Christian)

Vian, Boris 1920-1959 .... TCLC 9
See also CA 106; DLB 72

Viaud, (Louis Marie) Julien 1850-1923
See Loti, Pierre
See also CA 107

Vicar, Henry
See Felsen, Henry Gregor

Vicker, Angus
See Felsen, Henry Gregor

Vidal, Gore
1925- ..... CLC 2, 4, 6, 8, 10, 22, 33, 72
See also AITN 1; BEST 90:2; CA 5-8R;
CANR 13; DLB 6; MTCW

Viereck, Peter (Robert Edwin)
1916- .... CLC 4
See also CA 1-4R; CANR 1; DLB 5

Vigny, Alfred (Victor) de
1797-1863 .... NCLC 7
See also DLB 119

Vilakazi, Benedict Wallet
1906-1947 .... TCLC 37

Villiers de l'Isle Adam, Jean Marie Mathias
Philippe Auguste Comte
1838-1889 .... NCLC 3; SSC 14
See also DLB 123

Vincent, Gabrielle a pseudonym ...... CLC 13
See also CA 126; CLR 13; MAICYA;
SATA 61

Vinci, Leonardo da 1452-1519....... LC 12

Vine, Barbara .... CLC 50
See also Rendell, Ruth (Barbara)
See also BEST 90:4

Vinge, Joan D(ennison) 1948-...... CLC 30
See also CA 93-96; SATA 36

Violis, G.
See Simenon, Georges (Jacques Christian)

Visconti, Luchino 1906-1976....... CLC 16
See also CA 81-84; 65-68; CANR 39

Vittorini, Elio 1908-1966 ...... CLC 6, 9, 14
See also CA 133; 25-28R

Vizinczey, Stephen 1933-.......... CLC 40
See also CA 128

Vliet, R(ussell) G(ordon)
1929-1984 .... CLC 22
See also CA 37-40R; 112; CANR 18

Vogau, Boris Andreyevich 1894-1937(?)
See Pilnyak, Boris
See also CA 123

Vogel, Paula A(nne) 1951-......... CLC 76
See also CA 108

Voight, Ellen Bryant 1943- .... CLC 54
See also CA 69-72; CANR 11, 29; DLB 120

Voigt, Cynthia 1942- .... CLC 30
See also AAYA 3; CA 106; CANR 18, 37,
40; CLR 13; JRDA; MAICYA;
SATA 33, 48

Voinovich, Vladimir (Nikolaevich)
1932- .... CLC 10, 49
See also CA 81-84; CAAS 12; CANR 33;
MTCW

Voltaire
1694-1778 ... LC 14; DA; SSC 12; WLC

von Daeniken, Erich 1935- .... CLC 30
See also von Daniken, Erich
See also AITN 1; CA 37-40R; CANR 17

von Daniken, Erich .... CLC 30
See also von Daeniken, Erich

von Heidenstam, (Carl Gustaf) Verner
See Heidenstam, (Carl Gustaf) Verner von

von Heyse, Paul (Johann Ludwig)
See Heyse, Paul (Johann Ludwig von)

von Hofmannsthal, Hugo
See Hofmannsthal, Hugo von

von Horvath, Odon
See Horvath, Oedoen von

von Horvath, Oedoen
See Horvath, Oedoen von

von Liliencron, (Friedrich Adolf Axel) Detlev
See Liliencron, (Friedrich Adolf Axel) Detlev von

Vonnegut, Kurt, Jr.
1922- ...... CLC 1, 2, 3, 4, 5, 8, 12, 22, 40, 60; DA; SSC 8; WLC
See also AAYA 6; AITN 1; BEST 90:4; CA 1-4R; CANR 1, 25; CDALB 1968-1988; DLB 2, 8; DLBD 3; DLBY 80; MTCW

Von Rachen, Kurt
See Hubbard, L(afayette) Ron(ald)

von Rezzori (d'Arezzo), Gregor
See Rezzori (d'Arezzo), Gregor von

von Sternberg, Josef
See Sternberg, Josef von

Vorster, Gordon 1924- .... CLC 34
See also CA 133

Vosce, Trudie
See Ozick, Cynthia

Voznesensky, Andrei (Andreievich)
1933- .... CLC 1, 15, 57
See also CA 89-92; CANR 37; MTCW

Waddington, Miriam 1917- .... CLC 28
See also CA 21-24R; CANR 12, 30; DLB 68

Wagman, Fredrica 1937- .... CLC 7
See also CA 97-100

Wagner, Richard 1813-1883. ...... NCLC 9
See also DLB 129

Wagner-Martin, Linda 1936- .... CLC 50

Wagoner, David (Russell)
1926- .... CLC 3, 5, 15
See also CA 1-4R; CAAS 3; CANR 2; DLB 5; SATA 14

Wah, Fred(erick James) 1939- ...... CLC 44
See also CA 107; 141; DLB 60

Wahloo, Per 1926-1975 .... CLC 7
See also CA 61-64

Wahloo, Peter
See Wahloo, Per

Wain, John (Barrington)
1925- .... CLC 2, 11, 15, 46
See also CA 5-8R; CAAS 4; CANR 23; CDBLB 1960 to Present; DLB 15, 27; MTCW

Wajda, Andrzej 1926- .... CLC 16
See also CA 102

Wakefield, Dan 1932- .... CLC 7
See also CA 21-24R; CAAS 7

Wakoski, Diane
1937- .... CLC 2, 4, 7, 9, 11, 40
See also CA 13-16R; CAAS 1; CANR 9; DLB 5

Wakoski-Sherbell, Diane
See Wakoski, Diane

Walcott, Derek (Alton)
1930- .... CLC 2, 4, 9, 14, 25, 42, 67, 76; BLC 3
See also BW; CA 89-92; CANR 26; DLB 117; DLBY 81; MTCW

Waldman, Anne 1945- .... CLC 7
See also CA 37-40R; CAAS 17; CANR 34; DLB 16

Waldo, E. Hunter
See Sturgeon, Theodore (Hamilton)

Waldo, Edward Hamilton
See Sturgeon, Theodore (Hamilton)

Walker, Alice (Malsenior)
1944- .... CLC 5, 6, 9, 19, 27, 46, 58; BLC 3; DA; SSC 5
See also AAYA 3; BEST 89:4; BW; CA 37-40R; CANR 9, 27; CDALB 1968-1988; DLB 6, 33; MTCW; SATA 31

Walker, David Harry 1911-1992. ... CLC 14
See also CA 1-4R; 137; CANR 1; SATA 8; SATA-Obit 71

Walker, Edward Joseph 1934-
See Walker, Ted
See also CA 21-24R; CANR 12, 28

Walker, George F. 1947- .... CLC 44, 61
See also CA 103; CANR 21, 43; DLB 60

Walker, Joseph A. 1935- .... CLC 19
See also BW; CA 89-92; CANR 26; DLB 38

Walker, Margaret (Abigail)
1915- .... CLC 1, 6; BLC 3
See also BW; CA 73-76; CANR 26; DLB 76; MTCW

Walker, Ted .... CLC 13
See also Walker, Edward Joseph
See also DLB 40

Wallace, David Foster 1962- .... CLC 50
See also CA 132

Wallace, Dexter
See Masters, Edgar Lee

Wallace, Irving 1916-1990 .... CLC 7, 13
See also AITN 1; CA 1-4R; 132; CAAS 1; CANR 1, 27; MTCW

Wallant, Edward Lewis
1926-1962 .... CLC 5, 10
See also CA 1-4R; CANR 22; DLB 2, 28; MTCW

Walpole, Horace 1717-1797. .... LC 2
See also DLB 39, 104

Walpole, Hugh (Seymour)
1884-1941 .... TCLC 5
See also CA 104; DLB 34

Walser, Martin 1927- .... CLC 27
See also CA 57-60; CANR 8; DLB 75, 124

Walser, Robert 1878-1956 .... TCLC 18
See also CA 118; DLB 66

Walsh, Jill Paton .... CLC 35
See also Paton Walsh, Gillian
See also CLR 2; SAAS 3

Walter, Villiam Christian
See Andersen, Hans Christian

Wambaugh, Joseph (Aloysius, Jr.)
1937- .... CLC 3, 18
See also AITN 1; BEST 89:3; CA 33-36R; CANR 42; DLB 6; DLBY 83; MTCW

Ward, Arthur Henry Sarsfield 1883-1959
See Rohmer, Sax
See also CA 108

Ward, Douglas Turner 1930- .... CLC 19
See also BW; CA 81-84; CANR 27; DLB 7, 38

Ward, Peter
See Faust, Frederick (Schiller)

Warhol, Andy 1928(?)-1987. .... CLC 20
See also BEST 89:4; CA 89-92; 121; CANR 34

Warner, Francis (Robert le Plastrier)
1937- .... CLC 14
See also CA 53-56; CANR 11

Warner, Marina 1946- .... CLC 59
See also CA 65-68; CANR 21

Warner, Rex (Ernest) 1905-1986. ... CLC 45
See also CA 89-92; 119; DLB 15

Warner, Susan (Bogert)
1819-1885 .... NCLC 31
See also DLB 3, 42

Warner, Sylvia (Constance) Ashton
See Ashton-Warner, Sylvia (Constance)

Warner, Sylvia Townsend
1893-1978 .... CLC 7, 19
See also CA 61-64; 77-80; CANR 16; DLB 34; MTCW

Warren, Mercy Otis 1728-1814. ... NCLC 13
See also DLB 31

Warren, Robert Penn
1905-1989 .... CLC 1, 4, 6, 8, 10, 13, 18, 39, 53, 59; DA; SSC 4; WLC
See also AITN 1; CA 13-16R; 129; CANR 10; CDALB 1968-1988; DLB 2, 48; DLBY 80, 89; MTCW; SATA 46, 63

Warshofsky, Isaac
See Singer, Isaac Bashevis

Warton, Thomas 1728-1790. .... LC 15
See also DLB 104, 109

Waruk, Kona
See Harris, (Theodore) Wilson

Warung, Price 1855-1911. .... TCLC 45

Warwick, Jarvis
See Garner, Hugh

Washington, Alex
See Harris, Mark

Washington, Booker T(aliaferro)
1856-1915 .... TCLC 10; BLC 3
See also BW; CA 114; 125; SATA 28

Wassermann, (Karl) Jakob
1873-1934 .... TCLC 6
See also CA 104; DLB 66

Wasserstein, Wendy
1950- .... CLC 32, 59; DC 4
See also CA 121; 129; CABS 3

Waterhouse, Keith (Spencer)
1929- .... CLC 47
See also CA 5-8R; CANR 38; DLB 13, 15; MTCW

Waters, Roger 1944- .... CLC 35
See also Pink Floyd

Watkins, Frances Ellen
See Harper, Frances Ellen Watkins

Author Index

Watkins, Gerrold
See Malzberg, Barry N(athaniel)

Watkins, Paul 1964- . . . . CLC 55
See also CA 132

Watkins, Vernon Phillips
1906-1967 . . . . CLC 43
See also CA 9-10; 25-28R; CAP 1; DLB 20

Watson, Irving S.
See Mencken, H(enry) L(ouis)

Watson, John H.
See Farmer, Philip Jose

Watson, Richard F.
See Silverberg, Robert

Waugh, Auberon (Alexander) 1939- . . CLC 7
See also CA 45-48; CANR 6, 22; DLB 14

Waugh, Evelyn (Arthur St. John)
1903-1966 . . . . . . CLC 1, 3, 8, 13, 19, 27,
44; DA; WLC
See also CA 85-88; 25-28R; CANR 22;
CDBLB 1914-1945; DLB 15; MTCW

Waugh, Harriet 1944- . . . . CLC 6
See also CA 85-88; CANR 22

Ways, C. R.
See Blount, Roy (Alton), Jr.

Waystaff, Simon
See Swift, Jonathan

Webb, (Martha) Beatrice (Potter)
1858-1943 . . . . TCLC 22
See also Potter, Beatrice
See also CA 117

Webb, Charles (Richard) 1939- . . . . . . CLC 7
See also CA 25-28R

Webb, James H(enry), Jr. 1946- . . . . CLC 22
See also CA 81-84

Webb, Mary (Gladys Meredith)
1881-1927 . . . . TCLC 24
See also CA 123; DLB 34

Webb, Mrs. Sidney
See Webb, (Martha) Beatrice (Potter)

Webb, Phyllis 1927- . . . . CLC 18
See also CA 104; CANR 23; DLB 53

Webb, Sidney (James)
1859-1947 . . . . TCLC 22
See also CA 117

Webber, Andrew Lloyd . . . . CLC 21
See also Lloyd Webber, Andrew

Weber, Lenora Mattingly
1895-1971 . . . . CLC 12
See also CA 19-20; 29-32R; CAP 1;
SATA 2, 26

Webster, John 1579(?)-1634(?) . . . . DC 2
See also CDBLB Before 1660; DA; DLB 58;
WLC

Webster, Noah 1758-1843 . . . . NCLC 30

Wedekind, (Benjamin) Frank(lin)
1864-1918 . . . . TCLC 7
See also CA 104; DLB 118

Weidman, Jerome 1913- . . . . CLC 7
See also AITN 2; CA 1-4R; CANR 1;
DLB 28

Weil, Simone (Adolphine)
1909-1943 . . . . TCLC 23
See also CA 117

Weinstein, Nathan
See West, Nathanael

Weinstein, Nathan von Wallenstein
See West, Nathanael

Weir, Peter (Lindsay) 1944- . . . . CLC 20
See also CA 113; 123

Weiss, Peter (Ulrich)
1916-1982 . . . . CLC 3, 15, 51
See also CA 45-48; 106; CANR 3; DLB 69,
124

Weiss, Theodore (Russell)
1916 . . . . CLC 3, 8, 14
See also CA 9-12R; CAAS 2; DLB 5

Welch, (Maurice) Denton
1915-1948 . . . . TCLC 22
See also CA 121

Welch, James 1940- . . . . CLC 6, 14, 52
See also CA 85-88; CANR 42

Weldon, Fay
1933(?)- . . . . CLC 6, 9, 11, 19, 36, 59
See also CA 21-24R; CANR 16;
CDBLB 1960 to Present; DLB 14;
MTCW

Wellek, Rene 1903- . . . . CLC 28
See also CA 5-8R; CAAS 7; CANR 8;
DLB 63

Weller, Michael 1942- . . . . CLC 10, 53
See also CA 85-88

Weller, Paul 1958- . . . . CLC 26

Wellershoff, Dieter 1925- . . . . CLC 46
See also CA 89-92; CANR 16, 37

Welles, (George) Orson
1915-1985 . . . . CLC 20, 80
See also CA 93-96; 117

Wellman, Mac 1945- . . . . CLC 65

Wellman, Manly Wade 1903-1986 . . CLC 49
See also CA 1-4R; 118; CANR 6, 16;
SATA 6, 47

Wells, Carolyn 1869(?)-1942 . . . . . TCLC 35
See also CA 113; DLB 11

Wells, H(erbert) G(eorge)
1866-1946 . . . . TCLC 6, 12, 19; DA;
SSC 6; WLC
See also CA 110; 121; CDBLB 1914-1945;
DLB 34, 70; MTCW; SATA 20

Wells, Rosemary 1943- . . . . CLC 12
See also CA 85-88; CLR 16; MAICYA;
SAAS 1; SATA 18, 69

Welty, Eudora
1909- . . . . . . CLC 1, 2, 5, 14, 22, 33; DA;
SSC 1; WLC
See also CA 9-12R; CABS 1; CANR 32;
CDALB 1941-1968; DLB 2, 102;
DLBY 87; MTCW

Wen I-to 1899-1946 . . . . TCLC 28

Wentworth, Robert
See Hamilton, Edmond

Werfel, Franz (V.) 1890-1945 . . . . . TCLC 8
See also CA 104; DLB 81, 124

Wergeland, Henrik Arnold
1808-1845 . . . . NCLC 5

Wersba, Barbara 1932- . . . . CLC 30
See also AAYA 2; CA 29-32R; CANR 16,
38; CLR 3; DLB 52; JRDA; MAICYA;
SAAS 2; SATA 1, 58

Wertmueller, Lina 1928- . . . . CLC 16
See also CA 97-100; CANR 39

Wescott, Glenway 1901-1987 . . . . CLC 13
See also CA 13-16R; 121; CANR 23;
DLB 4, 9, 102

Wesker, Arnold 1932- . . . . CLC 3, 5, 42
See also CA 1-4R; CAAS 7; CANR 1, 33;
CDBLB 1960 to Present; DLB 13;
MTCW

Wesley, Richard (Errol) 1945- . . . . . . CLC 7
See also BW; CA 57-60; CANR 27; DLB 38

Wessel, Johan Herman 1742-1785 . . . . LC 7

West, Anthony (Panther)
1914-1987 . . . . CLC 50
See also CA 45-48; 124; CANR 3, 19;
DLB 15

West, C. P.
See Wodehouse, P(elham) G(renville)

West, (Mary) Jessamyn
1902-1984 . . . . CLC 7, 17
See also CA 9-12R; 112; CANR 27; DLB 6;
DLBY 84; MTCW; SATA 37

West, Morris L(anglo) 1916- . . . . . CLC 6, 33
See also CA 5-8R; CANR 24; MTCW

West, Nathanael
1903-1940 . . . . TCLC 1, 14, 44
See also CA 104; 125; CDALB 1929-1941;
DLB 4, 9, 28; MTCW

West, Owen
See Koontz, Dean R(ay)

West, Paul 1930- . . . . CLC 7, 14
See also CA 13-16R; CAAS 7; CANR 22;
DLB 14

West, Rebecca 1892-1983 . . CLC 7, 9, 31, 50
See also CA 5-8R; 109; CANR 19; DLB 36;
DLBY 83; MTCW

Westall, Robert (Atkinson)
1929-1993 . . . . CLC 17
See also CA 69-72; 141; CANR 18;
CLR 13; JRDA; MAICYA; SAAS 2;
SATA 23, 69; SATA-Obit 75

Westlake, Donald E(dwin)
1933- . . . . CLC 7, 33
See also CA 17-20R; CAAS 13; CANR 16

Westmacott, Mary
See Christie, Agatha (Mary Clarissa)

Weston, Allen
See Norton, Andre

Wetcheek, J. L.
See Feuchtwanger, Lion

Wetering, Janwillem van de
See van de Wetering, Janwillem

Wetherell, Elizabeth
See Warner, Susan (Bogert)

Whalen, Philip 1923- . . . . CLC 6, 29
See also CA 9-12R; CANR 5, 39; DLB 16

Wharton, Edith (Newbold Jones)
1862-1937 . . . . . . TCLC 3, 9, 27, 53; DA;
SSC 6; WLC
See also CA 104; 132; CDALB 1865-1917;
DLB 4, 9, 12, 78; MTCW

Wharton, James
See Mencken, H(enry) L(ouis)

Wilson, A(ndrew) N(orman) 1950- . . **CLC 33**
See also CA 112; 122; DLB 14

Wilson, Angus (Frank Johnstone)
1913-1991 . . . . **CLC 2, 3, 5, 25, 34**
See also CA 5-8R; 134; CANR 21; DLB 15;
MTCW

Wilson, August
1945- . . . . . **CLC 39, 50, 63; BLC 3; DA;**
DC 2
See also BW; CA 115; 122; CANR 42;
MTCW

Wilson, Brian 1942- . . . . **CLC 12**

Wilson, Colin 1931- . . . . **CLC 3, 14**
See also CA 1-4R; CAAS 5; CANR 1, 22,
33; DLB 14; MTCW

Wilson, Dirk
See Pohl, Frederik

Wilson, Edmund
1895-1972 . . . . **CLC 1, 2, 3, 8, 24**
See also CA 1-4R; 37-40R; CANR 1;
DLB 63; MTCW

Wilson, Ethel Davis (Bryant)
1888(?)-1980 . . . . **CLC 13**
See also CA 102; DLB 68; MTCW

Wilson, John 1785-1854 . . . . **NCLC 5**

Wilson, John (Anthony) Burgess 1917-1993
See Burgess, Anthony
See also CA 1-4R; CANR 2; MTCW

Wilson, Lanford 1937- . . . . **CLC 7, 14, 36**
See also CA 17-20R; CABS 3; DLB 7

Wilson, Robert M. 1944- . . . . **CLC 7, 9**
See also CA 49-52; CANR 2, 41; MTCW

Wilson, Robert McLiam 1964- . . . . . **CLC 59**
See also CA 132

Wilson, Sloan 1920- . . . . **CLC 32**
See also CA 1-4R; CANR 1

Wilson, Snoo 1948- . . . . **CLC 33**
See also CA 69-72

Wilson, William S(mith) 1932- . . . . . **CLC 49**
See also CA 81-84

Winchilsea, Anne (Kingsmill) Finch Counte
1661-1720 . . . . **LC 3**

Windham, Basil
See Wodehouse, P(elham) G(renville)

Wingrove, David (John) 1954- . . . . . **CLC 68**
See also CA 133

Winters, Janet Lewis . . . . **CLC 41**
See also Lewis, Janet
See also DLBY 87

Winters, (Arthur) Yvor
1900-1968 . . . . **CLC 4, 8, 32**
See also CA 11-12; 25-28R; CAP 1;
DLB 48; MTCW

Winterson, Jeanette 1959- . . . . **CLC 64**
See also CA 136

Wiseman, Frederick 1930- . . . . **CLC 20**

Wister, Owen 1860-1938 . . . . **TCLC 21**
See also CA 108; DLB 9, 78; SATA 62

Witkacy
See Witkiewicz, Stanislaw Ignacy

Witkiewicz, Stanislaw Ignacy
1885-1939 . . . . **TCLC 8**
See also CA 105

Wittig, Monique 1935(?)- . . . . **CLC 22**
See also CA 116; 135; DLB 83

Wittlin, Jozef 1896-1976 . . . . **CLC 25**
See also CA 49-52; 65-68; CANR 3

Wodehouse, P(elham) G(renville)
1881-1975 . . . **CLC 1, 2, 5, 10, 22; SSC 2**
See also AITN 2; CA 45-48; 57-60;
CANR 3, 33; CDBLB 1914-1945;
DLB 34; MTCW; SATA 22

Woiwode, L.
See Woiwode, Larry (Alfred)

Woiwode, Larry (Alfred) 1941- . . . . **CLC 6, 10**
See also CA 73-76; CANR 16; DLB 6

Wojciechowska, Maia (Teresa)
1927- . . . . **CLC 26**
See also AAYA 8; CA 9-12R; CANR 4, 41;
CLR 1; JRDA; MAICYA; SAAS 1;
SATA 1, 28

Wolf, Christa 1929- . . . . **CLC 14, 29, 58**
See also CA 85-88; DLB 75; MTCW

Wolfe, Gene (Rodman) 1931- . . . . **CLC 25**
See also CA 57-60; CAAS 9; CANR 6, 32;
DLB 8

Wolfe, George C. 1954- . . . . **CLC 49**

Wolfe, Thomas (Clayton)
1900-1938 . . . **TCLC 4, 13, 29; DA; WLC**
See also CA 104; 132; CDALB 1929-1941;
DLB 9, 102; DLBD 2; DLBY 85; MTCW

Wolfe, Thomas Kennerly, Jr. 1931-
See Wolfe, Tom
See also CA 13-16R; CANR 9, 33; MTCW

Wolfe, Tom . . . . **CLC 1, 2, 9, 15, 35, 51**
See also Wolfe, Thomas Kennerly, Jr.
See also AAYA 8; AITN 2; BEST 89;1

Wolff, Geoffrey (Ansell) 1937- . . . . . **CLC 41**
See also CA 29-32R; CANR 29, 43

Wolff, Sonia
See Levitin, Sonia (Wolff)

Wolff, Tobias (Jonathan Ansell)
1945- . . . . **CLC 39, 64**
See also BEST 90:2; CA 114; 117; DLB 130

Wolfram von Eschenbach
c. 1170-c. 1220 . . . . **CMLC 5**

Wolitzer, Hilma 1930- . . . . **CLC 17**
See also CA 65-68; CANR 18, 40; SATA 31

Wollstonecraft, Mary 1759-1797 . . . . . . **LC 5**
See also CDBLB 1789-1832; DLB 39, 104

Wonder, Stevie . . . . **CLC 12**
See also Morris, Steveland Judkins

Wong, Jade Snow 1922- . . . . **CLC 17**
See also CA 109

Woodcott, Keith
See Brunner, John (Kilian Houston)

Woodruff, Robert W.
See Mencken, H(enry) L(ouis)

Woolf, (Adeline) Virginia
1882-1941 . . . . . . **TCLC 1, 5, 20, 43; DA;**
SSC 7; WLC
See also CA 104; 130; CDBLB 1914-1945;
DLB 36, 100; DLBD 10; MTCW

Woollcott, Alexander (Humphreys)
1887-1943 . . . . **TCLC 5**
See also CA 105; DLB 29

Woolrich, Cornell 1903-1968 . . . . **CLC 77**
See also Hopley-Woolrich, Cornell George

Wordsworth, Dorothy
1771-1855 . . . . **NCLC 25**
See also DLB 107

Wordsworth, William
1770-1850 . . . . **NCLC 12, 38; DA; PC 4;**
WLC
See also CDBLB 1789-1832; DLB 93, 107

Wouk, Herman 1915- . . . . **CLC 1, 9, 38**
See also CA 5-8R; CANR 6, 33; DLBY 82;
MTCW

Wright, Charles (Penzel, Jr.)
1935- . . . . **CLC 6, 13, 28**
See also CA 29-32R; CAAS 7; CANR 23,
36; DLBY 82; MTCW

Wright, Charles Stevenson
1932- . . . . **CLC 49; BLC 3**
See also BW; CA 9-12R; CANR 26;
DLB 33

Wright, Jack R.
See Harris, Mark

Wright, James (Arlington)
1927-1980 . . . . **CLC 3, 5, 10, 28**
See also AITN 2; CA 49-52; 97-100;
CANR 4, 34; DLB 5; MTCW

Wright, Judith (Arundell)
1915- . . . . **CLC 11, 53**
See also CA 13-16R; CANR 31; MTCW;
SATA 14

Wright, L(aurali) R. 1939- . . . . **CLC 44**
See also CA 138

Wright, Richard (Nathaniel)
1908-1960 . . . . **CLC 1, 3, 4, 9, 14, 21, 48,**
74; BLC 3; DA; SSC 2; WLC
See also AAYA 5; BW; CA 108;
CDALB 1929-1941; DLB 76, 102;
DLBD 2; MTCW

Wright, Richard B(ruce) 1937- . . . . . . **CLC 6**
See also CA 85-88; DLB 53

Wright, Rick 1945- . . . . **CLC 35**
See also Pink Floyd

Wright, Rowland
See Wells, Carolyn

Wright, Stephen 1946- . . . . **CLC 33**

Wright, Willard Huntington 1888-1939
See Van Dine, S. S.
See also CA 115

Wright, William 1930- . . . . **CLC 44**
See also CA 53-56; CANR 7, 23

Wu Ch'eng-en 1500(?)-1582(?) . . . . **LC 7**

Wu Ching-tzu 1701-1754 . . . . **LC 2**

Wurlitzer, Rudolph 1938(?)- . . . **CLC 2, 4, 15**
See also CA 85-88

Wycherley, William 1641-1715 . . . . **LC 8, 21**
See also CDBLB 1660-1789; DLB 80

Wylie, Elinor (Morton Hoyt)
1885-1928 . . . . **TCLC 8**
See also CA 105; DLB 9, 45

Wylie, Philip (Gordon) 1902-1971 . . . **CLC 43**
See also CA 21-22; 33-36R; CAP 2; DLB 9

Wyndham, John
See Harris, John (Wyndham Parkes Lucas)
Beynon

Literary Criticism Series
Cumulative Topic Index

This index lists all topic entries in the Gale Literary Criticism Series *Classical and Medieval Literature Criticism, Contemporary Literary Criticism, Literature Criticism from 1400 to 1800, Nineteenth-Century Literature Criticism,* and *Twentieth-Century Literary Criticism.*

German, 427-50
American, 450-66
French, 466-74
and modern history, 474-82

Yellow Journalism NCLC 36: 383-456
overviews, 384-96
major figures, 396-413
the role of reporters, 413-28
the Spanish-American War, 428-48
Yellow Journalism and society, 448-54

Young Playwrights Festival
1988—CLC 55: 376-81
1989—CLC 59: 398-403
1990—CLC 65: 444-48

TCLC Cumulative Nationality Index

ISBN 0-8103-2431-8